FIFTH EDITION

BANK MANAGEMENT
Text and Cases

GEORGE H. HEMPEL
Southern Methodist University

DONALD G. SIMONSON
University of New Mexico

John Wiley & Sons, Inc.

New York • Chichester • Weinheim • Brisbane • Singapore • Toronto

EDITOR	Marissa Ryan
MARKETING MANAGER	Rebecca Hope
SENIOR PRODUCTION EDITOR	Kelly Tavares
COVER DESIGN	David Levy
INTERIOR DESIGN	Nancy Field
ILLUSTRATION EDITOR	Anna Melhorn

This book was set in Times Roman by Achorn Graphics and printed and bound by Hamilton Printing. The cover was printed by Lehigh Press.

This book is printed on acid-free paper. ∞

Library of Congress Cataloging in Publication Data:
Hempel, George H.
 Bank management : text and cases. — 5th ed. / George H. Hempel,
Donald G. Simonson.
  p. cm.
 Includes index.
 ISBN 0-471-16960-9 (cloth : alk. paper)
 1. Bank management. 2. Bank Management—Case studies.
I. Simonson, Donald G. II. Title.
HG1615.H45 1998
332.1'068—dc21

98-28268
CIP

ISBN 0-471-16960-9

Printed in the United States of America

10 9 8 7 6 5 4

Preface

The evolution in the principles of managing financial institutions has been dramatic. It was not very long ago that all but the large money market institutions could rely on comfortable homilies about banking a loyal, geographically bound customer base. They could take for granted a certain funding base of depositors who had few other outlets for their money and of local credit customers who depended on them as their singular banking connection. The greatest change has been the way that competitive and financial market forces have penetrated into customer relationships. Scarcely any significant banking transactions take place without the need to assess actual or potential competition. Thanks to the rapid spread of nationwide banking, managers in previously isolated local markets now contend with national, as much as local, competition. Furthermore, managers are aware that they must understand and adapt to the influence of an efficient financial market, and they must test their local transactions against pricing signals generated by the market. Changes in the financial markets themselves have been equally dramatic. Phenomena like financial restructuring, a stream of innovative new financial instruments, and derivative markets that create opportunities to redistribute risk challenge the adaptivity of managers. Banks find that problem solving using entrenched rote procedures or depending on the knowledge and character of a dominant CEO is no longer adequate. Problem solving has become more analytical and informed by financial markets and modern financial theory.

In turn, these developments are forcing a dramatic evolution in the teaching of the financial management of financial institutions. At one time, some instructors taught this subject as an exclusively situation-based one. The concept was that you could deduce good management practice on a case-by-case basis, studying a mix of situations that presented themselves to managers in rich institutional settings. Well-conceived cases called for students to apply sound logic in the preparation of creative solutions. When cumulated, enough such case situations certainly helped to round out students. But it was not sufficient.

To be sure, contextual learning cannot be abandoned in a predominantly institutional course. Missing, however, are analytical and theoretical devices to unify the series of institutional topics. In this book our aim is not to ignore the institutional setting of banking but to present it in a framework that recognizes the vast bridge to financial markets and theory that has developed quite recently. These developments provide a great opportunity for teachers to enhance their courses of study with powerful intuitions. The fifth edition of *Bank Management: Text and Cases* is committed to bringing this opportunity to fulfillment.

WHO WILL PROFIT FROM USING THE BOOK?

This book uniquely appeals to undergraduate and graduate courses in financial institution management as well as seminars for practicing bankers. At universities, it is helpful for students using the book to have completed the introductory course in finance at either the graduate or undergraduate level, along with the usual supporting courses in accounting, statistics, and economics. However, students without a complete formal exposure to these background courses can still succeed, for we introduce the fundamentals of topics that would ordinarily be built from these supporting courses. The book is appropriate for elective courses that qualify for majors or concentrations in finance, accounting, and general management. Professionals have used the materials for specialized study in a number of areas, including bank performance analysis, credit management, asset and liability management, and, recently, the fundamentals and applications of derivatives. Each of these areas is supported with lively case materials.

NEW IN THE FIFTH EDITION

In this edition, we continue to leverage the wisdom and insight offered in past editions of the book. As in earlier editions, we continue to explain the management of profit and risk in funding, lending, liquidity, capital, securities, and coordinated asset and liability activities. However, the fifth edition is extensively ''re-engineered'' to meet the needs of these rapidly changing subjects. The book now incorporates technical finance in five new chapters and appendices. The following lists some of the most extensive changes in scope and topics.

- A new Chapter 4 provides a thorough introduction to valuation in banking based on fixed-income and business finance theory.
- A new Chapter 5 extends and carefully paces the analysis of asset and liability management, with emphasis on insights about its interaction with yield curve behavior. We also emphasize basis risk.
- Chapters 13, 14, and 15 present the complete analytics of forwards, futures, options (especially option-like banking products), and interest rate swaps and the markets in which these instruments trade. We integrate derivative products into bank hedging and product pricing.
- Technical appendices to the five new chapters with banking applications provide potential for attractive and challenging graduate student projects.
- The number of chapters on credit has been reduced from four to three: these chapters now are based on a unifying model that clarifies the structure and stepwise management of bank credit risk.
- The number of cases has been reduced from 27 to 20 select cases in this edition:

these include several classic cases from prior editions and seven completely new cases. Several of the new cases present inside looks at actual applications of derivatives to manage banking products, balance sheet structure, and currency risk.

- A rich collection of end-of-chapter problems has been added: most of these are student-tested computational problems that encourage students to learn-by-doing applications of principles articulated in the chapter.

- A more student-friendly format has been added in which many chapters now incorporate frequent ''vignette'' examples to reinforce the significance of text discussions.

STRATEGY OF THE BOOK

This revision has been written to provide considerable instructional flexibility. Our experience with many instructors of bank management indicates that they use a variety of routes to achieve successful student learning. This has led us to conclude that a book on the management of financial institutions should include elements of business financial theory along with the practical institutional material that distinguishes financial businesses from nonfinancial ones. Instructors who emphasize practical and traditional information will find as strong a support base in the book as instructors who emphasize the applicability of financial principles to financial institutions.

If a book without analytical rigor is insufficient, neither is a book sufficient that excludes practical content. Our experience indicates that students emerging from introductory courses in finance and accounting sometimes assume that the nature of these subjects is merely computational. Using end-of-chapter problems and case exercises, we seek to raise computation to a higher level that requires inference. In the absence of practical background materials, it is difficult to infer what is going on at the institutional level.

Similarly, the book offers flexibility in the level of analytical rigor. The chapters on value, asset and liability management, forwards and futures, options, and swaps all progress from patient introductions of fundamentals to more challenging applications and, finally, to appendices that contain advanced and often rigorous concepts and applications that appeal to graduate finance students. These include topics such as deriving risk premiums through strip curve interpolation, using convexity measurement, detailing loan pricing from Eurodollar strips, using binomial option models to find prices for option-embedded banking products, pricing swaps off of the futures market, inferring swap pricing from the swap curve, and comparing various currency hedging techniques.

The purpose of this book is to present the concepts and techniques that will help bank managers be successful in this challenging period. This book is based on thoroughly updated and comprehensive text materials, new sets of end-of-chapter exercises to reinforce the learning of key points in chapters, and a complement of 20 well-researched cases. This opening chapter presents an introduction to the changing nature of bank management. The remainder of the text is divided into four parts. In the first part, Chapters 2 through 5, we deal with basic materials on the changing nature of banking, measuring bank performance, and the market foundations of value in banking. Chapter 2 familiarizes the reader with the balance sheets and income statements of financial institutions, and with special banking nuances such as accounting for loan losses, sources and uses of funds, ''gap'' repricing schedules, off-balance sheet items, banking risks, and risk-return tradeoffs. Chapter 3 provides tools for evaluating banks' financial performance, including enhancements to risk and return measures discussed in the preceding chapter. We analyze Uniform Bank Performance Reports as the crucial performance report card available on every banking firm. Chapter 4 lays out the theory drawn from financial markets for understanding how value is created in financial firms and discusses how banks create value as nominal contractors. It focuses on the time value of money to demonstrate how sensitivity to the interest rate environment affects values in banking. Chapter 5 reviews how banks control earnings exposure to financial markets, integrates the theory of the term structure of interest rates with asset and liability gap strategies and shows how markets inform banks about risk premiums.

Part Two, Chapters 6 to 9, covers many of the key elements of bank asset, liability, and capital management. Chapter 6 discusses such topics as deposit and borrowing sources of funding, effects of the growing funding spread, effects of size and type of bank on the funding decision, risks associated with funding decisions, contingency funding, and strategies for attracting funds in the ever changing money markets. It also includes a section on measuring and using the cost of funds. Chapter 7 discusses the calculation of reserve requirements and how banks apply corporate cash management principles to manage reserves. It reviews how a bank measures and manages its liquidity needs. Chapter 8 covers the management of bank security portfolios. The chapter starts with a description of traditional and newly evolving securities that banks may own and discusses how such securities are priced. The dynamics of security valuations are examined, followed by a discussion of such topics as how a bank should inventory its investment needs, formulate investment policies, and develop investment strategies. Chapter 9 covers the purposes of bank capital, methods of appraising capital adequacy, allocation of capital to product lines, determination of total capital needs, and implications of risk-based capital requirements.

Part Three, Chapters 10 through 12, discusses the lending function of commercial banks in considerable detail. Chapter 10 presents the structure of credit risk in banks and how a bank should organize to manage the risk of credit operations to minimize losses within the constraints of policy and regulation. In Chapter 11, we examine the fundamentals of managing credit selection risk and underwriting risk, including creating loan agreements, monitoring loan performance, and pricing and rating loans. The chapter culminates in a discussion of loan portfolio risk management, namely, managing intrinsic and concentration risks. Chapter 12 focuses on consumer and real estate lending, including management of loan selection risk. A special section covers types of loans and regulatory provisions that affect consumer lending.

Part Four, Chapters 13 through 15, presents a thorough and innovative treatment of the derivative models and products used and sold by banks. Specific uses of derivatives in bank pricing, bank risk reduction, and customer accounts are demonstrated throughout this material. Chapter 13 covers the fundamentals of forward and futures contracts and hedging and pricing rules. It covers situations of riskless arbitrage; micro-anticipatory hedges; strip hedges of fixed rate loans; and macro hedging the duration gap with Eurodollar and Treasury bond futures. In Chapter 14, we present the fundamentals of exchange-traded and OTC options. Topics include hedging bank portfolios, pricing product optionality, pricing fixed-rate loan commitments, standby letters of credit, and loan portfolio insurance. We evaluate swaps in Chapter 15. Areas covered include hedging with plain vanilla swaps, arbitrage-free swap pricing using Eurodollar swaps, the swap curve, basis swaps, and pros and cons of swaps versus futures.

Chapter 16 discusses the increasing importance of global banking for banks and for the world economy, and covers international banking activities in foreign exchange, interbank deposits, swaps, and other markets. A special section presents the use of derivative securities in currency hedging.

ACKNOWLEDGMENTS

We are grateful for the interest of those who have used past editions of this book. We are indebted to bankers and professors who have provided their expertise and experience to comment on its development. We believe this edition will honor the bond we have enjoyed with past users. In addition, we hope the book reaches a new wave of users who are alert to the pervasive influence that the remarkable developments in financial markets is having on bank management.

This book has a rich legacy. Its origins go back to one of the first widely used casebooks in financial institutions management developed in the early 1960s by the late Alex Robichek and Alan Coleman. Alan contributed a great deal to the success of earlier editions of this book. The text component of the book has its roots in the successful book developed by the late Howard Crosse of the now-defunct Franklin National Bank in the early 1970s. Subsequently, George Hempel teamed with Howard to produce a widely used successor text. George, Alan and I collaborated for many years in the launching and maturation of *Bank Management: Text and Cases* through four editions. While the fifth edition benefited from George's intellectual energy, he was unable to participate in its completion owing to health reasons and his untimely death.

George appreciated and I continue to appreciate the special interest and support of colleagues at Southern Methodist University and the University of New Mexico. For many years, we both benefited from the work, spirit and friendship of Kay McKee, the Southwestern Graduate School of Banking, who provided support in typing and organizing past editions.

Finally, I thank Marsha for her patience and grace in the making of this fifth edition.

Donald G. Simonson
Anderson Schools of Management
University of New Mexico
Albuquerque, New Mexico 87131

September, 1998

DEDICATION

The fifth edition is dedicated to George Hempel and his wife, Elaine Hempel. George H. Hempel died in June 1998. His contributions to the development of learning in banking are well known. Hundreds of scholars and bankers and thousands of students have been lifted through association with George as a scholar, teacher and complete human being.

"Nature sustains itself through three precious principles, which one does well to embrace and follow. These are gentleness, frugality and humility. When one is gentle, he has no fear of retaliation. When one is frugal, he can afford to be generous. When one is humble, no one challenges his leadership."

Lao Tzu, *Tao Teh King*

Contents

PART ONE

MEASUREMENT, ANALYSIS AND THEORY OF VALUE CREATION	1

CHAPTER 1

The Changing Nature of Banking in the U.S.   3

Role of Commercial Banking in the U.S. Economy   3
Historical Background: Current Regulation and Structure   6
Resulting Bank Regulation in the United States   21
Resulting Banking Structure   24
An Approach to Bank Management in This Challenging Environment   31
Discussion Questions   31

CHAPTER 2

Understanding a Bank's Financial Statements   35

Understanding a Bank's Balance Sheet   35
Understanding a Bank's Income Statement   41
Supplementary Information   44
Data for a Typical Bank?   47
An Introduction to Loan Loss Accounting   47

Off-Balance Sheet Information   48
Nonfinancial Information   51
Sources and Quality of Information   51
End of Chapter Problems   54

CHAPTER **3**

Evaluating a Bank's Returns, Risks and Overall Performance   58

Using Basic Ideas from Business Finance   58
Key Return and Risk Measures for a Sample Bank   63
Return-Risk Trade-Offs   69
Analysis of Key Return-Risk Trade-Offs   74
Comprehensive Ratio Analysis for Financial Firms   77
The Components of Net Interest Margin   87
Improving Risk Measurement and Management   91
The Appropriate Trade-Off Between Risks and Return   94
Uniform Bank Performance Reports   96
End of Chapter Problems   97

CHAPTER **4**

Foundations of Value in Banking   103

Banks Enter ''Nominal Contracts''   104
Time Value of Money and Interest Rate Sensitivity   104
Balance Sheet Maturity Mismatching   107
Measuring Interest Rate Sensitivity: Duration   111
Arithmetic Calculation of Duration   113
The Duration Gap   115
Using Convexity to Modify Duration Analysis   118
Yield to Maturity   119
Summary and Conclusions   121
End of Chapter Problems   122

Appendix 4A: *Combining Convexity and Duration Estimates of Price Change*   126
End of Appendix Problems   128

CHAPTER **5**

Asset and Liability Management and the Yield Curve   129

Managing with Discount Rate Expectations   130
Gap Management   134
Gap Management and Basis Risk   138

Simulation Systems   138

Gap Strategies and Interest Rate Benchmarking   141

Summary and Conclusions   144

End of Chapter Problems   145

Appendix 5A: *Theories of the Term Structure of Interest Rates*   148

Interest Rate Expectations   148

Liquidity Premium Theory   150

Market Segmentation and Preferred Habitat Theories   151

Appendix 5B: *Risk Premiums and the Term Structure*   152

Bootstrapping   153

Yield Curve Interpolation   153

End of Appendix Problems   156

Case 1 First National Bank   157

Case 2 Lincoln National Bank   173

Case 3 Quaker National Bank   183

Case 4 Peralta National Bank   191

Case 5 Norwest Corporation   200

PART TWO

Asset, Liability, and Capital Decisions   207

CHAPTER 6
The Acquisition and Cost of Bank Funds   209

Types and Changing Composition of Deposits   209

Types and Composition of Borrowed Bank Funds   214

The Funding Spread as a Source of Profitability   216

Funding Availability and Strategy for Different Types of Banks   217

Measuring and Using the Cost of Funds   219

Using Cost-of-Funds Measures   228

Risks Associated with Raising Funds   230

Introduction to Basic Funding Strategies   233

CHAPTER 7
Measuring and Providing Reserves and Liquidity   242

Determining A Bank's Reserve Needs   242

Meeting Required Reserves and Managing the Money Position   246

Measuring a Bank's Liquidity Needs   253

Filling a Bank's Liquidity Needs   262

Matching Liquidity Sources to Liquidity Needs   264

Meeting Contingency and Future Liquidity Needs   268
End of Chapter Problems   270

CHAPTER **8**

Managing the Security Portfolio   274

Asset Priority Model   274
Portfolio Objectives   275
Debt Instruments   277
Managing the Security Portfolio   286
Total Return: Trading and Swapping Bonds   293
Accounting Classification of Securities   296
Portfolio Management and Business Cycles   298
Evaluating Securities with Uncertain Cash Flows   303
Implementing Investment Policies and Strategies   303
Summary   304
End of Chapter Problems   305

Appendix 8A: *Alternative Investment Instruments Used by Banks*   307

CHAPTER **9**

Managing Bank Capital   322

Determining Capital Adequacy   322
Managing Capital and Lines of Business   331
Sustainable Internal Growth   339
Raising Capital Externally   343
End of Chapter Problems   354

Appendix 9A: *A Process for Planning Financial Needs*   356

Case 6 Shawnee National Bank   360
Case 7A Hillside Bancorp (A)   368
Case 7B Hillside Bancorp (B)   376
Case 8 Aspict Bankshares Corporation   379

PART THREE

MANAGING LOANS AND THE LOAN PORTFOLIO   387

CHAPTER **10**

The Bank Credit Organization   389

Loan Risks and Losses   390
Managing Credit Risk   391

The Credit Organization   394
Loan Committees and the Loan Approval Process   395
Loan Policy and Procedures Formulation   397
Controlling Loan Losses   403
Pricing Policy   409
Unethical Conduct and Conflicts of Interest   409
Common Reasons for Loan Losses   409
Legal and Regulatory Controls on Lending   410
Summary   414
End of Chapter Problems   415

Appendix 10A: *Are Bank Loans Competitive?*   416

CHAPTER **11**
Credit Selection, Underwriting and Portfolio Diversification   418

Selection Risk Analysis   418
Covenants and Pricing   423
Risk Rating and Monitoring   429
Managing Portfolio Risk   431
Types of Loans   432
Loan Sales and Securitization   446
Summary   452
End of Chapter Problems   453

Appendix 11A: *Financial Ratio and Credit Selection Analysis*   455
Appendix 11B: *Bases for Loan Pricing*   473

CHAPTER **12**
Consumer Lending   475

Commercial Bank Consumer Credit   476
Automobile Lending   477
Revolving Credit   478
Home Equity Credit   478
Mobile Home Financing   479
Securitization of Consumer Loans   479
Interest Charge Considerations   480
Credit Analysis in Consumer Lending   482
Credit Evaluation Systems   486
Reporting the Credit Decision   490
Banks and Credit Card Finance   491
Real Estate Loans   494
Consumer Loan Losses and the Bankruptcy Code   500

Bankruptcy Reform   501

Criticism and Reform of the 1978 Bankruptcy Code   502

Consumer Regulation and Compliance   503

Summary   505

End of Chapter Problems   506

Case 9 Lobo Mill Products Company   507

Case 10 Questor Inc.   509

Case 11 Global Machinery and Metals Compnay, Inc.   513

Case 12 Bergner Construction Company   517

Case 13 Calbank Leasing Corporation   522

Case 14 Edward Edwards Company (A)   529

PART FOUR

HEDGING AND PRICING WITH DERIVATIVES AND INTERNATIONAL BANKING   533

CHAPTER **13**

Financial Futures and Forwards: Hedging and Pricing   535

Overview of Derivatives   535

The Basics and Forwards of Futures Contracts   537

Forward Prices   541

Microhedging   544

Macrohedging   550

Foreign Exchange Forwards and Futures   555

Summary   556

End of Chapter Problems   557

CHAPTER **14**

Interest Rate Options: Hedging and Pricing   559

Option Basics   560

Exchange-Traded Interest Rate Options   563

Hedging a Bond Portfolio   565

Options Pricing Models   566

Interest Rate Options   568

Caps, Floors, and Collars   573

Other Contingent Claims Products   575

Summary   582

End of Chapter Problems   582

Appendix 14A: *Black-Scholes Model and Put-Call Parity*   586

CHAPTER **15**
Interest Rate Swaps: Hedging and Pricing   **588**

The Basics of Interest Rate Swaps   589
Basis Swaps   592
Swaps, FRAs and Futures   594
Swap Pricing   597
Summary   600
End of Chapter Problems   601

Appendix 15A: *Adjusting the Swap Rate for Convexity*   604
Appendix 15B: *The Swap Curve*   606

CHAPTER **16**
International Banking   **609**

Bank Foreign Exchange (FX) Risk Management   610
Foreign Exchange Rates   611
Interest Rate Parity   618
Structure of the Foreign Exchange Market   620
The Eurocurrency Markets   621
Bank Financial Management in a Foreign Environment   622
International Loans   624
International Lending by U.S. Banks   628
Legal Forms of International Banking Organizations   628
Summary   630
End of Chapter Problems   631

Case 15 Edward Edwards Company (B)   633
Case 16 KeyCorp   635
Case 17 Region Financial Corporation   641
Case 18 City Federal Savings and Loan Association   649
Case 19 Grantland Bank   658

Index   671

PART ONE

MEASUREMENT, ANALYSIS, AND THEORY OF VALUE CREATION

Chapters 2 through 5 in this part of the book present the accounting and financial principles needed to undertake a serious study of the functioning and management of financial institutions. Chapter 2 explains the structure and rationale underlying the balance sheets and income statements of financial institutions. This chapter untangles crucial but less understood banking nuances such as accounting for loan losses, sources and uses of funds, repricing or gap schedules, off-balance sheet items, banking risks, and risk-return trade-offs. Chapter 3 provides tools for analyzing and critiquing a bank's financial performance, including enhancements to risk and return measures discussed in Chapter 2. We analyze Uniform Bank Performance Reports as the crucial performance report card available on every banking firm. Chapter 4 lays out the conceptual foundations of financial theory drawn from business finance and from financial markets. Central to this topic is value creation in financial firms. It focuses on the time value of money to demonstrate how sensitivity to the interest rate environment affects values in banking. Chapter 5 reviews how banks control earnings exposure to financial markets, integrates the theory of the term structure of interest rates with asset and liability gap strategies, and shows how markets inform banks about risk premiums. ■

The Changing Nature of Banking in the United States

There is no question about it: The management of a commercial bank has become increasingly challenging. Views on the appropriate managerial attitudes and techniques of just a decade or so ago are dramatically different. Managers of only two decades ago find today's banking environment and management attitudes strange and unfamiliar. The markets that banks tap for money have changed dramatically. Many old regulatory protections and outdated restrictions on the geographic scope and product offerings of banks have almost disappeared. The new banking business relies on electronic delivery of its products and services, supported by information systems and telecommunications. To traditional bank managers, the increasing complexities of banking are worrisome. To many others, however, modern complexities present opportunities to be rewarded by innovative management. This book will give both active and aspiring bank managers insight into concepts and techniques for this dynamic period in the venerable history of the banking profession.

By focusing on the macro-banking environment, this introductory chapter differs from the remainder of the text. Hereafter, we emphasize the micro-financial concepts and techniques that are found most effective in managing financial institutions. The present chapter briefly discusses the economic role of commercial banks and historical events leading to the unique and sometimes puzzling regulatory and banking structure in the United States. Then we present an overview of the current regulation of banks in the United States and today's banking structure. We conclude with an outline of the primary topics covered in this book.

ROLE OF COMMERCIAL BANKING IN THE U.S. ECONOMY

You can begin to understand the critical roles of financial intermediaries by looking at the flow of money in the U.S. economy.[1] Figure 1.1 shows the three ways that the flows

[1] The economic role of financial intermediaries is discussed in greater depth in *Two Faces of Debt* (Federal Reserve Bank of Chicago, 1994) and George H. Hempel and Jess B. Yawitz, *Financial Management of Financial Institutions* (Upper Saddle River, N.J.: Prentice-Hall, 1977).

FIGURE 1.1   Simplified graph of financial flows in the U.S. economy

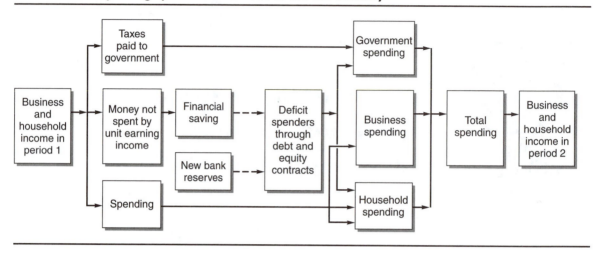

of income to businesses and households for a period can be used. First, a part of this income is taxed by government units. Then, the remaining "disposable" amount is either spent or saved (invested) by the unit earning the income. Thus all income is used up in the form of taxes, spending, or saving. Taxes are paid to governments and the governments spend them. The spending of governments becomes part of the total spending that finds its way into income received by businesses and households in the next period. As businesses and households spend their income, the money spent provides still other businesses and households with income in the following period. By not spending all of their income, some of these units become "surplus" units who, as savers, lend out their unspent funds for various periods of time to "deficit" units that want to spend more than they earned. As deficit-spending governments, businesses, and households acquire borrowed funds, they quickly use them, returning them to the spending stream.

Some of the transfers of funds from surplus units to deficit users of funds might be accomplished directly with no middleman—that is, through direct transactions between a single surplus unit and a deficit unit. However, as you might imagine, it is an unlikely coincidence that the different transaction requirements of two individual units can be matched as to the amount, maturity, legal character, marketability, liquidity, divisibility, redeemability, and risk of the transactions. For example, a person may have just a small amount of funds and may only want an asset with short maturity that she will be able to convert to cash easily. On the other hand, the person she proposes to lend to may desire a large amount of funds for a long period of time, with the assurance that he will not have to pay the money back for a long period of time.

The difficulties of matching these two persons' specific transaction requirements are avoided by creating two alternative types of channels for moving funds from savers to borrowers. The two channels are *open financial markets* and *financial intermediaries*. For open financial markets to work, there must be a large number of deficit units, each of whom requires large amounts of funds. Facilitators called brokers and dealers create and issue standardized debt or equity contracts for these units and distribute them to investors

FIGURE 1.2   The intermediation process

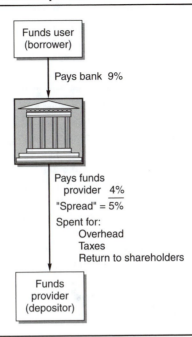

in open financial markets. The liquidity and marketability of such securities are vastly enhanced by the existence of *secondary markets* (e.g., the New York Stock Exchange) for trading securities. Deep and liquid financial markets allocate funds in an economy on the basis of the issuers' profitability and ability to pay and are vital for encouraging economic efficiency.

Financial intermediaries come into play when the requirements and characteristics of savers and borrowers are specialized or when they require specialized services.[2] Financial intermediaries create two "submarkets" to facilitate the flow of funds between savers and borrowers (see Figure 1.2). In one type of submarket, intermediaries acquire assets by purchasing primary securities directly from borrowers (for example, loans); in the second submarket, they sell their own liabilities (for example, deposits) to saving units. In this way, a financial intermediary is able to tailor its asset and liability structure to satisfy the desires of both the ultimate borrowers and ultimate lenders in the economy. By holding diversified portfolios of assets, intermediaries are able to reduce the risk to surplus unit customers (depositors) beyond the ability of these customers to diversify their holdings and reduce the risk on their own. Intermediaries also assist borrowers to obtain funds in amounts and forms they could not duplicate on their own.

Thus, in a highly developed financial system like the U.S. system, savers/investors

---

[2] Brokers or agents are also institutions that serve as go-betweens and receive commissions for their services. Typically, they do not hold financial assets for a long period themselves. Their services help match surplus and deficit units but do not overcome the differences that may exist between surplus and deficit units.

can choose among a wide variety of alternative financial assets, including buying the primary securities of deficit units in open financial markets or, alternatively, selecting among numerous types of liabilities offered by financial intermediaries. In addition, borrowers can usually get purchasing power in the form they desire, either by raising funds en masse from savers/investors in open markets or, when they require specialized credit services, by contracting with a financial intermediary. The resulting efficiencies stimulate both capital accumulation and economic growth.

Of all the many kinds of financial intermediaries—insurance companies, pension funds, mutual funds, and others—commercial banks conduct the largest share of financial intermediation in the U.S. economy. Bank assets are predominantly financial and consist of contracts for future payments owed to them by borrowers such as households, nonfinancial businesses, and governments. Commercial banks issue contractual obligations in the form of deposits or borrowed money to obtain funds for purchasing their financial assets. A bank raises capital by selling stock or by accumulating retained earnings. Capital represents a relatively minor source of funds but is vital for supporting the bank's risk-taking.

The role of banking can, therefore, be stated very simply: Banks fill the diverse desires of both the ultimate borrowers and lenders in our economy. They compete with other banks, other financial intermediaries, and open financial market transactions. In general, they compete with any other entity that also pursues the goals of fulfilling diverse financial desires of surplus and deficit units. Banks succeed in this competition only if they perform their intermediation role as well as, and hopefully better than, other institutions.

Competing Successfully

Financial intermediation starts with raising funds by issuing financial obligations that promise to pay interest or to provide services to funds providers (surplus units). Then, they pool the funds and convert them into loans that can be sold, along with other services, to funds users (deficit units) who pay interest in return. In addition to intermediating funds, intermediaries provide nonmonetary services to both types of customers (funds providers and funds users) in order to enhance the appeal of doing business with them. In conducting this apparently simple process, however, financial intermediaries incur large overhead expenses that they must recover from their customers.

Figure 1.2 depicts a bank that pays its depositors 4 percent and earns 9 percent from its borrowers, apparently pocketing the 5 percent difference called the "spread." However, if you think about it, you can see that the spread represents an expense that is unique to doing business with financial intermediaries. In contrast, transactions in open financial markets cost only a small fraction of this amount. You might say that the 5 percent spread cost of intermediation amounts to a "tax" on transactions conducted through banks which does not exist in transactions in open financial markets. In our example, we need to ask where the 5 percent difference goes. Obviously, the bank does not pocket it in petty cash. Rather, the bank uses it to pay skilled employees, as well as the expenses of supplies, computers, furnishings, and occupying physical facilities; to pay legal tax obligations; and, certainly not least, to pay a competitive return to its investors.

How the bank spends this 5 percent intermediation "tax" is of little consequence to potential bank customers. Of greater consequence to customers is that, as a group, bank transactions cost considerably more than the minimal cost transactions in open financial markets. This cost differential is a fundamental challenge to managers of financial intermediaries. Managers ought to expect their customers in aggregate to ask the question: "Why should we pay the middleman expenses passed along to us by financial intermediaries, while transactions costs in open financial markets are nearly zero?" In substance, bank customers demand to know "what's in it for us?" Intermediaries have to justify their higher cost of doing business in order to justify their existence.

Intermediaries survive, despite their higher costs, because they create value for their customers. Savers benefit from intermediaries' liquid "on demand" payments services (examples are checking and wire transfers of funds) as well as low risk or riskless (due to deposit insurance) investment services. They also benefit because financial intermediaries capture and organize information on the payments and investments needs of savers/depositors to develop additional valuable services. Borrowers benefit because intermediaries analyze their needs for funds, qualify them as creditworthy, and extend them credit. Credit services are based on the skills of collecting and organizing information about potential borrowers. Intermediaries use this information to screen and analyze borrowers, structure credits suitable for their means, monitor their ongoing debt payment ability, and, finally, to re-tailor credit arrangements if borrowers' financial circumstances deteriorate.

Credit services are especially valuable to those units that cannot qualify for open financial market credit. Financial markets are not able to gather and process detailed information necessary to conduct small-size credit transactions. In addition, research suggests that banks *certify* the financial strength of borrowers that primarily use open markets. The bank connection serves to confirm such borrowers' financial reputations. Finally, all users benefit from the special role financial intermediaries, and especially banks, play in creating new money. The loans and deposits created by banks add to the total amount of money in the system.

In short, the expenses of intermediated financial transactions must be justified by the value added for services provided to customers; in essence, the 5 percent spread in the above example must be paid back in the form of valuable services to all classes of customers. The bank in the example cannot pass along a 5 percent "tax" to its customers if its customers do not perceive that the bank services are worth it. The bank must create at least 5 percent worth of value for customers. If it does not, it must (1) reduce its costs and become more efficient, or (2) accept a lower return for its shareholders, or (3) offer a level of service that justifies the expense. The more the bank's services compete with transactions that are feasible for open financial markets where expenses are minimal, the less it can charge for such services.

To be sure, the need to produce customer added value has a positive side. If the bank offers a level of service or creates unique services that produce a high degree of added value for its customers, a 5 percent spread may be too little. Customers may place a higher value on the services of a dynamic intermediary and a higher spread (profit) may be justified! For example, an intermediary might make an especially faithful commitment to understanding a business borrower's needs and to supporting the borrower under uncertain future conditions. This institution is entitled to a higher interest rate on its loans than an intermediary with a lesser commitment. In the end, value is created by intermediaries' employees. In the coming banking environment, the value added concept increasingly will be applied to employees who will be compensated in line with the value they create for their customers.

The difficulty of successfully performing the financial intermediation role does not end with satisfying the needs of customers. Intermediaries must also balance the requirements of bank owners and bank regulators. As noted in the earlier example, there must be an adequate difference between what the bank earns from funds users and what it pays funds providers for the funds (plus overhead costs) in order for it to make an acceptable profit. As if keeping surplus units, deficit units, and owners satisfied is not enough, bank management must also be concerned with a fourth group, bank regulators. In general terms, regulators are interested in limiting the risks a bank takes in obtaining and employing funds. Limiting risks, however, limits banks' abilities to pay a high return on deposits, to lend at low costs, and to earn an adequate spread between these two factors to satisfy the returns shareholders expect. In a competitive environment, a bank management that can keep these four economic groups satisfied has done a remarkable job.

HISTORICAL BACKGROUND: CURRENT REGULATION AND STRUCTURE

The history of the regulation and structure of commercial banks in the United States offers a lesson in the central issues of banking systems.[3] For background on these issues, we briefly describe historical events that have led to the current (1999) regulation and banking structure. Available data on the number of banks and total banking assets in the United States in selected years from 1811 through 1997 are summarized in Table 1.1.

Experimentation in a Young Nation

Upon achieving its independence, the United States set about to reduce its dependence on banks domiciled in other countries. The new government relegated the chartering and control of banks to state governments. The states generally permitted banks to branch within the chartering state and allowed them to issue bank notes. Such notes comprised a substantial part of the early monetary supply of the United States.

In 1791, Congress established the First Bank of the United States and granted it a 20-year charter. This government-owned bank was formed to add credibility to the bank notes used as currency. It was authorized to branch in all states and to compete with the previously chartered state banks. The bank failed to extend sufficient credit (make loans), however, and concern in Congress about centralizing financial power in the bank led Congress to allow the First Bank's charter to expire in 1811. The bank's assets and liabilities were assigned to existing and newly chartered state banks. The state banks were generally poorly managed, and they permitted an excessively rapid expansion of credit and bank notes. A crisis ensued when a faltering economy precipitated numerous bank failures. As a result of this crisis, the Congress created the Second Bank of the United States in 1816, again with a 20-year charter, to restore confidence and safety in the U.S. banking system. As before, this Second Bank could branch throughout the country and compete, with many special advantages, with state banks. Also, the new Bank again centralized banking powers and restored conservative lending in a rapidly expanding nation. As re-

---

[3] The historical development of banks and bank regulation is covered in D. R. Dewey, *Financial History of the United States* (New York: Longman, 1934); Raymond W. Goldsmith, *Financial Intermediaries in the American Economy Since 1900* (Princeton, N.J.: Princeton University Press, 1958); Paul B. Trescott, *Financing American Enterprise* (New York: Harper & Row, 1963); H. R. Kroos and M. R. Blyn, *A History of Financial Institutions* (New York: Random House, 1971); and James L. Pierce, *The Future of Banking* (New Haven: Yale University Press, 1991).

TABLE 1.1   Number and Total Assets of Commercial Banks[a]

Year	Number of Banks	Total Assets (dollars in millons)
1811	88	$ 42
1820	307	103
1830	329	110
1866	1,391	1,673
1880	3,355	3,399
1900	13,053	11,388
1920	30,909	53,094
1930	24,273	74,290
1940	15,076	79,729
1950	14,676	179,165
1960	13,999	230,046
1970	14,199	518,220
1980	15,120	1,704,000
1981	15,213	1,781,700
1982	15,329	1,972,100
1983	15,380	2,113,100
1984	15,023	2,348,900
1985	14,797	2,581,600
1986	14,559	2,763,400
1987	13,987	2,998,300
1988	13,398	3,101,200
1989	12,816	3,283,900
1990[a]	12,343	3,389,500
1991	11,921	3,430,700
1992	11,462	3,505,700
1993	10,958	3,706,200
1994	10,450	4,010,500
1995	9,940	4,312,700
1996	9,528	4,578,300
1997	9,215	4,869,500

[a] Only insured commercial banks are included after 1990. In 1998, the number of uninsured banks was probably less than 60, with assets in all of these totaling less than $1 billion.

SOURCES: *The Statistical History of the United States from Colonial Times to the Present* (Stamford, Conn.: Fairfield Publishers, 1974); *Statistical Abstracts of the United States;* Board of Governors of the Federal Reserve System, Federal Reserve Bulletin, FDIC Quarterly Banking Profile.

sentment of the bank's powers arose in the hinterlands, however, Congress once again permitted the charter to expire in 1836. At this point, the United States reverted to a privately owned, state-chartered banking system.

Beginning Foundations—From the Civil War to the Depression

While a significant number of banking failures occurred in the later 1830s, Table 1.1 demonstrates that both the number and size of banks, all state-chartered at this time, increased sharply in the mid-1800s. The need to finance the Civil War led to passage of the *National Banking Act* in 1864. One clear intention of the Act was to force the larger banks in northern states to convert from state charters to national charters. The Congress granted national banks special tax advantages, but, in return for the favor, the banks had to buy government bonds. Since the National Banking Act, in what is known as the ''dual'' banking system, banks have been able to choose between a national banking charter and a state charter.

The period from the end of the Civil War through the early 1900s is known as the era of wildcat banking. Commercial banks controlled over 90 percent of all financial intermediation. It was easy for a new bank to enter the industry because national and state authorities tried to outdo one another in creating bank charters under their aegis. Just as entry was easy, it also was easy to exit the industry. More than 20 percent of the nation's banks failed in major financial panics of the mid-1870s and mid-1890s. Once banks met the chartering requirements, they faced little regulatory scrutiny. There was no central authority to regulate the growth of the money supply—primarily bank notes and the rapidly increasing demand deposit (checking) accounts—and the money supply expanded or collapsed depending on economic conditions and banks' willingness to lend.

A prosperous society forgave the banking foibles of this era because the real economy was growing at a brisk 6 percent annually. However, the great financial panic of 1907 produced severe banking turmoil and quickly exhausted the country's patience. In response to public outcry, an alarmed federal government appointed a task force to create a safer banking system for the nation. This initiative resulted in passage by the Congress of the *Federal Reserve Act of 1913*. This Act created the Federal Reserve System, a banker's bank with 12 district banks charged with setting reserve requirements for bank deposits, supplying emergency liquidity to its members, setting lending rates at which it would lend to its members, and controlling interest rates and the money supply. The Act required all national banks to become members of the Federal Reserve, while membership was made optional for state banks.

In its early years, the Federal Reserve was unsuccessful in realizing some of the Act's macroeconomic and banking objectives. Indeed, many historians believe that rather than stabilizing monetary growth and the economy, the Federal Reserve contributed to the economic downturn and eventual collapse of financial markets and institutions that began in 1929. Up to this time, U.S. banks exercised broad financial product powers akin to those of universal banks. Commercial banks dominated other financial intermediaries— they held over half of all intermediary assets and liabilities—and they formed holding companies and other banking groups to gain broad geographic and product influence.

Emphasis on Safety: From the Depression into the Early 1960s

For Americans used to modern banking conveniences, it is hard to imagine what banks were like between the early 1930s and 1960. Banks were highly restricted by rules and regulations passed by the U.S. Congress following the collapse of the banking system during the Great Depression of the 1930s. The Congress passed laws that largely cast banks as passive receptacles for local deposits and cautious dispensers of short-term business loans to local borrowers. Traumatized by the nation's financial collapse during the Great Depression, the Congress felt compelled to pass laws to enforce and perpetuate a conservative approach to banking.

Since the Depression, the computerization of information coupled with modern telecommunications has forced enormous changes on the financial services industry. Banks now compete on a national and worldwide scale. Instead of gathering local deposits, large banks tap financial resources from a vast pool of domestic and international funds through the global money markets. And rather than rely on short-term business lending, banks offer many types of loans and engage in investment banking, insurance, stock and bond brokerage, and leasing, and they securitize loans and sell them to other institutions.

Nevertheless, changes in the conservative 1930s New Deal legislation have been very gradual, and the legislation still controls important aspects of banking competition. To appreciate the purpose of the tough 1930s legislation, you need to understand how fractional reserve banking works. This aspect of traditional banking presents what is unquestionably the most basic of banking risks. In fractional reserve banking, banks acquire *demand* liabilities (transaction deposits), set aside a small fraction of them as *prudential reserves* to cover normal withdrawals, and then use the rest for illiquid loans. The risk comes into play when depositors lose confidence in banks' ability to accommodate them when they want to withdraw their funds.

If many depositors suddenly wanted their funds all at once, the bank would be forced to sell some of its loans. It follows that, to have confidence in a bank, one must have confidence that the bank can liquidate its loans or other assets on short notice. When depositors lost confidence in the quality and liquidity of banks' assets—as they did in the financial crisis of the late 1920s and early 1930s—they became panicky and withdrew their funds. To deal with depositor runs during the Depression years and to stem cash outflows, banks cut off lending and tried to get cash by selling off their existing loans. The pressures of selling loans and withholding new credit from borrowers plunged the financial markets into a self-perpetuating downward spiral.

As a result of the market's collapse, 9,600 banks failed between 1930 and 1933. President Roosevelt's first executive act upon taking office was to rush passage of the Emergency Banking Act through the Congress. Pursuant to this Act, passed on March 9, 1933, the nation's 17,000 banks were closed for a six-day "bank holiday." After six days 12,000 banks were reopened, but 2,000 were closed permanently and 3,000 more were opened at a later date. Over the ensuing two years, as part of the administration's *New Deal* initiatives, the Congress and the President passed legislation that created a *federal safety net* aimed at protecting the public by protecting banks:[4]

The main elements of this program were:

1. The Federal Deposit Insurance Acts of 1933 and 1934: these Acts created the Federal Deposit Insurance Corporation and the deposit insurance fund.

2. The Glass-Steagall Act of 1933: this Act separated investment banking from commercial banking, and, among other provisions, it placed restrictions on the payment of interest on deposits. It sheltered banks from competitive forces.

3. The Securities Exchange Acts of 1933 and 1934: these Acts created the Securities Exchange Commission and tightly regulated the issuance and trading of securities.

4. The Federal Reserve Act of 1935: this Act strengthened and centralized control

---

[4] In retrospect, many scholars challenge the wisdom underlying this flurry of legislation. For example, Charles W. Calomiris, "Deposit Insurance: Lessons from the Record," *Economic Perspectives,* Federal Reserve Bank of Chicago, May/June 1989, 10–30.

of the Federal Reserve in Washington, D.C., and ensured that the Fed would be a reliable source of liquidity to troubled banks.

Congress was greatly concerned about "overbanking" and "destructive competition" among banks. They intended that the safety net would support bank profitability and would protect banks from competition. The new legislation did this by sharply restricting the qualifications for bank charters, thus limiting the formation of new banks. It required national banks to observe the chartering and branching restrictions of the states in which they were established. Furthermore, it set ceilings on bank deposit interest rates, including the prohibition of interest on demand deposits, because Congress believed that interest rate competition for deposits compelled banks to seek high-risk loans to sustain their profits. (The Federal Reserve implemented interest rate ceilings under its *Regulation Q*.)

Congressional legislation also gave banks exclusive rights to checking accounts and gave them monopoly access to the Federal Reserve's check clearing facilities. In addition, banks received exclusive access to Federal Reserve discount loans and to federal insurance for deposits (along with the savings and loan associations). Ultimately, by design, this package of protective legislation isolated banks from the financial system with the aim of assuring they would be profitable. It sought to confine them to conservative and traditional banking. Congress meant for banks to be immune to market forces.

1960s' Erosion of New Deal Banking

The New Deal concept for the protection of banks seemed to work well for several decades. Bank failures were quite rare for 50 years afterward. However, the banks' protection from financial market forces began to be seriously compromised in the 1960s. In 1960, banks held about 40 percent of the system's assets and dominated the U.S. financial system. By 1998, this share declined to about 20 percent. The decline in banks' market share was caused by the evolution of an intensely competitive global financial environment and by a series of events that gradually defeated many of the 1930s reforms.

In 1962, City National Bank of New York City (now Citibank) made an important inroad into New Deal protections when it introduced the *negotiable certificate of deposit (NCD)*. This instrument created the opportunity for corporate money managers to invest their idle cash in large multimillion dollar Citibank deposits. The NCD was available in any fixed maturity from 14 days to one year. Citicorp and, soon, other money center banks, established a secondary market for these certificates to permit buyers to resell the certificates to other holders if they needed the funds before maturity.

The innovative NCD attracted a large volume of temporarily idle corporate funds, broke the large banks' exclusive dependence on deposits based on close customer relationships, and freed the banks to tap the open marketplace to fund their growth. In the process, however, it exposed banks to open market competition because large banks aggressively competed with one another for corporate funds that previously languished in noninterest-bearing deposit accounts at each other's banks.[5]

A high rate of inflation and volatile interest rates during the middle and late 1960s added mightily to the decline of bank dominance of the financial system. The fast pace of fiscal spending on social programs and the war in Viet Nam forced interest rates to

---

[5] Marcia Stigum, *The Money Market: Myth, Reality and Practice* (Homewood, Ill.: Dow Jones-Irwin, 1995).

rise sharply above regulatory ceilings on bank deposits in 1966 and again in 1969. Because of the interest rate ceilings, banks could not raise their deposit rates enough to keep up with escalating market interest rates. It appeared to some that the Federal Reserve's rate ceilings were part of the Fed's anti-inflation strategy to choke off banks' flow of credit to business in order to slow down the economy.

In a phenomenon known as *disintermediation,* depositors pulled funds out of banks in favor of higher yielding direct investments in financial markets. Short of funds, banks were forced to curtail lending to large corporate customers, creating a *"credit crunch."* Banks reneged on loan commitments and caused irreparable damage to their reputations as dependable conduits of credit for large corporate borrowers. Large corporate customers learned to bypass banks in favor of simpler and cheaper alternative credit in the commercial paper market. The new borrowing pressure of funds-starved corporations stimulated a 250 percent expansion of commercial paper between 1965 and 1969.

Driven by interest rate restrictions on their deposits, large banks for the first time became aware that they did not need to rely on depositors for growth but could sustain their own growth by raising funds throughout the world. The most significant funding alternatives were Eurodollars (deposit liabilities of U.S. banks that are held and exchanged in Europe and other foreign economies) and commercial paper issued through their holding companies. The Federal Reserve imposed restrictions on Eurodollars in the form of reserve requirements, but the Fed usually was a step behind the banks' latest funding innovations.

Finally, the Federal Reserve suspended interest rate ceilings on negotiable CDs in 1970.[6] This move presaged further liberalization of the antiquated 1930s' interest rate controls on deposits. Funding in national and international markets had an important side effect: Banks began to use their new experience and widening vision to generate loans on a large scale outside of their geographic market and traditional customer base.

In the meantime, banks effectively had obliterated many of the barriers the New Deal had set up to insulate banking from financial markets. Now, for example, banks whose asset quality was suspected of deterioration were exposed to the possibility of "silent" runs by the sophisticated investors who provided banks' *managed liabilities,* including negotiable CDs, Eurodollars, and commercial paper. Unlike traditional depositors, banks' new creditors were price sensitive and had no customer loyalty to individual banks.

Breakthrough in Information Production

The negotiable CD, created by Citibank to serve corporate money managers, pioneered the development of the field of corporate cash management. The NCD sensitized corporate treasurers to the prospect of earning attractive returns on previously idle funds and, in the end, accelerated the loss of bank corporate customers. Cash management techniques, assisted by the growing use of computers, diverted a huge volume of noninterest-bearing deposits out of banks and into higher earning short-term money market instruments.

By computerizing their loans and deposits, banks were better able to analyze their loan customers. They used computers to build large customer databases and to automate their lending activities. In addition, computers helped banks evaluate customers' creditworthiness by analyzing customers' deposit flows.

[6] Ibid.

But computerization also made banks more vulnerable to nonbank competition. In an earlier era, banks' exclusive systems of screening and monitoring loan applicants allowed them to monopolize privileged information on customers. This exclusive grip on customer information gave banks domination of the loan market.[7] However, nonbanks' access to computers reduced banks' control of information and weakened banks' dominant position as corporate lenders. Debt rating agencies learned to use computers to mobilize data on corporations and to rate them as issuers of commercial paper or fixed-income securities (corporate bonds). As a result, the commercial paper market and other direct sources of finance rapidly increased nonbanks' share of credit services. Banks lost their exclusive hold on information.

Continued Erosion of New Deal Legislation: Problems of the 1970s

The events of the 1960s and 1970s drove banks to search for new types of loans. Their share of large corporation lending was shrinking at the same time they were discovering new money market sources of funds. This left banks with large unused lending capacity. Fortunately or not, beginning in 1973 significant lending opportunities arose because of a dramatic increase in worldwide petroleum prices. Unexpectedly, the petroleum exporting nations raised petroleum prices and earned additional hundreds of billions of dollars. They deposited much of their windfall profits in large European and U.S. money center banks, flooding the banks with funds.

The banks quickly found they could recycle these funds back into the world economy by lending to eager businesses and governments in the less developed nations (LDCs). However, in their rush to invest these excess funds, banks failed to recognize and control the extraordinary risks of such loans. They did little to monitor the LDCs' sometimes corrupt and frequently ill-planned use of loan funds. Meanwhile, world interest rates rose rapidly in the late 1970s and drove interest charges above rates that LDCs were able to pay. As the 1970s closed, losses on LDC loans rose dramatically at U.S. money center banks.

Market forces and information technology next assaulted the banks' and thrift institutions' monopoly on consumer deposits. In the mid-1970s, Merrill Lynch made a major breakthrough by developing the computer technology for introducing the Cash Management Account (CMA). This product operated as a *money market mutual fund* (MMMF). The MMMFs offered consumers superior market rates of return on their money in contrast to Regulation Q-restricted savings and time deposit rates. Although the MMMFs were not insured, they invested savers' funds safely in short-term, low-risk government securities and high grade commercial paper. This innovation not only offered market-competitive returns, but it also permitted customers to write checks against investment shares they held in the account. Other brokerage firms copied the Merrill Lynch CMA and taught consumers that deposit-rate restricted banks could not compete with the MMMFs' earnings rates. Consumers quickly drew down their bank accounts.

As inflation and interest rates soared in 1979 and 1980, the deposit-rate disadvantage of banks and savings and loan associations (S&Ls) hindered their ability to compete with

---

[7] The significance of information in banking is explained in Eugene Fama, ''What's Different About Banks?'' *Journal of Monetary Economics* (June, 1985), 29–39.

money market mutual funds for money. The institutions lobbied Congress for relief from the Regulation Q restrictions. Regulation Q interest rate ceilings especially impacted the S&Ls because they depended on low-cost deposits to fund their assets which consisted primarily of low-earning long-term mortgages. Rising interest rates and the loss of deposits to the money market mutual funds drove the entire savings and loan industry underwater. Alarmed by the plight of banks and the S&Ls, Congress passed the *Depository Institutions Deregulation and Monetary Control Act of 1980* (DIDMCA) to modify the New Deal's legislated restrictions on deposit rates. DIDMCA mandated the staged dismantling of interest rate ceilings through 1985, authorized interest payments on NOW (*negotiable orders of withdrawal*) transactions accounts, and raised federal deposit insurance limits, previously $40,000 per account, to $100,000.[8]

High rates of inflation and interest persisted, however, and increased the threat to the savings and loan industry. A concerned Congress then passed the *Garn-St. Germain Act of 1982*. This Act accelerated the deregulation of interest on consumer deposits and authorized depository institutions to offer *money market deposit accounts* that bore market rates of interest competitive with MMMFs. In addition, the Act attempted to overcome the S&Ls' narrow dependence on real estate mortgages by expanding the thrifts' asset powers to permit limited investment in commercial loans, real estate development, and below investment-grade corporate securities popularly known as ''junk bonds.''[9]

1980s: The Thrift Industry Debacle[10]

In the early 1980s, the Congress's move to repeal key New Deal legislative restrictions on depository institutions coincided with the Reagan administration's efforts to deregulate business in general. Unfortunately, the sentiment behind this joint legislative and executive thrust proved to be extremely naive about the ''free lunch'' of federally insured deposits. The administration tried to reduce the examination staffs of thrift regulatory agencies, especially the now defunct Federal Home Loan Bank Board, just at a time when S&Ls needed the close attention of examiners to enforce their safety. For their part, regulators were reluctant to interfere with troubled S&Ls and hoped that, given enough time, they would regain profitability by undertaking high-risk project investments with high returns. To prop up troubled S&Ls, regulators devised unsound Regulatory Accounting Principles (RAP) accounting measures to create the appearance of sufficient capital where there was too little or no true capital.

In addition to lax regulation, other factors presaged disaster for the S&Ls. With interest rates on insured deposits now competitive with or exceeding rates on money market instruments and MMMFs, S&Ls easily attracted new funds. With easy access to funds, quite a few S&Ls became too aggressive. They channeled their unconstrained pools of insured deposits into high-risk investments in which they had no experience. These investments included land development and large-scale commercial real estate projects newly authorized under the Garn-St. Germain Act of 1982.

---

[8] One scholar estimated that the S&L industry was $150 billion underwater in 1980. See Edward J. Kane, *The Gathering Crisis in Federal Deposit Insurance* (Cambridge, Mass.: MIT Press, 1985).

[9] A summary is in Gillian Garcia et al., ''The Garn-St. Germain Depository Institutions Act of 1982,'' *Economic Perspectives,* Federal Reserve Bank of Chicago, 6 (April 1983), 3–31.

[10] An important source analyzing events surrounding the debacle is Lawrence J. White, *The S&L Debacle: Public Policy Lessons for Bank and Thrift Regulation* (New York: Oxford University Press, 1990).

In addition, investment bankers introduced *brokered deposits,* a new consumer investment device for funneling enormous sums into the S&Ls. Investment bankers packaged retail investments structured as portfolios of $100,000 certificates of deposit obtained from the S&Ls that paid the highest rates nationwide. Compared with the previous $40,000 insurance limit, placing funds at the $100,000 limit was a more economical size and made it feasible for the investment bankers to package and broker the CDs. The brokerage houses were able to sell shares in the CDs to their clients as fully insured and absolutely safe investments. The most aggressive S&Ls benefited most because, by paying above-market interest rates, it was easy for them to attract money from wide and far to invest in high-risk commercial real estate projects. Fully insured, the CD holders were indifferent to the risks taken by the S&Ls.

The combination of insured depositors, who channeled large sums of money to aggressive S&Ls, and the S&Ls' often extremely high-stakes investments and inadequate or indulgent regulators created a mountain of uncollectible loans and direct investments. Troubled S&Ls presented a *moral hazard* to regulators and taxpayers. Confronted with near certain failure, the managers of these S&Ls tended to ''gamble for restitution'' by investing heavily and desperately in improbable high-risk ventures. They hoped for a miraculous payoff, but, typically, their ventures turned into expensive failures. The managers' gambles were rational. The upside was a small chance of a success that would save their firms and well-paid positions. The downside was a likely failure at no cost to the managers: the costs would be absorbed by the federal deposit insurance funds of the Federal Savings and Loan Insurance Corporation (FSLIC) or, if insurance funds were depleted, the taxpayer.

By the late 1980s, widespread failures or consolidations with other institutions eliminated about two-thirds of the S&L industry. In time, resolutions of failed institutions consumed thrift deposit insurance funds and the FSLIC failed. It was not until the early 1990s that the Congress finally allocated funds to cover the remaining resolution costs, resulting in losses to taxpayers of between $200 and $300 billion.

1980s: Banking Problems

While the banks suffered from problems like those of the S&Ls, the effects of these problems were tempered by banks' asset diversification programs and a stronger tradition of commercial bank regulation. Nevertheless, bank failures rose to post-Depression record levels: from 1985 to 1992 there were 1,304 failures, or about 186 bank failures per year. In an earlier period, from 1934 to 1984, the nation had experienced only 756 bank failures, or about 15 per year.

The proximate cause of the failures was the banks' poorly conceived lending programs in an industry that generally had relaxed credit standards. Compromises in the quality of lending came about, first of all, because big banks had lost their primary business of lending to large corporations. To replace this business, the banks shifted into high-risk LDC loans and downscale loans to ''middle market'' borrowers. Smaller regional banks tended to meet this competition by reducing their own credit standards. In the late 1970s, as world petroleum prices soared, many banks pursued high-stakes lending to oil and gas field developers in the Southwest. In addition, the 1970s–early 1980s energy bubble and a liberal 1980 tax act that favored real estate developers spawned a great boom in commercial real estate development that was financed largely by banks. The ensuing collapse of oil prices in 1982 dried up the oil-exporting nations' cash flows and their ability to pay their large bank loans. These difficulties were signaled by the Mexican government's default on its huge bank debts, which severely impacted numerous large banks in the United States and Europe. The Mexican default, followed by Poland's default, led to a round of LDC debt postponements and the stretching out of their loan payments. The plunge in oil prices drove many oil and gas producers into bankruptcy and rendered their bank loans unpayable. The energy industry's crash, overbuilding, and the reversal of the real estate-favored provisions of the tax code in 1986 caused widespread failure of real estate development projects and a wave of defaults by developers on their bank loans.

The simultaneous effects of failed loans to LDCs, energy producers, and commercial real estate developers put U.S. banking under tremendous stress. In 1984, the Continental Illinois National Bank of Chicago, the tenth largest U.S. bank and a large money center bank, essentially failed. Continental's problems surfaced with the failure of the Penn Square Bank in Oklahoma City. This once-tiny shopping center bank had grown explosively by originating billions of dollars in loans for oil and gas exploration and upstreaming the loans to Continental Bank and several other very large correspondent banks. By trusting Penn Square Bank's questionable loan underwriting standards and acquiring billions of dollars worth of the upstart bank's loans, Continental permitted a near fatal lapse in its risk management procedures. The collapse of world oil prices in 1982 plunged much of Continental's energy loans into default. The bank's large base of money market creditors anticipated the deterioration in the bank's loans and rapidly began to pull out their funds, creating a severe liquidity crisis.

In a controversial step to prevent the probable failure of the bank, the Federal Reserve bailed out these creditors by providing a massive injection of funds into the bank. As the bank's insurer, the Federal Deposit Insurance Corporation shored up the bank's equity base by purchasing $1 billion of preferred stock, pending the bank's expected recovery over an eight-year period. The federal banking agencies justified their urgent rescue efforts based on the doctrine of "essentiality." In applying this doctrine, the regulators declared that Continental Bank was "*too big to fail*." By this the regulators meant that the bank's failure would be an unacceptable threat to the nation's financial stability. They believed the failure would have widespread impact on bank customers, and they feared that money market lenders would withdraw support from other large banks with loans of dubious quality.[11] Shortly after this episode, the Comptroller of the Currency formalized and expanded the too-big-to-fail guarantee by telling the Congress that "the government won't currently allow any of the nation's 11 largest banks to fail."

The rescue of the Continental Bank from near failure was a seminal case in regulatory and legislative interference with market forces. According to some observers, the regulatory authorities acted improperly because the rescue signaled to creditors and customers that they could count on the government to protect their interests in such cases in the future. Critics believed that the regulators should have permitted Continental to fail as an inducement for other institutions, their creditors, and customers to exercise prudence in managing, funding, and patronizing banks in an impartial and unforgiving marketplace. Continental's failure would also have encouraged investors and creditors of other large banks to monitor and discipline the policies adopted by those banks.

---

[11] Scholars tend to challenge this view and argue that the system would have been better off if Continental had been allowed to fail. Scholars expected a failure to force similar institutions to be more disciplined in managing their asset quality. See George G. Kaufman, "The Truth About Bank Runs," in C. England and T. Huertes, eds., *The Financial Services Revolution* (Boston: Kluwer Academic Publishers, 1988).

In addition, Illinois' archaic banking laws prohibited the state's banks from establishing branches. Without branches, Continental Bank could not attract a significant amount of stable retail deposits. This forced the bank to depend too much on an unstable funding base of hot money raised from money market creditors. Thus the branching restriction harmed Continental's liquidity and contributed to its near failure. The availability of stable retail funds through a branching system would likely have staved off the threat of illiquidity.

Following Continental Bank's informal, if not legal, failure, large numbers of other banks also fell victim to deteriorating loan portfolios. There was an epidemic of failures among small and large banks that had accumulated concentrations of loans in energy-dependent Texas, Oklahoma, and Louisiana. In Texas, nine out of the ten largest banks failed. In many U.S. cities, especially in New England, defaults on construction and development loans in overbuilt real estate markets caused more banks to fail.

Faced with the growing losses in many banks, the FDIC and the Federal Reserve practiced *regulatory forbearance* by holding back on enforcing capital adequacy rules that would have forced otherwise failed banks to close. They hoped that regulatory forbearance would give the banks time to regain profitability and to recover. Instead of saving failed banks, however, forbearance drove the ultimate cost of failure considerably higher. Banks that continued to operate with deficient capital or with stopgap "public" capital provided by emergency Federal Reserve advances, continued to produce large losses.[12] Ultimately, by the time the FDIC resolved (closed or merged) these living-dead banks (so-called zombies), the costs had increased well above what they would have been if the banks had been closed when insolvency was first detected.

The commercial banking industry continued to lose market share during the 1980s, in large part because the proliferation of information technology opened financial services to competition from nonbank providers. Activities that previously were performed in a "general store" environment of banks shifted toward more efficient institutions that specialized in investment products, credit cards, business lending, and consumer finance or other narrow lines of business.

At the end of the 1980s, bankers and others increasingly blamed the banks' shrinking share of financial business on 1930s era legislation and on newly restrictive bank supervision. Indeed, because of the 1980s loan disasters, federal banking regulators sharply tightened their examination standards and supported even more restrictive legislation for banks. New legislation reinforced the already existing *Community Reinvestment Act* (CRA), setting forth rules to ensure that banks would offer socially desirable services such as extending credit to revitalize low-income communities. In addition, CRA and the *Home Mortgage Disclosure Act* introduced antidiscriminatory reporting measures to protect minorities' access to credit and other banking services.

Whatever their merit, these inhibiting regulatory factors did not apply to nonbank financial services firms. Bankers complained that, as a result of the negative competitive effects of regulation, unregulated nonbanks gained market share at the expense of banks' market share.

In business lending, commercial finance companies made large gains in the types of loans banks specialized in—those that required a large component of information gath-

---

[12] See Donald G. Simonson and George H. Hempel, "Running on Empty: Accounting Strategies to Clarify Bank and S&L Capital Value," *Stanford Law and Policy Review,* Spring (1990), Vol. 2, pp. 92–101.

ering and monitoring of less known corporate and down market borrowers. Also, banks came under heavy competitive pressures in the retail lending market because of innovation and growth in markets for securitized loans.[13] By 1997, securitized residential mortgage loans made up over 40 percent of mortgage activity, and securitized credit cards, automobile loans, boat loans, and others were increasingly common. Special credit card banks owned by such nonbank firms as Sears, J.C. Penney, and American Express invaded bank credit card businesses.

Meanwhile, money market funds continued to soar in popularity and steadily eroded banks' competitive positions in liability product markets. Finally, debt and equity mutual funds as well as insurance annuities were becoming the investment vehicles of choice, far outstripping the growth of time and savings deposits in banks. By 1998, banks' share of financial sector assets had fallen below 20 percent.

1990s: Another Flurry of Federal Legislation

The Congress was slow to grasp the meaning of the epidemic of failures among S&Ls and banks during the 1980s. In part, this oversight was due to the forbearance measures practiced by federal regulators which concealed the poor condition of zombie institutions. In addition, agency heads and career politicians sought to avoid being connected to large-scale failures "on their watches." In 1987, Congress finally recognized the plight of the FSLIC, whose insurance reserves were depleted in payouts to depositors of failed S&Ls. In part to assist the FSLIC, Congress passed the *Competitive Equality Banking Act.* The hallmark of this Act was a hotly debated and, it later became apparent, extremely inadequate $10.8 billion allocation for recapitalizing the FSLIC.

Congress began to act with a greater sense of urgency as the problems of depository institutions and the federal deposit insurance funds became more obvious. In 1989, Congress passed the *Financial Institutions Reform, Recovery, and Enforcement Act* (FIRREA) as a measure for "reregulating" depository institutions.[14] The Act provided $50 billion to be used to close unresolved S&Ls. It also eliminated the Federal Home Loan Bank Board and transferred supervision of thrift institutions to the Comptroller of the Currency. Further, it eliminated the FSLIC and transferred S&L deposit insurance to a new fund, the Savings Association Insurance Fund or SAIF, under the FDIC. Bank deposit insurance remained in a separate fund, the Bank Insurance Fund or BIF, under the FDIC. FIRREA also set up a mammoth liquidation unit, the Resolution Trust Corporation, for divesting assets acquired by the government in the process of shutting down S&Ls and for selling off troubled S&L businesses to healthy banks and S&Ls. FIRREA raised deposit insurance premiums that were charged to insured institutions and set tough standards for appraising real estate and other regulatory functions.

By 1991, Congress and the Bush administration had taken a more realistic and complete measure of the disaster that had befallen banks and thrifts. Congress passed the *Federal Deposit Insurance Corporation Improvement Act* (FDICIA) in December of that year. In addition to providing another $70 billion to resolve failed institutions, this far-

---

[13] Charles Cumming, "The Economics of Securitization," Federal Reserve Bank of New York, *Quarterly Review* (Autumn 1987).

[14] R. Dan Brumbaugh and Robert E. Litan, "A Critique of the FIRREA and the Financial Strength of the Commercial Banks," in J. R. Barth and R. D. Brumbaugh, eds., *The Reform of Federal Deposit Insurance* (New York: HarperCollins, 1992).

reaching Act sought to reform the "free lunch" beneficently doled out by the American system of federal deposit insurance.[15] At first, the administration wanted legislation that would remedy deposit insurance directly by such means as reducing the $100,000 insurance limit or limiting the number of accounts—each insured to $100,000—that individual depositors would be permitted.

In the end, FDICIA took an *indirect approach* to deposit insurance reform through a system of "prompt intervention." This system established a target level of bank capitalization and a schedule of regulatory sanctions and restrictions on bank activities that became increasingly punitive when a bank's capitalization level declined. Prompt intervention provided for the actual closure of an institution within 90 days if its capital fell to 2 percent of assets or less. Prompt intervention thus preserves some value (or avoids negative values) in a dying institution when the FDIC takes it over. Finally, to raise the reserves in the BIF and SAIF funds to statutory levels, FDICIA imposed a large increase in insurance premiums for banks and an especially onerous increase for thrifts.

FDICIA prohibits federal agencies from forbearing in the closure of a failing institution by declaring it too-big-to-fail (as in the case of Continental Bank), unless there is a consensus finding among the FDIC, Federal Reserve, and the Treasury that a large institution's failure poses *systemic risk*. Furthermore, the Act provides for safety and soundness standards in which regulatory authorities require a high standard for internal bank controls on credit, officer compensation, other management functions, and bank director qualifications. The banking industry greeted passage of FDICIA with hostility and complained vociferously about the Act's tough-sounding "intrusive" provisions. In retrospect, however, it appears that Congress's intentions were to discipline the banking industry to maintain its insurability and to prevent the industry from imposing costs on taxpayers for future banking emergencies.

Major federal regulatory legislation passed in recent years breaches the venerable geographic restrictions on banking that have existed explicitly since the 1920s. The *Interstate Banking and Branching Efficiency Act of 1994* opened the door to nearly unimpeded nationwide banking. It removed barriers to interstate consolidations of banks by bank holding companies, authorized interstate consolidations of affiliated or newly acquired banks, and permitted interstate *de novo* branching if individual states expressly authorize it. This act was inspired by the claim that the patchwork structure of U.S. banking renders it highly inefficient because it prevents banks from expanding over wide regions or, for that matter, the nation as a whole. In addition, both banking scholars and politicians believe that such inefficiencies cause banks to continue to lose market share to nonbanks. These critics also believe that legal limits on geographic expansion prevent individual banks from achieving the size they need to compete with giant foreign rivals in pursuit of international financial business.

In addition, advocates of interstate expansion argue that it permits greater geographic and product diversification, which is likely to protect big banks from economic adversities arising in isolated regions, such as the depression that struck the energy-producing states of the Southwest in the 1980s. Moreover, the advocates claim that permitting a single centralized headquarters organization to manage perhaps thousands of limited local branches will generate large overhead savings. Experts have estimated such savings at

---

[15] For an important discussion of deposit insurance reform, see Barth and Brumbaugh, eds., *The Reform of Federal Deposit Insurance*.

anywhere from $14 to $23 billion, much of which presumably will be passed through as lower prices to consumers and business users of banks. Finally, interstate banking is said to permit big banks to develop large core funding which, unlike the 1980s' Continental Bank case, provides deep liquidity and reduces dependence on hot money market sources of funds.

Partly because of freer geographic expansion and a drive to achieve greater scale efficiencies, the banking industry has consolidated steadily throughout the 1990s. The industry's historically significant component of community banks—nominally those with less than $1 billion in assets—shrank dramatically. As the total number of banks in the United States fell from over 14,000 in 1980 to 9,024 in 1998, the number of banks in the under $1 billion asset size range decreased from 12,500 with 54 percent of U.S. banking assets, to 8,661 with 21 percent of assets. At the other extreme, banks with more than $10 billion in assets increased from 6 in number and 32 percent of all bank assets in 1980 to 65 in number and 60 percent of assets. In the 1990s, a half-dozen very large banking companies with assets in excess of $100 billion—among them Chase Manhattan, Citicorp, and BankAmerica-NationsBank—were emerging at the top of the banking structure pyramid, each with a presence in many or most markets in the United States.

The 2000s: New Powers and Technologies

At the end of the 1990s, Congress appeared to be on the brink of sweeping legislation to neutralize the last vestiges of the archaic banking legislation that had been on the books since the 1930s. These steps are expected to thoroughly revamp the larger financial services industry. Existing legislation has been a major stumbling block to reform. The 1933 Glass-Steagall Act severely restricts banks from engaging in securities underwriting and prohibits mergers between banks and securities firms. In addition, it prevents banks from underwriting and selling insurance, although many insurance products are incidental to banking activity (for example, underwriting homeowners' insurance for banks' mortgage customers).

Glass-Steagall also restricts ownership structure in banking. Banking companies cannot affiliate with insurance companies, securities brokers/dealers, and investment bankers, and banks cannot hold or be held by nonfinancial commercial or industrial businesses. The Bank Holding Company Act of 1956 and its amendments of 1963 and 1970 give the Federal Reserve authority to restrict banking companies to activities that, in the Fed's judgment, are ''closely related to banking.'' Because the Federal Reserve often has interpreted this language restrictively, banks have been hampered from meeting the genuine needs of the financial marketplace or from competing in financial services in which they might be successful.

As this text was going to press, it appeared that most, if not all, of these barriers to growth and efficient delivery of financial products would be challenged and perhaps reformed by Congress. Banking firms feel these reforms are especially urgent in light of the fast-breaking developments in technology at the turn of the millennium that radically transform the way banking services are delivered.

Most experts believe that the technology-induced change in financial services to date is only the tip of the iceberg. Currently, nonbanking firms like Intuit and Microsoft market software that delivers online banking services to the home 24 hours a day. Customers can inquire about their account information, transfer funds between accounts, pay bills, and reconcile various accounts. Developing electronic marketplaces such as the internet facilitate buying and selling insurance and mutual funds. In the future banks will no longer be the sole source or ''gatekeeper'' for financial services.

Future competition in banking will not be based so much on being an efficient processor of traditional banking transactions as it will require capturing and using information contained in the transactions themselves. Information permits the bank to monitor its customers' activities and needs—for example, observing that the customer is taking risks that the bank might help the customer to hedge. The growing familiarity of consumers and businesspersons with technology is a powerful force for change. If banks fail to match the software and other innovations that are being introduced at the turn of the century, banks' customers are likely to be drawn to the nonbanking providers.

Recap of Key Legislation

Table 1.2 summarizes the major provisions of 12 major legislative acts affecting banks in the United States today. Most of the original acts have been amended. For example, the Bank Holding Company Act was permissive until the early 1930s when legislative

---

TABLE 1.2   Major Provisions of Legislation Affecting Banks

- National Banking Act (many amendments)—created the Comptroller of the Currency, which charters, examines, and supervises banks that choose to become national rather than state banks.
- Federal Reserve Act (many amendments)—created a system of 12 Federal Reserve banks to control the supply of money and credit and supervise state-chartered banks that are members of the Federal Reserve. Control now is centralized in the Board of Governors and the Open Market Committee. Supervises bank holding companies.
- Edge Act—allows commercial banks to open subsidiary offices in other states to transact international business.
- Bank Holding Company Act (many amendments)—defines a holding company and states the criteria the Board of Governors of the Federal Reserve System must apply to determine a holding company's nonbank activities.
- Federal Deposit Insurance Act (many amendments)—created the FDIC, which insures deposit accounts in member banks up to $100,000 (at present). Examines and supervises state banks.
- Glass-Steagall Act—requires separation of investment activities and commercial banking.
- McFadden Act—prohibited interstate banking (later legislation eliminated most of the effect of this legislation).
- Depository Institution Deregulation and Monetary Control Act of 1980–authorized NOW accounts; provided for the phaseout of Regulation Q; increased FDIC insurance to $100,000; altered the competitive relationship between banks and other financial institutions; created the Depository Institutions Deregulation Committee (DIDC).
- Depository Institutions Act of 1982 (Garn-St. Germain)—authorized money market accounts; required the end of the interest rate differential favoring thrifts; gave broader asset powers to S&Ls and thrift institutions.
- Financial Institutions Reform, Recovery, and Enforcement Act of 1989 (FIRREA)—reformed the regulatory structure of S&Ls; provided the structure and financing (inadequate) for bailout of the S&L industry; added acceptable levels of penalties for some regulatory standards (particularly capital adequacy); and called for a comprehensive study of deposit insurance.
- Federal Deposit Insurance Corporation Improvement Act of 1991 (FDICIA)—made a number of reforms addressing the safety and soundness of deposit insurance funds, supervision, accounting, prompt regulatory action, least-cost resolution, and federal insurance for state-chartered depository institutions. The act also expands regulation of foreign banks, implements changes in consumer protection laws, and provides for netting procedures to reduce the systemic risks within the borrowing system.
- Interstate Banking and Branching Efficiency Act of 1994—removed barriers to interstate consolidation of banks by bank holding companies; authorized interstate consolidations of affiliated or newly acquired banks; and permitted interstate *de novo* branching. Individual states could opt in or out of most provisions and set effective dates. (By 1998 most states had "opted in," and rules were effective in many states.)

amendments restricted the geographic and product powers of banks. The Act then became more permissive with amendments passed in 1970. All of the listed legislation, with the exception of the McFadden Act, affects bank regulation and structure today.

RESULTING BANK REGULATION IN THE UNITED STATES

The historical events and legislation described above explain today's current plethora of bank regulatory agencies and regulation. There are three federal agencies—the Comptroller of the Currency, created by the National Banking Act; the Federal Reserve System; and the Federal Deposit Insurance Corporation—and independent regulatory agencies in each of the 50 states. The primary objective of bank regulation is to ensure the safety and soundness of the banking system. Areas of responsibility overlap, yet the duties of the diverse regulatory agencies are generally carried out smoothly and efficiently. Indeed, the pluralism of bank regulatory authority in the United States *may* have led to a regulatory environment superior to one charted by a single authority.

The Federal Reserve (Fed) has unique macroeconomic responsibilities relating to growth, stability, employment, and inflation. The Fed uses open market operations; sets discount and reserve requirement rates; and exercises moral persuasion to try to achieve its goals in these macroeconomic areas. Although these actions have a large impact on how banks perform, technically they are considered to be functions of the Federal Reserve's role as the central bank, and not regulatory or supervisory functions per se. On the other hand, as a supervisory agent the Federal Reserve, along with the other two federal agencies and the 50 states, has extensive bank regulatory authority. This authority encompasses a wide variety of functions relating to the operation of banks, including:

1. The chartering of banks.
2. The insurance of bank deposits (generally to $100,000 per account).
3. The issuance and enforcement of regulations.
4. The review and analysis of banks' periodic reports of condition, earnings, and expenses.
5. The periodic examination of banks and the requirement that bank management take steps to correct unsatisfactory or unsound conditions found through such examinations.
6. The approval of proposed changes in the scope of corporate functions exercised by individual banks and of proposed changes in their capital structures.
7. Authorization for the establishment of branches and the exercise of trust powers.
8. The approval of bank mergers and consolidations.
9. The organization and regulation of bank holding companies.
10. The regulation of bank service corporations.
11. The liquidation of banks.
12. General responsibilities, such as promoting competition, protecting consumers, and encouraging social programs.

Not all functions are performed by each of the four types of regulatory agencies, but they are all the responsibility of at least one of the agencies. In the following discussion, we summarize the broad aspects of the regulatory environment in which commercial banks must operate.[16]

The diffusion of bank regulatory authority does not mean that banks are not closely regulated. Banking is more closely regulated in the United States than in any other developed country in the world. At the same time, no other country has as many banks relative to its population. These facts are not unrelated. On the contrary, the degree and character of bank regulation in the United States spring directly from the nature of the U.S. banking structure (covered in the next section of this chapter).

As noted earlier, the diversity of U.S. banking structures arose in response to the conflicting desires of different segments of the public. Despite the recent trend toward consolidation, there are still thousands of small banks chartered by both states and the federal government that for the most part are locally owned and operated. Left to their own, often inadequate devices in the past, hundreds of small banks failed. However, the United States apparently wanted to preserve this diverse structure without sacrificing banking safety. The U.S. system of bank regulation, therefore, has developed over the years in response to the desire to have a banking system that is both sound and responsive to the credit needs of small and large customers alike in a dynamic economy. One basic responsibility of bank regulatory authorities should be to ensure the continuance of a responsible bank regulatory system.

A distinctive feature of banking in the United States is the way it limits banking activities through detailed regulation and law. All banks derive their powers from the banking laws, which are, in this sense, permissive. On the other hand, banking laws such as the Glass-Steagall Act specifically limit the powers granted and are thus essentially restrictive. The restrictions are designed to prevent, if possible, U.S. banks from making the mistakes that caused widespread bank failures in the past.

Both state and federal regulatory authorities are concerned with regulation and supervision. They administer the banking laws, promulgate and interpret regulations issued thereunder, and exercise impersonal and objective judgments regarding bank policies to further the public interest. They use the examination process to review both the legality and soundness of an individual bank's operations.

As stated, the historical development of the American banking structure has given rise to a multiplicity of regulatory agencies at both the state and federal level. Under the concept of dual banking, national banks are chartered and supervised by the Office of the Comptroller of the Currency, whereas state banks are chartered and supervised primarily by the banking authorities of the respective states. Most state-chartered banks, however, have come under one form or another of federal supervision and regulation. With the establishment of the Federal Reserve System, those state-chartered banks that became members submitted voluntarily to many of the legal restrictions imposed on national banks and to examination and supervision by the Board of Governors of the Federal Reserve System.

With the advent of federal deposit insurance, nearly all the remaining state banks accepted supervision by the Federal Deposit Insurance Corporation (FDIC) as a condition of insurance. There are now fewer than 60 nonmember, noninsured commercial banks that are subject to no direct federal supervision.

---

[16] More complete descriptions of the regulatory structure for banks are contained in Part 10 of the *Bankers Handbook,* William H. Baughn and Charles E. Walker, eds. (Homewood, Ill.: Dow-Jones-Irwin, 1989), and in *Bank Supervision* (St. Louis, Mo.: Federal Reserve Bank, 1995).

Moreover, the jurisdictions of the three federal regulatory agencies overlap, and individual banks are subject to the rules of more than one agency. National banks, for example, while chartered and supervised solely by the Comptroller of the Currency, are required to be members of the Federal Reserve System and to qualify for deposit insurance under the FDIC. Both of these latter agencies have the power to examine national banks (a power seldom exercised), but both review reports of examinations made by national bank examiners. National banks are also subject to some state laws, such as those governing branching authority and legal holidays.

The crisscrossing of regulatory responsibility is further illustrated by the rules regarding changes in banking structure. All holding company transactions, including those involving nonmember banks, are subject to the jurisdiction of the Board of Governors of the Federal Reserve System. The establishment of *de novo* branches requires the approval of the chartering authority, state or national, and, for state banks, the additional approval of either the Board of Governors or the FDIC, depending on member or nonmember insured status. Merger applications follow the same course, except that each of the three federal agencies must seek the advice of the other two as well as the Department of Justice regarding the anticipated effects on competition within the affected markets of the merged banks.

Bank Examination

The three federal regulatory agencies and the state agencies are responsible for bank examination, the foundation of bank regulation. American banking is highly competitive because of the diversity and large number of banks in the country. In most communities there are two or more sources of banking services. Usually, some of them offer highly customized products and services, while others offer more commodity-like products and services. Bank examinations in the United States are designed primarily to protect depositors from unsound banking practices rather than to provide a substitute for competition. Bank examinations, completed by any of the four major types of regulatory agencies, are based on the review and appraisal of earning ability, asset quality, capital adequacy, liquidity, and management ability.

Two factors that give rise to the need for examination are inherent in banking. The first involves the bank's loans and investments, which lead to the creation of demand deposits. Since these demand deposits make up the major portion of the nation's money supply, the quality of bank credit underlies the value of money. The second factor is the nature of the financial intermediary role that banks fulfill in the economy. Banks receive savings and demand deposits that are highly liquid. The banks invest these deposits in other, less liquid assets. To prevent a liquidity crisis, banks must hold some liquid assets, have adequate capital, and maintain professional management.

The focus of bank examination has seemed to shift in recent years. In the mid- and late 1980s, international standards for an adequate amount of capital relative to risk-weighted assets was developed; their standard seemed similar to a system discontinued by the Federal Reserve in the early 1960s. Then FDICIA added mandatory penalties when capital fell below certain levels. The risk-weighting scheme and penalties in capital regulation are covered in detail in Chapter 9; the ultimate penalty was that the bank would lose its charter if Tier 1 (primarily equity) capital to risk-weighted assets fell below 2 percent and was not increased within 90 days. Many regulators and supporting academics believed that such a focus was the major foundation of bank regulation and examination. Interestingly, the rather arbitrary standards have not been tested. In the prosperous late 1990s, most banks have faced a problem of too much rather than too little capital.

A second shift in the focus of examination was incomplete as of 1999. Some regulators seem to believe that banks which have their own well-defined risk management systems meet the safety and soundness requirements. Definitions, rules, and standards remain hazy at this time; new requirements will be untested should difficult conditions return.

Three major concerns about the diversity and practices of our regulatory system deserve special mention. First, rivalry and feuding among the chief bank regulatory agencies have made bankers uncertain about how to handle many important banking functions. Areas of regulatory disagreement include bank holding companies, limited-service banks, loans to other countries, disclosure of financial condition, entry into insurance and investment banking, and brokered deposits. Overlapping responsibilities, bureaucratic power plays, and different opinions make rational decisions much harder. Some bankers, however, prefer this diversity, because they say that they can always find one regulatory official who agrees with them on most issues.

The second major area of concern is that FDIC deposit insurance might encourage excessive risk. Since the risk of failure is passed on, with explicit insurance up to $100,000 and possibly higher implicit insurance or guarantees (e.g., the Continental Illinois Bank bailout), banks may take higher risks without incurring higher costs in the quest for high returns. For the last decade, academics have generally criticized such subsidies and the possible excessive risks to which they may lead. Recently, many bankers and legislators have joined the ranks of the concerned. The Federal Deposit Insurance Corporation Improvement Act (FDICIA), passed in December 1991, represents an initial attempt to address this concern. As with the rigid capital standards, the jury is still out. Most banks have now exceeded their minimum deposit insurance requirements and are not paying premiums for insurance at this time. The late-1990s, a period of record high bank profits and low bank losses, has not tested the adequacy of the insurance fund or decided if insurance leads to excessive risk-taking.

The third area of concern is that current examinations often seem to emphasize social priorities rather than safety and soundness. Banks appear to be singled out as the private institutions that must help achieve some laudable public social objectives. While it is hard to argue against issues of the public's welfare such as equal opportunity to poor or minority borrowers, one wonders why banks are singled out and if an unsafe and unsound bank could be of much assistance in meeting such goals.

Joint consideration of some problems by the various regulatory bodies has been a positive trend. For example, representatives from each of the major bank regulatory groups met to establish bank capital requirements. In addition, the Federal Financial Institutions Examination Council has been given a broader role in coordinating regulatory initiatives. This council includes representatives from the Federal Reserve, FDIC, Comptroller, and state bank supervisory groups. In our opinion, more consistent and uniform bank regulation should lead to better bank management.

RESULTING BANKING STRUCTURE

Today many banks compete on a regional, national, and international scale, tapping financial resources in a highly mobile supply of funds that move rapidly and voluminously through global financial markets. Most banks offer a vast spectrum of deposit and loan products, and a rising number engage in insurance, stock and bond brokerage, leasing, and the securitization of loans. These changes in banking are part and parcel of the quantum changes in the financial world itself, and are driven by the increasing efficiency, computerization of information, and telecommunication capabilities. One has to believe that more changes are forthcoming. However, even though a picture of banking today will be obsolete tomorrow, the current banking structure needs to be reviewed before management techniques can be reviewed and evaluated.

UNIT, BRANCH, AND ELECTRONIC BANKING

Figure 1.3 depicts the changes in the number of banks (defined as units examined separately) as compiled by the Federal Deposit Insurance Corporation from 1980 through 1996. In the early 1980s, the number of banks increased because more banks received new charters than failed or were part of some form of combination. The number of banks began declining in 1983 as failures and combinations grew and the number of new charters declined. Although the rate of decline has slowed recently, with very few failures and faster growth in the number of new charters, the number of banks has declined each year from 1985 through 1996.

Table 1.3 presents data on the banking structure as of December 31, 1996. There were 9,528 entities identified as insured commercial banks at the end of 1996, down from a post–World War II peak of close to 15,380 in 1983. This is the number of entities examined, and it overstates effective economic units because holding companies may own

FIGURE 1.3   Structural changes among FDIC-insured commercial banks, 1980–1996

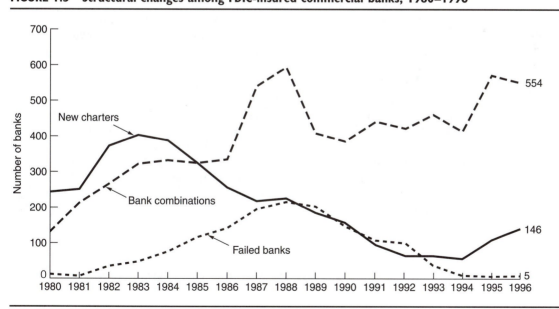

SOURCE: *Quarterly Banking Profile*, FDIC, Washington, D.C. 1997.

TABLE 1.3   Data on Banking Structure, December 31, 1996[a]

Structure	Number of Banks
National banks (examined by Comptroller of the Currency)	2,843
Federal Reserve member banks—national banks plus (state banks examined by Federal Reserve)	949
Bank covered by FDIC—all Federal Reserve members plus (examined by state and FDIC)	5,736
State non-FDIC banks (examined by state banking authority)	58 est.
Total banks	9,586
Branch offices (of 6,108 banks)	52,317
Total banking offices	61,903

	Number[b]	Banks Controlled
One-bank holding companies	4,567[c]	4,564
Multibank holding companies	829	3,140
Total holding company banks	5,396	7,714

[a] Fifty states and the District of Columbia.

[b] After eliminating tiered one- and multibank holding companies.

[c] A few banks are partially owned by two one-bank holding companies.

SOURCE: Federal Reserve System and Federal Deposit Insurance Corporation, 1997.

and control several units that are examined separately. These figures understate the number of banking offices, which stood at above 60,000 because of the large number of branches. Furthermore, branches exclude automatic teller machines (ATMs), point of sale terminals (POSs), unmanned branches in supermarkets and stores, home computer terminals, and other methods of delivering financial services that used to be done at banking offices. In spite of these complexities, it seems worthwhile to define and introduce trends in unit banking, branch banking, and electronic banking.

Most banks in the United States have traditionally been unit banks—single-office institutions primarily serving their local communities. Of the 9,528 insured commercial banks in the United States at the end of 1996, 3,420 were unit banks, down sharply from 9,375 at the end of 1971. Although still accounting for over 30 percent of all commercial banks, the unit bank might well be placed on the endangered species list. The tide toward multiple-office banking is running strong. The number of branch banking offices increased from 4,613 in 1948 to 10,605 in 1960, 23,362 at the end of 1971, and 52,317 at the end of 1996.[17] This increase has resulted from state and federal laws that allow intra- and interstate branching, the establishment of new branches in growing communities, and the absorption of previously independent banks through mergers. The pros and cons of multiple-office banking and bank mergers are still in the forefront of bank policy considerations today.

While state and federal legislation has become more and more permissive regarding

---

[17] Data from the Federal Deposit Insurance Corporation, 1997.

branch banking, technological developments seem to be pointing in the opposite direction. Some bankers believe that "brick and mortar" branches will soon become one of the least efficient ways of delivering banking services. Evidence is scattered at the present time. There are now several one-office banks that accept deposits and make loans electronically over the internet.

Bill Gates of Microsoft and Scott Cook of Intuit have labeled banks as "dinosaurs" that will be replaced by low-cost high-tech providers of similar financial services. Banks, often with extensive branching systems, have closed branches, extended unmanned automatic teller machines, point of sale terminals, and loan kiosks. Many of the manned branches that have been opened are in leased areas in grocery, discount, and department stores.

Interpreting these new developments for unit, branch, and electronic banking is not easy. Predicting the demise of most branches and even banking offices seems premature. We may recall that in the late 1970s and early 1980s many bankers, regulators, and academics predicted there would be a "checkless society" by the early 1990s. Nevertheless, the structure for delivering bank services is very fluid at the present time, and bank management must carefully evaluate their decisions in this area.

The Bank Holding Company

Bank holding companies are another integral part of our current banking structure, but there are questions about the future role of these entities. There are two general types of bank holding companies, one-bank and multibank. Prior to the 1970 amendments, one-bank holding companies did not fall within the definition of the Bank Holding Company Act amendments in 1956 and were, therefore, not subject to the specific control of the Board of Governors of the Federal Reserve System. Under our current laws, a one-bank holding company is created when an existing bank organizes a holding company of which the bank becomes a subsidiary. Multibank holding companies own a controlling interest in the stock of two or more banks. Many smaller banks (with assets under $500 million) have formed one-bank holding companies to gain tax or capital advantages, or both, from that form of organization. The holding company form of organization appeals to larger banks for two additional reasons. Multibank holding companies can be used to acquire additional banks (particularly important in the few states still limiting nationwide branching), and either type can be used to form or acquire additional subsidiaries in financially related activities.

The Board of Governors, under the authority of the 1970 amendments, has established a "laundry list" of such permissible activities. Table 1.4 lists activities that have been found permissible by regulation or order and activities that have been specifically denied. Numerous other financial activities have been neither approved nor denied.[18]

At the end of 1996, bank holding companies controlled 7,714 banks, and approximately 5,000 subsidiaries engaged in, or were authorized to engage in, various other activities. Not all of these subsidiaries are currently active. At that time, there were 5,396 holding company groups in the United States controlling 92 percent of the assets of all commercial banks. Of these, 4,567 were one-bank holding companies.[19]

---

[18] The American Bankers Association provided this list.
[19] Board of Governors of the Federal Reserve System.

TABLE 1.4   Permissible and Denied Nonbanking Activities by Bank Holding Companies

Permitted by Regulation	Permitted by Order	Denied by Federal Reserve
1. Extensions of credit[a] Mortgage banking Finance companies—consumer, sales, and commercial Credit cards Factoring	1. Issuance and sale of traveler's checks[a,c]	1. Insurance premium funding (combined sales of mutual funds and insurance)
2. Industrial bank, Morris Plan bank, industrial loan company	2. Buying and selling gold and silver bullion and silver coin[a]	2. Underwriting life insurance not related to credit extension
3. Servicing loans and other extensions of credit[a]	3. Issuing money orders and general-purpose, variable denominated payment instruments[a,b,c]	3. Real estate brokerage[a]
4. Trust company[a]	4. Futures commission merchant to cover gold and silver bullion and coins[a,b]	4. Land development
5. Investment or financial advising[a]	5. Underwriting certain federal, state, and municipal securities[a,b]	5. Real estate syndication
6. Full-payout leasing of personal or real property[a]	6. Check verification[a,b]	6. General management consulting
7. Investments in community welfare projects[a]	7. Financial advice to consumers[a,b]	7. Property management
8. Providing bookkeeping or data-processing services[a]	8. Issuance of small-denomination debt instruments[b]	8. Computer output microfilm services
9. Acting as insurance agent or broker primarily in connection with credit extensions[a]		9. Underwriting mortgage guaranty insurance[d]
10. Underwriting credit life, accident, and health insurance		10. Operating a savings and loan association[b,e]
11. Providing courier services[a]		11. Operating a travel agency[a,b]
12. Management consulting for unaffiliated banks[a,b]		12. Underwriting property and casualty insurance[b]
13. Sale at retail of money orders with a face value of not more than $1,000, traveler's checks, and savings bonds[a,b]		13. Underwriting home loan life mortgage insurance[b]
14. Performing appraisals of real estate[a]		14. Orbanco: Investment note issue with transactional characteristics
15. Audit services for unaffiliated banks		
16. Issuance and sale of traveler's checks		
17. Management consulting to nonbank depository institutions		

[a] Activities permissible to national banks.

[b] Added to list since January 1, 1975.

[c] To be decided on a case-by-case basis.

[d] Board orders found these activities closely related to banking but denied proposed acquisitions as part of its "go slow" policy.

[e] Operating a thrift institution has been permitted by order in Rhode Island and New Hampshire only.

Under the current legislative structure, multibank holding companies have usually been pushed into one of two different patterns of organization and decision making. First, some holding companies operate very much like a branching system. Although each bank has a separate board of directors, the subsidiary board tends to have little power. All banks have the same name and same functions (e.g., investment loan rates and deposit rates are done entirely at the holding company level).

The second pattern emphasizes that the distinctive feature of any form of bank holding company lies in its ability to realize many of the benefits and render most of the services of widespread branch banking organizations while retaining the decentralization of management that can preserve the "local touch." Each banking unit of this form of holding company system typically is managed by a board of directors composed of local citizens who retain a substantial measure of autonomy in forming lending policies and dealing with local management problems. Without a substantial grant of local autonomy, the outstanding citizens and business leaders of the various communities could hardly be induced to serve as directors, because in most cases they hold only a nominal stock interest in the bank or the holding company. Given enough local authority, they regard their directorships as a form of community service.

The relationship of the holding company to its subsidiary banks in this holding company pattern is largely that of an informed and helpful stockholder. This role combines many of the functions often rendered to country banks by their city correspondents, with provision for effective group action in such fields as accounting, loan participation, purchasing, or investment analysis. In short, this form of holding company has covered many staff functions for its constituent banks; it also tends to encourage healthy rivalry among its units. Such competition provides stimulus for experimentation and can lead to a diversity of approaches that are less likely to be found in a branch organization, where final management authority stems from one top-management team and a single board of directors.

The future of the bank holding company has numerous crosscurrents. The Federal Reserve, which uses its supervision of holding companies and their activities as its key bank regulatory mechanism, seems to favor continuing the bank holding company as a key banking structure. The other two federal regulatory agencies and most state agencies tend to point out the inefficiencies of bank holding companies. Duplicate directors, officers, reports, and regulatory responsibilities are inefficiencies that may make banks less competitive with nonbanks.

Banks favoring the holding company organization cite advantages such as the ability to acquire other related products and services and to build up "firewalls" between insured banking products and other products that the FDIC will not insure. Recent trends in other U.S. industries and in large banking organizations in other countries might argue against using holding companies for nonbank products and services. In the United States for 1998, the number of nonbank corporate spin-offs exceeded the number of mergers and acquisitions. (While some argue this is a way to keep lawyer and investment banker fees up, economic reality indicates that it is very difficult for management to control several nonrelated businesses. The sum of the parts is worth more than the total business, and shareholders rather than the firm can diversify their holdings.) Some large banking institutions in other countries are following a similar strategy of selling off lines of business that do not have synergies with their core banking business.

Correspondent Banking in the United States

The correspondent banking system is an entirely informal arrangement whereby a smaller bank maintains deposit balances with larger banks headquartered in nearby cities and looks to them for a wide variety of services and assistance. The city banks, in turn, keep correspondent balances with still larger banks in the principal money centers. Before the establishment of the Federal Reserve System, all checks were collected through this network of correspondent banks (often by roundabout routing). The correspondent system served as a means of mobilizing the supply of credit and channeling it to areas where and when it was needed. Thus, correspondent banks provided liquidity and credit fluidity to a diverse economy. Country banks could deposit their idle funds with their correspondents, who invested them in money market loans (theoretically, at least). Then, at times of peak demand for seasonal agricultural credit, the country banks not only could draw down their balances but also could borrow from their correspondents. The inadequacies of these arrangements, which did not include a central bank, were evident in recurring panics and finally led to the establishment of the Federal Reserve System. Nevertheless, without correspondent relationships, the early credit needs of the country could hardly have been met.

Today, correspondent banks are still active in the collection of checks and still supply credit to the smaller banks for the balances that the latter maintain. In addition, correspondent banks perform many services that would otherwise be unobtainable for smaller (downstream) banks and their customers. Large (upstream) banks give investment advice, provide safekeeping for customers' securities, arrange for the purchase and sale of securities, arrange international financial transactions, trade in federal funds, participate in loans too large for the small banks, sell participation in large loans to small banks with surplus funds, and provide a wide range of other services.

Most large correspondent banks are members of the Federal Reserve System. They indirectly channel the benefits of the system to nonmember banks, and they provide services to member banks (such as giving investment advice) that would be inappropriate for the central bank to perform.[20] The correspondent banking system extends economies of scale to smaller banks. Small banks experience infrequent demands for some services, such as international financial transactions, but generally must be able to offer such services to customers. Returns would rarely compensate the initial investment required for small-scale production of these services. Larger banks, however, have sufficient demand from the public and from other commercial banks to provide these services profitably and at a lower unit cost to their customers. Aside from direct expenses incurred in providing these services or the fees required for data processing, correspondents rarely charge customer banks. Instead, they are compensated for the services by the deposit balances that small banks hold with them.[21]

---

[20] One of the primary advantages Federal Reserve membership gave larger banks was the ability to pass on many benefits of systems membership to their smaller correspondents. The Depository Institution Regulation and Monetary Control Act of 1980, which requires the Federal Reserve to price its services to members, to allow nonmembers to receive some ''Fed'' services, and increasingly to encourage nonmember banks to hold reserves at the Fed, is changing this aspect of correspondent relationships.

[21] By far the largest share of these compensating correspondent balances is held as demand deposits. A recent survey found that fewer than 6 percent of the banks favored a fee arrangement. This general preference for demand deposits as compensation for correspondent services may exist partly because nonmember banks can normally count correspondent balances toward reserve requirements. Many banks, however, charge fees for computer services.

One new player has evolved in the correspondent banking relationship. So-called bankers' banks have been formed in numerous states. The primary business of these banks is to accept deposits from and make deposits to other banks. Their bank customers typically own most or all of the stock of the bankers' bank. Most bankers' banks are members of the Federal Reserve and compete with the Federal Reserve and larger banks in providing correspondent-like services to their shareholder banks.

The volume of interbank deposits provides some indication of the usage of correspondent services. In 1896, correspondent balances represented 10 percent of total demand deposits in commercial banks. These balances climbed to 13 percent in 1913, just before the organization of the Federal Reserve System, and then fell gradually to 7 percent in 1928. They reached roughly 12 percent of total demand deposits in the late 1940s, declined to 9 percent by the early 1960s, and then rose to approximately 11 percent by early 1976. The rather sharp increase in the late 1960s and 1970s appears to have been caused by the increasing need for correspondent services and the substantial increase in loan participation among correspondent banks. By 1997 this percentage had dropped back to below 8 percent. This decline probably resulted from higher interest rates during the 1980s, which encouraged banks to minimize idle balances. In addition, the Depository Institution Deregulation and Monetary Control Act of 1980 encouraged nonmember banks to hold reserves at the Federal Reserve.[22] Bankers' banks in many states have grown rapidly from a small base because many of their bank customers felt that banks headquartered outside of their geographic area neither understood nor cared about their needs. Competition has tended to reduce the cost of and profit from correspondent relationships.

AN APPROACH TO BANK MANAGEMENT IN THIS CHALLENGING ENVIRONMENT

Where does the combination of a difficult economic environment, a changing regulatory environment, increasingly sharp competition, a virtual technological revolution, concerns about recent trends in banking, and continuing changes in the money and capital markets leave the banking industry? The environment for bank management decisions will clearly be a challenging one in the coming years. Although the number of newly chartered banks will continue growing, there will be numerous acquisitions and mergers in the banking and depository industries. The number of banks will probably decline 20 to 30 percent more in the first decade of the 2000s, and the decline in other depository institutions may be even greater. The banking structure will continue changing, and delivery systems for banking services will change markedly. Well-managed banks can and will be very successful during such times.

END OF CHAPTER PROBLEMS

1.1 Examine the latest annual report of a major U.S. bank. Based on the bank's income statement, what is the "spread" earned by the bank between what it pays to providers

---

[22] *All Bank Statistics,* 1896–1995 (Washington, D.C.: U.S. Board of Governors of the Federal Reserve System, 1959); Federal Reserve Bulletins, 1956–1977.

of funds and what it charges its borrowers? In what proportions is this spread applied to the following:

a. bank overhead expenses

b. provisions for future losses on the bank's loans

c. taxes

d. returns to shareholders

1.2 Explain how the "fractional reserve" method of banking made banks vulnerable before the 1930s New Deal banking legislation.

1.3 List the primary elements of the 1930s New Deal banking reforms and define the federal "safety net" for banks. What seemed to be Congress's reasoning concerning how the 1933–1935 legislation would help and protect banks?

1.4 Describe what caused the conservative 1930s banking legislation and regulations to begin to erode in the 1960s and 1970s. List specific causes and comment especially on how the barriers between financial institutions and open financial markets were breached.

1.5 Describe the main elements that led to the large-scale failures of the savings and loan associations and, to a lesser extent, commercial banks.

1.6 Describe the role of "moral hazard" in the cost of resolving failed institutions. What is the significance of "too-big-to-fail" for banking regulation?

1.7 What public policy arguments can you give to prevent banking regulators from having and utilizing the authority to decide if and when a financial institution is too-big-to-fail?

1.8 What role did the U.S. system of deposit insurance play in the large number of failures of banks and S&Ls in the 1980s and early 1990s? What steps did the Congress take to solve (or try to solve) the need for reform of the deposit insurance system?

1.9 What arguments can be made for overturning the historical prohibitions on unfettered geographic expansion for banks? Why did public policy retain its narrow geographic limits on bank expansion?

1.10 Review the evaluation factors that are the focus of bank examinations. What must examiners do when visiting the examined bank site to ascertain the bank's status with regard to these factors? Name the two chartering bodies for U.S. commercial banks. If a bank wanted to form a holding company, to what regulatory body would it apply?

1.11 A flurry of new banking legislation was enacted in the late 1980s and early 1990s. However, the mid- and late 1990s were relatively free of distress for financial institutions. Suppose conditions of the late 1980s were to return. Discuss your belief about how the performance of the banking system would differ today, given that this recent legislation is now in place.

Understanding a Bank's Financial Statements

In this chapter we introduce and briefly explain the primary data used in evaluating a bank. To facilitate this task, we detail the balance sheet and income statement of an example bank—First National Bank—and we discuss supplementary financial information and qualitative factors that may affect a bank's performance. In addition, we describe and clarify financial reporting topics that can often be confusing, such as loan loss accounting, repricing schedules, and off-balance sheet items. Finally, sources of banking information are listed. Readers familiar with this introductory material can skip this chapter without loss of continuity and proceed directly to Chapter 3.

UNDERSTANDING A BANK'S BALANCE SHEET

Table 2.1 presents balance sheets for First National Bank for 1999, 2000, and 2001. You should immediately observe that these data reflect average daily balances and not end-of-year figures. While end-of-year figures are useful in certain situations, we prefer using average balances for measuring a bank's performance to avoid distortions that occur when we generalize results based on only one particular day.

In broad terms, the data on First National Bank's assets show how the bank used the funds it has attracted. The bank's liabilities and net worth itemize the specific sources of funds. Liabilities are nonowner claims on the bank's assets. The net worth or equity capital is the value of the bank's assets minus the value of its liabilities. Because many bank assets and liabilities are still valued at cost or adjusted as they approach their maturity value rather than by their market values, many analysts worry about the validity of the resulting net worth.

TABLE 2.1   First National Bank's Average Balance Sheet (dollars in thousands)

	1999 $	1999 %	2000 $	2000 %	2001 $	2001 %
ASSETS						
Cash and due from institutions	26,948	6.05%	28,053	6.04%	29,521	6.14%
Short-term instruments						
Fed funds sold and repos	4,879	1.09%	867	0.19%	1,102	0.23%
Other interest-bearing instruments	189	0.04%	563	0.12%	609	0.13%
Securities						
Held to maturity	36,719	8.24%	35,097	7.56%	32,147	6.68%
Available for sale	106,417	23.87%	100,364	21.61%	98,983	20.58%
Trading account assets	0	0.00%	0	0.00%	0	0.00%
Loans						
Commercial loans	86,481	19.40%	92,571	19.93%	94,918	19.73%
Consumer loans	82,107	18.42%	94,810	20.41%	103,367	21.49%
Real estate loans	53,817	12.07%	56,481	12.16%	63,249	13.15%
Other loans	23,176	5.20%	28,694	6.18%	28.793	5.99%
Leases	8,950	2.01%	8,794	1.89%	9,806	2.04%
Less: Reserve for loan losses	−3,412	−0.77%	−2,987	−0.64%	−3,249	−0.68%
Net loans and leases	251,119	56.34%	278,363	59.94%	296,884	61.73%
Premises and fixed assets	13,468	3.02%	14,468	3.12%	14,845	3.09%
Other real estate owned	786	0.18%	421	0.09%	273	0.06%
Goodwill and other intangibles	0	0.00%	0	0.00%	0	0.00%
All other assets	5,231	1.17%	6,237	1.34%	6,604	1.37%
Total assets	445,756	100.00%	464,433	100.00%	480,968	100.00%
LIABILITIES AND CAPITAL						
Demand deposits	61,733	13.85%	63,781	13.73%	66,389	13.80%
Interest-bearing deposits						
NOW and other transaction accounts	93,417	20.96%	95,911	20.65%	98,271	20.43%
Savings accounts	86,238	19.35%	87,396	18.82%	89,043	18.51%
Time certificates (CDs under $100,000)	121,895	27.35%	124,386	26.78%	129,807	26.99%
CDs, $100,000 and over	28,025	6.29%	29,683	6.39%	31,269	6.50%
Other interest-bearing deposits	8,469	1.90%	9,214	1.98%	9,806	2.04%
Borrowed funds						
Fed funds purchased and repos	843	0.19%	5,188	1.12%	4,800	1.00%
Other borrowed funds	8,324	1.87%	10,284	2.21%	11,131	2.31%
All other liabilities	4,649	1.04%	4,416	0.95%	4,160	0.86%
Subordinated debt	0	0.00%	0	0.00%	0	0.00%
Equity capital						
Preferred stock						
Common stock	12,000	2.69%	12,000	2.58%	12,000	2.49%
Surplus	8,000	1.79%	8,000	1.72%	8,000	1.66%
Undivided profits	12,163	2.73%	14,174	3.05%	16,292	3.39%
Total liabilities and capital	445,756	100.00%	464,433	100.00%	480,968	100.00%

Asset Accounts

The following paragraphs provide a brief description of the principal bank asset accounts.

Cash and due from institutions generally include four categories of cash assets:

1. Currency and coin held in the bank's vault.

2. Deposits with the Federal Reserve Bank, which are used to meet legal reserve requirements and may also serve as a balancing account for checking clearance, transactions in Treasury securities, wire transfers, and so on.

3. Deposits with correspondent banks, which Fed nonmember banks can use to help meet legal requirements and all banks can use to compensate their correspondents for services performed.

4. Cash items in the process of collection, that is, items deposited in the Federal Reserve or correspondent banks for which credit has not been received. Since a bank does not earn interest on any of these four categories of cash assets, they are labeled nonearning assets and banks generally exert considerable effort to minimize their cash assets.

Short-term instruments include interest-bearing short-term assets such as federal funds sold (excess reserves that one bank lends to another), securities purchased under agreement to resell (reverse repurchase agreements), and other bank certificates of deposit. Such short-term instruments have obvious appeal to banks with extra funds for a short period; however, some banks use these short-term assets continuously as a way of employing attracted funds.

Securities refers to any eligible type of debt securities that a bank owns. They may be of any maturity and are valued at market value (for securities available for sale) or at what the bank paid for them plus or minus an amortized adjustment toward the maturity value of the principal (for securities held to maturity). The largest amount of securities held by most banks is securities of the U.S. government—Treasury bills, notes, and bonds. Many banks do have sizable holdings of securities of U.S. government agencies, such as the Federal Home Loan Bank. Some banks also hold either corporate debt or debts of foreign governments or businesses. More and more banks are also holding asset-backed debt securities, such as mortgage-backed securities or derivative securities, such as obligations stripped of their interest payments. Other securities held by many banks include general obligation or revenue bonds issued by states or their political subdivisions. The interest on such bonds may be partially exempt from federal income taxes. However, the 1986 Tax Reform Act eliminated most of the tax exemption on most state and local issues purchased after August 1986. Realized appreciation or depreciation on these bonds' principal value, however, is subject to such taxes. Banks are not permitted to buy securities that the large private rating agencies, such as Standard & Poor's or Moody's, rate below *investment grade* (for example, below Moody's Baa rating). Banks are not permitted to buy corporate stocks.

Banks must classify their debt securities as either (1) hold-to-maturity (HTM), (2) available-for-sale (AFS), or (3) trading securities (defined below). HTM securities can be valued on the balance sheet at original cost adjusted for amortization toward the securities' par or redemption value. To qualify for HTM, the bank must prove that it has both the intent and the ability to hold the bond until maturity. AFS securities must be valued at market, and any paper gains or losses are credited to or debited from the bank's capital position. However, gains or losses are not applied to the income statement. AFS securities are those that the bank may choose to sell if future business conditions put pressure on its liquidity.

Trading account assets include any of the preceding securities (usually Treasury securities) or other marketable assets that are held primarily for resale within relatively short periods, usually with the intent of profiting from short-term price movements. These assets must be valued at market rather than at book value, and gains or losses in value must be reported as ordinary gains or losses on the income statement as well as attributed to the capital position.

Loans are the primary earning assets of most any bank. The bank lends funds to a customer and in return gets a promissory note from the customer promising to pay interest, at either a fixed or a variable rate, and to repay the principal balance of the loan. Loans are usually categorized by type of user and by use of the funds. The three major categories for most banks are as follows.

1. Commercial loans, which are short- or intermediate-term loans to businesses typically for seasonal buildup of accounts receivable or inventory or for permanent working capital or plant and equipment.

2. Consumer loans, which include automobile loans, other consumer durable loans, home improvement loans, credit card loans, and other installment and single-payment loans to finance personal expenditures.

3. Real estate loans are used to finance single and multifamily residences, construction, and commercial real estate such as office buildings, retail outlets, and factories. Most long-term loans made prior to the early 1980s were amortizing and fixed-rate; however, many recent real estate loans have been variable-rate or a rate that is renegotiable every few years.

Other types of loans include agricultural loans, loans to banks and other financial institutions, loans to brokers and dealers, and any other loans that do not fit into the preceding loan categories.

Leases consist of the outstanding balances on leases of assets owned directly or indirectly by the bank. Lease payments are made by the lessor to the bank. While treatments of depreciation, residual ownership, and tax liability are different with lease contracts, most aspects of a lease are similar to a term loan.

The reserve for loan losses, a *contra-asset account* (i.e., "negative asset"), represents the balance in the valuation portion of a bank's bad debt reserve. A bank builds up this reserve to absorb future loan losses. Contributions to the reserve constitute a non-cash expense charged against income, and, because they are tax deductible, banks must estimate them according to strict Internal Revenue Service tax rules. This reserve is decreased when loans are charged off and removed from the balance sheet. The valuation reserve is subtracted from total loans to arrive at a bank's net loans.

Net loans and leases are total loans and leases less any unearned income and the reserve for loan losses. Since 1976, only net loans have been reported as bank assets.

Premises and fixed assets include all the bank's premises, facilities, equipment, furniture, fixtures, and leasehold improvements. These items are on the books at their depreciated book value and are classified as nonearning assets because they usually do not directly create an income stream.

Other real estate owned refers to all real estate owned by the bank, excluding bank premises and equipment. Most of this category is real estate acquired through foreclosure when customers default on loans secured by the real estate. Thus, the account may signal trouble in the loan portfolio.

Goodwill and other intangibles are usually the present value of expected future income in excess of the normal return, for example, a strong reputation and favorable location. They are generally recorded as the part of the value of an acquisition that exceeds the book value of the net assets acquired.

All other assets is simply a catchall category of other assets not large enough to warrant a separate account, such as customer liability to the bank on acceptances, prepaid expenses, and balances held with other institutions. If the items become significant, they will appear as a separate balance sheet item.

Liabilities and Capital Accounts

The liabilities and capital side of a bank's balance sheet separates all the bank's sources of funds into appropriate categories. The categories can be based on the form of the organization supplying the funds, such as individual, partnership, and corporation deposits versus public deposits, or on the form of the contract, such as passbook savings versus money market deposits. The following paragraphs emphasize the broad forms of the contract, but the descriptions include some of the principal forms of the organization using each contract.

Demand deposits by law are noninterest-bearing checking accounts of individuals, partnerships, corporations, and governmental units. The majority of these accounts generally come from businesses (partnerships or corporations) because (1) businesses are not eligible for interest-bearing checking accounts and often are required to leave compensating demand deposit balances with the bank as part of a loan agreement, (2) individuals are usually eligible for interest-bearing checking accounts, and (3) governmental units keep most of their deposits in interest-bearing accounts.

NOW and other transaction accounts are checking accounts of individuals and partnerships that receive interest as long as they meet the specifications set by the bank. The proper legal title for these accounts is Negotiable Order of Withdrawal (NOW) accounts. Prior to March 31, 1986, they were subject to Regulation Q limits set by the Depository Institutions Deregulation Committee.

Savings accounts represent interest-bearing deposits of individuals and partnerships that have no specified maturity. They do not have contractual provisions requiring the depositor to give written notice of an intention to withdraw funds. These accounts include passbook savings, which have been in use for over seven decades, and money market accounts, which were created in December 1982 to provide banks with an instrument that was eligible to pay ''money market'' interest rates that would compete effectively with money market mutual funds. Most banks pay rates that vary according to an average rate on a short-term money market instrument and will probably continue to use minimum sizes and maximum free withdrawals to market this account.

Time certificates (CDs under $100,000) are time deposits evidenced by nonnegotiable instruments that specify the interest rate and the maturity date, which must be seven days or longer. These certificates are not subject to rate ceilings, and there are usually interest penalties if the deposits are withdrawn prior to maturity. They are generally priced at a fixed rate and held by individuals, but they can be held by businesses, and some have floating rates—often tied to those of similar-maturity Treasury securities.

Certificates of deposit (CDs $100,000 and over) are larger accounts than time certificates and are often negotiable, with maturities of 14 days or greater. They can be either fixed or variable obligations. The negotiable CDs are denominated in amounts ranging from $100,000 to $100 million, with $1 million being the standard trading unit and three months to one year the most popular maturity range. Principal purchasers are treasurers of large businesses; however, state and local governments and wealthy individuals also have purchased significant amounts.

CDs are considered "flight money" and, therefore, represent a less secure form of funding because amounts over $100,000 are not federally insured and the depositor is highly alert to any deterioration in the bank's reputation for financial strength.

Other interest-bearing deposits is a catchall category of time and savings deposit accounts. The primary category of public deposits is usually time deposits of state and local governments. In many states, securities must be pledged as collateral for such deposits. Other time deposits include time deposits of commercial banks, other financial intermediaries, and foreign governments and financial institutions.

Short-term borrowing includes *federal funds and repurchase agreements* (repos). Federal funds are the excess reserves of banks that are purchased on an unsecured basis by a bank or possibly another institution that has a reserve deficiency. The purchases are often made on a daily basis but generally can be easily renewed. For the banking system, federal funds purchased are roughly equal to federal funds sold, and the rate on federal funds is determined by the amount of excess reserves available versus the demand for this form of funding. Repurchase agreements, or repos, are the sale of securities under an agreement to repurchase. They are a form of short-term borrowing that represent a bank's obligation to buy back securities that it has temporarily sold. Because the purchaser owns the securities during this period, these repos constitute, in effect, secured borrowing. *Other short-term borrowing* forms include discount borrowings from the Federal Reserve, Eurodollars, and commercial paper.

All other liabilities is another catchall category for remaining liabilities. Items usually found in this category include accrued taxes and expenses, dividends payable, liabilities on acceptances, trade payables, and other miscellaneous liabilities.

Subordinated debt includes bank capital notes and debentures with maturities exceeding one year. These notes or debentures are not insured and may be either straight (nonconvertible) or convertible into the bank's common stock. Subordinated debt is a source of funds and may also be treated as part of capital if the debt meets certain requirements. The requirements usually include subordination to deposits and other liabilities, minimum average maturity when issued (usually eight to ten years), and minimum remaining maturity (usually two years).

Equity capital represents the difference between the book value of a bank's assets and its liabilities. It includes up to four possible categories—preferred stock, common stock, surplus, and undivided profits. *Preferred stock* pays a fixed or variable dividend that is not a tax-deductible expense; therefore, banks do not often use preferred stock. The *common stock* account is the total par or stated value of all the bank's outstanding shares. The *surplus* account can be increased by the sale of common stock at a premium above its par value and by transfers from the undivided profits account. The surplus account may also include equity reserves. Equity reserves include contingency reserves (the emphasis generally on reserves that are not a tax-deductible expense), such as reserves for security gains or losses and the contingency portion of provisions for possible loan losses. The *undivided profits* account is similar to the retained earnings account for most nonfinancial businesses. After-tax net income increases undivided profits, and cash or stock dividends and capital transfers reduce undivided profits. The book value of a bank's common stock is the summation of the common stock, surplus, and undivided profits.

UNDERSTANDING A BANK'S INCOME STATEMENT

The income statement measures bank performance over a period of time. It tells what was occurring between two year-end balance sheets. Table 2.2 contains the 1999, 2000, and 2001 income statements for First National Bank. The structure of these income statements is very purposeful. Interest-related accounts are shown first because of the financial character of banks and other financial services firms—most assets and liabilities are financial contracts. Interest income on a bank's earning assets is the primary source of bank income, whereas the interest expense required to obtain the funds employed by the bank usually is the bank's primary cost category. The focus on interest-related items gives an immediate picture of the rewards of financial intermediation. Also, as we discuss in Chapters 3 and 4, it permits the analyst to isolate that part of performance that is directly affected by *changes* in market interest rates. Ultimately, management has to try to answer the question: What effect will unexpected changes in interest rates have on net income?

Other income and expense items are not directly affected by unexpected changes in market interest rates. Still, other income items, such as service charges, fees, sale of other financial services, and net trust income, are important sources of revenues for most banks. Other expenses, most notably the costs associated with the bank's employees and its premises and equipment, are usually significant expenditures for a bank.

A description of the income statement items listed in Table 2.2 follows.

Interest income on short-term instruments, securities, tax-exempt securities, commercial loans, real estate loans, other loans, and leases is the interest the bank receives on each of these specific asset categories. All interest income, less associated expenses, is taxable, with the exception of some of the interest income on securities of state and local governments which may be partially exempt from federal income taxes.

Interest expense on NOW and other transaction accounts, savings accounts, CDs of $100,000 and over, time certificates, short-term borrowing, other liabilities, and subordinated debt includes the interest expense on each specific deposit or liability category. Every category of interest expense is a deductible expense for determining a bank's income taxes.

Net interest income is the difference between interest income (revenues) and interest expense. It measures how much total interest income on all earning assets exceed total interest expense on all sources of funding.

Provision for loan losses is the amount charged against earnings to establish a reserve sufficient to absorb expected loan losses. Internal Revenue Service rules set the maximum amount that can be a tax-deductible expense and that can be included in the valuation reserve account on the balance sheet. Management, based on its knowledge of the quality of the loan portfolio and the opinions of the regulatory authorities, may charge more or less than the maximum tax-deductible amount if it believes this amount is more appropriate for possible loan losses.

TABLE 2.2   First National Bank's Income Statements for Specified Years Ended December 31 (in thousands of dollars)

	1999	2000	2001
INTEREST INCOME			
Short-term instruments	265	71	91
Securities	9,324	8,412	7,999
Commercial loans	7,960	8,480	8,761
Consumer loans	9,220	10,817	11,595
Real estate loans	4,693	4,818	5,509
Other loans	2,128	2,778	2,689
Leases	889	897	973
Total interest income	34,481	36,274	37,618
INTEREST EXPENSE			
NOW and other transaction accounts	2,391	2,302	2,565
Savings accounts	3,605	3,767	3,856
Time certificates (under $100,000)	6,509	6,704	7,087
CDs $100,000 and over	1,578	1,674	1,785
Other interest-bearing deposits	447	499	517
Borrowed funds	490	868	918
Other liabilities and sub notes	0	0	0
Total interest expense	15,020	15,814	16,728
NET INTEREST INCOME	19,461	20,460	20,890
Provision for loan losses	570	535	720
NET INTEREST INCOME AFTER PROVISION	18,891	19,925	20,170
NONINTEREST INCOME			
Deposit service charges	2,649	2,744	2,812
Other noninterest income	1,546	1,828	2,203
Total noninterest income	4,195	4,572	5,015
NONINTEREST EXPENSES			
Salaries and benefits	9,040	9,237	9,452
Premises and equipment expense	2,218	2,401	2,734
Other noninterest expense	3,980	4,041	4,318
Total noninterest expenses	15,238	15,679	16,504
NET OPERATING INCOME	7,848	8,818	8,681
SECURITIES GAINS (LOSSES)	−85	0	123
APPLICABLE INCOME TAXES	2,521	2,943	2,895
EXTRAORDINARY GAINS (LOSSES)	0	0	0
NET INCOME	5,242	5,875	5,909
CASH DIVIDENDS PAID	3,600	3,600	3,720

Net interest income after provision is net interest income less the provision for loan losses. It represents an attempt to adjust the net interest income downward by a proxy measure for the credit risk taken to obtain interest income.

Deposit service charges include income from maintenance fees and various activity fees that most banks charge on their deposit accounts under a certain size. Businesses usually receive a credit against these charges based on their average balances, whereas fees on individual deposits are often waived if a minimum balance requirement is met.

Other noninterest income includes the net income from the bank's trust department (if it has one), commissions on insurance premiums, income from direct lease financing, commissions on mutual funds sales, trading account income, safety deposit rental fees, and miscellaneous noninterest income sources. Fees for originating loans or guaranteed lines of credit are often included in this category.

Salaries and benefits represent the total compensation paid to all officers and employees of the bank. This compensation includes not only salaries and wages but also unemployment and social security taxes paid, contributions to retirement or pension plans, cost of medical or health services, and other fringe benefits provided officers and employees.

Premises and equipment expense consists of depreciation on premises, computers, and equipment, the rental or leasing cost of offices, computers and other machines, and taxes on premises and equipment.

Other noninterest expense is a general category for a bank's remaining noninterest operating expenses. This account usually includes such expenses as advertising, premiums on deposit insurance and fidelity insurance, directors' fees, supplies and postage, and costs associated with temporary employees. This category now includes security gains or losses from the sale, exchange, redemption, or retirement of investment securities above or below the value at which these securities are carried on the bank's books.

Net operating income (before taxes) is the difference between total interest and noninterest income and total expenses. Although banks pay the existing corporate income tax rates, net operating income is usually adjusted slightly to determine taxable income. Adjustments are usually to subtract the interest on tax-exempt securities from net operating income before taxes; however, other adjustments may be needed if the bank uses other tax avoidance techniques.

Securities gains (losses) represent the realized gains or losses from the actual sales of any securities during the time period. Security gains are generally taxable at the bank's ordinary income tax rate, and losses can be used to reduce taxable income.

Applicable income taxes include federal and any state and local taxes on the bank's taxable income.

Extraordinary gains (losses) represent gains or losses on unusual and typically nonrecurring events. These events may or may not be taxable and are usually reported net of any taxes.

Net income or after tax income is taxable income, including security gains or losses and extraordinary items, less the estimated federal, state, and local income taxes payable for that year. Some bank regulators and analysts favor using net operating income after taxes as the primary dollar measure of a bank's income. This is computed by eliminating nonoperating events, such as significant gains or losses on the sale of securities or extraordinary gains or losses.

SUPPLEMENTARY INFORMATION

Items from a bank's balance sheet and income statement are generally accompanied by other information useful in evaluating bank performance. Table 2.3 is an example of useful supplementary data that are usually available in a bank's annual report, its 10-K report, or bank reports available on the internet. The supplementary items are as follows.

Earning assets refers to all assets earning an explicit interest return. Cash and due from banks and bank premises and equipment are the two major asset categories that are not earning assets.

Risk assets are earning assets subject to either credit risk or interest rate risk. Some banks still calculate risk assets as earning assets less all government securities. However, First National Bank uses a more appropriate designation of earning assets less all short-term instruments and investment securities maturing within one year.

TABLE 2.3 First National Bank's Supplementary Information (in thousands of dollars, except last four rows)

	1999	2000	2001
Earning assets (average)	402,735	418,241	432,974
Risk assets (average)	370,217	386,751	400,788
Maturities of securities			
Under one year	32,518	31,490	32,186
One to five years	56,401	50,136	46,214
Over five years	54,217	53,835	52,730
Insider loans	6,289	8,104	7,846
Loan losses less recoveries	580	442	720
Noncurrent (over 90 days) loans			
Commercial loans	277	287	352
Consumer loans	509	740	1,013
Real estate loans	156	119	177
Other loans and leases	0	60	60
Core deposits	371,752	380,688	403,316
Liquid assets	37,586	32,920	33,897
Unused commitments	24,138	25,860	27,172
Off-balance sheet derivatives	0	0	0
Purchased mortgage service rights	0	0	0
Noncore funding	37,192	45,155	47,200
Interest rate sensitivity (one year)			
Repricing assets	192,435	221,784	220,980
Repricing liabilities	217,942	235,165	239,366
Mutual fund sales	0	0	1,408
Number of offices	7	9	9
Number of employees	245	249	256
Number of common shares	1,200,000	1,200,000	1,200,000
Market price per share	36.42	41.27	46.35

Maturities of securities classify a bank's investment securities into selected maturity categories. This information is helpful in understanding the interest sensitivity of the securities portfolio and the potential appreciation or depreciation of this portfolio if interest rates change.

Insider loans are loans to members of the board of directors or top management and to businesses in which such persons have a substantial ownership interest.

Loan losses less recoveries represent the actual loan losses the bank has recognized during the year less any recoveries of previous loan losses.

Noncurrent (over 90 days) loans are loans on which interest or principal payments or both have not been paid at the contracted time. Usually, a bank allows a short grace period (e.g., 60 or 90 days) before it classifies a loan as noncurrent. Noncurrent loans differ from classified loans, provisions for possible loan losses, and loan losses, although all these categories give some idea of the credit quality of a bank's loan portfolio. Many banks also report nonperforming loans or renegotiated loans.

Unused commitments are firm commitments to extend loans or to complete other transactions usually at an agreed rate and for a set period of time.

Off-balance sheet derivatives refer to a wide array of securities whose value is derived from an underlying security. Many of these derivatives, such as swaps and options, are not included on a bank's balance sheet.

Purchased mortgage service rights are the right to collect principal and interest on mortgages owned by another institution. The purchasing bank receives fees for collecting such payments and sending them to the owning institution.

Noncore funding are impersonal (noncustomer) deposits and borrowing which the bank has basically purchased by paying a competitive rate. Such liabilities are more vulnerable to withdrawal than core (customer) deposits and borrowings.

Interest rate sensitivity refers to a comparison of the sensitivity of cash flows on assets and liabilities to changes in interest rates. Interest-sensitive assets (liabilities) are any category of assets (liabilities) on which interest income (expense) will change in the specified time period in response to interest rate changes. The time period of such sensitivity should be identified. Many banks measure rate sensitivity for several time periods (e.g., 30 days, 90 days, six months, and one year) because of sizable time differences in sensitivity between assets and liabilities. A dollar gap (difference between sensitive assets and sensitive liabilities), as well as the ratio of sensitive assets to sensitive liabilities, is often calculated.

Mutual funds sales are the principal amount of mutual funds sold at the bank during the year. Banks generally receive a selling commission.

Number of offices refers to the number of branches and manned offices of the banks. Unmanned offices, ATMs, and stand-alone computing units are not included.

Number of employees should be the number of full-time officers and employees plus the full-time equivalent of a bank's part-time employees. Temporary employees generally are not included.

Number of common shares are the number of shares of common stock that are issued and outstanding. They are used to calculate earnings, book value, and market value per share.

Market price per share is available for larger banks whose shares are actively traded. Data may not be available or not as meaningful if a bank is the nondominant member of a bank holding company or if the bank is small and does not have an active market for its shares.

TABLE 2.4 Comparative Financial Data for Selected Banks (dollar data in thousands of dollars)

	Heritage	American	Overton	Mellon	Comerica
TOTAL ASSETS ($)					
Percent of total assets	75,535	70,908	756,436	37,330,293	27,051,459
Cash and due from institutions	1.75%	5.01%	9.84%	7.16%	4.85%
Fed funds sold and rev repos	0.00%	0.00%	0.00%	1.45%	0.47%
Other short-term instruments	0.00%	0.01%	0.00%	2.12%	0.10%
Securities	17.80%	21.71%	31.08%	16.29%	12.85%
Trading account assets	0.00%	0.00%	0.10%	0.93%	0.07%
Net loans and leases	71.57%	68.03%	54.92%	61.48%	77.49%
Premises and fixed assets	1.83%	3.82%	2.53%	1.33%	0.84%
Other real estate owned	0.13%	0.23%	0.14%	0.14%	0.07%
Goodwill and intangibles	1.43%	0.14%	0.00%	4.18%	0.23%
All other assets	5.48%	1.06%	1.38%	4.95%	3.04%
Total	99.99%	99.98%	99.99%	100.03%	100.01%
Demand deposits	15.23%	12.45%	31.30%	19.89%	16.25%
Interest-bearing deposits	65.79%	75.14%	54.08%	55.97%	44.48%
Fed funds purchased and repos	0.62%	3.22%	7.74%	4.50%	5.68%
Other borrowed funds	7.72%	0.55%	0.29%	5.43%	22.56%
All other liabilities	0.68%	1.08%	0.36%	2.96%	1.28%
Subordinated debt	0.00%	0.00%	0.00%	2.62%	2.55%
Preferred stock	0.00%	0.00%	0.00%	0.00%	0.00%
Common stock	0.82%	1.41%	0.19%	0.45%	0.22%
Surplus	1.83%	3.03%	1.21%	2.40%	2.36%
Undivided profits	7.31%	3.11%	4.83%	5.81%	4.62%
Total	100.00%	99.99%	100.00%	100.03%	100.00%
INCOME STATEMENT ($)					
Interest income	5,645	5,804	48,789	2,306,153	2,006,988
Interest expense	2,207	2,549	16,558	1,113,487	1,000,737
Net interest income	3,438	3,255	32,231	1,192,666	1,006,251
Provision for loan losses	104	366	1,194	−16,998	102,831
Net interest income after provision	3,334	2,889	31,037	1,209,664	903,420
Noninterest income	799	823	10,190	1,382,391	387,829
Noninterest expenses	2,279	2,587	29,292	1,710,938	837,373
Net operating income	1,854	1,125	11,935	881,117	453,876
Security gains (losses)	3	0	88	5,799	13,396
Applicable income taxes	673	380	3,773	317,978	155,893
Extraordinary gains (losses)	0	0	0	0	0
Net income	1,184	745	8,250	568,938	311,379
SUPPLEMENTARY INFO ($)					
Earning assets	67,506	63,643	651,341	30,421,858	24,592,857
Long-term assets (5+ years)	6,999	1,833	107,348	6,881,972	5,065,273
Insider loans	60	11	15,675	295,662	570,781
Loan losses less recoveries	17	363	256	9,751	68,701
Noncurrent loans	5	193	6,232	158,366	109,008
Unused commitments	12,065	8,018	137,046	27,147,023	18,908,757
Off-balance sheet derivatives	0	0	0	38,242,035	11,505,366
Purchased mortgage service rights	0	0	0	739,993	22,018
Volatile liabilities	10,817	8,397	112,313	10,719,504	8,976,183
SUPPLEMENTARY INFO (#)					
Number of offices	2	5	16	432	273
Number of employees	33	40	437	19,625	6,085

DATA FOR A TYPICAL BANK?

Up to this point, you might imagine that most commercial banks had similar balance sheets, income statements, and supplementary information. This is certainly not the case. Table 2.4 presents the balance sheets, income statements, and selected supplementary information from a recent year for five commercial banks: American Heritage Bank in El Reno, Oklahoma; American National Bank of Sorpy County, Nebraska; Overton Bank and Trust in Fort Worth, Texas; Mellon Bank in Pittsburgh, Pennsylvania; and Comerica Bank in Detroit, Michigan.

Some characteristics are in line with what you might expect—the very large banks (Mellon and Comerica) with their expertise made extensive use of off-balance sheet derivatives, while the small institutions did not use derivatives. The very large banks, through their access to global financial markets, tended to use more wholesale funding, while the smaller banks used primarily customer funding. There are exceptions even to these generalizations. For example, American Heritage had more borrowed funds on a percentage basis than Mellon, and Overton had more federal funds purchased and repos than either Mellon or Comerica.

Other characteristics in Table 2.4 vary widely. For example, the proportion of assets in federal funds sold, securities, loans and leases, long-term assets, demand deposits, and equity capital varied without any pattern related to size. Our beginning conclusion is that while size may permit more expertise and access to financial markets, the determining factors for many characteristics depend on a bank's strategic plans and the lines of business the bank chooses to emphasize. In Chapter 3, we will analyze return and risk measures for the five banks in Table 2.4 in order to shed more light on the question: Is there a typical bank?

AN INTRODUCTION TO LOAN LOSS ACCOUNTING

Although a thorough analysis of loan loss accounting is a legal and accounting nightmare, the basics can be clarified by a simple example. The reconciliation of the loan loss reserve accounts for First National Bank in 2001 appears in Table 2.5. Figure 2.1 gives an illustration of the data in Table 2.5. The reserves for loan loss balances are year-end balance sheet figures rather than the average balances found in Table 2.1. The provision for loan losses figure can be found in the income statement in Table 2.2. The figure for actual loan losses less recoveries is part of the supplementary information in Table 2.3.

TABLE 2.5 First National Bank's Reconciliation of Loan Loss Accounts (in thousands of dollars)

Reserve for loan losses, Dec. 31, 2000		3,124
Loan losses during 2001	480	
Recoveries from previous loan losses	12	
Loan losses less recoveries		−468
Provision for loan losses		720
Reserve for loan losses, Dec. 31, 2001		3,376

FIGURE 2.1   Simplified illustration of how loan loss accounting works

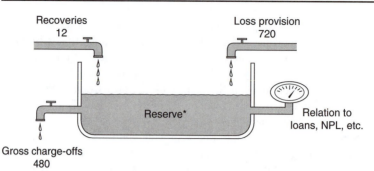

*Reserve was 3,124 on December 31, 2000. Recoveries increased the reserve by 12 in 2000, but charge-offs reduced it by 480. To hit the targeted reserve of 3,376, the Provision for loan losses—an income statement expense—had to be 720.

First National Bank had a reserve for loan losses of $3,124 million as of December 31, 2000. During the year, this reserve would be decreased by the actual loan losses First National charged off and increased by any recoveries of loans previously charged off. Toward the end of the accounting period (here we assume it is an annual period, but for most banks it is quarterly), First National makes an additional provision for loan losses to bring the period-ending reserve to the desired level. This provision is an expense item on the income statement and is usually deductible as an expense establishing taxable income.

The desired level of the ending reserve for loan losses should be based primarily on management's knowledge of the current loan portfolio. Specifically, management must continually review problem loans and overall portfolio quality, current and expected economic and financial conditions, loss experience relative to outstanding loans, and examinations by internal and outside auditors and the regulatory authorities to determine the adequacy of this reserve.

OFF-BALANCE SHEET INFORMATION

During the late 1980s and 1990s, banks developed new means of doing business that did not appear on their balance sheets as assets and liabilities. Later we will see that these off-balance sheet items may have a significant impact on bank returns and risk. At this point, some of the more common off-balance sheet activities are introduced and possible sources of information are disclosed.

There are two broad categories of off-balance sheet information. The first consists of activities that generate income or expenses without the creation or holding of an underlying asset or liability. A simple example would be cases in which the bank acted as a broker (taking a fee for arranging for funds to be provided to borrowers without making loans or raising deposits) rather than as a dealer (making and holding loans and the funding source). Other banking services, such as cash management, that generate fee income without requiring assets or liabilities also fit in the category.

The second category of off-balance sheet activities involves the bank's commitments and contingent claims. A commitment means that the bank commits to some future action

TABLE 2.6   Primary Types of Off-Balance Sheet Commitments and Contingent Claims

1. Financial guarantees
   a. Standby letter of credit
   b. Lines of credit
   c. Revolving loan commitments
   d. Note issuance facilities
   e. Securitization with recourse
2. Trade finance
   a. Commercial letters of credit
   b. Acceptance participations
3. Investment activities
   a. Forward commitments
   b. Financial futures
   c. Interest rate swaps
   d. Options
   e. Currency swaps

and receives a fee for making such a commitment. A contingent claim is an obligation by a bank to take action (e.g., to lend funds or buy securities) if a contingency is realized. The claim does not appear on the balance sheet until it is exercised (e.g., the loan is made or the security is purchased). The bank, however, usually has underwritten an obligation of a third party and has increased income and taken risk.

Table 2.6 shows some more common commitments and contingent claims grouped into three subcategories: (1) financial guarantees, (2) trade finance, and (3) investment activities. A financial guarantee is an undertaking by a bank (the guarantor) to stand behind the obligation of a third party and to carry out that obligation if the third party fails to do so. For example, in standby letters of credit, the bank must pay the beneficiary if the third party defaults on a financial obligation of the performance contract. A line of credit is a nonfee, informal agreement between a bank and a customer that the bank will typically make a loan up to the maximum agreed amount to that customer unless conditions have changed materially. In contrast, a revolving loan agreement is a formal agreement between the bank and a customer that obligates the bank to lend funds according to the terms of the contract. Note issuance facilities—Euronotes, revolving underwriting facilities (RUFs), and standby note issuance facilities (SNIFs)—and securitization of assets with recourse are other examples of financial guarantees.

Trade finance includes commercial letters of credit and acceptance participations, both of which are used to finance international trade. A letter of credit involves a bank's guarantee that its customer will pay a contractual debt to a third party. An acceptance participation is all or part of a banker's acceptance (a time draft the originating bank has agreed to pay at maturity) that has been purchased and for which the purchasing bank has a contingent liability.

Investment activities that do not appear on a bank's balance sheet include derivative instruments such as forward commitments, financial futures, interest rate swaps, options (puts, calls, collars), and currency swaps. Chapters 13, 14, and 15 provide institutional arrangements and formal analyses of all these instruments and shows that the other off-balance sheet commitments and contingent claims similarly can be conceived and analyzed as derivatives. A bank usually receives a fee or changes a risk position immediately for an activity that does not appear on the balance sheet now but for which the bank may

TABLE 2.7   Schedule RC-L—Commitments and Contingencies
Please read carefully the instructions for the preparation of
Schedule RC-L

Dollar Amounts in Thousands	C360		
	Bil	Mil Thou	
1. Commitments to make or purchase loans or to extend credit in the form of lease financing arrangements (report only the unused portions of commitments that are fee paid or otherwise legally binding)..			1.
2. Futures and forward contracts (exclude contracts involving foreign exchange):			
a. Commitments to purchase..............................			2.a.
b. Commitments to sell			2.b.
3. When-issued securities:			
a. Gross commitments to purchase			3.a.
b. Gross commitments to sell....................................			3.b.
4. Standby contracts and other option arrangements:			
a. Obligations to purchase under option contracts ...			4.a.
b. Obligations to sell under option contracts............			4.b.
5. Commitments to purchase foreign currencies and U.S. dollar exchange (spot and forward)			5.
6. Standby letters of credit:			
a. Standby letters of credit:			
(1) To U.S. addressees (domicile)......................			6.a.(1)
(2) To non-U.S. addressees (domicile)................			6.a.(2)
b. Amount of standby letters of credit in Items 6.a.(1) and 6.a.(2) conveyed to others through participations			6.b.
7. Commercial and similar letters of credit...................			7.
8. Participations in acceptances (as described in the instructions) conveyed to others by the reporting bank			8.
9. Participations in acceptances (as described in the instructions) acquired by the reporting (nonaccepting) bank			9.
10. Securities borrowed..			10.
11. Securities lent..			11.
12. Other significant commitments and contingencies (list below each component of this item over 25% of Schedule RC, Item 28, "Total equity capital").....			12.

Memoranda

1. Loans originated by the reporting bank that have been sold or participated to others during the calendar quarter ending with the report date (exclude the portions of such loans retained by the reporting bank; see instructions for other exclusions).............			M.1.
2. Notional value of all outstanding interest rate swaps			M.2.

SOURCE: Adapted from Schedule RC-L by the Federal Financial Institutions Examination Commission.

have to take future actions. Other aspects of off-balance sheet investment activities are described in further detail in Chapters 8 and 14.

Table 2.7 is a copy of the Federal Financial Institutions Examining Committee Schedule RC-L on which banks report nonbalance sheet commitments and contingencies. These commitments and contingencies may have a significant effect on the return and capital adequacy measures discussed in the following chapter. One of the most important aspects of the recently adopted risk-backed capital rules is the requirement that capital be held for most off-balance sheet items.

NONFINANCIAL INFORMATION

Nonfinancial information also affects a bank's overall financial condition. A checklist of such information was developed by Michael Knapp and is summarized in Table 2.8. Although many of the items are self-explanatory, a few deserve further explanation. For example, recent dismissal of an audit firm or significant management turnover may indicate internal conflict regarding the quality of financial or operating policies. Outside directors who lack experience, expertise, or interest may encourage dominant management personalities of untested abilities who may dictate weak lending, investment, or funding policies. Poor loan documentation and overvalued or nonexistent collateral are frequent shortcomings at poorly managed banks. The key point is that information such as that listed in Table 2.8 is an important supplement to a bank's financial information.

SOURCES AND QUALITY OF INFORMATION

The sources of banking information range from the bank's annual financial reports to the detailed financial analysis available in the Uniform Bank Performance Reports. Consulting

TABLE 2.8 Checklist of Nonfinancial Information Affecting a Bank's Financial Condition

1. Is the bank insured by the FDIC?
2. Is the bank audited by a CPA firm?
3. Has the bank recently changed independent auditors?
4. Have there been significant management changes in recent years?
5. How much banking experience and general business experience do the outside directors possess?
6. Do the outside directors appear to have significant influence on the bank's operations?
7. Does the bank have a loan review committee?
8. What is the general quality and financial strength of correspondent banks?
9. Does the bank use a conservative method of defining nonperforming loans?
10. Does the bank offer substantial interest rate premiums to depositors?
11. Have bank regulators recently required the bank to sign administrative agreements or cease-and-desist orders?

SOURCE: Michael C. Knapp, "Avoiding Problem Banks," *Journal of Accountancy* (May 1985): 103.

firms, industry associations, and computer-based services also provide important information for evaluating a bank's performance.

Much more detailed information and quantitative analytical analysis of a bank are available for all insured commercial banks in the Uniform Bank Performance Reports. These reports provide a detailed five-year financial profile for the requested bank and a similar profile for a "peer" group and are prepared from quarterly call report data by the Federal Financial Institutions Examination Council. The contents of a typical Uniform Bank Performance Report are explored in Chapter 3. A number of consulting firms also specialize in bank analysis. Most of the data used by consulting firms come from computer CD-ROMs of quarterly call report data.

The bottom portion of Table 2.9 lists some of the more widely used sources of general banking information. The American Bankers Association is the largest industry trade group and has periodicals and studies on various aspects of banking. The FDIC Information Service provides the public with current information on the banking industry and banking data. The Bank Administration Institute is a nonprofit organization that funds and publishes research of interest to bankers and their customers. INNERLINE and the Money Market Monitor are two computer-based services that track the financial health of banks and market interest rates. The only daily banking paper published in the United States is the *American Banker*. It reports on innovative banking services and provides constant surveillance of legislative and judicial actions that significantly influence the industry.

The quality of information, particularly financial information, on a bank also deserves mention at this point. Three areas of concern are briefly discussed here: (1) the use of point-of-time data, (2) the use of book value data, and (3) the discretion allowed in determining some key data. Most of the annual and quarterly report data by banks are given at a particular point of time. Because many financial assets and liabilities are short term or can be bought, sold, or repaid in a short period, some point-of-time data may be misleading. Most bank analysts prefer daily averages of balances in assets and liabilities for many measures of banking performance.

Second, banking financial information is generally stated in book value rather than market value terms. This is particularly surprising because most banking assets and liabilities are financial ones that are generally more amenable to valuation (market values exist or can be estimated from very similar instruments) than the nonfinancial assets and liabilities of other businesses. About the only balance sheet item most banks provide market value information on (in footnotes to financial statements) is their security holdings. Other key assets, such as loans, and liabilities, such as long-term borrowings, are expressed in book value terms, with no hints about market values. Since the book value of common equity is the difference between the book value of assets and the book value of liabilities, one has to wonder what book value of common equity measures.

Finally, numerous types of bank financial information are affected by accounting rules, tax rules, and management decisions. For example, the provision for loan losses and the resulting reserve for loan losses, described earlier in this chapter, is probably affected more by accounting rules, tax rules, and management decisions than by economic realities. Why do some banks have reserves against 60 percent of their nonperforming loans (another rather arbitrary number), while other banks have reserves against only 20 percent of their nonperforming loans? Also, why, in the spring of 1987 did most large banks suddenly deem necessary a momentous increase in reserves against losses on loans to less developed countries? Changes in the rules or management interpretation of such

TABLE 2.9 Primary Sources of Banking Information

Source	Information Provided	Availability
Financial Information		
Annual financial report	Basic financial statements and supplemental disclosures	By request from bank
Quarterly call report	Reports of condition and income—contain essentially the same information supplied in a bank balance sheet and income statement	By request from Data Base, Federal Deposit Insurance Corporation, 550 17th Street N.W., Washington, D.C. 20429 (small fee for copying and postage)
Annual Form 10-K (bank holding companies)	Securities and Exchange Commission—required financial statements and other extensive financial disclosures, including nature and extent of foreign loans and related-party transactions	By request from the bank holding company. Included in annual report.
Financial Analysis		
Uniform Bank Performance Report	Detailed 15- to 20-page comparative analytical report	By request from Federal Financial Institutions Examination Council, 1776 G Street N.W., Suite 701, Washington, D.C. 20006 ($45 per report)
Bank analysts	In-depth information and reports on specific banks	Keefe, Bruyette & Woods, 2 World Trade Center, 85th Floor, New York, N.Y. 10048 Sheshunoff & Company, P.O. Box 13203, Capitol Station, Austin, Tex. 78711 Financial Institutions Analysts and Consultants, Inc., 3 Embarcadero Center, Suite 1830, San Francisco, Calif. 94111
General Information		
American Bankers Association	Information and studies on the banking industry	ABA Public Information Office, 1120 Connecticut Avenue N.W., Washington, D.C. 20036
FDIC Information Service	General information on the banking industry and current status of the availability of information on specific banks	FDIC, Corporate Communications Office, 550 17th Street N.W., Washington, D.C. 20429
Bank Administration Institute	Various research studies in the banking field	60 Gould Center, Rolling Meadows, Ill. 60008 (varying fees)
INNERLINE	Online access to call report data base	American Banker, State Street Plaza, New York, N.Y. 10004 (fee schedule available on request; least expensive rate is $30 per month)
Money Market Monitor	Online access to database containing current interest rates on money market certificates and jumbo CDs by over 200 U.S. banks	American Banker ($7.50 per use accessed via INNERLINE)
American Banker	Overview of current banking events and financial market data	Daily financial newspaper ($675 annually)

SOURCE: Michael C. Knapp, "Avoiding Problem Banks," *Journal of Accountancy* (May, 1985), p. 101.

rules may make some aggregate information questionable and comparison between banks highly suspect.

END OF CHAPTER PROBLEMS

2.1 Prepare a December 31 balance sheet from the following information:

	Million
Investment securities	$ 130
Demand deposits	170
Federal funds purchased	105
Total (gross) loans	644
Cash and due from banks	98
Savings and time deposits	555
Net loans	636
Bank premises and equipment	33
Other assets	10
Accumulated retained earnings	43
Federal funds sold	22
Other borrowed funds	12
Other real estate owned	4
Allowance for loan and lease losses	8
Capital surplus	30
Long-term debt	10
Other liabilities	8

2.2 EquiBank's long-term debt and stockholders' equity for December 31, 1999 is shown in the following list. The bank had 1 million shares outstanding.

	Million
Long-term debt	$ 5
Preferred stock	20
Common stock (par $1)	1
Surplus	12
Accumulated retained earnings	32

During the year 2000, EquiBank issued 200,000 additional new common shares at a price of $50 per share. The bank generated $8 million of net income and paid $5 million in dividends. It repaid $1 million of the principal on long-term debt. Prepare the same accounts as of December 31, 2000 to reflect these changes during the year.

2.3 Develop a bank's income statement based on the following data and determine the bank's net income:

Salaries and benefits expense	$ 2,340,683
Interest from business loans	5,448,274
Trust department income	660,339
Interest on savings and time deposits	3,679,880
Occupancy expense	776,425

Service charge income	221,568
Interest on consumer loans	4,056,296
Interest on long-term CDs	504,390
Provision for loan losses	790,392
Miscellaneous expense	923,786
Interest on borrowed funds	1,332,585
Interest from taxable securities	1,940,395

The bank pays a 34% tax rate.

2.4 Bank X made a provision for loan losses of $3.5 million, took loan charge-offs of $5 million, and had recoveries of $1,750,000 during the year 1999. At the *end* of 1999 (that is, December 31, 1999), the bank's balance sheet reserve for loan losses was $2 million. What was the bank's apparent reserve for loan losses at the end of the prior year (December 31, 1998)?

2.5 Robobank's allowance for loan losses from its balance sheet for the years ending 2001 and 2002 is:

	12/31/01	**12/31/02**
Allowance for loan losses	$49,235,000	$55,335,000

During the year 2002, Robobank took a provision for loan losses charge of $15 million against its income. Determine the apparent amount of *net loan charge-offs* during 2002.

2.6 In early January, Advalorem Bank decided to set its allowance for loan losses at 1.50 percent of total loans by the end of December of the same year. Its allowance for loan losses was $40 million; total loans were $3 billion and loans were expected to grow 12 percent during the year. Advalorem Bank estimated that it would charge off $20 million during the year but also would recover $6 million on previously charged-off loans. What provision for loan losses should the bank make against income during the year?

2.7 X-Bank is trying to determine if it should acquire tax-exempt industrial revenue securities. Following are income statement data for the bank:

Interest income	
Loans	9,023
Taxable securities	2,345
Tax-exempt securities	1,198
Interest expense	8,460
Noninterest income	883
Noninterest expense	4,090

X-Bank pays a tax rate of 40 percent. Calculate the bank's net income after taxes. (Assume there is no TEFRA [Tax Equity and Fiscal Responsibility Act] adjustment to tax-exempt interest.)

2.8 a. In Problem 2.7, assume X-Bank is holding $25,000 in tax-exempt securities on its balance sheet. What is the average *tax-equivalent interest income on tax-exempt securities* already on X-Bank's balance sheet?

b. Assume the earnings rate (market yield) on the tax-exempt industrial revenue securities proposed for acquisition is 5.5 percent and assume X-Bank was paying positive taxes on its income and could fully utilize the tax exemption. Calculate the *tax-equivalent interest yield* on these securities.

2.9 Following is Buena Vista Savings Bank's balance sheets for the years ending 1999 and 2000:

			($000)	
	1999	2000	Sources	Uses
Assets				
Cash and due from banks	240,000	320,000	————	————
Federal funds sold	100,000	286,000	————	————
Investment securities	934,000	1,321,000	————	————
Gross loans and leases	3,700,000	3,507,000	————	————
Less: Allowance for losses	50,000	49,000		
Net loans and leases	3,650,000	3,458,000	————	————
Premises, fixed assets	81,000	73,000	————	————
Other real estate owned	6,000	10,000	————	————
Other assets	53,000	45,000	————	————
Total assets	5,064,000	5,513,000		
Liabilities and shareholders' equity				
Transactions deposits	1,611,000	1,739,000	————	————
Time and savings accounts	2,451,000	2,799,000	————	————
Core deposits	4,062,000	4,538,000		
Time deposit of $100M or more	476,000	416,000	————	————
Federal funds purchased	36,000	86,000	————	————
Other borrowed funds	65,000	48,000	————	————
Other liabilities	22,000	24,000	————	————
Common stock	22,000	22,000	————	————
Surplus	113,000	113,000	————	————
Retained earnings	268,000	266,000	————	————
Total liabilities and share-holders' equity	5,064,000	5,513,000		
Totals			**Sources** ————	**Uses** ————

a. Determine Buena Vista's flows of funds by completing the above table of sources and uses during the year 2000. Recall that increases in assets and decreases in liabilities and equity are uses of funds; decreases in assets and increases in liabilities and equity are sources of funds, that is:

$$\text{Uses: } \Delta A\uparrow \text{ and } \Delta L\&E\downarrow$$
$$\text{Sources: } \Delta A\downarrow \text{ and } \Delta L\&E\uparrow$$
$$\text{and Total Sources = Total Uses}$$

b. Discuss the apparent major activities based on your sources and uses of funds solution. What were Buena Vista's major sources, uses, and shifts in mix of assets and liabilities? What insights can you give regarding the possible causes of Buena Vista's activities?

c. Calculate Buena Vista's *net federal funds position* during the year 2000.

2.10 Market interest rates rose throughout the year 20X2. The income statements for ZimBank for 20X1 and 20X2 showed the following:

	20X1	**20X2**
Interest income	8,000	8,800
Interest expense	4,200	5,500
Net interest income	3,800	3,300

Discuss the *interest rate sensitivity* of the cash flows on the firm's assets and liabilities. How does the interest sensitivity of the assets compare with that of the liabilities? Describe what you believe to be *the dollar gap* between assets and liabilities (positive or negative); explain. What result would you expect if interest rates had fallen during 20X2 instead?

CHAPTER 3

Evaluating a Bank's Returns, Risks, and Overall Performance

In the previous chapter we accomplished an important purpose: we introduced bank financial statements along with a few specialized accounting techniques. These form the business language of financial institutions. Although absolutely fundamental to recording and measuring how banks perform, the details of bank accounting are just that: details. In this chapter, we show how institutions use accounting information to manage their profitability and risks. Our investment in taking the time to learn the details of accounting for financial institutions will reap rewards as we apply accounting information to this crucial task.

In all probability, to continue profitable operations in the early 2000s, banks will have to take and manage higher risks. During this decade environmental factors, especially deregulation and the access to new product powers, will challenge all firms offering financial services. A *sine qua non* of survival will be the individual institution's ability to measure and analyze the risks it must take to produce acceptable returns. A bank's performance will affect its valuation in the market, its ability to acquire other banks or to be acquired at a good price, and its ability to be funded in the deposit and financial markets. Although a bank cannot change its past performance, thorough evaluation of this performance is the necessary first step in planning for acceptable future performance.

USING BASIC IDEAS FROM BUSINESS FINANCE

All too often, bankers conclude that commercial banks are so different from nonfinancial businesses that most of the concepts developed in analyzing such businesses are not appropriate for commercial banks. Such a conclusion is unwarranted. Although banks are unique in certain ways, most of the primary concepts developed for profit-oriented, private corporations are generally appropriate for analyzing commercial banks.

Attaining the Primary Objective

Analysts describe the activities of a business in either operating or financial terms. In operating terms, a business firm buys raw materials and combines them with capital and labor to produce goods or services. The firm sells these goods or services to others at prices high enough to yield returns above the cost of the raw materials, capital, and labor. In financial terms, the business obtains funds through creditors and owners, and spends them for raw materials, labor, and fixed assets. Sales follow and the firm recovers its funds as customers make payments, hopefully in excess of the amount spent.

The basic tenet of financial theory holds that management's first objective is to maximize the value of the owners' investment. For large, publicly held businesses operating in efficient capital markets, this objective requires maximizing the market price per share. In an efficient market, returns are commensurate with the calculated risks taken by the firm. This idealized result falls short for small firms whose shares are not traded actively. Managers of typical small firms whose shares seldom trade cannot rely on a reading from an efficient market to assist in making decisions about tradeoffs between returns and risks. Nevertheless, the firm's management (which for small firms is often its owners) tries to maximize the value of the owners' investment by seeking the highest returns for the risk level deemed appropriate by the owners.

Beginning Return Measures for a Company

To see if a firm's management has achieved its objectives, we must analyze the company's return and risk measures. Table 3.1 presents a simplified balance sheet, an income statement, and an introductory profitability analysis for the ABC Manufacturing Company. We begin the analysis with a return-on-equity, or ROE, model as illustrated in Table 3.2. The ROE model, widely known as the DuPont model, disaggregates return on equity into several basic components in order to isolate the sources of a firm's profitability. We then analyze the components to identify areas in which a business may want to improve.

Additional Information Needed

We need to conduct a more in-depth profitability analysis to evaluate the quality of ABC's returns. Ideally, we would calculate risk measures such as variability of sales, nature of costs, coverage of fixed operating and financial costs, and variability of the firm's returns versus returns on a diversified portfolio. We then compare the firm's return and risk measures with those of similar-size firms in the same industry. One should observe higher returns if the firm takes a higher degree of risk. In the end, an optimal balance between returns and risks should maximize the value of the owners' investment in the firm.

Parallels with Banking

Like a nonfinancial business, a financial institution obtains funds from creditors and owners; spends them on raw materials, labor, and capital; and hopes to recover funds in excess of the amount spent. For financial firms, the raw material purchased is funds rather than iron ore, clothing, or food, and the product sold is funds packaged in a usable form such as loans, instead of steel, clothing, or groceries. As in nonfinancial businesses, a bank

TABLE 3.1   ABC Manufacturing Company

Average Balance Sheet for 1998

Assets		Liabilities and Net Worth	
Cash	$ 500,000	Current liabilities	$ 3,000,000
Accounts receivable	3,000,000	Long-term debt	2,000,000
Inventory	2,000,000	Common stock	1,000,000
Plant and equipment	4,500,000	Retained earnings	4,000,000
	$10,000,000		$10,000,000

Income Statement for Year 1998

Revenue (or sales)	$20,000,000
Cost of goods sold	15,000,000
Gross operating income	5,000,000
Selling and administrative expenses	3,000,000
Net operating income	2,000,000
Interest	400,000
Taxable income	1,600,000
Taxes (34%)	544,000
Net income	$ 1,056,000

Profitability Analysis

Gross margin $= \dfrac{\text{Gross operating income}}{\text{Revenue}} = \dfrac{5{,}000{,}000}{20{,}000{,}000} = 25\%$

Net margin (before interest and taxes) $= \dfrac{\text{Net operating income}}{\text{Revenue}} = \dfrac{2{,}000{,}000}{20{,}000{,}000} = 10\%$

Net margin (after interest and taxes) $= \dfrac{\text{Net income}}{\text{Revenue}} = \dfrac{1{,}056{,}000}{20{,}000{,}000} = 5.28\%$

Asset utilization (assets turnover) $= \dfrac{\text{Revenues}}{\text{Assets}} = \dfrac{20{,}000{,}000}{10{,}000{,}000} = 2\times$

Return on assets $= \dfrac{\text{Net income}}{\text{Assets}} = \dfrac{1{,}056{,}000}{10{,}000{,}000} = 10.56\%$

Leverage multiplier $= \dfrac{\text{Assets}}{\text{Equity}} = \dfrac{10{,}000{,}000}{5{,}000{,}000} = 2\times$

Return on equity $= \dfrac{\text{Net income}}{\text{Equity}} = \dfrac{1{,}056{,}000}{5{,}000{,}000} = 21.12\%$

TABLE 3.2   Return-on-Equity Model

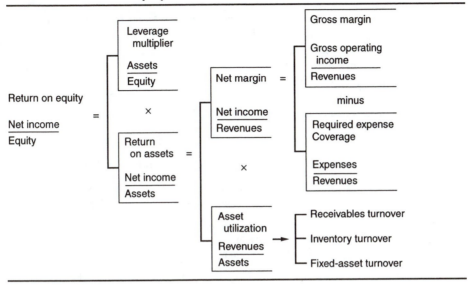

manager's objective is to maximize the value of the owners' investment. For publicly held banks, the behavior of the market price for the banks' stock reveals the rewards for risks the banks take. For small institutions that are not publicly traded, management must seek the highest returns for the risk levels set by the owners and top management.

A Simplified Bank Example

The simplified financial information on XYZ Commercial Bank in Table 3.3 illustrates some of these similarities. Note that, like ABC Manufacturing, XYZ Bank has short- and long-term assets and that funds were obtained from current liabilities, long-term liabilities, and either issued or retained common equity. The proportions of assets and liabilities are often different for banks than for manufacturing businesses because banks have just a small investment in fixed assets, such as premises. Also, their funding differs: they have comparatively little equity capital and substantially larger amounts in short-term financial assets and liabilities. XYZ Bank's income statement includes revenue and expense items similar to those of ABC Manufacturing. We apply the same basic profitability analysis in Table 3.3 that can be applied to the XYZ Bank example.

Let's review the meaning of each return measurement in Table 3.3 and then compare the results with the parallel results for ABC Manufacturing Company. The correct place to begin is with the *return on equity,* which divides net income after all expenses and taxes by common equity capital (par value, paid in surplus, undivided profits, and capital reserves). Return on equity is the closest an accounting measure comes to revealing how well managers have done in maximizing shareholder wealth; it tells how much has been earned on the book value of common shareholders' investment in the bank. Implicitly, ROE embeds revenue generation, operational efficiency, financial leverage, and tax planning.

A bank's return on equity is derived from its *return on assets* and its *leverage multi-*

TABLE 3.3   XYZ Commercial Bank

Average Balance Sheet for 1998

Assets		Liabilities and Net Worth	
Cash and due from banks	$ 8,000,000	Current liabilities	$ 70,000,000
Short-term loans and securities	60,000,000	Long-term liabilities	23,000,000
Long-term loans and securities	30,000,000	Common stock	1,000,000
Premises and equipment	2,000,000	Undivided profits	6,000,000
	$100,000,000		$100,000,000

Income Statement for Year 1998

Revenues—interest	$9,000,000
Interest expenses	4,000,000
Net interest income	5,000,000
Overhead—people and premises	3,000,000
Net operating income	2,000,000
Taxes (34%)	680,000
Net income	$1,320,000

Profitability Analysis

Interest margin $\dfrac{\text{Net interest income}}{\text{Earning assets}} = \dfrac{5,000,000}{90,000,000} = 5.6\%$

Net margin (after tax) $\dfrac{\text{Net income}}{\text{Revenues}} = \dfrac{1,320,000}{9,000,000} = 14.7\%$

Asset utilization $\dfrac{\text{Revenues}}{\text{Assets}} = \dfrac{9,000,000}{100,000,000} = 9.0\%$

Return on assets $\dfrac{\text{Net income}}{\text{Assets}} = \dfrac{1,320,000}{100,000,000} = 1.32\%$

Leverage multiplier $\dfrac{\text{Assets}}{\text{Equity}} = \dfrac{100,000,000}{7,000,000} = 14.3\times$

Return on equity $\dfrac{\text{Net income}}{\text{Equity}} = \dfrac{1,320,000}{7,000,000} = 18.86\%$

plier. Return on assets is net income divided by total assets and should reflect bank management's ability to utilize the bank's financial and real resources to generate net income. Many regulators believe return on assets is the best measure of bank efficiency. Since return on assets is lower for financial intermediaries such as commercial banks than for most nonfinancial businesses, most intermediaries must make heavy use of financial leverage (fixed- or limited-cost funding) to raise return on equity to a level that will compete with nonfinancial firms for owners' capital. We calculate the leverage multiplier to be applied to return on assets by dividing assets by common equity.

We can decompose return on assets into the product of *net (or profit) margin* and the *asset utilization (or yield).* Asset utilization—revenues divided by assets—reflects how effectively management has invested in earning assets by calculating the overall yields earned on the assets. Net margin—net income divided by revenues—represents what is left out of one dollar's revenue after all costs have been deducted. It is affected by the interest margin—the difference between interest income on assets and interest expense for funds—and by the burden (or overhead). We define *net burden* as noninterest expense net of noninterest income.

The overall results in Table 3.3 indicate that the XYZ Bank had lower asset utilization and return on assets than ABC. However, the higher leverage multiplier makes the resulting return on equity competitive with that of ABC Manufacturing. This would, of course, have to be true if the two types of businesses were to compete in the markets for new equity capital.

Just as we needed additional information to analyze ABC's performance, we need more in-depth profitability analysis for a qualitative evaluation of the bank's returns. Risk measures, similar to such measures for nonfinancial businesses as well as some that are specific to banks and similar financial institutions, should be calculated. We should then compare the bank's return and risk measures with those of similar banks. As with nonfinancial firms, banks generally earn higher returns if they take higher risks. The bank's management tries to maximize the value of the owners' investment in the bank by balancing the tradeoffs between the risks and returns. Bank management should keep such parallel concepts in mind when analyzing the key measures of returns they make and the risks they take.

KEY RETURN AND RISK MEASURES FOR A SAMPLE BANK

In this section, we present Smithville Bank as a simplified example of a commercial bank in a hypothetical environment to illustrate further how to measure bank returns and risks and how to evaluate their interrelationships.

To keep this example basic, we assume that the bank can obtain funds in only five ways: (1) transaction deposits consisting of demand deposit (checking) and NOW accounts; (2) short-term time and savings deposits consisting of passbook savings, money market deposit accounts, and time deposits maturing within 180 days; (3) long-term time deposits, which mature in over 180 days; (4) money borrowed from other sources; and (5) equity capital representing the owners' investment and earnings retained in the bank. Similarly, we assume that, after meeting its cash and premises requirements, the bank employs the funds it obtains in one of only five ways: (1) short-term high-quality debt securities maturing within 180 days, (2) long-term high-quality debt securities maturing in over 180 days, (3) good-quality loans whose rate varies with changes in interest rates,

TABLE 3.4   Hypothesized Environment

	Rates
Reserve and cash requirements	
Transaction deposits	15%
Time deposits	4%
Potential earnings available	
Short-term securities	5%
Long-term securities (currently)	7%
Long-term securities (held)	8%
High-quality, variable-rate loans	7%
Medium-quality, variable-rate loans	9%
Fixed-rate loans (currently)	8%
Fixed-rate loans (held)	9%
Expenses in environment	
Transaction deposits	3%
Short-term time deposits	4%
Long-term time deposits	5%
Borrowings	4%
Other expenses (net of other income)	$2 million
Income tax rate	34%

(4) medium-quality loans whose rate varies with changes in interest rates, and (5) good-quality fixed-rate loans.

Table 3.4 presents the basic conditions in the hypothetical environment in which Smithville Bank must operate. Although we do not mean for this environment to represent any particular time period, the reserves, revenues, and expenses are not materially different from those that existed in the late 1990s. Furthermore, the relationships between interest rates are reasonably representative of many periods of time. Short-term securities yield 5 percent versus 7 percent on long-term securities because of the greater price fluctuations (interest rate risk) on the long-term securities. Loans yield more than securities because of their greater credit risk. In addition, higher-quality loans yield less than medium-quality loans, and variable-rate loans yield less than fixed-rate loans. On the cost side, transaction deposits cost less than time deposits but have higher required reserves and may cause more liquidity pressures on assets. Long-term time deposits cost more than short-term ones because of interest rate risk.

The Bank's Financial Statements

Table 3.5 summarizes the balance sheet and income statements for Smithville Bank. We assume that Smithville Bank has obtained $30 million in transaction deposits (demand deposits and NOW accounts), $30 million in short-term time and savings deposits, and $30 million in longer-term time deposits. Furthermore, the bank has borrowed an additional $3 million and has equity capital totaling $7 million. The bank employed these funds in legal reserves and other cash accounts of $6.9 million—15 percent of $30 million in transaction

TABLE 3.5   Smithville Bank

Balance Sheet (dollars in thousands)

Assets		Liabilities and Net Worth	
Cash and due from banks	$ 6,900	Transaction deposits	$ 30,000
Short-term securities	15,000	Short-term time deposits	30,000
Long-term securities	15,000	Long-term time deposits	30,000
High variable loans	20,000	Borrowings	3,000
Medium variable loans	20,000	Equity capital	7,000
Fixed-rate loans	20,000		$100,000
Premises and other assets	3,100		
	$100,000		

Income Statement (dollars in thousands)

Revenues	$6,950
Interest expenses	−3,720
Other expenses (net)	−2,000
Operating income	$1,230
Taxes	− 418
Net income	$ 812

deposits plus 4 percent of $60 million in time deposits—and in premises and other assets worth $3.1 million. The bank invested $15 million in liquid short-term securities and lent $20 million, respectively, in high-quality variable-rate loans, low-quality variable-rate loans, and fixed-rate loans. It invested the remaining $15 million in long-term securities. Fortunately, the $15 million of long-term securities and $20 million of fixed-rate loans had been invested in higher rate environments and had average yields of 8 and 9 percent, respectively.

We calculate the income statement for Smithville Bank from the account balances in Table 3.5 and rates available in the environment. For example, revenues are calculated as follows:

Category	Balance	×	Yield	=	Revenue
Cash and due from banks	$ 6,900		0%		$ 0
Short-term securities	15,000		5%		750
Long-term securities	15,000		8%		1,200
High variable loans	20,000		7%		1,400
Medium variable loans	20,000		9%		1,800
Fixed-rate loans	20,000		9%		1,800
Premises	3,100		0%		0
Total revenues					$6,950

Note carefully that, although returns on long-term securities and fixed-rate loans average 8 and 9 percent, respectively, new additions to these accounts will earn only 7 and 8 percent, respectively. We calculate interest expenses in a similar fashion:

Category	Balance	×	Cost	=	Expenses
Transaction deposits	$30,000		3%		$ 900
Short-term deposits	30,000		4%		1,200
Long-term deposits	30,000		5%		1,500
Borrowing	3,000		4%		120
Total interest expenses					$3,720

The operating income is the total revenues less the total interest expenses and other expenses. The net income is the operating income less income taxes, assumed in this example to be 34 percent.

Measuring Returns

How well has this bank performed? Has it earned acceptable returns? What risks has it taken to achieve these returns? Table 3.6 shows how to calculate 10 introductory profitability and risk measurements for Smithville Bank. The profitability measurements and their relationships are similar to those appearing in Table 3.2. The first profitability measurement is the interest margin expressed in percentage terms—interest income minus interest expense divided by earning assets, where earning assets consists of all securities and loans. Net margin is net income minus both interest expense and other expenses, divided by revenues. Then, net margin times asset utilization—interest plus noninterest revenues divided by assets—equals the return on assets. It is important to note that the proportion of assets invested in earning assets strongly affects asset utilization. The product of return on assets multiplied by the leverage multiplier—assets divided by equity—yields return on equity. Thus, return on equity is the most important measurement of profitability because it integrates how well the bank has performed on all other profitability categories and indicates how competitive a bank can be in raising private sources of capital in a market economy.

Measuring Risks

Risk measures are related to the profitability measurements because a bank must take risks to earn adequate returns. We describe four categories of risk measurement in this section. (For introductory risk measurements for Smithville Bank, see Table 3.6.)

Liquidity Risk   Liquidity risk measures show the relationship of a bank's liquidity needs for meeting deposit outflows and loan increases versus its actual or potential sources of liquidity from either selling an asset it holds or acquiring additional liabilities. For the sample bank, we can approximate this risk by comparing a proxy of the bank's liquidity needs, deposits, with a proxy for the bank's liquidity sources in the form of short-term securities. Although both variables are only rough approximations (funding loan demand may be a major liquidity need, and purchasing liabilities may be an important

TABLE 3.6   Introductory Return and Risk Measurements (Smithville Bank figures)

Category	Equation		Calculations		Results
Interest margin	$\dfrac{\text{Int. inc.} - \text{int. ex.}}{\text{Earning assets}}$	=	$\dfrac{6{,}950 - 3{,}720}{90{,}000}$	=	3.59%
Net margin	$\dfrac{\text{Net income}}{\text{Revenues}}$	=	$\dfrac{812}{6{,}950}$	=	11.68% ×
Asset utilization	$\dfrac{\text{Revenues}}{\text{Assets}}$	=	$\dfrac{6{,}950}{100{,}000}$	=	6.95% =
Return on assets	$\dfrac{\text{Net income}}{\text{Assets}}$	=	$\dfrac{812}{100{,}000}$	=	0.81% ×
Leverage multiplier	$\dfrac{\text{Assets}}{\text{Equity}}$	=	$\dfrac{100{,}000}{7{,}000}$	=	14.29× =
Return on capital	$\dfrac{\text{Net income}}{\text{Equity}}$	=	$\dfrac{812}{7{,}000}$	=	11.60%
Risk Measures					
Liquidity risk	$\dfrac{\text{Short-term securities}}{\text{Deposits}}$	=	$\dfrac{15{,}000}{90{,}000}$	=	16.67%
Interest rate risk[a]	$\dfrac{\text{Int. sens. assets}}{\text{Int. sens. liabilities}}$	=	$\dfrac{55{,}000}{63{,}000}$	=	0.87%
Credit risk	$\dfrac{\text{Medium loans}}{\text{Assets}}$	=	$\dfrac{20{,}000}{100{,}000}$	=	20.00%
Capital risk	$\dfrac{\text{Capital}}{\text{Assets}}$	=	$\dfrac{7{,}000}{100{,}000}$	=	7.00%

[a] Short-term securities and all variable-rate loans are interest-sensitive assets, whereas transaction deposits, short-term time and savings deposits, and borrowings are treated as interest-sensitive liabilities. Transaction deposits are treated as interest sensitive because more and more of such deposits are interest-bearing deposits.

source of liquidity), this relationship is a beginning indicator of most banks' liquidity risk. Investment in short-term securities involves a sacrifice of the greater profitability of long-term securities for the liquidity of short-term ones. The reverse would be the case if long-term securities were increased. Thus, a larger liquidity ratio for the sample bank indicates a less risky, but also less profitable, bank.

Interest Rate Risk   The bank's interest rate risk is related to the changes in asset and liability returns and values caused by movements in interest rates. A beginning measurement of this risk is the ratio of interest-sensitive assets to interest-sensitive liabilities. Particularly in periods of wide interest rate movements, this ratio reflects the risk the bank is willing to take that it can predict the future direction of interest rates. If a bank has a ratio above 1.0, the bank's returns will be lower if interest rates decline and higher if they increase. Given the difficulty of predicting interest rates, some banks conclude that they can minimize interest rate risk with an interest sensitivity ratio close to 1.0. Such a ratio may be difficult for some banks to achieve and often can be reached only at the cost of lower returns on assets, such as short-term securities or variable-rate loans.

Credit Risk   The credit risk of a bank is defined as the risk that the interest or principal, or both, on securities and loans will not be paid as promised. In the Smithville Bank example, credit risk is estimated by relating the proportion of assets that are medium-quality loans. The better measure would be the relative amount of past-due loans or loan losses, but such data are not available in this example. Credit risk is higher if the bank has more medium-quality loans, but returns are usually higher too. Returns tend to be lower if the bank chooses to lower its credit risk by having a smaller portion of its assets in medium-quality loans. Note that this measure is only available internally. If one is analyzing a bank from external data, such qualitative data are not available and one must use summary measures such as noncurrent loans, loan losses, and loss reserves as proxies for credit risk.

Capital Risk   The capital risk of a bank indicates how much asset values may decline before the position of its depositors (or the deposit insurer such as the FDIC) and other creditors is jeopardized. Thus, a bank with a 10 percent capital-to-assets ratio could withstand greater declines in asset values than a bank with a 5 percent capital-to-assets ratio. We measure the capital risk of Smithville Bank by examining the percentage of the bank's assets that are covered by its equity capital. The capital risk is inversely related to the leverage multiplier and, therefore, to the return on equity. When a bank chooses to take more capital risk (assuming this is allowed by its regulators), its leverage multiplier and return on equity, *ceteris paribus,* will increase. If the bank chooses (or is forced to choose) to lower its capital risk, its leverage multiplier and return on equity will decrease.

Setting Objectives for Returns and Risks

Clearly, returns are increased by increasing one or more of the four primary risks a bank may take. Obviously, bank management would prefer the highest returns for a given level of risks and the lowest risks for a given level of returns. Two questions remain for the bank manager: What degree of total risk should a bank take to increase returns, and how much of which type of risk should a bank take?

The answers to these questions are difficult and not exact. For assistance a bank can look at its past performance and determine whether it is satisfied with the profitability obtained and the risks taken. The bank can compare return and risk measurements for similar individual banks or peer groups of banks with its own similar measures. If the bank's stock is actively traded, it can take actions to try to maximize its market price. Exact answers are hard to come by. Each bank has its own characteristics, such as the nature of a bank's market, the level of competition it faces, the areas in which it has special management expertise, and the stance of its regulators, that affect its desired return-risk tradeoffs.

The following three steps should prove helpful. The first step for bank management is to assess how other similar individual banks and groups of banks have made their risk-return decisions. Any bank can obtain information on other individual banks or peer

TABLE 3.7   Performance Objectives for Smithville Bank

Return Measures	Objective	Actual
Interest margin	4.00%	3.59%
Net margin	12.50%	11.68%
Asset utilization	8.00%	6.95%
Return on assets	1.00%	0.81%
Leverage multiplier	15.00×	14.29×
Return on equity	15.00%	11.60%
Risk Measures		
Liquidity risk	23.00%	16.67%
Interest rate risk	1.00	0.87
Credit risk	20.00%	20.00%
Capital risk	6.67%	7.00%

groupings from the FDIC, Federal Reserve, Comptroller's Office, or numerous private bank service companies. Banks' regulatory reports include a comparison with peer group banks. The second step is to compare a bank's performance (return and risk) measurements with those of selected similar banks. Significant variances in these measurements should be justified. There are many reasons for differences, such as different markets or different management philosophies; however, many banks may find one or several areas for improvement. The final step is to set reasonable (challenging but attainable) objectives, given a bank's past performance, the performance of its peers, and its environment.

Comparison with Objectives

Assume that after careful study of its past performance and that of its peers, Smithville Bank decided on the performance objectives shown in the first column of Table 3.7. These objectives should be compared with the bank's actual performance for the period being examined (see Table 3.6). Smithville Bank's return on equity was below its objective, and the return composition for achieving this target was slightly different from those objectives. The bank's interest margin and resulting return on assets were below the objectives, and a below-target leverage multiplier brought the return on equity even further below its objective.

Analysis of the risk measures shows that the bank's liquidity and interest rate risks were above its objectives. Smithville Bank could get closer to its return-on-equity objective only by taking even higher risks in these areas, as well as taking a greater capital risk to provide a higher leverage multiplier. The bank appears to be vulnerable to substantial increases in either interest rates or loan demand. Based on the preceding analysis, Smithville Bank might set future goals such as increasing its net interest margin, increasing liquid assets, and balancing its interest rate sensitivity position. Such actions would be expected to increase the value of the shareholders' investment in the bank.

RETURN-RISK TRADEOFFS

Two additional Smithville Bank examples illustrate the difficulty in achieving conflicting goals and the tradeoffs between returns and risks taken by nearly every commercial bank.

It is assumed that in the year following the initial example (see Table 3.5), Smithville's deposits grew by $10 million and its capital by $1 million, while available returns and expenses remained the same (see Table 3.4). The bank's management set its highest priorities on increasing the bank's liquidity position and on making the bank less vulnerable to interest rate fluctuations. To achieve these objectives, the bank chose to place all the newly attracted funds, less those required as reserves and cash, into short-term securities. The resulting balance sheet, income statement, and return-risk measures are shown in Table 3.8.

Results of Lower Risk

Smithville Bank's management decisions improved its risk position measurably. The bank's liquidity risk, credit risk, and capital risk were all better than the targeted objectives. Its interest-sensitivity position moved from 0.87 to 0.96—toward its targeted goal of 1.00. However, the other side of the bank's performance, its returns, had deteriorated. Both the interest margin and the net margin declined appreciably because the bank's use of the funds it obtained emphasized more liquid, variable-return securities whose yields were lower than those of other alternatives. The resulting return on assets and on capital fell to 0.78 percent and 10.81 percent, respectively, even further below the bank's goals of 1.00 and 15.00 percent. Thus, Smithville Bank was unable to obtain its risk objectives without hurting its return performance significantly. The bank's owners would probably be unhappy with such management decisions.

Results of Improving Returns

Using the same figures (Smithville's deposits grow by $10 million and its capital grows by $1 million, with available returns and expenses the same as those in Table 3.4), the second example assumes that the bank's management decided to emphasize increasing returns. The bank chose to invest the newly attracted funds, less those required as reserves, in the two asset categories that produced the highest returns. The resulting balance sheet, income statement, and return-risk measures are shown in Table 3.9.

Management, Owner, and Regulatory Perspectives

The new management decisions improved Smithville Bank's returns appreciably. The interest margin improved slightly, and the net margin and asset utilization rate improved significantly. The resulting return on assets and return on capital increased to 1.00 and 13.88 percent, respectively, and were closer to the bank's objectives of 1.00 and 15.00 percent. The costs to obtain these increased returns were taking risks considerably higher than those in the previous year and higher than the bank's objectives. Smithville's liquidity deteriorated further; its earnings were even more sensitive to interest rate movements; and it had taken slightly above-average credit risk. The bank's capital risk improved slightly from the previous year; however, the resulting lower leverage multiplier reduced return on equity. The bank's owners might be happy with the higher returns, but other parties, such as large depositors and regulators, might become concerned about the risks the bank had taken to obtain these returns.

**TABLE 3.8   Emphasis on Liquidity and Balanced Interest Sensitivity
(for Smithville Bank)**

Balance Sheet (dollars in thousands)

Assets		Liabilities	
Cash and due from banks	$ 7,300	Transaction deposits	$ 30,000
Short-term securities	25,600	Short-term time deposits	35,000
Long-term securities	15,000	Long-term time deposits	35,000
High variable loans	20,000	Borrowings	3,000
Medium variable loans	20,000	Equity capital	8,000
Fixed-rate loans	20,000		
Premises	3,100		
	$111,000		$111,000

Income Statement (dollars in thousands)

Revenues	$7,480
Interest expenses	−4,170
Other expenses	−2,000
Operating income	1,310
Taxes (34%)	− 445
Net income	$ 865

Introductory Return and Risk Measures

Return Measures	Objective	Previous	Emphasizing Liquidity
Interest margin	4.00%	3.59%	3.29%
Net margin	12.50%	11.68%	11.56%
Asset utilization	8.00%	6.95%	6.74%
Return on assets	1.00%	0.81%	0.78%
Leverage multiplier	15.00×	14.29×	13.88×
Return on equity	15.00%	11.60%	10.81%
Risk Measures			
Liquidity risk	23.00%	16.67%	25.60%
Interest rate risk	1.00	0.87	0.96
Credit risk	20.00%	20.00%	18.02%
Capital risk	6.67%	7.00%	7.21%

Additional Return-Risk Tradeoff Situations

With the aid of a personal computer, management can try many variations of the Smithville Bank example—changing the bank's liability structure, increasing or decreasing its capital position, varying the external environment so that rates are higher or lower, and so forth. Four such situations are summarized in Table 3.10. The results are always similar. To

TABLE 3.9   Emphasis on Profitability (for Smithville Bank)

Balance Sheet (dollars in thousands)

Assets		Liabilities	
Cash and due from banks	$ 7,300	Transaction deposits	$ 30,000
Short-term securities	15,000	Short-term time deposits	35,000
Long-term securities	15,000	Long-term time deposits	35,000
High variable loans	20,000	Borrowings	3,000
Medium variable loans	25,500	Equity capital	8,000
Fixed-rate loans	25,100		
Premises	3,100		
	$111,000		$111,000

Income Statement (dollars in thousands)

Revenues	$7,853
Interest expenses	−4,170
Other expenses	−2,000
Operating income	1,683
Taxes (34%)	− 572
	$1,111

Introductory Return and Risk Measures

Return Measures	Objective	Previous	Emphasizing Returns
Interest margin	4.00%	3.59%	3.66%
Net margin	12.50%	11.68%	14.14%
Asset utilization	8.00%	6.95%	7.07%
Return on assets	1.00%	0.81%	1.00%
Leverage multiplier	15.00×	14.29×	13.88×
Return on equity	15.00%	11.60%	13.88%
Risk Measures			
Liquidity risk	23.00%	16.67%	15.00%
Interest rate risk	1.00	0.87	0.86
Credit risk	20.00%	20.00%	22.97%
Capital risk	6.67%	7.00%	7.21%

increase its returns, the bank must take additional risk. Conversely, lower risk means lower returns.

Liquid, Low-Capital Situation   The first situation summarized in Table 3.10 is based on the assumption that regulatory authorities allow the liquid version of Smithville bank (see Table 3.8) to have a lower equity capital position and, therefore, a higher leverage multiplier. It is assumed that the liquid Smithville Bank is required to hold $2 million

TABLE 3.10   Additional Risk-Return Situations for Smithville Bank

	Objective	(1) Liquid Low-Capital Bank	(2) Profitable High-Capital Bank	(3) Shifting Fund Sources Bank	(4) Rapid Purchased-Growth Bank
Return Measures					
Interest margin	4.00%	3.21%	3.74%	3.42%	3.50%
Net margin	12.50%	10.85%	14.82%	12.52%	15.79%
Asset utilization	8.00%	6.74%	7.07%	7.03%	6.98%
Return on assets	1.00%	0.73%	1.05%	0.88%	1.10%
Leverage multiplier	15.00×	18.50×	11.10×	13.88×	13.00×
Return on equity	15.00%	13.53%	11.64%	12.20%	14.32%
Risk Measures					
Liquidity	23.00%	25.60%	15.00%	17.00%	18.36%
Interest rate risk	1.00	0.94	0.92	0.98	0.90
Credit risk	20.00%	18.02%	22.97%	19.82%	20.00%
Capital risk	6.67%	5.41%	9.01%	7.21%	7.69%

less equity capital and replaces this $2 million through borrowing. Although return on assets is lower because of the cost of borrowing the additional $2 million, return on equity is significantly higher than that for the liquid situation in Table 3.8 because of the higher leverage multiplier. Risks are the same, except that capital risk is considerably higher than the 6.67 percent objective.

Profitable, High-Capital Situation   The second situation summarized in Table 3.10 assumes that the regulatory authorities require $2 million of additional equity capital for the high-profit, high-risk version of Smithville Bank. (The original data for this revision appear in Table 3.9.) The asset structure is left unchanged from Table 3.9, but borrowing falls to $1 million and capital is raised by $2 million. With the lower leverage multiplier, the return on capital falls from 13.88 to 11.64 percent, and, except for lower capital risks, all the risk measures remain high. Raising capital lowered profitability and did not improve the bank's liquidity, interest sensitivity, or credit risk situation.

Shifting Fund Sources Situation   In the third situation, it is assumed that Smithville Bank's sources of funds changed appreciably. Transaction deposits fell to $20 million, and the bank was able to remain the same size by attracting $5 million more in short-term and savings deposits and $5 million more in long-term time deposits. The funds attracted were invested approximately equally in five categories of earning assets. The results in this situation are worrisome. Profits are below average (the return on equity is 12.20 percent), and liquidity risk, interest rate risk, and capital risk are all higher than the target objectives.

Rapid Purchased-Growth Situation   The fourth and final situation depicts the case in which Smithville Bank decides to grow rapidly, from $111 million to $130 million in the following year. Funds are attracted by aggressive bidding to obtain $5 million in new short-term time and savings deposits, $5 million in new long-term time deposits, and $7 million in new borrowings. For this situation, capital is increased to $10 million, and approximately equal amounts are invested in each of the five categories of earning assets. The results, as summarized in Table 3.10, indicate that Smithville Bank exceeded targeted profits, liquidity, and interest rate risk. A bank having above-average growth clearly needs to consider the effects on its return-risk position of how the growth is financed and how the funds obtained are employed.

ANALYSIS OF KEY RETURN-RISK RATIOS

In this section, we compute and analyze the key risk-return measures discussed in Chapter 2 for First National Bank, using information presented in Chapter 2. Table 3.11 illustrates the calculation of the basic ratios measuring the bank's returns and risks it has taken to obtain these returns. We are able to modify two risk measures because more information is available than was available for the sample Smithville Bank. We now measure liquidity risk by comparing the difference between liquid assets (short-term instruments and securities maturing within a year) and short-term borrowing (a proxy for how much of the bank's borrowing capacity is used) to total deposits. This time we measure credit risk by dividing noncurrent loans by net loans.

Once such calculations are completed, the next concern is the interpretation of the resulting return-risk ratios. Several sources may serve as a beginning basis for comparison. First, trends in a bank's own return-risk measures over time often provide useful insights. Second, it is possible to identify areas of strength and weakness by comparing a bank's return-risk measures with the same measures for analogous banks. Reasonably similar banks could include individual banks of like size and serving comparable markets or an entire grouping of peer banks of similar size and in comparable markets. Averages and various percentile groupings of return-risk measures for peer groupings are available from the three national regulatory agencies and numerous service companies. They are available on the internet (http://www.smu/~swgsb), and the peer group of similar banks can be easily constructed. Finally, a bank can compare its return-risk measures with its own planned targets or objectives for such measures. Interpreting comparisons with any of these sources should be done carefully. Even favorable trends in a bank's own return-risk ratios may still be at an undesirable level. Totally identical individual banks or groupings of banks are difficult, if not impossible, to find. A bank's planned objectives are typically based on its own and its peer group's performance in recent years, which may still be at an unacceptable level. In addition, the directors and top management of a bank may choose different strategies and tradeoffs between return and risk from peer banks to achieve an acceptable level of performance. Clearly, comparative ratios are only the first step in analyzing a bank's key return-risk ratios.

The skill required and complexities of analyzing a bank's key return-risk ratios can be illustrated by trying to interpret the trends in Table 3.11. We can also compare First National Bank's key ratios with the average ratios for peer banks of similar size and in regions and markets similar to those of First National, which appear in Table 3.12. In the case of its interest margin, First National would probably be somewhat concerned with

TABLE 3.11 First National Bank Return-Risk Ratios

	1999	2000	2001
Interest margin	$\dfrac{\text{Interest income} - \text{Interest expense}}{\text{Earning assets}} = \dfrac{34{,}439 - 15{,}021}{402{,}735} = 4.82\%$	$\dfrac{36{,}278 - 15{,}814}{418{,}241} = 4.89\%$	$\dfrac{37{,}617 - 16{,}728}{432{,}974} = 4.82\%$
Net margin	$\dfrac{\text{Net income}}{\text{Revenues}} = \dfrac{5{,}239}{38{,}674} = 13.55\%$	$\dfrac{5{,}874}{40{,}845} = 14.38\%$	$\dfrac{5{,}908}{42{,}632} = 13.86\%$
Asset utilization	$\dfrac{\text{Revenues}}{\text{Assets}} = \dfrac{38{,}674}{445{,}756} = 8.68\%$	$\dfrac{40{,}854}{464{,}433} = 8.80\%$	$\dfrac{42{,}632}{480{,}968} = 8.86\%$
Return on assets	$\dfrac{\text{Net Income}}{\text{Assets}} = \dfrac{5{,}239}{445{,}756} = 1.18\%$	$\dfrac{5{,}874}{464{,}433} = 1.26\%$	$\dfrac{5{,}908}{480{,}968} = 1.23\%$
Leverage multiplier	$\dfrac{\text{Assets}}{\text{Equity}} = \dfrac{445{,}756}{32{,}163} = 13.86\times$	$\dfrac{464{,}433}{34{,}174} = 13.59\times$	$\dfrac{480{,}968}{36{,}292} = 13.25\times$
Return on equity	$\dfrac{\text{Net income}}{\text{Equity}} = \dfrac{5{,}239}{32{,}163} = 16.29\%$	$\dfrac{5{,}874}{34{,}174} = 17.19\%$	$\dfrac{5{,}908}{36{,}292} = 16.28\%$
Liquidity risk	$\dfrac{\text{Liquid assets} - \text{Short-term borrowing}}{\text{Total deposits}} = \dfrac{37{,}595 - 9{,}167}{399{,}777} = 7.11\%$	$\dfrac{32{,}920 - 15{,}472}{410{,}371} = 4.25\%$	$\dfrac{33{,}847 - 15{,}931}{424{,}585} = 4.22\%$
Interest rate risk	$\dfrac{\text{Interest-sensitive assets}}{\text{Interest-sensitive liabilities}} = \dfrac{192{,}435}{217{,}942} = 88.30\%$	$\dfrac{221{,}784}{235{,}165} = 94.31\%$	$\dfrac{220{,}980}{239{,}366} = 92.32\%$
Credit risk	$\dfrac{\text{Past-due loans}}{\text{Net loans}} = \dfrac{942}{251{,}119} = 0.38\%$	$\dfrac{1{,}206}{278{,}363} = 0.43\%$	$\dfrac{1{,}602}{296{,}884} = 0.54\%$
Capital risk	$\dfrac{\text{Equity}}{\text{Assets}} = \dfrac{32{,}163}{445{,}756} = 7.22\%$	$\dfrac{34{,}174}{464{,}433} = 7.36\%$	$\dfrac{36{,}292}{480{,}968} = 7.55\%$

TABLE 3.12   Return-Risk Ratios for Peer Banks of First National Bank

	1999	2000	2001
Interest margin	5.07%	5.11%	5.09%
Net margin	13.86%	14.03%	13.91%
Asset utilization	8.74%	8.82%	8.79%
Return on assets	1.21%	1.24%	1.22%
Leverage multiplier	14.39×	14.27×	14.23×
Return on equity	17.43%	17.66%	17.40%
Liquidity risk	6.78%	6.69%	6.81%
Interest rate risk	93.78%	95.22%	96.47%
Credit risk	0.32%	0.41%	0.46%
Capital risk	6.95%	7.01%	7.03%

the fact that its interest margin was below peer average from 1999 to 2001. The below-average interest margins might not cause great concern if the bank's other costs, such as salaries and occupancy costs, were below average. Often more retail-oriented (consumer-oriented) banks have high interest margins and high other costs. Wholesale (large business customer) banks often have relatively lower margins but considerably lower other costs.

First National Bank's net margin, which reflects both its interest margin and its ability to cover all other costs, including taxes, is closer to its peers but still is cause for concern. The bank's net margin declined from 2000 to 2001. Clearly, other costs in addition to interest expense still remained relatively high. Techniques for investigating this problem will be discussed later in this chapter.

First National's asset utilization was slightly above peer in 2001 and was rising. This tends to verify that First National's problem was expense control rather than failure to earn an adequate gross yield on assets. The return on assets that resulted from the low net margin and the average asset utilization fell from slightly above average in 1999 to below that of peer banks in 2000. A below-peer-average leverage multiplier further hurt First National's return on equity because of the low return on assets. The bank's return on equity was below that of its peer banks in all three years.

Examination of First National Bank's risk position produced some surprising results. Because of its lower than average returns, the bank would be expected to take lower risks. The opposite proved true for three of the four primary risk categories. First National Bank appeared to be taking a higher-than-peer liquidity risk in 1999 and 2000. Its liquid assets fell, and its short-term borrowings appeared high relative to its deposits and the liquidity ratio, recognizing these variables for its peer banks. First National experienced a rapid growth in interest-sensitive liabilities in 2000. By 2000 the bank's interest rate risk (interest-sensitive assets divided by interest-sensitive liabilities) had fallen to 0.92. This net liability sensitivity indicates that the bank is hoping for a decline in the level of interest rates. First National's credit risk (measured by noncurrent loans) is also above the similar measurement for its peers. Finally, its capital risk is slightly lower; that is, the bank's equity capital is a larger proportion of assets than it is for its peer banks.

In summary, analysis of the key risk-return ratios for First National Bank indicates that the bank's slightly lower return on equity is caused primarily by a below-average interest margin without compensating lower expenses. Better control of interest and noninterest expenses should be a top priority in coming years. Of equal concern is the conclusion that the bank is taking above-average risk in three of the four primary risk categories. First National appears to be gambling that interest rates will fall and that its liquidity needs will be relatively small. The bank's only area of strength is its slightly above-average equity capital to assets. Using the preceding analysis as a starting base, we can develop supplemental ratios to enable First National to understand its performance in greater depth and to serve as a guide to specific future actions.

COMPREHENSIVE RATIO ANALYSIS
FOR FINANCIAL FIRMS

Table 3.13 presents a master set of financial ratios used in the banking industry. Five classifications are shown: key profitability ratios, including those embedded in the ROE model; liquidity risk ratios; credit quality risk ratios; interest rate risk ratios; and capital risk ratios. The risk-related ratios are more detailed and meaningful than the broadly conceptual ratios we discussed earlier for Smithville Bank. Some of these ratios require more detailed data, such as those provided for First National Bank in Table 2.3. Although trends, targets, and peer group figures are helpful as a basis for evaluating such supplemental ratios, we do not present them here. We will apply ratios from Table 3.13 to identify specific strengths and weaknesses. The solutions for most of the ratios in the case of First National Bank are shown in Table 3.14.

Before applying the ratios from Table 3.13, however, we list an account-by-account analysis of First National Bank's income statement in Table 3.14. This is presented in the same four basic categories of the income statement: interest income, interest expense, noninterest income, and noninterest expense. These results provide a detailed picture of some of the factors that underlie the bank's net margin and return on assets. The first category measures the yields on each type of earning asset. First National is able to see the trends in yields on various earning assets, to examine how its gross returns compare with those of its peers on specific assets, and to identify assets on which yields might be improved. The second category looks at the interest cost of the bank's various sources of funds. Competitive funds pricing as well as a favorable mix of funding sources is important in obtaining a good net interest margin.

The third category quantifies noninterest sources of income to examine a bank's performance in earning income from sources other than interest on its earning assets. Although noninterest income is relatively small for most banks, small improvements in this account can be the margin of success for a bank. Furthermore, most bank analysts feel that noninterest income will be a growing contributor to bank returns in future years. The final category emphasizes control of the components of overhead or noninterest expense, such as salaries and occupancy expenses. Rising or above-average costs can be indicative of potential problem areas. Controlling noninterest expense has been vital for many banks in achieving high performance.

In addition, the bank's asset and liability composition shown earlier in Table 2.1 provides useful supplemental information to the bank's key return-risk ratios. The current environment and a bank's specific market obviously affect a bank's particular asset mix and liability mix. To be sure, bank management decisions also impact mix. It is helpful to analyze these compositions in conjunction with yields on specific assets and costs of

TABLE 3.13   Part A. Profitability Measures for Financial Institutions

Ratio Name	Definition	Comment
1. Net (or profit) margin	$\dfrac{\text{Net income}}{\text{Operating revenue}}$	Percent net income remaining after all costs deducted from (interest income + noninterest income)
2. Asset utilization	$\dfrac{\text{Operating revenue}}{\text{Total assets}}$	Total revenues produced by assets. Productivity of assets.
3. Return on assets	$\dfrac{\text{Net income}}{\text{Total assets}}$	Rate of return on total assets.
4. Leverage multiplier	$\dfrac{\text{Total assets}}{\text{Common equity}}$	Value of assets supported by $1 of common equity.
5. Return on equity	$\dfrac{\text{Net income}}{\text{Common equity}}$	Rate of return to common shareholders. Main accounting measure of shareholder wealth.
6. Earnings power	$\dfrac{\text{Earning assets}}{\text{Total assets}}$	Proportion of assets invested in earning assets.
7. Noninterest expenses-to-total assets	$\dfrac{\text{Noninterest expense}}{\text{Total assets}}$	Basic measure of efficient use of overhead.

TABLE 3.13 *(Continued)*
Part A (continued). Profitability Measures for Financial Institutions

Ratio Name	Definition	Comment
8. Net noninterest expenses-to-total assets	$\dfrac{\text{Noninterest expense} - \text{Noninterest income}}{\text{Total assets}}$	Efficient use of overhead accounting for expenditures to create noninterest income.
9. Efficiency	$\dfrac{\text{Noninterest expense}}{\text{Net interest income} + \text{Noninterest income}}$	Comprehensive measure of efficiency. Reflects "input" (numerator) over "output" (denominator).
10. Interest margin (total assets)	$\dfrac{\text{Net interest income}}{\text{Total assets}}$	Net interest yield on assets. Overall net interest yield on the intermediation process.
11. Interest margin (earning assets)	$\dfrac{\text{Net interest income}}{\text{Earning assets}}$	Net interest yield on earning assets. Net interest yield on assets tied to the intermediation process.
12. Yield on earning assets	$\dfrac{\text{Interest income}}{\text{Earning assets}}$	Gross rate of return on earning assets.
13. Cost rate on total funds	$\dfrac{\text{Interest expense}}{\text{Total liabilities} + \text{Equity}}$	Gross interest cost on aggregate funds.
14. Cost rate on interest bearing funds	$\dfrac{\text{Interest expense}}{\text{Interest-bearing liabilities}}$	Average interest cost of liabilities that bear interest cost.
15. Spread	Yield on earning assets − Cost rate on interest-bearing funds	Net earned on interest-bearing funds invested in earning assets. Approximate return on marginal earning assets.

TABLE 3.13 *(Continued)*
Part B. Ratios for Measuring Financial Risks in Financial Institutions

Ratio Name	Definition	Comment
Liquidity Risk Ratios		
1. Core deposits-to-assets	$$\frac{\text{Core deposits}}{\text{Total assets}}$$	Availability of most stable funds used to finance assets
2. Liquid assets-to-earning assets	$$\frac{\text{Short-term investments } (<1 \text{ year})}{\text{Earning assets } - \text{ S-t investments}}$$	Most liquid assets available to cover investment in earning assets
3. Net loans-to-deposits	$$\frac{\text{Net loans \& leases}}{\text{Total deposits}}$$	Share of deposits locked into loans (most nonliquid assets)
4. Net loans-to-core deposits	$$\frac{\text{Net loans \& leases}}{\text{Core deposits}}$$	Share of loans supported by the most stable funds
5. Net-loans-to-assets	$$\frac{\text{Net loans \& leases}}{\text{Total assets}}$$	Share of assets allocated to least liquid assets
6. Net noncore funding dependence	$$\frac{\text{Noncore liabilities } - \text{ S-t investments}}{\text{Earning assets } - \text{ S-t investments}}$$	Dependence on funds that are volatile (noncore) net of liquid assets to fund earning assets
7. Securities maturing < 1 year	$$\frac{\text{Securities maturing } < 1 \text{ year}}{\text{Total assets}}$$	Securities with cash inflows in 1 year (minimum loss exposure); portion of assets

TABLE 3.13 *(Continued)*
Part B (continued). Ratios for Measuring Financial Risks in Financial Institutions

Ratio Name	Definition	Comment
Credit Quality Ratios		
1. Net charge-offs-to-gross loans and leases	$$\dfrac{\text{Charge-offs} - \text{Recoveries of previously charged-off loans}}{\text{Gross loans \& leases}}$$	Proportion of loan portfolio charged off
2. Loss reserves-to-gross loans and leases	$$\dfrac{\text{Allowance for loan \& lease losses}}{\text{Gross loans \& leases}}$$	Share of loan portfolio reserved for losses
3. Loss reserves-to-noncurrent loans	$$\dfrac{\text{Allowance for loan \& lease losses}}{\text{Nonaccruing loans}}$$	Share of noncurrent loans reserved
4. Provision for loan losses-to-gross loans and leases	$$\dfrac{\text{Provision for loan loss expense, this period}}{\text{Gross loans \& leases}}$$	Provision expense set aside as share of gross loans and leases
5. Noncurrent loans + OREO-to-gross loans and leases + OREO	$$\dfrac{\text{Nonaccruing loans} + \text{OREO}}{\text{Gross loans \& leases} + \text{OREO}}$$	Share of "nonperforming" assets vs. loan portfolio

TABLE 3.13 *(Continued)*

Part B (continued). Ratios for Measuring Financial Risks in Financial Institutions

Ratio Name	Definition	Comment
Interest Rate Sensitivity Ratios		
1. Repriceable assets-to-total assets: 3 months 1 year	$\dfrac{\text{Assets interest rate sensitive within time horizon}}{\text{Total assets}}$	Assets subject to repricing if market rates change: maturing, floating rate, or paid before contract maturity
2. Repriceable liabilities-to-total assets: 3 months 1 year	$\dfrac{\text{Liabs. interest rate sensitive within time horizon}}{\text{Total assets}}$	Liabilities subject to repricing if market rates change: maturing, floating rate, withdrawn before contract maturity
3. Dollar gap	Int. rate sens. assets − Int. rate sens. liabs.	Rate sensitivity difference: horizon, e.g, 3 months or 1 year
4. Gap-to-assets ratio	$\dfrac{\text{Int. rate sens. assets} - \text{Int. rate sens. liabs.}}{\text{Total assets}}$	Share of balance sheet exposed to interest rate risk
5. Gap-to-equity ratio	$\dfrac{\text{Int. rate sens. assets} - \text{Int. rate sens. liabs.}}{\text{Total equity}}$	Capacity of equity to cover loss due to interest rate risk
6. Sensitivity ratio	$\dfrac{\text{Interest rate sensitive assets}}{\text{Interest rate sensitive liabilities}}$	Ratio relationship of RSA to RSL. If > 1, firm is asset sensitive; if < 1, liability sensitive

TABLE 3.13 *(Continued)*
Part B (continued). Ratios for Measuring Financial Risks in Financial Institutions

Ratio Name	Definition	Comment
Capital Adequacy Ratios		
1. Capital ratio: (capital-to-assets)	$\dfrac{\text{Total capital}}{\text{Total assets}}$	Overall measure of capital strength.
2. Equity capital ratio	$\dfrac{\text{Common equity}}{\text{Total assets}}$	Capital strength contributed by common shareholders.
3. Capital-to-risk assets	$\dfrac{\text{Capital}}{\text{Assets subject to default and assets with} > \text{1-year maturity}}$	Capital coverage of assets subject to loss.
4. Tier one capital ratio	$\dfrac{\text{Tier one capital}}{\text{Risk-weighted assets}}$	Highest quality capital (mostly common equity) coverage of assets weighted by risk. BIS (Basle) requirement: min. 4%.
5. Tier two capital ratio	$\dfrac{\text{Tier two capital}}{\text{Risk-weighted assets}}$	Total capital coverage of assets weighted by risk. BIS (Basle) requirement: min. 8%.

TABLE 3.14   First National Bank's Ratio Analysis

	1999	2000	2001
Yield on earning assets			
Short-term instruments	5.23%	4.97%	5.32%
Securities	6.51%	6.21%	6.02%
Commercial loans	9.20%	9.16%	9.32%
Consumer loans	11.23%	11.41%	11.22%
Real estate loans	8.72%	8.53%	8.71%
Other loans	9.18%	9.68%	9.34%
Leases	9.93%	10.20%	9.92%
All loans & leases	9.91%	9.98%	9.95%
All earning assets	8.56%	8.67%	8.69%
Cost of funds			
NOW and other transaction accounts	2.56%	2.40%	2.61%
Savings accounts	4.18%	4.31%	4.33%
Time certificates	5.34%	5.43%	5.46%
CDs, 100,000 and over	5.63%	5.64%	5.71%
Other interest-bearing deposits	5.28%	5.42%	5.27%
All interest-bearing deposits	4.30%	4.31%	4.41%
Borrowed funds	5.35%	5.61%	5.76%
All interest-bearing funds	4.33%	4.37%	4.47%
All earning assets	3.73%	3.78%	3.86%
Noninterest income			
Service charges/revenues	6.85%	6.72%	6.60%
Other noninterest income/revenues	4.00%	4.48%	5.17%
Total noninterest income/earning assets	1.04%	1.09%	1.16%
Noninterest expense			
Provision for loan losses/revenues	1.47%	1.31%	1.69%
Salaries and benefits/revenues	23.37%	22.61%	22.17%
Salaries and benefits per employee	$36,898	$37,096	$36,922
Assets ($ thousands) per employee	$1,819	$1,865	$1,879
Premises and equipment/revenues	5.74%	5.88%	6.41%
Other expenses/revenues	10.29%	9.89%	10.13%
Noninterest expenses/earning assets	3.78%	3.75%	3.81%
Annual growth rates			
Assets		4.19%	3.56%
Loans (net)		10.85%	6.65%
Deposits		2.65%	3.46%
Capital		6.25%	6.20%
Composition of assets			
Earning assets/total assets			
Details appear on balance sheet		(See Table 2.1)	
Composition of liabilities			
Details appear on balance sheet		(See Table 2.1)	

TABLE 3.14   *(Continued)*
First National Bank's Ratio Analysis

	1999	2000	2001
Supplemental profitability ratios			
Earnings power	90.35%	90.05%	90.02%
Noninterest expense-to-total assets	3.42%	3.38%	3.43%
Net noninterest expense-to-total assets	2.48%	2.39%	2.39%
Efficiency	64.42%	62.64%	65.53%
Interest margin (total assets)	4.37%	4.41%	4.34%
Interest margin (earning assets)	4.83%	4.89%	4.82%
Yield on earning assets	8.56%	8.67%	8.69%
Cost rate on total funds	3.37%	3.41%	3.48%
Cost rate on interest-bearing funds	4.33%	4.37%	4.47%
Spread	4.23%	4.30%	4.22%
Supplemental liquidity risk ratios			
Core deposits-to-assets	83.40%	81.97%	83.86%
Liquid assets-to-earning assets	9.33%	7.87%	7.83%
Net loans-to-deposits	62.81%	67.83%	68.31%
Net loans-to-core deposits	67.55%	73.12%	73.61%
Net non-core funding dependence	0.11%	3.18%	3.33%
Supplemental credit quality ratios			
Net chargeoffs-to-gross loans & leases	0.23%	0.16%	0.24%
Loss reserves-to-gross loans & leases	1.34%	1.06%	1.08%
Loss reserves-to-noncurrent loans	3.62%	2.48%	2.03%
Provision for loan losses-to-gross LL	0.22%	0.19%	0.24%
Noncur lns+OREO-to-gross LL+OREO	0.68%	0.58%	0.62%
Supplemental interest rate risk ratios			
Repriceable assets-to-total assets: 3 mos	43.17%	47.75%	45.94%
Repriceable liabilities-to-total assets: 3 mos	48.89%	50.63%	49.77%
Dollar gap: 3 mos	($25,507)	($13,381)	($18,386)
Gap-to-assets	(5.72%)	(2.88%)	(3.82%)
Gap-to-equity	(79.31%)	(39.16%)	(50.66%)
Sensitivity ratio	0.883	0.943	0.923
Supplemental capital adequacy ratios			
Capital (leverage) ratio	7.22%	7.36%	7.55%
Equity capital ratio	7.22%	7.36%	7.55%
Capital-to-risk assets	8.69%	8.84%	9.06%
Tier one capital ratio	unknown	unknown	unknown
Tier two capital ratio	unknown	unknown	unknown

specific funds. For example, specific costs of fund sources for First National Bank appear to be acceptable. However, changes in the composition of liabilities from low-cost sources, such as demand deposits and savings accounts, to high-cost sources, such as borrowings and large CDs, have caused the bank's cost of funds to grow.

We can get helpful insights on both returns and risks by examining the annual growth rates of selected items, the next category of supplemental measures in Table 3.14. For example, rapid loan growth leads to higher returns as well as higher risk. The bank's asset growth has outstripped its deposits growth and caused it to rely on borrowed funds extensively. The growth rate of capital in relation to the growth rate of assets and loans often dictates the bank's future capital position. (Chapter 9's discussion on bank capital will cover this relationship in detail.)

Master Set of Ratios: Table 3.13

We can gain greater insight into First National Bank's performance using the master set of ratios shown in Table 3.13. The commentary in the table on each ratio helps to explain the ratio's meaning. In addition to the ROE model variables, crucial supplemental profit-ability ratios measure earnings power, use of bank overhead (noninterest expense), and overall yields on assets and costs of funds. Earnings power reveals how fully a bank employs its funds in interest-yielding assets.

The use of bank overhead is measured in several ways. Noninterest expense-to-assets is not sufficient unto itself. Net noninterest expense-to-assets recognizes that, while some institutions have higher overhead percentages, this might be justifiable if the extra expense is used to create a larger flow of noninterest income. This ratio acknowledges the adage that "it takes money to make money." The efficiency ratio is, however, the most complete measure of overhead use. This ratio postures overhead as the input to banking activities (the numerator) and net interest income plus noninterest income as the output (the denominator) being produced by overhead. Clearly, smaller values of the efficiency ratio indicate greater efficiency. As an *ad hoc* standard, many profitable institutions lowered this ratio toward 50 percent by the end of the 1990s. In comparison, First National's ratios in the low to mid-60s suggests that its efficiency lags.

Although the ratios representing liquidity, credit quality, interest rate, and capital risks are defined and explained in Table 3.13, we need benchmarks for evaluating their "goodness." One type of benchmark is *serial* in the sense that we can observe the trend in each ratio's time series to monitor changes over the three years. None of First National's ratio trends is cause for alarm. However, in the two types of loans-to-deposits ratios we observe a trend toward being more fully loaned up (and therefore, less liquid). In addition, small increases in net noncore funding dependence show a slight increase in reliance on borrowed funds and large CDs that are more subject to flight. Consistent with larger non-core funding is a small increase in the costs of funds. There are no trends in credit quality, interest rate sensitivity, and capital adequacy that would cause us to be concerned.

The other type of benchmark needed to evaluate financial ratios is *cross-sectional.* This benchmark compares an institution with a peer group of institutions that are similar in size and markets served. This is perhaps the most powerful of the two benchmarks. Unfortunately, we do not have such information for First National Bank. However, the end of chapter problems set provides an opportunity to apply this important technique.

Variations in Acceptable Bank Performance

In the preceding chapter, we demonstrated the wide differences in asset and liability compositions and sources of revenues and expenses among five reasonably successful banks. Table 3.15 contains a selected group of performance measures for these five banks—American Heritage Bank in El Reno, Oklahoma; American National Bank of Sarpy

**TABLE 3.15 Performance Measures for Selected Banks
(all numbers are percentages)**

	Heritage	American	Overton	Mellon	Comerica
Yield on earning assets	9.14	9.32	8.51	7.43	7.99
Cost of funding earning assets	3.57	4.09	2.89	3.59	3.98
Net interest margin	5.57	5.23	5.62	3.84	4.01
Noninterest income/earning assets	1.29	1.32	1.78	4.46	1.54
Noninterest expense/earning assets	3.69	4.16	5.11	5.51	3.33
Net operating income/assets	1.70	1.07	1.24	1.52	1.10
Return on assets	1.70	1.07	1.25	1.53	1.13
Return on equity	17.23	14.98	19.03	18.06	16.50
Net loans & leases/deposits	88.33	77.68	64.33	81.05	127.60
Loss reserve to loans	0.83	0.99	1.23	1.36	1.38
Noncurrent loans to loans	0.01	0.40	0.15	0.69	0.52
Net charge-offs to loans	0.04	0.75	0.07	0.04	0.33
Loan loss provision/net charge-offs	612	101	466	−174	150
Volatile liabilities/total liabilities	15.90	12.81	15.83	31.43	35.76
Fed funds sold/assets	0.00	0.00	0.00	1.45	0.47
Borrowed funds/assets	8.34	3.78	8.03	9.93	31.01
Equity capital/assets	9.96	7.55	6.23	8.66	7.20

County, Papillion, Nebraska; Overton Bank & Trust in Fort Worth, Texas; Mellon Bank headquartered in Pittsburgh, Pennsylvania; and Comerica Bank in Detroit, Michigan.

The differences among the selected performance measures are revealing. Clearly, banks often differ in environment, product lines, strategies, access to financial markets, and so on. Comparing two similar-size banks, American Heritage Bank and American National Bank, may be as ludicrous as comparing American Heritage Bank with the much larger Mellon. Comparison of the larger banks, Mellon and Comerica, may be equally misleading. Mellon has highly developed retail funding, lending, and customer investment sources, whereas Comerica borrows large amounts of funds and lends primarily to midsize business customers. Overton and Mellon, banks of very different sizes, have relatively high noninterest expenses associated with retail banking systems that have relatively low funding costs. Our conclusion is that one must be cautious when comparing one bank with another bank of similar size or one bank with all banks in the same size category. The good news is that there are numerous ways for practically any size bank to achieve an acceptable return!

THE COMPONENTS OF NET INTEREST MARGIN

Understanding the sources of profits in financial institutions requires a critical look at the primary businesses they conduct. In traditional terms, there are two primary businesses:

FIGURE 3.1   Three components of net interest margin

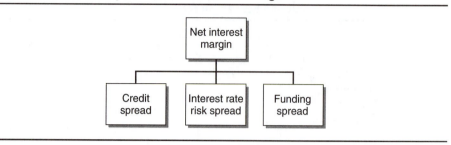

the business of raising funds and the business of selecting earning assets in which to invest the funds. Institutions should strive to make a profit on both of these businesses. We know this may sound like hair-splitting, but beneath the concept of testing for the profitability of funding as well as of selecting assets, there lies a fundamental insight.

The point can be shown as follows. Suppose we were to ask the traditional banker of the 1970s the following two questions: ''How much profit do you earn on your lending function?'' and ''How much do you earn on your deposit-taking function?'' Chances are we would receive an answer that challenged the premise of the questions: ''We can only make money on making loans; taking deposits *costs* us money.''

Advances in accounting techniques among large banks, particularly in the art of *funds transfer pricing,* have led to an understanding that profits should be made on both sides of the financial intermediation equation: raising funds and selecting assets. The focus of funds transfer pricing (FTP) is to ascertain the effective cost and profit for funds that are invested in earning assets. FTP dissects the bank's net interest margin into its component parts. This dissection, in addition to the primary businesses of funding and investing in assets, takes into account a third business conducted by financial institutions: the taking of interest rate risk by mismatching the interest rate sensitivity of assets and liabilities. We will devote much of Chapters 4 and 5 to more comprehensive analyses of interest rate risk.

As shown in Figure 3.1, profitability in the three businesses of banking is captured in the three components of net interest rate margin: the *credit spread,* the *funding spread,* and the *interest rate risk spread.*

This three-way analysis of net interest margin is based on financial market tests of the profitability of an institution's yield on assets, cost of funds, and mismatch of asset and liability maturities. The financial market presents an alternative venue for investing and funding. If the rate of return on an investment in long-term loans cannot beat the rate of return on long-term securities in the financial market, it is not profitable to make the loans. This is especially so if the loans bear greater default risk than comparable investment in default-free securities. It is crucial to standardize maturity before making comparisons of market investment with bank credit activities. For example, five-year loans must be compared to five-year securities. Standardizing maturity is necessary because, in the financial market, interest rates differ for different investment maturities; most often long-term securities bear a higher interest rate than short-term securities. The relationship of interest rates and maturities of securities is depicted in the *yield curve.* We will discuss the yield curve and the related theoretical concept of the term structure of interest rates in Chapter 5 and Appendix 5A.

FIGURE 3.2   Yield curve basis for measuring three components of net interest margin

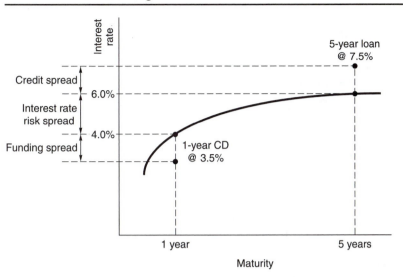

Figure 3.2 illustrates the FTP process and how it leads to measures of credit spread, funding spread, and interest rate risk spread. First, you should observe that the yield curve is shown as a concave relationship between market interest rates and maturity. As is often the case, in Figure 3.2 short-term maturities bear lower interest rates than long-term maturities; thus, there is an upward-sloping yield curve. Moreover, our yield curve is *risk-free*. This is because we based it on interest rates for U.S. Treasury securities; the yield curve illustrates the interest rate structure for default-free assets. The only assets that may never default are Treasury securities; all others bear some degree of credit risk. The case of Cerrillos National Bank will demonstrate how the components of net interest margin are measured.

EXAMPLE The lending division of Cerrillos National Bank originates a $10 million five-year loan and charges its risky borrower 7.5% percent. Simultaneously, Cerrillos National's funding division acquires $10 million in one-year deposits. The two transactions are not related to one another; however, they occur at the same time and, therefore, under the same yield curve conditions.

An officer in Cerrillos' finance division plots the five-year loan in Figure 3.2 above the five-year maturity point on the risk-free yield curve. He knows that the profitability of this loan must meet the test of the financial market: Cerrillos Bank could have chosen to invest in five-year risk-free Treasury securities for a yield of 6.0 percent. Instead, the bank chose a risky five-year loan yielding 7.5 percent. The finance division officer determines that the *credit spread* for this transaction is the difference between the loan rate and the same-maturity yield curve rate for a 1.5 percent profit that he credits to Cerrillos National's lending division. He figures that the 1.5 percent spread is compensation for the fact that the lending group is taking credit risk. In addition, the lenders get compensated for providing crucial banking services such as analyzing and certifying the customer's

TABLE 3.16   **Details of the Components of Net Interest Margin**

Yield on 5-year loans:	7.50%	
− Opportunity yield on 4-year investment	6.00	(FTP price)
Credit spread		**1.50%**
Opportunity yield on 5-year investment	6.00	
− Opportunity cost on 1-year funds	4.00	(FTP price)
Interest rate risk spread		**2.00%**
Opportunity cost on 1-year funds	4.00	
− Cost for 1-year CDs	3.50	
Funding spread		**0.50%**
Net interest margin		**4.00%**

creditworthiness, applying their skills to structure a loan agreement that is appropriate for the customer, and standing by to revise the agreement in the event the customer gets into trouble.

Similarly, the finance division officer measures the profitability of acquiring the one-year CDs. He plots them in Figure 3.2 below the one-year maturity point on the yield curve. Again, he applies a financial market test of this transaction: Cerrillos Bank could have chosen to buy funds in the market for 4.0 percent, but the funding division came up with new deposits, paying 3.5 percent to its depositors. Our finance officer credits the funding division with a *funding spread* profit on this transaction of 0.5 percent.

Finally, he realizes that the combination of the above funding and lending transactions produces interest rate risk for Cerrillos National, which is the responsibility of the finance division. As an institution, the bank chose to acquire short-term liabilities and long-term assets. In effect, the bank chose to mismatch the maturities of assets and liabilities. The interest rate risk of such a mismatch is that short-term interest rates may rise in the near future. An interest rate rise would eventually lead to higher funding costs as the shorter-term CDs are rolled over. However, the longer-term loans continue yielding 7.5 percent for five years. Moreover, a rise in interest rates constitutes an opportunity cost; Cerrillos is stuck with its earlier loan yield and cannot free up the money invested in the loans to take advantage of the evolving higher rates. Recall that we identified interest rate risk as one of three primary businesses for financial institutions. Just as credit risk and funding (liquidity) risk should be compensated, so should interest rate risk. In Figure 3.2, the interest rate risk is the acquisition of one-year funds and investment in five-year assets. Because the yield curve is upward sloping, Cerrillos National's finance division is compensated 2 percent, the difference in five-year and one-year risk-free interest. Table 3.16 summarizes all three spread measures that make up the 4 percent net interest margin earned on these transactions.

The Cerrillos National case describes three separate transactions. The institution's lending personnel should be recognized for creating a 1.5 percent spread but not, as our traditional banker would have claimed, for creating the whole 4.0 percent profit. Personnel responsible for attracting and servicing depositors should be recognized for creating a 0.5 percent spread but not, as our traditional banker would have claimed, for simply incurring costs. Finally, then, the financial personnel have created a 2 percent spread as compensation for assuming interest rate risk.

IMPROVING RISK MEASUREMENT AND MANAGEMENT

In the challenging environment of the early 2000s, banks will have to take considerable risks to earn a reasonable return. The measurement and management of such risks is one of the most important aspects of bank financial management. Beginning measures of risk were discussed in the preceding chapter and at the beginning of this chapter. This section elaborates on the types of risks a bank must take to be profitable and on the measurement of such risks. Many of the subsequent chapters in this book emphasize the management of the various risks in banking.

Figure 3.3 shows one way to classify the risks a bank must take to achieve acceptable returns. There are four broad classes of risk: (1) environmental risks, which the bank must take as a regulated firm that is a key part of the payments system in the United States; (2) management risks, which are caused by the people managing a bank; (3) delivery risks, which are taken as the bank delivers financial services; and (4) financial risks, which are taken in managing the balance sheet. Environmental risk is a catchall category that refers to risks the bank must guard against but over which it has, at best, limited control. Legislative risk refers to changing the laws that affect commercial banks. Economic risks are associated with national and regional economic factors that can affect bank performance materially, whereas competitive risks arise because most bank products and services can be offered by more and more financial and nonfinancial firms. Finally, regulatory

FIGURE 3.3   Classification of banking risks

Banking Characteristics	Risk Class	Risk Category
Environment	Environmental risks	Legislative risk Economic risk Competitive risk Regulatory risk
Human resources	Management risks	Defalcation risk Organizational risk Ability risk Compensation risk
Financial services	Delivery risks	Operational risk Technological risk New-product risk Strategic risk
Balance sheet	Financial risks	Credit risk Liquidity risk Interest rate risk Leverage risk International risk

risk involves living with some rules that place a bank at a competitive disadvantage and the ever-present danger that legislators or regulators will change the rules in a manner unfavorable to the bank.

Management risks include the risk of dishonesty by an officer or employee; the risk that the bank will not have an effective organization; the risk that management lacks the ability to make good decisions consistently; and the risk that the bank's compensation plans do not provide appropriate management incentive.

Four major risks are associated with the delivery of financial services. Operational risk, sometimes called burden risk, is the bank's ability to deliver its financial services in a profitable manner. Both the ability to deliver services and the ability to control the overhead associated with such delivery are important elements. Technological risk refers to the risk of current delivery systems becoming inefficient because of the development of new delivery systems. New-product risk is the danger associated with introducing new products and services. Lower than anticipated demand, higher than anticipated cost, and lack of managerial talent in new markets can lead to severe problems with new products. Strategic risk refers to the bank's ability to select geographic and product areas that will be profitable for the bank in a complex future environment.

There are five primary categories of financial risks. Credit risk, also called default or asset quality risk, is the probability of receiving cash flows from assets when promised. Liquidity risk, or funding risk, indicates the bank's potential ability to fund its financial needs. Interest rate risk refers to the potential negative effect on the net cash flows and values of assets and liabilities resulting from interest rate changes. Leverage risk, also called capital risk, is a function of the capital cushion a bank has to protect its depositors and borrowers from declines in asset value. Finally, international risk can include fluctuations in currency exchange rates and country risk beyond ordinary credit risk. The interaction between these risks should be apparent. For example, a bank that has little risk of declines in net asset values and that has low credit and interest rate risks can afford to take more leverage risk.

Figure 3.4 contains traditional and possible lead measures of the four categories of financial risk. We discussed the traditional measures in this chapter; and we discuss lead measures at a later point. The management techniques used to control these financial risks are listed in Figure 3.4 and are discussed in several other chapters in the book as well.

Credit risk is taken, at least to some degree, by nearly all banks and may lead to serious problems or failure if excessive or poorly managed. Traditional measures, such as loans to assets, nonperforming loans to loans, loan losses to loans, and reserves for losses to loans, were previously discussed. These measures are somewhat deficient because they lag in time behind the returns gained by taking higher credit risk. Potential lead indicators for credit risk include loan concentration in geographic or industry areas, rapid loan growth, high yields on categories of loans, and the ratio of loan loss reserves to nonperforming loans. Although none of these measures is a perfect predictor, weaknesses in one, and particularly more than one, may be a sign of future credit problems. Techniques for managing credit losses include selecting credits with an appropriate credit philosophy and culture and the use of analysis, credit scoring, and a credit organization that controls transaction risks. In addition, banks must manage aggregate loan or loan portfolio risk. Credit management topics are discussed in Chapters 10 through 12 of this book.

Traditional measures of liquidity risk, such as the loan-to-deposit ratio or the proportion of liquid assets to deposits, generally tend to focus on the liquidity of assets on the

FIGURE 3.4   Measuring and managing financial risks

Financial Risk	Traditional Measures	Lead Measures	Management Techniques

1. Credit risk	Loans/assets
	Nonperforming
	   loans/loans
	Loan losses/loans
	Reserves for losses/
	   loans
		Loan concentration
		Loan growth
		High lending rates
		Reserves to nonper-
		   forming loans
			Credit analysis
			Internal credit
			   scoring
			Credit controls
			Portfolio risk assess-
			   ment

2. Liquidity risk	Loans/deposits
	Liquid assets/
	   deposits
		Purchased funds
		Borrowing cost
		Liquid assets
		Borrowings/deposits
			Liquidity plan
			Contingency plan
			Cost/pricing models
			Development of fund-
			   ing sources

3. Interest rate risk	Interest-sensitive
	   assets/interest-
	   sensitive liabili-
	   ties
	Gap
		Gap buckets
		Duration
		Dynamic gaps
		Rate shocks
			Dynamic gap man-
			   agement
			Duration analysis
			Simulation
			Rate shocks

4. Leverage risk	Equity/deposits
	Equity/assets
	Capital/assets
		Risk-adjusted
		   assets/equity
		Growth in assets vs.
		   growth in equity
			Capital planning
			Sustainable growth
			   analysis
			Dividend policy
			Risk-adjusted capi-
			   tal adequacy

balance sheet. More progressive or lead measures should focus more on actual or potential cash flows to meet cash needs. For example, how much a bank has in purchased or volatile funds may be indicative of the bank's need for liquidity and of how much of its potential borrowing reserve the bank has used. The same may be true for a bank that has to pay higher than average borrowing costs. The difference between liquid assets (positive for liquidity sources) and borrowings (use of a bank's borrowing potential) related to some proxy for potential liquidity needs (e.g., volatile funds) may be a good lead indicator of liquidity risk. Management techniques for controlling liquidity risk include a liquidity plan, a contingency plan, a good cost-pricing model, and the continuous development of funding sources. These and other liquidity and funding management techniques are discussed in Chapters 6 and 7.

Interest rate risk has traditionally been measured by the ratio of interest-sensitive assets to interest-sensitive liabilities or the gap or difference between interest-sensitive assets and interest-sensitive liabilities. Problems with these traditional measures include difficulty in selecting the maturity to use as the criterion for sensitivity, concern that reinvestment and changing rates may affect interest sensitivity quickly, and failure to consider the valuation effects of rate changes. More progressive or lead measures of interest rate risk include gap measures at several different maturity times, or "buckets"; dynamic gap measures based on selected reinvestment and rate assumptions; duration and convexity measures for the bank's assets, liabilities, and off-balance sheet items, interest rate simulations, and rate shock measures. Management techniques for protecting the values of financial institutions and controlling and managing interest rate risk are discussed in Chapters 4 and 5. The theory and modern applications of financial derivatives, namely, forwards, futures, options, and swaps to risk management and to pricing banking assets, are covered in Chapters 13, 14, and 15.

Traditional measures of leverage risk or capital adequacy usually emphasize equity capital as a percentage of assets and may also include equity-to-deposits or capital-to-assets ratios. The weaknesses of these measures include emphasis on static balance sheet values, no recognition of differences in risk among various assets, no recognition of off-balance sheet items, and the use of book rather than market values for both assets and equity. Improved and lead measures of capital risk might include comparisons of risk-adjusted or risk-weighted assets with equity or total capital, measures recognizing off-balance sheet items as part of capital adequacy, and measures comparing the growth in assets or risk-adjusted assets to the growth in equity capital. Measurement and management of leverage risk start with capital planning and include such techniques as sustainable growth analyses, dividend policy effects, and recognition of risk-adjusted capital adequacy. These and similar techniques for controlling and managing leverage risk are discussed in Chapter 9.

THE APPROPRIATE TRADEOFF BETWEEN RISKS AND RETURNS

The tradeoffs between risk and return have already been discussed and were illustrated in the Smithville Bank example earlier in this chapter. Without question some risks have to be taken to get adequate returns. The big question is how many.

Figure 3.5 presents one approach to answering this tradeoff question. The basic emphasis is that bank management should try to maximize the value of the owners' investment in the bank. This value maximization involves both returns and risks and the balance between the two. Return variables include not only the return measures covered, such as ROA and ROE, but also the timing of returns and future return prospects. The quality or riskiness of returns is related to the size, timing, and future prospects of returns. Returns can be increased and made faster by taking more financial and operating risks. Timing of returns and future prospects are affected by the operating risk and, to a lesser degree, the financial risks. The environmental risks typically do not increase returns but serve as constraints on return and risk decisions.

Management of larger banks or holding companies whose stock trades in an active market should use the market price of its bank's common shares as a guide to balancing risk-return tradeoffs. A bank's market price should represent its returns times some multiple that the market places on these returns. The multiple probably depends primarily on the risks the bank has undertaken to obtain its returns and the future prospects of the bank. The bank should take on additional risks if the market price increases, because the increase in returns more than offsets the lower return multiple resulting from the higher risks the bank has taken. If the market price declines, the previous lower returns, but lower risk and higher multiple is the preferable alternative.

For banks whose stock is not actively traded, the following equations might provide some guidance. Maximization of value to owners is estimated by discounting net cash benefits to shareholders. This condition can be expressed algebraically as:

FIGURE 3.5 Elements of goal of maximizing value to owners

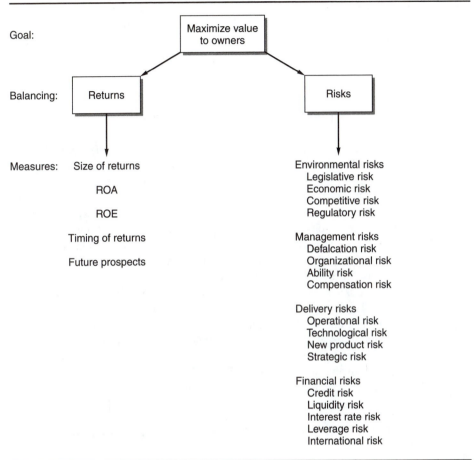

$$W = B_1/(1 + r)^1 + B_2/(1 + r)^2 + B_3/(1 + r)^3 +] \cdot [ ] \cdot [ ] \cdot [+ B_n/(1 + r)^n \tag{3.1}$$

where W is the wealth position of its shareholders; B denotes the net cash benefits to the shareholders in periods 1, 2, 3, . . . , and n; and r is the appropriate rate of discount that reflects both the timing and the risk associated with the net cash receipts.

The key variables constituting B and r are shown in the following equations:

$$B = R - (C + O + T) \tag{3.2}$$

$$r = I + p \tag{3.3}$$

In Equation 3.2, R denotes the gross receipts from the financial institution's assets, C represents the costs of its financial liabilities, O is the overhead costs associated with R and C, and T is the taxes the bank must pay. Depreciation and other noncash costs are generally a relatively small percentage of O, so net cash benefits and net income are reasonably similar for most financial institutions. In Equation 3.3, I is an estimated riskless interest rate that reflects the time value of money, and p is the appropriate risk premium associated with the assets and liabilities of the bank. By substituting Equations 3.2 and 3.3 into Equation 3.1, the following is obtained:

$$W = R_1 - (C_1 + O_1 + T_1)/[1 + (I + p)^1] + R^2 - (C_2 + O_2 + T_2)/[1 + (I + p)^2]$$

$$+] \cdot [ ] \cdot [ ] \cdot [+ R_n - (C_n + O_n + T_n)/[1 + (I + p)^n]$$

(3.4)

The interdependent nature of these variables should be evident. R represents the flow of benefits from the stock of assets, and C represents the flow of negative benefits (costs from the stock of liabilities) that the bank has created to obtain funds. O, which has both fixed and variable components, will depend at least partially on the nature of the asset and liability positions. For taxable institutions, T can be taken as a variable cost that is a function of $R - (C + O)$. While the riskless rate (I) is beyond the bank's control, it will tend to be strongly correlated with both R and C. Finally, p is a function of the interaction of the risks associated with the assets and liabilities portfolios. Conceptually, it is useful to think of the required return ($I + p$) determined by the market's perception of the riskiness of the bank's asset, liability, and capital composition.

To make prudent financial management decisions, bank managers must consider the combined impact of all relevant variables. For example, if management considers purchasing liabilities of 8 percent and investing the proceeds in assets earning 10 percent, it must take account of changes in O, T, and p from the transaction. It may well be that, in spite of the positive spread between R and C, the total effect, including increases in overhead, taxes, or risks, may reduce the wealth of the bank's shareholders.

UNIFORM BANK PERFORMANCE REPORTS

The Uniform Bank Performance Report (UBPR) is probably the most comprehensive information source for analyzing commercial banks. A UBPR is prepared quarterly for each insured commercial bank by the Federal Financial Institutions Examinations Council (FFIEC). The UBPR provides a detailed five-year financial report on a bank and a similar profile for a peer group of banks that can be used for comparative purposes. The FFIEC prepares these reports from a database of financial information from filed quarterly reports.

The three major sections and the principal subsections of each are listed in Table 3.17. The summary ratios section, page 1 of the UBPR, is used as an example. Notice that the summary ratios are grouped into five categories, with three measures reported for each ratio:

1. The selected bank's ratio.
2. Mean ratios for the peer group.
3. Percentile ranking of the requested bank's ratio within the peer group.

The most efficient use of a UBPR probably comes from studying this summary ratio section, identifying potential strengths and weaknesses, and then following upon specific items contained in the detailed analysis in the three remaining sections. Analysts who wish to interpret the detailed UBPR measures will be helped considerably by the *UBPR*

TABLE 3.17   Typical UBPR's Table of Contents

Section	Page
1. Summary ratios	1
2. Income information	
Income statement-revenues and expenses	2
Noninterest income and expense and yield	3
3. Balance sheet information	
Balance sheet: assets, liabilities, and capital	4
Commitments and contingencies	5
Balance sheet: percentage of composition of assets and liabilities	6
Analysis of loan and lease loss reserve and loan mix	7
Analysis of past due, nonaccrual, and restructured loans and leases	8
Maturity and repricing distribution	9
Liquidity and investment portfolio	10
Capital analysis	11

User's Guide (revised 1996), which is available from the FFIEC and can be accessed on the internet.

UBPR users should also be aware of at least three weaknesses of these reports. First, the reports are prepared from a regulatory point of view. Any available market price, per share data, or return-on-equity measures that are important from the shareholder's perspective are ignored. Second, the data are accounting data, which are generally based on historical costs and ignore values that are generally more important to decision makers. Third, the data are usually quarterly averages, which are neither daily averages nor year-end data that appear in many other banking reports. Often bank analysts end up with three sets of measures—one based on daily averages, one based on quarterly averages, and one based on year-end figures. In spite of such weaknesses, UBPRs remain one of the key sources for evaluating bank performance.

END OF CHAPTER PROBLEMS

3.1 Use the data below to construct the return-on-equity (or DuPont) model for StarFirst Bank and Trust.

Total assets	$ 50,000,000,000
Shareholders' equity	4,500,000,000
Interest income	5,000,000,000
Net income	700,000,000
Noninterest income	600,000,000

3.2 Assume that the following relationships apply for Community Bank:

Operating revenues/total assets	13.50%
Return on assets (ROA)	1.72%
Return on equity (ROE)	18.20%

Calculate Community Bank's equity multiplier and profit margin.

Please apply data for the balance sheet of Buena Vista Savings Bank given in Problem 2.9 and the following income statement in working Problems 3.3 through 3.6.

Balance Sheet	($000) 12/31/2000	Income Statement	($000) Year 2000
Assets			
Cash and due from banks	320,000	Interest income:	
Federal funds sold	286,000	Interest on federal funds	8,525
Investment securities	1,321,000	Interest on investment securities	77,247
Gross loans and leases	3,507,000	Interest on gross loans and leases	322,918
Less: Allowance for losses	49,000	Total interest income	408,690
Net loans and leases	3,458,000	Interest expense:	
Premises, fixed assets	73,000	Interest on transactions deposits	45,653
Other real estate owned	10,000	Interest on time and savings deposits	112,088
Other assets	45,000	Interest on time deposits >100M	21,809
Total assets	5,513,000	Interest on federal funds purchased	2,794
		Interest on other borrowed funds	2,718
Liabilities and shareholders equity		Total interest expense	185,062
Transactions deposits	1,739,000	Net interest income	223,628
Time and savings accounts	2,799,000	Provision for loan losses	26,943
Core deposits	4,538,000	Noninterest income	72,368
Time deposits of $100M or more	416,000	Noninterest expense	
Federal funds purchased	86,000	Salaries and benefits	157,238
Other borrowed funds	48,000	Occupancy expense	28,428
Other liabilities	24,000	Miscellaneous	16,355
Common stock	22,000		202,021
Surplus	113,000	Net income before taxes	67,032
Retained earnings	266,000	Taxes	14,304
Total liabilities and shareholders equity	5,513,000	Net income	52,727

3.3 a.) Compute the 2000 values for the return-on-equity model:

	2000	
Ratio	Buena Vista	Peer Group
Return on equity	_____	15.00%
Return on assets	_____	1.44%
Equity multiplier	_____	10.4X
Profit margin	_____	14.8%
Salaries and benefits/operating revenue	_____	27.23%
Occupancy expenses/operating revenue	_____	7.94%
Miscellaneous expenses/operating revenue	_____	3.12%
Asset utilization	_____	9.7%

b.) Briefly comment on Buena Vista's profitability structure. Do you observe any strengths and weaknesses?

c.) Suppose Buena Vista's loans, equity, interest income, interest expense, and non-interest income and expense all increased 50 percent in 2001. How would that affect the accuracy of your ratio analysis? (Consider how our ratios based on a single year differ from ratios based on averages of the beginning and ending balance sheets.)

d.) Several elements of profit margin include salaries and benefits, occupancy, and miscellaneous expense. Calculate these expense ratios and compare them with those of Buena Vista's peers. Which help to explain the difference between BV and its peers?

3.4 a.) Calculate Buena Vista's (i) net interest margin (earning assets or EA) and (ii) net interest margin (total assets or TA). Observe that the difference between these two ratios is explained by the "earnings power" ratio Earning assets/Total assets. Determine this ratio for Buena Vista.

	2000	
Ratio	**Buena Vista**	**Peer Group**
Net interest margin (EA)	_____	5.22%
Net interest margin (TA)	_____	4.80%
$\dfrac{\text{EA}}{\text{TA}}$	_____	0.92

b.) Compare Buena Vista's results with those of its peers. What key factors cause interest margins to differ from one institution to the next?

c.) Which is most affected by interest margin: profit margin or asset utilization? (*Hint:* Remember that the calculation of asset utilization does not incorporate expense items).

3.5 a.) Calculate the following ratios for Buena Vista involving interest yields and interest cost rates. What is the role of the ratio Earning assets/Total assets in explaining the difference between the two interest yield calculations?

	2000	
Ratio	**Buena Vista**	**Peer Group**
Yield on total assets	_____	8.17%
Yield on earning assets	_____	8.88%
Cost rate on total funds	_____	3.84%
*Cost rate on interest bearing funds	_____	4.79%
**Spread	_____	5.04%
Yield on investment securities	_____	6.01%
Yield on gross loans and leases	_____	9.10%
Cost rate on transaction deposits	_____	3.23%

* Assume one-half of Buena Vista's transaction deposits are interest bearing.

** Yield on earning assets minus cost of interest-bearing funds.

Cost rate on T&D deposits	_____	4.42%
Cost rate on CD>100M	_____	5.28%

b.) Discuss the different roles of the yield and cost components in explaining differences in net interest margin between Buena Vista and its peers; that is, are Buena Vista's yield ratios favorable versus those of its peers? Its cost ratios? Why does Buena Vista lead or lag in net interest margin?

3.6 a.) Calculate the following "efficiency" ratios for Buena Vista.

	2000	
Ratio	**Buena Vista**	**Peer Group**
Noninterest expense/assets	_____	3.23%
Net noninterest expense/assets	_____	2.28%
Efficiency ratio	_____	0.616

b.) Compare these ratios with those of Buena Vista's peers. Considering these results and your results from Problem 3.1, part d, discuss more generally how Buena Vista's management of overhead compares to that of its peers.

3.7 Buena Vista has determined that $666,000 of investment securities are short-term (less than one-year maturity). Calculate the liquidity ratios shown below:

Ratio	**Buena Vista**	**Peer Group**
Core deposits-to-assets	_____	74.30%
Liquid assets-to-earning assets	_____	25.80%
Net loans-to-deposits	_____	76.40%
Net loans-to-core deposits	_____	89.80%
Net loans-to-assets	_____	68.20%
Net noncore funds dependence	_____	5.50%

b.) Compare these ratios with those of Buena Vista's peers. Discuss the underlying reasons that Buena Vista's liquidity differs from that of its peers.

3.8 a.) During the year 2000, Buena Vista charged off $24,000 on loans and recovered $13,000 on previously charged-off loans. Noncurrent loans on December 31, 2000 were $40,000. Calculate credit quality ratios for Buena Vista in the following table:

Ratio	**Buena Vista**	**Peer Group**
Net chargeoffs-to-gross loans and leases	_____	1.10%
Loss reserves-to-gross loans and leases	_____	1.51%
Loss reserves-to-noncurrent loans	_____	2.45X
Provision for loan losses-to-gross loans and leases	_____	0.95%
Noncurrent+OREO-to-gross loans and leases+OREO	_____	2.04%

b.) Discuss Buena Vista's loan quality compared to that of its peers. What appears to be strengths? What are weaknesses?

3.9 Complete the balance sheet and revenue information in the following table for Mid-West Savings using the following financial data:

Net loans/deposits:	72%
Core deposits/assets:	73%
Net federal funds:	−$66,000
Asset utilization:	10%
Return on equity:	15.29%
Cash and due from banks/total deposits:	8.00%

Balance Sheet

Cash and due from banks	_____	Demand deposits	500,000
Federal funds sold	42,000	Time & savings deposits	_____
Investment securities	_____	CDs>100M	_____
Net Loans and leases	_____	Federal funds purchased	_____
Other assets	18,000	Common surplus	20,000
Total assets	_____	Accumulated retained earnings	_____
Interest income	90,000	Total liabilities and equity	_____
Noninterest income	8,000	Net income	13,000

3.10 First Bank's ROE was a disappointing 2.5 percent last year. To improve it, management will move the firm's equity/assets ratio to 8 percent, achieve a $2,000 net income before taxes, and establish an asset utilization ratio of 12 percent on operating revenues of $20,000. The firm's new tax rate will be 34 percent. With these changes, what will be First Bank's return on equity? What will be its return on assets?

SMITHVILLE BANK EXERCISE

OBJECTIVE

To become familiar with bank balance sheet and income statement relationships, identify the effects of financial changes on bank return/risk tradeoffs and understand the meaning of interest sensitivity.

REQUIREMENTS

1. Derive a new balance sheet and income statement modeled on Table 3.5 and calculate profitability and risk ratios as in Table 3.6 for Smithville Bank after the changes described below.

2. Describe and discuss as favorable or unfavorable the changes in profitability ratios versus risk ratios compared to Smithville's beginning ratios position in Table 3.6. (You should appreciate that the risk ratios are grossly simplified; more credible ratios were examined in the chapter.)

Starting with the hypothesized environment shown in Table 3.4 and the Smithville Bank balance sheet in Table 3.5, assume the following *new* environment:

A. Changes in Smithville's Balance Sheet

New Funds Raised (Sources of Funds)
$1 million in equity capital
$2 million in transaction deposits
$3 million in short-term time deposits
$4 million in long-term time deposits
$5 million in borrowings

Changes in Assets (Uses of Funds)   After satisfying reserve requirements and investing an additional $5 million in long-term securities, invest equal parts of the remaining funds in medium-variable loans and fixed-rate loans. (Assume that short-term maturing and "repriceable" assets and liabilities—for example, transaction deposits—are rolled over [replaced] in the new environment. Nonmaturing items retain their original earnings or cost rates.)

B. Change in the Hypothesized Environment

Potential earnings available:

Short-term securities	7%
Long-term securities (new)	8.5%
Long-term securities (held)	8%
High-quality, variable rate loans	8.5%
Medium-quality, variable rate loans	10.5%
Fixed-rate loans (new)	10%
Fixed-rate loans (held)	9%

Interest expense:

Transaction deposits	4%
Short-term time deposits	6%
Long-term time deposits (held)	5%
Long-term time deposits (new)	6%
Borrowing	6.5%

Other items remain as in the original "hypothesized environment" (see Table 3.4): remember *other expenses.* Long-term items held before changes in interest rates are not "interest rate sensitive."

CHAPTER 4

Foundations of Value in Banking

At this point, we must examine the most important financial concept of all: How economic value is created in banking. Consider this example. A bank contemplates expanding its assets by entering a high-return, high-risk loan market. Is this a good idea? Some managers feel that "bigger" is better. But in this case, bigger could create losses in excess of the returns. We need to know if the new loan business will add value to the bank; it may increase the bank's assets, but that is not the point.

This bank may be lost if it tries to make a value-additive decision using the primary accounting data we discussed in Chapters 2 and 3. Value is a *forward*-looking concept. Up to now we have been applying accounting data to analyze *past* bank performance. Such data are *backward* looking. They give us *historical* values of assets and liabilities, not forward-looking values.

EXAMPLE Five years ago Camelot Bank acquired long-term government bonds at par for $10 million. Interest rates have risen during the intervening five years and if Camelot decided to sell the bonds today, it would realize only $9 million. However, Camelot's balance sheet still shows the "value" of the bonds as $10 million.[1]

A recent chairman of the Securities Exchange Commission dismissed historical accounting data as fantasy (he called them "once upon a time" accounting). His statement might seem rash. After all, do not traditional accounting data give us important information on bank activities?

The chairman's complaint was not that accounting data are not useful; rather, he believed that the data do not give us vital information on *economic* values. Worse, they disguise the impact that changes in real-world market conditions have on economic values in banking. So in that sense, the chairman was right: the data do not tell us how well

---

[1] Under recent accounting rulings (Financial Accounting Standard 115), bonds must be classified "held to maturity" bonds to be valued at original cost or "available for sale" bonds to be marked according to market values.

management's past decisions have stood up under new market conditions. We need to determine economic values to measure economic performance and to make sound management decisions.

BANKS ENTER "NOMINAL CONTRACTS"

The items we account for on banks' balance sheets are called *nominal contracts*. This is fancy terminology for what appears on the two sides of the balance sheet—assets and liabilities. But the terminology emphasizes value in future terms: Bank asset contracts obligate customers to make future cash payments to the bank, and bank liability contracts obligate the bank to make future cash payments to customers.

Clearly, then, the economic values of asset and liability nominal contracts do not come from historical monetary values. Rather, the values of assets and liabilities should be viewed as *present values*. The time value of money principle defines present values as the values of future cash flows to be received or paid, discounted by the rate of return investors expect to earn during the period of each particular cash flow.

Several factors may cause present values to change unexpectedly. For bank assets, the main factor is default risk. If a large customer's business suffers a reversal, the customer may not pay his loan in a timely fashion. Another factor is payment timing risk; for example, a customer might pay off her mortgage unexpectedly. Usually, such a change in payment behavior is bad news because it tends to reduce the value of the mortgage to the bank. We will look deeper into the issues of loan default and unexpected changes in customer repayment patterns in other chapters. For now we will focus on interest rate effects on value.

This chapter addresses changes in banking values due to changes in financial market conditions. We will be especially alert to value changes that are caused by changes in *market risk,* defined as value changes that arise from changes in interest rates.

TIME VALUE OF MONEY AND INTEREST RATE SENSITIVITY

The value (price) of a government bond is found from:

$$P_0 = \sum_{t=1}^{n} \frac{CF_t}{(1 + r)^t} + \frac{R_n}{(1 + r)^n} \tag{4.1}$$

where P_0 = present bond price, CF_t = cash flow received by investor at time t, n = time of the final cash flow (maturity), r = risk-free discount rate per period, and R_n = the final payment that redeems the par value of the bond. The term $1/(1 + r)^t$ is the present value of \$1 to be received at time t.

Investors who buy a 6 percent coupon bond with only one year to maturity receive a single \$60 coupon at the end of the year as well as the \$1,000 redemption or par value payment. The bond's price, assuming a market discount of 6 percent, is:

$$P_0 = \frac{\$60}{(1 + .06)^1} + \frac{\$1,000}{(1 + .06)^1} = \$1,000 \tag{4.2}$$

If the market discount rate rises instantaneously to 7 percent, the bond's value becomes:

$$P_0 = \frac{\$60}{(1 + .07)^1} + \frac{\$1,000}{(1 + .07)^1} = \$990.65 \qquad (4.3)$$

That is, a rise in the interest rate causes the bond's price to decrease. Conversely, a fall in the interest rate to 5 percent causes the price to increase.

$$P_0 = \frac{\$60}{(1 + .05)^1} + \frac{\$1,000}{(1 + .05)^1} = \$1,009.52 \qquad (4.4)$$

Assume instead that the bond in our example has a maturity of five years and pays $60 at the end of each of the next five years. Again, assume the market discount rate is 6 percent. The example bond's price is:[2]

$$P_0 = \sum_{t=1}^{5} \frac{\$60}{(1 + .06)^t} + \frac{\$1,000}{(1 + .06)^5} = \$1,000.00 \qquad (4.5)$$

Now, let's assume the market interest rate on our government bond rises to 7 percent; then we get:

$$P_0 = \sum_{t=1}^{5} \frac{\$60}{(1 + .07)^t} + \frac{\$1,000}{(1 + .07)^5} = \$959.00 \qquad (4.6)$$

On the other hand, if the market interest rate falls to 5 percent:

$$P_0 = \sum_{t=1}^{5} \frac{\$60}{(1 + .05)^t} + \frac{\$1,000}{(1 + .05)^5} = \$1,043.29 \qquad (4.7)$$

We say that the values of longer-term bonds are more *interest rate sensitive* than short-term ones. This means that assets with longer-term cash flows, holding the coupon rate constant, produce larger decreases or increases in value when market discount rates rise or fall. In Table 4.1, the last column shows the sensitivities of one-year and five-year bonds and also considers the sensitivity of a 6 percent coupon bond with 30 years to

---

[2] The $\sum_{t=1}^{5} \$60/(1 + .06)^t$ term of this equation comprises five coupon payments made in each of five years, discounted by the term $(1/(1 + .06)^t)$ applicable to each year $(t = 1, 2, 3, 4, 5)$. A direct, so-called *closed form* calculation for this summation is $C/r\, [1 - 1/(1 + r)^n]$.

TABLE 4.1   Interest Rate Sensitivities Based on Maturity

	$r = 6\%$	$r = 7\%$	Percent Change
1-year	$1000.00	$990.65	−0.94%
5-year	$1000.00	$959.00	−4.10%
30-year	$1000.00	$875.10	−12.40%

maturity. Furthermore, you can compare these bonds' sensitivities with the sensitivity of the very long-term 30-year bond. The last row of Table 4.1 shows the sensitivity of this bond.

It is obvious from Table 4.1 that interest rate sensitivity increases with maturity. But it increases at a decreasing rate. In other words, long-term bonds are more interest sensitive, but the increase in sensitivity gets smaller the longer their maturity. This peculiarity is caused by interest compounding. You can observe this relationship in Table 4.1. When you compare the five-year bond with a bond with four years shorter maturity (the one-year bond), the five-year bond is 4.36 times more sensitive to a 1 percent rise in interest rate than the 1-year bond with four years shorter maturity (4.10% divided by 0.94%). Now, contrast the five-year bond with the sensitivity of a bond that has 25 years longer maturity. Notice that the 30-year bond is only 3.02 times more sensitive (12.40% divided by 4.10%). For the short-term bond with a four-year difference in maturity, the ratio of sensitivity is 4.36; for the long-term bond with a 25-year difference in maturity, the ratio of sensitivity is only 3.02.

Compounding creates another peculiarity in valuation. Interest sensitivity is *asymmetrical*. By this we mean that the loss from a 1 percent increase in the interest rate *is not the same* as the gain from a 1 percent decrease in the rate. For example, the table shows that the price of a five-year, 6 percent coupon bond declines 4.10 percent when market rates rise from 6 to 7 percent. On the other hand, our earlier calculation shows that the bond's price *rises* to $1,043.29 or by 4.33 percent when the market rate *falls* from 6 to 5 percent. Prices rose by a larger amount for a decrease in interest than they fell for the same increase in interest.

We can illustrate this graphically with a bond *price curve* portraying the relationship between bond prices and market interest rates. Figure 4.1 presents the price curve for the five-year, 6 percent coupon bond. In general, the curvature or *convex* shape of the price curve is greater the smaller the coupon. *Zero-coupon bonds*—which are simple bonds that make just one payment during their life—are the most curved (i.e., the most *convex*). The asymmetry of price changes is captured in the curve's convex shape. If price curves were not curves but were straight lines instead, the price changes would be symmetrical.

Now, consider bonds with the same coupons but with different maturities. The curvature and the asymmetry increase rapidly the longer the bonds' maturity. Or consider bonds with the same maturity but with different coupons. Curvature increases a bit the smaller the coupon, but it's not as important as maturity in terms of its effect on asymmetry.

Bond traders feel that the degree of curvature of price curves is absolutely indispens-

FIGURE 4.1   Price curve for 5-year, 6 percent coupon bond

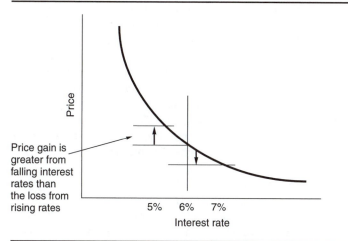

able to the valuation of fixed-income securities. We present a more formal discussion of the critical curvature property of bond pricing in an appendix to this chapter.

BALANCE SHEET MATURITY MISMATCHING

The market value of a financial institution's balance sheet is the value of its assets minus the value of its liabilities. It is critical for a financial services firm to understand how this value can be impacted by interest rate sensitivity. If interest rate movements have a different effect on assets than they do on liabilities, the value of the firm must change. This difference in effect is caused by differences in the maturities of assets and liabilities known as maturity *mismatching,* a normal situation for financial services (FS) firms' assets and liabilities. If a firm mismatches maturities by a large magnitude, changes in interest rates can change balance sheet value dramatically.

Most banks are mismatched because of the unique nature of the markets they serve. Banks seldom are able to gather portfolios of assets and liabilities with the same cash flow patterns. Even if they are able to, bank management may decide there is a profit advantage in deliberately mismatching. The following example uses information from Table 4.1 to give important insight into the effect of changing interest rates on the value of a mismatched FS firm.

EXAMPLE   Edmundson Investments, Inc. has a very simple balance sheet. However, Edmundson mismatched its balance sheet because it borrowed $1 million of one-year funds at 6 percent interest and then used these funds to purchase $1 million of five-year bonds, also at 6 percent interest. We learned in Table 4.1 that, given an interest rate rise to 7 percent, the value of the five-year asset with a 6 percent coupon has a four times greater decrease in value than the decrease in value of the one-year 6 percent debt. If Edmundson were forced to liquidate its balance sheet immediately after the rise in rates, it would receive only $959,000 on its $1 million investment in five-year bonds but would have to repay $990,650 on its one-year borrowings, creating a net loss of $31,650.

Instead of liquidating, suppose Edmundson decides to hold the portfolio to the bonds' maturity of five years. Now if interest rates rise, the firm still has a problem. Its borrowings will come due at the end of the first year, and, because interest rates have gone up, Edmundson will have to re-borrow at the now higher rate. Meanwhile, the earnings on its assets are locked in for four more years at a rate that is now below the market. Edmundson should anticipate taking annual losses in net interest income for four more years.

Another way to look at it is Edmundson's lost opportunity. Because its borrowed funds are locked up in a five-year asset, Edmundson cannot use the funds to take advantage of the market's new 7 percent earnings rate. The firm is married to an asset with inferior earnings.

Banks have the same kind of asset-liability mismatch risk as Edmundson Investments. Their fundamental balance sheet management problem is that they tend to pay for long-term assets with demand liabilities such as transactions deposits. Such funds can be withdrawn with little or no warning. In the history of banking, if depositors felt that their bank's assets were of poor quality, they all would try to cash in their deposits at the same time. To satisfy depositors' demands for funds, banks were forced to liquidate their assets at fire sale values well below the assets' original cost.

Deposit insurance has removed the risk of such bank runs. Since the introduction of federal deposit insurance in 1933, banks are no longer forced to liquidate assets. But banks still must deal with balance sheet mismatching in an environment of volatile interest rates. As we will see, balance sheets based on market valuation make the effects of interest rate movements abundantly clear.

EXAMPLE Treadwater Bank is started up by enthusiastic investors who put in $1 million in equity capital. The new bank raises an additional $9 million in one-year certificates of deposit (CDs) bearing 6 percent interest. The bank now invests all $10 million in a five-year term loan, also yielding 6 percent. Treadwater has no other costs or revenues. Here is how historical cost accounting represents Treadwater's balance sheet.

Assets		Liabilities and Equity Capital	
Loans	$10,000,000	Deposits	$9,000,000
		Equity Capital	1,000,000
	$10,000,000		$10,000,000

We will show Treadwater how to create a market value balance sheet that reflects changes in future earnings and cash flows due to interest rate changes. Table 4.2 shows five years of Treadwater's projected earnings statements. Initially, it is assumed there are no changes in the market interest rate. Interest income is $600,000 per year consisting of 6 percent earnings on $10 million loans; interest expense of $540,000 is based on $9 million of liabilities. Because interest rates are constant, Treadwater's liabilities are rolled over at 6 percent interest at the end of each year. Happily, Treadwater Bank's investors earn $60,000 each year.

These earnings underlie Treadwater's market value balance sheet. Note that Table 4.2 omits important information because it does not recognize the residual values of assets,

TABLE 4.2   Treadwater Bank's Five-Year Projected Earnings with Constant 6 Percent Interest Rate

	1st Year	2nd Year	3rd Year	4th Year	5th Year
Int. income	$600,000	$600,000	$600,000	$600,000	$600,000
Int. expense	540,000	540,000	540,000	540,000	540,000
Net earnings	$ 60,000	$ 60,000	$ 60,000	$ 60,000	$ 60,000

liabilities, and capital. At the end of the five years, borrowers will pay off their loan principal, creating a $10 million cash inflow to the bank. Depositors will cash out their investment for the last time and cause a cash outflow of $9 million from the bank. The difference in these two "terminal year" cash flows will be a net $1 million inflow to investors.

The following values will appear on Treadwater's current (time = 0) market value balance sheet:

$$\textbf{Assets } A_0 = \sum_{t=1}^{5} \frac{\$600,000}{(1 + .06)^t} + \frac{\$10,000,000}{(1 + .06)^5} = \$10,000,000$$

$$-\textbf{ Liabilities } L_0 = \sum_{t=1}^{5} \frac{\$540,000}{(1 + .06)^t} + \frac{\$9,000,000}{(1 + .06)^5} = -\$9,000,000 \quad (4.8)$$

$$= \textbf{Equity Capital } E_0 = \sum_{t=1}^{5} \frac{\$60,000}{(1 + .06)^t} + \frac{\$1,000,000}{(1 + .06)^5} = \$1,000,000$$

Although these values are derived by different means than those of the historical accounting ("once-upon-a-time") balance sheet, the two balance sheets come out the same as long as interest rates do not change.

Now, let's suppose interest rates rise on five-year loans and one-year CDs from a level of 6 percent to 7 percent and that the rise occurs immediately after the investors start up the bank. Assume that everyone expects one-year interest rates to remain at 7 percent for the next five years.[3] Table 4.3 presents annual income statements for this situation.

Treadwater's asset-liability mismatch situation is described as *liability sensitive*. This is because its short-term liabilities are subject to rolling over (*repricing*) in one year at a higher interest rate, but the interest rate on its long-term assets is fixed for a much longer time. Note that the negative impact on earnings from a sustained rise in interest rates does not affect the bank's first year's earnings of $60,000 because commitments were made before CD interest rates changed. The negative change is effective starting the second year.

The current historical (book value) balance sheet is unchanged by events that occur after items are put on the balance sheet and does not reflect the rise in interest rates. This

---

[3] The discussion of the "yield curve" in Chapter 5 will show how interest rates expected in the future are connected with the pattern of present interest rates.

TABLE 4.3   Treadwater's Five-Year Projected Earnings with Initial 6 Percent Interest Rate and Rates Rise Immediately to 7 Percent

	1st Year	2nd Year	3rd Year	4th Year	5th Year
Int. income	$600,000	$600,000	$600,000	$600,000	$600,000
Int. expense	540,000	630,000	630,000	630,000	630,000
Net earnings	$ 60,000	−$ 30,000	−$ 30,000	−$ 30,000	−$ 30,000

balance sheet continues to value investors' capital at $1 million. However, Treadwater's *market value* balance sheet does reveal the effects of interest rate movements. Market values discount cash flows beyond the present ($t = 0$) by the higher new one-year interest rate.

Assets

$$A_0 = \frac{\$600,000}{(1+.07)} + \frac{\$600,000}{(1+.07)^2} + \frac{\$600,000}{(1+.07)^3} + \frac{\$600,000}{(1+.07)^4} + \frac{\$10,600,000}{(1+.07)^5} = \quad \$9,589,980$$

− Liabilities

$$L_0 = \frac{\$540,000}{(1+.07)} + \frac{\$630,000}{(1+.07)^2} + \frac{\$630,000}{(1+.07)^3} + \frac{\$630,000}{(1+.07)^4} + \frac{\$9,630,000}{(1+.07)^5} = -\$8,915,888 \quad (4.9)$$

= Equity Capital

$$E_0 = \frac{\$60,000}{(1+.07)} + \frac{-\$30,000}{(1+.07)^2} + \frac{-\$30,000}{(1+.07)^3} + \frac{-\$30,000}{(1+.07)^4} + \frac{\$970,000}{(1+.07)^5} = \quad \$ \ 674,092$$

After the increase in interest rates, Treadwater's market value balance sheet becomes:

Assets		Liabilities and Equity Capital	
Loans	$9,589,980	Deposits	$8,915,888
		Equity Capital	674,092
	$9,589,980		$9,589,980

Because of their long maturities, the value of Treadwater's five-year loans is much more sensitive to interest rates and has been hit sharply by the expectation of higher future interest rates. But because deposits are rolled over each year after the interest rate changes, their value has been affected much less. The net result is that the value of investors' stake in Treadwater—the bank's economic value—has declined from $1,000,000 to $674,092, a loss of $325,908.[4] Treadwater shareholders are no longer happy.

---

[4] The term *market value accounting* may be misleading when applied to the equity value of the firm. Stock market participants think in terms of firms' "capitalization" value, that is, the value in the stock market of all the firm's outstanding stock. Capitalization value also includes the values of attributes that include, but also go well beyond, the bank's currently held assets and liabilities. An important additional element is the market's valuation of earnings from future operations (operating value) and of future business that may be attracted because of accumulated goodwill (franchise value).

The economic value of the balance sheet—what we have been calling the *market value balance sheet*—is the *mark-to-market value* of assets minus the *mark-to-market value* of liabilities. Investors' returns come from two sources: earnings—the accounting perspective—and the change in the value of the firm—the economic perspective. A moment's reflection should make it clear that interest rate sensitivity (think of it as *the risk of exposure to changes in market interest rates*) shows up in both earnings (accounting) effects and economic balance sheet valuation effects. Combined, these two elements—change in earnings and the change in economic values—comprise *total interest rate risk.*

$$\text{Total returns} = \text{Earnings} + \text{Changes in value}$$
$$\text{Total interest rate risk} = \text{Earnings risk} + \text{Economic (value) risk}$$

Managers, being practical people focused on immediately visible results, naturally zero in more narrowly on short-term results in the form of current earnings and downplay the economic value effects we have been examining. Bank regulators have been concerned enough by this tendency to encourage a more complete managerial perspective on interest rate risk. As a result, beginning in 1990, federal regulators began to require financial institutions to track total returns and not just the interest rate risk to short-term earnings.[5]

By now it should be clear that the two dimensions of interest rate sensitivity, earnings and economic or balance sheet value, are one and the same. Long-run earnings discounted to the present simply collapse into the market value balance sheet. A focus on short-term earnings to the exclusion of longer-term earnings is myopic and only captures part of the value and risk of FS institutions. Implicitly, we defined interest rate risk as the effect of changes in interest rates on either (1) the value of a single asset, (2) the value of a portfolio of assets, or (3) the difference in the values of a portfolio of assets and a portfolio of the liabilities that finance the assets. The last difference, asset values minus liability values, is the equity value (or economic value) of the balance sheet.

Obviously, it is risky to mismatch asset and liability maturities on bank balance sheets. However, it is not possible to quantify this risk on the basis of asset and liability maturities. For example, Table 4.1 shows that a 30-year asset's sensitivity is 13.2 times that of a one-year asset [12.40%/0.94% = 13.2], not the 30 times ratio of their maturities. The concept of *duration* permits us to make a far more accurate characterization of interest rate sensitivity than we are allowed with maturity.

MEASURING INTEREST RATE SENSITIVITY: DURATION[6]

Single-Payment Assets

The value of a financial asset with a single payment of C_n dollars to be received in n years is:

---

[5] This requirement was first formalized in the Office of Thrift Supervision's Thrift Bulletin 13 and the Office of the Comptroller of the Currency's Examination Bulletin 90-1.

[6] This section applies formal mathematics and can be bypassed without much cost to beginning finance students. Skip to the next section.

$$P_0 = \frac{C_n}{(1 + r)^n} \tag{4.10}$$

We can define the asset's interest rate sensitivity as the partial derivative of P_0 with respect to r.

$$\delta P_0 = \frac{-nC_n}{(1 + r)^{n+1}} \, \delta r \tag{4.11}$$

Dividing both sides of this equation by P_0 gives the percentage change in P_0.

$$\frac{\delta P_0}{P_0} = \frac{-n\delta r}{1 + r} \tag{4.12}$$

This equation gives the price (or value) volatility for a single-payment asset. Because we are using calculus, the latter equation applies to only infinitesimal changes in r. Equation 4.12 can be restated to give a reasonable approximation when changes, Δ, in r are finite, but still small.

$$\frac{\Delta P_0}{P_0} = \frac{-n\Delta r}{1 + r} \tag{4.13}$$

Equations 4.12 and 4.13 show that there is an approximately linear relationship between the proportional change in P_0 ($\delta P_0/P_0$ or $\Delta P_0/P_0$) and r. Suppose that r was initially 10 percent and Δr was a positive 1 percent. Further assume two single-payment assets, one of which has a maturity of one year and the other a maturity of five years. Substituting in Equation 4.13:

$$\frac{\Delta P_0}{P_0} = \frac{-(1)(.01)}{1.10} = -0.91\% \text{ for the one-year asset} \tag{4.14}$$

and

$$\frac{\Delta P_0}{P_0} = \frac{(-5)(.01)}{1.10} = -4.55\% \text{ for the five-year asset} \tag{4.15}$$

The significance of these results is that the five-year asset's price is five times more volatile than the price of the one-year asset (-4.55% is five times -0.91%). Thus, the assets' volatilities are directly represented by their maturities. However, as we will see, it is only in the case of single-payment assets that maturity n is an exact index of the assets' respective interest rate risks.

Multipayment Assets

The index n of a single-payment asset is also its *duration*. However, maturity and duration are equal only for single-payment assets. Duration can be derived as an index of interest rate risk for multipayment assets as well. Here is where duration and maturity part ways. Duration is a reliable index for multipayment assets but maturity is not.

Let P_0 be the value of an n-maturity asset that generates a series of n cash flows, C_t.

$$P_0 = \frac{C_1}{1+r} + \frac{C_2}{(1+r)^2} + \frac{C_3}{(1+r)^3} + \cdots \frac{C_n}{(1+r)^n}$$

$$= \sum_{t=1}^{n} \frac{C_t}{(1+r)^t} \tag{4.16}$$

The differential of this equation for infinitesimal changes in r is

$$\delta P_0 = - \left[\frac{(1)C_1}{(1+r)^2} + \frac{(2)C_2}{(1+r)^3} + \cdots + \frac{(n)C_n}{(1+r)^{n+1}} \right] \delta r \tag{4.17}$$

Divide this equation by P_0 to obtain

$$\frac{\delta P_0}{P_0} = - \left(\frac{1}{P_0}\right) \left[\frac{(1)C_1}{(1+r)} + \frac{(2)C_2}{(1+r)^2} + \cdots + \frac{(n)C_n}{(1+r)^n} \right] \frac{\delta r}{1+r} \tag{4.18}$$

which can be written as

$$\frac{\delta P_0}{P_0} = - \left[\frac{\displaystyle\sum_{t=1}^{n} \frac{(t)C_t}{(1+r)^t}}{\displaystyle\sum_{t=1}^{n} \frac{C_t}{(1+r)^t}} \right] \frac{\delta r}{1+r} \tag{4.19}$$

Here, the term in brackets is duration (D). Now, Equation 4.19 can be written as

$$\frac{\delta P_0}{P_0} = \frac{-D\delta r}{1+r}$$

ARITHMETIC CALCULATION OF DURATION

Equation 4.19 gives the estimated price (or value) volatility for multipayment assets. An approximation for the price changes of a bond when the interest rate changes by a small, finite amount is:

$$\frac{\Delta P_0}{P_0} = \frac{-D\Delta r}{1+r} = D_M \Delta r \tag{4.20}$$

It is conventional to modify duration by standardizing it on $(1+r)$. Sensibly enough, this result is popularly known as *modified duration*.

TABLE 4.4   Duration and Modified Duration for 6 Percent Coupon, Five-year Bond Priced at Par

(1) Year	(2) Cash Flow	(3) Present Value of $1 at 6%	(4) Present Value of Cash Flow	(5) Weighted Cash Flows: (1) × (4)
1	60	0.9434	$ 56.60	$ 56.60
2	60	0.8900	$ 53.40	106.80
3	60	0.8396	$ 50.38	151.13
4	60	0.7921	$ 47.53	190.10
5	1060	0.7473	$ 792.09	3,960.45
			$1,000.00	$4,465.08

Duration (D) = Weighted cash flows/present value (price) = $4,465/$1,000
$$= \underline{4.465} \text{ years}$$

Modified duration (D_M) = $\dfrac{D}{(1 + r)}$

$$= \underline{4.212} \text{ years}$$

$$\text{Modified duration} = D_M = \frac{D}{(1 + r)} \tag{4.21}$$

Notice that this expression is identical in form for either single-payment or multipayment securities. As an index of interest rate risk, the duration (D) of a multipayment asset is analogous to the maturity (n) of a single-payment asset. Duration is simply an index of interest rate risk that captures the cash flow pattern of complex (multipayment) assets. It is comprised of the present value of cash flow weights applied to the timing of the cash flows.

Table 4.4 presents a sample calculation of the duration of our earlier five-year bond that pays a $60 coupon each year and returns the entire $1,000 principal in year 5. The bond is discounted at a market interest rate of 6 percent. Note that the bond's duration of 4.46 years is, as expected, less than its maturity.

As a linear operator, duration provides a convenient estimator of interest sensitivity. For example, if the market rate shifts from 6 percent to 7 percent, apply the estimated price volatility Equation 4.20 for the estimated change in the bond's value:

$$\frac{\Delta P_0}{P_0} = -4.465 \left(\frac{.01}{1.06} \right) = -4.212\% \tag{4.22}$$

For this interest rate shift, the estimate for ΔP_0 is −$42.12, which indicates an estimate that the bond's price will fall from $1,000 to $957.88. As a caution, however, if the change in interest rate is large, one must be concerned with the effect of curvature in the price curve (convexity), a subject we address later in the chapter.

Duration helps to resolve another interest rate sensitivity problem known as the *coupon effect.* The coupon effect is another reason that bond maturity is not a workable index of sensitivity.[7] For a given maturity bond, *the smaller the coupon the greater the price change for a change in interest rates.* The coupon effect occurs because the redemption value at maturity makes up a larger share of the cash flows for small coupon securities (that is, the cash flows are more "back-end loaded") than it does for large coupon ones.

Duration distinguishes between these two levels of coupons for bonds with the same maturity. In the duration calculation, the distribution of cash flows for a small coupon bond magnifies the weight of the redemption value in relation to the weight of the coupons. For example, duration for a 6 percent coupon, five-year bond at a market discount rate of 6 percent equals 4.465 years (see Table 4.4), whereas the duration of a 12 percent coupon, 5-year bond is 4.14.

THE DURATION GAP

Duration can help us understand how a financial institution's balance sheet net asset value—the market value of balance sheet equity—is affected by changes in interest rates. It turns out that the critical factor is the duration mismatch of assets and liabilities and not the maturity mismatch. We can derive the duration of an entire portfolio of assets or of liabilities from information on the portfolio's future cash flows and market discount rates.

A bank can control the interest rate exposure of its equity value by approximately matching the duration of its portfolio of assets with that of its portfolio of liabilities. When a bank is nearly duration matched, general interest rate movements should have roughly identical effects on the values of its assets and liabilities, thereby offsetting the effect on equity value.

In the following example, we will develop and examine the use of *duration gap,* defined as the measure of the mismatch between the aggregate durations of assets and liabilities. We will see that, in theory at least, duration gap provides a unitary index of equity value's exposure to interest rates.

EXAMPLE Table 4.5 presents an abbreviated balance sheet for Snow Bank and the durations in years of each of the bank's asset and liability classifications. Snow Bank found the duration of total assets, $D_A = 1.125$, and of total liabilities, $D_L = 0.572$, by dollar weighting the durations of each category of the bank's assets and liabilities. The estimated price volatility Equation 4.20 is applied to both assets and liabilities.

$$\frac{\Delta A}{A} = -D_A \left(\frac{\Delta r}{(1 + r)} \right)$$

$$\frac{\Delta L}{L} = -D_L \left(\frac{\Delta r}{(1 + r)} \right)$$

---

[7] Duration was described long before the 1970s by Frederick R. Macaulay in *Some Theoretical Problems Suggested by the Movement of Interest Rates, Bond Yields, and Stock Prices in the United States since 1856* (New York: National Bureau of Economic Research, 1938). Other scholars proposed variations in the years following Macaulay's work and its rather recent rediscovery by the practical world of Wall Street.

TABLE 4.5   Interest Rate Exposure to Snow Bank's Balance Sheet

	Present Economic Value	Years Duration	Economic Value after 2% Rate Increase
Assets			
Securities			
Liquid	$ 150	0.5	$ 148.6
Investment	100	3.5	93.6
Loans			
Floating	400	0	400.0
Fixed-rate	350	2.0	337.3
Total assets	$1,000	1.125	$ 979.5
Liabilities and net worth			
Transaction deposits	$ 400	0	$ 400.0
CDs and other time deposits			
Short-term	350	0.4	347.5
Long-term	150	2.5	143.7
Net worth	100		88.3[a]
Total liabilities and net worth	$1,000	0.572	$ 979.5

[a] Decreased 11.7%.

Transposing these two expressions gives

$$\Delta A = -D_A A \left(\frac{\Delta r}{(1 + r)} \right)$$

and

$$\Delta L = -D_L L \left(\frac{\Delta r}{(1 + r)} \right) \qquad (4.23)$$

where A = market value of assets
L = market value of liabilities
D_A = duration of assets
D_L = duration of liabilities

The change in equity value of the bank (E) is found from the balance sheet accounting identity expressed in the form of changes in the market values of assets, liabilities, and equity.

$$\Delta A = \Delta L + \Delta E,$$

or

$$\Delta E = \Delta A - \Delta L \qquad (4.24)$$

Substituting from Equation 4.23 into Equation 4.24 gives

$$\Delta E = -D_A A \left(\frac{\Delta r}{(1+r)} \right) + D_L L \left(\frac{\Delta r}{(1+r)} \right)$$

$$= -(AD_A - LD_L) \left[\frac{\Delta r}{(1+r)} \right] \tag{4.25}$$

and dividing through by A gives

$$\frac{\Delta E}{A} = \left(D_A - \frac{L}{A} D_L \right) \left[\frac{\Delta r}{(1+r)} \right] \tag{4.26}$$

Equation 4.26 is the estimated value volatility for the entire balance sheet. Snow Bank's duration gap is:

$$DG = \left(D_A - \frac{L}{A} D_L \right) \tag{4.27}$$

In this expression the duration of liabilities is weighted by the ratio of the market values of liabilities to assets. This adjusts for the fact that the difference in these two magnitudes affects the relative amounts each will change with a change in interest rates.

A more compact form of Equation 4.26, solved directly for ΔE, gives

$$\Delta E = -DG \left[\frac{\Delta r}{(1+r)} \right] A \tag{4.28}$$

The market value balance sheet in Table 4.5 shows Snow Bank's economic values before and after a hypothetical 2 percent general rise in interest rates. Snow Bank calculated the duration in years for each of several portfolios of assets and liabilities. For instance, the bank's $150 million short-term (liquid) securities portfolio is found to have a duration of 0.5 year. Based on present values of the assets and liabilities before and after the 2 percent increase in interest rates, the bank determines that equity value will fall $11.7 million, from $100 million to $88.3 million. With our knowledge of Snow Bank's aggregate asset and liability durations, we use the duration gap to estimate this exposure.

From Equation 4.27 and using the dollar-weighted durations of assets and liabilities, the duration gap for the bank in Table 4.5 is

$$DG = \left(D_A - \frac{L}{A} D_L \right)$$

$$= 1.125 - \left(\frac{900}{1,000} \right) \times 0.572 = 0.610 \tag{4.29}$$

How accurate is the duration-based estimate in relation to the direct calculation of
−$11.7 million noted earlier? According to Equation 4.28, given a 2 percent increase in
interest rate and assuming an initial rate (r) of 10 percent, the estimated change in equity
value is

$$\Delta E = -DG\left[\frac{\Delta r}{(1+r)}\right]A$$

$$= -0.610 \times \frac{.02}{(1+0.10)} \times \$1,000,000,000 = -\$11,100,000$$

(4.30)

Notice that the approximate change in equity value of $11.1 million given in Equa-
tion 4.30 is somewhat less than the $11.7 million calculated directly in Table 4.5. Recall
that the changes in value can be assumed to be linear with changes in interest rates for
only infinitesimal changes in interest rates. The large 2 percent change assumed in Table
4.5 produces a nonlinear result.

In addition to duration gap, analysts use the *duration of equity* to estimate interest
rate effects on equity value. Equity duration reflects the leveraging of asset and liability
durations, based on equity value. For example, in Table 4.5 we multiply the weighted
average asset duration of 1.125 by the ratio of assets to equity ($1,000/$100) and the
weighted average liability duration of 0.572 by the ratio of liabilities to equity ($900/
$100). The resulting duration of equity is

$$D_E = 1.125\left(\frac{1,000}{100}\right) - 0.572\left(\frac{900}{100}\right) = 6.102$$

(4.31)

or, simply, 10 times DG. This result follows naturally from the leverage factor (A/E) =
($1,000/$100) = 10.

Equity exposure now can be written as

$$\Delta E = -D_E\left[\frac{\Delta r}{(1+r)}\right]$$

(4.32)

USING CONVEXITY TO MODIFY DURATION ANALYSIS

Not surprisingly, equity values change nonlinearly with large changes in interest rates.
We encountered nonlinearity in the changes in price or value with changes in interest
rates throughout our discussion of market risk. Nonlinearity, described in our earlier discussion in terms of the convex shape of the price-interest relationship and illustrated in
Figure 4.1, is the normal case. Duration, on the other hand, describes a linear relationship
between price and interest rates. This strict linearity is depicted in Figure 4.2. It is no
wonder that errors result when we apply duration methodology to estimate the curvilinear
price-interest rate relationship.

As we found earlier, the degree of nonlinearity—the convex shape of the price
curve—differs because of the dissimilar cash flow patterns of different bonds. Analo-
gously, the extent of nonlinearity in the values of banks' balance sheets in response to

FIGURE 4.2   Duration and convexity describe the price curve

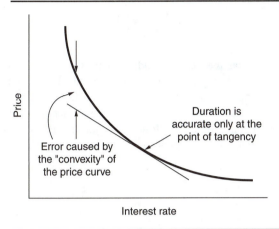

changes in interest rates differs because each bank's unique mix of assets and liabilities produces different patterns of cash inflows and outflows. The amount of nonlinearity affects the size of the error in simple linear duration equations.

This error is illustrated in Figure 4.2, which reproduces the bond price curve of Figure 4.1. Figure 4.2 shows the duration relationship as the slope of a straight line tangent to the price curve at the present interest rate. The duration error gets quite large for large changes in interest rates: the larger the assumed change in interest rates, the further duration drifts from the "true" price curve. Appendix 4A presents the formal methodology for estimating the duration error caused by the convex shape of price curves.

YIELD TO MATURITY

In Equation 4.1 we implied that the risk-free discount rate remains constant in relation to the timing or maturity of bond cash flows. For example, Equation 4.5 discounted all five years of cash flows for a five-year bond with the same discount rate. Once again, in our discussions of duration and convexity (see Appendix 4A), we assumed a constant discount rate. Let's refer now to this constant rate as the *yield to maturity*. We will show the practical sense of this designation.

In truth, the level of interest rates is not constant over time but varies with the maturity of the cash flows. The relationship between yield and the timing of securities' cash flows is known as *the term structure of interest rates*. We will show that *yield to maturity* is intimately connected to (you might say it embeds) this relationship.

Equation 4.33 shows how one values a typical bond that pays coupons semiannually. We discount the half-year coupon payments for such bonds at a six-month discount rate equal to one-half of the annual discount rate, $r/2$.[8]

---

[8] While this convention is convenient, it is not mathematically satisfactory. A mathematically preferred version is $[(1 + r)^{1/2} - 1]$.

$$P_0 = \sum_{t=1}^{2n} \frac{CF_t}{\left(1 + \dfrac{r}{2}\right)^t} + \frac{R_{2n}}{\left(1 + \dfrac{r}{2}\right)^{2n}} \tag{4.33}$$

We identify the value r as the annual yield to maturity (that is, r without a time subscript). n is the number of whole years and $2n$ is the number of semiannual periods. CF_t is the semiannual coupon. Yield to maturity contains the different discount rates ("yields") that apply to the dates of each bond cash flow. In other words, it blends these several discount rates into a single rate.[9] The following modifies Equation 4.33 to allow for the time-dependent differences in discount rates.

$$P_0 = \sum_{t=1}^{2n} \frac{CF_t}{\left(1 + \dfrac{r_t}{2}\right)^t} + \frac{R_{2n}}{\left(1 + \dfrac{r_n}{2}\right)^{2n}} \tag{4.34}$$

where r_t now carries the time subscript t (or $2n$ in the case of the redemption payment at maturity) in order to recognize that the discount rate varies with time; the general case is $r_1 \neq r_2 \neq \ldots \neq r_n$. Assume a 6 percent coupon, three-year bond that pays \$30 semiannually and where annual market discount rates differ for every six-month period. We represent the array of annual discount rates for six-month periods as $(r_{0.5}, r_1, r_{1.5}, r_2, r_{2.5}, r_3) = (4\%, 5\%, 6\%, 7\%, 8\%, 9\%)$.

$$
\begin{aligned}
P_0 = {} & \frac{\$30}{(1.02)} + \frac{\$30}{(1.025)^2} + \frac{\$30}{(1.03)^3} + \frac{\$30}{(1.035)^4} \\
& + \frac{\$30}{(1.04)^5} + \frac{\$30}{(1.045)^6} + \frac{\$1,000}{(1.045)^6} = \$927.15
\end{aligned}
\tag{4.35}
$$

Based on this price and Equation 4.33, Equation 4.36 reiterates the solution to derive r, the unique yield to maturity; r is determined by the interaction of bond cash flows and the discount rates that apply to the timing of the cash flows as elaborated in Equation 4.35.

$$\$927.15 = \sum_{t=1}^{6} \frac{\$30}{\left(1 + \dfrac{r}{2}\right)^t} + \frac{\$1,000}{\left(1 + \dfrac{r}{2}\right)^6} \tag{4.36}$$

The solution for $r/2 = 4.408\%$ and, thus, $r = 8.816\% \cong 8.82\%$.

At times, financial market practitioners may use yield to maturity carelessly to represent the yield on securities of a given maturity without regard to differences in the size and timing of the securities' cash flows. For example, they might generalize the yield on three-year government securities to be 8.82 percent. In reality, other three-year government

---

[9] In the terminology of interest rate mathematics, a security's yield to maturity is its internal rate of return.

securities with different sets of cash flows have unique yields to maturity. For example, consider a 12 percent coupon, three-year bond that pays $60 semiannually.

$$P_0 = \frac{\$60}{(1.02)} + \frac{\$60}{(1.025)^2} + \frac{\$60}{(1.03)^3} + \frac{\$60}{(1.035)^4}$$
$$+ \frac{\$60}{(1.04)^5} + \frac{\$60}{(1.045)^6} + \frac{\$1,000}{(1.045)^6} = \$1,086.41$$

(4.37)

Applying Equation 4.33 with price equal to $1,086.41 produces a yield to maturity (r) for this bond of 8.67 percent, not 8.82 percent as found earlier for the 6 percent coupon bond. We can avoid this confusion by not referring to a single yield on different sets of time-variant cash flows simply because they happen to have the same final maturities. To be correct, one should refer to a set of yields (discount rates) in which each one corresponds to the specific time of each future cash flow.

Individual securities may be treated as unique portfolios of cash flows. In general, the yields to maturity of two securities with the same final maturity are the same only if the timing, size, and risks of the cash flows of one exactly match the other. If these cash flow factors differ, we cannot determine the correct valuation of both securities using the same yield to maturity.

In summary, yield to maturity is the unique discount rate which, when applied to all of a security's cash flows, correctly produces the security's price. In a sense, yield to maturity flattens the maturity or duration structure of interest rates.[10] However, such structures typically are not flat; in general, it is incorrect to assume the yields to maturity are equal for securities with equal maturities but have different cash flow patterns. Each future cash flow should be viewed as a zero-coupon bond to be discounted at the market rate corresponding to the time at which it will be paid or received.

SUMMARY AND CONCLUSIONS

In this chapter, we emphasized the value of financial institutions' balance sheets and how this value is affected by the financial environment, mainly interest rates. Interest rate effects raise issues of *interest sensitivity*.

1. The valuation of simple government bonds provides a basic building block of an institution's balance sheet. In the general case of annual coupon bonds, value is found from

$$P_0 = \sum_{t=1}^{n} \frac{CF_t}{(1 + r_t)^t} + \frac{R_n}{(1 + r_n)^n}$$

2. Bond values are sensitive to changes in discount or market interest rates. The degree of sensitivity depends on the structure of the cash flows, especially their maturity and size.

---

[10] Recall that maturity and duration are the same only in the case of single-payment (zero-coupon) securities.

3. Financial institutions deal in nominal contracts, which derive value from their discounted cash flow streams. We combine the discounted cash flow values of individual assets and liabilities into a *market value balance sheet.* These balance sheet values are sensitive to interest rate, default, and other risks; as such, they differ significantly from historical accounting *book value balance sheets.*

4. We introduce *duration* and *convexity* as short-hand measures for analyzing the impact of interest rates on assets and liabilities. Simplified, duration is expressed in

$$\frac{\Delta P_0}{P_0} = \frac{-D\Delta r}{1 + r}$$

5. The notion of duration gap is applied to balance sheets in order to determine the impact of interest rates on entire balance sheets.

$$DG = \left(D_A - \frac{L}{A} D_L \right)$$

$$\Delta E = -DG \left[\frac{\Delta r}{(1 + r)} \right] A$$

6. For assets with multiple payments, the rate of discount is known as the yield to maturity. This measure blends the discrete discount rates that differ for each maturity of an asset's multiple cash flows.

END OF CHAPTER PROBLEMS

4.1 Assume the following movements in market interest rates:
- Increase from 8% to 10%
- Decrease from 8% to 6%

Create a table of two price changes in dollars and percentage each for four bonds, given the above interest rate movements. The bonds are as follows:
- 3-year zero-coupon bond
- 3-year, 12% annual coupon bond
- 30-year zero-coupon bond
- 30-year, 12% coupon bond

a.) Compare and comment on differences in the magnitude of the price changes between these bonds. Discuss your findings concerning the relative influence of maturity and coupon on this magnitude. Which has the greatest influence, maturity or coupon? Why?

b.) Calculate the ratio of price changes for same-coupon (zero or 12%) bonds (i.e., 30-year zero over 3-year zero; 30-year, 12% coupon over 3-year, 12% coupon).

c.) Calculate the ratio of price changes for same-maturity bonds (e.g., 3-year zero over 3-year, 12% coupon; 30-year zero over 30-year, 12% coupon).

d.) The *asymmetry* in price changes is a clue to the curvature or "convexity" of bonds. Rank the four securities in terms of their convexity. (*Hint:* Determine differences in percentage price changes for each bond between the rising rate scenario and the falling rate scenario.)

4.2 The balance sheet of Palace Avenue Trust (PAT) is structured as follows:

Assets:
- $5 billion in 4-year loans.
- $3 billion in 1-year securities.
- $2 billion in 2-year securities.

Liabilities & equity
- $9 billion in 1-year CDs.
- $1 billion in book value of common equity.

All items (loans, securities, and CDs) bear interest at 9 percent. There are no other revenues or expenses and no taxes. As balance sheet items mature, they will be re-placed or rolled over into items identical to the original items (i.e., same new maturity) except at then-current interest rates. After four years, PAT will liquidate all asset principal, pay off all liability principal, and pay any net proceeds to its share-holders.

Determine the economic value of Palace Avenue Trust assuming:

a.) Market interest rates remain at 9 percent for four more years. PAT shareholders discount future cash flows at 9 percent.

b.) Market interest rates on all items rise tomorrow to 10 percent and remain at that level for the next four years. PAT shareholders discount future cash flows at 9 percent.

4.3 Milan Floss holds six different pure discount securities in his portfolio. Five of them yield a single payment of $100 at dates, respectively, one, two, three, four, and five years from now; none of the securities has payments before maturity. The one-year security earns an interest rate of (is discounted from $100 at) 8 percent; the two-year earns a rate of 9 percent; the three-year, 10 percent; the four-year, 11 percent; and the five-year, 12 percent. The sixth security pays $1,000 in the fifth year only and also earns the five-year rate of (is discounted at) 12 percent.

a.) Find the total market value of Floss's portfolio.

b.) Based on the market value you found in a.) and all securities' cash flows, find the yield to maturity on the entire portfolio. *Note:* Floss's portfolio is identical to a single five-year 10 percent coupon bond. Comment on how your yield to maturity compares to the different interest rates across the years.

c.) Suppose Floss held only the five single $100 payment securities. What is the yield to maturity for this portfolio?

4.4 Find the yield to maturity for the following two Treasury notes, given their coupons and prices. These notes pay interest semiannually. Assume that it is February 1998 and that a semiannual coupon has just been paid (the notes mature in exactly eight years).

$$5\tfrac{5}{8}\text{s of Feb 06 price} = 101{:}5$$

$$9\tfrac{3}{8}\text{s of Feb 06 price} = 125{:}13$$

Note: Bond designations give annual coupon value in percentages of 100 (e.g., 5⅝s is 5.625 or 2.8125 semiannually) and maturity date (e.g., Feb 06 denotes maturity date is February 2006). Note and bond prices are expressed in 1/32s (101:5 is 101.1563).

    a.) Determine the yield to maturity for each bond.

    b.) It is possible that the yields to maturity differ despite the fact that the notes are both default risk free and mature at the same time. Discuss reasons why this might occur. Indicate which note you believe *should* be expected to have the highest yield to maturity.

4.5 Suppose in Problem 4.4 yields on eight-year Treasury securities instantly move up to 7.00 percent (annual rate).

    a.) Find the new prices for the two bonds.

    b.) What were the percentage changes in their prices? Based on your answer, state a theorem concerning the relationship between price volatility and coupons for same-maturity fixed-income securities.

4.6 Calculate, preferably using an electronic spreadsheet, the duration of the notes in Problem 4.4, using the market yields you found as discount factors. Compare your duration results with the volatility of prices found in Problem 4.5. (Remember that duration is an index of price volatility.)

4.7 In March 2000, a five-year security is issued by a Government Sponsored Enterprise (GSE) priced at 100 with a final maturity of March 2005. The security bears a 6 percent coupon, payable semiannually at $3 per $100, and is callable starting in March 2001 (one year hence). If called, the security would be redeemed for 102. Current market yields on such securities that are noncallable are 6 percent semiannually compounded.

    a.) Suppose you are prescient and know there is a 0.5 probability that interest rates on such securities will rise to 7 percent immediately and will remain there indefinitely—in which case the security will never be called—and a 0.5 probability that rates will fall to 5 percent immediately and remain there indefinitely—in which case the security will be called at the first call date. How much should you, as a prescient investor, be willing to pay for the security?

    b). In a.) above, the issuer, GSE, is acquiring a *call option.* From your calculations as a prescient investor, what is a reasonable estimate of the value of this option to you?

4.8 Refer to the example given in the text of this chapter of Treadwater Bank's balance sheet consisting of $10 million five-year loans yielding 6 percent and $9 million one-year certificates of deposit also bearing 6 percent interest. Treadwater's expected income statement was presented in Table 4.2.

    a.) Determine the duration of Treadwater's assets and liabilities. (Remember to account for the residual values at the end of five years.)

    b.) On the basis of a.) above, calculate Treadwater's duration gap (*DG*). Based on your value for *DG*, estimate the change in equity value from an across-the-board 1 percent increase in interest rates.

    c.) Determine the duration of equity, assuming interest rates remain at 6 percent over five years.

4.9 The asked prices in May 1998 for two Treasury securities are shown below. These securities are noncallable and pay semiannually; assume a semiannual payment was just paid (i.e., there is no accrued interest).
- The 10¾ May 03 Treasury bond, asked price: 124:03
- The 6½ May 05 Treasury note, asked price: 106:09

a.) Calculate the yield to maturity for each security.

b.) Assume the yield to maturity of both securities rises a full 1 percent. Calculate the new asked prices.

c.) Calculate the securities' durations. Then assume "the" interest rate increases a full 1 percent. Determine the duration-estimated new prices. Compare with your results in b.).

Combining Convexity and Duration Estimates of Price Change

Duration permits the analyst to estimate the price sensitivity of bonds to changes in the interest rate. However, the duration-based estimate inevitably contains an error because of the curvature of the bond price curve. Figure 4.2, reproduced here as Figure 4A.1, illustrates this error as a drift in the price curve from the linear shape due to the convex shape of the price curve. The following discussion refines the duration estimate by supplementing duration with an estimator for *convexity*.

Together, the second, third, and higher derivatives of value with respect to the interest rate (recall that duration is based on the first derivative) account for virtually all of the convex shape of the price curve. These higher order derivatives are found in the Taylor Series expansion around P_0 that approximates the mathematical relationship between price and interest rate.

$$\delta P_0 = \frac{\delta P_0}{\delta r}\, \delta r + \frac{1}{2}\frac{\delta^2 P_0}{\delta r^2}\, \delta r^2 \\ + \cdots + \frac{1}{n}\frac{\delta^n P_0}{\delta r^n}\, \delta r^n \tag{4A.1}$$

In combination with the first derivative (the basis of duration), estimators based on these higher-order derivatives anticipate most of the total change in price even when interest rates change erratically— for example, when there seems to be no or little connection between the changes in interest rates for

different maturity bonds. The addition of more estimators permits the analyst to more accurately track price changes due to complicated—and not unusual—changes in interest patterns.

However, the second derivative alone captures most of the effects of nonlinearity. To keep matters simple, we will ignore derivatives higher than the second. The second derivative in Equation 4A.1 is:

$$\frac{\delta^2 P_0}{\delta r^2} = \left(\frac{1}{(1+r)^2}\right) \\ \times \left[\frac{(1)(2)C_1}{(1+r)} + \frac{(2)(3)C_2}{(1+r)^2} \right. \\ \left. + \cdots + \frac{(n)(n+1)C_n}{(1+r)^n} \right] \tag{4A.2} \\ = \left(\frac{1}{(1+r)^2}\right) \sum_{t=1}^{n} \frac{(t^2+t)C_t}{(1+r)^t}$$

Dividing Equation 4A.2 by P_0 gives the value for *convexity:*

$$\text{Convexity} = D_2 = \frac{1}{P_0}\left(\frac{1}{(1+r)^2}\right) \\ \times \sum_{t=1}^{n} \frac{(t^2+t)C_t}{(1+r)^t} \tag{4A.3}$$

Note that Equation 4A.3 closely resembles text

FIGURE 4A.1   Duration and convexity as estimators of the price curve

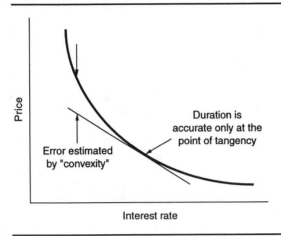

Equation 4.19 for duration, except for the divisor $(1 + r)^2$. The present values of cash flows in the numerator, instead of being multiplied simply by time of receipt, are multiplied by time squared plus time.

Table 4A.1 presents the calculation of convexity for a 6 percent coupon, five-year bond at a market rate of 6 percent. Modified duration and convexity enable us to solve the first two terms of the Taylor Series expansion (Equation 4A.1) so that we can estimate the price change for bonds. How effective is the addition of convexity when estimating the price change for a bond?

Earlier we found the modified duration of the 6 percent coupon, five-year bond example to be

$D_M = 4.212$. Duration estimated price change due to 1 percent increase in interest rate is:

$$\Delta P_{0,D_M} = -D_M(\Delta r)(P_0)$$
$$= -4.212 \times (+.01) \times \$1,000 = -\$42.12$$

Substituting convexity into the second term of the Taylor Series, we see that the additional convexity-estimated price change due to 1 percent increase in interest rate is:

$$\Delta P_{0,D_2} = \left(\frac{1}{2}\right)(D_2)(\Delta r)^2(P_0)$$

$$= \left(\frac{1}{2}\right)(22.919)(0.01)^2(\$1,000) = +\$1.146$$

Table 4A.1   Convexity Calculation for 6 Percent Coupon, Five-year Bond Priced at Par

Year (t)	Cash Flow	Present Value of $1 at 6%	Present Value of Cash Flow	PV Cash Flows X ($t^2 + t$)
1	60	0.9434	$ 56.60	$ 113.21
2	60	0.8900	$ 53.40	320.40
3	60	0.8396	$ 50.38	604.53
4	60	0.7921	$ 47.53	950.51
5	1060	0.7473	$ 792.09	$23,762.81
			$1,000.00	$25,751.46

$$D_2 = \frac{1}{P_0}\left(\frac{1}{(1 + r)^2}\right)\sum_{t=1}^{n}\frac{(t^2 + t)C_t}{(1 + r)^t} = \frac{25,751.46}{1000.00}\left(\frac{1}{(1 + .06)^2}\right) = 22.919$$

Total estimated price change is:

$$\Delta P_0 = -\$42.12 + \$1.15 = -\$40.97$$

Recall that the true price change calculated in text Table 4.1 was $-\$41.00$. Thus, a duration estimate alone produced an error of $-\$1.12$ [equal to $-\$42.12 - (-\$41.00)$]. The duration plus convexity estimate produced an error of $+\$0.03$ [equal to $-\$40.97 - (-\$41.00)$]. Convexity compensated for 103 percent of the price curve error.

END OF APPENDIX PROBLEMS

4A.1 For the securities in Problem 4.9, calculate convexity. Assume "the" interest rate increases a full 1 percent. Determine the duration-plus-convexity-estimated new prices. Compare with your results for b.) and c.) in Problem 4.9.

4A.2 A 6 percent coupon, five-year bond (semiannual payments) is currently selling to yield 9 percent (par value is 100). The bond's price volatility can be estimated from:

Duration (half-years) = 8.69

$$\text{defined as} \quad - \left[\frac{\sum\limits_{t=1}^{n} \dfrac{(t)C_t}{(1 + r)^t}}{\sum\limits_{t=1}^{n} \dfrac{C_t}{(1 + r)^t}} \right]$$

Convexity (half-years) = 83.392

$$\text{defined as} \quad \frac{1}{P_0} \left(\frac{1}{(1 + r)^2} \right) \sum\limits_{t=1}^{n} \frac{(t^2 + t)C_t}{(1 + r)^t}$$

$$= \frac{1}{P_0} \frac{\delta^2 P_0}{\delta r^2}$$

Based on these values for the bond's duration and convexity, estimate the price change in this bond (base prices on par = 100) for a 1 percent annual (0.50% for one-half year) rise in the required yield on the bond. Compare the actual calculated price change in the bond with this estimate. What percent of the actual price change is captured in the duration + convexity estimate? (As described in Appendix 4A, the first two terms of the Taylor Series around P_0 are:

$$\delta P_0 = \frac{\delta P_0}{\delta r} \delta r + \frac{1}{2} \frac{\delta^2 P_0}{\delta r^2} \delta r^2$$

Hints: It is not necessary to calculate duration and convexity, for they are already calculated above. Demonstrate how to apply these terms and to manipulate the above Taylor Series equation.

CHAPTER 5

Asset and Liability Management and the Yield Curve

Chapter 4 properly establishes how the values of financial firms change with interest rates. They might change for other reasons, too, such as poorly managed loan quality or failure to serve their customers' needs. But the logic that interest rate behavior impacts bank valuation is inescapable. After all, most of the products that banks deal in are priced in relation to general interest rates. The composition and duration of these products define banks' balance sheets and, it is there—on the balance sheets—that interest rate changes map into changes in value.

Up to this point, however, we have been very naïve in our portrayal of interest rates. In this chapter we expand our description of "the" interest rate into a larger complex of interest rates that differ from one another because of duration (or maturity). We will review means of explaining why short-term interest rates differ in level and behavior from long-term rates. You should see that the need for such an explanation is obvious: the cash flows of financial institutions occur over the short term, long term, and many terms in between.

Our other task in the present chapter is to return to our earlier discussion of how interest rates affect period earnings. We pointed out in the previous chapter that value changes—which we designated as economic effects—were only part of the effects of interest rates. Although valuation is the theoretically correct focus, it would be foolhardy to ignore the gravity with which managers, analysts, and regulators view near-term earnings. The difference in how earnings are affected and how value is affected is a matter of immediacy. That is, earnings effects depend on those cash flows that are most immediately affected by short-term interest rates. This chapter blends these two topics: (1) how duration determines the level and behavior of different interest rates and (2) how the outlook for interest rate level and behavior affects earnings.

For the moment, we refer to interest rates synonymously with discount rates. We are reverting to the language of Chapter 4 where we refered to the rates of discount on institutions' cash flows.

MANAGING WITH DISCOUNT RATE EXPECTATIONS

Why do discount rates differ from one another? This is a question that concerns everyone involved in debt markets. In Chapter 4, we identified duration or maturity as a major cause. In addition to maturity, we can easily name several other factors that cause discount rates to differ from one another. These include differences in market liquidity, default risk, taxability, and call risk (the risk that duration may turn out to be shorter than stated). For now, we will hold these other factors constant. Later chapters examine liquidity, default, and taxability in some detail. Appendix 5B contains a formal presentation of the measurement of call risk.

In this section we show how today's relationship between rates and maturity helps investors to decide where interest rates are going in the future. Bankers use such information to manage the rate sensitivity of their balance sheets.

Discussions about interest rates and duration—the term structure of interest rates—usually are based on securities that are devoid of all risks but maturity risk. The primary source of such securities is the U.S. Treasury. In short, you can consider such securities to be identical in all important ways except duration. U.S. Treasury securities allow you to isolate duration as a unique cause of differences in interest rates. Appendix 5A discusses a body of three contending theories of the term structure developed by financial economists. Each theory has a different explanation of why maturity causes interest rates to differ.[1] Of these theories, the one that describes how investors make educated guesses (theorists say "form expectations") about future interest rates is most important to practitioners. Before explaining how investors form expectations about future rates, we describe the *yield curve*. It may come as some relief to know that the yield curve is not a theory but is simply a graphical representation showing the relationship between security yields and maturities or durations.

The Yield Curve

Figure 5.1 presents a recent listing of U.S. Treasury *strip* securities reported by the *Wall Street Journal* at the close of the market on March 11, 1996. This report appears daily in the *Wall Street Journal.*[2] Strip securities are either single-coupon payments or at-maturity redemption payments "stripped" from ordinary U.S. Treasury notes and bonds. They make no payments until their payment at maturity, and, consequently, they qualify as *pure discount securities* whose maturities uniquely are the same as their durations. They produce pure discount rates that correspond to the timing of single cash flows. As a result, yields on Treasury strips can be used to develop a true duration structure of interest rates.

The yield curve plots the current yields on either U.S. Treasury coupon or strip securities against their maturities. Figure 5.2 shows interest rate movements for U.S. Treasury bills, notes, and bonds with the passage of time. This figure reveals that interest rates

---

[1] One could refer to the "duration structure of interest rates" and properly define the term of a security to be the duration of its cash flows or, if the security makes only one payment, the timing of its sole cash flow. As a rule, we will refer to "term structure" because this description is well established as part of the language of financial markets.

[2] The Treasury Department designates its securities as *bonds* when the original maturity is greater than 10 years, *notes* when original maturities are over one year to ten years, and *bills* when original maturities are one year or less. Bonds and notes are coupon securities. Bills are sold at a discount from face value.

FIGURE 5.1   U.S. Treasury Strip Securities

U.S. TREASURY STRIPS

Mat.	Type	Bid	Asked	Chg.	Ask Yld.
May 96	cl	99:03	99:04	....	5.17
May 96	np	99:04	99:04	....	5.14
Aug 96	cl	97:27	97:27	+ 1	5.14
Nov 96	cl	96:17	96:18	+ 1	5.27
Nov 96	np	96:16	96:17	+ 1	5.33
Feb 97	cl	95:06	95:06	+ 3	5.38
May 97	cl	93:26	93:27	+ 3	5.49
May 97	np	93:24	93:25	+ 2	5.55
Aug 97	cl	92:15	92:16	+ 4	5.53
Aug 97	np	92:13	92:14	+ 3	5.59
Nov 97	cl	91:03	91:04	+ 4	5.63
Nov 97	np	91:00	91:02	+ 3	5.68
Feb 98	cl	89:25	89:26	+ 5	5.65
Feb 98	np	89:22	89:24	+ 4	5.70
May 98	cl	88:14	88:15	+ 4	5.71
May 98	np	88:13	88:15	+ 5	5.72
Aug 98	cl	87:01	87:03	+ 6	5.77
Aug 98	np	86:31	87:01	+ 5	5.80
Nov 98	cl	85:26	85:29	+ 6	5.77
Nov 98	np	85:22	85:24	+ 6	5.83
Feb 99	cl	84:15	84:18	+ 7	5.82
Feb 99	np	84:13	84:15	+ 7	5.85
May 99	cl	83:05	83:08	+ 6	5.87
May 99	np	83:03	83:06	+ 7	5.89
Aug 99	cl	81:29	82:00	+ 6	5.88
Aug 99	np	81:26	81:28	+ 8	5.92
Nov 99	cl	80:25	80:28	+ 8	5.87
Nov 99	np	80:17	80:20	+ 7	5.95
Feb 00	cl	79:15	79:18	+ 7	5.91
Feb 00	np	79:08	79:11	+ 8	5.98
May 00	cl	78:10	78:13	+ 8	5.91
May 00	np	78:06	78:09	+ 8	5.95
Aug 00	cl	77:03	77:06	+ 10	5.94
Aug 00	np	76:27	76:30	+ 8	6.01
Nov 00	cl	75:29	76:00	+ 10	5.96
Nov 00	np	75:22	75:25	+ 9	6.02
Feb 01	cl	74:22	74:26	+ 12	5.98
Feb 01	np	74:16	74:20	+ 12	6.03
May 01	cl	73:16	73:19	+ 12	6.01
May 01	np	73:09	73:13	+ 12	6.07
Aug 01	cl	72:09	72:12	+ 13	6.05
Aug 01	np	72:02	72:05	+ 13	6.10
Nov 01	cl	71:03	71:07	+ 13	6.07
Nov 01	np	70:29	71:00	+ 13	6.13
Feb 02	cl	69:30	70:02	+ 14	6.10
May 02	cl	68:26	68:30	+ 13	6.12
May 02	np	68:20	68:23	+ 11	6.17
Aug 02	cl	67:18	67:22	+ 14	6.16
Aug 02	np	67:13	67:17	+ 14	6.20
Nov 02	cl	66:12	66:17	+ 14	6.20
Feb 03	cl	65:05	65:09	+ 15	6.25
Feb 03	np	65:03	65:07	+ 15	6.27
May 03	cl	64:02	64:06	+ 16	6.28
Aug 03	cl	62:30	63:03	+ 16	6.30
Aug 03	np	62:29	63:01	+ 16	6.31
Nov 03	cl	61:28	62:00	+ 16	6.33
Feb 04	cl	60:24	60:28	+ 16	6.36
Feb 04	np	60:26	60:30	+ 17	6.35
May 04	cl	59:20	59:24	+ 17	6.40
May 04	np	59:20	59:24	+ 17	6.40
Aug 04	cl	58:17	58:22	+ 18	6.43
Aug 04	np	58:19	58:23	+ 18	6.42
Nov 04	cl	57:15	57:20	+ 18	6.46
Nov 04	bp	57:12	57:16	+ 17	6.48
Nov 04	np	57:17	57:22	+ 18	6.45
Feb 05	cl	56:15	56:19	+ 18	6.48
Feb 05	np	56:19	56:23	+ 18	6.45
May 05	cl	55:14	55:19	+ 17	6.50
May 05	bp	55:11	55:16	+ 16	6.52
May 05	np	55:25	55:30	+ 18	6.44
Aug 05	cl	54:16	54:21	+ 17	6.51
Aug 05	bp	54:10	54:15	+ 17	6.55
Aug 05	np	54:29	55:02	+ 18	6.43
Nov 05	cl	53:19	53:24	+ 18	6.52
Nov 05	bp	54:06	54:11	+ 18	6.40
Feb 06	cl	52:18	52:23	+ 17	6.55
Feb 06	bp	53:10	53:15	+ 18	6.41
May 06	cl	51:20	51:25	+ 17	6.57
Aug 06	cl	50:24	50:29	+ 17	6.58
Nov 06	cl	49:27	50:00	+ 17	6.60
Feb 07	cl	48:31	49:04	+ 18	6.61
May 07	cl	48:02	48:07	+ 18	6.63
Aug 07	cl	47:07	47:12	+ 18	6.65
Nov 07	cl	46:12	46:17	+ 18	6.66
Feb 08	cl	45:17	45:22	+ 19	6.68
May 08	cl	44:22	44:27	+ 19	6.70
Aug 08	cl	43:28	44:01	+ 19	6.71
Nov 08	cl	43:02	43:07	+ 19	6.73
Feb 09	cl	42:05	42:10	+ 19	6.76
May 09	cl	41:14	41:19	+ 18	6.77
Aug 09	cl	40:22	40:27	+ 19	6.78
Nov 09	cl	39:31	40:04	+ 19	6.79
Nov 09	bp	39:14	39:19	+ 18	6.89
Feb 10	cl	39:07	39:12	+ 18	6.81
May 10	cl	38:16	38:21	+ 18	6.82
Aug 10	cl	37:26	37:31	+ 18	6.83
Nov 10	cl	37:04	37:09	+ 18	6.84
Feb 11	cl	36:13	36:18	+ 18	6.85
May 11	cl	35:25	35:30	+ 18	6.86
Aug 11	cl	35:05	35:10	+ 18	6.86
Nov 11	cl	34:17	34:22	+ 17	6.87
Feb 12	cl	33:28	34:01	+ 17	6.88
May 12	cl	33:09	33:14	+ 17	6.89
Aug 12	cl	32:21	32:26	+ 17	6.90
Nov 12	cl	32:02	32:07	+ 16	6.91
Feb 13	cl	31:15	31:20	+ 16	6.92
May 13	cl	30:29	31:02	+ 16	6.92
Aug 13	cl	30:12	30:17	+ 17	6.93
Nov 13	cl	29:27	29:31	+ 18	6.93
Feb 14	cl	29:09	29:14	+ 18	6.94
May 14	cl	28:25	28:30	+ 18	6.94
Aug 14	cl	28:08	28:13	+ 19	6.95
Nov 14	cl	27:24	27:29	+ 19	6.95
Feb 15	cl	27:08	27:13	+ 19	6.96
Feb 15	bp	27:17	27:22	+ 18	6.90
May 15	cl	26:25	26:29	+ 19	6.96
Aug 15	cl	26:09	26:14	+ 19	6.97
Aug 15	bp	26:13	26:18	+ 18	6.94
Nov 15	cl	25:26	25:31	+ 18	6.97
Nov 15	bp	25:30	26:03	+ 19	6.95
Feb 16	cl	25:11	25:16	+ 18	6.98
Feb 16	bp	25:14	25:19	+ 17	6.96
May 16	cl	24:28	25:01	+ 18	6.99
May 16	bp	25:05	25:09	+ 18	6.93
Aug 16	cl	24:13	24:18	+ 18	6.99
Nov 16	cl	23:31	24:03	+ 17	7.00
Nov 16	bp	24:07	24:12	+ 17	6.95
Feb 17	cl	23:16	23:20	+ 16	7.01
May 17	cl	23:03	23:08	+ 17	7.01
May 17	bp	23:08	23:12	+ 17	6.98
Aug 17	cl	22:22	22:26	+ 17	7.02
Aug 17	bp	22:27	22:31	+ 17	6.98
Nov 17	cl	22:09	22:14	+ 18	7.02
Feb 18	cl	21:29	22:01	+ 17	7.02
May 18	cl	21:17	21:21	+ 17	7.02
May 18	bp	21:22	21:26	+ 18	6.99
Aug 18	cl	21:04	21:09	+ 17	7.02
Nov 18	cl	20:25	20:30	+ 18	7.02
Nov 18	bp	20:29	21:02	+ 17	6.99
Feb 19	cl	20:13	20:18	+ 17	7.02
Feb 19	bp	20:18	20:22	+ 17	6.99
May 19	cl	20:02	20:06	+ 17	7.02
Aug 19	cl	19:23	19:27	+ 17	7.02
Aug 19	bp	19:29	20:01	+ 17	6.98
Nov 19	cl	19:12	19:17	+ 17	7.02
Feb 20	cl	19:02	19:07	+ 17	7.02
Feb 20	bp	19:06	19:11	+ 18	6.99
May 20	cl	18:24	18:29	+ 17	7.01
May 20	bp	18:27	19:00	+ 17	6.99
Aug 20	cl	18:14	18:18	+ 17	7.01
Aug 20	bp	18:17	18:21	+ 17	6.99
Nov 20	cl	18:04	18:08	+ 17	7.01
Feb 21	cl	17:27	17:31	+ 17	7.00
Feb 21	bp	18:01	18:05	+ 17	6.96
May 21	cl	17:18	17:22	+ 17	7.00
May 21	bp	17:22	17:26	+ 16	6.97
Aug 21	cl	17:08	17:12	+ 16	7.00
Aug 21	bp	17:12	17:16	+ 16	6.97
Nov 21	cl	17:00	17:04	+ 16	6.99
Nov 21	bp	17:04	17:08	+ 16	6.96
Feb 22	cl	16:24	16:28	+ 16	6.98
May 22	cl	16:16	16:20	+ 16	6.97
Aug 22	cl	16:08	16:12	+ 16	6.96
Aug 22	bp	16:13	16:17	+ 16	6.93
Nov 22	cl	16:01	16:05	+ 16	6.95
Nov 22	bp	16:06	16:10	+ 16	6.91
Feb 23	cl	15:28	16:00	+ 16	6.93
Feb 23	bp	16:01	16:05	+ 16	6.89
May 23	cl	15:22	15:26	+ 16	6.91
Aug 23	cl	15:15	15:19	+ 16	6.89
Aug 23	bp	15:21	15:25	+ 16	6.85
Nov 23	cl	15:08	15:12	+ 16	6.88
Feb 24	cl	15:03	15:07	+ 16	6.86
May 24	cl	14:28	15:00	+ 16	6.85
Aug 24	cl	14:22	14:26	+ 15	6.83
Nov 24	cl	14:14	14:17	+ 15	6.84
Nov 24	bp	14:19	14:23	+ 15	6.80
Feb 25	cl	14:14	14:18	+ 15	6.77
Feb 25	bp	14:19	14:23	+ 15	6.74
Aug 25	cl	14:14	14:18	+ 15	6.65
Aug 25	bp	14:19	14:23	+ 15	6.62
Feb 26	cl	14:25	14:29	+ 16	6.46
Feb 26	bp	14:31	15:03	+ 17	6.42

SOURCE: *Wall Street Journal*, March 12, 1996.

differ according to maturity; short-term interest rates usually are less than long-term. The differences do not reflect differences in factors such as liquidity, default risk, taxability, and callability because U.S. Treasury securities are equivalent in all but maturity. They are highly liquid because they are very actively traded and there is a large volume of most issues with maturities as far out as 30 years. In addition, they are default free, uniformly taxed, and do not have call features.[3]

[3] The U.S. Treasury has not issued callable securities since 1986.

FIGURE 5.2   Interest Rate Movements, U.S. Treasury Securities

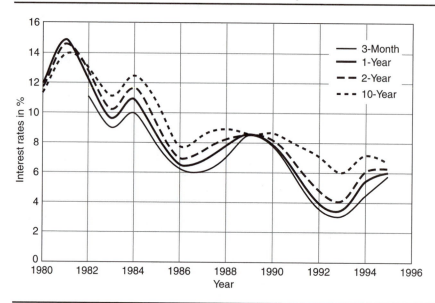

Figure 5.3 shows *yield curves* for three different dates. The yield curve graphically represents the term structure of interest rates on a specific date. It is created by plotting maturity on the horizontal axis and yield on the vertical axis. The characteristic shape of yield curves is upward-sloping, as in Figure 5.3, although, historically, in times of rapid inflation and abnormally high economic growth it has sloped downward.

The shape of the yield curve gives investment managers, including asset and liability managers, valuable information. For example, asset and liability managers consider the yield curve for December 31, 1994 in Figure 5.3 to be "banker friendly" because its steeply positive (upward) slope gives a large yield spread between short and long maturities and many banks invest in assets with maturities that are longer than their liabilities. It might appear to bankers that this yield curve automatically provides the gift of an attractive earnings spread simply for mismatching asset maturities with shorter liability maturities.

Interest Rate Expectations

To explain how investors make guesses about future interest rates requires that we understand the *forward interest rate*. This rate reflects where investors in aggregate think interest rates are going. We will find that the forward rate can be determined with a simple mathematical calculation. Most important, this mathematical result is presumed to be equal to the interest rate that today's investors expect to occur at some date in the future. This is powerful information because it identifies investors' expectations. As a consequence, the forward rate proves to be a vital decision-making tool for bankers, investors, and traders.

The forward rate serves as a *benchmark rate* for such useful purposes as identifying incorrectly priced fixed-income securities and setting the interest sensitivity of a bank's

FIGURE 5.3   Yield Curves, U.S. Treasury Securities

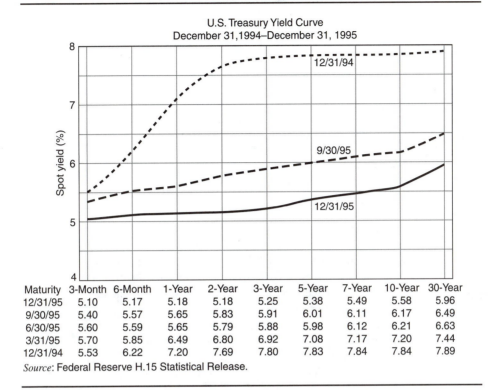

U.S. Treasury Yield Curve
December 31,1994–December 31, 1995

Maturity	3-Month	6-Month	1-Year	2-Year	3-Year	5-Year	7-Year	10-Year	30-Year
12/31/95	5.10	5.17	5.18	5.18	5.25	5.38	5.49	5.58	5.96
9/30/95	5.40	5.57	5.65	5.83	5.91	6.01	6.11	6.17	6.49
6/30/95	5.60	5.59	5.65	5.79	5.88	5.98	6.12	6.21	6.63
3/31/95	5.70	5.85	6.49	6.80	6.92	7.08	7.17	7.20	7.44
12/31/94	5.53	6.22	7.20	7.69	7.80	7.83	7.84	7.84	7.89

Source: Federal Reserve H.15 Statistical Release.

balance sheet. Appendix 5B shows that the forward rate also helps to determine the risk premium offered on assets that contain default risk or call risk.

The forward rate is calculated from the current term structure of interest rates. The calculation is based on the premise that investors with the same time horizon should expect to earn the same returns. Suppose two equally astute investors plan to invest in risk-free debt securities for exactly one year but they buy securities with different maturities. In theory, there is no reason to assume that one investor will best the other in earnings.

Let's assume our investors plan to be in the market for two years. They have the same objective: They aspire to maximize returns over a two-year horizon. Investor A acquires a two-year note and holds it for two years. Investor B acquires a one-year note knowing that one year from now he will have to roll his investment over for an additional year. Neither investor is prescient. However, both should assume that their respective investment strategies will produce the same result. It's not important that, after the facts, the results probably will not be the same. What is important is that at the moment of investing, they *expect* the result to be the same. Consider the following example.

EXAMPLE   Gillian St. George is an investment manager for a large industrial institution. She is looking for a way to invest a large amount of funds for exactly two years and observes that the current term structure offers a one-year spot rate of 6 percent and a two-

FIGURE 5.4   Yield Curve Segment

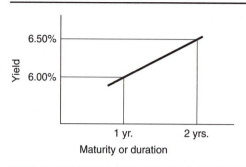

year spot rate of 6.50 percent. Figure 5.4 shows the yield curve for this situation. Obviously, by locking in her investment for two years, Ms. St. George assures herself of earning 6.50 percent per year. Randall Pecoque, an investment manager for a competing firm, also has a two-year investment horizon for an equally large amount of funds. However, Mr. Pecoque is attracted to a one-year initial investment and can only be sure of earning 6 percent for the first year. Why would Pecoque be willing to forego the sure 6.5 percent rate for two years? The only feasible reason is that he *expects* to roll over his investment at the end of the year at a *future rate* of a minimum of 7 percent or more to earn at least 6.5 percent per year [(6.0% + 7.0%)/2 = (6.5% + 6.5%)/2]. The resulting 7 percent calculation, founded on today's term structure, is the *forward rate of interest.*

St. George must expect that Pecoque's strategy is no better than hers. For the moment, suppose she comes to believe that the future one-year rate will exceed 7.0 percent, rendering her two-year return inferior to the rollover strategy. She, and others like her, will avoid the two-year security in favor of the one-year. But this action will put buying pressure on the one-year, forcing its price up and its yield down. Meanwhile, the absence of demand for the two-year security will reduce its price, driving its yield up. Eventually, things should stabilize when neither strategy dominates the other. Pecoque goes through a similar mental exercise. He must expect that his strategy is at least equivalent to St. George's. If he does not expect so, he will apply buying pressure that will rectify the term structure.

Almost unwittingly, the buying and selling actions we described illustrate *arbitrage.* Arbitrage occurs when market participants buy or sell to make a profit on differences in the value of two essentially equal assets or transactions. It entails opportunistic buying and selling of the kind we described for Gillian St. George and Randall Pecoque. *Arbitrageurs'* actions correct the inherently unstable prices in the market.

GAP MANAGEMENT

At the "risk" of being repetitious, interest rate risk can be described as the potential for earnings and balance sheet market values to decrease owing to changes in interest rates. In Chapter 4, our discussion of interest rate risk focused on economic or value risk. We investigated the balance sheet market value model and duration as methods for quantifying economic risk. We now round out the discussion by showing how financial institutions manage earnings risk stemming from interest rate changes.

In Chapter 3, we characterized *earnings risk* for Smithville Bank using a comparison between interest rate sensitive assets and interest rate-sensitive liabilities called "gap." Furthermore, in discussing Treadwater Bank's market value model in Chapter 4, we observed how rising interest rates turned Treadwater's annual earnings series negative because its liabilities were more interest sensitive than its assets. Here, we discuss how financial firms formalize the presentation and analysis of gap as an indicator of earnings risk.

Table 5.1 presents a recent interest rate sensitivity or *gap* report for Norwest Corporation, a large banking firm operating in all 50 states of the United States. Management has time-classified all of its balance sheet items into categories of rate or *repricing* sensitivity to changes in short-term interest rates. Suppose general interest rates rose today and stayed at the new level of rates indefinitely. Norwest would expect cash flows on $16.813 billion of its total $39.182 billion loans and leases to change (reprice) during the next six months. Cash flows on the remaining loans would not change in the next six months. The firm would expect another $3.103 billion to reprice between six months and one year, and so forth. Implicitly, it expects sensitive cash flows to change in the same direction and proportion as the change in interest rates.

TABLE 5.1 Interest Rate Sensitivity Report, Norwest Corporation

Norwest Corporation and Subsidiaries Interest Rate Sensitivity *In millions, except ratios* *Average Balances for December 1996*	*Repricing or Maturing*				
	Within 6 Months	**6 Months to 1 Year**	**1 Year to 3 Years**	**3 Years to 5 Years**	**After 5 Years**
Loans and leases	$16,813	3,103	5,966	2,863	10,437
Investment securities	2,218	2,088	2,700	1,935	8,166
Loans held for sale	2,659	—	—	—	—
Mortgages held for sale	5,881	—	—	—	—
Other earning assets	4,251	—	—	—	—
Other assets	—	650	—	—	10,102
Total assets	$31,822	5,841	8,666	4,798	28,705
Noninterest-bearing deposits	$ 4,134	63	268	178	8,832
Interest-bearing deposits	16,508	3,733	4,770	981	9,633
Short-term borrowings	8,230	—	—	—	—
Long-term debt	3,938	709	2,266	2,321	4,154
Other liabilities and equity	1	—	188	—	8,925
Total liabilities and equity	$32,811	4,505	7,492	3,480	31,544
Swaps and options	$(3,860)	196	1,153	866	1,645
Gap*	(4,849)	1,532	2,327	2,184	(1,194)
Cumulative gap	(4,849)	(3,317)	(900)	1,194	—
Gap as a percent of total assets	(6.1)%	(4.2)	(1.2)	1.5	—

* [assets − (liabilities + equity) + swaps and options]. The gap includes the effect of off-balance sheet instruments on the corporation's interest sensitivity.

Altogether, Norwest expects cash flows on $31.822 billion of assets and $32.811 billion of liabilities to change with interest rates in the coming six months. The difference in these magnitudes—($0.989 billion)—is designated the six-month gap. In theory, if interest rates rise, more liabilities will reprice upward than assets, causing a *decline* in net interest margin. The six-month to one-year gap is ($5.841 − $4.505) = +$1.336 billion and, with rising interest rates, eventually would contribute *positively* to net interest margin. If short-term rates fell, the results would be reversed; the negative six-month gap would produce favorable results for net interest, and the six-month to one-year gap would produce unfavorable results.

The bottom portion of the gap report in Table 5.1 includes the effect of *swaps* and *options* on interest sensitivity. These types of *derivative* instruments help the bank to manage its interest sensitivity. Derivative instruments such as these do not appear on the balance sheet. We will treat thoroughly the valuation and pricing of derivatives in Chapters 13, 14, and 15. Finally, common gap measures are shown at the very bottom of Norwest's report and include the periodic gaps described in the previous paragraph, the cumulative gaps (adding prior gaps to later gaps), and gap as a percentage of total assets.

It is not easy to make the connection from gap information such as that in Table 5.1 to the exposure of earnings to interest rates. The lack of a clear connection is a major fault of this measurement technique. However, we can approximate the earnings exposure, albeit crudely, as follows:

$$\Delta \text{ net interest margin } \$ = \text{gap} \times \Delta \text{ interest rate, or}$$

$$\Delta NIM\$ = G\Delta r$$

For the six-month gap, given a 1 percent rate increase:

$$\Delta NIM\$ = -\$0.989 \text{ billion} \times \Delta 0.01 = -\$989,000$$

Also,

$$\Delta \text{ net interest margin } \% = \text{gap/earning assets} \times \Delta \text{ interest rate, or}$$

$$\Delta NIM\% = \frac{G}{EA}\Delta r$$

For the six-month gap, given a 1 percent rate increase:

$$\Delta NIM\% = -1.24\% \times \Delta 0.01 = -0.0124\%$$

You ought to be suspicious of these results. The rate-sensitive items in the six-month gap, or any other period, do not all reprice at the same time. Perhaps they reprice at a uniform rate over the six-month period—on average, at the midpoint (three months) of the period. In this case, the full earnings effect of a rate change on six-month gap items would be effective only for an average of nine months of the coming year.

There are several concerns about the validity of gap reports:

1. It is not clear what time period is appropriate for determining the rate sensitivity of assets and liabilities.

2. For sensitivity purposes, you cannot readily classify items that have no stated maturity or pay no interest, for example, transactions deposits. The tendency is to classify such items as nonrate sensitive, such as demand deposits, which is seldom completely correct. A portion of such accounts is rate sensitive. Customers are prone to withdraw zero interest accounts when interest rates rise because such accounts bear increasingly greater high opportunity costs.

3. Bank management probably is not expert in predicting the direction, magnitude, and timing of interest rate movements.

4. Bank management may not have the control it needs to flexibly adjust assets and liabilities to obtain a desired gap. Expertise in derivative instruments might be of assistance here, but such expertise is not widely spread.

5. Interest rates on different balance sheet items may not change by the same magnitude.

6. Managing strictly with short-term gap may ignore reinvestment risk and possible significant changes in the values of bank assets and liabilities. Long-term cash flows may be mistakenly considered insensitive. As we observed in Chapter 4 in the case of Treadwater Bank, when interest rates change, the changes in the value of long-term cash flows often greatly exceed those of short-term cash flows.

Types of Earnings Risk

Norwest's gap report is typical of reports prepared by nearly every banking firm. Unfortunately, such reports do not efficiently capture the totality of interest rate risk. Here are five types of interest rate risk that affect earnings.

1. *Repricing or gap risk:* This risk is reflected in the description of the previous paragraph and the gap report.

2. *Basis risk:* The risk that repricing is not perfect or uniform for different items. For example, a given asset might reprice twice as fast as a given liability for the same change in general rates.

3. *Yield curve risk:* The risk that rates of different maturities may change by different magnitudes; for example, three-month rates might rise 200 basis points, while three-year rates simultaneously rise only 50 basis points. The above discussion of yield curves and the discussion in Appendix 5A imply that changes of different magnitudes indeed are not the exception; rather, they are normal.

4. *Option risk:* The risk that the payment patterns for assets or liabilities will change when interest rates change. Examples are prepayments on home mortgages when customers discover refinancing rates have become more attractive, fixed-rate loan commitments, caps on loan rates, and callable bonds. Chapter 14 presents formal methods of valuing and pricing such *embedded* options.

5. *Reinvestment and refunding risk:* The risk of unknown future interest rates on, respectively, net positive and net negative cash flows, created when short-term cash flows are not matched.

Gap reports especially are not competent to deal with risks 3 and 4, yield curve risk and option risk. These risks are better measured through the computer simulation method discussed in the next section. The gap report gives a semblance of information on the risks noted in items 1 and 5. Financial firms can attempt to deal with item 2, basis risk, using either gap or simulation.

GAP MANAGEMENT AND BASIS RISK

Interest rates on different assets and liabilities are likely to change by different magnitudes, even when they have the same duration. We must incorporate such basis risk into gap analysis. Unfortunately, the means of doing so is not straightforward. Financial firms especially need to understand the differential pricing behavior of their customer-based products. One approach is to develop a percentage change relationship between, say, each type of deposit account, and changes in a short-term reference rate—say, the rate on 91-day Treasury bills. With such information we can transform balance sheet interest sensitivity analysis into income terms to show how much annual earnings are exposed to interest rate movements.

EXAMPLE   Table 5.2 presents an example of how Lincoln National Bank uses regression analysis to examine changes in the weekly rates it pays on money market deposit accounts (MMDAs) and changes in the 91-day Treasury bill rate. The result we are looking for is the statistical measure, correlation coefficient. In Table 5.2, this value is 0.273, implying that the MMDA rate changes by 27.3 percent of changes in the 91-day bill: alternatively, the MMDA changes 27.3 basis points for a 1 percent change in the T-bill.

EXAMPLE   With a glow of satisfaction over her analysis of the MMDA correlation with T-bill rates, the asset and liability manager at Lincoln National Bank sets about to examine all of the bank's accounts in a similar fashion. She determines sensitivity correlations with general changes in a reference market rate for each account. She then creates a balance sheet that converts the gap for the degree of sensitivity of each type of account. With this corrected balance sheet gap, the manager calculates the bank's annual earnings at risk. Table 5.3 presents the results of her earnings-at-risk statement for Lincoln National Bank.

   The asset and liability manager's adjustments reveal an entirely different picture of interest rate sensitivity than that presented by the raw gap analysis. What appeared to be a gap of negative $90.4 million is actually a gap of about positive $51.2 million.

SIMULATION SYSTEMS

Earnings simulation models are an increasingly practical tool for asset and liability management and control, thanks to many bankers' familiarity with personal computers. Thoughtful simulation modeling can overcome the lack of insight and misleading information that are characteristic of simple gap management. Simulation software can easily manipulate the huge volume of forward data required by the simulation technique. *Forward data* are the bank's estimates of new business activity, including prepayments on existing and future loans and deposits, under alternative interest rate and other environmental scenarios. Simulation models produce complete earnings results iteratively for different product demand and interest rate scenarios. This gives banking firms a picture of

TABLE 5.2 Sensitivity Analysis, Lincoln National Bank's Money Market Deposit Account vs. 91-day T-bill

Date	90-Day Treasury	MMDA Account	Date	90-Day Treasury	MMDA Account
01/03/97	5.20	4.50	07/04/97	5.19	4.40
01/10/97	5.16	4.50	07/11/97	5.13	4.32
01/17/97	5.15	4.50	07/18/97	5.21	4.35
01/24/97	5.18	4.45	07/25/97	5.22	4.35
01/31/97	5.18	4.45	08/01/97	5.25	4.40
02/07/97	5.13	4.40	08/08/97	5.29	4.50
02/14/97	5.14	4.40	08/15/97	5.31	4.50
02/21/97	5.11	4.40	08/22/97	5.25	4.50
02/28/97	5.19	4.40	08/29/97	5.26	4.50
03/07/97	5.23	4.45	09/05/97	5.17	4.48
03/14/97	5.22	4.45	09/12/97	5.13	4.46
03/21/97	5.31	4.50	09/19/97	5.09	4.50
03/28/97	5.39	4.50	09/26/97	4.98	4.50
04/04/97	5.31	4.50	10/03/97	5.07	4.50
04/11/97	5.27	4.50	10/10/97	5.10	4.50
04/18/97	5.30	4.55	10/17/97	5.07	4.50
04/25/97	5.34	4.55	10/24/97	5.12	4.50
05/02/97	5.29	4.55	10/31/97	5.18	4.55
05/09/97	5.21	4.50	11/07/97	5.28	4.60
05/16/97	5.20	4.50	11/14/97	5.29	4.60
05/23/97	5.25	4.50	11/21/97	5.29	4.60
05/30/97	5.09	4.45	11/28/97	5.27	4.60
06/06/97	5.08	4.45	12/05/97	5.27	4.60
06/13/97	5.01	4.40	12/12/97	5.23	4.55
06/20/97	5.05	4.40	12/19/97	5.26	4.55
06/27/97	5.10	4.40	12/26/97	5.41	4.68

Correlation coefficient, % change: 0.273

earnings sensitivity, given the present and future balance sheets, under alternative yield curve forecasts.

EXAMPLE Table 5.4 shows a set of simulated earnings results for Bank of Utah. ALCO ordered the finance division to test two alternative funding strategies. One strategy emphasized a short-term, variable-rate funding program, and the other emphasized a long-term, fixed-rate funding program. In running its computer simulations, the division mapped the different balance sheet details of each funding program against interest rate forecasts of upward- and downward-shifting yield curves.

The finance division's results alert ALCO to a large earnings exposure associated with the long-term funding program. While the earnings improvement of $13 million in a rising-rate scenario is superior to any outcome for the short-funding alternative, ALCO decides that Bank of Utah's downside earnings risk of negative $20.8 million under the

TABLE 5.3   Lincoln National's Earnings at Risk Based on Basis Risk Estimation

	Balance Sheet Gap (A)	Correlation Coefficient (B)	Income Gap (A) × (B)
Rate-Sensitive Assets			
Fed funds sold	14,300	95%	13,858
Short-term investments	19,695	95%	18,710
Treasuries	8,488	80%	6,790
U.S. agencies	6,311	85%	5,364
Municipals	266	77%	205
Commercial loans—floating	13,071	100%	13,071
Commercial loans—fixed	1,323	85%	1,125
RE mortgages—floating	55,764	90%	50,188
RE mortgages—fixed	3,096	80%	2,477
Installment—floating	3,621	100%	3,621
Installment—fixed	4,016	75%	3,012
Home equity line of credit	14,026	100%	14,026
Total rate-sensitive assets	143,977		132,174
Rate-Sensitive Liabilities			
Demand deposits	76,987	16%	12,318
Savings	18,986	45%	8,544
MMDA	78,177	27.3%	21,342
CDs < $100,000	34,167	60%	20,500
CDs > $100,000	20,900	65%	13,585
Fed funds purchased	1,713	95%	1,627
Repurchase agreements	2,577	85%	2,190
FHLB borrowings	852	100%	852
Total rate sensitive liabilities	234,359		80,958
Rate-sensitive gap	(90,382)		51,216
Total assets	275,672		
Gap: % total assets	−32.8%		+18.6%

Change in reference rate	Estimated change in net interest margin
Increase 2%	1,024
Increase 1%	512
Decrease 1%	(512)
Decrease 2%	(1,024)

long-term funding program is unacceptable. Result: Cancel plans for marketing long-term CDs and of borrowing term funds from the Federal Home Loan Bank.

With well-developed software, institutions can elevate earnings simulation to any degree of sophistication desired. At a minimum, the software should readily handle basis (spread) risk and correlated interest rate risk (rate sensitivity of prepayments of assets or early withdrawals of liabilities). In the early years of bank simulation modeling, modelers limited their objective to animating the basic static gap report. This resulted in the so-

TABLE 5.4   Bank of Utah Earnings Simulation

	Change in Earnings	
	Upward Shift in Yield Curve	Downward Shift in Yield Curve
Short-term funding	($6.0 million)	$10.5 million
Long-term funding	$13.0 million	($20.8 million)

called *dynamic gap,* or forward gap, which simulated the static gap that would occur in the future. To arrive at this forward gap, much of the same forward data used in a complete simulation had to be input. Unlike the forward earnings emphasis of simulation, however, the emphasis was on gap for gap's sake. That is, instead of focusing on earnings, it focused on future repricing mismatches at each time bucket.

Simulation is not as simple as gap analysis. It relies on many detailed data, which fortunately, are readily handled with modern desktop computers. Simulation requires asset-liability managers to specify unique relationships between balance sheet volume, mix, and spreads for each interest rate scenario. To be correct, they have to specify these relationships definitively and not assume, given numerous possible interest rate scenarios, that everything else remains constant. In other words, one cannot just apply a new set of yields and rates to a set of asset and liability volumes and proportions that are constant for all rate scenarios. In the real world, bank balance sheets change dramatically with the radically different business conditions implied by different interest rate environments. Falling interest rates, for example, might imply declining loan demand, prepayment of loans, rising securities volume, declining purchased funds, and so forth. Most smaller banks do not have the time or expertise to specify their simulation exercises so finitely. Large banks are more likely to derive valuable insights from simulation, but only if they are willing to provide the expertise needed to specify volume, mix, and spread dynamics knowledgeably.

GAP STRATEGIES AND INTEREST RATE BENCHMARKING

You ought to expect the two central topics of this chapter—the term structure of interest rates and gap management—to be connected. Unfortunately, the two are more in conflict than they are in agreement. Most financial economists rely on expectations theory to explain the term structure of interest rates. They find the arbitrage proof of expectations theory to be especially powerful in explaining pricing in securities markets. The proof is straightforward and intuitive enough to appeal not just to academicians but to financial market practitioners, bankers, and even financially unsophisticated customers.

First, let's see how a bank customer might apply the theory. Later, we will explain why the principles of gap management are in conflict with this appealing explanation of interest rate behavior.

EXAMPLE Novákoff Banky offers two types of time deposits, a three-month certificate yielding annual 5.00 percent and a six-month certificate yielding annual 5.50 percent. How should a maximizing depositor with $10,000 to invest and a six-month investment horizon decide between the two? If you apply the thinking underlying the term structure of interest rates, the decision depends on the investor's expectation for the three-month yield to be offered three months from now. If he believes the yield will be greater than 6.00 percent, he should select today's three-month certificate at 5 percent and roll it over in three months. The reason is that he expects the average of the two rates to exceed the six-month rate of 5.50 percent. In other words, the depositor—who might be completely unsophisticated about financial markets—instinctively determines the three-month forward rate three months from now.

Sophisticated or not, the depositor must have a personal hunch about the future course of interest rates and whether or not the future three-month rate will exceed 6.00 percent. We designate the latter as the *benchmark* interest rate. This implies that market participants should not focus simply on the issue of whether interest rates will rise or fall. As in the case of our depositor, the issue is not even the direction of future interest rates. The issue is *whether a specific future rate will be above or below the benchmark rate.*

Now let's apply the reasoning about benchmarks to the task of asset and liability management. The task of asset and liability management is more complicated because managers must consider not just investing. Rather, they must consider investing and borrowing decisions simultaneously; clearly, they must manage both sides of the balance sheet. Chapter 3 and the gap discussion earlier in this chapter described what we now might call the naïve rule of asset and liability ''gap'' management. According to the rule, if financial institution managers believe interest rates are going to rise, they should structure their balance sheets to be asset sensitive to changes in interest rates. An asset-sensitive structure under changing interest rates should result in more assets repricing than liabilities. If interest rates rise, therefore, the interest revenues on assets should increase more rapidly than the interest costs on liabilities.

EXAMPLE Adirondack Trust Company must make simultaneous investment and borrowing decisions concerning the acquisition of $10 million in new loans funded with $10 million in new certificates of deposit (CDs). The loans and the CDs are both available in either one-year or three-year maturities (Table 5.5). The interest rates on the assets and CDs are higher for three-year maturities than for one-year maturities. Adirondack Trust receives a constant earnings spread of 4 percent on assets above liabilities of the same maturity. The spread is not germane to the underlying principle we wish to make: We just want to be sure Adirondack will make a profit!

Suppose the CFO at Adirondack believes interest rates will rise over the next three years. Accordingly, the gap rule calls for the institution to create an asset-sensitive relationship between assets and liabilities; in this instance, $10 million one-year loans will be funded by $10 million three-year CDs. Now assume that one-year interest rates on loans and CDs rise as shown in Table 5.6.

TABLE 5.5 Adirondack Gap Management Example: Rates Available on Loans and Liabilities

	1-Year	3-Year
Loans	10.00%	12.00%
CDs	6.00%	8.00%

TABLE 5.6   One-Year Interest Rates During Three-Year Asset and Liability Management Horizon

	This Year	Next Year	In 2 Years
Loans	10.00%	11.50%	13.00%
CDs	6.00%	7.50%	9.00%

TABLE 5.7   Net Interest Income for Asset-Sensitive Adirondack Trust

	Year 1	Year 2	Year 3
Interest income: rates 10%, 11.5, 13%	$1,000,000	$1,150,000	$1,300,000
Interest expense: 3 year rate 8.00%	800,000	800,000	800,000
Net interest income	$ 200,000	$ 350,000	$ 500,000

TABLE 5.8   Net Interest Income for Liability-Sensitive Adirondack Trust

	Year 1	Year 2	Year 3
Interest income: 3-year rate 12.00%	$1,200,000	$1,200,000	$1,200,000
Interest exp. rates 6%, 7.5%, 9%	600,000	750,000	900,000
Net interest income	$ 600,000	$ 450,000	$ 300,000

Adirondack Trust's net interest income for the three years, as shown in Table 5.7, comes to a total of $1,050,000.

Now, instead of creating an asset-sensitive balance sheet structure, suppose Adirondack's CFO acts contrary to the gap rule and creates a liability-sensitive structure. She does this by investing in three-year loans and funding them with one-year CDs that will be rolled over at an increasing interest cost at the end of years one and two. Adirondack Trust Company's new net income, detailed in Table 5.8, totals $1,350,000 for the three years, or $300,000 more than the allegedly superior strategy of creating an asset-sensitive structure when interest rates are rising.[4]

The surprising result is that net interest income improves when Adirondack Trust's balance sheet is structured to be liability sensitive. However, this result contradicts the gap rule which dictates that you must create an asset-sensitive structure when interest rates are expected to rise. Interest rates did, in fact, rise, but asset sensitivity produced inferior results. The explanation for this outcome is clear. Adirondack's CFO did not use forward rate benchmarking as a guide for structuring the firm's balance sheet. Had she done so she would have set as her benchmark the implied two-year (forward) rate for loans.

---

[4] This result is not perfectly accurate because we did not discount the future net interest income streams. However, present value analysis does not materially change the difference between the asset-sensitive and liability-sensitive cases.

Based on the rate structure for one-year versus three-year loans, the benchmark two-year forward rate was approximately 13 percent the one-year at a spot rate of 10 percent and the two-year at a forward rate of 13 percent matches the three-year at a spot rate of 12 percent: that is, $[(10\% + 13\% + 13\%)/3 = (12\% + 12\% + 12\%)/3]$. The actual average one-year rate for years two and three turned out to be 12.25 percent, which was well below the 13 percent benchmark. The fundamental issue for Adirondack Trust Company's CFO is the same as it was for the depositor discussed above: does the CFO believe the future rate will be above or below a benchmark rate? It is not sufficient simply to prognosticate the direction (up or down) of the rate; she needed to locate her rate projection with reference to the benchmark rate.

If asset and liability managers want to adopt a gap rule, the rule can now be restated as follows. When management believes the future interest rate will rise by less than today's corresponding forward rate (the *benchmark rate*) in a rising interest rate environment, it should create a balance sheet that is liability sensitive. (In the depositor example, the depositor should take the six-month CD.) When management believes the rate will rise above the forward rate, it should create asset sensitivity. (The depositor should take the three-month CD.) If management accepts the forward rate as the most likely future interest rate, it should seek a balanced asset and liability structure with zero interest rate sensitivity.

SUMMARY AND CONCLUSIONS

Theories about the term structure of interest rates attempt to explain the relationship between interest rates and maturity. Most important is the formation of investors' expectations, which allows us to equate the future expected *spot rate* with the calculated *forward rate*. The yield curve is a graphical depiction that plots interest rates against their maturities. Ideally, term structure and the construction of the yield curve employ Treasury *strip rates,* which are considered *pure discount rates.*

Interest rate expectations have a special place in financial institutions and markets. The predictions made from today's forward rates do not have to be correct. What is important is that, at the moment, investors' choices are reflected in the forward rate. Expectations set the standard for structuring the balance sheet interest sensitivity of financial firms. Therefore, earnings sensitivity gap management addresses matching of the near-term repricing volumes of assets and liabilities. In contrast to duration matching, it tends to ignore the interest elasticity of long-term assets and liabilities. Banks that wish to stabilize earnings should do so by controlling short-term gap matching. If they wish to stabilize the market value balance sheet, they should do so by matching asset and liability durations.

Bankers may focus on matching gap sensitivity rather than matching duration because they are oriented to short-term earnings objectives, not balance sheet market values. This bias toward earnings would not hold up if banks and thrifts adhered to market value balance sheet principles. If they did so, the impact of interest rate movements on the values of loans, securities, and various funding sources would immediately be clear. Duration would be more widely used in a world where accounting values were marked to the market values than it is now. One drawback to duration, however, is that it is rather technical and, therefore, difficult to explain to nonfinancial managers.

In any event, the practical value of duration appears to be limited. Duration values are unstable over time. Future cash flows change, defaults occur, reinvestment opportunities vary, and assumptions about future business may fail to hold. As a result, to be correctly matched, asset and liability durations must be continually rebalanced and readjusted.

In fairness, these criticisms also apply to simulation. Proponents of simulation argue that the nature of simulation overcomes uncertainties related to changing cash flows, defaults, future business assumptions, and so forth. They can easily revise these variables from model run to model run. This iterative procedure produces a range of simulation results that reveal realistic uncertainties in future outcomes. Proponents claim that only in this way can risk be properly evaluated. You have to be cautious about such reassurances, however, because the relationships *between* the variables surely change from one interest rate scenario to the next.

Using the forward rate as a benchmark, we disprove the strict gap rule that managers always profit from structuring the balance sheet to be asset (liability) sensitive when interest rates are expected to rise (fall). Instead, the rule should acknowledge that asset (liability) sensitivity is correct when the interest rate is expected to rise or fall to a level above (below) the benchmark forward rate.

END OF CHAPTER PROBLEMS

5.1 Following are current prices for pure discount, $1,000 par value bonds of different maturities as of January 1, 2010.

    a.) Calculate the spot interest rates for each bond.

Bond Maturity	Price
1 year	$943.40
2 years	881.66
3 years	816.30
4 years	748.80

    b.) Assume the expectations theory is valid. Based on your results in part a.), determine the forward one-year, two-year, and three-year rates expected one year later on January 1, 2011.

5.2 In part a.) below, assume that the yield curve adjusts to the forward rates found in problem 5.1b.). This case has a persistence factor of 0, meaning that the yield curve perfectly evolves into its forward rates.

    a.) What would be the one-year rates of return on investments made in January 2010, respectively, for the one-year, two-year, three-year, and four-year bonds? (*Hint:* Find the January 2011 values of the bonds, subtract the January 2010 investment prices given in Problem 4.10, and divide the difference by the investment prices. The one-year security simply matures in January 2011).

    b.) Assume now that interest rates do not move from their spot rates of January 2010. This case has a persistence factor of 1, meaning that current spot rates persist. What would be the one-year rates of return on investments?

    c.) Assume a persistence factor of 0.5 in which the yield curve evolves to a point halfway between those defined by persistence factors of 0 and 1. What would be the one-year rates of return on the investments?

Please use the following information for Problems 5.3 and 5.4:

In early 2000, RoboBank decided to analyze the profitability of business it put on its books in January 1998, including rollovers that have occurred since. Items booked in January 1998 totaled $150 million as follows:

Assets

$100 million two-year business loans as follows:

- $70 million fixed rate @ 2% over comparable Treasury rate.
- $30 million variable rate @ 1.5% over Treasury.
- $50 million, 30-year mortgages @ 1% over Treasury

Liabilities

- Funded the above with $150 million three-month deposits @ 0.5% *under* Treasury.

In January 2000, RoboBank rolled over the $100 million maturing business loans at the same pricing basis as in January 1998. Also, $30 million mortgages were prepaid at this time, and the proceeds were invested in two-year Treasuries. Throughout the two years, the bank continued to fund with three-month deposits by continuously rolling over into three-month deposits on the same pricing basis. Yield curve data for each January are as follows.

Yield Curve

	Jan. 1998	Jan. 1999	Jan. 2000
3-month Treasuries	3.0%	6.0%	5.0%
2-year Treasuries	4.5%	7.0%	5.0%
30-year Treasuries	7.0%	8.0%	5.5%

5.3 Calculate the expected annual net interest income and net interest margin at January 1998 (for the year 1998) as well as the two following Januarys (for the years 1999 and 2000) using the yield curve data given.

5.4 What are the implications of your results in Problem 5.3 for managing the bank's assets and liabilities (especially maturities and pricing) under changing interest rates and yield curve movements. Discuss the bank's net interest margin in terms of a breakdown of net interest margin into (1) credit spread, (2) funding spread, and (3) "gap" spread based on lending long and funding short (see Chapter 3, "The Components of Net Interest Margin"). How do these components of net interest margin vary with changes in interest rates and in the shape of the yield curve?

5.5 Midvale Bank has assets of $600 million. It has determined that its three-month gap-to-assets ratio is negative 11.5 percent. What dollar impact will a 2 percent increase in interest rates have on Midvale's net interest income? (Ignore basis risk.)

5.6 VerBrugge Bank and Trust Company analyzed its unadjusted three-month gap as follows:

	1 Day to 3 Months $Millions
Rate-Sensitive Assets	
Liquid investments	$ 860
Investment securities	300
Loans	2,340
	3,500

Rate-Sensitive Liabilities

Demand deposits	1,300
Saving deposits	400
Money market deposit accounts	2,150
Borrowed funds	850
	4,700
Gap	−1,200
NIM impact: ±1%	±12 million

VerBrugge's asset and liability manager is nervous about how basis risk might affect these figures and conducts a correlation analysis. He determines correlations of response for each account to a reference short-term interest rate to be, for assets: Liquid investments, 0.95; Investment securities, 0.70; Loans, 0.90: for liabilities: Demand deposits, 0.20; savings, 0.40; MMDAs, 0.60; borrowings, 0.90.

Determine the dollar effect on VerBrugge's net interest income from changes in the reference rate of ±1 percent and ±2 percent.

5.7 Following are gap numbers for Insular Bank's 0–6 month, 6-month to 1-year, and over 1-year rate-sensitivity gaps:

Time Bucket	Gap	Cumulative Gap
0–6 month	−2,000	−2,000
6-mo. to 1-year	+1,350	−650
Over 1-year	+650	0

Assume a 1 percent increase in the reference rate. Estimate the effect on net interest income for the coming 1-year period. Assume that repricing occurs at a uniform rate within each time bucket; that is, on average, repricing occurs at the midpoint of each time period. (The full effect on earnings does not occur until halfway through the period.)

Theories of the Term Structure of Interest Rates

Implicitly, as the text of this chapter pointed out informally, we are interested in term structure information beyond the observed interest rate spreads for maturity as depicted graphically in the yield curve. The term structure embeds information that directly affects the prices of fixed-income securities. Almost all financial economists contend that the term structure reflects a consensus about investors' expectations for the future course of interest rates, that is, future *spot* interest rates. In this appendix we show more formally that investors and traders use their expectations about future spot rates to determine the relationship between the prices of different securities and other financial assets like bank loans.

Interest Rate Expectations. Investors determine the term structure according to where they think interest rates are headed in the future. Over one hundred years ago, Irving Fisher proposed that one can impute investors' interest rate expectations from the current term structure of interest rates.[5] He concluded that the rate of return earned for a specific period of investment ought to be the same no matter the differences in investors' maturity strategies.

Assume a two-year investment horizon. Investors who buy a one-year security and roll it over into another one-year security one year from now should achieve the same rate of return as investors

who simply buy a two-year security and hold it for the two-year investment period. Alternatively, another class of investors might buy a three-year security and sell it at the end of two years. All three types of investors should expect to realize the same return.

As we pointed out in the chapter, the conclusion that investment maturity strategies should not matter depends on an *arbitrage* proof. Arbitrage describes the process whereby traders buy or sell to exploit inconsistencies in prices between two comparable deal structures or items (say, the same commodity sold in separate markets) to make profits. This opportunistic buying and selling corrects mispricing in the market. For example, arbitrageurs force to the same price any two investment packages that are expected to produce the same yield. The arbitrage proof supports Fisher's conclusion that maturity strategies are irrelevant. We show how arbitrage transforms a straightforward mathematical calculation of forward rates into theoretical future spot rates.[6]

Embedded in the term structure is a set of *forward rates*, where $f_{n,t}$ is the forward n-period rate beginning at time t. For example, $f_{2,3}$ is the forward two-year rate three years from now. The $f_{n,t}$s are

---

[5] Irving Fisher, ''Appreciation and Interest,'' *Publications of the American Economics Association,* 11 (August 1896).

[6] The calculated forward rates do not, of course, tell us much about *actual* future spot rates. Interest rates realized at a future date may not resemble today's expected future rate for the same date.

FIGURE 5A.1   Yield Curve Segment

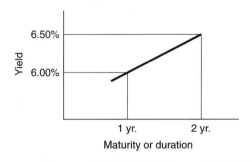

simply the result of mathematical computation and are not behavioral results. However, we can impute investors' expectations for spot rates at some future date by calculating the forward rate for the same date.

Investors with a two-year investment horizon who buy a one-year security today and roll it over into another one-year security a year from now will earn r_1 (the one-year spot rate) this year and *expect* to earn $f_{1,1}$ next year. Of course these investors cannot observe $f_{1,1}$ now but can only form expectations for next year's earnings rate. They expect this sequence of two one-year securities to earn a combined annual yield of $[\{(1 + r_1)(1 + f_{1,1})\}^{1/2} - 1]$ for two years. However, they will follow this investment strategy only if they believe this yield will be at least equal to or exceed the annual yield available on strategies that employ other maturities. For example, investors compare this strategy with an investment strategy of buying and holding the two-year security to earn r_2 for each of the two years.[7]

$$(1 + r_1)(1 + f_{1,1}) \geq (1 + r_2)^2 \quad (5A.1)$$

Solving directly for the one-year forward rate,

$$f_{1,1} \geq \frac{(1 + r_2)^2}{(1 + r_1)} - 1 \quad (5A.2)$$

For the investor to be indifferent to alternative maturity strategies, Equation 5A.2 must be an equality. If it is not, the price relationship between securities is inconsistent; arbitrage will take place in which investors will buy the underpriced security and sell the overpriced one. Ultimately, the forward rate and the relevant spot rates must be in balance.

As in the chapter, assume a term structure of interest rates consisting of a one-year spot rate of 6 percent and a two-year spot rate of 6.50 percent. This implies the yield curve shown earlier in Figure 5.4 and reproduced here as Figure 5A.1.

The one-year forward rate one year from now will be

$$f_{1,1} = \frac{(1.065)^2}{(1.06)} - 1 = 7.00\% \quad (5A.3)$$

In general, the term structure is comprised of many one-period forward rates and can be determined from spot rates in the following formulation

$$(1 + r_n)^n = (1 + r_{n-1})(1 + f_{1,n-1}) \quad (5A.4)$$

from which we can solve for the forward one-year rate $n - 1$ periods from now.

$$(1 + f_{1,n-1}) = \frac{(1 + r_n)^n}{(1 + r_{n-1})^{n-1}} \quad (5A.5)$$

Forward rates are not esoteric values; they are readily available to financial decision makers. They appear indirectly every day in the *Wall Street Journal* embedded in the yield data on Treasury strip securities. For example, in May 1996, Treasury strip rates were $(r_1, r_2, r_3, r_4) = (5.65\%, 6.03\%, 6.23\%, 6.32\%)$. Based on Equation 5A.5, at that time one-year forward rates imputed for different future times

---

[7] Also, the one-year-at-a-time investors would compare this strategy against buying the three-year security and selling it after two years. This unnecessarily complicates the presentation above. Basically, investors would require that $(1 + r_1)(1 + f_{n,t}) \geq [(1 + r_3)^2((1 + \mathscr{P}_{1,2} - P_3)/P_3)]^{2/3}$ where $\mathscr{P}_{1,2}$ is the expected price (i.e., the *forward* price) of the three-year security in two years (it will be a one-year security two years from now) and P_3, is the present price.

were $(f_{1,1}, f_{1,2}, f_{1,3}) = (6.41\%, 6.63\%, 6.59\%)$. These one-year rates were expected for May 1997, May 1998, and May 1999, respectively. The data also imply that two-year forward rates expected for May 1997 and May 1998 were $(f_{2,1}, f_{2,2}) = (6.52\%, 6.61\%)$.

Bond market traders effectively take positions in forward rates by buying and selling bonds of different maturities. Suppose new information—for example, an unexpected monetary action by the Federal Reserve—causes traders to believe that the future one-year spot rate one year from now will be 7.25 percent instead of the 7.00 percent forward rate implied in the term structure described above. The traders would "short" the forward rate by selling two-year securities (which contain the one-year forward rate) and buying one-year securities. This selling and buying pressure leads to adjustments in the prices and yields of the two securities in which two-year prices will fall, one-year prices will rise, or both.

Large differences between forward and expected future spot rates are unlikely, however. Markets like the market for U.S. Treasury bonds or the market for bonds of large corporations are *efficient* because they have deep supplies of bonds that are traded continuously. Bond prices reflect all important valuation information and adjust almost instantaneously to new information. If differences in forward and expected future spot interest rates arise, arbitrage immediately closes the differences before investors at large can profit.

Liquidity Premium Theory. Two additional theories of the term structure suggest that forces other than interest rate expectations play a role in determining the term structure. The first is liquidity premium theory, which holds that, in addition to expectations, forward rates reflect investors' demands for a yield premium to induce them to buy longer-term securities. Earlier, we found that the longer the maturity (duration), the greater securities' market risk. Because of this risk, investors prefer short-term securities. Borrowers, on the other hand, prefer the comfort of long-term borrowing to put off the repayment of principal. In theory, a "liquidity premium" on longer-term debt is required to bring investors and borrowers together. Let $L_{n,t}$ be the forward liquidity premium for yields on n-period securities issued at time t. Liquidity premiums increase with increasing duration.

$$L_{1,t} < L_{1,t+1} < \ldots < L_{1,n-1} \quad (5A.6)$$

where $L_{1,n-1}$ is the liquidity premium applied to the one-year forward rate corresponding to the last cash flow for an n-maturity security. Proponents claim that the prevailing positive slope observed for yield curves is based on time-dependent liquidity premiums embodied in the forward rate. If true, this conclusion is crucial for bank asset and liability management.

If a pattern of increasing liquidity premiums exists, bankers ought to mismatch their balance sheet structure to be liability sensitive by funding long-term assets with shorter-term liabilities. Also, they should extend the duration of their securities portfolio to obtain higher yields. For example, bankers should purchase two-year securities instead of one-year securities. This is because, on average, the future one-year rollover rate would produce a smaller yield than the one-year forward rate. By purchasing the two-year security, bankers would capture the forward one-year rate along with its liquidity premium. Unfortunately, these strategies conflict with our discussion above in which "pure" expectations determine forward rates and maturity strategies are not relevant for improving yields.

There is no clear evidence that liquidity premiums exist universally.[8] However, they may exist in the market for short-term U.S. Treasury securities. Several researchers have found that forward rates are larger than the actual spot rates that occur subsequently for the same time period.[9] For example, they compare the three-month forward rate implied in the six-month Treasury bill on January 1 with the spot three-month rate subsequently observed on April 1. Suppose the three-month and six-month bills yielded 6.50 percent and 7.00 percent, respectively, in January, which implies a forward three-month rate for April of 7.50 percent. Further suppose that, later, on April 1, the three-month spot rate is 7.25 percent. A comparison of the three-month forward rate of 7.50 percent calculated back in January suggests a 25-basis point (0.25%) annualized three-month premium for purchasing the original six-month bill instead of the three-month bill. Re-

---

[8] Eugene F. Fama, "Forward Rates as Predictors of Future Spot Rates," *Journal of Financial Economics* 3, no. 4 (1976), 361–77.

[9] Stanley Diller, "Liquidity Premiums in Treasuries," *Economic Research*, Goldman Sachs (1976); Alden Toevs and David Mond, "Liquidity Premiums and Maturity Strategies," Morgan Stanley (1987).

searchers have found that this experiment, repeated monthly over many years, reveals a significant reward for purchasing the less liquid six-month bill instead of the three-month.

However, evidence in support of the existence of liquidity premiums seems to be limited to short-term U.S. Treasury securities. Researchers do not find significant liquidity premiums in other markets such as the bank negotiable certificate of deposit, commercial paper, or Eurodollar markets. One reason researchers offer is that the U.S. Treasury is less attuned to the discipline of the marketplace. The Treasury might not be a fully cost-conscious issuer of debt, but, instead, its preconceived strategies for managing the maturity structure of its debt may dominate cost considerations.

Market Segmentation and Preferred Habitat Theories. The third theoretical explanation of the term structure holds that interest rates are segmented and are determined by buying and selling activity that is isolated in several maturity sectors. Market segmentation theory posits that narrow market sectors exist because highly restrictive rules based on regulation, investment law, and institutional preferences force market participants to confine the maturities of purchases and sales of securities. Institutional investors seek to match the term of their debt obligations to the timing of their future revenue streams.

For example, a microchip manufacturer builds a plant on which revenues will be spread over many years. The firm will try to issue long-term debt that can be serviced as these deferred revenues are earned. An insurance firm seeks long-term investments on which income is timed to the firm's expected long-term payouts to its insured.

Preferred habitat theory modifies the view that autonomous supply and demand behavior strictly segments markets and partitions the determination of interest rates. Although investors and debt issuers prefer their own *habitats,* they can be induced to switch over to adjacent maturity sectors if sufficient incremental yields are offered.[10] Yield differences are thought to persist (thus, a structure based on term) even if they are not sufficiently differentiated from yields required to induce many participants to leave their preferred habitats. Partial segmentation of interest rates will exist to attract some portion of those who are willing to buy and sell across maturity sectors.

---

[10] Franco Modigliani and Richard Sutch, ''Innovations in Interest Rate Policy,'' *American Economic Review* 56 (May 1966): 178–97.

Risk Premiums and the Term Structure

Discussion of the term structure of interest rates in the chapter and in Appendix 5A examined differences in market rates of interest caused by the term to maturity. Previously, we noted that term, expressed as duration, is an index of a security's market risk. Increases in duration increase the volatility of security prices in relation to interest rate movements.

To complete our discussion of term structure of interest rates, this section introduces two additional reasons that market rates of interest differ—default or credit risk and what is called *option risk*. This section seeks to link the measurement of these components of risk to the term structure. We examine credit risk in Chapter 11, and we create models for pricing option risk in Chapter 14.

Credit risk is simply the risk that the payment schedule on a risky asset will be interrupted by the debtor's inability to pay. Nonpayment can range from a simple delay in a scheduled payment to the total collapse of the debtor's cash flow and eventual liquidation of the debtor's business.

Option risk occurs in assets that contain features such as call options (known as "embedded" interest rate options). Option-embedded assets have asymmetrical payoffs. If interest rates rise in the future, the payoff for the asset with a call option will be negative and similar in size to that for an option-free asset. On the other hand, if interest rates fall, gains on the option-embedded asset (the option "goes into the money") are cut off because the issuer will call the asset before its maturity.

The assets with option risk most used in banks are callable bonds, home mortgages, and mortgage-backed securities. Each permits repayment before maturity. Lenders have the risk that debtors will pay off their bonds or mortgages when market rates fall sufficiently below their contractual interest rates to merit the cost and effort to refinance. This forces the lender to accept liquidation of loans with yields above the present market and to reemploy funds at a less favorable rate.

Financial institutions are in the business of contracting for such risky financial assets in order to earn *risk premiums*. The institutions' managers are experts at risk reduction—controlling risks to make them acceptable in relation to the premiums earned. Despite their best efforts, managers cannot eliminate risk and must accept some remaining level of it. A critical part of this management task is to assess whether the risk premiums earned are an adequate reward for the remaining risk.

To determine risk premiums, we hold other factors constant, including term (duration) risk, other than credit risk or option risk. The risk premium on a risky asset can be approximated as the difference between the yield on the asset and the yield on a risk-free asset. However, it is difficult to hold term risk constant because it is difficult to find pure risk-free discount assets—such as zero coupon securities formed from stripping U.S. Treasury securities—whose cash flows match exactly the timing or duration of the cash flows of the risky asset.

The first step in determining risk premiums,

therefore, is to find risk-free yields for the dates on which the cash flows occur for the risky asset. Our task is to create a risk-free yield-to-duration curve. Market analysts apply two practical methods to create such a curve,[11] *bootstrapping* and *interpolation*. Bootstrapping is used when there are too few data on zero-coupon or Treasury strip securities to form a reliable duration structure of interest rates.

Bootstrapping. Often, data on coupon bonds are more readily available than data on zero-coupon securities. Bootstrapping uses coupon security prices to estimate yields on later zero-coupon securities. The procedure is an iterative one that repeatedly applies shorter maturity yields to impute zero-coupon rates on longer maturity par coupon securities. The process starts with a short-term security that has only one remaining period to maturity. The security pays one final coupon along with the payment of terminal principal in one period.

Let $P_{0,1}$ be the present (time $= 0$) price of a one-period coupon bond and C_1 be the dollar value of the remaining coupon. Note that, for a par value bond, $P_{0,1} = 100$. We solve for r_1, the zero-coupon rate (the one-period security has only one payment date) in the following:

$$P_{0,1} = 100 = \frac{100 + C_1}{(1 + r_1)} \qquad (5B.1)$$

Knowing r_1 and the dollar value of C_2, the coupon for a two-period coupon security, we derive the two-period zero-coupon rate r_2 by solving Equation 5B.2:

$$P_{0,2} = 100 = \frac{C_2}{(1 + r_1)} + \frac{100 + C_2}{(1 + r_2)} \qquad (5B.2)$$

Armed with knowledge of r_1, r_2, and C_3, the coupon on the three-year security, we solve iteratively for r_3, the three-period zero-coupon rate. We continue this process until we determine all zero-coupon rates through r_n:

$$100 = \sum_{t=1}^{n-1} \frac{C_t}{(1 + r_t)^t} + \frac{100 + C_n}{(1 + r_n)^n} \qquad (5B.3)$$

Notice that this derivation assumes that zero-coupon rates are directly related to one another through the equations and that there are no liquidity premiums for longer-term yields. Table 5B.1 shows zero-coupon rates derived by bootstrapping a set of par bonds with annual coupons.[12] The bonds represent maturities for every year out to five years. The one-year coupon is 6 percent, and coupons increase by 1 percent for every year to maturity.

Solving Equation 5B.4 for the two-year zero coupon yield,

$$100 = \frac{7}{1.06} + \frac{107}{(1 + r_2)^2}$$

$$(1 + r_2)^2 = \frac{107}{93.396226} = 1.1456566 \quad (5B.4)$$

$$r_2 = 1.070353 - 1 = .070353$$

Table 5B.1 demonstrates that an upward-sloping yield curve based on coupon bonds produces zero-coupon rates that grow progressively larger than the corresponding coupon rates. In general, upward-sloping coupon bond yield curves understate zero-coupon rates. Contrarily, downward-sloping coupon yield curves overstate zero-coupon rates.

Yield curve interpolation. As the example above shows, bootstrapping to find zero-coupon rates is rather work intensive. In addition, it does not necessarily provide zero-coupon data for the exact payment dates that allow us to examine the risk premiums on risky securities. Interpolation is a straightforward method of approximating zero coupons for any series of dates.

There are three steps in the method. First, construct a yield curve based on zero-coupon rates on U.S. Treasury *strip* securities. Second, through interpolation, find the U.S. Treasury strip yields for all the dates on which cash flows (coupon and redemption payments) occur for the risky asset. Finally, estimate the risk premium by equating the asset's price to the present value of the asset's cash flows discounted by their corresponding risk-free

---

[11] More sophisticated models for mathematically fitting the term structure include J. McCulloch, "Measuring the Term Structure of Interest Rates," *Journal of Business* 44 (1971): 19–31; and John C. Cox, Jonathon E. Ingersoll, Jr., and Stephen A. Ross, "A Re-examination of Traditional Hypotheses about the Term Structure of Interest Rates," *Journal of Finance* 36, no. 4 (September 1981): 769–99.

[12] This example is based on Ira G. Kawaller and John F. Marshall, "Deriving Zero-Coupon Rates: Alternatives to Orthodoxy," *Financial Analysts Journal* (May/June 1996): 51–55.

TABLE 5B.1   Bootstrapping to Estimate Zero-Coupon Rates

Maturity (years)	Annual Coupon Rate	Zero-Coupon Rate
1	6.00%	6.0000%
2	7.00%	7.0353%
3	8.00%	8.1111%
4	9.00%	9.2439%
5	10.00%	10.4562%

rates plus the risk premium. Solve this equation for the risk premium.

Table 5B.2 constructs the interpolated yield curve. In the table we determine the exact maturities in days and list the asked prices and yields of certain coupon strips from Figure 5.1 in the chapter. The strips represent maturities for every quarter from May 1996 through May 2001 as of March 11, 1996. The fourth column lists the calculated maturities in days for each security based on:

$$P_0 = \frac{100}{\left(1 + \dfrac{r_t}{2}\right)^m} \quad (5B.5)$$

where m is the fractional number of one-half year periods until payment.[13] Equation 5B.5 is solved for m, and then m is converted into days by multiplying by 182.5 days (one-half year). Column 5 lists the dates on which the maturities fall. Column 3 reveals the yields on single cash flows that occur on the maturity dates. For example, cash flows that will occur on May 12, 1996 have a market discount rate of 5.17 percent; cash flows of August 12, 1999 have a discount of 5.88 percent; and so forth. Because Treasury cash flows are promises of the U.S. government, there is no risk of default. In addition, Treasury strips are not callable and thus do not have option risk. The discount rates differ from each other only because of investors' expectations for future interest rates and because of their aversion to greater price volatility as the maturity of the cash flows increase.

The next step is to find, through interpolation,

the U.S. Treasury strip yields on all the specific dates of the risky asset's cash flows. We base an example on Federal Home Loan Bank (FHLB) System bonds due on March 26, 2001 with a 6.87 percent coupon. These bonds have insignificant credit risk because, as a Government Sponsored Enterprise (GSE), it is extremely unlikely that the Congress would permit FHLB bonds to default. However, they have option risk because they are callable after six months and present a risky situation to investors. Investors know that if future interest rates decline, the FHLB will call in the bonds and repay investors at a time when earning rates for reinvesting their funds in the market have deteriorated.

Column 7 in Table 5B.2 shows the number of days from March 11, 1996—the announcement date for the bonds—until coupon payments and the final principal payment are paid on the FHLB bonds. Column 6 lists the payment dates.[14] Then, by interpolation, the U.S. Treasury yields are formed for each of these dates in column 8. For example, the interpolated yield for the first coupon of $6.87/2 = $3.435 per $100, is:

$$5.14\% + (5.27\% - 5.14\%)$$

$$\times \left(\frac{199 - 157}{245 - 157}\right) = 5.20\% \quad (5B.6)$$

The numerator in the brackets is the number of days after the latest Treasury strip payment (August

---

[13] m can be found using a financial calculator or from

$$m = \frac{\ln(100) - \ln(P_0)}{\ln\left(1 + \dfrac{r_t}{2}\right)}$$

[14] On March 11, 1996 the 6.87 percent FHLB of March 26, 2001 was a "when issued" bond. Investors make commitments obliging them to take down when issued bonds at the future issue date (which is the "settlement date"), in this case March 26, 1996. The bond's value, however, is based on yield curve conditions at the time of commitment, March 11, 1996. When issued bond commitments may be traded before issuance.

TABLE 5B.2   Option Risk Premium: 6.87% Coupon, FHLB Bonds Due March 26, 2001

1	2	3	4	5	6	7	8	9
Maturity	Asked Price, $P_0{}^a$	Asked Yield, $r_t{}^a$	Maturity (days)[b]	Implied Pay-ment Dates	Date FHLB Coupon Paid	Days to Payment	Interpl'd Strip Yield	Option-ADJ. Spread
May 96	99.13	5.17%	63	5/12/96				6.07%
Aug 96	97.84	5.14%	157	8/14/96	9/26/96	199	5.20%	6.04%
Nov 96	96.56	5.27%	245	11/11/96				6.17%
Feb 97	95.19	5.38%	339	2/13/97	3/26/97	380	5.43%	6.28%
May 97	93.84	5.49%	428	5/13/97				6.39%
Aug 97	92.50	5.53%	522	8/14/97	9/26/97	564	5.58%	6.43%
Nov 97	91.13	5.63%	611	11/11/97				6.53%
Feb 98	89.81	5.65%	704	2/12/98	3/26/98	745	5.68%	6.55%
May 98	88.47	5.71%	794	5/13/98				6.61%
Aug 98	87.09	5.77%	887	8/14/98	9/26/98	929	5.77%	6.67%
Nov 98	85.91	5.77%	975	11/10/98				6.67%
Feb 99	84.56	5.82%	1,067	2/10/99	3/26/99	1,110	5.84%	6.72%
May 99	83.25	5.87%	1,157	5/11/99				6.77%
Aug 99	82.00	5.88%	1,250	8/12/99	9/26/99	1,294	5.88%	6.78%
Nov 99	80.88	5.87%	1,339	11/10/99				6.77%
Feb 00	79.56	5.91%	1,433	2/11/00	3/26/00	1,476	5.91%	6.81%
May 00	78.41	5.91%	1,524	5/13/00				6.81%
Aug 00	77.19	5.94%	1,615	8/11/00	9/26/00	1,660	5.95%	6.84%
Nov 00	76.00	5.96%	1,706	11/10/00				6.86%
Feb 01	74.81	5.98%	1,798	2/10/01	3/26/01	1,841	5.99%	6.88%
May 01	73.59	6.01%	1,890	5/13/01				6.91%

[a] *Wall Street Journal*, March 12, 1996.

[b] $m \times 182.5$ where $m = \dfrac{\ln 100 - \ln P_0}{\ln\left(1 + \dfrac{r_t}{2}\right)}$ = one-half year periods.

14, 1996, from column 7, Table 5B.2) to the first FHLB bond coupon; the denominator is the number of days between Treasury strip payments (November 11, 1996 "minus" August 14, 1996).

The final step—once the Treasury strip yields on the FHLB payment dates are found—is to solve for the risk premium. We set the asset's price equal to the present value of the asset's cash flows discounted by their corresponding discount rates. The discount rates combine the risk-free Treasury strip yields and the risk premium (the unknown "X" in Equation 5B.7).

$$100 = \frac{\$3.435}{\left(1 + \dfrac{0.0520 + X}{2}\right)^1} + \frac{\$3.435}{\left(1 + \dfrac{0.0543 + X}{2}\right)^2}$$

$$+ \frac{\$3.435}{\left(1 + \dfrac{0.0558 + X}{2}\right)^3} + \frac{\$3.435}{\left(1 + \dfrac{0.0568 + X}{2}\right)^4}$$

$$+ \frac{\$3.435}{\left(1 + \dfrac{0.0577 + X}{2}\right)^5} + \frac{\$3.435}{\left(1 + \dfrac{0.0584 + X}{2}\right)^6} \quad (5B.7)$$

$$+ \frac{\$3.435}{\left(1 + \dfrac{0.0588 + X}{2}\right)^7} + \frac{\$3.435}{\left(1 + \dfrac{0.0591 + X}{2}\right)^8}$$

$$+ \frac{\$3.435}{\left(1 + \dfrac{0.0595 + X}{2}\right)^9} + \frac{\$103.435}{\left(1 + \dfrac{0.0599 + X}{2}\right)^{10}}$$

where X is the risk premium and equals 0.90 percent, or 90 basis points. X is assumed to be constant over all time periods. In cases such as this where we assume the risk premium is due solely to option risk, the resulting yield in excess of the Treasury yields on a security with matched cash flow payment dates is known as the *option-adjusted spread*.

END OF APPENDIX PROBLEMS

5B.1 Appendix 5B notes that "downward-sloping coupon bond yield curves overstate zero coupon rates." Bootstrap a zero-coupon yield curve to prove this proposition for a coupon bond curve with coupons $(C_1, C_2, C_3, C_4, C_5)$ = (10%, 9%, 8%, 7%, 6%). Show your calculations and tabulate the results.

5B.2 Find the yield premium accorded to a recent "when issued" callable government agency (Fannie Mae, Federal Home Loan Bank, etc.) medium-term note issued on the date of the note's offering to compensate for the note's callability. (See recent *Wall Street Journal*, section C, "New Securities Issues—Corporate." Such issuances appear on most days.) For example, notes when issued on, say, March 15, 2000 and maturing on March 25, 2007 will have coupon payment dates of September 25, 2000, March 25, 2001, September 25, 2001, . . . , March 25, 2007. Use the interpolation methodology described in Appendix 5B and the U.S. Treasury strip yields for the "when-issued" date (see *Wall Street Journal*, section C, "Treasury Bonds, Notes and Bills") much as in Figure 5.1 of the chapter text.

Note: The yield premium above expresses the price of your note's call option.

CASE

1

FIRST NATIONAL BANK OF PARK CITIES

INTRODUCTION

Mr. Tom Turner had long wanted to organize and direct a new community-oriented commercial bank. He had never seriously explored the possibility of such an entrepreneurial experience, however, since nearly all his banking affiliations had carried him toward large, well-established bank holding companies.

Nonetheless, from time to time, Turner had mentioned his interests to business associates and friends in his residential community, an independent incorporated town entirely surrounded by the city of Dallas. He continued to receive enough encouragement and enthusiasm from his friends to believe that his goal of directing a new independent bank might indeed be feasible and that significant financial support might be available to him.

By mid-1983, Turner began spending part of his time studying and researching the possibility of a new bank in the Park Cities area within Dallas, and exploring specific investment interest among his friends and business colleagues.

By the end of 1983, Turner had developed a preliminary strategy for a new community bank, and he had identified a group of some 15 to 20 organizers and investors who had expressed serious interest in the project.

In the early stages of his explorations of this venture, Turner had identified several key questions and judgmental issues that would have to be resolved if this effort was to move forward. Some of the principal early considerations were as follows:

1. Was there a real need and a profitable opportunity for another new bank in the Dallas–Park Cities area, given the many new financial institutions that had already been opened in recent years?
2. How much capital would be required for such a venture, and how difficult would it be to earn a competitive rate of return on that necessary capital base?
3. How difficult might the competitive environment prove to be, and how could Turner make his projected bank a uniquely different institution, meeting customers' needs in ways that would justify the opening of still another community bank in Dallas?

4. What kind of strategic plan and marketing effort would be required to "sell" the projected new bank to its community?
5. What would be the management requirements of such a venture, including the formation of a board of directors, and the operating challenges and problems that such a new enterprise might encounter?
6. Should the proposed new bank seek a national or a state (Texas) bank charter?

Some of the answers to these questions gradually became clearer as Turner continued to study the possibilities and as interested potential investors began to express their ideas and suggestions. The following data summarize some of the preliminary planning and analytical data that Turner assembled as he became increasingly serious about the formation of a new bank.

THE PROPOSED BANK'S GEOGRAPHIC LOCATION

The proposed Park Cities Bank would be located on the southwest corner of the intersection of Hillcrest Avenue and University Boulevard in Dallas, Texas. The market area encompasses the two cities of Highland Park and University Park (the Park Cities) and a portion of the city of Dallas. The area extends approximately 1.6 miles north, 1.9 miles south, 0.7 mile east, and 1.8 miles to the west from the proposed location.

This site would be especially attractive because it represents a combination of two towns that form an inner-city community within Dallas and because three of the boundaries (north, east, and west) are major traffic arteries in Dallas and form natural barriers for the marketplace. The southerly boundary has been chosen because residents of the Park Cities tend to identify and conduct their retail and banking business within their community.

The primary market area for the deposits and loans is outlined in Exhibit 1, which shows the bank's potential market area in relation to the Dallas/Fort Worth metroplex and the central portion of the city of Dallas.

The proposed bank would be well located in its market area, providing convenient access for the entire community through two major north-south thoroughfares. Moreover, there would be numerous retail establishments surrounding the proposed bank's site. Customers who patronized those stores would be able to complete their shopping and banking at one convenient location. Finally, the new bank would be located across the street from the Southern Methodist University campus, one of the market area's largest employers. The organizers believed the bank could attract the university's administration, faculty, staff, and students as customers.

THE MARKET ECONOMY

Population, Housing, and Income Characteristics

The market area for the projected new institution would span two of Texas's most vibrant cities, Highland Park and University Park. Known as the Park Cities, they cover approximately 6 square miles and are completely surrounded by the city of Dallas. They are among the most affluent communities in the state. In 1980, for example, median family income in Highland Park was $52,742, and in University Park it was $33,763. In contrast, median family income in the state of Texas as a whole for that year was $19,619 and for the United States it was $19,928. Thus, median family income was 168.8 percent higher in Highland Park and 72.1 percent higher in University Park than in Texas as a whole. The area's residents are, generally speaking, very successful and affluent.

Population figures for the Park Cities indicate a stable population base. The cities of Highland Park and University Park have been completely developed for many years and, consequently, are not expected to experience sharp increases in population growth. Community stability coupled with considerable residential redevelopment and renovation of existing homes has created one of the most desirable residential areas in the Dallas metroplex.

Exhibit 2 provides income and housing data for the Park Cities, and it summarizes current population estimates for Highland Park and University Park. A solid indicator of the area's general affluence is its housing values. In 1982, the State Property Tax Board confirmed the average value of a single-family residence in the Highland Park Independent School District (whose boundaries closely parallel those of the proposed bank's market area) to be $226,000.

Employment and Commercial Activity

Although the (new) projected bank's market area economy would be anchored in its own retail and commercial activity, the location under study would be convenient to all primary employment centers in Dallas. To the east, the Central Expressway corridor contains approximately 4.9 million square feet of office space; to the south, the Dallas Central Business District has over 16 million square feet; the Turtle Creek Corridor, which passes through the center of the proposed market area, contains 1.5 million square feet of office space; on the west, the Stemmons Freeway area has over 6 million square feet of office space; north of the market area, the LBJ/Far North Dallas area comprises over 7 million square feet of office space.

Retail Sales

Retail sales for the cities of Highland Park and University Park in 1982 were estimated to be $62,017,135 and $107,723,720, respectively. (See Exhibit 3.) These figures reflect a 97 percent increase over 1978 sales in Highland Park and a 64 percent increase in University Park. The yearly increase in estimated retail sales figures summarized in Exhibit 3 demonstrates an outstanding retail growth trend for the Park Cities. There are nine retail shopping centers located within the proposed bank's market area.

At the northern boundary market area is one of Dallas's largest regional shopping malls—NorthPark Shopping Center. Built in 1973, NorthPark has over 1 million square feet. The mall caters to Dallas's more affluent consumers; its anchor tenants are Neiman-Marcus, Woolf Brothers, and Lord & Taylor.

THE COMPETITIVE ENVIRONMENT

A major area of concern to Tom Turner, however, was the intense competition coming from both new and established banks. The market area was currently served by 10 banks, 3 of which were organized in 1982 and opened in early 1983. An eleventh bank had recently received charter approval and was currently in organization. There was also a new charter application currently pending in the Comptroller of the Currency's office.

All of these market-area banks provide a reasonably full range of services to area residents. Each of them would, of course, compete with the proposed bank. In addition, many other financial institutions in Dallas County would offer some competition for the projected institution because of previously established banking connections, long term in many cases, by Park Cities residents.

At year's end 1982, deposits in these directly

competing banks totaled $1,083,516,000; total loans were $806,212,000. These figures represent a 144.6 percent increase in deposits and a 177.5 percent increase in loans since 1977. (See Exhibit 4.) The organizing group for the Park Cities Bank fully realized that competition for such an affluent customer base would be intense. Accordingly, they could not just offer "me too" banking services and expect to attract customers without somehow differentiating the new bank from all the others. The real challenge, therefore, would be to design a marketing and customer services program that would make the new bank stand apart.

Deregulation of Financial Institutions

The Garn-St. Germain Depository Institutions Act of 1982, signed into law on October 15, 1982, brought about significant changes in the competitive environment for financial institutions. Mr. Turner realized that provisions of the legislation would affect the marketplace for *de novo* banks, and for all other banks. New provisions of the law dealing with chartering thrift institutions, liberalizing investment opportunities, raising lending limits to individual customers, and expanding insurance activities of bank holding companies all would have effects on bank competition. Moreover, the establishment of new deposit accounts, the ability of thrift institutions to make commercial loans, and the phasing out of interest rate ceilings on time and savings deposits under Regulation Q signaled major changes that would directly affect newly established banks.

In any event, Turner and the other organizers recognized that competition from existing and new banks in the market area, as well as from new competitors to banks generally, would present perhaps the greatest challenge to any new bank's profit potential.

Of the 11 banks in the market area, 4 were newly chartered and therefore likely to offer substantial competition for the proposed bank. Of these, Central National Bank is located on the east side of North Central Expressway, with only difficult access to the proposed market. Grand Bank-Central, Oak Lawn Bank, and Sherry Lane National Bank, however, are located on the west side of North Central Expressway and would be expected to provide vigorous competition in the southern and western portions of the proposed bank's market.

The organizers were confident that the convenience of the Park Cities bank location to all parts of its market area would reduce the competitive impact from Grand Bank-Central and Oak Lawn Bank. Nonetheless, they realized that they would have to implement an aggressive marketing strategy for the proposed bank that would include extensive outreach throughout the market area, highlighting the new bank's competitive rates and its full line of services.

Nearly all of the probable organizers had longstanding ties to the Park Cities. It was their intention, therefore, to make use of their substantial professional and social contacts to attract loan and deposit business. Moreover, sale of the new bank's common stock to residents and enterprises throughout the Park Cities was expected to strengthen the bank's relationship to its market area and, thereby, its competitive effectiveness.

In addition to the 11 banks in the immediate area, there are 12 S&L offices, 1 credit union, and 3 mortgage or insurance companies. In short, competition would be intense.

PLANS AND STRATEGIES FOR OPERATION

The organizers' goal was to create a profitable and growing bank to service the needs of the residents, employees, and businesses in the market area. To achieve this result, a strong deposit base would have to be secured, a sound investment and lending strategy developed, and a stable asset-liability mix created. To achieve these preopening goals, the organizers discussed designating preliminary committees with differing responsibilities. These committee members were considered likely members of a future board of directors.

A building committee would oversee the planning and construction of the bank facility and would supervise the purchase of office furniture and equipment. A personnel committee would assist in the selection of a vice-president, cashier, and other staff personnel. An operations committee would examine operating systems and consider the various security measures needed to protect the bank's assets. A loan committee would establish the bank's lending policy. Once the bank opened, this group would serve as the standing loan committee. An investment committee would determine the bank's investment strategy. These groups would have responsibility for managing the bank's portfolio prior to opening (after raising the initial capital) and continuing with this responsibility once the bank began operating. An asset-liability committee would provide oversight supervision for the bank's assets and liabilities.

Finally, a marketing committee would study how common stock could be sold, how a public relations campaign plan might be organized, how to maximize value from the bank's opening ceremonies, and how to market the new bank continually to its publics.

Sources of Deposits

The prime sources of deposits for the bank would be the residents, employees, and businesses in the bank's market area. It was hoped that the probable organizers and board of directors together with the bank's marketing strategies would ensure access to these target markets.

The organizers had diverse business and financial interests that represented a majority of the important aspects in the market area's economy. Consequently, they would be in a position to contact individuals and companies, and encourage such potential customers to become depositors and to move some or all of their banking relations to the new institution. Mr. Turner proposed that each organizer-director be responsible for generating $1 million in deposits during the first operating year.

Marketing campaigns would be directed to the area's business and professional community. The organizers also intended to use advertising and public programs to communicate the proposed bank's services. They believed that recent legislation creating new deposit accounts would enable the Park Cities bank to compete effectively with money market funds for deposits.

Lending and Investment Strategies

The loan policy would need to meet all of the communities' needs. To begin operations, however, the founders expected to receive some assistance from correspondent banking relationships in obtaining the initial loans. It was anticipated that most of the loan portfolio would soon be originated by the bank itself. Mr. Turner planned to solicit and originate loans through the directors, the customer base, advertising, and direct contact with the local community through an officer call program.

In outlining a loan policy, Mr. Turner considered the following loans to be possibilities:

1. Interim construction loans.
2. Loans secured by marketable bonds, generally not to exceed 95 percent of the market value of U.S. government and federal agencies, 85 percent of state and political subdivisions, and 80 percent of the market value of corporate obligations.
3. Loans secured by marketable securities listed on a recognized stock exchange, not to exceed 75 percent of the market value.
4. Loans secured by over-the-counter stocks with adequate margins.
5. Loans secured by time or savings deposits with interest rates charged not less than 1 percent more than those earned on the deposits where such deposits are with the bank.
6. Loans to professional men and women (i.e., doctors, lawyers, dentists, and CPAs).
7. Participation loans.
8. Floor-plan loans which a significant banking relationship could develop.
9. Loans to business concerns secured by equipment, generally for 36 to 60 months, not to exceed the equipment's estimated useful life.
10. Aircraft loans at 75 percent of cost or appraised value, whichever is less.
11. Loans to companies secured by inventory with a margin of at least 50 percent. The inventory value and marketability must be determined and monitored.
12. Loans to companies secured by assignment of acceptable accounts receivable with a 30 percent margin. Accounts receivable would be from companies whose financial strength and payment record are known to be favorable.
13. Unsecured loans to businesses that exhibit a satisfactory balance sheet and earnings statement. These loans would largely be short term and self-liquidating.
14. Unsecured loans to individuals who are commercial customers.

A proposed investment policy had been developed along the following lines:

1. U.S. Treasury securities and U.S. government agency obligations would be the principal taxable portfolio component, as distinct from corporate bonds.
2. Maturities of taxable securities generally would be no longer than 7 years, and the average life of such securities would be 4.5 years or less.
3. U.S. government-guaranteed securities (taxable or tax-exempt) would be included within the guidelines that apply to taxable securities.
4. The quality of all tax-exempt securities would be no lower than "A" as established by major rating services or, in the absence of ratings, in the opinion of recognized bond dealers.
5. Investments would also consist of local and state obligations with maturities not to exceed 10 years.

6. Intermediate- and long-term bonds would be acquired as long as the average maturity of the tax-exempt portfolio did not exceed 10 years and the intermediate maturity did not exceed 7 years.

7. Tax-exempt securities of Texas issuers would be emphasized as far as practical.

8. Attention would be focused at all times on diversification in the investment portfolio.

Diversification should include geographical and industrial categories.

Asset-Liability Mix

The asset-liability mix proposed by the bank organizers would, it was hoped, minimize risk due to interest rate fluctuations. Mr. Turner planned to maintain a rate-sensitive asset (RSA) to rate-sensitive liability (RSL) ratio of between 0.8 and 1.2. This policy was intended to stabilize the bank's long-run earning power. When a board-designated committee believed interest rates would rise, it could take actions to increase the RSA/RSL ratio toward 1.2. On the other hand, the committee could decide to decrease the RSA/RSL ratio toward 0.8 when it concluded that rates might decline.

Physical Facilities

The organizers were considering permanent facilities that would be located on approximately 23,000 square feet at the southwest corner intersection of Hillcrest Avenue and University Boulevard. The bank would lease space in a projected 30,000-square-foot, two-story building. Mr. Turner anticipated that the opening needs would total 7,500 square feet with an option to expand, eventually occupying the entire building. The bank would initially be operating four teller stations, reserving space to add two more future teller positions.

Assumptions Used to Determine Pro Forma Balance Sheets and Income Statements

The pro forma balance sheets and income statements developed by Mr. Turner were derived by forecasting total deposit levels for the first three years and then constructing income statements based on assumptions about cost and operating ratios. Deposits were projected based on average market-area income, the growth and development of area residential and commercial markets, and the other banks' experience in Dallas County. (See Exhibits 5 to 7.)

The key assumptions were as follows:

1. Deposits and expenses would be accrued uniformly throughout the year. This would permit averages to be used in determining the profit-loss statement. Since the bank would have its initial capital invested in government securities at opening, it was assumed that investment securities would average $5.18 million for the first year.

2. Loans and discounts were estimated to yield 13.5 percent throughout the three-year period. Investment securities would yield an estimated 11 percent for the three years. The average cost of time deposits was assumed at 8.5 percent for the period. NOW accounts were estimated to cost 5.25 percent, and Super NOW accounts would average 8.5 percent. These rates were estimated from recent interest levels and average rates forecast during the three-year period.

3. Employee wages and benefits were increased from the initial base at 10 percent annually. The level of wages and the annual increases were determined from discussions by the organizers about appropriate levels necessary to attract competent employees in the Dallas County market.

4. The demand-deposit/time-deposit ratio was 20 to 80 percent. This assumption was based on area bank experience and the anticipation that time deposits would continue to constitute a larger fraction of total deposits.

5. The loan-to-deposit ratio was forecast at 60, 65, and 70 percent, respectively, for the first three years. These ratios reflected the experience of newly chartered urban banks in Texas.

6. The first-year $20 million deposit forecast was large for suburban banks. The organizers believed, however, that this level of deposits was realistic because (a) the market was the most affluent in Dallas; (b) the bank's marketing plan assigned an "obligation" level of $1 million in deposits that each organizer would, it was hoped, be able to attract during the first year; and (c) Mr. Turner had served as the principal banker for business firms and individuals that he believed would shift deposits to the new institution.

7. Although Mr. Turner expected to attract public funds, the amount and timing of these deposits would be highly variable. Accordingly, no such funds were incorporated in the pro forma forecasts.

A short biographical comment on each of the bank's probable organizers follows.

Tom E. Turner Mr. Turner was currently serving full-time coordinating the bank's organizing effort. He graduated from the University of Texas (BBA-

General Business) and the Southwestern Graduate School of Banking at Southern Methodist University. He was previously employed by InterFirst Bank Dallas, entering the executive training program in 1963 and becoming a vice-president in the Correspondent-Southwest Division of that bank in 1965.

In 1973, Mr. Turner joined BancTexas, Dallas. At the time of his resignation in May 1983, Mr. Turner was a senior vice-president, serving as the group head of the bank's Correspondent Division/National and as a member of the Senior Credit Policy Committee and the Senior Loan Committee. In these positions, he was responsible for loan and deposit portfolios in excess of $100 million, and he supervised a 15-person staff.

A resident of the Park Cities, Mr. Turner brought over 21 years of banking experience in Dallas to the investing group. As an executive officer of important Dallas banks, he had been actively involved in the formation of lending policies and in the careful scrutiny of credit applications. Furthermore, he had experience in serving the needs of individuals and businesses located within the proposed bank's market area.

In his prior position, Mr. Turner was responsible for managing the accounts of several bank directors and the personal accounts of major business customers. Turner believed that serving the financial needs of executives would prove very helpful in developing the proposed bank's services.

Webber W. Beall, Jr. Mr. Beall was a partner in the law firm of Touchstone, Bernays, Johnston, Beall & Smith. He graduated from Southern Methodist University (BBA-Accounting) in 1954 and Southern Methodist University School of Law (LLB) in 1959. Mr. Beall's knowledge of the market-area residents, both socially and professionally, would enable him to contribute to business development and the profit potential of the proposed bank.

William P. Carr, Jr. Mr. Carr was an owner of Carr Petroleum Corporation, Inc., a family-owned oil and gas business operating properties in Texas, New Mexico, and Kansas and drilling on properties located in these states, as well as in Colorado and Nebraska. Mr. Carr graduated from the University of Texas in 1963 (BS-Economics). Prior to his current position, he was an investment banker with First Southwest Company. He served on numerous

boards of business, educational, and charitable institutions.

Edward F. Doran Mr. Doran is the co-owner and co-manager of Doran Chevrolet-Peugeot, Inc. He is a graduate of Southern Methodist University (BBA-General Business). He was very knowledgeable about the market area's business and residents and was in a good position to attract customers to the proposed bank.

R. William Gribble, Jr. Mr. Gribble was the owner of Gribble Oil Corporation, an independent oil and gas production company. He is a graduate of the University of Texas (BS-Geology) and the University of Oklahoma (BS-Geological Engineering). Mr. Gribble intended to support the new bank with his business and personal accounts while assisting in bringing new customers to the institution.

Harrell S. "Buddy" Hayden Mr. Hayden was the managing partner of Hayden & Smith Co., a commercial real estate sales and leasing company. He is a graduate of the University of Texas (BBA-Marketing). He was a past president of the Greater Dallas Board of Realtors and had served on the Texas Association of Realtors' board of directors. Mr. Hayden had actively participated in the bank's site selection. He was a lifelong resident of the Park Cities.

James E. Herring Mr. Herring was president and chairman of the board of Marcom International, Inc., a commodity trading and commodity futures brokerage. Mr. Herring attended the University of Houston and is a graduate of the University of Texas (BBA-Finance) and Harvard Graduate School of Business. Mr. Herring served as a director of Tascosa National Bank of Amarillo from 1970 to 1979.

Henry D. Lindsley III Mr. Lindsley was the chairman of the board of Higginbotham-Bartlett Company of New Mexico, a retail lumber and hardware concern. He is a graduate of the University of Texas (BBA). Mr. Lindsley had served as a director of First National Bank of Brownsville (Texas). He and his family were lifelong residents of Dallas.

Edwin J. Luedtke, Jr. Mr. Luedtke was a partner in the firm of Luedtke, Aldridge, Pendleton, Inc., a commercial real estate development and brokerage company. He is a graduate of Rice University (BA and BS) and the University of Virginia (MBA).

Michael A. McBee   Mr. McBee was a partner in an oil and gas exploration and production company. He is a graduate of the New Mexico Military Institute. Mr. McBee and his family were lifelong residents of Dallas.

Donald J. Malouf   Mr. Malouf was an attorney serving as president of the law firm Malouf, Lynch & Jackson, a professional corporation. He is a graduate of the University of Texas (BA and MBA) and Southern Methodist University School of Law (LLB). Mr. Malouf had prior experience as a director of other financial institutions.

Robert A. Massad   Mr. Massad was the president of MAS/TER Realty, Inc., a full-service real estate company engaged in the brokerage, development, management, and acquisition of real estate in the Dallas area. He is a graduate of Southern Methodist University (BBA-Banking and Finance). Mr. Massad had a great deal of experience in analyzing and financing the acquisition of real estate in the Dallas area.

Matthew C. Roberts III   Mr. Roberts was a self-employed investor. He is a graduate of Southern Methodist University (BS-Geology). Mr. Roberts had been active in the Dallas-Park Cities area all of his life. Moreover, he had served as a director of Terrell State Bank (now InterFirst Bank-Terrell) for over 14 years.

Wade C. Smith   Mr. Smith was an attorney and the managing partner of the firm Touchstone, Bernays, Johnston, Beall & Smith. He is a graduate of the University of Texas and the University of Texas School of Law and has been consistently active in community activities in both Dallas and the Park Cities.

Tom J. Stollenwerck   Mr. Stollenwerck was an attorney and partner in the firm Touchstone, Bernays, Johnston, Beall & Smith. He is a graduate of Southern Methodist University and Southern Methodist University School of Law.

John C. Vogt   Mr. Vogt was the president of International Supply Co., Inc., a wholesale distributor of plumbing, utility, and industrial supplies. He is a graduate of the University of Texas. He was a resident of the Park Cities and was a member of numerous civic and charitable area organizations.

The organizing group, under Tom Turner's leadership, was greatly encouraged by the prospects for a new bank in the Park Cities area. The members believed that as much as $5 million in common stock could be raised from the organizers and some area residents to launch this new venture. They realized, however, that there were some real risks attached to this undertaking. In particular, they were concerned about the level of competition, which was currently strong and growing; the challenges in marketing and selling a new bank to the Park Cities community, given the presence of several other well-sponsored new banking organizations; and finally, the attractiveness of the return on investment for this new institution. Although they had gathered the necessary data and had completed a preliminary charter application, the group was still uncertain whether the final decision should be made to invest this large amount of capital and to proceed with the venture.

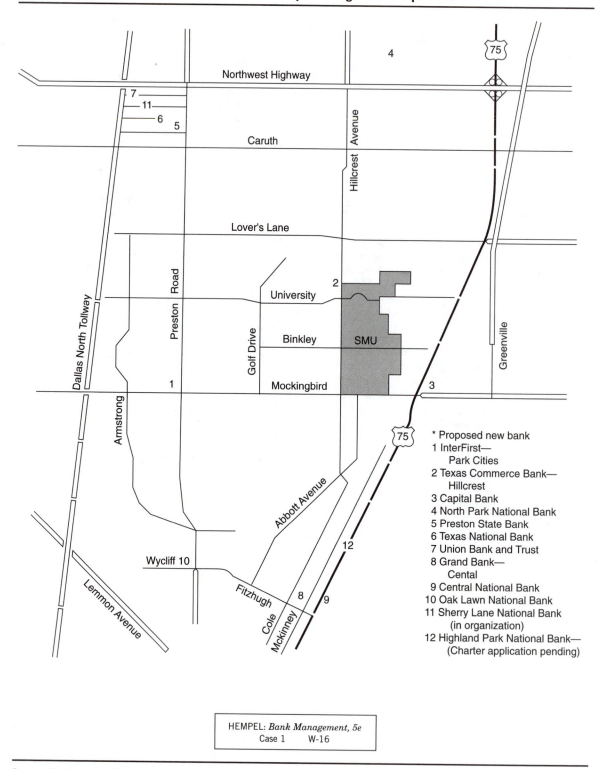

* Proposed new bank
1 InterFirst—
  Park Cities
2 Texas Commerce Bank—
  Hillcrest
3 Capital Bank
4 North Park National Bank
5 Preston State Bank
6 Texas National Bank
7 Union Bank and Trust
8 Grand Bank—
  Cental
9 Central National Bank
10 Oak Lawn National Bank
11 Sherry Lane National Bank
  (in organization)
12 Highland Park National Bank—
  (Charter application pending)

HEMPEL: *Bank Management, 5e*
Case 1   W-16

SOURCE: Southwestern Graduate School of Banking.

EXHIBIT 2   First National Bank of Park Cities—Economic Data for the Park Cities

	City of Highland Park	City of University Park
Demographics		
Total population, 1980 final census	8,909	22,254
Estimated population, Jan. 1, 1983	8,950	23,300
Households, 1980	3,702	8,597
Average household size, 1980	2.41	2.24
Income		
Median family income, 1980	$52,742	$33,763
Housing		
Total housing units, 1980	3,950	9,040
Vacant units, 1980	248	443
Occupancy rate (percent), 1980	93.7	95.1
Single-family units, 1980	3,132	7,458
Multifamily units, 1980	818	1,578
Median housing value, 1980	$200,100	$126,900

SOURCE: U.S. Bureau of the Census, 1980, and North Central Texas Council of Governments.

**EXHIBIT 3   Estimated Retail Sales for the Cities of Highland Park
and University Park**

Year	University Park	Percent Change	Highland Park	Percent Change
1982	$107,723,720	+ 7.45	$62,017,135	+22.94
1981	100,251,400	+ 4.41	50,443,090	+ 6.50
1980	96,019,811	+23.69	47,364,877	+18.93
1979	77,626,933	+18.27	39,825,047	+26.80
1978	65,632,793	—	31,406,769	—

SOURCE: Texas Comptroller of Public Accounts, Sales Tax Office.

EXHIBIT 4 Selected Market-Area Banks, Loan and Deposit Summary 1977–1982

	1982		1981		1980		1979		1978		1977	
	Deposits	Loans	Deposits	Loans	Deposits	Loans	Deposits	Loans	Deposits	Loans	Deposits	Loans
InterFirst Bank-Park Cities	$ 214,320,000	$160,635,000	$173,333,000	$119,762,000	$137,809,000	$ 93,819,000	$ 97,232,764	$ 73,234,716	$ 81,569,070	$ 62,993,882	$ 70,034,774	$ 46,363,461
Texas Commerce Bank-Hillcrest	80,485,000	53,646,000	65,079,000	24,735,000	57,967,955	31,310,212	55,139,881	29,000,460	52,020,788	22,772,425	52,466,301	28,689,923
Capital Bank	83,125,000	50,794,000	68,888,526	45,017,412	55,658,207	32,012,366	48,417,032	29,980,232	31,381,372	22,890,986	23,885,127	16,150,610
North Park National Bank	262,233,600	175,878,600	225,921,000	154,200,000	188,671,254	104,854,507	143,249,554	82,278,323	103,998,109	65,985,780	81,134,537	46,334,174
Grand Bank-Central	In organization											
Preston State Bank	391,260,818	330,594,007	372,024,313	273,547,621	344,662,965	228,574,392	294,920,225	214,707,936	237,812,309	178,236,720	205,081,288	143,460,301
Texas National Bank	14,630,173	9,440,030	In organization									
Union Bank and Trust	37,461,347	25,224,417	29,335,600	12,812,637	22,609,540	9,988,313	20,850,157	16,952,675	13,845,990	11,016,694	10,379,483	9,586,010
Central National Bank	In organization											
Oak Lawn Bank	In organization											
Sherry Lane National Bank	In organization											
Highland Park National Bank	Charter pending											
Total Market-Area Banks	$1,083,516,000	$806,212,000	$934,582,000	$630,075,000	$807,380,000	$500,558,000	$659,810,000	$446,155,000	$520,627,000	$363,896,000	$442,981,000	$290,584,000

SOURCE: *Texas Banking Red Book*, 1978–1983, Banker's Digest, Inc.; FDIC Call Reports.

EXHIBIT 5   First National Bank of Park Cities—Pro Forma Balance Sheet (dollars in thousands)

	Year-end Balance						Average Balance for Income Generation		
	First Year	Percentage	Second Year	Percentage	Third Year	Percentage	First Year	Second Year	Third Year
Cash and due from banks	$ 2,175	(9)	$ 3,562	(10)	$ 4,637	(10)			
Investment securities	8,633	(36)	9,894	(29)	10,605	(24)	5,180	9,264	10,250
Loans	12,000	(50)	19,500	(56)	28,000	(62)	6,000	15,750	23,750
Fixed assets	679	(3)	598	(2)	517	(1)			
Other assets	716	(3)	1,020	(3)	1,332	(3)			
Total assets	$24,203	(100)	$34,574	(100)	$45,090	(100)			
Demand deposits	$ 4,000	(17)	$ 6,000	(17)	$ 8,000	(18)	2,000	5,000	7,000
Time and savings deposits	16,000	(66)	24,000	(69)	32,000	(71)	8,000	20,000	28,000
Total deposits	$20,000	(83)	$30,000	(87)	$40,000	(89)	10,000	25,000	35,000
Other liabilities	475	(2)	678	(2)	884	(2)			
Common stock	2,000	(8)	2,000	(6)	2,000	(4)			
Surplus	2,000	(8)	2,000	(6)	2,000	(4)			
Undivided profits	(272)	(−1.1)	(104)	(−0.3)	206	(0.5)			
Total capital funds	$ 3,728	(15)	$ 3,896	(11)	$ 4,206	(9)			
Total liabilities and capital	$24,203	(100)	$34,574	(100)	$45,090	(100)			

Note: Because of rounding, percentages do not always equal 100%.

EXHIBIT 6   First National Bank of Park Cities—Operating Income and Expense (dollars in thousands)

	First Year	Second Year	Third Year
Operating Income			
Interest and fees on loans	$ 810	$2,126	$3,206
Interest on investment securities	570	1,019	1,125
Other operating income[a]	160	230	310
Total operating income	$1,540	$3,375	$4,641
Operating Expense			
Officer salaries and benefits	$ 235	$ 289	$ 358
Employee salaries and benefits	195	320	487
Interest on deposits	680	1,700	2,300
Net occupancy expense[b]	276	276	276
Provision for loan losses	60	158	238
Other expenses[c]	247	464	594
Total operating expense	$1,693	$3,207	$4,253
Subtotal: Income minus expense	$ (153)	$ 168	$ 388
Income taxes	—	—	78
Net operating income (loss)	(153)	168	310
Beginning capital funds	$4,000	$3,728	$3,896
Less organization expense[d]	(119)	—	—
Add/subtract net operating income/loss	(153)	168	310
Ending capital funds	$3,728	$3,896	$4,206
Number of officers	4	5	6
Number of other employees	13	20	29

[a] Includes service charges, insufficient check fees, exchange fees, and so on.

[b] Includes rental of building, amortization of leasehold improvements, and furniture and equipment expense.

[c] Includes stationery, printing, postage, data processing, accounting, examination fees, advertising, telephone, and so on.

[d] Includes Mr. Turner's salary, in addition to the Comptroller's filing fee, and the attorney's and economist's fees.

**EXHIBIT 7   First National Bank of Park Cities—Information on Loans and Deposits
(dollars in thousands)**

	First Year	(%)	Second Year	(%)	Third Year	(%)
Loan Detail						
Real estate loans	$ 2,400	(20)	$ 3,900	(20)	$ 5,600	(20)
Commercial loans	4,800	(40)	7,800	(40)	11,200	(40)
Installment loans	4,200	(35)	6,825	(35)	9,800	(35)
Other loans	600	(5)	975	(5)	1,400	(5)
Total	$12,000		$19,500		$28,000	
Demand Deposit Detail						
NOW accounts	$ 200	(5)	$ 300	(5)	$ 400	(5)
Regular checking	1,800	(45)	2,700	(45)	3,600	(45)
Corporate and business checking	2,000	(50)	3,000	(50)	4,000	(50)
Public funds	—	(0)	—	(0)	—	(0)
Total	$ 4,000		$ 6,000		$ 8,000	
Time and Savings Deposits Detail						
Automatic transfers	—	(0)	—	(0)	—	(0)
Regular passbook savings	$ 800	(5)	$ 1,200	(5)	$ 2,000	(6)
Money market deposits and Super NOW accounts	10,400	(65)	15,600	(65)	18,000	(56)
Money market CDs less than $10,000	800	(5)	1,200	(5)	2,000	(6)
CDs over $10,000	800	(5)	1,200	(5)	2,000	(6)
CDs over $100,000	3,200	(20)	4,800	(20)	8,000	(25)
Public funds	—	(0)	—	(0)	—	(0)
Total	$16,000		$24,000		$32,000	

EXHIBIT 8   First National Bank of Park Cities—National Bank Charters Compared to State Bank Charters

1. STATUTORY REQUIREMENTS

National Bank

The Comptroller of the Currency ("Comptroller") charters national banks pursuant to the standards set forth in the National Bank Act of 1864, the Federal Deposit Insurance Act of 1935, and the Community Reinvestment Act. The Comptroller's decision is based upon objective facts and subjective judgment. The National Bank Act delineates the procedure necessary to obtain a charter.

The broad statutory factors considered by the Comptroller in deciding whether to approve or disapprove applications to organize new banks are derived from the Federal Deposit Insurance Act and include: (12 C.F.R. #5.20(b))

1. The bank's future earnings prospects.
2. The general character of its management.
3. The adequacy of its capital structure.
4. The convenience and needs of the community to be served by the bank.
5. The financial history and condition of the bank.
6. The compliance with the National Bank Act.
7. Whether the corporate powers are consistent with the Federal Deposit Insurance Act.

Although a literal reading of the National Bank Act requires the Comptroller to grant a charter if the statutory standards are met, the Comptroller's discretion to deny a charter is unquestioned.

The Act provides that a national bank may be organized by five or more natural persons who enter into articles of association specifying the objectives for which the association is formed. The organizers also prepare an organization certificate stating the name of the association, which must include the word "national," the place of operation, the amount of capital stock, the number of shares, the names and addresses of shareholders, the number of shares held by each shareholder, and the fact that the certificate is made to enable the persons to organize a bank under the national banking laws (12 C.F.R. #27, 28).

The initial capital of a national bank is the amount of its unimpaired common stock plus the amount of preferred stock outstanding and unimpaired. The statutory minimum capital of a national bank depends upon the population of the city where the bank is located (12 U.S.C. #51).

Population of City	Capital Requirement for National Bank
1. 6,000 or fewer inhabitants	Not less than $50,000
2. 6,001–50,000 inhabitants	Not less than $100,000
3. More than 50,000	Not less than $200,000

However, this statutory minimum is deemed inadequate by the Comptroller; generally at least $1 million in capital is required before authorization to commence business (12 C.F.R. #5.20(c)(3)(iii)).

State Bank (Texas Civil Statutes)

Art. 342-300. Application for and Granting of Charters Approval

A. Applications for a state bank charter shall be granted only upon good and sufficient proof that all of the following conditions presently exist:

1. A public necessity exists for the proposed bank.
2. The proposed capital structure is adequate.
3. The volume of business in the community where such proposed bank is to be established is such as to indicate profitable operation of the proposed bank.

EXHIBIT 8   *(Continued)*

4. The proposed officers and directors have sufficient banking experience, ability, and standing to render success of the proposed bank probable.
5. The applicants are acting in good faith.

The burden to establish said conditions shall be upon the applicants.

B. Applicants desiring to incorporate a state bank shall file with the Banking Commissioner an application for charter upon official forms prepared and prescribed by the Commissioner. All persons subscribing to the capital stock of the proposed bank shall sign and verify under oath a statement of such stock subscribed, and which statement shall truly report the number of shares and the amount to be paid in consideration; the names, identity, title, and address of any other persons who will be beneficial owners of such stock or otherwise share an interest or ownership in said stock, or who will pay any portion of the consideration; whether said stock is to be pledged as security for any loan; whether a loan has been committed or is intended for the subscription and purchase of said stock, and if so, the name and address of such person or corporation which is intended to loan funds for said purchase; the names of any cosigners, guarantors, partners or other persons liable for the repayment of any loan financing the purchase of such stock. Provided, however, that the verified statement of subscribers to stock shall be confidential and privileged from public disclosure prior to the final determination by the Board of the application for a charter, unless the Board shall find that public disclosure prior to public hearing and final determination of the charter application is necessary to a full development of the factual record.

C. The Commissioner shall require deposit of such charter fees as are required by law and shall proceed to conduct a thorough investigation of the application, the applicants and their personnel, and the charter conditions alleged. The actual expense of such investigation and report shall be paid by the applicants, and the Commissioner may require a deposit in an estimated amount, the balance to be paid in full prior to hearing of the application. A written report of the investigation shall be furnished to the State Banking Board and shall be made available to all interested parties at their request.

D. Upon filing of the application, the Commissioner shall promptly set the time and place for public hearing of the application for charter, giving the applicants reasonable notice thereof. Before the 10th day preceding the day on which the hearing is held, the Commissioner shall publish notice of the hearing in a newspaper of general circulation in the county where the proposed bank is to be located. After full and public hearing the Board shall vote and determine whether the necessary conditions set out in Section A above have been established. Should the Board, or a majority of the Board, determine all of the said conditions affirmatively, then the application shall be approved; if not, then the application shall be denied. If approved, and when the Commissioner receives satisfactory evidence that the capital has been paid in full in cash, the Commissioner shall deliver to the incorporators a certified copy of the Articles of Association, and the bank shall come into corporate existence. Provided, however, that the State Banking Board may make its approval of any application conditional, and in such event shall set out such condition in the resolution granting the charter, and the Commissioner shall not deliver the certified copy of the Articles of Association until such condition has been met, after which the Commissioner shall in writing inform the State Banking Board as to compliance with such condition and delivery of the Articles of Association.

Article 342-301. Powers

Subject to the provisions of this Code, five (5) or more persons, a majority of whom are residents of this state, may incorporate a state bank, with any one or more of all the following powers:

(a) To receive time and demand deposits at interest or without interest; to lend money with or without security at interest; and to buy, sell, and discount bonds, negotiable instruments and other evidences of indebtedness.

(b) To act as fiscal agent or transfer agent and in such capacity to receive and disburse money and to transfer registered and countersigned certificates of stock, bonds, or other evidences of indebtedness.

EXHIBIT 8 *(Continued)*

(c) To act as trustee under any mortgage or bond issue and to accept and execute any trust not inconsistent with the laws of this state.

(d) To act under the order or appointment of any court of record, without giving bond, as guardian, receiver, trustee, executor, administrator and, although without general depository powers, as depository for any moneys paid into court.

(e) To purchase, invest in, and sell bills of exchange, bonds, mortgages, and other evidences of indebtedness, and to lend money and to charge and collect interest thereon in advance or otherwise.

(f) To receive savings deposits with or without the payment of interest.

(g) To receive time deposits with or without the payment of interest.

(h) To issue, sell and negotiate notes, bonds and other evidences of indebtedness, and, in addition, to issue and sell, for cash or on an installment basis, investment certificates, creating no relation of debtor and creditor between the bank and the holder, to be retired solely out of specified surplus, reserves, or special retirement account, and containing such provisions relative to yield, retirement, penalties, withdrawal values, and obligations of the issuing bank as may be approved by the Commissioner.

A state bank shall have all incidental powers necessary to exercise its specific powers.

Article 342-303. Capital, Surplus, and Reserve Requirements
Repealed by Acts 1981, 67th Leg., eff. May 20, 1981.

Art. 342-304. Articles of Association
The articles of association of a state bank shall be signed and acknowledged by each incorporator and shall contain:

1. The name of the corporation.
2. The city or town and the county of its domicile.
3. Such of the powers listed in Article 1 of this Charter as it shall choose to exercise.
4. The capital and the denomination and number of shares.
5. The number of directors.
6. The period of duration, which may be perpetual.

2. NATIONAL OR STATE CHARTERS

National Bank

Advantages	Disadvantages
Free use of check-clearing facilities	Must hold stock in the Federal Reserve System equal to 3% of its capital and surplus, and such amount must be kept in nonincome-producing status
Use of the Federal Reserve discount window	
Automatically become members of FDIC	
	Not permitted to lend on unimproved real estate
	Can make loans to a single customer up to only 15% of capital and surplus if it is unsecured; 25% if it is secured

EXHIBIT 8   *(Continued)*

State Bank

Advantages	Disadvantage
May count correspondent balances as a part of its reserve requirement and still produce income from those reserves	Must elect membership and be approved by FDIC
Is permitted to lend on unimproved real estate	
Can make loans to a single customer up to a level equal to 20% of capital and surplus	

CASE 2

LINCOLN NATIONAL BANK

INTRODUCTION

Jeff Vigil pushed his chair back from the desk where he had been absorbed in analyzing the bank's changing financial structure. It was January 1996 and the bank was making good money now. But Jeff's natural caution had him thinking about how the good times at the bank in the mid-1980s precipitated the hard times and large loan losses of the late 1980s. "We're smarter now," Jeff thought, "and there's been a change in management. But let's not fail to learn from the past." With that thought, he set about reviewing the possible exposures the bank might have at present.

Exhibit 1 contains several key pages from Lincoln National's Uniform Bank Performance Report for December 1995. Lincoln National Bank held $233 million in assets (UBPR04)[1] in a thriving tourist city with a market area of 100,000 people. The bank was closely held by two shareholder groups in a tiered holding company structure; one of the groups controlled 60 percent of the stock. The bank's charter dated from the 1860s. The city had experienced a sustained tourist boom and influx of new residents for nearly a decade. The new residents, both part time and full time, enjoyed incomes and pensions that were considerably higher than those received by most local residents. Recently, the newcomers had fueled a boom in housing values and the construction of new homes. Many of them purchased local housing as their second homes.

CREDIT HISTORY

Vigil joined the bank as CFO early in 1991 when the bank's earnings had started to rebound (UBPR02). At the time, however, noncurrent loans as a percentage of total loans was over 5 percent and placed the bank in the top 10 percent of its peers in this category. The credit quality picture brightened at this time (UBPR01) when the bank's new management installed strong credit policies and controls and temporarily reduced lending activity (gross loans and leases—UBPR04). The bank's large OREO (other real estate owned) portfolio declined rapidly through 1995 (UBPR04), and large gains were taken on the sale of OREO property on two occasions, including a $240,000 gain in 1994. Finally, in 1994, the bank reversed $300,000 of its loss allowance into income (provision—UBPR02) at the behest of regulators who deemed it excessive.

Following recovery from its bad loans, the bank's loan portfolio began to grow rapidly—including a 30 percent growth in 1995 (UBPR04)—driving interest income (UBPR01). The bank has long been a leader in commercial real estate lending. It prices loans to this market at variable rates of 300 basis points over the bank's base rate. The bank's reputation historically has been that of a well-to-do busi-

[1] Uniform Bank Performance Report (Exhibit 1) page references appear throughout the case. As a UBPR familiarization exercise, the reader should find data at these references to verify the facts cited in the case narrative.

nessman's bank, and it has always enjoyed the business of downtown merchants (some of whose businesses were quite "tourist sensitive"). Starting in 1994, Lincoln National accelerated its large position in home mortgage lending (real estate loans—UBPR04) by offering highly competitive interest rates. Bank officers began making persistent calls on real estate brokers, and the bank launched a campaign of advertising its strongly competitive loan rates in local newspapers and real estate circulars. Responding to market demand, the bank placed most of its recent home mortgage business at fixed rates. Whereas previously the bank sold most loans into the secondary market, it now began to hold more loans on the balance sheet. In addition, in 1994, Lincoln National introduced its home equity line of credit which quickly generated good volume (UBPR05). Also in 1994, the bank offered an unsecured line of credit which customers could access simply by writing a check against the line. These two products experienced increasing delinquencies, causing the bank to withdraw its unsecured consumer line of credit product (UBPR05).

FUNDING POLICIES

Lately, the boom in lending had tended to dry up excess funds. In 1995, core deposit growth funded only $0.8 million of $41.2 million loan growth (UBPR04). To meet loan growth, the bank aggressively sold off securities holdings (UBPR04). In spring 1995 the bank borrowed from the Fed discount window for the first time in many years. In addition, as Fed funds sales plummeted (UBPR04), the bank obtained a large increase in the Fed funds line, with its primary correspondent in the state's largest city. Coincident with funding pressures, the bank joined the Federal Home Loan Bank (FHLB) of Dallas in 1994, and in 1995 it started to borrow significant amounts of longer-term funds of up to ten years maturity to support portfolio mortgages (other borrowings > 1 yr.—UBPR06).

Lincoln's deposit base produces low interest expense (UBPR01) based on an unusual number of small business and long-term individual depositors with ample balances in transaction accounts (demand deposits and all NOW & ATS accounts—UBPR06). The bank never attempts to lead the market in deposit rates and, on certain accounts, tries to remain near the market's bottom. For example, rates on large CDs are below market and are not advertised, although the bank does execute re-purchase agreements for large customer accounts at rates above Fed funds. On the other hand, the bank promptly resets its rates on money market and NOW accounts. Excess funds, when available, are sold through the FHLB into the overnight liquidity market at a discount from the Fed funds rate.

Lincoln National operates seven branches compared with its larger cross-town rival bank affiliate of a large multiregional banking company, which operates only three branches. In part, this results in much higher personnel expense as a percent of average assets (UBPR03). The bank's pride in its employees is shown by its above-average personnel expense *per employee* (UBPR03) and its generous benefits package, averaging nearly 30 percent of salaries. The bank has operated a trust department for many generations. By 1996, over $200 million in trust assets were under the management of a staff of 12 employees. Trust generated nearly $1 million in revenue, giving the bank above-average noninterest income (UBPR01). In other activities during 1994, Lincoln National installed a wide area network and a new teller system, remodeled its 20-year-old operations center, and moved its real estate loan department to a new location. In the early 1990s, the bank replaced an old computer mainframe with a turnkey AS400 processing system designed for community bank needs. The bank's operations center was returned to its home city after several years in the large city an hour and a half away where the bank had maintained a now defunct branch. A local branch was closed in 1991, causing losses owing to the buyout of a facility rental agreement.

ALCO PROCESS

Lincoln National Bank's asset and liability management objective is "to control and maximize overall profitability while maintaining sound liquidity and capital adequacy with prudent management of risk." Asset and liability committee (ALCO) membership includes the president, chief financial officer, senior retail banking officer, senior lending officer, senior trust officer, marketing director, controller, and assistant controller. The CFO chairs the committee, and members who cannot attend any given meeting must find a replacement for themselves. The ALCO process is controlled by several formal written bank policies for asset and liability management, investments, cash management, liquidity management, and dividends.

Controls

Included in the asset and liability management policy are several quantified guidelines that specify maximums, minimums, or target ranges for certain critical "ALCO ratios." These are listed in Exhibit 2. Interest rate sensitivity is measured and controlled in two dimensions: gap ratios and sensitivity of net interest income to an interest rate shock. In the case of gap ratios, the policy sets a target range of 0.8 to 1.2 for the one-year cumulative ratio of rate-sensitive assets to rate-sensitive liabilities, and a target range of −15 percent to +15 percent for the one-year cumulative ratio of gap-to-assets. In addition, the policy stipulates a limit on the interest rate sensitivity of net interest income. Simulated annual net interest income must not vary by more than 25 percent of projected net interest income in reaction to an across-the-board interest rate shock of 200 basis points.

Other guidelines include minimum liquidity of 15 percent (see Exhibit 3 for Liquidity Report), loans to deposit ratio between 65.0 and 80.0 percent, maximum large CDs to total deposits of 25 percent, and maximum public deposits to total deposits of 10 percent.

ALCO Input

ALCO meets once a month and reviews the following reports:

- Minutes from the prior meeting
- Three-page gap report including detailed gap, average rates, and a condensed gap (Exhibit 4)
- ALCO ratios report (Exhibit 2)
- Securities listing (par values, maturities, unpledged securities, unrealized gain/loss on portfolio)
- Recent securities transactions report detailing current month purchases and maturities
- In addition, ALCO receives a report on changes

in demand patterns for various maturities of small CDs.

ALCO Output

ALCO manipulates the maturity structure of its securities portfolio as a principal tool for controlling interest rate sensitivity. ALCO may also vary the volume of fixed rate (as opposed to adjustable rate) mortgages for this purpose. A so-called mini ALCO subcommittee, consisting of two or more ALCO members, meets on an as-needed basis and makes all investment decisions. There is no single designated investment officer. An outside portfolio management service provides recommendations concerning portfolio management.

In addition, ALCO members meet weekly as an interest rate subcommittee. At these meetings, the subcommittee reviews deposit interest rates and decides on changes in rates to be offered. This subcommittee uses a rate tracking report to monitor the local deposit prices of competitor banks in the community.

One major committee that operates somewhat independently of ALCO is the bank's senior loan committee. However, the senior lending officer is an important participant of both committees.

Budget Process

The annual budget or "plan" is prepared with a computer model that applies three alternative interest rate scenarios (rising rates, flat rates, and falling rates). Senior management selects the scenario that it thinks is most likely to occur. Management does not believe in revising the budget once it is established, regardless of the subsequent course of interest rates. However, a 200-basis-point rate shock is applied to the selected budget to ascertain the sensitivity of net interest income and conformance to interest sensitivity guidelines (see Exhibit 2).

EXHIBIT I Lincoln National Bank Summary Ratios

CERT # 2239 DSB # 10350340
CHARTER # 1750 COUNTY:

SUMMARY RATIOS

	12/31/95			12/31/94			12/31/93			12/31/92		12/31/91	
	BANK	PEER 07	PCT	BANK	PEER 07	PCT	BANK	PEER 07	PCT	BANK	PEER 07	BANK	PEER 07
AVERAGE ASSETS ($000)	219922			205207			192604			178714		179365	
NET INCOME ($000)	2994			2504			2920			1916		1174	
NUMBER OF BANKS IN PEER GROUPS	932			948			949			969		930	

EARNINGS AND PROFITABILITY

PERCENT OF AVERAGE ASSETS:

	BANK	PEER 07	PCT	BANK	PEER 07	PCT	BANK	PEER 07	PCT	BANK	PEER 07	BANK	PEER 07
INTEREST INCOME (TE)	8.27	7.83	73	6.84	7.13	33	6.44	7.13	16	7.49	7.86	8.96	9.07
− INTEREST EXPENSE	2.42	3.20	11	1.77	2.52	08	1.75	2.56	06	2.36	3.31	3.77	4.73
NET INTEREST INCOME (TE)	5.85	4.61	91	5.07	4.59	76	4.69	4.52	62	5.13	4.53	5.19	4.32
+ NONINTEREST INCOME	1.36	0.86	81	1.55	0.90	84	1.84	0.96	88	1.48	0.90	1.35	0.85
+ MEMO: FEE INCOME	0.25	0.18	70	0.27	0.19	69	0.25	0.20	65	0.17	0.18	0.16	0.17
− NON-INTEREST EXPENSE	5.05	3.51	89	4.94	3.65	87	4.61	3.65	79	4.87	3.59	5.20	3.51
= PROVISION: LOANS & LEASE LOSSES	0.00	0.14	15	−0.15	0.13	02	0.02	0.20	15	0.20	0.34	0.33	0.37
= PRETAX OPERATING INCOME (TE)	2.16	1.84	67	1.83	1.75	53	1.91	1.69	60	1.54	1.55	1.01	1.33
+ REALIZED GAIN/LOSS SECS	0.00	0.00	74	0.00	0.00	77	0.00	0.02	44	0.13	0.04	0.00	0.02
= PRETAX NET OPERATING INC (TE)	2.16	1.84	67	1.83	1.73	54	1.91	1.74	58	1.67	1.64	1.01	1.39
NET OPERATING INCOME	1.36	1.18	66	1.22	1.12	59	1.42	1.12	74	1.07	1.05	0.65	0.89
ADJUSTED NET OPERATING INCOME	1.33	1.23	59	1.08	1.16	42	1.53	1.18	77	1.11	1.14	0.40	0.97
ADJUSTED NET OPERATING INCOME	1.35	1.22	61	1.15	1.15	49	1.42	1.19	68	1.11	1.13	0.50	0.96
NET INCOME	1.36	1.19	66	1.22	1.12	59	1.52	1.16	79	1.07	1.06	0.65	0.90

MARGIN ANALYSIS:

	BANK	PEER 07	PCT	BANK	PEER 07	PCT	BANK	PEER 07	PCT	BANK	PEER 07	BANK	PEER 07
AVG EARNING ASSETS TO AVG ASSETS	92.94	92.96	48	92.56	92.68	47	92.83	92.45	54	91.96	92.45	90.86	92.52
AVG INT-BEARING FUNDS TO AVG AST	68.72	75.40	16	69.08	75.67	15	69.63	76.58	16	70.75	77.86	73.03	78.59
INT INC (TE) TO AVG EARN ASSETS	8.90	8.44	72	7.39	7.72	30	6.94	7.73	13	8.15	8.53	9.86	9.80
INT EXPENSE TO AVG EARN ASSETS	2.60	3.44	09	1.91	2.72	06	1.88	2.77	05	2.56	3.59	4.15	5.12
NET INT INC-TE TO AVG EARN ASSET	6.30	4.97	90	5.48	4.96	76	5.05	4.91	59	5.58	4.91	5.71	4.67

LOAN & LEASE ANALYSIS

	BANK	PEER 07	PCT	BANK	PEER 07	PCT	BANK	PEER 07	PCT	BANK	PEER 07	BANK	PEER 07
NET LOSS TO AVERAGE TOTAL LN&LS	0.05	0.16	30	−0.02	0.16	14	−0.16	0.25	03	0.27	0.44	0.93	0.50
EARNINGS COVERAGE OF NET LOSS(X)	60.60	21.70	80	NA	19.39		NA	13.84		10.80	8.86	2.27	6.77
LN&LS ALLOWANCE TO NET LOSSES(X)	32.08	9.65	83	NA	9.34		NA	6.81		9.16	4.34	2.42	3.55
LN&LS ALLOWANCE TO TOTAL LN&LS	1.39	1.41	50	1.86	1.47	75	2.42	1.57	84	2.57	1.59	2.35	1.45
NON-CURRENT LN&LS TO GROSS LN&LS	0.17	0.74	15	0.08	0.77	08	1.25	1.08	60	2.12	1.34	4.23	1.61

LIQUIDITY

	BANK	PEER 07	PCT	BANK	PEER 07	PCT	BANK	PEER 07	PCT	BANK	PEER 07	BANK	PEER 07
VOLATILE LIABILITY DEPENDENCE	4.96	0.25	67	−4.85	2.39	24	−1.72	−1.16	47	−6.53	−2.26	−7.63	−2.82
NET LOANS & LEASES TO ASSETS	74.42	60.00	93	63.27	60.34	58	55.97	58.01	41	51.43	57.50	59.14	59.40

CAPITALIZATION

	BANK	PEER 07	PCT	BANK	PEER 07	PCT	BANK	PEER 07	PCT	BANK	PEER 07	BANK	PEER 07
TIER ONE LEVERAGE CAPITAL (***)	8.21	8.53	44	8.15	8.43	46	7.99	8.10	47	7.63	7.76	7.36	7.48
CASH DIVIDENDS TO NET INCOME	43.42	29.15	66	43.93	28.18	69	34.25	25.80	61	41.75	23.16	64.14	30.22
RETAIN EARNS TO AVG TOTAL EQUITY	9.40	8.14	83	8.57	8.09	51	12.79	8.42	79	8.22	8.16	3.32	5.82
RESTR+NONAC+RE ACQ TO EQCAP+ALLL	2.84	5.24	36	3.46	6.59	36	12.00	9.53	62	32.84	13.16	83.64	14.44

GROWTH RATES

	BANK	PEER 07	PCT	BANK	PEER 07	PCT	BANK	PEER 07	PCT	BANK	PEER 07	BANK	PEER 07
ASSETS	11.12	9.05	60	4.30	4.99	49	5.38	5.50	52	7.94	6.02	−7.85	5.78
TIER ONE CAPITAL (***)	9.75	9.98	50	8.78	9.83	42	13.65	10.54	67	8.62	10.08	3.36	7.42
NET LOANS & LEASES	30.71	10.16	90	17.90	10.14	74	14.69	7.14	73	−6.14	4.23	−3.21	2.86
TEMPORARY INVESTMENTS	−21.26	52.92	14	43.98	−16.91	82	−50.56	0.98	15	1.16	−8.47	1.39	5.90
VOLATILE LIABILITIES	145.48	21.04	95	1.50	18.74	34	−38.60	6.75	06	5.27	−10.02	11.91	−10.02

(***) TIER ONE CAPITAL FOR 12/31/93 EXCLUDES FASB 115 NET UNREALIZED HOLDING GAIN ON AVAILABLE-FOR-SALE SECURITIES.

EXHIBIT I *(Continued)*

INCOME STATEMENT — REVENUES AND EXPENSES ($000)

	12/31/95	12/31/94	12/31/93	12/31/92	12/31/91	PERCENT CHANGE 1 YEAR
INTEREST AND FEES ON LOANS	15330	10992	9476	10331	12349	39.47
INCOME FROM LEASE FINANCING	0	0	0	0	0	NA
FULLY TAXABLE	15323	10969	9446	10291	12299	39.69
TAX-EXEMPT	7	23	30	40	50	−69.57
ESTIMATED TAX BENEFIT	3	11	15	20	26	
INCOME ON LOANS & LEASES (TE)	15333	11003	9491	10351	12375	39.35
U.S. TREAS & AGENCY SECURITIES	2389	2223	1915	2008	2904	7.47
TAX-EXEMPT SECURITIES INCOME	160	102	13	3	8	56.86
ESTIMATED TAX BENEFIT	76	49	6	1	4	
OTHER SECURITIES INCOME	114	209	885	917	449	−45.45
INVESTMT INTEREST INCOME (TE)	2739	2583	2819	2929	3365	6.06
INTEREST ON DUE FROM BANKS	33	219	1	18	19	−62.10
INT ON FED FUNDS SOLD & RESALES	33	225	92	89	308	−85.33
TRADING ACCOUNT INCOME	0	0	0	0	0	NA
TOTAL INTEREST INCOME (TE)	18189	14030	12404	13388	16067	29.64
INTEREST ON CD'S OVER $100M	479	197	237	347	777	143.15
INTEREST ON ALL OTHER DEPOSITS	3976	3271	2997	3768	5863	21.55
INT ON FED FUNDS PURCH & REPOS	616	158	135	89	51	289.87
INT BORROWED MONEY (+NOTE OPT)	247	0	0	0	0	NA
INT ON MORTGAGES & LEASES	0	0	0	9	23	NA
INT ON SUB NOTES & DEBENTURES	0	0	0	0	43	NA
TOTAL INTEREST EXPENSE	5318	3626	3369	4213	6757	46.66
NET INTEREST INCOME (TE)	12871	10404	9035	9175	9310	23.71
NONINTEREST INCOME	2991	3186	3548	2644	2426	−6.12
ADJUSTED OPERATING INC (TE)	15862	13590	12583	11819	11736	16.72
NON-INTEREST EXPENSE	11116	10129	8884	8709	9319	9.74
PROVISION: LOAN & LEASE LOSSES	0	−300	30	360	600	100.00
PROV: ALLOCATED TRANSFER RISK	0	0	0	0	0	
PRETAX OPERATING INCOME (TE)	4746	3761	3669	2750	1817	26.18
REALIZED G/L HLD-TO-MATURITY SEC	0	0	0	238	0	NA
REALIZED G/L AVAIL-FOR-SALE SEC	0	0	NA	NA	NA	NA
PRETAX NET OPERATING INC (TE)	4746	3761	3669	2988	1817	26.18
APPLICABLE INCOME TAXES	1672	1197	909	1050	613	
CURRENT TAX EQUIV ADJUSTMENT	80	60	22	22	30	
OTHER TAX EQUIV ADJUSTMENTS	0	0	0	0	0	
APPLICABLE INCOME TAXES (TE)	1752	1257	931	1072	643	
NET OPERATING INCOME	2994	2504	2738	1916	1174	19.57
NET EXTRAORDINARY ITEMS	0	0	182	0	0	
NET INCOME	2994	2504	2920	1916	1174	19.57
CASH DIVIDENDS DECLARED	1300	1100	1000	800	753	18.18
RETAINED EARNINGS	1694	1404	1920	1116	421	20.66

EXHIBIT I (Continued)

UBPR page 03

NONINTEREST INCOME AND EXPENSE ($000) AND YIELDS

NONINTEREST INCOME & EXPENSES	12/31/95 BANK	PEER 07	PCT	12/31/94 BANK	PEER 07	PCT	12/31/93 BANK	PEER 07	PCT	12/31/92 BANK	PEER 07	12/31/91 BANK	PEER 07
FIDUCIARY ACTIVITIES	956			917			1104			1017		1015	
DEPOSIT SERVICE CHARGES	1184			1122			1009			998		879	
TRADING COMMISSIONS & FEES	0			0			0			0		0	
FOREIGN EXCHANGE TRADING	0			0			0			0		0	
OTHER FOREIGN TRANSACTIONS	0			0			0			0		0	
OTHER NONINTEREST INCOME	851			1147			1435			629		532	
NONINTEREST INCOME	2991			3186			3548			2644		2426	
MEMO: FEE INCOME	544			544			489			295		287	
PERSONNEL EXPENSE	5971			5435			4682			4545		5008	
OCCUPANCY EXPENSE	1457			1354			1218			1166		1255	
OTHER OPER EXP (INCL INTANGIBLES)	3688			3340			2984			2998		3056	
TOTAL OVERHEAD EXPENSE	11116			10129			8884			8709		9319	
O/H & INTEREST ON MORTG & LEASES	11116			10129			8884			8718		9342	
DOMESTIC BANKING OFFICES (#)	8			8			8			8		8	
FOREIGN BRANCHES (#)	0			0			0			0		0	
ASSETS PER DOMESTIC OFFICE	29405			26544			25448			24148		22371	
NUMBER OF EQUIVALENT EMPLOYEES	158			152			129			130		133	
PERCENT OF AVERAGE ASSETS													
PERSONNEL EXPENSE	2.72	1.73	93	2.65	1.73	91	2.43	1.71	91	2.54	1.65	2.79	1.62
OCCUPANCY EXPENSE	0.66	0.52	71	0.66	0.52	71	0.63	0.52	71	0.65	0.52	0.70	0.51
OTHER OPER EXP (INCL INTANGIBLES)	1.68	1.23	81	1.63	1.34	74	1.55	1.37	74	1.68	1.35	1.70	1.32
TOTAL OVERHEAD EXPENSE	5.05	3.51	89	4.94	3.65	87	4.61	3.65	86	4.87	3.60	5.20	3.51
O/H & INTEREST ON MORTG & LEASES	5.05	3.51	89	4.94	3.65	86	4.61	3.66	86	4.88	3.60	5.21	3.51
OVERHEAD LESS NONINTEREST INCOME	3.69	2.56	90	3.38	2.67	82	2.77	2.60	82	3.39	2.61	3.84	2.58
OTHER INCOME & EXPENSE RATIOS:													
AVG PERSONNEL EXP PER EMPL ($000)	37.79	33.23	75	35.76	32.17	72	36.23	30.77	72	34.96	29.73	37.65	28.28
ASSETS PER EMPLOYEE ($MILLION)	1.49	2.07	10	1.40	1.95	10	1.58	1.90	10	1.49	1.88	1.35	1.83
MARGINAL TAX RATE	36.92	36.30	59	33.43	36.22	16	24.18	35.62	16	35.88	36.03	35.39	36.30
YIELD ON OR COST OF:													
TOTAL LOANS & LEASES (TE)	9.83	9.59	60	8.75	8.83	47	8.93	8.88	47	9.90	9.54	10.95	10.74
TOTAL LOANS	9.83	9.58	61	8.74	8.81	48	8.92	8.85	48	9.88	9.50	10.92	10.69
REAL ESTATE**	9.69	9.33	63	8.57	8.76	44	9.01	8.93	44	10.22	9.66	10.93	10.64
COMMERCIAL, TIME, DEMAND, OTH**	11.76	9.89	91	9.00	8.68	65	8.29	8.21	65	8.86	8.67	10.62	10.23
INSTALLMENT**	9.06	9.58	33	8.68	9.18	35	9.58	9.82	35	10.95	10.77	11.81	11.53
CREDIT CARD PLANS	14.83	14.02	58	19.26	13.80	92	11.84	14.05	92	12.20	14.66	13.13	15.03
MEMO: AGRICULTURAL LNS IN ABOVE	NA	9.93		NA	8.76		NA	8.40		NA	9.03	NA	10.64
TOTAL INVESTMENT SECURITIES (TE)	5.94	6.36	23	4.76	5.86	23	4.07	6.22	07	5.23	7.32	7.65	8.46
U.S. TREASURIES & AGENCIES	5.80	6.07	30	4.84	5.49	15	4.77	5.80	14	6.31	6.95	7.85	8.15
STATE & POLITICAL SUB (800K)	5.08	5.57	30	4.18	5.58	11	3.28	5.96	11	9.52	6.53	11.00	6.95
STATE & POLITICAL SUB (TE)	7.51	8.04	36	6.20	8.08	15	4.99	8.65	15	14.48	9.51	16.71	10.08
OTHER DEBT SECURITIES	NA	6.61		6.06	6.26	47	6.66	6.44	47	6.54	7.35	8.07	8.22
EQUITY SECURITIES	6.42	0.17	61	3.52	5.47	16	3.04	5.10	16	3.64	5.42	5.47	5.84
INTEREST-BEARING BANK BALANCES	4.98	5.78	26	4.64	4.19	66	0.93	3.84	66	1.93	5.25	3.77	7.31
FEDERAL FUNDS SOLD & RESALES	5.27	5.83	06	4.33	4.09	74	2.83	2.97	74	3.20	3.45	5.69	5.60
TOTAL INT-BEARING DEPOSITS	3.24	4.20	04	2.52	3.30	05	2.51	3.34	05	3.33	4.26	5.12	6.04
TRANSACTION ACCOUNTS	1.78	2.23	22	1.64	2.09	18	1.46	2.23	18	2.03	2.96	3.71	4.54
MONEY MARKET DEPOSIT ACCOUNTS	2.97	3.29	32	2.48	2.71	27	2.21	2.72	27	2.84	3.43	4.49	5.16
OTHER SAVINGS DEPOSITS	2.64	2.78	38	2.37	2.62	27	2.14	2.78	27	2.70	3.50	4.25	4.94
LARGE CERTIFICATES OF DEPOSIT	5.41	5.52	39	3.59	4.07	19	3.33	3.86	19	4.53	4.80	6.43	6.72
ALL OTHER TIME DEPOSITS	5.18	5.43	28	3.91	4.20	31	4.16	4.25	31	5.14	5.27	6.86	6.96
FEDERAL FUNDS PURCHASED & REPOS	6.31	5.62	78	3.62	4.06	32	2.66	2.94	32	3.07	3.53	4.92	5.60
OTHER BORROWED MONEY	6.59	5.24	79	NA	3.55		NA	2.55		NA	2.55	NA	4.04
SUBORDINATED NOTES & DEBENTURES	NA	8.48		NA	8.11		NA	7.87		NA	8.24	11.94	9.21
ALL INTEREST-BEARING FUNDS	3.52	4.25	10	2.56	3.34	06	2.51	3.34	06	3.32	4.24	5.14	6.02

EXHIBIT I   (Continued)

	12/31/95	12/31/94	12/31/93	12/31/92	12/31/91	PERCENT CHANGE 1 QTR	PERCENT CHANGE 1 YEAR
ASSETS:							
REAL ESTATE LOANS	150618	111584	96993	74771	83773	3.99	34.98
COMMERCIAL LOANS	10069	9289	10421	20922	17865	3.07	8.40
INDIVIDUAL LOANS	15242	15910	9157	6506	6974	-2.99	-4.20
AGRICULTURAL LOANS	2150	0	0	73	45	NA	NA
OTHER LN&LS IN DOMESTIC OFFICES	NA	113	204	NA	NA	370.46	+##
LN&LS IN FOREIGN OFFICES	NA	NA	NA	NA	NA	NA	NA
GROSS LOANS & LEASES	178079	136896	116775	102272	108657	4.28	30.08
LESS: UNEARNED INCOME	0	0	0	298	260	NA	NA
LN&LS ALLOWANCE & ATRR	2470	2547	2825	2621	2547	-4.04	-3.02
NET LOANS & LEASES	175609	134349	113950	99353	105850	4.41	30.71
U.S. TREASURY & AGENCY SECURITIES	33367	45737	50003	29315	31835	-8.24	-27.05
MUNICIPAL SECURITIES	2846	3524	1786	0	42	1.50	-19.24
FOREIGN DEBT SECURITIES	0	0	0	0	0	NA	NA
ALL OTHER SECURITIES	2811	1315	14287	26806	12282	48.26	113.76
INTEREST-BEARING BANK BALANCES	195	6821	4900	688	329	4.84	-97.14
FEDERAL FUNDS SOLD & RESALES	0	0	0	18300	8000	NA	NA
TRADING ACCOUNT ASSETS	0	0	0	0	0	NA	NA
TOTAL INVESTMENTS	39219	57397	70976	75109	52488	NA	NA
TOTAL EARNING ASSETS	214828	191746	184926	174462	158338	NA	NA
NONINT CASH & DUE FROM BANKS	14162	13432	12107	11184	11607	33.91	5.43
ACCEPTANCES	0	0	0	0	0	NA	NA
PREMISES, FIX ASSTS, CAP LEASES	3915	3751	3191	3295	3443	3.52	4.37
OTHER REAL ESTATE OWNED	321	394	610	2240	2972	0.00	-18.53
INV IN UNCONSOLIDATED SUBS	0	0	0	0	0	NA	NA
OTHER ASSETS	2734	3029	2757	2009	2611	-1.34	-9.74
TOTAL ASSETS	235960	212352	203591	193190	178971	3.99	11.12
AVERAGE ASSETS DURING QUARTER	232555	213441	200155	184349	175954	4.34	8.96
LIABILITIES:							
DEMAND DEPOSITS	51818	51340	48023	45340	33927	2.46	0.93
ALL NOW & ATS ACCOUNTS	46504	54688	51532	41505	40499	4.18	-14.96
MONEY MARKET DEPOSIT ACCOUNTS	31613	28399	28385	25999	24090	13.81	11.32
OTHER SAVINGS DEPOSITS	15639	16961	15862	14230	11962	-1.04	-7.79
TIME DEP UNDER $100M	39731	33150	32872	34058	38463	5.59	19.85
CORE DEPOSITS	185305	184538	176674	161132	148941	5.04	0.42
TIME DEP OVER $100M	16916	5351	5761	6423	10964	44.92	216.13
DEPOSITS IN FOREIGN OFFICES	0	0	0	0	0	NA	NA
TOTAL DEPOSITS	202221	189889	182435	167555	159905	7.51	6.49
FEDERAL FUNDS PURCHASED & RESALE	3697	4594	4037	9535	4195	-30.91	NA
OTHER BORROWINGS INCL MAT < 1 YR	3800	0	0	0	0	-1.03	145.48
VOLATILE LIABILITIES	24413	9945	9798	15958	15159	-3.27	NA
OTHER BORROWINGS WITH MAT > 1 YR	5623	1059	1130	2031	1919	0.29	31.63
ACCEPTANCES & OTHER LIABILITIES	1394	0	0	0	0	4.06	10.84
TOTAL LIABILITIES (INCL MORTG)	216735	195542	187602	179121	166019	NA	NA
SUBORDINATED NOTES & DEBENTURES	0	0	0	0	0	3.30	14.37
ALL COMMON & PREFERRED CAPITAL	19225	16810	15989	14069	12952	3.99	11.12
TOTAL LIABILITIES & CAPITAL	235960	212352	203591	193190	178971		
MEMORANDA:							
OFFICER, SHAREHOLDER LOANS (#)	1	0	0	0	1	NA	NA
OFFICER, SHAREHOLDER LOANS ($)	1284	341	494	2	1543	176.13	276.54
NON-INVESTMENT ORE	321	394	610	2240	2972	0.00	-18.53
HELD-TO-MATURITY SECURITIES	13292	20975	66076	56121	44159	-18.78	-36.63
AVAILABLE-FOR-SALE SECURITIES	25732	29601	0	NA	NA	4.18	-13.07
ALL BROKERED DEPOSITS	0	0	0	0	0	NA	NA

EXHIBIT I *(Continued)*

UBPR page 05

OFF-BALANCE SHEET ITEMS

OUTSTANDING ($000)	12/31/95	12/31/94	12/31/93	12/31/92	12/31/91	PERCENT CHANGE 1 QTR	PERCENT CHANGE 1 YEAR
HOME EQUITY (1-4 FAMILY)	6720	3046	101	161	373	14.79	70.30
CREDIT CARD	6	62	65	120	108	-89.66	-90.32
COMMERCIAL RE SECURED BY RE	6424	9973	7670	4392	5157	-6.70	-35.59
COMMERCL RE NOT SECURED BY RE	0	1012	542	826	906	-100.00	-100.00
ALL OTHER	10724	12515	14550	8750	8195	-31.13	-14.31
SECURITIES UNDERWRITING					0	NA	NA
MEMO: UNUSED COMMIT W/MAT GT 1 YR	119	1341	977	369	623	891.67	-91.13
STANDBY LETTERS OF CREDIT	0	99	201	563	168	-100.00	-100.00
AMOUNT CONVEYED TO OTHERS	0	0	0	0	0	NA	NA
COMMERCIAL LETTERS OF CREDIT	1027	1001	357	0	0	87.41	2.60
PRINCIPAL BALANCE OF MTG POOLS	0	0	0	0	0	NA	NA
AMOUNT OF RECOURSE EXPOSURE	0	0	0	0	0	NA	NA
ALL OTH OFF-BALANCE SHEET ITEMS	0	0	0	0	0	NA	NA
OFF-BALANCE SHEET ITEMS	24901	28608	23486	14812	14907	-16.31	-12.96

OUTSTANDING (% OF TOTAL)	12/31/95 BANK	PEER 07	PCT	12/31/94 BANK	PEER 07	PCT	12/31/93 BANK	PEER 07	PCT	12/31/92 BANK	PEER 07	12/31/91 BANK	PEER 07
HOME EQUITY (1-4 FAMILY)	2.85	1.06	81	1.86	0.99	70	0.05	0.95	25	0.08	0.93	0.21	0.83
CREDIT CARD	0.00	0.32	47	0.03	0.29	49	0.03	0.26	51	0.06	0.26	0.06	0.26
COMMERCIAL RE SECURED BY RE	2.72	1.79	69	4.70	1.67	86	3.77	1.40	83	2.27	1.14	2.88	1.00
COMMERCL RE NOT SECURED BY RE	0.00	0.00	84	0.48	0.00	95	0.27	0.00	92	0.43	0.00	0.51	0.00
ALL OTHER	4.54	4.80	48	5.89	4.76	62	7.1	4.27	77	4.53	3.96	4.58	3.90
TOTAL LN&LS COMMITMENTS	10.12	9.73	54	12.95	9.50	72	11.26	8.74	66	7.38	8.14	8.24	7.88
SECURITIES UNDERWRITING	0.00	0.00	99	0.00	0.00	99	0.00	0.00	99	0.00	0.00	0.00	0.00
STANDBY LETTERS OF CREDIT	0.00	0.43	09	0.05	0.43	13	0.10	0.44	19	0.29	0.44	0.09	0.46
AMOUNT CONVEYED TO OTHERS	0.00	0.00	96	0.00	0.00	95	0.00	0.00	95	0.00	0.00	0.00	0.00
COMMERCIAL LETTERS OF CREDIT	0.44	0.00	94	0.47	0.00	94	0.18	0.00	89	0.00	0.00	0.00	0.00
PRINCIPAL BALANCE OF MTG POOLS	0.00	0.00	97	0.00	0.00	98	0.00	0.00	98	0.00	0.00	0.00	0.00
AMOUNT OF RECOURSE EXPOSURE	0.00	0.00	97	0.00	0.00	98	0.00	0.00	98	0.00	0.00	0.00	0.00
ALL OTH OFF-BALANCE SHEET ITEMS	0.00	0.00	93	0.00	0.00	92	0.00	0.00	90	0.00	0.00	0.00	0.00
OFF-BALANCE SHEET ITEMS	10.55	10.58	50	13.47	10.45	69	11.54	9.78	62	7.67	9.12	8.33	8.84

EXHIBIT 1   (Continued)

BALANCE SHEET — PERCENTAGE COMPOSITION OF ASSETS AND LIABILITIES

ASSETS, PERCENT OF AVG ASSETS	12/31/95 BANK	12/31/95 PEER 07	12/31/95 PCT	12/31/94 BANK	12/31/94 PEER 07	12/31/94 PCT	12/31/93 BANK	12/31/93 PEER 07	12/31/93 PCT	12/31/92 BANK	12/31/92 PEER 07	12/31/92 PCT	12/31/91 BANK	12/31/91 PEER 07
TOTAL LOANS	71.12	61.13	83	61.07	60.11	51	54.78	58.69	38	56.41	59.17	38	62.03	61.09
LEASE FINANCING RECEIVABLES	0.00	0.00	81	0.00	0.00	80	0.00	0.00	79	0.00	0.00	79	0.00	0.00
LESS: LN&LS ALLOWANCE & ATRR	1.15	0.87	79	1.32	0.89	83	1.40	0.91	84	1.39	0.88	84	1.56	0.83
NET LOANS & LEASES	69.97	60.34	82	59.74	59.32	48	53.38	57.93	36	55.02	58.41	36	60.47	60.41
INTEREST-BEARING BANK BALANCES	0.68	0.05	86	2.14	0.06	93	0.07	0.09	60	0.38	0.16	60	0.18	0.25
FEDERAL FUNDS SOLD & RESALES	0.00	2.93	04	2.62	2.45	56	3.60	3.54	52	5.38	3.80	52	3.44	4.04
TRADING ACCOUNT ASSETS	0.00	0.00	98	0.00	0.00	97	0.00	0.00	95	0.00	0.00	95	0.00	0.00
HELD-TO-MATURITY SECURITIES	8.30	11.78	37	14.05	16.56	41	33.80	28.29	65	29.20	26.97	65	23.40	24.44
AVAILABLE-FOR-SALE SECURITIES	12.31	13.04	48	12.31	9.68	62	NA	NA		NA	NA		NA	NA
TOTAL EARNING ASSETS	91.26	91.46	45	90.86	91.46	40	90.85	91.39	41	89.98	91.15	41	87.49	90.94
NONINT CASH & DUE FROM BANKS	5.58	4.46	76	5.90	4.44	80	5.50	4.42	72	5.41	4.55	72	6.99	4.71
PREMISES, FIX ASSTS & CAP LEASES	1.71	1.88	44	1.63	1.84	42	1.66	1.81	45	1.83	1.76	45	2.01	1.80
OTHER REAL ESTATE OWNED	0.16	0.13	59	0.27	0.19	65	0.77	0.34	74	1.53	0.42	74	1.89	0.35
ACCEPTANCES & OTHER ASSETS	.29	1.55	30	1.34	1.56	34	1.22	1.46	29	1.26	1.50	29	1.61	1.59
SUBTOTAL	8.74	8.54	54	9.13	8.54	59	9.15	8.61	58	10.03	8.86	58	12.50	9.06
TOTAL ASSETS	100.00	100.00		99.99	100.00		100.00	100.00		100.01	100.00		99.99	100.00
STANDBY LETTERS OF CREDIT	0.03	0.44	09	0.05	0.45	12	0.31	0.45	41	0.22	0.45	41	0.19	0.50
LIABILITIES, PERCENT OF AVG ASST														
DEMAND DEPOSITS	22.68	15.04	84	23.52	15.08	87	22.80	14.41	87	22.13	13.47	87	18.49	13.06
ALL NOW & ATS ACCOUNTS	21.97	11.47	96	25.50	12.25	97	23.09	12.12	97	22.92	11.39	97	22.70	10.04
MONEY MARKET DEPOSIT ACCOUNTS	12.92	10.84	64	13.79	12.13	61	13.74	12.87	57	13.35	12.99	57	15.09	12.11
OTHER SAVINGS DEPOSITS	7.34	10.73	32	8.05	12.34	31	7.62	12.27	29	6.99	10.73	29	6.26	8.81
TIME DEP < $100M	16.03	27.34	16	15.92	24.88	20	17.23	25.96	20	19.53	29.17	20	21.61	32.39
CORE DEPOSITS	80.96	79.95	56	86.78	81.36	85	84.99	82.11	69	84.92	81.78	69	84.16	79.81
TIME DEP OVER $100M	4.28	7.42	21	2.66	6.27	14	3.57	6.22	27	4.27	7.12	27	6.66	9.18
DEPOSITS IN FOREIGN OFFICES	NA	0.76		NA	1.19		NA	0.68		NA	2.15		NA	1.17
TOTAL DEPOSITS	85.24	88.27	23	89.44	88.61	55	88.56	89.22	39	89.18	89.74	39	90.82	89.83
FEDERAL FUNDS PURCH & REPOS	3.65	0.80	83	2.08	0.89	71	3.03	0.62	82	2.33	0.65	82	0.82	0.69
OTHER BORROWINGS INCL < 1 YR	0.84	0.12	85	0.00	0.17	50	0.00	0.22	48	0.00	0.17	48	0.00	0.15
VOLATILE LIABILITIES	8.77	9.77	44	4.74	8.94	19	6.60	8.72	36	6.59	9.35	36	7.48	11.33
OTHER BORROWINGS > 1 YR	1.58	0.00	91	0.00	0.00	80	NA	NA		NA	NA		NA	NA
ACCEPTANCES & OTHER LIABILITIES	0.55	0.73	29	0.50	0.63	34	0.72	0.67	58	1.15	0.75	58	1.14	0.91
TOTAL LIABILITIES (INCL MORTG)	91.86	91.40	57	92.02	91.64	58	92.31	91.85	61	92.66	92.27	61	92.77	92.46
SUBORDINATED NOTES & DEBENTURES	0.00	0.00	96	0.00	0.00	95	0.00	0.00	94	0.00	0.00	94	0.20	0.00
ALL COMMON & PREFERRED CAPITAL	8.14	8.58	43	7.98	8.32	42	7.69	8.12	39	7.34	7.69	39	7.03	7.50
TOTAL LIABILITIES & CAPITAL	100.00	100.00		100.00	100.00		100.00	100.00		100.00	100.00		101.01	100.00
MEMO: ALL BROKERED DEPOSITS	0.00	0.00	87	0.00	0.00	88	0.00	0.00	88	0.00	0.00	88	0.00	0.00
INSURED BROKERED DEP	0.00	0.00	87	0.00	0.00	88	0.00	0.00	88	0.00	0.00	88	0.00	0.00

EXHIBIT 2   Lincoln National Bank ALCO Ratios December 31, 1995
(in thousands where applicable)

	December	Target Range or Guideline
Rate-sensitive assets/		
Rate-sensitive liabilities		
90 days	0.50	
180 days	0.65	
One year	0.89	0.8 to 1.2
Five years	1.16	
GAP		
RSA less RSL/total assets		
90 days	(25.17)%	
One year	(6.73)%	(15)% to 15%
Five years	10.56%	
Net interest income after tax at risk with 200-basis-point change in rates[a]	$454	$650
Net interest margin	6.31%	6.28%
Liquidity ratio	13.25%	15.0% minimum
Loans/deposits (Avg)	86.31%	65.0% to 80.0%
Large CDs/total deposits (Avg)	4.99%	25.0% maximum
Public CDs/total deposits (Avg)	0.65%	10.0% maximum
Investment portfolio		
Average maturity (years)	3.06	
Unrealized gain or (loss)	(8)	

[a] If the gap ratio is positive, rising rates will cause an increase in income, and falling rates will cause a decrease. If gap ratio is negative, rising rates will cause a decrease in income, and falling rates will cause an increase.

EXHIBIT 3   Lincoln National Bank Liquidity Report December 31, 1995

Liquid Assets	
Cash and due	$ 14,162
Unpledged and overpledged gov't sec. (mkt)	4,106
Fed funds sold	0
Cash management funds	500
LESS:	
Smaller of due from & due to time deposits	0
Fed funds purchased	3,697
Required reserve (excluding vault cash)	2,245
Net liquid assets	$ 24,710
Adjusted Liabilities	
Total liabilities	216,735
LESS:	
Smaller of due from & due to time deposits	0
Fed funds purchased	3,697
Long-term borrowings	5,623
Secured liabilities: state & gov't subdivisions	20,896
NET LIABILITIES	$186,519
LIQUIDITY RATIO: liquid assets/net liabilities	13.25%

CASE 3   QUAKER NATIONAL BANK

INTRODUCTION

At the end of 1997, Quaker National Bank had total resources of $410 million. It served its market area with 11 offices and a staff of 295 full-time equivalent officers and employees. Early in 1998, Mr. Matthew Killian, executive vice-president of Quaker Bank, was reviewing the financial data he had assembled for the asset and liability management committee (ALCO). Mr. Killian had joined the bank the previous November, along with Mr. Bryce Wilson, who was named chairman of the board and chief executive officer. Shortly after the two men had assumed their new positions, Mr. Wilson instructed Mr. Killian to respond to the report of national bank examiners, dated October 17, 1997, which was highly critical of the bank's policies and procedures for monitoring and controlling its risk position. Mr. Wilson asked Mr. Killian to review the bank's performance and, as soon as he completed his evalua-

tion, to present his recommendations for corrective measures to the ALCO.

In late 1996, national examiners had introduced a new program of "supervision by risk." The Office of the Comptroller of the Currency (OCC) handbook identified nine types of banking risk: credit, liquidity, market, interest rate, foreign exchange, strategic, transaction, compliance, and reputation risks. The theory behind the OCC's program was to refocus field examinations around assessments of the quantity of banks' risk-taking and their risk management procedures. The new examination procedures applied to banks with assets over $1 billion or with assets of special complexity. Although Quaker National was smaller and therefore not subject to these examination procedures, a similar emphasis on risk assessment seemed to be entering the examinations of larger community banks like Quaker.

In the October exam, the examiners had found

much to criticize. They specifically made note of three areas of concern. First, they judged the bank's exposure to credit, interest rate, and liquidity risks to be excessive in relation to its capital strength and earnings performance. Second, the bank funded approximately 25 percent of its assets through large CDs, more than twice the peer bank average of about 12 percent. Finally, the bank's financial reports and written policy statements regarding interest rate and liquidity risk management did not provide the data and specific guidelines needed to make well-reasoned asset and liability management decisions.

During the past few weeks, Mr. Killian had worked on evaluating Quaker's recent operating performance and its financial condition. He was also occupied with designing an information system of financial reports that would be useful in managing the bank's resources and that would meet the examiners' criticism.

For his analysis of Quaker's performance, Mr. Killian put together the financial data of eight banks for the last two years, 1996 and 1997. While none of the eight banks competed with Quaker National, each was about the same size, with total assets that ranged from about $300 million to just under $600 million. Also, the banks selected as the basis of a suitable peer group were located in areas with economic and demographic characteristics similar to those of Quaker's market. The balance sheet and income statement data for Quaker and the peer group banks are shown in Exhibits 1 and 2. Exhibit 3 contains key financial ratios for Quaker and its peers.

The two primary financial reports designed by Mr. Killian for management's use in making asset and liability management decisions were an interest rate sensitivity report (Exhibit 4) and a liquidity report (Exhibit 5). Mr. Killian felt that the reports would improve management's ability to monitor and understand Quaker's risk position.

In preparing for the ALCO meeting at which he would discuss his findings and present his recommendations, Mr. Killian talked to each member of the committee and obtained their views on the outlook for the local and national economies in 1998. The consensus estimate of the ALCO members was that interest rates would trend downward until the end of the second quarter and would begin a slow but steady increase during the last half of the year. Mr. Killian's summary of this forecast appears in Exhibit 6.

EXHIBIT I   Quaker National Bank Average Balance Sheet (dollars in thousands)

	1997			1996		
	Quaker		Peers	Quaker		Peers
	$	%	%	$	%	%
Cash and due from banks	27,424	7.03	6.87	25,869	7.16	6.97
Interest-bearing bank balances	8,348	2.14	3.10	7,299	2.02	2.98
Federal funds sold and resales	10,884	2.79	5.24	9,683	2.68	4.95
Investment Securities						
U.S. Treasuries & Federal agencies	35,226	9.03	12.17	35,913	9.94	12.96
State and local government securities	24,654	6.32	7.93	26,628	7.37	9.04
Other securities	5,930	1.52	1.75	4,805	1.33	1.21
Total investment securities	65,810	16.87	21.85	67,346	18.64	23.21
Loans and Leases						
Commercial	96,589	24.76	17.06	90,867	25.15	17.03
Real estate	69,516	17.82	23.51	56,218	15.56	21.59
Consumer	82,935	21.26	14.87	74,247	20.55	14.89
Other loans	16,306	4.18	4.29	17,776	4.92	4.82
Lease financing	1,053	.27	.35	831	.23	.31
Total loans and leases	266,399	68.29	60.08	239,939	66.41	58.64
Less reserve for losses	3,199	.82	.73	2,746	.76	.66
Net loans and leases	263,200	67.47	59.35	237,193	65.65	57.98
Bank premises and equipment, net	7,295	1.87	1.69	7,045	1.95	1.84
Other assets	7,139	1.83	1.90	6,865	1.90	2.07
Total assets	390,100	100.00	100.00	361,300	100.00	100.00
Total earning assets	351,441	90.09	90.27	324,267	89.75	89.78
Noninterest-bearing demand deposits	67,058	17.19	17.14	63,264	17.51	17.32
Interest-bearing demand deposits	29,375	7.53	8.24	29,012	8.03	8.80
Regular savings	21,104	5.41	7.89	18,860	5.22	8.07
Money market deposit accounts	44,159	11.32	18.39	38,876	10.76	15.96
Time deposits under $100,000	82,857	21.24	23.86	77,788	21.53	24.57
Time deposits $100,000 and over	90,032	25.13	11.49	88,048	24.37	11.68
Total deposits	342,585	87.82	87.01	315,848	87.42	86.40
Federal funds purchased	14,551	3.73	4.77	15,211	4.21	5.15
Other liabilities	7,295	1.87	1.24	6,937	1.92	1.37
Total liabilities	364,431	93.42	93.02	337,996	93.55	92.92
Shareholders' equity	25,669	6.58	6.98	23,304	6.45	7.08
Total liabilities and equity capital	390,100	100.00	100.00	361,300	100.00	100.00

EXHIBIT 2   Quaker National Bank Income Statement—Taxable-Equivalent Basis—Percentage of Average Total Assets (dollars in thousands)

	1997 Quaker		1997 Peers	1996 Quaker		1996 Peers
	$	%	%	$	%	%
Interest income						
Loans and leases	30,467	7.81	6.80	30,156	8.35	7.27
Investment securities	7,001	1.79	2.33	7,677	2.12	2.64
Intrest-bearing bank balances	689	.18	.27	718	.20	.29
Federal funds sold	775	.20	.38	794	.22	.42
Total interest income	38,932	9.98	9.78	39,345	10.89	10.62
Interest expense						
Interest on deposits	18,828	4.83	4.70	19,835	5.49	5.40
Interest on short-term borrowings	989	.25	.34	1,156	.32	.39
Total interest expense	19,817	5.08	5.04	20,991	5.81	5.79
Net interest margin	19,115	4.90	4.74	18,354	5.08	4.83
Provision for loan losses	2,146	.55	.43	1,770	.49	.41
Adjusted net interest margin	16,969	4.35	4.31	16,584	4.59	4.42
Noninterest income	3,511	.90	.94	3,324	.92	.97
Noninterest expense						
Personnel	6,671	1.71	1.61	6,540	1.81	1.70
Occupancy and equipment	2,302	.59	.52	2,276	.63	.57
Other noninterest expense	5,110	1.31	1.24	4,914	1.36	1.28
	14,083	3.61	3.37	13,730	3.80	3.55
Net overhead	10,572	2.71	2.43	10,404	2.88	2.58
Income before income taxes	6,397	1.64	1.88	6,178	1.71	1.84
Applicable income taxes	2,849	.73	.84	2,746	.76	.82
Net income	3,548	.91	1.04	3,432	.95	1.02

EXHIBIT 3 Quaker National Bank Key Financial Ratios—Average Balances and Taxable-Equivalent Income

	1997		1996	
	Quaker	Peer Group	Quaker	Peer Group
Profitability Measures				
1. Return on assets	.91%	1.04%	.95%	1.02%
2. Net profit margin	8.36	9.70	8.04	8.80
3. Asset yield or utilization	10.88	10.72	11.81	11.59
4. Return on equity capital	13.82	14.90	14.73	14.41
5. Leverage or equity multiplier	15.20×	14.33×	15.50×	14.12×
Spread Management (% of earning assets)				
6. Net interest margin	5.44%	5.25%	5.66%	5.38%
7. Adjusted net interest margin	4.83	4.77	5.11	4.92
8. Net overhead burden	3.01	2.69	3.21	2.87
Asset Management (% of assets)				
9. Fed. funds sold & int.-bearing bk. balances	4.93%	8.34%	4.70%	7.93%
10. U.S. Treasuries & Federal agencies	9.03	12.17	9.94	12.96
11. State and local government securities	6.32	7.93	7.37	9.04
12. Net loans and lease financing	67.47	59.35	65.65	57.98
13. Bank premises and equipment	1.87	1.69	1.95	1.84
Liability Management (% of assets)				
14. Noninterest demand deposits	17.19%	17.14%	17.51%	17.32%
15. Interest-bearing demand deposits	7.53	8.24	8.03	8.80
16. Regular and money market savings	16.73	26.28	15.98	24.03
17. Time deposits under $100,000	21.24	23.86	21.53	24.57
18. Time deposits $100,000 and over	25.13	11.49	24.37	11.68
19. Short-term borrowings	3.73	4.77	4.21	5.15
Expense Control				
20. Interest expense/assets	5.08%	5.04%	5.81%	5.79%
21. Interest expense/int. paying liabilities	6.83	6.75	7.84	7.80
22. Assets per FTE employee (thousands $)	$1,322	$1,485	$1,216	$1,352
23. Personnel expense/assets	1.71%	1.61%	1.81%	1.70%
24. Other operating expenses/assets	1.90	1.76	1.99	1.85
25. Provision for loan losses/assets	.55	.43	.49	.41
Asset Yield Enhancement				
26. Interest income/assets	9.98%	9.78%	10.89%	10.62%
27. Interest income/earning assets	11.08	10.83	12.13	11.83
28. Noninterest income/assets	.90	.94	.92	.97
29. Loan income/loans and leases	11.44	11.32	12.57	12.40
30. Yield on investment securities	10.64	10.66	11.40	11.37
Credit Quality (% of loans and leases)				
31. Net charge-offs	.64%	.52%	.60%	.47%
32. Past-due & nonaccrual loans & leases	1.93	1.58	1.89	1.71
Liquidity Measures				
33. Temporary investments/assets	10.64%	15.07%	11.02%	16.15%
34. Volatile liabilities/assets	28.86	16.26	28.58	16.83
35. Net loans & leases/core deposits	107.62	78.59	104.12	77.60

EXHIBIT 3   (Continued)

	1997		1996	
	Quaker	**Peer Group**	**Quaker**	**Peer Group**
Interest Sensitivity Measures (% of assets)				
36. Assets repricing in one year	51.92%	51.95%	53.06%	52.24%
37. Liabilities repricing in one year	60.37	57.83	59.84	55.04
38. One-year GAP	(8.45)	(5.88)	(6.78)	(2.80)
Capital Adequacy and Loan Loss Coverage				
39. Equity capital/assets	6.58%	6.98%	6.45%	7.08%
40. Net loans & leases/equity capital	10.25×	8.50×	10.18×	8.19×
41. Loan loss reserve/loans and leases	1.20%	1.22%	1.14%	1.13%
42. Cash dividends/net income	33.34	38.64	33.90	34.67
43. Internal capital generation rate	9.21	9.14	9.74	9.41

GLOSSARY OF SELECTED TERMS

Adjusted net interest margin. The yield realized on earning assets less total interest expense and the provision for loan losses divided by average earning assets.

Asset yield or utilization. Total operating income (interest income on a taxable-equivalent basis plus noninterest income) divided by average total assets.

Core deposits. Interest-bearing and noninterest-bearing demand deposits, regular savings, money market savings, and CDs under $100,000.

Earning assets. Interest-bearing assets including total loans and leases, investment securities, Federal funds sold, interest-bearing deposits with other banks, and other money market instruments.

FTE employees. Full-time equivalent employees.

Gap. The difference between rate-sensitive assets and rate-sensitive liabilities over a specified time period.

Internal capital generation rate. The annual rate of increase in common stockholders' equity that results from retained earnings. The rate is computed by multiplying the return on average common stockholders' equity by the earnings retention rate (the percentage of earnings retained).

Leverage or equity multiplier. Average total assets divided by average common stockholders' equity.

Net charge-offs. The difference between gross loan charge-offs and recoveries on loans.

Net interest margin. The difference between the yield realized on earning assets (on a taxable equivalent basis) and total interest expense divided by average earning assets.

Net loans and leases. Gross loans less unearned income and the loan loss reserve.

Net overhead. The difference between noninterest income and noninterest expense divided by average earning assets.

Net profit margin. Net income after taxes divided by total operating income (on a taxable equivalent basis).

Nonaccrual loans and leases. Loans and leases on which interest accruals have been discontinued, usually due to the borrower's financial difficulties.

Noninterest expense. All operating expenses other than interest expense and the provision for loan losses, including salaries, fringe benefits, and occupancy costs.

Noninterest income. All income other than interest and fees on earning assets, including trust department income, deposit service charge income, and other service charges.

Personnel expense. Salaries, wages, and officers' and employees' benefits.

Return on assets. Net income after taxes divided by average total assets.

Return on equity capital. Net income after taxes divided by average common stockholders' equity.

Taxable equivalent. Income, chiefly on state and local government securities, that is exempt from federal income tax, is restated to a taxable equivalent basis by dividing such income by $(1 - t)$, where t is the full statutory tax rate. All yield calculations reflect this adjustment.

Temporary investments. Interest-bearing deposits with banks, Federal funds sold, trading account securities, and investment securities with remaining maturities of one year or less.

Volatile liabilities. Large CDs and other time accounts in amounts of $100,000 and more, Federal funds purchased, repurchase agreements, foreign office deposits, interest-bearing demand notes issued to the U.S. Treasury, and other liabilities for short-term borrowed funds.

EXHIBIT 4   Quaker National Bank—Interest Rate Sensitivity Report, December 31, 1997

	1–7 Days	8–30 Days	31–60 Days	61–90 Days	91–120 Days	121–150 Days	151–180 Days	181–365 Days	Over 365 Days	Total
Cash and due from banks									$ 28,795	$ 28,795
Interest-bearing bank balances		$ 1,557							45,696	8,765
Investment securities	$ 2,625	505	$ 832	$ 3,929	$ 1,662	$ 785		$ 7,467		69,101
Federal funds sold and resales	11,428		2,148	3,074		7,586				11,428
Commercial loans	59,187	4,180	3,762	4,026	3,226	2,262	$ 1,978	8,762	13,635	101,418
Real estate loans	10,532	1,284	1,052	1,708	1,131	1,137	1,125	6,766	48,257	72,992
Consumer loans	296	3,527	4,104	7,208	4,710	4,692	4,753	17,536	40,256	87,032
Other loans and lease financing	696	536	880	1,048	1,413	1,218	2,094	3,600	6,742	18,227
Other assets									15,156	15,156
Total assets	$85,064	$ 11,689	$ 12,778	$ 20,993	$ 12,142	$ 17,680	$ 9,950	$ 44,131	$198,537	$412,964
Noninterest-bearing demand deposits									70,411	70,411
Interest-bearing demand deposits		18,506							12,338	30,844
Regular savings		234	415	508	465	509	281	3,766	15,981	22,159
Money market deposit accounts		46,367								46,367
Time deposits under $100,000	714	2,558	22,575	4,602	2,445	6,795	2,661	19,626	25,024	87,000
Time deposits $100,000 and over	1,565	14,267	10,046	21,842	18,024	11,734	6,587	16,943	1,925	102,933
Federal funds purchased	15,279									15,279
Other liabilities									7,660	7,660
Shareholders' equity									26,952	26,952
Loan loss reserve									3,359	3,359
Total liabilities and equity capital	$17,558	$ 81,932	$ 33,036	$ 26,952	$ 20,934	$ 19,038	$ 9,529	$ 40,335	$163,650	$412,964
Periodic GAP	$67,506	$(70,243)	$(20,258)	$ (5,959)	$ (8,792)	$ (1,358)	$ 421	$ 3,796	$ 34,887	0
Cumulative GAP	$67,506	$ (2,737)	$(22,995)	$(28,954)	$(37,746)	$(39,104)	$(38,683)	$(34,887)		
Cumulative GAP as percent of assets	16.35%	(.66%)	(5.57%)	(7.01%)	(9.14%)	(9.47%)	(9.37%)	(8.45%)		
Cumulative GAP as percent of equity capital	250.47%	(10.16%)	(85.32%)	(107.43%)	(140.05%)	(145.09%)	(143.53%)	(129.44%)		

EXHIBIT 5   Quaker National Bank Liquidity Report for Maturing and Volatile Funds—First Quarter, 1998 (dollars in thousands)

	Maturing Funds	Volatile Funds	Loan Demand/ Deposit Growth
Assets			
Interest-bearing bank balances	$ 6,318		
Investment securities	8,352		
Federal funds sold	11,428		
Principal payments			
Commercial loans	15,172		
Real estate loans	6,606		
Consumer loans	15,135		
Other loans and lease financing	2,658		
Total	$65,669		
Liabilities[a]			
Non-interest-bearing demand deposits		$ 8,300	
Interest-bearing demand deposits		2,100	
Regular savings	1,157		
Money market deposit accounts		3,500	
Time deposits under $100,000	22,837		
Time deposits $100,000 and over	47,720		
Federal funds purchased	15,279		
Total	$86,993	$13,900	
Estimated new loan demand			$35,000
Estimated new core deposits[a] (excluding large CDs)			$21,000

[a] All deposit amounts are adjusted for required cash reserves.

EXHIBIT 6   Quaker National Bank—Asset and Liability Management Committee Consensus View of Local and National Economic Conditions

LOAN DEMAND

Loan demand in 1998, especially in real estate and consumer credit card activity, will pick up in our market area in response to increased population as three major national firms—an electronics company, an automotive parts and accessories manufacturer, and a building materials supplier—will open new facilities and hire about 2,700 employees during the year. Nationally, we believe the economy will flatten out in the first two quarters, followed by an actual slowdown in the latter half of 1998.

INTEREST RATES

In spite of an economic slowdown in the United States, business activity is stronger than anticipated in our region. Following a short-term scare from the collapse in some Asian financial markets, the Fed will avoid tightening monetary policy (real money growth may have been extremely small during 1997) and could increase money growth during 1998 to stem a possible further slowdown. Short-term interest rates will fall 100 to 200 basis points and then rise from 50 to 100 basis points above those levels. New York prime should average 8.00, while three-month Treasury bill and CD rates should move to 4.50 to 5.00 percent. Long government bonds will fluctuate between 5.00 and 6.00 percent. All rate bets are off if there is a recession moving into 1999, in which case all interest rates will continue to fall.

Quaker National Bank will pay competitive deposit rates at the high end to enlarge its base of core deposits. It will not match rates offered by some of the thrifts in our market area but will pay rates above those of our bank competitors.

CASE 4

PERALTA NATIONAL BANK

INTRODUCTION

The Asset and Liability Committee (ALCO) of Peralta National Bank gathered promptly in the bank's board room at 8:00 A.M. on October 26, 1992, for its regular monthly meeting. The committee members gradually had become aware that the bank was developing an unusual mix of assets. Loan demand was very weak, and, increasingly, the bank was compelled to find appropriate investment instruments in the national money and bond markets for the bank's large supplies of available funds. During 1991 and 1992, the bank experienced substantial increases in its core deposits when it acquired several branches of a failed thrift institution in its region that was being liquidated by the FDIC. Today's meeting was important because the bank's available funds had continued to grow in the third quarter of 1992, while loans continued to retreat. As a result, the bank's loans-to-deposit ratio stood well below the range that had been targeted by the board of directors.

ALCO

The members of ALCO included the following:

Chairman of the board,	Ed Chalmers
President,	Dwight Jamison
Executive vice-president and chief lending officer,	George Svoboda
Senior vice-president, chief of operations and branch administration,	Lucille Van Order
Senior vice-president and investments officer,	Anna Martinez
Senior vice-president and controller,	Arnold Weitzman

ALCO (sometimes called the *funds management committee*) was responsible for the overall financial direction of the bank. In this role it controlled the attraction and application of the bank's funds. At its monthly meetings the committee reviewed the status of the bank's liquidity, interest rate sensitivity, investment and loan portfolios, deposit activity and pricing, and capital. ALCO's considered decisions were referred for action to three separate committees for loans, investments, and pricing. ALCO's activities were monitored by the bank's board of directors. All decisions pertaining to the bank's capital position were made by the board.

ECONOMIC AND INTEREST RATE CONDITIONS

Chairman Ed Chalmers called the meeting to order and asked Arnold Weitzman to distribute the agenda (Exhibit 1). The meeting began with a discussion of national and local economic and interest rate conditions, led by Dwight Jamison. The discussion focused on the continuing steep positive slope of the yield curve. Jamison directed the committee's attention to the interest rate report shown in Exhibit 2. He noted that short-term interest rates, represented by the three-month Treasury bill, recently had declined to 3 percent, while the yields on long-term Treasury securities such as the 30-year bond were 7.5 percent or more. He seemed optimistic that short-term interest rates would remain low. He reminded the committee that the Federal Reserve had lowered the discount rate repeatedly in the past several months, and he observed that the Fed seemed determined to hold rates down to prevent any interruption of the economic recovery.

However, Jamison cautioned that the presidential election to be held the coming week, on November 3, might change the present outlook. Several prominent economists believed that if the Democratic candidate were elected—and it seemed that he would be—a fiscal stimulus package of increased government spending might ignite inflationary forces and drive interest rates higher. If that happened, he warned, "the stage is set for deposit interest rates to rise rapidly. Banks that are investing in long-term securities with today's low-cost, short-term deposits could have a lot of difficulty."

Chalmers joined in with the observation that the steep upward-sloped yield curve could not continue forever, and he speculated that one of two things would occur: either the low, short-term interest rates would pull down the long-term rates or the high, long-term rates would force the short-term rates to surge. Chalmers commented that financial theory supported the latter result; short-term rates must eventually rise. He said, "It is just a matter of time before short-term rates take off."

BANK PERFORMANCE

Arnold Weitzman, the bank's controller, distributed the bank's income statements, balance sheets, and ratio analysis (Exhibits 3, 4, and 5, respectively). The committee noted with satisfaction that the bank's profitability remained strong. However, Weitzman explained that although bank profits were up for the total nine-month period of 1992 through September, results for the third quarter, as well as for October, were below the bank's profit plan. "The August, September, and October figures show that we are not sustaining the unprecedented net interest margins we made in the first two quarters of this year."

Loan quality was very high, and virtually no losses had been experienced for the past three years. George Svoboda, who had joined the bank several years ago as its chief lending officer, could not avoid gloating over the vast improvement in loan quality. "When I arrived here three and a half years ago, this bank's loan policies were out of control. With the huge losses it had taken, the bank was almost dead in the water. The turnaround in our loan quality is truly remarkable."

President Jamison countered, "George, we may not be taking losses, but it looks to me like we are not taking *loans* either! We seem to have developed a large liquidity position and have no place to invest it. We have finally rebuilt our capital from the disasters in real estate lending this bank experienced in the late 1980s. Is it not time to use our capital for making loans to business? After all, the purpose of our capital is to support that kind of risk taking."

LOAN ACTIVITY

Since his arrival as head loan officer at Peralta National Bank, George Svoboda had insisted that the bank adopt a comprehensive loan policy and a rigorous structure of loan analysis and approval. The loan policy set strict documentation requirements, and loans were reviewed periodically to ascertain that borrowers were performing as agreed and that loan file data were current. The policy required the board to set the desired mix of commercial, consumer, agricultural, and real estate loans. A new approval process for loan requests consisted of controls at three levels. First, individual loan officers were given approval authority levels that did not require committee action. These ranged from $10,000 for junior officers to $100,000 for President Jamison and Chief Lending Officer Svoboda. Second, the senior loan committee met at least twice weekly to review requests for large loans and lines of credit. This committee also considered any requests that raised the aggregate borrowing of a customer to more than $100,000. Finally, at the third level of approval, loan requests that raised a single borrower's aggregate borrowings above $500,000 were submitted to the board of directors' loan committee. Recently, real estate loans had constituted about 10 percent of the loan portfolio, which fell far short of the board's desired 25 percent target. Also, the bank's 52 percent loan-to-deposit ratio was well below the board's desired ratio of 65 to 75 percent.

Svoboda reported a continuing shortage of what he considered good-quality loan requests. "In fact," he commented, "since the beginning of this year, we have had quite a few of our strong borrowers reduce or pay off their loans. As you know, we are extremely liquid, but until loan demand becomes more vigorous, I suggest we invest excess funds in short-term, readily marketable securities. The time will come when our borrowers will expect us to have funds immediately available."

Svoboda observed that most economists were predicting slow, if any, loan growth through the first half of 1993. "Our largest borrowers agree," he said.

They are telling us to expect their funding needs to accelerate in the second half of next year. In the meantime, even though the loan portfolio is shrinking, we are still receiving high income because of our new premium pricing policy of charging for loan risk as fully as possible. Concerning the restoration of our capital position, it is true that we have made progress. Our risk-based capital to risk-weighted assets is 11 percent and exceeds the board's minimum 10 percent limit. Also, we have nearly achieved the board's leverage capital limit of 7 percent. However, our capital ratios remain well below those of our peers. I believe we must protect the bank's capital by remaining cautious until highly qualified borrowers return.

SECURITIES ACTIVITY

Peralta Bank's investment policy required the purchase and sale of investment securities with maturities of greater than one year to be submitted to ALCO for approval. The stated objectives for management of the investment portfolio were as follows:

1. To ensure an adequate degree of safety of invested funds.
2. To provide liquidity.

3. To act as a primary asset pool for the management of interest rate risk.
4. To maximize the return on invested funds.
5. To provide a mix of securities that meets collateral requirements for public deposits.

Anna Martinez, the investment officer, reported that since August, inflows of funds from loan payoffs and a large volume of maturing securities had been reinvested in Treasury bills, interest-bearing interbank deposits, and short-term tranches of mortgage pass-through securities called *planned amortization classes (PACs)*. In addition, the bank had developed a large position in federal funds sales. Martinez explained that in her opinion, the decline in net interest margin recorded since August was due to the shift from high-yielding loans and securities to low-yielding short-term securities. "However," she explained, "the bank's interest sensitivity position has improved." Martinez distributed the interest sensitivity analyses prepared by her department (Exhibits 6 and 7). Referring to Exhibit 5, she noted, "We are slightly more liability sensitive than our peer banks, but we have twice the volume of assets repriceable in three months as our peers." Regarding the interest sensitivity report shown in Exhibit 6, she commented, "Actually, I am not satisfied that we report the interest sensitivities of our core deposits correctly—especially our demand and NOW deposits. Do we seriously believe that all of these are truly repriceable in one to three months? Why are they not all shown in the long-term categories?"

Concerning the shape of the yield curve, Martinez argued, "The present yield curve is the steepest that any of us can remember. This is the time to invest in long-term bonds and mortgage-backed securities. The spread between deposit rates at less than 3 percent and 30-year Treasury bond yields at 7.5 percent or—even better—mortgage-backed securities at 8.5 percent is a sure thing. And if interest rates do start to move up, these spreads of $4\frac{1}{2}$ to $5\frac{1}{2}$ percent give us a huge cushion against increases in the cost of our deposits. I believe we could move our whole federal funds position into long-term securities such as guaranteed mortgage agency securities—Ginnie Maes or Freddie Macs."

THE DEBATE

Lucille Van Order, the bank's operations officer, had been silent until now. On hearing Martinez's comments, she spoke up concerning the risks of the potential effects of rising interest rates on deposit pricing and long-term securities. "After all, if we are forced to become more competitive on deposit rates and we are locked into long-term securities, our net interest income is going to be damaged." Van Order reminded the committee about the bank's policy for managing interest sensitivity. The policy prohibited the bank from taking interest rate positions that could impair the bank's planned net interest income by more than 5 percent if interest rates changed by 1 percent. Referring to Exhibit 7, Van Order noted that the bank's simulation model indicated that a 1 percent rise in interest rates would reduce November's net interest income by 5.4 percent, an amount that exceeded the 5 percent limit on interest rate risk exposure established as policy by the board of directors. She stated that, in her opinion, a larger movement in interest rates would do even more serious damage to net interest income.[1]

At this point, several members of the committee began talking at the same time in animated tones. Jamison cautioned against extending investment maturities beyond five years, noting that "we may not earn 7½ percent or 8½ percent but 6 percent or 7 percent still would give us an ample spread over 3 percent deposits and we would not be locked in to 30-year securities."

Svoboda countered, observing, "We are going to need those deposits later next year. If interest rates rise, we will have to raise our deposit prices to meet them or we will be left high and dry when our major loan accounts come looking for funds. The best alternative is to invest in short-term securities to just match off the deposits. Besides, this

will keep our interest rate sensitivity from getting out of control."

Anna Martinez stated, "Maybe I have some alternatives that can keep everyone satisfied, and serve both our return and risk objectives." She produced an offering statement (Exhibit 8) for mortgage-backed offerings the bank had received yesterday afternoon. Ms. Martinez said, "These are government agency issues and so they have no credit risk. The first two issues reprice monthly and the third annually, which would improve our interest rate risk position. And since we have a reputable investment banker making the offerings, we know that the average life calculations are accurate." The looks on the faces around the room hinted to Anna that the real debate was about to start.

[1]Investment Department staff members prepared the matrix shown in Exhibit 7 every month, using the bank's computer simulation model. The matrix quantifies interest rate risk for the current month as well as the coming year. In addition to presenting current net interest income sensitivity, it reveals the bank's future net interest income sensitivity from a static perspective. This static view shows what the interest rate risk will be at future dates if the present balance sheet items are permitted to run off contractually between the present and the future dates shown.

To create the interest rate risk matrix, the bank simulates its expected base net interest income for future dates under a no-rate-change scenario. Then it determines the extent of income variations on the residual assets and liabilities, given certain changes in rates. The bank considers the assumption of immediate rate shocks (shown as positive 1, 2, 3, and 4 percent, as well as negative 1 and 2 percent) to be naive because it involves the instantaneous movement of rates at all maturities. The bank prefers instead the more realistic gradual changes shown. In addition, the bank tests for changes in basis—the risk that the relationship between rates on different financial instruments with equal maturities may vary.

EXHIBIT 1   Agenda for Asset and Liability Committee Meeting of October 26, 1992

I. Outlook for local and national economy and interest rates
II. Review of bank's performance
   a. profitability
   b. loan quality
   c. capital
   d. interest rate sensitivity
   e. liquidity
III. Loan activity report
IV. Securities portfolio status; proposed transactions
V. Deposit pricing committee report
VI. Proposed action steps

EXHIBIT 2   Yield Curve (as of 10/26/92)

Maturity	Interest Rate
3 months	2.971%
6 months	3.297
1 year	3.516
2 years	4.340
3 years	4.888
5 years	5.883
7 years	6.428
10 years	6.842
30 years	7.664

EXHIBIT 2   *(Continued)* **Blue Chip Financial Forecasts**

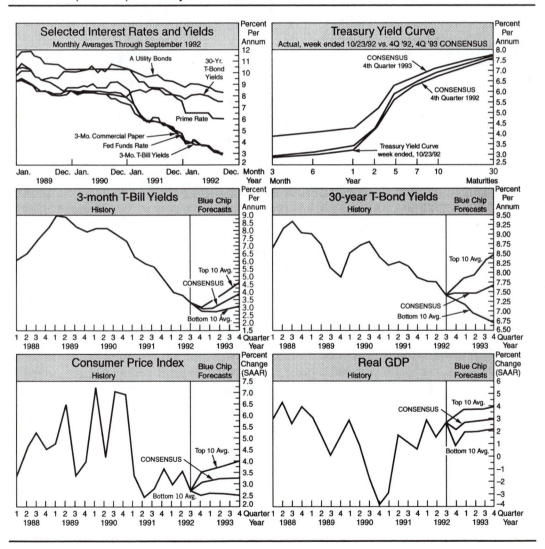

EXHIBIT 3   Peralta National Bank Balance Sheets (dollars in thousands)

	9/30/92	12/31/91	12/31/90	12/31/89
Assets				
Cash and due from banks	$ 8,020	$ 11,510	$ 12,630	$ 12,910
Investments	76,042	71,955	54,162	55,449
Federal funds sold	41,030	200	0	7,390
Gross: Loans and leases	137,128	163,070	150,269	127,742
Less: Allowance	2,360	2,300	2,270	1,900
Net loans and leases	134,768	160,770	147,999	125,842
Premises, fixed assets	11,870	7,570	8,040	3,170
Other assets	13,310	13,090	12,000	2,610
Total assets	$285,040	$265,095	$234,831	$207,371
Liabilities				
Demand and NOW deposits	$111,910	$ 92,980	$ 78,460	$ 78,040
Money market deposits	97,520	95,960	75,630	71,390
Savings deposits	24,580	19,520	15,410	13,690
Time deposits < $100,000	22,820	25,780	23,900	14,190
Time deposits > $100,000	7,020	11,310	25,700	14,500
Total deposits	263,850	245,550	219,100	191,810
Other liabilities	1,030	1,650	1,030	1,790
Equity capital	20,160	17,895	14,701	13,771
Total liabilities & capital	$285,040	$265,095	$234,831	$207,371

EXHIBIT 4   Peralta National Bank Income Statements (dollars in thousands)

	Three Quarters Ending 9/30/92	12/31/91	12/31/90	12/31/89
Interest and fees on loans	$12,379	$17,366	$17,689	$15,913
Interest on investments—TE	5,181	6,134	5,541	4,087
Total interest income—TE	17,560	23,500	23,230	20,000
Total interest expense	6,831	11,917	12,263	9,036
Net interest income—TE	10,729	11,583	10,967	10,964
Noninterest income	3,840	5,540	4,410	3,470
Adjusted operating income—TE	14,569	17,123	15,377	14,434
Overhead expense	9,770	11,500	10,190	10,160
Provision: Loan and lease losses	60	0	400	240
Pretax net operating income	4,739	5,623	4,787	4,034
Applicable income taxes + tax equivalent adjustment	1,960	2,370	2,110	1,670
Net income	$ 2,779	$ 3,253	$ 2,677	$ 2,364

EXHIBIT 5   Peralta National Bank Ratio Analysis (all numbers are percents)

	9/30/92[a]		12/31/91		12/31/90	
	PNB	Peer	PNB	Peer	PNB	Peer
Income Statement (% of Assets)						
Total interest income—TE	8.45	8.17	9.26	9.07	10.25	9.52
Total interest expense	3.28	3.77	4.70	4.93	5.41	5.42
Net interest income—TE	5.17	4.40	4.56	4.14	4.84	4.10
+ Noninterest income	1.85	0.53	2.18	0.53	1.95	0.56
− Overhead expense	4.70	2.79	4.53	2.84	4.49	3.12
− Provision: Loan & lease losses	0.03	0.13	0.00	0.17	0.00	0.00
Securities gains/losses	0.00	0.02	0.00	0.01	0.00	0.00
= Pretax net oper. income	2.29	2.02	2.21	1.66	2.30	1.36
Applicable income taxes + tax equiv- alent adjustment	0.94	0.68	0.94	0.58	0.93	0.43
Net income	1.35	1.34	1.27	1.08	1.37	0.93
Profitability						
Net int. inc./avg. earn. assets	6.02	4.69	5.37	4.42	5.30	4.43
Return on average assets	1.35	1.34	1.27	1.08	1.37	0.93
Return on average equity	19.41	13.42	19.81	10.87	22.33	9.63
Net overhead	2.85	2.26	2.35	2.31	2.54	2.56
Efficiency	0.67	0.57	0.67	0.61	0.66	0.67
Liquidity						
Volatile liab. dependence	−16.71	−5.73	1.49	−13.23	12.48	−18.87
Net loans & leases to assets	47.28	54.42	61.51	55.78	63.99	56.67
Net loans & leases to deposits	51.97	60.23	66.41	62.95	71.00	65.48
Loan Quality						
Net loss to avg. loans & leases	0.00	0.17	0.02	0.31	0.02	0.34
Loans & leases allowance to loans & leases	1.56	1.76	1.30	1.75	1.40	1.82
Noncurrent loans & leases to loans & leases	0.32	1.13	0.90	1.28	0.20	1.35
Capital						
Tier I leverage capital	6.98	9.90	6.67	9.49	6.16	9.15
Tier I & tier II capital to risk-wt. assets	11.01	19.11	10.31	18.58	9.67	18.02
Retained earnings to avg. equity	11.40	8.09	13.42	5.63	6.18	5.07
Dividends to net income	55.60	18.77	46.04	40.42	74.95	33.18
Interest Rate Sensitivity (% of Assets)						
Assets repriced in 3 months	42.11	23.92				
Liabilities repriced in 3 months	59.02	39.47				
Net 3-month position	−16.91	−15.55				
Assets repriced in 6 months	49.80	46.79				
Liabilities repriced in 6 months	64.11	62.47				
Net 6-month position	−14.31	−15.68				

[a]These data are annualized.

EXHIBIT 6   Peralta National Bank Interest Sensitivity Analysis (dollars in thousands)

	September 30, 1992						
	0–30	31–90	91–182	183–1 yr	1–2 yrs	>2 yrs	Total
Interest Sensitive Assets							
Fed funds sold	$ 41,030						$ 41,030
Securities	24,221	$ 8,044	$10,983	$ 5,634	$16,355	$10,805	76,042
Floating rate loans	30,688	4,806	2,862	6,124	30	88	44,598
Fixed:							
Commercial lns.	3,075	3,588	4,616	2,439	3,301	22,180	38,199
Consumer lns.	510	2,617	2,478	4,128	9,023	15,044	33,800
Credit cards						1,829	1,829
Agricultural loans	375	868	623	487	1,649	1,568	5,570
Real estate loans	107	178	260	341	1,049	11,197	13,132
Allowance for loan losses						(2,360)	(2,360)
Total	$100,006	$20,101	$21,822	$19,153	$31,407	$60,351	$251,840
Interest Sensitive Liabilities							
Fed funds purchased							
Demand & NOW	$ 14,439	$23,879	$ 9,200		$3,342	$61,050	$111,910
Savings & MM	122,100						122,100
CDs < 100	1,986	2,142	4,876	$ 4,363	3,535	5,918	22,820
CDs > 100	2,050	1,584	463	1,445	918	560	7,020
Other liabilities							
Total	$140,575	$27,605	$14,539	$ 5,808	$ 7,795	$67,528	$263,850
GAP	−40,569	−7,504	7,283	13,345	23,612	−7,177	
% GAP	−14.23%	−2.63%	2.56%	4.68%	8.28%	−2.52%	
CUM GAP	−40,569	−48,073	−40,790	−27,445	−3,833	−11,010	
% C GAP	−14.23%	−16.86%	−14.30%	−9.62%	−1.34%	−3.86%	

EXHIBIT 7   Peralta National Bank Rolling 12-Month Interest Rate Risk

Percent Change in Net Interest Margin Because of:
Immediate Rate Shock

Occurring on	11/1/92	2/1/93	5/1/93	8/1/93	11/1/93
(parallel rate shock)					
4.00%	−31.6%				
3.00%	−21.1%				
2.00%	−12.0%				
1.00%	−5.4%	−5.3%	−4.7%	−0.5%	+2.3%
Base net interest income	$10.2 mm	$10.6 mm	$11.1 mm	$11.3 mm	$11.5 mm
Projection (annual)					
−1.00%	10.8%				
−2.00%	15.6%				
Yield Curve Variations					
Gradual +2% over 2 yrs.	−3.4%				+1.8%
Gradual +4% over 2 yrs.	−7.4%				−0.4%
Short rates +2%—2 yrs.	−5.2%				−0.8%
Long rates −2%—2 yrs.	−0.3%				−1.7%
Basis Risk					
Gradual +2% over 2 yrs.	−5.2%				−12.0%
Gradual +4% over 2 yrs.	−5.4%				−12.0%

EXHIBIT 8   Market Offerings (October 25, 1992)

	Description	Coupon	Average Life (yrs.)	Price	Yield (%)
Floating	CMO Floating Rate Class F				
	1 Mo Libor + 50 − Monthly	3.75%	3.5	100.00	3.75
Floating	CMO Floating Rate Class G				
	11th District COFI + 100 − Monthly	5.60%	2.4	100.00	5.60
Floating	GNMA ARM				
	1 Yr CMT + 150 − Annual	5.50%	8.5	100.00	5.50
Fixed	FNMA 7 Yr Balloon	6.50%	4.6	100.50	6.33
Fixed	FNMA 15 Yr	7.00%	6.0	100.875	6.80
Fixed	FNMA 30 Yr	7.50%	8.2	98.25	7.86

CASE 5

NORWEST CORPORATION

INTRODUCTION

In early 1997, Norwest Corporation was celebrating a historic achievement in the year just past when its net income exceeded $1 billion for the first time in history. The firm's 1996 earnings totaled $1.154 billion on year-end assets of $80 billion (see Exhibits 1 and 2). The corporation was the twelfth largest banking company in the United States. The firm had over 53,000 employees, and the market capitalization of its stock was in excess of $16 billion. The firm was proud of its 3,449 business offices—Norwest employees called them "stores"—which were distributed across all 50 states. The corporation had three major components: Norwest Banks, with offices in 16 states; Norwest Mortgage, which claimed to finance one out of every 15 mortgages in the United States; and Norwest Financial, a consumer finance subsidiary with 3.6 million customers.

FUNDING PATTERN

Norwest's three business components provided the firm with an enormously diverse base of earning assets, including net loans and leases of $38 billion (Exhibit 1). Much of the asset base consisted of consumer products, including installment loans, sales finance contracts, and credit card loans. Norwest held a large portfolio of mortgage servicing rights. In addition, the firm had a diverse presence in business lending. Its typical small office, often located outside of large cities, was active in small business lending, Small Business Administration (government-guaranteed) loans, and, in larger offices, financing for middle market companies. In addition, specialized subsidiaries in "asset-based" business credit and equipment leasing helped to round out its loan portfolio. Finally, the firm held a total of nearly $19 billion in investment securities, some of which the firm used flexibly to adjust its asset and liability position.

Norwest Corporation benefited from an especially solid funding base. Because of the firm's retail thrust and network of small offices, 58 percent of the corporation's total funding consisted of core deposits, including demand deposits, regular savings and NOW accounts, money market checking, and consumer savings certificates. The core funds represented an unusually high percentage of funds according to industry standards. These funds provided highly stable and low-cost funding. While many core deposit rates increased when market interest rates increased, they did so with a lag and then moved slowly. Short-term borrowing, consisting of federal funds purchased, repurchase agreements, negotiated private financing, and commercial paper issued by Norwest Mortgage and Norwest Financial, accounted for another 11.6 percent of financing. Other sources of funds included about 4 percent in purchased deposits—CDs of more than $100,000 and foreign deposits—long-term debt accounting for another 18.5 percent, and a moderate amount from equity sources (mostly retained earnings).

INTEREST RATE SENSITIVITY

As is often the case, the direction for interest rates in early 1997 was uncertain. Rates had been quite stable throughout 1996, although, as the year ended, market experts grew cautious about the Federal Reserve's intentions. Some assumed the Fed would raise rates soon to try to get ahead of possibly upcoming inflationary pressures. As 1997 began, there was already evidence that there would be upward pressure on rates during the first quarter. Norwest's financial executives explained how the corporation's system for asset and liability management dealt with interest-sensitivity risk.[1]

Asset and Liability Management

The goal of the asset and liability management process is to manage the structure of the balance sheet in order to provide the maximum acceptable levels of interest-sensitivity risk and liquidity. The focal point of this process is the corporate Asset and Liability Management Committee (ALCO). This committee forms and monitors policies governing investments, funding sources, off-balance sheet commitments, overall interest-sensitivity risk, and liquidity. These policies form the framework for

---

[1] The following description appears in Norwest Corporation 1996 Annual Report published by Norwest Corporation.

management of the asset and liability process at the corporate and affiliate levels. The corporation's interest-sensitivity position is managed as a function of balance sheet trends, asset opportunities, and interest rate expectations, and the corporation is normally well within policy risk limits at any given time.

Definition of Interest-Sensitivity Risk

Interest-sensitivity risk is the risk that future changes in interest rates will reduce net interest income or the net market value of the corporation's balance sheet. Two basic ways of defining interest rate risk in the financial services industry are commonly referred to as the accounting perspective and the economic perspective. The corporation draws on aspects of each perspective to provide a more complete picture of interest rate risk than would be provided by either perspective alone.

The accounting perspective focuses on the risk to reported net income over a particular time frame. Differences in the timing of interest rate repricing (repricing risk or "gap" risk) and changing market rate relationships (basis risk) determine the exposure of net income to changes in interest rates.

The economic perspective focuses on the risk to the market value of the corporation's balance sheet, the net of which is referred to as the market value of balance sheet equity. The sensitivity of the market value of balance sheet equity to changes in interest rates is an indication of both the level of interest rate risk inherent in the institution's current position and longer term horizon earnings trends. Assessing interest rate risk from the economic perspective focuses on the risk to net worth arising from all repricing mismatches (gaps) across the full maturity spectrum.

Measurement of Interest Rate Risk

Measurement of interest rate risk from the accounting perspective has traditionally taken the form of the gap report, which represents the difference between assets and liabilities that reprice in given time periods. While providing a rough measure of rate risk, the gap report provides only a static (i.e., point-in-time) measurement, and it does not require basis risk or risks that vary either asymmetrically or nonproportionately with rate movements.

The corporation uses a simulation model as its primary method of measuring earnings risk. The simulation model, because of its dynamic nature, can capture the effects of future balance sheet trends, different patterns of rate movements, and changing relationships between rates (basis risk). In addition, it can capture the effects of embedded option risk by taking into account the effects of interest rate caps and floors, and varying the level of prepayment rates on assets as a function of interest rates. The simulation model is used to determine the one- and three-year gap levels that correspond to the limits within which the corporation has placed earnings at risk to interest rate movements.

Measurement of interest rate risk from the economic perspective is accomplished with a market valuation model. The market value of each asset and liability is calculated by computing the present value of all cash flows generated. In each case the cash flows are discounted by a market interest rate chosen to reflect as closely as possible the characteristics of the given asset or liability.

Management of Interest Rate Risk

In the most current simulation, net income was forecasted using various interest rate scenarios. A most likely scenario, in which short rates remain constant but long rates increase somewhat, was used as the base case for comparison of other scenarios. If short rates increase 200 basis points above the base case over the next 12 months, accompanied by a smaller increase in long rates, the effect will be to decrease net income by approximately $40 million relative to the base case. If short rates decrease 200 basis points below the base case over the next 12 months, accompanied by a lesser decrease in long rates, the effect will be to increase net income by approximately $63 million. This analysis takes into account the effect of derivative products that are used to hedge balance sheet instruments, as well as the effect of interest rates on prepayment speeds of mortgages and mortgage-backed securities. However, under the rate scenarios considered, net income would not be affected by impairment of capitalized mortgage servicing rights.

The market valuation model is used to measure the sensitivity of the market value of equity to a wide range of interest rate changes. The process of modeling market valuation risk continues to evolve in the financial services industry, including structuring the modeling process, defining policy limits, and interpreting the results.

Changes in Interest Sensitivity

Exhibit 3 presents the corporation's interest-sensitivity gaps for December 1996. The cumulative

202   Case 5

gap within one year was $(3,317) million, or (4.2) percent of assets. This compares with a one-year gap of $(2,762) million, or (3.8) percent of assets, in December 1995. The cumulative gap within three years was $(990) million, or (1.2) percent of assets, in December 1996, compared to $(1,603) million, or (2.2) percent of assets, in December 1995. The relatively small changes in the gaps in percentage terms are due to a number of offsetting changes in the balance sheet during the year, including increases in the investment portfolio and demand deposits. The current interest-sensitivity position makes the corporation's earnings slightly vulnerable to rising rates and neutral to falling rates.

In addition to adjusting the prices and levels of assets and liabilities, the corporation utilizes off-balance sheet derivative financial instruments to manage interest rate risk. The corporation primarily enters into interest rate swaps, interest rate caps and floors, futures contracts, and options as part of its overall risk management activities. Certain of these derivative financial instruments synthetically change the repricing or other characteristics of underlying assets and liabilities hedged. The corporation principally utilizes interest rate swaps to hedge certain fixed-rate debt and certain deposit liabilities and to convert these funding sources to floating rates. Interest rate floors, futures contracts, and options on futures contracts are principally used to hedge the corporation's portfolio of mortgage servicing rights. The floors provide for the receipt of payments when interest rates are below predetermined interest rate levels. The unrealized gains (losses) on the floors and futures contracts are included, as appropriate, in determining the fair value of mortgages servicing rights, offsetting lost future servicing revenue related to increased levels of prepayments associated with lower interest rates.

The corporation's net cash flows from off-balance sheet derivative financial instruments used to manage interest rate risk added approximately $56.9 million to net interest income in 1996, compared with $7.1 million in 1995 and $12.3 million in 1994. This resulted in an impact on net interest margin of nine basis points in 1996, compared with one basis point in 1995 and two basis points in 1994.

Based on interest rate levels at December 31, 1996, total estimated future cash flows related to the corporation's derivative financial instruments, including interest rate swaps and floors hedging capitalized mortgage servicing rights, are expected to approximate $74 million in 1997, $55 million in 1998, $52 million in 1999, $32 million in 2000, $23 million in 2001, and $59 million thereafter.

QUESTIONS

1. Discuss limitations in the reliability of the interest rate-sensitivity gap. As implied in the case, the methodology is to classify assets and liabilities in terms of the time to certain repricing events (maturity, adjustment upon a change in market rates, amortization of a portion of principal, expected prepayment of certain assets, and early withdrawal of liabilities before maturity). What factors would you cite to show weaknesses in the precision of and methodology for creating the interest rate-sensitivity gap report?

2. Assume an immediate and sustained 1 percent across-the-board rise in interest rates. Based on a review of Exhibit 3, discuss how one would use interest rate-sensitivity gap information to estimate the impact of rising interest rates on the earnings of Norwest Corporation.

3. Describe in your own words Norwest's methodology for determining "accounting risk" and "economic risk" and the distinctions between them.

4. What would you suppose to be some practical difficulties in the art of earnings simulation modeling? Why is it a preferred method for measuring interest rate risk?

5. What difficulties do you suppose Norwest faces in creating a reliable "market value model?"

6. Suppose Norwest strongly believes interest rates will rise materially in 1997 and estimates that the rise will cause a drop in earnings. Discuss the practical steps it could take to reduce the size of the earnings reduction. Describe both on-balance sheet measures and off-balance sheet measures the corporation might take.

EXHIBIT I Norwest Corporation and Subsidiaries Consolidated Balance Sheets

In millions, except shares At December 31,	1996	1995
Assets		
Cash and due from banks	$ 4,856.6	4,320.3
Interest-bearing deposits with banks	1,237.9	29.4
Federal funds sold and resale agreements	1,276.8	596.8
Total cash and cash equivalents	7,371.3	4,946.5
Trading account securities	186.5	150.6
Investment securities (fair value $745.2 in 1996 and $795.8 in 1995)	712.2	760.5
Investment and mortgage-backed securities available for sale	16,247.1	15,243.0
Total investment securities	16,959.3	16,003.5
Loans held for sale	2,827.6	3,343.9
Mortgages held for sale	6,339.0	6,514.5
Loans and leases, net of unearned discount	39,381.0	36,153.1
Allowance for credit losses	(1,040.8)	(917.2)
Net loans and leases	38,340.2	35,235.9
Premises and equipment, net	1,200.9	1,034.1
Mortgage servicing rights, net	2,648.5	1,226.7
Interest receivable and other assets	4,302.1	3,678.7
Total assets	$80,175.4	72,134.4
Liabilities and Stockholders' Equity		
Deposits		
Noninterest-bearing	$14,296.3	11,623.9
Interest-bearing	35,833.9	30,404.9
Total deposits	50,130.2	42,028.8
Short-term borrowings	7,572.6	8,527.2
Accrued expense and other liabilities	3,326.2	2,589.5
Long-term debt	13,082.2	13,676.8
Total liabilities	74,111.2	66,822.3
Preferred stock	249.8	341.2
Unearned ESOP shares	(61.0)	(38.9)
Total preferred stock	188.8	302.3
Common stock, $1⅔ par value–authorized 500,000,000 shares: Issued 375,533,625 and 358,332,153 shares in 1996 and 1995, respectively	625.9	597.2
Surplus	948.6	734.2
Retained earnings	4,248.2	3,496.3
Net unrealized gains on securities available for sale	303.5	327.1
Notes receivable from ESOP	(11.1)	(13.3)
Treasury stock—6,830,919 and 5,571,696 common shares in 1996 and 1995, respectively	(233.3)	(125.9)
Foreign currency translation	(6.4)	(5.8)
Total common stockholders' equity	5,875.4	5,009.8
Total stockholders' equity	6,064.2	5,312.1
Total liabilities and stockholders' equity	$80,175.4	72,134.4

See notes to consolidated financial statements.

EXHIBIT 2 **Norwest Corporation and Subsidiaries Consolidated Statements of Income**

In millions, except per common share amounts Years Ended December 31,	1996	1995	1994
Interest Income on			
Loans and leases	$4,301.5	3,955.8	3,071.2
Investment securities	36.2	83.8	71.5
Investment and mortgage-backed securities available for sale	1,170.1	1,065.3	835.9
Loans held for sale	254.3	195.7	111.4
Mortgages held for sale	468.5	366.2	257.2
Money market investments	63.0	35.7	21.9
Trading account securities	24.7	14.8	24.6
Total interest income	6,318.3	5,717.3	4,393.7
Interest Expense on			
Deposits	1,324.9	1,156.3	863.4
Short-term borrowings	454.1	515.8	290.3
Long-term debt	838.0	775.9	436.4
Total interest expense	2,617.0	2,448.0	1,590.1
Net Interest Income	3,701.3	3,269.3	2,803.6
Provision for credit losses	394.7	312.4	164.9
Net interest income after provision for credit losses	3,306.6	2,956.9	2,638.7
Noninterest Income			
Trust	296.3	240.7	210.3
Service charges on deposit accounts	329.5	268.8	234.4
Mortgage banking	821.5	535.5	581.0
Data processing	72.5	72.4	61.6
Credit card	122.2	132.8	116.5
Insurance	279.6	224.7	207.4
Other fees and service charges	294.4	230.3	182.3
Net investment securities gains (losses)	—	0.6	(0.2)
Net investment and mortgage-backed securities available for sale losses	(46.8)	(45.1)	(79.0)
Net venture capital gains	256.4	102.1	77.1
Trading	35.3	39.9	(18.1)
Other	103.7	45.5	65.0
Total noninterest income	2,564.6	1,848.2	1,638.3
Noninterest Expenses			
Salaries and benefits	2,097.1	1,745.1	1,573.7
Net occupancy	316.3	254.4	227.3
Equipment rentals, depreciation and maintenance	327.7	272.7	235.4
Business development	227.9	172.2	190.5
Communication	285.2	225.0	184.8
Data processing	163.0	136.2	113.4
Intangible asset amortization	161.5	124.7	77.0
Other	511.0	452.0	494.3
Total noninterest expenses	4,089.7	3,382.3	3,096.4
Income Before Income Taxes	1,781.5	1,422.8	1,180.6
Income tax expense	627.6	466.8	380.2
Net Income	$1,153.9	956.0	800.4
Average common and common equivalent shares	369.7	331.7	315.1
Per Common Share			
Net Income			
Primary	$ 3.07	2.76	2.45
Fully diluted	$ 3.07	2.73	2.41
Dividends	$1.050	0.900	0.765

EXHIBIT 3   Norwest Corporation and Subsidiaries Interest Rate Sensitivity

In millions, except ratios Average Balances For December 1996	*Repricing or Maturing*				
	Within 6 Months	6 Months– 1 Year	1 Year– 3 Years	3 Years– 5 Years	After 5 Years
Loans and leases	$16,813	3,103	5,966	2,863	10,437
Investment securities	2,218	2,088	2,700	1,935	8,166
Loans held for sale	2,659	—	—	—	—
Mortgages held for sale	5,881	—	—	—	—
Other earning assets	4,251	—	—	—	—
Other assets	—	650	—	—	10,102
Total assets	$31,822	5,841	8,666	4,798	28,705
Noninterest-bearing deposits	$ 4,134	63	268	178	8,832
Interest-bearing deposits	16,508	3,733	4,770	981	9,633
Short-term borrowings	8,230	—	—	—	—
Long-term debt	3,938	709	2,266	2,321	4,154
Other liabilities and equity	1	—	188	—	8,925
Total liabilities and equity	$32,811	4,505	7,492	3,480	31,544
Swaps and options	$ (3,860)	196	1,153	866	1,645
Gap*	(4,849)	1,532	2,327	2,184	(1,194)
Cumulative Gap	(4,849)	(3,317)	(990)	1,194	—
Gap as a percent of total assets	(6.1)%	(4.2)	(1.2)	1.5	—

*[Assets − (Liabilities + Equity) + Swaps and options] The gap includes the effect of off-balance sheet instruments on the corporation's interest sensitivity.

PART TWO

ASSET, LIABILITY, AND CAPITAL DECISIONS

P art Two of this book, consisting of Chapters 6 through 9, discusses the basic methods for obtaining and using funds (excluding lending, which is covered in Part Three). Chapter 6 analyzes how banks determine the funds they want to acquire through depository relationships and borrowing; Chapter 7 covers decisions involving the bank's reserve (or money) position and its liquidity position; Chapter 8 discusses management of the bank's security portfolio; and Chapter 9 examines obtaining and managing the bank's capital position. ∎

CHAPTER 6

The Acquisition and Cost of Bank Funds

The ability to attract funds at a reasonable cost has become one of the key ingredients of commercial bank management in recent years. For many years after the Depression of the 1930s, banking could be labeled as an industry that emphasized the use of funds. Bank management focused on how to lend and invest the surplus funds that banks were easily able to attract. Although the use of attracted funds is still important, changing conditions, such as the shortage of savings, increased competition for these scarce savings, and increasing loan demands, force banks to place increased emphasis on attracting funds. This shift is demonstrated by the more creative and intensive use of existing sources of funds and by the aggressive development of new sources of funds during the 1970s and much of the 1980s. By the late 1980s, declining loan demand and pressures to increase capital positions lowered funding needs, and banks were able to lower their cost of funding. The prosperity of the late 1990s which led to strong loan growth appears to have intensified pressure on banks to attract adequate amounts of funds at a reasonable cost.

This chapter addresses this challenging situation in six sections: (1) trends in the primary types of funds that banks attract; (2) banks' profits from lower funding costs on time and savings deposits in the mid-1990s; (3) different types of funding by different types and sizes of commercial banks; (4) techniques for measuring the cost of and resulting potential profit from these funding sources; (5) risks associated with acquiring various types of bank funds; and (6) bank strategies for acquiring funds.

TYPES AND CHANGING COMPOSITION OF DEPOSITS

The changing trends in total bank funds may provide future challenges to bank management. However, it is the marked and continuing changes in the composition of bank funds sources that have caused dramatic changes in bank management in the 1980s and 1990s.

TABLE 6.1　Primary Sources of Funds for Commercial Banks (at the end of 1997)

Principal Sources of Bank Funds	Primary Ownership				Maturity	
	Individuals	Business	Government	Interbank	None	Typical Range
Demand deposits	x	x	x	x	x	
NOW accounts	x		x		x	
Special NOW accounts	x				x	
Passbook or statement savings deposits	x				x	
Money market deposits	x		x		x	
Time deposits under $100,000	x					Seven days to one year
Time certificates	x					14 days to eight years
Individual retirement and Keogh time deposits	x				x	
CDs	x	x	x			14 days to one year
Federal funds				x		Day or term
Repurchase agreements	x	x	x	x		Day to 1 year
Other borrowings (Eurodollars, bankers' acceptances, etc.)	x	x		x		Day to 270 days
Capital notes	x	x		x		Over five years

Table 6.1 categorizes and describes the principal types of nonequity sources of funds for commercial banks according to primary ownership, nature of interest paid, and maturity. Table 6.2 and Figure 6.1 indicate the net amount of funds in the major categories of funds in selected years from 1950 through 1996. Interbank sources of funds—deposits of other banks, deposits in the process of collection, and federal funds transactions between affiliates—are eliminated from the figures in Table 6.2 and Figure 6.1. Each source of bank funds is briefly described; then the overall pattern of bank funding and its implications for bank returns and risks are discussed.

Demand Deposits

Demand deposits are noninterest-bearing transaction deposits that have no maturity and must be paid by banks when a negotiable instrument, generally in the form of a check or an electronic impulse, is presented. Since demand deposits have no explicit interest cost, they are generally a bank's lowest-cost source of funding. However, increasing costs of processing demand deposit transactions have raised the effective overall cost of demand deposits to close to, if not higher than, the cost of passbook savings. Table 6.2 and Figure 6.1 further illustrate that the demand deposits fell from 63.3 percent of all commercial bank net sources of funds in 1950 to under one-sixth of these sources by 1997. The declining importance of demand deposits in the last three decades can be attributed to more efficient cash management by individuals, businesses, and governmental units; significantly higher interest rates; and the appearance of competitive instruments, such as NOW

TABLE 6.2   Noncapital Domestic Net Sources of Funds for All Insured Commercial Banks, Excluding Interbank Deposits

End of Year	(Dollars in Billions)				(As a Percentage of Total Deposits and Borrowings)			
	Demand Deposits[a]	Savings Deposits[b]	Time and Other Deposits[a]	Borrowing	Demand Deposits[a]	Savings Deposits[b]	Time and Other Deposits[b]	Borrowing
1947	61.8	34.7		.5	63.7	35.8		.5
1960	94.6	53.5		1.4	63.3	35.8		.9
1962	101.5	79.7		3.6	54.9	43.1		2.0
1964	108.3	103.6		2.5	50.5	48.3		1.2
1966	112.9	139.8		4.6	43.9	54.3		1.8
1968	131.5	175.3		8.5	41.7	55.6		2.7
1970	135.2	97.2	133.8	18.6	35.1	25.2	34.8	4.8
1972	158.4	129.2	196.3	36.4	30.5	24.8	37.7	7.0
1974	185.9	146.1	255.8	52.8	28.5	22.5	40.8	8.1
1976	225.8	190.3	293.1	67.0	29.1	24.5	37.8	8.6
1978	252.3	220.9	395.2	114.7	25.7	22.5	40.2	11.7
1980	302.1	201.2	558.7	161.5	24.7	16.4	45.7	13.2
1981	348.2	223.7	662.5	231.0	23.7	15.3	45.2	15.8
1982	370.9	304.7	723.7	255.3	22.4	18.4	43.7	15.4
1983	389.5	462.6	682.0	265.7	21.6	25.7	37.9	14.8
1984	414.3	503.5	727.4	281.0	21.5	26.1	37.8	14.6
1985	450.9	589.1	755.9	310.4	21.4	28.0	35.9	14.7
1986	472.3		1,751.1	359.0	18.3		67.8	13.9
1987	479.1		1,853.6	361.4	17.8		68.8	13.4
1988	479.4		1,952.2	380.9	17.0		69.4	13.5
1989	483.4		2,065.1	418.7	16.3		69.6	14.1
1990	488.9		2,161.0	384.7	16.1		71.2	12.7
1991	480.4		2,207.2	379.1	15.7		72.0	12.3
1992	540.6		2,157.9	406.5	17.4		69.5	13.1
1993	571.8		2,182.1	497.8	17.6		67.1	15.3
1994	572.3		2,302.1	591.1	16.5		66.4	17.1
1995	612.0		2,415.6	666.7	16.6		65.4	18.0
1996	664.3		2,532.9	715.9	17.0		64.7	18.3

[a] Net demand deposits were total domestic demand deposits other than domestic commercial interbank and U.S. government less cash items in the process of collection through 1980. After 1980, figures are total demand deposits because adjustments are not available.

[b] Interbank deposits are excluded from both savings and time deposits. NOW, Super NOW, and money market accounts are classified as savings deposits.

SOURCES: *Federal Reserve Bulletins*, selected issues; FDIC Quarterly Banking Profile (Washington, D.C.: FDIC, selected years).

FIGURE 6.1   Net Sources of Bank Noncapital Funds, 1960–1996

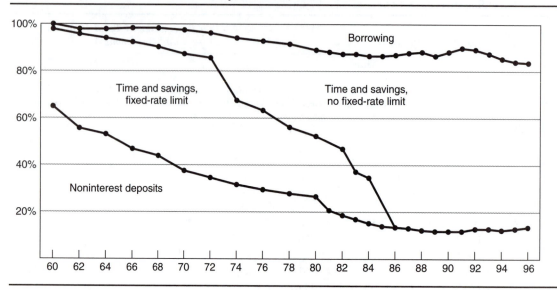

accounts and money market instruments at banks and other financial institutions, money market funds, and cash management accounts.

NOW and Special NOW Accounts

NOW accounts are interest-bearing checking accounts on which Regulation Q rate maximums were dropped on March 31, 1986; they have no maturity and must be paid by banks upon demand. Although limited amounts of NOW accounts were outstanding in the New England states in the late 1970s, they were not legalized throughout the United States until January 1, 1981. Special NOW accounts, with no rate limits, became available to individuals on January 5, 1983. The typical difference between NOW and Special NOW accounts at banks is that Special NOW accounts pay higher rates but usually have higher minimum balances and restrictions on activity. There are no legal requirements for rates, minimum balances, or activity. NOW accounts are included with transaction deposits, and Special NOW accounts are included with savings deposits in current federal statistics.

Savings Deposits

Savings deposits are interest-bearing deposits without specific maturity. A check or other order of withdrawal cannot be written directly on most savings accounts, but withdrawals can be made whenever the depositor desires, and it is easy to shift funds to a transaction account on which checks may be written. These accounts have no fixed maturity, and individuals keep track of their balances through passbooks or periodic bank statements. Passbook savings deposits may be the lowest overall cost source of funds currently available to commercial banks; however, the low interest rate often paid severely restricts the growth of these types of deposits.

Money market deposit accounts are savings deposits of individuals and partnerships. This type of deposit was created in December 1982 to provide banks with an instrument that could compete effectively with money market mutual funds. There are no rate maximums, and regulatory limits on minimum size and maximum free withdrawal were removed on December 31, 1985. Most banks pay rates that vary according to an average rate on a short-term market instrument, and will probably continue to use minimum sizes and maximum free withdrawals to market this account. Money market accounts grew rapidly throughout the 1980s, but lower relative rates slowed the growth of money market deposit accounts in the 1990s.

Table 6.2 shows that total savings deposits fell from roughly 25 percent of the net total funds as late as 1976 to slightly above 16 percent at the end of 1980. In the early 1980s several savings deposit forms—most notably money market accounts—were not subject to Regulation Q. Since March 31, 1986, savings deposits have not been subject to Regulation Q or any size or activity limits, and savings deposits have grown as a share of total noncapital funds.

Time Deposits

Time deposits differ from savings deposits primarily because they have a predetermined maturity date, and withdrawals prior to that date are often subject to interest penalties. In the early 1980s, total time deposits were consistently above 40 percent of the total noncapital sources of funds (see Table 6.2). In contrast, time and savings deposits combined were only 36 percent of all net deposits as late as 1960.

There are several categories of time deposits. The first category, CDs of $100,000 or more, is primarily large negotiable CDs of corporations. The majority of these are fixed rate, with no rate limit, although some variable-rate CDs are included in the total. They have a fixed maturity that usually ranges between 14 and 270 days at the time of issue. There is an active market for large negotiable CDs, and, economically, they are more like borrowings than deposits. A second category, other time deposits of $100,000 or more, is not subject to rate limits; these deposits are nonnegotiable, can have fixed or flexible maturities, and are deposited by individuals, partnerships, corporations, and municipalities. The third major category, time deposits under $100,000, is a catchall category that includes savings certificates with many varying terms, individual retirement and Keogh time deposits, several types of public time deposits, and miscellaneous and other time deposits. These deposits have no rate limit and no regulatory size minimum.

Other Classifications of Deposits

Brokered deposits are both small and large time deposits obtained by banks from intermediaries seeking insured-deposit accounts on behalf of their customers. Deposit brokers appeared in the early 1980s, when depositors began to face increased risk of loss because of bank failure. An often cited example of this risk was the failure of Penn Square Bank in July 1982. For the first time since the Great Depression, federal regulators liquidated a large bank, as opposed to allowing it to be merged or acquired by a solvent bank with no loss to depositors.

Brokers entered deposit markets to bring together depositors (sellers) seeking insured accounts with banks and other depository institutions (buyers) demanding lower-cost, insured-deposit funds. Electronic funds transfer technology enabled brokers cost-effectively to ''split'' $1 million, for example, into 10 fully insured $100,000 deposit accounts at 10 different depository institutions. Alternatively, brokers could offer smaller depositors better yields than otherwise could be obtained by pooling their deposits and selling ''shares'' in ''participating'' large CDs offering higher yields than smaller CDs.

Bank regulators generally have opposed the use of brokered deposits. Regulators seem to believe that since insured depositors are less likely to discipline bank management by withdrawing their funds or charging higher rates on deposits, bank safety and soundness might be compromised to the extent that banks used nationally brokered deposits to grow excessively or to take excessive loan risks. As of early 1998, banks with fully insured brokered deposits in excess of either their total capital (including reserves) or 5 percent of their total deposits must provide monthly reports of the volume, interest rates paid, and usage of such deposits to the FDIC.

Public deposits are demand, savings, or time deposits of governmental units. Treasury tax and loan accounts are interest-bearing, demand-type accounts of the U.S. government. Most other governmental units, such as agencies and state and local units, have both noninterest-bearing demand deposits and savings or time deposits. Competition is often intense for such deposits, and many public bodies require a bidding process to make sure their governmental unit gets the highest rate. The federal government and many state and local units still require qualified securities to collateralize the uninsured part of their deposits.

Correspondent deposits or deposits of other banks are a significant source of funds for some upstream correspondent banks. Most correspondent deposits are demand deposits that are left by one bank in another because the latter offers services such as check clearance, international transactions, investment advice, and loan participations. Money earned on such deposits pays the upstream bank for the services. Less than 10 percent of correspondent deposits are savings or time deposits because interest payments would pay for the deposits rather than the upstream bank's services.

TYPES AND COMPOSITION OF BORROWED BANK FUNDS

Table 6.2 and Figure 6.1 show that less than 1 percent of total net sources of commercial bank funds consisted of net borrowings as late as 1960. By 1997 borrowing sources constituted over 18 percent of the total noncapital bank sources of funds. Table 6.3 contains brief descriptions of some of the major borrowing sources of bank funds.

The largest source of borrowed funds for commercial banks are federal funds purchased and securities sold under agreement to repurchase (repos). Most federal funds are one-day purchases of another bank's excess reserves. Security dealers, large businesses, and the Federal Reserve are also able to supply these one-day reserves, so that for commercial banks, total federal funds purchased usually exceed the amount of federal funds sold. There is also a limited amount of federal funds purchased and sold between banks maturing in periods longer than one day.

Repos provide funds to banks during the period when securities are temporarily sold to another bank, a business, an individual, or other potential temporary purchaser. The temporary selling period typically ranges between 1 and 89 days, and the purchaser has title to the securities until the repo is repurchased. Repos usually have a rate slightly

TABLE 6.3   Brief Descriptions of Nondeposit Short-Term Funding Forms

Funding Form	Characteristics
Borrowing from Federal Reserve (discounts or advances)	Credit extended on a short-term basis by a Federal Reserve Bank to a bank or other depository institution. Rate is set by the Fed and is called the *discount rate*, with penalty rates for frequent or unusually heavy users. Security (securities or acceptable loans) required for either discounts or advances.
Federal funds purchased	Purchase of another bank's excess reserves on daily or short-term basis. Other side of federal funds sold. Purchased through correspondent or informal phone market at existing federal funds rate. Banks that are continual users often subject to informal limit by sellers. Unsecured; therefore, funds seller checks credit of borrowing bank.
Securities sold under agreement to repurchase (repos)	Temporary sale of government or other securities in which bank has received funds from purchase and agreed to rebuy securities at predetermined price. In effect, short-term (often daily) secured borrowing from purchaser.
Eurodollar and other foreign sources	Eurodollars are deposits in U.S. banks held outside the United States with maturities ranging from overnight to a year. Active secondary market with at least one overseas branch is essential to continual involvement. Rates set in international market. Other foreign sources also used by very large banks. Bank must not engage in activities or assume risks that could potentially blemish its name.
Bankers' acceptances	A time draft drawn on a bank by either an exporter or an importer to finance international business transactions. The bank may discount the acceptance in the money market to (in effect) finance the transaction.
Other liability forms	Includes commercial paper (large, short-term unsecured promissory notes sold through the bank or its holding company), promissory notes, bills payable, mortgages payable, ineligible acceptances, and so on. Key element is that bank can raise funds through such forms if bank pays going market rate and lender has confidence in bank.

below the existing federal funds rate because they are effectively collateralized by the security sold, whereas federal funds are usually unsecured. Some banks use small-denomination, "retail" repos; however, the total dollar amounts obtained through this source is relatively small.

Commercial banks also use a variety of other borrowing forms, such as discounts and advances from the Federal Reserve, bankers' acceptances, commercial paper, and Eurodollars, as sources of funds. These are described in Table 6.3. Many of these sources are available primarily to larger banks. Eurodollars and other international sources generally require an international office.

TABLE 6.4   Components of Net Interest Margin

a. Yield Spread and Funding Spread

	1992	1996
3-month Treasury rate	3.44%	5.01%
Yield on earning assets	8.34%	8.20%
Cost of funds/earning assets	3.68%	3.93%
Net interest margin	4.66%	4.27%
Yield spread	4.90%	3.19%
Funding spread	0.24%	1.08%
Net interest margin	4.66%	4.27%

b. Rates Paid by Banks on Savings and Small Time Deposits Relative to Yields on Treasury Securities, 1996

Category of Deposits	Interest Rate	Treasury Security of Comparable Maturity	Yield
Savings deposits	2.89%	3-month Treasury bill	5.01%
Small time deposits with maturity of:			
7 to 91 days	4.06%	3-month Treasury bill	5.01%
92 to 182 days	4.56%	6-month Treasury bill	5.08%
183 days to 1 year	4.94%	1-year Treasury note	5.21%
More than 1 year to 2½ years	5.14%	2-year Treasury note	5.84%
More than 2½ years	5.39%	3-year Treasury note	5.99%

THE FUNDING SPREAD AS A SOURCE OF PROFITABILITY

In Chapter 3 we introduced two components of the net interest margin—yield spread and funding spread. Table 6.4 has selected data on the spread between cost of funding and the three-month Treasury rate in 1992 and 1996. It also has detail by maturity categories for 1996. Figure 6.2 shows the trend in the 90-day CD rate, a market rate, and the rates on other checkable deposits (primarily NOW accounts) and savings deposits.

For 1992 (which was representative for the late 1980s and early 1990s), the average rates that banks paid on savings and time deposits were slightly above the three-month Treasury rate. The 90-day CD rate was very close to the other checkable deposit, and savings account rates (Treasuries vs. CDs) rose relative to the rate that banks paid on other checkable deposits and savings accounts. By 1996, Table 6.4 indicates the rates paid by banks on savings, and small time certificates were substantially lower than the yields on Treasury securities with comparable maturities.

Two other trends were notable between 1992 and 1996—bank profitability grew strongly, but the growth of bank deposits slowed considerably. The reason for the slower growth of deposits is probably the higher rates by competitors. R. Alton Gilbert examined the impact of relatively lower deposit rates on bank profits. He assumed the rates paid on each category of savings and small time deposits were the same as those of Treasury securities of comparable maturities in 1992 and 1996. These hypothetical rates were multiplied by the average amount in each type of deposit account (no adjust-

FIGURE 6.2   Deposit Interest Rates

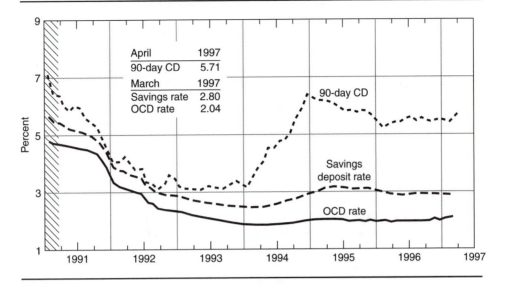

ment in amount was made because of higher deposit rates). Gilbert found that net income before taxes as a percentage of total assets would have been reduced from 1.32 percent to 1.28 percent in 1992 and from 1.86 percent to 1.36 percent in 1996. Gilbert concluded that most of the rise in profitability of the banking industry from 1992 to 1996 can be attributed to the relatively low rates that banks paid in savings and small time deposits in 1996.[1]

In trying to explain how banks continued to attract savings and small time deposits (albeit at slower growth) in 1996, Gilbert stated: "The bank customers who continue to hold these deposits appear to have relatively strong attachments to banks and to Federal Deposit Insurance, and they are willing to accept deposit rates that are below those on alternative investments, such as money market mutual funds."[2]

FUNDING AVAILABILITY AND STRATEGY FOR DIFFERENT TYPES OF BANKS

While there is substantial variation among banks even in similar size groupings, we can make some broad generalizations about the composition of funding by size of bank and type of products and services emphasized by the bank. The top part of Table 6.5 presents the 1996 funding characteristics for three different size groupings of commercial banks— those with assets under $100 million; those with assets from $300 million to $1 billion; and those with assets over $10 billion.

---

[1] R. Alton Gilbert, "Bank Profit on Low Rates on Time and Savings Deposits," *Money Trends* (St. Louis: Federal Reserve Bank of St. Louis, June 1997).

[2] Ibid.

TABLE 6.5   Effects of Bank Funding Composition

a. By size groupings, 1996

	Under $100 Million	$300 Million to $1 Billion	Over $10 Billion
Performance Characteristics			
Yield on earning assets	8.30%	8.32%	8.01%
Cost of funds/earning assets	3.66%	3.62%	4.10%
Funding spread (vs. 3-month Treas.)	1.35%	1.39%	0.91%
Net interest spread	4.64%	4.70%	3.91%
Net noninterest expenses	2.59%	2.26%	1.50%
Return on assets	1.16%	1.26%	1.12%
Funding Composition			
Demand deposits to total deposits	15.39%	17.70%	22.66%
Savings and time deposits to total deposits	84.61%	82.30%	77.34%
Total deposits to total liabilities	96.85%	88.05%	69.36%
Volatile liabilities to total liabilities	12.77%	20.57%	41.91%
Fed funds and repos/total liabilities	1.08%	6.62%	8.32%
All borrowed funds/total liabilities	2.11%	10.49%	24.72%
All borrowed funds/equity capital	20.01%	106.87%	310.48%

b. By individual banks, 1996

	Oaks	American	Barnett	Morgan
Performance Characteristics				
Yield on earning assets	8.61%	9.14%	8.47%	6.25%
Cost of funds/earnings assets	1.61%	3.57%	2.99%	4.74%
Funding spread (vs. 3-month Treas.)	3.40%	1.44%	2.02%	0.27%
Net interest spread	7.00%	5.57%	5.49%	1.51%
Net noninterest expenses	2.36%	2.40%	2.34%	−0.03%
Return on assets	2.70%	1.70%	1.49%	0.78%
Funding Composition				
Demand deposits to total deposits	47.28%	18.80%	20.05%	4.81%
Savings and time deposits to total deposits	52.72%	81.20%	79.95%	95.19%
Total deposits to total liabilities	99.47%	89.98%	93.72%	32.66%
Volatile liabilities to total liabilities	3.74%	15.91%	11.11%	64.83%
Fed funds and repos/total liabilities	0.00%	0.69%	4.31%	5.04%
All borrowed funds/total liabilities	0.00%	9.12%	4.39%	57.63%
All borrowed funds/equity capital	0.00%	82.43%	46.70%	949.96%

The average small bank depicted in the top part of Table 6.5 uses customer savings and time deposits as its primary funding source. This size group made less use of volatile liabilities and borrowing. The positive impact of the low funding cost was offset by the higher net noninterest expenses (dominated by salary, premises, and equipment) to attract these lower cost funds. For midsize banks, yields, cost of funds, and interest spread were similar. The main advantage of being midsized seemed to be the ability to spread the net noninterest expenses over a larger asset base—2.26 percent versus 2.59 percent for the smaller banks. The resulting ROA of 1.26 percent was above the ROA for the small or larger bank groups. Finally, the larger banks had significantly higher funding cost (because of more borrowing and other expensive funding sources). The lower funding spread and lower yields on earning assets overcame the low net noninterest expenses. The resulting ROA was 1.12, the lowest of the three size groupings.

The bottom part of Table 6.5 illustrates the effects of the funding composition for a sample of four individual banks. There are large variations in products offered and in sources of funding. Oaks Bank in Dallas, Texas, is the traditional type of small bank with approximately $60 million in assets. It has a large net funding spread, few volatile liabilities, and no borrowed funds. Oaks Bank is very profitable. There are, however, a number of smaller banks, such as American Heritage Bank of El Reno, Oklahoma, and American National Bank of Sarpy County, Nebraska which use borrowings and volatile liabilities fairly extensively. American Heritage Bank is used as an example. Its funding spread is much lower than that of Oaks Bank, with similar net noninterest expenses; its resulting ROA, while very good, is considerably below that of Oaks Bank.

Although larger banks usually have much more extensive ability to use financial markets and numerous borrowing sources than smaller banks, their use of volatile liabilities and borrowings vary all over the map. Morgan Guaranty of New York, a large wholesale bank, borrows over half of its total funding sources. Its funding spread is very low versus that of nearly all banks in the United States, and only its negative noninterest expense kept its 1996 ROA close to acceptable. At the same time, there are numerous larger retail banks which, even though they have extensive borrowing possibilities, have chosen to use customer deposits as their primary funding source. Banks such as Barnett Bank, for example, nearly always have large funding spreads that are at least partly offset by higher net noninterest expenses. American Heritage with assets under $100 million looks more like the ''traditional'' large bank than Barnett with assets in excess of $40 billion.

MEASURING AND USING THE COST OF FUNDS

Why should a bank be interested in measuring its cost of funds? Three reasons stand out. First, a bank will generally seek the lowest-cost combination of funds sources available in its market. Other things being equal, a bank will have higher returns when its cost of funds is lower without taking significantly higher risks. Second, a reasonably accurate cost of funds measure is an essential ingredient in determining the returns a bank must obtain on its earning assets. Third, the types of sources of funds a bank obtains and the employment of these sources have a significant impact on the bank's liquidity risk, interest rate risk, and capital risk.

There are several methods of measuring the cost of funds for a bank. Examples and an evaluation of the three most widely used methods—historical average cost, marginal cost of specific sources of funding, and a weighted average expected cost of all sources as a proxy for marginal cost—are presented for First National Bank. Tables 6.6, 6.7, and 6.8 contain balance sheets, income statements, and supplementary information for First National through 1997. Table 6.9 contains projections for the bank's fund resources, the amount of these attracted funds the bank can employ for 1996, and expected future costs of specific funds sources.

TABLE 6.6   First National Bank's Average Balance Sheet (dollars in thousands)

	1995 $	1995 %	1996 $	1996 %	1997 $	1997 %
ASSETS						
Cash and due from institutions	26,948	6.05%	28,053	6.04%	29,521	6.14%
Short-term instruments						
Fed funds sold and repos	4,879	1.09%	867	0.19%	1,102	0.23%
Other interest-bearing instruments	189	0.04%	563	0.12%	609	0.13%
Securities						
Held to maturity	36,719	8.24%	35,097	7.56%	32,147	6.68%
Available for sale	106,417	23.87%	100,364	21.61%	98,983	20.58%
Trading account assets	0	0.00%	0	0.00%	0	0.00%
Loans						
Commercial loans	86,481	19.40%	92,571	19.93%	94,918	19.73%
Consumer loans	82,107	18.42%	94,810	20.41%	103,367	21.49%
Real estate loans	53,817	12.07%	56,481	12.16%	63,249	13.15%
Other loans	23,176	5.20%	28,694	6.18%	28,793	5.99%
Leases	8,950	2.01%	8,794	1.89%	9,806	2.04%
Less: Reserve loan losses	−3,412	−0.77%	−2,987	−0.64%	−3,249	−0.68%
Net loans and leases	251,119	56.34%	278,363	59.94%	296,884	61.73%
Premises and fixed assets	13,468	3.02%	14,468	3.12%	14,845	3.09%
Other real estate owned	786	0.18%	421	0.09%	273	0.06%
Goodwill and other intangibles	0	0.00%	0	0.00%	0	0.00%
All other assets	5,231	1.17%	6,237	1.34%	6,604	1.37%
Total assets	445,756	100.00%	464,433	100.00%	480,968	100.00%
LIABILITIES AND CAPITAL						
Demand deposits	61,733	13.85%	63,781	13.73%	66,389	13.80%
Interest-bearing deposits						
NOW and other transaction	93,417	20.96%	95,911	20.65%	98,271	20.43%
Savings accounts	86,238	19.35%	87,396	18.82%	89,043	18.51%
Time certificates	121,895	27.35%	124,386	26.78%	129,807	26.99%
CDs, $100,000 and over	28,025	6.29%	29,683	6.39%	31,269	6.50%
Other interest-bearing deposits	8,469	1.90%	9,214	1.98%	9,806	2.04%
Borrowed funds						
Fed funds purchased and repos	843	0.19%	5,188	1.12%	4,800	1.00%
Other borrowed funds	8,324	1.87%	10,284	2.21%	11,131	2.31%
All other liabilities	4,649	1.04%	4,416	0.95%	4,160	0.86%
Subordinated debt	0	0.00%	0	0.00%	0	0.00%
Equity capital						
Preferred stock	0	0.00%	0	0.00%	0	0.00%
Common stock	12,000	2.69%	12,000	2.58%	12,000	2.49%
Surplus	8,000	1.79%	8,000	1.72%	8,000	1.66%
Undivided profits	12,163	2.73%	14,174	3.05%	16,292	3.39%
Total liabilities and capital	445,756	100.00%	464,433	100.00%	480,968	100.00%

TABLE 6.7   First National Bank's Income Statements for Specified Years Ended December 31 (in thousands of dollars)

	1995	1996	1997
INTEREST INCOME			
Short-term instruments	265	71	91
Securities	9,325	8,412	7,999
Commercial loans	7,960	8,480	8,761
Consumer loans	9,221	10,818	11,596
Real estate loans	4,693	4,818	5,509
Other loans	2,128	2,778	2,689
Leases	889	897	973
Total interest income	34,479	36,273	37,617
INTEREST EXPENSE			
NOW and other transaction accounts	2,391	2,302	2,565
Savings accounts	3,605	3,767	3,856
Time certificates (under $100,000)	6,509	6,704	7,087
CDs $100,000 and over	1,578	1,674	1,785
Other interest-bearing deposits	447	499	517
Borrowed funds	490	868	918
Other liabilities and sub notes	0	0	0
Total interest expense	15,021	15,814	16,728
NET INTEREST INCOME	19,458	20,459	20,889
Provision for loan losses	570	535	720
NET INTEREST INCOME AFTER PROVISION	18,888	19,924	20,169
NONINTEREST INCOME			
Deposit service charges	2,649	2,744	2,812
Other noninterest income	1,546	1,828	2,203
Total noninterest income	4,195	4,572	5,015
NONINTEREST EXPENSES			
Salaries and benefits	9,040	9,237	9,452
Premises and equipment expense	2,218	2,401	2,734
Other noninterest expense	3,980	4,041	4,318
Total noninterest expenses	15,238	15,679	16,504
NET OPERATING INCOME	7,845	8,817	8,680
SECURITIES GAINS (LOSSES)	−85	0	123
APPLICABLE INCOME TAXES	2,521	2,943	2,895
EXTRAORDINARY GAINS (LOSSES)	0	0	0
NET INCOME	5,239	5,874	5,908
CASH DIVIDENDS PAID	3,600	3,600	3,720

TABLE 6.8   First National Bank's Supplementary Information (in thousands of dollars, except last four rows)

	1995	1996	1997
Earning assets (average)	394,255	413,824	428,014
Risk assets (average)	361,737	382,334	395,828
Maturities of securities			
Under one year	32,518	31,490	32,186
One to five years	56,401	50,136	46,214
Over five years	54,217	53,835	52,730
Insider loans	6,289	8,104	7,846
Loan losses less recoveries	580	442	720
Noncurrent (over 90 days) loans			
Commercial loans	277	287	352
Consumer loans	509	740	1,013
Real estate loans	156	119	177
Other loans and leases	0	60	60
Unused commitments	24,138	25,860	27,172
Off-balance sheet derivatives	0	0	0
Purchased mortgage service rights	0	0	0
Volatile liabilities	40,012	51,225	53,500
Interest rate sensitivity (one year)			
Repricing assets	192,435	221,784	220,980
Repricing liabilities	217,942	235,165	239,366
Mutual fund sales	0	0	1,408
Number of offices	7	9	9
Number of employees	245	249	256
Number of common shares	1,200,000	1,200,000	1,200,000
Market price per share	36.42	41.27	46.35

Historical Average Cost

The first method of measuring the bank's cost of funds, historical average cost, is probably still the most common. The weighted average cost of funds for First National Bank is calculated in Table 6.10. The interest cost in dollars ($16.728 million for First National Bank) is either available or can be calculated by multiplying the average amount in each type of funding account by the average cost of the funds during the period (the year 1997 in this example). The weighted average interest cost, 3.76 percent, is calculated by dividing the dollar interest cost by the total deposits and borrowed funds, $444.516 million. The weighted average interest cost for interest-bearing funds (4.42 percent in this example) is calculated by including only interest-bearing funds in the denominator.

Such weighted average cost of funds measures may be helpful in evaluating past funds acquisition performance, but they suffer from four shortcomings. First, some bank funds have to be invested in assets that do not earn returns, such as required reserves, correspondent balances, and fixed assets (e.g., premises). Since the proportion not earning returns varies with different forms of funding, adjustments need to be made both in costs and in the resulting returns that need to be made to cover the interest costs. Second, the cost of funds should include other expenses associated with attracting funds, such as op-

TABLE 6.9   Information for Estimating Required Yields on Sensitive Assets for First National Bank (dollars in millions)

1. The bank's holdings of vault cash, deposits with the Federal Reserve and other banks, and other cash items in 1998 are expected to be:
   20 percent of noninterest-bearing demand deposits
   12 percent of interest-bearing NOW and other transaction deposits
    3 percent of savings and time deposits
2. The bank's investment in premises and equipment and other nonearning assets is expected to be 4 percent in 1998.
3. During 1998, the bank expects its assets will average $500 million. The average amount and investable amount of the various fund sources are projected as follows (amounts in millions of dollars):

	Average Amount	Percentage Usable	Amount Investable
Demand deposits, noninterest	$ 70	76%	$ 53.00
NOW and other transaction accounts	105	84%	88.00
Savings accounts	92	93%	86.00
Time certificates	130	93%	121.00
CDs, $100,000 and over	31	93%	29.00
Other interest-bearing deposits	10	96%	10.00
Short-term borrowings	20	96%	19.00
Other liabilities (noninterest)	4	96%	4.00
Stockholders' equity	38	96%	36.00
Total sources of funds	$500		$446.00

4. The bank's target rate of return on equity is 15 percent after taxes. Its marginal income tax rate is 34 percent; therefore, the pretax return is $0.15/(1 - 0.34)$ or 22.73 percent.
5. Costs of each type of funding (percentage):

	Interest Cost 1997	Est. Interest Cost 1998	Net Processing Cost 1998
Demand deposits, noninterest	0.0%	0.0%	4.8%
NOW and other transaction accounts	2.6	3.0	2.7
Savings accounts	4.3	4.5	1.0
Time certificates	5.5	5.7	0.5
CDs, $100,000 and over	5.7	6.0	0.2
Other interest-bearing deposits	5.3	5.5	0.2
Short-term borrowings	4.6	5.5	0.1
Other liabilities (noninterest)	0.0	0.0	0.0
Stockholders' equity	22.0	22.7	0.0

6. Expenses other than interest for 1998 are estimated to be $8.8 million in net processing costs and $3.5 million in net other costs (other expenses of $9.0 million less other income of $5.5 million) for total net noninterest expenses of $17.8 million.
7. Forecast average assets for 1998 (in million of dollars):

	Interest Sensitive	Nonsensitive	Total
Cash and due from banks		32	32
Short-term securities and instruments	32		32
Long-term securities		114	114
Loans	200	100	300
Bank premises and equipment		15	15
Other assets (nonearning)		7	7
Total			500

8. Projected returns on short-term securities purchased in 1998 is 5.0 percent and projected returns on loans is 11 percent.

TABLE 6.10   Historical Weighted Average Cost Measures (dollars in thousands)

Type of Funds	Average Amount	Interest Cost	Interest
1. Demand deposits	$ 66,389	0.00%	$ 0
NOW and other transaction accounts	98,271	2.61%	2,565
Savings accounts	89,043	4.33%	3,856
Time certificates	129,807	5.46%	7,087
CDs, $100,000 and over	31,269	5.71%	1,785
Other interest-bearing deposits	9,806	5.27%	517
All borrowed funds	19,931	4.61%	918
Totals	$444,516		$16,728

$$\text{Weighted avg interest cost } \frac{\text{Interest cost } 16,728}{\text{All deposits and borrowings } 444,516} = 3.76\%$$

$$\text{Weighted cost interest-bearing funds } \frac{\text{Interest cost } 16,728}{\text{Interest-bearing funds } 378,127} = 4.42\%$$

2. Earnings requirements based on weighted average cost of funds
   a. To cover interest expense:

$$\frac{\text{Interest cost}}{\text{Earning assets}} = \frac{16,728}{428,014} = 3.91\%$$

   b. To break even:

$$\frac{\text{Interest + noninterest expenses}}{\text{Earning assets}} = \frac{16,728 + 11,489}{428,014} = 6.59\%$$

   c. To earn 15% return on equity (tax rate = 34%):

Earnings to cover ROE = % ROE before taxes × Equity/Earning assets

$$= \frac{0.15}{1 - 0.34} \times \frac{36,292}{428,014} = 1.93\%$$

Required to cover expenses and ROE = 6.59% + 1.93% = 8.52%

Sources: Tables 6.6, 6.7, and 6.8.

erating and advertising expenses. Third, there are numerous questions about whether the cost of equity funds should be included in this cost of funds measure and, if so, how. Finally, historical costs can be extremely unreliable as a guide in choosing funds to attract or as an asset pricing guide if interest rates are changing markedly over time, as they did in the 1980s.

Improvements in Historical Average Cost Measures

Adjustments are made in the lower part of Table 6.10 to overcome the first three of these shortcomings. In Section 2a of the table, interest cost divided by earning assets adjusts for funds that have to be employed in nonearning assets and shows the return, 3.91 percent, the bank must earn on its earning assets to cover its interest expenses. The so-called breakeven yield on earning assets is calculated in 2b, the total interest expense and net other expenses (noninterest expense less noninterest income) divided by earning assets. This calculation shows how much the bank must earn, 6.59 percent, to cover all its expenses. Finally, one way to recognize the cost of stockholder equity is presented in Section 2c. The before tax ROE is multiplied by equity divided by earning assets. This earning requirement (1.93 percent) is added to the return required to cover all expenses in order to indicate the return required on earning assets, 8.52 percent, for the bank to earn 15 percent after taxes (22.73 percent before taxes) on its equity capital. The same results could have been obtained by the following computation (amounts in thousands):

Interest expenses	$ 16,728
plus All other expenses (net)	$ 11,489
plus Equity return ($36,292 × 0.2273)	$ 8,249
Total	$ 36,466
divided by	
Earning assets	$428,014
Required earnings rate on earning assets to earn 15% ROE	8.52%

In spite of these adaptations, the historical average cost measures seem useful primarily in assessing a bank's past performance. For example, to help explain a bank's earning performance, a bank's actual returns on earning assets can be compared with its breakeven yield and the yield required to earn a specified return on capital. If a bank wants guidance about which type of funds to attract, whether or not to take on new assets, or pricing its loans, historical average costs may be very misleading. For example, when rates are rising, the historical average cost of funds is less than the cost of replacing these funds, and the bank might be led into making new loans at unprofitable yields. The reverse could be true when rates fall. If predictions about fluctuating rates in the 2000s are at all accurate, it would seem that a better measure of the cost of bank funds would be essential for a bank to attain reasonable profitability.

Marginal Cost of Funds

The second measure of the bank's cost of funds, the marginal cost of funds, is a direct result of the deficiencies in using the historical average cost cited earlier. The basic idea is that the bank would use its marginal cost, the cost paid to produce one additional unit of usable funds, to determine the acceptable return on the additional assets purchased with such funds. Also, the bank would seek to attract the lowest-cost source of funds. At first glance these concepts seem easy to implement, but figuring the full cost of a new dollar of funds is difficult, especially if it is necessary to estimate the impact of one source of funds on the cost of other sources.

The simplest approach is to determine a single source of funds a bank wants to use, compute its marginal cost, and use that cost as a basis for pricing new assets. Presumably, the single source selected would be the cheapest one available to the bank. For example, let us assume that First National Bank hopes to use NOW and other transaction accounts to finance its asset expansion. The interest cost of these funds is projected to be 3.0 percent, 16 percent of the attracted funds will be employed in nonearning assets, and the cost of acquiring and servicing such accounts is 2.7 percent. Usually, the overall cost of a single marginal source is calculated as follows:

Marginal return on funds

$$\text{from single source} = \frac{\text{Interest costs} + \text{Other costs}}{1 - 16\% \text{ in nonearning assets}} = \frac{3.0 + 2.7}{1 - 0.16} = 6.79\%$$

Two problems limit the usefulness of this measure. First, the cost of a single source may need to be adjusted to compensate suppliers of other sources of funds for the added risk created by using the single source. For example, if First National's ratio of debt to equity rose because of the added NOW and other transaction accounts, uninsured depositors and other creditors and shareholders might demand a higher return. Community National's cost of attracting and holding NOW accounts might be 8.29 percent—the 6.79 percent computed cost plus a 1.5 percent premium—because of the higher cost of other sources. A reasonably precise measurement for such a premium seems impossible.

Second, few banks use a single source of funds over a very long period of time. Often several sources provide significant amounts of new funding. One alternative promoted by some banks to overcome this weakness is to use the cost of the most expensive marginal source of funds as the bank's marginal cost of funds.

Pooled Marginal Cost of Funds

A second alternative is to use an average marginal cost calculation similar to that summarized in Table 6.10 for First National Bank. In Table 6.11 it is assumed that First National is expected to grow by close to $20 million in 1998, primarily through five sources of financing. The interest costs, all other costs, and percentage in nonearning assets expected

TABLE 6.11   Pooled Marginal Costs of Funding (dollars in millions)

Types of Funds	(1) Amount of Increase	(2) Percentage Earning Assets	(3) Earning Assets Amount	(4) Interest & All Other Costs	(5) Total $ Cost (1) × (4)
Demand deposits, noninterest-bearing	$ 4	76%	$ 3.04	4.8%	$0.192
NOW and other transaction accounts	7	84%	5.88	5.7%	0.399
Savings accounts	3	93%	2.79	5.5%	0.165
Time certificates	0	93%	0	6.2%	0
Short-term borrowings	4	96%	3.84	5.6%	0.224
Supporting equity	2	96%	1.92	22.7%	0.454
Total	$20		$17.47		$1.434

$$\text{Marginal cost} = \frac{\text{Total \$ cost}}{\text{Total amount}} = \frac{1.434}{20} = 7.17\%$$

$$\text{Required return on earning assets} = \frac{\text{Total \$ cost}}{\text{Investable funds}} = \frac{1.434}{17.47} = 8.21\%$$

SOURCES: Tables 6.5, 6.6, 6.7, 6.8, and 6.9.

in 1998 came from Table 6.9. The return required on earning assets to cover this "pooled" cost of funds, 8.21 percent in Table 6.11, was found by dividing the total dollar cost of the funds attracted by the amount of funds that could be invested in earning assets. Although the accuracy of this measure might be improved by using the amount each category of funds was expected to rise or fall in 1998, the pooled marginal cost of financing is very sensitive to estimations (or misestimations) of sources of funding in the future.

Weighted Average Projected Cost

A final way to estimate the cost of funds is to use the weighted average projected cost of all funds sources as an estimation of the marginal cost. Financial theory suggests that if it is assumed that a bank has been financed with the lowest overall cost of funds, its marginal cost of funds should be equal to its weighted average projected cost of funds. It is important to note that the resulting number is *not* a weighted average cost of funds figure, but rather an estimation for the bank's marginal cost of funds if the bank is efficiently financed. Table 6.12 illustrates the calculation of the required overall returns on earning assets based on the projected average cost of funds for 1998. The overall cost of acquiring funds can be estimated by dividing the summation of total dollar acquisition costs, $34.64 million (in column 3) in this example, by the average assets, $500 million (in column 1). The return required on earning assets to cover the cost of funds is calculated

TABLE 6.12   Weighted Average Projected Cost of Funds as Estimation of Marginal Cost of Funds (dollars in millions)

Types of Funds	(1) Average Amount	(2) Interest and Net Processing Costs	(3) Total $ Cost
Demand deposits, noninterest-bearing	$ 70	4.8%	$ 3.36
NOW and other transaction accounts	105	5.7%	5.99
Savings accounts	92	5.5%	5.06
Time certificates	130	6.2%	8.06
CDs, $100,000 and over	30	6.2%	1.86
Other interest-bearing deposits	10	5.7%	0.57
Short-term borrowing	20	5.6%	1.12
Other liabilities	5	0.0%	0.00
Stockholders' equity	38	22.7%	8.63
Total	$500		$34.65

$$\text{Weighted average projected cost of funds} = \frac{34.65}{500.0} = 6.93\%$$

$$\text{Required return on projected earning assets to cover cost of funds} = \frac{34.65}{446.0} = 7.77\%$$

$$\text{Required return on projected earning assets to cover cost of funds plus noninterest items} = \frac{38.15}{446.0} = 8.55\%$$

SOURCES: Tables 6.5, 6.7, 6.8, and 6.9.

by dividing the dollar acquisition cost, $34.64 million, by the projected earning assets, $446 million.

Which Cost Measure Is Most Appropriate?   Which cost of funds measurement should a bank use? Any of the four measures discussed is appropriate, depending on the purpose of the cost-of-funds figure. The historical average cost of funds is useful in assessing past performance. Marginal cost of specific funds may be helpful in deciding which form of funds the bank should try to attract. It is also important to measure all marginal costs. For example, a bank may believe demand deposits are the cheapest source because they have no explicit interest cost. However, if the acquisition of $1 million in demand deposits costs $200,000 in advertising, personnel calling, and operational costs, demand deposits may be a high-cost source of funds. Furthermore, cost adjustments for changing risks due to a change in funding sources are very difficult to measure. Finally, either the marginal cost of pooled funding or the weighted average projected cost of funds as an estimation of the marginal cost of funding may be acceptable as asset-pricing guides. The weighted average projected cost of funds is used in the example that follows.

USING COST-OF-FUNDS MEASURES

Average Return Required on Earning Assets

It is assumed that the objective of First National Bank is to obtain an interest margin sufficient to cover other costs and to earn an adequate return on the owner's investment. However, costs other than those required to attract funds and income other than interest income have been ignored in the calculations. These cost and income figures can be incorporated by adding in all costs other than the acquisition costs already incorporated, net of all noninterest income items ($9.0 million less $5.5 million) divided by earning assets ($446 million), which is 0.78 percent, to the previously calculated required return (7.77 percent).

This resulting required return to cover total net costs of 8.55 percent includes an after tax return to equity holders of 15 percent. This return, adjusted to a before tax rate by dividing by 1 minus the marginal bank income tax rate, was treated as a cost of funds similar to other sources. If the forecasted interest rates were approximately correct and the bank earned above 8.55 percent on its assets, the residual after tax return on equity would be above 15 percent, and vice versa. The concern is how to employ earning assets, which are a mixture of sensitive and nonsensitive assets, so that they will yield an average of 8.55 percent or above.

Effects of Rate Sensitivity of Assets

First National Bank is used in Table 6.13 to demonstrate a simplified worksheet that can be used to calculate the yields required on newly priced, interest-sensitive assets. The key principle of the worksheet is that to obtain the targeted return on equity, the bank must earn 8.55 percent on its earning assets of $446 million, or $42.75 million. The yields on nonsensitive loans and long-term securities are known, and the dollar returns of $10 million and $5.54 million, respectively, should be reasonable estimates. Estimated dollar returns on rate-sensitive loans and short-term securities are more complex. In the case of

TABLE 6.13 Worksheet for Calculation of the Yield Required on Newly Priced Sensitive Loans (dollars in millions)

Asset Category	Forecasted Average for 1998	Yield on Nonsensitive Assets	Yield on Sensitive Assets (Old)	Yield on Sensitive Assets (New)	Average Yield	Return (Dollars)
Short-term securities	$ 32		5.4%	5.0%	5.2%	$ 1.66
Long-term securities	114	6.0%			6.0	6.84
Loans (nonsensitive)	100	10.0%			10.0	10.00
Loans (sensitive)	200		10.0%	(3)[a]	(2)[a]	(1)[a]
Total earning assets	446				8.55%	$42.75
Nonearning assets	54				0	0
Total assets	$500				8.55%	$42.75

[a] Number in parentheses indicates calculation of the answer in Table 6.14.

short-term securities, First National felt that its securities, which were yielding 5.4 percent at the start of the year, would mature about evenly during the year and that the average yield on newly purchased securities would be 5 percent. The average yield on the $32 million of short-term securities would then be 5.2 percent, or $1.66 million.

A calculation similar to that performed on short-term securities can be performed for rate-sensitive loans if the rates on currently outstanding loans are known; if there are reasonable estimates of the repricing, renewal, and maturity profiles of these loans; and if the average rate on newly priced loans can be forecast. A slightly different approach is taken: the current rate and repricing profile are estimated, and the required yield on newly priced sensitive loans to earn 15 percent on equity is calculated. Table 6.14 shows

TABLE 6.14 Calculation of the Yield Required on Newly Priced Sensitive Loans (dollars in millions)

1. Total dollar return on all assets		$42.75
Dollar returns on:		
Short-term securities	$ 1.66	
Long-term securities	6.84	
Nonsensitive loans	10.00	
Cash, premises, etc.	0	18.50
Required dollar return on sensitive loans:		$24.25

2. Required average yield on all sensitive loans:

$$\frac{24.25}{200.00} = 12.13\%$$

3. Required yield on newly priced sensitive loans:

$$\frac{24.25 - 10.00}{200.00 - 100.00} = \frac{14.25}{100.00} = 14.25\%$$

that the calculations can be made by first finding the required dollar yield on sensitive loans by subtracting the returns on short-term and long-term securities and nonsensitive loans from the total return required on all assets. The required average yield on sensitive loans can then be calculated by dividing the required dollar yields on sensitive loans by the average amount of sensitive loans. Finally, if sensitive loans will be repriced about evenly during the year, the required yield on newly priced sensitive loans can be calculated by subtracting the dollar yield at the old sensitive rate and the average amount at the old rate from the numerator and denominator, respectively. The resulting dollar amount divided by the average amount repriced during the year is the average required percentage yield on newly priced sensitive loans (14.25 percent for First National).

Two final comments about using this type of model seem appropriate. First, the real world is more complex than this simplified model. For example, the growth rates of different types of loans vary, and loan prepayments and extensions occur. This type of model, however, may be made considerably more complex than this simplified example. The authors have worked with banks that have considerably more complex computerized models, which are based on the same basic ideas. Second, even the simplified model presented in this section can be flexibly used. For example, a bank can forecast all rates for the coming year and project the resulting rate of return on equity. Or a bank can solve for the minimum new yield it requires on sensitive short-term securities, given the dollar return on all other earning assets (including newly priced sensitive loans).

The required yield on newly priced sensitive loans can then be compared with the bank's estimates of competitive market rates for the coming year. If market rates are expected to be lower than the required yield, as was the case for the First National example, the bank will probably earn less than the targeted 15 percent on equity, unless the asset-liability structure is changed or more risk is taken to get increased returns. The bank is likely to earn above 15 percent on equity if expected market rates exceed the required yield on newly priced sensitive loans.

RISKS ASSOCIATED WITH RAISING FUNDS

Different sources of funds may affect the risks of a bank in different ways. With a goal of achieving the highest value for the stockholders' investment, bank management must consider the risks as well as the costs of the various types of bank sources of funds. This section examines how bank sources of funds affect the primary financial risks of banking—liquidity risk, interest rate risk, credit risk, and capital risk.

Liquidity Risk

The liquidity risk associated with bank sources of funds is primarily the probability that depositors or lenders will want to withdraw their funds from the bank. The risk of outflow of such funds differs markedly, depending on the type of deposit, and seems to have changed as economic conditions have changed. The conventional banking wisdom of the 1940s and 1950s generally regarded demand deposits as the most vulnerable source of outflows at most banks. Savings and time deposits, dominated by passbook savings, were thought to be very stable sources of funds. Nondeposit liabilities were an insignificant source of funds for most banks. The primary liquidity pressures on a bank, therefore, came from fluctuations in demand deposits.

By the mid-1960s, the situation had changed appreciably. As interest rates rose, many bank customers managed their demand deposit balances tightly so that transaction needs and compensating balances for loans were the major reasons for such deposits. The probability of large declines for all demand deposits in a bank seemed to subside. Savings and time deposits grew rapidly and became more vulnerable to deposit outflows because Regulation Q put most deposits at a competitive disadvantage with open market instruments when interest rates rose. Therefore, the disintermediation of these deposits caused a liquidity problem for banks during credit tightness in 1966, 1969, and 1974. By the early 1970s, banks were willing to buy relatively more expensive deposit or nondeposit liabilities in order to escape the high liquidity risk associated with deposits that were subject to Regulation Q rate limits.

The gradual lifting of Regulation Q and the creation of new deposit and liability forms in the late 1970s and 1980s again changed the liquidity risks associated with a bank's sources of funds. Corporate demand deposits remained at transaction and compensating balance levels and tended to be subject to limited liquidity risk. Consumer demand deposits, which faced competition from money market funds, and interest-bearing NOW accounts, which could be competitively priced by other banks and thrift institutions, increased the liquidity risk. Passbook or statement savings declined steadily in the last few years because of competition from mutual funds, NOW accounts, money market accounts, and Regulation Q limits that were considerably below open market rates.

Bank savings and time deposits were no longer subject to Regulation Q ceilings after March 31, 1986. Thus, banks are now able to compete with other financial institutions and open market instruments. Since these savings and time deposits have been an increasingly important source of bank funds, commercial banks have probably lowered the liquidity risks associated with *their source of funds.* In the 1970s, bank management was more concerned with managing quantity than price, which was often fixed by regulation. In the 1990s, banks were able to get and keep the quantities of funds they desired if they were willing and able to pay the price.

In spite of the increased flexibility in buying deposits and other funds, some banks have faced liquidity problems because of this deposit attraction. Two potential sources of deposit-induced liquidity problems are reviewed here. First, a bank may overemphasize the use of impersonal purchased deposits or funds and cause concerns of confidence among actual and potential depositors and creditors. Why should an impersonal depositor with deposits exceeding the FDIC insurance limit of $100,000 leave money in a risky bank, even if the depositor receives an above-average rate? The Continental Illinois Bank crisis in 1984 illustrates this point. It is estimated that roughly three-fourths of Continental's funds were from large, uninsured, generally impersonal depositors or creditors. It should not be surprising that many of these depositors and creditors chose to withdraw their funds when the quality of the bank's loan portfolio was perceived to have deteriorated.

Second, brokered deposits, packaged deposits of $100,000 each from many clients of brokerage firms, may represent a unique type of liquidity risk. Since these deposits are insured by the FDIC, they go to the highest rate payer. Brokered deposits may be a temporary source of funds for fast-growing or high-risk commercial banks that temporarily hide the bank's more basic problems. Since these deposits may exacerbate future liquidity pressures, there is regulatory and legislative pressure to limit their use.

In summary, two factors stand out as determining causes of the liquidity risks associated with the withdrawal of funds. First, does the bank have the earnings ability to pay competitive rates? Second, does the bank have the recognized quality that will enable it to use the needed amounts of impersonal, purchased deposits or funds?

Interest Rate Risk Associated with Funding

The interest rate risk associated with bank sources of funds depends heavily on the interest sensitivity of the assets financed by these funds. For example, if savings certificates, which are repriced every six months, are used to purchase either federal funds (which are repriced daily) or five-year government bonds, the bank is taking an interest rate risk. The appropriate management technique is to compare the interest sensitivity over time of all sources of funds with the interest sensitivity over time of the assets financed by these funds. It should be emphasized that liquidity risk and interest rate risk may be different for different sources of funds and that there are broad ranges of interest sensitivities among sources of funds.

Variable-rate CDs are an example of a source of funds on which interest rates may vary with changes in market rates but which may pose little liquidity risk over the life of the CD. The same is true for most other nonlimit-rate time deposits, as long as the bank is willing to pay the going market rate. The menu of interest-sensitivity forms available among bank sources of funds is broad. Federal funds purchased and repos are rate sensitive on a daily basis; large CDs are sensitive to rate changes in a few days to a few months; money market accounts may be sensitive to rate changes each week; longer-term CDs may not be rate sensitive for several years; and capital notes may not be rate sensitive for 20 to 25 years. If the needed sources of funding for the desired interest-sensitivity position are not available at reasonable costs, a bank should consider the use of derivative hedging instruments, such as interest rate futures, interest rate swaps, and interest rate options.

In summary, a bank's choice among the funds sources available would seem to depend on the interest cost of the source, other acquisition costs of the source, and its contribution to the liquidity and interest-sensitivity balance of the bank.

Interactions with Credit Risk

A bank's sources of funds do not have a direct effect on its credit risk because depositors or lenders of funds are taking the risk that the bank will not pay them. Two indirect effects, however, are possible. A higher cost of funds may be a side effect of depositors or lenders of funds becoming worried about a bank's ability to pay its claims on time. For example, the problems of Seafirst, Continental Illinois Bank, and InterFirst in 1983 and 1984 raised their cost of funds appreciably. Because of credit concerns about energy and real estate loans, the so-called Texas premium raised the cost of funds for banks in that state nearly 1 percent in the late 1980s. Second, if a bank has a high cost of funds, it may be encouraged to take higher credit risks in its struggle to maintain its profit margin. Deposit insurance partially mitigates the impact of these two indirect effects.

Interactions with Capital Risk

Finally, a bank's sources of funds have a direct impact on the capital risk and leverage of a bank. A bank's equity costs much more than its deposits and borrowings because of the greater uncertainty associated with the return on equity and because the return on equity, whether earnings or cash dividends, is not a tax-deductible expense. Thus, a bank may lower its cost of funds by increasing its leverage. As capital risk becomes more pronounced, however, these gains may be illusory. The cost of other sources of funds may rise as capital risk becomes appreciable. In addition, other bank activities, such as new branches and acquisitions, may be curtailed if regulatory authorities feel the bank's capital risk is too high.

INTRODUCTION TO BASIC FUNDING STRATEGIES

A bank must develop strategies for acquiring funds after it has decided what effects the various types of funds will have on its cost of funds and risks. In a broad sense, this means using the marketing concept to determine consumer needs and then communicating to the consumer how the bank will serve these needs. In the following sections, several particularly important strategies in acquiring funds are examined—delivery systems, product development, market segmentation, product differentiation, and product attraction.

Delivery Systems

One change that will affect the funding strategies of most banks is the dramatic changes in the systems for delivering bank services. Table 6.15 looks at the current and probable future delivery systems for banks' deposit and loan products. This chapter emphasizes funds attraction, although lending delivery systems also will have an impact on the attraction of funds in the future.

The appropriate delivery systems for a bank obviously depend on the types of customers the bank wants. We list what we think are the typical target customer markets for the various delivery systems. In the next few years, we believe the bank lobby, limited-service ATMs, and banking-by-mail will decline in importance. We predict that direct deposit, on-line home banking on personal computers and internet banking will be rapidly growing delivery media. Increases or decreases in other delivery systems—for example, branching networks—will depend on the types of customer markets the bank wants to service, and so on.

Product Development

The first step in product development is to identify bank customers' wants and needs. Once these are identified, a bank should develop and manage its products to fulfill these desires. Although there are some limitations on the product line of every bank—imposed by size, location, regulations, and managerial capabilities—a major shortcoming of most banks is their narrow conception of bank products. Many banks have said in effect that their "products" are making loans and accepting deposits. Banking products should include rendering (at a profit to the bank) all the financial services the customer can use. The willingness (accompanied by regulatory and legislative approval) to develop and market new financial products is one key to banking success in the 2000s.

Product development strategies may be divided into two groups. First, there are those that relate to each individual product—its means of identification, product quality and features, and price. Second, for its whole line of products, the bank must form strate-

TABLE 6.15   Delivery Systems for Deposit and Loan Products

Delivery Systems	Target Market Today	Probable Future Usage
• The bank lobby	Older consumers	Declining rapidly
• The drive-in	All transaction consumers	Still popular
• Branching networks	Varies by market	Increasingly sales centers instead of service centers
• Supermarket branches	Younger consumers	Convenient, low cost
• Limited-service ATMs	All volume consumers	Matured
• Multipurpose ATMs	All consumers	The next wave
• Limited-service ATM card	All consumers	Continued growth
• Debit/ATM card	More affluent markets, credit card users, and volume check writers	Rapid growth
• Personal service card	All consumers	2000+ product
• Credit cards	Increasingly a niche market game	Still growing
• Checks	Baby boomers and older	Now declining
• Direct deposit	All consumers	Rapid growth
• ACH/electronic payments and funds transfer	All consumers	Rapid growth
• Bank-by-mail	None	Matured
• Personal phone service	Affluent consumers	Growing
• Automatic bank-by-phone	All consumers	Growing rapidly
• Personal loan-by-phone	All borrowers	Jury is still out
• Automatic loan-by-phone	All borrowers	Jury is still out
• Credit lines activated via phone, ATM, and check	Affluent consumers	Growth potential
• On-line PC banking	Younger, better educated and/or more affluent markets, but rapidly expanding to other markets	Finally taking off
• Internet banking	Same as above	The next frontier

gies covering the product assortment, the essential supporting services, hours of business, and bank location and layout. Some of the basic policy aspects of bank product development for both groups are described briefly in the following paragraphs.

Market Segmentation

Strategies that have proved useful for nonbanking firms include market segmentation, product differentiation, and image. Market segmentation is the isolation of certain sectors of the total market and the creation of new products so uniquely designed for this sector that no immediate competition exists. This strategy may prove profitable for all banks competing with other financial institutions. One problem with such a strategy for an individual bank is the speed with which other banks can copy most new banking products. This condition leads to the need for product differentiation. Often the purpose is to appeal to different market segments with an essentially standardized product. Such product differentiation is a difficult task, and effectively establishing a sense of difference often requires heavier than usual advertising and promotional expenditures.

Many banks have adopted a combination of these strategies for product development. They strive to develop new products to fill customers' wants in some market segments, to match their competition's new product when it appears desirable to do so, and to differentiate their products in the eyes of their customers.

Commercial banks must also develop new financial services to compete successfully with other financial institutions and other institutions offering financial services. Ideas for new banking products may just happen, but they will occur more often if customers' desires are studied and if sensitivity to their potential needs is cultivated among bank employees. Product ideas can come from customers, directors, employees, competing banks, other financial institutions, or trade magazines. Once the ideas are obtained, the development and selection process must start. As many as 50 to 100 new product ideas may yield only one banking product that will ultimately be marketed successfully.

Product Differentiation and Image

Even if a bank is able to bring new banking products into the market or successfully copy the products of a competitor, it will be likely to face competition from similar products within a relatively short time. Creative pressures will force a need for product identification that often requires at least some differentiation. The brand name, trademark, trade character, slogan, and other identification devices common to manufactured goods all have potential application to bank marketing. They may be employed for individual products or for the entire bank.

The bank's image is related to these identification devices. A bank's image is a complex collection of attitudes and awarenesses on the part of customers and potential customers. All trademarks, brand names, and contacts with bank facilities and bank personnel must combine to create a favorable image in the customer's mind. When a large part of the product is an intangible feeling of confidence, security, and trust, as it is with many bank services, a favorable image is essential. The question of how an individual bank may raise specific types of funds is now addressed.

Product Attraction

Although individual banks do not have absolute control over the level of their deposits, they can nevertheless influence the amount they hold. Because deposits and other fund sources are so important to the profitable operation of a bank, most banks tend to compete aggressively for them. Some of the factors determining the level of deposits in a bank cannot be affected significantly by the bank. For example, monetary and fiscal policy, Regulation DD, and the level of general economic activity are exogenous factors that an individual bank must recognize but cannot control. The individual bank can control in varying degrees an intermediate group of factors (e.g., the size and physical location or locations of the bank). Finally, the individual bank determines such factors as its physical features and personnel, its marketing effort, the interest rates it pays on savings and time accounts, the type of loans it is willing to make, and the level of services it offers its depositors. The major factors contributing to the attraction of principal types of deposits are discussed next.

Corporate Demand Deposits

At this time, banks are not permitted to pay interest on corporate demand deposits; therefore, each bank must compete primarily on the basis of services rendered the depositor. It has long been held that the failure to charge for a service is not a payment of interest, and this concept has led to the theory of supporting or compensating balances.

As corporate depositors, particularly the larger ones, have become more sophisticated, and as alternative uses of money have become more profitable, corporate treasurers have learned to seek a specific quid pro quo in terms of services for every dollar of their corporation's demand deposits.

The most essential service compensated for by demand deposits is the collection and payment service in all its various forms. Every business that draws checks needs a bank account; those who receive checks need a bank to provide the collection function. The best service is rendered by the bank that can collect checks most quickly, thereby making funds available to the depositor earlier. Out of this need for faster collection has sprung a whole art of *funds mobilization,* in which the Federal Reserve System has cooperated fully. These facilities include arrangements for sending large cash letters directly by wire or air mail to Federal Reserve Banks in other districts (postage paid by the Federal Reserve) or to correspondent banks in major cities, bypassing the Reserve System entirely. Special carrier services have been established to bring checks into major cities more quickly than they can be delivered by mail. Lock-box arrangements have proliferated. Some large banks have special departments whose function is to advise the corporate treasurer on the most effective way to mobilize cash for short-term investment.

Ideally, banks should carefully calculate the costs of these services and make sure that the value of the related deposits compensates them for these costs as well as an adequate profit margin. This is usually done by calculating a service charge representing the actual cost plus profit margin and offsetting this charge, in whole or in part, by an earnings credit for balances maintained at the bank. This credit is related to some money market rate representing the value of the funds in the bank. Both the service charges and the earnings credits are competitive rates.

The bank's true net cost of the services it renders to depositors represents its cost of money for those deposits. Faced with higher costs in other markets for funds, most banks are willing to compensate the demand depositor by providing services at a charge somewhat less than the net cost. Some banks waive service charges entirely, figuring that the cost of servicing those accounts is less than the interest they would have to pay on savings or time deposits.

It is very easy, however, to become trapped by this philosophy, and a bank can easily find itself rendering a number of services while double-counting the value of the same demand deposit account. The aggregate cost of these services may well exceed the value of the deposit. It becomes increasingly important, therefore, to look at each account relationship as a whole, and in recent years computer programs have been developed to enable banks to measure the relative total profitability of an account relationship. This involves coordinating in one computer printout all the services performed and their cost, the average collected balances maintained by a given customer (including other related accounts he or she may control) and their value, and credit usage, if any. Small banks can use a microcomputer to look at smaller numbers of large deposit accounts in this fashion.

The bank's willingness to lend money is of almost equal importance in attracting demand deposits, particularly business accounts. Credit availability is an essential need for most businesses at one time or another and is a constant need for some. When funds are in short supply (as they are predicted to be in the foreseeable future), banks will give preference to those customers who maintain demand deposit accounts with them. The offer of credit accommodation is a primary factor in deposit solicitation. For this reason, banks frequently offer "solicitation" lines of credit to businesses with no present need to borrow. By the same token, businesses maintain deposit balances in anticipation of their possible future borrowing needs. One outstanding example of this relationship is the so-called backup line of credit supporting a corporation's sale of commercial paper. A company actively using commercial paper to finance its current needs will obtain and advertise the availability of its unused bank lines of credit. The unused lines are typically supported by demand deposit balances of at least 10 percent of the credit available.

In short, the willingness to lend is another vital service that banks perform for corporations or individuals who maintain or control demand deposit balances. At times when money is extremely scarce, this relationship between deposit balances and credit availability seeps down even to the consumer lending field. For example, nondepositors may seek home mortgage loans in vain.

Transaction Deposits of Individuals

Individuals' transaction deposits offer a broad spectrum of opportunities. Individuals can choose to receive interest on their transaction deposits through NOW and Special NOW accounts. Special NOW accounts usually have a minimum size and a limit on checking activity. Noninterest-bearing demand deposits usually have lower or no balance requirements and often offer more services to the depositors. Services for individuals with noninterest-bearing demand deposits have proliferated in recent years. Most banks have established automated tellers, with which a customer with a "money card" and a secret account number can make deposits or withdraw small amounts of cash 24 hours a day, seven days a week, at scattered and convenient locations. Some banks have instituted systems to allow their customers to pay their bills by telephone. The customer states his or her account number and a personal identification number and then instructs the bank to pay designated amounts to specific payees. The customer can also designate the date on which he or she wishes the payments to be made.

The basic relationship between demand deposits and services rendered is essentially the same whether the depositor is an individual, a business corporation, or a municipality. The most successful bank will be the low-cost producer that can market its services at the lowest price and still maintain an adequate profit margin.

NOW and Special NOW Accounts

NOW and Special NOW accounts are available only to individuals. These accounts used to have either rate limitation, activity limitation, or size minimums, but these regulations were removed on March 31, 1986. In such a deregulated environment, banks have to pay rates and offer services that are reasonably competitive with those for similar accounts at thrift institutions and at money market funds. At the same time, a bank should carefully price the complete NOW or Super NOW package to include interest rates, number of transactions permitted without charge, service fees, and minimum size so that the effective cost of the attracted funds is not too high to earn an adequate return.

Advertising and promotional expenditures, as well as a competitive rate package, will continue to be important in attracting NOW and Super NOW accounts. Slight differences in rates are not generally perceived as an overriding concern by most individuals, and once accounts are opened, individuals appear to be hesitant to change to another bank or institution. By 2000, the authors predict that there will be no distinction between NOW and Special NOW accounts. Indeed, many individuals may have a single account that pays an interest rate dependent on the average size and activity in the account.

Passbook Savings Deposits

The passbook or statement savings market has been primarily a market of convenience. The primary emphasis of commercial bank advertising in this field has been on ''one-stop'' or ''full-service'' banking. The fact that commercial banks, even when they are in close competition with strong thrift institutions, still have large amounts of savings deposits is evidence of the effectiveness of this marketing technique. It has become less effective in recent years, since thrift institutions and banks have been permitted to have NOW accounts. Furthermore, the rapid growth of money market mutual funds has cut heavily into bank passbook and statement savings deposits.

As of March 31, 1986, rate limits on passbook savings were removed. To compete effectively in the passbook savings market (with or without an actual passbook), banks will have to go beyond mere convenience and offer competitive rates and additional services. A bank might offer lower or no charges on checking account facilities to savings deposit customers in some relation to the size of their savings accounts. It might offer a vacation club or special-purpose accounts. Some people save for various reasons; the interest earned is not the only reason for saving. The reason may be general or specific, but the process should be made easy, attractive, and convenient. In spite of all efforts, the passbook or statement savings of individuals in most banks will probably continue declining and be replaced by NOW and money market deposit accounts in future years.

Money Market Deposits

Money market deposits are a special category of savings deposits that have grown rapidly since they were first permitted in late 1982. Most banks place some minimum size on these accounts, and the rate paid may vary with the size. Rates are usually changed weekly in line with some money market index. While rate is the dominant factor in attracting these types of funds, promotion of deposit insurance, convenience, and transferability with other bank accounts have also assisted banks in competing for such deposits. This form of deposit may also be combined with NOW and Special NOW deposits into single account deposits by 2000.

Time Deposits

There are several categories of time deposits. The first category, *negotiable CDs of $100,000 or more,* has attracted the largest amounts of funds of any deposit category.

These are primarily for corporations and are not subject to interest rate limits. These certificates represent a fruitful source of funds, especially for large banks that lack a large retail deposit base. To be effective in the impersonal CD market, a bank must be large enough and sufficiently well known for its certificates to be traded at reasonable rates in the secondary market.

Although most corporate treasurers will, in theory, buy the certificates of any recognized bank at the highest rate obtainable, if rates are comparable, they are more likely to acquire the certificates issued by one of their banks of account. In times of tight money, banks may put considerable pressure on treasurers with whom they have established contact. By the same token, the treasurer with funds to invest will call a number of banks and "shop the market." Actual rates are often negotiated slightly off the posted rates for large blocks of funds of especially desirable maturities. From the deposit attraction standpoint, it is important that the banker get to know as many treasurers and other shoppers for such funds as possible. Although rate is always the primary factor, personal acquaintance is definitely a plus if several competitive rates are equal.

A second category, *other time deposits of $100,000 or more,* is not subject to rate limits, is not negotiable, can have fixed or flexible maturities and is purchased by individuals, partnerships, corporations, and municipalities. The majority of these larger time deposits are issued by small or moderate-sized banks to their customers who from time to time have excess cash to invest. Customer-related time deposits of $100,000 and over must be at competitive rates but are kept at the bank primarily by the other relationships the customer has with the bank. Although excessive brokered deposits may lead to liquidity problems (see the previous section) and regulation limits the acceptable amount of brokered deposits, this deposit source should not be completely ignored. Brokered deposits *in moderate amounts* may make sense, and in spite of rates slightly above those of competitors may be less expensive than some other deposit forms. There is little if any acquisition cost, and maturities and terms may be structured to a bank's specific needs.

Time deposits under $100,000 is a catchall category for remaining time deposits. Many of these deposits are called *time certificates.* These certificates are issued in a variety of forms to suit the needs and tastes of various classes of customers. They are usually sold in minimum denominations of $1,000. Interest may be paid by check on a monthly or quarterly basis or, in some cases, accumulated to maturity. For customers who cling to the passbook concept, such certificates may be issued in the form of a special passbook. Some certificates are issued with rates tied to Treasury securities with various maturities. Although the interest cost on these certificates will vary over time, the money raised through such deposits will be more permanent because these certificates will always be competitive with market securities. Advertising has been essential in informing the public of the forms of savings certificates a bank is emphasizing.

A majority of *individual retirement and Keogh accounts* fall into this category of time deposits. Such accounts offer banks a relatively new (expanded in 1982 but limited again by the 1986 tax legislation) means for attracting funds. Low- and middle-income individuals, as well as high-income individuals not covered by another retirement plan, can deduct an IRA contribution of up to $2,000 to establish their taxable income. All individuals, including high-income individuals with another retirement plan, benefit from tax-sheltered income on eligible IRA investments. If attractively priced, IRAs should represent a relatively permanent source of funds. IRAs give banks the opportunity to innovate new competitive products with little regulatory constraint. Early ideas regarding interest rates have included rates fluctuating slightly above various-maturity Treasury bill rates or rates set for up to one year. Advertising expenditures to try to attract these deposits have been relatively large for the more aggressive banks.

Public Deposits

There are several types of public deposits. Treasury tax and loan accounts are interest-bearing, demand-type accounts of the U.S. government. It is relatively easy for a bank to become a qualified depository. To keep its prorated share of these deposits for over a day or so, the bank must formally agree to pay a rate based on the market repurchase agreement rate. Qualified securities must be pledged for the uninsured part of these deposits. To attract state or municipal demand deposits, the financial services provided for the state or municipal unit is an important consideration. Attracting state and municipal time deposits depends on factors similar to those affecting large-denomination CDs. In some states, such deposits must go to the institution that bids the highest rate. Competition for state and municipal time deposits can be intense, and banks should be careful that, in the rates they bid, they recognize reserve and pledging requirements and an adequate return on capital. Repurchase agreements in which the bank agrees to rebuy securities it has sold to the political unit are an alternative way of attracting funds from these units. Many states still require pledging of securities against demand and time deposits of the state and its municipalities.

Correspondent Deposits

Deposits of other banks are a significant source of funds for some upstream, correspondent banks. (Over half of a few banks' demand deposits are from other banks.) Demand balances are left by one bank in another bank because the latter offers services such as check clearance, international entry, investment advice, and loan participation. The services offered should be significant enough to attract other banks; however, the depository bank should be sure it is making a profit on the funds attracted.

Nondeposit Sources

Banks should also have fund attraction strategies for nondeposit sources of funds. Some forms, such as federal funds purchased and commercial paper, clearly depend on a willingness to pay the going rate. Nonprice strategies are also important. Repurchase agreements depend on the bank having acceptable securities or other assets that can be sold subject to repurchase. A bank may be able to borrow more federal funds if it has good correspondent relations and a strong capital position. Eurodollar and other foreign sources may be encouraged by foreign offices and connections with foreign banks and businesses.

Future Possibilities

It appears that one-account banking may gain popularity in the early 2000s. One version of such an account would be a flexible format in which each customer would have deposits over a certain amount automatically transferred to a variable-rate account. A more complex version would let the customer specify time horizons over which funds would be left with the bank. The customer would receive rates based on the specified maturities, with large penalties for maturity violations. Banks should begin developing this deposit product and plans to promote it as soon as possible.

The evolution of new delivery systems is clearly well under way and will affect the way banks fund themselves. In-lobby banking, banking by mail, and limited-purpose ATMs seem to be declining in use. Most banks aggressively use multipurpose ATMs at the present time as a method of attracting funds. A growing number of banks are beginning to use point-of-sale (POS) terminals as part of their strategy for attracting funds. Questions still remain about the cost-effectiveness of some ATM and POS terminals and about sharing and switching systems and charging customers for such electronic terminals. Home banking (on-line personal computer banking) is an even newer electronic method for attracting funds. Some proponents believe that over half of all banking transactions will be done at home by the early 2000s. Attractive and cost-effective systems are now available. Finally, banking on the internet, though still in its infancy, appears likely to be the wave of the future in attracting funds.

CHAPTER 7

Measuring and Providing Reserves and Liquidity

Management's discretion in how it employs its funds differs according to the purpose. Regulatory decision determines the minimum amount of cash and deposits banks must hold with Federal Reserve Banks, whereas management choice determines the amount held in liquid securities. In this chapter, we consider how a bank measures its reserve needs and what assets and borrowings the bank can use to meet these needs. We then show how several types of liquidity needs can be determined, and we present methods of meeting them. Some of the discussion on meeting liquidity needs by borrowing funds complements discussion on this topic covered in the preceding chapter.

DETERMINING A BANK'S RESERVE NEEDS

A bank's need for legal reserves is set by regulatory requirements and by the types of funds attracted by the bank. Reserve requirements are expressed as percentages of the types of funds attracted times the amount of funds attracted in the particular category as delineated in Regulation D of the Federal Reserve. Historically, national banks, which must be members of the Federal Reserve, and state banks that have chosen to be Fed members have always been required to meet reserve requirements. The reserve requirements for state banks that are not members of the Federal Reserve (nonmember banks) were formerly set by the regulatory authority in each state. However, by 1988 legislation equalized reserve requirements for nonmember banks and other depository institutions.

As of year-end 1997, banks with reservable liabilities of less than $4.4 million were not required to maintain reserves. These banks only need to report annually on the amount of their (potentially) reservable liabilities. Banks with reservable liabilities between $4.4 million and $59.3 million report their reservable liabilities and must meet their specified reserve requirements on a quarterly basis.[1] The remaining banks—those with reservable liabilities over $59.3 million—must report on reservable liabilities weekly and must meet their reserve requirements over a two-week period. Since most banks fall into this third category, we will describe meeting reserve requirements for this category only. As of January 1, 1998, the level of reserves required for all banks with assets in excess of $59.3 million is shown in Table 7.1.[2]

Member banks must use Form 2900, shown in Table 7.2, to report their transaction accounts, other deposits, and vault cash to their Federal Reserve Bank for a week that starts on Tuesday and ends on the following Monday. Deposits are recorded as of the end of each business day. A bank that is open Monday through Friday will record the same amount for its deposits on Friday, Saturday, and Sunday of a statement week. If a bank is also open on Saturday, then only its Saturday and Sunday deposit totals will be the same. Deposits and vault cash are recorded on a seven-day basis, with the total for the week appearing in column 8 regardless of the days the bank conducts business. The figures contained in Form 2900 are based on a sample small bank not located in a financial center.

Table 7.3 illustrates the calculation of this sample member bank's reserve needs for two weeks (the *maintenance period*) starting on Thursday, October 15, 1998, two days after the first Tuesday covered by the bank's transaction deposits. To keep it simple, we assume the data are the same for each of the two weeks. For nontransactions deposits, emergency liabilities, and vault cash reported on Form 2900 (Table 7.2), the calculation is lagged 17 days. Thus, most banks (those with total deposits of $59.3 million or more) report their deposits and vault cash on a weekly basis. Reserve needs are figured for a two-week period, which is nearly contemporaneous for transaction deposits and has a 17-day lag for other deposits and vault cash. Demand balances due from depository institutions in the United States and cash items in the process of collection are subtracted from total transaction deposits to find the transaction amounts subject to reserves. In the example, the first $4.4 million of transaction accounts are not subject to reserves; the next $49.3 million of transaction accounts are multiplied by the 3 percent requirement, with the remaining transaction accounts subject to 10 percent reserves. The amount of reserves on transaction accounts is added to reserves based on lagged savings and time deposits and other obligations subject to reserves (at a 0 percent rate in 1998). Vault cash (also lagged) is subtracted from this total amount of reserves to determine the reserves to be maintained at the Federal Reserve directly or on a pass-through basis during the reserve week ending two weeks later.

Figure 7.1 illustrates the calendar timing for determining the reserve requirements for the sample bank for the reserve maintenance period of October 15 to 28, 1998. The requirements for this period are based on the bank's transaction deposits during October 13 to 26 and on other deposits during September 15 to 28. Reserves required to be held in the following two weeks (October 29 to November 11) will be based on transaction deposits held during October 27 to November 9 and on other deposits held during September 29 to October 12, and so on. In addition, the Federal Reserve allows member banks

[1] For exempt depository institutions (there are only a small number), the breaking point for quarterly versus weekly reporting is $48.2 million instead of $59.3 million.

[2] Regulation D itself, with detailed descriptions and answers to typical questions, appears in *Federal Reserve Requirements* (Washington, D.C.: Federal Reserve Board of Governors, 1988). *Amendments to Regulation Reserve Requirements* (Washington, D.C.: Federal Reserve Board of Governors) was published in 1998.

TABLE 7.1   Reserve Requirements for Commercial Banks, December 31, 1997[a]

Type of Deposit and Deposit Intervals[b]	Percent of Deposits
Net transaction accounts[c,d]	
$0–$4.4 million	0
Next $49.3 million	3
Over $53.7 million	10
Nonpersonal time and savings deposits[e]	0
Eurocurrency liabilities[f]	0
Ineligible acceptances and obligations by affiliates	3–10[g]

[a] Reserve requirements in effect on December 31, 1997. Required reserves must be held in the form of deposits with Federal Reserve Banks or vault cash. Nonmembers may maintain reserve balances with a Federal Reserve Bank indirectly on a pass-through basis with certain approved institutions.

[b] The Garn-St. Germain Depository Institutions Act of 1982 (Public Law 97-320) required that $2 million of reservable liabilities (transaction accounts, nonpersonal time deposits, and Eurocurrency liabilities) of each depository institution be subject to a zero percent reserve requirement. The board is to adjust the amount of reservable liabilities subject to this zero percent reserve requirement each year for the succeeding calendar year by 80 percent of the percentage increase in the total reservable liabilities of all depository institutions, measured on an annual basis as of June 30. No corresponding adjustment is to be made in the event of a decrease. On December 31, 1997, the exemption was $4.4 million. In determining the reserve requirements of depository institutions, the exemption shall apply in the following order: (1) net NOW accounts (NOW accounts less allowable deductions), (2) net other transaction accounts, and (3) nonpersonal time deposits or Eurocurrency liabilities starting with those with the highest reserve ratio. With respect to NOW accounts and other transaction accounts, the exemption applies only to such accounts that would be subject to a 3 percent reserve requirement.

[c] Transaction accounts include all deposits on which the account holder is permitted to make withdrawals by negotiable or transferable instruments, payment orders of withdrawal, and telephone and preauthorized transfers in excess of three per month for the purpose of making payments to third persons or others. However, money market deposit accounts and similar accounts subject to the rules that permit no more than six preauthorized, automatic, or other transfers per month, of which no more than three can be checks, are not transaction accounts. (Such accounts are savings deposits subject to time deposit reserve requirements.)

[d] The Monetary Control Act of 1980 requires that the amount of transaction accounts against which the 3 percent reserve requirement applies be modified annually by 80 percent of the percentage increase in transaction accounts held by all depository institutions, determined as of June 30 each year. Effective December 31, 1997, the amount was $49.3 million.

[e] In general, nonpersonal time deposits are time deposits, including savings deposits, that are not transaction accounts and in which a beneficial interest is held by a depositor that is not a natural person. Also included are certain transferable time deposits held by natural persons and certain obligations issued to depository institution offices located outside the United States. For details, see section 204.2 of Regulation D.

[f] Net borrowings from related foreign offices, gross borrowings from unrelated foreign depository institutions, loans to U.S. residents made by overseas branches of domestic depository institutions, and sales of assets by U.S. depositor institutions to their overseas office.

[g] Treated as an addition to net transaction accounts.

TABLE 7.2 Report of Transaction Accounts, Other Deposits, and Vault Cash

FR 2900
OMB No. 7100-0087
Hours per response: 1.0 to 12.0
Approval expires August 1994

For the week ended Monday, _____ 19 ____.

You must file a *Report of Certain Eurocurrency Transactions* if your institution had any foreign borrowings during the reporting period.

This report is required by law [12 U.S.C. §§248(a), 461, 603, and 615]. The Federal Reserve System regards the information provided by each respondent as confidential. If it should be determined subsequently that any information collected on this form must be released, respondents will be notified.

PLEASE READ INSTRUCTIONS PRIOR TO COMPLETION OF THIS REPORT.

Report all balances as of the close of business each day to the nearest thousand dollars.

ITEMS	For FRB Use Only	Column 1 Tuesday Mil	Thou	Column 2 Wednesday Mil	Thou	Column 3 Thursday Mil	Thou	Column 4 Friday Mil	Thou	Column 5 Saturday Mil	Thou	Column 6 Sunday Mil	Thou	Column 7 Monday Mil	Thou	Column 8 Total Mil	Thou	Ref
A. TRANSACTION ACCOUNTS																		
1. Demand deposits:																		
a. Due to depository institutions	2698	12	221	12	166	12	147	12	144	12	144	12	144	12	162	85	128	A.1.a
b. Of U.S. Government	2280	8	150	8	162	8	164	8	150	8	150	8	150	8	164	57	090	A.1.b
c. Other demand	2340	28	205	28	214	28	241	28	205	28	205	28	205	28	241	197	516	A.1.c
2. ATS accounts and NOW accounts/share drafts, and telephone and preauthorized transfers	6917	30	010	30	242	30	240	30	210	30	210	30	210	30	241	211	363	A.2
3. Total transaction accounts (must equal sum of Items A.1 through A.2 above)	2215	78	586	78	784	78	792	78	709	78	709	78	709	78	808	551	097	A.3
B. DEDUCTIONS FROM TRANSACTION ACCOUNTS																		
1. Demand balances due from depository institutions in the U.S.	0063	2	190	2	194	2	191	2	192	2	192	2	192	2	191	15	342	B.1
2. Cash items in process of collection	0020	4	231	4	230	4	230	4	235	4	235	4	235	4	230	29	626	B.2
C. 1. TOTAL SAVINGS DEPOSITS (including MMDAs)	2389	48	214	48	038	48	165	48	215	48	215	48	215	48	355	337	417	C.1
D. 1. TOTAL TIME DEPOSITS	2514	42	565	42	531	42	531	42	506	42	506	42	506	42	526	297	671	D.1
E. 1. VAULT CASH	0080		506		512		498		492		492		492		493	3	475	E.1
F. MEMORANDUM SECTION																		
1. All time deposits with balances of $100,000 or more (included in Item D.1 above)	2604	8	614	8	314	8	414	8	714	8	714	8	714	8	823	60	307	F.1
2. Total nonpersonal savings and time deposits (included in Items C.1 and D.1 above)	6918	24	872	24	961	24	821	24	857	24	857	24	857	24	901	174	126	F.2

If your institution had no funds obtained through use of ineligible acceptances or through issuance of obligations by affiliates, please check this box and do not complete Schedule AA. ☑

SCHEDULE AA: OTHER RESERVABLE OBLIGATIONS BY REMAINING MATURITY Ineligible Acceptances and Obligations Issued by Affiliates:	For FRB Use Only															Total		Ref
1. Maturing in less than 7 days	2245		0		0		0		0		0		0		0		0	A.A.1
2. Maturing in 7 days or more (**Nonpersonal Only**)	6919		0		0		0		0		0		0		0		0	A.A.2

TABLE 7.3   Calculation of Required Reserves (for October 15–28, 1998)[a]

	Amount (dollars in thousands)	Required Reserves (%)	Reserve (dollars in thousands)
Transaction Accounts (Oct. 13–26)			
Total transaction accounts	$78,728		
Less deductions	6,424		
Subject to reserves	$72,304		
Zero percent reservable	4,400	0	$ 0
Low reserve amount	49,300	3	1,429
Remaining amount	18,604	10	1,860
Other reservable transaction obligations	0	10	—
Total transaction reserves			$3,339
Savings and Time Deposits (Sept. 15–28)			
Nonpersonal savings and time deposits	$24,875	0	—
Eurocurrency transactions	0	0	—
Other reservable obligations	0	3–10	—
Total other accounts and obligations			$ 0
Total reservable deposits and obligations			$3,339
Vault cash (Sept. 15–28)			608
Daily average balance, to be maintained at Federal Reserve directly or on pass-through basis (before consideration of carryover)			$2,731

[a] Based on data in Tables 7.1 and 7.2.

to carry a reserve excess or deficiency into the following two-week reserve period. This provision gives a bank permission to end a reserve maintenance period in either an excess or deficient position up to 2 percent. The bank carries this position into the next two-week period where it is applied to that period's new reserve requirement. An excess or deficiency cannot be carried over to the second two-week period following the week in which the excess or deficiency occurs.

MEETING REQUIRED RESERVES AND MANAGING THE MONEY POSITION

Banks' "money positions" consist of four basic asset accounts, as follows.

1. *Currency and coin* (or vault cash) consists of money that the bank holds to meet its daily transaction needs. When the bank has more vault cash than it needs, it deposits the excess in its Federal Reserve Bank or a correspondent bank. When the bank has less vault cash than it needs, it draws currency and coin from the Fed or correspondent bank.

2. *Due from the Federal Reserve* represents the bank's deposits with its Federal Re-

FIGURE 7.1   Timing Sequence of Measuring and Filling Reserve Needs

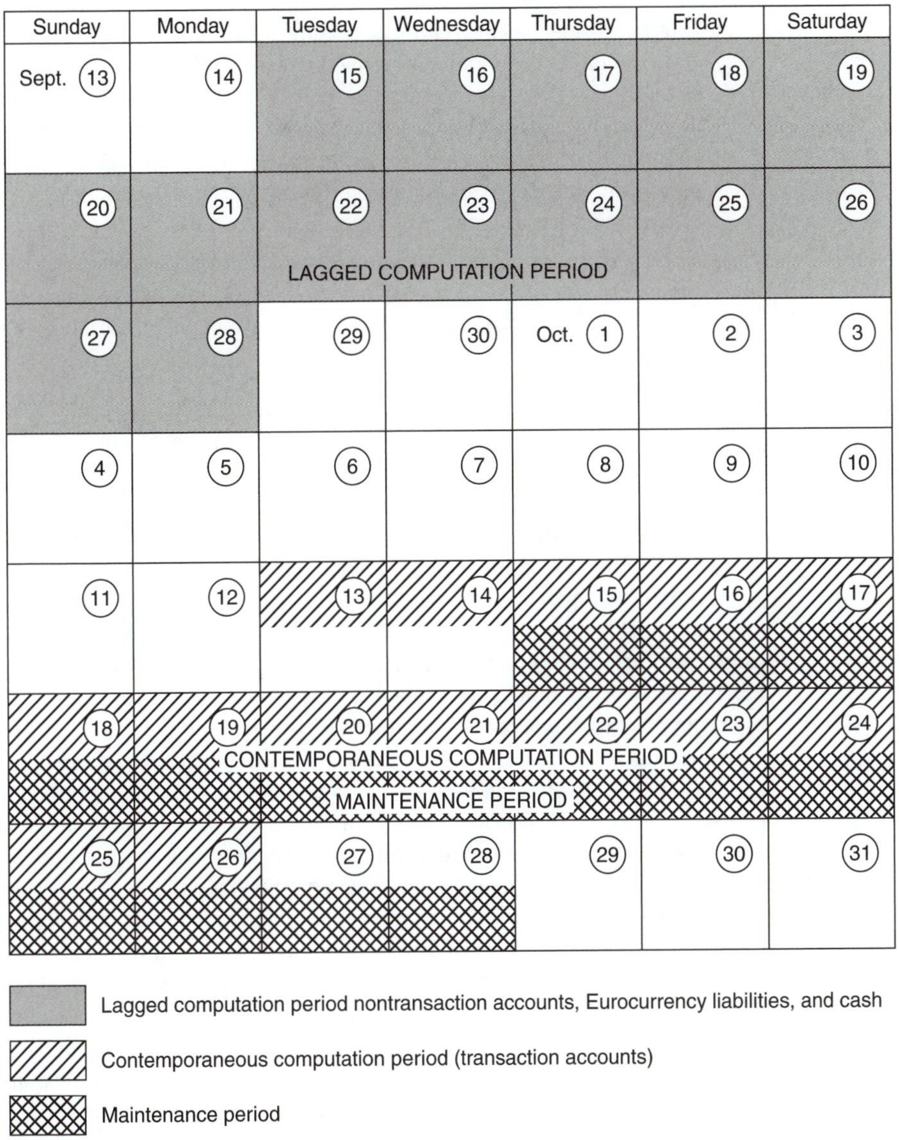

Sunday	Monday	Tuesday	Wednesday	Thursday	Friday	Saturday
Sept. (13)	(14)	(15)	(16)	(17)	(18)	(19)
(20)	(21)	(22)	(23)	(24)	(25)	(26)
(27)	(28)	(29)	(30)	Oct. (1)	(2)	(3)
(4)	(5)	(6)	(7)	(8)	(9)	(10)
(11)	(12)	(13)	(14)	(15)	(16)	(17)
(18)	(19)	(20)	(21)	(22)	(23)	(24)
(25)	(26)	(27)	(28)	(29)	(30)	(31)

LAGGED COMPUTATION PERIOD

CONTEMPORANEOUS COMPUTATION PERIOD

MAINTENANCE PERIOD

Lagged computation period nontransaction accounts, Eurocurrency liabilities, and cash

Contemporaneous computation period (transaction accounts)

Maintenance period

serve Bank. This account is the basic reserve account of banks that are members of the Federal Reserve. The net of check clearings and electronic funds transfers is ultimately taken from or added to this account. This account can be increased by purchasing federal funds, borrowing funds from the Federal Reserve, increasing depository currency and coins, and redeeming Treasury securities as they mature. Methods for decreasing the Federal Reserve account include selling federal funds, reversing purchases of federal funds, repaying borrowing from the Federal

Reserve, withdrawing coin and currency, and directly purchasing Treasury securities.

3. *Due from other commercial banks* consists of all deposits the bank has in other commercial banks. Nonmember banks must hold reserves directly (or indirectly through pass-through accounts) in their Federal Reserve Banks. Member and nonmember banks usually hold balances with other commercial banks, but these accounts do not qualify as legal reserves. Correspondent banks compensate banks that place balances with them by providing services such as loan participations, international transactions, and investment advice.

4. *Cash items in process of collection* represent checks deposited in Federal Reserve Banks or correspondent banks for which credit has not yet been received. Recognized as ''float,'' the size of these cash items depends on the volume of checks and the time it takes to clear the checks.

As we demonstrated in Chapter 4, bank management's primary objective should be to maximize the value of the owners' investment in the bank. Since the assets represented by the bank's money position are generally nonearning assets, management's objective should be to minimize the amount invested in such assets without taking excessive risk. The means of achieving this objective can be divided into three groups: cash items in the process of collection, nonreserve correspondent balances, and required reserves.

In general, management should strive to process and collect cash items as rapidly as possible. This may involve working evenings to process checks earlier, using electronic funds transfer effectively, and flying checks by courier to key collection cities. Management must ascertain that the marginal benefits—return on assets changed from nonearning to earning assets—exceed the marginal costs of speeding up the collection process.

Management should compare the cost of holding demand deposit balances at correspondent banks that are not used to meet reserve requirements with the value of services provided by the correspondent. Large correspondent banks usually provide check collection services for their ''downstream'' correspondent banks. In return for the resulting deposit balances, correspondent banks may perform a number of services. These include such services as giving investment advice, holding securities in safekeeping, arranging for the purchase and sale of securities, trading federal funds, arranging international financial transactions, participating in loans too large for smaller banks, and selling participations in loans to banks with surplus funds. They should be capable of providing such services at a cost that is lower than the recipient bank's cost of producing the services in-house, and yet providing them should contribute to the profits of the correspondent bank. The cost of holding funds in correspondent balances is the returns the bank foregoes by not investing the funds in earning assets. Such costs should not exceed the benefits from the services received.

The final category, required reserves, should be regarded as the dues (explicit cost) required to conduct a banking business. Dues above the required amount earn either no return or a return significantly below what the bank can earn on other earning assets. The bank should manage the required reserve portion of its money position by just holding the required reserves amount in vault cash, deposits at the Federal Reserve bank, and pass-through accounts to the Federal Reserve.

Required reserves are the dues required to be a bank and are used by the Federal Reserve to implement monetary policy by controlling the money supply. *Required reserves are not liquid assets,* which can be used to meet loan demands or deposit outflows. Indeed, vault cash and deposits at the Federal Reserve that are required as reserves would seem to be about as nonliquid as bank premises. The interaction between reserves and liquidity is strong. The reserve position of a bank serves as the clearing account for liquidity needs, such as new loans and deposit outflows, and the liquidity position is a buffer for its money position. However, both needs must be met separately.

In managing its money position, a bank must meet its reserve requirements within the time constraints discussed in the preceding section. Random demands for loans and fluctuations in supplies of funds may force it either to buy funds at a higher than optimal price because it needs funds quickly or to employ funds at a lower than optimal return because it has excess reserves to invest immediately. The leeway provided by knowing reserve requirements in advance does not greatly simplify the problem because the balances themselves are subject to change each day. Having determined the bank's requirement at opening time, the money-position manager needs to keep track of all important transactions that affect the reserve balance during the day and to take steps to counteract any adverse effects.

The principles of managing the money position are virtually the same in large and small banks. It is the number rather than the nature of the transactions that greatly complicates the task for larger banks in money centers. For the larger banks, especially those serving the New York City money and securities markets, the management of reserve positions is a continuous task. The rapidity with which funds flow through the money market banks reflects the payment for most of the nation's security transactions, as well as the financing of brokers and dealers. This rapidity results from the high degree to which national corporations have consolidated their balances in the money centers, as well as how fully they keep them invested. Finally, the balancing adjustments of all the country banks and the settlement of the federal funds markets are made on the books of banks in the money centers.

The basic problems involved in managing a money position can be more readily seen in the analysis of procedures used in Tables 7.1, 7.2, and 7.3. Our example procedures are adequate for a small bank not located in a financial center. Table 7.4 presents a sample worksheet that such a bank might use to manage its money position. The bank starts by adding its *estimated* contemporaneous reserves for transaction deposits for the October 13 to 26 period to known reserve requirements (based on September 15 to 28 figures) for other deposits and idle cash. Note that balances with the Federal Reserve for Friday, Saturday, and Sunday do not change. Column 2 shows "potential" balances with the Federal Reserve before any specific actions by bank management to affect the balances. This results in a potential excess or deficiency (column 3). However, this magnitude can be changed by federal funds transactions, borrowing from the Federal Reserve, and direct transactions on Treasury securities, with the resulting estimated actual excess or deficiency appearing in column 8 and accumulated in column 9.

The estimated contemporaneous reserves will be revised when transaction deposits for October 13 to 19 are reported, and they will be finalized when transaction deposits for October 20 to 26 are calculated. It is the bank's responsibility, and not the Federal Reserve's, to make these transaction deposit estimates and to make sure the final required balance is consistent with the contemporaneous transaction deposit reserves. Banks have generally done a good job since contemporaneous reserves were implemented starting in the mid-1980s.

The bank's analyst places any surplus or deficit position up to 4 percent of daily average reserve requirements from the previous two-week period on the worksheet in

TABLE 7.4 Worksheet for Computing Reserve Position

Reserve Balances for: Day	Date	Required Balances with Federal Reserve Banks[a] (1)	Potential Balances with Federal Reserve Bank (2)	Potential Excess or Deficiency (3)	Federal Funds Actions — Federal Funds Purchased (4)	Federal Funds Actions — Federal Funds Sold (5)	Other Adjustments Affecting Reserve Position[b] (6)	Closing Balances with Federal Reserve Bank (7)	Actual Excess or Deficiency (8)	Accumulated Excess or Deficiency +30 (9)[e]
Thurs.	Oct. 15	2,731	2,884	+153				2,884	+153	+183[c]
Fri.	Oct. 16	2,731	2,790	+59		200		2,590	−141	+42
Sat.	Oct. 17	2,731	2,790	+59		200		2,590	−141	−99
Sun.	Oct. 18	2,731	2,790	+59		200		2,590	−141	−240
Mon.	Oct. 19	2,731	2,529	−202				2,529	−202	−442
Tues.	Oct. 20	2,731	2,286	−445				2,286	−445	−887
Wed.	Oct. 21	2,731	2,538	−193	379			2,917	+186	−701
Thurs.	Oct. 22	2,731	2,656	−75	300			2,956	+225	−476
Fri.	Oct. 23	2,731	2,665	−66	200			2,865	+134	−342
Sat.	Oct. 24	2,731	2,665	−66	200			2,865	+134	−208
Sun.	Oct. 25	2,731	2,665	−66	200			2,865	+134	−74
Mon.	Oct. 26	2,731	2,797	+66				2,797	+66	−8
Tues.	Oct. 27	2,731	2,758	+27				2,758	+27	+19
Wed.	Oct. 28	2,731	2,817	+86		200		2,617	−114	−95[d]

[a] Usually estimated on October 15, October 20 (October 13 to 19 figures available) and finalized on October 27 (October 20 to 26 figures available).
[b] Such as borrowing from the Federal Reserve and payments for and receipts from direct transaction in Treasury securities.
[c] Allowable excess in reserve balances equal to 30 brought forward and added to first day's excess (or deficiency).
[d] Allowable excess or deficiency in reserve balances to be carried forward.

Table 7.4 at the head of columns 3, 8, and 9. These amounts are included only in the excess or deficiency figures because they do not, of course, affect the actual amounts of deposits on record. Without the carryover provision, reserve surpluses would be wasted, since reserves earn no interest. Similarly, shortfalls in reserve holdings can also be carried into the next period. Negative carryovers are not permitted for two or more consecutive periods.

A glance at the final column of the worksheet will tell the bank's money manager just where the bank stands at the opening of business each day.[3] This person then needs to calculate the effects of the debits and credits that he or she believes will be posted to the reserve account during each day. As a result, he or she is in a position to project the current and cumulative average balances as of the close of business the same day. On the basis of this projection, a decision can be made regarding what actions, if any, will be necessary to keep this position in reasonable balance. Table 7.5 provides a suggested format for making these calculations. For small banks with only moderate deposit fluctuations, not much more is needed. For larger banks seeking to keep excess reserves to the barest minimum, a closer scrutiny of daily transactions is necessary.

The bulk of the credits and debits affecting a small nonmoney center bank's accounts is usually evident in the clearing figures each morning (checks presented to it and checks forwarded by it for collection) or is the result of transactions, such as securities purchases and sales, that the bank has originated. In sharp contrast is the situation of banks that operate in the money centers or that carry substantial amounts of due-to-bank balances. During the course of each day, these banks are subject to immediate and unpredictable demands in the form of interbank transfers and other payments arranged in federal funds by their depositors.

Nevertheless, even for a small to medium-sized bank, the unpredictable can loom large in the management of its reserve position. The volatility of large deposit accounts can cause money position management to go awry as the result of unexpectedly large withdrawals or even large deposits that cannot be used. Alert money managers will therefore attempt to keep a close watch over their larger depositors and will take notice of the transactions that may affect the reserve position not only on a particular day but later in the reserve-computation period as well. The money-position manager should scan large deposits and withdrawals daily for clues to future deposit movements and should attempt to get advance notice of future transactions from the financial officers of important corporate customers. At the same time, the manager should maintain a calendar of maturing CDs and securities and large loan repayments to incorporate into the daily adjustments of the reserve position. The money-position manager should also receive a brief daily memorandum of the sources of funds available and a list of correspondent balances and liquidity instruments. Most large banks require that branch managers and department heads report large transactions to the money desk as soon as these transactions become known.

In addition to gathering data, the money market manager seeks to match reserve requirements with actual reserve positions. At the start of the statement period, a bank

---

[3] Since the Federal Reserve is open only five days a week, no transactions are recorded over the weekend; hence the reserve balance that the bank achieves Friday afternoon will also be its deposit balance for Saturday and Sunday. When holidays occur on Mondays or Fridays, the position is carried a day longer. For example, if a holiday falls on a Monday, the Federal Reserve being closed, the bank's reserve position as of Friday will apply not only to Saturday and Sunday but also to Monday. Hence, locking into a surplus reserve position over a holiday weekend is one method of helping meet reserve requirements for a period.

TABLE 7.5   Estimated Money Position Calculations, Thursday, October 22   (dollars in thousands)

	Previous	Current	Cumulative
Accumulated actual excess or deficiency			(−)701
Required reserves tonight		2,731	
Reserve position last night	2,538		
Transactions affecting reserves today:			
Other credits			
Yesterday's immediate cash letter		2,181	
Deferred items available today		885	
Security sales available today		737	
Currency and coin in transit		100	
Credit in local clearings		—	
Other		—	
Total other credits		(+)3,903	
Other debits			
Remittances charged today		3,206	
Securities purchased charged today		—	
Notes due today		—	
Tax and loan account call		100	
Currency and coin orders		—	
Debits in local clearings		55	
Other		—	
Total other debits		(−)3,361	
Net credits minus debits		(+)118	
Potential balances tonight persuant to net check clearings		2,656	
Potential excess or deficit tonight		(−)75	(−)776
Adjusted today:			
Credits			
Transfers from bank account		—	
Borrowing from Federal Reserve		—	
Federal funds bought		300	
Securities sold for "cash"		—	
Total credits		300	
Debits			
Transfer from reserve account		—	
Federal funds sold		—	
Total debits		—	
Net adjustments		(+)300	
Adjusted excess or deficiency		(+)225	(−)476

should make a rough forecast of its expected reserve position for each day in the coming period. The manager of the reserve position must then plan out the bank's activity during the period on the basis of the mean forecast of reserve positions and the possible deviations from the mean forecast that might be experienced.

If the projected deposit balances at the Federal Reserve are as shown in Table 7.4, the bank will probably need to buy federal funds (or borrow from the Federal Reserve) sometime during the period to meet its reserve requirements. However, if the possible deviations from these expected levels are small, the reserve manager may decide to wait until close to the end of the period and then (since the reserve deficiency is not expected to be large) enter the market and buy funds if necessary. Since the distribution of possible outcomes is small and the expected deficit is also small, the manager can wait until more information is available before acting.

On the other hand, if there is a great deal of uncertainty about the upcoming week, the reserve manager may want to borrow federal funds early in the period and establish a cushion of reserves so as to avoid borrowing a large amount at the last minute. In this case, the bank will sell federal funds toward the end of the period if the reserve position has evolved to be much closer than forecast. The bank will act defensively in this time period, sacrificing returns to be able to satisfy legal reserve requirements.

MEASURING A BANK'S LIQUIDITY NEEDS

A bank's liquidity needs consist of immediate obligations, such as deposit withdrawals or legitimate loan demands, that the bank must meet to continue its functions as a financial intermediary. Depositors and creditors must have confidence in the value of their bank's assets in order to trust the bank with their funds. Because it is difficult to know how much confidence quality-sensitive depositors and creditors have in a bank, it is difficult to measure banks' liquidity needs and ability to meet such needs.

Traditional analysis measures liquidity using ratios based on static balance sheet data. Several such ratios are tabulated in Chapter 3. The analyst separates bank assets into liquid (easily convertible into cash without appreciable loss) and nonliquid components. The analyst then divides the bank's liabilities and net worth into core (stable) and noncore (vulnerable to unexpected withdrawal). Short-term investments are available to pay off noncore funds withdrawals.

The most sophisticated ratio for representing bank liquidity is the noncore funds dependence ratio. (This ratio appeared in Table 3.15 along with several other common liquidity ratios.) The noncore dependence ratio indicates how dependent a bank is on volatile sources to finance its nonliquid earning assets, after subtracting short-term investments.

$$\frac{\text{Noncore liabilities} - \text{Short-term investments}}{\text{Earning assets} - \text{Short-term investments}}$$

Such ratios do not give the complete picture we need to assess a bank's liquidity risk because they ignore the dynamic nature of liquidity needs and sources. In the following paragraphs, the dynamic nature of liquidity is stressed. A bank's liquidity needs are measured over time; then liquidity sources are matched with these changing needs.

TABLE 7.6   Illustration of Liquidity Needs for Sample Bank (dollars in thousands)

1. Starting Position

Assets		Liabilities and Capital	
Reserves	$ 17,100	Transaction accounts	$100,000
Securities	75,000	Savings and time deposits	170,000
Loans	200,000	Borrowings	10,000
Other assets	7,900	Capital	20,000
	$300,000		$300,000

2. Period of Low Liquidity Need

Assets		Liabilities and Capital	
Reserves	$ 18,000	Transaction accounts	$105,000
Securities	84,100	Savings and time deposits	180,000
Loans	200,000	Borrowings	5,000
Other assets	7,900	Capital	20,000
	$310,000		$310,000

3. Period of High Liquidity Need

Assets		Liabilities and Capital	
Reserves[a]	$ 15,600	Transaction accounts	$ 90,000
Securities[a]	46,500	Savings and time deposits	160,000
Loans	220,000	Borrowings[a]	20,000
Other assets	7,900	Capital	20,000
	$290,000		$290,000

[a] $20,000 decline in deposits and $20,000 increase in loans financed by additional borrowings of $10,000, lower monetary position of $1,500, and sale of $28,500 of securities.

Table 7.6 illustrates the changing liquidity needs for a sample bank. This bank holds cash reserves equal to 9 percent of transaction accounts and 3 percent of time and savings deposits. The bank's initial position is given in panel 1 of Table 7.6. Panel 2 depicts a recessionary situation when the bank has low liquidity needs. Its deposits actually grew in relation to the starting position, but its new loan demand was flat. In contrast, under economic boom conditions indicated in panel 3 of Table 7.6, the bank encountered high liquidity needs because of rapid loan growth accompanied by a decline in deposits. A $10,000 increase in borrowings and $28,500 generated from the sale of securities produced most of the liquidity needed by the bank. A small amount was provided by the lower required monetary position of $15,600.

Bank management has an important task to measure and meet its liquidity needs. The example of Table 7.6 conclusively points out that management should measure liquidity needs *dynamically*. Long-run profitability will suffer when banks hold too much in low-earning liquidity sources in relation to its needs for such liquidity. On the other hand, too little liquidity can lead to severe financial problems and even failure. We now turn to methods for measuring dynamic liquidity.

Measuring Dynamic Liquidity Needs

Thus far in this chapter we have established that detailed management of the money position is crucial daily or hourly, in the case of large regional and money center banks. At this point we address how managers can accurately estimate short-term, cyclical, and trend needs for liquidity. To do so, banks are guided by their past experience and knowledge of events likely to affect liquidity needs. Next we discuss how to measure these liquidity needs dynamically. Then we will investigate the appropriate sources for filling these liquidity needs.

The short-term or seasonal liquidity needs of a bank may arise from several sources. For example, seasonal factors often affect deposit flows and loan demand. Since loans are generally to deposit customers, seasonal increases in loans tend to occur when deposits are at seasonal lows, and vice versa. For example, a bank in a farming community might find high liquidity needs when its loan demand rises and its deposits fall in the spring to meet farmers' funding needs for planting and fertilizing crops. After the crops are sold in the fall, loans fall while deposits increase. Banks that depend a lot on one or a few types of customers may find seasonal liquidity needs particularly important. Most seasonal fluctuations can be estimated on the basis of past experience.

Large depositors and large borrowers may influence the short-term liquidity needs of an individual bank disproportionately. The extent of these customers' influence is in direct relationship to the bank's size. The short-term funding needs of important customers can strongly affect bank liquidity in the short run. Some customers' needs are highly predictable, such as the school district that has $5 million in CDs that are scheduled to pay for a new school building when they mature. The short-term needs of other customers may be very difficult to predict, such as the loan needs of a volatile business that may use its $10 million line of credit (borrowing authority) to finance inventory. Much of the estimation of this type of short-term liquidity need is determined by detailed information about the needs and intentions of large customers.

Let's analyze the short-term liquidity needs of Fifth National Bank. Data for this bank are presented in Tables 7.7 and 7.8 and illustrate the measurement of short-term liquidity needs. A condensed balance sheet is given for the end of 1998 in panel 1 of Table 7.7. In panel 2, Fifth National has (1) classified loans as volatile (large customers subject to rapid loan increases or decreases) and other loans (primarily subject to seasonal fluctuations); (2) classified savings and time deposits as vulnerable (subject to large withdrawals or increases) and other deposits (estimated to grow $1 million each month in 1999); and (3) computed a cash position based on a required 9 percent reserve on all transaction accounts and a 3 percent reserve on all time and savings deposits. Bank management has estimated monthly patterns for volatile loans and vulnerable deposits. The seasonal indexes for transaction accounts and other loans that appear in Table 7.8 were estimated from Fifth Bank's seasonal deposit fluctuations over the past several years.

The appropriate seasonal index (index for month/index for December) was multiplied by the December transaction accounts and other loans to estimate the dollar amounts in these categories. The various categories of loans and deposits in Table 7.8 are added and used in Table 7.7 to project the bank's estimated liquidity needs from December 31, 1998, to the end of each month in 1999. An estimated balance sheet for the month of

TABLE 7.7   Measuring Seasonal Liquidity Needs of Fifth National Bank

1. Balance Sheet at End of Year
December 31, 1997 (dollars in thousands)

Assets		Liabilities and Capital	
Reserves	$ 17,100	Transaction accounts	$100,000
Securities	75,000	Vulnerable time deposits	20,000
Loans (volatile)	20,000	Other savings and time deposits	150,000
Loans (other)	180,000	Borrowings	10,000
Other assets	7,900	Capital	20,000
	$300,000		$300,000

2. Monthly Loan and Deposit Fluctuations

End of Month	Total Loans	Total Deposits	Estimated Liquidity Needs[a]
January	$192,800	$273,000	$+10,200
February	193,200	278,000	+14,800
March	205,000	269,000	−6,000
April	223,000	263,000	−30,000
May	212,200	262,000	−20,000
June	198,400	264,000	−4,400
July	191,200	271,000	+9,888
August	199,800	273,000	+3,200
September	210,600	273,000	−7,600
October	214,200	273,000	−11,200
November	210,600	272,000	−8,600
December	210,000	277,000	−3,000

3. Balance Sheet, Time of Highest Liquidity Need
April 30, 1998 (dollars in thousands)

Assets		Liabilities and Capital	
Reserves[a]	$ 16,350	Transaction accounts	$ 94,000
Securities	45,750	Vulnerable time deposits	15,000
Loans (volatile)	25,000	Other savings and time deposits (trend)	154,000
Loans (other)	198,000	Borrowings	10,000
Other assets	7,900	Capital	20,000
	$293,000		$293,000

[a] Total loans and deposits for the month minus total at the start of the year without adjustment for required reserves. Minus (−) means that liquidity is needed, and plus (+) means added liquidity from the end of the year.

TABLE 7.8   Seasonal Indexes and Calculation of Monthly Loans and Deposits for Fifth National Bank (dollars in thousands)

End of Month	Loans (Volatile)	Loans (Other)		Transaction Accounts		Vulnerable Time Deposits	Other Time and Savings Deposits
		Index	Amounts	Index	Amounts		
January	$20,000	96	$172,800	102	$102,000	$20,000	$151,000
February	25,000	94	169,200	106	106,000	20,000	152,000
March	25,000	100	180,000	101	101,000	15,000	153,000
April	25,000	110	198,000	94	94,000	15,000	154,000
May	25,000	104	187,200	92	92,000	15,000	155,000
June	22,000	98	176,400	98	98,000	10,000	156,000
July	22,000	94	169,200	104	104,000	10,000	157,000
August	27,000	96	172,800	105	105,000	10,000	158,000
September	27,000	102	183,600	104	104,000	10,000	159,000
October	27,000	104	187,200	98	98,000	15,000	160,000
November	27,000	102	183,600	96	96,000	15,000	161,000
December	30,000	100	180,000	100	100,000	15,000	162,000

highest liquidity needs appears at the bottom of Table 7.7. It is assumed that the liquidity needs from the $23 million increase in loans and $7 million decrease in deposits were financed by the sale of $29.250 million of securities and a $750,000 drop in required reserves. (The methods of filling liquidity needs are discussed in detail in a later section.)

Although the example in Tables 7.7 and 7.8 is highly simplified, it illustrates the basic methods for estimating the bank's short-term liquidity needs. Loans and deposits need to be categorized according to their seasonal or other short-term potential fluctuations. There may be as many as 20 to 30 categories of loans and deposits, and many banks use weekly rather than monthly data. Numerous prepared computer software programs to estimate short-term liquidity needs are available for personal computers, and many banks have created their own software programs for estimating liquidity needs.

Cyclical liquidity needs of a bank are much more difficult to estimate. These needs often are out of the control of any individual bank. Economic recession or boom and interest rate movements, particularly when banks may be constrained from changing their own rates because of political pressure or regulation, can cause significant liquidity pressures. Furthermore, the timing of such cyclical pressures can be very difficult to predict. A bank that provides for all potential cyclical liquidity needs would probably end up holding primarily low-earning liquid assets at the cost of significantly lower profitability. The lower risk of this high liquidity position would probably not offset the negative impact of these lower returns.

The impact of cyclical liquidity needs can be illustrated by looking back at Fifth National Bank in Table 7.7. Assume that a cyclical boom creates a 25 percent, $50 million increase in loans. Fifth National will be compelled to sell most of its securities and to borrow heavily just at a time when interest rates are high and security prices are low. Similar liquidity pressures might occur because of large deposit outflows, caused by business factors or by a loss of confidence in a bank's ability to repay its debt. Such a loss of confidence is apt to occur when a bank reports large loan losses or takes large losses on unsuccessful gambles involving interest rate speculation or foreign exchange trading. It is doubtful that Fifth National Bank would survive deposit outflows and lender loss of confidence of a magnitude similar to that experienced by Continental Illinois Bank in 1984.

As mentioned earlier, cyclical liquidity pressures are usually difficult to predict. The following methods may give some helpful indications about the magnitude of cyclical liquidity needs. First, cyclical vulnerability to loans may be partially estimated for many banks by looking at the proportion of lines of credit currently used versus the highest use of lines in a previous cyclical boom. For example, if 40 percent of a bank's lines of credit is currently used and if 62 percent was the highest past usage of such lines, the bank might estimate an increase of 22 percent of its total lines as the cyclical liquidity needs from such lines.

Second, correlation patterns between deposit flows and selected indicators, such as the level of rates, changes in rates, and rate ceilings, may provide guidelines for deposit inflows and outflows. Third, a bank's vulnerability to deposit outflows and lack of confidence by lenders should be realistically evaluated. For example, Continental Illinois had over two-thirds of its deposits and borrowings from such nonpersonal sources as large corporate CDs and foreign sources. Large deposits and borrowings from foreign sources were clearly vulnerable to cyclical (or any other) confidence-shattering news. A bank should carefully evaluate its funding diversification, the probable loyalty of its major funding sources, and the risks the bank is taking in areas such as credit risk, interest rate risk, and capital risk, which might blemish the bank's name.

Finally, certain statistical programs (in computer software packages) can remove seasonal and trend effects from a time series of loan and deposit accounts. The residuals should give a rough estimation of the type of cyclical liquidity pressures these accounts were subject to in the past. Thus, if large CDs had fallen 10 to 15 percent in past cyclical periods or confidence crises, the bank might try to make sure it had the ability to meet liquidity needs for 15 percent of its current large CDs.

Trend liquidity needs are required by banks for liquidity demands that can be predicted over a longer time span. These longer-term liquidity needs are generally related to the secular trends of the community or markets that a bank serves. In rapidly expanding areas, loans often grow faster than deposits. A bank in such a situation needs sources of liquidity to provide funds for loan expansion.

In stable communities, on the other hand, deposits may show a steady rise, while loans remain virtually unchanged. In such cases, the longer view of liquidity requirements may enable the bank to keep more fully invested than it otherwise would. In either case, to gauge the bank's needs for longer-term liquidity, a bank's management must attempt long-range economic forecasting as the basis on which it can reasonably estimate loan and deposit levels for the next year and perhaps five years ahead.

Figure 7.2 illustrates a methodology a bank might use to plan its trend to longer-term liquidity needs. The bank starts by classifying every asset on its balance sheet as liquid (convertible into usable funds within less than 90 days with little, if any, loss if the asset is sold) or nonliquid. The accounts listed to the left of the liquidity and nonliquidity columns in Figure 7.2 are representative of the asset types that would fall into each category. Next, the sources of funds, liabilities, and capital are divided into two categories—volatile (subject to withdrawal because of seasonal, rate, or other pressures) and stable. The accounts listed to the right of the volatile and stable columns are representative

FIGURE 7.2   Illustration of Trend Liquidity Planning for a Bank

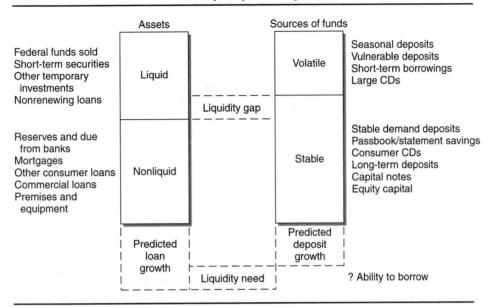

of the types of liabilities and capital that would fall into each category. The difference between liquid assets and volatile sources is termed the liquidity gap. The gap is positive if liquid assets exceed volatile sources and negative if the reverse is the case.

The broken lines in Figure 7.2 represent expected fund flows during the next period that are added to the balance sheet totals. The primary increase in assets usually comes from loan growth, whereas deposit growth represents the primary source of funds for the bank depicted in Figure 7.2. If predicted loan growth exceeds predicted deposit growth, the bank has a liquidity need that may be covered by reducing a positive liquidity gap or by purchasing funds. (Methods for meeting liquidity needs are discussed in a later section.) On the other hand, if predicted deposit growth exceeds predicted loan growth, the bank can improve its liquidity position or seek to employ the excess liquidity in higher-return assets.

Figure 7.3 illustrates a method for combining short-term and trend liquidity pressures into a unified model for measuring liquidity needs. Again Fifth National Bank is used as the example, but the bank's growth in 1998 and its predicted growth as well as its past and predicted seasonal pattern are the basis for charting liquidity needs. Although the charts in Figure 7.3 are simplified to serve as illustrations, a personal computer can be used for more elaborate calculations as well as for tracing more detailed charts.

The volatility of Fifth National Bank's deposits is shown in the chart for month-end deposits at the top of Figure 7.3. (For most banks with over $100 million in assets, this chart should be the summation of several charts for specific categories of deposits and should cover successive reserve-computation periods.) A trend line drawn through or near the low points should indicate the trend of stable deposits. The amount of deposits above this baseline represents the bank's seasonal liquidity needs caused by deposits sub-

FIGURE 7.3   Charting Liquidity Needs

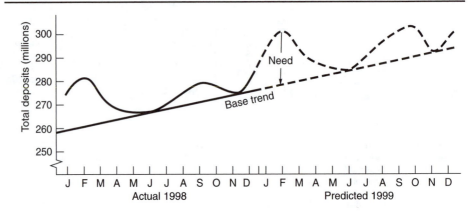

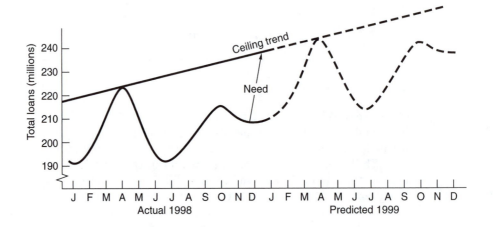

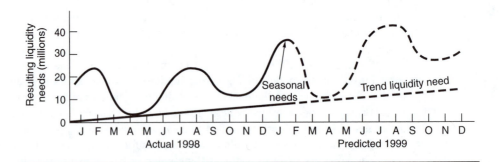

ject to withdrawal. More complex charts or calculations would recognize liquidity needs for volatile deposits and would be the total of such deposits less the percentage of required reserves held against them. As deposits decline, the release of reserves provides a small part of the requisite liquidity.

The middle chart in Figure 7.3 depicts the liquidity needs from rising and fluctuating loan demands. Part of this demand may be seasonal and can be depicted in a chart of month-end totals. (As with deposits, larger banks will have charts or calculations for several types of loans and will use successive reserve computation periods.) A trend line, drawn through or near the high points, represents the ceiling trend to which loans may be expected to rise periodically or seasonally. The amount by which loans are below the ceiling at any given time represents the bank's potential liquidity needs to meet seasonal loan demands.

The lowest chart in Figure 7.3 traces the combined seasonal and trend liquidity needs for Fifth National Bank. Trend liquidity is calculated by subtracting the changes in the deposit trend line from the changes in the loan trend. If loan growth exceeds deposit growth, there will be a liquidity need; if the reverse is true, there will be a liquidity excess. For example, if the trend line of deposits rose from $250 million to $270 million and the loan trend line rose from $220 million to $250 million in the same period, there would be a trend liquidity need of $10 million. Total seasonal liquidity needs would be the total of deposit deviations from the base trend and loan deviations from the ceiling trend. These seasonal liquidity needs would be added to the trend liquidity previously calculated to trace the bank's total need for liquidity.

Although this method is relatively straightforward, there are numerous practical problems. First, it is difficult to isolate which part of past fluctuations in loans and deposits are seasonal, cyclical, and trend. Second, forecasting future seasonal patterns and trends based on the past is hazardous at best. Seasonal patterns may change. The trend in deposits may change because of regulatory or competitive actions the bank cannot control. Trends in loans may change because of such actions, economic conditions, or changes in bank lending policies. Third, the method ignores cyclical liquidity needs or liquidity crises due to a lack of confidence, which are often the least predictable and can be the most harmful, if not at least partially recognized. Most banks, using methods similar to those illustrated in the charts in Figure 7.3, add some more liquidity needs for forecasting error and unpredictable cyclical needs. The question is, how much? In spite of such problems, the method seems to offer a bank significant information on its liquidity needs.

Contingent liquidity needs are caused by unusual events that are difficult, if not impossible, to predict. Examples include an unexpected outflow of deposits caused by a rumor about the bank, an unusual increase in loan demand, or the closing of an extensively used funding source. By their very nature, contingency liquidity needs are impossible to forecast accurately. At the same time, every bank should have a plan (and most regulators require a plan) to remain liquid in case some contingency does occur.

Rules of thumb for assessing contingency liquidity needs vary greatly. For example, a retail community bank might believe it should have the ability to cover a contingent deposit outflow of 20 percent. An urban wholesale bank might believe it should have the ability to meet 70 percent of its lines of credit (even though 40 percent is the norm). A larger bank that uses nondeposit sources extensively might believe it should be able to cover the disappearance of one of its primary borrowing sources. A bank's primary regulatory body is often a good source for establishing contingency liquidity needs.

FILLING A BANK'S LIQUIDITY NEEDS

Providing for a bank's liquidity needs is often as complex as estimating those needs. Many banks have some estimates of their liquidity needs but do not have adequate policies and procedures for meeting these needs. Various sources that can be used to fill a bank's liquidity needs are described; then methods for matching liquidity needs and sources are discussed.

Traditional Sources of Liquidity

The primary traditional sources of liquidity fall into two basic categories. The first category consists of assets in which funds are temporarily invested with the assurance that they either will mature and be paid when liquidity is needed or will be readily salable, without material loss, in advance of maturity. The second category includes the various methods by which banks can borrow or otherwise obtain funds. Large CDs are an example of a classification conflict between deposits, which presumably are used to measure liquidity needs, and funds borrowed to provide liquidity. A general rule of thumb for smaller and medium-sized banks in such conflicts could be to classify deposits that can be readily purchased or sold in an ongoing market as sources of liquidity and to include all other deposits in measuring liquidity needs. Such a rule of thumb for some very large banks might be misleading because a significant proportion of their deposits comes from purchased sources. These sources are permanent as long as the bank can maintain the confidence of the lender and afford to pay the going market rate.

Most of the primary traditional sources of liquidity are briefly described in Table 7.9. The rule of thumb is that assets must be of high credit quality and either of short maturity or very marketable, with little chance of loss. The amount of liquid assets may be limited by the bank's willingness to hold such assets, which generally earn less than loans or less liquid securities. The use of borrowings or other increases in liabilities to fund liquidity needs is typically limited in one or more ways. Large money center banks and super regional banks that use purchased liabilities extensively as a source of funds are limited primarily by how much the money market and its participants think such banks can use. Confidence of the money markets is the key variable. Regional banks may have limited access to some markets and will probably have lower limits on their total usage of purchased liabilities. Once again, lender confidence is an essential ingredient. The access of smaller banks to some markets is closed, and they may find that their usage of borrowed funds is limited to how much their correspondent banks and the Federal Reserve are willing to lend them. These types of limits indicate that banks of any size should have considerable unused borrowing capacity if they plan to borrow to fund liquidity needs.

Emerging Sources of Liquidity

In addition to these traditional sources, banks use numerous other emerging methods to meet liquidity needs. Four widely used methods have emerged in recent years. One method applies underwriting of highly standardized loans, particularly home mortgages, for resale in well-organized secondary markets. We discuss this process and the government- and nongovernment-supported secondary market for mortgages in Chapter 12. Another method is to *securitize* standardized loans, such as installment loans, credit card loans,

TABLE 7.9   Potential Traditional Sources of Bank Liquidity

Asset Stores of Liquidity

Cash and due from	A bank's money position is a source of liquidity only if (1) there are excess reserves, (2) there are extra balances in correspondent accounts or checks not credited, or (3) deposits drop, freeing an amount equal to the decline times the percentage reserve requirement.
Federal funds sold	Excess reserves of a bank usually sold to another bank to provide earning assets to selling bank. Most mature daily but can be easily renewed; "term funds" are also short-maturity funds with a good market. Unsecured.
Short-term U.S. government securities	Treasury bills and notes or bonds close to maturity are widely used sources of liquidity because they are short term and tend to be bought and sold in active markets. Thought to have no risk of nonpayment.
Commercial paper, bankers' acceptances, and negotiable CDs	Obligations of private borrowers that are bought and sold through money market dealers. Generally traded on a discounted basis, and most issues have a fairly active secondary market. Still high quality (i.e., risk of nonpayment very low).
Other marketable securities	Short-term government agency and state and local obligations having slightly higher yields than government securities, and yield and secondary markets similar to those for commercial paper, CDs, etc. Must be high quality (range available) if used for liquidity.
Securities purchased under agreement to resell (repos)	Temporary purchase of government or other securities in which seller has agreed to repurchase securities at fixed price and set time in the future. Difference between sale and purchase prices is return received by holder.
Other liquid assets	Other creditworthy securities, loans, or assets if their maturity conforms with the bank's liquidity needs and if the bank will have no compunction about reducing the size of such assets if necessary.

Purchased Forms of Liquidity

Borrowing from Federal Reserve (discounts or advances)	Credit extended on a short-term basis by a Federal Reserve Bank to a bank or other depository institution. Rate, set by Fed, is called discount rate, with penalty rates for frequent or unusually heavy users. Collateral (securities or acceptable loans) required for either discounts or advances.
Federal funds purchased	Purchase of another bank's excess reserve on daily or short-term basis. Other side of federal funds sold. Purchased through correspondent or informal phone market at existing federal funds rate. Banks that are continual users often subject to informal limit by sellers. Unsecured; therefore, funds seller checks credit of borrowing bank.
Securities sold under agreement to repurchase	Temporary sale of government or other securities in which bank has received funds from purchaser and agreed to rebuy securities at predetermined price. In effect, short-term (often daily) secured borrowing from purchaser.
Large CDs	CDs in minimum amounts of $100,000 that can be issued to corporate treasurers with excess cash. Larger issues may be marketable. Bank must bid at least going market rate. Since unsecured and since insurance limited to $100,000, corporate treasurers check soundness of bank.
Public deposits	Treasury tax and loan accounts may be retained if bank is willing to pay market rate and has pledgeable securities. Many state and local time deposits go to the bank bidding the highest rate. Often limited by amount of securities available for pledging against public deposits.
Eurodollar and other foreign sources	Eurodollars are deposits in U.S. banks held outside the United States with maturities ranging from overnight to a year. Active secondary market with overseas branch essential to continual involvement. Rates set in international market. Other foreign sources also used by very large banks. Bank must not engage in activities or assume risks that could potentially blemish its name.
Other liability forms	Other liability sources of liquidity include capital notes, ineligible acceptances, commercial paper sold through holding companies, etc. Key element is that bank can raise funds through such forms if bank pays going market rate and lender has confidence in bank.

or mortgages. Chapter 11 gives a detailed description of loan securitization and reviews the economics of this approach.

A third method is to purchase intermediate or long-term securities that have the option of being sold at a set price in the future. The option feature removes the price fluctuation risk (albeit, at lower interest income to the bank; in Chapter 14 we show how such reduced income can be analyzed as the price of the option) and makes the long-term securities liquid.

Still another method is for the bank to use capital market obligations (such as preferred stock or capital notes) to finance its liquidity needs. Clearly, bank financial managers must become more and more innovative in providing sources of liquidity.

MATCHING LIQUIDITY SOURCES TO LIQUIDITY NEEDS

Banks must choose among various assets, liabilities, and the new emerging sources of liquidity to fill their liquidity needs. The wide variety of potential and actual choices used in providing for liquidity is often a bewildering menu of solutions. The choice among the variety of sources of liquidity should depend on several factors: (1) purpose of liquidity needed, (2) access to financial (money) markets, (3) management philosophy, (4) costs and characteristics of the various liquidity sources, and (5) interest rate forecasts.

Purpose of the Liquidity Needed

The reason that liquidity is needed can affect the source of liquidity used to fill that need. Seasonal liquidity needs, increasing loans, and/or deposit outflows tend to be reasonably repetitive in extent, duration, and timing. Forecasts of seasonal needs can usually be based on past experience, and most banks should be reasonably confident in making such forecasts. Therefore, only moderate risk is apparently associated with the use of purchased forms of liquidity to cover seasonal liquidity needs. Unless the bank has low earning maturity assets (Federal funds sold might be an example), purchased funding (e.g., Federal funds purchased or large CDs) are often the favored liquidity choice. There should be a high probability that subsequent cash inflows will provide the funds to repay these purchased forms. The Federal Reserve seems to recognize this in its lending policies by having less stringent requirements for discounts and advances that are clearly for seasonal purposes. The potential gain from using purchased forms to meet seasonal liquidity needs is that the loan and investment portfolios can be structured on the basis of fund availability at seasonal highs. Since loans and investments usually earn higher returns than liquid assets, earnings should be higher from using purchased funds than from building up liquid assets during periods of low seasonal needs.

On the other hand, the use of purchased funds to meet cyclical needs seems less appropriate. Cyclical needs are much more difficult to predict, and when and whether borrowings can be repaid may be a serious concern. The contribution of purchased forms in providing liquidity needs during a cyclical boom may be limited and is likely to be very costly. Loan demands tend to run high in such periods, and liability sources (1) tend to become expensive, (2) may be limited by the market's lack of confidence in a bank's ability to repay its obligations, and (3) may be restricted to only larger and better-known banks. For all but very large banks with good access to broad money market sources, holding liquid assets in slow periods to meet rising loan demand in boom times seems preferable to using purchased funds. By holding an adequate amount of liquid assets—an approach that may involve some loss of current income during the early stage of a cyclical expansion—most banks will avoid higher costs and possibly far greater capital losses (from the sale of depreciated bonds) during the later stages of expansion. Put in more precise terms, the essence of liquidity management is to equate the probable earlier loss of income with the subsequent higher fund cost and possible capital losses. Even large banks with many sources of borrowing should not overemphasize purchased funds for cyclical needs. The reputation of such banks is critical in determining access to the money markets, and overemphasis on purchased funds can hurt that reputation.

Meeting longer-term liquidity needs can be more complex. Loan growth exceeds deposit growth for most banks with longer-term liquidity needs. Such net growth can be financed by selling liquid assets or purchasing funds. The problem is that the supply of salable liquid assets and the amount of borrowing permissible are limited in size. Thus, a bank that sells all its liquid assets cannot use this source to finance a continuing excess of loans relative to deposits. A bank that aims for rapid growth is likely to have some limit on how much of its funding sources can be purchased funds. This limit will vary widely, depending on bank size and entry into various financial markets, but there is some limit. The message would seem to be that a bank must finally limit its longer-term liquidity needs. Three potential strategies are to find more permanent deposit sources, to make standardized loans that are sold or securitized practically as the loans are made, or to limit bank loans in some meaningful way.

Finally, any bank should limit its use of purchased forms of liquidity enough to have a borrowing reserve if future unpredicted liquidity needs occur. This may mean that a smaller bank will seldom use purchased funds, keeping its limited ability to borrow as a liquidity or borrowing reserve. A large bank that believes it can purchase additional funds of up to 100 percent of its core deposits may restrict this source to 75 percent in order to have a borrowing reserve for future unexpected liquidity needs. Some banks claim they have assets they can sell or securitize as their source of contingent liquidity need. We question this source because the sale or securitization must be at the current market rate, which could mean a large loss.

Access to Money Markets

The preceding paragraphs have alluded to differences in access to money markets. This factor is the second primary determinant of the sources of liquidity that banks use to fill their liquidity needs. Many small banks are limited to borrowing from the Federal Reserve or purchasing federal funds through a larger correspondent. Most members of this group of banks want to avoid borrowing from the Federal Reserve unless the borrowing is classified as seasonal. Furthermore, the use of Federal funds is often limited to between 75 to 125 percent of the borrowing bank's capital base. The result of such limited access to sources of purchased liquidity forms is that most banks in this category use the sale or securitization of assets as their primary source of liquidity. The small borrowing reserve that exists is not used but is left available for unpredicted liquidity needs.

At the opposite extreme are money center banks and super regional banks. If reasonably managed, such banks usually have access to a variety of purchased forms in both domestic and international financial markets. These forms include large negotiable CDs, commercial paper, banker's acceptances, and Eurodollars. Furthermore, the total combined size of all purchased forms available to such large banks tends to be much larger in relation to total assets and capital than that for smaller banks. Large banks, therefore, are usually able to choose between liquid assets that may be sold and purchased forms of liquidity. The other determinants of filling liquidity should have a strong impact on this choice.

Diversification of funding sources is also essential to these large banks. Some lenders are more sensitive than others with respect to which banks they will lend money. The most sensitive lenders will cease lending at the first sign of a problem, whereas others tend to be more forgiving. The same attribute applies to markets (e.g., the domestic money market tends to be more sensitive than the Eurocurrency markets). By diversifying its funding sources, a bank can take advantage of differences in sensitivity to credit quality across lenders and markets.

Many banks fall between the two size extremes. Purchased sources include not only funds borrowed from the Federal Reserve and federal funds but also such forms as large CDs and public funds put up for bid. Such medium-sized banks generally lack access to the commercial paper market and most international markets and have relative borrowing limits between those of the small and large banks. Although there is considerable variation in the sources used to provide for liquidity needs, a typical pattern seems to be to use purchased forms for seasonal needs and liquid asset sales to meet other liquidity needs.

Managerial Philosophy

A bank's management philosophy is the third primary determinant of a bank's sources of liquidity. This philosophy consists of a set of implicit or explicit liquidity guidelines established by top management. The primary liquidity guideline is the extent to which the bank is willing to rely on sources of funds that might disappear in difficult times. A bank that makes little or no use of purchased funding sources for liquidity needs (i.e., one that relies exclusively on its liquid assets) reflects a conservative management philosophy.

At the other end of the spectrum is the bank that seeks out purchased funds from any available source, as long as the total cost of such funds is less than the net rate of return the bank is earning by investing them. Such a bank generally relies heavily on outside sources of funds and reflects an aggressive management philosophy. At the same time, aggressive management must realize that the bank's reputation is critical in determining its access to money market sources. Managements with aggressive liquidity philosophies must neither engage in activity nor assume risks that could potentially blemish the institution's name in the money markets. Most banks in the United States fall somewhere between these two extremes; however, management philosophy has a profound effect on the methods individual banks use to provide for their liquidity needs.

The decision to make many loans in standardized forms so that they can be sold or securitized is also partly a management philosophy question. Bank management at some banks, even a few large ones, is philosophically against either standardization or the selling or securitization of any loans. On the other hand, the majority probably use selling or securitization as a source of liquidity for financing some types of their loans. For example, the authors know a small bank where each mortgage the bank makes is instantaneously securitized with a pension fund.

Cost and Characteristics of Various Liquidity Sources

The fourth primary determinant of the liquidity sources a bank should use is the cost and characteristics of the various liquidity sources. Usually, the bank will choose the lowest-cost, available source that achieves the given liquidity need. This lowest-cost principle is subject to the overall constraints imposed by access to financial markets and by the bank's management philosophy. In the case of assets the bank is considering selling to provide for liquidity needs, the ''cost'' is the income given up during the life of the assets adjusted for any gain or loss, tax effects, and brokerage fees. When considering purchased forms, the cost includes not only interest cost but also reserve requirements, processing costs, insurance fees, and other factors.

In addition to directly comparing costs, banks should look at differences in costs for different time periods. For example, a bank facing a seasonal increase in loans may finance these loans with either large CDs or repurchase agreements. One fundamental difference between the two instruments is that repurchase agreements are commonly renewed on a daily basis, sometimes even with different customers. Moreover, because they involve the literal sale and repurchase of securities, repos require a great deal of paperwork. Thus, the total costs of repurchase agreements are largely variable, rising steadily as a function of the length of time for which the funds are needed. In contrast, issuing CDs involves the bank with high fixed costs (including insurance premiums and nonearning reserves) but no variable costs; once the CDs are issued, no further expenses are incurred. Thus, other considerations aside, the bank should tend to finance a loan expansion of a few days' duration with repurchase agreements and a loan expansion of several weeks' duration with CDs.

It is equally important to evaluate both selling or securitizing an asset and buying a deposit or borrowing form as a source of liquidity. For example, if a bank wants to match fund (i.e., fund an asset with a source of funds of similar maturity) a six-month loan, it should evaluate the effect of selling a six-month Treasury security or buying a six-month CD. The bank should ask what effect these and other alternative liquidity sources have on income and risk.

Interest Rate Forecast

The bank's opinions on the future course of interest rates may also affect the choice among alternatives for meeting liquidity needs. Using the previous CDs versus repos example, if interest rates were expected to rise, the cost of CDs would become lower than that of repos at a shorter maturity. Because the repos would have to be rolled over at higher and higher rates, total costs would rise at an increasing rate. Under such circumstances, the bank would prefer to lock in the current low CD rate for all but its most temporary needs. That is, only if the bank needed the funds for a very short time period would it prefer to use repurchase agreements. Alternatively, if interest rates were expected to fall in the future, the total costs of bank borrowing through repurchase agreements would rise at a decreasing rate. In this case, the bank would prefer to avoid a comparatively long-term commitment at the currently high CD rate and instead would prefer to stay in repos to take advantage of the expected lower rates in the future. Thus, in periods when the bank expects interest rates to rise, the tendency is to raise funds through longer-term instruments. In periods when rates are expected to fall, the tendency is to utilize very short-term sources of funds, such as federal funds and repurchase agreements.

The shape of the yield curve (maturities versus yields for securities with similar credit risks as covered in Chapter 5) for both liquid assets and potential borrowed sources may also affect the choice among the various sources of liquidity. For example, if the yield curve for Treasury bills has a positive slope (which is the normal situation), the yield of a longer-term bill for the period held (remember that one year is the maximum maturity) is usually higher than the yield for a bill with a maturity that matches the holding period. On the funding side, longer-maturity funds usually cost more than shorter-maturity funds. However, in periods of crises, it is reassuring to management to know that the longer-maturity funds will remain with the bank. A liquidity premium may exist on both the asset and funding side.

MEETING CONTINGENCY AND FUTURE LIQUIDITY NEEDS

Meeting Contingency Liquidity Needs

Every bank should have a contingency liquidity plan that should enable the bank to meet its contingency needs (discussed earlier). As in meeting other liquidity needs, the primary sources are selling an asset or increasing a liability to provide the needed liquidity. Meeting contingency liquidity needs is particularly difficult because the size of such needs is difficult to predict and because contingency liquidity needs typically arise at the worst possible time for the bank.

A bank needs to keep two facts in mind when looking at potential asset sources to meet contingency needs. First, many bank assets can be sold when the need for funds is truly extreme. The bank's building, branch offices, subsidiaries, and some loans and mortgages are assets most banks would not ordinarily sell to meet seasonal or cyclical liquidity needs, but they may be considered in developing plans to meet contingent liquidity needs. Securitization of many standard loans is a similar possibility. The amount of loss or the potential taxation of gains on the sale or securitization of such assets must be considered. Second, the sale or securitization of such assets is often a one-time event, and it may take many years to build up new assets of the type sold. For example, a consumer credit card subsidiary can be sold once. The beneficial cash flows will no longer accrue to the selling bank, and it would probably take many years to rebuild such an asset to its original earning capacity.

These factors have encouraged many banks, particularly larger ones, to emphasize the development of liability sources to meet contingency liquidity needs. It is generally suggested that a bank should work hard in developing several potential liability sources to meet contingency liquidity needs. For example, a smaller bank might develop fed funds lines of credit with several of its upstream correspondent banks. In addition, such a bank should have pledgeable collateral at its Federal Reserve Bank, so that the commercial bank can borrow there if contingency liquidity needs arise. A larger bank, which usually has access to a much broader group of sources, should have several liability sources open for its use at all times. Correspondent bank and Federal Reserve sources should be available. Large corporate and public sector accounts should be courted—both for current business and as an emergency source of funds. Open market sources, such as commercial paper, notes, and securitized assets, should be developed as potential sources for such larger banks. In addition, Eurodollar and other foreign deposits might be courted as potential sources of liquidity. The main message is that banks of all sizes should spend considerable time and effort in developing potential liability sources to meet contingency liquidity needs.

Liquidity crisis management requires a careful, professionally prepared plan. The liquidity crisis plan has three fundamental elements. The first is a program for promoting good communications from the bank's lenders to the funding manager and from the funding manager to the bank's institutional investors and rating agencies. The second element consists of fire drill-type exercises for testing and establishing the marketability of bank assets. Of special interest to large wholesale banks is the possibility for liquidity enhancement available in an ongoing and comprehensive program of loan securitization or liquification by direct negotiation with a network of investors cultivated over time. The final element consists of steps to broaden, deepen, and stabilize markets for the bank's liabilities.

The emphasis on each of these elements is the prevention of a liquidity crisis and not damage control. Preparedness is the sole weapon available for preventing crises. In the event that a liquidity crisis does befall the bank, however, a liquidity crisis plan centered on good communications and positioning in both asset and liability markets provides the best chance for survival.

Meeting Future Liquidity Needs

It is easy to become pessimistic about the liquidity situation of banks. Aggregated figures show that liquid assets have decreased and that purchased deposits plus borrowed funds have increased markedly for commercial banks in the last couple of decades. Furthermore, the probability that liquidity problems will arise as a result of the lender's and markets' lack of confidence in a bank's ability to repay debt obligations appears to have risen in the late 1980s. At the same time, three positive aspects about bank liquidity have emerged in recent years—more realistic regulatory liquidity assessment, the disappearance of rate ceilings on funding sources, and the development of interest rate hedging instruments, which allow banks to separate liquidity risk from interest rate risk.

As recently as the early 1990s, the primary regulatory authorities tended to look at static balance sheet measures of liquidity. Typically, the amount of unpledged, short-term securities was compared with some proxy for liquidity needs, such as total deposits. If this ratio met a preestablished target, the bank was deemed to be liquid. The static and arbitrary nature of this type of liquidity measure coupled with the rapidly changing nature of banking weakened the usefulness of regulatory liquidity evaluations.

The emerging approach used by the three federal regulatory authorities seems much more reasonable. The examiner asks bank management for the bank's information on its liquidity needs and its ability to meet those needs. If the examiner believes the bank's system for assessing liquidity provides appropriate information and the bank's liquidity is adequate, the bank meets the regulatory requirements. If the bank's method for measuring liquidity is weak, the examiner compares his or her calculation of the bank's short-term liquidity needs with the bank's ability to meet such needs. Liquidity needs include estimated credit demands, probable deposit volatility, and borrowed funds that must be repaid. Sources of meeting these needs include securities maturing in less than a year, other securities with market values exceeding book value, and other assets that appear to be readily sellable with little loss. The examiner is satisfied if sources exceed needs. If needs exceed sources, the examiner will consider the bank's ability to sell securities under agreement to repurchase (repos) and the bank's ability to borrow (e.g., federal funds) before making the final regulatory liquidity decision.

The disappearance of rate ceilings on funding sources was documented in Chapter 6. Over 90 percent of bank interest-bearing funds were subject to rate ceilings in the late 1970s, but virtually none has been subject to any rate ceilings since 1986. No longer will liquidity crunches, or deposit outflows, be created when rates on open market instruments exceed Regulation Q rate limits on bank deposits. Banks with reasonable credit reputations and an ability to pay the going market rate should be able to purchase liquidity.

Finally, the new risk management tools analyzed in Chapters 13–15, including financial futures, options, caps, floors, and interest rate swaps, share the common feature of allowing for the differentiation of liquidity risk and interest rate risk. Using these tools enables banks to manipulate the effective interest rate maturity of embedded assets and liabilities without altering the balance sheet. Liquidity can be managed separately and does not need to be sacrificed for the sake of managing interest rate risk.

END OF CHAPTER PROBLEMS

7.1 A bank finds that it has been too conservative in managing its funds position during the current reserve requirement accounting period. There are five days remaining in the accounting period, and the bank has an accumulated excess reserve position of $800 million. For the remaining five days the bank expects daily credit and debit adjustments for net check clearings and other factors to be a wash, that is, neither excess nor deficit. What kind of transaction (purchase or sale) and how much should daily Federal funds transactions be until the end of the accounting period to end the period at breakeven (neither excess nor deficit accumulated funds)? Assume the same size of transaction for all five days.

7.2 During the current two-week reserves maintenance period, Left Bank has estimated its daily average required reserve balances with its Federal Reserve Bank to be $6 million. The bank's cumulative reserve deficiency going into Friday was $600,000, and its *potential* balances with the Federal Reserve on Friday night are $6.4 million. Left Bank sells $1 million in the Federal funds market on Friday afternoon. Determine the bank's cumulative reserve position (excess or deficiency) on Monday morning at the start of business. (*Hint:* Recall that balances with the Federal Reserve Bank for Friday, Saturday, and Sunday do not change.)

7.3 SensiBank began the day with accumulated excess reserves of $1.262 billion above its cumulative required reserves (i.e., an excess). During the day net check clearings amounted to a debit (−) of $824 million. Also during the day, payments totaling $212 million were received on maturing government securities in SensiBank's investments portfolio, $36 million in currency and coin was credited to the bank's account, and the bank repaid $150 million of notes it had issued last year to investors. At the end of the day, SensiBank's money desk sold $441 million in federal funds. What is the cumulative excess or deficiency position at the end of the day, accounting for all of the above adjustments?

7.4 Shawnee Bank intentionally began the last Monday of its two-week required reserves maintenance period with an accumulated reserve deficiency of $70 million. The bank's money desk manager assumed, on the basis of past check clearing activity for this period, that a $60 to $65 million reserve buildup would occur on Monday, thereby offsetting most of the deficiency with only two days left until *settlement Wednesday*. To her surprise, only $10 million of the expected reserve credits materialized on Monday. Unfortunately, she was constrained from purchasing a sufficient amount of federal funds by a bank policy that put a cap on such purchases during any 14-day maintenance period, and she had already used most of this cap. Her remaining alternatives for overcoming the accumulated deficit by Wednesday were:

a.) Borrow from the Federal Reserve Bank.

b.) Borrow with repurchase agreements using the bank's unpledged securities as collateral.

c.) Issue new CDs.

d.) Sell off short-term securities.

e.) Sell off high-coupon investment securities.

f.) Cancel outstanding call loan to security brokers.

Discuss the pros and cons, including comparative costs, of using these various sources of funds.

7.5 The balance sheets for Extol Bank and Vora Bank are shown below for the years 20X0 and 20X1 (millions of dollars). During the year 20X1, loan demand rose rapidly and drove up interest rates. Determine and describe how each bank met its loan demand. (*Hint:* Observe sources and uses of funds.) Which bank entered 20X1 with greater liquidity? Discuss how the banks' beginning balance sheet position might have affected the profitability of each bank during 20X0 and during 20X1.

	Extol Bank		Vora Bank	
	20X0	**20X1**	**20X0**	**20X1**
Cash items	8	6	6	6
Short-term securities	20	12	6	2
Long-term securities	20	20	28	22
Net loans	52	65	60	84
Total assets	100	103	100	114
Transactions deposits	25	22	20	17
Core savings and time deposits	67	68	65	62
Borrowed funds	0	4	5	24
Equity	8	9	10	11
Total liabilities and equity	100	103	100	114

7.6 In early 1982, a few perceptive money market investors (i.e., holders of federal funds debt and repurchase agreements) suspected that Continental Illinois National Bank was lending too much money to oil and gas developers without proper credit quality controls. Such investors are notoriously sensitive to any deterioration in their debtors' positions; depositors and other creditors were much less sensitive. (Eventually, in 1984, this bank was made infamous as the recipient of the largest ever government bailout of a bank.) From its balance sheets of 1981 and 1982, discuss how and whether Continental adjusted to money market pressures in 1982. (Illinois state law prevented the bank from establishing branches and therefore from competing effectively in the market for consumer deposits.) Did the perceptive money market investors appear to cause Continental to be more cautious in its funding policies? In general, did Continental modify its activities in 1982 to become more conservative?

	$ Millions	
	12/31/1981	**12/31/1982**
Cash and interest-bearing deposits	7,985	3,860
Investments portfolio	2,408	1,985
Net loans	31,517	33,744
All others	4,871	3,226
Total assets	46,781	42,815
Transaction, time, and savings deposits	5,019	4,787
Large negotiable CDs	9,607	8,632
Foreign deposits	14,316	14,862
Federal funds and repo agreements	8,804	6,763
Long-term debt	824	1,240
All other liabilities	6,516	4,832
Equity	1,695	1,699
Total liabilities and equity	46,781	42,815

7.7 Swift Community Bank forecasts that its market for loans will boom in the next five years. Simultaneously, deposit growth will fall far short of loan growth, creating a need for borrowed funds. The bank currently holds $100 million in loans, has $140 million in core deposits, and a zero net federal funds position. Assume that, over the next five years, loans will grow at a compounded annual rate of 20 percent and deposits will grow at a rate of 5 percent. Any shortfalls in funding will be made up in the federal funds market. Assume all other balance sheet items remain the same as today.

a.) What is Swift Bank's current loan-to-deposit ratio?

b.) What will be Swift Bank's net federal funds position five years from now?

c.) What will be Swift's loan-to-deposit ratio five years from now?

7.8 Chet Adkins, Secura Savings Bank's chief financial officer, conducts a detailed analysis to determine assets that are liquid versus those that are nonliquid and which liabilities are core (stable) versus those that are noncore (maturing soon and subject to nonrenewal at maturity or, in the case of deposits, subject to withdrawal) during his liquidity planning horizon.

Assets	$Millions	Classification	
Cash items	100	20%	liquid
Securities	350	70%	liquid
Net loans	500	5%	liquid
Fixed and other assets	50	0%	liquid
Total	$1,000		
Liabilities & Equity			
Transaction deposits	300	90%	core
Time and savings deposits < $100M	450	78%	core
Certificate of deposit > $100M	100	20%	core
Borrowed funds	70	0%	core
Equity	80	100%	core
Total	$1,000		

In addition, Mr. Adkins anticipates that over the liquidity horizon Secura must have cash to fund new loan demand of $90 million but will acquire cash of $15 million in the form of new core deposits. Determine Secura Savings Bank's liquidity position.

7.9 In 1996, BankAmerica Corporation reported the following cash flows:
- **a.)** additions to deposits = $7.58 billion
- **b.)** repurchases of common and preferred stock = $1.72 billion
- **c.)** investment security maturities, prepayments, and calls in excess of securities purchases = $0.61 billion
- **d.)** loan sales and securitizations and sales of OREO = $5.78 billion
- **e.)** loan originations, purchases of loans, and other assets and short-term investment = $19.62 billion
- **f.)** issuances of long-term debt and stock, net of principal repayments = $2.41 billion
- **g.)** dividends paid = $0.97 billion
- **h.)** cash inflows from income and other operating activity = $1.04 billion

Purchased funds (either additional purchases or repayment of short-term funds) were used to cover the difference between cash inflows and cash outflows. Determine BankAmerica's purchased funds transactions during 1996. (*Hint:* Sum up items that represent cash inflows and subtract those that represent cash outflows.)

7.10 Cole Community Bank serves an agricultural area and is subject to seasonal liquidity pressures. On December 31, as shown in the condensed balance sheet below, CCB's total deposits were $200 million, and its total loans were $150 million. Cash items include legal reserves and float equal to 8 percent of core deposits, plus any excess funds.

Balance Sheet: December 31

Assets		Liabs. & equity	
Cash items	$ 16,000,000	Core deposits	$200,000,000
Securities	54,000,000	Borrowed funds	0
Loans	150,000,000	Equity	20,000,000
Total	$220,000,000	Total	$220,000,000

A trend rate of growth in deposits is expected to be $2 million in each month of the coming year, and a trend rate of growth in loans is $1 million in each month. CCB uses an index based on its past experience to account for seasonal volatility components in loans and deposits. (These components are *in addition* to trend growth components.) December's loans and deposits are indexed at 100. Subsequent months' seasonal components are based on each month's index multiplied by the December balance.

	Loan Index	Core Deposit Index
January	97	102
February	102	103
March	112	98
April	120	95
May	126	92
June	116	96

Excess funds are added to cash items, and any deficiency in funds is borrowed. Securities and capital do not change. Create balance sheets for the months of January–June and determine the month of greatest liquidity need.

CHAPTER 8

Managing the
Security Portfolio

To this point, most of our discussion has dealt with products that banks originate through customer relationships. In this chapter we focus on banks' security portfolios, which consist of debt instruments that banks buy outright in financial markets instead of through customer relationships. This difference highlights fundamental distinctions about securities. First, banks can make large-scale investments in securities almost instantaneously, unlike the gradual process that it takes to accumulate an investment in customer-based products such as consumer loans or home mortgages. They can divest themselves of securities just as quickly. This rapid turnaround makes securities a powerful tool for applying a quick fix to balance sheet interest-rate sensitivity. Another critical distinction about securities is that, instead of exercising influence on the price (interest rate) they receive from customers such as borrowers, banks must accept the price the market offers on securities. Investment securities pay the bank a limited (usually fixed) return until the assets (usually a debt instrument) mature.

ASSET PRIORITY MODEL

In order to understand the role of securities in banks' balance sheets, it helps to review the banks' four traditional priorities in the use of their funds. These priorities follow a special hierarchy. First, banks must use a fraction of their deposit funds to satisfy legal reserve requirements. Second, they use funds to make adequate provisions for their liquidity needs, such as the purchase of liquid securities. (Banks sometimes provide liquidity by borrowing from money markets, but most banks, including money center and large regional banks, meet most of their liquidity needs through operating cash flows and by holding liquid assets.) The third priority is to serve the loan demands in their market areas, which may range from a small community for a local bank to the entire globe for an international bank. Typically, loans are tailored to the needs and capacities of customers and, therefore, have higher yields than securities. Lending itself is an important source for attracting deposits. Lastly, banks invest whatever funds remain, after they serve the first three priorities, in their security portfolios.

We can therefore see that it is in the nature of banking that investment securities come last. Securities constitute the residual use of funds after more fundamental needs are addressed. Inevitably, this leads to problems of timing in banks' purchase and sale of securities. In recessions and periods of slow economic growth when loan demands and interest rates tend to be at low levels, most banks accumulate large amounts of excess funds and invest them in securities. In the ensuing boom periods, when loan demands and interest rates tend to be at high levels, banks usually are short of funds and do not have excess funds to purchase securities. More likely, in periods of high loan demand, they may be forced to sell securities at a loss in order to finance loan growth. Later in the chapter, we examine strategies for mitigating the problems resulting from investing funds in securities at the ''wrong'' times.

Periods of high loan demands, inflation, and high and volatile interest rates, such as the late 1970s and early 1980s, raise a special concern about banks' security portfolio management. Under such boom circumstances, most bank managers concentrate on making loans and, secondarily, on acquiring funds to finance the loans. In such periods, the conventional approach is to use the security portfolio as a source of liquidity and, therefore, to purchase only short-term securities. As a result, many high-earnings-performance banks in the early 1980s boom period built large loan portfolios and held few long-term securities.

This was a clear indication that many banks tended to underestimate the importance of more comprehensive management of the security portfolio. As interest rates fell after 1985 into the early 1990s, banks began to take gains by selling longer-term, high-coupon securities. The profits on security sales temporarily made a bank's net income higher, but the bank had to invest the proceeds of securities sales either in same-quality securities with less future income or in higher risk loans with income that just maintained the income level of the original securities. Again, management of the security portfolio was subordinated to other pressures in the bank. In the middle to late 1990s, when loan demand grew sharply, many banks again reduced their security portfolios even though interest rates on long-term securities were relatively high.

PORTFOLIO OBJECTIVES

Such portfolio management methods are suboptimal when you take a more comprehensive view of banks' objectives in managing their security portfolios. Table 8.1 presents rankings of banks' declared portfolio objectives based on a recent survey involving 56 banks. The highest ranked objective, except for banks in the $5–$10 billion assets range, was using the security portfolio to manage interest rate risk. Securities permit banks to adjust interest-rate sensitivity very quickly because they can be bought or sold instantly and in any maturity (duration). Second in importance, according to these banks, was liquidity management. Most banks use the security portfolio as their primary source of liquidity and to reduce liquidity risk. As the table suggests, this is true even among large banks with access to many markets for purchased funds.

Third, and nearly equal in rank to liquidity, is income production for yield. The security portfolio is an important contributor to banks' earnings. In 1997, a period with

TABLE 8.1   Ranking of Security Portfolio Objectives, 56-Bank Survey[a]

Objective	All Banks[b]	Size Group Asset Size ($billions)[b]				
		<$5	$5–10	$10–25	$25–50	>50
Manage Interest Rate Risk	1.84	1.88	2.50	1.95	1.55	1.13
Liquidity Management	2.60	2.38	2.00	2.79	2.82	2.86
Income for Yield	2.65	2.63	2.75	2.78	2.36	2.71
Manage Credit Risk	4.44	4.00	3.63	4.29	5.20	5.40
Total Return	4.45	4.63	4.56	4.35	4.64	4.13
Manage Risk-Based Capital	5.50	6.38	4.75	5.39	5.60	5.50
Securities Gains	6.10	6.25	6.14	6.29	6.09	6.33

[a] *Investment Portfolio Performance: Survey Results,* BAI Foundation, Bank Administration Institute, Chicago, Illinois 1995.

[b] Average rankings based on 1 = most important; 7 = least important.

high loan demand, banks' securities portfolios nevertheless accounted for over one-fourth of the total revenue of all banks in the United States.[1] Because securities are acquired and managed far more cheaply than loans,[2] it is likely that the security portfolio's contribution to banks' net income is even greater than its contribution to total revenues. Another important objective in portfolio management is to mitigate credit risk. Securities range from risk-free to a level of modest credit risk competitive with the credit risk of good-quality bank loans. The fifth category listed is total return. This recognizes a recent, nontraditional objective to measure the effectiveness of security portfolio management in terms of both interest earnings and capital gains. The sixth objective is to use the securities portfolio to manage risk-based capital. Most securities held by banks have a zero or very low risk weight. As a consequence, banks may choose to employ excess funds in securities rather than in loans to avoid higher capital requirements (Chapter 9 explains how regulations require banks to hold more capital for higher risk assets such as loans). The final objective listed in Table 8.1, securities gains, recognizes the aggressive objective of actively trading securities with the intention of capturing short-term gains in securities' prices.

The security portfolio also provides collateral for public deposits, supports Federal Reserve discount borrowing, supplies collateral for repurchase agreements, and dresses up the balance sheet for customers and regulators. All of these objectives suggest that the subject of this chapter, managing the security portfolio, is worth careful attention.

This chapter is divided into two sections. The first section covers the types of securities banks usually purchase and methods of measuring returns and risks on such securities. The second section covers the five steps a bank's management should follow in actively managing its security portfolio.

[1] *FDIC Quarterly Banking Profile* (Washington, D.C.: FDIC, 1998).

[2] See *Functional Cost Analysis: National Average Reports,* various years. Published annually by the Federal Reserve Board of Governors.

DEBT INSTRUMENTS

Our discussion in this chapter will pertain to debt securities only because, in general, commercial banks in the United States cannot own equity securities. In this section we discuss crucial properties of the debt instruments commonly held in commercial banks. These include maturity or duration, taxability, and interest rate risk.

Banks acquire security portfolios that contain securities with a wide range of durations. Those with the shortest durations are the numerous types of money market instruments banks buy. These are frequently in the form of pure discount securities and have maturities (durations) ranging from one day to one year. In addition, short-term securities include securities that may have had long-term original maturities but are now within one year of their maturity. Banks also choose from among numerous intermediate and long-term securities. Chapter 4 explained that the risk of interest rate movements to such securities' market values increases with their duration. Short-term securities bear little of this kind of risk.

Securities differ in the taxability of their income and security gains and losses. In general, security gains increase taxable ordinary income, and losses decrease taxable ordinary income. Most interest income is taxed. However, income on Treasury and many U.S. agency issues and on in-state state and local issues is not subject to state and local income taxes. Also, interest income on all state and local bond issues prior to August 1986 is exempt from federal income tax as is income on smaller, post–1986 general obligations after deducting 20 percent of the average cost to finance them.

Debt instruments bear *four types of risk.* The first is that the bank may be forced to sell a security that does not have broad marketability. Price concessions are often made in order to sell the security and may significantly decrease the security's return. This is *marketability risk. Interest rate risk* derives from changes in the general level of interest rates. Changes in the market value of outstanding securities are inversely related to changes in interest rates and to the instruments' duration. Also, as we observed in Chapter 4, the magnitude of changes in market value for a given change in rate depends on the size of securities' coupons. Price volatility is greatest for pure discount (zero-coupon) bonds. Interest rate risk also includes reinvestment risk, the risk to earnings because changes in interest rates alter the market rate at which securities' cash inflows can be reinvested. Short-term investments are particularly vulnerable to reinvestment risk. In addition, the payment patterns of securities are subject to change when interest rates change. For example, falling interest rates may cause debtors to prepay their obligations unexpectedly before the obligations mature. Appendix 5B examined the interest premium investors should earn on instruments that have the potential to prepay, such as callable securities. A third risk is *credit risk* (or default risk). It is important for banks to examine the possibility of nonpayment of interest or principal on most debt securities except those that are obligations of the federal government. Federal government securities are designated risk free.

Finally, all debt securities bear *purchasing power risk.* If interest or principal payments received in the future are not able to purchase as much as current dollars used to purchase debt instruments, the investor suffers a loss of purchasing power. The investor must attempt to overcome this loss by requiring a higher interest return or by having dollar liabilities that are paid in lower-purchasing-power dollars, or both. It is difficult to separate interest rate and purchasing power risk because they are positively correlated. That is, nominal (market) interest rates contain a premium for anticipated inflation, and they adjust with changes in inflationary expectations. We can convert nominal rates of return (r_n) to real rates (r_r) according to the following:

$$r_r = \frac{1 + r_n}{1 + p^*} - 1 \tag{8.1}$$

where p^* is the actual rate of change in the general price level over the holding period. We can simplify this to

$$r_r = r_n - p^* \tag{8.2}$$

Securities may have many other characteristics that differentiate them. For example, some are callable and others may have specific or implicit buyback options (*put options*). Increasingly, new types of debt instruments are being created with specific terms that distinguish them from generic securities.

Short-Term Instruments

Following are descriptions of instruments most commonly held by banks. These are summarized in Table 8.2.

TABLE 8.2 Short-Term Instruments Purchased by Commercial Banks

Security	Issuer	Brief Description
Federal funds sold	Other commercial banks	Excess reserves of a bank usually sold to another bank to provide earning assets to selling bank; most mature daily but can be easily renewed; "term funds" are also short-maturity funds with a good market; unsecured
Treasury bills	Federal government	Highly marketable debt with no credit risk; sold on discount basis
Agency notes	Government agencies	Obligations of federal agencies; very high quality and nearly as marketable as federal debt
State and local notes	State and local governments	Short-term tax or bond anticipation obligations of state and local governments; interest is generally tax exempt for banks but not for most other investors
Commercial paper	Business or finance companies	High-quality business promissory notes; sold on discount basis
Negotiable CDs	Commercial banks and other financial institutions	Large interest-bearing deposits that can be traded before maturity
Bankers' acceptances	Businesses backed by commercial bank	Paper used to finance international trade, backed by commercial bank to improve credit quality
Securities purchased under agreement to resell (repos)	Commercial banks or businesses	Temporary purchase of government or other securities in which seller has agreed to repurchase securities at fixed price and set time in the future; difference between sale and purchase prices is return received by holder
Broker call loans	Securities brokers	Loans created when securities dealers borrow from bank to finance securities position of their clients

Federal funds sold are short-term sales of funds to other banks through the Federal Reserve System. Acquiring banks use them to meet their reserve requirements at the Federal Reserve. Federal funds sold represent the excess reserves that are offered in the market at competitively determined interest rates to banks needing funds to meet reserve requirements. The market for federal funds is predominantly short term, for over 80 percent of total federal fund transactions are made with overnight maturity. Typically, banks lend federal funds on an unsecured basis, although they may require collateral to secure the sale. The credit risk of an unsecured bank depends on the financial condition of the borrowing bank. The federal funds market is important because it is the core of the overnight credit market in the United States, and many other money market rates are tied to the current and expected federal funds rates.

Treasury bills are short-term obligations of the U.S. government. The U.S. Treasury auctions three- and six-month discount bills every week, and it auctions one-year discount bills monthly. The discount prices of Treasury bills are determined by sealed auction bids and are sold in minimum amounts of $10,000 and in additional $5,000 increments. These securities are free from default risk, since they are the direct obligation of the U.S. government. There is a very active market for Treasury bills and, therefore, no marketability risk of ownership. Interest income is subject to federal income tax but is exempt from state and local taxes.

Federal agency notes are the credit obligations of federally sponsored agencies that obtain their funding requirements by selling either debt or pass-through securities in the money and capital markets. A few agencies, for example, the Government National Mortgage Association, are owned by the government and have no credit risk. Other agencies, however, are wholly owned by the private sector and hence do not have the credit guarantee of the federal government. Federally sponsored credit agencies finance their loan programs and secondary market purchases by issuing notes and pass-through securities. Interest on these securities is usually exempt from state and local taxes. Discount notes are also a popular form of issuance. The maturities of discount notes range from overnight to 360 days, but the maturity of a particular note depends on which agency has issued the debt. The sponsored agencies typically pay lower returns than other private borrowers as a result of the unique features of the agencies and their generally low level of credit risk. There is an active secondary market for most agency notes, similar to that for Treasury securities, so that the marketability risk of these securities is minimal.

State and local notes are short-term municipal securities and are obligations of state and local governments, and of the districts and authorities they create, to be repaid by the issuer's ability to tax or borrow or by the cash flow generated from a specific project. State and local notes with original maturities of less than one year are classified as short-term obligations. The interest on these obligations is exempt from federal tax and can be exempted from state and local taxes in the state of issue for individuals and most other potential purchasers except those using borrowed money to purchase the obligations. The actual yield to an investor will depend on the investor's marginal tax rate. However, banks, nearly all of which pay tax-deductible interest on money borrowed to acquire the notes, cannot exempt an amount equal to the average cost of the funds they raise to finance these notes. Because the note interest is tax-exempt to other investors, their initial coupon rate and market yields are below those of taxable obligations. This low interest rate tends to make these notes less appealing to banks than to investors that can utilize the full tax exemption. The credit risk of these securities is determined by the financial condition of the issuer and is borne by the investor. The secondary market is often thin and is made by dealers who underwrote the original issue. Thus, marketability risk is a concern, since the secondary market for municipal obligations is not as liquid as that for other investment alternatives.

Commercial paper is the short-term, unsecured borrowing of both financial and nonfinancial corporations used to meet short-term working capital needs. Commercial paper is issued in bearer form and is issued in maturities tailored to meet the needs of the issuing corporation. Maturities typically range from 1 to 270 days. Commercial paper is generally issued on a discount basis, with interest fully taxable. The yield on commercial paper is typically close to that of large negotiable CDs and bankers' acceptances. Since these obligations are generally short term, and most paper is issued with 5- to 45-day maturities, interest rate risk is not pervasive. However, there is not an active secondary market, and liquidity risk can be a problem. Commercial paper also has the credit risk of the underlying issuer of the obligation. Rating agencies such as Standard and Poor's or Moody's provide credit ratings that correlate well with the premium investors require for bearing the credit risk.

Negotiable CDs are CDs issued by banks that have a defined face amount, interest rate, and maturity but have features that allow them to be traded in a secondary market. Banks issue most large CDs in negotiable form to provide easy marketability. Their maturities range from a minimum of seven days to 12 months. The most popular maturities are one, two, three, and six months. Rates on negotiable CDs are quoted on an interest-bearing basis, and interest is subject to full taxation. Yields are typically found to be at a premium to Treasury bills of similar maturities. This is due to the underlying credit risk for exceeding the $100,000 FDIC insurance limit and the fact that, unlike Treasury bills, they are not exempt from state and local taxes. Although there is an active secondary market for negotiable CDs, it does not have the depth or breadth of the Treasury market.

Bankers' acceptances (BAs) are highly marketable short-term money market instruments that are used primarily to finance international trade. The BA represents a commercial bank's unconditional guarantee to pay a specified amount at a specified time. BAs are issued in maturities that range from 30 to 270 days and generally are structured to match the flow of goods and services that are being financed by the underlying transaction. These securities are issued at a discount, and the interest earned is subject to full taxation. Yields on BAs are generally similar to those on large negotiable CDs. The credit risk of a BA is minimized, since it has the unconditional guarantee of the accepting bank and is the secondary liability of the drawer or initiator of the transaction for the full face amount. BAs are traded in a highly active secondary market; thus, the marketability risk and interest rate risk of this type of security are minimized.

Repurchase agreements ("repos") involve borrowing funds by selling securities temporarily and with the agreement to repurchase them at a given time, within one year, at a specified price. As investors in this market, banks conduct *reverse repos* and temporarily *buy* borrowers' securities. The securities underlying this transaction are typically Treasury and agency obligations. Transactions often are overnight but may be for as long six months. Interest paid on repos is fully taxable, and the rate paid is determined by the initial selling price and by negotiation. As an investment, repos are close substitutes for federal funds but pay a somewhat lower rate because they are collateralized. There is virtually no credit risk in this transaction. Also, interest rate risk is avoided by requiring additional collateral when interest rate movements cause the value of the original collateral to decline.

Broker call loans, though technically loans, are true money market securities. They are created when securities brokers borrow from banks to finance the securities positions of their clients for short intervals, collateralizing the loans with securities salable on stock exchanges. They provide attractive yields, often in excess of one percentage point over interest rates on commercial paper or BAs. Call loans are so-called because investors may call them with only 24-hours' notice.

Long-Term Debt Securities

Banks invest in long-term debt securities primarily to obtain higher interest income. Currently (1998), they carry (on their books) the value of the securities they own in one of three ways: (1) "trading account" securities, which are periodically marked to market values with gains or losses in value counted as part of income as well as credited to and debited from capital; (2) "available for sale" securities, which are periodically marked to market value with gains or losses attributed to an equity reserve account but not included as part of income; and (3) held-to-maturity securities, which are valued at cost (plus or minus any question of discount or amortization of premium) with gains or losses not recognized. A description of the primary characteristics of long-term securities follows, and Table 8.3 gives a summary.

TABLE 8.3   Long-Term Securities Purchased by Banks

Security	Issuer	Brief Description
Treasury notes and bonds	Federal government	Longer-term interest-bearing notes and bonds that are obligations of the federal government
Agency bonds	Government agencies	Longer-term interest-bearing bonds of federal agencies
General obligations	State and local governments	Bonds backed by full faith, credit, and taxing power of issuing unit; interest may be partially tax exempt (subject to TEFRA and tax reform limits)
Revenue	State and local governments	Bonds backed by revenues from specific projects or tax source; interest on new issues is subject to 100 percent TEFRA
Corporate bonds	Businesses	Interest-bearing long-term business debt with varying degrees of quality and marketability
Mortgage-backed bonds	Consumers (packaged)	Interest-bearing long-term debt backed by grouping of mortgages and guarantee of government agency
Other asset-backed bonds	Consumers and businesses (packaged)	Interest-bearing long-term debt backed by the cash flows from a group of loans (e.g., installment loans, credit card loans), usually credit enhanced
Floating rate notes	Government agencies and businesses	Notes (generally intermediate maturities) that pay a floating rate of interest (based on some rate index) during some or all of their life
Preferred stock	Businesses	Stocks of businesses that have claim on income and assets above common stock (but below debt). Available in fixed or floating rate. Only 30 percent of dividend is taxable.
Derivatives	Varied	Securities that are a part of an issued security (e.g., principal only) or whose value is derived in some way from another security (e.g., options)

Treasury Notes and Bonds   The lack of credit risk on U.S. Treasury securities and the highly efficient market for such securities explain the importance of Treasury securities to the commercial banking system. Income from all Treasury securities is subject to federal income taxes but is exempt from state and local income taxes. Marketable Treasury securities may be used as security for deposits of public monies and for loans from Federal Reserve Banks.

The three basic types of marketable Treasury securities are bills, notes, and bonds. The characteristics of Treasury bills were discussed in the section on short-term securities. The primary difference between notes and bonds is their maturity. Treasury notes are issued with a maturity of not less than 1 year and not more than 10 years. These notes are available in minimum denominations of $10,000 in either registered or bearer form. Interest is paid on the registered bearer notes semiannually when the appropriate coupon is surrendered. Treasury bonds mature more than 10 years after the date of issuance. Bonds are available in either registered or bearer form and pay interest semiannually. Treasury bonds cover a wide range of maturities; maturity selections by buyers are based on portfolio requirements and on the willingness to assume interest rate risk. Nearly all Treasury issues are noncallable.

Agency Obligations   The amount of outstanding securities that is not a direct obligation of the Treasury but that, in one way or another, involves federal sponsorship or guarantee has increased rapidly in recent years. Yields on securities of federal agencies are generally somewhat higher than yields on Treasury securities of similar maturity. Although most agency securities are not the direct obligations of the federal government, they are regarded in the investment community as being of a credit quality nearly equal to that of Treasury securities. It is generally felt that the U.S. government would not allow a default on any of these bonds. Agency issues are, therefore, treated as noncredit risk assets and usually may be carried separately from risk assets in a bank's statement of condition. Although all agency securities are subject to federal income taxes, most of them are exempt from state and local income taxes. In addition, agency securities may be used as collateral to secure the fiduciary, trust, and public funds of the U.S. government and of many state and local governments. Some agency issues have slight marketability risk. The interest rate risk on agency securities is similar to that on Treasury securities; and some agency securities are callable.

State and Local Government Bonds   The increasing demand of state and local governments for funds has resulted in a rapidly growing market for state and local securities. The interest payments on this type of indebtedness used to be exempt from federal income taxes and are usually still exempt from income taxes imposed within the state of issue. Commercial banks used to be the dominant purchaser of state and local bonds; however, reduced taxable earnings primarily from increased loan losses at some banks, other methods of reducing taxes, and reduction of tax exemption on state and local securities to banks have caused banks' dominance to decline.[3]

[3] Commercial bank holdings of state and local securities fell from about 50 percent of all state and local securities outstanding in the early 1970s to about 1 percent at the end of 1997. The drop in banks' share of state and local securities—particularly among larger banks—reflects expansion into leasing, lending subject to foreign tax credits, and other activities that reduce the availability of taxable income that could be sheltered by state and local securities. Loan losses by some banks in 1982–1987 also made tax-exempt income less desirable. Passage of TEFRA and tax reform legislation in 1986 has kept banks from gaining exemption to federal income taxes on larger state and local issues purchased after August 1986.

Intermediate and longer-term state and local bonds can be divided into three broad categories. Bonds in the first category, *housing authority bonds,* are issued by local housing agencies to build and administer low-rent housing projects. Although the bonds are issued under the auspices of local housing agencies, the Housing Act of 1949 provided that the full faith and credit of the United States is pledged to the payment of all amounts agreed to be paid by the local agencies.

A bond is considered a *general obligation* if all the property in a community can be assessed and taxed at a level that will produce the revenues necessary to pay the debt. The primary tangible tax base is real estate on which the taxing authorities possess a lien equivalent to a first mortgage. Sales taxes, income taxes, and governmental subsidies are also important state or local revenue sources. The pledge of full faith and credit by a state or local unit usually includes a promise to levy taxes at whatever level debt service payments require.

Revenue bonds, the third type of bonds, are payable solely from the earnings of a designated public project or undertaking. This type of bond includes all obligations not payable from or guaranteed by the general taxing power of the state or local government. The revenue supporting these bonds may come from (1) specifically dedicated taxes, such as those on cigarettes, gasoline, and beer; (2) tolls for roads, bridges, airports, or marine port facilities; (3) revenues from publicly owned utilities; (4) rent payments on buildings or office space; or other specific sources. Some banks have become heavy purchasers of industrial revenue bonds or pollution-control bonds, which are secured by revenues promised to the issuing unit by large corporations. Banks have also purchased recently popular issues, such as single-family mortgage revenue bonds and revenue bonds issued by non-profit organizations—primarily hospitals.

The housing authority bonds, which are guaranteed by the federal government, are virtually free of credit risk. The credit risks inherent in other types of state and local debt are related to the governmental unit's ability and willingness either to pay its obligations or to revise its capitalization. With general obligation bonds, the ability to pay is contingent mainly on the economic background of a community, the diversity of industry, the stability of employment, and so on. The ability to pay revenue bonds can generally be ascertained by comparing operating income with debt service requirements. This ability to pay could be changed by recapitalization, the issuance of additional debt with a credit position, and a claim on taxing power or earnings equal to or superior to those of the existing bonds. Issues of revenue bonds usually specify the extent to which additional debt may be undertaken. There is usually no such protection for general obligation bonds.

Marketability risk varies widely among state and local issues and may be quite high for smaller issues. Interest rate risk is primarily a function of maturity, as is true of Treasury and agency securities. Two other characteristics of state and local debt are especially pertinent for commercial banks. First, nearly all general obligations have serial maturities. A bank could, therefore, buy one issue with maturities in several years. Second, the 1982 Tax Equity and Fiscal Responsibility Act (TEFRA) allowed deductions for only 85 percent of the interest cost on funds used to buy state and local securities. The Deficit Reduction Act of 1984 further reduced that share to 80 percent. The Tax Reform Act of 1986 prohibited banks from deducting interest costs or carrying larger issues of state and local securities purchased after August 1986. The bonds of issuers of general-purpose obligations totaling less than $10 million annually are still subject to the 80 percent TEFRA. These types of issues are called bank-qualified bonds and tend to have lower yields because of this classification.

Corporate Bonds   A corporate bond is an obligation (usually long term) of a private corporation. Although a governmental body may generally be assumed to have a continuing existence, a private corporation is subject to the vicissitudes of a market economy. The credit risk assumed by purchasers of corporate bonds is, therefore, a serious consideration; the failure of the enterprise may result in permanent and total loss. Marketability risk and interest rate risk are similar to those of state and local issues. Most corporate bonds are callable.

Banks have not purchased corporate bonds much in the past because there have been only brief interludes in recent history when the tax-equivalent yield on state and local bonds did not exceed the yields on corporate bonds of equal quality. The market for corporate bonds was composed primarily of institutions subject to minimal or no federal income taxation. In the 1980s, however, there were enough banks with no taxable income so that the banking industry had become a factor in the corporate bond market. The worry in the 1990s has been that banks may purchase junk bonds (below investment grade) or bonds subject to event risk, such as leveraged buyouts. Bank regulators have developed rules to eliminate or severely limit such security holdings.

Other Bank Portfolio Instruments

The late 1980s and 1990s have seen less traditional bank portfolio instruments replace most state and local securities as the commercial banks' primary new investment purchases. Tremendous growth has taken place in commercial bank holdings of mortgage-backed securities and, to a lesser extent, other asset-backed securities. In addition to lowered or no tax exemption for state and local securities, a combination of attractive yield spreads, low credit risk, fairly stable prepayment rates, and favorable risk-based capital requirements have made mortgage-backed securities the most popular new portfolio instrument for many commercial banks. At the end of 1997, commercial banks held slightly over $400 billion of mortgage-backed securities, or nearly 20 percent of that market. Banks must realize that these and other new instruments have complicated risks that should be carefully analyzed. Mortgage-backed securities and some of the other new bank portfolio instruments are described in the following paragraphs.

Two mortgage-backed instruments made their initial appearance in the late 1970s: Government National Mortgage Association (GNMA) fully modified *mortgage-backed pass-through securities* and the Federal Home Loan Mortgage Corporation (FHLMC) *mortgage participation certificates*. The cash flow to pay debt service on both securities comes from the selected groups of mortgages backing the security. The GNMA pass-throughs represent a share in a pool of Federal Housing Administration (FHA) or Veterans Administration (VA) mortgages. GNMA guarantees the timely payment of principal and interest on these securities, and this guarantee is backed by the full faith and credit of the U.S. government. The participation certificates represent undivided interests in specified residential conventional mortgages underwritten and owned or partly owned by the FHLMC. These securities are not guaranteed by the U.S. government, but the FHLMC itself does guarantee debt service payments. Early prepayment by mortgagers has typically caused the average maturity of these instruments to be less than the 12-year basis used for determining initial yield quotations.

In addition to the government-sponsored agencies, private institutions have issued mortgage pass-through certificates. These are participants in a pool of trusteed mortgages that may be either conventional, FHA, or VA; they are not guaranteed by the issuing institution. Banks also may buy securities backed by the cash flows from credit cards or installment loans. Typically, mortgages and other asset-backed securities are issued through major underwriters for public distribution, and many have active secondary markets.

Another potential security is the *mortgage guaranteed or insured by the federal government.* FHA-issued and VA-guaranteed mortgages may be purchased by commercial banks from several federal agencies, as well as from other banks or nonbank financial intermediaries. The government-sponsored Federal National Mortgage Association and GNMA have contributed to the development of a national secondary mortgage market, purchasing and making purchase commitments where and when investment funds are in short supply and selling when and where investment funds are available. Even with the efforts of these agencies, however, the liquidity of guaranteed or insured mortgages may be limited in periods of restrictive monetary conditions.

There are several *derivative securities* from mortgage-backed and other securities. The derivative securities redistribute the cash flows from the backing securities into different tranches. One form, called *collateralized mortgage obligations* (CMOs), consists of maturity tranches in which investors can buy the short-, intermediate-, or longer-term cash flows from the backing security. Short average-life CMO tranches have been particularly popular for banks, for they seem to provide a better match against the short maturity of interest-bearing liabilities. Among these, sequential pay and planned amortization classes (PACs) were perceived as the closest alternative to the commercial banks' traditional holdings in Treasury and agency notes. Another form (called STRIPS, for Separate Trading of Registered Interest and Principal Securities) divides the cash flows into income stream (called IOs) and principal stream tranches (called POs). The structure and pricing of mortgage-backed derivative securities is explained in the appendix to this chapter.

Floating-rate notes are also a relatively new security. Although variable-rate securities have been around for nearly a decade, the exchangeable variable-rate note made its debut in 1984. The interest rate on such notes typically floats (is reset each quarter) for five years and then becomes fixed for five years. The governmental or corporate borrower can exchange the variable-rate notes for those with a fixed rate of interest based on Treasury rates.

Preferred stocks and adjustable-rate preferred stocks are a relatively new vehicle that has proved to be a good investment for some banks. Traditional preferred stock has a fixed dividend rate, while adjustable-rate preferred stock is usually repriced annually at a preselected basis point spread below one or several predetermined interest rate indexes. Some stocks are repriced every seven weeks through a dutch auction mechanism in which the highest bidder (lowest dividend) gets the stock. The major appeal of these and similar preferred stocks is that 70 percent of the dividend is exempt from corporate income taxes. A simplified example of an adjustable-rate preferred stock with a yield 100 basis points below the intermediate-term Treasury yield illustrates this appeal. If the Treasury yield is 9 percent, the preferred yield is 8 percent, and the bank has a 34 percent marginal income rate tax, the after tax yield of the Treasury is $9 \times (1 - 0.34)$, or 5.94 percent, and that of the preferred is $8 - (8 \times 0.3 \times 0.34)$, or 7.18 percent. Banks that are prohibited from holding preferred stocks invest in these and other preferred stocks through their holding companies.

In addition, numerous combinations and permutations of the preceding instruments have become available for banks and others to buy in the early 1990s. For example, banks can buy *zero-coupon* state and local bonds or corporate bonds, which do not pay coupon interest but have predetermined appreciation to maturity. There is no reinvestment risk on these bonds, so the yield is certain if the bond is held to maturity. State and local bonds and corporate *bonds with put options,* which let the bank sell them back to the government or company for the full face value after a set period of time (usually two to five years), appeared in the early 1980s.

Off-balance sheet financial instruments—financial futures, options, and interest rate swaps—are discussed in Chapters 13, 14, and 15.

MANAGING THE SECURITY PORTFOLIO

Management of the security portfolio differs among commercial banks because of differences in size, location, condition, loan demand, and managerial capabilities. There are, however, basic steps to sound and flexible bank security portfolio management. The process starts with establishing general criteria and objectives. Next, broad predictions are made about the economy and interest rates. Then, the bank inventories its security portfolio needs. Next, management decides on basic policies and strategies for managing the security portfolio and finally, delegates portfolio authority while still maintaining control.

1. Establish General Criteria and Objectives

Policies for managing the security or investment portfolio actually are often a subpart of the bank's asset and liability management (ALM) policy. The Federal Financial Institutions Examination Council provides guidance in its description of portfolio policy:[4]

A written description of authorized securities investment, trading (covered in a separate policy) and held for sale activities including goals and objectives the institution expects to achieve through such activities. Written description of the way management intends to achieve policy goals and objectives addressing management's plans for each type of securities that will be used. . . . It should be consistent with . . . overall business plans. . . . It should take into account factors such as asset and liability position, asset concentrations, interest rate risk, market volatility, management capability and desired rate of return.

Written policies provide continuity of approach over time, as well as concrete bases for appraising investment portfolio performance. It cannot be emphasized enough that portfolio policies become clear only when the people concerned in their formulation and execution have agreed on their exact wording. All policies, of course, should be reviewed periodically to consider changing circumstances.

The first section of the written portfolio policy should be a clear statement of the objectives of the security portfolio. (See the discussion of portfolio objectives earlier in this chapter.) Institutions should state portfolio objectives carefully to provide continuing and mutual understanding of these objectives. Objectives should be challenging but achievable, understandable, and measurable.

---

[4] This statement was promulgated on February 10, 1992.

2. Coordinate Investment Decisions with Expected External Environment

It is difficult to forecast key elements of the external environment, such as growth of the economy, interest rates, inflation, and unemployment. Nevertheless, forecasting general trends in key economic indicators is an important step in managing the security portfolio. In nearly every security decision—for example, the decision of whether to buy long-term or short-term bonds—there is an implicit forecast of the external environment. Security management decisions should be consistent with an explicit forecast; security decisions that contain an implicit forecast may or may not be consistent with what the security portfolio manager believes will happen. Decisions should be made with adequate safeguards to protect the bank in the case of incorrect predictions.

3. Inventory the Security Needs of the Institution

After the bank establishes broad objectives and forecasts the external environment, it must formulate specific portfolio policies suited to the characteristics and conditions of its bank. Management should investigate several areas to take an appropriate inventory of the security management of the bank.

Determining Need to Control Interest Rate Sensitivity   The bank must evaluate the interest sensitivity of its assets and liabilities gathered in its market. Often, it is partly captured by the interest rate sensitivity of the loans it makes and the funds it attracts in servicing its market. Accurate interest sensitivity measurement, including gap techniques, duration analysis, and market value modeling (we discussed these measures in Chapters 4 and 5), is an integral part of deciding what contribution the security portfolio can make in achieving the bank's desired total interest rate exposure. Off-balance sheet forms such as financial futures, options, or interest rate swaps may also be used to help achieve the desired overall position (we discuss futures, options, and swaps in Chapters 13, 14, and 15, respectively).

Coordinating Investment and Liquidity Planning   One of the first concerns in inventorying portfolio needs is to decide how the bank's investment strategy should be coordinated with its liquidity position. We discussed measuring liquidity needs in Chapter 7.

Evaluating Pledging Requirements   Banks must determine their pledging requirements against their public deposits. The types of securities acceptable for pledging vary greatly with the type of public deposits. For example, Treasury securities are the only collateral acceptable for securing some public deposits. Other public deposits can be secured by Treasury securities, agency securities, or state and local securities of the same state or municipality depositing the funds.

Assessing the Risk Position   Banks must determine their needs for securities transactions to manage interest rate risk. Banks should actively exploit the greater discretion they have in selecting securities than they have in, say, acquiring loans. Suppose a bank's assets are dominated by long-term loans such as home mortgages and, further, that these assets are financed with unstable short-term funds. To overcome the interest rate gap created by this borrow short–lend long position, the bank might choose to emphasize short-term security investment in order to match the rate sensitivity of short-term funds. Alternatively, a bank with a large portfolio in floating-rate business loans and a large position in noninterest sensitive core deposits might invest discretionary funds in long-term securities in order to match the long-term nature of its deposits. In addition, securities can be used to diversify risk solely on the asset side of the balance sheet. For example, if a bank aggressively has filled loan demands in a robust loan market, it should probably limit risk in the investment portfolio.

A second consideration is to set portfolio policy according to the bank's capital. If capital is more than enough to support the bank's existing assets, the bank should consider additional leveraging by increasing the size of the portfolio. If management believes that the cost of raising new capital exceeds the benefits from a higher-risk portfolio, the bank should take little risk in its investment portfolio. If management believes that the after tax benefits from a higher-risk portfolio exceed the cost of raising new capital, it should consider raising additional capital.

Finally, banks' expertise in investments dictates portfolio strategy. Those that do not have the necessary expertise may seek the advice of large correspondent banks or consultants. Nevertheless, it is advisable for an inexpert bank to limit the securities risks it takes. At minimum, it should compare the costs of hiring the necessary expertise with the additional after tax returns it might generate. The bank will be better off providing the necessary expertise if the incremental returns exceed the additional costs.

Determining the Tax Position   The bank should estimate its net taxable income and calculate the amount of additional tax-exempt income it could profitably use. Tax-exempt income should not exceed current operating earnings. Even if a bank had a portfolio large enough to provide all the tax-exempt income it could use, it should not eliminate all taxable income. There should be enough taxable income to provide for maximum legal tax-free transfers to the reserve for loan losses and to absorb actual losses. In addition, the bank should consider the losses it wishes to take in bond switching and swapping operations. (We discuss these operations later in this chapter.)

The tax considerations for small banks with incomes of less than $100,000 will usually be different from those affecting large banks because of the disparity in their effective tax rates. Factors other than taxes often determine the investment policies of small banks. For large banks, tax considerations may weigh heavily in determining portfolio policy. Larger banks can use many legal means to reduce or avoid taxes, such as leasing, lending subject to foreign tax credits, timing of loan or security losses, and accelerated depreciation. Large banks should compare such alternatives with shielding income using tax-exempt securities. Tax legislation passed in 1986 limits securities with tax-exempt income to smaller municipal issues (general-purpose obligations with issues limited to $10 million a year) and to municipal issues acquired before August 1986. The alternative minimum income tax further mitigates the usefulness of tax-exempt income. Management's objective is still to reduce taxes to the extent permitted under existing law without compromising the bank's obligation to make sound loans in its marketplace and to support risk assets with adequate capital funds.

Estimating the Need for Diversification   The bank should determine the industrial and geographical distributions of its loans and its state and local securities acquired for collateral or community relations. It should limit new investment to areas in which it is already concentrated. The bank must weigh advantages gained by diversification against its lack of knowledge of new issues it has not held previously.

4. Formulate Policies and Strategies for Managing the Security Portfolio

Policies and strategies must be consistent with the bank's written portfolio objectives, its economic forecast, and its inventory of needs. They must allow adequate flexibility for management discretion as conditions change. We discuss specific policies and strategies and examine how to integrate security portfolio management with total asset and liability management.

Size of the Security Portfolio   The bank should determine the size of its portfolio based on (1) the amount of available funds after liquidity requirements, including meeting the loan demands of it market, (2) pledging requirements, and (3) the profitability of securities compared with competing forms of employing bank funds such as loans. Some institutions designate part of the portfolio as *core.* After providing for liquidity needs, the bank identifies some or all of the remaining portfolio as a core that management will not use to meet liquidity needs. This is essentially the *hold-to-maturity* designation in accounting for securities.[5] The bank can be more aggressive with regard to type of security, maturity, and other strategies, knowing it is not counting on selling the portfolio at an inopportune time.

Investment Media and Quality Levels   With flexible portfolio policies and strategies pertaining to security media and quality, the bank can select securities for the portfolio that matches its portfolio *needs.* The first portfolio need affecting investment media is the level and acceptable form of the bank's pledging requirements. The bank must have an adequate amount of acceptable securities—Treasury, U.S. agency, or state and local securities—to meet the requirements for public deposits in its political jurisdiction. When more than one type of security can be used to meet the pledging requirements, the choice will depend on the bank's risk and tax positions. In practically all banks, policymakers should insist that the pledged securities be those eligible securities that the bank is least likely to want to sell. Substitution for pledged securities, though possible, may be a costly and time-consuming process.

The bank's risk position has strong impact on the policies affecting the investment media and quality level of the bank. Banks that take large lending risks in relation to their capital position or banks that lack managerial expertise should limit their purchases to Treasury securities, agency obligations, AAA- or AA-rated state and local securities or AAA- or AA-rated corporate bonds, and federally insured or guaranteed mortgages. Such a policy, along with appropriate maturity policies, restricts investment portfolio risk and can be implemented with limited managerial expertise and effort. Many small banks should adopt this policy because their small senior management core is unlikely to have the requisite expertise.

On the other hand, banks that have the necessary managerial talent and time and are in a position to take additional risks in their investment portfolio should be less restrictive in their quality limits. Such banks should be able to purchase lower-quality bonds, which usually have higher yields. Before prudent policy allows the purchase of state and local securities or corporate bonds rated below AA, the board of directors and senior

---

[5] The next section reviews recent changes in security accounting requirements and their influence on portfolio management.

management should make sure that talent and time are available for the required credit analysis by the bank staff.

Banks should examine their tax positions to determine if they should hold tax-exempt state and local securities acquired before the August 1986 tax reform. If the yields on tax-exempt state and local obligations are 10 to 20 percent below the yields on other obligations of comparable quality, bank policy can emphasize holding state and local obligations, providing the bank's marginal income is taxed at the 34 percent or higher rate. Some smaller state and local issues are still exempt from income taxes but have limited marketability. If income is taxed at marginal rates below 20 percent, policy should emphasize switching to taxable securities, including taxable municipals.

Finally, if gains from diversification outweigh the unfamiliarity of securities that are new to the bank, investment policy should indicate acceptable industries or geographic areas.

Maturity Policies and Strategies   Maturities may present two types of policy problems: the establishment of a maximum maturity limit, if considered sound policy, and the scheduling of maturities within the portfolio. The latter is closely related to the bank's appraisal of the economic climate. Arranging and rearranging portfolio maturities also forces the portfolio manager to make decisions regarding taking profits and losses, with their own special tax considerations. These aspects of the maturity problem are all interrelated but can perhaps be understood more readily if they are examined separately.

There are two risk-related reasons that some banks limit the maximum acceptable maturities in their portfolio. First, the quality of state or local securities and corporate bonds may vary over time. A bank that lacks sufficient managerial expertise or time to evaluate the probability of deterioration in the quality of some securities in its portfolio can reduce its exposure to this risk by setting some fairly short-term limits on the maturities of such securities. The second reason pertains to interest rate movements. If interest rates rise, the prices of long-term bonds deteriorate much more than the prices of short-term bonds. Instead of being able to purchase bonds at higher yields or meet expanding loan demands at profitable rates, the holders of long-term bonds are stuck with securities with large, unrealized capital losses.

Commercial bank experience with longer-term bonds generally was unfavorable in the 1970s and early 1980s because of the upward trend in interest rates. Prices of previously purchased bonds deteriorated, and higher yields than those on held securities seemed to be continually available. The reverse was true from mid-1982 through 1992, when interest rates generally trended down and prices of longer-term bonds rose substantially. Interest rates rose (and bond prices fell) moderately during most of the mid-1990s. Still, if a bank is purchasing longer-term securities with the expectation of holding them to maturity, one could readily counsel, ''Never buy a yield that you are not willing to live with.'' In light of the uncertainties of a rapidly changing world, such advice might well limit portfolio commitments to no longer than three years. Even that is a long time to look ahead.

On the other hand, one should not lose sight of the full sweep of history and the long periods in the past during which the secular trend of interest rates was down. Should policymakers be convinced that this particular phase of history was in the process of repeating itself, there would be ample justification for extending maturities beyond 10 or 15 years. And to a certain extent, current tax laws soften the effect of realized losses on investments.

Clearly, one should not be doctrinaire. If the bank lacks managerial expertise or effort in the investment portfolio area or if management expects interest rates to rise and loan demand to be as strong as it was in the late 1970s and early 1980s, it probably should set a fairly short maximum maturity (between three and seven years) for the bulk of its portfolio investments. On the other hand, if the bank has the managerial competence *and* is willing to accept some security losses and to recognize the higher risks and returns generally associated with longer-term bonds, no maximum maturity limit seems necessary. Over the long run, the higher risks associated with these bonds should result in larger profits.

Scheduling maturities within the investment portfolio is undoubtedly the most difficult and exacting task of portfolio management. Other policies can be established, periodically reviewed, and occasionally adapted to new circumstances. Maturity policy, in contrast, requires constant review and decision making. Obviously, as funds become available for investment. The ideal course of action in portfolio management would be to hold short-term securities when interest rates are likely to rise and to lengthen maturities when rates are expected to decline. The risk is that such expectations may prove to be incorrect. Probably the most important determinants of maturities are the interest sensitivity and duration of the bank's nonportfolio assets and liabilities. The scheduling of maturities within the investment portfolio should help the bank achieve its desired overall interest sensitivity and duration positions. Portfolio maturities should not be dominated solely by such considerations, however, because maturities of other assets and liabilities can be partially managed and because off-balance sheet hedging instruments, such as financial futures, options, and interest rate swaps, are available. Within established interest sensitivity and duration constraints, there are three major philosophies for scheduling maturities: cyclical maturity determination, spaced or staggered maturities, and a "barbell" maturity structure.

From the previous discussion, it would appear that the strategy is tantamount to shortening maturities when business conditions (and the demand for credit) are expected to improve and lengthening maturities when the first signs of a recession appear. There are several problems in applying this theoretical ideal. First, even in cyclical periods such as the 1960s, bank portfolio managers found themselves under heavy pressure to produce profits (and thereby encouraged to buy longer-term securities) when interest rates were low. When interest rates were high (and expected to decline), banks tended to have only limited amounts to invest in any maturity. Second, business cycles do not always act as the textbooks say they should. For example, the 1970s might be described as 10 years of stagflation and fluctuating, rising interest rates, with only limited vestiges of traditional cyclical movements. As of 1999, the economy had grown for over six years with inflation and unemployment both at low levels. Third, portfolio management can be seen to be closely integrated with economic forecasting, which some observers consider to be a dubious art at best.

Because of the many uncertainties involved in such an ideal approach, banks have frequently been counseled to solve the problem of maturity distribution by spacing maturities more or less evenly within the maximum range. In this way, the bank will assure itself of at least average yields, or a little better. It will not be gambling on changes in the level of rates or the state of the economy. As long as the yield curve is rising, the reinvestment of maturing assets at the longest end of the maturity schedule will assure the bank of maximum income on a portfolio of which the average maturity will be relatively short. Figure 8.1 illustrates a staggered portfolio in which maturing bonds are invested in bonds that mature in 10 years.

Banks using the barbell maturity structure tend to strengthen their liquidity position

FIGURE 8.1   Ten-Year Staggered-Maturity Portfolio Distribution of Bonds by Maturity

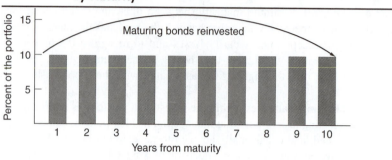

by investing a part of their investment portfolio in short-term liquid securities. The remainder of the typical barbell portfolio usually consists of high-yield, very-long-term bonds. Figure 8.2 illustrates a barbell portfolio. Advocates of this maturity philosophy reason that the greater liquidity and higher returns more than compensate for any additional risks. Barbell portfolios tend to be trading portfolios, and it is typical for the long-term proportion of the portfolio to be largest when interest rates are high and for the short-term portion

FIGURE 8.2   A 30 Percent Short-Term Barbell Portfolio Distribution of Bonds by Maturity

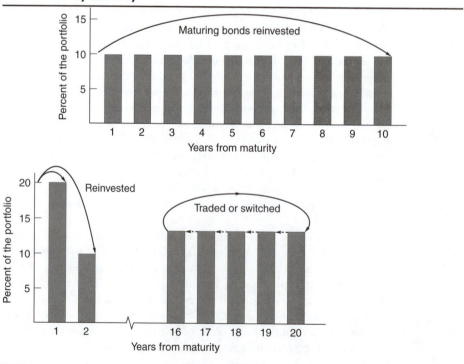

of the portfolio to grow when rates are low. Managerial expertise is clearly a prerequisite for the barbell maturity structure.

For bank management that lacks managerial competence in the investment area or that does not wish to take the trouble to frame a more flexible portfolio policy, average results obtained through regularly spaced (staggered or laddered) maturities are undoubtedly better than what might result from a purely haphazard or intuitive approach to the problem. Spaced maturities are probably an acceptable solution for the small bank. The barbell structure or other flexible approaches are generally preferable for bank managements that have the necessary competence and are willing to exercise judgment. It certainly does not make sense for such managements to invest the proceeds of maturity securities in the longest-term bonds permitted by the bank's policy at a time when the economy is obviously in a slack condition, when banks hold excess reserves, and when money rates are abnormally low.

Not even the most competent investment managers, of course, will be able to call every turn, nor do they need to do so. Alert and informed managers can take advantage of events that have already occurred. They do not need to gamble on the future.

TOTAL RETURN: TRADING AND SWAPPING BONDS

Traditional portfolio managers buy securities and hold them in the bank's portfolio until they mature. However, this is not the way to achieve an optimal risk-return trade-off. There are times to buy and times to sell and then to buy something else. Both large and small banks can take advantage of the broad movements in the securities markets.

Ultimately, one crucial test of portfolio performance is the measure over an investment horizon of the *total return*. As suggested in Table 8.1 at the beginning of the chapter, for many banks total return is one of the key objectives of the security portfolio. Such an objective is more aggressive than portfolio management practices of the past. It is not necessary to make total return the sole measure of performance, but, increasingly, it should be one mandatory way, among others, to audit the effectiveness of portfolio management. Banks now establish benchmarks as a basis for evaluating actual realized total return.

EXAMPLE At the beginning of 1998, Bank of Coronado (BC) launched a three-year $100 million bond investment program. The bank planned to liquidate the program at the end of 2000. BC's investment policy prohibited the investment manager from investing in bonds with maturities greater than seven years. At the time, Bank of Coronado considered two separate strategies: the short-term (S-T) strategy consisted of buying one-year discount securities and rolling them over each year for three years; the long-term (L-T) strategy consisted of investing in and holding a seven-year, 6 percent coupon bond throughout the period.

Table 8.4 shows the three-year annual total returns for the two strategies, as well as a maximum total return benchmark based on optimal trading strategies under the two interest rate scenarios. BC assumed that transactions are restricted to purchases and sales of only these two securities and that they could only occur on the first day of each year. The bank formulated the optimal trading strategy by assuming perfect foresight about interest rates. It formulated the optimal trading strategy, using interest rate scenario 1 as an example, as follows: the portfolio manager acquires the 6 percent coupon bonds at the beginning of 1998; sells them after long-term rates fall to $4\frac{1}{2}$ percent at the beginning of

TABLE 8.4 Short-Term and Long-Term Total Returns vs. Maximum Return Benchmark

	1/1/1998	1/1/1999	1/1/2000	1/1/2001	Return Benchmarks	[a]Actual Ttl. Return: Pct. Benchmark
Interest rate scenario 1						
S-T: 1-year rate	4.0%	2.0%	6.0%	6.0%	4.14%	55%
L-T: Long-term rate	6.0%	4.5%	7.0%	7.0%	4.92%	66%
Optimal total return					7.49%	
Interest rate scenario 2						
S-T: 1-year rate	4.0%	8.0%	4.0%	4.0%	5.82%	53%
L-T: Long-term rate	6.0%	8.0%	7.0%	7.0%	4.92%	45%
Optimal total return					10.90%	

[a] Return on short-term or long-term strategy expressed as percentage of total return on optimal strategy.

1999; invests the proceeds in 2 percent one-year securities until the beginning of 2000 and reinvests the funds, with interest, in the 6 percent coupon bonds (maturity has declined to five years) after market yields rise to 7 percent; and liquidates this position at the beginning of 2001.[6]

Bank of Coronado has determined that the strict S-T strategy would achieve 55 percent and 53 percent of the benchmark (optimal trading) strategy total returns for, respectively, rate scenarios 1 and 2. The strict L-T buy-and-hold strategy achieves 66 percent and 45 percent of the benchmark.

We should make an important distinction between trading and swapping. The objective of *trading* operations is to make gains on the movement of security prices and requires constant monitoring of the market with frequent purchases and sales. As such activity implies, trading requires a high level of market expertise, an attribute that is not available to many banks. *Bond swapping* involves active portfolio management that responds to opportunities brought about by changes in economic conditions and related changes in interest rates and the yield curve. Unlike trading, this does not require a constant presence in the market. However, bond swapping has the potential for adding appreciably to portfolio total returns over time.

SWAP EXAMPLE Portfolio managers use bond swaps to take advantage of changes in market rates and the tax effects of taking gains or losses. You can analyze a swap transaction exactly as you would analyze the replacement of a productive asset with a new asset in project capital budgeting. You should recall that capital replacement decisions require a complete incremental analysis. Two examples involving Bank of Chula Vista illustrate the elements in such an analysis. The first example involves taking an initial loss and

---

[6] The transactions are: acquire $100 million face value of seven-year securities at the beginning of 1998 and sell for $107.73681 million at the beginning of 1999, invest the sale proceeds plus the $6 million coupon in a 2 percent one-year security and collect $113.73681/0.98 = $116.058 million at the beginning of 2000, reinvest these funds in the 6 percent coupon securities (now five-year and selling for 0.959 of par) at a market yield of 7 percent, acquiring $121.020 million in par value, sell for $116.921 million, and collect coupon payment of $121.020 million × 0.06 = $7.2612 million for total liquidation value of $124.182 million at the beginning of 2001. The resulting rate of return is ($124.182 million /$100 million)$^{1/3}$ − 1 = 7.49 percent.

TABLE 8.5   Valuation of Bank of Chula Vista's Proposed Bond Swap, Initial Loss

	Cash Flows				
	1/1/1999	1/1/2000	1/1/2001	1/1/2002	1/1/2003
Interest, new 12% bond	$ 98,371	$ 98,371	$ 98,371	$ 98,371	$ 98,371
− Int. lost, old 7% bond	(70,000)	(70,000)	(70,000)	(70,000)	(70,000)
− Amortization of loss	(36,048)	(36,048)	(36,048)	(36,048)	(36,048)
= Δ taxable income	(7,677)	(7,677)	(7,677)	(7,677)	(7,677)
Δ Taxes (tax saved)	(3,071)	(3,071)	(3,071)	(3,071)	(3,071)
Δ After tax income	(4,606)	(4,606)	(4,606)	(4,606)	(4,606)
Δ Maturity value					180,239
Δ Cash flow[a]	31,442	31,442	31,442	31,442	(148,797)
PV, discount @ 12% NPV = $11,069	$ 28,073	$ 25,065	$ 22,380	$ 19,982	($ 84,431)

[a] Includes adding back noncash (amortization) charges.

reinvesting to obtain a positive increment in future interest income. The second involves an initial gain with reduced future interest income.

EXAMPLE: (Initial loss). Several years ago the Bank of Chula Vista paid par value for $1 million of bonds with 7 percent annual coupons bonds. At present, January 1, 1998, the bonds have five years to maturity, and in the years after it was purchased, market interest rates on such five-year bonds have risen to 12 percent. As a result, the current market value of Chula Vista's bonds is $819,761. The bank now contemplates selling the bonds at the loss and purchasing $819,761 of new five-year 12 percent annual coupon bonds at par value. (We assume Bank of Chula Vista can buy fractional positions in the new bond.) New annual interest income will be $819,761 × 0.12 = $98,371. Losses on the sale of the original 7 percent bonds can be amortized and deducted from taxable income on a straight-line basis over their remaining life as follows: ($1,000,000 − $819,761)/5 = $36,048 per year.[7] The Bank of Chula Vista pays marginal taxes of 40 percent.

Table 8.5 shows that the swap immediately would add economic value (net present value) in the amount of $11,069. If it does not violate tax rules such as prohibitions against "wash sales," this swap is a value-enhancing transaction for Bank of Chula Vista.[8]

EXAMPLE: (Initial gain). In 2005, the Bank of Chula Vista (BCV) sells $1 million, 12 percent coupon bonds with five years remaining maturity. BCV paid par for these bonds several years ago, but now, given that rates have declined to 7 percent, they are selling for $1,205,010. The bank now purchases $1,205,000 of new five-year 7 percent annual coupon bonds at par value. (Again, assume Bank of Chula Vista can buy fractional positions in the new bond.) New annual interest income will be $1,205,010 × 0.07 = $84,351.

[7] Also, loss amortization can be based on "the yield curve" method, an actuarially correct, but more complex, method than the straight-line method.

[8] The rule on "wash sales" nullifies tax benefits in such a swap if the institution acquires a substantially identical security within 30 days of the sale of the original security.

TABLE 8.6   Valuation of Bank of Chula Vista's Proposed Bond Swap, Initial Gain

	Cash Flows				
	1/1/2005	**1/1/2006**	**1/1/2007**	**1/1/2008**	**1/1/2009**
Interest, new 7% bond	$ 84,351	$ 84,351	$ 84,351	$ 84,351	$ 84,351
− Int. lost, old 12% bond	(120,000)	(120,000)	(120,000)	(120,000)	(120,000)
− Amortization of gain	41,002	41,002	41,002	41,002	41,002
= Δ taxable income	5,353	5,353	5,353	5,353	5,353
Δ Taxes	2,141	2,141	2,141	2,141	2,141
Δ After tax income	3,212	3,212	3,212	3,212	3,212
Δ Maturity value					205,010
Δ Cash flow[a]	(37,790)	(37,790)	(37,790)	(37,790)	167,220
PV, discount @ 7%	($ 35,318)	($ 33,007)	($ 30,848)	($ 28,830)	$ 119,226
NPV = −$8,777					

[a] Includes adding back noncash (amortization) charges.

Gain on the sale of the 12 percent bonds will be amortized and added to taxable income on a straight-line basis over their remaining life as follows:
($1,205,010 − $1,000,000)/5 = $41,002 per year.

Table 8.6 shows that this swap reduces the Bank of Chula Vista's economic value by $8,777 and, so, would not be pursued. Taking gains may make sense in a few situations when the bank wishes to smooth income or increase book capital. The usual guide is to not take gains unless the proceeds are reinvested to shorten overall maturities.

ACCOUNTING CLASSIFICATION OF SECURITIES

A revolutionary recent rule in accounting for securities, Financial Accounting Standard (FAS) 115, has had a dramatic effect on security portfolio management. The Financial Accounting Standards Board passed FAS 115 in 1993 after considerable pressure from the Securities Exchange Commission to reform accounting standards pertaining to equity and debt securities.[9] The rule, which became effective at the beginning of 1994, requires that changes in security market values must be accounted for on certain securities but exempts other securities from market valuation. Historically, financial institutions carried all of their securities at amortized cost (except for *trading* securities) without regard to the securities' actual market valuations. FAS 115 requires institutions to face the reality of economic valuations of a portion of their holdings.

The purpose underlying FAS 115 is to encourage the management of portfolios based on economics and to discourage portfolio manipulation that exploited obsolete cost-basis accounting. Previously, institutions pursued "gains trading," a distorted management technique that encouraged banks to sell securities with price gains—the "winners"—in order to report larger profits, and to hold securities with price losses—the

[9] You may recall from Chapter 4 that a past SEC chairman criticized the historical cost method of valuation as "once-upon-a-time" accounting.

''losers''—to avoid recording the losses. Much of the time, these selling and holding decisions were made without any regard for economic merit.

FAS 115 establishes three classes of security holdings as follows:

1. Hold-to-maturity (HTM)
2. Available for sale (AFS)
3. Trading

When a bank acquires securities, it must classify them into one of these three categories. The classification should be reassessed at each reporting period.

Hold-to-Maturity Securities

The values of securities classified as HTM are reported at amortized cost, just as all securities were reported before FAS 115. Thus, neither gains nor losses need to be reported. To qualify as HTM, the bank must have the ability and intent to hold them until maturity. As long as securities are classified HTM, they are not available to sell in response to changes in interest rates or prepayment risk, availability of new alternative investments, liquidity needs, and changes in funding needs. Alternatively, certain events constitute the reasons that HTM securities might be sold or transferred to AFS. These include:

a. Significant deterioration in credit quality.
b. Changes in law that reduce tax exemption of a security.
c. Major reorganization, such as a merger, that changes the holding institution's interest rate or credit risk.
d. Major increase in regulatory capital requirements that might require downsizing.
e. Significant increase in risk weight of a security for capital purposes.
f. Unusual and unanticipated events that allow the sale of a given HTM security without calling into question the status of other HTM securities.

At times, sales of HTM securities can be viewed as their effective maturity and, therefore, technically are not sales. Examples are (1) sales when the security is within three months of maturity or call date and (2) when 85 percent of principal has been collected (either through amortization or prepayment).

As a practical matter, HTM securities should include certain tax-exempts, securities that qualify for pledging against public deposits, long-term corporates, pass-through mortgage securities, and long-duration tranches of CMO securities.

Available for Sale Securities

AFS securities are those that are not accounted for as HTM or trading. Unrealized gains and losses on AFS securities are included in a separate component of shareholders' equity and thus affect banks' reported capital. Such gains and losses are not included in periodic earnings. Only interest income is included in earnings. AFS securities are purchased without the intent or ability to hold-to-maturity and so provide flexibility in portfolio management as well as bank balance sheet management. They are used for active portfolio management to produce maximum total returns balanced with their role in providing liquidity and as vehicles for adjusting interest rate risk. Because changes in market value have a direct impact on bank capital, banks prefer more liquid, shorter-duration securities such as Treasury and Agency securities, short-term CMOs such as PACs, floating-rate instruments, and adjustable-rate mortgages.

Trading Securities

Unrealized gains and losses on securities classified as trading are included in earnings. Trading securities are purchased and sold in the short term, primarily for the purpose of generating profits on short-term differences in price. Banks carry a variety of security types in their trading portfolio. For example, longer-term Treasury securities provide the "price action" banks seek in trading accounts. They have little interest in trading highly liquid, short-term securities. Certain "high-risk" securities such as certain mortgage derivative or other asset-backed securities also provide sought-for price action. They cannot be held as HTM. High-risk mortgage securities are those that meet certain tests of riskiness. For example, they may have an expected average life over 10 years and may be subject to large adjustments in price or expected life upon certain prescribed hypothetical shifts in the yield curve.

The differential effects of FAS 115 on reported capital and earnings have influenced the way banks manage their security portfolios. These effects are illustrated in the case of Santamero Bank and Trust Company.

EXAMPLE In 1998, Santamero Bank and Trust Company (SBT), a firm with $3.5 billion in assets, was concerned about the effects of FAS 115 on its reporting of earnings and capital in 1999. The firm prepared two forecasts for 1999's results. One forecast assumed no change in interest rates; the second "worst-case" forecast assumed rising rates and projected losses on the security portfolio as follows:

	($million) Par Value	No Change in Interest Rates	Interest Rates Rise	Gain (Loss)
Hold-to-Maturity	$200	$200	185	(15)
Available for Sale	500	500	470	(30)
Trading	100	100	90	(10)
Reported Capital	350	350	310	(40)

Table 8-7 shows the results from changes in earnings and reported capital.

In the case of the projected rise in interest rates, SBT's earnings will fall to a small fraction of the no-change case because of losses passed through from the trading portfolio. In addition, SBT's capital ratio will fall 140 basis points below the no-change case because of charges to capital from losses on both trading and AFS portfolios. HTM securities suffer a paper loss that is not passed through to either income or capital.

PORTFOLIO MANAGEMENT AND BUSINESS CYCLES

Earlier in this chapter we described how banks' hierarchical use of funds, in which the security portfolio is treated as the residual use, creates a dilemma for the management of the portfolio. As the lowest priority or residual use of funds, security investments and

TABLE 8.7   Santamero Bank and Trust's Forecast Income, ROA and Capital Ratio

	Forecast: 1999 ($million)	
	No Change in Rates	**Rising Interest Rates**
Interest income		
$2,000 loans	180	190
$200 HTM securities	16	16
$500 AFS securities	35	35
$100 Trading portfolio	7	7
Total interest income	238	248
Interest expense	90	100
Net interest income	148	148
Gain (loss) on trading	0	(10)
Net other expense	100	100
Net income	48	38
− dividends	35	35
Retained earnings	13	3
Return on assets	1.37%	1.09%
Capital ratio[a]	10.37%	8.97%

[a] Capital includes initial $350 plus 1999 retained earnings income minus AFS and trading losses.

sales often are poorly timed. Typically, timing issues are driven by the business (or interest rate) cycle. We explore these issues next.

Cyclical Peaks

Periods of high loan demand often coincide with high interest rates caused by the Federal Reserve's monetary restraint. During such periods, rising interest rates drive the market values of many banks' security portfolios below their acquisition or book values. (Portfolio managers refer to this condition as being "under water.") Although banks are short of liquidity in these circumstances, many are loath to recognize large losses created by liquidating longer-term securities. Moreover, they are inclined to place any available funds into short-term securities where they will be easily accessed when needed to meet ongoing loan demands.

However, this is the ideal time to sell long-term securities and take tax losses and to place available funds in long-term securities. The reasons are simple. First, the losses will tend to be offset by normally profitable operations during periods of strong loan demand. Second, funds generated by security sales can be used to lengthen maturities in anticipation of lower interest rates and future higher security prices.

Portfolio management's willingness to extend maturities depends on its confidence that the business cycle and interest rate high points are peaking. With sufficient confidence, the manager should employ several strategies. These can be stated as rules. First, invest available funds at the long end of the portfolio and, second, "refund in advance" by selling short-term issues and reinvesting the proceeds in long-term bonds. These two strategies entail taking losses to lengthen the portfolio in order to gain from the coming onset of lower interest rates. The last rule is to switch securities into alternative but same-maturity securities when this will improve yield and long-term profit potential. Although more limited in objective, the tax loss aspect of this strategy tends to free up cash that can contribute to long-run profitability. This is especially true for banks that employ a barbell portfolio policy.

Despite the benefits listed above, many banks do not sell aggressively for losses in periods of high interest rates. Historically, this was because managers were reluctant to report reduced net income for fear that shareholders would object. It is not easy to explain to shareholders that reductions in current profits are to their advantage over the long run. Recent changes in accounting rules for securities is another reason managers forego such sales. The new rules we described in the previous section require that the bank partially report paper losses on securities that the bank seems willing to sell. If the bank sells certain securities at a loss, regulators may require that the values of similar securities still on the books be adjusted for unrealized losses. Finally, banks are inhibited from loss sales because taxable income is ultimately limited. Losses are valuable only to the extent that they reduce taxes at a high marginal tax rate, such as 35 percent. Finally, since losses reduce income, they also reduce the rate at which bank capital is formed through retained earnings, potentially prompting supervisory authorities to require a bank to raise more capital.

Cyclical Bottoms

Just as periods of peak loan demand tend to coincide with high interest rates, so periods of weak loan demand coincide with a low interest rate and a steep, positively sloped yield curve environment. When the economy is clearly in recession and interest rates are bottoming out, the security portfolio is likely to produce price gains above bonds' purchase prices. At such times, bank management does not feel liquidity pressures and incorrectly may prefer to invest in long-term securities where yields are highest. This strategy appears to be attractive because it helps the bank counter its earnings shortfall due to insufficient loan demand.

Such a strategy is ill-advised for security portfolio management purposes. Generally, at the bottom of the interest rate cycle, banks should keep their new investments short. In addition, they might offset the immediate income they forego by avoiding long-term investments if they take profits by selling their longer bonds. However, there is a caveat concerning taking profits on such sales.

Taking profits always seems more desirable than absorbing losses, but it can be wrong merely to take profits and reinvest in comparable (or longer) maturities. There are two challenges to this practice. First, the gain on securities that are sold is taxable and leaves less money working than before the sale when, in effect, the full market value of the security was working for profit. Second, if the portfolio manager is convinced that the economy (and interest rates) is close to the bottom, which should prompt the bank to take profits, the manager also should shorten maturities in anticipation of a coming rise in rates. The general rule should be: ''Do not take profits without shortening maturities.''

We should make one final point about profit taking. Portfolio managers recognize that profits (after taxes) taken in times of low interest rates should not be looked on as permanent additions to the bank's capital. Rather, they are more inclined to view, and account for, such profits as reserves against future security losses, where they will be

FIGURE 8.3 Cyclical Maturity Management of the Security Portfolio

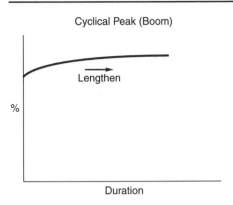

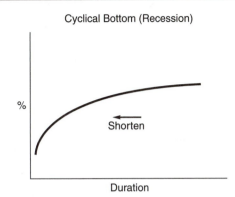

Bank Priorities
• Invest short-term to provide liquidity
• Avoid loss: do not sell long-term securities

Portfolio Management Priorities
• Use available funds to extend maturities
• Sell long-term, take losses, reinvest long-term

Bank Priorities
• Invest long-term to enhance income
• Take security gains, extend maturities

Portfolio Management Priorities
• Invest available funds short-term to provide future liquidity
• Sell long-term, take gains, reinvest short-term

available to absorb the losses when the next turn in interest rate levels provides new profit possibilities.

Figure 8.3 illustrates these points concerning security portfolio management at the extreme point of cycles. While common sense underlies these strategies and rules, they are highly idealized. One never truly knows when one is experiencing a cyclical peak or trough, although experience improves one's estimate of when these events are occurring. Still, this discussion sets up a valuable foil for understanding the profits and risks involved in cyclical movements of loan demand, interest rates, and yield curves. In each instance, we pit the desires and priorities of a bank in its primary role as a lender against the strategies a portfolio manager would follow to maximize the performance of the security portfolio.

EXAMPLE Reginald Hack, portfolio manager for Bank of the Southwest (BSW), is reviewing the bank's security portfolio performance over the latest complete business and interest rate cycle. Following are interest rates for short-term securities and five-year securities (BSW's policy maximum maturity) at the extremes of the cycle. BSW began with $50 million par value, five-year, 9 percent coupon bond in its portfolio. An additional $100 million became available at the peak of the cycle. To keep it simple, the bank's environment is tax free.

	Interest Rates	
	Peak	**Bottom**
Short term	12%	3%
5-year, 9% coupon bond	11%	6%

Hack's transactions and income at the peak were:

	Income
• Hold $50 million par value, 5-year, 9% coupon bond:	$ 4.500 million
• Invest $100 million available funds in 12% short-term security	12.000 million
Income at peak	$16.500 million

His transactions at the bottom were:

	Income
• Reinvest the $100 million in 5-year, 6% coupon bond	$ 6.000 million
• Sell the $50 million par, 5-year, 9% coupon bond for $56.391 million (market rate is 6%); gain of	6.359 million
• Invest $56.391 million in 5-year, 6% coupon bond	3.384 million
Income at bottom	$15.743 million
Total income	$32.243 million

In looking back, Hack calculated what the portfolio's performance would have been if he had observed optimal portfolio management rules. In this case, his transactions would have been: Hypothetical transactions at the peak:

	Income
• Sell $50 million par value, 5-year, 9% coupon bonds for $46.304 (market rate is 11%); take loss	$(3.696 million)
• Invest $46.304 million in 5-year, 11% coupon bond	5.093 million
• Invest $100 million in 5-year, 11% coupon bond	11.000 million
Income at peak	$12.397 million

Hypothetical transactions at the bottom:

	Income
• Sell $146.304 par value, 5-year, 11% coupon bonds for $177.118 million (market rate is 6%); take gain	$30.814 million
• Invest $177.118 million in 3% short-term securuity:	5.314 million
Income at bottom	$32.128 million
Total hypothetical income	$48.525 million

While the example simplifies the process into pure extreme transactions, the loss in not taking gains and in shortening during rate peaks is obvious. Overall, bank priorities produce $16.282 million less annualized income ($48.525 million minus $32,243 million) than portfolio management priorities. Such actions provide liquidity at a steep price.

EVALUATING SECURITIES WITH UNCERTAIN CASH FLOWS

The market rate at which an earning asset's cash inflows are reinvested has a large impact on the asset's realized yield. The problem becomes more complex when the timing of the cash flows, especially prepayments, is uncertain. Examples are corporate or agency bonds that are callable at the issuer's option or mortgage-backed securities on which the mortgages backing the securities may be refinanced at the borrower's option.

Practical investors calculate the yield-to-call for callable bonds that sell at a premium above their call price.[10] The appropriate technique for mortgage-backed derivative products is complex and not practical for the average investor. It becomes more attractive to refinance when mortgage rates fall; however, the decision is made by numerous individual borrowers. Investment bankers and others who sell mortgage-backed securities estimate what will happen to principal and interest cash flows under various scenarios of interest rate changes. These estimates can be used to predict what realized yields will be under various rate scenarios. Generally, banks that purchase mortgage-backed securities are better off if yields remain fairly stable. Chapter 14 presents formal techniques for solving such issues for banking assets with embedded options.

IMPLEMENTING INVESTMENT POLICIES AND STRATEGIES

There are five key elements in implementing investment policies and strategies successfully. Two of these elements—determining investment objectives and putting portfolio objectives in writing—have been discussed. The other three—identifying the purpose and makeup of the portfolio, complying with regulatory rules, and delegating investment authority with adequate controls—are discussed here.

Identifying the Portfolio

The *investment account* usually refers to all security holdings of a bank. It is common practice for bank management to provide directors and owners with a list of the bank's security holdings, showing book values, market prices, and range of maturities. The list is generally subdivided into U.S. government securities, state and municipal securities, and other securities. Few attempts are made, however, to distinguish the liquidity position from the investment portfolio—that is, to identify those securities held specifically for the purpose of liquidity and those held for long-term investment.

Length of maturity alone will not be the distinguishing feature, because under certain circumstances (in anticipation of rising rates, for example), a portion of the investment portfolio could well be held temporarily in short-term issues. The real distinction is the purpose for which the securities are held. Liquidity assets are used to meet estimates of potential deposit withdrawals and increased loan demands. The investment portfolio, by contrast, represents the investment of surplus funds for income. The distinction between securities available for sale or held to maturity may also be useful in this context.

---

[10] Appendix B to Chapter 5 examined the method for identifying the premium paid in the market for call features on bonds.

Complying with Regulatory Rules

The relative importance of securities in most banks' asset structures has increased regulatory interest in securities activities by commercial banks. Most of the regulatory bodies seemed particularly concerned about policies and practices involving new derivative products, such as mortgage- or other asset-backed derivative securities. Regulatory treatment has varied among the various regulatory bodies. Finally, in 1991 the Federal Financial Institutions Examination Council adopted a supervisory policy statement on securities activities that should make supervision similar among the various regulatory bodies.

Delegating Authority But Maintaining Control

The delegation of authority and retention of control are essential parts of security portfolio policy. In this area the board of directors has the ultimate responsibility, and it should share responsibilities for policy determination with members of senior management. The portfolio manager should be in charge of day-to-day management and may recommend major courses of action or policy changes to the board and senior management.

A bank's investment policy should delegate specific authority to designated officers to purchase or sell securities up to certain amounts, just as a bank's loan policy should permit the bank's lending officer to commit the bank for stated amounts. Opportunities for profitable switching or trading that might be evident to the investment officer, or that might be called to his or her attention by a correspondent bank, a dealer, or an investment advisory service, do not last long in the market. If decisions must be referred to an investment committee, or even to a chief executive officer who may be away from the bank at the moment, portfolio opportunities will be irretrievably lost. A sound policy, therefore, will set trading limits, based on the size of the bank and the investment officer's knowledge and experience, within which he or she should have full discretion. It is relatively simple to compare the results of trading, say every six months, with what would have resulted had no purchases or sales been made. Such a comparison should be a clear indication of the investment officer's acumen.

Compensation plans in the investment area should also recognize good performance. It is important to remember that performance includes assessment of both returns and risks taken.

SUMMARY

Security portfolio management should recognize differences in size, location, condition, and managerial capabilities among banks. There are, however, five basic steps that should lead to sound, flexible security policies and strategies. Security portfolio policies should be in writing and should start with a statement of the objectives of the security portfolio. After the objectives have been established, the bank should make its forecast for the economy and interest rates. Next, the bank should inventory its own investment needs by identifying the portfolio, estimating pledging requirements, assessing the risk position, determining the tax position, coordinating with the bank's interest-sensitivity position, and estimating the need for diversification. After inventorying its needs, the bank should establish policies and strategies affecting the size, risk, maturity, and marketability of the investment portfolio that are consistent with these needs. Finally, bank policies should delegate authority for action commensurate with responsibility and should reward outstanding performance. All these steps should be coordinated with overall asset-liability management. One of the most important contributions of the security portfolio is that it permits impersonal flexibility in balancing a bank's overall liquidity and interest-sensitivity position.

END OF CHAPTER PROBLEMS

8.1 A portfolio manager invests $1 million in a 30-year, 7 percent coupon bond and pays par value. She holds the bond for two years, when rates on such bonds have fallen to 5 percent, and sells it (now a 28-year bond). What total return did she earn?

8.2 Maverick Bank believes it should manage its security portfolio for total return. As a check on the profitability of this strategy, determine the five-year annual total returns for two opposing strategies:

   i. (naïve strategy): Invest only in one-year discount bonds, rolling over at the end of each year.

   ii. (prescient strategy): Invest in one-year discount bonds at the beginning of years in which long-term rates subsequently increase; invest in 10-year, 8 percent coupon bonds at the beginning of years in which long-term rates subsequently decrease; sell coupon bonds in advance of subsequent long-term rate increases.

Transactions occur only once each year at the beginning of the year. Maverick's five-year annual projection of short-term and long-term interest rates is shown in the following listing. There are no taxes.

Beginning of Year	One-Year Rate	Long-Term Rate
1999	6%	10%
2000	7%	8%
2001	3%	7%
2002	3%	9%
2003	5%	8%
End year 2003	5%	8%

8.3 Swiebruken Bank uses a barbell portfolio strategy (see text Figure 8.1). The short-term component had a maximum one-year maturity and, as it matured, was continuously rolled over into new one-year discount securities. The long-term component had a distribution of three-, four-, and five-year 7 percent coupon securities. Each year, when the shortest-term security aged to a two-year maturity, it was sold and the proceeds were reinvested in a new five-year security. In January 1999 the bank had $200 million invested in one-year securities (short-term component) and $100 million each in the three-, four-, and five-year securities.

Based on the yield curve forecasts for Problem 8.2, determine the annual dollar returns and total return on this portfolio. There are no taxes.

8.4 Evaluate the following bond swap for Fargo Savings (FS). FS will sell $10 million par value of 10-year, 6 percent coupon bonds (purchased several years ago at par value) in a market yielding 9 percent on such bonds. The proceeds will be rolled into new 10-year, 9 percent coupon bonds at par.

Losses will be amortized on a straight-line basis: income and gains or losses are subject to a tax rate of 34 percent.

Alternative Investment
Instruments Used by Banks

When banks are short of loans, they seek to make up for unavailable loan revenues by acquiring longer-term capital market investment alternatives. With nontraditional capital market investment, banks must accept not only interest rate (or price) risk but also credit and prepayment risk. Among banks, the most popular of these "nontraditional" instruments is mortgage-backed securities of which U.S. banks held $346 billion at the end of 1997.

Table 8A.1 lists several kinds of nontraditional investment instruments available to bank portfolio managers.

MORTGAGE DERIVATIVES

A secondary mortgage market was first conceived by the federal government with the creation of the Federal National Mortgage Association (FNMA or Fannie Mae) in 1938. This government-sponsored corporation was chartered to purchase mortgages from lenders and resell them to investors. Its purpose was to provide home buyers with capital to overcome regional shortages of funds. In due course, FNMA and two subsequently founded government agencies—the Government National Mortgage Association (GNMA or Ginnie Mae) and the Federal Home Loan Mortgage Corporation (FHLMC or Freddie Mac)—began buying home loans from lenders, packaging them into securities, and providing explicit (in the case of GNMA) or implicit (in the cases of FNMA and FHLMC) guar-antees on the packages. The securitization and guarantee of home mortgages through vehicles such as participation certificates offered by the agencies greatly enhanced the flow of loans for housing finance. In the late 1990s nearly 50 percent of all mortgages were securitized.

Mortgages and mortgage-backed securities (MBS) constitute callable investments because mortgagors are granted the option to pay off their mortgages before maturity. Confronted with an indeterminate term on mortgage securities, investors demand a yield premium above the yield available on noncallable securities of similar credit and price risk. MBSs are analogous to a sinking fund bond with an unknown retirement formula.

The factors that determine mortgage prepayment rates are well known, but unfortunately, they are subject to variation. Demographic factors are relatively more predictable than interest rate factors. Demographic data, such as the geographic region of the mortgaged houses and the occupation and age of the mortgagors, determine mortgagors' mobility and, therefore, a fairly constant basic rate of prepayment. In addition, mortgagors are inclined to prepay and refinance their homes when market interest rates on new mortgages fall sufficiently below the coupon rates on their existing mortgages. For securitized pools of mortgages, the constant prepayment rate (CPR) varies markedly for different combinations of the pools' coupon rates and the current market interest rate on new mortgages.

TABLE 8A.1   Alternative Investments Used by Banks

Mortgage derivatives
    Fixed-rate mortgage-backed securities, 15 years
    Fixed-rate mortgage-backed securities, 30 years
    Adjustable-rate mortgage-backed securities
    Collateralized mortgage obligations (CMO)
        • sequential class
        • planned amortization class
        • targeted amortization class
    Interest only–principal only securities (IO-PO)
    Real estate mortgage investment conduits (REMIC)
Small Business Administration–guaranteed loan pools
Mutual funds
Government investment certificates
Corporate debt securities

Prepayment Effects on Yields.   Most of the more than $1 trillion international market for MBS includes mortgages that grant mortgagors nearly unlimited prepayment privileges. Figure 8A.1 refers to a typical historical period to illustrate the effects of changes in mortgage interest rates on the CPRs and cash flows of a 30-year, fixed-rate FHLMC mortgage bearing a coupon of 10 percent. As panel A in Figure 8A.1 indicates, the interest rate on fixed-rate, 30-year mortgages fell over 100 basis points during 1992. As the market rates fell, many holders of 10 percent and higher-rate mortgages found that they could profitably pay the loan fees and other transaction costs to refinance their mortgages at market rates. Typically, mortgage holders refinance when the market rate falls approximately 1½ to 2% below the rate on their mortgages. Panel B in Figure 8A.1 depicts the resulting rapid rise in the CPR over a six-month holding period. These rates actually continued to rise after October 1992 as market rates fell to levels close to 7 percent. An extremely rapid rate of prepayments produced a radical change in the cash flow pattern of MBS, which resulted in a large amount of prepaid principal being received prematurely by investors, as shown in Figure 8A.2. Bank and thrift institution holders of these securities incurred significant reinvestment penalties because they had to reinvest these cash flows at a time when reinvestment rates were low.

In summary, the interaction of market rates, CPR, and prices on MBS is a known and rather predictable phenomenon. The CPR increases when the current market rate falls below a security's coupon rate by about 1½ to 2 percent or more. The pattern of prepayments can be forecast with reasonable accuracy for different interest rate environments. Once prepayment rates are forecast, the prices on MBS can be calculated in a straightforward manner. With higher CPRs, cash flows accelerate, shortening the duration; on premium-priced securities, yields are reduced. The accelerated cash flows we examined for the FHLMC 10s in panel B of Figure 8A.1 shortened this security's duration to 1.90 years and reduced its yield. The dramatically shortened duration of these securities qualified them as short-term investments despite the roughly 320 months remaining to final maturity. Therefore, when investors compared this FHLMC security in October 1992 with competitive investment opportunities, they should have looked to investment alternatives on the short-term end of the yield curve.

Premium MBS Investment Analysis.   To assess the potential benefit of purchasing a government agency-backed premium MBS, investors compare its performance with that of U.S. Treasury securities of comparable maturities. The MBS must provide an adequate yield spread over Treasury yields to compensate investors for the risk of prepayment. To be comparable, the Treasury security should have the same duration as the MBS. Normally, duration serves as a measure of the price sensitivity of securities. However, prepayment risk on a premium MBS subjects it to changes in yield and duration as market rates change, rendering duration unsatisfactory

FIGURE 8A.1   Mortgage Rates and MBS Prepayments

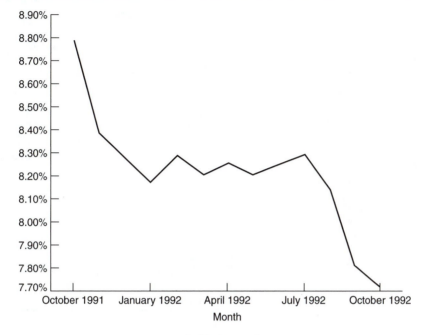

A. Mortgage rates

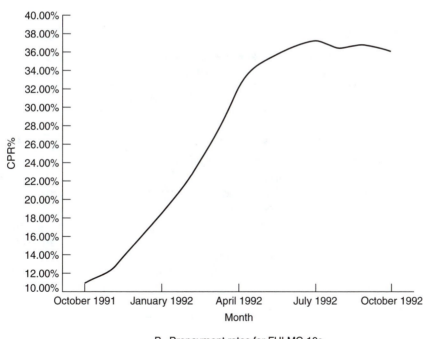

B. Prepayment rates for FHLMC 10s

FIGURE 8A.2   Principal and Interest Payments

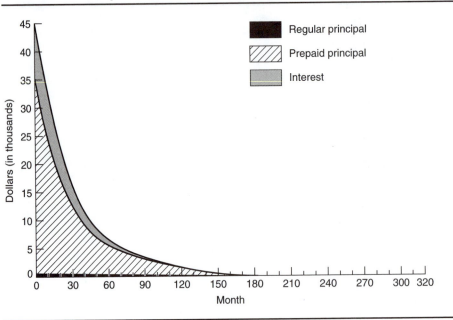

FIGURE 8A.3   Premium MBS Rates of Return[a] Compared to Various Treasury Securities Return on 11.5% GNMAs for a Six-Month Holding Period

Monthly Constant Prepayment Rate	Price at Sale								
	105.5	106.0	106.5	107.0	107.5	108.0	108.5	109.0	109.5
0.5%	6.66%	7.56%	8.46%	9.36%	10.26%	11.16%	12.06%	12.96%	13.86%
1.0%	6.28	7.15	8.03	8.90	9.77	10.65	11.52	12.39	13.27
1.5%	5.91	6.76	7.61	8.46	9.30	10.15	11.00	11.84	12.69
2.0%	5.56	6.38	7.20	8.02	8.84	9.66	10.49	11.31	12.13
2.5%	5.20	6.00	6.80	7.60	8.38	9.19	9.99	10.78	11.58
3.0%	4.86	5.63	6.41	7.18	7.95	8.73	9.50	10.27	11.04
3.5%	4.53	5.28	6.03	6.78	7.52	8.27	9.02	9.77	10.52
4.0%	4.20	4.93	5.65	6.38	7.10	7.83	8.56	9.28	10.01
4.5%	3.88	4.59	5.29	5.99	6.88	7.40	8.10	8.81	9.51
5.0%	3.57	4.25	4.93	5.62	6.30	6.98	7.66	8.34	9.03

[a] Rate of return is defined as the sum of the capital gain (loss), the cash flow (principal and interest), and the reinvestment earnings all divided by the value of the original investment.

SOURCE: U.S. League Investment Services.

as a measure of price sensitivity. (One investment banker has called the duration measure a "rubber ruler" when applied to MBS.)

Given the uncertainty of MBS durations, we can estimate some realistic outcomes on premium MBSs and several possible alternative investments in U.S. Treasury securities. Figure 8A.3 shows six-month holding period rates of return on a premium GNMA 11.5 percent security, assuming various CPRs and initial prices. In Figure 8A.4, parts A, B, and C of the figure show rates of return under constant, falling, and rising market rates for the GNMA (priced initially at 107.5) and on one-, two-, and three-year Treasury securities. We assume an initial money market rate of 5.5 percent. In Figure 8A.4, part A, rates remain constant and prices remain flat over the six-month holding period. Under these con-

ditions, the GNMA yields 8.0 percent, somewhat more than the yields on each of the Treasury securities. The GNMA yield is based on an assumption of a rather fast 3 percent monthly CPR.

If market rates decline 100 basis points, as in part B of Figure 8A.4, the rates of return on the one-, two-, and three-year Treasuries increase substantially because of price appreciation. For the GNMA, assuming an increase in CPR to 3.5 percent and a price rise to 108.5, the rate of return rises moderately to 9.02 percent. If market rates rise 100 basis points instead, as Figure 8A.4, part C, the rates of return on all three Treasuries issues fall well below money market rates. If the GNMA 11.5's price falls to, say, 106.5 and its monthly CPR declines to 2.0 percent, the GNMA will produce an annualized yield of 7.2 percent, or considerably more than the

FIGURE 8A.4   Premium MBS Rates of Return Compared to Those of Various Treasury Securities

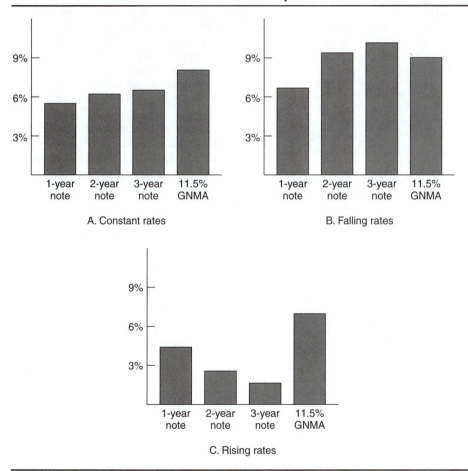

TABLE 8A.2   Rate Reset Characteristics

	FHLMC	FNMA	GNMA
Index	1-year Treasury bill	11th FHLB District cost of funds	1-year Treasury bill
Spread over index	200 basis points (b.p.)	200 b.p.	150 b.p.
Rate cap, annual	2%	2%	1%
Lifetime cap over initial rate	6%	6%	5%
Reset frequency	Annually	Annually	Annually

Treasury notes. Typically, the GNMA security provides the best defensive position in a bearish (rising-rate) market. It also outperforms comparable Treasury securities in a constant-rate environment. As a caution, however, the outcomes described for the GNMA 11.5s resulted from assumptions we made about how the speed of prepayments was affected by various market rates of interest. As market conditions change, shifts in prepayment rates change the nature of MBS. The key to successful investment choices requires an understanding and a careful analysis of projected prepayments.

Adjustable-Rate MBS.   In addition to the large volume of securitized, fixed-rate mortgages, there is a smaller but growing volume of securitized adjustable-rate mortgages (ARMs). The volume of new ARMs is highly cyclical and tends to increase most when mortgage rates are falling.

The pricing of ARM securities is considerably more volatile than the pricing of comparable Treasury securities, with maturities equal to the ARM rate reset intervals. Like fixed-rate mortgages, ARMs may carry not only the risks of default (conventional MBS), interest rate risk, and liquidity risk, but also prepayment risk. In addition, however, be-

cause ARMs rates can only be reset up to a contractual cap set on their adjustability, they possess *basis risk*—defined for these purposes as the risk that rate adjustment caps may prevent ARM securities from being adjusted with increases (decreases) in the underlying index (in this case, the Treasury bill rate plus 150 basis points and an annual adjustment cap of 1 percent). Now suppose that the one-year Treasury bill rate rises from 7.5 to 9.5 percent. The ARM security, with an initial rate of 9.0 percent, is limited this year to an adjustment to 10.0 percent. Barring further changes in the Treasury bill rate, it will take another full year before the ARM rate can be set at 11.0 percent, its expected spread over the Treasury bill.

The rate-resetting characteristics of the ARMs issued by FHLMC, FNMA, and GNMA are described in Table 8A.2. Repayment risk presents a threat to the value of ARM securities purchased at a premium. Table 8A.3 presents the relationship between ARM securities yields and various projected constant prepayment rates.

Multiclass Securities.   Securitization of pools of single-family home mortgages has forced investors and analysts to understand and quantify

TABLE 8A.3   FNMA Adjustable-Rate MBS

Gross Coupon[a]	Price	*Projected Yields for Various CPRs*					
		0%	5%	10%	15%	20%	30%
8.0	102½	7.82	7.68	7.54	7.38	7.21	6.83
9.0	102½	8.82	8.69	8.53	8.37	8.19	7.18
10.0	102½	9.83	9.69	9.53	9.36	9.18	8.79
11.0	102½	10.85	10.70	10.53	10.36	10.17	9.77

[a] Eleventh FHLB District cost of funds + 125 basis points.

the insidious problem of prepayment risk. In the 1980s, new generations of securitized mortgages were introduced to address prepayment risk by redistributing it among various classes. These derivative securities—collateralized mortgage obligations (CMOs) and stripped mortgage-backed securities (SMBSs)—created securities with unique risk-return characteristics.

CMOs separate mortgage pools into short-, medium-, and long-term classes called *tranches*. These tranches clarify for investors the repayment rate to be expected on mortgage-backed investments. Investors who seek a rapid return on their funds can buy a short-term tranche, say, a three-year CMO. Long-term investors can acquire a portion of a 20-year tranche. Each class is assigned a fixed, floating, or zero interest rate; a fixed principal amount; and a set of payment conditions. Short-term CMO investors sustain relatively little prepayment risk and receive a corresponding return; long-term investors bear relatively greater prepayment risk and, consequently, are paid a premium rate. Generally, CMOs are packaged in "vanilla" or sequential-pay tranches that pay out the underlying principal only after previous classes have been retired. Therefore, short-term tranche investors receive all of their principal before medium-term investors do, and, as a

result, are subject to a lower price sensitivity risk. Figures 8A.5 and 8A.6 illustrate the basic structure and allocation of cash flows as well as the outstanding principal balances of a typical CMO or real estate mortgage investment conduit.

REMICs present still another variation of the problem of prepayment risk and its effect on the investment properties of the affected securities. REMICs are an extension of the basic CMO type of contract. They were created on January 1, 1987, by the Tax Reform Act of 1986, which removed various Internal Revenue Service regulations that imposed burdensome costs on CMO issuers and investors. REMIC legislation removed barriers to entry for certain multiclass MBS issuers and expanded the demand for multiclass securities by financial institutions. Today virtually all multiclass securities are issued in REMIC form.

The cash flows associated with CMOs and REMICs are distributed according to the securities' tranche structure, as noted earlier. The cash flows occur as follows:

1. Interest payments are made simultaneously to all bond classes. (The actual interest cash flow to any zero accrual bonds is applied to repayment of principal.)

FIGURE 8A.5   Building Blocks for REMICs

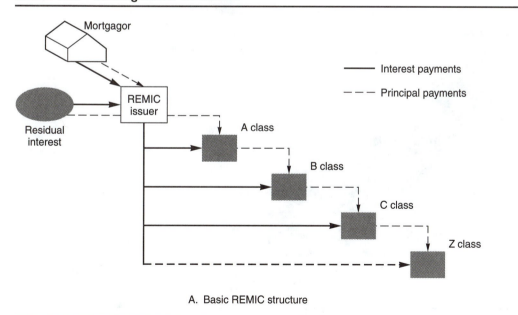

A. Basic REMIC structure

FIGURE 8A.6   **Cash Flows and Principal Balances for REMIC Classes**

Allocation of cash flows among REMIC classes

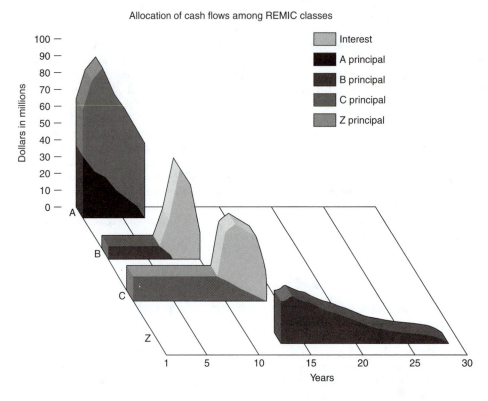

Outstanding REMIC principal balances

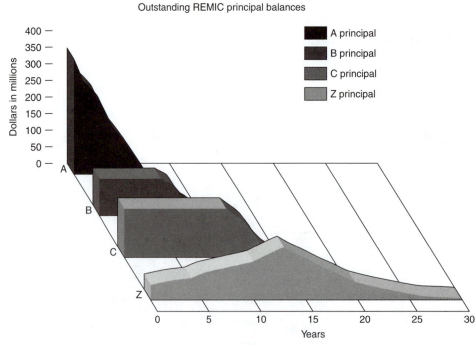

FIGURE 8A.6 *(Continued)*

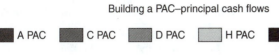

Building a PAC–principal cash flows

A PAC   C PAC   D PAC   H PAC   Companion tranches

80% PSA

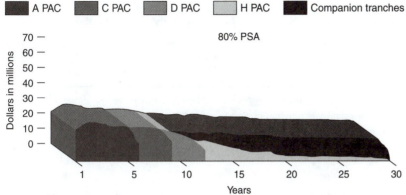

165% PSA

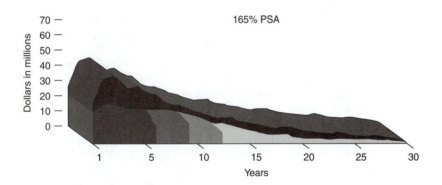

250% PSA

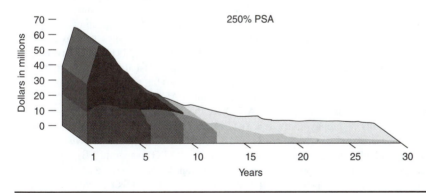

TABLE 8A.4   Multiclass Securities—Average Life and Prepayment Rates

Prepayment Speed[a]	A Tranche		B Tranche		C Tranche		Z Tranche (0 Coupon)		Residual Equity	
	Projected Maturity[b]	Average Life[c]	Projected Maturity[b]	Average Life[c]	Projected Maturity[b]	Average Life[c]	Projected Maturity[b]	Average Life[c]	Projected Maturity[b]	Average Life[c]
100%	4.5	2.45	6.5	5.45	10	8.33	29	15.78	None	3
200%	3	1.59	4	3.45	7.5	5.59	29	13.98	None	2.5
300%	2	1.25	3	2.56	5.5	4.24	29	9.44	None	2

[a] Prepayment speeds represent percentages of the Public Securities Association standard prepayment model.

[b] Number of years by which the bonds should be completely retired.

[c] Average life is the average time to the receipt of principal weighted by the size of each principal payment.

SOURCE: U.S. League Investment Service, Inc.

2. Principal repayments are used to retire the bond tranches sequentially. All principal payments on the collateral are directed first to retiring the shortest-maturity (designated *A-class*) bonds.
3. After these bonds are completely retired, principal payments on the collateral are directed to retirement of the next-shortest (*B-class*) bond. This process continues until all the bonds are retired.
4. Payments to owners of residual equity are made periodically. After the required interest and principal payments have been made to bondholders, any excess cash flow can be paid on a pro-rata basis to owners of equity interests.

The primary source of residual cash flow is the positive spread between the bond coupons and the coupons on the underlying collateral. Other sources include income from investing monthly cash flows pending distribution to bondholders and excess prepayments.

Table 8A.4 shows the changes in the average life of each tranche, the zero-coupon (terminal years' principal) bond, and residual equity as prepayment rates vary. The prepayment measure used for CMOs and REMICs is based on the Public Securities Association estimates for prepayment speed (PSA speed) and average life of the class affected. The average life declines most rapidly for longer-term tranches and for the zero-coupon bond as prepayment rates accelerate. Yield declines associated with changing lives are smaller for shorter-term tranches.

CMOs may also be packaged with PACs (planned amortization classes) and TACs (targeted amortization classes), which are similar to sinking fund bonds. A PAC, instead of producing interest cash flows until the principal is paid back for a given tranche, pays out principal on specific payment schedules. The CPR on the collateral underlying the PAC is held constant as long as the PSA speeds remain within a given protected range known as the *PAC band*. The PACs are issued within the REMIC structure with companion or support tranches. The support tranches absorb excess cash flows and make up for shortfalls. Because the support tranches bear most of the prepayment risk of the pool, their lives vary greatly. PACs are also purchased with different average lives, but they offer reduced volatility and provide the greatest certainty of cash flows of all MBSs. TACs are similar to PACs except that protection is provided only against increasing prepayments and early retirement. In other words, if CPRs speed up, companion tranches will absorb cash flows to prevent retirement of the TAC; but if CPRs slow, the average life of the TAC increases. Usually, TACs are not issued as isolated securities but are incorporated as support classes within PAC structures. Figures 8A.6 and 8A.7 show the principal cash flows of a PAC and a TAC at various prepayment speeds.

SMBSs, sometimes referred to as *interest only–principal only* (IO-PO), separate MBS into principal payments and interest payments. IO segments perform better in sustained rising-rate environments because their cash flow patterns are heavily loaded toward the early years and the cash flows become available for reinvestment at higher and higher rates. PO segments perform well in falling-rate environments. This property of IOs, whereby IO prices are positively related to interest rates, has increased investors' interest in them as a natural hedge against the decline in prices on normal securities when interest rates rise.

FIGURE 8A.7   TAC REMIC Structure Principal Cash FLows

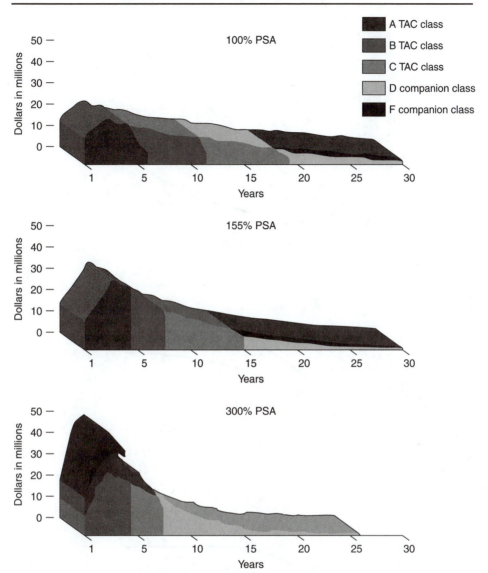

FIGURE 8A.8   Cumulative Cash Flows for $100,000 Mortgage

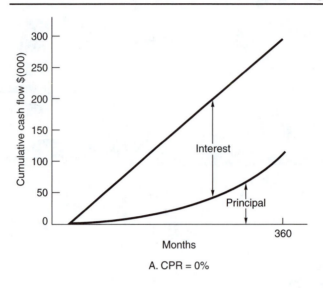

A. CPR = 0%

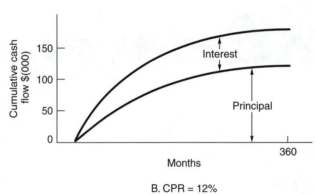

B. CPR = 12%

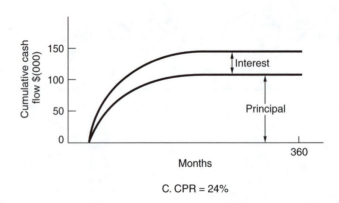

C. CPR = 24%

FIGURE 8A.9 Price Volatility of Pools, IOs, and POs

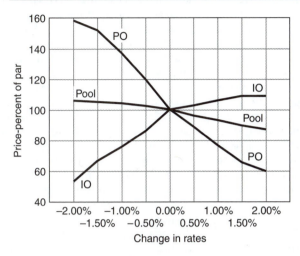

A. Pool of 9% mortgages

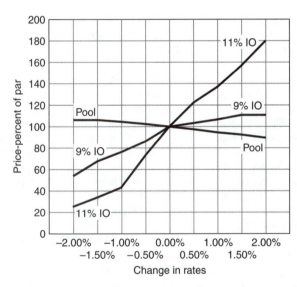

B. 9% IO versus 11% IO

To appreciate the hedging capability of IOs, we analyze interest and principal cash flows on a $100 million pool of mortgages, given alternative CPRs. Panel A, Figure 8A.8, shows the cumulative cash flows that will result if no changes in CPRs occur. By the time the mortgage matures, the borrower has paid in almost twice as much interest as the principal originally borrowed. Because there is no pre-payment of principal, interest payments accumulate rapidly, becoming the dominant component of cash flows.

Panels B and C of Figure 8A.8 show the cumulative cash flows generated by this mortgage pool with, respectively, a 12 percent and a 24 percent CPR. Prepayments of principal cause a smaller ac-cumulation of interest payments. With principal payments, on the other hand, differences in prepayment rates change the timing of the receipt of payments but do not change the total payment; obviously, $100 million must be paid. However, with respect to the IO, neither the timing of receipt nor the total amount of the cash flow is guaranteed. Thus, the purchaser of the IO who assumes a CPR of 12 percent can experience wide variance in total returns with swings in the prepayment rate.

The volatility in the timing and size of the IO is reflected in Figure 8A.9. This figure shows that the price volatility of either the IO or the PO component will exceed the price volatility of the whole mortgage. The relatively greater price sensitivity of the IO, combined with its positive price–interest rate relationship, makes it useful for hedging. For example, assume that a 9 percent mortgage pool is priced at par (the points of intersection in Figure 8A.9) and has a 6 percent CPR. Now if interest rates rise 2 percent, causing a decline in CPR to 4 percent, the price of the pool decreases to approximately 88.3 percent of par. If, alternatively, interest rates fall 2 percent (accompanied by an increase in the assumed CPR to 21 percent), the pool's price increases to 106.2 percent of par. In contrast, the IO portion of the mortgage undergoes a much wider swing in price. If, for example, the IO strip is priced at 54.5, given a 6 percent CPR assumption, it may increase in price to 60.1, or by 10.7 percent with a 2 percent rise in rates. If rates decline 2 percent, on the other hand, the IO's price will decrease to 28.8, or by 47 percent. Note that the price of the mortgage is the sum of the prices of its IO and PO components.

The performance of the IO strip as a hedge vehicle improves with the price volatility of the instrument. For instance, Figure 8A.9 contrasts the price volatility of an IO strip from a pool of 11 percent mortgages with the volatility of an IO strip from a 9 percent pool.

As interest rates increase, the prepayment speeds

of the 11 percent mortgages will decrease more rapidly from much higher levels. This results in greater price appreciation on the 11 percent IO strip. Conversely, as interest rates fall, the prepayment speed on the 11 percent collateral will pick up much faster, thereby depressing the IO's price very quickly.

IO and PO strips clearly have the potential for price depreciation and negative holding period returns. Investors must analyze the effect of prepayment risk by simulating the impact of varying prepayment assumptions on the mortgage collateral supporting the payments of interest or principal.

The hedging character of IO strips may not be as attractive as investors might assume. If interest rates decline even for a short period of time, prepayments will occur and will permanently deplete the basis of future interest payments. Even if interest rates rise later, reducing prepayment rates, earlier high rates of principal reduction will reduce future interest payments.

SMALL BUSINESS ADMINISTRATION LOAN POOLS

In addition to MBS, bank portfolio managers have access to securities backed by Small Business Administration (SBA) guaranteed loan pools. These pools are backed by the full faith and credit of the U.S. government. They vary in stated maturity from 5 to 25 years. Prepayments on the pools are subject to significant change. Rates on pools are adjusted to a published prime rate at a spread ranging from −100 to +200 basis points. Table 8A.5 lists some typical SBA-pool-backed security offerings.

DEBT SECURITIES MUTUAL FUNDS

Another, less commonly used investment vehicle for banks' investment portfolios is debt securities

TABLE 8A.5   Typical SBA Loan Pool Offerings

Quarterly Adjustable	Price	CPR (%)	Yield	Average Life (years)	Maturity (years)
Prime + 0.875	106.75	6%	8.34%	9.2	20
Prime + 0.875	104.75	6	8.01	5.3	10
Prime + 0.875	103.50	6	7.96	2.9	5
Prime − 0.125	103.00	6	7.95	9.8	22
Prime − 0.125	102.75	6	7.87	6.1	15

mutual funds. These funds are typically open-end mutual funds that purchase and manage a portfolio of debt securities funded by a continual sale of shares to investors. In addition, such mutual funds offer immediate redemption of shares on demand. A mutual fund serves as a conduit. It pays no taxes on the interest and capital gains flowing through to its investors. Investors benefit from mutual fund holdings because of the funds' diversification and professional management of a portfolio of debt securities. Mutual fund shares simply reflect the risk and return characteristics of the securities they hold in their portfolios. Mutual funds comprising intermediate-term debt securities, for example, typically produce yields and exposure to interest rate risk commensurate with an intermediate position on the yield curve.

Mutual funds that invest in longer-term debt instruments, such as MBS, similarly exhibit the risks of a portfolio of such securities. When managed successfully, mutual funds have the potential to deliver a more consistent flow of income with less variance of principal than can be achieved by direct investment. On the other hand, some debt securities mutual funds may target high returns and may adopt strategies to lengthen maturities and purchase premium-priced securities that may increase the volatility of their share values. Finally, the size of the fund allows fine tuning and some economies of scale that are not available to the smaller portfolios of individual institutions.

CHAPTER 9

Managing Bank Capital

Capital is the foremost financial requirement for chartering a bank. Equally important, a sufficient amount of it must be present on a bank's balance sheet in order for the bank to continue ongoing operations. The amount of a bank's capital puts a limit on the losses it can bear.

Thus, capital plays an all-important role in both starting a bank and ensuring its survival. The subject of capital is a focal point in the banking industry. Directors and managers of banks, customers, and regulatory authorities are all concerned about banks' ability to attract and maintain adequate capital. Bank capital management has become as much a matter of legal requirement in the public interest as it is a matter of management's discretion. The crucial legal requirements include recent capital rules that determine capital requirements according to the risk of each bank's activities as well as explicit capital ratio requirements mandated in the Federal Deposit Insurance Improvement Act of 1991. As a result, when capital is concerned, bank management must play by a complicated set of public rules.

This chapter treats the difficult question of how bank managers define ''adequate capital'' compared to how regulators define it. It also analyzes the factors that determine a bank's internal or sustainable growth. Finally, the chapter evaluates the various forms, old and new, of capital that can be raised externally by a commercial bank and introduces capital management techniques to utilize capital more effectively.

DETERMINING CAPITAL ADEQUACY

How much capital is appropriate for an individual bank? Three primary factors affect the appropriate amount of capital for an individual bank: (1) the functions of bank capital, (2) the advantages of leverage to owners, and (3) capital adequacy as measured by regulators.

Functions of Bank Capital

The first factor is the most difficult to quantify: how much capital is needed to fulfill the functions capital is supposed to perform? The primary function of bank capital is to support or absorb risk. Losses are absorbed by capital. From the viewpoint of bank creditors such as holders of banks' long-term bonds and providers of federal funds and other short-term creditors from the money markets, capital protects them from loss. Banks that operate at higher levels of risk, for example, those that conduct aggressive lending programs, should have more capital than low-risk institutions. If risk-averse creditors perceive that a bank has insufficient capital for the degree of risk it takes, they will avoid lending to the bank. To remain creditworthy, therefore, banks must be sure that their capital at least matches the risks they take.

The functions of a bank's capital are similar to its function in a nonfinancial corporation.

EXAMPLE In Table 9.1, the ABC Manufacturing Company finances roughly one-half of its assets in the form of debt and one-half in equity capital. Equity capital assists ABC Manufacturing in several ways: it provides a substantial proportion of the funds used to finance the firm's assets, it serves as a cushion or a potential loss absorber to satisfy creditors as to the safety of lending to ABC, and it indicates that ABC may be an attractive equity investment as well. Furthermore, it assures ABC's customers and suppliers that the firm is sound, able to weather business downturns, and most likely will continue operations without the imminent threat of bankruptcy.

EXAMPLE The balance sheet of XYZ Commercial Bank in Table 9.1 consists of more short-term assets than ABC Corporation. As a result, XYZ Bank attracts considerably more funds from short-term creditors such as depositors and money market lenders. The

TABLE 9.1 Illustration of the Functions of Capital

ABC Manufacturing Company			
Assets		**Liabilities**	
Cash	$ 50	Current liabilities	$ 300
Accounts receivable	300	Long-term debts	200
Inventory	200		
Plant and equipment	450	Equity capital	500
	$1,000		$1,000

XYZ Commercial Bank			
Assets		**Liabilities**	
Cash	$ 100	Current liabilities	$ 700
Short-term loans and investments	600	Long-term liabilities	220
Long-term loans and investments	260		
Facilities and equipment	40	Equity capital	80
	$1,000		$1,000

relative amount of capital for XYZ Bank is considerably lower than ABC Manufacturing's capital. However, the primary functions—to encourage depositors, other creditors, and potential shareholders; to improve confidence among customers and suppliers; and to finance a portion of assets—are roughly the same.

A special feature of banks is that, unlike manufacturing firms like ABC, the providers of a large share of their funds are insured by a federal agency, the Federal Deposit Insurance Corporation. At times, such as happened during the late 1980s, some banks do not have sufficient private capital on their books to protect against losses to creditors. When this occurs, the Federal Reserve and the FDIC hold off closing insolvent institutions, in effect providing *de facto* capital to cover insured depositors. At times when the FDIC believes the loss of uninsured creditors' confidence might jeopardize a bank's future, it protects uninsured depositors and creditors as well. In cases of actual failure, the FDIC does not always pass along losses to uninsured creditors. Thus, in the past, banks have been supported by ''public capital''—deferring the closure of insolvent institutions and, when they do close them, paying off uninsured creditors with insurance funds.

Thus, the notion that bank capital protects uninsured depositors in the event of insolvency and liquidation contains an element of truth but may overstate the case. Capital adequacy in the sense of balance sheet net asset values is just one measure of a bank's soundness, and a static one at that. Increasingly, regulators recognize that the quality of a bank's earnings and the bank's management systems for producing and protecting its future earnings is a more dynamic measure. You can easily become highly abstract in discussing what capital is. One might reasonably assert that markets served and customer bases cultivated over years constitute one of the most fundamental elements of bank capital.

Still, regulators and other stakeholders are conditioned to referring to balance sheet capital. One secondary reason for this is that regulators have used capital to restrain unjustified expansion of bank assets. Regulatory capital requirements may prevent a bank from growing beyond the ability of management to manage. In turn, this may improve the quality of the bank's assets, control the bank's ability to leverage its growth, and lead to stronger bank earnings on assets. Indeed, capital requirements have been used to prevent unjustified expansion in several recent bank holding company decisions. One warning is that to rely solely, or even primarily, on bank capital requirements to achieve all of these tasks does not address all of the issues.

The Need for Leverage to Improve the Returns to Owners

The second of the three primary factors affecting the appropriate amount of capital for an individual bank is the need for financial leverage to increase returns for the bank's owners. Tables 9.1 and 9.2 illustrate the importance of financial leverage. The ABC Manufacturing Company was 50 percent equity financed, which meant that the firm had a leverage multiplier of 2 times. A 7 percent after tax return on assets by ABC, approximately the average return on assets for manufacturing companies in 1998, translates into a 14 percent return on equity for ABC Manufacturing.

How can XYZ Commercial Bank, which earns only 1.1 percent on its assets (the average for U.S. banks in 1997 was over 1.2 percent), satisfy its owners and still attract additional equity investment? To do so, XYZ Bank requires significantly more leverage, which means fewer assets financed by equity and a higher leverage multiplier, in order to compete with ABC Manufacturing for equity in the financial markets. In Table 9.2 we

TABLE 9.2   Effects of Financial Leverage on Returns on Equity

	ABC Manufacturing Company[a]	XYZ Commercial Bank[a]	Typical Small Bank[b]	Typical Large Bank[b]
Assets	$1,000	$1,000	—	—
Equity	500	70	—	—
Net income	70	11	—	—
Equity-to-assets ratio	50.0%	8.0%	9.4%	7.3%
Return on assets	7.0%	1.1%	1.3%	1.0%
Leverage multiplier	2.0×	12.5×	10.7×	13.7×
Return on equity	14.0%	13.8%	13.9%	13.7%

[a] From Table 9.1.

[b] Estimated from the Quarterly Banking Profile (Washington, D.C.: FDIC, 1997).

assume that 8 percent of XYZ Bank's assets are financed by equity, about the average for banks in 1997. The resulting leverage multiplier of 12.50 times translates into a competitive return on equity of 13.8 percent.

This example indicates that in order to attract and keep owners, commercial banks must, and in the real world do, have the financial leverage resulting from low levels of equity in relation to assets. Thus, particularly from the owners' point of view, the appropriate amount of equity capital is an amount that is small enough to produce at least an adequate return on equity capital and yet to have enough to absorb risk. Three factors keep bank owners from using excessive financial leverage to increase their bank's return on capital.

First, market constraints keep creditors from lending excessive amounts to banks in relation to the money provided by bank owners. Free market economists believe that a bank's ability to attract both capital and noncapital funds should be the primary determinant of the bank's capital position. This position ignores important market imperfections, including realities such as a high level of government monitoring, inefficient exchange of information on small customers, and deposit insurance. These factors especially affect the ability of smaller banks to attract funds. Nevertheless, the market does limit the amounts of capital and noncapital funds available to most banks, and it may do so with reasonable efficiency for the larger ones.

Second, excessive leverage may be inconsistent with the goal of maximizing the market value of stock. For example, if a bank earning $2.00 per share can increase earnings per share to $2.10 by using additional leverage, it should increase leverage only if the market price per share increases. If, for example, the price-earnings multiple fell from 10 to 9 because of the greater risk, the bank would be wise to avoid the additional leverage because its stock price would fall from $20 to $18.90 per share despite the bank's larger earnings.

Third, regulatory capital rules force banks to keep amounts of capital that these rules deem adequate to protect depositors and the banking system. While regulatory constraints often are the most common factors that limit the use of financial leverage by commercial banks, capital resources have abounded in the relative economic calm of the late 1990s. When regulatory constraints are more binding, however, they may conflict with owners' desires for more leverage and higher returns. Regulators usually want more equity capital, whereas owners generally favor less equity capital.

The special characteristics of senior capital, debt, and preferred stock are also important. If a debt or preferred stock issue is accepted as capital by regulatory authorities, the issue increases the bank's capital position. However, the same debt or preferred issue also increases financial leverage and the resulting leverage multiplier of the bank. This dual advantage—increased safety *and* increased earnings to owners—encouraged the use of senior capital by banks in the 1960s and 1970s. Factors such as high interest rates, repayment and refinancing difficulties, and regulatory concerns weakened this dual advantage substantially in the 1980s; however, conditions in the early 2000s may again be favorable for senior capital.

The effect of bank size on the acceptable and permissible levels of financial leverage is also a concern. Table 9.2 shows the effect of financial leverage on a typical small bank and a typical large bank. The typical small bank usually has a higher return on assets and a higher percentage of equity to assets. More equity capital means a lower than average leverage multiplier, which lowers the higher return on assets to nearly an average or below-average return on equity. The typical large bank usually has a lower than average return on assets and a lower than average percentage of equity to assets, which produces a higher leverage multiplier, and a close to average return on equity because of the greater leverage.

Several factors can be cited as causes for differences in equity-to-assets ratios and leverage due to bank size. For example, large banks have greater management depth. The higher return on assets and the greater market concentration risk of many small banks lead one to the conclusion that they should be required to have a higher percentage of equity to assets than large banks. This larger capital base is not a major problem as long as small banks are able to earn an above-average return on assets. This is not always the case. In the 1980s, small banks' returns on assets declined, while the average return on assets for large banks improved slightly.

The FDIC figures for U.S. commercial banks with assets under $100 million are as follows:

Small Bank Leverage Effects

	1960	1970	1980	1990	1997
Return on assets	0.70%	0.89%	1.15%	0.70%	1.25%
Leverage multiplier (assets/equity)	13.3×	13.5×	12.7×	11.4×	9.1×
Return on equity	9.3%	12.0%	14.6%	8.0%	11.4%

The capital for large banks, with over $10 billion in assets, varied greatly. As late as 1960, large banks had more capital in relation to assets than average banks. The FDIC figures are as follows:

Large Bank Leverage Effects

	1960	1970	1980	1990	1997
Return on assets	0.95%	0.69%	0.52%	0.39%	1.18%
Leverage multiplier (assets/equity)	11.2×	18.2×	27.8×	19.0×	14.5×
Return on equity	10.7%	12.6%	14.6%	7.4%	17.2%

The reciprocal of the leverage ratio, the ratio of equity capital to assets, had fallen from 9.0 percent in 1960 to 3.6 percent in 1980 but had climbed back to 7.8 percent in 1997. One feasible explanation of the low equity-to-assets ratios of large banks in the 1980s and early 1990s is that these banks use arbitrage more extensively than most small banks. An extreme example would be a large bank that purchases and sells large amounts of federal funds daily, often with correspondent banks, at a very low spread between the bid (purchase) and asked (sale) prices. Or a large bank could purchase some type of deposits that it covers with similar maturity assets at a small margin. Small margins on arbitrages are usually justifiable only if little or no additional capital is needed. Such arbitrage transactions tend to build up a large bank's asset size, reduce its return on assets, and reduce its ratio of equity capital to assets. As regulators increased the capital requirements on large banks in the 1980s, these banks responded by reducing low-margin arbitrages, using securitization, and taking as many transactions as possible off the balance sheet. Return on assets and the ratio of equity to assets improved markedly, but return on equity improved less because of the lower leverage multiplier.

By the mid-1990s, banks faced a different capital problem. Helped by much higher earnings, bank equity-to-asset ratios were rising sharply. Most banks exceeded regulatory requirements by a substantial margin, but the resulting lower leverage multipliers (assets/ equity) meant lower returns on equity. The problem of low capital in the late 1980s rapidly changed to a problem of too much capital from the point of view of the reduced leveraging of the return on equity.

Regulatory Capital Adequacy Criteria and Concerns

The third factor affecting the appropriate amount of capital for an individual bank is the amount of capital a bank's regulators believe is adequate. Bank regulators are responsible for protecting depositors' funds and the safety of the banking system. Although other factors such as liquidity and interest sensitivity are as important, if not more important, in achieving such objectives, capital adequacy has been a primary concern of regulators for many years.

Federal and state laws prescribe the minimum amount of capital required for the organization of a new bank. The minimum is usually related to the population of the bank's locality. In recent years, as a matter of practical policy, supervisory authorities have usually required new banks to start with more than the legal minimum amount of capital.

Both federal and state laws also have minimum capital requirements for the establishment of branches (where permitted). These legal requirements have little real significance for banking today. They were enacted at a time when banks generally were much smaller. They have not been revised upward.

With respect to member banks of the Federal Reserve System, the basis for determining capital adequacy is detailed in Section 9 of the Federal Reserve Act and in Regulation H of the Board of Governors of the Federal Reserve. The regulation requires that the net capital and surplus of a member bank shall be adequate in relation to the character and condition of its assets and to its deposit liabilities and other corporate responsibilities. The regulation leaves the exact nature of the relationship between capital adequacy and the character and condition of the bank to the judgment of the responsible regulatory authority.

In late 1981, the three federal regulatory bodies announced new measures for evaluating capital adequacy. The FDIC stated that equity capital of 6.0 percent or more of total assets is acceptable for FDIC member banks of all sizes. Banks in a strong financial position might fall between 6.0 and 5.0 percent of equity to total assets, whereas any bank below 5.0 percent would be considered undercapitalized. Equity capital consisted of the total of all common stock accounts, 100 percent of equity reserves, a reserve for loan losses, noncallable preferred stock, and debt that must be converted into common stock less 100 percent of doubtful loans and 50 percent of classified loans.

The comptroller and the Federal Reserve jointly announced a slightly different new method for measuring capital adequacy, stating that most banks' total capital must relate to their total assets as a specified percentage (generally between 6 and 7 percent), depending on the bank's size and financial strength. Total capital consisted of primary capital plus secondary capital. Primary capital was the same as the FDIC's equity capital. Secondary capital included callable preferred, convertible (nonmandatory) debt, and subordinated debt. Debt was reduced 20 percent in value for each year between five years from maturity and its maturity date. Total secondary debt could not be more than 50 percent of primary debt.

In 1985, the three bank regulatory agencies finally agreed to similar capital adequacy guidelines. Banks and bank holding companies of all sizes were supposed to have primary capital of at least 5.5 percent of adjusted total assets and primary and secondary capital of at least 6 percent of total assets. Although a few minor differences still existed, this was the first time banks and holding companies had achieved a reasonable understanding of all regulators' definitions of adequate capital.

The history of capital regulation is long and arduous. For the most part, banking regulators vacillated somewhere between imposing rigidly defined accounting measures and applying liberal standards that considered capital adequacy uniquely for each institution according to its risk exposure and other circumstances. Starting in the mid-1980s, bank regulators became concerned with at least three conditions. First, the capital-to-assets ratios used did not differentiate banks with high-risk assets and those with low risk. In theory, a capital ratio standard encouraged banks to take higher risks because capital requirements were the same for Treasury bills as they were for high-risk consumer loans. Second, some banks began to use off-balance sheet items extensively—derivative instruments, commitments, letters of credit, and so forth—to improve both return on assets without impacting capital-to-assets ratios. Risk in off-balance sheet activity was ignored in capital adequacy standards. Third, U.S. banks appeared to be at a competitive disadvantage to foreign banks because of the higher capital requirements imposed on most U.S. banks.

In January 1987, these and similar concerns caused the three U.S. federal regulatory agencies, in conjunction with the Bank of England, to release for public comment a proposed risk-based capital adequacy framework. In 1988, the Bank for International Settlement, consisting of bank regulators in the United States and England and bank regulatory agencies in 10 other developed, free-world countries, adopted reasonably similar risk-based capital adequacy frameworks.

Under the basic framework approved in the United States, a weighted average measure of total assets is calculated, with the weights corresponding to four different categories of assets grouped according to their risk. The key measure of capital adequacy became a risk-asset ratio calculated as follows:

$$\text{Risk-asset ratio} = \frac{\text{Qualified capital}}{\text{Weighted risk-based assets}}$$

TABLE 9.3   Summary of Risk Weights and Major Risk Categories for Risk-Adjusted Capital Requirements

Risk Category	Weight	General Description
On-balance sheet items		
No risk	0%	Vault cash and balances held with the central bank, domestic national government-guaranteed export loans, gold, and direct claims on the U.S. Treasury and U.S. government agencies
Low risk	20%	Cash items in the process of collection, short-term claims on U.S. depository institutions and foreign banks, general obligation municipal bonds or claims so guaranteed by U.S. government-sponsored agencies, all claims (including repurchase agreements) fully collateralized by 0% and 20% risk assets, and other low-credit-risk claims
Moderate risk	50%	One- to four-family residential mortgages, credit equivalents of foreign exchange and interest rate contracts, municipal revenue securities, and other securities in which the government is a shareholder or contributing member
Standard risk	100%	Long-term claims on U.S. depository institutions and foreign banks, securities issues by foreign governments, fixed assets and all other assets, such as assets typically found in bank loan portfolios
Off-balance sheet items		
	0%	Unused portion of loan commitments with less than one year original maturity and any unconditionally cancellable loan for which a separate credit decision is made with each draw
	20%	Commercial letters of credit and other self-liquidating, trade-related contingencies
	50%	Transaction-related contingencies such as a letter of credit backing nonfinancial performance, unused loan commitments with greater than one year original maturity, and revolving underwriting facilities, note issuance facilities, and so on
	100%	Direct credit substitutes, standby letters of credit, and assets sold with recourse

SOURCE: Summarized from regulators' requirements.

where the weighted-risk-asset base is the sum of four categories of on-balance sheet risk assets, as shown in Table 9.3, weighted by the appropriate percentage (0, 20, 50, or 100 percent) plus the off-balance sheet items weighted by the appropriate percentage (0, 20, 50, or 100 percent). Table 9.4 describes eligible capital and lists the minimum guideline ratios effective at the start of 1998.

Table 9.5 presents a simple example comparing conventional versus risk-adjusted capital ratios. Requirements imposed on individual banks are also affected by on-site examinations of banks' quality and diversity of assets, liquidity, earnings level and stability, management control of risk, and other factors. Thus, the risk-based approach to capital adequacy attempts to link capitalization to bank exposure to risk, with emphasis on loan risk in particular and probability of default in general.

TABLE 9.4   Risk-Based Capital—Types, Ratios, and Minimum Guidelines

A. Eligible Capital
  1. Core (Tier I)
      a. Common tangible equity
      b. Perpetual preferred stock and qualified, mandatory convertible debt up to 25%
      c. Minority interest in equity of consolidated subsidiaries
  2. Total (Tier II—limited to 100% of Tier I)
      a. Nonspecific loan loss reserve up to 1.25% of risk-adjusted assets (RAA)
      b. Perceptual preferred stock not included in Tier I
      c. Mandatory convertible debt not included in Tier I
      d. Long-term subordinated debt—limited to 50% of Tier I and a phased-out, straight-line basis in the last five years of life
      e. Limited-life preferred stock—included with and treated like long-term subordinated debt

B. Risk-Based Capital Ratios

$$\text{Tier I ratio} = \frac{\text{Core capital}}{\text{Risk-adjusted assets}}$$

$$\text{Tier II ratio} = \frac{\text{Total capital}}{\text{Risk-adjusted assets}}$$

C. Minimum Guidelines Effective 12/31/98
Minimum Ratios

Tier I	4.0%
Tier I & II	8.0
Shareholders' equity/RAA	4.0

TABLE 9.5   Comparison of Conventional versus Risk-Adjusted Capital Ratios

Asset Category	Amount	Weight	Risk-Weighted Amount
No risk	$ 10,000,000	0%	$ 0
Low risk	30,000,000	20%	6,000,000
Moderate risk	30,000,000	50%	15,000,000
Standard risk	60,000,000	100%	60,000,000
Off-balance sheet items[a]	(20,000,000)	100%[a]	20,000,000
Total assets[a]	$130,000,000		
Risk-weighted assets			$101,000,000

    Assuming bank had $8,000,000 in primary capital:
      Primary capital to total assets: 8,000,000/130,000,000 = 6.15%
      Primary capital to risk-adjusted assets: 8,000,000/101,000,000 = 7.92%

[a] Off-balance sheet items are not part of the bank's total assets in the traditional capital-to-asset ratio calculation. It is assumed that the off-balance sheet items of this bank were in the 100% weighting category.

There are several concerns about risk-weighted capital requirements. One concern is the initially exclusive focus on credit risk and the failure to address interest rate risk and liquidity risk. For example, the same capital is required for an asset with a 20-year maturity as for a 20-day asset, perhaps issued by the same borrower. In addition, banks may adopt strategies—for example, selling mortgages and buying mortgage-backed securities—that reduce risk-weighted capital requirements without a seemingly significant reduction in overall risk. Finally, a bank with only long-term GNMA securities, an asset with large prepayment option risk, would have no risk-weighted capital requirements.

In addition to the risk-weighted capital requirements, banks must observe a minimum 4 percent leverage ratio of core (Tier I) capital to tangible assets. Equity is net of intangible assets such as accounting goodwill. Banks with significant interest rate risk are required to have capital above the minimum risk-weighted requirements. The now-defunct Office of Thrift Supervision established interest-rate-risk-related capital requirements in early 1991, and commercial bank regulators followed suit.

A major capital rule was passed in 1991 as part of the wide-ranging Federal Deposit Insurance Corporation Improvement Act. Designated as the ''prompt intervention'' rule, it specified sanctions on the activities of banks that fell short of the capital adequacy rules. A key purpose of the prompt intervention regulation was to prevent regulators from using their discretion to keep banks open even after they had become insolvent. Such practices in the late 1980s and early 1990s resulted in burgeoning losses as dying institutions were permitted to continue hemorrhaging losses. Banks with (1) over 10 percent Tier I and Tier II capital to risk-weighted assets, (2) over 6 percent Tier I capital to risk-weighted assets, and (3) over 5 percent equity capital to total assets would be classified as well capitalized and would need little if any regulatory permission for activities such as acquisitions, opening new branches, and so on. Banks with (1) under 4 percent Tier I and Tier II capital to risk-weighted assets, (2) under 2 percent Tier I capital to risk-weighted assets, or (3) under 2 percent equity capital to total assets would be classified as critically undercapitalized and would have 90 days to remedy their capital deficiency. If the capital deficiency is not remedied, according to law the bank must be closed. Banks falling between these two extremes will be subject to greater and greater regulatory scrutiny when these three capital ratios decline. Table 9.6 illustrates the requirements for all five categories.

Ironically, the emergence of highly specific capital rules coincided with substantial improvements in the economic environment that have made most concerns about capital moot. After a period in 1990 when over 1,000 banks would not have met the prompt intervention standards of well- and adequately capitalized, when the rule went into effect in December 1992 fewer than 100 banks were in the lowest capital category. That number had fallen to less than 20 by 1998. Indeed, in the late 1990s, the problem most banks face is too much capital (a low leverage multiplier) rather than too little capital. Furthermore, Figure 9.1 shows that equity capital has risen relative to total assets throughout the 1990s. Slower asset growth relative to retained earnings growth has been a major cause of this trend.

MANAGING CAPITAL AND LINES OF BUSINESS

You have to be careful about becoming too focused on regulatory requirements for capital. Banks must adhere to these standards to obey administrative laws. However, regulatory adherence is only the beginning of capital management. The crucial responsibility of man-

TABLE 9.6   Bank Classifications According to Capital Ratios under Prompt Corrective Action (FDIC Improvement Act of 1991)

Category	Risk-Based Capital		Leverage Tier I/ Assets
	Tiers I and II	Tier I	
1. Well capitalized: Significantly exceeds required capital standards. *Restrictions:* None.	>10%	>6%	>5%
2. Adequately capitalized: Meets minimum standards. *Restrictions:* Cannot underwrite insurance where state law permits. Requires approval of FDIC to accept brokered funds.	>8%	>4%	>4%
3. Undercapitalized: Fails to meet minimum standards. *Restrictions:* As in 2 above and close monitoring by regulatory agency; capital restoration plan; asset growth restricted; needs approval for acquisitions, branching, new activities.	<8%	<4%	<4%
4. Significantly undercapitalized: Significantly below required minimum standard. *Restrictions:* As in 3 above and must sell new stock to recapitalize; restrictions on transactions with affiliates, as well as on interest paid on deposits and management compensation; must divest troubled affiliates.	<6%	<3%	<3%
5. Critically undercapitalized: Less than 2% leverage capital ratio. *Restrictions:* As in 4 above and prohibition of interest payments on subordinated debt. Placed in receivership or conservatorship within 90 days.			<2%

agement is to utilize the financial institution's capital as effectively as possible. Capital is the bank's ultimate scarce resource. Without it, business cannot go on. Poorly utilized, capital becomes redundant, at best, and barren, at worst, and fails to serve its owner. In a relatively free enterprise system, investors "vote with their feet." If their investments are underserved in one capacity, figuratively they will walk out by selling and reinvesting where their capital will be better served.

We will discuss *line of business* reporting systems used by progressive banks to answer the following questions about each of its activities:

- Which activities are viable?
- Which activities need correction or improvement?
- Which activities deserve greater emphasis and material support in the future?
- Which activities should be eliminated?

Capital Allocation

As we will see, consistent with this chapter's focus on capital, to make these determinations banks assign their capital to absorb the risk in each of their activities. In doing so,

FIGURE 9.1   Aggregate Capitalization Increases

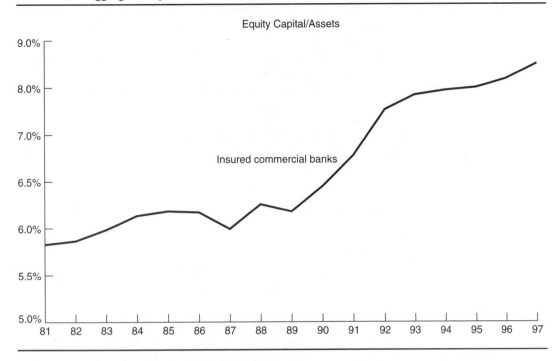

Equity Capital/Assets

they explicitly acknowledge and try to quantify the risk in terms of the capital required to absorb it. We will use the example of BankAmerica Corporation to demonstrate the broad implications of managing capital in this way.

EXAMPLE   At the end of 1996, BankAmerica Corporation held total assets of $251 billion and common equity of $18 billion. Table 9.7 presents a breakdown of Bank of America's business into five operating sectors or *lines of business:* Consumer banking, U.S. commer-

TABLE 9.7   BankAmerica Corporation Line of Business Capital, Income, and ROE

	($Billions)		
Line of Business	Common Equity	Net Income	Return on Equity
Consumer banking	7.3	1.23	16.9%
U.S. commercial and international	5.1	0.98	19.2%
Middle market	1.5	0.33	21.5%
Commercial real estate	0.7	0.24	34.3%
Wealth management	0.5	0.08	17.3%
Other, not allocated	2.9	−0.14	−5.1%
Total corporate	$18.0	$2.72	16.00%

cial and international banking, middle market banking, commercial real estate, and wealth management. The ''other'' category listed represents residual assets not associated with any of the five business lines. BankAmerica credits net income to each of these lines. Furthermore, as reported in Table 9.7, the firm has allocated its capital across these lines of business on a risk-adjusted basis. Finally, as a measure of productivity, the firm calculates return on equity for each line of business. Assuming BankAmerica Corporation is able to make the necessary accounting allocations, we see that the result of this reporting system gives unmistakable evidence of where its capital is most productive and where it is less so.

As you might have concluded, a complete line of business reporting system requires specialized accounting systems to determine factors underlying the report. For each line, the systems must account for:

a. Capital required

b. Revenues generated

c. Funds used

d. Overhead consumed

Capital Required

An accounting system must determine how to allocate capital to each division. While this seems a horrendous task, there are guidelines that facilitate it. Capital is assigned to a business line in two parts. These account for losses that are expected and losses that are unexpected. Of these two, banks already are accustomed to dealing with expected losses They simply assign provisions for loan losses based on historical experience and known characteristics of the assets in the particular business. For example, BankAmerica's Consumer Division can estimate reliably how many customers will fail to pay and periodically assign loss reserves accordingly.

Dealing with unexpected losses is more abstract because the institution must draw upon perceptions of risk and associated losses they may never have experienced. Here, managers of the business line must develop scenarios to conjure events that pose special losses. For example, perhaps the Consumer Division manages the bank's operations center, processing many millions of electronic and paper data daily. What are the risks and losses that might follow a fire or a hurricane that shuts down the center for a period of time? Scenario analysis must include probabilistic analysis: for example, at what level of probability of an operations center disaster should capital be assigned? Is a one chance in 1,000—or in 10,000—that such a disaster will strike in any given year sufficient to assign capital? Whatever the outcome of such an analysis, the bank must decide if and how much capital it should assign for such events.

For another example, how should the Consumer banking line assign capital to defaults on its credit card loan portfolio? Expected losses—say 3 percent of outstanding loans—are covered by loss reserves based on good knowledge of default statistics. However, what is the probability of a national economic scenario that might drive defaults to bank-threatening levels, say 10 percent? The way such information is quantified is to set a probability limit on disaster scenarios. Bank managers use the language of probability in setting such limits—for example, ''a 3-sigma event.'' Sigma refers to the standard deviation in the normal probability distribution. A 3-sigma event has one chance in over

400 of occurring. A 10 percent credit card loss scenario might be viewed as a 3-sigma event, and capital would be assigned to this business accordingly.

Revenues Generated and Funds Used

Banks rely on well-developed *funds transfer pricing* systems to estimate the line of business revenues and costs of raising funds. You will do well to refer to the discussion on the *components of net interest margin* covered in Chapter 3. As we noted there, the analysis of revenues credited to lines of business and uses of funds by the lines is based on financial market tests of the profitability of an institution's yield on assets, cost of funds, and mismatch of asset and liability maturities. The financial market test is used to standardize maturities so that bank businesses that generate assets are charged for using funds at a rate tied to the asset's maturity.

Overhead Consumed

Finally, the lines of business are charged for their use of bank overhead including personnel, plant, furnishings, and so forth. While beyond the scope and interest of our present discussion, such systems consist of well-developed cost accounting methods for allocating the expenses of organizationally lower bank support units to the business line units.

Capital Management

It is instructive to compare the capital allocation decisions bank management makes with the capital adequacy rules set forth in administrative regulations.

EXAMPLE Table 9.8 presents capital data for two commercial banks, each with $10 billion in assets and $600 million in capital. These banks emphasize different product lines. Bank A has 30 percent of its assets in national commercial loans, 20 percent in home

TABLE 9.8   Capital Allocation Systems versus Risk-Based Capital Requirements

Balance Sheet	Bank A			Bank B		
	$Million	Risk-Based Capital	Management Allocation	$Million	Risk-Based Capital	Management Allocation
National loans	$ 3,000	300	90	$ 1,000	100	30
Home mortgages	2,000	100	60	2,000	100	60
Consumer loans	1,000	100	120	3,000	300	360
Other assets	4,000	240	240	4,000	240	240
Total	$10,000	740	510	$10,000	740	690
Deposits	8,000			8,000		
Borrowed funds	1,260			1,260		
Capital	740			740		
Total	$10,000			$10,000		

mortgages, and only 10 percent in consumer installment loans. Bank B has only 10 percent of its assets in national commercial loans, 20 percent in home mortgages, and 30 percent in consumer installment loans. Each bank has concluded, based on past and expected payment records, that national commercial loans and home mortgages require only 3 percent capital, while consumer installment loans require 12 percent capital. Both banks wish to meet the *well-capitalized* prompt intervention standards under FDICIA requiring 10 percent risk-based capital.

Under risk-based capital rules, to obtain a well-capitalized classification, both Banks A and B must hold $740 million in capital or somewhat in excess of what they judge to be the capital requirements of their businesses. Moreover, while the rules assign the same capital requirements, the banks would claim that their asset mixes differ in risk and, therefore, capital required to absorb the risk. Bank A has a decidedly lower asset risk profile but must hold the same capital as Bank B.

If banks believe they have a capital shortage or "excess" capital, they can take several types of management actions. These are summarized in Table 9.9. The first two options—slow or increase growth and decrease or increase riskiness of assets—are vital to the bank's financial and strategic plans, and capital management should be one of many factors determining such decisions. The third decision, increasing or decreasing internal generation, depends on the net income of the bank and how much it pays out in dividends. Since we assume the bank will earn the highest net income possible consistent with its risk parameters, dividend payout becomes the dominant capital management technique. We discuss factors affecting a bank's dividend policy in the following paragraphs. We have already discussed one side of the fourth and final factor—raising capital externally. However, the other side—repurchasing external capital—was used extensively in the late 1990s and will be evaluated after dividend policy.

The dominant motive in a bank's dividend policy decision should be to maximize the value of the stockholders' return, which, in turn, should benefit the bank. For the present investor to feel comfortable about his or her investment, a bank's dividend policy should be dependable, and the bank should make assurances that past dividend actions will be continued in the future. For the potential investor, a consistent dividend policy history is an important factor in evaluating the worth of the bank's stock. Probably the most important element in a bank's dividend policy is establishing a payout (dividends as a percentage of earnings) policy so that dividends will increase as earnings (hopefully)

TABLE 9.9 Potential Management Actions to Solve Capital Problem

Bank Has Capital Shortage	Bank Has "Excess" Capital

1. Slow growth of assets and liabilities
     a. sell fixed assets
     b. sell or securitize loans
	1. Increase growth of assets and liabilities
	     a. internal opportunities
	     b. acquisitions

2. Decrease risk mix of assets	2. Increase risk mix of assets

3. Increase internal generation
     a. increase net income
     b. decrease dividend payout
	3. Decrease internal generation
	     a. decrease net income (X)
	     b. increase dividend payout

4. Raise capital externally
     a. issue new stock
     b. sell notes or debentures
	4. Reduce external capital
	     a. repurchase stock
	     b. retire notes or debentures

increase. The level and pattern of a bank's dividends are also key elements on which investors rely to help determine the total return that can be expected from their investments and whether or not they will invest at all in a particular bank. If an investor is confident that he or she understands a bank's dividend policy, the investor may place a higher value on that bank's stock.

The level of cash dividends should be set so that the bank can maintain that level over various types of business and economic conditions. Should business or economic conditions be such that earnings and profits are squeezed temporarily, cash dividends should be at a point where the bank is capable of maintaining them for a reasonable period of time until conditions improve. On the other hand, in times of favorable business conditions, dividends should not necessarily be increased immediately. If conditions change and the increased level of dividends cannot be sustained, then a reduction in dividends will be necessary. Cutting dividends is a negative sign to investors and reflects a pessimistic view of the future by management. Management usually views an increase in dividends as expected prosperity; thus investors would anticipate the continuance of the higher dividend level. A good rule to follow, therefore, is that an increase in the dividend level should lag somewhat behind actual increases in earnings in order for management to be sure that it can maintain that level.

With regard to the dividend pattern, consistency is also desirable. Just as with the level of dividends, where fluctuation in the amount of the cash dividend paid is undesirable, the regularity with which this dividend is paid is also important. The income-oriented investor will usually prefer more frequent payments of cash dividends, such as quarterly or semiannually, as opposed to annually. Closer-spaced dividend payments also help increase the investor's confidence because the greater frequency of these payments will set up a definite pattern more rapidly.

In deciding on the level and pattern of dividends, management must consider several factors. These factors include fulfilling the investor's objectives, determining whether the bank has a shortage or excess of capital, the rate of return a bank can earn on its capital (as opposed to the rate that an individual could earn in an alternative situation), the bank's earnings stability, and the bank's plans for future growth. Dividend payouts for all insured commercial banks decreased slightly in the 1960s and 1970s, probably because of the large capital needs to finance growth and the relatively poor market for most bank stocks. In the 1980s, this trend was reversed. The increases in dividend payouts appeared to be the result of depressed earnings for many banks. However, some banks believed that higher dividend payouts would lead to higher stock market prices. The dividend increases that accompanied rising earnings for many banks in the late 1990s indicate that at least some bankers conclude that they have excess capital and that cash dividends paid by publicly held banks tend to have a positive effect on common stock prices.

The excess capital of many banks in the middle and late 1990s was further verified by the large number of stock repurchases in that period. For example, 23 of the 25 largest U.S. banks in 1996 used stock repurchase plans.

There are four repurchase vehicles. First are the *exchange offers* of cash or debt at a fixed price which shareholders can choose to accept. The difficulty of setting an appropriate price (with subsequent under- or overtendering) has discouraged many banks from using this vehicle. A second vehicle is the *dutch auction "self" tender* in which shareholders can offer any number of shares within a range of specified prices. The bank chooses which prices are acceptable and repurchases all offers within that price range. In the third method, *privately negotiated repurchases,* ''blocks'' of shares are repurchased directly from large shareholders or institutional investors on a negotiated basis. This method is not widely used because not all shareholders are treated equally, and there may be potential lawsuits. Fourth are purchases of the bank's shares on the open market. These *open market purchases* are the most used vehicles to repurchase shares. The repurchases are governed by SEC rules 10B-18, under which the bank announces its intention to repurchase a dollar amount of stock from time to time, through its market makers, at market prices.

Table 9.10 shows the result of any of these four vehicles for repurchasing shares. In the example we assumed the bank bought back $160 million of shares at their book value of $16 per share. The repurchase of stock increased return on equity, earnings per share, and book value per share. Furthermore, the repurchase probably enhanced the value of the remaining common shares because earnings per share are growing faster. Not surprisingly, many of the large, overcapitalized banks proudly announced stock repurchase plans each year in the mid 1990s.

Although stock repurchases are often a good capital management strategy, possible concerns should at least be considered. The first concern is the concept that you should sell stock when market prices are high and buy back stock when market prices are low. Assume in Table 9.10 that the bank bought back the shares at 200 percent of book value. Because fewer shares are bought back, the gains in earnings and book value are much less. Second, undisciplined stock repurchases could inflate stock prices to levels that could prove evanescent if, for whatever reason (economic downturn, regulator action) banks were obliged to back away. Third, stock repurchased today is gone if better opportunities—unique opportunities, acquisitions, or buying back the bank's stock at lower prices—occur in the future.

For banks with excess capital a reasonable rule might be: Buy back your stock if

TABLE 9.10   Example of a Stock Repurchase (in millions of dollars)

Bank Without Repurchase
(shares outstanding: 100 million)

	Assets	Equity	Income	Dividends	ROE	Equity/Assets	Earnings per Share	Book Value per Share
1997	$20,000	$1,600	$200	$80	12.50%	8.00%	$2.00	$16.00
1998	21,500	1,720	215	86	12.50%	8.00%	2.15	17.20
1999	23,100	1,849	231	92	12.49%	8.00%	2.31	18.49

Assume repurchased 10 million shares @ $16.00 book value; total outlay of $160 million. Opportunity cost of $160 million projected at 10% (6.6% after taxes).

Pro Forma Impact of Repurchase
(shares outstanding: 90 million)

	Assets	Equity	Income	Dividends	ROE	Equity/Assets	Earnings per Share	Book Value per Share
1997	$19,840	$1,440	$198	$79	13.75%	7.26%	$2.20	$16.00
1998	21,340	1,559	213	85	13.66%	7.31%	2.37	17.32
1999	22,940	1,677	229	92	13.67%	7.31%[a]	2.54[b]	18.63[c]

[a] ROE is 9.45% higher with repurchase.

[b] Earnings per share is 9.96% higher with repurchase.

[c] Book value per share is 0.76% higher with repurchase.

you believe (1) there is a high probability that market price will continue to increase; (2) no acquisition opportunities are available at reasonable prices (say for less than 15 times earnings); and (3) spreads of better than 50 basis points are not available in the capital markets. As long as everything stays the same and the bank's stock price never goes down, repurchasing the stock will prove to be the best alternative use of capital. If share prices fall or there are profitable investment (growth) opportunities in the future, stock re-purchases may be a poor use of today's excess capital.

SUSTAINABLE INTERNAL GROWTH

If retained earnings are sufficient to fill the bank's needs, they are usually the best form of bank equity capital to use. A general rule is that if a bank can finance all of its capital needs internally without hurting its owners or its stock price, it should do so. Retained earnings are not a free source of capital. (The cost of retained earnings includes the higher value of cash dividends received today versus those received in future years and possibly a lower stock price because of lower cash dividends.) However, they are generally less costly than selling new issues of common equity stock and are subject to direct management control.

The three variables that combine to determine how much of a bank's growth can be sustained through the retention of earnings are (1) the amount of capital the bank and its regulators determine to be adequate, (2) the earnings the bank is able to generate, and (3) the proportion of these earnings that is retained in the bank.

The relationship between the proportion of capital that is deemed to be adequate and how much growth can be financed internally is illustrated in Table 9.11. Retained earnings of $1 million would finance asset growth of $14.3 million (from $100 million to $114.3 million) if the bank determined that its present 7 percent capital-to-assets requirement were appropriate. In Example 2 of Table 9.11, the same $1 million would support $16.7 million in asset growth if its capital-to-assets requirement were maintained at 6 percent. The lower the capital requirement, the larger the amount of growth a given amount of retained earnings would finance. In Example 3 we show that if the capital-to-assets requirement fell from 7 to 6 percent during the year, $1 million of retained earnings would still finance $16.7 million of asset growth, but an additional $16.7 million of asset growth would be supported by the decline in the capital requirement. An increase in the capital required would, of course, reduce the total internally financed asset growth.

The second variable, the earnings a bank is able to generate, should have a direct effect on how much growth the bank is able to finance internally. If the bank used in Example 1 of Table 9.11 were able to earn enough to retain $1.1 million instead of $1 million during the year, the growth financed internally would be proportionately 10 percent, or $1.43 million, greater.

The third variable, the proportion of a bank's earnings that is retained, has a similar direct effect on how much growth the bank is able to finance internally. Assume that the bank in Table 9.11 had earned $1.5 million and paid cash dividends of $0.5 million. Reducing the dividend payout so that cash dividends would fall to $0.4 million would increase retained earnings to $1.1 million, and the growth financed internally would be proportionately greater.

Table 9.12 applies the formulas for calculating sustainable growth to an example bank situation. Equation (c) is the most common formula for calculating sustainable

TABLE 9.11   The Effects of Required Capital Levels of Internally Financed Growth (dollars in millions)

Example 1		
Start of year for bank with 7% capital-to-assets requirement:		
Assets 100	Deposits and borrowings	93
	Capital (7%)	7
End of year, same capital requirement, $1 retained earnings:		
Assets 114.3	Deposits and borrowings	106.3
	Capital (7%)	8
Example 2		
Start of year for bank with 6% capital-to-assets requirement:		
Assets 100	Deposits and borrowings	94
	Capital (6%)	6
End of year, same capital requirement, $1 retained earnings:		
Assets 116.7	Deposits and borrowings	109.7
	Capital (6%)	7
Example 3		
Start of year for bank with 7% capital-to-assets requirement:		
Assets 100	Deposits and borrowings	93
	Capital (7%)	7
End of year, required capital falls to 6%, $1 retained earnings:		
Assets 133.3	Deposits and borrowings	125.3
	Capital (6%)	8

growth. For the example bank, Equation (c) shows that its assets could grow 9.89 percent before its capital-to-assets ratio of 6.8 percent (a leverage multiplier of 14.71 times) would decline. The formulas can also be applied to solve for the required ROA to support a target annual asset growth rate or to calculate the cash dividend payout that will support a target annual asset growth. The example bank in Table 9.12 needed an ROA of 1.21 percent to support asset growth of 12 percent with a 6.8 percent equity capital ratio (equity capital to total assets) and a 40 percent payout. With an ROA of 1 percent and a 12 percent target asset growth rate, the example bank could pay out 28.57 percent of earnings without hurting its 6.8 percent equity capital ratio.

Finally, Equation (c) can be solved for the equity capital ratio that will result from a capital asset growth rate, an expected ROA, and a planned dividend payout ratio. In Table 9.12 the example bank's equity capital ratio would decline to 5.71 percent if the bank had an annual asset growth rate of 12 percent, an ROA of 1.02 percent, and a cash dividend payout of 40 percent.

TABLE 9.12 Calculating a Bank's Capacity for Asset Growth

Bank Situation

Average total assets	$500,000,000
Average equity capital	34,000,000
Expected net profit margin	8.50%
Expected yield on average total assets	12.00%
Expected return on average total assets	1.02%
Leverage multiplier	14.71×
Expected return on average equity capital	15.00%
Cash dividend payout percentage	40.00%

1. *The annual growth rate in assets that can be supported by internally generated equity capital* is called the sustainable growth rate. This rate can be determined by any one of the following four equations:

(a) $SG = \dfrac{(PM)(AY)(1 - D)}{EC/TA - (PM)(AY)(1 - D)}$

(b) $SG = \dfrac{(PM)(AY)(LM)(1 - D)}{1 - (PM)(AY)(LM)(1 - D)}$

(c) $SG = \dfrac{(ROA)(1 - D)}{EC/TA - (ROA)(1 - D)}$

(d) $SG = \dfrac{(ROE)(1 - D)}{1 - (ROE)(1 - D)}$

where

SG = sustainable growth rate, or the annual rate of increase in average total assets that can be supported by internally generated equity capital

PM = profit margin, or net income after taxes divided by total operating income

AY = asset yield, or total operating income divided by average total assets

D = percentage of after tax net income paid in cash dividends

EC = average equity capital

TA = average total assets

LM = leverage multiplier, or average total assets divided by average equity capital

ROA = return on average total assets, or net income after taxes divided by average total assets

ROE = return on average equity capital, or net income after taxes divided by average equity capital

Solving Equation (c):

$$SG = \dfrac{(0.0102)(1 - 0.40)}{0.068 - (0.0102)(1 - 0.40)}$$

$$= 9.89 \text{ percent}$$

TABLE 9.12   *(Continued)*

Proof (dollars in thousands)

Average total assets, next year	$500,000
	× 1.0989
	$549,450
Required average equity capital	$549,450
	× 0.068
	$ 37,363
Required increase in average equity capital	$37,363 − $ 34,000
	= $ 3,363
Projected net income after taxes	$549,450
	× 0.0102
	$ 5,604
Retained earnings	$ 5,604
	× 0.60
	$ 3,363

2. *The ROA should support the expected annual growth rate of average total assets.* If the expected annual growth rate of average total assets is 12 percent for this bank, the ROA required to support that growth is

$$\text{ROA} = \frac{(\text{EC/TA})(\text{SG})}{(1 + \text{SG})(1 - \text{D})}$$

$$= \frac{(0.068)(0.12)}{(1.12)(1 - 0.40)}$$

$$= 1.21 \text{ percent}$$

3. *The cash dividend payout percentage should support the expected annual growth rate of average total assets.* For this bank, with a desired ratio of equity capital to total assets of 6.8 percent, an expcted ROA of 1.02 percent, and a 12 percent expected annual growth rate of average total assets, the cash dividend payout percentage is

$$\text{D} = 1 - \left[\frac{(\text{EC/TA})(\text{SG})}{(\text{ROA})(1 + \text{SG})} \right]$$

$$= 1 - \left[\frac{(0.068)(0.12)}{(0.0102)(1.12)} \right]$$

$$= 28.57 \text{ percent}$$

4. *The equity capital ratio (EC/TA) should sustain the expected annual growth rate of average total assets.* To sustain an annual growth rate of 12 percent in average total assets, with an ROA of 1.02 percent and a cash dividend payout of 40 percent, the bank's equity capital ratio will decline to

$$\text{EC/TA} = \frac{(\text{ROA})(1 - \text{D})}{\text{SG}} + (\text{ROA})(1 - \text{D})$$

$$= \frac{(0.0102)(1 - 0.40)}{0.12} + (0.0102)(1 - 0.40)$$

$$= 5.71 \text{ percent}$$

A bank's target or planned growth can be compared with its internally supported growth resulting from its earnings, dividend payout, and capital requirements. Returns required for sustainable growth were generated for 7 and 6 percent capital-to-asset ratios in Table 9.13. For target capital to assets of 7 percent, if a bank earned 0.83 on its assets and paid out 60 percent of these earnings as dividends, it could sustain asset growth of 5 percent internally. Earnings of 0.85 percent on assets and a 25 percent payout would sustain growth of 10 percent. For a capital target of 6 percent, earnings of 0.84 on assets and a dividend payout of 35 percent would sustain growth of 10 percent.

Rapidly growing commercial banks with capital needs clearly exceeding the amount of earnings that can be retained face a complex policy decision. If the bank's management believes that dividends will not significantly affect the market price of the bank's stock, the preferable policy is to pay a modest cash dividend and use typically low-cost retained earnings to finance as much of the expansion as possible. On the other hand, if management believes that dividends will have an *appreciably* positive effect on the bank's stock price, the bank may gain from paying higher dividends and raising more of its needed equity capital by selling higher-priced common stock.

RAISING CAPITAL EXTERNALLY

Although raising capital externally has not been a major problem for most banks in the late 1990s, a few rapidly expanding banks have needed more capital than they were able to generate internally.

When a bank finds that it may need additional external capital, it must decide whether all of its capital should be common equity capital or whether senior securities (subordinated debt or preferred stock) should be used to fill some of its capital needs. Table 9.14 describes the principal forms banks can use to raise capital needs externally.

Should All Capital Be Common Equity?

The comptroller and the Federal Reserve appear to have conceded that, in spite of their objections to capital notes and long-term debentures, the availability of these forms adds needed flexibility to bank management. And although these regulators do not encourage the use of notes and debentures, they do accept such issues. First, such debt instruments add to the basic regulatory purpose of bank capital by providing additional protection for bank depositors and others who would be adversely affected by bank failure. Second, in some market situations a bank cannot sell new common equity because there are no potential buyers or situations in which existing bank stockholders would be severely penalized (generally because the common stock price is significantly below the book value) if regulators were to insist on an injection of new common equity funds.

Noncallable preferred stock and mandatory convertible debt are now accepted as Tier I capital by three federal regulatory authorities under the new risk-weighted capital rules. (The other forms of senior capital in Table 9.14 are Tier II capital.) The restraints against using preferred stock generally come from bank management, which notes that dividends on preferred stock are not tax deductible, as is interest on indebtedness. As a result, financial leverage is usually more favorable for debt issues than for preferred stock issues. Nevertheless, preferred stock should be considered if (1) the bank does not pay income taxes; (2) the bank cannot sell either debt or common stock at anything close to

TABLE 9.13 Return on Assets Required for Sustainable Growth Rates Without External Financing

	Example 1: Target Leverage (Growth %) of 14.28× or 7.00%						
Dividend Payout %	5.00	7.50	10.00	12.50	15.00	17.50	20.00
5.00	0.35	0.51	0.67	0.82	0.96	1.10	1.23
10.00	0.37	0.54	0.71	0.86	1.01	1.16	1.30
15.00	0.39	0.57	0.75	0.92	1.07	1.23	1.37
20.00	0.42	0.61	0.80	0.97	1.14	1.30	1.46
25.00	0.44	0.65	0.85	1.04	1.22	1.39	1.56
30.00	0.48	0.70	0.91	1.11	1.30	1.49	1.67
35.00	0.51	0.75	0.98	1.20	1.41	1.60	1.79
40.00	0.56	0.81	1.06	1.30	1.52	1.74	1.94
45.00	0.61	0.89	1.16	1.41	1.66	1.90	2.12
50.00	0.67	0.98	1.27	1.56	1.83	2.09	2.33
55.00	0.74	1.09	1.41	1.73	2.03	2.32	2.59
60.00	0.83	1.22	1.59	1.95	2.28	2.61	2.92
65.00	0.95	1.40	1.82	2.22	2.61	2.98	3.33
70.00	1.11	1.63	2.12	2.59	3.04	3.48	3.89
75.00	1.33	1.95	2.55	3.11	3.65	4.17	4.67
80.00	1.67	2.44	3.18	3.89	4.57	5.21	5.83
85.00	2.22	3.26	4.24	5.19	6.09	6.95	7.78
90.00	3.33	4.89	6.37	7.78	9.13	10.43	11.67
95.00	6.67	9.77	12.73	15.56	18.27	20.86	23.33

	Example 2: Target Leverage (Growth %) of 16.67× or 6.00%						
Dividend Payout %	5.00	7.50	10.00	12.50	15.00	17.50	20.00
5.00	0.30	0.44	0.57	0.70	0.82	0.94	1.05
10.00	0.32	0.47	0.61	0.74	0.87	0.99	1.11
15.00	0.34	0.49	0.64	0.78	0.92	1.05	1.18
20.00	0.36	0.52	0.68	0.83	0.98	1.12	1.25
25.00	0.38	0.56	0.73	0.89	1.14	1.19	1.33
30.00	0.41	0.60	0.78	0.95	1.12	1.28	1.43
35.00	0.44	0.64	0.84	1.03	1.20	1.37	1.54
40.00	0.48	0.70	0.91	1.11	1.30	1.49	1.67
45.00	0.52	0.76	0.99	1.21	1.42	1.62	1.82
50.00	0.57	0.84	1.09	1.33	1.56	1.79	2.00
55.00	0.63	0.93	1.21	1.48	1.74	1.99	2.22
60.00	0.71	1.05	1.36	1.67	1.96	2.23	2.50
65.00	0.82	1.20	1.56	1.90	2.24	2.55	2.86
70.00	0.95	1.40	1.82	2.22	2.61	2.98	3.33
75.00	1.14	1.67	2.18	2.67	3.13	3.57	4.00
80.00	1.43	2.09	2.73	3.33	3.91	4.47	5.00
85.00	1.90	2.79	3.64	4.44	5.22	5.96	6.67
90.00	2.86	4.19	5.45	6.67	7.82	8.93	10.00
95.00	5.71	8.37	10.91	13.33	15.65	17.87	20.00

TABLE 9.14 Types of Capital That Banks May Issue

Type	Description
Capital notes	Usually smaller-denomination subordinated debt at fixed rate(s) with original maturities of 7 to 15 years. Can be sold to bank customers (retail capital notes).
Capital debentures	Generally larger (in denomination and total size) subordinated debt at fixed rates and with original maturity of over 15 years. A few issues have no interest payment and are sold at a deep discount.
Convertible debt	Subordinated debt that is usually convertible at the option of the debt holder into common stock of the bank at a predetermined price. Interest is usually 10 to 20% below the rate on straight debt; conversion price is 15 to 25% above stock market prices. A few convertible issues have mandatory conversion.
Variable-rate debt	Subordinated debt on which the interest rate varies with some interest rate index.
Option-rate debt	Subordinated debt initially issued as variable-rate debt but convertible into fixed-rate debt at the option of the debt holder during at least some period of the life of the debt.
Leasing arrangements	Financial lease, sale, leasebacks, etc., most of which are capitalized and some of which qualify as capital in a manner similar to debt capital.
Preferred stock	Stock paying a fixed-rate (nondeductible for corporate income tax) dividend, with a claim on income and assets ahead of common stock.
Adjustable-rate preferred stock	Similar to preferred stock, but dividends have no fixed rate. Instead, dividends are adjusted according to some agreed-upon indicator. Includes preferreds with dividends repriced at some percent or basis difference from other yield indices, repriced every seven weeks through a dutch auction mechanism, or repriced based on some measure or facet of bank performance.
Convertible preferred stock	Preferred stock that is convertible at the option of the holder into common stock of the bank at a predetermined price. Issued at a lower rate and a higher conversion price than straight issues. Used for some acquisitions and mergers.
Common stock	Residual but unlimited claim on income and assets of bank; voting shares that elect board of directors who appoint management. Common stock may be issued; however, some new shares are sold through dividend reinvestment plans, employee stock option plans (ESOPs), and employee stock option trusts (ESOTs).

what it believes are reasonable prices; and (3) preferred stock rates, which can be fixed or variable, are now low because of the 70 percent corporate tax exclusion on dividends.

A bank should evaluate three factors when deciding whether all capital should be equity capital: (1) the availability of the various forms of external capital, (2) the need for flexibility in issuing capital in future years, and (3) the financial effects of the various forms of capital, such as leverage, immediate dilution, and earnings per share over longer periods.

The first two factors are dependent on the size of the bank. Most community banks will find that long-term debentures and preferred stock are not available to them because such securities are attractive only to institutional investors, which would not purchase these types of securities from banks that have less than $100 million in total assets. A market for some forms of senior capital—small-denomination capital notes, convertible debentures, and debt placed directly with a correspondent bank—may be available, however, to many community banks.

Some community banks have been successful in selling a moderate amount of capital notes in denominations as low as $500 to depositors or friends of the bank at a rate of interest somewhat higher than they pay on long-term savings certificates but below the general market rate for other debt securities. This approach can be an attractive method of raising some additional capital. Although the buyer's investment is difficult to justify in economic terms (except perhaps that earnings are more than those on savings certificates), experience has shown that buyers can sometimes be found. Even so, it is unlikely that the typical community bank can rely on its ability to sell notes whenever it chooses, and meeting maturities on notes already sold could increase the bank's need for common equity at some future date.

The option to sell convertible debentures is also available to some community banks. These debentures typically are sold locally in small denominations to the bank's friends, customers, and stockholders—the same group that would also buy additional common stock in the bank. In addition, direct placement of senior debt with a correspondent bank appears to be an effective and relatively reliable channel for community banks. Bank regulatory authorities have criticized this source, however, because it simply circulates funds within the banking system and fails to add capital strength to the system.

As a bank becomes larger, a separate market develops for its senior securities. Some institutional investors do not buy common stock from banks but instead consider the bank's capital notes or debentures as an investment. A market for the preferred stock of large banks has also developed among certain corporate institutional investors because of the 70 percent corporate tax exclusion. Senior securities of banks compete in the marketplace with similar securities of other companies. Through security analysis, these securities are appraised as to quality and value. Since the market associates size with marketability, and possibly with quality, the larger the bank, the better the market for its senior securities. A larger bank, therefore, generally has the option of issuing senior securities. Any bank considering this option should evaluate the financial effects of the various forms of capital. Even if senior capital is financially favorable, it is generally not wise to borrow up to the regulatory limit in order to preserve financial flexibility in the future.

The availability of new common equity capital at anything like a reasonable price varies widely among banks. Sufficient amounts of reasonably priced common stock are available to most community banks located in small and medium-sized cities and towns. In such situations, ownership of shares in a local bank is often a source of pride and marks a contribution to the local community. Problems such as maintaining control, ensuring widespread ownership, and moderating the desire to be on the bank's board of directors seem more common than finding willing buyers for new stock issues.

Large money market centers and regional banks face different problems. They must compete in an impersonal national market for common equities. A bank may find its common stock selling at a low price, either because the entire stock market is depressed or because the market is pessimistic about banks in general.

The availability of new common equity capital may be most limited for small and medium-sized banks in larger cities. These banks do not have the national markets of the larger banks or the community interest and prestige of banks located in smaller communities. Even in the best of times, such banks must work to develop a market for their stock, and there are times when such banks cannot sell common stock.

The need for flexibility in issuing capital in future years may further restrict the use of available senior capital. New equity capital may not be available at a reasonable price, or senior capital may produce more favorable financial results for a bank, or both. While most bank capital should be common equity, external capital does not have to be restricted to equity capital.

Financial Effects of Senior Capital

Senior capital has two potential financial advantages over common stock as a source of capital. First, the issuance of senior capital results in lower immediate dilution of earnings per common share, unless the financing cost exceeds the amount the bank is earning on shareholders' equity. Second, in the long run, senior capital usually increases the earnings per share on common stock because it introduces favorable financial leverage, which means that the returns earned on these funds exceed their fixed costs.

For example, assume that the bank in Table 9.15 earns 1.0 percent before taxes on total assets and has a tax rate of 34 percent. Having grown rapidly, the bank now has $500 million in assets but only $30 million in capital funds. The bank examiners suggest that the bank is at the regulatory minimum and that it should raise $5 million in additional capital. The present capitalization consists of 1 million shares of $10 par-value stock and $20 million in surplus, undivided profits, and reserves. Assume further that the bank has three alternative methods of raising the additional capital: (1) selling 166,667 shares of common stock at $30 a share (approximately nine times earnings); (2) selling $5 million of preferred stock with an 8 percent dividend rate; and (3) selling $5 million of subordinated debentures with a 10 percent coupon. Immediately after any of the financing alternatives, the bank will have assets of $505 million and capital of $35 million.

The first section of Table 9.15 illustrates the immediate dilution of earnings per share under the three alternatives. Debt and preferred stock cause less dilution than common stock, and the dilution of earnings per share is higher for preferred stock than for debt because the 8 percent preferred dividend is not a tax-deductible expense. There is favorable financial leverage from using both the preferred stock and the debt, but the financial leverage is more favorable with the tax-deductible interest.

The second section of Table 9.15 illustrates what would happen if the bank's assets increased by an additional $75 million over time. Note that the new capital has assisted in financing new assets that contribute to higher earnings. For example, earnings per common share would be $3.28 if the additional capital had been raised by the issuance of common stock and $3.50 if the additional capital had been raised by the issuance of 10 percent debentures or 8 percent preferred stock, respectively. This example portrays favor-

TABLE 9.15   Earnings Results for Alternative Methods of Raising Capital

	Present Capital	Additional Capital Financed with Common Stock (at $30 per share)	Additional Capital Financed with 8% Preferred Stock	Additional Capital Financed with 10% Subordinated Debentures
Earnings on Existing Assets				
Earnings on assets (1.0%)	$5,000,000	$5,050,000	$5,050,000	$5,050,000
Less: Interest	0	0	0	500,000
Net income before tax	$5,000,000	$5,050,000	$5,050,000	$4,550,000
Less: Taxes (at 34% rate)	1,700,000	1,717,000	1,717,000	1,547,000
Net income after tax	$3,300,000	$3,333,000	$3,333,000	$3,003,000
Less: Preferred dividends	0	0	400,000	0
Net for common stock	$3,300,000	$3,333,000	$2,933,000	$3,003,000
Divided by: Number of shares	1,000,000	1,166,667	1,000,000	1,000,000
Earnings per share	$3.30	$2.86	$2.93	$3.00
Earnings on Increased Assets				
Earnings on assets (1.0%)	$5,750,000	$5,800,000	$5,800,000	$5,800,000
Less: Interest	0	0	0	500,000
Net income before tax	$5,750,000	$5,800,000	$5,800,000	$5,300,000
Less: Taxes (at 34% rate)	1,955,000	1,972,000	1,972,000	1,802,000
Net income after tax	$3,795,000	$3,828,000	$3,828,000	$3,498,000
Less: Preferred dividends	0	0	400,000	0
Net for common stock	$3,795,000	$3,828,000	$3,428,000	$3,498,000
Divided by: Number of shares	1,000,000	1,166,667	1,000,000	1,000,000
Earnings per share	$3.80	$3.28	$3.43	$3.50

able financial leverage. The highest earnings per share, of course, would result if no additional capital were raised; however, the bank was seeking a more adequate capital position.

The conclusions that can be derived from Table 9.15 rest primarily on four important variables: (1) the amount the bank can earn on its total capital (or assets with a given proportion of capital) before income taxes, (2) the fixed cost of the senior capital, (3) the effective income tax rate, and (4) the proportion of total capital that is senior capital. Table 9.16 shows the effect on earnings per common share from Table 9.15 when any one of these variables is changed after the additional capital has been raised and assets have increased by an additional $75 million.

Alternative 1 in Table 9.16 shows the earnings per share as they appeared under the assumptions for the second section of Table 9.15. Alternative 2 shows that when earnings on assets rise, the positive effect of financial leverage, given the same fixed cost for the preferred stock or debt, is even greater. On the other hand, when the return on assets falls, the leverage becomes less favorable—that is, earnings per share were higher when common stock was used—as shown in Alternative 3. Taken together, Alternatives

TABLE 9.16   Effect of Changing an Important Variable of Earnings per Common Share

Variable Changes from Table 9.15[a]	Additional Capital Financed with Common Stock	Additional Capital Financed with Preferred Stock	Additional Capital Financed with Subordinated Debentures
1. No change	$3.28	$3.43	$3.50
2. Earnings on assets rise to 1.5% before taxes	$4.92	$5.34	$5.41
3. Earnings on assets fall to 0.5% before taxes	$1.64	$1.51	$1.58
4. Cost of debt falls to 6%; preferred to 4%	$3.28	$3.63	$3.63
5. Cost of debt rises to 14%; preferred to 12%	$3.28	$3.23	$3.37
6. Tax rate is 50%	$2.49	$2.50	$2.65
7. Tax rate is 0%	$4.97	$5.40	$5.30
8. Senior capital (when used) was $10 million rather than $5 million[b]	$3.28	$3.79	$3.96

[a] The specific variable mentioned is the only one allowed to change. All other variables were left the same as in Table 9.15 (assuming that additional capital was raised by one of the three methods and that assets have increased an additional $75 million). Taxes were left at an average rate of 34%.

[b] When senior capital was used, the equity account was reduced from $30 million to $25 million (800,000 shares). Regulators probably would not accept this much senior capital, but the relatively large amount illustrates the effects more clearly. All other variables were left the same as in Table 9.15.

2 and 3 demonstrate the greater variability of earnings per share when more financial leverage is used.

Alternative 4 shows that if the dividend or interest cost for preferred stock or debt is lower, the earnings per common share are greater. In Alternative 5, higher dividends or interest costs for preferred stock or debt result in lower earnings per common share. In Alternative 5, the increase of 4 percent in the preferred dividend and interest cost means that the leverage from using preferred stock was unfavorable, while the leverage from using debt was much less favorable with the higher interest cost.[1]

Alternatives 6 and 7 examine the impact of different income tax rates. The higher income tax rate in Alternative 6 hurts returns no matter what form of capital is used; however, the pain is less for debentures on which interest is a tax-deductible expense. For Alternative 7, in which there was no corporate income tax, the preferred stock provides more favorable leverage because tax deductibility of interest does not help the debentures. Finally, Alternative 8 shows that greater use of senior capital results in higher earnings

[1] These results make the naive assumption that the price of the common stock remains the same. The market price of common stock will tend to be higher (meaning fewer shares sold to raise the same amount of capital) when interest rates are lower, and the price of common stock will tend to be lower (more shares for the same amount) when interest rates are higher.

per share when financial leverage is favorable. Earnings per share are more volatile, and negative financial leverage is always a possibility when more senior capital is used.

Bank debt instruments, even if not currently required for capital, may also have several advantages over long-term deposits as a source of funds. First, if they meet certain requirements, debt instruments are not subject to reserve requirements; second, because these instruments have fixed maturities, there is less need for liquidity reserves, and most of the proceeds can be invested in longer term, higher-yielding assets; third, the handling and placing costs associated with debt instruments may be lower than the cost of acquiring additional time deposits; and finally, the funds acquired through debt instruments are not subject to the deposit insurance costs of the FDIC.

Balancing the advantages and disadvantages to determine the appropriate amount of senior capital is a difficult task. Small to moderate-sized banks need some financial flexibility. They are generally advised to meet all their capital needs with equity and to issue senior capital only when their capital needs exceed expectations or when the market for their stock is unusually poor. The primary sources, when small or medium-sized banks do decide to issue senior capital, will probably be principal correspondent banks or the banks' existing customers.

Most larger banks should seriously consider the use of some senior capital to meet part of their capital needs. In addition to the advantages of favorable financial leverage, senior capital does not reduce ownership control if current shareholders are unwilling or unable to invest in new common stock. Many larger commercial banks and their holding companies are subject to the 34 percent corporate income tax and should use subordinated debentures as their source of senior capital.[2]

The amount to be used will depend partially on the current and expected cost of such debentures in relation to the bank's pretax return on its entire capital base. In theory, banks should use senior capital up to the point where the market value of the common shareholders' investment is maximized. The advantages, such as higher earnings per common share, will be weighed against the higher risks, greater variability of earnings, and higher probability of bankruptcy. One rule of thumb is that a bank should use debt within reasonable limits as long as its earnings on total senior and equity capital exceed the current cost of debt by approximately 50 percent or more. Bank managers should limit indebtedness to between one-half and three-fourths of the maximum amount acceptable to regulatory authorities in order to assure themselves of some financial flexibility. The limit should be broad and flexible because of the economies of issuing debt in large blocks.

Newer Forms of Senior Capital

In the 1980s and 1990s, there was tremendous expansion in the forms of securities issued by corporations. (For example, in 1985 alone, corporations issued over 40 new forms of

---

[2] Because preferred dividends must be paid from net earnings after taxes, and because interest on debt capital is normally deductible from earnings before taxes, preferred stock will be attractive only to banks that have a low effective income tax rate or that pay no income taxes. The earnings per share figures in Table 9.16 show that preferred stock produces the same after tax earnings as similar-cost debt in the no-tax situation. Preferred stock might be attractive in such a situation because of its lower priority and generally smaller charges (because repayment or sinking funds are not usually required). In low-tax situations, interest payments on debt capital may not be deductible from earnings before taxes if the Internal Revenue Service can associate tax-exempt income with the proceeds of the debt issue. Also, preferred dividends may be lower than interest on debt issues because corporate owners have to pay taxes on only 30 percent of preferred dividends received.

securities.) Although bank regulators have closely scrutinized many of these newer forms, banks and bank holding companies have found some forms that regulators find acceptable as part of bank capital. Convertible securities and some of the newer forms are evaluated here.

Convertible securities nearly always have significantly lower interest or dividend costs than do similar nonconvertible securities. The lower cost of convertibles does not by itself mean that convertibles are "cheaper" than nonconvertibles. A proper appraisal of the cost differences to the issuer of using convertibles or nonconvertibles also must take into account the potential dilution that can result from conversion. (For this reason, a few issuers of convertibles hope that these issues will not be converted.) Whatever the long-term cost differences might be, the lower interest or dividend payments of convertibles may prove advantageous to the issuing bank, particularly in tight money periods.

Convertible securities have several other potential advantages. First, with a call provision, the bank has the flexibility of determining whether an issue selling above the call price will be converted. This flexibility gives the bank a wider range of choices in future financial decisions. Second, in a few situations, the conversion privilege may be necessary as a sweetener to enable a bank to sell a debt or preferred issue. Third, convertible securities may be preferable to common stock in a few situations where the bank is owned by only a few shareholders. Conversion normally does not take place immediately, but rather over time. Therefore, convertibles offer the controlling group an opportunity to meet immediate capital needs while obtaining the time to acquire firmer control before conversion takes place. Also, control may be more of a problem when earnings are decreasing than when the bank is prospering. Conversion normally will not take place unless the bank prospers. Hence, when bank performance is less than satisfactory and the threat of loss of control is greatest, the controlling group is most sheltered from the threat of conversion.

The overall potential advantages of convertibles as a commercial bank's financial strategy are convincing. One can imagine a rapidly growing bank issuing convertibles at a favorable cost, forcing conversion a few years later at a higher price, and then selling a new convertible issue because of the enlarged common equity base. A slower growing bank, on the other hand, might gain from the lower interest cost, greater flexibility, and better control of the convertible issue over the entire life of the issue.

There is another issue in the question of convertible securities that must be addressed. One might argue that convertible bonds are not advantageous because they are both a senior security and a right to convert to stock. Under the assumption of efficient capital markets, the gains of (in effect) selling common stock above its current price coupled with a lower interest cost would be offset by potential disadvantages to the bank. For example, if bank performance were not satisfactory, the bank would still be forced to make fixed-cost interest payments, which would not be true if the bank had sold common stock. On the other hand, if the bank did very well, it might wish it had waited to sell common stock at an even higher price. The problem with such arguments is that everyone does better with hindsight. Furthermore, the wide fluctuation of premiums on convertible issues under different market conditions and the lower margin requirements on purchases of convertibles raise some questions about the assumption of efficient capital markets. Individual banks may also have special conditions that make convertible issues more favorable to them than to the typical bank in the general market.

Banks have also cited two practical considerations as disadvantages of convertibles. First, earnings per share must now be stated on both a primary basis and a fully diluted basis. The negative connotation of this accounting ruling is that earnings are stated on an as-if-diluted basis even before conversion takes place. If actual and potential shareholders base their investment decision on the fully diluted earnings figure, the hoped-for advantages of favorable leverage may not be fully recognized in the market price of the bank's common stock.

Second, some observers maintain that there is no proper time to issue convertibles. Proponents of this argument hold that common stock should be sold if the bank's common stock is considered to be overvalued. The required equity capital is more likely to be raised on more favorable terms at the present time than in a future period. On the other hand, if the bank believes its common stock is undervalued, the best financial decision is to issue straight debt or preferred stock. Common stock can be sold later when the price of the stock rises to its normal level.

Mandatory convertible issues, whose conversion is mandatory by the end of a certain period of time, are a variation of regular convertibles. Regulatory authorities prefer this form because the convertibles cannot mature. Regulators classify mandatory convertibles as Tier I capital. Some of these issues have been sold; however, mandatory convertibles have been sold on less favorable terms than regular convertibles, and the bank and security holders lose flexibility with such sales.

Variable-rate debt and option-rate debt are among the other new capital-raising alternatives. Variable-rate debt makes particular sense in situations in which fixed-rate debt would increase a bank's interest rate risk. Option-rate debt is usually variable-rate debt that can be converted into fixed-rate debt at the option of the debt holder during at least some of the life of the debt. This option increases the price of the debt, which reduces the interest cost to the bank.

The limited number of banks that have no taxable income and have large tax losses to carry forward should consider preferred stock. The 70 percent dividend exclusion for corporate income taxes makes preferred dividend rates lower than yields on bonds. The cost of preferred stock will be less than the cost of debt if the bank has low or no taxes. To escape potential interest rate risk, preferred stock should either be callable or issued at an adjustable (tied to some interest rate index) rate. A noncallable, adjustable-rate preferred stock qualifies as primary capital. One interesting form of adjustable-rate preferred stock has its dividend repriced every seven weeks through a dutch auction mechanism.

External Common Stock Issues

Common stock has to be issued when a new bank is formed. Common stock may also be the appropriate form of raising external capital to finance growth. When a new bank is organized, its capital stock is usually sold to a small group of interested investors. Additional stock may later be offered to this group and their friends; however, if the bank grows rapidly and needs larger amounts of additional common stock, it may have to offer its stock to the public. The pricing of a bank's book value, earning power, and dividends are compared with the prices of actively traded stocks of similar-sized banks for the determination of a reasonable stock price. It is not generally advisable for the issuing bank to try to squeeze the last dollar out of such an offering. The presence of a group of initial shareholders who are satisfied with the appreciation in the market price of their stock will encourage higher common stock prices in future years. The initial public offering should be priced in the popular range for new issues. A stock split may be used to adjust the price of previously issued shares if their value is not between $10 and $30 per share.

Once the stock is reasonably actively traded, the offering price of new issues will be determined primarily by the market price of outstanding shares. In addition to improving its operating efficiency, the bank may take several steps to improve its market price. First, it should foster an effective dividend policy. Second, it should try to publicize the bank and its activities as much as possible (e.g., in the news media and in financial analysts' meetings). It is imperative that the senior management and director always be honest and realistic in presenting information about the bank. The investment community is very slow in forgetting unjustifiably optimistic predictions. The directors and senior management should also use stock splits to keep the market price of the stock in an attractive price range, which is between $20 and $60, according to most financial analysts. (Stock dividends can also be used for this purpose. Stock dividends tend to be smaller than splits, and they force the bank to capitalize a portion of its undivided profits. Smaller stock dividends provide shareholders with a lower-cost opportunity to sell a small portion of their holdings but are more expensive to effect than stock splits.)

Price information is usually available for the issues of larger banks or bank holding companies that are traded on one or more stock exchanges or are traded actively in the over-the-counter market. If a medium-sized bank's stock is not listed on the National Association of Security Dealers Automated Quotation Service (NASDAQ), the bank should try to build its shareholder base, trading activity, and dealer support (some banks could get on NASDAQ just by getting one or two more dealers to make a market in their stock) to obtain this listing. Advantages of the NASDAQ listing include the widespread publication of stock price quotations and the immediate availability of bid and asked quotations for dealers.

Even the smaller bank, while unable to obtain the NASDAQ listing, should try to make stock price information available. If the bank or a local dealer makes the market, the bank should make sure that the local press gets and publishes the quote on the stock price daily. For infrequently traded stocks of such banks, establishing a reasonable value for the stock is a major problem. Two techniques that a few smaller banks have used successfully to establish a reasonable price are (1) using preemptive rights offerings of new shares to existing shareholders and (2) holding periodic stock auctions in which those who wish to buy or sell shares can bid for them or place them in an auctionlike setting.

Other strategies that might improve the bank's market price and its ability to raise equity capital include dividend reinvestment plans (which allow shareholders to reinvest cash dividends automatically in new shares) and purchase by a bank or holding company of some of its own shares. Bank directors and senior management should be flexible in evaluating the probable costs and benefits of these alternative strategies.

Even if a bank's board and its management use the strategies appropriate to their situation and work hard to increase the market's earnings multiple for the bank's stock, the bank's management may believe the market price of the bank's stock to be vastly understated. Often the depressed price is the result of conditions beyond the bank management's control. For example, in the late 1980s the multiples for nearly all bank stocks were depressed because of concern about loans to less developed countries, well-publicized banking problems and failures, proposed legislation affecting banks, and other concerns. What should the astute banker do in this hostile environment, particularly if the bank's stock is selling below its book value?

If the bank does not urgently need additional capital, the answer is relatively simple: Do not raise additional equity capital at this time, but do everything possible to strengthen the bank's earnings multiple in future periods in which new capital may be needed. If the bank needs additional capital, it has three options. First, it may decide not to raise additional capital but instead work to improve the bank's capital ratios by selling or securitizing assets, slowing asset and deposit growth, or retaining a higher proportion of earnings. Regulatory authorities tend to be relatively lenient in such situations if the bank is clearly following such a strategy. A second option is to sell senior capital instead of issuing new shares of common equity. There are limits on the proportion of senior capital a bank may have in its capital structure, and a few banks have used up their ability to exercise this option. The third option is to issue common stock in spite of obviously hostile conditions. In September 1975, for example, the Crocker National Corporation sold 1.5 million shares of its common stock at roughly 75 percent of its book value. This was the first time a major banking institution had offered shares at a price below the book value of its shares. Crocker was forced into this position because $170 million (approximately 30 percent) of its $565 million of capital supporting $6.3 billion in loans was already in debt securities. Crocker's existing shareholders may have been more willing to accept a dilution in their average earnings per share than many bank shareholders because the bank had recently brought in a new top management team, headed by a former Citibank vice-chairman, Thomas B. Wilcox. Since that time, a limited number of other banks have sold new common issues at below book value.

A different version of this third option would be to issue debt or preferred stock that is convertible into common stock. The hoped-for scenario would be that the bank's common stock price would eventually recover, and the bank would have, in effect, sold common stock at 15 to 30 percent above its market price when the capital was raised. Several banks followed this option in the early 1990s.

END OF CHAPTER PROBLEMS

9.1 On an electronic worksheet, create a matrix of bank return-on-equity values for a series of equity leverage ratios (across the columns of your matrix) and a series of return-on-asset ratios (down the rows). Use the following series:
- Equity leverage in increments of 1 percent beginning with 5 percent and ending with 14 percent
- Return-on-assets in increments of 0.2 percent beginning with 0.2 percent through 3.0 percent

Comment on the trade-offs between ROE and leverage. What is the fallacy in assuming low ROAs combined with high leverage?

9.2 Interstate Bank had $1 billion in assets at the beginning of 2000. With Interstate Bank's static asset mix, it was clear that it would have to maintain equity capital amounting to 6 percent of its assets to meet regulatory rules. Within this constraint, management wanted to increase assets as fast as possible. The bank's only other source of funds was deposits. The bank projected that its return-on-assets would equal 1.2 percent per year and dividend payout would always be 40 percent of earnings. Make projections of Interstate Bank's balance sheets (assets, deposits, and capital) for the beginning of 2001, 2002, and 2003.

9.3 Botticelli Bank's assets are listed below:
- **a.** Find the minimum amount of Tier I and Tier II capital Botticelli Bank must have to meet the 10 percent well-capitalized risk-based capital level.
- **b.** Given your results in (a) above, what will be Botticelli's Tier I leverage ratio?

Asset	$ Million	Risk Weights	Weighted Assets
Cash	$ 150	0	_____
Treasury securities	300	0	_____
Agency securities	200	20	_____
Fed funds sold	260	20	_____
Mortgages	800	50	_____
Business loans	600	100	_____
Allowance for loan loss	$ (60)		
Premises and equipment	50	100	_____
Goodwill	100		
	$2,400		

9.4 Haight-Asbury Trust Company's goal statement indicates that the firm seeks to earn 25 percent on equity before taxes and to be classified under capital rules as well capitalized. What spread in basis points must the firm earn after expenses on assets that have a 100 percent risk-weighting factor (such as commercial or consumer loans)? *Hint:* Well-capitalized banks must satisfy a 10 percent risk-weighted capital requirement.

9.5 Determine the risk-based and Tier I leverage capital ratios for Amadeus Federal Savings:

Balance Sheet

Cash and due from banks	$ 7,000	Core deposits	$ 95,000
Treasury securities	8,000	Borrowed funds	22,000
Government-sponsored agency securities	10,000	Long-term subordinated debt	5,000
Federal funds sold	8,000	Perpetual preferred	3,000
Commercial and con- sumer loans	60,000	Limited life preferred	1,000
Home mortgages	36,000	Common equity	9,500
Allowance for loan losses	(2,800)		
Premises and equipment	4,000		
Goodwill	3,500		
Other assets	1,800		
Total	$135,500	Total	$135,500

9.6 Mitternecht Bank of Commerce earns 2 percent before taxes on assets of $1 billion. The bank's capital consists of $60 million in common equity. One million shares of common stock are outstanding. Mitternecht intends to issue $10 million in new capital but is concerned over the dilution effects the issue might have on earnings to shareholders. The bank is considering three methods of raising the capital.

  i. Issue 100,000 shares for $100 per share.
 ii. Issue 6.5 percent perpetual preferred stock.
iii. Issue subordinated debentures bearing 9 percent interest.

Mitternecht pays a 34 percent tax rate.

  a. Determine the earnings per share (after taxes) under each plan, assuming the present level of assets.
  b. Repeat (a) above assuming pretax ROA rises to 3 percent.
  c. Repeat (a) above assuming pretax ROA falls to 0.5 percent.
  d. Suppose the subordinated debt rate rises to 12 percent and preferred to 8 percent. Compare earnings per share.

A Process for Planning Financial Needs

The first step in financing a bank's capital needs is to develop an overall financial plan. The amount of capital needed is affected by the bank's financial plan, and the plan is constrained by the amount of capital the bank has raised. The financial planning process starts with a careful analysis of the bank's present position and performance. Next, the bank should predict several key variables, use these variables to develop overall financial projections, and see if the financial results of these projections are consistent with the bank's plans and policies. The sensitivity of these overall results to changes in key variables should also be carefully examined. The bank should then analyze these results, with emphasis on the question of how much capital will be necessary to produce the desired results.

ANALYZING A BANK'S PERFORMANCE

A bank should know where it has been—its accomplishments and failures, its strengths and weaknesses—before it projects its future course. The bank must analyze all of the primary aspects of its performance, even when the principal objective is to measure its capital needs. The methods used for analyzing a bank's past performance were discussed in detail in Chapter 3. The key risk-return measurements for a bank should be compared with those for peer banks in this first step of capital planning.

PREDICTING SELECTED KEY VARIABLES IN THE FUTURE

After a complete analysis of the bank's past performance has been made, the next step is to select a few key variables for the bank and to predict the levels of these variables for targeted future periods. It is important that the predictions for these variables be more than mere extrapolations of past data. They should represent strategic plans that include reasonable policy goals and objectives, as well as observation of trends from past periods.

Selecting a limited number of key variables can be a difficult task. One variable that is usually emphasized is the predicted level of deposits. When predicting the amount of deposits, a bank should consider factors affecting deposit growth that can be controlled (such as promotional efforts, services offered, and rates paid on savings) and factors that cannot be controlled (such as population growth, competition, and economic conditions). Deposits often must be separated by the form of deposit (demand, saving, and time) and by the type of depositor (business, individual, and public) in order to pick up the differences in factors affecting their growth. Furthermore, some banks have the ability to control their level of time deposits and other purchased obligations by changing their rates in the marketplace. Such banks may want to predict demand and passbook deposits and then treat the level of their time deposits as a residual based primarily on their projections of profitable loan and investment opportunities (assuming that they can always purchase the funds required).

Another commonly used key variable is the predicted level of the bank's loans. Both controllable variables (such as the rates charged on various types of loans) and noncontrollable variables (such as local economic conditions and the national business cycle) can affect how much a bank has in its loan portfolio. Often a bank will predict loans equal to a target percentage of deposits. However, this prediction assumes that a bank can cut off loans to customers when demand is strong or can find new loan customers when demand is weak. Both of these predictions seem highly suspect, and it is preferable to predict a range of loan-to-deposit relationships, depending on the national and local economic conditions during the period for which loans are predicted.

Generally, the other key variable or variables should be any other factors that set limits on the bank's progress during the prediction period. The limiting variable may be the adequacy of trained personnel, the target for the spread to be earned on employed assets, the rate of opening new branches, or some other factor. The important criterion is that the variables will allow the bank to perform some basic activity, such as increasing deposit or loan growth in a different way than would be possible without that variable.

Once the key variables have been selected, the bank must estimate what will happen to them during the prediction period. Selecting the prediction period is itself a difficult task. Very short-term predictions, such as a month, may be subject to random fluctuations and are usually too short-term and small to have a large impact on capital needs. Longer-term predictions, such as 10 years, are subject to so many changes in noncontrollable factors that to take current actions is unrealistic. The most meaningful time period for predicting the key variables is probably annually for the next three to five years. As an overall projection is developed, it may be necessary to change the predictions for one or more of the key variables or even to change a key variable itself. The availability of capital, which

seems to be a key variable for at least some banks, is not included as a key variable for the initial overall projection. Instead, the need for capital is established by the overall projection; then the question of the availability of capital is examined carefully.

Developing an Overall Projection from the Key Variables. The next step, once predictions have been made for the key variables, is to develop pro forma balance sheets and projected income statements for the prediction period. Because these statements are interrelated, they must be developed jointly. (When available, a personal computer should be used to make these predicted statements.) The relationships calculated in analyzing the bank's past performance can be very useful during this step. Prior experience serves as a useful guide to necessary relationships in developing an overall projection and as a check on the reasonableness of assumptions. Bank management should have good reasons for projecting figures that depart significantly from prior experience. Generally, the overall number of categories should be kept as low as possible without materially harming the accuracy of the projection.

The first step in constructing the pro forma balance sheet should be to estimate the bank's major sources of funds. The deposit accounts can be predicted from forecasted growth rates for demand, time, and savings deposits and from the predicted dollar amount of public deposits. The other liabilities account is often a key variable in larger banks in which various forms of liabilities (such as Federal funds or Eurodollars) are purchased. For smaller banks, unless specific information exists, the other liabilities account is often small and may be estimated to remain constant or to grow at about the same rate as deposits and capital.

In predicting the capital accounts, the planner must remember that assets will increase because of additional capital (usually from retained earnings) and new deposits or increases in other liabilities. The amount of retained earnings for a period depends on the level of a bank's earnings in that period, which is partially a function of the amount of earning assets and the bank's cash dividend payout. The uncertainties and interdependencies associated with these variables usually do not materially weaken the financial plan because the amount of retained earnings is only a small proportion of the total additional funds in most time periods. Initially, then, banks can safely use either of two methods to predict the capital accounts: (1) leave total capital at the preceding year's-end level (less any scheduled debt repayments) or (2) allow total capital to increase by the increase in earnings estimated from the predicted income statement less any planned cash dividends. No changes should be made on the initial projection except for scheduled debt repayments or an estimation of retained earnings. (In a later step, specific financing to meet additional capital needs will be reflected in the balance sheet.)

The next step in constructing the pro forma balance sheet is to estimate the uses of the funds from the various sources. The amount in cash and due from banks is estimated by multiplying the various categories of deposits by the reserve requirements for these categories and adding that amount to the minimum correspondent balances and float.

The loan category is often the most difficult to predict. A bank may have a target amount of loans or a desired loan-to-deposit ratio, but factors such as national, regional, and local economic conditions may make the target difficult to attain. Fortunately, flexibility in security holdings can cushion the lower income if loan demand is low and can provide some extra funds if loan demand is higher than predicted.

The category of fixed assets changes as a result of additions to fixed assets less depreciation on existing equipment. If the amount in this category does not change much, capital expenditures can be assumed to be roughly equivalent to depreciation. Because noncash expenses (such as depreciation) charged against revenues are relatively small for a bank, changes in this category are significant only if the bank plans major physical expansion.

The other assets account is a catchall category that can be predicted from prior experience, and the investments account is generally used as a balancing residual. That is, it is the difference between total (deposit and other) sources of funds and the previously discussed asset categories (cash and due from banks, loans, fixed assets, and other assets).

All of the predictions for balance sheet accounts are rough estimates, but if the predictions for the key variables are reasonable, the overall forecast will be accurate enough for thoughtful capital planning. Care must be taken at every step to keep the balance sheet in balance. The pro forma balance sheet for the first year provides the base for building the following year's projections; this process continues until each year's projection has been completed.

When average or year-end balances are readily obtainable, average balances are preferable. If an attempt is made to calculate precise earnings on assets and interest on deposits, average figures will have to be considered. One simple alternative is to use an average of beginning and year-end figures for this purpose. A bank with significant seasonal variations, however, will have to use daily, weekly, or monthly average figures.

SENSITIVITY ANALYSIS AND A RANGE FOR THE PROJECTIONS

As the bank continues to make projections year after year, it will probably acquire increasing confidence in those projections. Still, many factors outside a bank's control affect its projections. In preparing to react to an array of possible developments, bank management must envision how sensitive its key variables are to changes beyond the bank's control and the effect of changes in these key variables on the overall forecast. For example, what would happen if a bank's deposits grew at a 20 percent compound rate annually instead of a predicted 10 percent rate? What would be the impact of a substantial drop in loan demand? Bank managers should test only those key variables that they are uncertain about and that might have a significant impact. For example, substantial changes in deposit growth may be important for a bank, but changes in equipment prices may have only a modest effect. One useful technique is to test the key variables by changing them by the greatest amount management thinks is possible and then following the consequences through the projection. If the projected statements are done on a personal computer, changing key variables or the environment by using a group of what-if situations is relatively easy.

If management believes that some key variables may be off by a wide margin and that future events might call for different plans and decisions, two more overall projections should be prepared to bracket the range of possibilities. One projection should be pessimistic, assuming that the identified key variables are at the lower end of reasonable expectations. Capital and other plans and strategies may be appreciably different under this pessimistic outlook. The other projection should be optimistic, assuming that the identified key variables are at the upper end of reasonable expectations. This projection is likely to place greater pressure on the bank's ability to raise external capital. In fact, capital requirements could become so great that the availability of capital becomes an important limiting variable in the overall projection.

DETERMINING CAPITAL NEEDS FROM PROJECTIONS

The final step in the financial planning process is to determine the capital needs based on the bank's projections. The preferred method is to determine what capital management believes is adequate to support the bank's projected assets, deposits, and other liabilities. This amount can then be compared with the bank's actual capital at the start of the year (less any capital repayments) and with its earnings (less anticipated cash dividends). If the amount of capital deemed adequate exceeds the available capital, then management should consider lowering cash dividends or raising capital from external sources. If the available capital exceeds the adequate level of capital, the bank might consider raising its cash dividends or buying back some of its stock. These alternatives were considered in the Section in Chapter 9, Sustainable Internal Growth.

SHAWNEE NATIONAL BANK

INTRODUCTION

Shawnee National Bank, a large unit bank located in Kansas City, Missouri, had total resources in early December 1996 of over $1.4 billion (see Exhibit 1). As with other weekly reporting institutions subject to the reserve requirements of the Federal Reserve, the balances that Shawnee National is required to maintain as reserves are based on the average of its daily transaction deposit account balances during a 14-day *computation* period. The reserves required by the Fed must be maintained on an average daily basis during a 14-day *maintenance* period that begins on a Thursday and ends on the second Wednesday thereafter, sometimes called *Settlement Wednesday*. Because the requirement is an average for the period, bank managers are able to exercise judgment concerning the appropriate level of their reserve balances on a day-to-day basis during the maintenance period. At the end of a maintenance period, leeway of up to 4 percent above or below the average total reserve requirement will carry forward into the next maintenance period.

The bank must determine the net daily average reserves that need to be maintained at the Federal Reserve Bank. For a 14-day computation period that ends three days before the related maintenance period begins, the bank's average daily cash balance (vault cash) is compiled. This average cash balance is confirmed on the Fed's Daily Position reports and is carried forward and applied against the gross average reserves required in the corresponding maintenance period.

Since the early 1980s, the computation period for compiling the transaction account balance has ended only two days prior to the end of the 14-day maintenance period, giving rise to so-called contemporaneous reserve requirements. At the close of business on Monday of a Settlement Week, Shawnee National has only Tuesday and Wednesday to bring into line the daily average reserves held at the Fed with the net required reserves for the maintenance period. Even with a good online accounting system, this nearly concurrent requirement can present a considerable challenge for the bank's money-desk manager. Numerous noncontrollable transactions (e.g., net checking transac-

tions initiated directly or indirectly by the bank's depositors) and controllable transactions (e.g., Federal funds purchases and sales) affect a bank's balances at its Federal Reserve Bank each day. Shawnee National must keep track of both its transaction deposits and its net reserve balances throughout each business day, reconciling the average daily amounts with the Fed. The Fed's reserve requirements in December 1996 were 10 percent for net transaction balances.[1]

Exhibit 2 contains a summary of Shawnee National's accumulated reserve position for the reserve maintenance period ending Wednesday, December 18, 1996. The associated computation period for transaction accounts ended Monday, December 16, and for vault cash (as a credit) it ended Monday, December 2.

Shawnee National's overall cash position[2] reflected a large number of individual investment, loan, and liquidity decisions made by the bank's officers throughout the year. As a basis for planning, a staff economist forecast the level of deposits and expected loan demand on a continuous basis for periods of three months, six months, and one year. Once these sources and applications of funds had been estimated and the bank had made its forecast of interest rates for the coming months, the bank could then determine its target asset and liability composition and make asset and/or liability management decisions to move toward that position.

As 1996 began, the U.S. economy was growing at a steady pace, and the low rate of price increases seemed to indicate that inflation was under control. Through 1996, loans at commercial banks grew at a pace of more than 8 percent. In this positive economic environment, Shawnee's lending program

---

[1]The Garn-St. Germain Depository Institution Act of 1982 grants a total exemption to the first $3 million or so of reservable deposits. The next amount of reservable deposits, called a *tranche level*, is subject to only a 3 percent reserve requirement. These adjustments give a relative advantage to a smaller institution. All net transaction amounts above the tranche are reservable at 10 percent. In previous years, other liability accounts have been reservable at various percentages. The level of the exemption and the tranche change annually.

[2]A commercial bank's *cash position* is defined as the sum of cash in the vault, deposits due from correspondent banks and from the Federal Reserve Bank, and terms in the process of collection.

had turned increasingly aggressive. Earlier in the 1990s, loan demand seemed almost nonexistent, and the bank moved a significant share of its investment portfolio into long-term issues (see Exhibit 3) to take advantage of long-term interest rates that were quite high compared to short-term rates, leaving it rather illiquid in 1994 when loan demand began to surge. Thus, the only significant exposures to the bank, according to the bank's financial officers, were pressure on the bank's liquidity and the possibility that the bank might see long-term interest rates rising. For now, whenever excess funds became available, Shawnee's management preferred to invest them in short-term securities at interest rates of 5.00 to 5.50 percent and to avoid further investment in longer-term securities which, by December 1996, were yielding 6.00 to 6.25 percent.

After the bank's deposit, loan, liability, and investment objectives had been estimated and short-run policies established, Seth Bradley, a vice-president, managed the daily cash position to adjust for short-run cash fluctuations and to ensure that the bank maintained the required minimum balances with the Federal Reserve Bank. Bradley's objective was to minimize the cost of meeting the bank's reserve requirements at the Fed and to invest any temporarily excess funds as profitably as possible.

The month of December was an unusual period for accumulating excess funds. Strong seasonal sales between Thanksgiving and Christmas by several large national mail-order firms located in Shawnee National's market area bolstered local retail activity. The bank's peak period in deposits generally occurred by Christmas, after which it declined rapidly (see Exhibit 4). This rapid decline after Christmas was due to various payments by area agribusinesses for tax management, as many used cash basis accounting.

On Friday, December 18, Bradley sold $8.0 million in federal funds, thereby deliberately creating an accumulated reserve deficiency of approximately $35 million (see Exhibit 2) for Monday morning.[3] He assumed that a $25 million to $30 million reserve buildup would occur on Monday, thereby offsetting the multiple effect of Friday's sale of federal funds. A large part of this growth in the reserve balance at the Fed was expected to come from immediate credit at the Federal Reserve on one-day items. These items consisted of checks drawn on other banks that Shawnee National forwarded to the Kansas City Clearing House and to its correspondent banks. These checks would increase Shawnee's transaction deposits and, at the margin, its average

required reserves for the last day of the contemporaneous computation period. But most important, when these checks were cleared, the full amount of the checks became usable funds on deposit in Shawnee's Federal Reserve account. Bradley further assumed that the bank would experience its typical small reserve drain on Tuesday.[4] Then, with a moderate purchase of federal funds, the average reserve balances for the maintenance period would closely approximate the legal requirements.

By mid-morning on Monday, December 21, Bradley realized that his assumptions were not proving correct. The bank opened on Monday with an accumulated reserve deficiency of $35.4 million for the reserve maintenance period that would end on Wednesday, December 23. The large immediate credits to the bank's account at the Federal Reserve had not materialized. A number of factors were responsible:

1. Incoming deposits over the weekend were smaller than expected.
2. A smaller than normal surplus was incurred at the Kansas City Clearing House.
3. A large correspondent bank withdrew funds one day early when in fact the courier plane delivering cash letters to Shawnee had been delayed by blizzard conditions.
4. Several important depositors made larger than normal withdrawals.
5. An adverse arithmetical error of $3 million was made in the general books department.

During Monday the bank experienced slower than usual growth in its reserve balance at the Fed. When combined with Sunday night's unfavorable events, this resulted in only $12.1 million in noncon-

---

[3] Federal fund sales (loans) on Friday are for three days; thus, the impact on average daily reserves of the net sale of $8.0 million for three days is the equivalent of selling $24.0 million for one day. Federal funds are reserve balances that a commercial bank may either loan or borrow from other banks to adjust its reserve position. These loans are generally made on an unsecured overnight basis, with repayment expected at the beginning of the next business day. Sales and purchases also can be made for somewhat longer periods. The federal funds rate is determined by the forces of supply and demand for such funds within the commercial banking system.

[4] Shawnee National's proof and transit department worked each Friday and Sunday night to process the heavy volume of banking-by-mail transactions. As a result, incoming items arriving over the weekend were cleared more promptly than those by other banks in the area, and Shawnee National generally experienced a peak in usable funds on Monday. This peak typically declined on Tuesday and Wednesday as other banks completed the processing of weekend mail.

trollable factors rather than the $30 million Bradley had expected (see Exhibit 2). Even though the normal noncontrollable factors on Tuesday of −$1 million would most likely change to +$3 million, Bradley realized that by the close of business on Tuesday, the bank could have an accumulated reserve deficiency of as much as $45.6 million. A deficiency of this size would be difficult to overcome through normal adjustments such as borrowing on its federal funds lines or selling short-term Treasury securities.

On Monday afternoon, Bradley decided that the reserve position at the Fed required immediate attention before the close of business that day. There were several alternatives from which Bradley could choose in order to adjust the bank's reserve position.

DISCUSSION OF ALTERNATIVES

Purchase of Federal Funds

To adjust its deficit balances at the Federal Reserve Bank, Shawnee National most often resorted to purchase of federal funds. Shawnee National's policy, however, was to limit net federal funds purchases to no more than $20 million. The bank did not want to be either an excessive net seller or buyer of federal funds. Bradley considered the use of federal funds as a "fine adjustment" in the bank's reserve position. Since short-term adjustments in reserve balances usually ranged from $5 million to $10 million, federal funds provided the bank with a convenient means either of profitably employing excess reserves or of offsetting small reserve deficits. The bank's limited use of federal funds sometimes made it necessary either to extend reserve adjustments over a longer period or to make more permanent adjustments.

Borrowing from the Federal Reserve

The accumulated reserve deficit could be made up by borrowing from the Federal Reserve Bank. Shawnee National Bank, however, looked upon the use of such borrowing as a privilege. Earlier, on Wednesday, December 2, temporary tightness in the federal funds market drove the offered rate to 7 percent, more than double the rates prevailing at that time. Bradley had found it necessary for Shawnee National to borrow at the discount window as federal funds became unavailable at reasonable rates. Moreover, during the last week of December, the annual additional short-term loan demand by

regional agribusinesses for tax management was usually met in part by a seasonal advance at the discount window. Bradley preferred, therefore, to avoid using the discount window during this week.

Borrowing by Means of Repurchase Agreements

Shawnee National could sell part of its government or agency portfolio and agree to repurchase it at some future date at a predetermined price or yield. The cost of this form of secured borrowing tended to be lower than that of unsecured forms. There were two potential problems: (1) nearly $74 million of U.S. government and agency securities, as well as $88 million of state and municipal securities, were already pledged to cover government deposits and (2) the maturities of repos were generally overnight, although they could be as long as several months. In Bradley's opinion, the use of this form might cause the bank to shift permanently to liabilities other than deposits as a source of funds.

Other Means of Borrowing

Bradley felt that the bank might obtain the needed funds by offering CDs with rates ranging from 0.25 to 0.50 percent above the existing market rate for comparable CDs. Since Shawnee National was classified as a well-capitalized bank, with its 6.34 percent leverage ratio, he concluded that restrictions on paying higher than prevailing market rates on CDs did not apply. He was concerned, however, about the difficulties some regional banks in the farm belt had experienced in issuing CDs and about the potential maturity of the CDs that Shawnee would offer. Bradley did not generally consider other forms of borrowing, such as the Eurodollar market and ineligible acceptances.

Sale of Short-Term Securities

If the adjustment of the reserve position required funds for more than a few days, short-term securities normally could be sold to provide the necessary funds. However, Bradley knew that a majority of the short-term securities were pledged as collateral for public deposits. He hoped to be able to retain most of the bank's short-term securities until maturity (see Exhibit 4).

Brokerage Collateral Loans or Other Loans Callable on Demand

Brokerage collateral loans or other callable loans were usually arranged through Shawnee National's correspondent banks in New York. When the bank negotiated a brokerage collateral loan, it indicated the length of time it wished to employ its funds. Although such loans were callable on demand, the bank would not normally recall the funds until the agreed time had expired.

Selling a Portion of the Investment Portfolio

On November 30, 1996, Shawnee National's investment portfolio (securities with maturities of over one year) was approximately $270 million (see Exhibit 4). Over half of the securities were pledged as collateral for public deposits, and most of the remaining securities could only be sold at losses. "It may be bad for the bank to take losses at this time," mused Bradley.

He also realized that he would have to try to make some assessments of Shawnee National's liquidity needs for the remainder of December 1996, especially related to the date in Exhibits 2 and 3. Because of recent discussions among the bank's senior officers, he wondered how the regulatory authorities (the Comptroller of the Currency) would view Shawnee National's liquidity position. The bank's liquidity situation had been a subject of spirited debate among the bank's senior management, with opinions divided as to whether overall liquidity was too high or too low.

Bradley also was unsure about whether he should talk further with senior management regarding the bank's short-term deposit, loan, and investment objectives before he decided on specific actions in managing the reserve position. He was not convinced that he should have sold the $8.0 million

of federal funds on Friday, December 18, thus deliberately creating a reserve deficiency.

By mid-afternoon on Monday, December 21, the accumulated reserve deficiency for the period was approximately $40 million. Bradley had not decided which of the several alternatives he should choose to reduce or eliminate the deficiency. He knew that he must evaluate the available alternatives, given the preceding considerations, and take action before the close of business on Monday afternoon.

COST OF ALTERNATIVES

Bradley wrote down the following cost estimates of the alternatives he believed were available at that time:

Alternatives	Income Lost	Added Expense
1. Purchase of federal funds		5.2–5.4%
2. Borrowing from the Federal Reserve		5.0%
3. Borrowing by means of repurchase agreements		5.3–5.5%
4. Other means of borrowing (including CDs)		5.3–5.5%
5. Sale of short-term securities		6.5–6.7%
6. Cancellation of $20 million brokerage participation with New York correspondent		7.5%
7. Selling part of the bank's investment portfolio		?

EXHIBIT 1   **Shawnee National Bank Statement of Condition, November 30, 1995–1996 (dollars in thousands)**

Resources	11/30/95	11/30/96
Cash and due from banks	$110,358	$118,835
U.S. government and agency securities	106,180	127,161
State, county, and municipal bonds	188,428	186,945
Federal Reserve Bank stock	1,070	1,560
Loans and discount, net	876,437	956,324
Accrued interest receivable	6,724	7,427
Customers' liability under letters of credit and acceptances	11,761	12,717
Bank premises, furniture, and fixtures	26,301	29,256
Other resources	613	1,124
Total resources	$1,327,872	$1,441,349
Liabilities		
Transactions deposits	$301,823	$334,258
Saving deposits	274,793	287,162
Time deposits	615,534	679,121
Other liabilities	35,424	33,234
Capital notes	16,100	15,600
Capital stock	9,104	9,104
Surplus	28,490	30,159
Undivided profits	46,604	52,711
Total liabilities and capital	$1,327,872	$1,441,349

EXHIBIT 2 Shawnee National Bank Worksheet for Computing Maintenance Period Reserve Position (as of Monday, December 16, 1996, at 2:30 P.M.) (dollars in millions)

Required Balances at Fed[a]	(1) Beginning Balance at Fed	(2) Controllable Factors Affecting Reserves	(3) Noncontrollable Factors [Net] Affecting Reserves	(4) Fed Funds Purchased (Sold) [Net]	(5) Other Factors Affecting Reserves[d]	(6) Closing Balances with Fed	(7) Net Reserves Required at Fed[e]	(8) Daily Reserve Excess (Deficiency)	(9) Accumulated Reserve Excess (Deficiency)
WED 12/09						36.7			(0.4)
1 THU 12/10	36.7	(4.9)[b]	(4.0)	c		27.8	37.2	(9.4)	(9.4)
2 FRI 12/11	27.8		6.3	c		34.1	37.6	(3.5)	(12.9)
3 SAT 12/12	34.1					34.1	38.0	(3.9)	(16.8)
4 SUN 12/13	34.1					34.1	38.3	(4.2)	(21.0)
5 MON 12/14	34.1		28.4	c		62.5	38.4	24.1	3.1
6 TUE 12/15	62.5		(5.9)	(6.8)		49.8	38.6	11.2	14.3
7 WED 12/16	49.8		4.7	(7.4)		47.1	38.7	8.4	22.7
8 THU 12/17	47.1		(13.5)	c		33.6	38.9	(5.3)	17.4
9 FRI 12/18	33.6		(3.7)	(8.0)		21.9	39.2	(17.3)	0.1
10 SAT 12/19	21.9					21.9	39.5	(17.6)	(17.5)
11 SUN 12/20	21.9					21.9	39.9	(17.9)	(35.4)
12 MON 12/21	21.9		12.1[f]			34.0[f]	40.1[f]	(6.1)[f]	(41.5)[f]
13 TUE 12/22	34.0[f]		3.0[f]			37.0[f]	40.4[f]	(3.4)[f]	(44.9)[f]
14 WED 12/23	37.0[f]		3.0[f]			40.0[f]	40.7[f]	(0.7)[f]	(45.6)[f]

[a] Maintenance period runs from Thursday, December 5, through Wednesday, December 18, 1996, based on a contemporaneous computation period of Tuesday, December 3, through Monday, December 16, 1996.

[b] Purchase of U.S. government securities.

[c] Insignificant net amount.

[d] Borrowing from the Fed window, payments for and receipts from direct Treasury security transactions, etc.

[e] The reserve balance is the average required reserves at the Fed based on cumulative daily deposit data for the computation period plus an additional $0.4 million that was the prior period's deficiency.

[f] Estimated if no adjustments are made.

EXHIBIT 3 Shawnee National Bank Maturity Distribution of Securities at Book Value, November 30, 1996 (dollars in thousands)

Maturity (Years)	U.S. Government Obligations	Federal Agency Obligations	State and Municipal Obligations	Total
1	16,038	10,690	17,932	44,660
2	2,101	10,921	16,529	29,551
3	1,566	3,172	15,072	20,350
4	5,031	11,613	13,572	30,216
5	16,401	13,854	15,070	45,325
6	13,095	10,746	12,145	35,986
7	0	0	9,051	9,051
8	0	3,219	13,138	13,357
9	0	0	12,190	12,190
10	0	1,974	9,144	11,118
11–15	0	6,200	21,245	27,445
15–20	0	0	20,540	20,540
Over 20	0	0	11,317	11,317
Total	54,232	72,929	186,945	314,106

EXHIBIT 4   **Shawnee National Bank Reservable Transaction Accounts, December 1993–1995 and December 1–13, 1996 (dollars in millions)**

Day of Month	1993	1994	1995	1996
1	321	291	344	—
2	291	305	—	390
3	253	—	—	401
4	—	—	349	409
5	—	341	366	416
6	278	350	370	421
7	288	354	375	—
8	307	364	388	—
9	315	361	—	422
10	341	—	—	437
11	—	—	391	440
12	—	376	393	449
13	344	372	405	460
14	363	377	406	—
15	366	381	411	—
16	375	384	—	—
17	380	—	—	—
18	—	—	424	—
19	—	403	379	—
20	396	379	345	—
21	358	370	343	—
22	321	388	310	—
23	291	396	—	—
24	253	—	—	—
25	—	—	—	—
26	—	—	379	—
27	252	375	345	—
28	278	338	343	—
29	270	297	310	—
30	283	274	—	—
31	280	—	—	—

CASE 7A

HILLSIDE BANCORP (A)

INTRODUCTION

Phil Forbes sat comfortably on the leather sofa in Jeff Stevens' office. He fumbled with a notepad and pencil as Jeff plopped down in the chair behind his desk.

It was early in January 1997. Forbes had started with Hillside National Bank five years earlier, and his progression to vice-president for finance fit the career path that Stevens, the bank's president, had mapped out for him. Over the five years, the bank had grown slowly but steadily to just over $160 million in assets. Hillside's population of 27,000 was stable, with little visible prospect for increasing.

The bank had remained profitable and rather trouble-free over the years under Jeff's leadership. Jeff was well liked in the community, and he was a detailed-minded executive where credit controls and other internal matters were concerned.

MARCY STATE BANK

Jeff immediately leveled with Phil Forbes on the business at hand—the opportunity to buy Marcy State Bank in the nearby town of Marcy. "I want you to check their numbers carefully so that I can reassure the board that we'll have no surprise need for capital beyond what we need to complete the cash purchase." Jeff went on to explain that Hillside Bancorp, the legal holding company framework for Hillside National Bank, would be the acquirer, and that the corporation's regulators would require a capital injection of $1.2 million into the holding company in order to complete the transaction.

"The majority shareholder wants to work with us," Jeff continued. "The firm price is $2.4 million, the current book value of the bank. We know that recent acquisitions of small banks in the state have been priced at 1.2 to 1.8 times book and in a range of 6 to 10 times earnings. Our loan people and I have been looking at their loan portfolio, and there are some problems. But then we expected problems, considering that they never managed to put together a decent lending group up there. And when you consider the real estate shakeout in Marcy over the past couple of years, that bank certainly could be worse off than it is."

It was clear to Phil that the opportunity to ac-quire Marcy State might provide a one-time chance for Hillside Bancorp to dramatically improve its prospects for the future. (An abbreviated balance sheet for Hillside Bancorp, the holding company parent of Hillside National, is shown in Exhibit 1.) Increasing competition in Hillside from two independent banks and an affiliate of a large multistate banking firm probably would prohibit much growth for Hillside National. The bank had done about all it could for now to strengthen its competitive position. By contrast, according to several directors, the community of Marcy had great potential.

Marcy was an attractive community situated on the tree-lined shore of a large recreational lake about 30 miles west of Hillside. The town had a population of 9,000 year-round residents, although a growing segment of the population, including three of Hillside National's directors, consisted of high-season residents who owned second homes in Marcy. The town's growth had been interrupted in the early 1990s by the failure of a large resort developer in town and the related glut of new luxury homes. Recently, however, a gradual resumption of growth indicated that the effects of these misfortunes had moderated and that more rapid growth soon would follow. Real estate prices had firmed and, in some cases, were rising.

There were a total of three banks in Marcy. One was equal in size to Marcy State and was affiliated with a moderate-sized holding company with headquarters in the state capital. Another was a *de novo* bank, chartered two years ago, that already held $15 million in deposits. But Hillside National Bank's target, Marcy State, a $38 million bank, had a checkered past. It was chartered 15 years ago, and it seemed to hire and fire a president every year or two. Also, the present ownership had felt compelled to provide a modest capital injection in early 1996.

FINANCIAL BACKGROUND

Exhibits 2A and 2B present two years of balance sheet and income statement data, including the just completed statements for December 31, 1996. Several facts about the bank's financial condition were especially germane to the proposed acquisition:

1. Phil figured that loan writeoffs, on the high side, would be just over $1 million in 1997 and that the bank's lending activity would retrench, resulting in initial overall shrinkage in the loan portfolio during 1997.

2. Phil considered that the application of purchase accounting rules to the acquisition would result in markdowns of Marcy State's loan values and book equity value. He figured the downward adjustment of equity would be fully offset by the creation of approximately $750,000 in goodwill and by the recognition of a core deposit base intangible asset of $250,000.

3. At the proposed acquisition date (January 15, 1997), the bank would have a net-operating loss carryforward of approximately $1.3 million, the use of which would be available for the next 15 years.

PROJECTING THE FUTURE

Phil Forbes knew that the board would want reasonable assurance that no further capital injections would be required in the near term. Hillside National's holding company was adequately capitalized for now, but under the proposed acquisition, it was expected that half of the purchase price would have to be injected into the holding company in the form of fresh (cash) capital. Two members of the board with significant share holdings agreed that their pro rata share of the cash injection "would be a stretch."

Exhibit 3 presents Forbes' pro forma balance sheet and income statements for 1997 and 1998. He knew the bank would have to meet the risk-based and leverage capital standards specified under the "prompt corrective action" regulation of the Federal Deposit Insurance Corporation Improvement Act of 1991. Exhibit 4A gives an abbreviated schedule of the risk weight classifications under risk-based capital standards. The minimum ratios under the prompt corrective action rules shown in Exhibit 4B indicate that examiners would expect the bank to maintain at least an 8 percent risk-based capital ratio as well as a 4 percent Tier I leverage capital ratio. However, more than 98 percent of banks in the United States maintained at least a 10 percent risk-based capital ratio. He knew bank supervisors could require more capital for a bank they considered in trouble. Exhibit 5 can be used to apply the risk-based capital requirements to Phil Forbes's projections.

EXHIBIT 1   Hillside Bancorp—Balance Sheet, December 31, 1996

Assets		Liabilities and Equity	
Cash	$ 100,000	Accounts payable	$ 200,000
Equity invested in subsidiary bank	12,000,000	Notes payable	8,000,000
Other assets	100,000	Shareholders' equity	4,000,000
Total	$12,200,000	Total	$12,200,000

EXHIBIT 2A   Marcy State Bank—Statement of Condition (dollars in thousands)

	December 31, 1995	December 31, 1996
Cash and due from banks	$ 6,400	$ 2,600
Investment securities	8,500	6,500
Federal funds sold	0	2,200
Loans	26,450	25,960
Allowance for loan losses	(350)	(960)
Premises and equipment	900	900
Other real estate owned	300	400
Other assets	700	500
Total assets	$42,900	$38,100
Demand deposits	9,800	6,600
Interest-bearing checking accounts	2,900	3,000
Money market deposits	8,600	8,200
Savings accounts	1,300	1,000
CDs < $100M	5,700	7,800
CDs > $100M	9,800	8,300
Total deposits	$38,100	$34,900
Other liabilities	1,800	800
Shareholders' equity	3,000	2,400
Total liabilities and equity	$42,900	$38,100

EXHIBIT 2B   Income Statement (dollars in thousands)

	Year Ended 12/31/95	Year Ended 12/31/96
Interest income	$3,500	$3,500
Interest expense	1,800	1,900
Net interest income	1,700	1,600
Provision for loan losses (PLL)	460	840
Net interest income after PLL	1,240	760
Noninterest income	370	320
Noninterest expenses		
Salaries and benefits	690	710
Occupancy, furnishings, and equipment	410	370
Other	1,090	830
Total noninterest expense	$2,190	$1,910
Net income (loss) before taxes	(580)	(830)
Income taxes (credit)	(40)	(70)
Net income (loss)	($540)	($760)

EXHIBIT 3A   Marcy State Bank—Pro Forma Statement of Condition (dollars in thousands)

	December 31, 1997[a]	December 31, 1998[a]
Cash and federal balances (cat. 1)	$ 1,800	$ 2,000
Placements with banks (cat. 2)	600	600
Investment securities		
Treasuries (cat. 1)	1,800	2,000
Govt.-sponsored agencies (cat. 2)	1,900	2,000
Federal funds sold (cat. 2)	3,000	1,000
Loans (also see footnote below)		
Residential mortgages (cat. 3)	14,000	16,000
Consumer and commercial (cat. 4)	10,000	11,600
Allowance for loan losses	(200)	(200)
Premises and equipment (cat. 4)	900	900
Other real estate owned (cat. 4)	500	600
Intangible assets	225	200
Goodwill	725	700
Other assets (cat. 4)	500	600
Total assets	$35,750	$38,000
Demand deposits	6,000	6,000
Interest-bearing checking accounts	3,000	3,000
Money market deposits	9,500	10,700
Savings accounts	1,200	1,200
CDs < $100M	7,900	8,300
CDs > $100M	4,810	5,120
Total deposits	$32,410	$34,320
Other liabilities	800	700
Stockholders' equity	2,540	2,980
Total liabilities and equity	$35,750	$38,000

[a] Loan commitments expected to total $3 million on December 31, 1997, and $4.5 million on December 31, 1998. Original maturities were over 1 year.

EXHIBIT 3B   Marcy State Bank—Pro Forma Income Statement (dollars in thousands)

	Year Ended 12/31/97	Year Ended 12/31/98
Interest income	$3,440	$4,020
Interest expense	1,620	2,120
Net interest income	1,820	1,900
Provision for loan losses (PLL)	250	200
Net interest income after PLL	1,570	1,700
Noninterest income	350	380
Noninterest expenses		
Salaries and benefits	680	650
Occupancy, furnishings, and equipment	400	390
Other	700	600
Total noninterest expense	$1,780	$1,640
Net income (loss) before taxes	140	440
Income taxes (credit)	0	0
Net income (loss)	$ 140	$ 440

EXHIBIT 4A   Risk-Weighting Categories for Risk-Based Capital Standard

Category 1 (0% risk weight)
    Cash
    Federal balances
    Federal Reserve Bank stock
    Treasuries/guaranteed U.S. govt. agency debt
Category 2 (20% risk weight)
    Collateralized loans
    Due from nonofficial banks
    Government-sponsored agency debt
    General obligation bonds
Category 3 (50% risk weight)
    Revenue bonds
    Residential mortgages
Category 4 (100% risk weight)
    Commercial and consumer loans
    Other loans
    Other assets
    Other real estate owned
    Furniture, fixtures, and equipment
Off-balance sheet items
    Loan commitments, maturities > 1 year (50% conversion factor [c.f.])
    Standby letters of credit (100% c.f.)
    Risk participation in bankers' acceptances (100% c.f.)
    Interest rate swaps, options (100% c.f.)

Total capital must be 8.00% of risk-weighted assets; up to 1.25% of this requirement can be loan loss reserve.

It is anticipated that Marcy State Bank will make up its capital requirements exclusively with stockholders' equity and allowable loan loss reserves.

Goodwill and other intangible assets are not admissible as capital.

EXHIBIT 4B   Eligible Capital for Risk-Based Capital Requirements

1. Core capital (Tier I)
    a. Common tangible equity
    b. Perpetual preferred stock and qualified, mandatory convertible debt up to 25%
    c. Minority interest in equity of consolidated subsidiaries
2. Tier II: limited to 100% of Tier I
    a. Nonspecific loan loss reserve up to 1.25% of risk-adjusted assets (RAA)
    b. Perpetual preferred stock not included in Tier I
    c. Mandatory convertible debt not included in Tier I
    d. Long-term subordinated debt—limited to 50% of Tier I on a phased-out straight-line basis in the last five years of life
    e. Limited-life preferred stock—included with and treated like long-term subordinated debt
3. Risk-based capital ratios:

$$\text{Tier I ratio} = \frac{\text{Tier I capital}}{\text{Risk-Adjusted Assets}}$$

$$\text{Tier I and II ratio} = \frac{\text{Tier I} + \text{Tier II capital}}{\text{Risk-Adjusted Assets}}$$

$$\text{Leverage ratio} = \frac{\text{Tier I capital}}{\text{Tangible assets}}$$

EXHIBIT 4C   Bank Classification According to Capital Ratios under Prompt Corrective Action (FDIC Improvement Act of 1991)

	Risk-Based Capital		Leverage Tier I/ Tangible Assets
	Tiers I and II	Tier I	
1. Well capitalized: Significantly exceeds required capital standards. *Restrictions:* None.	>10%	>6%	>5%
2. Adequately capitalized: Meets minimum standards. *Restrictions:* Cannot underwrite insurance where state law permits. Requires approval of FDIC to accept brokered funds.	>8%	>4%	>4%
3. Undercapitalized: Fails to meet minimum standards. *Restrictions:* As in 2 above and close monitoring by regulatory agency; capital restoration plan; asset growth restricted; needs approval for acquisitions, branching, new activities.	<8%	<4%	<4%
4. Significantly undercapitalized: Significantly below required minimum standard. *Restrictions*: As in 3 above and must sell new stock to recapitalize; restrictions on transactions with affiliates, as well as on interest paid on deposits and management compensation; must divest troubled affiliates.	<6%	<3%	<3%
5. Critically undercapitalized: Less than 2% leverage capital ratio. *Restrictions:* As in 4 above and prohibition of interest payments on subordinated debt. Placed in receivership or conservatorship within 90 days.			<2%

EXHIBIT 5   Risk-Based Capital Requirements—Marcy State Bank—Pro Forma Statement of Condition (dollars in thousands)

	December 31, 1997	December 31, 1998	Weight	12/31/97 Risk-wtd.	12/31/98 Risk-wtd.
Cash and federal balances	$ 1,800	$ 2,000	0.00%	_____	_____
Placements with banks	600	600	20.00%	_____	_____
Investment securities					
Treasuries	1,800	2,000	0.00%	_____	_____
Govt.-sponsored agencies	1,900	2,000	20.00%	_____	_____
Federal funds sold	3,000	1,000	20.00%	_____	_____
Loans					
Residential mortgages	14,000	16,000	50.00%	_____	_____
Consumer and commercial	10,000	11,600	100.00%	_____	_____
Allowance for loan losses	(200)	(200)	—	_____	_____
Premises and equipment	900	900	100.00%	_____	_____
Other real estate owned	500	600	100.00%	_____	_____
Intangible assets	225	200	—	_____	_____
Goodwill	725	700	—	_____	_____
Other assets	500	600	100.00%	_____	_____
Total assets	$35,750	$38,000			
Loan commitments at $3 million, $4.5 million on 12/31/97, 12/31/98			50%	_____	_____
Total Risk-Weighted Assets				═══	═══
Demand deposits	$ 6,000	$ 6,000			
Interest-bearing checking accounts	3,000	3,000			
Money market deposits	9,500	10,700			
Savings accounts	1,200	1,200			
CDs < $100M	7,900	8,300			
CDs > $100M	4,810	5,120			
Total deposits	$32,410	$34,320			
Other liabilities	800	700			
Stockholders' equity	2,540	2,980			
Total liabilities and equity	$35,750	$38,000			

Qualifying Capital:	*12/31/97*	*12/31/98*
Stockholders' equity		
+ Loan loss reserve[a]	+ _____	_____
− Intangible assets	− _____	_____
− Goodwill	− _____	_____
Total		
Risk-wtd. capital ratio = (Tiers I & II)	═══	═══
Leverage ratio[b] =	═══	═══

[a] Maximum allowed is the lesser of:
  1. 1.25% of risk weighted assets, or
  2. Allowances for loan losses on the balance sheet.

[b] Leverage ratio $= \dfrac{\text{Tier I capital}}{\text{Tangible assets}}$

CASE 7B

HILLSIDE BANCORP (B)

INTRODUCTION

A year had passed since Hillside Bancorp acquired Marcy State Bank in January 1997. The new owners were disappointed over large unanticipated loan losses, necessitating a substantial provision against income. Still, they were very aggressive in reserving for and taking writeoffs. As a result, the new owners were confident that all of Marcy State Bank's loan problems had been identified.

Economic conditions in Marcy continued to improve; home sales were increasing at prices above last year's. The city's share of sales tax revenues actually exceeded budget by 7 percent for the year. Several new specialty retail shops opened earlier in the year and enjoyed good sales volumes.

At Marcy State, several other unexpected events had occurred, including a large increase in noninterest expense due to several factors. These included recognition of certain abandoned improvements to a branch closed during the year 1997, high legal expenses, the buyout of the former president's employment contract, and recognition of certain costs incurred under the bank's data processing agreement, scheduled to terminate on June 30, 1998. The bank's actual financial statements for 1997 are shown in Exhibit B1.

Phil Forbes had been informed that examiners from the state and the FDIC were preparing an order demanding that Marcy State increase its capital. He knew that the capital plan he was creating for submission to the examiners would have to take into account the bank's new circumstances. He believed that, with Hillside National's highly professional support, Marcy State Bank's losses had been largely recognized by now. He began to prepare a new pro forma balance sheet for 1998.

FORBES'S TASKS

Phil Forbes would have to follow these steps:

1. Compare actual 1997 balance sheet and income statement results (Exhibit B1) with pro forma 1997 statements prepared in early 1997 (case A). Among other things, determine the apparent actual writeoffs in 1997 (case B) and compare with the implicit expected writeoffs in the pro forma statements (case A).

2. Develop revised pro forma financial statements for 1998 (Exhibit B1). Determine how much additional capital Hillside Bancorp should inject under its new capital plan.

3. Ascertain whether Marcy State Bank will meet the risk-based capital and leverage (or primary) capital requirements (Exhibit B2, capital worksheet).

EXHIBIT B1-A   Marcy State Bank—Statement of Condition 1997 (dollars in thousands)

	Actual December 31, 1997[a]
Cash and balances at Fed	$ 1,700
Placements with banks	700
Investment securities	
Treasuries	1,300
Government-sponsored agencies	1,900
Federal funds sold	3,000
Loans	
Residential mortgages	14,000
Consumer and commercial	6,000

EXHIBIT BI-A   (*Continued*)

	Actual December 31, 1997[a]
Allowance for loan losses	(150)
Premises, furnishings, and equipment	800
Other real estate owned	1,500
Intangible assets	225
Goodwill	725
Other assets	600
Total assets	$32,300
Demand deposits	5,800
Interest-bearing checking deposits	2,600
Money market deposits	9,300
Savings accounts	1,200
CDs < $100M	6,200
CDs > $100M	4,840
Total deposits	29,940
Other liabilities	800
Stockholders' equity	1,560
Total liabilities and equity	$32,300

[a] Loan commitments totaled $4 million at 12/31/97 (original maturities were over 1 year).

EXHIBIT BI-B   Marcy State Bank—Income Statement 1997 and Revised Pro Forma for 1998 (dollars in thousands)

	Actual 1997	Pro Forma 1998
Interest income	$3,200	_____
Interest expense	1,640	_____
Net interest income	1,560	_____
Provision for loan losses	500	_____
Net interest income after PLL	1,060	_____
Noninterest income	360	_____
Noninterest expenses		
Salaries and benefits	740	_____
Occupancy, furnishings, and equipment	400	_____
Other	920	_____
Total noninterest expense	2,060	_____
Net income (loss) before taxes	(640)	_____
Income taxes (credit)	0	_____
Net income (loss)	$ (640)	_____

EXHIBIT B2   Marcy State Bank—Statement of Condition 1997, Revised pro forma for 1998 and Capital Worksheet (dollars in thousands)

	Actual December 31, 1997	Pro Forma: 12/31/98 (revised)	Weight	Risk-Weighted Assets	
				Actual 12/31/97	Pro Forma 12/31/98
Cash and balances at Fed	$ 1,700	_____	0%	_____	_____
Placements with banks	700	_____	20	_____	_____
Investment securities					
Treasuries	1,300	_____	0	_____	_____
Government-sponsored agencies	1,900	_____	20	_____	_____
Federal funds sold	3,000	_____	20	_____	_____
Loans					
Residential mortgages	14,000	_____	50	_____	_____
Consumer and commercial	6,000	_____	100	_____	_____
Allowance for loan losses	(150)	_____		_____	_____
Premises, furnishings, and equipment	800	_____	100	_____	_____
Other real estate owned	1,500	_____	100	_____	_____
Intangible assets	225	_____		_____	_____
Goodwill	725	_____		_____	_____
Other assets	600	_____	100	_____	_____
Total assets	$32,300	_____			
Loan commitments at $4 million on 12/31/97			50		
Total Risk-Weighted Assets				_____	_____
Demand deposits	5,800	_____			
Interest-bearing checking accounts	2,600	_____			
Money market deposits	9,300	_____			
Savings accounts	1,200	_____			
CDs < $100M	6,200	_____			
CDs > $100M	4,840	_____			
Total deposits	29,940				
Other liabilities	800	_____			
Stockholders' equity	1,560	_____			
Total liabilities and equity	$32,300	_____			

Qualifying Capital	*12/31/97*	*12/31/98*
Stockholders' equity		
+ *Allow for loan losses	+ _____	_____
− Intangible assets	− _____	_____
− Goodwill	− _____	_____
Total		
Risk-wtd. capital ratio = (Tiers I & II)	══════	══════
Tier I risk-weighted capital ratio = Tier I capital/(r-w assets−allow*)	══════	══════
Leverage ratio = Tier I capital/assets	══════	══════

*Minimum of 1.25% risk-weighted assets or actual allowance

CASE 8

ASPICT BANKSHARES CORPORATION

INTRODUCTION

In April 1997, Doug Wolford, CEO of Aspict Bankshares Corporation (ABC), was considering a capital plan in light of the firm's ongoing acquisition program. Wolford had been recruited into the top job at ABC in 1989 in the midst of a period of great strain for depository institutions. At the time, widespread failures were decimating the savings and loan industry and commercial banks were failing at a rate of over 200 per year. Under Wolford's guidance, the firm began to pick up small blocks of deposits by acquiring local branches of savings and loan companies that were in the process of dissolution under federal regulators. Through this program, Aspict grew from a modest one-bank holding company with $89 million in assets in 1989 to a company with $287 million in assets as of March 31, 1997, including a nationally chartered bank ($186 million assets) and nonbanking subsidiaries active in venture capital and livestock credit.

ABC served a market located in several communities, all of which were within 50 miles of a metropolitan area of about 1.5 million in population. The bank specialized in small business and agricultural credit as well as retail banking, although lately it began to build a substantial portfolio of real estate mortgages. Twenty-five percent of Aspict's stock was held by family members of the bank's original owner who founded the bank before the Great Depression.

PROGRESS ON PRESENT ACQUISITION

A stock purchase agreement had been drawn up to acquire Gramarcy State Bank, a local competitor with $65 million in assets, for $10,770,000, although regulatory approval still needed to be obtained. Exhibit 1 presents a pro forma combined statement for the consolidated holding company that would result from the acquisition. (Regulatory rules required bank holding companies with more than $150 million in assets to report all holdings on a consolidated basis.) Exhibit 2 shows the accounting adjustments required to effect the consolidation of the proposed new banking subsidiary. These adjustments include the revaluation of the book values

of the to-be-acquired bank's securities and bank premises to fair market values. In addition, the exhibit records an intangible asset in the amount of the excess of the purchase price over the restated value of the acquired assets. Finally, it reflects adjustments made to investment securities (federal funds) for the holding company's cash payment for the purchase, paid to the owner-sellers of Gramarcy State Bank.

Wolford knew that the pro forma consolidated organization must meet three types of regulatory capital standards. Slight variations of these standards were applied to banks throughout the industrialized world. The standards included (1) the Tier 1 risk-weighted ratio, (2) the Tier 1 plus Tier 2 risk-weighted ratio, and (3) the total tangible assets Tier 1 leverage ratio (Tier 1 capital divided by tangible assets). The more that banking firms fell short of the minimum ratios, the more they were exposed to regulatory restraints on their activities. The required levels for each of these ratios are outlined in Exhibit 3. Although capital ratios that meet "adequately capitalized" standards in Exhibit 3 were acceptable, it was widely recognized that regulators were only comfortable with "well-capitalized" ratios, a designation achieved by over 98 percent of banks in the United States. Exhibit 4 provides a calculation worksheet for determining the pro forma capital schedule and the risk-weighted assets for the consolidated holding company. Intangible assets are not allowable as capital and are deducted from calculations of capital, risk-weighted assets, and total assets. Exhibit 5 presents a pro forma combined income statement for 12 months ending March 31, 1998.

CAPITAL PLANNING

As indicated in Exhibit 1, the acquisition of Gramarcy State Bank would expand Aspict's asset footings to $345 million. In addition, Wolford and his staff were negotiating the acquisition of a suburban branch with $28 million in deposits from a large multiregional bank that had a strong position in the metropolitan area. ABC was also embarking on

Case 8 was prepared in collaboration with Carla Brooks, KPMG Peat Marwick, Dallas, Texas.

the application for a *de novo* branch in a community near its suburban headquarters. However, Wolford knew that the board was committed to finding still other acquisitions to expand the organization's franchise in the wider region around the metropolitan area.

In reviewing these present and planned acquisitions, Wolford had growing concerns over the firm's ability to generate the required capital base for its banking holdings. Wolford, an "outsider" to the controlling family, understood that the family did not wish to have its holdings diluted by the issuance of more common shares. Moreover, the family did not have the liquid resources that would allow it to add significantly to its present holdings, although, so far, the family was pleased with ABC's growth under Wolford.

Potentially, a capital shortfall at the bank level could be remedied by issuing subordinated debt or preferred stock through the holding company and injecting capital downstream as equity into the bank subsidiaries. However, this would not necessarily solve the capital problem at the holding company level.

Wolford was uncertain about whether the organization's capital needs would be best served with Tier 1 or Tier 2-type capital. Tier 1 capital would support both the Tier 1 to risk-weighted assets ratio and the leverage ratio. Still, if common stock issuance were not feasible, Wolford knew that perpetual noncumulative preferred stock, allowed as Tier 1 capital, would not be as attractive to investors as perpetual preferred that was cumulative (but only allowed as Tier 2 capital at the bank level). The issuance of subordinated debt, allowable only as Tier 2 capital, was restricted to no more than 50 percent of total Tier 1 capital.

The market for the apparent level of capital needed by Aspict was a "custom" market. Issuances of preferred stock and subordinated debt in the range above $15 or $20 million were of the right size to attract interest among regional investment bankers who often succeeded in placing such issues with wealthy individual investor clients. In addition, at that issuance size, long-term institutional investors such as insurance companies, pension funds,

and mutual funds at times had expressed interest in banking securities. However, Wolford worried that with an issuance of $20 million or more, a substantial period would ensue in which the firm would be heavily overcapitalized and underleveraged.

Preferred stock issuances under the $15 to $20 million size would probably require Wolford or board members with prominent connections to "hit the street" by soliciting possibly dozens of individual subscriptions from more modest investors. Wolford thought he could persuade a wealthy friend or two to commit up to $1 million apiece, but an experience he had earlier in his career of chartering a new bank suggested he also could wind up trying to sell the new security in numerous blocks as small as $25,000 to $50,000 each. The thought of a seemingly interminable series of one-on-one breakfasts and lunches for the purpose of selling the organization's capital loomed as an unwelcome claim on his time, especially since he wanted the organization to continue its ambitious plans for growth.

WOLFORD'S TASK

Wolford understood that he had to prepare crucial decisions for the board. He broke his tasks down into the following steps:

1. Determine Aspict Bankshares Corporation's Tier 1, Tier 2, and total capital. Compute risk-weighted assets (Exhibit 4).

2. Compute the three different regulatory capital ratios for ABC.

3. Determine the additional capital needed by ABC to meet the "well-capitalized" levels of Exhibit 3. If the firm did not expect further expansion by acquisition or new branching, how should it raise this additional capital?

4. Given ABC's expected growth between now and the year 2000, how should it meet its requirements for more capital? That is, how much additional capital, when, and in what form? Wolford knew he would have to create pro forma income statements over the interim years and incorporate the expected retained earnings into capital.

EXHIBIT 1   Pro Forma Combined Balance Sheet After Acquisition of Gramarcy State Bank

This schedule reflects the pro forma combined balance sheet after adjustments for the period ending March 31, 1997. All entries in the adjustment column are footnoted and explained in Exhibit 2 following.

	Consolidated BHC 3/31/97	Gramarcy State Bank 3/31/97	Adjustments	Pro Forma Consolidated BHC
ASSETS				
Cash	2,537	880		3,417
Securities issued by the United States government and its agencies	14,596	16,928	(304)	31,220
All other claims on the United States government and its agencies	15,705	1,488		17,193
Claims on government-sponsored agencies	46,341	9,183	(486)	55,038
General obligation claims on state and local governments	11,118	663	63	11,844
Claims on depository institutions (including demand deposits)	24,028	15,590	(10,770)	28,848
Revenue bonds	1,775	409		2,184
Commercial and consumer loans (net of unearned income)	124,933	14,936		139,869
Loan claims on government-sponsored agencies	17,141			17,141
Qualifying 1–4 family mortgages	18,117	3,416		21,533
Less: Allowance for loan and lease losses	(1,497)	(498)		(1,995)
	158,694	17,854	0	176,548
Bank premises, furniture, fixtures	6,689	716	459	7,864
Other assets	4,197	1,029		5,226
Intangible assets	1,568	0	3,773	5,341
TOTAL ASSETS	287,248	64,740	(7,265)	344,723
LIABILITIES				
Demand deposits	40,496	8,774		49,270
Time deposits	224,109	48,406		272,515
Total deposits	264,605	57,180		321,785
Interest, taxes, and other liabilities		—		0
Federal funds purchased and securities sold under agreement to repurchase	—	—		0
Other borrowed money with original maturity of one year or less	3,170	—		3,170
Other liabilities	1,878	295		2,173
TOTAL LIABILITIES	269,653	57,475		327,128
CAPITAL				
Subordinated notes and debentures	0	—		0
Stockholders equity				
Preferred stock	0	—		0
Common stock	167	600	(600)	167
Surplus	2,542	900	(900)	2,542
			(5,497)	
Retained profits	16,166	6,287	(790)	16,166
Net unrealized gains (losses), AFS	(1,280)	(522)	522	(1,280)
Other capital and contingency reserves				
TOTAL EQUITY CAPITAL	17,595	7,265	(7,265)	17,595
TOTAL LIABILITIES, SUBORDINATED NOTES AND DEBENTURES, AND EQUITY CAPITAL	287,248	64,740	(7,265)	344,723

EXHIBIT 2   Adjustments to Create Post-Acquisition Consolidated Balance Sheet

Adjustments	Debit	Credit
General obligation claims on state and local governments	63	
Bank premises	459	
Retained earnings	790	
Securities issued by the United States government and its agencies		304
Claims on government-sponsored agencies		486
Net unrealized holding gains (losses), AFS		522
To record purchase accounting adjustments		
Common stock	600	
Surplus	900	
Retained earnings	5,497	
Intangible assets	3,773	
Investment securities		10,770

To record purchase of Gramarcy State Bank by First National Bank.

EXHIBIT 3   Bank Classifications According to Capital Ratios under Prompt Corrective Action (FDIC Improvement Act of 1991)

	Risk-Based Capital		Leverage
	Tiers 1 & 2	Tier 1	Tier 1/ Assets
1. Well capitalized: Significantly exceeds required capital standards. *Restrictions:* None.	>10%	>6%	>5%
2. Adequately capitalized: Meets minimum standards. *Restrictions:* Cannot underwrite insurance where state law permits. Requires approval of FDIC to accept brokered funds.	>8%	>4%	>4%
3. Undercapitalized: Fails to meet minimum standards. *Restrictions:* As in 2 above and close monitoring by regulatory agency; capital restoration plan; asset growth restricted; needs approval for acquisitions, branching, new activities.	<8%	<4%	<4%
4. Significantly undercapitalized: Significantly below required minimum standard. *Restrictions*: As in 3 above and must sell new stock to recapitalize; restrictions on transactions with affiliates, as well as on interest paid on deposits and management compensation; must divest troubled affiliates.	<6%	<3%	<3%
5. Critically undercapitalized: Less than 2% leverage capital ratio. *Restrictions:* As in 4 above and prohibition of interest payments on subordinated debt. Placed in receivership or conservatorship within 90 days.			<2%

EXHIBIT 4   Pro Forma Capital Schedule: Consolidated BHC

Part A: Qualifying Capital

Tier 1:	Common Stock and Surplus	_____	
	Perpetual preferred with noncumulative dividends and related surplus	_____	
	Undivided profits	_____	
	Other	_____	
	Net unrealized gains (losses), AFS	_____	
Less:	Goodwill and ineligible intangibles[a]	_____	
Total Tier 1			_____
Tier 2:	Subordinated debt[b]	_____	
	Intermediate term (original maturity ≥ 5 years) preferred stock[b]	_____	_____
			Limited to 50% of Total Tier 1
	Subtotal	_____	
	Long-term preferred stock[b] (original maturity ≥ 20 years)	_____	
	Perpetual preferred stock	_____	
	Allowance for loan and lease losses (1.25% of total risk-weighted assets)[c]	_____	
	Other	_____	
	Subtotal	_____	
Total Tier 2 capital Limited to 100% of total Tier 1			_____
Total Tier 1 and Tier 2			_____
	Less: Investments in unconsolidated subsidiaries		_____
Total capital			=========

[a] Included, but is not limited to, deposit, tax attributes, or any other intangibles.

[b] Subject to discount by a fifth of the original amount in each of the last five years prior to maturity.

[c] Must not exceed actual balance sheet amount.

Part B: Risk-Weighted Assets Estimation

	Pro Forma Consolidated BHC
Cash	_____
Securities issued by the United States government and its agencies	_____
Subtotal A (0% risk weight)	_____
All other claims on the United States government and its agencies	_____
Security and Loan Claims on government-sponsored agencies	_____

EXHIBIT 4   *(Continued)*

	Pro Forma Consolidated BHC
General obligation claims on state and local governments[a]	
Claims on depository institutions (including demand deposits)	

Risk-Weighted Assets Estimation

Subtotal B (20% risk weight)	
Revenue bonds	
Qualifying 1–4 family mortgages	
Subtotal C (50% risk weight)	
All other balance sheet tangible assets = Tangible assets + allowance for LL − subtotals A, B and C	
Net unrealized gains (losses), AFS (100% risk weight)	
Off-balance sheet	
Commitments (50% risk weight)	
All other off-balance sheet items (guarantees, standby L/Cs, repos, and sales with recourse that do not appear on the balance sheet, etc.) (100% risk weight)	
Gross risk-weighted assets:	

Claims refer to loans to, securities issued by, loans or securities guaranteed by, and loans collateralized by securities issued by or guaranteed by the entity in question.

* Collateral consisting of general obligation securities issued by or guaranteed by state and local governments or securities issued by banks does not qualify a loan for inclusion in the 20% category.

Part C: Adjusted Total Assets
(For Leverage Ratio Calculations)

Total assets—Charter bank	
Less: Purchase price	
Plus: Total assets acquired institution	
Plus: Purchase accounting adjustments*	
Less: Disallowed intangible assets	
Less: Losses not charged off	
Less: Premium for this transaction	
Net unrealized gains (losses), AFS	
Equals: Adjusted total assets	

*These totaled 3,505.

Part D: Ratio Calculations

Tier 1 capital/Adjusted total assets =	
Tier 1 capital/Risk-weighted assets =	
Tier 1 and 2 capital/Risk-weighted assets =	

EXHIBIT 5   Pro Forma Combined Income Statement for the 12 Months Ending March 31, 1998

	First National Bank	Gramarcy State Bank	Combined
Interest Income			
Real estate loans	5,500	700	6,200
Installment loans	825	575	1,400
Credit card and related plans	150	25	175
Commercial loans	3,025	700	3,725
Due from banks	10	150	160
Taxable securities	20	0	20
Tax-exempt securities	425	100	525
U.S. government securities	2,350	1,400	3,750
Other domestic debt securities	100	0	100
Equity securities	25	0	25
Federal funds sold	175	200	375
Total Interest Income	12,605	3,850	16,455
Interest Expense			
NOW accounts	675	250	925
Money market accounts	400	150	550
Other savings deposits	550	100	650
Certificates of deposit > $100,000	975	275	1,250
Certificates of deposit < $100,000	1,750	500	2,250
Federal funds purchased	0	0	0
Total Interest Expense	4,350	1,275	5,625
Net Interest Income	8,255	2,575	10,830
Provision for loan losses	300	0	300
Noninterest Income			
Service charges	1,400	550	1,950
Other fee income	275	25	300
Other noninterest income	75	50	125
Total Noninterest Income	1,750	625	2,375
Realized gains (losses) on AFS securities	(200)	0	(200)
Noninterest Expense			
Salaries and employee benefits	3,725	900	4,625
Premises and fixed assets	975	200	1,175
Other noninterest expense	2,700	800	3,500
Total Noninterest Expense	7,400	1,900	9,300
Income before taxes/extraordinary items	2,105	1,300	3,405
Applicable income taxes	755	450	1,205
Net Income	1,350	850	2,200

EXHIBIT 5   (*Continued*)

Ratio assumptions used to create the pro forma combined income statement for the
12 months ending March 31, 1998.

	As a % of Average Assets
Interest income	6.75%
Interest expense	2.30%
Net interest income	4.45%
Noninterest income	0.97%
Noninterest expense	3.81%
Provision for loan and lease losses	0.12%
Realized gains (losses) on AFS	0.08%
Applicable income taxes	0.52%
Net income	0.98%

NOTE: Even though interest rates have increased since the pro forma income statement was prepared, the net interest margin is expected to be maintained.

PART THREE

MANAGING LOANS AND THE LOAN PORTFOLIO

The previous chapters of this book described the measurement and analysis of overall bank performance and examined specifics of managing liquidity, investments, funds attraction, and capital. We consider these topics to be subordinate to banks' lending activities. Lending is a bank's toughest challenge. With this in mind, the three chapters of this section are devoted to the management of the lending function.

Chapter 10 presents the structure of credit risk in banks. It examines one aspect of the risk in credit transactions: how banks organize to manage the risk in credit operations. The key organizing principle is to design an institutional infrastructure that minimizes losses within the constraints of policy and regulation. The emphasis is on safely processing one loan at a time.

Chapter 11 examines the two other aspects of managing credit transactions risk. It reviews the fundamentals of managing credit selection risk, including qualitative and quantitative analysis. The chapter then discusses managing underwriting risk including creating the loan agreement, monitoring loan performance, pricing, and rating loans for risk. It goes on to describe means of managing aspects of portfolio risk, namely, intrinsic risk and concentration risk. The chapter ends with a presentation of the various types of loans banks make to the nonconsumer private sector.

Chapter 12 concentrates on consumer and real estate lending, including aspects of loan selection, types of loans, and regulatory provisions that affect such lending. ∎

CHAPTER 10

The Bank
Credit Organization

Ironically, industrialists sometimes fail to identify the basic nature of their businesses. For example, managers of General Motors Chevrolet Division and the Mercedes-Benz Division of the Daimler-Benz Company probably assume that their core business is making automobiles. However, few automobile aficionados would agree that the core businesses of these two companies are identical. It is Chevrolet's business to satisfy the basic transportation needs of individuals and families, whereas Daimler-Benz's business is to provide luxury.

By the same token, the core business of banks is not, as bankers might assume, taking deposits and making loans. Successful bank lending is based not on making loans but on minimizing the risk in collecting them. Thus, the true core business of banking is *the profitable management of risk.*

Banks' survival and ability to compete depend foremost on their ability to profitably manage *credit risk.* Historically, banking crises in the United States and in the rest of the world have occurred when a group of banks create loans of poor quality. True, banks may occasionally get into trouble because of insufficient liquidity, unexpected interest rate movements, and so forth. But when banks *fail,* they do so because of poor-quality loans.

Lending is based on the two fundamental products of banking: money and information. Banks obtain these products from customers themselves by offering customers valuable services. They package money and information about their borrowers together with valuable banking services to create loan agreements and then, in effect, sell the loan agreements back to their customers. The trick is to create loan agreement packages and management systems that maximize banks' chances of getting the money back.

We observe in Appendix 10A that the scope of bank lending is changing. Still, national data indicate the central role lending plays in banks. At the present time, nearly $3 trillion in bank loans are outstanding. Interest and fees on these loans contribute over two-thirds of banks' total operating income. Bank lending is cyclical and reflects the robustness of economic conditions. At the end of the 1990s, loans accounted for 60 percent of banks' total assets. Early in the decade, however, loans had declined to slightly less than 50 percent of banks' total assets.

Bank loans finance diverse groups in the economy. Manufacturers, distributors, service firms, farmers, builders, home buyers, commercial real estate developers, consumers, and others all depend on bank credit. The ways in which banks allocate their loanable funds strongly influence the economic development of communities and the nation. Bankers find that it is in their own best interests to supply credit within the communities they serve because credit helps communities to grow, thus expanding the market for banking products. In addition, bank regulators prompt banks to comply with the Community Reinvestment Act, which requires banks to evaluate their communities' credit needs closely and to service and stimulate local economic activities.

Every bank bears a degree of risk when it lends to private borrowers such as businesses and consumers, and, without exception, every bank experiences some loan losses when certain borrowers fail to repay their loans as agreed. Whatever the degree of risk taken, loan losses can be minimized by organizing and managing the lending function in a highly professional manner.

LOAN RISKS AND LOSSES

The trends in lending show that banks' lending opportunities have declined among low-risk borrowers. As we described earlier, commercial paper, securitization, and nonbank competition have pushed banks toward riskier classes of borrowers to replace these traditional borrowers. For example, large, stable corporate borrowers that once were the mainstays of banks' loan portfolios have shifted to open market sources like commercial paper and the bond market in order to lower their transactions costs. Banks have been seeking to replace this business with smaller, less stable borrowers.

Recent banking history shows how critical it is for banks to control lending risks. Poor loan quality was the main factor in the large number of U.S. bank failures a decade or so ago, which culminated in an average of nearly 200 failures per year from 1987 to 1992.

Figure 10.1 shows *net loan losses* as a percentage of loans outstanding for all U.S. banks from 1976 to 1997. Net loan losses are loans charged off during a year minus recoveries of principal on loans that were previously charged off. There is a clear relationship between net loan losses and years during and following recessions. For example, the decline in loan losses for several years beginning in 1976 followed the recession years of 1974 and 1975. Recession and its attendant poor economic conditions produce declines in firms' sales and profit margins. Falling sales generate unexpected increases in corporate inventories, and falling profits cause firms to attempt to cut overhead. These changes can be readily observed in a borrower's financial statements and may foretell a coming delinquency.

Beginning in about 1983, loan losses for the banking system began a sharp rise that finally flattened out in 1987. This rise in losses was not related to national economic conditions but rather to concentrations of loans in some banks among weak borrowers in the Third World and in energy, farming, and real estate. These sectors suffered from a combination of causes, including disinflationary trends that followed the severe inflation of 1979–1982, declines in export markets, and a reaction to earlier aggressive international lending by certain banks. The pattern of the 1980s caused well-managed banks to imple-

FIGURE 10.1   Loan Losses: Percent of Loans

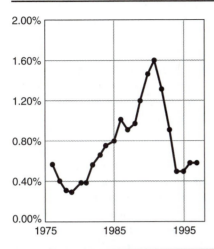

ment and enforce sounder loan policies and to use their loan review functions to detect inappropriate concentrations of loans that might expose them to pyramiding losses. The rise in loan losses resumed from 1988 to 1991 following overinvestment in commercial real estate and the approach of the recession of 1990–1991. Subsequently, loan losses declined rapidly from their 1991 peak as economic factors strengthened through 1998.

In a study of national banks that failed in the mid-1980s, the Comptroller of the Currency found that the consistent element in the failures was the inadequacy of the banks' management systems for controlling loan quality. In reporting its findings, the Comptroller's office listed several basic faults in lending procedures, including the following:

1. Inattention to loan policies.
2. Overly generous loan terms and lack of clear standards.
3. Disregard of banks' own policies.
4. Unsafe concentration of credit.
5. Poor control over loan personnel.
6. Loan growth beyond the banks' ability to control quality.
7. Poor systems for detecting loan problems.
8. Lack of understanding of borrowers' cash needs.
9. Out-of-market lending.

MANAGING CREDIT RISK

This section discusses the principles of managing the risks of bank lending.

Credit Philosophy and Culture

Managing credit risk requires a clear *credit philosophy* in order to set management's priorities with respect to the marketplace. Banks' credit philosophies may range from an emphasis on consistent performance of the highest quality loan portfolio based on highly conservative underwriting standards to an emphasis on aggressive loan growth and market share with highly flexible underwriting standards. The bank's lending philosophy is established in a formal written loan policy.

Next, the credit philosophy and loan policy must be supported and communicated with an appropriate *credit culture.* An effective credit culture exists when the actual behavior of every individual in the loan organization is closely aligned with management's priorities. Finally, credit culture is reflected in the loan organization's systems and procedures that implement management's priorities and minimize errors and poor lending decisions.

Figure 10.2 shows the profit and risk of the possible range of credit philosophies, supported with a credit culture continuum over this range. Figure 10.2A indicates that *expected* returns increase when banks emphasize growth and flexible loan standards. Panel 10.2B shows, however, that the volatility of *actual* returns increases as philosophical priorities shift toward growth and flexibility. A priority that emphasizes loan quality is the lower-risk one and produces stable earnings. The growth and flexibility set of priorities is the higher-risk one and is associated with "acceptable" loan quality and expectations of superior but unstable earnings.

FIGURE 10.2   Returns and Risk for Credit Philosophy and Culture

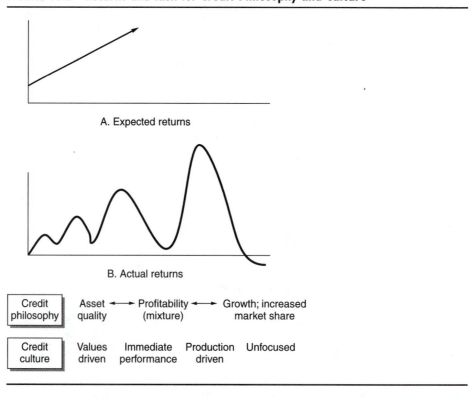

A. Expected returns

B. Actual returns

| Credit philosophy | Asset quality | ← Profitability → (mixture) | Growth; increased market share |

| Credit culture | Values driven | Immediate performance | Production driven | Unfocused |

FIGURE 10.3   The Structure of Bank Credit Risk

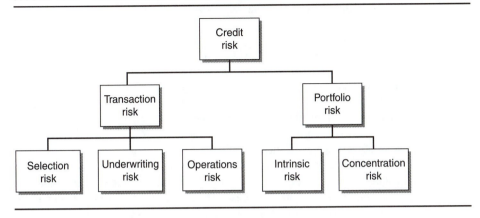

Credit Risk Management Strategy

Once the credit philosophy and culture have been set, the bank must design its credit risk management strategy. Figure 10.3 illustrates the structure of bank credit risk.[1] Overall credit risk is divided into two basic parts—*transaction risk* and *portfolio risk.* Transaction risk is the risk taken as the bank accumulates loans one loan at a time. The rest of this chapter as well as parts of Chapter 11 concern transaction risk.

Chapter 11 also considers portfolio risk. It will show how portfolio risk is divided into *intrinsic risk* and *concentration risk.* Intrinsic risk arises from factors that are unique to specific borrowers or industries—for example, a particular borrower's or industry's customer base, its geographic market, its financial leverage, and so forth. Concentration risk stems from the dollar amounts or proportions of banks' loan portfolios accumulated in single affiliated borrowers or industries or in narrow types of loans (e.g., energy, commercial real estate, less developed countries, highly leveraged transactions), as well as certain geographic areas.

We address transaction risk in three components: *selection risk, underwriting risk, and operations risk.* Chapter 11 covers the first of these—selection risk—by discussing the bank's systems of credit investigation and analysis. It also discusses underwriting risk in terms of the bank's standards for underwriting loans—for example, the terms written into its loan agreements, the kinds of collateral it accepts, and so forth.

In this chapter we review how banks solve problems of operations risk with the types of credit organizations they create to administer the credit function. We explain the need for and the formulation of a *loan policy* to steer banks toward the desired makeup and control of their loan portfolios. We include the *loan approval* process in the discussion of loan policy. Then we discuss *loan review and monitoring* of the loan portfolio, including the use of *risk rating systems.* We also cover the technical aspects of problem loan administration, basically the legal and pecuniary protection of the loan portfolio. Finally, we ex-

---

[1] This framework was first suggested in John E. McKinley and John R. Barrickman, *Strategic Credit Risk Management* (Philadelphia: Robert Morris Associates, 1994).

plain the indirect controls on the loan portfolio that result from regulation and the examination of banks by various bank supervisory agencies.

THE CREDIT ORGANIZATION

The organizational structure of the lending function varies with a bank's size and type of business. An officer of a small bank may perform all of the detailed work associated with making a loan, including credit investigation and analysis, negotiation, customer contact, periodic review of the loan file, and even, at times, collection. In larger banks, individual loan officers specialize in consulting and negotiating with customers, and there is greater compartmentalization of support functions such as credit analysis, loan review, and loan collection. The next chapter will explain the main tasks of loan officers.

Figure 10.4 shows a representative loan organization for a medium-sized bank. An important checks-and-balances feature of lending organizations is to have the loan review department and the audit department report directly to the board of directors via appropriate directors' committees. This arrangement preserves the independence of these functions and protects them from the undue influence of the officers who make loans and who may not want to face up to potentially adverse information about their loan customers.

Loan Divisions

The various loan divisions shown in Figure 10.4 perform the basic functions of generating loan business and supporting customers. In larger banks, the divisions usually are orga-

FIGURE 10.4   A Typical Lending Organization in a Medium-Sized Bank

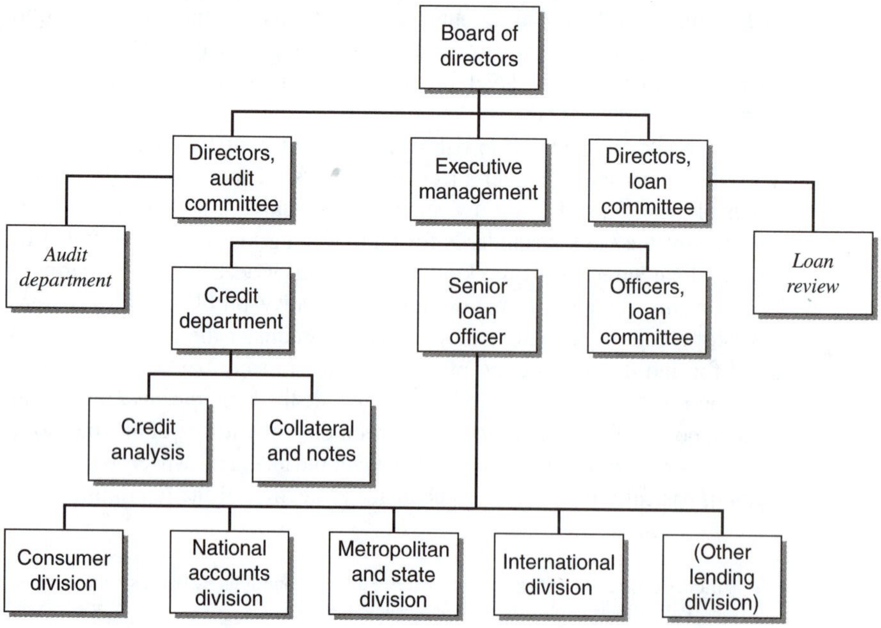

nized along geographic, industry, or product lines. Large banks develop lending expertise in such specialized businesses as energy, mining, public utilities, specialized lines of manufacturing, or commercial real estate. Separate loan divisions are necessary to service the special needs of these industries. At the same time, national and regional loan divisions that cut across different industries are needed to serve geographically dispersed customers.

Credit Department

The primary mission of the credit department is to evaluate the creditworthiness and debt payment capacity of present loan customers and new loan applicants. (This evaluation process is covered in detail in the next chapter.) Because of the technical nature of its credit evaluation function, the credit department is an excellent place to train new loan officers. Trainees are exposed to a variety of good and not so good loan cases on which they assist loan officers in making credit decisions.

The credit department may also be responsible for loan review, although in larger banks this function is likely to be handled by a separate department. Credit departments are sometimes responsible for collections of past-due loans. This function is usually handled by specialists within the department.

Collateral and Note Department

A crucial and complex loan function is the perfection of the bank's security interest in collateral offered in support of a loan. A later section of this chapter presents the details and documents that are used to take a security interest in collateral offered by prospective borrowers. The legal complications and paperwork generated in this function often justify its separation from other activities in a unit such as the collateral and note department. This department also performs the discount function: the monitoring and crediting of payments received on outstanding notes.

LOAN COMMITTEES AND THE LOAN APPROVAL PROCESS

Loan Committees

Two or three committees deal with major credit decisions: an officers' loan committee, a directors' loan committee, and, for banks with an excessive number of troubled loans, a "special assets" committee. These committees are commissioned to approve only those loans that conform to loan policy. Loans above certain minimum sizes are sponsored by individual loan officers before the officers' loan committee, consisting of the bank's most experienced loan officers. This committee's duties are as follows:

1. Review major new loans.
2. Review major loan renewals and ascertain the reasons for renewal.
3. Review delinquent loans and determine the cause of delinquency.
4. Ensure compliance with stated bank policy.
5. Ensure full documentation of loans.
6. Ensure consistency in the treatment of loan customers.

The officers' committee meets frequently—daily in large banks and perhaps only once a week in small banks. The committee serves as a check on, not a substitute for, the individual loan officer's judgment.

The directors' loan committee reviews major loans approved by the officers' committee. It is usually composed of the bank's president, the most senior loan officers, and two or more external members of the board of directors. The committee makes a final judgment on the officers' loan committee decisions, giving closer scrutiny to the largest credits. It is especially concerned with conformance to bank loan policy and avoidance of violating law and policies that control insider loans. The directors' loan committee also reviews significant past-due loans and credit problems.

Finally, a special assets committee is created in banks that have experienced a significant increase in regulator-criticized loans. This committee monitors the progress of problem loans and tries to determine how to work out the loans through creative cooperation with distressed borrowers and through persistent collection efforts.

Loan Approval Process

The three fundamental elements of the loan approval process are:

1. Delegation of authority
2. Uniform presentation format and standards
3. The actual loan decision

Delegation of Authority   Banks differ in how they structure the delegation of authority. A decentralized process gives relatively large loan limits to their loan officers, with the ability to combine their limits with other officers to approve most of the acceptable loan applications. Usually, officers with more senior titles have higher approval limits than their junior colleagues. Other banks grant smaller loan limits, do not permit combining of loan limits, and rely mostly on loan committees to approve loans. The first system results in greater customer responsiveness and productivity; the second system has the advantages of greater consistency and safety.

Uniform Presentation Format and Standards   It is vital that loan presentations be uniform and focused. To make sure this is the case, loan committees use a single standardized cover sheet that summarizes the key elements of the loan decision. Attachments to the cover sheet include spread sheets, balance sheet and other projections, credit analysis, and comments by the originating loan officer. The cover sheet should present concise comments on the following:

1. Description of the client's business and position in its market and industry.
2. Assessment of management.
3. Purpose of the loan request.
4. Repayment schedule and source of repayment.
5. Secondary sources of repayment including collateral values and guarantors.
6. History of past borrowing with the bank.
7. Required monitoring steps, including timing of submissions of financial statements.
8. Sponsoring officer's comments, including consistency with policy.

The summary cover sheet isolates factors that must be discussed for every loan, making committee time more efficient and reducing digressions that may contain personal biases.

The Loan Decision   Most loans presented to the loan committee receive approval. This is not to say that the loan committee's work is perfunctory. Rather, loans are normally approved because officers do not submit requests that are clearly at variance with policy or profitability standards. Also, the officer is likely to have done a substantial amount of work to ensure that the loan will be acceptable. Nonetheless, loan committees frequently can improve the transaction by openly discussing the loan's merits, the ways to administer it, and the additional requirements that might be placed on the borrower.

LOAN POLICY AND PROCEDURES FORMULATION

Loan Policy

The composition and quality of a bank's loans should reflect its loan policy. The policy should in turn reflect the bank's lending philosophy and culture, indicating priorities, specifying procedures, and means of monitoring lending activity. As such, it provides guidance and focus to the bank's lending activities. To ensure that such direction is unambiguous and is communicated to all concerned, the loan policy must be in written form. Indeed, the Comptroller of the Currency puts great emphasis on a written loan policy being handed down from the board of directors to management. From the comptroller's viewpoint, a written loan policy should obtain three results:

1. Produce sound and collectible loans.
2. Provide profitable investment of bank funds.
3. Encourage extensions of credit that meet the legitimate needs of the bank's market.

Loan policies may change over time. For example, immediately after World War II, most banks considered consumer loans to be inappropriate.[2] However, as the demand for consumer durable goods and housing increased, the resulting attractive interest rate spreads on consumer and mortgage finance encouraged banks to shift loan funds to these markets. For a decade or so during the late 1970s and early 1980s, many large banks adopted policies to seek loans aggressively in Third World countries. This policy thrust was abruptly interrupted when, starting in 1982, many less developed nations failed to meet loan repayment schedules. In many banks loan policies moved into another, similarly trendy loan market in commercial real estate in the early and mid-1980s. This market was boosted artificially by new tax incentives for investment in real estate and by regulatory encouragement. A sweeping change in policy was forced upon banks when, beginning in the 1980s, low-cost nonbank lenders acquired an increasing share of the market for top-rated corporate loans. As a result of this nonbank competition, many banks redirected their efforts to smaller and higher-risk middle-market corporate borrowers.

---

[2] The postwar evolution of bank lending policies is reviewed in D. A. Hayes, ''Bank Lending Policies: Domestic and International'' (Ann Arbor: Division of Research, Graduate School of Business Administration, University of Michigan, 1977).

In addition, loan policies vary over the credit cycle. In periods of tight money, banks are able to expand lending rapidly and may have to restrict their loan growth. In contrast, when funds are plentiful and the economy is weak, banks may require their borrowers to show greater balance sheet and earnings strengths than during boom periods. To find solid loans during such periods, some banks may decide to lend outside their normal market areas. Clearly, the loan policy should be adaptable to changes in cyclical and secular circumstances. It is crucial that loan policies be updated routinely to reflect current circumstances and to maintain their relevance as control tools. A well-managed bank may review its loan policy on an annual basis to ensure that the policy adequately addresses the types of risks the bank is willing to take in its dynamic market area.

Loan Policy Outline

The elements of a written loan policy are as follows:

1. Introduction
2. Objectives
3. Strategies
4. Lending authorities and approvals
5. Credit standards

The loan policy contains general policy statements that specify in broad terms the mission of the bank's credit function and the desired qualities of the loan portfolio.

Introduction   The introduction to the loan policy expresses the bank's credit philosophy. In broad terms it should reconcile the bank's commitment to loan quality with the degree of aggressiveness the bank seeks in its lending activities. In addition, the introduction should present the bank's loan policy as a guide, with exceptions permitted where fully justified. It reminds loan personnel that they are responsible for gaining a thorough knowledge of the policy as well as for recommending desirable revisions to existing policy.

Objectives   The objectives section of the loan policy statement sets forth the bank's external and internal missions. Included are statements about its perceived business role in its trade area, perceived market niche, desired profitability, and maintenance of public confidence. It might quantify loan growth and earning objectives, including the desired size of the loan portfolio in relation to total deposits or total assets.

Strategies   A meaningful loan policy will express risk management strategies in concrete terms. Banks' loans comprise a portfolio of loan types, geographical areas, and risk. In the case of portfolio risk, the desired loan mix should be quantified: for example, short-term business loans, 20–30 percent; consumer loans, 40–50 percent; real estate loans, 15–20 percent; term commercial loans, 10–15 percent. In practice, a desired percentage range of loans by type will prove to be more flexible. Portfolio mix expresses the diversification the bank seeks in its loan placements. Diversification reduces the portfolio risk associated with large concentrations of loans in a single category. Banks in one-industry communities sometimes have few chances to diversify their loans. For them, participation with correspondent banks might be a good way to achieve geographical diversification. This section of the policy statement may also describe the maximum amount the bank is willing to lend to any one customer; this is the bank's so-called in-house limit. This limit might be set at, say, 60 or 80 percent of the bank's legal lending limit. (Legal limits are described later in this chapter under "Legal and Regulatory Controls on Lending.") Finally, the types of loans and borrowers that the bank considers to be undesirable should be mentioned.

The bank's liquidity strategy should be indicated because it acts as a constraint on lending activity and because liquidity is partly determined by the maturity structure of the loan portfolio. The desired size of the loan portfolio expresses the bank's intended aggressiveness in expanding its loan portfolio. A highly aggressive loan policy comes with both good news and bad news. The good news is that a large loan portfolio may increase bank earnings. The bad news is that an aggressive policy may lead to lower credit standards, marginal loans, and large loan losses.

Lending Authorities and Approvals   The loan policy should establish lending limits for all loan officers and for combinations of officers and loan committees. Bankers regard increases in an individual's lending authority as a privilege that must be earned empirically. Limits for individuals will normally be predicated on their experience and length of service as lenders. Secured loans will carry higher limits than unsecured loans for comparable purposes, and seasonal working capital loans may carry higher limits than term loans. Individual officers' lending authorities for any one borrower are determined by totaling all of the borrower's existing loans, credit lines, and credit requests under consideration. Joint authorities might be used to approve larger loans than the officers involved would be permitted to approve individually, although in such cases it should be made clear that each officer is responsible for monitoring the performance of the loan. Division heads (e.g., commercial, real estate, or dealer) or branch heads should be held responsible for loans made by their subordinate officers. Individual officers' limits also depend on the bank's capital base and its ultimate legal, or in-house, loan limit. For example, a vice-president in a bank with $50 million in assets may have a loan limit of $50,000, whereas an officer of identical rank in a $10 billion bank may have a $500,000 limit.

Credit Standards   The written loan policy states the types of loans the bank considers desirable.

a. Short-term credit.   Desirable loans routinely include meeting the demand for short-term loans to business customers in the trade area to the extent that resources and opportunities permit. For such working capital-type loans, a minimum out-of-the-bank period (say 30 to 90 days each year) should be specified. Nonworking capital short-term loans should indicate a specific source of repayment.

Other, less conventional loans are also discussed in the policy statement. Cautions should appear about lending to new businesses that are not well capitalized or backed by a strong private guarantor or a federal guarantor such as the Small Business Administration or Farm Home Administration.

b. Undesirable loans.   Among the types of loans banks might avoid are loans to acquire a business or to buy out stockholders in the borrower's present business. The funds from such capital loans effectively replace part of a firm's equity with debt. The borrower normally expects to repay the loan from earnings of the business, which may drain the business of needed equity funds. In addition, in new-acquisition borrowing, the borrower is usually less familiar with the business than the former owner, so that future profits may slip below their historic level. The policy may limit such loans to cases in which the borrower's other resources are ample or in which former owners guarantee the loan.

So-called bridge loans are often cited as contrary to bank loan policy. Such loans "bridge" a firm's needs until it can raise additional permanent funds. The bank's exposure is especially great when repayment depends on a small firm's ability to sell stock under uncertain future market conditions.

c. Speculative loans.   Speculative loans also are frequently proscribed by policy unless the borrower can qualify independently on the basis of his or her normal business performance. If a borrower has depleted working capital funds through speculative activity, loans to replenish the working capital normally will not be permitted.

d. Trade area.   Loan policy should designate both a primary and a secondary trade area to instruct loan officers on the bank's geographic priorities. Banks understand their own trade areas best and are more apt to misjudge the quality of loans originating outside their areas. Loan officers are less alert to the economic deterioration of communities outside their trade areas. Banks should (1) define the area to be serviced routinely by each of their officers, (2) set limits on loan participation with other bank customers outside the area, and (3) process any other loans as an exception to policy. Trade area definitions must comply with the Community Reinvestment Act. This act is discussed in Chapter 12.

The extent of a trade area obviously depends on the size and special characteristics of banks. The trade area for large money center banks is not limited geographically but is national and international in scope. In addition, geographic limits are less important to many regional banks with lending expertise in narrow fields, such as oil and gas, meat packing, electronics, or public utilities, or to regional banks that have major relationships with corporations with national and international locations.

e. Acceptable collateral.   Loan policy should indicate both desirable and unacceptable types of collateral. It should further indicate circumstances in which unsecured lending is prohibited. The quality and liquidity of collateral must be verified, and maximum loan-to-collateral-value ratios should be applied before a secured loan is approved.

f. Appraisals.   Responsibilities and procedures for appraisals should be specified, including the time intervals between reappraisals. Special attention must be paid to regulations covering appraisals under the Financial Institutions, Reform, Recovery and Enforcement Act (FIRREA), passed in 1989 (see Chapter 12). This legislation contains specific parameters governing the frequency and quality of appraisals. FIRREA also establishes special requirements on the credentials of independent appraisers.

Principles and Procedures

Written principles and procedures are a mandatory extension to the written loan policy and can be organized in two parts. The first part describes technical principles and procedures to be followed in structuring and administering the loan portfolio. The second part introduces the detailed procedures and parameters that apply to each of the various types

TABLE 10.1   Principles and Procedures of Loan Administration

I. CREDIT ADMINISTRATION
    A. Insurance protection
    B. Documentation standards, security interest
    C. Problem loan collections and charge-offs
    D. Legal constraints and compliance
    E. Loan pricing
    F. Borrower financial information, other monitoring
    G. Ethical issues, conflicts of interest
    H. Loan review
II. PROCEDURES AND PARAMETERS
    A. Real estate mortgage loans[a]
        1. Loan description
        2. Purpose of proceeds
        3. Preferred maturities
        4. Appraisal standards
        5. Pricing: rates, fees, compensating balances
        6. Minimum and maximum amounts
        7. Insurance requirements
        8. Perfection of collateral
        9. Channels of approval for policy
    B. Accounts receivable lending
    C. Inventory lending
    D. Term loans
    E. Securities purchase loans
    F. Agricultural loans
    G. Small business loans
    H. Consumer loans
    I. Home equity loans
    J. Credit Card loans
    K. Purchased loans

[a] Elements 1–9 and others also pertain to each other loan category (sections B–K).

of loans made by the bank. Table 10.1 outlines these two aspects of principles and procedures. The following discusses the first part.

Insurance Protection   Most borrowers are exposed to risks that threaten their ability to repay their bank loans. Life insurance on key personnel is especially important to protect against loss caused by the death or disability of the borrower or one of the borrower's indispensable employees. A catastrophic fire or flood may interrupt the borrower's business or destroy the loan collateral.

The procedures policy should indicate the types of borrowers who must be insured. The policy must designate the bank as loss payee, or, when the cash value of a life insurance policy is offered as protection, this must be properly assigned to the bank in a binder issued by the insurer. An increasingly common form of protection is the credit life policy written by the bank. Credit life is simply term life insurance written on consumer loan customers. It pays off outstanding balances due the bank in the event of the customer's death.

A somewhat different form of protection is obtained through reinsurance. If the borrower defaults, reinsurance pays off and the insurance company pursues collection on its own behalf on the bank's defaulted note. Reinsurance premiums are rather costly, and the bank's policy should indicate what classes of borrowers, if any, should be subject to reinsurance programs.

Documentation Standards   Procedures policy should prescribe uniform credit files and documentation procedures. Such requirements are routine for most medium-sized and larger banks. Too often, however, documentation procedures in many small banks are determined by the preferences of individual loan officers. Customers' credit files should be organized around an effective documentation system that promotes uniformity and almost certainly results in lower loan losses, especially when coupled with a well-designed loan review program (discussed in the next section). The credit files are administered by the credit department.

A uniform loan documentation checklist should be required for each credit file. The documents listed include only those most frequently used in lending transactions:

1. The basic loan agreement.
2. The credit application.
3. The borrower's financial statements.
4. Credit reports.
5. Evidence of perfection of security interests (e.g., UCC-1 financing statement).
6. Assignment of rents or leases on real estate or other productive property.
7. The borrower's life or casualty insurance policies (showing the bank as the loss payee).
8. Corporate borrowing resolution or partnership agreement.
9. Subordination agreement.
10. Continuing guarantee.
11. Financial statements on the guarantor.
12. Correspondence.
13. Copies of existing and paid-off promissory notes.

Although most of this list is self-explanatory, we will comment on several aspects. The *basic loan agreement* is the pivotal loan document used to describe the conditions of the loan transaction. This agreement ties all the loan documents together. It spells out the ground rules, procedures, and mechanics, including the terms of repayment, as well as loan covenants. (Loan covenants are covered in Chapter 11.)

Other data and documents pertaining to the credit file should also be included in the loan documentation. Of special concern is item 5—*perfection of security interests*—which pertains to documents that establish the bank's legal claim to collateral in the event of default. This item accounts for much of the attention banks give to its documentation. It is discussed in detail in the next section; the law governing security interests is covered by Article 1 of the Uniform Commercial Code.

Item 8—the *corporate borrowing resolution or partnership agreement*—indicates those employees of the borrowing firm who are authorized to commit the borrower to indebtedness. Loan officers must confirm that the name of the person who signs a loan agreement appears on the appropriate borrowing authorization instrument. The loan officer should obtain a certified copy of the instrument for the credit file. Item 9—a *subordination agreement*—is used when it is necessary to subordinate a prior loan and lender to the present loan agreement with the bank. In cases in which a corporate borrower's loan is backed by a guarantor, such as a *suretyship,* the credit line should contain the signed personal guarantee document, called a *continuing guarantee.* A continuing guarantee is often required of a firm's majority stockholders to ensure that the loan is protected against the possibility of corporate insolvency. Without a guarantee, stockholders might permit their insolvent corporation to abandon its debt obligations.

It would be difficult to exaggerate the need for careful loan documentation. It is needed to protect the bank in the event of a default and to enforce the bank's secured position in borrowers' collateral. A crucial dimension of loan documentation is to use the documents to monitor the performance of a loan to ensure that the borrower complies with the loan agreement and that deterioration in the borrower's financial condition does not go unnoticed. The early recognition of a borrower's problem that might create a cash flow interruption and a default may permit the bank to protect its position before a major loan loss occurs.

Banks conduct loan previews before loan funds are disbursed. Loan previews examine all materials pertaining to a pending loan in order to ensure that documentation is complete; that the loan conforms to policy, laws, and regulations; and that a workable security interest in collateral has been obtained.

CONTROLLING LOAN LOSSES

Securing Collateral

A bank takes a legal security interest in borrower collateral to gain the right to sell the collateral assets and apply the proceeds to the loan if the borrower cannot repay the loan as agreed. Most bank loans to businesses are made on this basis. Although short-term loans to high-quality borrowers are not secured, most long-term loans are secured. In fact, the loan policies of many banks treat unsecured term loans as an exception. Large banks are more liberal in granting unsecured loans to large prime borrowers because such borrowers tend to have stronger equity support, more stable cash flows, and more certain investment opportunities.

Banks follow precise procedures to establish and document their legal claim to the proceeds of collateral assets in the event of default. Different procedures and documents are required for *real,* as opposed to *personal,* property. There is also a difference in the procedures for securing personal property, depending on whether the property remains in the possession of the bank or the borrower. Figure 10.5 presents a schematic diagram of the methods and documents for gaining an enforceable security interest.

Real Property   When real estate collateral (land and improvements, including structures) is offered, the bank must record the associated mortgage with a public agency such as the county clerk. This recording or "filing" protects the bank against subsequent claims by third parties. A title search is required to establish the existence of defects in the title in the form of other possible claims on the real estate. A major concern is the status of taxes and assessments on the real estate. These items are senior to all other claims; ideally, the borrower should be current on them. Title companies sell title insurance to protect the bank against loss due to defects that were not disclosed by the title search.

In addition to matters of title, there are other routine considerations in real estate-

FIGURE 10.5   Methods and Documents for Taking Security Interest

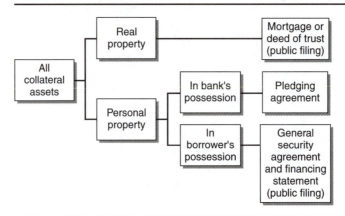

secured lending. A professionally prepared appraisal is necessary to document the real estate's value in the present market or in case of possible liquidation. A certified survey is required to ascertain the secured property's physical location and dimensions and to ensure that improvements are properly located on the borrower's (and not infringing on someone else's) property. Evidence of insurance on the property is needed, including the designation of the bank as payee in the event of loss.

Personal Property in the Bank's Possession   A security interest in the borrower's property is perfected when the bank or its agent takes physical possession of it. The borrower completes a pledge agreement, which authorizes the bank to hold the collateral and to derive cash from it in the event of default. Because the asset is already in the bank's possession, it is not necessary to file a pledge agreement publicly.

There are several considerations in dealing with the more common types of collateral secured under pledge agreements. When negotiable securities are held as loan collateral, the borrower must execute a stock power assignment. The stock power simply authorizes the bank to sell the stock upon default of the loan. Stock loans are subject to Regulation U, under which the Federal Reserve Board controls the margin financing of stock purchases. The bank must report the purpose of stock loans and observe additional restrictions if the purpose is to purchase stock on margin.

Loans secured by the cash value or face value of a life insurance policy require a special pledge agreement to assign the policy to the bank. To be valid, the bank's security interest in the policy must be formally acknowledged by the issuing insurance company.

Banks commonly take a security interest in a savings account or CD belonging to an owner or a stockholder of a borrowing firm. If the borrower's deposit is in another financial institution, that institution must formally acknowledge the assignment. This third-party notice perfects the lending bank's claim. To secure a borrower's deposits within the lending bank, a pledge agreement is important to block the borrower's possible withdrawal of the funds.

Personal Property in the Customer's Possession   Under the Uniform Commercial Code, a bank perfects its security interest in collateral property held by the borrower with a public filing of a *general security agreement*. The general security agreement simply grants the bank a security interest. It is accompanied by a *financing statement* that describes the collateral and gives the legal names and addresses of the borrower and the bank. The financing statement officially "places the world on notice" of the collateral position granted to and taken by the bank. To survive beyond their normal five-year expiration term, financing statements must be renewed by the filing of a *continuation statement.*

The Loan Review Function

It is said that banks never make bad loans; at least, they are not bad at the time they are made. However, banks find that invariably a small portion of their loans become delinquent and eventually must be written off. This basic risk of the lending function is not entirely bad; banks would be remiss in not bearing such risk in the course of underwriting a variety of business enterprises and consumer needs. When a bank does not experience at least a few loan losses, this is likely a sign that it is passing up profitable opportunities. Nevertheless, well-managed banks should do all they can to minimize loan losses.

Most banks conduct loan reviews to reduce losses and monitor loan quality. Loan reviews consist of a periodic audit of the ongoing performance of some or all of the active loans in the bank's loan portfolio. Its essence is credit analysis, although, unlike the credit analysis conducted by the credit department as part of the loan approval process, credit analysis in loan review occurs after the loan is on the books. To fulfill its basic objective of reducing loan losses, the following points should be emphasized in loan review:

1. To detect actual or potential problem loans as early as possible.
2. To provide an incentive for loan officers to monitor loans and to report deterioration in their own loans.
3. To enforce uniform documentation.
4. To ensure that loan policies, banking laws, and regulations are followed.
5. To inform management and the board about the overall condition of the loan portfolio.
6. To aid in establishing loan loss reserves.

The true purpose of loan review is a source of some confusion. Most bankers would cite an "early warning" purpose wherein loan review provides the basic defense against deteriorating credit quality. They would claim that loan review can detect, in timely fashion, the changes in credit quality that can occur quickly in loan agreements. Gregory Udell argues, however, that the infrequency of review and, for some loans, the absence of review (discussed later in this section) inherent in formal loan review systems make it impossible to always catch early deterioration in loans.[3] Udell argues persuasively that the fundamental purpose of loan review is to reinforce a "credit culture" within the lending organization. The credit culture relies on loan officers, not the loan review department, as the basic defense against deteriorating credit quality. Indeed, banking regulators refer to loan officers as the "first line of defense" against credit problems.

The rationale for depending on the credit culture is that loan officers are privy to

---

[3] Gregory F. Udell, *Designing the Optimal Loan Review Policy* (Madison, Wis.: Herbert V. Prochnow Educational Foundation, 1987).

crucial information about borrowers' financial condition, and they are the first persons in the bank to know about changes in credit quality. Thus, correct loan review procedures attempt to overcome the disincentives for loan officers to monitor their loans. The disincentives include time and energy taken away from other tasks, the fear of discovering quality deterioration that might reflect poorly on loan officers' original credit judgments, and the personal friendships and bonding that often occur between loan officers and their corporate borrowers.

The credit culture must offset such disincentives by establishing a climate in which it is clear that lenders are accountable for devoting appropriate attention to monitoring credit quality. Loan officers are viewed as responsible for communicating changes in the quality of their loans. Loan review reinforces this responsibility by detecting, after the fact, how diligently loan officers reported changes in quality. The net result is that loan review has the function of monitoring loan officers (who are responsible for monitoring the loans), not loan performance itself.

Loan Review Procedures

The procedures for loan review should be formalized in written form in the loan policy. In general, all the materials needed for loan review should be in the credit files set up for each loan made. Historically, the process required the arduous task of manually handling many files. Today, however, banks store most credit file data on computers.

The scope of a bank's loan review operation is partly a matter of bank size. Some large banks establish a separate loan review staff directly under executive management to ensure its independence from loan personnel. There is a compelling logic to this approach, because the chief executive officer is ultimately accountable for loan quality and can act directly to remedy deficiencies. Medium-sized banks may make the review operation an additional duty of the credit department or assign it to the audit department. The smallest banks often do not have a loan review program, or they depend on loan officers to conduct the loan review as time permits. Loan officers should, of course, monitor their own loans continuously. In addition, however, it is vital that there be an independent loan review to, in effect, monitor the loan officer. Within the formal loan review system itself, loan officers should not review their own loans; human nature prevents people, including loan officers, from being objective when reviewing their own work.

Whatever means are used to conduct loan reviews, the following points should be covered:

1. Financial condition and repayment ability of the borrower.
2. Completeness of documentation.
3. Consistency with the loan policy.
4. Perfection of the security interest on collateral.
5. Legal and regulatory compliance.
6. Apparent profitability.

Most banks are unable to review every loan on their books on a regular basis. Some banks review all loans in excess of a certain cutoff value and review only a random sample of loans below the cutoff. The frequency of review of individual loans is determined by the size and quality of the loan; large, poor-quality loans are reviewed most frequently.

Many banks have a loan grading or risk rating system that establishes the quality and, therefore, the frequency of review of each loan. Table 11.4 in the next chapter presents an example of such a system.

As a general rule, each year a bank should review at least as much of its loan portfolio as its regulator would review in an examination. For example, 70 percent of the commercial loan portfolio might be reviewed in a year's time, along with a random sampling of homogeneous loan pools such as consumer and residential loan portfolios.

Correcting Problem Loans

The loan policy should require diligence on the part of all loan personnel to detect and attempt to correct problem loans. Although loan review personnel are important in the early detection of problem loans, individual loan officers frequently have special ongoing knowledge to contribute. Loan officers attempt to maintain good rapport with their borrowers. If the borrower's business deteriorates, the loan officer frequently will find that this rapport deteriorates as well. Any unexplained change in the borrower's attitude toward the loan officer or the bank may be a clue to the borrower's financial difficulties. Unexpected declines in deposit balances and the occurrence of overdrafts are signs of such difficulties.

Other clues include late payments of principal and interest and abnormal delays by the borrower in submitting periodic financial statements as required in the loan agreement. Delays might indicate a reluctance to submit unfavorable financial results to the bank. In the event of such delays, the loan officer should immediately inquire about the reasons. Payment delinquencies also must be followed up quickly because they frequently indicate that the borrower is undergoing a financial crisis.

Other indicators of trouble include the following:

1. Disturbing trends in financial statements.
2. Management turnover.
3. Cancellation of insurance.
4. Security interest filed against the borrower by other creditors.
5. Notice of a lawsuit, tax liens, or other legal action against the borrower.
6. Deteriorating relations with trade suppliers.
7. Death or illness of principals.
8. Marital difficulties of principals.
9. Loss of key source of revenue.
10. Deterioration of labor relations.
11. Natural disaster.
12. Rapid growth.

When a problem loan is detected, the responsible loan officer should take immediate corrective action to prevent further deterioration and to minimize potential loss. The preferred solution to a problem loan is to negotiate a plan of action with the borrower to try to protect both the bank and the borrower from possible loss. The plan of action is actually a revised loan agreement. It should set forth a new repayment schedule, provide covenants limiting the customer's activities, establish requirements for the customer to report operating and financial activities for the bank to monitor, and specify the extent of the bank's authority to concur in management decisions. Often banks operate a special assets division that takes charge of such problem loans. There are at least two important advantages in operating a special assets division. First, the loan is administered by officers who specialize in situations that involve actual or potential litigation; second, the loan relationship can be managed more objectively. Both of these advantages act to reduce the potential loss to the bank.

Problems with secured loans may arise when the collateral is inadequate. The market value of certain types of collateral, such as securities, may fall below the loan value. Also, the loan may have been inadequately secured at the outset because of either improper documentation or an excessive loan-to-value ratio. An obvious solution would be to obtain additional collateral in the form of marketable securities, cash value of life insurance, receivables, inventory, or even real estate equity.

A problem loan might be remedied through the addition of guarantees or endorsements. The extent of the improvement in the bank's position is directly related to the financial strength of the guarantors.

Loan officers must be especially alert to detect fraud such as false financial statements, false documents, securities, and titles for collateral. In the event of bankruptcy, proof that fraud was used in obtaining a loan may be the basis for gaining legal access to a borrower's resources ahead of other creditors.

In any case, the earlier the bank's officers detect pending loan problems, the more likely they will be able to take action to protect the bank's position by requiring the borrower to provide additional security or, perhaps, by encouraging the borrower to refinance the loan at another institution. Whatever the solution, early detection of problems reduces potential losses to the bank.

Borrower's Financial Statements

Loans should always be supported by concrete financial data. The data may consist of a small consumer borrower's personal financial statement or a multinational corporate borrower's unqualified audited financial statement studied by professional analysts, CPAs, and attorneys. The loan policy should establish certain guidelines for such data. Normally, common dated balance sheets and income statements for at least the immediate past three years are required of commercial borrowers.

For small banks that deal regularly with small businesses, the professionalism of the borrower's financial statements can be expected to vary a great deal. Small businesses often present statements prepared by an owner who has no formal training in accounting. Statements prepared by professional accountants may be compiled, indicating that they are derived solely from the company's accounts without audit. Even professionally audited statements may contain broad disclaimers as to the integrity of certain information presented. When financial data are insufficient, the loan officer should ask the customer for clarification. For example, it is frequently necessary to clarify how receivables, inventory, or equipment are valued and whether or not they have been pledged for other purposes. Also, the delinquency of trade payables or the maturity of other debt may need clarification. Written clarifications of such issues should be part of the credit file.

Personal financial statements should be required of all co-makers, guarantors, or endorsers. Details of real estate owned, stocks and bonds, mortgages, loans, and other debt maturities should be included so that the borrower's personal net worth is clearly indicated.

PRICING POLICY

Interest rates charged on loans may depend on considerations, such as the following:

1. The bank's cost of funds (sometimes including the cost of equity funds).
2. The riskiness of the borrower.
3. Compensating balances and fees.
4. Interest rates charged by competitors.
5. Usury ceilings.
6. Other banking relationships with the borrower.

Chapter 11 deals with many of these considerations in its discussion of the pricing and profitability of commercial loans. General guidelines should be included as part of the loan policy's principles and procedures. For example, the bank's own prime loan rate—the interest rate quoted to the bank's most creditworthy borrowers—should be explained. Most small or medium-sized banks' prime rates are based on a national prime rate but are modified according to their customer base and market competitive situation. Legal challenges to the prime rate concept (discussed in Chapter 11) are nullifying its use at many banks. Bank pricing policy for single-pay, balloon maturity loans (*bullet* loans) versus fully amortized loans might be indicated. In addition, lawful exceptions to established usury ceilings are sometimes detailed for the benefit of loan officers.

UNETHICAL CONDUCT AND CONFLICTS OF INTEREST

The success of any bank depends partly on its customers' confidence that the bank's employees will not exploit their unique positions of trust for unethical gain. Bankers deal more directly and routinely with money than perhaps any other professional group. The exchange of money is the basis, and not just the outcome, of customer interaction. Bankers also deal with highly sensitive and confidential information related to their customers. As a result, the potential for conflict of interest is unusually serious.

Loan policy statements frequently list improper activities or relationships that loan officers should avoid. Such a list should include acceptance of gifts of value or loans from customers or loan applicants, investment in a customer's business or other uses of privileged information for personal gain, and improper use of credit information on a customer. On the last point, many banks use the Robert Morris Associates Code of Ethics for the Exchange of Credit Information to govern the exchange of credit information. The code prescribes controls on the creditors' sharing between themselves of their credit experiences with customers without unduly violating the customers' right to privacy.

Conflicts of interest may also arise between the commercial loan division and the trust department when the loan division has inside information on a firm whose securities are held by the trust department. Policy should prohibit the trust department's access to such files.

COMMON REASONS FOR LOAN LOSSES

Well-managed banks regularly conduct what might be called an ''autopsy'' on loans that resulted in losses for the bank. This step is the strongest feedback available on the effec-

TABLE 10.2   Twenty Common Reasons for Loan Losses

1. Collateral overvalued, improperly margined; failure to get appraisal.
2. Dispersal of funds before documentation finished.
3. Officer making "good ole boy" loans, bypassing the loan committee, personal friendship of loan officer with borrower.
4. Loan to a new business with an inexperienced owner-manager.
5. Renewing a loan for increasing amounts, with no additional collateral taken.
6. Repeatedly rewriting loan to cover delinquent interest due.
7. Not analyzing borrower's cash flows and repayment capacity.
8. Failure of officer to review loan's status frequently enough.
9. Funds not applied as represented; diverted to borrower's personal use (no attempt to verify to what purpose money was applied).
10. Funds used out of the bank's market area; poor communications with borrower.
11. Repayment plan not clear or not stated on the face of the note.
12. Failure to receive or infrequent receipt of borrower's financial statements.
13. Failure to realize on collateral because borrower raised nuisance legal defenses.
14. Bank's failure to follow its own written policies and procedures.
15. Bank president too dominant in pushing through loan approvals.
16. Ignoring overdraft situation as a tip-off to borrower's major financial problems.
17. Failure to inspect borrower's business premises.
18. Lending against fictitious book net worth of business, with no audit or verification of borrower's financial statement.
19. Failure to get or ignoring negative credit bureau reports or other credit references.
20. Failure to call loan or to move against collateral quickly when deterioration becomes obviously hopeless.

SOURCE: Unpublished survey, Western States School of Banking, Albuquerque, New Mexico.

tiveness of loan policies, documentation, loan officers, and the loan review function. Invariably, losses reflect on parts of the lending function that may require correction or revision. While a thorough review of failed credits is painful, it probably teaches lending personnel about the importance of controls on the lending function better than any hypothetical exercise could possibly do. Table 10.2 lists common causes for loan failures that were uncovered in loan autopsies recently conducted in a sample of 60 small to medium-sized banks.

LEGAL AND REGULATORY CONTROLS ON LENDING

Historically, commercial banking has been one of the most tightly regulated industries in the United States. There are several reasons. First, banking risks must be minimal because banks are pivotal in our payments system, and because taxpayers ultimately guarantee banks' deposits and must pay for losses from an epidemic of bank failures, just as they did for the massive failures of S&Ls in the late 1980s and early 1990s. In the case of the payments system, the public's confidence in the nation's monetary system and its currency depends on the safety of its banks. Second, commercial banks are instruments of national monetary policy. Tight control over banks ensures an elastic currency by enforcing desired and more predictable behavior by banks. Third, memories of past banking panics and failures make special precautions politically appealing. In the case of the taxpayer's guarantee of bank deposits, the taxpayer is protected by the banking industry-supported system of deposit insurance. The taxpayer relies on regulatory control of the bank's loan quality to avoid drains on deposit insurance resources. Finally, incentives and controls are sometimes placed on the banks' power to create credit in order to allocate credit to socially desirable ends.

Although not all of these reasons directly address the bank lending function, they do result in prominent regulation of the loan portfolio, from which most of the risk in banking is derived.

Legal Provisions

Regulatory constraints on lending activity are reflected in enacted legislation and interpretive decisions of supervisory agencies. Regulations that deal with limited types of loans (commercial, consumer, real estate) are discussed in Chapters 11 and 12.

Loans to single affiliated borrowers are limited to prevent the concentration of a bank's assets. In the case of national banks, the 1982 Depository Institutions Act established a complex mechanism for limiting loans to single borrowers or a combination of borrowers who are in a common enterprise or who are otherwise financially interdependent. Generally, the limit is 15 percent of the bank's capital and surplus, plus an additional 10 percent for loans fully secured by readily marketable collateral. Still higher limits are possible for loans to a combination of certain organizations and their subsidiaries. For the purpose of defining capital, eligible notes and debentures have been included since the early 1960s. There are several exceptions to these limits, including drafts or bills of exchange used to finance domestic and international trade. In addition, goods secured by shipping documents are exempt, and those secured by warehouse receipts are partially exempt.

The Financial Institutions Regulatory Act of 1978 tightly restricted loans to insiders (executive officers, directors, and principal shareholders). In 1983, insider borrowing rules were relaxed somewhat. Executive officers were permitted to borrow 2.5 percent of bank capital and surplus, with a ceiling of $100,000. Under the "insider abuse" clause of the Federal Deposit Insurance Corporation Improvement Act of 1991 (FDICIA), banks may not extend credit to their executive officers, directors, and principal shareholders on preferential terms such as low interest rates and insufficient collateral but must apply the terms offered to outside borrowers. Moreover, loans to such insiders must not bear more than nominal risk. FDICIA requires that all loans to insiders be approved in advance by the bank's board of directors. This law limits the amount of aggregate credit extended to insiders and their affiliated interests to the amount of the bank's unimpaired capital and surplus. Exceptions may be made for community banks with under $100 million in deposits if the board believes that this provision would impede the flow of credit in the bank's community. In such cases, the aggregate credit to insiders cannot exceed two times the bank's unimpaired capital and surplus. Loans to bank examiners are illegal.

Regulation U sets margin restrictions on credit granted to acquire or carry securities and is intended to prevent speculation in securities markets. The regulation does not apply to loans secured by stocks, assuming that loan proceeds are not to be used to acquire stocks.

National banks are limited in the size of their real estate loan portfolios to the largest of either capital and surplus or 70 percent of time and savings deposits. Loans on real estate are confined to improved farm, business, and residential properties.

Many states have usury laws that establish ceilings on interest rates charged consumers and small businesses by state banks. National banks are permitted to charge up to 1 percentage point above the Federal Reserve discount rate. A federal preemption of state usury ceilings was effective during most of the period from the late 1970s through the mid-1980s, permitting banks to earn market rates of interest on previously restricted loans.

Supervisory Examination of Loan Quality

In-bank examination by federal or state regulatory authorities has as its primary goals the evaluation of the following:

1. The bank's liquidity and solvency.
2. The bank's compliance with banking laws and regulations.
3. The quality and liquidity of the bank's assets.
4. The sufficiency of internal controls and safeguards.
5. The adequacy of capital.
6. The soundness of management's policies.

The evaluation of each of these factors directly or indirectly involves the quality of the loan portfolio. Indeed, since it typically contains the majority of bank assets, the loan portfolio probably occupies more examiner time than all the other examination procedures combined. Considering that several thousand person-hours might be spent on a single examination of a $1 billion bank, depending on the extent of the bank's problems, it is clear that the loan portfolio receives considerable examiner attention. The examiner's summary evaluation regarding the condition of the bank and the soundness of its management is influenced heavily by the examiner's assessment of the bank's loans.

Loan examination, in its broadest aspects, requires an evaluation of the bank's lending policy and the administration of the whole loan portfolio. Problems in the loan portfolios of many banks often stem from inexperienced and poorly paid managers at the top. Loan problems also arise because of inadequate internal loan review systems in which loan officers, management, and directors are not alerted to deteriorating loans in need of follow-up and correction. Other problems occur because of failure to ascertain how loan proceeds are to be used, failure to establish clear loan repayment programs, failure to obtain sufficient credit information, and overdependence on collateral.

Ultimately, however, the examiner's evaluation of the loan portfolio comes down to appraisal of individual loans. Some of the evaluation process is quite mundane and includes detailed steps such as proving each note to the general ledger, verifying the accuracy of collateral described in the note, recording loan details on the examiner's line card, and verifying that loan proceeds have been disbursed in the manner intended in the note.

Other aspects of the evaluation process are less mundane and require the examiner to have substantial experience, judgment, perceptiveness, and analytical ability in evaluating the risk of a loan. The measurement of loan risk must be based primarily on the borrower's willingness and ability to perform as agreed in the loan negotiation. Consideration is given to the character, capacity, financial responsibility, and record of the borrower. Tests are made to determine if the borrower's actual and potential earning or liquid assets will cover interest payments and enable the loan principal to be repaid on the agreed schedule.

After a detailed review and discussion of individual loans with bank officers, the examiner provides the bank with a listing of all loans warranting "criticism." Generally, criticized loans have above-average levels of risk or present risks at the time of the examination that the bank would not ordinarily undertake. Criticized loans are further broken down into the following categories:

1. *Other assets especially mentioned* (OAEM) are assets that are currently protected but *potentially weak.* The risks to these loans may be relatively minor, yet constitute an unwarranted risk in light of the circumstances surrounding them.

2. *Substandard* loans are inadequately protected by the net worth and paying capacity of the borrower or the pledged collateral. The bank will likely sustain some loss if deficiencies are not corrected.

3. *Doubtful* loans have all the weaknesses of substandard loans but have deteriorated so much that they have a high probability of substantial loss.

4. *Loss* loans are considered uncollectible and are of little or no value as a bank asset.

After deriving a list of criticized loans, the examiner assesses the adequacy of the bank's reserve for loan losses. The examiner's list of criticized loans is used as the basis for determining the adequacy of the reserve. As shown in the following example, the examiner applies an estimated loss percentage to each category of criticized loans. The total of these calculations is the amount of the *required reserve,* according to the examiner. If the total is equal to or less than the bank's actual loan loss reserve, the examiner considers the bank to be *adequately reserved.* If the required reserve is greater than the bank's actual loan loss reserve, the bank is *underreserved,* and the bank will be compelled to debit its current earnings and credit its loan loss reserve in an amount sufficient to raise the loan loss reserve to the required level estimated by the examiner.

Criticized Loan Category	Estimated Loss Amount	Percentage	Reserve Requirement
OAEM	$1,000,000	2	$ 20,000
Substandard	3,000,000	10	300,000
Doubtful	1,000,000	50	500,000
Loss	500,000	100	500,000
Totals	$5,500,000		$1,320,000
Less: Actual loan loss reserve			820,000
Amount underreserved			$ 500,000

In this example, the bank would be required to charge its earnings with a $500,000 provision for loan losses. Such a charge would come as an unpleasant surprise to the bank's shareholders and directors. To avoid such a situation, bankers are well advised to criticize their bank's loans realistically. The example also highlights the importance of detecting problem loans as early as possible.

There is good evidence that examiners are rather successful in evaluating and classifying problem loans. Of the loans they examine, they manage to classify most of those that are subsequently charged off (although not all the loans they classify are charged off). In a long-term study of the classification of loans by examiners in a sample of 12 banks, it was found that of the charged-off loans that had been previously examined, 87 percent were adversely classified. Examiners also appear to be successful in assigning loans to the substandard, doubtful, and loss classification categories according to their relative risks of default. In the aforementioned 12-bank sample, higher charge-off rates occurred for the lowest classification categories; 10 percent of substandard, 58 percent of doubtful, and 95 percent of loss classifications were eventually charged off.[4]

SUMMARY

Effective organization and control of the lending function are vital to the profitability and solvency of every bank. The lending function is perhaps the most diverse and complex activity in banking. Moreover, for most banks, it is the function involving risk to management, depositors, and stockholders.

The key tool for control and for communicating the bank's lending goals and strategies is the written loan policy. A formal loan policy is handed down from the board of directors to the loan officers for implementation; that is, loan officers' lending authority is derived from the directors. Bank directors are ultimately responsible for the quality and condition of the loan portfolio, and, as in all matters pertaining to the bank, they must answer to stockholders and bank regulatory authorities for deficiencies. Regulators expect the directors to conduct a regular internal examination of the loan portfolio in order to assess the quality and documentation of the loans, to review specific large credits, to ensure that proper loan approval policies and other policies are being followed, and generally to evaluate the performance of loan officers.[5]

Inherent in loan policy is the directors' attitude toward risk taking. Taking risks is a natural part of lending to consumers, businesses, farmers, and others, and inevitably losses will occur. The bank can do much to minimize loan losses in relation to the risks it does take, however, through a loan policy that mandates complete and uniform loan information and documentation; prompt action on delinquencies; secondary protection in the form of insurance on borrowers; and adequate collateral, profitable pricing, and, most important, loan review.

Small banks tend to rely on the bank examiner to perform their loan review or credit examination. Although examiners appear to be quite proficient in classifying problem loans, regulatory examinations were less frequent in the 1980s in relation to earlier periods. Examination personnel had not increased at the same pace as bank assets or new regulations and compliance requirements. However, a serious spate of troubled banks with problem loans in the mid-1980s added pressure for greater examination capacity. It appears that, in the future, banks of all sizes will need to provide for a professional and uniform internal loan review function. This function should be independent of the loan divisions and the loan approval channels.

[4] Kenneth Spong and Thomas Hoenig, ''Bank Examination Classifications and Loan Risk,'' *Economic Review,* Federal Reserve Bank of Kansas City (June 1979), pp. 15–25.

[5] Margaret A. Hoffman and Gerald C. Fischer. *Credit Department Management* (Philadelphia: Robert Morris Associates, 1980).

In the next chapter we discuss credit analysis, which is perhaps the most basic loan function in minimizing loan losses. Through credit analysis, the bank attempts to determine a borrower's ability to repay legitimate extensions of credit. By refusing credit to a potential borrower who, on analysis, cannot demonstrate sufficient financial strength, the bank hopes to improve its chances of avoiding unnecessary losses in its loan portfolio.

END OF CHAPTER PROBLEMS

10.1 Discuss the loan quality checks and balances that are built into the loan organization structure of typical banks. Is there a difference in loan committees fulfilling a review function versus a decision-making function on proposed loans?

10.2 What is the function of the loan policy? Why do regulators insist that loan policies be written?

10.3 Loan policies often list types of legal loans that are undesirable, even if they are made to profitable borrowers. List five types of such loans. What are the common ingredients of these types?

10.4 In the Penn Square Bank failure of 1982, poor or missing documentation was cited on many of the bank's loans and on many loans the bank sold to other banks. From historical accounts of the failure (see any financial newspaper or magazine account written at the time or since), find several quotations of examiners and correspondent banks regarding the quality of Penn Square's loan documentation.

10.5 The upsurge of bad loans in the mid-1980s has made loan review crucial, yet some bankers object to the cost of this "nonproductive" function. Discuss the economies of loan review in a small bank that is under pressure to hold down its overhead expenses.

10.6 Discuss the value of the following as indicators of a bank's loan quality:
   a. Reserve for loan losses (balance sheet).
   b. Provision for loan losses (income statement).
   c. Net loan charge-offs (loans charged off minus recoveries on previously charged-off loans).

10.7 Should banks require all borrowers to submit financial statements that are audited by CPAs?

10.8 Banks employ "workout specialists," who excel at collecting bad loans. Compare and contrast the technical and personal characteristics of workout specialists with those of regular loan officers.

10.9 What factors make it difficult for banks to apply the same credit standard to bank directors and senior managers that they apply to regular borrowers?

10.10 Examiners sometimes adversely classify loans that a bank's management considers sound and collectible. What circumstances might produce this difference of opinion?

10.11 What is the effect on bank capital adequacy when examiners adversely classify loans? Should the effect be the same on highly profitable banks as it is on banks with poor profits?

Are Bank Loans Competitive?

In the future, commercial bank lending may not be a perpetually growing business. Banks have encountered a great deal of competition in the market for loans to business. The stiffest competition comes from the intermediation of credit directly through the financial markets, such as the commercial paper market. Increasingly intense competition also comes from nonbank institutional providers of loans, such as finance companies. In addition, banks' lending costs may be too high, particularly under the recently established risk-based capital rules described in Chapter 9. The new capital rules require more capital to back loans to consumers and businesses than other types of bank assets. This bias of higher capital standards puts such loans at a cost disadvantage because of the high cost of capital. Finally, as we will show in later chapters, loans may decline as a proportion of total bank assets because of the trend toward loan securitization.

In light of such factors, some observers believe that the commercial banking system is in a "Darwinian struggle" to hold its share of the market for credit. To these observers, the system of allocating financial resources through commercial banks is less viable than it was 25 years ago. They portray bank lending as archaic because it involves ponderous decision making by committees, administered pricing, subordination to a broader customer relationship, and a high cost of bank funds (especially the cost of bank capital) to carry the loans on the bank's own balance sheet. In this view, bank lend-ing amounts to a clublike activity that imposes unnatural costs on the intermediation of loanable funds.

In contrast to bank lending is the system of loans created through the open markets. The open market system competes for business credit without the need for bureaucratic organizations. The open markets rely on investment bankers, not commercial bankers, not only to originate but also to trade credit agreements in the markets. In this system, pricing is far more efficient because loanable funds are allocated through impersonal open market bidding and trading activity.

Yet, despite the apparent efficiency of the open market, banks offer advantages and strengths as credit intermediaries that the open market does not. Banks have special skills for gathering and processing credit information that enable them to play a unique role in (1) screening undeserving loan applicants, (2) ensuring that credit is made available impartially and objectively, and (3) seeing to it that outstanding credit agreements are monitored and enforced. Banks have other advantages too. Historically, they have been able to fund loans at lower costs than nonbank intermediaries. Part of the lower cost is due to banks' relatively inexpensive sources of funds. First, depositors place a high value on deposit insurance, which may allow banks to raise deposit funds at below-market interest rates. Second, banks attract substantial amounts of demand deposits that do not bear interest. In addition, banks have an advantage in monitoring loans because, typically, their borrowers maintain deposit accounts with them. This enables banks to observe the behavior of borrowers' cash flows and their ability to repay loans.[6]

Banks' information advantage may be decreasing, however. New technologies for storing and transmitting data have reduced the costs of information and communication by a factor of perhaps 20 in the last 20 years. As a result, information has become widely available at very low cost. In addition, large banks in highly competitive deposit markets find it is too expensive to fund loans on their balance sheets with deposits and equity capital. Nondiscretionary costs of deposit insurance premiums and reserve requirements raise deposit costs to somewhat more than their stated rates. Equity cost rates are much higher, and regulatory capital requirements ensure that banks incur a significant cost of equity to carry loans on their balance sheets. Thus, large banks are finding that it is cheaper to fund the loans they originate by quickly selling them to remove them from their balance sheets. Alternatively, banks may use certain qualified loans as collateral to back securities they issue in the financial markets. This latter approach is a process known as *securitization.* Banks began to securitize many types of loans in the 1980s, including home mortgage loans, automobile and consumer loans, and even business loans.

In the final analysis, it seems clear that banks are no longer competitive in the market for large amounts of high-quality credit. In this market, there is far less need for bankers' unique information-gathering advantages for screening borrowers and for structuring and monitoring loan agreements. Large borrowers are attracted to the commercial paper market which, in recent years, has accounted for 15 percent or more of total business credit. Commercial paper can be issued quickly and in widely varied amounts, beginning at $1 million. Credit rating agencies provide their own valuable monitoring services for commercial paper borrowers. Despite the advantages of open market borrowing, however, large borrowers do not find banks completely irrelevant to their needs. Even the strongest of borrowers are motivated to seek a credit relationship with banks because such relationships increase operating flexibility and appear to add value to the borrowing firms. A banking relationship may add value by signaling to the borrowing firm's investors that the firm has the advantage of being scrutinized and expertly advised by a bank.[7] Thus, although banks are not the lowest cost source of funds for large, high-quality firms, a more limited relationship with banks proves to be valuable to such firms.

The borrowing firms that are most likely to have the most valuable relationships with banks tend to be smaller firms and firms that produce products and services for less stable or less established markets. The lending bank is required to develop a great deal of information on the creditworthiness of these firms and to be highly flexible about how it structures and monitors the loan. And, if things go awry, the bank stands ready to resolve the borrower's distress. Traditionally, banks excel in performing such functions. However, in recent years, commercial finance companies have taken a share of this business away from banks, accounting in the late 1990s for nearly 20 percent of business borrowing. Commercial finance companies fund their lending activities in the commercial paper market. They specialize in asset-based loans such as loans secured by accounts receivable, inventory, or equipment. In addition to financing purchases of such assets, companies can pledge existing working capital and equipment to obtain finance company lines of credit. However, many firms are not naturally positioned to borrow from finance companies. For example, service companies do not hold sufficient collateral to obtain asset-based loans.[8]

---

[6] This point is developed in Eugene F. Fama, "What's Different about Banks?" *Journal of Monetary Economics* (January 1985), pp. 29–39.

[7] See, for example, Christopher James, "Some Evidence on the Uniqueness of Bank Loans," *Journal of Financial Economics* (December 1987), pp. 217–235.

[8] See the discussion in Sean Becketti and Charles Morris, "Are Bank Loans Still Special?" *Economic Review,* Federal Reserve Bank of Kansas City (Third Quarter, 1992), pp. 71–84.

CHAPTER 11

Credit Selection, Underwriting, and Portfolio Diversification

Figure 10.3 of Chapter 10 depicted the structure of credit risk, and Chapter 10 examined operations risk as a component of risk in credit transactions. In this chapter we want to move beyond operational issues into the actual creation of credit by banks. We now want to show how banks manage the transaction risks of selecting and then underwriting (structuring) credit and how they cope with intrinsic and concentration risks in developing loan portfolios.

This chapter introduces four fundamental lines of inquiry in credit selection and discusses the resources and procedures used in credit investigation; describes underwriting as a negotiation process and reviews the considerations that determine the structure— term, collateral, covenants, and pricing—of the loan; presents loan risk rating systems as the key tool for measuring transaction risk; discusses loan portfolio design and the elements of portfolio risk, namely, intrinsic risk and concentration risk; gives a taxonomy of types of commercial loans and describes special categories of credit, including asset-based loans, agricultural credit, guaranteed small business loans, and lease financing; and reviews the sale and securitization of loans, an activity that enables banks to remove loans from their balance sheets to reduce their cost and to intensify the utilization of capital. An optional appendix at the end of the chapter reviews the basics of credit analysis, including financial ratio and statement analyses, aspects of working capital analysis, and financial forecasting. A second appendix presents background on indexes or bases used in the pricing of loans.

SELECTION RISK ANALYSIS

Credit selection is the process of assessing the risk of lending to a business or an individual. This chapter evaluates risk against the benefits the bank expects to derive from making the loan. The direct benefits are simply the interest and fees earned on the loan and, possibly, the deposit balances required as a condition of the loan. Indirect benefits consist of the initiation or maintenance of a relationship with the borrower that may provide the bank with increased deposits and with demand for a variety of bank services. Then this chapter covers the ways in which banks underwrite the loans they make in order to control risk and provide benefits commensurate with the risk.

Selection risk has both qualitative and quantitative dimensions; the qualitative dimensions are generally more difficult to assess. The steps in qualitative risk assessment consist primarily of gathering information on the borrower's record of financial responsibility, determining the borrower's true purpose for borrowing funds, identifying the risks confronting the borrower's business under future industry and economic conditions, and estimating the degree of commitment the borrower is expected to have regarding repayment. The quantitative dimension of credit risk assessment consists of the analysis of historical financial data and the projection of future financial results to evaluate the borrower's capacity for timely repayment of the loan and, indeed, the borrower's ability to survive possible industry and economic reversals.

The essence of credit selection analysis can be captured in four basic credit factors or lines of inquiry:

1. The borrower's character and soundness.
2. The intended use of loan funds.
3. The primary source of loan repayment.
4. Secondary sources of repayment.

Character and Soundness

The paramount factor in a successful loan is the honesty and goodwill of the borrower. Dishonest borrowers do not feel morally committed to repay their debts. A determined, skilled, and dishonest borrower usually can get credit through misrepresentation. Because loan officers must spread their time over many loan relationships, they do not have time to uncover elaborate schemes to defraud the bank.

To be sure, default does not always occur because of the borrower's moral failing and willful neglect. Equally important are intelligence, personal discipline, and managerial skills and instincts. These qualities may be easier to evaluate than blatant dishonesty— but not much easier. Loan officers must devote ample time in attempting to determine the competence of borrowers.

Finally, perhaps the subtlest task loan officers face is to discover the true quality of a borrower's business or project. Even competent and essentially honest borrowers are motivated to represent their plans and prospects in the best possible light when they are applying for funding. Without being deceitful, they often will not reveal their innermost fears or doubts. Thus, the loan officer tends to receive only part of the information needed to make a balanced credit decision. More than any other factor, it is this *asymmetry* in credit information volunteered by borrowers that compels loan officers to analyze carefully other, more objective information.

The bank must protect itself from dishonest, incompetent, or overly subjective borrowers by thoroughly investigating the borrower's credit background. The borrower's previous credit relationships can be evaluated from records of the local credit bureau, suppliers, past banking relationships, and customers. If the borrower has built a record of prompt payment of interest and principal, it is likely that future loans will be similarly serviced.

If the borrower has been routinely late in paying past debts, the reasons should be determined. If previous creditors have experienced losses, the loan officer should almost automatically reject the application.

Use of Loan Funds

On first impression, the borrower's need and proposed use for funds seem perfectly clear. In many commercial loans, however, this is frequently not the case. More often than not, determining the true need and use for funds requires good analytical skills in accounting and business finance. An understanding of the loan's intended use helps the analyst to understand whether the loan request is reasonable and acceptable.

Ostensibly, most business loans are made for current asset additions to working capital. However, the specific purpose for the loan may be substantially different. For example, the loan proceeds may actually provide emergency funds to meet the firm's payroll, or be used to pay overdue accounts to suppliers, or may replace working capital that was depleted to purchase fixed assets or funds depleted through operating losses. A common need for funds arises when borrowers extend trade credit inappropriately, causing collections to slow down. The analyst should also determine whether working capital needs are seasonal or permanent. Frequently, short-term loans are made to finance working capital needs that initially appear seasonal but subsequently prove to be permanent needs arising from sales growth trends. As a result, short-term loans often become de facto term loans that support permanent increases in accounts receivable, inventory, and fixed assets.

Assets financed by longer-term term commercial loans should meet the legitimate needs of the borrower's business. An asset purchased in the hope of profiting from its resale is speculative. Banks ordinarily do not lend for such a purchase because it does not contribute to the economic needs of the business.

Primary Source of Repayment

The analyst's accounting and finance skills are crucial in determining the borrower's ability to repay a loan from cash flow. For seasonal working capital loans, cash flows are generated by means of the orderly liquidation of the seasonal buildup in inventories and receivables. In term loans, cash flows are generated from earnings and noncash expenses charged against earnings (depreciation, depletion, and so forth). The analyst must ascertain the timing and sufficiency of these cash flows and evaluate the risk that cash flows may fall short.

Sources of repayment other than cash flows from operations should be viewed with caution. The borrower may plan on a future injection of investor capital to repay the loan. Unfortunately, if the firm fails to produce attractive profits, outsiders usually withhold future investment in the firm. The customer may be depending on borrowing (*takeout* funds) from another institution to repay the bank. Unless a formal commitment exists from another institution, this source suffers from the same limitation as a planned equity injection. An exception is the interim construction loan in which another, long-term lender has formally committed to provide takeout funds. Otherwise, the future sale of a fixed asset is not a reliable source of loan repayment. If the borrower is either unwilling or unable to sell the asset at the time of the loan, a future, possibly forced, sale of the asset to repay the loan is highly speculative.

Secondary Sources of Repayment

In general, cash flow from business operations is the most dependable source of loan repayment. However, if sufficient cash flows fail to materialize, the bank can prevent a loss if it has secured a secondary source of repayment.

Collateral should always be viewed as a secondary, not a primary, source of repayment. Banks hope to avoid foreclosing on collateral because foreclosure entails much time and expense. Collateral value should cover, in addition to the loan amount and interest due, the legal costs of foreclosure and interest during foreclosure proceedings. Collateral is the preferred secondary source of repayment.

Other secondary sources are guarantors and co-makers. However, collection from guarantors and co-makers often requires expensive litigation and results in considerable ill will between the bank, borrower, and guarantor.

Sources of Credit Information

The purpose of credit investigation is to acquire enough information to determine the loan applicant's willingness and capacity to service the proposed loan. The investigation should develop an understanding of the nature of the borrower in terms of the four basic credit factors just discussed: the borrower's character, the true purpose of the loan, the primary source of repayment, and the secondary sources of repayment. There are three fundamental sources of information: customers, internal bank sources, and external sources available through institutions outside the bank.

Customer Interview   Despite the possible lack of objectivity, the loan customer ordinarily provides the most important information needed in a credit investigation. The prospective borrower should indicate the use, type, and amount of loan requested, designate the proposed source and plan of repayment, provide pro forma financial data, identify the collateral or guarantors, name other previous and current creditors, list primary customers and trade suppliers, identify the firm's accountant, indicate the principal officers and shareholders, and give personal and business histories. The borrower also should provide documents needed to establish the lending relationship, including such items as the latest three or more years of business financial statements, personal financial statements, personal income tax returns, borrowing authorities, evidence of insurance, and continuing guarantees.

Lenders can quickly gather a wealth of supporting information using well-planned questions during the interview. What are the characteristics of the borrower's market? How are the products sold and distributed to the market? How important is price, quality, or service in selling the product? What is the production process? Are labor relations a problem? Who are the principal owners and executives, and what are their experience and educational backgrounds? Who would be in charge in the event that the present chief executive officer became unavailable? Does the firm have a strategic planning program? How will future markets of opportunity differ from those of today, and what resources will be needed to serve them? These and related questions serve to build the lender's comprehensive grasp of the strengths and weaknesses of a loan applicant.

Internal Sources of Information   If a loan customer has existing relationships with the bank, a great deal of information is internally available to the bank about the customer's willingness and capacity to service the proposed loan. The investigator should study credit files on any current or previous borrowings, examine checking account activity, and review other deposits previously or currently held. These sources will indicate the degree of the bank's satisfaction with past payment performance, and they may reveal any tendency to overdraw deposit accounts. These sources will also identify primary customers, suppliers, and other creditors with whom the borrower has had financial transactions.

Values shown on a borrower's personal financial statement usually require validation. For example, bank accounts and CDs can be verified from bank statements. Ownership of stock, bonds, or mutual funds can be verified from stock and bond certificates or brokerage account statements. The value of a home or of other real estate can be verified with qualified appraisals or property tax statements. The validation of personal liability is equally important and usually is done from external sources, as described in the next subsection.

Income tax returns are very useful for validating almost every aspect of a borrower's personal finances, including income sources, assets, and liabilities. Special schedules that form part of income tax returns provide details on expenses claimed as deductions, income from investment and employment, and gains and losses on investment activities. Schedules on income averaging; income from rents, royalties, estates, or trusts; and depreciation expense on property all combine to provide a complete picture of the applicant's income and expense that is difficult to construct from other sources.

External Sources of Information   Several service agencies provide credit reporting on businesses and business principals:

Business Information Report, published by Dun and Bradstreet, summarizes the financial history and current payment status of businesses. This basic credit report provides a composite credit rating, describes the promptness of trade payments by the subject firm, and indicates the highest credit balance carried during the most recent year. Other details include balance sheets, sales and profit records, insurance coverage, lease obligations, biographical information on principals, the firm's history, and its recent business trends.

The Credit Interchange Service of the National Association of Credit Management (NACM) is a national subscription service that provides information on a firm's current trade payment habits. The NACM sponsors local associations of trade suppliers and financial institutions, which share their credit listings and records on their payment experiences with businesses in their market areas.

Credit bureaus are local, regional, and national organizations that produce payment and employment information on individuals. Although this information source is generally used in connection with a consumer loan request, it may be used to obtain the payment history of principals in a business. Banks and other financial institutions are legitimate credit references and should be consulted. In the exchange of commercial credit information, bank officers are expected to govern themselves according to principles such as those set forth in the Robert Morris Associates Code of Ethics for the Exchange of Credit Information. This code describes ethical standards for confidentiality and accuracy in making and replying to credit inquiries.

A variety of commercial publications provides descriptive written and statistical information. These include *Moody's Industrial Manuals, Polk's City Directories, Standard and Poor's Corporation Records, Thomas' Registers,* and other special-purpose directories. Articles on individual firms or industries are published in many trade publications and may be found through the *Business Periodical Index* at any library. Official public information sources include filings of titles and mortgages, registration of corporation status, and business licenses.

COVENANTS AND PRICING

In this section we address key considerations in the structuring of loans—covenants and pricing.

Loan Covenants

Every business loan bears the risk that the loan's purpose will go awry or that the borrower's financial condition will deteriorate and jeopardize repayment of the loan. These risks increase with the length of time a loan is outstanding. Loan agreements set up a conflict between borrowers and lenders.[1] Intuitively, it should be clear that borrowing firms or, more precisely, their shareholders have an incentive to take on risky activities in the expectation of a payoff commensurate with the risk. If the activities fail totally, the borrowing firms' shareholders' stake is wiped out and the lending bank is left with a worthless claim. On the other hand, even if the borrower succeeds beyond its wildest dreams, banks do not earn excess returns. The borrower's shareholders enjoy extraordinary returns while its lenders recover only a set amount of interest and principal. To protect against such risk, banks write restrictive covenants into loan agreements. Term loans usually are set up with the most extensive loan covenants, although there are standard boilerplate covenants that are part of all loan agreements.

Affirmative versus Negative Covenants   There are two types of covenants in most term loan agreements: affirmative and negative. *Affirmative covenants* set out the borrower's obligation to submit financial statements regularly, to maintain adequate insurance, to certify compliance with provisions of the loan agreement periodically, to pay principal and interest as scheduled, and to conform to other requirements for reporting on company activities. *Negative covenants* range from requiring the borrower to maintain reasonable financial health to outright restraints or prohibitions on the borrower's activities. Because negative covenants might restrict or impose costs on the borrower, they are the subject of other intense negotiations.

There may be many negative covenants in a term loan agreement or just a few. The banker must determine, in each case, the types of covenants to include and how they should be quantified.

Objectives of Covenants   In framing loan agreement covenants, bankers must first decide what they want to control and achieve. Covenants may be classified by their objectives as follows:

1. Cash flow control.
2. Trigger call or restructuring of the loan.
3. Balance sheet control.

---

[1] A comprehensive analysis of loan and bond covenants is presented in Clifford W. Smith, Jr., and Jerold B. Warner, ''On Financial Contracting,'' *Journal of Financial Economics* (June 1979).

The most common objective is *cash flow control* in order to ensure that cash flow from the borrower's operations will be available to service the interest and principal of the loan. For term loans, the most important factor in cash flow is profits. The banker reviews the firm's business plan and the way in which the loan proceeds will be used. If the firm's plans are considered too risky, the banker might use loan covenants to force a modification, such as reducing the amount that the firm will invest in a high-risk venture or even prohibiting the firm from entering a new, high-risk market or product line.

It is not enough that a borrower's future profits seem assured. The banker may insist on covenants that prevent dividend payments, excessive capital investments, or repayment of debts owed to other lenders in order to guarantee that future cash flows will repay the bank's loan.

A *trigger* type of loan covenant establishes critical financial thresholds that, when violated, trigger the bank's right to some form of protective recourse. For example, if the borrower fails to maintain minimum profitability or a minimum net working capital level, the bank might gain the right to call the entire loan. The call protects the bank against deterioration in the value of the firm's working capital: If the firm cannot repay the loan on call, the bank's recourse lies in the firm's assets. Alternatively, a call on the loan permits the bank to revise the agreement, whether by changing the loan interest rate, increasing collateral requirements, or writing stricter covenants.

Balance sheet control covenants are aimed at restricting future actions by the firm that will weaken the balance sheet. A firm may compromise its balance sheets in reaction to unexpected changes in its business situation. Banks use covenants to limit further indebtedness or depletion of current assets and so prevent an unacceptable debt-to-equity ratio, current ratio, or other balance sheet standards.

Pricing

A critical risk in underwriting credit is the failure to price loans profitably, commensurate with the loans' risk and the bank's costs of funds, operations, and loss provisions. Loans represent the central activity of banking and are the basis of most banks' relationships with their major customers. As a consequence, loan prices, including loan interest rates, fees, and compensating balances, are banks' dominant source of revenue. If a bank chronically underprices loans, it will never be adequately compensated for the losses on loans that inevitably occur.

The way a bank prices its products says a lot about its strategies for delivering them. Figure 11.1 shows a spectrum of product delivery strategies. Banks must select a delivery strategy along this spectrum. At one extreme, they might choose to deliver a product at its commodity price. This price implies a strategy to compete based on lowest price.

Products that are priced as commodities are highly generic, with no value added by bank services. In Chapter 10 we noted the two fundamental products in banking: money and information. These products are obtained from customers themselves and are truly commodities. If a bank resells money or information to other customers without adding valuable services, it is simply selling commodities and it must compete by lowering the price.

To get customers to pay more, banks compete by packaging the commodities of money and information together with valuable banking services. Banks need to know not only how much its lending services cost but also how much they are worth to their customers. The price for services should not exceed their applied value to the customers. From

FIGURE 11.1   The Product Delivery Spectrum

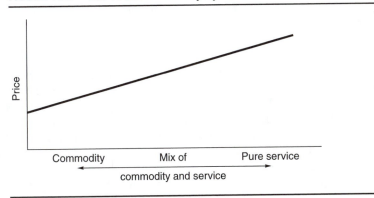

the customer's viewpoint, services that have marginal prices at or below the marginal (perceived) benefits are worth the price.

Banks cannot expect to add much perceived value to lending services for their largest and most creditworthy borrowers and should expect to lend at near commodity prices. Such customers have alternative sources of funds from the commercial paper market, foreign banks, and nonbank institutions. Unlike weaker and more local borrowers, large prime customers tend not to tie their borrowing needs to their needs for other bank services.

Banks estimate their customers' elasticities of demand and price the loans or services they sell customers so that the price-quality combination maximizes net revenue. Large creditworthy borrowers have infinitely elastic demand for funds; none will borrow at above-market rates, and all will try to borrow at below-market rates.

Loan pricing for the majority of borrowers is conditioned by a strong customer relationship. Banks emphasize cross-selling their customers a broad range of products and banking services. To such borrowers, loan rates are nominally established at a spread above the base cost of funds. However, the focus of concern is the yield on the total activities, including loans, associated with the relationship.

Spread Pricing Model   Typically, loan rates are set at a spread over banks' costs. The cost of bank funds is the transfer price charged by the funds-gathering function of the bank. The transfer price is the cost for market sources of funds that match the duration of the loan. The lending division then prices the loan at a markup (spread) over the cost of such funds plus other allocated noninterest costs, including loan officer time and other costs. The typical cost benchmark for funds might be the interest rate offered on the bank's short-term CD or perhaps a blended cost based on a mix of the CD rate and an overnight rate such as the Federal funds rate or repurchase agreement rate. By duration-matching the loan with its funding source, the bank removes the interest rate risk from the lending division of holding the loan in the division's portfolio. Thus, the lending division's performance is based on the credit risk of loans it originates and not on the interest rate risk, a task for which the division is not trained.

Alternatively, the bank may view the transfer price of its funds for financing the loan to be the weighted average of its deposit and other sources of funds. In this case, the funds-gathering function of the bank transfers the *pooled* rate on all funds. Whether it uses a duration-matched or a pooled transfer price, the price should be based on the marginal, not average, cost of funds. Clearly, the interest rate to be charged the borrower on a specific new loan will be at the margin and will be independent of the historic rates on the bank's existing loans. The value of the bank's funds, no less, should be based on marginal costs.

Given the appropriate value or transfer price of funds, the spread is then determined by the bank's target return on the funds it used to finance the loan, plus a premium for the credit risk involved. Table 11.1 presents a model applied to the spread pricing of such a loan. In meeting the bank's spread target, the customer is credited with bank income generated from servicing and commitment fees (lines 2 and 4 in Table 11.1) and with the value of deposit balances held by the borrower in the bank (line 6). The value of bank funds (line 1) may be set equal to the all-in cost of bank liabilities or to the earnings rate on risk-free assets such as Treasury bills. The borrower's deposit balances are adjusted downward to account for the fact that reserve and float requirements reduce the usability of these funds (resulting in usable funds equal to 85 percent of total funds, shown in line 6 of the table). The desired spread of 4 percent over the bank's cost of funds shown in line 7 might be appropriate for a small, somewhat high-risk borrower. Comparable spreads in the case of high-quality, large corporate loans are much smaller than in this example and would produce a lower loan interest rate.

Cost Accounting Systems   Clearly, models such as spread pricing assume that the bank has a good understanding of its costs (for example, the cost for providing services in line 2 of Table 11.1). Many banks are latecomers in developing and accepting cost accounting techniques. Historically, banks have applied a majority of their staffs and their creative efforts to procuring low-cost deposits and servicing depositors without charge. The slow-to-die tradition of not charging to recover the costs of many deposit-related services retarded the development of accounting systems to determine banks' costs for those services.

In recent years, large banks have developed sophisticated cost accounting systems. Other banks participate in the Federal Reserve System's Functional Cost Analysis program or use the data generated by this program as a reference point for cost-dependent decision making. The functional cost analysis program collects uniform cost and income data from a group of participating Federal Reserve member banks. The data are structured to indicate the profitability and cost characteristics of various functional activities in banks.

TABLE 11.1   Spread Loan Pricing Model

1. Value of bank funds	6.00%
2. Servicing fees, net of costs	0.35
3. Commitment fee on average unused portion	0.50
4. Commitment fee income = unused portion × (3): 1/3 × 0.75% =	0.25
5. Collected balances: percent of loan usage	11.00
6. Value of balances = (5) × usable portion × value of funds: 11% × 0.85 × 6%	0.56
7. Desired spread over value (cost of funds)	4.00
8. Loan price = (1) + (7) − (2) − (4) − (6) = 6.00% + 4.00% − 0.10% − 0.25% − 0.56% =	9.09%

Noninterest Aspects of Loan Pricing: Direct Factors   In our previous discussion, we neglected explanations of loan pricing aspects other than the explicit interest rate charged. However, there are important considerations in pricing loans other than direct interest charges. Foremost among the noninterest factors of loan pricing are compensating balance requirements and commitment fees. Both of these factors directly affect banks' yield on loans.

Compensating Balances   Compensating balance requirements obligate the borrower to hold demand deposits or low-interest time deposits as part of a loan agreement. Balance requirements are also sometimes set on loan commitments. The balance requirement on loans usually requires that balances average an agreed-on percentage of the loan amount. An alternative way of setting the balance requirements is with reference to a percentage of a minimum, not an average, balance. The predominant use of an average requirement allows the borrower to draw balances down to well below the average requirement when loan funds are applied to their intended purpose and then to raise the average balance as funds accumulate to well above the average requirement, pending repayment of the loan.

Average balance requirements range from 10 to 20 percent, with 15 percent perhaps being most common. At times, balance requirements are applied to both the loan and the total commitment. For example, "10 and 10" indicates balances of 10 percent on the loan and 10 percent on the total commitment. This results in a 20 percent requirement on the loan and 10 percent on the unused commitment.

One rationale for compensating balance requirements is that they ensure that borrowers will remain as customers on both sides of the balance sheet, that is, as both borrowers and providers of funds. Banks obviously do not want their borrowers to redeposit loan proceeds at another institution. Another rationale is that compensating balances permit banks to pay implicit interest that they are prohibited from paying explicitly under Regulation Q. The implicit interest arises from the fact that banks can charge lower loan rates because borrowers' balances have considerable value to them. It is also argued that the compensating balance requirement simply adds discipline to the borrower's management of working balances, much of which the borrower would maintain on deposit in any case. Finally, compensating balances reflect a traditional belief that the central function of banks is to take deposits. At the extreme, this belief states that loans are made to ensure the availability of deposits in the present and the future.

The cost to the borrower of compensating balance requirements can be directly reflected in the cost of a loan. If a borrower needs $80,000 but must retain an average compensating balance of 20 percent, the borrower must obtain a $100,000 loan. If the loan rate is 16 percent, or a cost to the borrower of $16,000 in interest charges annually, the effective rate on the $80,000 portion of the loan usable by the borrower is then 20 percent ($16,000 divided by $80,000). These factors apply only if the borrower would otherwise maintain a zero deposit balance—a most unlikely event. The actual amount of redundant borrowing is the amount by which the required average balance exceeds the amount that the borrower would otherwise maintain.

Compensating balances are criticized as being an inefficient pricing mechanism because, although they raise the effective borrowing costs, banks must hold idle reserves against the additional deposits and therefore cannot fully invest them in earning assets. This rationale strikes some borrowers and bankers as questionable. In some instances, among banks that have moved toward unbundled and explicit pricing, balance requirements have been replaced by fees or higher loan rates. Banks that substitute fees or higher rates for balances reflect their belief in lending, rather than deposit taking, as the bank's central function; they do not hold the traditional belief that lending is primarily a tool for obtaining deposits. Their concerns are, first, to generate good loans and, second, as skillful liabilities managers, to obtain deposits or purchased sources of money to fund the loans.

Nevertheless, in periods of tight money and high interest rates, compensating balances tend to become more attractive to banks than fees. During such times, the balances ought to provide the banks with higher yields, because interest rates increase on banks' earning assets, where the cost to banks for handling compensating balances is relatively unaffected. However, borrowers attempt to economize on demand deposits as interest rates rise, and they are inclined to resist restrictive balance requirements.

Commitment Fees Formal loan commitments arise mostly for revolving credits and, to a lesser extent, for term loans and short-term credits. They set forth a bank's firm obligation to provide a specified amount of credit in the future at a specified price or pricing formula. Unlike the informal loan commitment on seasonal short-term credit, the formal commitment also frequently specifies the fee to the borrower for making future credit available. In essence, the commitment fee is the price for a call on future credit.

Commitment fees on revolving credits are more prevalent because of the delay and relative unpredictability of the takedown by the customer. For the usual commitment period of two to five years, fees on the unused portion average about 0.5 percent. They may increase to as much as 0.75 percent during periods of tight money and may fall below 0.5 percent in periods of slack loan demand.

In theory, commitment fees are related to the bank's cost of preparing to meet borrowers' future calls for credit, either by maintaining liquidity on its balance sheet or, alternatively, by preserving its own capacity to borrow funds. There are logical explanations for both kinds of costs. The bank may feel compelled to hold assets in short-term government securities to ensure that it has liquidity for backing up commitments to meet borrowers' future calls for loan funds. By maintaining liquidity in this way, the bank foregoes returns on higher-yielding assets and, instead, holds low-yielding liquid assets. Alternatively, the bank may maintain its own borrowing capacity in the money markets to meet future calls on credit. In this case, the bank foregoes borrowing in the money markets and investing in earning assets currently in order to ensure its ability to borrow in the future when loan commitments are called.

Noninterest Aspects of Loan Pricing: Indirect Factors Indirect noninterest factors in loan pricing include collateral requirements, loan maturity limits, and loan covenants. In our discussion of loan pricing so far, we have ignored the effect of these factors or have assumed that they remain constant for every loan. In fact, these indirect factors are important variables in any loan negotiation. If the terms involving collateral, maturity, and loan covenants become more restrictive, the risk to the bank is reduced and the effective cost to the customer increases. Highly restrictive terms ought to ease other, more direct, pricing elements. Specifically, shortened loan maturities, increased collateral, and more restrictive loan covenants should result in lowering some or all of the direct pricing elements of loan rates, commitment fees, and compensating balance requirements.

In addition, the indirect noninterest pricing factors are frequently used as a means of rationing loan funds, particularly during periods of tight money when banks struggle to find sufficient funds. To qualify for a larger loan at the going rate of interest, certain borrowers are required to put up more collateral and accept shorter loan maturities and stricter covenants. Borrowers subject to these forms of credit rationing are generally those with few, if any, alternative sources of funds. These borrowers can be thought of as perceived-value customers. They are prepared to pay any price up to the value they perceive the credit to be worth and do not have the ability to play off prices against competitor lenders. If indirect or direct pricing factors are too restrictive, that is, too costly, perceived-value customers became rationed out of the loan market altogether.

RISK RATING AND MONITORING

Chapter 10 and this chapter have discussed how a bank copes with the credit transaction risks of credit operations, selection, and underwriting. These are the risks the bank incurs in making one loan at a time. It remains for the bank to measure the resultant risk.

Risk Rating Systems

Every bank uses a risk rating system to measure the risk of their loans. Risk ratings force the loan personnel to quantify the risk perceived in their loans. The risk must be assessed and the rating assigned at the time the loan is made and then revised during the life of the loan if its credit quality changes materially. The degree of monitoring required for a loan is in proportion to its rated risk.

Risk rating systems are imperfect and contain both objective and subjective elements. Objective aspects, for the most part, are based on financial statement data and apply weights to certain financial ratios that reflect liquidity, leverage, and earnings. Despite the requirement that risk be quantified, risk rating systems always have a subjective dimension that attempts to capture intangibles such as the quality of management, the borrower's status within its industry, the market strength of products or services, and the quality of financial reporting. These subjective items inevitably result in inconsistencies. Still, any system is better than simply omitting the measurement of loan risk.

Table 11.2 reproduces a subjective risk rating system proposed by Edgar M. Morsman, Jr.[2] In practice, most banks use risk rating systems with more than the five classes represented in Table 11.2. Some use as many as ten classes. The lower rating classes should be parallel to examiner ratings. (For a review of examiner ratings, see Chapter 10.) For example, a Class IV loan rating in Table 11.2 equates to "other loans especially mentioned."

Watch List and Migration Analysis

Loans that become rated in the lower categories of the risk rating system constitute the "watch list." As the name implies, watch-listed credits bear special attention to prevent their becoming losses. The watch list is a vital aid for understanding the total loss exposure. The bank's future performance is tied up intimately in the watch list. Lenders are encouraged to "watch-list" problem loans before the loans actually are in default. This requires

---

[2] See pages 62 and 63 in Edgar M. Morsman, *Effective Loan Management* (Philadelphia: Robert Morris Associates, 1983). The review schedules were added by the authors.

TABLE 11.2   A Loan Risk-Rating System

Class I (highest quality)

Businesses with high liquidity, excellent financial conditions, history of stable and predictable earnings, available sources of alternative funding, strong management, favorable industry trends. Loans adequately secured with certificates of deposit, government securities, cash value of life insurance, etc. Individuals have substantial net worth concentrated in highly liquid assets with well-defined primary and secondary sources of repayment.
Review schedule: annual

Class II (good quality)

Businesses with most of the characteristics described in class I. However, certain characteristics are not quite as strong, such as more cyclical earnings and less availability of alternative funding in periods of economic distress. Individuals have substantial net worth which may be concentrated in less liquid assets such as real estate or stock in closely held but strong companies. Present and future earnings potential is strong, and the secondary source of repayment is readily apparent with an adequate secondary source available.
Review schedule: 6 months

Class III (satisfactory quality)

Companies with fair liquidity and a reasonable financial condition which falls within acceptable tolerances of similar companies in the RMA *Annual Statement Studies.* Earnings may be erratic, and satisfactory payment is expected but not assured under all conditions. Loans are frequently secured by collateral such as receivables and inventory where conversion to cash is difficult and uncertain. Alternative funding sources are normally restricted to competitor banks. Individuals have marginal liquidity and net worth but reasonable earnings with a reliable primary source of repayment. Secondary sources of repayment are less obvious and are restricted to such possibilities as mortgage refinancing.
Review schedule: 3 months

Class IV (below-average quality)

Businesses with poor liquidity, high leverage, and erratic earnings or losses. The primary source of repayment is no longer realistic, and asset or collateral liquidation may be the only source of repayment. Loans are marginal and require continuing and close supervision by the responsible loan officer. Asset-based revolving credit supplying working capital for an indefinite period. Close monitoring of collateral by personnel with sufficient expertise is required. Individuals have no liquidity, marginal net worths and a speculative primary source of repayment with no secondary source identified. Loans classified "other loans especially mentioned" by examiners. Loans where the information in the credit file is insufficient to draw any conclusion as to quality.
Review schedule: 30 days

Class V (poor quality)

Collateral, net worth, and cash flow are insufficient to support the level of borrowing, and sources of repayment are not readily identifiable. Without constant and intense supervision, the real possibility of partial or full loss exists. Individuals have insufficient net worth or earnings to support the loan. Additional collateral must be obtained, and there is a distinct possibility of loss. Loans classified "substandard," "doubtful," and "loss" by examiners.
Review schedule: 30 days or less

them to monitor closely not only past-due loans but also current loans that are known to be potential past-dues because of deterioration in the credit. On the other hand, not all past-due loans are to be watch-listed. Some are good-quality loans in which the borrower's payment behavior has become careless.

At the bottom of the watch list, most risk rating systems include a category equivalent to the examiners' "loss" rating. When a loan rating falls to loss, it should be immediately charged off. Generally, loans that reach 90 days past-due should be classified loss and charged off.

Migration analysis is the method for longitudinal tracking over time the outcomes of loans in the same risk classes. To estimate loss potential, banks analyze how loans of given risk classes are ultimately resolved, including those that become charged off. The method is especially important for loans rated in watch-list risk classes because it is from these classes that future charge-offs are most likely to occur.

Migrations of loans to different risk classes or charge-offs should be tracked over three or more years in order to best understand their eventual disposition, based on their present risk ratings. For example, the analysis should determine the proportion of loans in a risk class such as class IV in Table 11.2, which are ultimately paid in full, carried as a "bankable" loan, remain in class IV, fall to class V, or become charged off. The result is crucial information on how future earnings and return-on-equity objectives are likely to be affected by the present size of the watch list. Finally, by studying the watch list and migration analysis, banks can estimate highly realistic values for loan loss provisions and loss reserves.

MANAGING PORTFOLIO RISK

Our discussion of credit risk to this point has been mainly about transaction risk. We defined transaction risk as the risk of making one loan at a time in creating a portfolio of loans. Lenders' training is primarily in unitary transactions, which naturally focuses them on maximizing the probabilities of getting paid back on individual loans. The theory of loan portfolio management, on the other hand, requires rating the risk of each loan, pooling loans of like risk, and determining through migration analysis the destiny of the whole population in given risk classes. This view on portfolio management assumes correlation risks that affect the whole portfolio.

We now want to expand our perspective on risk to the risk of the whole portfolio. The accumulation of individual loan risks is not the same as portfolio risk. In broad terms, this is because of diversification. Portfolio theory explains that the returns on diversified assets are not perfectly correlated. As a result, the total risk of the portfolio is somewhat less than the summation of each asset's risk.

The structure of risk suggested by McKinley and Barrickman in Figure 10.3 reveals that portfolios of loans contain two other kinds of risk: *intrinsic risk* and *concentration risk*.[3] Both of these risk classifications qualify as correlation risks—that is, the risk that portfolio assets are not well diversified and that their returns can be expected to be highly correlated.

Intrinsic Risk

Lending to certain kinds of businesses or industries is inherently more risky than others. We define such risk as intrinsic. This risk is different from concentration risk. A high concentration in one kind of loan—for example, consumer loans—may readily entail less

---

[3] Supra, p. 36.

risk than a lower concentration in another kind—say, construction loans. Banks can more safely build a concentration in the former than in the latter.

That certain businesses or industries make for riskier loans is a simple truism. It can be demonstrated by examining the historic loss exposure of such lending and by analyzing factors endemic to their future operations. Historic loss exposure is primarily a matter of prior experience of lenders serving the risky sectors. In addition, one should review past financial vulnerability such as the longitudinal record of profitable operations, cost structure and cyclicality of demand, volatility of earnings, and financial leverage. Factors that will affect future operations include probable product demand, strength and concentration of customer base, competitive pressures, and regulatory and legal risks.

Concentration Risk

Concentration risk is the risk that the performance across many loans is highly correlated. It stems from the lack of diversification in geography, industry, and individual borrowers. When there is insufficient diversification, banks are exposed to accumulations of transaction risk and intrinsic risk.

Concentration risk is controlled by setting concentration limits. The bank might limit lending to affiliated borrowers by setting *house limits* as a percentage of capital or setting maximum exposure to high-risk industries or businesses.

Risk Profile

A portfolio risk profile is determined from transaction risk, intrinsic risk, and concentration risk. Traditionally, as loans are accumulated one at a time, lenders are taught to focus on transaction risk. However, transaction risk does not equate to portfolio risk. McKinley and Barrickman describe intrinsic risk as ''a more effective measure of the probability of portfolio deterioration.'' Concentration risk gives clues to the possible *magnitude* of the deterioration.[4]

TYPES OF LOANS

Although they are highly flexible and diverse, we can classify bank loans according to their maturity, type of collateral, and other special features. This section classifies bank loans into four types: short-term loans, bridge loans, revolving credit loans, and term loans. At any particular time, individual borrowers may have any number of each type of loan. This simple classification permits us to focus on the ways banks structure each type.[5]

Short-Term Loans

Source of Repayment   Well over half of bank commercial loans are made for a short term, that is, for periods of less than a year. Most of these loans are for financing increases in inventory for seasonal borrowers. The loan is repaid when the borrower's

---

[4] Supra, p. 42.

[5] Parts of the following discussion of loan types are based on Edgar M. Moorsman, Jr., ''Commercial Loan Structuring,'' *Journal of Commercial Bank Lending* (November 1991).

inventory is sold and its receivables are collected. Short-term loans also finance borrowers with short-lived and project-oriented needs for funds—for example, service businesses such as accounting or engineering design firms.

Analysis   Retailers and manufacturers are regular users of seasonal working capital lines of credit. Through a line of credit, a bank indicates its intention to provide credit up to the amount of the line. The lender analyzes borrower-prepared projected monthly balance sheets and income statements. The projections show the need for funds for financing seasonal bulges in working capital as inventory, sales, and receivables expand in sequence. This sequence is known as the *working capital cycle.* The projections should reveal the expected peak loan need, the timing of takedowns, the link between bank and supplier credit, and the amount and time of the bank's maximum reliance on inventory support of its loan.

Facility   A loan facility is defined as the structure and terms established in a loan agreement. In the case of lines of credit, the facility is very flexible and overcomes the need to extend a series of short-term loans. The borrower takes down only part of the line as the need arises. As a result, the borrower is not left to borrow redundant funds. Interest is charged only on the amount actually borrowed, and the loan is repaid as cash flows back into the firm with the usual seasonal decline in sales, inventory, and receivables.

Normally, as a condition of the credit line, the agreement requires that the customer be out of debt to the bank for some period of time during the year. This required *rest period* is usually 30 to 90 consecutive days and is intended to provide confirmation that the customer's need for funds is not continuous and permanent. If the need appears to be continuous and permanent, the bank may seek to increase the collateral and otherwise restructure the loan. Seasonal lines of credit can "revolve" in the sense that amounts repaid can be reborrowed within the line. However, they generally do not revolve; amounts repaid are seldom reborrowed. Lines of credit should not be confused with loan commitments. Commitments are enforceable obligations to advance funds under agreed-upon terms. By contrast, lines of credit can be revoked without the consent of borrowers.

A letter of agreement may be used to specify the line amount; define how the proceeds against a line are to be used; restrict the use of funds for other purposes, such as the purchase of fixed assets or the repayment of other debt; and spell out the expiration date. Despite their lack of enforceability, credit lines normally are honored faithfully by banks. Even an infrequent failure to honor its lines would risk a bank's reputation and its standing with present and potential customers. If the borrower's soundness deteriorates, lines of credit are subject to reduction or even cancellation. On the other hand, formal commitments obligate the bank to advance funds as established in a formal loan agreement, unless the borrower fails to fulfill the terms and conditions set forth.

Normally, the total of banks' open lines exceeds their practical capacity to honor all of them simultaneously. An "oversold" position such as this is a reasonable posture for a bank to take because it is virtually impossible that all line-of-credit customers would try to take down a large part of their lines at the same time. A bank can hedge against such an occurrence and preserve flexibility by structuring forward agreements informally so that they are not legally binding.

Collateral   Line-of-credit borrowings usually are secured with inventory, accounts receivable, or fixed assets. The use of a formula for advancing funds against a borrowing base (defined later in this chapter) is not normal for seasonal borrowing. Because inventory values often are difficult to determine, the bank is most exposed when the borrower's seasonal inventory reaches its peak. In addition, however, as the inventory is sold, the lender must be concerned with the quality of receivables. This concern requires an understanding of the firm's credit policy, including how the firm checks on the credit of its own customers, how it sets customers' credit limits and denies credit, its collection procedures, and other considerations.

Bridge Loans

Source of Repayment   Another type of short-term loan is the bridge loan. Such loans can be thought of as project-type loans that bridge a period of time up to a specific event that generates sufficient funds for repayment of the loan. For example, money center and regional banks lend large sums to investment bankers to bridge their underwriting and placement of securities issues until the issues can be sold to investors. Sales to investors generate the funds needed to pay off the banks. Interim construction and real estate loans are normally short-term loans to builders or land developers for the purpose of acquiring and improving real estate. Such loans are secured by the subject real estate and are conditional on a commitment of long-term takeout funds from a permanent lender. The takeout funds are the source of repayment at project completion for the bank making the bridge loan. Interim construction lending is the norm for the construction of single-family and multifamily housing, office buildings, shopping centers, warehouses, hotels, and restaurants, as well as for land development. Another type of bridge loan is one that spans the period until an issue of long-term debt or equity can be completed. On completion of the issue, the proceeds are used to retire the bridge loan.

Analysis   The bridge loan lender must make two kinds of evaluations. First, the lender must determine the probability that the bridge event will occur as projected; for example, the lender should assess the probability that construction takeout funds will, in fact, be forthcoming. Second, the lender must analyze the borrower's ability to repay the loan if the projected event does not occur—for example, if the construction takeout commitment is not fulfilled.

Facility   Bridge loan maturities are tailored to the timing of the payoff event. If repayment is not completed at the time of the event, the lender must conclude that a failure has occurred.

Collateral   When a bridge loan finances the acquisition or building of an asset for immediate resale, the collateralization usually is as simple as taking a security interest in the asset itself. If the bridge loan is for financing or bridging a security underwriting, the lender ensures that repayment is made directly from the proceeds of the security offering. However, the lender must determine if the borrower can repay from other sources if the sale or refinancing event does not succeed.

Revolving Credit Loans

Revolving credit loans finance the expansion of current assets or the retirement of current liabilities. This type of credit often is called *asset-based* lending because the amounts borrowed are tied to a *borrowing base* formula that limits the outstanding amount to a margin percentage on the borrower's receivables, inventory, or, in extractive industries, reserves owned. This credit is the long-term equivalent of short-term line-of-credit loans entailing a commitment to advance funds up to a maximum line for longer terms, that is, for as much as five years. The need for funds arises most often because the borrower cannot fund its increasing sales from internal sources such as retained earnings.

Source of Repayment   During the life of the revolving credit loan, repayment is derived from collections from the borrower's customers. With revolving credit, however, further advances are made when the borrowing firm periodically increases its inventories. Thus, repayment is indefinite and often remains so until the loan is converted to a term loan with a definite repayment schedule. Whether or not conversion to a term loan is appropriate depends on the likelihood that long-term earnings will be adequate to repay the loan. Another source of repayment may be refinancing with an alternative lender or through a securities offering to market investors. The risk of nonrepayment is greater for revolving credit than for other types of loans because of the borrower's unresolved earnings power and the duration of the borrower's need.

Analysis   It is imperative to analyze the operating capabilities of revolving credit borrowers because such borrowers maintain a tenuous balancing act that matches the bank's financing to growing inventories, sales, and collections. This requires sharp internal controls and reporting systems. Debt ratios usually are higher than average and must be managed wisely so that financing costs are tolerable. The lender must determine how the borrower can demonstrate long-term earnings power capable of methodically repaying the current loan.

Facility   Revolving credit loans are made on a revocable basis. A loan agreement specifies the credit limit available and the conditions under which funds are advanced and repaid. Advances are made against evidence of adequate working collateral, with reports on the status of the collateral submitted frequently.

Collateral   Normally, revolving credit advances are made against a borrowing base of eligible receivables and inventories. Advances support the growth of inventories or the decrease in current liabilities, such as the reduction of excessive trade credit outstanding. Experienced lenders determine the quality of inventories and receivables and, therefore, the margins to be applied in a borrowing base advance formula. As a general rule, commodity-like raw materials inventories qualify for a higher advance rate than an end product from the borrower's conversion process. Commodity-like products are more likely to be sold to manufacturers who need similar raw materials. Alternatively, such inventories can usually be returned to the supplier, net of a restocking charge. By contrast, goods-in-process inventories may not be accepted as collateral at all because the bank is likely to find it extremely difficult to supervise the finishing of production in a failed firm. Also, finished goods inventories usually are less valuable than raw material inventories because finished goods inventories, especially specialized goods, often are difficult to liquidate. Lenders must also be wary of any category of inventories subject to obsolescence or spoilage.

Of the two, receivables constitute better collateral, whereas inventories must be viewed on a highly discounted liquidation basis. However, even though receivables generally are better collateral, the lender should margin them conservatively, usually providing an advance rate of 60 to 95 percent, to discount past-due accounts of customers and to deduct profit margins in order to restrict the recognition of value to actual value added to products sold net of the profit margin and of returns and allowances.

Term Loans

Term loans are loans (other than consumer and real estate loans) with maturities over one year. Often they finance the purchase of fixed assets or the broad expansion of production capacity, but they may also be made to finance a change in company control or an acquisition or to take out a revolving credit loan.

For some highly rated companies with access to the bond market, term loans offer a viable "privately placed" alternative source of long-term funds. Their advantage over bonds is that term loans can be executed *quickly, flexibly,* and with *low issuance costs.* Because term loans are negotiated directly with a bank, an agreement can be reached more quickly and can be tailored to the specific case of the borrower, whereas a public bond issue must go through a lengthy registration process with the SEC. Typically, bonds are burdened with extensive terms or "boiler plate" to conform to the expectations of a broad bondholder public. Also, unlike the 20- to 30-year maturities usually associated with bonds, most term loans have intermediate maturities of less than 10 years.

Source of Repayment   The repayment source for term loans must consist of stable, long-term sources of cash flow. In the long run, sufficient earnings power is imperative, although cash flows arising from depreciation tax shelters may be a significant source for capital-intensive borrowers with high rates of depreciation. For loans made to finance fixed assets, repayment should be scheduled before the end of the useful life of the asset.

Analysis   The analysis of term loan borrowers focuses on what might be called the *long-term income statement.* The lender must understand the company's long-term earnings potential. This implies a broad-based analysis of the firm's products and management, its industry, and its competitive strength within the industry. Long-term earnings projections are required, as well as sensitivity analyses that test the effects of unfavorable developments in sales volumes, profit margins, asset turnover rates, and direct and overhead expense ratios. In lending on specific fixed assets, it should be determined whether the assets will produce sufficient profitability to warrant their purchase.

Facility   Term loans typically are outstanding for a specified period of time and are amortized with payments of interest and principal on a quarterly or, ideally, monthly basis. Monthly payments have the advantages of more frequent compounding of the interest rate earned. They also provide the bank with more frequent confirmation that the borrower is remaining current on its debt and that its ability to repay has not deteriorated. A formal loan agreement is prepared, with terms and covenants spelling out the duties of the bank and the borrower, including certain rights that accrue to the bank if the borrower fails to comply with the requirements of the agreement. Loan proceeds are normally disbursed when the loan agreement is closed or shortly thereafter. In reality, term loans provide intermediate term credit; maturities are usually limited to 10 years and are predominantly in the two- to five-year range.

Collateral The term bank loan is normally secured by the borrower's fixed assets, including a mortgage on land and structures or a perfected security interest on equipment. Working capital is less often used for collateral in term loans but is used to support seasonal or revolving credit loans. The collateral value of secured assets is the assets' liquidation value, usually under assumed distress conditions.

Third-Party Credits

Within the four generic types of loans described above, there are credit arrangements that involve contracting with third parties. The most common of these are as follows.

Guarantees As noted in Chapter 10, guarantees of loans to small corporations are often required of major stockholders to prevent stockholders from using limited corporate liability to shield themselves from their firm's debt obligations. In general, loans should not be made on the strength of a guarantee; they should be based on the business source of repayment. The bank's position may be strengthened somewhat if the proposed guarantor signs as a co-maker instead. This may prevent litigation that could arise in loans with guarantors if the guarantors choose to contest a possible later restructuring of the loan.

Accounts Receivable Financing Accounts receivable financing is a form of collateralized lending with a particularly intimate link between the loan and its collateral. The bank lends money against an agreed percentage (50 to 90 percent) of accounts receivable assigned to it. The borrowing firm usually continues its regular credit and collection functions, and its customers are not notified of the assignment of their debt to the bank. Collections are automatically paid down on the loan, and new loan funds are granted as new receivables are generated.

This type of financing has advantages for both the bank and the borrower. It gives the bank access to the readily convertible collateral of weaker borrowers who otherwise might not provide a viable loan market. Credit is well controlled since receivables financing permits borrowing only as the borrower generates sales. It also provides for automatic repayment of the loan as collections come in.

Accounts receivable financing gives relatively weak borrowers access to credit they otherwise might not obtain. The credit is *evergreen* in that no rest period is required. The amount of credit is more or less tailored to the borrower's rolling needs, particularly because financing reacts to expanding sales, thus supporting the necessary buildup of inventories. However, the cost of accounts receivable financing is higher than the cost paid by a borrower that is qualified for unsecured lending.

Banks proceed cautiously because of the unusual reliance on the collateral in receivables financing. The collateral needs to be examined carefully and continually to ensure performance and to eliminate ineligible receivables from the borrowing base.

Factoring Accounts receivable financing is often confused with factoring. In factoring, a bank or a commercial factor purchases selected accounts receivable from its customer at a percentage of their face value. In a strict sense, then, factoring is not a form of collateralized lending but rather an outright purchase of the customer's assets. The bank notifies the borrower's debtors to remit all payments directly to the bank and not to the customer. Generally, the customer is required to maintain a cash reserve against losses due to buyers' claims against the customer firm.

TABLE 11.3   Accounts Receivable Financing versus Factoring

	Accounts Receivable Financing	Accounts Receivable Factoring
Credit function performed by	Borrower	Bank
Collection function performed by	Borrower	Bank
Proceeds allowed via	Loan	Purchase
Cash reserve required	No	Yes
Account ownership	Borrower	Bank
Debtor notification	No	Yes
Cost	Lower	Higher

Table 11.3 summarizes the differences between accounts receivable financing and factoring.

Inventory Financing   For our purposes, inventory financing can be defined as any loan that is secured by inventory and scheduled to be repaid from the sale of that inventory. Like accounts receivable financing, it is a highly specialized lending service to business; it is often combined with accounts receivable financing. Lending against inventory is a high-risk venture because such financing is usually extended to businesses that are financially weak. Also, the lender frequently encounters problems related to the valuation and marketability of inventory, as well as difficulties in physical control of the inventory.

There are several forms of inventory lending. All of the borrower's inventories can be used as security on a loan under a *floating lien.* However, the seller is not constrained from selling inventories, so that the bank cannot control specific inventory items. The floating lien may be used to provide continuing security on receivables created when the inventory is sold.

Trust Receipt Financing   Also known as *floor plan finance,* this form of financing is vitally important in many retail businesses and involves transitory legal ownership of inventory by the bank. Typically, the borrower is provided funds with which to pay for goods received from suppliers. The borrower holds the goods in trust for the bank by issuing the bank a trust receipt. As sales occur, the borrower transmits the proceeds to the bank. Contracts from the borrower's credit sales are also frequently sold to the bank, so that the bank, in effect, provides continuous financing.

Trust receipts can be issued only on specifically identifiable goods. The goods must be easily verified when the bank runs its audit of the customer's inventory. Trust receipts are most convenient when used to finance new- and used-automobile dealers, other durable consumer goods retailers, and machinery dealers.

Warehousing Finance   This financing facilitates inventory lending by providing controls on the disposition of a borrower's inventories. Two different warehousing arrangements are used: the public warehouse and the field warehouse. The *public warehouse* is owned and operated remotely from the borrower's site by an independent third party in the storage business. The *field warehouse* is controlled by an independent third-party operator on the borrower's site and is more suitable when the goods handled are too bulky to relocate or when goods are moved in and out with great frequency.

In both public and field warehouse arrangements, the independent third party receives and stores the inventories and provides the bank with warehouse receipts. The bank then creates a deposit for the borrower at an advance rate, typically in the range of 50 to 80 percent of the value of the receipted goods. As the borrower's customers submit orders for the goods, the bank releases goods to make the sales, and the proceeds of the sales are remitted directly to the bank to repay the loan. The costs of warehouse financing are quite high and become prohibitive for smaller operations. Banks undertake a major risk in warehouse financing because of the difficulty of verifying the quality of goods on which they acquire warehouse receipts. Fraud has also played a prominent part in warehouse finance. The great salad oil scandal of the early 1960s, in which banks advanced millions of dollars against warehouse receipts for which no goods existed, stands as testimony to the inherent risk of this type of loan.

Participation Agreements   Banks sometimes find it beneficial to sell or *participate* part of a commercial loan to another bank or other lender. Alternatively, banks frequently have opportunities to acquire a participation in loans originated by others. The basis of participation is established either as pro rata or lifo. The *pro rata* basis entitles the participant to a set proportion of the loan, without distinction as to subordination. The *lifo* basis, in effect, layers participants for subordination purposes. Each participant is lined up ahead of or behind other participants, based on their order of entry. State and federal laws and regulations often govern the role of participation agents for banks.

In many large participated commercial loans, a *multilender loan agreement* often is used. This agreement sets forth the identities of each participating lender on all loan documents and indicates the proportional interest each has in the agreement, as well as the collateral supporting the loan. This permits each lender to hold its own promissory note. In addition, a formal agreement establishes the lead bank as the *managing agent* and the other participants as *co-agents,* and it clarifies the rights and obligations of the managing bank in administering the loan and the participation agreement.

The net effect of such formalization of participation agreements is that each participant acquires a direct contractual relationship with the borrower that does not depend on the lead bank. This arrangement has the obvious advantage of protecting the participant against the possible failure of the lead bank.

Guaranteed Small Business Loans

Small businesses represent enormous potential for bank lending, particularly for small banks. There are an estimated 14 million small business firms operating in the United States, and most of these firms must shop for borrowed funds at some time. In total, 99 percent of all firms in the United States are small, but they employ 57 percent of the private work force and account for 50 percent of domestic private production.

Unfortunately, because small firms are riskier borrowers than large, well-established firms, they have few alternative sources of credit. Historically, banks have loaned predominantly to the low-risk minority of small business firms. Business finance companies traditionally have loaned to select higher-risk firms at substantially higher interest rates than those on bank loans. However, with the establishment of the Small Business Administration (SBA) in 1953, another credit alternative became available in the form of guaranteed loans.

SBA Loan Guarantee Program   The SBA offers a loan guarantee program in which a participating bank can obtain a guarantee up to 90 percent of the principal of a qualified small business loan. Currently, the SBA extends its 90 percent guarantee to a principal value of up to $500,000. Recent estimates show that the total volume of SBA-guaranteed loans made annually was approaching $10 billion at the end of the 1990s. However, until recently, many banks believed that participation in the SBA loan guarantee program was too inefficient to make it worth their effort. SBA guarantees were restricted to a narrow range of loan purposes. In addition, the SBA tied the interest rates on guaranteed loans closely to a base rate it determined in relation to its own borrowing rate and other factors. SBA application procedures and lengthy loan approval times further deterred bank participation.

Recently, however, SBA pricing and procedure rules have been greatly loosened and simplified. Interest rates on floating-rate loans can now be set up to 2.25 to 2.75 percent (depending on the maturity) over the prime rate. Loan types now vary from long-term, fixed-asset financing (504 programs) to a pilot program line of credit with guarantees for up to five years (known as the *Green Line* program). Moreover, the approval process has been speeded up, partly through simplification and partly because the SBA now certifies participating banks to conduct the SBA's credit evaluation. This latter step eliminates the delays of sending the application forms to the SBA, waiting for the SBA to conduct its own evaluation, and waiting for the SBA to advise the bank of its approval or denial. These factors, and the increased liquidity due to the development of a secondary market, make SBA-guaranteed loans increasingly viable and profitable.

The present application procedure for SBA-guaranteed loans requires the borrower to complete several forms, including a detailed cash flow analysis. Although they appear quite technical, the requirements are no more stringent than those required by a conscientious bank loan officer from a borrower in applying for a conventional loan. The SBA typically responds with its decision in 7 to 10 days.

Secondary Market   The SBA-guaranteed portions of loans are readily marketable. Qualified institutional investors are often eager to bid on the guaranteed portions at prices that provide them yields close to those of government-issued securities. Banks retain the nonguaranteed portions of the loans and continue to service them for an attractive fee. The economics of this transaction often are quite favorable to the originating bank.

To illustrate this process, suppose that the bank makes a $500,000 SBA 90 percent guaranteed loan and sells the guaranteed portion of $450,000. Furthermore, suppose that the loan is priced at a fixed rate of 2 percent over a prime rate of 6 percent at a time when short-term U.S. Treasury bills are yielding 4.5 percent. Investors might thereby bid for the 90 percent guaranteed portion at a price that yields 5 percent. At that yield to investors, the bank will collect a guaranteed spread of 3 percent (8 − 5 percent) on the entire guaranteed portion of the loan just for servicing the loan. In addition, the bank will continue to earn 8 percent on the nonguaranteed 10 percent of the loan that it still owns. As shown in Table 11.4, this arrangement yields a 35 percent overall return on bank funds invested in the loan.

Although the loan terms appear extremely favorable to the bank, the rates and servicing spreads shown are achievable. In addition, compensating balances requirements might

TABLE 11.4 Yield on a $500,000 SBA-Guaranteed Loan Sold in the Secondary Market

Income

$450,000 at 3% = $13,500
 50,000 at 8% = $\underline{\quad 4,000}$

Total $17,500

Bank funds invested = $50,000

Gross yield to bank $= \dfrac{\$17,500}{\$50,000} = 35\%$

be included in the final loan agreement. The inclusion of compensating balances as an offset to the net amount of bank funds invested would increase the yield to the bank even more.

The extraordinary yields possible with making and selling SBA guarantees illustrate the distortion that results from market intervention. In the present case, public policy implemented through the SBA calls for diverting funds to high-risk, small firms from other uses of funds. The high yields indicated provide a powerful incentive for banks to allocate funds to SBA-guaranteed loans to small businesses.

The marketability of SBA-guaranteed loans received a boost when the SBA began to securitize these loans. As with securitization in the mortgage and consumer markets, the SBA pools loans and sells pay-through-type securities that are supported and serviced by the underlying loan pool. Toward the end of this chapter we review loan securitization in greater depth, including the prepayment and pricing characteristics of loans that are securitized.

The ability to sell SBA loans provides banks with immediate liquidity and frees up bank funds to make additional loans. The guaranteed portions of SBA loans are government obligations and can be eliminated from the bank's loan portfolio for the purpose of determining legal capital requirements. Also, the guaranteed portions do not have to be counted against regulatory loan limits. Thus, regulators permit loans to be made that are larger than legal lending limits because the government guarantees amounts in excess of the limits.

Lease Financing

Lease financing by banks is a unique means of funding a firm's need for capital equipment without actually lending to the firm. Like term loans, leases typically give the lessee firm the use of an asset over most of the asset's life and, in addition, include the right to purchase the asset at the expiration of the lease term. The distinction between a term loan to purchase equipment and a lease covering the same equipment is formalized in the Federal Reserve's Regulation Y, which restricts leasing by bank holding companies to situations in which the lease is the "functional equivalent to an extension of credit." Types of assets that are commonly leased include the following:

1. Computers
2. Production machinery

3. Transportation equipment

4. Pollution control equipment

5. Medical equipment

6. Materials-handling machinery

7. Oil drilling equipment

Financial versus Operating Leases   The principle of leasing recognizes that it is the use of an asset that gives it value, and not ownership of the asset. In a lease agreement, the lessor owns equipment that it makes available for the lessee's use in return for rental fees and possibly other benefits. There are two basic types of leases—financial and operating; however, banks can offer only financial leases.

In a *financial lease,* the lessor expects to recover the entire acquisition cost of the leased asset plus a profit. The lessor's proceeds include the rental fees, salvage value, and, either directly or indirectly, tax benefits due to investment tax credits and tax deferrals from accelerated depreciation. Financial leases are not cancelable by either party, and they are usually *net* leases, which means that the lessee is responsible for maintenance, insurance, and applicable taxes. To qualify as a financial lease (and not a sale) under the rules of the Internal Revenue Service (IRS), the lease should include (1) an option for the lessee to buy the asset, usually at fair market value, (2) a lease term not exceeding 30 years, and (3) rental payments that provide a reasonable rate of return to the lessor. Qualification as a financial lease and not a sale, according to the IRS, is necessary to enable the lessee to deduct as expense the full amount of rental payments. An *operating lease,* on the other hand, can be canceled and does not bind the lessee for a long period. Its term is significantly shorter than the asset's economic life. Also, unlike the arrangement with the financial lease, the lessor is responsible for maintenance, insurance, and applicable taxes.

For many years, banks could not hold an equity position in real earning property. Finally, in 1963, the Comptroller of the Currency authorized national banks to own and lease real property. Subsequently, the Federal Reserve extended the same privilege to bank holding companies. Bank acquisitions of real earning assets can occur only in response to a customer's request to enter into a financial lease agreement. Banks are specifically forbidden to acquire real assets in anticipation of unidentified customers' leasing needs.

Forms of Bank Participation in Lease Financing   Direct-lease financing by banks takes place in two basic forms: straight leases and leveraged leases.

Straight Leasing.   The most straightforward form of leasing is the direct lease, in which the bank provides 100 percent financing. The customer firm develops specifications for an asset needed in its operations. The customer then determines the manufacturer or dealer that is best able to supply the asset and makes arrangements for a purchase. Next, the bank acquires the asset, which is delivered to the customer; simultaneously, the bank completes an agreement to lease the asset to the customer.

Most often, this type of leasing negotiation evolves out of a total banking relationship with an established customer. However, some leasing deals are developed by brokers who bring together a client needing to lease equipment and a bank willing to participate. A broker relationship might be especially good for a bank that does not have loan officers experienced with leasing.

Banks also get involved in a modified form of lease financing through leasing companies. In this approach, the bank does not take an ownership position in the asset. The leasing company acquires the asset, using bank loan funds, and then leases the asset to a client. The lessor pledges the asset against its loan through a security agreement and also pledges the lease revenues.

Leveraged Leasing. A somewhat more sophisticated form of leasing in which banks may engage is leveraged leasing. Typically, a bank holding company affiliate acts as the lessor and sets up an ownership trust, which acquires an asset to be leased. The holding company provides only a small part of the funds for purchase of the asset, and the trust borrows the remaining funds from an institutional lender such as an insurance company. The holding company funds represent the equity investment and must be at least 20 percent of the cost of the asset. In other words, the purchase is leveraged with up to 80 percent borrowed funds.

The institutions providing the debt funds to the trust do not have recourse to the holding company bank (lessor). They look to the lessee's ability to make rental payments and to the collateral value of the asset. To the bank holding company, the profitability of leveraged leasing is heavily affected by the tax benefits of owning the asset. The principal tax benefits are the investment tax credit and the tax deductibility of accelerated depreciation and interest on borrowed funds. In relation to the amount of equity invested, these benefits are multiplied by leveraging with debt. Generally, the tax benefits of ownership are more significant to the bank holding company than to the lessee, and the benefits are passed through to the lessee in the form of lower lease rental payments. For example, a public hospital (nontaxable) lessee would benefit from leveraged leased medical equipment because of tax advantages that accrue to the lessor and are passed on through reduced costs of leasing. On the other hand, if the lessee is able to take full advantage of the tax benefits, there may be little financial advantage in leveraged leasing.

Agricultural Loans

For about 28 percent of all commercial banks, farm loans are significant, exceeding 25 percent of their loan portfolios. These rural-area banks hold more than half of all commercial bank farm loans. However, farm-related lending accounts for only about 5 percent of the loans made by the banking industry as a whole.

Although farm loans are not a major factor in the banking industry, banks are a major part of the market for farm credit. In 1996, bank loans to farmers and to financial agricultural production totaled $49 billion, which constituted 25 percent of the market for farm credit. Of this debt, $40 billion, or four-fifths, was non-real estate debt; banks' market share of farm real estate debt was comparatively minor. Non-real estate farm debt is dominated by production loans that finance the crop cycle; funds needed for the planting season are not repaid until the crop is harvested and marketed. Farmers sometimes delay the sale of crops by storing them in the hope of getting a better price later on. This frequently results in further demand for loan funds to carry the unsold crops and to finance ongoing operations. Farm capital equipment is another source of loan demand. Increasingly, sophisticated and expensive farm mechanization has added considerably to farm term loans.

Farm Credit Evaluation   The history of troubled farm loans in the late 1970s and early 1980s provides lessons that apply for the future. Banks are at risk in agricultural lending if their loan officers lack experience with farm problems. Lenders should examine this costly era for farm credit in order to better judge the risks of adverse commodity prices, crop failure, and poor financial planning by the farmer.

In evaluating the farmer's ability to service bank debt, it is important to consider the farmer's financial leverage. One measure of financial leverage is the debt-assets ratio, which shows what proportion of the farm's assets is subject to the claims of debt holders rather than the claims of the owners.

In the early 1980s this ratio deteriorated dangerously. The stage was set for this deterioration by a tremendous growth in both farm debt and equity values beginning in the mid-1960s. The parallel rise in both debt and equity values resulted in a steady debt-assets ratio until 1980 and concealed farmers' and lenders' exposure to declining farm income in the 1980s.

Overall, total farm debt from all lenders grew from $54.4 billion in 1970 to a peak of $204.8 billion in 1985. Agriculture experienced an extraordinary boom in the inflationary environment of the 1970s. Farm exports and domestic demand flourished, and both farmers and lenders were euphoric over the apparently endless rise in crop prices, farm income, and land values. With record returns on farm assets in the mid-1970s, farmers and investors began to bid aggressively on farmland, driving the average price for an acre of farmland from $189 in 1970 to $628 by 1979. During the same period, farm equity rose from $262 billion in 1970 to $849 billion in 1979. As noted, the rise in equity supported more and more debt, and farmers borrowed heavily to invest in equipment, buildings, and especially land.

In the early 1980s, export markets for agriculture dried up, and poor crop production in several years severely strained farmers. Interest rates soared and put further pressure on farmers' debt service capability. Prices for farm acreage fell, reducing farm equity from a high of $1,065 billion in 1979 to $530 billion in 1986. With decreasing asset values, debt-asset ratios escalated to a record 24 percent by 1985 from an average of 16 percent during the 1970s and rendered many farmers technically insolvent. According to the Department of Agriculture, in 1985 one-third of all farmers were in serious financial trouble. These farmers accounted for nearly two-thirds of all farm debt, putting farm lenders at serious risk. It was estimated that 12 percent of all farmers failed in 1985.

Although an apparently strong debt-assets ratio suggests that a farm is solvent, as it did for many farmers in the 1970s, it does not reveal the cash flow problems that a farmer often faces. A second and more meaningful measure of financial leverage in the short run is the ratio of interest to return on assets. This measure, the reciprocal coverage ratio, gives a more dynamic view of the farmer's cash flow and ability to service debt from current income. For the farm industry, this ratio rose dramatically throughout the 1970s and was especially high in the early 1980s, when interest rates were high. This trend signifies the increased share of the return on farm assets going to creditors for interest payments. Unfortunately, the interest-return ratio is unstable because the farmer's return on assets is relatively volatile, owing to the uncertainties of weather and crop prices. As the ratio increases, generally the lender's cushion against such uncertainties is seriously eroded. The ratio of interest to return on assets rose from 8 percent in 1970 to about triple that level in the 1980s.

Not surprisingly, then, the farm crisis was transmitted to agricultural banks and other farm lenders. Charge-offs of non-real estate farm loans peaked at 3.4 percent of outstanding farm loans at banks. Over 200 agriculture-dependent banks failed because of farm loan problems in the 1980s. Meanwhile, farmland values, which were the basis of many

TABLE 11.5 Farm Debt Outstanding, Recent Year

	Amount (dollars in billions)	Percent
Total Debt		
Banks	41.3	26.2
FCS	45.5	28.9
Life insurance companies	10.2	6.5
FmHA	23.9	15.2
Individuals and others	36.3	23.1
Total	157.3	100.0
Real Estate Debt		
Banks	11.7	13.1
Federal land banks	35.0	39.1
Life insurance companies	10.2	11.4
FmHA	9.5	10.6
Individuals and others	23.1	25.8
Total	89.4	100.0
Non–Real Estate Debt		
Banks	29.6	43.7
PCAs	10.6	15.6
FmHA	14.4	21.2
Individuals and others	13.2	19.5
Total	67.8	100.0

ill-advised bank credit extensions, fell back toward the preinflationary levels of the mid-1970s.

Farm Loan Competition   Table 11.5 shows the amount and share of farm debt held by various lenders, including commercial banks. The major nonbank financial institutional lenders are described in this section. Individuals and others are nonfinancial institutional lenders whose extensions of farm credit stem from their primary, nonfinancial business. Much of farms' non-real estate credit arises from trade receivables.

The *production credit associations* (PCAs) are a major part of the federally supervised cooperative Farm Credit System (FCS). This system is regulated by the Farm Credit Administration through 12 regional Farm Credit Districts. The system consists of three cooperative lending groups:

1. Twelve federal land banks and 388 local federal land bank associations that finance farm real estate.
2. Thirteen banks for cooperatives, which lend to farmers' supporting operations, such as marketing, supply, and business service cooperatives.
3. Thirty-seven federal intermediate credit banks (FICBs) and 315 local PCAs.

The FCS's role in non-real estate farm lending is performed by the 315 PCAs. The

PCAs are borrower-owned cooperatives that lend short- and intermediate-term funds to farmers for crop and livestock operations. The PCAs are funded by the FICBs, which, in turn raise their funds through bond issues in the national financial markets.

The Farmers Home Administration (FmHA) is a federal government agency that engages in direct lending to farmers and guarantees farm loans originated by commercial banks. The FmHA was authorized under the Emergency Agricultural Credit Act of 1979 (amended in 1980) to lend funds to farmers who are temporarily unable to acquire funds from their normal lenders at reasonable rates. Like the FICBs, the FmHA raises its funds in the national capital markets.

The Commodity Credit Corporation (CCC) is a federal government agency that is involved in a unique aspect of farm lending. The CCC is an instrument of the government's price support and farm income policies, and provides price support and crop storage loans. Lending by the CCC fluctuates erratically, depending on commodity prices. If market prices fall below the amount per bushel that the CCC is willing to provide, farmers rush into the CCC program. This happened during the 1982–1986 period of depressed crop prices.

Since 1975, and as indicated in Table 11.5, the FCS has been the largest lender to agriculture, a position it wrested from commercial banks. Along with banks, the FCS experienced a serious crisis in the mid-1980s. By 1986, 14.4 percent of its outstanding loans and 42.9 percent of the FmHA's loans were delinquent. The federal land banks alone lost $2.1 billion in 1985.

The net effect on banks of the government-supported credit agencies is indirect. Before the aggressive lending via federal agencies in the 1970s, commercial banks tended to supply a rather steady stream of credit to the farm sector. This supply of credit was restricted by the limited investment opportunities available. With rising commodity prices and a boom in exports, however, the federal agencies fueled an explosive growth in farm debt. As a result, farm investment in modern equipment, irrigation systems, and land exceeded the value of the resulting gains in productivity. In the 1980s, when the farm economy deteriorated owing to high interest rates, declining food and commodity prices, inflation, and the collapse of export markets, farmers could not support the huge debt overload taken on during the boom. All lenders suffered enormous losses. It is possible, however, that the crisis experienced in commercial banks would have been avoided had not government-supported credit lured farmers into assuming unprecedented burdens of debt.

Beginning in 1985, farm debt began to decline as farmers sought a way out of their excessively leveraged position. Between 1985 and 1996, farm credit market debt decreased by over $12 billion.

LOAN SALES AND SECURITIZATION

Banks engage in another type of off-balance sheet activity when they sell loans. Loans are sold either outright, to pension funds and other banks, or via securitized pools of mortgages, consumer loans, or commercial loans for sale to secondary market investors. Bank pooling of mortgage loans for sale as mortgage-backed securities (MBS) began in about 1970. The sale of consumer and commercial loans, however, is a recent and revolutionary phenomenon in which banks are liquidating what were historically considered nonmarketable assets.

The volume of both types of sales—MBS and conventional loan sales—began to boom in the mid-1980s. Annual sales volumes in the mid-1990s indicated that as much as $4 trillion worth of MBS was sold by all sellers, with loan sales by commercial banks accounting for about one-quarter of the total.

Mortgage-Backed Securities

The market for MBS is dominated by issues bearing government guarantees. The largest issuer is the GNMA, which authorizes pass-through securities that are serviced by the cash flows from a pool of mortgages originated by GNMA-approved lenders. GNMA guarantees these mortgages against default but accepts only Federal Housing Authority (FHA), Veterans Administration (VA), or Farmer Home Administration (FmHA) mortgages.

FNMA and FHLMC purchase mostly conventional mortgages from banks and issue MBS. FHLMC's securities are guaranteed pass-throughs called *participation certificates* (PCs). In 1980, FHLMC began to offer its PCs for mortgages held on lending institutions' balance sheets. This move permitted many institutions to mobilize heretofore inert assets and to refresh their liquidity. The volume of PCs also boomed as a result of this action.

The private-sector MBS market evolved more gradually than the government-guaranteed market. Private activity began to boom in the early to mid-1980s, when a new type of intermediary called the *private mortgage conduit* appeared. Conduits act as an intermediary between mortgage originators and investors and serve to pool the mortgages of many small lenders. The conduits issue pass-through securities to the originating lenders, providing them with greater liquidity and diversification. Private MBS issuers suffer a disadvantage, however, compared with public agency issues because, unlike the latter, they do not offer a guarantee. Private issuers have responded by offering their own guarantees, including sinking fund set-asides, and have made private MBS issues nearly as attractive as government-backed issues.

Consumer Loan Sales

Beginning in the mid-1980s, commercial banks began to apply the principles of the secondary mortgage market to create securities pools backed by their loans to consumers. The banks' reasoning was the same as for securitized mortgage loans: to transform risky, illiquid loans such as credit card receivables into much less risky and more liquid securities. These types of asset-backed securities were originally offered in 1985. The market for such securities has grown dramatically from $9 billion in 1987 to perhaps $70 billion in 1997.

Such securities allow the banks to make consumer loans and then quickly move them off the balance sheet to reduce their capital requirements. The two most common forms of consumer loan pools have become popularly known as CARs (certificates of automobile receivables) and CARDs (certificates for amortizing revolving debt). Similar loan pools have been formed with backing by boat loans, truck leases, and others, but CARs and CARDs have been the most widely accepted because of investors' preferences, because of the homogeneous nature of the underlying loans, and because historical data on default and prepayment rates are more available and reliable.

CARs are generally backed by a pool of four- to five-year automobile installment loans. These securities have an average life of about two years. CARs have been highly successful, in part, because banks have considerable experience with such loans, making it easier to identify the securities' risk. However, from the banks' perspective, the short-term nature of the loans backing the securities means that origination and securitization costs must be recovered over a relatively short period of time. As a result, the securitization process puts pressure on the loans' profitability.

CARDs, on the other hand, are backed by the revolving debt from credit card receivables and generally have a longer life than CARs, averaging two to seven years. CARDs may offer investors better protection than CARs because they are supported by highly liquid, *revolving* loans. Bank issuers can tailor the securities' maturities and offer speedy liquidation. An example of a CARD is Citibank's Citi Credit Card Trust, which securitized $2.2 billion of the bank's $13.4 billion in credit card receivables from 1988 to 1990.

Securities sold for investment into pools such as Citibank's are created by forming a portfolio of good-quality performing loans. A backup pool of loans is earmarked to replace loans that are paid down. As shown in Figure 11.2, a trust is then formed to receive the loans' principal and interest payments. PCs are sold to investors (usually at $1,000 par value) based on the cash flows from the loans, although some capital may be placed up front by the bank in a spread account. The PCs are sold to the investors at a yield below the assets' (loans') yield, usually at a spread over the Treasury rate of about 100 basis points. This large earnings spread tends to reduce the bank's required capital contribution and increases liquidity. As shown in Figure 11.2, the excess flows are available for reinvestment in the bank's loan portfolio.

Table 11.6 shows the hypothetical earnings on a credit card securitization program. The bank generates a net flow of 3.395 percent on its loans, and investors receive attractive

FIGURE 11.2   Cash Flows for Credit Card Securitization

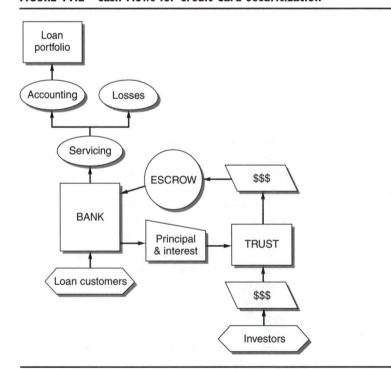

TABLE 11.6 Yield on a Credit Card Securitization Program

Bank Income	
Loan yield	17.66%
Less: charge-offs	3.25%
Net yield	14.41%
Expenses	
Servicing	1.25%
L/C fee	0.25%
Trust fee	0.50%
Interest on PCs	9.00%
Total expenses	11.00%
Excess	3.41%
To escrow (spread acct.)	0.015%
Net flow	3.395%

returns on a low-risk investment. The example is based on a $100 million CARD pool with a three-year maturity that yields 8.5 percent. In the mid-1990s, revolving card debt backing such pools averaged a yield of 17.66 percent.

Because such loan pools are not backed by federal agency guarantees, as most mortgage-backed instruments are, CARs and CARDs are set up with credit and collateral enhancements that exceed the par value of the security by 10 to 15 percent. This ensures that principal payments are not lost in cases of delinquency and default. Some trusts automatically repay principal once a level of default is reached. Additional principal insurance for these securities may be obtained through L/Cs.

Commercial Loan Sales

In the strictest sense, the sale of commercial loans by banks is an old practice. For a long time, banks have sold participations in loans they originate to peer or correspondent banks. A recent call report verified the popularity of this practice and indicated that over 8,000 banks out of a sample of 11,461 sold loans sometime during the mid-1990s.

A new dimension to commercial loan sales has emerged, however, through the sales of outstanding single loans to a wide variety of bank and nonbank investors. Volume estimates for this type of activity in 1985 reached as high as $50 billion at one point during the 1980s. Commercial loan sales differ from MBS, CARs, and CARDs. Typically, they involve single loans rather than pools. As a rule, they are sold without recourse. Loan sales activity is most prominent among money center banks, with the nine largest U.S. bank participants accounting for about 40 percent of the volume. Most loans sold are of short maturity, with about one-third of the volume in overnight loans. Another one-third of the volume is in loans with maturities of up to 30 days. Most commercial loans sold are credits produced more or less routinely from loan commitments to major, high-quality corporations.

Many of the banks selling loans, including virtually all money center banks, use a technique known as *stripping,* in which only the short-term obligations of longer-term loans are sold to loan buyers. This approach enhances the quality (reduces the risk) of the sale because the buyer avoids the loan's longer-term exposure to default and the possibility of a refinancing crisis at the loan's maturity.

Medium- to long-term loan sales have been slower to develop because of the customized nature and greater credit risk of longer-term loans. In addition, the special customer relationships that exist in the longer run, including the portfolio of bank services the customer uses, make longer-term credits difficult to detach for sales to more impersonal markets.

Originating banks almost always retain the servicing of loans sold, and frequently they play a role—at the buyer's request—in resolving disputes or claims due to defaults. The clear documentation of loans is crucial to their salability. Short-term loans are easier to structure according to standardized documentation. Longer-term loans are more difficult to standardize because the uniqueness of loan terms increases in proportion to the loans' maturities.

Benefits of Loan Sales and Securitization

Recent research has sought to explain the perceived advantages to banks that sell loans outright or securitize them for sale through investment bankers. One prominent theme is that loan sales permit avoidance of regulatory "taxes." According to this reasoning, loans that are warehoused on banks' balance sheets are subject to regulatory taxes that invariably occur when banks finance assets. Loans that are sold are relieved of financing requirements and therefore do not create such taxes. Regulatory taxes include reserve requirements and deposit insurance premiums on the issue of deposits and capital requirements that periodically force the issue of equity. In addition, because equity is not tax deductible, the returns the bank must earn for equity holders are subject to corporate income taxes. All these taxes, reserve requirements, deposit insurance premiums, capital requirements, and corporate income taxes provide an incentive for banks to focus on selling loans they originate instead of holding them on their balance sheets.

It is easy to quantify the costs imposed by regulatory taxes on warehoused loans. The financing cost can be expressed as follows:

$$\text{Cost of deposits and equity to finance loans} = ck_e/(1 - t) + (1 - c)(k_d + IP)$$

where c is the bank's required capital ratio, k_e is the after tax cost of equity (the return required by equity holders), t is the corporate income tax rate, k_d is the interest cost of deposits, and IP is the deposit insurance premium.

In addition, deposits are subject to a reserve requirement (RR) that must be set aside in nonearning reserves. For every dollar raised to finance loans, therefore, only $c + (1 - c)(1 - RR)$ can be used. The reserve requirement raises the cost of loan financing as indicated by the following equation:

Financing cost for warehoused loans =

$$ck_e/(1 - t) + (1 - c)(k_d + IP)/[c + (1 - c)(1 - RR)]$$

Suppose that a bank that warehouses loans must compete for funds by paying 5 percent to depositors and returning 15 percent after tax to equity holders. If the required capital ratio (*c*) is 0.10 percent, the tax rate (*t*) is 34 percent, the deposit insurance premium (*IP*) is 0.250 percent, and the reserve requirement (*RR*) is 3 percent, then

$$0.10(0.15)/(1 - 0.34) + (1 - 0.1)(0.05 + 0.0025)/[0.1 + (1 - 0.1)(1 - 0.03)] = 0.0713$$

Now assume that investors expect only a 5 percent return on the purchase of loans, that is, an amount equal to the return on deposits. In this example, banks would be unable to compete by warehousing rather than selling loans because they would require an additional 213 basis points—the unfavorable excess over money market financing rates.

There are several other reasons that explain why banks are willing to sell loans. Loan sales may permit banks to diversify their loan portfolios. Banks may specialize in originating certain loan types, or their portfolios may be too concentrated geographically. Loan sales permit them to off-load certain loans and to acquire other types of assets.

A compelling motive for loan sales is to improve bank liquidity management. A leading example of this motive is the thinking developed by Bankers Trust Company. This banking firm views loan sales as a continuous part of its asset and liability management process.

In the view of Bankers Trust's management, the *absence* of loan liquification techniques mismatches efforts at balance sheet management. Balance sheet management, as practiced in most regional and money center banks, typically combines operation of a loan warehousing facility with aggressive pursuit of liabilities. Funds are acquired aggressively to build immobile loan portfolios, necessitating special care to control costs, market risk, and interest rate risk. In these banks, liability management is active and asset management is comparatively passive. The tactics of the asset and liability management committee are tuned to the bank's liabilities. Even the development of interest rate risk management tools, such as swaps, options, and loan price caps, is an attempt to solve problems resulting from aggressive liability management.

In contrast, Bankers Trust urges a more balanced approach. The firm believes that asset and liability management should be balanced by addressing investor markets through loan sales and deposit sales, respectively. Both types of sales are conducted continuously to maximize the risk-adjusted yield on the total loan portfolio: Liquidity is demanded of the asset side as well as the liability side of the balance sheet. Bankers Trust's style of active asset management centers on the efforts of loan product managers. These officers focus intensely on loan documentation standards to ensure loan liquidity and salability. For further portfolio flexibility, the product managers are also responsible for reconfiguring existing assets to make them salable.

Loan liquification is seen as an inseparable part of the bank's global strategy, with links to investors in Hong Kong, London, and New York. The Bankers Trust concept puts investor markets (buyers of the loan product) in the same loop as the loan product managers. Loans are structured as products to be participated out to the world markets. The firm benefits from greater funds flexibility and responsiveness to borrowers, and it gains greater market efficiency by matching users of capital with pools of capital.

Through loan sales, according to Bankers Trust, bank capital is used more intensely and bank liquidity is enhanced. Moreover, the bank increases its underwriting income to offset the pricing pressures on conventional loan business that all large banks are experiencing. Loan salability also enhances diversification by giving the bank access to borrowers who otherwise may not be acceptable to its portfolio by reason of concentration limits or exposure policies.

Regulatory Issues

Important regulatory problems surrounding bank loan sales remain to be solved. Can loan sales be structured, through creative origination and selling techniques, to avoid significant recourse to the bank? If not, loan sales will certainly cause a call on bank capital. In addition, recourse might mean that the proceeds from loan sales will be treated as deposits and as reservable, adding to the cost of selling loans for the purpose of regenerating funds. On the other hand, should not sales with recourse be viewed as superior to collateralized borrowing (which in most instances need not be reservable)? Answers to these questions are being formulated by the Financial Accounting Standards Board, by the Comptroller of the Currency, and in the marketplace as each gains experience with loan sales. Clearly, the most troublesome regulatory questions have to do with the implications for the capital adequacy of selling institutions. At present, it appears that the supervisory examining apparatus is not equipped to deal with this kind of off-balance sheet activity.

New capital requirements on loan sales with recourse appear to restore the regulatory tax that banks hope to escape when they sell loans. Nevertheless, other incentives appear sufficient to ensure the continuation and growth of loan sales activity. For some large banks, it seems clear that loan sales reduce liquidity risk. This type of banking risk exists simply because no bank has complete match funding; in aggregate, liabilities mature at times that are different from those of assets. Conventionally, liquidity risk becomes a crisis when investors stop accepting a bank's liabilities. But banks that master the knowledge and techniques for liquidating loans enjoy an extra liquidity reserve.

SUMMARY

Banks overcome selection risk with careful assessment of both hard and soft facts about the borrower's credit background. They ascertain the reason for borrowing, identify a source of repayment that is related to the successful business operations of the borrower, and identify a secondary source such as collateral, guarantor, or other possible sources.

Credit analysis requires the cooperation of the borrower and of informants both inside and outside the bank. Subjective judgment must be used in evaluating a borrower's trustworthiness and, therefore, his or her moral commitment to repay the loan as agreed.

The borrower's ability to repay is mostly a matter of financial analysis. Historical financial analysis is two-dimensional. Time series analysis is used to spot evolving financial strengths and weaknesses with the perspective of the passage of time. Cross-sectional analysis permits the analyst to determine how effectively the borrower has performed in relation to other firms with like market opportunities and risks. Cash flow analysis demonstrates the dynamic funds needs of the firm.

Banks' underwriting standards must be well considered to overcome risk. This requires skills in securing collateral, negotiating covenants, pricing in accordance with risk, rating the riskiness of each loan, monitoring, and conducting migration analysis. In addition to transaction risk, loan portfolios are subject to correlation risks stemming from insufficient diversification. These include intrinsic risk—the risk of portfolio deterioration from clusters of loans to high-risk industries or lines of business—and concentration risk—the risk of massive portfolio deterioration due to inappropriately large aggregations of loans to single borrowers, industries, or geographic areas.

Most banks actively seek to make business loans. In the past, banks offered only short-term, self-liquidating credit. Such loans were usually for temporary additions to working capital that would soon be sold off to generate cash for repayment of the loans. This type of loan included a requirement that borrowers pay off their loans sometime during the year. Borrowers often refinanced their loans at other banks to meet this *clean-up* rule and then later returned to the bank of origin to renew the loan. Bankers call such loans *evergreen loans.*

Evergreen loans engaged banks in term lending despite their intentions to grant short-term loans. From such beginnings, many banks have shifted aggressively to longer-term credits to finance plant and equipment. This shift has produced dramatic changes in bank lending principles by tying loans to borrowers' long-term profitability as a primary source of repayment and by routinely tying loans to collateral as a secondary source of repayment. Large banks in particular provide revolving credits, revolving credit commitments, and term loans structured to meet intermediate-term financing needs of business.

A crucial dimension of term credits is the negotiation of covenants. Restrictive or negative covenants can be classified into three categories according to their objectives. The objective of cash flow covenants is to protect cash flows for loan repayment. They can be used to restrict the borrower's actions that introduce unacceptable risks to earnings or to restrict uses of cash flow other than for loan repayment. Trigger covenants protect the bank from the borrower's financial deterioration by establishing minimum financial standards that, when violated, authorize the bank to call or restructure the loan. Balance sheet covenants protect the loan by restraining the borrower from taking actions that would unduly weaken the balance sheet and jeopardize the value of collateral assets.

For most borrowers, loan interest rates are typically set on a prime-plus basis to account for the risk associated with the credit. However, banks are increasingly pricing loans in the context of a total customer relationship. Customer profitability analysis explicitly prices and tracks the costs of individual (unbundled) services rendered, in addition to the usual loan and deposit aspects of the relationship.

Compensating balances and commitment fees directly affect loan yield and the cost to the customer of borrowing. Some argue that compensating balance requirements are an anachronism left over from an era when the main focus of banking was taking deposits. Although balance requirements are being replaced by fees in some banks, they will undoubtedly persist in some banks into the future.

END OF CHAPTER PROBLEMS

11.1 Why are banks counseled not to lend money on the strength of collateral alone?

11.2 Develop a list of questions that a loan officer might present to a prospective borrower to gain a comprehensive understanding of the borrower's business.

11.3 Why do loan officers usually assign priority to the importance of the four basic credit factors indicated in the text, namely, the borrower's character, use of loan funds, primary source of repayment, and secondary sources of repayment? What arguments can you give for alternatively ranking sources of repayment ahead of the use of funds?

11.4 How would you evaluate the primary source of repayment on a loan to a business for the purchase of a corporate aircraft?

11.5 Using data in the annual report for a corporation, fill in the spreadsheets given in Tables 11A.1 and 11A.2 in Appendix 11A. Complete one year only.

11.6 List and discuss the services offered by several key credit reporting agencies.

11.7 From a corporation's annual reports, compute financial ratios for three years, including liquidity, leverage, activity, and profitability ratios. Discuss the trends of the firm's strengths and weaknesses.

11.8 How does the definition of liquidity differ from the two alternative views of net working capital?

11.9 Using balance sheet and income statement data from a corporate report, construct a statement of cash provided from operations.

11.10 In credit analysis, how would the emphasis differ for a seasonal, self-liquidating loan versus a term loan to be repaid over several years?

11.11 Distinguish between open lines of credit and commitments that are usually associated with revolving credit agreements.

11.12 Discuss the pros and cons of a business making term loans from a bank as opposed to issuing its bonds in the open capital markets.

11.13 What are the key documents used by banks to take a security interest in collateral under the Uniform Commercial Code? Review the purposes of these documents.

11.14 What are the features that distinguish accounts receivable financing and factoring?

11.15 Trace the cash flows that occur when a bank provides floor plan financing for a dealer in new automobiles.

11.16 What are the characteristics that distinguish public warehousing finance from field warehousing finance?

11.17 Describe and give examples of negative loan covenants for the purpose of
  a. Cash flow control.
  b. Calling of a loan for noncompliance.
  c. Balance sheet control.

11.18 (See Appendix 1B.) How does the prime rate differ from the base rate? What caused many banks to abandon the use of prime rate loans?

11.19 How should bank shareholders' return on equity be incorporated into loan pricing formulas?

11.20 Determine the true cost of funds to a borrower on a loan that has
  a. A 10 percent interest rate on borrowed funds.
  b. An 8 percent compensating balance on borrowed funds and a 4 percent balance on the unborrowed portion of the commitment.
  c. A 0.5 percent commitment fee on unborrowed funds.
  d. An average 50 percent usage of the commitment.

11.21 All else equal, will borrowers prefer to leave compensating balances or to pay commitment fees when interest rates are abnormally high? Why?

Financial Ratio and Credit Selection Analysis

The more technical part of credit analysis and its use in making loan decisions has to do with concrete methods of analysis of financial statements. These methods of analysis generally rely on financial ratios calculated from various combinations of balance sheet and income statement accounts. Financial ratios may relate balance sheet accounts to one another, relate income statement accounts to one another, or cross-relate balance sheet and income statement accounts. Financial ratios are usually separated into categories based on the intended purposes or characteristics of the firm. The following are five frequently used classifications:

1. Common size ratios.
2. Profitability ratios.
3. Liquidity (short-term solvency) ratios.
4. Financial leverage (long-term solvency) ratios.
5. Activity or turnover ratios.

Short-term lenders are concerned foremost with liquidity ratios and, to a lesser extent, with activity ratios. Long-term lenders are interested mainly in profitability and financial leverage ratios.

Common size ratios are perhaps the simplest form of financial ratio. They express each balance sheet account as a percentage of total assets and each income statement account as a percentage of total revenue to create common size statements. The purpose of common size statements is to reduce firms of different sizes to a common basis and reveal underlying differences in their allocation of assets, sources of funds, and expenses.

Profitability ratios give the firm's profitability in relation to some investment base or to net sales. They attempt to measure the overall operational efficiency of the firm's management. The following three ratios—return on equity, return on assets, and profit margin—are most commonly used, although many others can be constructed.

Return on equity

$$= \frac{\text{Net income available to common stock}}{\text{Common stock equity}}$$

Return on equity is a summary measure of how effectively common stockholders' funds have been employed, including the effectiveness of the use of financial leverage. The numerator is after tax income less any preferred dividends. The denominator is the average of balance sheet equity over the period of income and is usually derived by averaging the equity at the beginning and end of the period.

$$\text{Return on assets} = \frac{\text{Net income after tax}}{\text{Average total assets}}$$

Return on assets indicates the efficiency with which management employed the total capital resources available to it. It is a better measure of operating performance than return on equity because the latter is affected by the degree of financial leverage. The denominator can be formed by averaging the beginning and ending values of total assets.

$$\text{Profit margin} = \frac{\text{Net income after tax}}{\text{Net sales}}$$

Profit margin measures the profit per dollar of net sales. Its complement (1 − Profit margin) indicates the expense incurred to generate $1 of revenue and reveals the effectiveness of cost controls and pricing policies.

Liquidity ratios indicate the firm's capacity for meeting its short-term liabilities as they become due. Two ratios are usually evaluated, the current ratio and the quick ratio.

$$\text{Current ratio} = \frac{\text{Current assets}}{\text{Current liabilities}}$$

The current ratio indicates the extent to which the claims of short-term creditors are covered by assets that can be readily converted into cash without loss. High current ratios suggest a high margin of safety for short-term creditors. However, the ratio does not consider differences in the quality of receivables and inventories.

Quick (acid-test) ratio

$$= \frac{\text{Current assets} - \text{Inventories}}{\text{Current liabilities}}$$

Concern over the quality of liquidity of inventories is purged in the quick ratio. Only the "quick" assets of cash, marketable securities, and receivables are included. For many industries in which inventory values may be suspect, the quick ratio is a more reliable measure of liquidity than the current ratio.

Because of their role as short-term lenders, banks have sought more reliable measures of liquidity than the static data reflected in the current and quick ratios. One such measure is the cash flow interval ratio, which relates quick assets to the firm's daily operating expenditures and other known cash disbursements. It indicates the number of days of net funds expenditures covered by quick assets. The cash budget, discussed earlier in this chapter, can be used in daily form to derive daily cash disbursements.

Financial leverage ratios indicate (1) the degree to which creditors, rather than owners, are financing a firm and (2) the firm's ability to meet long-term interest and principal payments on debt. From a lender's viewpoint, the amount of equity represents a cushion against operating losses or against a decline in the value of the firm's assets. As a result, lenders prefer to hold financial leverage within safe limits. On the other hand, the use of debt permits owners to control a firm with less personal investment. Assuming that borrowed funds can be invested to earn a rate of return greater than their cost, owners are motivated to increase financial leverage. Three ratios are commonly used to analyze the degree of financial leverage—debt ratio, interest coverage ratio, and fixed-charge coverage ratio.

$$\text{Debt ratio} = \frac{\text{Total debt}}{\text{Total assets}}$$

The debt ratio represents the portion of assets being financed by creditors. It is a measure of the financial risk of the firm. Generally, the more debt in the firm's financial structure, the more volatile its earnings and the greater the risk to owners and creditors.

Interest coverage ratio

$$= \frac{\text{Pretax income} + \text{Interest}}{\text{Interest expenses}}$$

The interest coverage ratio indicates the margin of safety that earnings provide creditors in relation to interest charges. A more liberal measure that is sometimes of value includes depreciation in the numerator to reflect the coverage provided by total cash flow.

Fixed-charge coverage ratio

$$= \frac{\text{Pretax income} + \text{Interest} + \text{Lease payments}}{\text{Interest} + \text{Lease expenses}}$$

The fixed-charge coverage ratio simply extends the interest coverage ratio to account for contractual commitments under leasing agreements. Here again, depreciation may be added to the numerator to obtain the coverage of fixed charges by cash flow and not just income. In both types of coverage ratios, the cyclical volatility of earnings must be analyzed to determine the appropriate coverage multiple.

Activity ratios indicate the intensity with which various assets are used to achieve a given sales level. In effect, they test for the operating efficiency of specific groups of assets. We will next discuss four of the more widely used activity ratios—average collection period, inventory turnover, fixed-asset turnover, and cash-to-cash cycle.

Average collection period

$$= \frac{\text{Accounts receivable}}{\text{Sales per day}}$$

When compared with the credit policy and terms granted by the firm, the average collection period measures the quality of credit extended and the effectiveness of collections. It indicates, on average, the time the firm must wait to collect after making a sale. Another important analysis of accounts receivable is the receivables' aging schedule, which classifies the proportion of receivables according to the period of time they have been outstanding, such as 1 to 30 days, 31 to 60 days, and over 60 days. The average collection period and the aging schedule together indicate the degree of liquidity of receivables. Relatively short collection periods combined with an aging schedule with very few overdue accounts suggest liquid and high-quality receivables.

$$\text{Inventory turnover ratio} = \frac{\text{Cost of sales (annual)}}{\text{Average inventory}}$$

The inventory turnover ratio indicates the effectiveness of management's inventory controls. It measures the number of times per year that the firm rolls over its entire investment in inventory. If the turnover of inventory is too high, it may indicate a less than optimal inventory level, which would re-sult in stockouts and lost sales. A too low turnover may indicate poor purchasing, production, and handling controls or obsolete merchandise. The cost of sales is used in the numerator, since inventory is usually valued at cost.

$$\text{Fixed-asset turnover} = \frac{\text{Net sales}}{\text{Average net fixed assets}}$$

Fixed-asset utilization is measured by the rate at which the product value flows through the firm's plant and equipment. Low rates of flow or turnover indicate below-capacity operations; a high rate of flow may reflect inadequate investment in plant and equipment. Differences in depreciation policies distort this ratio so that appropriate adjustments must be considered.

$$\text{Cash-to-cash cycle} = \frac{\text{Average cash}}{\text{Net sales per day}}$$
$$+ \text{Average collection period}$$
$$+ \frac{\text{Average inventory}}{\text{Cost of sales per day}}$$

The cash-to-cash cycle measures the turnover rate of working capital. As shown in Figure 11A.1, it represents the time required for a single dollar to move through the working capital cycle. First, funds are invested in operating cash balances, then they are converted to inventories by means of purchases of labor and material, next they are transformed into receivables as inventory is sold on credit, and fi-

FIGURE 11A.1   Cash-to-Cash Cycle (dollars in thousands)

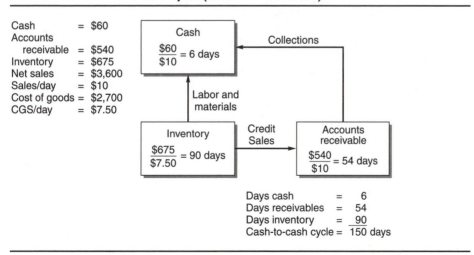

nally, they are returned to cash as receivables are collected.

SOURCES OF COMPARATIVE FINANCIAL DATA

Unfortunately, financial ratios cannot easily be analyzed in isolation because there are no reliable absolute standards to determine what their values should be. As a result, financial ratios must be analyzed in two basic comparative modes: cross-sectional and time series. Cross-sectional analysis compares the firm's ratios with those of peer firms in its industry for the same period or point in time. This section mainly discusses cross-sectional analysis and the use of comparative financial data of similar firms.

Time series analysis is concerned with the historical trend of the firm's ratios; that is, it measures the firm against itself at different points in time. Time series analysis can detect trends that may indicate potential problems before they occur. For example, the analyst may find that a firm experiencing rapid sales growth has a steadily falling profit margin because of a rising trend in its cost of goods sold. Without a time series perspective, the euphoria of rapid growth might conceal a dangerous deterioration in profit margins.

Analysts use several sources of comparative financial ratios in both time series and cross-sectional analysis. *Statement Studies,* published annually by Robert Morris Associates, is the most familiar such source to bankers. A common size balance sheet and income statement and a series of liquidity, leverage, activity, and profitability ratios are presented for several hundred types of businesses. The ratios are derived from a sample of over 40,000 sets of statements submitted by bank loan officers throughout the nation. The ratios are reported by firm size so that a small firm can be compared with other small firms in its industry and a large firm can be compared with large firms. The most recent three years of time series data are given for the entire sample of firms in each line of business. In addition, three stratified values are reported for each ratio: upper quartile, median, and lower quartile. The distributional data for ratios give the analyst a better sense of the difference between a loan applicant's ratios and those of its peers.

Dun and Bradstreet publishes *Key Business Ratios in 125 Lines of Business.* This publication reports 14 ratios and, like the annual *Statement Studies,* gives the interquartile ranges. It does not,

however, provide the ratios by firm size categories, nor does it report recent historical or time series data.

The *Almanac of Business and Industrial Financial Ratios,* published by Prentice Hall, reports financial ratios for 170 lines of business and industries. The sample of firm data is taken from Internal Revenue Service corporate tax filings and is quite accurate and complete. However, the data are available only with a two- to three-year lag.

RATIO INTERRELATIONSHIPS: THE DUPONT SYSTEM

Crucial information about a firm's financial condition is revealed in several financial ratios, not just one. A combination or a system of financial ratios can reveal a great deal about the sources of a firm's profit performance. No single ratio can explain more than one facet of the firm's performance.

The DuPont system of analysis breaks the summary profitability ratio return on equity into its constituent leverage, profit margin, activity, and common size ratios. This system enables the analyst simultaneously to view the key relationships governing a business enterprise. Return on equity (ROE) may be defined as follows:

$$\text{ROE} = \frac{\text{Total assets}}{\text{Equity}} \times \frac{\text{Net income after taxes}}{\text{Total assets}}$$

ROE is simply a multiple of total assets/equity—the dollars of assets supported by a single dollar of equity in the firm—and return on assets (ROA). ROA can be defined as follows:

$$\text{ROA} = \frac{\text{Sales}}{\text{Total assets}} \times \frac{\text{Net income after taxes}}{\text{Sales}}$$

The term sales/total assets is the activity ratio called *total assets turnover,* and the term net income after taxes/sales is the profitability ratio called *profit margin.*

Total assets can be further divided into the assets' side of the common size balance sheet, and the net income after taxes can be shown as the residual from the common size income statement. Figure 11A.2 graphically presents the complete system.

Robert Morris Associates (RMA) cautions that the statistics be regarded only as a general guideline and not as an absolute industry norm. This is due to limited samples within categories and different methods of operations by companies within the

FIGURE 11A.2   DuPont System of Analysis

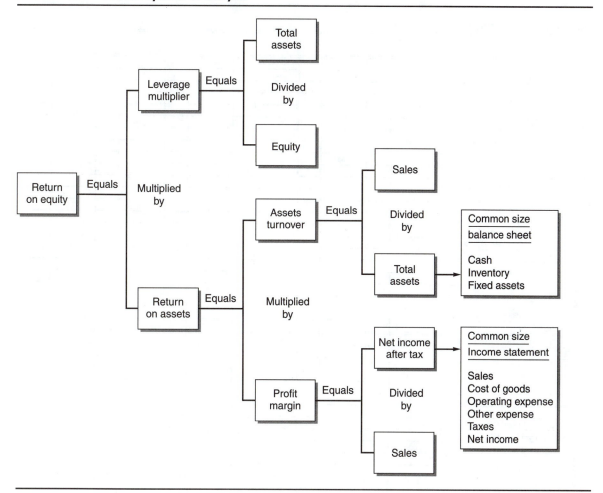

same industry. RMA recommends that the figures be used only as general guidelines in addition to other methods of financial analysis.

SPREADSHEETS AND STATEMENT SPREADING

Bankers generally use so-called spreadsheets for recording a credit applicant's financial information (Tables 11A.1 and 11A.2). Spreadsheets permit the analyst to organize financial data in a consistent manner. This frequently requires that certain data submitted by the applicant be reclassified to match the bank's purposes. For example, an item included as a current asset in the applicant's statement might

be reclassified as noncurrent on the spreadsheet if the credit analyst has doubts about its liquidity. An example of such an item might be a note due from one of the business's officers or principals.

The spreadsheet is arranged to allow easy comparison of current and historical trends and is readily updated, as the columns are completed from left to right. Spreadsheets typically are structured to permit entry of up to five years of financial statement history.

Columns are provided for common size ratios for each balance sheet and income statement account. Space is provided for several key financial ratios and for analysis of changes in net worth and working capital. Supplementary forms are often used to enter a time series of other key ratios.

TABLE 11A.1   General Spread Form

GENERAL SPREAD FORM

NAME

AUDITED STATEMENT									
STATEMENT DATE									
CASH									
MARKETABLE SECURITIES									
NOTES RECEIVABLE									
ACCOUNTS RECEIVABLE									
INVENTORY									
ALLOW. FOR DOUBT. ACCT.									
TOTAL CURRENT ASSETS									
FIXED ASSETS—NET									
NON-MARKETABLE SECURITIES									
NON-CURRENT RECEIVABLES									
PREPAID AND DEFERRED EXPENSES									
INTANGIBLES									
TOTAL NON-CURRENT ASSETS									
TOTAL ASSETS									
CURRENT MTY OF TERM DEBT									
NOTES PAYABLE									
ACCOUNTS PAYABLE									
ACCRUED EXPENSE & MISC.									
INCOME TAX LIABILITY									
TOTAL CURRENT LIABILITIES									
SUBORDINATED DEBT									
TOTAL LIABILITIES									
MINORITY INTEREST									
DEFERRED INCOME/RESERVES									
TREASURY STOCK									
PREFERRED STOCK OUTSTANDING									
COMMON STOCK OUTSTANDING									
CAPITAL SURPLUS									
RETAINED EARNINGS (DEFICIT)									
NET WORTH									
TANGIBLE NET WORTH									
WORKING CAPITAL									
EXCESS CUR. ASSETS OVER TOT. LIAB.									
CURRENT RATIO									
CASH. MKT. SEC. & A/R TO CURR. LIAB.									
A/R COLLECTION PERIOD—DAYS									
NET SALES TO INVENTORY									
COST OF SALES TO INVENTORY									
INVENTORY TO WORKING CAPITAL									
SR DEBT TO (TANG. N.W. & SUB. DEBT)									
NET PROFIT (LOSS) TO AVG. NET WORTH									

TABLE 11A.2   Income Statement Analysis

NAME										
PERIOD COVERED (MONTHS)										
STATEMENT DATE										
NET SALES										
COST OF SALES										
GROSS PROFIT										
SELLING EXPENSES										
GENERAL & ADMINISTRATIVE EXP.										
TOTAL OPERATING EXPENSES										
OPERATING PROFIT										
OTHER INCOME (EXPENSE)—NET										
NET PROFIT (LOSS) BEFORE TAXES										
INCOME TAXES										
NET PROFIT (LOSS) AFTER TAXES										
ADDITIONAL DATA										
DIVIDENDS—PREFERRED STOCK										
DIVIDENDS—COM. STOCK or WITHDRAW										
OFFICER REMUNERATION										
INTEREST EXPENSE										
OTHER CHANGES IN WORTH										
CONTINGENT LIABILITIES										
LEASE OBLIGATIONS										
ANALYSIS OF CHANGES IN WORTH OR SURPLUS										
AT BEGINNING OF PERIOD										
ADD NET PROFIT										
DEDUCT DIVIDENDS OR WITHDRAW										
WORTH OR SURPLUS REPORTED										
ANALYSIS OF WORKING CAPITAL										
AT BEGINNING OF PERIOD										
ADD. NET PROFIT										
NON-CASH CHARGES										
MISCELLANEOUS										
TOTAL ADDITIONS										
DEDUCT:										
DIVIDENDS/WITHDRAWALS										
PLANT EXPENDITURES										
MISCELLANEOUS										
TOTAL DEDUCTIONS										
NET CHANGE (+ OR −)										
AT END OF PERIOD										
W/C AS ABOVE										
INVENTORY										
EXCESS OF W/C OVER INVENTORY										
ANALYST INITIALS										

TABLE 11A.3   TV and Appliance Retailer—Comparative Balance Sheet (dollars in thousands)

	12/31/88	Percentage of Total Assets	12/31/89	Percentage of Total Assets	12/31/90	Percentage of Total Assets	Local Competitor 1990	RMA Ratios
Assets								
Cash	$ 11	6%	$ 12	5%	$ 16	6%	5%	11%
Accounts receivable	22	13	48	21	41	14	19	21
Inventory	122	69	147	65	203	72	66	46
Total current assets	155	88	207	91	260	92	90	78
Net fixed assets	21	12	21	9	24	8	10	22
Total assets	$176	100%	$228	100%	$284	100%	100%	100%
Liability and equity								
Accounts payable	$ 16	9%	$ 10	4%	$ 4	1%	2%	12%
Flooring finance	112	64	127	56	149	53	63	34
Total current liabilities	128	73	137	60	153	54	65	46
Long-term debt	23	13	57	25	94	33	8	10
Total equity	25	14	34	15	37	13	27	44
Total liabilities and equity	$176	100	$228	100	$284	100	100	100

CREDIT ANALYSIS RATIONALE: A CASE EXAMPLE

The calculation of financial ratios provides the basis of most technical, quantitative credit analysis. For the uninitiated reader, this appendix contains a review of some commonly used financial ratios. This section demonstrates, through a simple case example, the kind of analytical reasoning used in credit evaluation. Tables 11A.3, 11A.4, and 11A.5 present, respectively, balance sheets, income statements, and key financial ratios for three years for a small television and appliance retailer. In addition, each table includes the most recent comparable data on a local competitor and on the sample of TV and appliance retailers from RMA's *Statement Studies*.

Even a cursory look at the common size balance sheets and income statements reveals a great deal about the character of the loan applicant's business. Table 11A.3 shows that the accounts receivable make up only 14 percent of the firm's 1990 assets, compared with 19 percent for its local competitor and 21 percent for the RMA firms. From these comparative data, the firm appears to have good control of its credit sales. It also appears to be overinvested in inventory, which represents 72 percent of its assets versus 66 percent for the local competitor and 46 percent for RMA firms. This suggests that the firm stocks slow-moving items or has a more complicated product mix, or both. On the other hand, the firm has less invested in fixed assets.

The firm's funds come predominantly from floor-plan and long-term debt. Both categories of debt far exceed in importance the same sources for RMA firms, although the local competitor firm relies even more heavily on floor-plan debt. The applicant's accounts payable appear to be relatively small for this line of business and suggest little conflict with trade creditors. The firm's equity base is dramatically smaller than those of other firms, offering much less protection to its creditors.

Table 11A.4 shows that the firm's 1990 cost of sales in relation to total income is 81.7 percent, compared with a cost of sales in the 70 percent range for other firms. In this retail business, an unusually high cost of sales suggests the likelihood of underpricing—the use of price cutting as a sales tool. Operating expenses, consisting of the sum of wages and salaries, sales expense, and other operating expense, totaled only 15 percent of income in 1990, compared with 26 percent for the local competitor and 25 percent for RMA firms. This indicates an exceptionally low-cost operation capable of supporting somewhat lower product prices. Unfortunately, all other (nonoperating) expenses nearly wiped out the firm's remaining revenues, so that the net income compared unfavorably with that of other firms.

The common size balance sheet and income statement highlight some key differences among firms in a similar line of business. However, common size ratios occasionally are misleading. If one

TABLE 11A.4   TV and Appliance Retailer—Comparative Statement of Income (dollars in thousands)

	1988	Percentage of Total Income	1989	Percentage of Total Income	1990	Percentage of Total Income	Local Competitor 1990	RMA Ratios
Income	$713.4	100.0%	$866.2	100.0%	$911.7	100.0%	100.0%	100.0%
Less: Cost of sales	592.2	83.0	706.2	81.5	745.1	81.7	70.5	71.3
Gross profit	$121.2	17.0	$160.0	18.5	$166.6	18.3	29.5	28.7
Operating Expenses								
Wages and salaries	$ 46.4	6.5	$ 60.1	6.9	$ 54.7	6.0	17.7	
Sales expense	19.6	2.7	24.3	2.8	39.7	4.4	4.2	25.2
Other operating expense	30.0	4.2	41.6	4.8	42.1	4.6	4.1	
Operating profit	$ 25.2	3.5	$ 34.0	3.9	$ 30.1	3.3	3.5	3.5
All Other Expenses	$ 15.9	2.2	$ 21.3	2.5	$ 22.9	2.5	0.5	0.7
Profit before taxes	9.3	1.3	12.7	1.5	7.2	0.8	3.0	2.8
Income taxes	2.4	0.3	3.9	0.5	4.4	0.5	0.4	
Net income	$ 6.9	1.0	$ 8.8	1.0	$ 2.8	0.3	2.6	2.8

TABLE 11A.5   TV and Appliance Retailer—Financial Ratio Analysis

	1988	1989	1990	Local Competitor 1990	RMA Ratios
Liquidity					
Current	1.2	1.5	1.7	1.4	1.7
Quick	0.3	0.4	0.4	0.4	0.7
Leverage					
Debt to total assets	0.86	0.85	0.87	0.72	0.54
Interest coverage	1.7	2.0	1.2	2.6	3.5
Fixed charge coverage	1.4	1.5	1.1	2.3	N/A
Activity					
Inventory turnover	5.4×	5.2×	4.3×	4.9×	5.7×
Average collection period (days)	14	15	18	20	27
Fixed assets turnover	34×	41×	39×	30×	13×
Cash-to-cash cycle (days)	87	90	109	101	98
Profitability					
Profit margin on sales	1.0%	1.0%	0.3%	2.6%	2.8%
Return on (average) total assets	4.6%	4.6%	1.1%	7.4%	6.8%
Return on (average) net worth	32.6%	29.8%	7.9%	26.2%	17.5%

asset account is grossly large, other asset accounts appear relatively small in ratio terms, even though they are about the amount expected in dollar terms. For example, a firm's total assets may be so inflated by gross overinvestment in, say, fixed assets that all other asset proportions, such as the inventory common size ratio, are dwarfed and falsely appear insufficient. Thus, liquidity, leverage, activity, and profitability ratios are necessary to complete a clear analytical picture.

Table 11A.5 shows that the firm's current ratio of 1.7 is in line with that of the RMA firms and exceeds that of the local competitor. However, the firm's quick ratio of 0.4 is well below the RMA quick ratio. Together the current and quick ratios indicate that the firm's balance sheet liquidity depends predominantly on inventory. If inventory is obsolete or otherwise not readily marketable, the firm would have great difficulty meeting its short-term obligations. It should be noted that there is no provision for the current portion of long-term debt, a current liability. If a portion of long-term debt is to be repaid currently, the firm's liquidity would be further squeezed.

The firm's 1990 debt ratio of 0.87 indicates that, in relation to its peers, it offers a very small equity cushion for its creditors. Only 13 percent of its funds come from its owners, whereas 28 percent of its local competitor's funds and 46 percent of RMA firms' funds came from owners. The 1990 interest coverage ratio of 1.2 and the fixed charge ratio of 1.1 are far short of those of the other firms. This indicates insufficient earnings or excessive interest payments, or a combination of the two.

Inventory turnover of 4.3 times in 1990 for the firm compares unfavorably with 4.9 times for the local competitor and 5.7 times for RMA firms, again suggesting excessive investment in inventory. A similarly unfavorable comparison exists for the firm's cash-to-cash cycle of 109 days versus 101 days and 98 days, respectively, for its competitor and the RMA firms. This factor, when considered along with the firm's favorable average collection period of 18 days, is further indicative of an abnormally large inventory. Specifically, the short average collection period demonstrates that receivables are not the cause of the long cash-to-cash cycle and implies that the cause is too much inventory. The firm's fixed-asset turnover of 39 times compared with 30 times and 13 times for its peers indicates that relatively little is invested in illiquid buildings and equipment.

Table 11A.5 shows that the firm's profitability lags far behind that of its peers. Its return on sales of 1.0, 1.0, and 0.3 percent for the last three years compares poorly with its competitor's 2.6 percent and the RMA firms' 2.8 percent. As determined from its common size income statement, this poor performance is due to the extreme underpricing of its merchandise. A similarly unfavorable return on assets, bottoming out at 1.1 percent in 1990, further reflects poor earnings and may indicate excessive investment in assets, particularly inventory. Despite poor earnings performance, the firm's return on net worth figures for 1988 and 1989 are biased upward, in relation to those of its peers, because of the small amount of equity in the firm (the denominator in the return-on-net-worth ratio). If the firm operates at a loss in the future, its return on net worth will be dramatically biased negatively by the small amount of equity.

Financial analysis alone is not always sufficient to determine the creditworthiness of a firm. As a loan applicant, the firm would have to provide additional information such as the purpose of the loan and how the loan would affect the financial statements and ratios. However, the previous evidence indicates that the historical earnings, liquidity, inventory management, pricing, and equity support of the firm are all deficient. In the case of the TV and appliance retailer, financial analysis creates substantial doubt about the advisability of extending credit to the firm.

WORKING CAPITAL ANALYSIS AND FINANCIAL PROJECTIONS

Concept of Net Working Capital. Historically, the major role of banks in commercial lending has been to finance nonpermanent additions to working capital, defined simply as all current assets. Such additions enable a business to increase its cash balances and inventory in anticipation of seasonal bulges in sales and temporarily to extend larger amounts of credit to its customers as an aftereffect of such sales. Working capital loans are said to be self-liquidating because repayment occurs with an orderly reduction in inventories as sales rise, followed by reductions in receivables after collections are made on credit sales. The repayment of these traditional commercial loans is largely independent of long-term profitability and long-term cash flows.

The measure known as *net working capital,* de-

FIGURE 11A.3   Net Working Capital

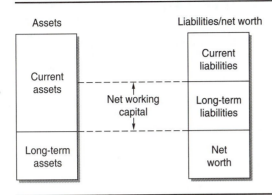

fined as current assets minus current liabilities, indicates the amount of a firm's working capital that is financed by long-term or so-called permanent sources of funds. This relationship is illustrated in Figure 11A.3. The assets and the liabilities/net worth sides of the balance sheet are represented by two bars. Each bar is divided into short-term and long-term items. Net working capital is a good indicator of a firm's liquidity because it identifies the part of a firm's most liquid assets that is supported by reliable (long-term) funds; that is, it is the amount of current assets that is not subject to claims by holders of current liabilities. Everything else being equal, a loan officer would have greater confidence in a borrower with a large net working capital position than one with little net working capital.

A corollary measure of liquidity is *net liquid assets,* which is a rough indication of the absolute dollar amount of liquidity in the firm. It is derived by subtracting from current assets the amount invested in inventory and all current liabilities. Inventory is subtracted because its liquidity often is suspect.

Sources and Uses of Funds Analysis.   In evaluating a working capital loan proposal, it is not enough simply to determine a borrower's net working capital position for one historic point in time. The loan officer should attempt to understand the dynamics in the borrower's balance sheet as seasonal activity ebbs and flows. Historical comparisons of the firm's balance sheet in a base period with its balance sheet during peak business activity will demonstrate how working capital is provided and used in operations. Table 11A.6 shows comparative January 1990 and June 1990 balance sheets for a wholesaler of garden

supplies whose sales and funds requirements usually peak in June. The differences between January 1990 and June 1990 in each account are recorded at the right as either a source or a use of funds. Decreases in assets and increases in liabilities constitute sources of funds, whereas increases in assets and decreases in liabilities are uses of funds.

In the case of Garden Wholesalers, the net working capital improved hardly at all from January to June 1990. A total of $535,000 was used for a net increase in current assets ($550,000 in uses and $15,000 in sources), of which $525,000, or nearly all of it, was financed by increases in current liabilities. Nearly three-fourths of the increased current liabilities were provided by bank funds in the form of $385,000 in notes payable, and a little over one-fourth was provided by trade credit in the form of $140,000 in new accounts payable to suppliers. Garden Wholesalers' cash flows from depreciation (assumed to be $5,000) and retained earnings were rather insignificant sources of funds for financing additions to working capital.

Financial Projections.   The sources and uses of funds analysis can also be used to make simple financial projections. Suppose that in the following January, Garden Wholesalers' bank attempts to determine the firm's need for funds for the peak of the coming season. The loan officer should review all the factors affecting sales and funds flows, including economic conditions, industry and local market conditions, the impact of potential regulation, and the characteristics of the firm's operation. From these factors it can be determined that by June 1991 receivables will increase by $425,000, inventories by $350,000, and accounts payable by

TABLE 11A.6   Comparative Balance Sheets—Sources and Uses of Funds, Garden Wholesalers (dollars in thousands)

	January 1990	June 1990	January to June Sources	Uses
Assets				
Cash	30	15	15	—
Accounts receivable	150	450	—	$300
Inventory	300	550	—	250
Current assets	480	1,015	15	550
Net fixed assets	180	175	5	—
Total assets	$660	$1,190		
Liabilities and Net Worth				
Accounts payable	$ 60	$ 200	$140	—
Notes payable	0	385	385	—
Current liabilities	60	585	525	0
Long-term debt	200	190	—	10
Common stock	50	50	—	—
Retained earnings	350	365	15	—
Total liabilities and net worth	$660	$1,190		
Total sources and uses			$560	$560

$230,000. Also, a $100,000 addition to fixed assets, $5,000 in depreciation, and $20,000 in retained earnings will occur. Finally, an estimate of change in cash balances and a partial repayment of long-term debt are included. Table 11A.7 shows that, starting with the end of the January 1991 balance sheet, the forecasted uses exceed the forecasted sources, indicating a need for new external funds of $675,000 (including refinancing of January's notes payable). The sources of the new funds are assumed to be a $575,000 bank loan and a $100,000 addition to long-term debt; the latter is considered to be the source of financing for the addition to fixed assets. Net working capital will increase nominally from $440,000 to $455,000.

A more detailed projection is probably warranted in the form of a cash budget. Preparation of a cash budget requires projecting specific cash inflows and cash disbursements on a monthly or even more frequent basis. The cash budget more closely identifies the amounts and timing of specific draws against a credit line extended by a bank or, alternatively, it identifies periods of excess cash in which

short-term money market investments can be considered.

Table 11A.8 shows a monthly cash budget for Garden Wholesalers for the same period covered in the balance sheet projection in Table 11A.7. The cash budget is divided into three parts: cash inflows, cash disbursements, and a cash and loan summary. It projects monthly additions to and subtractions from the firm's balances and reflects bank borrowings to replenish cash balances. Note that the June cash balance and bank loan concur with the respective accounts on the pro forma June 1991 balance sheet in Table 11A.7. In addition, the cash budget directly reflects transactions indicated in the sources and uses analysis in Table 11A.7, such as the long-term debt repayment, issuance of new bonds, and payments on the addition to fixed assets. Still other cash budget entries are more directly related to the pro forma income statement (not shown), and the sum of every month's profit or loss is ultimately reflected in pro forma $20,000 additions to retained earnings shown in Table 11A.7.

Although the pro forma income statement is not

TABLE 11A.7   Financial Projection, New Funds Requirements for Garden Wholesalers (dollars in thousands)

	January 31, 1991	January to June 1991 (Projected) Sources	January to June 1991 (Projected) Uses	June 30, 1991 (Projected)
Assets				
Cash	$ 30	—	—	$ 30
Accounts receivable	175	—	425	600
Inventory	350	—	350	700
Current assets	555	0	775	1,330
Net fixed assets	170	5	100	265
Total assets	$725			$1,595
Liabilities and Net Worth				
Accounts payable	$ 70	$230	—	$ 300
Notes payable	45	? → 575	$ 45	$ 575
Current liabilities	115	230		875
Long-term debt	180	? ← 100	10	270
Common stock	50	—	—	50
Retained earnings	380	20	—	400
Total liabilities and net worth	$725	255	930	$1,595

930
−255
675
(new funds needed
to balance)

| **Net Working Capital** | **$440** | | | **$455** |

shown, most of its ingredients are implicit in the sources and uses projections and the monthly cash budget. Sales for January 31 to June 30, 1991, are not shown in the previous example, although they generally lead the cash collections shown in Table 11A.8 by a more or less regular time period. The firm's cost of goods sold can be derived from the beginning inventory level plus additions to inventory minus ending inventory. Additions to inventory usually can be derived from purchases plus employee wages. Operating expenses and taxes constitute other expense items. The aggregate of sales, cost of goods sold, and other expense items provides the information needed to develop a pro forma income statement consistent with the pro forma balance sheet and cash budget.

Simply stated, the cash budget or cash flow analysis gives estimates of the borrower's cash inflows and outflows for a short interval of time. The example of Garden Wholesalers indicated the pattern of cash needs and subsequent loan take-downs as the firm approached its seasonal peak of activity. The example can easily be extended further into the future as the firm's activity subsides, generating cash for repayment of the loan. A more complete cash budget then shows when and whether the loan can be repaid.

Cash Flow from Operations.   It should be obvious by now that cash flow does not appear directly on balance sheets or income statements. However, in the final analysis, lenders must rely on cash flow

TABLE 11A.8   Cash Budget for Garden Wholesalers, 1991 (dollars in thousands)

	February	March	April	May	June
Cash Inflows					
Collections	$100	$ 75	$305	$369	$476
Issue bonds	—	100	—	—	—
Cash Disbursements					
Accounts payable	70	110	150	200	220
Operating expenses	20	20	20	20	20
Wages	100	130	170	250	300
Taxes paid	—	—	23	—	22
Repayment on long-term debt	—	—	—	10	—
Additions to fixed assets	—	50	—	—	50
Cash and Loan Summary					
Net inflow (outflow)	(90)	(135)	(58)	(111)	(136)
Beginning cash	30	30	20	22	26
Loan increase (repayment)	90	125	60	115	140
Accumulated loan	135	260	320	435	575
Ending cash	$ 30	$ 20	$ 22	$ 26	$ 30

to repay loans. In the short run, there is often little similarity between net income and cash flow. Thus, it is perilous to count on net income as a source of repayment. This simple fact—income does not equal cash flow—frequently is puzzling to beginner analysts.

Although it is not revealed directly in balance sheets and income statements, cash flow from a firm's operations can be derived through adjustments to these financial statements. The adjustments unlock the accrual accounting convention that forms the basis of financial statements. Balance sheet noncash assets represent historical cash inflows and potential cash outflows. By unlocking this accrual convention, we reveal the implicit present cash flows. Changes in assets, liabilities, and net worth, along with events that create income and expense, all contain cash flow information.

The rules for converting accrual accounting to cash basis accounting are straightforward. To con-

vert revenues to receipts, one starts with revenues, subtracts increases in related assets, and adds increases in related liabilities. A symmetrical approach is followed to convert expenses (an accrual concept) to actual cash expenditures. In this case one starts with expenses, adds related increases in assets, and subtracts related increases in liabilities. Table 11A.9 summarizes these rules.

The example of Textile Distributors, Inc., demonstrates the adjustments needed to unlock cash flow information. Table 11A.10 presents balance sheets for year-end 1989 and year-end 1990 and a statement of income for 1990. Table 11A.11 gives an analysis of cash provided during 1990 and consists of adjustments that essentially unravel the accruals represented on the balance sheets. A careful study of Table 11A.11 will reveal its reasoning to anyone who is well acquainted with the logic of accrual accounting.

Consider Figure 11A.4, which diagrams the first

TABLE 11A.9   Converting Accrual Income to Cash Flow

To Get Cash	Related Assets	Related Liabilities
Receipts	Subtract	Add
Expenditures	Add	Subtract

TABLE 11A.10 Textile Distributors, Inc.—Balance Sheets and Income Statement

Balance Sheets

	December 31, 1989	December 31, 1990
Assets		
Cash	$ 88	$ 72
Accounts receivable	1,142	1,532
Inventory	212	392
Current assets	1,442	1,996
Net fixed assets	44	100
Total assets	1,486	2,096
Liabilities and Net Worth		
Accounts payable	$1,008	$1,332
Notes payable—bank	200	400
Accrued expenses	24	40
Current liabilities	1,232	1,772
Common stock	170	170
Retained earnings	84	154
Total liabilities and net worth	$1,486	$2,096

Income Statement
1990

Net sales		$5,483
Cost of goods sold		4,495
Gross profit		988
Less:		
Office salaries	$112	
Depreciation	23	
General and administrative	642	
Total operating expense		777
Operating income		211
Interest expense		38
Net income before taxes		173
Income taxes		70
Net income after taxes		103
Less dividends		33
Retained earnings		$ 70

TABLE 11A.11   Textile Distributors, Inc.—Cash Provided from Operations, 1990 (dollars in thousands)

Net Cash Received		
Sales	$ 5,483	
+ Beginning accounts receivable	+1,142	
	6,625	
− Ending accounts receivable	−1,532	
= Net cash received		$5,093
Cash Disbursed for Inventory		
Cost of goods sold	4,495	
+ Ending inventory	+ 392	
	4,887	
− Beginning inventory	− 212	
= Goods available for sale	4,675	
+ Beginning accounts payable	+1,008	
	5,683	
− Ending accounts payable	−1,332	
= Total cash disbursed inventory		4,351
Cash Disbursed for Expenses		
Total expenses	885	
− Noncash charges	− 23	
	862	
+ Beginning accrued expenses	+ 24	
	886	
− Ending accrued expenses	− 40	
	846	
− Beginning prepaid expenses	− 0	
	846	
+ Ending prepaid expenses	+ 0	
= Total expenses		846
Cash surplus or deficient		$ (104)

FIGURE 11A.4   Net Cash Received in 1990—Textile Distributors, Inc.

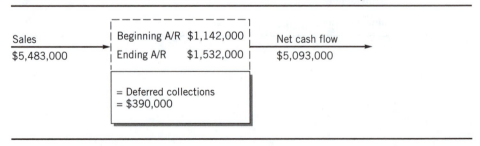

part of Table 11A.11, "Net Cash Received." Textile Distributors sells everything on credit. Therefore, sales do not fully correspond with cash received; rather, sales initially is added to accounts receivable. The accounts receivable account is better thought of as a deferred collections account. If accounts receivable increase during the period, as in Figure 11A.4, sales will overstate the net cash received because additional deferred collections are created.

Other adjustments are made in the second section, "Cash Disbursed for Inventory," to account for cash disbursed to produce goods and the accrual effects of changes in inventory and accounts payable. The third section, "Cash Disbursed for Expenses," can be used for similar adjustments to accrued expenses (liabilities), prepaid expenses (assets), accrued taxes, depreciation, interest, and other accrued items.

Note that overall, Textile Distributors' net cash flow during 1990 was a negative $104,000, despite a strong net income of $103,000. Clearly, a lender that depended on net income to reduce Textile's loan would have been greatly disappointed.

Long-Term Financial Requirements. The principle of sources and uses of funds analysis to obtain balance sheet projections is as valid for long-term as it is for short-term estimates of funds requirements. For long-term purposes, however, the emphasis is on overall financial needs and not simply on the financing of temporary additions to working capital. The approach is to project the balance sheet for some future period—say, three to five years from the present. The differences between the future and present accounts indicate how funds will be used (invested) in the interim and determine how much external financing will be required. The future balance sheet is established using at least two kinds of data. First, discrete planning data are usually

TABLE 11A.12 Three-year Balance Sheet Projection for a Manufacturing Firm (dollars in thousands)

	June 1990	June 1993	Sources	Uses
Assets				
Cash	$ 70	$ 50	$ 20	—
Accounts receivable	700	800	—	$ 100
Inventory	850	1,280	—	430
Current assets	1,620	2,130		
Fixed assets				
Gross	1,800	2,300	—	500
Accumulated depreciation	(300)	(450)	150	—
Net fixed assets	1,500	1,850		
Total assets	3,120	3,980		
Liabilities and Net Worth				
Accounts payable	250	320	70	—
Notes payable	300	610	310	—
Current liabilities	550	930		
Long-term debt (old)	1,300	1,000	—	300
Long-term debt (new)	—	348	348	—
Total long-term debt	1,300	1,348		
Common stock	200	200	—	—
Retained earnings	1,070	1,502	432	—
Total liabilities and net worth	$3,120	$3,980		
Total sources and uses			$1,330	$1,330

given, such as a planned dollar amount to be invested in new equipment or plant expansion. The second kind of data are derived by relating certain balance sheet accounts to key planning variables. For example, receivables and inventories may be a percentage of the sales anticipated in the future period. The ratios used to relate an account to sales may be derived from the firm's experience or may be equal to known norms in the firm's industry, such as those given in the RMA *Statement Studies*.

To illustrate, in Table 11A.12 we have constructed a balance sheet for three years into the future (June 1993) for a manufacturer, taking the actual June 1990 balance sheet as a base. The following guidelines are applied:

1. Sales will be $4.8 million during each of the next three years.
2. Minimum cash should be $50,000.
3. Receivables represent sales for the most recent 60 days (two months).
4. Inventories will turn over three times per year. Inventories are valued at the cost of goods, which will be 80 percent of sales.
5. Additions to fixed assets will total $500,000. Depreciation will be $50,000 per year.
6. Accounts payable will be equal to one-fourth of inventories.
7. Existing long-term debt will be retired at a rate of $100,000 per year.
8. After tax profits will total 5 percent of sales each year. Forty percent of profits will be paid out in dividends.
9. Net working capital must be at least $1.2 million.

Each June 1993 balance sheet account is derived either explicitly or implicitly from the guidelines. The explicit derivations are as follows:

1. Cash = $50,000 as specified.
2. Accounts receivable = 2 months/12 months/ year × $4.8 million sales = $800,000.
3. Inventory = 0.80 × $4.8 million sales/3 × turnover = $1.28 million.
4. Net fixed assets = $1.5 million (June 1990) + $500,000 additions = $50,000 depreciation × 3 years = $1.85 million.
5. Accounts payable = $1.28 million inventory × 1/4 = $320,000.
6. Notes payable = $2.13 million current assets − $320,000 payables − $1.2 million required net working capital = $610,000.
7. Total long-term debt = plug figure to balance the balance sheet after deducting $100,000 × 3 years of old debt retirement.
8. Retained earnings = $1.07 million (June 1990) + 0.05 after tax profit × $4.8 million sales × 3 years × 0.6 retention rate = $1.502 million.

The sources and uses data in Table 11A.12 reveal a lot about the financial dynamics of the firm over the coming three-year period. One debatable issue is the allocation of new debt between bank loans (notes payable) and new long-term debt. If the additions to working capital are considered permanent, the firm's banker might consider financing part or all of it through term lending in the future, or the banker might urge that other long-term sources, such as the bond market, be tapped.

Bases for Loan Pricing

PRIME RATE

The national lending prime rate is set by the large money market banks. The banks adjust the prime, with considerable public fanfare, to signal the softening or hardening of loan conditions. They do not necessarily synchronize the adjustment of the prime closely with changes in short-term open-market rates, such as the Federal funds rate.

Since the late 1970s, when as much as 90 percent of their loans were linked to the prime rate, money center banks have moved away from the prime rate as a benchmark used in loan pricing. As indicated in Table 11B.1, only one-fifth of business loans made by nine of the largest money center banks were based on the prime rate in a recent year. The remainder of their business loans shifted to one of several open market reference rates. This was due to new sources of competition for these loans, especially from foreign banks that sought loan business in the United States through their offshore branches and agencies. Thirty-seven percent of large business loans by money center banks were tied to the Federal funds rate, and about one-quarter was tied to other domestic money market rates, such as the CD or Treasury bill rate. Only a small fraction was tied to external interest rates such as the London Interbank Offering Rate (LIBOR).

For other large banks, the prime rate was still somewhat more important as a pricing benchmark rate, although the open market-based rate had increased significantly during the past 25 years. Slightly over half of small bank business loans re-mained linked to the prime rate, although here too, market-based pricing demonstrated a considerable gain.

The movement from large, prime-based short-term loans to pricing on money market base rates probably will never be reversed. The movement occurred, as noted earlier in the chapter, because of price competition from an expanding commercial paper market and from foreign banks, both of which were historically more open to unrestrained competition. Nevertheless, local banks' prime rates are still the basis of pricing most small loans, and many large revolving credits are frequently based on prime. In addition, the rates on certain consumer loans and many construction loans continue to be based on the prime rate.

Some smaller banks have given up the practice of quoting loan prices based on a prime rate because of publicity from court cases challenging prime rate lending practices during the 1980s. Plaintiffs claimed that banks misled customers by implying that the prime rate was the interest rate charged to their most creditworthy customers when, in fact, they made certain other loans at interest rates below their stated primes. Although the term *prime rate* is not clearly defined, it suggests the lowest commercial loan rate available. Some plaintiffs claimed that the defendant banks violated antitrust laws because they colluded to fix their prime rates at noncompetitive levels. In any case, the practice by large banks of quoting a national prime rate as an indicator of loan tightness, although not as a specific loan offer rate, continues to persist.

TABLE 11B.1   Pricing Business Loan Base Rates at U.S. Banks (percentage of loans)

Rate Basis	Nine Money Center Banks	Other Large Banks	Other Banks
Prime rate	21.1%	29.0%	54.0%
Federal funds rate	37.7	25.8	16.7
Other domestic money market rate	25.5	20.7	12.0
Foreign rate	4.3	9.4	6.2
Other	11.4	15.1	11.0

SOURCE: Thomas D. Simpson, "Developments in the United States Financial System since the Mid-1970s," *Federal Reserve Bulletin* (January 1988), pp. 1–13.

FLOATING RATES

When money market rates of interest fluctuated dramatically during the early 1980s, banks switched to floating rates on business loans. Fluctuating rates caused bank funding costs to rise as well, and had banks continued using fixed-rate loan pricing, they would have taken unacceptable losses. Floating-rate pricing ties loans to a base rate that responds to the movement of market rates in general or to a rate designated as the prime rate.

The first large-scale introduction of floating-rate loans dates from the early 1970s. At that time, large banks offered floating rates that were guaranteed not to exceed an average or absolute *cap*. This ceiling rate policy had the effect of partly protecting the bank against rising market rates and of giving the customer a guarantee against unlimited increases in rate. However, market rates unexpectedly rose to record heights in the mid-1970s, capping rates on many outstanding loans well below market and, in some cases, below the banks' changing cost of money. As a result, banks generally offer only a cap rate in conjunction with hedges based on financial derivatives such as financial futures and cap options.

As interest rates soared in the early 1980s, changes in the pricing of loans and deposits forced banks to focus on the interest sensitivity of their balance sheets for the first time. Key banking legislation had begun to remove interest rate restraints on bank deposits, and banks with large positions in fixed-rate loans found themselves exposed to interest rate risk when deposit rates rose sharply. These banks quickly adopted floating-rate loan pricing strategies.

Floating rates based on LIBOR (London Interbank Offered Rate) have become highly important. LIBOR is a widely quoted rate on short-term European money market credits. It largely determines the overseas lending rates of large U.S. banks, particularly when the spread between U.S. money market base rates and LIBOR rates favors the latter. In addition, U.S. banks' access to overseas sources of funds has recently made LIBOR an increasingly popular base rate among borrowers of regional and even small banks.

CHAPTER 12

Consumer Lending

The long-term secular growth of consumer credit since the Second World War reflects the steady rise of income and employment and the increased job security of millions of middle-class families. Growing and secure future personal income is a crucial criterion for extending credit to consumers because it allows them to acquire goods or services today based on tomorrow's income. On the other hand, recession or slow economic conditions such as occurred in the early 1990s creates uncertainty about consumers' future incomes and causes consumers to reduce their borrowing.

Overall, however, consumer debt has grown considerably more rapidly than personal income since the mid-1970s and has produced a secular rise in the ratio of consumer credit to disposable income. This ratio was a mere 5 percent in the mid-1970s. When the ratio reached 20 percent in 1990 (see Figure 12.1), it was feared that U.S. households were at risk of exceeding their debt capacity and that banks might experience massive consumer defaults. The ratio declined rapidly in the 1990–1991 recession and by 1994 was down to 11 percent. By early 1997 it had climbed to over 18 percent, again causing anxiety among some observers.

However, research tends to refute the notion that consumers are in danger of exceeding their ability to pay. Households consistently have maintained high levels of liquidity. Data show that the ratio of consumer installment credit outstanding to the amount of consumer-held liquid assets (meaning assets that are readily convertible into cash) has remained at around 20 percent for the past 25 years or so. This ratio falls moderately during recessions and rises somewhat during economic expansions.

The long-term growth of consumer lending reflects aggressive competition by banks and other financial institutions for consumer loan market shares. Recent growth in credit card and home equity credit has been especially impressive. These products make credit more attractive and more available to consumers. One researcher has concluded that, because of the existence of credit cards, home equity loans, and below-market interest rate financing from manufacturers, lenders have become less able to ration credit during pe-

FIGURE 12.1 Consumer Debt, Percentage of Disposable Income

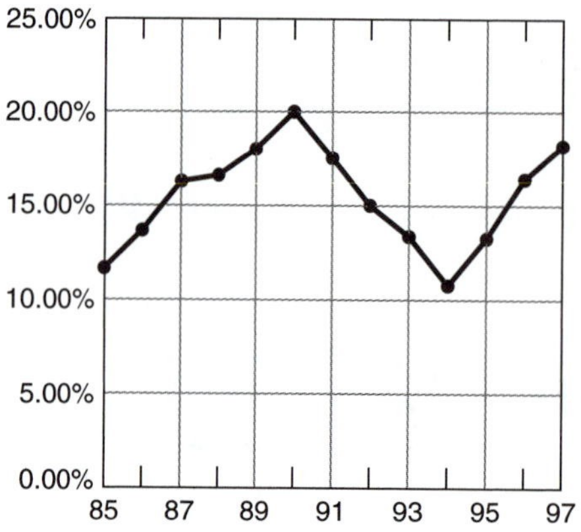

riods of credit restraint. In addition, market share has steadily shifted from high-cost finance companies and retailers to commercial banks.

Meanwhile, consumers have expanded their purposes for borrowing to include more purchases of luxury goods and services such as recreational possessions and activities. Concurrent with these developments is the rise in consumer debt delinquencies and personal bankruptcies. These changes do not necessarily portend major future losses for banks. They do, however, call for banks to maintain good controls on their consumer lending underwriting standards.[1]

COMMERCIAL BANK CONSUMER CREDIT

Table 12.1 shows that nonmortgage consumer debt held by U.S. commercial banks totaled $521.2 billion in 1997, or nearly 20 percent of the $2,773 billion in total loans held by

TABLE 12.1 Nonmortgage Consumer Debt Held by Commercial Banks, 1972 and 1997 (dollars in billions)

Nonmortgage Debt	1972	1997
Automobile	20.8	152.2
Revolving[a]	7.4	217.7
Other	37.0	151.3
Total	65.2	521.2

[a] Revolving debt includes credit card, revolving home equity, and other revolving debt.

[1] Charlene Sullivan, "Consumer Credit: Are There Limits?" *Journal of Retail Banking* (Winter 1986–1987), pp. 5–18.

TABLE 12.2   Debt for All U.S. Families by Type of Lender, 1989 and 1995

Type of Lender	1989	1995
Commercial bank	29.4%	35.1%
S & L (savings bank)	23.4%	11.3%
Credit union	3.3%	4.2%
Finance or loan co.	9.6%	21.0%
Brokerage	2.9%	1.9%
Real estate lender	13.3%	12.9%
Individual lender	6.8%	4.4%
All other	11.1%	9.2%
Total	100.0%	100.0%

SOURCE: *Federal Reserve Bulletin*, January 1997, p. 20.

banks. Over the 25-year period from 1972 to 1997, consumer debt grew an annual compound rate of nearly 9 percent.

Banks are the most frequently used suppliers of credit services to households. The recent survey reported in Table 12.2 shows that banks lead other depository institutions and nondepository sources in the percentage of household users as a source for credit, including bank credit cards, mortgages, motor vehicle loans, home equity or other credit lines, and all other types of credit.

About 36 percent of households now have at least one kind of credit relationship with nondepository institutions. This nondepository percentage appears to be growing as numerous large and highly diversified companies such as AT&T, General Electric, General Motors, the Fidelity Group of mutual funds, and insurance companies like Equitable, Prudential, and John Hancock have entered the credit card business and, to some extent, the mortgage business.[2]

AUTOMOBILE LENDING

Direct automobile loans are simply loans made to consumers for the purchase of an automobile, and the lender secures the loan through a chattel mortgage on the automobile. *Indirect* loans are automobile loans acquired from automobile dealers. In the latter arrangement, the consumer applies for a loan to the dealer, who conveys essential information regarding the consumer's creditworthiness to the bank. Typically, banks attempt to aid auto dealers in executing their transactions by indicating acceptance or rejection of such credit requests as quickly as possible. Banks acquire indirect loans from automobile dealers in ''packages.'' In the dealer relations of many banks, it is understood that the individual loans in a package will vary in quality; that is, dealers are normally permitted some borrowers of marginal creditworthiness for the size of the loan or collateral value involved. As a result, delinquencies and losses on indirect automobile loans run as high as twice

[2] David Lawrence, ''Consumer Banking: Still the Bank's Profit Center,'' *The Banker's Magazine* (March–April 1992), pp. 18–22.

those on direct loans. In addition, banks pay automobile dealers a rebate on loans provided by the dealers. Finally, in the interest of maintaining and promoting their dealer relations, banks frequently offer *floor-plan financing* to dealers at favorable rates, as well as financing support for dealers' automobile leasing programs. However, the attractiveness of the relationship changes over the business cycle; during periods of high loan demand, many banks downplay these support factors.

After several decades of generally rapid growth, automobile debt now declines periodically at commercial banks because of aggressive, below-market financing campaigns by automobile manufacturers. Both direct and indirect lending on new automobiles are affected by such campaigns. For both types of loans, maturities have consistently increased, as auto finance companies now routinely offer 60-month loans on new cars. In mid-1997, new loan maturities averaged 54 months for new cars and 48 months for used cars. Interest rates on new-car loans range between 2 and 2.5 percent over the banks' prime rates, and used-car loans run as much as 6 percent over prime.

REVOLVING CREDIT

Credit and debit card overdraft loans account for one of the highest rates of consumer debt growth. Credit card and debit card lending is based on preauthorized lines of credit that can be taken down as the consumer takes cash advances or makes purchases from any of the more than 1.5 million merchants who accept such cards. This easy access to credit through plastic cards has been helped dramatically by the rapid deployment of electronic banking devices. These devices include automated teller machines (ATMs), at which bank customers conduct direct deposit and cash withdrawal transactions, and point-of-sale (POS) machines at merchants' locations, which credit the merchants' accounts and either debit the cardholders' checking accounts or trigger an overline debit in payment for goods and services. As indicated in a later section of this chapter, in the past card-type lending was sometimes hampered by state usury laws that restricted the interest rates charged for this high-risk credit, and by laws that prohibit bank card issuers from charging the consumer an annual fee for card services. While these usury restraints were modified and liberalized in many states during the 1980s, there are recurring calls by consumer rights advocates to institute a federal ceiling on credit card fees and interest rates.

HOME EQUITY CREDIT

Personal revolving lines of credit can be extended either secured or unsecured. They may total as little as $1,000 but often amount to tens of thousands of dollars. When the loans are unsecured, the borrower must demonstrate considerable financial strength. A popular secured version of this type of credit is the line of credit secured by equity in the borrower's home. The home equity line of credit was widely offered by banks beginning in the mid-1980s, and its popularity was boosted sharply as a result of the Tax Reform Act of 1986. This law curtailed the deductions of interest expense on more traditional consumer loans, including auto, credit card, and other nonmortgage loans. The deductibility of interest on mortgage loans, however, continued to be available up to the purchase price of the home (plus improvements). In effect, then, the after tax cost of home equity credit fell relative to the after tax costs of other types of consumer credit. From bankers' points of view, home equity credit was a fortuitous replacement in their loan portfolios for automobile loans that, at times, declined dramatically.

In addition to their cost competitiveness, home equity loans have other positive qualities. The use of a home as collateral usually provides the bank with collateral that has the potential for appreciation. With automobile loans, on the other hand, rapid depreciation must be expected. Moreover, home equity lines are frequently drawn upon for home improvement, thereby further increasing the value of the collateral on which the loan is based.

A survey in the late 1980s determined that the appraised value of the average house supporting a home equity loan was $101,000 and the average outstanding balance on the first mortgage was $39,000, leaving available equity of $62,000. In addition, the loan-to-appraised-value limit applied by the average bank surveyed was 77 percent, indicating that, on average, $38,770 could be borrowed ($101,000 $\times$ 77 percent $-$ $39,000). Thus, there appears to be very good potential growth for home equity credit.

Most banks that provide home equity credit offer it on an open-ended (revolving), variable-rate basis. About one-half of issuing banks also offer a closed-end version of the product. Home equity credit usually is priced on a variable-rate basis, with the rate set at about 2 percent over the national or local prime rate. Compared with other sources of credit, taking tax deductibility into account, home equity lines of credit appear to be a relative bargain for consumers.

MOBILE HOME FINANCING

Mobile home financing is not unlike the financing of automobiles. Most mobile home financing is indirect as it is arranged through dealers. Bank relationships with mobile home dealers often include financing of their inventory.

Mobile home financing grew rapidly in the 1960s and 1970s with the explosive growth of the industry. The continuing high cost of conventional housing indicates that mobile home sales and mobile home financing will probably continue to grow, although the relatively poor credit quality of this market has resulted in a slight reduction of mobile home lending by commercial banks. Many mobile home borrowers do not have solid credit histories, and default and delinquency rates on these loans are relatively high. Compared with conventional home mortgages, mobile home loans have shorter maturities, normally 10 to 12 years, and interest rates 4 to 5 percent higher than those of home first mortgages. Table 12.3 lists the prevailing national interest rates for the predominant types of consumer credit in early 1997.

SECURITIZATION OF CONSUMER LOANS

A breakthrough in bank loan portfolio management occurred in 1985 when securities backed by automobile loans was the first securitization of consumer loans on bank balance sheets. In 1987, a bank issued the first securities backed by credit card receivables. *Securitization* is a method in which banks sell part of their loan portfolios in trust to back publicly issued securities sold to investors on the open market. In addition to automobile loans and credit card receivables, mobile home loans, boat loans, and unsecured personal loans have been securitized. In 1995, securitized consumer loans totaled $125 billion, up from

TABLE 12.3   Interest Rates for Types of Consumer Loans, February 1997

Type of Loan	Rate
Credit card	15.88%
New car loan	8.92%
Personal loan	13.46%

SOURCE: *Federal Reserve Bulletin*, June 1997, p. A36.

only $15 billion just eight years earlier. Of the total value of consumer loans originated by commercial banks in 1995, 20 percent was securitized. Securitization was discussed in greater detail in Chapter 11.

INTEREST CHARGE CONSIDERATIONS

Add-On Rates

For automobile loans and most other types of consumer installment loans, interest charges are quoted in terms of an *add-on* rate. The add-on rate is applied to the original loan principal and is charged over the life of the loan despite the amortization of principal by means of installment payments. For example, suppose that an add-on rate of 8 percent is charged on a $1,200, one-year loan to be repaid in monthly installments. The interest amount of $96 (8 percent of $1,200) is added up front on the amount borrowed, and monthly payments are determined by dividing principal plus interest, or $1,296, by 12 (the number of payments). Although interest in the amount of $96 is charged, the average outstanding loan balance during the year will be only $600. The resulting effective annual rate will be nearly 16 percent, or double the add-on rate quoted.

When more than one payment is made over the life of the loan, the add-on rate will always result in an effective rate that exceeds the nominal rate. This is because the borrower does not have the full use of the amount borrowed for the whole time period. Also, the more frequent the installment payments, the higher the effective rate. Installment loan rates must also be quoted in annual percentage rates (APRs), and the total dollar finance charge must be disclosed in accordance with truth-in-lending legislation and Regulation Z, discussed later in this chapter.

Bank Discount Rate

Another method for calculating loan interest is based simply on the amount to be repaid. The amount loaned is equal to the amount to be repaid minus the interest amount. Suppose that $1,200 is borrowed at 15 percent and repaid after one year. The interest amount will be 15 percent of $1,200, or $180. In the simple interest method, the $180 interest amount would be for the use of $1,200 over the entire year. In the bank discount method, however, the $180 would be deducted from $1,200, leaving $1,020 to be used for the year. The effective interest rate in this case would be 17.647 percent ($180 divided by $1,020), or considerably more than 15 percent. The bank discount method is sometimes used for single-payment consumer loans and for small business loans. Regulation Z requires the bank to disclose the true annual percentage rate.

State Usury Ceilings

As with credit card and other revolving loans, installment loan interest rates are subject to usury limits in many states. The usury ceilings usually specify limits on add-on, as well as true annual percentage rates. Lenders obviously cannot avoid legal interest limits by quoting on an add-on basis with the appearance of bargain rates. In the middle and late-1980s, a temporary federal preemption of state usury laws at times went into effect. With implementation of this legislation. Lenders were able to make consumer loans competitive with the then prevailing competitive high market interest rates. However, this legislation permitted individual states to override the federal preemption by reestablishing their own structures of usury ceilings.

Variable-Rate Consumer Loans

In the early 1980s, banks began to employ variable-rate pricing for installment loans in response to the soaring variable cost of bank funds in an era of high and volatile market rates of interest. At the time, variable rates were already well accepted by corporate borrowers, but their acceptance by consumers was uncertain. A prolonged period of generally falling interest rates beginning in early 1984, however, quickly won over consumers to variable rates. In the generally low interest rate era of the middle and late 1990s, variable-rate installment lending dominated fixed-rate lending by a considerable margin. In the future, if interest rates should begin a prolonged rise, it would be unlikely that consumers would continue to accept installment loans priced on a variable-rate basis.

Prepayment Penalties

The assessment of charges on consumer loans that are paid off early is an important aspect of consumer loan charges. A method must be used to refund unearned income to the consumer when a loan is prepaid. However, the bank is entitled to collect more than the interest that would be prorated to the length of time the loan is outstanding because of the high average loan balance during the early part of the loan period and because the bank incurs origination costs that it initially expected to recover over the full life of the loan.

The usual approach to determining the customer's rebate is the *Rule of 78s* method. The method varies the rebate amount according to the time at which prepayment occurs and is based on the sum of the installment period numbers. The finance charge in any one month that a prepayment occurs is a proportion of the sum-of-the-months' digits over the maturity of the loan. For a 12-month loan, the sum of the digits is

$$1 + 2 + 3 + \cdots + 12 = 78$$

thus the name *Rule of 78s*. In this case, the bank's total charge in the first month will be 12 times the amount charged in the twelfth month: 12/78 of the total finance charge is earned in the first month, 11/78 in the second month, and so forth, to 1/78 in the twelfth month. For example, if the customer repays the loan in the second month, the bank will earn 23/78 [(12 + 11)/78)] of the total finance charge. The method is appealing to bankers because it is relatively simple to compute.

The Rule of 78s is sometimes criticized as being arbitrary and unfair to the borrower.

The mathematically accurate method of computing loan prepayment charges is called the *actuarial method.* This method calculates the earned finance charge on the actual (declining) balance before prepayment occurred. Historically, bankers found the actuarial method to be too complicated and time-consuming, although hand held financial calculators and simple computer software now facilitate its use. In most cases, the Rule of 78s method does approximate the actuarial method reasonably well. However, the Rule of 78s is not a good approximating tool if the annual percentage rate is very high or the loan maturity is unusually long, or both.

CREDIT ANALYSIS IN CONSUMER LENDING

Banks' consumer lending activities involve handling a large number of customers. Each borrower represents a relatively small amount of loan business, and banks need to process a great many of these loans to generate a substantial dollar volume of nonmortgage consumer loan business. With such large numbers of borrowers, it is vital for bank management to exercise effective control over the consumer credit-granting process.

Most banks with large numbers of consumer credit applications supplement their analyses with *statistical credit scoring.* This automated analysis system is a means of evaluating applications using a form of score card that lists application characteristics such as income level, job tenure, residence ownership, and established credit with retailers or other lenders. The application is awarded point values for each characteristic, and the total number of points indicates whether or not the applicant qualifies for a loan. Acceptability is predicated on the bank's database of past applicants with similar creditworthiness profiles and the historical incidence of these applicants' success or failure in paying off loans from the bank. Statistical credit scoring models are described more fully in the next section.

Credit scoring is seldom used as the sole criterion for granting consumer credit. Other factors, such as debt payment capacity, present economic conditions, and collateral requirements, must meet the bank's underwriting standards. Subjective information—such as personality and the apparent character of the borrower, the potential for a profitable relationship in the future, and other extenuating and nonquantifiable factors—causes credit analysis to be a highly judgmental process. *Credit analysis* is the process by which both quantifiable and subjective factors are evaluated simultaneously and judged. The objective of this process is to minimize loan losses and nonperforming loans. The steps in consumer credit analysis are outlined in Table 12.4.

TABLE 12.4   Steps in Consumer Credit Analysis

1. Determine loan purpose and amount	3. Investigate and verify information
2. Obtain information	4. Analysis
a. Consumer credit	a. Financial statements
b. Personal financial statement	b. Cash flow
c. Income tax returns	5. Evaluate collateral, if required
d. Business financial statements	6. Price and structure the credit
	7. Negotiate with applicant

Loan Types

Nonmortgage consumer credit products are differentiated according to the purpose, amount, source of repayment, and term of the loan. The type of loan product suitable for a qualified applicant must be determined in the interview process. The following types of credit products are typically offered by an aggressive retail loan department:

1. Checking revolving overdraft line of credit.
2. Large personal revolving line of credit, including home equity credit.
3. Installment loan.
   a. Short term
   b. Long term
4. Single-payment loan.

Checking Overdraft Line   The checking revolving loan is usually restricted to small loan amounts, seldom over several thousand dollars, and offers protection against overdrafts. The borrower simply triggers the line by writing checks in excess of his or her account balance, usually with notice to the bank. The account bears a high rate of interest and is normally unsecured. A solid record of disciplined credit activity is required. Many banks consider the checking overdraft line of credit too aggressive and too risky.

Other Installment Loans   Installment loans are made for a fixed amount and may be either unsecured or secured. By definition, installment loans are repayable in two or more installments. Repayment schedules are set up to amortize the principal fully, usually on a monthly basis, over the life of the loan. Maturities typically are 3 to 5 years, although long-term installment credit may extend as far as 20 years. Although loans may be unsecured or secured, unsecured loans usually do not exceed three years or so in maturity.

Installment loans are often made to buy automobiles, which constitute the collateral. As noted earlier, at times automobile lending by banks declines sharply. Declines occur because of aggressive financing programs launched by automobile manufacturers in which below-market financing rates, occasionally even including zero rates, are offered as a sales tool. As described earlier, home equity is also used as collateral for installment loans. The purpose of such loans appears to be mostly home improvement and debt consolidation.

Single-Payment Loans   The support for a single-payment loan usually is a single source of repayment available at the time of maturity. Repayment typically does not come from regular income sources, but from sources such as maturing securities, including certificates of deposits or bonds, or from the planned sale of common stock or real estate. Since this type of loan depends a great deal on the validity of the source of repayment, the lender must be meticulous in verifying and validating the source.

Obtaining Information

As in commercial lending, the most valuable credit information available in consumer lending is supplied by the loan applicant. A bank asks nonmortgage consumer borrowers to provide this information on the bank's own standardized credit application forms. The form generally requires data on employment, income, living arrangements, marital status, assets owned, and outstanding debt.

On unsecured loans and secured loans over, say, $5,000, banks require a current personal financial statement. They should also require income tax returns and business financial statements on self-employed applicants. Income tax returns are filed on Internal Revenue Service Form 1040, which should be accompanied by supporting schedules that detail deductions and income from investments, dividends, businesses owned, rents, royalties, and other sources.

An important secondary source of credit information is credit reporting agencies. These agencies gather extensive data on consumers' credit histories, including a listing of outstanding debts, legal actions, and promptness of payment. Credit agencies compile these data from information supplied by creditors. Regulation B governs the way in which creditors maintain their customers' credit records and how they report the records to credit agencies or other inquirers. Originally, one intent of the regulation was to enable married women to build a credit record when credit is extended jointly to married couples. This Regulation B provision corrected a previously common practice of creditors that omitted a spouse (usually the wife) from the credit history on accounts for which the spouse was jointly liable. On the other hand, Regulation B prohibits creditors from associating a person with a spouse's bad credit history if he or she was not responsible for the debts of the spouse.

Investigation and Verification

Before banks can depend fully on primary financial documents submitted by the borrower, the information they contain must be verified. Personal financial statements are usually self-prepared, and they should be tested for accuracy and realism. Direct verification can be made by contacting present creditors about indebtedness reported by potential borrowers, employers, and other organizations with official knowledge of the borrower's income. On assets offered as collateral, legal searches should be conducted to determine if there are previous claimants who have filed under the Uniform Commercial Code. Appraisals on both real and personal property may be required to establish an estimate of collateral values.

Information and Equal Credit Opportunity   According to the Equal Credit Opportunity Act (ECOA) and Regulation B, under which the ECOA is implemented, borrowers have the right to withhold information that is irrelevant to the loan transaction. Because of the complexities of Regulation B, it is not always clear to bankers what information they are not permitted to require of consumer borrowers. To avoid requesting proscribed information, most banks model their loan application forms on a standard form published by the Federal Reserve Board that conforms with Regulation B.

In general, the information that is not required is that which might be used to discriminate against the applicant. Information concerning the borrower's marital status generally must not be required if the borrower applies for individual credit as opposed to joint credit. An exception is permitted for secured loans if, in the event of default, the bank's access to the collateral might be affected by the borrower's marital status. This is particularly important in community property states, where assets owned by a married person may also be owned by the person's spouse. In cases in which the bank can legally inquire about marital status, it cannot inquire whether the applicant is divorced. Such information might be used unfairly in judging the applicant's general stability.

The bank cannot require an applicant (often a separated or divorced person) to provide information on alimony, child support, or separate maintenance income unless the applicant wishes to offer the information in support of her (or his) creditworthiness. The bank may, however, require disclosure of the liability to pay alimony, child support, and separate maintenance, since such payments could impair the applicant's ability to repay the loan.

A bank cannot discriminate against female loan applicants because of their potential to bear children. A bank can, however, inquire about present dependents, including their ages and expenses. Regulation B prohibits inquiries about an applicant's race, color, religion, or national origin. The bank may not refuse credit to aliens because they are not citizens, although it may inquire about their immigration status to determine creditworthiness.

It might seem that Regulation B interferes with a bank's natural desire to know as much as it can about a loan applicant in order to be comfortable about its evaluation of creditworthiness. However, Regulation B probably does not prevent inquiries that are germane to the evaluation. It does attempt to block the use of extraneous information that might reinforce unreasoned and often subconscious biases that lenders sometimes develop. On the other hand, some bankers believe that they should avoid requiring too much information so that loan applicants will not feel that their privacy is being invaded. In this regard, requiring too much information may inhibit the bank's efforts to market its consumer lending service.

Cash Flow and Statement Analysis

As in commercial lending, the primary criteria for consumer credit are the borrower's financial standing and debt service capacity. Collateral pledged as a secondary source of repayment is used to reduce the risk and to help define the amount and maturity of the loan, but it is not a basis *per se* for making the loan.

Assets should be reviewed to determine how much liquidity they afford. On credit line loans, underwriting standards sometimes require liquid assets to equal or exceed the amount of the line. Diversification of assets is important to provide more stable values. The borrower's tangible net worth must be calculated, and intangible assets should be ruled out. Credit line borrowing might require that tangible net worth be three or more times the amount of the credit line. The borrower's total income should be from stable sources that are dependable. Secondary or collateral sources should be determined. A thorough understanding of the borrower's financial status is important in structuring the loan to fit the borrower's repayment capability and needs. When collateral is called for, the loan should be structured with an appropriate collateral value margin.

Ultimately, the primary concern in consumer loan analysis is to identify a specific source of repayment. The usual source is income from wages. This requires an evaluation of employment stability and of other claims on income, such as debt payment obligations and a reasonable level of subsistence. The process of determining if adequate resources are available to repay a loan is referred to as *cash flow analysis*.

The monthly debt-to-income ratio is used to determine the amount of income needed to meet the borrower's total monthly debt obligations:

$$\text{Debt-to-income ratio} = \frac{\text{Total monthly payments}}{\text{Gross monthly payments}}$$

The debt-to-income ratio compares the regular sources of income, exclusive of contingent or unverifiable income, to fixed monthly obligations. The latter includes items such as mortgage payments, installment and charge card payments, and monthly support and child care payments, in addition to the payment requirements of the proposed bank loan. The fixed obligations do not include normal daily living expenses. The underwriting standards of many banks require that the debt-to-income ratio not exceed 40 percent. On large credit line borrowings, gross income should be two or more times the amount of the credit line.

Balancing Loan Losses and Opportunities

Two basic types of errors can be made in evaluating loan applications, and they should be balanced to minimize overall losses. The first type of error is the obvious one of granting a loan to a borrower who ultimately does not pay satisfactorily. The bank risks the direct loss of income and, potentially, the loss of its funds when it lends to such customers. To prevent these losses, the bank can tighten its lending standards, but it does so at the risk of disqualifying good borrowers, which leads to the second type of error, eliminating good borrowers. Tightening credit standards may lead the bank to deny loans to applicants who would have paid exactly as agreed. This type of error can be offset by liberalizing the granting of credit, which increases the probability of including unsatisfactory borrowers. In the simplest terms, the bank's loan application evaluation system should achieve an acceptable trade-off of losses due to default and opportunity losses due to the rejection of borrowers who would have paid satisfactorily.

CREDIT EVALUATION SYSTEMS

We have discussed what might be called *judgmental credit analysis.* Here we summarize that system and describe in detail the alternative credit scoring system mentioned earlier and known as *statistical* or *empirical credit analysis.*

Judgmental Credit Analysis

The judgmental system of consumer credit analysis relies on the consumer loan officer's experience and insight when appraising a borrower's ability and willingness to repay. This evaluation is similar to the evaluation of a business loan at perhaps a lower level of sophistication. As in commercial lending, the consumer loan officer also must assess the applicant's character, use of funds, primary source of repayment, and any secondary or collateral sources of repayment.

In the judgmental method of credit analysis, character can be evaluated from the applicant's credit history and from the degree of dependability demonstrated through length and consistency of employment, length and type of residence, apparent sincerity, and other factors. The loan officer must be as objective as possible and, under the ECOA, must not apply subjective values or personal biases. In using judgmental systems, the ECOA prohibits taking into direct account the applicant's age, although the lender may consider age as a factor in the applicant's future income because age usually is a determinant of time to retirement and life expectancy. Prospective retirement and life expectancy are germane when setting loan maturity.

The applicant's income is almost always the primary source of the repayment of consumer loans. Income, as noted earlier, must be adequate in relation to the borrower's debts and other financial obligations. The loan officer must also evaluate secondary sources of repayment and establish the present and probable future value of collateral offered.

Empirical Credit Analysis

Empirical consumer credit analysis, referred to earlier as *credit scoring,* assigns point values to various applicant characteristics. The points are added up to award the applicant a numerical score, which is then compared with a predetermined accept-reject score, and credit is denied to those whose scores are below this level. An example of one bank's credit scoring system is given in Table 12.5. Note that each applicant characteristic used in a scoring system is weighted to have greater or less effect than other characteristics. For example, ''Time with present employer'' may have more influence than ''Own or

TABLE 12.5   Sample Credit Scoring System Characteristics and Weights

	Points		Points
1. Own or rent principal residence		e. Loan only	10
a. Owns/buying	40	f. None given	10
b. Rents	8	g. No answer	10
c. No answer	8	6. Major credit card/dept. store	
d. Other	25	a. Major CC(s) and department	
2. Time at present address		store(s)	40
a. Under 6 months	12	b. Major CC(s) only	40
b. 6 months–2 years	15	c. Department store(s) only	30
c. 2 years–$6\frac{1}{2}$ years	22	d. None	10
d. Over $6\frac{1}{2}$	35	7. Finance company reference	
e. No answer	12	a. One	15
3. Time with present employer		b. Two or more	10
a. Under $1\frac{1}{2}$ years	12	c. None	5
b. $1\frac{1}{2}$–3 years	15	d. No answer	10
c. 3 years–$5\frac{1}{2}$ years	25	8. Income	
d. Over $5\frac{1}{2}$ years	48	a. $0–15,000	5
e. Retired	48	b. $15,000–25,000	15
f. Unemployed with alimony/child		c. $25,000–40,000	30
support/public assistance	25	d. Over $40,000	50
g. Homemaker	25	9. Monthly payments	
h. Unemployed–no public assistance	12	a. $10–200	35
i. No answer	12	b. $200–500	25
4. Applicant's age		c. Over $500	10
a. Under 45 years	4	d. No payments	45
b. 45 years or older	20	e. No answer	10
c. No answer	4	10. Derogatory ratings	
5. Banking reference		a. No investigation	0
a. Checking and savings	60	b. No record	0
b. Checking	40	c. Two or more derogatory	−20
c. Savings	40	d. One derogatory	0
d. Loan and checking and/or	30	e. All positive ratings	15
savings			

rent principal residence.'' Under the ECOA, such systems cannot use race, color, religion, national origin, or immigration status.

Unlike judgmental systems, empirical systems of analysis can consider age, but only as a positive factor. In congressional testimony on the ECOA, it was determined that most creditors find that creditworthiness increases with age, and to prohibit the use of age in credit scoring systems would reduce the points usually awarded to older applicants. However, for credit scoring systems using age, the ECOA requires ''a demonstrably and statistically sound empirically derived credit system.'' There should be no age penalty for elderly applicants. When using age as an attribute of the applicant, Regulation B requires that credit scoring systems do the following:

1. Be based on data from an appropriate sample of creditors' applicants.
2. Separate creditworthy from noncreditworthy applicants ''at a statistically significant rate.''
3. Be periodically reevaluated as to their ability to predict good versus bad loans.

The appeal of a credit scoring system is that its allegedly pure objectivity precludes discriminatory evaluation of credit applications. However, this system requires highly sophisticated statistical tools, which make it expensive to derive and to revalidate periodically. The derivation is based on multivariate statistical methods of either multiple regression or a technique known as *multiple discriminant analysis* (MDA). This latter technique is an especially good solution to the credit scoring problem.

The objective of credit scoring is to predict from applicant characteristics whether a borrower is a good (creditworthy) or bad (not creditworthy) risk. MDA determines the statistical importance of each characteristic and how the characteristics can be combined to distinguish bad from good.

The statistical concept of MDA can be illustrated graphically. Figure 12.2 shows a three-dimensional diagram of a simple credit scoring system with only two applicant characteristics—''time with present employer'' on the Y-axis and ''income'' on the X-axis. In reality, credit scoring systems use as many as 10 to 15 characteristics. Unfortunately, they cannot be illustrated like the system in Figure 12.2 because each characteristic requires its own dimension; that is, 10 characteristics would require 10 dimensions to plot! The profiles of both bad and good past borrowers are plotted in two dimensions in Figure 12.2, with little ''o's'' designating bad and ''•'s'' designating good. The boundaries of each group are drawn to enclose a specified proportion of related points, such as 98 percent. Notice that the boundary enclosing 98 percent of one group also encloses a small proportion of the other group. Now we draw a straight line through the points at which the group boundaries intersect and project the line to the Z-axis. This is the line, condensed into a Z *score,* which best separates the bad group points from the good ones. Also, the bad and good group points themselves are projected onto the Z-axis, where they form frequency distributions of their Z scores. These distributions overlap, indicating the existence of a few bad borrowers in the good borrowers' group (Type 1 error) and a few good borrowers among the bad borrowers' group (Type 2 error). The cutoff Z score can be adjusted toward the origin in Figure 12.2 to liberalize credit granting. This adjustment would reduce the elimination of good borrowers but would also increase the acceptance of bad borrowers. Adjusting further away from the origin would reduce the acceptance of bad borrowers but would also eliminate more good borrowers.

The credit scoring system illustrated in Figure 12.2 combines the two characteristic profiles of good and bad borrowers into simple numbers. The line projected to the Z-axis

FIGURE 12.2   Illustration of a Credit Scoring System

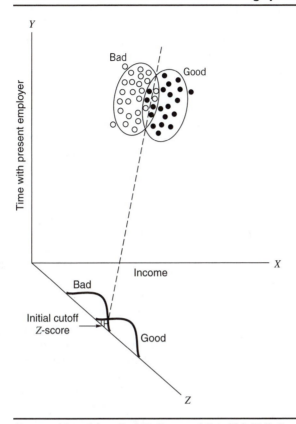

(SOURCE: Adapted from Paul E. Green and Donald S. Tull, *Research for Marketing Decisions.* Englewood Cliffs, N.J.: Prentice-Hall, 1970.)

that best discriminates between good and bad borrowers implicitly assigns unique weights to each of the two characteristics.

Statistically derived credit scoring systems have two technical flaws that are commonly cited. First, the borrower data used are historical and might be obsolete in detecting current predictors of creditworthiness. Second, the data consist of only those loan applications that have been accepted and omit applications that have been rejected. There can never be an actual record of the creditworthiness of rejected applications.

Judgmental versus Empirical Systems

In comparing the effectiveness of judgmental and credit scoring empirical systems for evaluating consumer loan applications, it is important to consider their ability to predict the creditworthiness of an applicant.[3] If creditworthiness can usually be predicted, the bank is protected against abnormal losses on its loans and is assured of a dependable flow of payments of interest and principal. However, there are other factors to consider in this

---

[3] A good reference on this topic is Gary G. Chandler and John Y. Coffman, ''A Comparative Analysis of Empirical versus Judgmental Credit Evaluation,'' *Journal of Retail Banking* (September 1979), pp. 15–26.

comparison. Perhaps equally important is management's control over the process of granting credit. Control factors such as consistency and objectivity are important to the bank's reputation and to its obligation to comply with laws and regulations.

Both systems are capable of using the same applicant characteristics. However, credit scoring assigns weights to each characteristic and reflects a hierarchy of their significance. In other words, credit scoring consistently weighs each characteristic according to its statistical importance in relation to other characteristics. Judgmental systems are subject to variation of the hierarchy of significance and, in addition, may consider certain intangible factors that cannot be quantified. Credit scoring considers only characteristics that historically have been associated with creditworthiness, whereas judgmental systems may use other factors, some of which may be contrary to regulations.

Credit scoring systems consider the multitude of creditworthiness characteristics simultaneously. Judgmental systems cannot do this because of the processing limitations of the human mind. Loan officers probably weight the information they do use differently from one applicant to the next.

The volume of credit granted and the amount of loan losses are difficult to control under judgmental credit evaluation. Control requires an explicit consumer loan policy that describes credit standards. Policy statements that refer to the many possible relevant characteristics of consumers are difficult to convey and to monitor. As a result, policy tends to be carried out inconsistently across consumer credit officers. Credit scoring, on the other hand, removes all issues of policy interpretation.

Judgmental methods of evaluation are better able to take into account present and future changes in economic conditions. An experienced analyst should be able to incorporate significant changes in the environment quickly in predicting a loan applicant's future creditworthiness. Credit scoring systems usually are less effective when major environmental changes are occurring. At such times, they suffer from the fact that they are based on customer data from an unrepresentative period in the past.

In practice, many banks use a combination of judgmental and credit scoring systems. Credit scoring isolates clearly noncreditworthy and clearly creditworthy applicants. The applicants that fall between these groups are then subjected to further information inquiries and to judgmental evaluation. For example, all applicants scoring below X are rejected, all scoring Y (higher than X) and above are granted credit, and all scoring between X and Y are evaluated further.

Finally, statistical credit scoring is expanding rapidly, even among small institutions. The primary reason is the tendency for institutions to view consumer lending in portfolio terms. They conceive of it as a statistical procedure in which losses are assured but are highly predictable. This precludes making extremely fine distinctions between borrowers. Thus, a crucial attraction of statistical scoring models is their ''automatic'' quality that fosters a high rate of loan production without large lending staffs.

REPORTING THE CREDIT DECISION

The final step in the consumer lending process is notifying the borrower of the decision. Of course, an affirmative decision by the bank is simply conveyed along with actual credit to the customer's deposit account or other means granting the customer access to funds.

If the loan application is unsuccessful, the bank is required under the Fair Credit Reporting Act of 1971 to report the denial of credit to the applicant. The bank either must provide the applicant with the reasons for the denial or must advise the applicant of his or her right to a statement of the principal reason or reasons. If the denial is based wholly or partly on information from a credit bureau, the bank must provide the name and address of the bureau. The bank does not have to reveal anything the credit bureau's report contains.

The Fair Credit Reporting Act enables consumers to trace the reasons for the denial of credit so that they can refute or challenge the accuracy of unfavorable information. The consumer is given the right to full disclosure of the contents of his or her credit bureau file.

BANKS AND CREDIT CARD FINANCE

Growth of Bank Credit Cards

In recent years, lending associated with bank credit cards has been the fastest growth area in consumer lending. Bank credit cards first became popular over 30 years ago. At that time, individual banks issued cards to their existing customers and recruited local merchants who agreed to accept them from the customers. Every day, participating merchants presented the bank with sales vouchers signed by their card-using customers. The merchants' bank accounts then received immediate credit, less the bank's discount. The arrangement provided benefits to all three parties. The bank collected fees derived from discounting merchants' sales vouchers and charged interest on cardholder balances that were carried beyond the grace, or free, period of 25 days or so. Cardholders enjoyed unquestioned credit from participating merchants, avoided the burden of carrying cash for large purchases, and did not have the hassle of uncertain acceptance of written checks. Merchants were pleased to expand their sales appeal to a growing pool of cardholders.

The local bank credit card plan had serious drawbacks, however. The card's usefulness was restricted to a circle of participating merchants in the card banks' market areas. In addition, bank card plans proliferated among competing banks, forcing merchants either to choose one plan to the exclusion of others or to operate with perhaps several parallel systems. These drawbacks were overcome in the late 1960s when two national credit card plans emerged to replace the local bank cards. These two plans—VISA and MasterCard—distribute their cards through a network of regional issuing banks, which, in turn, enlist smaller agent banks that further distribute the cards. Issuing banks retain control of the approval of new card applicants, including establishment of the credit limit assigned to each applicant. The issuing banks (not their agent banks) extend revolving credit to cardholders who do not wish to pay their monthly statements in full within the due date. In addition, issuing banks collect merchants' fees and incur the costs associated with operating the card system.

The appeal of VISA and MasterCard to consumers is their worldwide acceptance. Cardholders can purchase an almost unlimited array of goods and services from merchants throughout the United States and in many foreign countries. Increasingly, large retail chains with their own credit card systems are accepting the two major bank cards in order to remain competitive. The VISA and MasterCard cards are not only a convenient form of consumer credit, but they are also a convenient form of payment. In this regard, national bank cards are as acceptable and effective as currency.

An important and complex feature of the national bank card systems is the worldwide communications credit record maintained on card users. If transactions exceed the merchant's *floor limit,* merchants call into their card-issuing bank on their automatic dial-up stations for credit authorizations on card users. The issuing bank accesses the card user's file through telecommunications lines to determine whether the proposed purchase would put the card user over his or her credit limit and whether the card has been canceled or reported lost or stolen. The worldwide character of this credit interchange system permits authorization within seconds on card users from distant issuing banks.

In the mid-1990s, there were over 6,000 credit card issuers in the United States and more than 600 million active accounts based on over 1 billion cards outstanding. However, banks represented less than two-thirds of the credit outstanding on card credits. Various nonbank cards exist and, in addition, pursuant to the Competitive Equality Banking Act of 1987 *credit card banks* were authorized, permitting nonbanks to issue VISA or MasterCard credit cards. Recent card issuers include huge corporations such as AT&T, Ford Motor Company, Sears, Prudential Insurance, General Electric, Amoco, and others. However, the largest credit card contingent is the subsidiary banks set up by bank holding companies to specialize in credit card lending. At year-end 1996, these credit card banks accounted for more than 60 percent of credit card outstandings at all banks. In addition, these banks securitized one-half of their outstanding balances of credit card loans.

Issues in Credit Card Pricing

The pricing and other features of the two bank credit card programs, VISA and MasterCard, are similar. Merchant discount fees generally range from 1 to 6 percent, with high-volume merchants paying lower percentages. It is doubtful, however, that banks' revenue from merchant discounts exceeds the cost of providing immediate cash against merchant sales, absorbing credit risk, and performing monthly billing services.

In the past, the usury laws of many states governed what banks could charge consumers for the use of credit cards. Until recently, these laws prohibited banks from charging consumers annual fees for the use of their cards. In most states, banks were prohibited from levying a finance charge on card users who made full payment on their card purchases within a *grace period,* usually 25 days after billing.[4] Finally, usury statutes limited interest charges on revolving or unpaid balances.

As a practical matter, these price regulations were eliminated by the U.S. Supreme Court's *Marquette National Bank v. First of Omaha Service Corporation* (439 U.S. 99) decision in 1978. In this seminal case, the Court held that bank interest rates were restricted by the state in which the bank is located, not the state in which the customer is located. As a result, banks set up the card operations in states without interest rate ceilings.

The absence of an interest rate ceiling in South Dakota attracted the largest bank credit operation in the world when Citibank located its credit card operation there in 1980. By operating from a state that has no usury ceiling, Citicorp became free to set its own rate for its card users everywhere. Chase Manhattan Bank made a similar move to Delaware in 1981 when that state removed pricing statutes affecting credit cards.

Periodically, bank credit card pricing comes under fire because of what some observers perceive to be unfair pricing practices. This criticism often stems from the observation

---

[4] The grace period gives card users who make purchases early in the monthly cycle the use of the bank's funds for almost two months. This free period does not apply to card users who make partial payments on their outstanding balances; in cases of partial payment, retrospective finance charges are applied to the whole balance.

FIGURE 12.3   Profitability at Credit Card Banks, 1985–1996

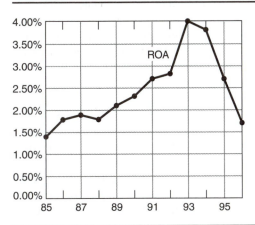

that interest rates on credit card outstanding balances do not decline when general market rates of interest decline. The most recent threat of an interest rate ceiling occurred in late 1991 when the President of the United States suggested that such a ceiling would make credit available more widely. In reality, bank credit card operations do appear to be highly profitable. We can gauge credit card profitability by looking at the profitability of the 40 large credit card banks. On average, 84 percent of their assets were credit card loans in 1996. Figure 12.3 shows the return on assets for these banks during 1985–1996. As shown, recent ROA figures have fallen well below 2 percent, in large measure because of increased provisioning for losses. Charge-off rates have risen quickly since 1994. As a basis for comparison, banks as a group do acceptably well if they earn 1.0 to 1.25 percent on total assets after taxes.

Highly educated and high-income consumers are most likely not to have revolving credit card balances, thus avoiding payment of finance charges. They use their bank card for its payment convenience, not as a means of gaining access to credit. As a result, banks must rely on income from their revolving credit card users to subsidize the free services given to nonrevolving users.

In sum, banks in many states are forced to give away credit card services to consumers who are most able to pay for them. In the interest of more equitable pricing, most banks now charge annual user fees or per-transaction fees. Another possibility is that banks will levy finance charges from the date of purchase. The effect of these changes is not clear. In general, such changes would probably reduce credit card use by nonrevolving users who do not presently pay monthly interest for card services.

Debit Cards

In the late 1990s, the use of debit cards was beginning to grow. Debit cards electronically debit the consumer's deposit account at the time of purchase and credit the merchant's account. Both types of cards—the credit card and the debit card—serve as a means of payment as readily as cash. However, debit cards have several efficiencies that credit cards do not possess. With debit cards, card users forego check writing, card-issuing banks need not prepare monthly billings, and, in the simplest debit card system, credit risk is eliminated. If enough consumers substitute debit cards for credit cards, ultimately banks' credit card lending might be reduced. It is likely, however, that banks will offer to tie debit cards to personal lines of credit in the form of overdraft protection. With this arrangement, if the consumer's debit card-based purchases exceed the funds in the consumer's bank account, a prearranged line of credit will be triggered. The size of the credit line for overdraft protection for a given consumer presumably will be identical to the credit limit on a credit card issued to that consumer. In either case, the bank will be exposed to the same risk of default. The total effect on the volume of consumer credit extended by banks remains to be seen.

It is also uncertain whether the two national credit card associations will dominate future debit card plans. Despite their success in gaining the worldwide acceptance of merchants, these associations are accepted reluctantly by their issuing banks. These banks would prefer to preserve more of their own identity instead of subordinating it to the MasterCard or VISA names. They also are reluctant to share with their local bank competitors the electronic transaction networks that will undoubtedly be the heart of future debit card plans.

REAL ESTATE LOANS

By far, the largest category of lending to consumers is for the purchase, development, and construction of real estate properties. Banks lend more for these purposes than any other type of lender.

In the third quarter of 1997, U.S. banks held $1,227 billion in loans secured by real estate of which $612 billion were one- to four-family residential mortgages outstanding, $96 billion were home equity loans, and $336 billion were commercial real estate loans, all exclusive of mortgages held by bank trust departments. Thus, one- to four-family residential properties account for one-half of bank mortgage loans. Mortgages on single-family residences make up most of these loans. Many banks appear to avoid permanent mortgage lending on large apartments and condominiums, preferring to leave such loans to life insurance companies or pension funds. Banks view apartments and condominiums as high risk and as requiring an imprudently large concentration of funds. To the extent that banks make such mortgages, they tend to be of relatively short maturity and at low loan-value ratios.

The $1,227 billion mortgage debt held by banks in 1997 included $360 billion in mortgage-backed securities. Altogether, loans secured by real estate accounted for 42 percent of total bank loans outstanding of $2,904 billion. However, the significance of mortgages in bank loan portfolios differed with the size of the bank. For large banks with assets of over $10 billion, mortgages represented 35 percent of loans; they also represented 60 percent of the average loans of small banks with assets of up to $1 billion. However, for some small banks, particularly those located in developing suburban locations, mortgages often constituted as much as 80 percent of their loan portfolios.

Residential mortgage loan originations fluctuate with the volume of new home construction and especially with the level of mortgage interest rates. Table 12.6 demonstrates that originations flourished in 1992 and 1993, when rates declined. As discussed later in this chapter, many mortgage loans are not held permanently by their originators. For example, mortgage bankers operate on turnover and quickly sell the mortgages they originate

TABLE 12.6   One- to Four-Family Mortgage Origination Activity, 1989–1994

	1989	1990	1991	1992	1993	1994
One- to four-family mortgage originations ($billions)	483	453	540	825	800	710
Mortgage interest rates (%)						
Fixed	10.12%	10.13%	9.24%	8.36%	7.97%	7.31%
Adjustable	8.80%	8.36%	7.10%	5.48%	5.16%	5.43%
Refinancings (percent of total)	19	16	30	38	38	20
Adjustable rate (percent of loans closed)	39	28	23	23	17	14

in the secondary market. At times, such as the 1992–1993 period, mortgage originations include a large number of refinancings as mortgagors pay off their old mortgages and simultaneously refinance their homes at lower interest rates. As shown in Table 12.6, refinancings surged during the low-rate period of 1991–1993.

The fraction of mortgages originated on an adjustable-rate basis reflects mortgagors' interest rate expectations. As shown in Table 12.6, when mortgagors perceive that interest rates are relatively high, they prefer adjustable-rate mortgages. At perceived low interest rates, they prefer fixed-rate mortgages.

Legal Restrictions

National banks must conform to the requirements of 12 U.S. Code 371 governing real estate loans. This section of the code considers a loan to be a real estate loan if it is secured either by a lien (mortgage, deed of trust, or other) or by a leasehold agreement on the subject real estate and if its original maturity is at least 60 months. The code requires the following:

1. A loan on unimproved real estate must not exceed 66.67 percent of the property's appraised value.
2. A loan on real estate improved by a building must not exceed 90 percent of the property's appraised value.
3. Real estate loans generally should be fully amortized within 30 years.
4. Total real estate loans must not exceed the bank's capital plus unimpaired surplus or the bank's time and savings deposits, whichever is greater.
5. Total second mortgages plus the amount unpaid on all prior liens must not exceed 20 percent of the bank's capital plus unimpaired surplus.

The loan-to-value restrictions set forth in the code do not apply to government-insured or government-guaranteed mortgages or to privately insured mortgages.

Government-Backed Mortgages

Many residential mortgages held by banks are *conventional* loans, meaning that they are not insured or guaranteed by a government agency. However, a growing proportion are not conventional and are supported by government agencies. The Federal Housing Administration (FHA) insures and the Veterans Administration (VA) guarantees payment of principal and interest on certain qualifying residential mortgages originated by banks and other private lenders. FHA or VA backing is available for loans that meet certain standards, set periodically by the agencies involved, including the following:

1. Maximum loan-value ratio.
2. Interest rate restriction.
3. Maximum loan size.
4. Minimum down payment.

Residences that are subject to FHA- and VA-backed mortgages must also meet certain construction and design standards. These features reduce the risk of the subject mortgages, make them more attractive to lending institutions, and thereby increase the flow of mortgage funds. These same features also make it possible for lenders to accumulate a bundle of guaranteed or insured, standardized mortgages for sale either to larger institutional investors, the Federal National Mortgage Association (FNMA, or "Fannie Mae"), or to the public by means of the Government National Mortgage Association (GNMA, or "Ginnie Mae"). The ability to package standardized loans helps banks to overcome the lack of marketability of small-denomination, single loans whose characteristics would otherwise be highly dissimilar.

Secondary Markets

The ability to sell their mortgages helps banks and S&Ls to avoid the problem of illiquidity associated with borrowing from short-term depositors and lending long term. Fannie Mae, a privately financed and managed association, developed the first resale market for mortgages. Although Fannie Mae was initially authorized to purchase and sell only FHA mortgages, it has become active in purchasing VA and, beginning in the 1970s, conventional loans. Fannie Mae does not create a pure secondary market, because it deals only in mortgages on which forward purchase commitments have been made. Banks and other institutions bid for Fannie Mae purchase commitments of a certain amount, and the commitment price is established at auction. Successful bidders acquire a commitment from Fannie Mae that assures them of a resale market for a bundle of loans to be made anytime up to the expiration date of the commitment.

Ginnie Mae is a government agency established in 1968 under the Department of Housing and Urban Development. Ginnie Mae shares with Fannie Mae the objective of making mortgages more liquid. Ginnie Mae developed the mortgage-backed *pass-through* security on which it guarantees the payment of principal and interest. To create a pass-through security issue, Ginnie Mae acquires pools of FHA and VA mortgages from banks and other lenders and uses the pools to back its securities. Payments to Ginnie Mae securities holders are passed through from payments made on the underlying pool of mortgages. Ginnie Mae's guarantee makes its securities attractive to investors who would not otherwise invest in the mortgage market. All of this activity increases the flow of money ultimately available to mortgage lenders.

The Federal Home Loan Mortgage Corporation (FHLMC, or "Freddie Mac"), created in 1970, accomplishes for conventional mortgages what Ginnie Mae accomplished for FHA and VA mortgages. Like Ginnie Mae, Freddie Mac sells participations in mortgage pools and guarantees payment of interest and principal. But unlike Ginnie Mae, Freddie Mac deals in conventional mortgages and has truly advanced the marketability of these nongovernment-supported loans. Freddie Mac does, however, require private insurance on most mortgages in which it deals.

Among them, the three federal credit agencies—FNMA, GNMA, and FHLMC—are the biggest buyers of mortgages. These agencies buy mortgages and pool them either to sell shares in the pool or to issue securities that are backed by the pool as collateral.

In addition to the three mortgage associations, there exists a substantial interinstitutional market. Banks, S&Ls, and mutual savings banks are able to sell bundles of mortgages to larger banks, insurance companies, and other institutional investors.

During the 1980s, a huge secondary market developed based on mortgage-backed securities and derivatives of these securities. The basic mortgage-backed market consisted of over $1.2 trillion in marketable securities in the mid-1990s and was continuing to grow. In Chapter 10 we discussed the investment properties of option-embedded securities such as mortgage-derivative securities. We confine the discussion here to the basic mortgage instrument and the credit or underwriting standards observed by mortgage lenders.

Credit Standards

Much of the impetus for developing the huge mortgage-backed securities market was the 1980s environment of turbulent interest rates and soaring costs of interest-sensitive bank funds. In this threatening environment, banks continued to originate mortgages but deemphasized the holding of mortgages, selling them whenever they could. In essence, the secondary mortgage market produced a separation of mortgage origination, which is a regional activity, from mortgage funding, which has become national. As a result, the marketability of mortgages has become so important to banks that their mortgage loan standards increasingly call for conformance to the standards of the secondary market. The standards of the national mortgage associations and of institutional investors, described earlier, profoundly influence banks' approach to mortgage lending.

Table 12.7 lists the primary credit underwriting standards recently observed by Freddie Mac, Fannie Mae, and the private mortgage insurance companies. The standards listed in Table 12.7 should not be viewed in absolute terms; a particularly favorable ratio may offset an unfavorable ratio. For example, lenders might accept a ratio of housing expense to owner's income that significantly exceeds 25 percent if the loan-value ratio is well below the maximum listed. This specific relationship is common in areas such as California, where housing values rose much faster than home buyers' incomes. If a home buyer's previous home has appreciated dramatically in price, he or she will probably be able to produce considerable equity for the purchase of the next home. In this case, a favorable loan-value ratio of 70 or 60 percent would offset an abnormally large housing-expense-income ratio of 40 percent or more.

Adjustable-Rate Mortgages

The standards listed in Table 12.7 are generally tied to traditional fixed-interest-rate and fixed-monthly-payment mortgages. Beginning in April 1981, however, legislators and federal regulators authorized wide use of the adjustable rate mortgage (ARM). Since then, during periods when market interest rates have been abnormally high, as in the early 1980s, ARMs have tended to dominate mortgage financing. During low-rate periods, such

TABLE 12.7   Credit Underwriting Standards for Mortgage Resale Organizations (1–4 family residential properties: effective 1993)

Standard	FHLMC	FNMA	Private Mortgage Insurance Co.
Maximum loan amount[a]	1 unit $203,150	1 unit $203,150	No maximum
	2 units $259,850	2 units $259,850	
	3 units $314,100	3 units $314,100	
	4 units $390,400	4 units $390,400	
Loan–value ratio			
1. Primary res. fixed	95%	95%	95%
ARM	90%	95%	95%
Refinance	90%		
2. Secondary res.	80%		
Refinance	70%		
3. Nonowner occupied	Not accepted	70%	90%
Down payment minimum	5%	5%	5% cash or land equity
ARM	Accepted with (1) Annual rate cap (1% or 2%) or (2) life rate cap (normal, 6%)[b]	Accepts full range of ARMs. Standard is 2% annual and 6% life rate cap	Acceptability based on adjusted rate index, frequency of adjustment, and payment increase
Maximum ratio of housing expense to gross income[c]	25–28%	28%	25–30%
Maximum monthly ratio of debt payment to income	33–36%	33–36%	33–38%

[a] Limits for FHLMC mortgages are 50% higher in Alaska, Guam, Hawaii and the Virgin Islands.

[b] If the loan–value ratio is greater than 75%, the borrower must qualify for the maximum rate in year 2.

[c] Expense includes principal, interest, taxes, and homeowners' association dues.

SOURCE: FHLMC, FNMA, Bank Administration Institute.

as the one beginning in 1986, the ARM has all but disappeared as mortgagors have sought to lock in low fixed rates. When interest rates rise, as from the 1986 low, however, and the difference between adjustable and fixed rates widens, as it did in 1987 and 1988, borrowers shift quickly to ARMs with the expectation that interest rates will eventually fall again. In the late 1980s, a period of gently rising interest rates, banks and other lenders introduced attractive adjustable-rate pricing features to lure still more borrowers to ARMs.

By the end of the 1980s, borrowers were more knowledgeable about ARMs than they had been earlier in the decade. They needed to be more knowledgeable because lenders began to offer pricing structures with a dizzying menu of features, such as teaser rates, several adjustment period options, different margins, a variety of lifetime and periodic adjustment caps, and possible convertibility. *Teasers* are initial discounts that reduce monthly payments substantially, typically for the initial year. The rate adjustment period for ARMs is normally one year. Some lenders, however, offer three-year ARMs for which the rate is reset every third year. In a way, the three-year ARM is a compromise between the fixed-rate mortgage and the standard one-year ARM because its rate holds constant for a full three years.

Lenders may also vary the *margin,* defined as the amount added to the adjustment index (usually the one-year Treasury bill rate). A higher margin is sometimes used to offset the cost to the lender of a teaser rate. Lenders may also vary the adjustment caps offered on an ARM. A 2 percent cap (the one most often used) restricts the annual rate adjustment to 200 basis points. One percent caps are less frequently offered but are still common.

Lifetime rate caps restrict the amount that the interest rate can increase during the life of the loan. A lifetime cap of 6 percent is perhaps the most common. Lifetime interest rate ceilings will be used on all ARMs in the future in conformance with the Competitive Equality Banking Act of 1987.

An innovation introduced in 1987 was the convertible ARM. This type of ARM permits the borrower to convert an ARM to a fixed rate during a window in the life of the loan (e.g., between the second and fifth years). The major attraction of convertibility is the low cost of effectively refinancing, thereby avoiding the expense of paying the origination costs on a new mortgage after prepaying an old one.

The advantage of a wide variety of pricing features on ARMs is the flexibility it gives lenders and borrowers in tailoring the loan to the borrower's needs. For example, an initial discount (teaser) might be combined with a high margin to accommodate a young, low-income borrower who expects a rapid increase in earning power. On the other hand, this flexibility runs counter to the needs of the secondary market, which thrives on standardization. The federal agencies are particularly focused on creating a standardized ARM product that will develop market liquidity and be readily understood by the investor. By the end of the 1980s, however, numerous pools of ARMs had been securitized, and a deepening of the secondary market for ARMs seemed assured.

Nonresidential Mortgages

Bank mortgages are made on commercial properties, consisting primarily of shopping centers, business and professional (e.g., medical or dental) office buildings, warehouses, hotels and motels, restaurants, and other commercial structures. Many such mortgages are direct extensions of banks' regular relationships with commercial customers (e.g., mortgage financing of a warehouse for a manufacturer who is a regular working capital loan customer).

In comparison with residential lending, most commercial mortgage financing by banks has shorter maturities (10 to 15 years) and smaller loan-value ratios (60 to 70 percent). Unlike residential mortgages, commercial mortgages have been based on variable interest rates for several years; typical rates float above the bank's prime rate.

Construction Loans

Many commercial properties are permanently financed by nonbank lenders, especially life insurance companies and, to a lesser extent, private pension funds. Nevertheless, banks do a substantial volume of interim lending to finance the construction of these properties, as well as residential projects. Construction financing is a relatively high-risk activity. It often involves a large loan commitment over a period of time long enough to cover the planning, building, and final acceptance by owners or permanent lenders. Construction time is subject to many contingencies, including poor weather, materials shortages, and labor stoppages; on large projects, the construction time may be several years. In addition, faulty construction and underestimation of costs are common. Finally, building contractors tend to be very modestly capitalized in relation to the value of their construction projects and are, therefore, less cushioned against insolvency.

Construction lending can be classified into two types: loans for which a permanent takeout commitment exists and loans without a takeout. In situations with a takeout commitment, a long-term lender such as a life insurance company agrees to advance permanent funding on completion and acceptance of the construction. Interim construction loans usually require regular supervision, including site inspections, commitment takedowns against construction progress, and assurance that subcontractor and other claimants are satisfied. Long-term takeout lenders usually are not equipped to offer these services.

Banks must treat a construction loan that is not backed by a takeout commitment as they would treat a high-risk working capital loan. In a sense, the process of converting construction materials into a finished product is similar to a typical manufacturing process. However, a collateral position is frequently awkward. Contractors must usually post a performance bond, and the project collateral is normally subject to the claim of the bond's underwriter.

Because of their risks, construction loans are priced above most bank commercial loans. Commitment fees are 1 to 1.5 percent (instead of the 0.5 percent typical on commercial loans), and loan interest rates float at 2 percent or more over the prime rate.

CONSUMER LOAN LOSSES AND THE BANKRUPTCY CODE

Historically, consumer loans tend to have the highest loss rates of all types of loans during periods of economic strength such as the mid-1990s. The data in Table 12.8 show that delinquency rates on consumer loans were mostly above those on loans for business purposes. However, in Table 12.8 consumer loan delinquency rates show greater stability in times of recession, as in 1991, and economic strength, as in 1996. Delinquencies on business types of loans are significantly more unstable. Still, banks must make a determined

TABLE 12.8   Delinquencies by Type of Loan

	Delinquency Rate	
Type of Loan	**1991**	**1996**
Credit card	5.3%	4.6%
Other consumer	3.6%	3.1%
Residential real estate	3.1%	2.4%
Commercial real estate	12.0%	3.2%
Commercial and industrial	6.0%	2.0%

SOURCE: Profits and Balance Sheet Developments at U.S. Commercial Banks in 1996," *Federal Reserve Bulletin*, June 1997, p. 475.

effort to try to recover principal and interest from seriously delinquent consumer borrowers.

Most consumers work conscientiously to stay current in repaying their loans. However, consumers who are under severe financial pressure can deter the collection effort of banks and other creditors by filing for bankruptcy under the Federal Bankruptcy Code. The code permits consumers to eliminate part of their indebtedness without being rendered destitute; that is, consumers are permitted to retain certain assets that will help them achieve financial rehabilitation.

BANKRUPTCY REFORM

For most of the twentieth century, bankruptcy procedures in the United States were governed by bankruptcy laws written in 1898. In 1978, Congress passed the Bankruptcy Reform Act, which modernized and consolidated into one consistent code the many amendments and court rulings since 1898. In part, the 1978 law attempted to remove the stigma of bankruptcy by identifying persons filing for bankruptcy as *debtors* instead of *bankrupts*. A stated objective of the Bankruptcy Reform Act was to ''better protect the American consumer and the unfortunate debtor.'' This objective was provided for in the new code by setting forth a generous list of debtor assets that are exempt from the claims of creditors when the debtor files for bankruptcy. This provision is intended to make it more feasible for financially distressed debtors to repay their debts voluntarily over time.

Two parts of the Bankruptcy Code provide relief for debtors while protecting certain of their assets. The first part, under Chapter 8 of the code, provides for liquidation of the debtor's assets to service debts. The second part, providing debtor relief, under Chapter 13, sets forth procedures for repayment planning based on the debtor's future earnings (the *wage earner plan*).

Chapter 8

Chapter 8 provides for conversion of the debtor's assets to cash and the pro rata distribution of the cash proceeds to creditors. The cash distribution results in a formal discharge of the debts. Certain debts, including taxes, alimony, child support, funds received through embezzlement, or debts incurred through misrepresentation, cannot be discharged. In relation to the previous outdated code, the new code significantly liberalizes the list of protected debtor's assets that are exempted from liquidation. These exempted, subsistence-related assets include a portion of home equity, a motor vehicle, and a limited amount of jewelry, household goods, funds in a retirement account, and tools of trade. Moreover, debtors may choose between federal and state exemption provisions, selecting the more favorable option. The liberal exemption of household goods in California, for example, is quite favorable to debtors in comparison with the federal provisions. However, most states have opted out of the federal statute by setting their own—typically lower—exemption levels.

Chapter 13

Chapter 13 provides for debtors to retain all of their assets while repaying their debts out of future earnings on the basis of a schedule approved by the court. Initially, the repayment schedule is distributed to all creditors who file a proof of claim with the courts. Secured creditors vote on the debtor's repayment plan. Unsecured creditors may not vote, but the value they receive under Chapter 13 must not be less than what they would receive under Chapter 8 liquidation, as estimated by the court. Unfortunately, the liberal asset exemptions of Chapter 8 usually result in no distribution at all to unsecured creditors. As a result, the repayment plans submitted to the creditors and the court under Chapter 13 often provide little or no payment to unsecured creditors. This loophole is highly controversial and appears to deny these creditors a fair remedy.

Once the debtor has paid off the creditors according to the plan, the court formally grants a discharge. The new code liberalizes the old code's wage earner plan concept by extending it to self-employed persons and by permitting unrestricted joint filings of married couples. Under another section of the code, Chapter 12, many of the concepts discussed earlier that protect consumers are extended to businesses. In order to file for Chapter 13 bankruptcy reorganization, a debtor must meet a ceiling amount of $350,000.

Creditors are prohibited or *stayed* from taking direct action against a debtor who has filed for bankruptcy or against his or her property. For example, if a borrower has filed for bankruptcy, a bank cannot use a setoff against its borrower's account, nor can the bank foreclose on a mortgage or repossess an automobile it financed for the debtor.

CRITICISM AND REFORM OF THE 1978 BANKRUPTCY CODE

Bankers contend that the 1978 Bankruptcy Code so liberalized bankruptcy procedures that it actually encouraged debtors to use the bankruptcy court to abandon their debts. In the opinion of one banker, "Congress may have inadvertently created a law by which most people in the United States could lawfully walk out on their debts while keeping all of their property." The rise of personal bankruptcy filings nationally following the effective date of the new code on October 1, 1979, seems to support this contention. The revised code, combined with the 1981–1982 recession, appeared to drive bankruptcy filings to a peak of 316,000 in 1981. By 1984, as the economy strengthened, bankruptcies fell to 284,000. However, they grew sharply after that, to a record 944,000 filings in 1991.

Statistical studies have demonstrated that of consumers who filed for a Chapter 8 set-aside of their debts, about 20 percent had the financial ability to repay their debts over several years.[5] In fairness, these consumers were candidates for servicing their debts under a court-approved Chapter 13 repayment schedule. Such abuses led to further reform of the code in 1984. One of the 1984 reforms—the "substantial abuse" test—allows the bankruptcy court to dismiss its earlier granting of Chapter 8 relief when it finds that a debtor's current income and expenses do permit the debtor to service his or her debts. However, the court cannot consider projections of the debtor's future income. Another reform simply lowers the amounts of property the debtor can exempt under Chapter 8.

The banking industry contends that bankruptcy proceedings are overdue for additional reform to provide better statistical information, simplify procedures for creditors, and eliminate growing abuses by debtors. One study concluded that about one-third of

---

[5] Credit Research Center, "Consumer's Right to Bankruptcy: Origins and Effect," and "Costs and Benefits of Personal Bankruptcy" (West Lafayette, Ind.: Credit Research Center, 1981).

bankruptcy petitions in a large western city had a possibly fraudulent basis. Reform proposals emphasize the need to provide creditors with more timely and complete notice and expedited procedures and to encourage greater use of Chapter 13 reorganizations in place of Chapter 8 liquidations.[6]

Bankers point out that the costs of writing off bad consumer debts must be passed along to other consumers. Otherwise, it is argued, banks could not afford to continue with their consumer lending programs. Another lesson is implied in the profusion of bankruptcies. That lesson is that bankers must realistically evaluate a consumer's ability to pay, and they must avoid making easy credit available to marginal borrowers.

CONSUMER REGULATION AND COMPLIANCE

During the decade beginning in the late 1960s, Congress passed a comprehensive regulatory legislation package to protect consumers in their dealings with financial institutions. Table 12.9 describes the most significant regulations and laws included in this package. As described previously in this chapter, Regulation B (Equal Credit Opportunity) and the Fair Credit Reporting Act are vital considerations in the process of credit investigation and analysis. Regulation Z (Truth in Lending) has had such a significant impact on bank compliance efforts that it warrants separate discussion in a later section. Several regulations deal primarily with housing and mortgage matters and are relevant to the discussion of real estate lending earlier in this chapter.

Banks have developed intricate systems of internal controls to be sure that they comply with these regulations. These controls ensure that documentation required by the new regulations is produced, and they set up mechanisms to monitor functional compliance.

Most banks employ a compliance officer, who is responsible to senior management, to ensure that the bank's compliance program is effective. Large banks may have several compliance officers. Small banks usually assign the compliance function to an officer who carries conventional banking responsibilities as well. Compliance programs create a lot of expense for banks. However, noncompliance is potentially much more expensive, because it can lead to severe pecuniary penalties and even prison sentences for managers who knowingly fail to observe consumer regulations.

A bank's policies and procedures in relation to regulatory compliance are generally set forth in a compliance manual. This manual contains the bank's policy statement on compliance; detailed procedures, including instructions to employees on completing loan and consumer disclosure forms; and instructions on the filing and retention of documents proving compliance. The compliance manual serves two basic purposes. First, its existence satisfies examiners who wish to see the bank's policies and procedures made explicit. Second, and probably more important, it serves as a control tool to instruct and inform bank personnel uniformly.

Truth in Lending

Originally passed by Congress in 1968, the Truth in Lending Act and the associated Regulation Z, enforced by the Federal Reserve System, represent a major compliance burden

---

[6] George Cleland, ''ABA Attacks a Growth Industry—Bankruptcy,'' *ABA Banking Journal,* Vol. 84 (May 1992), p. 14.

TABLE 12.9   Regulations and Laws Pertaining to Consumer Lending

Regulation AA (Consumer Inquiries and Complaints)
   Sets forth procedures for investigating and processing complaints by a consumer in relation to the denial of credit. (Applies to state member banks.)

Regulation B (Equal Credit Opportunity)
   Prohibits discrimination against a credit applicant on the basis of race, sex, color, marital status, religion, age, receipt of public assistance, and national origin in any credit transaction.

Regulation BB (Community Reinvestment)
   Forbids the arbitrary consideration of geographic factors or redlining in granting credit within the financial institution's local community. Redlining consists of blanket refusal to grant credit within circumscribed (redlined) neighborhoods deemed by the bank to be in physical and economic decline.

Regulation C (Home Mortgage Disclosure)
   Details reporting requirements of geographical data on mortgages to enable regulators to detect redlining practices. The 1989 amendments to the Home Mortgage Disclosure Act expand disclosure requirements on the disposition of loan applications and on the race or national origin, gender, and annual income of loan applicants and borrowers.

1989 Amendments to Home Mortgage Disclosure Act
   Expand disclosure on the disposition of loan applications and on the race or origin, gender, and annual income of loan applicants and borrowers.

Regulation E (Electronic Funds Transfer)
   Limits consumer liability for unauthorized use of lost credit or debit cards. Controls issuance of cards and specifies information to be supplied to consumer in using electronic transfer devices.

Regulation Z (Truth in Lending)
   Requires that consumers be given meaningful and consistent information on the cost of credit. Certain nonprice information must also be disclosed.

Fair Housing Act
   Prohibits discrimination in housing and housing credit on the basis of race, color, religion, national origin, or sex. This act preceded passage of the Equal Credit Opportunity Act, which defined several additional bases of discrimination. The Fair Housing Act prohibits redlining housing credit.

Fair Credit Reporting Act
   Grants consumers access to their credit bureau records, and entitles them to check the source of information and its accuracy. Denials of credit by banks on the basis of credit bureau information must be reported to consumers.

Real Estate Settlement Procedures Act
   Requires detailed statement of settlement costs on real estate transactions and reporting of borrowers' rights in the granting of mortgage credit.

on banks. The Truth in Lending Act, like much consumer protection legislation, was prompted by what Congress considered to be abuses by creditors. Congress believed that banks and other lenders were not giving consumers enough information about credit. It thought that the terminology used by lenders varied too widely, causing confusion and poor borrowing decisions by consumers. The Truth in Lending Act was designed to standardize the methods of disclosing loan terms to creditors, so that consumers could effectively shop for the best deal on a loan among alternative lenders. The act emphasized disclosure of key credit information in straightforward terms by focusing on the *finance charge* and the *annual percentage rate* (APR).

The finance charge simply expresses the total dollar amount of the cost of credit. This total includes not only interest costs but also ancillary charges, such as points[7] or credit insurance premiums. In addition to the finance charge, the lender must disclose prepayment penalties, charges in the event that the borrower defaults, and any security interest taken on collateral.

The second crucial provision of the Truth in Lending Act specifies standard rules for determining the APR. The APR is the simple annual rate computed by the actuarial method. For example, the lender cannot represent the add-on rate used in installment contracts as the APR. Unlike the add-on rate, the APR must be computed in such a way that any declining loan balance outstanding is recognized. In the case of credit card or other revolving-type credit, the APR is the monthly percentage finance charge multiplied by 12. For example, if an open-ended credit plan charges 1.75 percent per month on the unpaid balance, the APR will be 21 percent.

In general, lenders must "clearly and conspicuously" disclose all material terms of the loan and must do so before the credit is extended. The Truth in Lending Act further regulates credit advertising. Most important, the lender cannot advertise one feature of its credit offer without stating other details, such as the means of determining the finance charge and the actual APR.

The Truth in Lending Act contains provisions for certain civil penalties to force compliance. Initially, an automatic $100 minimum civil penalty was imposed for violations.

As passed in 1968, the Truth in Lending Act was so exacting in its requirements that consumers were confused about the technical details of statements of disclosure regarding loan terms. Many frustrated consumers failed to read the disclosure statements, making the technical details self-defeating. Furthermore, compliance by lenders was difficult under the disclosure requirements and ambiguities of the act, coupled with the Federal Reserve System's literal interpretations. Compliance was made even more difficult by the highly technical finding in over 15,000 civil lawsuits filed in federal courts under the Truth in Lending Act through 1980.

Finally, in 1980, Congress passed the Truth in Lending Simplification and Reform Act, which reduced some of the original disclosure requirements, exempted agricultural credit from the provisions of the act, and provided standard disclosure forms that ensured compliance if used by lenders.

SUMMARY

The granting of all types of credit to consumers by banks has grown dramatically in the past 30 or more years. This type of credit now makes up over one-third of the average bank's loan portfolio. Installment credit is used mostly for the purchase of household durables and automobiles. Revolving credit, especially that associated with credit or debit cards, is increasingly used to purchase a wide variety of personal goods and services. Card-type transactions are valued by consumers for their convenience as a virtual cash substitute as well as a source of credit.

---

[7] One point represents 1 percent of the total loan amount charged "on the front end" as a loan origination fee. For example, three points on a $10,000 loan equals $300.

The mix of consumer credit appears to be changing rapidly. Credit extended by means of credit cards and, increasingly, debit cards is expanding rapidly. The future growth of this form of consumer debt seems assured as electronic devices that utilize them proliferate. On the other hand, automobile loan lending as a proportion of total bank consumer lending probably has shrunk permanently as auto manufacturers have usurped the market for this type of loan.

Installment lending is characterized by low amounts per loan and large numbers of loans. Banks have to organize efficiently to receive, analyze, and evaluate loan applications and to advise consumers of their decisions. Formal credit scoring systems are an appropriate approach to efficient processing at banks with particularly high rates of installment loan applications. For large banks, the benefits of a credit scoring system probably outweigh the costs of maintaining and updating the system using the sophisticated statistical techniques on which such systems are based. However, no credit scoring system can be entirely devoid of judgment; applications that fall in the gray area need further individual attention. Small banks probably cannot justify a statistically verified scoring system tailored to their clientele. These banks will probably always need to depend primarily on judgment.

Consumer lending is further complicated by a host of federal consumer protection regulations that require careful compliance. Part of any major consumer lending program in a bank must be a system for monitoring and documenting the bank's adherence to consumer regulations. Regulation B (Equal Credit Opportunity Act) and Regulation Z (Truth in Lending Act), in particular, demand the bank's comprehension and careful implementation. Recognition of the complexity of such regulations is growing, and as a result, Congress is regularly promoting legislation to simplify them.

END OF CHAPTER PROBLEMS

12.1   Distinguish between direct and indirect automobile loans. Why should banks seek both types of this loan business, instead of just one or the other?

12.2   Determine the effective annual rate on a two-year loan of $1,200 with an 8 percent add-on rate, paid in monthly installments.

12.3   How does conversion to floating-rate consumer loans affect the interest sensitivity of bank balance sheets?

12.4   What is the purpose or rationale for the Rule of 78s?

12.5   Cite the purpose and some basic provisions of the Equal Credit Opportunity Act and its operational equivalent, Regulation B.

12.6   Summarize the pros and cons of judgmental and empirically based credit evaluation systems.

12.7   Why has the credit card system evolved from a system whereby many banks issued their own cards to one dominated by VISA and MasterCard?

12.8   What are the advantages of the proposed debit card over the present credit card? Why have debit cards been accepted so slowly?

12.9   Some observers claim that the 1978 Bankruptcy Reform Act encourages debtors to abandon their debts with the help of the bankruptcy courts. What provisions of the act might lend credence to this statement?

12.10   What are the main provisions of the Truth in Lending Act?

LOBO MILL PRODUCTS COMPANY

INTRODUCTION

Mr. Enriqué (Harry) Lobo almost never took the time to reflect on his business success—he was too busy! In a rare moment of reflection in the spring of 1998 he appreciated that the profits of his firm, the Lobo Mill Products Company, were rising briskly. Most of the profits were retained in the business. In addition, it looked like sales were increasing substantially again this year. Things change, Mr. Lobo thought. And he considered how circumstances now dictated that he would have to break off his firm's original banking relationship initiated 10 years ago.

The firm had borrowed nearly $125,000 from South Valley State Bank in Albuquerque, New Mexico, at the beginning of 1998 but found that its cash shortage emerged again a month or so later. South Valley Bank had "maxed out" at its lending limit and would not be able to meet larger loan requests in the future. A friend referred Mr. Lobo to Chemical National Bank of New Mexico, a large banking company with a national presence. Chemical had recently entered the Albuquerque market by acquiring one of the state's largest banks. Mr. Lobo had a pleasant first meeting with a Chemical National loan officer. This banker had good local experience, and Mr. Lobo decided to present her with a request for a loan of $325,000. Following this visit, the bank got busy on its investigation of Lobo Mill Products and Mr. Lobo.

BUSINESS CHARACTERISTICS

Mr. Lobo and a partner, Mr. Andrew Murphy, founded the Lobo Mill Products (LMP) Company in 1988. He bought out Mr. Murphy in 1994 and carried on in the business as sole proprietor. His business was the milling and wholesale distribution of wood products to builders' supply retail outlets and lumber yards throughout New Mexico and parts of southern Colorado. LMP gave discounts on quantity purchases and sold on terms of net 30 days.

Mr. Lobo competed vigorously on price by watching operating expenses and by making quantity purchases at large savings. Most of his products were used for home repair and remodeling. Typically, LMP made between 55 and 60 percent of its total annual sales in the six months of April through September. Comparative operating statements for 1995 through 1997 and for three months ending March 31, 1998 are shown in Exhibit 1.

Mr. Lobo was still a young man and had a reputation as a "take-charge" person. Suppliers told the bank's credit officers that Mr. Lobo was an indefatigable worker who put in a lot of hours. While Mr. Lobo had not completed his university studies, he was proud that he had installed the latest accounting, billing, and inventory control software. He was ably assisted by a woman with a degree in accountancy who was familiar with all of the administrative tasks, and she did many of them as well. LMP had seven other employees, including two truckers and three skilled woodworkers. These employees spoke well of Mr. Lobo and appeared to be highly loyal to the firm. Long-term employees were paid better than comparable workers in similar businesses. His wife's and his personal assets consisted mainly of equity in a home built in 1985, furnishings, and a new automobile. A mortgage of $35,000 remained on the home, although the home's value had grown to more than twice the original price he paid. He was fully paid up on a $50,000 ordinary life insurance policy payable to Mrs. Lobo.

FINDINGS OF THE INVESTIGATION

The bank's investigation, including discussions with LMP customers and suppliers, concluded that the firm had a continuous, ready market for its products and that the sales outlook was particularly favorable. The bank estimated that sales would fall in the range of $3.3 million to $4.2 million in 1998. The bank paid special attention to the firm's debt position and current ratio. The rate of inventory turnover was high, and losses on bad debts in past years had been quite small. Comparative balance sheet data are given in Exhibit 2. From dealing with similar businesses in the past, the bank knew that the usual terms of purchase in the trade were 2 percent, 10 days after arrival. Suppliers took 60-day notes when requested by good customers, but they did this rather unwillingly.

Chemical National's loan officer had several questions in her mind about LMP's request:

1. The business was clearly profitable, so why did Mr. Lobo require so much money? To evaluate Mr. Lobo's estimate of his loan requirement, she determined that she would forecast a year-end 1998 balance sheet assuming sales at the upper part of the $3.3 million to $4.2 million range.

2. She wondered what the detail of LMP's historic needs for funds would show. She decided to create a Statement of Cash Flows for prior years and the first quarter of 1998.

3. Though profitable, the firm may have problems in certain aspects of its operations or financing. She concluded that a ratio analysis would help her identify strengths, weaknesses, and trends.

4. Should she prepare a loan package for the bank officers' loan committee to recommend a loan? If so, what terms and conditions should be put on it?

EXHIBIT I   Lobo Mill Products Co. Operating Statements for the Years Ending December 31, 1995 through 1997 and for the Three Months Ending March 31, 1998 (dollar figures in thousands)

	1995	1996	1997	1st Quarter[a] 1998
Net sales	$1924	$2288	$3065	$ 806
Cost of goods sold				
Beginning inventory	289	252	367	468
Purchases	1589	2200	2779	874
	1877	2452	3146	1342
Ending inventory	252	367	468	634
Cost of goods sold	1625	2085	2678	707
Gross profit	299	203	387	99
Operating expenses	99	125	190	52
Net operating profit	200	78	198	47
Add: Purchase discounts taken	13	13	13	3
	213	91	211	50
Deduct: Sales discounts given	42	47	73	21
Net profit[b]	$ 172	$ 44	$ 138	$ 29
Drawings by proprietor	—	—	$ 73	$ 15

[a] In first quarter 1997, net sales were $655,200 and net profit was $33,800.

[b] Stated before provision for federal income tax liabilities. Owners of proprietorships must include in their personal income and pay taxes on it at the regular personal tax rate.

EXHIBIT 2   Lobo Mill Products Co. Comparative Balance Sheets as of December 31, 1995–1997 and March 31, 1998

	1995	1996	1997	1st Quarter 1998
Assets				
Cash	$ 146	$ 733	$ 9,256	$ 3,479
Accounts receivable net of reserve for bad debt	149,037	232,406	285,184	335,122
Inventory	252,213	367,682	466,848	633,511
Total current assets	401,396	600,821	761,288	972,112
Property—net of reserve for depreciation	15,504	19,781	29,718	26,939
Deferred charges	. . .	. . .	. . .	6,749
Total assets	$416,900	$620,602	$791,006	$1,005,795
Liabilities				
Notes payable—bank	. . .	. . .	. . .	124,800
Notes payable—employees for bonuses	. . .	. . .	. . .	12,584
Notes payable—Andrew Murphy	83,200	. . .	. . .	
Notes payable—trade	. . .	. . .	. . .	170,994
Accounts payable	149,396	355,480	450,941	359,674
Accrued expenses	. . .	8,944	18,704	2,345
Total current liabilities	232,596	364,424	469,646	670,397
Net worth[a]	184,304	256,178	321,360	335,398
Total liabilities and net worth	$416,900	$620,602	$791,006	$1,005,795

[a] H. Lobo invested an additional $27,300 in the business in 1996. Note that the "net worth" account in 1996 shows a larger increase than the retained earnings for 1996.

CASE 10   QUESTOR, INC.

INTRODUCTION

Catherine Logan was president of Questor, Inc., a manufacturer of valves and pipe fittings. In April 1999, she visited Felix Fernandez, a loan officer for Golden West Bank, with a loan request. She gave Mr. Fernandez Questor's financial statements for the years 1997 and 1998 and for the most recent three-month period ending March 31, 1999. In addition to providing her firm with credit, Ms. Logan indicated that she would be open to having Golden West Bank provide all of Questor's banking requirements.

She complained that her present bank had become careless in serving Questor's banking requirements and that the loan officers assigned to the account were being changed frequently, causing her great inconvenience. She was frustrated with having to explain Questor's needs and business every time there was a change in loan officers. Recently, the firm's line of credit agreement with its present bank had expired, and the bank seemed to be delaying action on the firm's request for a much needed moderate increase in the line.

Ms. Logan informed Mr. Fernandez that she believed Questor would need as much as $1 million during the next 12 months. She wanted part of the credit in 90-day notes and the rest on an intermediate-term basis. "Our sales volume continues to grow and our profits are good," she commented to Mr. Fernandez. "We have been in business for 15 years and, except for our first year, we have been profitable ever since. Our equipment is in good condition, and we will not have to expand our plant for at least three more years." Ms. Logan offered as references her current mortgage lender, Fairview Savings Bank, and several of her major suppliers. She did not suggest that Mr. Fernandez contact her present full-service bank, although she observed: "you may not get the complete story from them."

CREDIT INVESTIGATION

In the days following Mrs. Logan's visit, Felix Fernandez completed credit checks with Questor's major suppliers who reported a pattern of generally prompt payment. The highest credit reported by a single supplier was $150,000. However, Questor frequently was not able to take trade discounts, which all suppliers offered on a 2/10/net 30 basis.

Fairview Savings Bank reported a balance of $275,000 owed on an original $500,000 loan. The loan from Fairview Savings was secured by land and buildings owned by Questor. Payments of $25,000 per quarter were being made promptly.

Mr. Fernandez had not yet checked with Questor's present bank to discuss its experience with Questor. Golden West Bank was very interested in establishing a complete business relationship with Questor, but Mr. Fernandez was uncertain how to approach Questor's present bank and how to interpret what officers from that bank might tell him.

After Mr. Fernandez conducted his initial investigation, he called Catherine Logan to set up a second meeting at the bank. At the meeting, Ms. Logan made a specific request for a $1 million loan. In addition to the financial statements she provided earlier (Exhibits 1 through 3), she provided a personal financial statement (Exhibit 4). Mr. Fernandez had also received a ratio analysis on Questor from Golden West Bank's credit analysis department (Exhibit 5).

Ms. Logan indicated that Questor's inventory was composed of the following:

Raw material	40%
Work in process	20%
Finished goods	40%

Another loan officer advised Mr. Fernandez that the fractions of values that could be recovered on short notice for inventories of the type maintained by Questor Inc. were probably 50, 0, and 50 percent, respectively, for raw, in-process, and finished inventories.

Concerning Questor's accounts receivable, Mr. Fernandez wondered if those outstanding for more than 60 days could be collected. He was also concerned that Questor continued to sell to customers for whom receivables had been outstanding for more than 60 days. He wondered if he should assign any value at all to the receivables of such customers. Finally, he decided to appraise accounts receivable that were on time at only the cost of production

(cost of goods), about 70 percent of their book value. In this way, Questor would not get credit for its markup on its unpaid billings.

LOAN MEMORANDUM

In preparation for presenting the Questor loan request to Golden West's officers, loan committee, Mr. Fernandez turned his attention to creating a loan memorandum. The standard format favored by Golden West required that he address the following:

1. *Financial Needs:* Summarize pros and cons of the firm's financial health. Specify the amount of loan or line of credit to extend to Questor at this time. For this purpose, Mr. Fernandez decided to create an Excel model of Questor's expected financial needs in the intermediate term by forecasting its financial statements for the full years 1999, 2000, and 2001, based on continued growth and his expectations for the firm's key ratios. Such key ratios included average collection period, inventory turnover, accounts payable, and other key accounts he determined to be appropriate. He knew that special heed must be given to reducing Questor's accounts payable.

2. *Purpose:* Determine the purpose for the loan. What is the immediate purpose, and what is the longer-term purpose?

3. *Types and Terms of Borrowing:* Specify whether and how much of the total amount to be loaned will be divided between short-term and long-term or revolving; that is, if the loan is divided between two types of loans, how much will be loaned of each type?

4. *Collateral Value and Borrowing Base:* Assuming that the bank secures the loan with Questor's accounts receivable and inventories, determine how much value can be recovered if Questor fails to pay—that is, the "borrowing base." (Alternatively, determine how much Golden West Bank can safely lend against Questor's accounts receivable and inventories.)

5. *Repayment Terms and Source:* Establish a repayment schedule for each type of borrowing. Indicate the cash flows expected to be used to repay each type of borrowing. Identify the cash flow sources of repayment for each type of borrowing.

6. *Rate:* Establish the interest rate on each type of borrowing. (Specify in terms of points above the prime rate.)

7. *Guarantees, Covenants, and Other Restrictions:* Specify the covenants to be placed on Questor. Describe the guarantees or other restrictions.

EXHIBIT 1   Income and Expenses—Questor, Inc.

	Three Months 1999	1998	1997	1996
Sales revenue	$1,878,000	$6,400,000	$6,101,000	$5,400,000
Cost of goods sold	1,333,380	4,480,000	4,209,000	3,780,000
Gross profit	544,620	1,920,000	1,892,000	1,620,000
Operating expense	438,869	1,428,500	1,408,900	1,176,000
Net income before taxes and interest	105,751	491,500	483,100	444,000
Interest expense	26,875	107,500	110,000	120,000
Income taxes	27,606	134,400	130,584	113,400
Profit after taxes	$ 51,270	$ 249,600	$ 242,516	$ 210,600

EXHIBIT 2   Balance Sheet—Questor, Inc.

	March 31 1999	Dec. 31 1998	Dec. 31 1997	Dec. 31 1996
Cash	$ 67,800	$ 113,000	$ 139,320	$ 130,600
Accounts receivable	1,009,960	914,284	859,200	782,600
Inventory	1,780,000	1,357,600	1,315,200	1,111,800
Current assets	2,857,760	2,384,884	2,313,720	2,025,000
Land	100,000	100,000	100,000	100,000
Plant and equipment	614,000	610,000	602,700	598,000
Depreciation	($280,000)	($270,000)	($230,000)	($190,000)
Net plant and equipment	334,000	340,000	372,700	408,000
Total assets	$3,291,760	$2,824,884	$2,786,420	$2,533,000
Notes payable (bank)	$ 800,000	$ 800,000	$ 650,000	$ 650,000
Accounts payable	640,834	190,228	467,364	370,460
Accrued expenses	70,000	80,000	64,000	50,000
Current liabilities	1,510,834	1,070,228	1,181,364	1,070,460
Long-term debt	275,000	300,000	400,000	500,000
Total liabilities	1,785,834	1,370,228	1,581,364	1,570,460
Capital	100,000	100,000	100,000	100,000
Retained earnings	1,405,926	1,354,656	1,105,056	862,540
Total stockholders' equity	1,505,926	1,454,656	1,205,056	962,540
Total liabilities and equity	$3,291,760	$2,824,884	$2,786,420	$2,533,000

EXHIBIT 3   Accounts Receivable Aging (March 31, 1999)—Questor, Inc.

Customer	Credit Extended Since Feb. 28, 1999	Credit Extended During:			Before Dec. 1998
		Feb. 1999	Jan. 1999	Dec. 1998	
Bunson, J. C.	$ 33,000	$ 66,000			
Carpenter Co.	44,000				
Dalton Co.			$ 20,000		
Davidson Co.	15,000				
Fredrick Co.			15,000	$ 6,000	
Gaston, Inc.	45,000				
Hardy Sons					$25,000
Ivor	6,000	5,000		10,000	
Logan, Inc.	104,000				
Jefferson, Inc.	52,000	3,600			
Kessel Sons	54,000	30,000	60,000	6,000	2,000
Lamont Co.	10,000				
Lawrence Sons	35,600				
Massey, Inc.		15,000	30,000		34,000
Nestor	12,000				
Olympia	84,000				
Pinocle, Co.		4,000	10,000	10,000	10,000
Trenton, Inc.	45,000	8,000			
Trilogy	26,000	30,000		5,000	
Watson	(240)				
Other	40,000				
Total	$ 605,360	$161,600	$135,000	$37,000	$71,000
Total: all receivables	$1,009,960				

EXHIBIT 4   Personal Financial Statement for Catherine and Cyril Logan (April 1, 1999)

Assets		Liabilities and Equity	
Cash	$ 24,000	Notes payable—banks	$ 150,000
Marketable securities	108,000	Notes payable—Questor, Inc.	65,000
Loan receivables from Logan, Inc.	80,000	Mortgage on home	335,000
Residence	550,000	Total liabilities	550,000
Automobiles	44,000	Equity	1,821,926
Personal property	60,000		
Stock of Questor, Inc. (book value)	1,505,926		
Total assets	$2,371,926	Total liabilities and equity	$2,371,926

Salary (1998)	$150,000
Bonus (estimated)	30,000
Other	2,000
Total Income	$182,000

EXHIBIT 5   Financial Ratios—Questor, Inc.

	1999[a]	1998	1997	1996	Industry Ave. 1998
Liquidity Ratios					
Current ratio = Current assets/Current liabilities	1.892	2.228	1.959	1.892	2.100
Quick ratio = $\dfrac{\text{Current assets} - \text{Inventory}}{\text{Current liabilities}}$	0.713	0.960	0.845	0.853	1.000
Activity Ratios					
Average collection period = $\dfrac{\text{Accounts receivable}}{\text{Annual sales Rev./365 days}}$	49.07 days	52.14 days	51.40 days	52.90 days	49.00 days
Inventory turnover = $\dfrac{\text{Costs of goods sold}}{\text{Avg. inventory}}$	3.40×	3.35×	3.47×	—	3.60×
Financial Leverage Ratios					
Debt to equity = $\dfrac{\text{Total liabilities}}{\text{Total stockholders' equity}}$	1.19	0.94	1.31	1.63	1.50
Coverage of interest expenses = $\dfrac{\text{EBIT}}{\text{Interest expenses}^{b}}$	8.99	10.15	10.15	8.57	3.50
Profitability Ratios					
Gross profit margin = $\dfrac{\text{Sales revenue} - \text{Cost of goods sold}}{\text{Sales revenue}}$	29.00%	30.00%	31.01%	30.00%	30.70%
Net profit margin = $\dfrac{\text{Profit after taxes}}{\text{Sales revenue}}$	2.73%	3.90%	3.98%	3.90%	3.60%
Return on total assets = $\dfrac{\text{Profit after taxes}}{\text{Total assets}}$	6.23%	8.84%	8.70%	8.31%	5.07%
Return on equity = $\dfrac{\text{Profit after taxes}}{\text{Total stockholders' equity}}$	13.62%	17.16%	20.12%	21.88%	17.00%

[a] 1999 quarterly figures are annualized.

[b] Estimated Interest expenses = Interest-bearing liabilities × Assumed 10% average interest rate.

CASE 11

GLOBAL MACHINERY AND METALS COMPANY, INC.

INTRODUCTION

In early 1996 Mr. David Farmer, assistant vice-president at Motor City National Bank, Detroit, Michigan, was considering an expanded loan request from one of the bank's established customers—Global Machinery and Metals Company, Inc. (GMMC). David Farmer had only recently joined the Motor City Bank after two years of credit analysis and lending experience at a nearby competing institution. The GMMC account, which was established at the Motor City Bank about four years ago, had been brought to the bank by the officer whom Farmer had recently replaced. Hence, he had no prior contact or experience with the managers at GMMC, beyond his understanding that the account had been a satisfactory and profitable one for the bank since the relationship began in 1992.

Wayne Newton, one of the principals of GMMC,

approached David Farmer with a request for a material expansion in the company's credit facilities. Newton was asking for an increased line of credit to $1 million and an increase in the letter of credit (L/C) line to $1 million.

The GMMC credits currently approved were as follows:

1. Line of credit: $500,000 at prime plus 2 percent.
2. L/C: $750,000 at prime plus 2 percent, with a fee of 1 percent per annum at issue plus 1 percent at funding.

The preceding authorized credit lines, which had been increased in 1993, were secured by all accounts receivable and inventory. Advances against those lines were based on 50 percent of eligible accounts receivable and 40 percent of inventory in amounts not to exceed the total credit approved.

The L/C line had been in constant use since its establishment in 1992 at or near the authorized limit. The line of credit was zeroed out for about 60 days in 1993 and about 30 days in 1994, and was paid down to a low of $265,000 in 1995. Average usage in 1995 totaled $470,000. Mr. Newton told David Farmer that his current request for increased credit facilities resulted from the continued rapid expansion of GMMC sales. Newton indicated that he would appreciate the bank's prompt consideration and approval of his request for increased credit. (See Exhibits 1 and 2.)

GMMC was organized in 1973 as a sole proprietorship, owned and operated by Wayne Newton, who was 54 years of age. GMMC operated as a dealer for new and used machine tools. In 1988 Newton converted the firm to a corporation. At about the same time, he concluded that some diversification of product and activity would serve to reduce the firm's risk as well as increase its profitability. Accordingly, GMMC began importing finished steel products such as stainless steel rounds, angles, pipes, sheets, and plates, principally from Japan and, to a lesser extent, from Spain and Korea.

METALS DIVISION

The metals division, whose sales had shown rapid growth in recent years, sold stainless steel products to about 450 customers in the South and Southwest. One client accounted for about 10 percent of total division sales; nearly all other buyers were significantly smaller, with no other customer accounting for as much as 3 percent of volume. Sales were managed through five salesmen, primarily to

small and medium-sized distributors and fabricators. Mr. William Hardin, 46, directed the metals division and its sales staff. He operated in GMMC with a great deal of autonomy.

The GMMC metals division worked with three Japanese suppliers and one each in Spain and South Korea. The company could sell to its customers at prices approximately 20 percent less than competitors who offered equivalent U.S. made products. This price advantage had allowed GMMC to expand its metals division sales volume quite rapidly.

Recently, the company had begun building its inventory of stainless steel products in anticipation of voluntary industry import restrictions on supplies from Japan and Korea. Although GMMC enjoyed a significant price advantage on its imported stainless steel products, there were some important disadvantages to imported sources of supply. GMMC customers had to place their orders at least 60 days in advance of needed delivery. This put GMMC at some competitive disadvantage with domestic (U.S.) suppliers, who could respond to orders in four to six weeks. This situation led to apparent risks for GMMC related to any interruption of supply sources. For example, dock strikes, either in the country of origin or in the United States, could quickly affect supplies. Domestic sources of similar-quality stainless steel products would be available to replace imports, but at a substantially higher cost to GMMC. Almost all of the recent inventory growth had resulted from the growth of stainless steel sales plus recent purchases to hedge against possible import restrictions.

MACHINE TOOL DIVISION

Mr. Wayne Newton closely supervised the activities of the machine tool division. Three salesmen serviced approximately 400 accounts, which were primarily machine shops and small manufacturers. GMMC frequently purchased surplus used machinery, and from time to time the company even bought entire small manufacturing plants, using in these cases various joint-venture partners. Sales by GMMC, when a large-scale purchase was made, would either be at auction or to existing customers within about 30 days.

When used machinery was purchased, it would be shipped to the company's facility for repair or refurbishing if that proved necessary. GMMC had maintained an excellent reputation for selling quality used machinery, and profit margins on this business were excellent.

PRODUCT MIX

The product mixes for year-end 1993, 1994, and 1995 were as follows:

	1993		1994		1995	
	Sales	**Earnings**	**Sales**	**Earnings**	**Sales**	**Earnings**
Metals division	79%	73%	73%	66%	45%	(14%)
Machine tool division	21%	27%	27%	34%	55%	114%

The company's records indicated that about 66 percent of the machine tool division's sales in 1994 resulted from used machinery, which accounted for 75 percent of the division's profitability.

FACILITIES

The company owned office and warehouse space containing approximately 36,000 square feet. In addition, other warehouse and yard area was leased with annual payments of $25,000. The majority of GMMC's facilities had been constructed from materials acquired through purchase of closed manufacturing plants. Through use of company labor, the cost of facilities had been held to a minimum without sacrificing function.

STAFFING

The company employed a total of 18 people, none of whom was a union member. Messrs. Newton and Hardin drew annual salaries of $65,000 each. They also participated in a bonus program based on performance. Each of the two men earned a bonus of $50,000 in 1995. Common stock ownership was divided, with Mr. Newton owning 60 percent and Mr. Hardin holding 40 percent.

In his discussion at the bank, Mr. Newton summarized his credit requests to the bank officer, David Farmer, as follows:

GMMC wishes to increase its line of credit to $1 million to strengthen our ability to buy closed manufacturing plants or surplus machinery on short notice and to enable the company to enter larger joint venture deals. We anticipate an average use for 1996 of $700,000, with a minimum of $300,000. We also want to use a portion of the credit line to finance increased stainless steel inventory from time to time in anticipation of supply interruptions. Finally, the increase we ask in the letter of credit line, to $1 million from the present $750,000, will help us finance additional stainless steel inventory to meet our steadily growing demand.

Mr. Farmer promised to review these requests and to respond to Mr. Newton within the next few days.

EXHIBIT I   Global Machinery and Metals, Inc.—Balance Sheet

	12/31/93 (Unaudited)	12/31/94 (Unaudited)	12/31/95 (Audited)
Assets			
Current assets			
Cash	$ 54,500	$ 76,420	$ 62,370
Receivables net of allowance for doubtful accounts[a]	457,676	787,442	972,154
Inventories[b]	644,794	1,527,925	2,480,115
Prepaid expenses	6,608	7,677	10,802
Total current assets	1,163,578	2,399,464	3,525,441
Property, plant, and equipment (at cost)			
Building	54,800	54,800	54,800
Equipment, furniture, and fixtures	87,281	103,943	113,635
Leasehold improvements	18,760	23,434	23,434
Land	23,000	23,000	23,000
Less: Accumulated depreciation	(55,195)	(66,846)	(81,695)
Net property, plant, and equipment	128,646	138,331	133,174
Other assets	632	704	423
Total assets	$1,292,856	$2,538,499	$3,659,038
Liabilities			
Current liabilities			
Notes payable	$ 50,000	$ 320,000	$ 500,000
Liability on L/Cs	150,000	580,000	750,000
Trade accounts payable	388,730	746,572	1,093,557
Accrued interest and taxes	48,081	66,522	88,364
Federal income taxes payable	147,000	142,600	250,048
Total current liabilities	783,811	1,855,694	2,681,969
Equity			
Common stock, 2,000 shares authorized and issued	100,000	100,000	100,000
Retained earnings	409,045	582,805	877,069
Total equity	509,045	682,805	977,069
Total liabilities and equity	$1,292,856	$2,538,499	$3,659,038

[a] Bad debt expense:

1995	$16,863
1994	117
1993	1,053

The reserve for doubtful accounts totaled $12,114 as of 12/31/95.

[b] Inventories are stated at the lower of cost, first-in, first-out method, or market. Amounts of inventories used in computing cost of sales for periods covered by the financial statements are as follows:

12/31/95	$2,480,115
12/31/94	1,527,925
12/31/93	671,402

EXHIBIT 2   Global Machinery and Metals, Inc.—Statement of Income

	1993 (Unaudited)	1994 (Unaudited)	1995 (Audited)
Net revenues	$2,654,536	$4,330,934	$5,229,695
Costs and expenses			
Cost of goods sold	1,688,268	3,111,927	3,759,491
Selling, general and administrative expenses	582,804	849,151	873,670
Total cost and expenses	2,271,072	3,961,078	4,633,161
Revenue after costs and expenses	383,454	369,856	596,534
Other income (expense)			
Miscellaneous income	1,120	(11,286)	3,898
Interest income	(26,037)	(45,810)	(56,668)
Total other income	(24,917)	(57,096)	(52,770)
Income before federal taxes	358,537	312,760	543,764
Provision for federal income taxes	160,500	139,000	249,500
Net income	$ 198,037	$ 173,760	$ 294,264
Statement of Retained Income			
Retained earnings—beginning of period	$ 211,008	$ 409,045	$ 582,805
Net income	198,037	173,760	294,264
Retained earnings—end of period	409,045	582,805	877,069

CASE 12

BERGNER CONSTRUCTION COMPANY

INTRODUCTION[1]

In May 1988, Mr. Peter Davis, a newly appointed loan officer at Westside National Bank in Cleveland, Ohio, received a request from John Bergner, president of Bergner Construction Company, for an increase in his revolving credit line to $250,000. Bergner's borrowing relationships were presently established at FirstOhio Bank in Cleveland, where he had been a customer for the past five years. For various reasons, however, Bergner wanted to change banks and to increase his revolving line from $100,000 to $250,000, leaving his other credit needs unchanged. Mr. Bergner explained to Peter Davis that this additional credit was required to help finance a large construction project that his company had just been awarded by the Pepsi-Cola Bottling Company in Boulder, Colorado.

BERGNER'S OPERATIONS

Bergner Construction Company, located in Cleveland, Ohio, was a mechanical contracting business, specializing in specialty construction projects in food and beverage manufacturing facilities. The company was a "custom-built" contractor, using primarily stainless steel to build the vessels and piping necessary for assembly lines in food and beverage processing. Like most specialty contractors, Bergner's installations were largely on a project-by-project basis, for which it provided engineering design and construction expertise to its clients. Companies of this kind required relatively little complex, specialized production equipment, and most inventory was associated with specific jobs

[1] This case was written by Sumon Mazumdar, Department of Economics, Southern Methodist University, Dallas, Texas.

in progress. Accordingly, Bergner Construction was thinly capitalized, like many firms in this kind of construction work.

The company's president, John Bergner, was 40 years of age. He held a degree in mechanical engineering from Ohio State University. Bergner began his career as a foreman for a large construction company that manufactured specialty food and beverage facilities. Having gathered several years of valuable on-the-job industry experience, Mr. Bergner subsequently formed his own company, which was incorporated in 1982.

Mr. Bergner initially did business with the FirstOhio Bank of Cleveland, where his account was handled by Peter Davis. During the next five years, 1982–1987, a comfortable working relationship developed between the two men. Davis came to regard Bergner as an honest and energetic entrepreneur. The banker found it easy to do business with his client, who was a pleasant, outgoing person eager to expand his business.

In December 1987, Mr. Davis accepted a new position, with a higher salary and greater responsibility, at the Westside National Bank, also located in Cleveland. Accordingly, the construction company's account was transferred to another loan officer at FirstOhio in January 1988.

Bergner Construction Company had recorded a small net operating profit of $13,088 in 1987. During the first four months of 1988, however, the company's completed jobs slumped, leading to a loss of $53,556 for that period. Mr. Bergner explained to his new loan officer that this loss was due largely to problems encountered on one project, for which a former estimator had underestimated construction costs. These results did not truly reflect the firm's capabilities, in Mr. Bergner's opinion. He pointed out that his company had enjoyed a sales growth rate of 23 percent over the past two years, and projected sales by the end of 1988 were $1.3 million.

LOAN PROPOSAL

Bergner required a moderate increase in his credit line to cover these losses and to complete other projects that his firm had been awarded. He quickly learned, however, that the new loan officer at FirstOhio was quite reluctant to commit a larger line of credit for these purposes. Thus, in May 1988, John Bergner considered transferring his account to Westside National, where he hoped his business

would continue to be handled by Mr. Davis, with whom he had enjoyed a satisfactory and understanding relationship.

After an initial meeting at Westside National Bank, Mr. Davis recommended John Bergner's company at the bank's loan committee, stressing his honesty and positive business attitude. Davis strongly urged his bank to add Bergner's company as a new customer and to approve the credit request, which had, in effect, been declined by the FirstOhio Bank.

Peter Davis was a "character" lender. He felt most strongly that the integrity of the loan applicant was a crucial aspect of loan decisions. If he believed the applicant to be honest and knowledgeable about his business and if an adequate check of the applicant's credit history was satisfactory, Mr. Davis was often prepared to approve a loan, even if the client's financial statements might be considered somewhat weak.

In Bergner's case, the nature of the contract construction business implied a low capital base, a factor that Davis argued should be considered in this case. Moreover, in Davis's opinion, financial statements were often misleading. He had concluded that the current somewhat weak financial state of Bergner's business did not imply an inability to manage his credit responsibilities properly. Indeed, Davis's faith in Bergner's integrity persuaded him that the proposed loan would be repaid, consistent with the company's past performance. It was important to Bergner that the present loan request be granted, since he was extremely anxious to proceed with the large Pepsi-Cola contract in Colorado, which would require additional financing before the project could be undertaken.

Peter Davis's polished presentation and eloquent appeal, however, left the committee undecided, and the decision was deferred, in part by limited time in committee, until the next meeting of the Loan Committee three days hence. Davis requested the following specific credit arrangements:

1. The sum of $100,000, which would be CD secured, the proceeds of which would be used to pay off Bergner's outstanding debt at FirstOhio Bank.
2. A $250,000 revolving line of credit, to be secured by accounts receivable and inventory (replacing an existing line of $100,000 at FirstOhio). The company's inventory consisted mainly of work in progress and raw materials.

3. A total of $128,000 in various equipment loans. These loans were secured by filings on various pieces of equipment, such as trucks, cars, forklifts, air compressors, and other tools. These loans were already approved and funded at FirstOhio. The loans and related security arrangements would also be moved, but this represented no increase in balances outstanding on this equipment. In most cases, the bank financed 100 percent of the original cost of equipment purchased.

Bergner Construction Company had limited its operations to the midwestern market, generally within a 500-mile radius of Cleveland. Mr. Bergner had always been anxious, however, to expand his business, and especially to search for contracts in other parts of the country to achieve greater geographical diversification. Accordingly, he had successfully bid for a renovation project at a Pepsi-Cola bottling plant in Boulder, Colorado, winning the bid in April 1988.

John Bergner felt that this new project offered an ideal opportunity to broaden his company's business contacts. This job would also represent the largest single construction project that his company had ever undertaken ($400,000), and he projected a 15 percent pretax profit as part of his winning bid. Its successful completion would, he hoped, improve prospects for future profitability.

For all these reasons, then, in May 1988 Mr. Bergner wanted to change his banking relationship by asking Peter Davis to move the Bergner account and to increase his revolving credit line to $250,000. Since Davis was a new loan officer at Westside and Bergner also represented a new customer, the Loan Committee realized it should carefully consider this credit request. Moreover, the amount involved would be substantial for Westside Bank.

The thinly capitalized structure of Bergner Construction Company was not, in Davis's mind, a significant handicap, since the contractual nature of the business did not require expensive long-term commitments to capital items such as plant and equipment. The initial Loan Committee meeting, however, raised questions on this point.

Construction companies typically work on a project-to-project basis. If no single project is excessively dominant, then a loss on one does not imply that the firm's profit potential would be significantly affected.

Peter Davis was anxious to "sell" this new customer to the bank's Loan Committee, partly because of his confidence in Bergner and partly to show his new colleagues his approach to lending and loan decisions.

EXHIBIT 1   Balance Sheet—Bergner Construction Company (dollars)

	4/30/88		12/31/87		12/31/86	
Assets						
Current assets						
Cash	150,408		5,699		18,697	
CD	100,000		102,200		115,200	
Accounts receivable	419,628		80,047		55,346	
Inventory	135,044		62,068		11,137	
Total current assets		805,080		250,014		200,380
Fixed assets						
Furniture and fixtures	7,620		6,430		5,780	
Leasehold improvements	35,120		30,000		27,700	
Automobiles and trucks	73,079		65,570		49,052	
Accumulated depreciation	(69,414)		(40,011)		(23,500)	
Total fixed assets		46,405		61,989		59,032
Other assets						
Deposits	85,500		44,161		6,500	
Total other assets		85,500		44,161		6,500
Total assets		$936,985		$356,164		$265,912
Liabilities						
Current liabilities						
Accounts payable—taxes	1,104		1,071		903	
Accounts payable—trade	37,102		26,400		11,000	
Bank loans payable	100,000		61,000		6,000	
Accrued expenses	13,894		10,867		3,394	
Customer deposits	596,430		3,562		5,982	
Total current liabilities		748,530		102,900		27,279
Long-term liabilities						
Notes payable—equipment	153,408		169,147		159,771	
Total long-term liabilities		153,408		169,147		159,771
Total liabilities		901,938		272,047		187,050
Equity						
Capital	82,729		67,615		68,417	
Current year retained profit (loss)	(47,682)		16,502		10,445	
Total net equity		35,047		84,117		78,862
Total liabilities and equity		$936,985		$356,164		$265,912

EXHIBIT 2 Consolidated Income Statement—Bergner Construction Company

	1/1/88– 4/30/88	%	1/1/87– 12/31/87	%	1/1/86– 12/30/86	%
Income						
Contract sales	$571,173	97.0	$ 970,411	95.0	$707,607	90.0
Noncontract sales	17,665	3.0	51,074	5.0	78,623	10.0
Total income	$588,838	100.0	$1,021,485	100.0	$786,230	100.0
Cost of sales						
Noncontract cost	13,543	2.3	30,682	3.0	39,311	5.0
Noncontract cost—travel	29,854	5.1	63,130	6.2	78,623	10.0
Contract cost—material	209,626	35.6	306,445	30.0	196,557	25.0
Contract cost—labor	141,321	24.0	296,230	29.0	235,869	30.0
Lease cost	23,555	4.0	71,503	7.0	51,450	6.6
Contract cost—travel	17,720	3.0	40,860	4.0	31,449	4.0
Total cost of sales	435,619	74.0	808,850	79.2	633,259	80.6
Gross profit	$153,219	26.0	$ 212,635	20.8	$152,971	19.4
Operating expenses						
Depreciation	29,403	5.0	16,511	1.6	19,913	2.5
Travel and entertainment	34,788	5.9	59,820	5.9	29,719	3.8
Interest	24,617	4.1	11,700	1.1	15,789	2.0
Professional fees	5,422	0.9	5,822	0.6	13,027	1.7
Salaries	33,911	5.8	61,245	6.0	21,969	2.8
Taxes (other than FIT)	10,909	1.9	8,410	0.8	9,680	1.2
Automobile expense	8,312	1.4	5,321	0.5	7,502	0.9
Rent	20,172	3.4	6,940	0.7	6,953	0.9
Telephone	7,030	1.2	8,482	0.8	5,287	0.7
Insurance	19,420	3.3	7,484	0.7	3,895	0.5
Other	12,791	2.2	7,812	0.8	8,792	1.1
Total operating expenses	206,775	35.1	199,547	19.5	142,526	8.1
Operating income	(53,556)	−9.1	13,088	1.3	10,445	1.3
Other income	5,874	1.0	3,414	0.3	0	0
Net income	$ (47,682)	−8.1	$ 16,502	1.6	$ 10,445	1.3

EXHIBIT 3   Financial Ratios—Bergner Construction Company

	4/30/88	12/31/87	12/31/86
Liquidity			
Current ratio	1.07	2.42	7.34
"Acid test" ratio	0.89	1.82	6.93
Leverage			
Debt/total assets	0.96	0.76	0.70
Debt/equity	25.73	3.23	2.37
Activity			
Inventory turnover[a]	13.26×	22.09×	56.86×
Average collection period (days)[a]	86.70	28.60	25.69
Fixed asset turnover[a]	32.59×	16.88×	13.31×
Profitability			
Profit margin on sales	−8.1%	1.6%	1.3%
Return on total assets (ROA)[a]	−22.0%	5.3%	3.9%
Return on equity (ROE)[a]	−240.0%	20.2%	13.2%

[a] Annualized.

CASE 13

CALBANK LEASING CORPORATION

INTRODUCTION[1]

In mid-1991, Sam Farrell was trying to complete the structuring of a leveraged lease financing package for negotiation with a prospective client. He reflected with satisfaction on the final commitment he had received that morning from an investor who was willing to put equity funds into the project. Farrell knew it was not going to be a cut-and-dried negotiation. The client, California Investment Partnership, had taken some unusual initiatives before approaching Farrell, and, as a result, he was uncertain about the position he would take.

Sam Farrell was vice-president of marketing for CalBank Leasing Corporation (CLC) and was responsible for developing leasing packages for possible funding through his organization. CLC was a subsidiary of CalBank, N.A., located in Los Angeles, California, and one of the largest commercial banks on the West Coast. Farrell had met with the management team of California Investment Partnership (CIP) several weeks earlier to discuss the financing of capital equipment to be installed adjacent to an oil and gas development site with large heavy crude oil reserves near Bakersfield, California.

CLC and its parent, CalBank, held lease financing outstandings of nearly $800 million. The leasing portfolio was an important profit center that contributed 8 percent of the parent's bottom-line earnings in 1990. Most of the leases in the portfolio were outright leases funded through CalBank resources. However, the larger leases increasingly were handled through leveraged lease packages involving long-term debt financing by a third party. By policy, the bank favored leasing capital equipment, such as major pieces of production or construction equipment. Special-purpose structures to house production equipment and processes often were included. CLC avoided lease financing of other types of real property such as commercial buildings, real estate development, and other improvements to land.

THE PROPOSAL

CIP was in the process of assembling a project to install a "cogeneration" plant in one of the heavy oil fields near Bakersfield. The plant would produce

[1] C. Dana Bickford participated in the preparation of this case.

both thermal (steam) and electrical energy from the burning of raw crude oil. The capital investment required to complete the plant totaled $8 million, of which CIP was able to provide only $500,000. CIP's management team knew that their modest investment potential was insufficient to qualify for a project-type debt financing; they knew that most lenders would require the investment firm to put in 25 to 40 percent, or roughly $2 to $3 million.

As an alternative, Farrell explained the possibility of a leveraged lease package to be managed by CLC. Under this plan, CLC would attempt to structure and place a leveraged lease in which its parent, CalBank, N.A., would provide interim construction financing and CLC would find an equity investor who would be willing to commit $1.6 million, or 20 percent, to the project. It was this crucial part of the package that Farrell had secured that morning by getting a commitment from an equity investor.

The long-term debt component of the funding of the plant to be leased would be provided by a long-term lender such as a bank, insurance firm, or pension fund. According to Chester Leopold, chief operating officer for CIP, a long-term lender had already committed verbally to the permanent debt component of the financing, and a formal commitment letter would be available in a matter of days.

DESCRIPTION OF THE COGENERATION PROCESS

The term *cogeneration* applies to the joint production of thermal and electrical energy from a single plant. Cogeneration plants typically use a hydrocarbon fuel (such as gasoline, natural gas, or fuel oil) to produce electricity and thermal energy (steam) simultaneously. In the project being undertaken by CIP, the electricity produced would be sold to Pacific Gas and Electric, a large California public utility. Fuel for the process would be heavy crude oil produced just off the plant site and sold to CIP by the oil producer. The waste heat resulting from the generation of electricity would be captured and used to produce steam, which would be sold, in turn, to the oil producer. The producer would use the steam to enhance production of heavy crude in a nearby oil reservoir. Cogeneration facilities typically obtain 35 to 40 percent greater fuel efficiency than power plants that do not utilize the waste heat resulting from generating electricity.

CIP had negotiated a nine-year contract with the oil company to supply steam under a take-or-pay contract. In a take-or-pay contract, if for some rea-

son the oil company was unable to take deliveries of steam as agreed, the company would have to pay for the steam as if it had actually taken delivery. Conversely, if CIP was unable to provide the steam for some period of time during the life of the contract, the oil company would be obligated to continue payments set by a predetermined schedule. CIP would be obliged to provide the steam, once its production capability returned, either at the end of the contract or in the form of increased amounts during the remaining contract life, at the oil company's option.

CIP's contract with the oil company also provided for a fuel supply for the cogeneration plant. The oil company would provide CIP with raw crude oil to be used as the fuel source for the cogeneration plant's combustors. A unique aspect of the plant was that it would utilize a modified gas turbine that would burn the heavy crude oil produced from the oil field. The advantages of burning this type of fuel were its low cost compared to refined fuels and its availability on site from the reservoir under production.

CONTRACT FOR COGENERATION PLANT AND EQUIPMENT

Farrell was somewhat surprised to learn that CIP had already signed a turnkey installation contract with a European manufacturer, Industrias Popular Español (IPE), for the plant and equipment needed to complete the project. IPE warranted the performance of the installation in terms of power and steam output, as well as fuel consumption in conformance with CIP's specifications. Farrell considered it unusual that a commitment of this sort was so far advanced before the permanent financing of the project was finalized.

Chester Leopold further advised Farrell that IPE had already filled orders for most of the major pieces of the equipment. Both the equipment and the liability for the equipment appeared on CIP's latest interim financial statement provided for Farrell's review. IPE provided the data in Exhibit I as its estimate of the value and degree of completion.

All of the units were assembled at IPE's local warehouse. IPE had transferred title to the equipment to CIP so that CIP could offer the units as collateral in any financing. IPE held a second lien on the equipment pending payment in full for the plant.

In the event of a default under any bank or lease agreement, IPE agreed to make a best-effort attempt to sell the equipment as a package elsewhere. If this attempt were not successful, IPE would do its best to assist the bank in disposing of the equipment by other means.

When Farrell met with the CIP team several weeks ago, the CIP team indicated that they had already contracted with Pacific Gas and Electric to deliver power produced by the plant for a period of seven years from the date operations began. The contract appeared to be quite favorable to both parties.

Chester Leopold provided Farrell with an eight-year pro forma operations statement (see Exhibit 2). He also provided a detailed monthly operations forecast for 1992, shown in Exhibit 3. Sam Farrell had prepared an analysis of the expected performance of the lease, shown in Exhibit 4, for his successful presentation to the equity investor.

CIP MANAGEMENT

Chester Leopold had assumed responsibility for coordinating the financing for CIP. Leopold was 50 years old and previously had worked for three different West Coast banks after several years as a stockbroker for Merrill Lynch. He also served as a director of CIP.

Warren Blume, age 42, was in charge of the cogeneration activities for CIP. Blume had attended three universities and since 1976 had been active in research, evaluation, and development of cogeneration technology and its application to enhanced oil recovery operations.

Jacques LeBoux, age 42, was the president and founder of CIP. He was a foreign national but was educated in the United States. LeBoux had worked in project engineering jobs with various public and private companies both in the United States and abroad. From 1980 to 1986, he was the chairman of the board of his own land development, home building, and construction company in his native country. Since 1986, he had been exclusively involved with the diversification and growth of CIP. LeBoux was the only one of the partners who had accumulated a significant personal net worth. His financial statement is summarized as follows:

Jacques LeBoux, January 1991

Assets		Liabilities and Net Worth	
Cash	$ 200,000	Short-term notes	$ 300,000
Real estate	10,300,000	Mortgage	800,000
CIP investment	9,000,000	Long-term notes[a]	5,000,000
Personal residence	1,000,000	Total liabilities	$ 6,100,000
Notes receivable	1,500,000	Equity	15,900,000
Total assets	$22,000,000	Total liabilities and equity	$22,000,000

[a] Long-term notes are secured by income-producing properties and without recourse to Mr. LeBoux.

Chester Leopold summarized CIP's financial statement as follows:

California Investment Partnership, January 30, 1991

Assets		Liabilities and Net Worth	
Cash	$ 50,000	Accounts payable	$ 1,000,000
Accounts receivable	500,000	Supplier financing	3,600,000
Plant 1	9,000,000	Long-term debt	5,000,000
Plant 2 (work in progress)	5,800,000	Total liabilities	$ 9,600,000
Notes receivable partners	4,000,000	Partners' equity	9,750,000
Total assets	$19,350,000	Total liabilities plus equity	$19,350,000

THE LEASE PACKAGE

Farrell had obtained a commitment on the morning in question from an equity investor who agreed to participate in the leveraged lease outlined below. The relationships in the lease are diagrammed in Exhibits 5 and 6.

Equipment Cost

There is an $8 million all-in cost. A minimum of $7,750,000 would qualify as Section 38 property, which qualifies for a 10 percent investment tax credit and five years ACRS (Accelerated Cost Recovery System).

Lease Expiration Alternatives

1. The equipment may be returned to CLC.
2. CIP may purchase the equipment at its then fair market value.
3. The lease may be renewed at the then fair market renewal rent.

Other Provisions

1. The proposal is contingent on CIP's ability to secure senior financing in the amount of at least 80 percent of the final, all-in equipment cost, to include installation capitalized interest. The lease payment would be adjusted to reflect the interest rate obtained. At a fixed interest rate of 15.5 percent, the quarterly lease payment will equal 5.1563 percent of the total equipment cost.
2. As an additional incentive to enter into this transaction, CIP would pay CLC a minimum of 12 percent of its pretax profit each year during the lease term. If CIP failed to achieve pretax profits in any particular year, there would be no liability for that year.
3. The commitment is contingent on CLC's review and approval of the financial statements of all parties involved, the contracts between the parties, and mutually satisfactory documentation.
4. CLC will receive an up-front, nonrefundable fee of 1 percent of the lease amount, or $80,000.

FINANCING

CIP asked CalBank to provide an interim construction loan of approximately $3 million to move the equipment to the Bakersfield area and bring the plant to operational status. It was anticipated that the loan would be outstanding for 120 to 150 days while construction was under way. Repayment would come from funding of the lease by CLC and the long-term lender.

Farrell was not sure what to make of the unconventional sequence of events in which CIP had already arranged for fabrication of the cogeneration equipment and even held legal title to it prior to arranging for financing. Normally, all the details of a lease agreement would be documented carefully before such action took place. The funding then would occur when the lessee signed a letter of acceptance of the completed plant.

CIP had specifically requested that the construction loan be without recourse to any of the CIP partners. CIP requested funding under the interim construction loan within two weeks. Farrell and Leopold had an appointment with a senior loan officer at CalBank to discuss the interim financing. They knew they must press for an early decision because contracts in the lease commitment called for the plant to be on stream in five months. The construction period would take nearly four months.

In summary, the sources and applications of funds would be as follows:

Sources

Lease	$1,600,000
Long-term debt	6,400,000
CIP miscellaneous contributions	300,000
Total	$8,300,000

Uses

Payment to IPE	$3,600,000
Construction, moving, start-up costs	1,550,000
Repayment of interim construction loans	3,150,000
Total	$8,300,000

EXHIBIT 1   Estimate of Value

Equipment	Estimated Fair Market Value	Percentage Complete	Available Collateral
Turbines and generators	$3,700,000	100	$3,700,000
Recuperators	300,000	100	300,000
Boilers and scrubbers	1,300,000	30	396,000
Total	$5,300,000		$4,396,000

EXHIBIT 2   California Investment Partnership—Operations Forecast, 1992–1999 (dollars in thousands)

	1992	1993	1994	1995	1996	1997	1998	1999
Total revenue	$7,023	$10,535	$11,167	$11,837	$12,547	$13,300	$14,098	$14,943
Operating expense	4,022	6,033	6,395	6,779	7,185	7,617	8,074	8,558
G&A expense	1,500	2,250	2,385	2,528	2,680	2,841	3,011	3,192
Lease costs	1,650	1,650	1,650	1,650	1,650	1,650	1,650	1,650
Pretax profit/(loss)	($ 149)	$ 602	$ 737	$ 880	$ 1,032	$ 1,192	$ 1,363	$ 1,543

EXHIBIT 3   California Investment Partnership—Monthly Operations Forecast, 1992 (dollars in thousands)

Income Statement—Financial	Jan.	Feb.	Mar.	Apr.	May	June	Jul.	Aug.	Sept.	Oct.	Nov.	Dec.	Total	Percent
Revenue	371	315	578	559	747	657	679	679	723	578	559	578	7023	100.00%
Operating expenses														
Fuel costs	186	174	186	180	186	180	186	186	180	186	180	186	2199	31.31%
Direct payroll and benefits	39	39	39	39	39	39	39	39	39	39	39	39	469	6.68
Plant operating costs	101	101	101	101	101	101	101	101	101	101	101	101	1212	17.26
Power discount	8	7	13	13	13	12	12	12	13	13	13	13	142	2.02
Total operating expenses	335	321	339	333	339	332	338	338	333	339	333	339	4022	57.27%
Operating income	36	−7	238	226	408	325	341	341	390	238	226	238	3001	42.73%
Site overhead	0	0	0	0	0	0	0	0	0	0	0	0	0	0.00
Reserve-engine rebuild	0	0	0	0	0	0	0	0	0	0	0	0	0	0.00
Depreciation—20 years	40	40	40	40	40	40	40	40	40	40	40	40	480	6.83
General and administrative	35	35	35	35	35	35	35	35	35	35	35	35	420	5.98
Interest	76	76	76	76	76	76	76	75	74	73	73	72	898	12.79
Plant lease costs	105	105	105	105	105	105	105	105	105	105	105	105	1254	17.86
Income before CNC fees and tax	−220	−262	−17	−29	152	70	86	86	136	−14	−26	−13	−51	−0.73%
CNC fee	0	0	0	0	0	0	0	0	0	0	0	0	0	0.00
Profit before tax	−220	−262	−17	−29	152	70	86	86	136	−14	−26	−13	−51	−0.73%
Taxes on income	0	0	0	0	0	0	0	0	0	0	0	0	0	0.00
Profits after tax	−220	−262	−17	−29	152	70	86	86	136	−14	−26	−13	−51	−0.73%
Cash flow	−180	−222	23	11	192	110	126	126	176	26	14	27	429	6.11%

EXHIBIT 4 Leverage Lease Analysis for Equity Investors, Not Including 12 Percent Pretax Profit Kicker

End of Year	(1) Initial Equity Participation Less ITC[a] (Net)	(2) Lease Payment Receipt[b]	(3) Depreciation[c]	(4) Loan Interest Payment[d]	(5) Pretax Profit (2) − (3) − (4)	(6) Taxes (40 Percent)[e]	(7) Total Loan Payment[f]	(8) Cash Flows[g]
0	($800,000)							($ 800,000)
1		$1,650,000	$1,368,000	$1,240,000	($ 958,000)	($383,200)	$914.286	(121,086)
2		1,650,000	2,508,000	1,062,857	(1,920,857)	(768,342)	914,286	441,199
3		1,650,000	1,900,000	885,714	(1,135,714)	(454,286)	914,286	304,286
4		1,650,000	1,216,000	708,571	(274,571)	(109,828)	914,286	136,971
5		1,650,000	608,000	531,429	510,571	204,228	914,286	57
6		1,650,000	—	354,286	1,295,714	518,286	914,286	(136,858)
7		3,250,000	—	177,143	3,072,857	909,143[h]	914,286	1,249,428

[a] $1,600,000 − (0.1)(8,000,000) = $800,000.

[b] 5.1563% × $8,000,000 × 4. In year 7, add $1,600,000 for the assumed 20% residual value, which is taxed at the 20% capital gains rate.

[c] Per 1985 federal tax guide; Section 38 property with five-year ACRS and 10% ITC.

[d] Year 1: $8,000,000 × 0.155 = $1,240,000
Year 2: $6,757,143 × 0.155 = 1,062,857
Year 3: $5,714,286 × 0.155 = 885,714
Year 4: $4,571,429 × 0.155 = 708,571
Year 5: $3,428,571 × 0.155 = 531,429
Year 6: $2,285,714 × 0.155 = 354,286
Year 7: $1,142,857 × 0.155 = 177,143

[e] Parentheses indicate a tax credit.

[f] $6,400,000 ÷ 7 = $914,286 per year.

[g] (1) + (2) − (4) − (6) − (7)

Assumes that the tax benefits flow through to the investors.

[h] $1,650,000 − 177,143 = 1,472,857 × 0.4 = $589,143
Salvage value   1,600,000 × 0.2 = 320,000
         Total   = $909,143

EXHIBIT 5   Ownership and Initial Funding Diagram

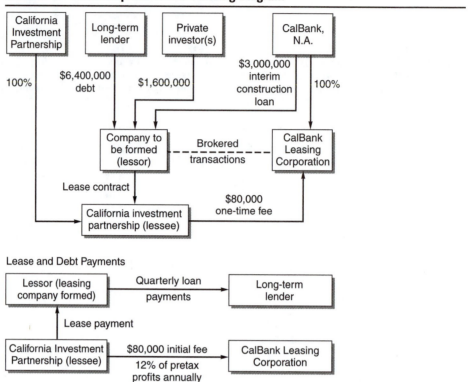

EXHIBIT 6   Contractual Relationships

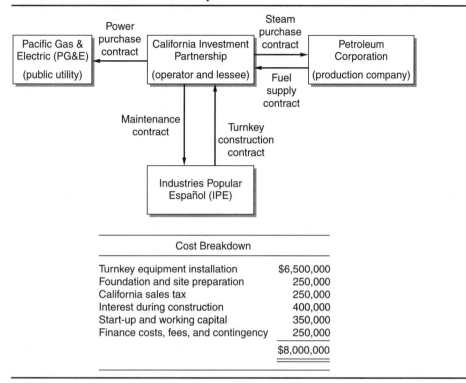

Cost Breakdown	
Turnkey equipment installation	$6,500,000
Foundation and site preparation	250,000
California sales tax	250,000
Interest during construction	400,000
Start-up and working capital	350,000
Finance costs, fees, and contingency	250,000
	$8,000,000

CASE 14

EDWARD EDWARDS COMPANY (A)

INTRODUCTION

Edward Edwards was a manufacturers' representative acting on a commission basis only. He sold decorative accessories, pictures, lamps, and garden accessories, and he engaged in direct importing of similar items for his own account. His territory covered Texas, Oklahoma, New Mexico, Missouri, Arkansas, Mississippi, Tennessee, and Louisiana. Edwards' business was not seasonal, and he had two employees in addition to himself. His business was located in rented showroom space in a multistory building in Dallas's industrial section. The showrooms covered 20,000 square feet, and the premises were orderly.

The business had been started 22 years ago in Oklahoma City and was moved to Dallas in 1993. Edwards was 50 years old. He had worked for his father, who was also a manufacturers' representative, for about eight years prior to forming his own company.

BANKING RELATIONSHIP

Edwards had been a customer at Third Bank of Dallas for the past 10 years. Since that time he had steadily used the letter of credit (L/C) services in the bank's international department. Third Bank of Dallas had issued its first L/C for Edwards' account some eight years ago for $16,000 on a 100 percent cash secured basis. Additional L/Cs were issued that same year on the same collateral basis, none of which individually exceeded $25,000. No more than that amount was outstanding at any time during the year.

The following year, Third Bank continued to service Edwards' L/C requirements covering his foreign purchases but changed its collateral position to one of being secured solely by shipping documents, including full sets of clean-on-board ocean bills of lading drawn to shipper's order and blank endorsed. Under this arrangement, individual CDs up to $40,000 were issued, all payable against shipping documents and sight drafts. At no time did such outstanding credits exceed $60,000 in the aggregate. Beginning in 1992, individual credits up to $50,000 were issued, and aggregate outstandings reached $120,000, all on the same basis noted previously.

Because of projected sales increases for the period 1995–1997, Edwards requested a $200,000 line to cover L/Cs payable against sight drafts when accompanied by ocean shipping documents, including bills of lading as noted previously. This line would also cover financing of sight draft L/C payments for up to 120 days. The line of credit was granted, and the bank's experience with Edwards proved entirely satisfactory.

Edwards continued to operate under this line from 1995 to 1997. In 1998, he again asked the bank to increase the line from $200,000 to $400,000 and requested that drafts under L/Cs be drawn payable at 120 days after sight, thus giving rise to a banker's acceptance. Edwards' request for this change in the use of drafts arose because the Japanese banks through which his sight draft L/Cs had been utilized were offering more attractive financing charges covering Japanese exports than were available in the United States.

The discount rate in Japan on acceptances of up to 120 days, together with Third Bank's acceptance commission on 120-day drafts, would be less than Edwards' borrowing rate at Third Bank. These credits would be utilized to provide the funds to meet sight draft payments under L/Cs. Edwards' unaudited financial statements for the past three years are summarized in Exhibits 1–3.

In discussions with Edwards, the bank indicated that it would study his request, including the liabilities and responsibilities that would be included in the issuance of L/Cs and the bank's subsequent acceptance of drafts associated with those L/Cs. In making a decision, the lending officer knew she must be aware of the bank's role as the issuing bank, accepting and paying L/Cs for Edwards' account.

EXHIBIT 1   Edward Edwards Company—Statement of Source and Application of Funds, Years Ended December 31, 1996, 1997, and 1998[a]

	1996		1997		1998	
Funds provided by:						
Net earnings		$179,320		$185,200		$200,060
Adjust for depreciation charges not requiring funds		9,260		9,350		1,750
Disposition of automobile		24,110		0		0
Disposition of investments		0		2,910		0
		$212,690		$197,460		$201,810
Funds applied to:						
Increase in working capital						
Working capital, end of year	$239,790		$303,920		$380,830	
Working capital, beginning of year	153,340	86,450	239,790	64,130	303,920	76,910
Acquisition of automobile		31,730		0		0
Acquisition of equipment		4,050		3,500		6,460
Increase in other assets and investments		24,130		0		51,580
Owner's net withdrawals and other		66,330		129,830		66,870
		$212,690		$197,460		$201,820

[a] All statements prepared from the books without audit.

EXHIBIT 2 Edward Edwards Company—Balance Sheet, December 31, 1996, 1997, and 1998

	1996		1997		1998	
Assets						
Current assets						
Cash—business account	$ 39,680		$ 53,170		$167,120	
Cash—personal account	104,210	$143,890	130,100	$183,270	118,480	$285,600
Trade accounts receivable		56,280		56,680		60,560
Merchandise inventory		155,000		175,020		223,100
Prepaid expenses		600		730		0
Total current assets		$355,770		$415,700		$569,260
Fixed assets						
Automobile—business	31,730		31,730		31,730	
Automobile—personal	27,510		27,510		27,510	
Office and showroom equipment	22,870		26,370		32,830	
Total—at cost	82,110		85,610		92,070	
Less accumulated depreciation	25,500	56,610	34,850	50,760	36,600	55,470
Other assets and investments						
Cash value of life insurance in force	37,450		37,450		41,950	
Contributions to retirement plan— General Motors	14,000		14,000		14,000	
Contributions to self-employed retirement plan	5,000		15,000		38,710	
Corporation stocks and bonds	117,800		94,950		133,000	
Deposits	350		350		350	
U.S. savings bonds	25,520		17,450		0	
United Science Fund Plan	0	200,120	18,000	197,200	20,760	248,770
		$612,500		$663,660		$873,500
Liabilities and Owner's Equity						
Current liabilities						
Trade accounts payable		$ 13,840		$ 9,720		$180,060
Insurance loan payable		3,770		3,770		2,760
Notes payable—bank		61,930		66,110		0
Payroll taxes		360		2,180		1,650
Income and self-employment taxes payable		36,090		29,900		3,940
Total current liabilities		115,990		111,770		188,410
Owner's equity						
Balance, January 1	$383,520		$496,520		551,890	
Net income	179,320		185,200		200,070	
Total	562,840		681,720		751,960	
Less owner's withdrawal and other	66,330	496,510	129,830	551,890	66,870	685,090
Total liabilities and owner's equity		$612,500		$663,660		$873,500

EXHIBIT 3   Edward Edwards Company—Statement of Earnings, Years Ended 1996, 1997, and 1998

	1996		1997		1998	
Net sales		$501,864		$814,200		$1,025,720
Cost of sales						
Inventory—beginning	$ 86,548		$155,004		$175,023	
Purchases	351,396		498,287		678,786	
Merchandise available for sale	437,944		653,291		853,808	
Less inventory—ending	155,004		175,023		223,096	
Cost of sales		282,940		478,268		630,713
Gross profit		218,924		335,932		395,016
Commission income		193,637		213,763		229,764
Rent subsidy		12,000		12,000		12,000
Miscellaneous income		0		1,142		0
Gross income		$424,561		$562,836		$636,780
Expenses						
Accounting and legal	6,000		12,600		8,250	
Advertising	3,206		9,608		12,096	
Automobile	7,355		6,992		5,736	
Bad debts charged off	4,976		11,714		3,299	
Customer contact	1,979		2,986		2,197	
Depreciation	9,262		9,345		1,755	
Dues and subscriptions	914		1,748		0	
Insurance	2,941		5,684		5,339	
Interest	4,381		7,099		7,023	
Office supplies	5,706		14,294		10,099	
Office and showroom rent	82,380		76,199		87,937	
Payroll taxes	1,781		1,556		3,110	
Repairs and maintenance	0		475		1,397	
Salaries	42,900		47,018		76,356	
Sales commissions	68,774		105,500		147,163	
Telephone	6,645		5,971		6,562	
Taxes—general	651		3,515		3,208	
Travel—lodging, meals, tips	8,618		8,915		11,060	
Travel—commercial fares	3,439		42,095		32,664	
Utilities	5,882		5,664		5,675	
Miscellaneous	508	268,295	2,330	381,239	5,789	436,715
Net operating income		156,266		181,597		200,065
Extraordinary income (expense)		23,058		0		0
Net earnings		$179,324		$181,597		$200,065

[a] No provision has been made in this statement for income tax accruing on the proprietor.

PART FOUR

HEDGING AND PRICING WITH DERIVATIVES AND INTERNATIONAL BANKING

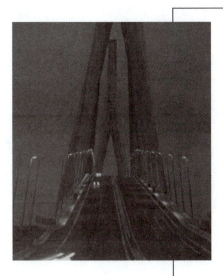

At the millennium, a recurring theme in bank management is the bridge between the institutional context of commercial banks and the vast financial markets that have developed especially rapidly in the United States and the United Kingdom. A central aspect of the growth of financial markets has been financial derivative instruments such as forwards, futures, options, and swaps. These instruments create highly efficient and convenient means for distributing the risk of institutions' contractual obligations, be they balance sheet items or, simply, financial agreements that have yet to be concretized into cash accountable items. In addition to their flexibility as devices for hedging financial risks, derivatives are efficient carriers of pricing information. As such, competent bankers use prices set on derivatives to be informed about how to price products sold in relationship banking. Chapters 13, 14, and 15 present aspects of, respectively, interest rate forward and futures contracts, interest rate options contracts, and interest rate swap contracts. Each chapter describes the subject instrument, introduces crucial institutional arrangements, and presents examples of risk hedging transactions. Each chapter concludes by presenting more advanced material on the use of the subject instrument in pricing a bank's relationship products. Chapter 16 closes this book by reviewing the foreign exchange market and currency derivative instruments. It develops special sections on international financial transactions, instruments, and institutions used to conduct international banking. ■

Financial Futures and Forwards: Hedging and Pricing

This section defines and analyzes three types of derivative instruments. More specifically, we examine the narrower segment of *financial* derivatives: futures, forwards, options, and swaps that are written on interest rates and foreign exchange.

OVERVIEW OF DERIVATIVES

Derivatives are so called because the values of forwards, futures, options, and swaps each are *derived* from some other instrument. The other instruments are called *the underlying*, and they include items such as corporate shares, fixed-income securities, currency, money market instruments, and stock or bond indexes. In a few words, derivatives are abstractions that depend on reference to something else. However, when we discuss derivatives, it does not require a great leap in abstraction. The whole field of finance is based on abstraction, and almost all of financial theory and analysis is organized around an abstraction called *the future*: it takes the form of future cash flows, rates for discounting future values, risk, and so forth.

Commercial banks in the United States are extraordinarily active users of derivatives. At the end of 1997, bank portfolios held a *notional amount* of derivatives equal to $26.0 trillion. Notional amounts are the amounts of underlying reference values such as those listed above. Notional amounts can be considered to be "pseudoprincipal." The derivatives themselves do not require the commitment of principal implied in the underlying reference values. Rather, derivatives create payment obligations derived from pseudo principal values. Nevertheless, the sheer size of this base implies enormous commitments on the part of banks. The $26.0 trillion notional value is more than five times the value of the banks' balance sheet assets.

Of the $26.0 trillion amount, two-thirds are contracts based on interest rates, and nearly all of the remaining one-third are contracts based on foreign exchange. Figure 13.1 indicates that in the six years from 1991 to 1997 the use of derivatives increased from

FIGURE 13.1   Derivative Contracts Held in the U.S. Banking System

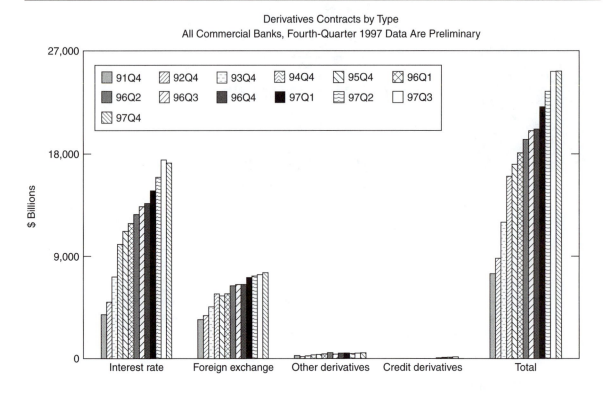

Derivative Contracts by Type ($ Billions)												
	91Q4	92Q4	93Q4	94Q4	95Q4	96Q1	96Q2	96Q3	96Q4	97Q1	97Q2	97Q3	97Q4
Interest Rate	3.637	4.872	7.210	9.924	11.064	11.820	12.817	13.257	13.427	14.642	15.602	17.270	17.065
Foreign Exchange	3.384	3.768	4.484	5.406	5.387	5.450	6.126	6.210	6.241	6.919	7.044	7.264	7.430
Other Derivatives	0.100	0.102	0.170	0.243	0.378	0.378	0.394	0.351	0.347	0.347	0.413	0.462	0.484
Credit Derivatives										0.10	0.20	0.30	0.55
TOTAL	7.330	8.764	11.673	15.774	16.541	17.847	19.036	19.818	20.036	21.847	23.325	25.024	26.044

a base of $7.3 trillion notional amount, a growth of 244 percent. Interest rate derivatives alone increased from $3.6 trillion to $17.1 trillion notional amount, a growth of 350 percent.

Derivatives are heavily concentrated among the largest banks. Eight commercial banks accounted for 95 percent of the total notional amount of derivatives in the banking system. The largest banks use more than 90 percent of their derivatives' holdings for trading purposes. Smaller regional banks tend to limit their use of derivatives for purposes of managing their own and their customers' risk.

Financial institutions use derivatives (1) to modify the repricing or maturity characteristics of certain assets and liabilities, (2) to price cash products, and (3) to trade for profit. In this chapter we study the role of futures and forward contracts in the first two types of uses: hedging and pricing. Normally, derivative positions are not recorded on the user institutions' balance sheets.

THE BASICS OF FORWARD AND FUTURES CONTRACTS

Forward and futures contracts set the terms today for transactions to take place in the future. There is nothing unusual about transactions today that involve the future: Financial institutions' decisions nearly always take a stake in the future. Institutions make loans by contracting forward for positions in the income streams of borrowers. They acquire long-term investment securities, as we noted in Chapter 4, by contracting forward for positions in future short-term interest rates embedded in the securities' yields. They sell deposits and investment products by contracting short positions to provide future payments and services. All of these are *cash* transactions based on future abstractions. They create a future risk-return structure in the form of portfolios of assets and liabilities that the institutions must manage. Forwards, futures, and other derivative products can be used to manage this risk-return structure.

Here is how forwards and futures differ from cash transactions. They call for the future exchange of cash in return for the delivery or receipt of currency, securities, or commodities at a price that is set today. In contrast, cash transactions typically require an immediate exchange of cash or credit and delivery of valuable assets such as funds or British pounds or bushels of corn. You have to be careful with such distinctions because cash transactions also embed future positions such as promises of future repayment of funds or currencies. A major difference is that at the time they are originated, positions in futures and forwards have no monetary value.

EXAMPLE Why should one enter an arrangement for forward delivery of securities, currency or commodities? Consider the case of a farmer who, in March, decides to sell his corn crop forward for delivery in September at $5 per bushel. If the price of corn falls to $4 per bushel by September, the farmer is entitled to sell corn for $5 and has protected the value of his crop. On the other hand, if corn prices rise to $6 in September, he still must sell for $5. By locking in the price back in the March planting season, the farmer missed an opportunity to receive a windfall $6 price, but he got the comfort of guaranteeing the value of his crop at harvest time. In short, he eliminated his price risk. The forward market enabled him to take a future position in goods that did not even exist when he made the contract.

Futures contracts are standardized as to size, quality, and date of delivery of goods, and for many types of futures, liquidity is ensured by a deep supply of contracts. Futures buyers and sellers seldom take or make delivery of the underlying asset but, instead, sell or buy offsetting contracts before the delivery date.

Forward contracts, as opposed to futures contracts, are individualized agreements between a buyer and a seller requiring delivery of an asset at a specified future date, with payment to be made upon delivery. For example, a public utility might enter a forward contract to receive a certain grade and amount of natural gas on specified dates during the heating season for future resale to its customers. Futures contracts accomplish roughly the same thing except that the contracts are *standardized* and their terms are enforced by a futures exchange. Parties to a forward contract are not limited by standardization. They are free to customize terms, such as the amount, quality and time of delivery of the deliverable asset.

For several reasons, however, this lack of standardization creates serious disadvantages to forwards. First, it may be difficult to find a trading partner that has an immediate corresponding need to exchange an identical amount of the same grade of asset at the same future delivery date. Second, with forward contracts, delivery often is called for, even though one may not want to take or make delivery. It is often sufficient for buyers and sellers simply to hold a temporary position in the asset underlying the forward contract without ever taking or making delivery.

EXAMPLE   Greenfields Bank, N. A. specializes in loans to dry land farmers whose major expense is for fuel used to operate their irrigation pumps. Greenfields decides to hedge against increasing gas prices by buying a forward contract in natural gas. The bank worries that rapid increases in gas prices will damage its farmer customers' solvency and capacity to repay the loans. Needless to say, the bank does not want to take delivery of the natural gas.

A third, and most important difference, between forwards and futures is *settlement risk*. Invariably, you can count on futures exchanges to solve the settlement risks of forward contracting. Trust between buyer and seller is not a concern with futures contracts because every day the futures contract is marked-to-market to recognize the change in value of the underlying asset. The exchange then requires that the losing party settle its losses every day. To guarantee that parties settle daily, the exchange sets a margin that traders must deposit in the form of good faith collateral (margin is not a down payment) such as cash, securities, or letters of credit. If one cannot meet a ''margin call,'' the exchange immediately closes out the position.

It is not that way in the forward market. At the outset, neither forward nor futures contracts have monetary value. As time passes, however, the market value of the underlying asset changes and creates a loss for one of the parties and a gain for the other. This makes for settlement risk in the forward market where there is no daily settling such as in the futures market. Once the market value changes, the losing counterparty loses motivation for complying with the contract. For example, a forward contract that calls for delivery of forward British pounds at $1.50/pound will have negative value to the buyer if the spot-exchange rate for the pound falls to $1.40 by the time of delivery. The buyer is now called upon to pay $1.50 at delivery for pounds that are worth only $1.40 in the market. It does not take genius to see that, absent daily settlement, the seller's risk is that the buyer may not take delivery. The buyer has everything to gain by not performing.

Interest rate futures contracts are written against the following instruments: U.S. Treasury notes and bonds, U.S. Treasury bills, federal funds, GNMA collateralized depository receipts, domestic CDs, and one-month and three-month Eurodollar time deposits and one-month LIBOR. Figure 13.2 reproduces daily trading information on many of these contracts. The last column in Figure 13.2 lists the *open interest,* which indicates the number of contracts outstanding for each type of contract. Combined, a buy and sell trade creates one contract of open interest.

FIGURE 13.2   Interest Rate Futures

INTEREST RATE

TREASURY BONDS (CBT)-$100,000; pts. 32nds of 100%

	Open	High	Low	Settle	Change	Lifetime High	Lifetime Low	Open Interest
Mar	111-14	111-18	110-29	111-09	− 4	120-00	99-26	473,566
June	110-29	111-02	110-13	110-25	− 4	118-21	99-16	20,658
Sept	110-12	110-15	110-02	110-11	− 4	117-21	100-18	5,322
Dec	....	....	....	109-29	− 4	118-08	100-08	3,755

Est vol 375,000; vol Tue 475,420; open Int 503,359, +17,362.

TREASURY BONDS (MCE)-$50,000; pts. 32nds of 100%

	Open	High	Low	Settle	Change	Lifetime High	Lifetime Low	Open Interest
Mar	111-19	111-19	110-28	111-08	− 6	116-17	105-29	10,442

Est vol 4,400; vol Tue 5,988; open Int 10,468, +121.

TREASURY NOTES (CBT)-$100,000; pts. 32nds of 100%

	Open	High	Low	Settle	Change	Lifetime High	Lifetime Low	Open Interest
Mar	108-19	108-21	108-10	108-17	....	113-09	104-15	321,819
June	107-30	108-01	107-25	107-30	....	111-04	104-19	11,718
Sept	....	....	....	107-15	....	110-15	107-12	180

Est vol 75,000; vol Tue 109,461; open Int 333,717, +3,075.

5 YR TREAS NOTES (CBT)-$100,000; pts. 32nds of 100%

	Open	High	Low	Settle	Change	Lifetime High	Lifetime Low	Open Interest
Mar	06-075	06-105	106-03	06-085	+ 1.00	8-115	103-30	167,208
June	05-315	106-01	105-27	106-00	+ 1.00	7-305	05-135	6,047

Est vol 42,500; vol Tue 56,035; open Int 173,255, −493.

2 YR TREAS NOTES (CBT)-$200,000; pts. 32nds of 100%

	Open	High	Low	Settle	Change	Lifetime High	Lifetime Low	Open Interest
Mar	03-087	103-09	03-065	03-082	+ .80	3-315	03-005	20,326
June	03-01	03-012	103-00	03-012	+ 1.00	3-245	02-265	150

Est vol 1,300; vol Tue 2,048; open Int 20,476, +91.

30-DAY FEDERAL FUNDS (CBT)-$5 million; pts of 100%

	Open	High	Low	Settle	Change	Lifetime High	Lifetime Low	Open Interest
Jan	94.700	94.705	94.700	94.705	+ .005	95.350	93.900	3,922
Feb	94.69	94.70	94.69	94.69	....	94.72	93.98	7,117
Mar	94.64	94.65	94.64	94.64	....	94.69	93.94	3,057
Apr	94.57	94.58	94.57	94.57	....	94.70	93.83	1,468
May	94.53	94.53	94.52	94.53	+.01	94.70	93.95	335

Est vol 1,597; vol Tue 3,074; open Int 16,052, +715.

MUNI BOND INDEX (CBT)-$1,000; times Bond Buyer MBI

	Open	High	Low	Settle	Change	Lifetime High	Lifetime Low	Open Interest
Mar	115-04	115-04	114-20	114-29	− 5	118-13	111-09	11,001

Est vol 2,500; vol Tue 3,863; open Int 11,124, +298.
The index: Close 116-00; Yield 6.02.

TREASURY BILLS (CME)-$1 mil.; pts. of 100%

	Open	High	Low	Settle	Chg	Discount Settle	Discount Chg	Open Interest
Mar	94.91	94.92	94.91	94.92	+ .02	5.08	− .02	4,760
June	94.74	94.76	94.74	94.76	....	5.24	....	2,732

Est vol 737; vol Tue 156; open Int 7,677, −3.

LIBOR-1 MO. (CME)-$3,000,000; points of 100%

	Open	High	Low	Settle	Chg	Discount Settle	Discount Chg	Open Interest
Feb	94.53	94.54	94.52	94.53	+ .01	5.47	− .01	19,248
Mar	94.46	94.48	94.46	94.48	+ .02	5.52	− .02	7,003
Apr	94.40	94.42	94.40	94.42	+ .02	5.58	− .02	2,717
May	94.36	94.37	94.36	94.37	+ .01	5.63	− .01	730
June	94.30	94.31	94.30	94.31	....	5.69	....	567
July	94.24	94.24	94.24	94.24	....	5.76	....	61
Aug	....	....	....	94.18	....	5.82	....	186

Est vol 17,102; vol Tue 6,617; open Int 30,764, −12,532.

EURODOLLAR (CME)-$1 million; pts of 100%

	Open	High	Low	Settle	Chg	Yield Settle	Yield Chg	Open Interest
Feb	94.41	94.43	94.41	94.41	....	5.59	....	11,640
Mar	94.37	94.38	94.36	94.37	+ .01	5.63	− .01	408,474
June	94.20	94.21	94.17	94.19	....	5.81	....	365,786
Sept	94.01	94.04	93.98	94.01	....	5.99	....	277,746
Dec	93.82	93.84	93.79	93.82	+ .01	6.18	− .01	191,821
Mr98	93.74	93.76	93.70	93.74	+ .01	6.26	− .01	158,433
June	93.66	93.66	93.61	93.64	+ .01	6.36	− .01	120,022
Sept	93.60	93.60	93.55	93.58	+ .01	6.42	− .01	94,191
Dec	93.47	93.50	93.45	93.48	+ .01	6.52	− .01	78,582
Mr99	93.49	93.49	93.44	93.47	+ .01	6.53	− .01	60,412
June	93.43	93.43	93.37	93.41	+ .01	6.59	− .01	62,157
Sept	93.37	93.37	93.32	93.35	+ .01	6.65	− .01	49,597
Dec	93.27	93.28	93.23	93.27	+ .02	6.73	− .02	41,308
Mr00	93.28	93.28	93.23	93.27	+ .02	6.73	− .02	38,253
June	93.22	93.22	93.17	93.21	+ .02	6.79	− .02	34,974
Sept	93.17	93.17	93.12	93.16	+ .02	6.84	− .02	30,955
Dec	93.06	93.09	93.04	93.08	+ .02	6.92	− .02	24,620
Mr01	93.06	93.09	93.04	93.08	+ .02	6.92	− .02	25,317
June	93.01	93.04	92.99	93.03	+ .02	6.97	− .02	20,319
Sept	92.99	93.00	92.95	92.99	+ .02	7.01	− .02	15,053
Dec	92.90	92.92	92.87	92.91	+ .02	7.09	− .02	9,996
Mr02	92.89	92.91	92.87	92.91	+ .02	7.09	− .02	5,000
June	92.85	92.87	92.83	92.87	+ .02	7.13	− .02	5,083
Sept	92.81	92.83	92.79	92.83	+ .02	7.17	− .02	5,216
Dec	92.74	92.76	92.72	92.75	+ .01	6.25	− .01	6,303
Mr03	92.73	92.75	92.72	92.75	+ .01	7.25	− .01	4,806
June	92.68	92.70	92.67	92.70	+ .01	7.30	− .01	3,942
Sept	92.64	92.66	92.63	92.66	+ .01	7.34	− .01	5,160
Dec	92.56	92.58	92.55	92.58	+ .01	7.42	− .01	4,014
Mr04	92.57	92.58	92.56	92.58	+ .01	7.42	− .01	2,051
June	92.52	92.53	92.51	92.53	+ .01	7.47	− .01	3,818
Sept	92.48	92.49	92.47	92.49	+ .01	7.51	− .01	3,082
Dec	92.40	92.41	92.39	92.41	+ .01	7.59	− .01	3,713
Mr05	....	....	....	92.42	+ .01	7.58	− .01	1,859
June	....	....	....	92.37	+ .01	7.63	− .01	2,321
Sept	....	....	....	92.33	+ .01	7.67	− .01	1,653
Dec	....	....	....	92.25	+ .01	7.75	− .01	1,188
Mr06	....	....	....	92.26	+ .01	7.74	− .01	2,195
June	....	....	....	92.21	+ .01	7.79	− .01	771
Sept	....	....	....	92.17	+ .01	7.83	− .01	538

Est vol 332,611; vol Tue 534,771; open Int 2,184,137, −12,763.

SOURCE: *Wall Street Journal,* January 16, 1997, C18.

There are two important facts to remember. First, open interest usually is largest for the *nearby contract*—the next contract due for delivery. The most *distant contracts*—those with delivery dates farthest in the future—have the least open interest, thus the least liquidity, and may not be efficiently priced. Second, open interest must go to zero by the end of the contract's life as traders enter reversing trades or, in rare instances, as they take or make delivery.

Margin and Settlement

One must understand settlement procedures in order to understand futures trading. Following is an example of margin requirements and futures settlement procedures for U.S. Treasury bill (T-bill) futures.

T-bill futures contracts call for delivery of a cash T-bill with $1 million in face value and a 90- to 92-day maturity. Delivery occurs on the Thursday, Friday, or Monday after the third Monday of the delivery month. The delivery month rotation for the International Monetary Market (IMM), the exchange with the most T-bill futures activity, is March, June, September, and December.

The T-bill contract is priced on a discount basis comparable to the price formula for cash T-bills (also called *spot* T-bills). Unlike the cash bill, however, the futures is quoted on an index basis, which is calculated as 100 minus the annual percentage discount that traders expect for the future three-month bill underlying the contract.[1] For example, an index of 94.00 implies a 6 percent annualized discount. As with bonds, the index and discount (price and interest rate) move in opposite directions: a rising discount rate corresponds to a falling index.

$$\mathcal{F}_{\text{T-Bill}} = \$1,000,000 \left[1 - d \times \left(\frac{t}{360} \right) \right] \tag{13.1}$$

where $\mathcal{F}_{\text{T-Bill}}$ = T-bill futures contract price
d = annualized discount rate

If d is 6 percent,

$$\mathcal{F}_{\text{T-Bill}} = \$1,000,000 \left[1 - 0.06 \times \left(\frac{90}{360} \right) \right] = \$985,000$$

T-bill futures calculations assume a 90-day maturity and a 360-day year. This results in a price movement of $25 corresponding to a single basis point change in discount or interest rates (called the value of a "tick" or the value of an 01). For example, solving Equation 13.1 for $d = 6.01$ percent results in a price of $984,975 or a $25 reduction for a 1 basis point increase in annualized discount. This value facilitates tracking daily settlement gains or losses on futures. The futures exchange merely multiplies the basis point change in discount rate by $25.[2]

Investors who enter a buy (long) or sell (short) position in futures must deposit "initial" margin with a broker to ensure that enough money will be on hand to cover losses in the event of adverse price changes. Margin acts as a performance bond to guarantee the performance of market participants.[3] If the broker is a clearing member firm, the broker in turn deposits margin with the exchange clearinghouse. The exchange "marks to the market" all open futures positions and requires investors to settle all gains and losses on a daily basis. If the open position incurs a loss on a given day, the exchange debits the investor's margin account for the amount of the loss.

When the value of a futures contract increases during the day, the margin accounts of customers holding short positions are debited. At the same time, the accounts of customers holding long positions are credited. If the losing customer's margin account is reduced

---

[1] The index is known as the IMM index for the International Monetary Market, the exchange where T-bill futures contracts were first introduced.

[2] Changes in the value of the futures differ from changes in the price of a deliverable cash T-bill because cash bills almost always have a 91-day maturity. Because of the difference in *day count*, $1 million worth of 91-day cash T-bills changes $25.28 for a 1 basis point change in discount. Everything else equal, this discrepancy slightly unbalances a T-bill futures hedge against price changes in the deliverable cash bill.

[3] The futures exchange sets the minimal maintenance margin, and then the initial margin is set at a multiple of it. For example, on the three-month Eurodollar contract, maintenance margin is $150 per contract, and the initial margin is fixed at 1.35 times this amount, or $203. Normally, brokers set higher margin requirements of their own.

to the level of the "maintenance" margin, the clearing firm promptly deposits additional funds known as "variation" margin. Futures exchanges establish, and sometimes revise, the amount of initial and maintenance margins required according to the contract's price volatility and maximum daily price change permitted by the exchange. The case of Cavaretta Securities, Inc. is an example of daily settlement.

EXAMPLE On March 1, Cavaretta Securities, Inc., a government securities dealer, acquires an inventory of $100 million in three-month Treasury bills which it will sell to a large institutional investor on March 3. Cavaretta finances the T-bills with a broker call loan at a rate that is reset only once a week. The firm buys 100 T-bill futures contracts to take advantage of possible declines in market rates over the three-day period.

Table 13.1 details the futures settlement procedures for the three days. On March 1,

TABLE 13.1 Futures Settlement Procedures for Cavaretta Securities

90-day Treasury bill futures:
Current margins are:
Initial margin = $1,200
Maintenance margin = $800

Mar 1: Cavaretta Securities buys 100 contracts (long)		
Entry price	94.92	
Closing price	94.79	
Ticks moved	−13	
Initial margin		$120,000
Settlement variation		
(−13) * $25 * 100 contracts		−32,500
Ending account balance		$ 87,500
Mar 2: *No trades*		
Previous day's close	94.79	
Close on 3/2	94.73	
Ticks moved	−6	
Opening margin		$ 87,500
Settlement variation		
(−6) * $25 * 100 contracts		−15,000
Ending account balance		$ 72,500
Mar 3: Cavaretta Securities liquidates position		
Previous day's close	94.73	
Liquidation price	94.95	
Ticks moved	+22	
Margin contribution		$ 7,500
Opening margin		80,000
Settlement variation		
(+22) * $25 * 100 contracts		+55,000
Ending account balance		$135,000
Profit computation		
−$32,500 − $15,000 + $55,000 = +$7,500		

Cavaretta goes long 100 T-bill futures contracts and liquidates the position on March 3. The table shows the flow of margin in and out of the account (the "settlement variation") based on the daily change in the futures price. On March 2, negative settlement variation reduces Cavaretta's account balance below the maintenance margin. This triggers a margin call and results in margin contribution on March 3 sufficient to raise the account to the level of the maintenance margin requirement before the exchange opens on that day.

FORWARD PRICES

Banks and other institutions mostly use two types of forward or futures contracts: those involving interest rates and those involving foreign currencies. We will show how interest rate forwards are priced; this result can then be applied to the pricing of futures contracts.[4]

The prices of forward contracts should have a logical connection to spot prices for the same assets. The only difference between them is time. Indeed, time is the main link in the pricing formula we will explore below.

The forward-spot relationship depends on the well-known principle of *arbitrage-free markets*. This principle requires that two proposed deals with the same payoffs be priced the same. If they are not priced the same, the price difference is eliminated by the buying and selling actions of arbitrageurs. *Pure* arbitrage has no risk because arbitrageurs do not put up any net investment—thus, *riskless arbitrage*.

An arbitrage-free situation exists when an asset's forward price is consistent with its spot price in a comparable cash deal. This situation requires that

$$\mathcal{F}_{n,t} = P_0(1 + r_t)^t \tag{13.2}$$

where $\mathcal{F}_{n,t}$ = the present forward price of an n-maturity asset for delivery at time t

P_0 = the spot price of the underlying asset

r_t = annual borrowing rate of interest until time t

t = time to expiration/delivery

Equation 13.2 does not constitute a proof of anything; rather, it describes a relationship that must hold because other relationships that contradict it cannot endure. Contradictory price relationships are disequilibria that will be arbitraged away. We develop a proof of Equation 13.2 using Treasury bill interest rate futures.

Arbitrage

Suppose the forward price in Equation 13.2 is momentarily greater than the spot price compounded by interest at rate r_t.

$$\mathcal{F}_{n,t} > P_0(1 + r_t)^t \tag{13.3}$$

---

[4] The relationship of forward and futures contract prices has been the subject of much academic study, most of which focuses on transactions that are unique to futures exchanges, in particular, settlement procedures that apply to futures but not to forwards. Though not fully resolved, research results indicate that forward prices probably can be applied to the pricing of futures. See J. C. Cox, J. E. Ingersoll, and S. A. Ross, "The Relation Between Forward and Futures Prices," *Journal of Financial Economics* 3 (January/March 1989), 145–166. Transaction costs, for example, sales commissions, are minor and usually are ignored.

TABLE 13.2   T-bill Futures Arbitrage Transactions

Date	Transaction	Cash Flow
March 20	Borrow $970,000 for 91 days at 6.25%	+$970,000
	Buy six-month T-bill for $970,000	−970,000
	Sell June T-bill futures for $986,000	0
	March 20 net cash flow	$0
June 19	June futures expires: Deliver 91-day T-bill	+$986,000
	Repay loan = $970,000(1.0625)$^{91/360}$	−984,979
	June 19 net cash flow	+$1,021

To exploit this situation, we sell the overpriced asset and buy the underpriced one. In such cases, we sell the forward contract today for $\mathscr{F}_{n,t}$, borrow P_0 dollars to buy the spot asset for P_0 and repay $P_0(1 + r_t)^t$ at the time of delivery, t.[5]

EXAMPLE   On March 20, 1997 the June T-bill futures is priced at $986,000, the six-month Treasury bill sells for $970,000 (91 days later in June it will become a 91-day bill), and the annual borrowing rate is 6.25 percent. The June futures contract delivers on June 19, 1997. Then

$$\$986,000 > \$970,000(1 + 0.0625)^{91/360} = \$984,979$$

The steps for conducting an arbitrage are presented in Table 13.2.

This arbitrage produces a guaranteed profit of $1,021 regardless of events after March 20. It is riskless because it does not require net commitment of capital. (The net cash flow for initiating the position on March 20 equals zero.) This situation cannot persist: arbitrageurs would flood the market with trades to profit from this situation and force the relative prices of the futures and the cash bill to adjust until it conformed with Equation 13.2.

EXAMPLE   Suppose

$$\mathscr{F}_{n,t} < P_0(1 + r_t)^t \tag{13.4}$$

In this case, the cash bill is overpriced, and/or the futures is underpriced. In the T-bill futures example, on March 20 investors buy the June futures, borrow a cash six-month bill, and sell (lend) it temporarily at interest.[6] Then, on June 19, they take delivery on the futures contract and use it to repay the bill borrowed in March. The price paid for delivery will be less than the loan funds returned with interest. Again, arbitrageurs will ensure that the pricing inequality will not last, and relative prices will revert to the situation described in Equation 13.2.

MICROHEDGING

The most important aspect of the relationship between spot and forward prices in Equation 13.2 is the light it sheds on why interest rate futures hedges largely succeed. While the

---

[5] The arbitrageur would finance the cash bill purchase with a repurchase agreement, selling the bill temporarily to someone who has excess short-term funds to invest and, later, paying back the purchase amount plus interest at the ''repo'' rate.

[6] This describes a ''reverse'' repurchase agreement that *earns* interest at the ''reverse repo'' rate.

TABLE 13.3   Asset and Liability Future Hedges

	Buy Futures (Long)	Sell Futures (Short)
Lengthen asset	X	
Shorten asset		X
Lengthen liability		X
Shorten liability	X	

position of the futures hedger remains open, changes in the futures' price correspond to the movement of market rates of interest. Hedging with interest rate futures protects against the unfavorable effects of interest rate movements on the market value of an asset or liability or the effects on net interest income. We classify interest rate futures hedges as either *cash* or *anticipatory*.

Financial institutions conduct two kinds of *cash* hedges—asset hedges and liability hedges. Asset hedges transform the effective interest rate maturity of an asset, and liability hedges transform the effective interest maturity of a liability. As shown in Table 13.3, to extend the maturity of an asset, investors buy (take a *long position*) the futures, and to reduce the maturity of an asset, investors sell (take a *short position*) the futures. To extend the effective maturity of a liability, investors sell the futures; to reduce the effective maturity of a liability, they buy the futures.

Hedgers who buy futures contracts (long hedgers) profit from falling current interest rates and the corresponding rise in the contracts' price. With rising cash prices, hedgers have the opportunity to take delivery of the underlying securities at their contracted futures price below the current market price. In practice, futures hedgers do not take or make delivery. Instead, they close their positions by selling the same contracts at a present high futures price to offset contracts bought earlier at a low contract price.

An *anticipatory* hedge is a hedge against a financial commitment a hedger plans to make in the future.

EXAMPLE   First Place Financial Corporation (FPFC) is highly sensitive to many banking matters but most of all to interest rates. On January 20, 1998, the word is out in the market that short-term interest rates will rise, and First Place is worried about rolling over $10 million of six-month CDs about ten weeks ahead on April 1. The present CD rate is 6.20 percent, and First Place would like to lock in this rate. At this soon-to-be-bargain rate, the CD interest expense for six months (183 days) would be[7]

$$\$10,000,000 \left[(0.062) \left(\frac{183}{360} \right) \right] = \$315,167$$

FPFC's transactions are outlined in Table 13.4. To hedge against the expected rise in the CD rate, First Place sells 20 June 1998 90-day Eurodollar futures contracts with a

[7] CD interest calculations are based on a 360-day year. In the case of First Place Financial, we base prospective interest expense on the number of days between April 1 (the rollover date) and October 1. Interest on bank CDs is paid at maturity.

TABLE 13.4 Anticipatory Hedge, First Place Financial Corporation's Six-Month CD Rollover

Date	Cash Transactions	Futures Transactions
January 20, 1998	Bank anticipates rollover of $10,000,000 six-month CDs on April 1. Expects rise in CD rate. Current CD rate = 6.20% $315,167	Bank sells 20 three-month Eurodollar futures at IMM index = 94.00 (Implied rate = 6%)
April 1, 1998	Bank completes rollover of $10,000,000 six-month CDs. CD market rate = 8.25% $419,375	Bank buys 20 three-month Eurodollar futures at IMM index = 92.00 (Implied rate = 8%)
	Change in CD interest cost: $10,000,000 \left[(0.0825 - 0.0620)\dfrac{183}{360} \right]$ $= \$104,208$	Gain on settlement variation: 200 bps × 20 contracts × $25 per bp = +$100,000

Cash (loss)	$104,208
Futures (gain)	100,000
Net loss	$ 4,208

contract face value of $1 million each on January 20. The futures are priced at an IMM index of 94.00, implying a discount of 6 percent. The company requires 20 contracts against the $10 million value of CDs because the maturities of the CDs and the futures differ. The dollar interest expense on a six-month CD changes slightly more than twice as much as the change in the value of one 90-day Eurodollar futures contract. In market terminology, this calls for a *hedge ratio* of 2.

FPFC holds these contracts through the CD rollover date of April 1, by which time the IMM index has fallen to 92.00 for an implied discount of 8 percent. The bank closes its short position by buying 20 June 1998 Eurodollar contracts. The decrease of 200 basis points in the IMM index results in positive settlement variation of $5,000 per contract, or a total of $100,000 for 20 contracts.

In the meantime, six-month CD interest rates move to 8.25 percent on April 1, which creates a CD interest expense for the coming six-month period through October 1 of

$$\$10,000,000 \left[(0.0825)\left(\frac{183}{360}\right) \right] = \$419,375$$

or an increase of ($419,375 − $315,167) = $104,208 above the prospective cost determined by First Place on January 20.

The futures hedge protected First Place Financial against most of the increase in its CD expense. The unhedged $4,208 of higher interest cost was caused by two factors. First, $1,667 was due to differences in settlement variation on the futures and CD interest calculations that are based on actual days of CD maturities. The 20 futures contracts gained $500 per contract in settlement variation for every basis point change, but interest expense increased $508.33 per basis point rate change on $10 million 183-day CDs. Second, First Place absorbed a $2,542 loss due to *basis risk*.[8] In this case, the IMM index for Eurodollar futures changed by only 200 basis points, while the six-month CD rate changed 205 points [(205 − 200) × $508.33 = $2,542].

In addition to offsetting its own liability sensitivity (negative repricing gap), a bank can employ this type of hedge as a vehicle for offering fixed-rate loans. Alternatively, the bank may offer a floating-rate loan and advise its borrower to hedge against rate increases on the floater and may assist by booking futures positions for the borrower's account.

When a bank lends on a fixed-rate basis to a customer, the bank foregoes benefits from potential increases in market rates during the life of the loan. The bank can sell a specified number of futures contracts and realize gains in a rising rate environment comparable to gains it would have received on a floating-rate loan. If interest rates decrease instead, the bank's losses on the futures contracts are offset by the fact that income on the fixed-rate loan does not fall with the decline in interest rates.

Strip Hedge to Price Fixed-Rate Loans

Earlier in this chapter, we pointed out that interest rate futures reflect explicit information about forward interest rates. Futures markets link short-term forward rates with present long-term ones. Among sophisticated financiers, quite a few strongly believe they can accurately and safely link a series of short-term forward rates to price fixed-rate loans.

Still, lending institutions favor floating-rate over fixed-rate loans because floaters help to match up the repricing of their assets with their normally large volume of variable-rate liabilities. On the other hand, they must be sensitive to their customers who, as a class, tend to favor fixed-rate loans to avoid uncertainties about the future interest expense when they pay floating rates.

EXAMPLE (complex) MicroCheap Electronics (MEC), a national discount electronic products retailer, is doing heavy inventory buying for the coming year. On December 17, MicroCheap asks ABC ROAM Bank's Chicago office to provide terms on a one-year $100 million fixed-rate loan to begin immediately.[9] ABC ROAM responds with a fixed-rate offer of 9 percent but, as an inducement to sell a floating-rate deal, suggests to MicroCheap that it might realize some savings at a loan rate that floats at 175 basis points (1.75 percent) over adjusted quarterly three-month LIBOR (London Interbank Offered Rate).

The present LIBOR rate is 6.25 percent. The present implied yields on Eurodollar CD futures for the period covered by the loan are 6.50, 6.75, and 7 percent, respectively, for the March, June, and September contracts.[10] To obtain a true interest rate, MicroCheap Electronics converts these rates to their *bond equivalent rates* as shown in Table 13.5.

Based on Table 13.5, MEC estimates the interest cost rate for the year:

---

[8] In Chapter 5, we dealt with basis risk as a crucial factor in asset and liability management. Basis risk refers to the spread between two prices (interest rates). It is the risk of loss due to a future change in basis.

[9] The example is structured similar to one in Fred Arditti, *Derivatives* (Boston: Harvard Business School Press, 1996).

[10] The Eurodollar CD futures contract (''the Eurodollar contract'') is based on the underlying Eurodollar CD which approximately pays LIBOR. In most all respects, the pricing conventions are similar to T-bill futures; it has a face value of $1 million, is traded on an index (IMM) basis, and has a 90-day maturity.

TABLE 13.5 Bond Equivalent Interest for Current Spot Rate and Eurodollar Futures, MicroCheap Electronics Loan

ED Futures Delivery Month	Discount	Bond Equiv. Yield (BEY)	BEY: 1% Rise in Discount
December (current)	6.25%	6.437%[a]	
March	6.50%	6.702%	7.750%
June	6.75%	6.964%	8.040%
September	7.00%	7.225%	8.280%

[a] Calculated as

$$\text{Price} = \$1,000,000 \left[1 - .0625 \left(\frac{90}{360} \right) \right] = \$984,375$$

$$\text{Discount} = \$1,000,000 - 984,375 = \$15,625$$

$$\text{BEY} = \frac{15,625}{984,375} \times \frac{365}{90} = 6.437\%, \text{ etc.}$$

Day counts for quarters following December 17, March 18, June 17, and September 16 are 90, 92, 92, and 91.

$$
\begin{aligned}
\text{Annual Cost Rate} &= (1 + y) \\[4pt]
&= \left[1 + (0.06437 + 0.0175) \left(\frac{90}{365} \right) \right] \\[4pt]
&\quad \times \left[1 + (0.06702 + 0.0175) \left(\frac{92}{365} \right) \right] \\[4pt]
&\quad \times \left[1 + (0.06964 + 0.0175) \left(\frac{92}{365} \right) \right] \\[4pt]
&\quad \times \left[1 + (0.07225 + 0.0175) \left(\frac{91}{365} \right) \right] \\[4pt]
&= 1.08583 \\[4pt]
y &= 8.583\%
\end{aligned}
$$

(13.5)

MicroCheap Electronics' projected cost for a floating-rate loan, given the forward rate information provided by the futures market, is 8.583 percent. Should MEC opt for the floating-rate offer at an estimated cost of 42 basis points below the fixed rate of 9 percent (9.00% − 8.583% ≈ 0.42)? MicroCheap knows that the actual floating rate, should future interest rates exceed the implied rates in the Eurodollar futures, may go well above the fixed-rate offer. Equation 13.5 is simply the expected value or mean (barring liquidity premiums in the market for Eurodollar CDs) of any number of possible outcomes.

Equation 13.5 builds an important link between the short-term financial market to the pricing of a fixed-rate longer-term loan. MicroCheap Electronics uses information in

FIGURE 13.3   Peeling a Eurodollar Strip; MicroCheap Electronics, Loan Hedge

∧	∧	∧	∧	
Dec	Mar	Jun	Sep	→
Sell 100- Mar	Del 100- Mar			
Sell 100- Jun		Del 100- Jun		
Sell 100- Sep			Del 100- Sep	
Borrow:				
@ 0.0819	@ 0.0845	@ 0.0871	@ 0.0898	

the form of implied forward interest rates to arrive at the yield of 8.583 percent. From ABC ROAM Bank's point of view, this is a valid market-based benchmark to inform the bank's pricing of the fixed-rate loan offer. The 9 percent fixed rate makes a charge to the customer equal to an overall risk premium of 217 basis points (175 basis points embedded in the floating rate plus a 42 basis point premium for fixing the rate). Is a 9 percent fixed rate competitive with an 8.583 percent floating rate, considering MicroCheap's preference for a fixed rate? Is the estimated 42 basis points fair compensation to the bank for taking the market risk of fixed-rate lending?

After short deliberation, MicroCheap Electronics opts for the floating-rate loan and simultaneously tries to lock in the rate at the estimate developed in Equation 13.5 by selling (shorting) a *strip* of 100 each of the March, June, and September Eurodollar futures contracts. These contracts will be closed sequentially at the loan's three quarterly LIBOR reset dates, March 18, June 17, and September 16. In effect, changes in the LIBOR rate between December 17 and March 18 will be hedged by the March contract, LIBOR changes between March 18 and June 17 by the June contract, and so forth. We graph this strategy for "peeling" the Eurodollar strip in Figure 13.3.

Suppose immediately after the loan agreement closes on December 17 that all discount rates rise by 1 percent and remain at that level throughout the life of the loan. MicroCheap Electronics receives an immediate cash flow consisting of settlement variation on the 300 open contracts equal to 100 bps × \$25 × 300 contracts = \$750,000. This settlement and the transactions throughout the year are recorded in Table 13.6. The day counts for the four quarters are 90, 92, 92, and 91, totaling a 365-day year.

Note that MicroCheap Electronics pays interest retrospectively at the end of each quarter based on the Eurodollar (ED) discount existing on the reset dates at the beginning of the quarter. In addition, we calculate the bond equivalent yield for the new ED discount rates following the rise in discount rates. These results appear in the last column of Table 13.5; the calculations are not shown but can easily be derived.

The effective borrowing rate is found as the yield to maturity of the cash flows in Table 13.6. Solve for y (interest cost rate) as follows:

$$\$100,000,000 = \frac{-750,000 + 2,018,712}{(1 + y)^{0.25}} + \frac{2,395,217}{(1 + y)^{0.50}}$$

$$+ \frac{2,467,616}{(1 + y)^{0.75}} + \frac{2,500,630}{(1 + y)}$$

$$+ \frac{100,000,000}{(1 + y)} \tag{13.6}$$

$$y = 8.86\%$$

TABLE 13.6   Borrow and Hedge Cash Flows, MicroCheap Electronics
$100 Million Loan

	Cash	Futures
Dec 17	Take down $100M loan: 3-month financing @ $(0.06437 + 0.0175) =$ 0.08187 (discount rates rise 1% on Dec. 17 after financing)	Sell 100- Mar ED contr. @ 93.50 Sell 100- Jun ED contr. @ 93.25 Sell 100- Dec ED contr. @ 93.00 Settlement variation = $750,000 (100 bps $\times$ $25/bp $\times$ 300 contracts)
Mar 18	3-month ED discount = 7.50% Pay Dec-Mar financing @ $(0.08187 \times 90/365 \times \$100M)$ $\qquad\qquad\qquad = \$2,018,712$	Del. 100 Mar ED contr. @ 92.50
Jun 17	3-month ED discount = 7.75% Pay Mar-Jun financing @ $((0.0775 + 0.0175) \times 92/365 \times \$100M)$ $\qquad\qquad\qquad = \$2,395,217$	Del. 100 Jun ED contr. @ 92.25
Sep 16	3-month ED discount = 8.00% Pay Jun-Sep financing @ $((0.0804 + 0.0175) \times 92/365 \times \$100M)$ $\qquad\qquad\qquad = \$2,467,616$	Del. 100 Dec ED contr. @ 92.00
Dec 17	Pay Sep-Dec financing @ $((0.0828 + 0.0175) \times 91/365 \times \$100M)$ $\qquad\qquad\qquad = \$2,500,630$	

The 8.86 percent rate compares favorably with a 9.70 percent rate that MicroCheap Electronics would have paid if the loan were not hedged and taking into account the 1 percent rise in interest rates.[11] It compares somewhat less favorably with the fixed-rate offer of 9 percent.

The effective rate of 8.86 percent is 28 basis points above the 8.58 percent estimated from the Eurodollar futures discounts at the beginning of the loan negotiation. Arditti suggests reasons for such differences.[12] Each quarter we hedge an amount equal to the total face value of the loan ($100 million) but do not hedge the accumulated interest. We also used 90-day ED contracts for each quarter, although the actual day count is somewhat longer for the last three quarters.

Finally, note how the result would change if the rise in the Eurodollar discount occurred gradually or at a later date, say March 18. In the latter case, the effective rate would have been larger because the settlement variation would have been deferred three months into the future and the present value of this positive cash flow would have been reduced.

MACROHEDGING

In the examples above, financial institutions (or their clients) used microhedging on a deal-by-deal basis to protect specific positions against unfavorable movements in interest

---

[11] To find the unhedged cost rate of 9.70 percent, proceed as in Equation 13.6, except remove the $750,000 settlement variation on the futures position on December 17.

[12] Arditti, *Derivatives,* 181.

rates. Regulators and auditors require clear specification of and accounting for derivative hedges. Microhedging strategies are very specific, and it is relatively easy to show how they reduce the risk of individual assets and liabilities and to account for them.

Macrohedges are not so straightforward. The main idea in macrohedging is for institutions to protect the equity value of their entire balance sheets or of entire portfolios of assets or liabilities. It is difficult to measure a balance sheet's interest rate exposure. This is primarily because balance sheet assets and liabilities contain many different kinds of risk, especially basis risk and embedded option risk.

We have encountered basis risk in earlier examples. It refers to the differential movement in the prices of items, often with the same maturity. In relation to banks' balance sheets, basis risk is a special problem, in part because banks originate their assets and liabilities in both open financial markets and relatively closed customer relationship markets. The pricing behaviors in these two types of markets are different and create differences in price sensitivity to interest rates. For example, certain depositors are notably unresponsive to the spread between interest rates on deposits and open market interest rates. On the asset side, loan customers may not be sensitive to small movements in interest rates but may be highly sensitive to service quality.

The issue of embedded option risk comes up, among other circumstances, when banks grant customers the right to prepay loans when rates fall. Alternatively, banks might grant customers the right to reset interest rates on certain deposits when rates increase but not when they decrease. Chapter 14 will present tools for evaluating these complex option features.

Difficulty aside, we must measure balance sheet equity risk in order to hedge it. Once we measure exposure and select the type of futures contract for hedging, we must determine a hedge ratio—the ratio of the value of futures contracts to the size of the exposure. Ultimately, the efficiency of the hedge depends on how fully the gain or loss on the futures compensates for the loss or gain in the equity value of the balance sheet or portfolio.

In Chapter 4 we presented two duration measures of the exposure of equity to interest rate changes. *Duration gap* was given by Equation 4.28 and is reproduced as Equation 13.7.

$$\Delta E = -DG\left[\frac{\Delta r}{(1 + r)}\right]A \qquad (13.7)$$

where $DG = (D_A - (L/A)D_L)$. We solved DG for the example balance sheet of Table 4.5 in Equation 4.29, shown here as Equation 13.8.

$$DG = 1.125 - \left(\frac{900}{1,000}\right) \times 0.572 = 0.610 \qquad (13.8)$$

Equity duration was presented in Equation 4.32 and is reproduced as Equation 13.9.

$$\Delta E = -D_E\left[\frac{\Delta r}{(1 + r)}\right]E \qquad (13.9)$$

From Equation 13.7, we estimated an approximate change in equity value of $-\$11.1$ million for an across-the-board 2 percent increase in interest rates.

$$\Delta E = -0.610 \times \frac{(+0.02)}{(1 + 0.10)} \times \$1,000,000,000 = -\$11,100,000 \qquad (13.10)$$

or $\Delta E = -\$5,550,000$ per 1 percent increase in interest rates.

where
$$DG = 0.610$$
$$D_A = 1.125$$
$$D_L = 0.572$$
$$D_E = 6.102$$

For firms with positive duration gap (positive equity duration), rising interest rates produce a loss. Such firms are designated asset sensitive. Firms with negative duration gap and (negative equity duration) experience loss when interest rates fall and are liability sensitive. Because the example firm is asset sensitive, the firm should construct a futures macrohedge to generate a gain when interest rates rise, offsetting its loss in equity value. On the other hand, when rates decline, the firm will lose on the futures hedge but gain in balance sheet equity value.[13]

The example firm must select the type of futures instrument to use for the hedge and then determine the hedge ratio and size of the hedge. The firm requires a short position to protect against rising interest rates. The most active and liquid futures markets are those for 20-year Treasury bonds and 91-day Eurodollar CDs.[14] The firm chooses the number of futures contracts that equates the futures gains or losses with the loss or gain in the equity value of the firm. The futures gain or loss is the number of futures contracts multiplied by the gain or loss per contract. We set

$$\Delta E = -(N \times \Delta F)$$

where
N = number of futures contracts
ΔF = gain or loss per futures contract

or

$$N = -\left(\frac{\Delta E}{\Delta F}\right) \qquad (13.11)$$

A negative N indicates a short position and a positive N is a long position.

---

[13] Douglas T. Breeden and Michael J. Giarla give an early description of macrohedging with futures. See "Hedging Interest Rate Risks with Futures, Swaps and Options," *Working Paper,* Duke University (September 1987).

[14] Compared to the Eurodollar futures market, the volume for other short-term futures contracts is almost not material. Eurodollar futures open interest on January 15, 1997 was 2,184,137 contracts compared to 7,677 for T-bill and 30,764 for one-month LIBOR contracts. For contracts on long-term underlying assets, the 20-year Treasury futures open interest on the Chicago Board of Trade was 475,420, also signifying a highly liquid market.

FIGURE 13.4 Treasury Bond Futures, Chicago Board of Trade

TREASURY BONDS [CBT]-$100,000; pts. 32nds of 100%

	Open	High	Low	Settle	Change	Lifetime High	Lifetime Low	Open Interest
Mar	111-14	111-18	110-29	111-09	—	120-00	99-26	473,566
June	110-29	111-02	110-13	110-25	—	118-21	99-16	20,658
Sept	110-12	110-15	110-02	110-11	—	117-21	100-18	5,322
Dec	—	—	—	109-29	—	118-08	100-08	3,722

Est vol 375,000; vol Tue 475,420; open int 503,358, +17,362

Earlier examples demonstrated that the price of the Eurodollar CD contract changes $25 per 1 basis point change in interest rates or $2,500 for a 1 percent (100 basis points) change. We estimated $\Delta E = -\$5,550,000$ for a 1 percent rise in interest rates. If the futures price changes correlate perfectly with changes in equity values, the number of Eurodollar contracts for the example firm should be set at[15]

$$N = -\frac{\$5,550,000}{\$2,500} = -2,220 \text{ contracts short}$$

Calculating the number of 20-year Treasury bond futures to hedge the example balance sheet is more complicated. The Chicago Board of Trade (CBT) quotes bond futures contracts for four maturity dates per year: March, June, September, and December. Figure 13.4 abstracts the CBT Treasury bond quotations from Figure 13.2. According to the first line in Figure 13.4, the contract amount is $100,000 and price quotations are in points and 32nds of 100 percent of par. The quotation for "Mar–Settle" of 111-09 means that the futures price closed at $111 + 9/32$ percent of face value for a contract price of $111,281.25.

For convenience, the contract assumes that a standard 8 percent semiannual coupon, 20-year bond is to be delivered against the contract. In actuality, exchange rules allow the seller to deliver any of a number of long-term T-bonds with a coupon other than 8 percent and with any maturity 15 years or more from the futures delivery date. The cash market value of bonds with other than 8 percent coupons must be translated to the 8 percent contract standard. The futures prices of bonds are multiplied by a "conversion factor" upon delivery to compensate for differences in the values of bonds delivered. This conversion factor is equal to the present value per $1 par value of the deliverable bond, discounted at 8 percent.[16]

For example, the conversion factor for a 9 percent coupon, 20-year bond is 1.063, which makes the March 1997 futures selling price $1.063 \times \$111,281.25 = \$118,291.97$. The seller determines the "cheapest bond to deliver" by comparing the converted futures

---

[15] To be consistent with the duration-based estimate for ΔE, we could base the value of ΔF on the modified duration of the Eurodollar futures contract. This contract has a duration of 0.25 year. For convenience, we base ΔF on its simple $25 per basis point settlement variation established earlier.

[16] The conversion factor is akin to the number of 8 percent, 20-year equivalent bonds contained in the bond being delivered.

price he will receive with the price he must pay on the cash market for the various bonds that are eligible for delivery. The advantage of this system is that there are too many deliverable bonds for any one trader to buy up in an attempt to create a "short squeeze." In nearly all cases, however, sellers do not actually deliver the bonds, but they offset their positions with opposite futures trades that are priced at the cheapest to deliver.

We base ΔF on the duration of the T-bond (cheapest to deliver) underlying the futures. The corollary to Equation 13.7 for ΔF is

$$\Delta F = -D_F \left[\frac{\Delta r}{(1 + r)} \right] (F_P) \tag{13.12}$$

where F_P = futures contract price
D_F = duration of futures contract

Substituting Equations 13.7 and 13.12 into Equation 13.11 and solving for N, we get

$$N = \frac{-DG(A)}{D_F(F_P)} \tag{13.13}$$

Duration for the March 1997 20-year T-bond futures is approximately 7.49:

$$N = \frac{-0.610(\$1,000,000,000)}{7.49(\$111,281.25)}$$

$$= -731.86 \approx 732 \text{ contracts short}^{[17]}$$

Now solve Equation 13.12 for a 1 percent rise in interest rates. Multiplying through by N gives

$$\Delta F(N) = \Delta E = -D_F \left[\frac{\Delta r}{(1 + r)} \right] (F_P)(N)$$

$$= -7.49 \left[\frac{+0.01}{1.10} \right] (\$111,281.25)(-732)$$

$$= +\$5,546,541$$

or approximately \$5.5 million, which is the negative of our earlier estimate of the change in equity value based on duration gap from a 1 percent increase in interest rates.

Duration-based hedging poses an issue in the accuracy of our macrohedge calcula-

[17] Treasury bond and note futures have a standard delivery amount of \$100,000, whereas shorter term futures such as the Eurodollar CD contract deliver \$1 million. The par values differ so much because of the wide difference in their volatilities. *Note:* To implement the above hedge, despite the relative smallness of the T-bond futures par value, it required only about one-third the number of contracts as the Eurodollar futures hedge.

tions. As Chapter 4 pointed out, duration assumes that price changes corresponding to interest rate changes are linear when, in fact, the price-interest relationship is convex. This becomes a problem in a futures hedge if the convexity of the cash position and the futures position differs significantly.

The problem is, as we noted in Chapter 4, that increases and decreases in interest rates do not produce symmetrical losses and gains. With positive convexity, prices rise more for a given decrease in interest than they fall for the same increase in interest. For example, the March 1997 T-bond contract in the example increases $8,166 in price for a 1 percent fall in interest rate and declines $7,262 for a 1 percent rate rise. Such asymmetry in price change is a positive factor for the cash side of the above hedge but a negative factor for a short futures hedge. As a seller of T-bond futures, the bank in the example benefits less from declining futures prices (rising interest rates) than it loses on rising prices (falling rates) for the same plus or minus increment in interest rates. Although the duration-based T-bond futures hedge probably will do a good job of offsetting losses with gains for small moves in interest rates, the precision of the hedge falls off for large interest rate movements.

Basis Risk

Futures hedges usually are distorted by *basis risk.* As noted earlier in this chapter, basis is the difference in cash price and price of the futures used to hedge the cash price. Basis risk is the risk that this difference will fluctuate. Basis risk is minimized by choosing futures contracts for the hedge that are highly correlated with the cash position. However, issues such as intra-balance sheet basis (basis for different cash items on the balance sheet) and option risk make it difficult to mirror changes in the cash position with futures.

Suppose we estimate that the equity value of the balance sheet will move 80 percent of the movement in the price of the selected T-bond futures (a correlation coefficient of 0.80). Rearranging Equation 13.11,

$$\Delta E(\rho) = (N^\rho \times \Delta F)$$

$$N^\rho = \frac{\Delta E(\rho)}{\Delta F}$$

(13.14)

where ρ = the cash-futures correlation
         N^ρ = number of contracts, modified by ρ

In the example hedge,

$$N^\rho = \frac{\Delta E(\rho)}{\left(-D_F\left[\dfrac{\Delta r}{(1+r)}\right](F_P)\right)}$$

$$= \frac{\$5,550,000(0.8)}{\left(-7.49\left[\dfrac{.01}{(1+0.10)}\right](\$111,281.25)\right)} = -585.5 \text{ contracts} \approx 586 \text{ contracts short}$$

FOREIGN EXCHANGE FORWARDS AND FUTURES

Financial institutions use forwards and futures to manage not just interest rate risk but also foreign exchange (FX) risk. Chapter 16 discusses the important factors that determine foreign exchange rates between two currencies and the rigorous pricing relationships between exchange rates, including the interest rate parity and purchasing power parity theorems. In addition, Chapter 16 reviews principles of FX hedging with forward and futures contracts. In the remainder of this chapter, we review the institutional settings of FX forwards and futures and compare them to interest rate forwards and futures.

We devoted more of our discussion to the futures markets for interest rates than to the forward market. This was because the market for interest rate futures is much more developed than the forward market for interest rates. The opposite is true in the case of foreign exchange for which a strong and successful forward market has existed for many years. An active futures market exists for several currencies too, but, overall, FX forward market activity dominates the FX futures market by a wide margin.

Major banks and other institutions are active makers of markets for forward foreign exchange. The forward market is worldwide and cannot be pinned down to a geographic location. Figure 13.5A presents the selling rates for spot and forward foreign exchange published in the *Wall Street Journal* for March 20, 1998. In addition to the spot rates for all currencies shown, it lists the rates for 30-, 90-, and 180-day forwards for the half-dozen most active currencies: British pounds, Canadian dollars, French francs, German marks, Japanese yen, and Swiss francs. In reality, forward contracts can be made for any specific number of days. This provides the flexibility to time the forward to the precise date of need.

Suppose, for example, that on July 1 an American importer acquires goods from a German manufacturer and must make payment in deutsche marks in 100 days on October 8. The importer can ask its bank to match this timing exactly and lock in deutsche marks by selling the importer a contract to buy the deutsche marks forward in 100 (or any other number) days. This exact matching is not available in futures markets where contracts mature only four times per year and are not available with maturity on or even near October 8. The nearest futures contract would not mature until December. With a long futures position, the importer is still exposed to differences in the spot rate on October 8 and the futures contract price. Timing mismatches may explain why few futures contracts are delivered but are offset well before maturity, while over 90 percent of forwards are delivered.

Businesses, such as the importer in the example, take foreign currency forward positions to hedge against currency exposures that arise in export or import transactions. Speculators, hoping to profit from short-run price movements, are even larger users of forward markets. The counterparty to the business's or speculator's forward contract is an institution such as a bank and not an exchange as in the case of futures markets. The difference is that when the futures exchange takes the role of counterparty, it breaks the direct connection between the long and the short counterparties. Institutions in both markets control the exposure they desire to take in each currency by adopting position limits for their "net books." Other differences in forward and futures FX are the same as those described for interest rate futures and forwards at the beginning of this chapter.

Figure 13.5B presents price quotations in the futures market for foreign exchange. Unlike the forward market, the futures market is specifically located at the International Monetary Market (the IMM) of the Chicago Mercantile Exchange (noted as CME in the

FIGURE 13.5 Foreign Exchange Forwards and Futures

EXCHANGE RATES
Friday, March 20, 1998

The New York foreign exchange selling rates below apply to trading among banks in amounts of $1 million and more, as quoted at 4 p.m. Eastern time by Dow Jones and other sources. Retail transactions provide fewer units of foreign currency per dollar.

Country	U.S. $ equiv. Fri	Thu	Currency per U.S. $ Fri	Thu
Argentina (Peso)	1.0001	1.0001	.9999	.9999
Australia (Dollar)	.6650	.6616	1.5038	1.5115
Austria (Schilling)	.07765	.07766	12.878	12.877
Bahrain (Dinar)	2.6518	2.6518	.3771	.3771
Belgium (Franc)	.02648	.02643	37.760	37.830
Brazil (Real)	.8818	.8818	1.1341	1.1341
Britain (Pound)	1.6690	1.6670	.5992	.5999
1-month forward	1.6665	1.6645	.6001	.6008
3-months forward	1.6616	1.6596	.6018	.6026
6-months forward	1.6544	1.6522	.6045	.6053
Canada (Dollar)	.7048	.7051	1.4189	1.4182
1-month forward	.7053	.7057	1.4178	1.4171
3-months forward	.7063	.7067	1.4159	1.4151
6-months forward	.7076	.7079	1.4133	1.4126
Chile (Peso)	.00207	.002211	453.05	452.35
China (Renminbi)	.1208	.1208	8.2792	8.2790
Colombia (Peso)	.0007343	.0007350	1361.87	1360.56
Czech. Rep. (Koruna)	....	....	....	....
Commercial rate	.02929	.02940	34.139	34.011
Denmark (Krone)	.1432	.1431	6.9817	6.9875
Ecuador (Sucre)	....	....	....	....
Floating rate	.0002176	.0002176	4595.00	4595.00
Finland (Markka)	.1801	.1800	5.5525	5.5561
France (Franc)	.1630	.1632	6.1360	6.1285
1-month forward	.1627	.1635	6.1474	6.1174
3-months forward	.1638	.1640	6.1041	6.0966
6-months forward	.1646	.1648	6.0749	6.0670
Germany (Mark)	.5459	.5457	1.8320	1.8325
1-month forward	.5468	.5467	1.8287	1.8292
3-months forward	.5487	.5486	1.8224	1.8229
6-months forward	.5514	.5513	1.8135	1.8140
Greece (Drachma)	.003094	.003085	323.20	324.17
Hong Kong (Dollar)	.1292	.1291	7.7420	7.7480
Hungary (Forint)	.004733	.004737	211.30	211.09
India (Rupee)	.02530	.02532	39.525	39.500
Indonesia (Rupiah)	.0001031	.00009756	9700.00	10250.00
Ireland (Punt)	1.3717	1.3704	.7290	.7297
Israel (Shekel)	.2780	.2782	3.5975	3.5940
Italy (Lira)	.0005548	.0005546	1802.50	1803.00
Japan (Yen)	.007666	.007652	130.44	130.69
1-month forward	.007699	.007684	129.88	130.13
3-months forward	.007765	.007750	128.79	129.03
6-months forward	.007866	.007852	127.13	127.35
Jordan (Dinar)	1.4134	1.4134	.7075	.7075
Kuwait (Dinar)	3.2733	3.2723	.3055	.3056
Lebanon (Pound)	.0006570	.0006570	1522.00	1522.00
Malaysia (Ringgit)	.2747	.2692	3.6400	3.7150
Malta (Lira)	2.5221	2.5221	.3965	.3965
Mexico (Peso)	....	....	....	....
Floating rate	.1168	.1167	8.5640	8.5660
Netherland (Guilder)	.4847	.4841	2.0632	2.0656
New Zealand (Dollar)	.5629	.5596	1.7765	1.7870
Norway (Krone)	.1314	.1313	7.6085	7.6143
Pakistan (Rupee)	.02296	.02296	43.560	43.560
Peru (new Sol)	.3600	.3602	2.7775	2.7760
Philippines (Peso)	.02642	.02616	37.845	38.225
Poland (Zloty)	.2912	.2900	3.4340	3.4480
Portugal (Escudo)	.005338	.005332	187.34	187.56
Russia (Ruble) (a)	.1640	.1641	6.0960	6.0940
Saudi Arabia (Riyal)	.2666	.2666	3.7513	3.7511
Singapore (Dollar)	.6217	.6196	1.6085	1.6140
Slovak Rep. (Koruna)	.02847	.02845	35.125	35.150
South Africa (Rand)	.2007	.2010	4.9815	4.9755
South Korea (Won)	.0006904	.0006784	1448.50	1474.00
Spain (Peseta)	.006439	.006439	155.30	155.30
Sweden (Krona)	.1256	.1251	7.9635	7.9960
Switzerland (Franc)	.6671	.6682	1.4990	1.4965
1-month forward	.6696	.6707	1.4935	1.4909
3-months forward	.6744	.6756	1.4828	1.4802
6-months forward	.6814	.6826	1.4675	1.4650
Taiwan (Dollar)	.03051	.03051	32.778	32.772
Thailand (Baht)	.02522	.02497	39.650	40.050
Turkey (Lira)	.00000421	.00000422	237720.00	237150.00
United Arab (Dirham)	.2723	.2723	3.6730	3.6730
Uruguay (New Peso)	....	....	....	....
Financial	.1003	.1003	9.9750	9.9750
Venezuela (Bolivar)	.001913	.001916	522.75	522.00
SDR	1.3413	1.3432	.7456	.7445
ECU	1.0847	1.0842	....	....

Special Drawing Rights (SDR) are based on exchange rates for the U.S., German, British, French, and Japanese currencies. Source: International Monetary Fund.

European Currency Unit (ECU) is based on a basket of community currencies.

a-fixing, Moscow Interbank Currency Exchange. Ruble newly-denominated Jan. 1998.

A. Spot and Forward Contracts

	Open	High	Low	Settle	Change	Lifetime High	Low	Open Interest
JAPAN YEN (CME)-12.5 million yen; $ per yen (.00)								
June	.7742	.7830	.7711	.7756	+ .0016	.9090	.7637	79,841
Sept	.7864	.7876	.7856	.7856	+ .0016	.8695	.7735	1,293
Dec	.7950	.7950	.7950	.7957	+ .0016	.8445	.7880	121
Mr99	....	....	....	.8059	+ .0016	.8315	.8065	1,478
Est vol 10,528; vol Th 29,982; open int 82,733, +9568.								
DEUTSCHEMARK (CME)-125,000 marks; $ per mark								
June	.5483	.5498	.5469	.5488	+ .0008	.5995	.5410	69,675
Sept	.5512	.5520	.5497	.5515	+ .0008	.5944	.5490	1,857
Est vol 12,057; vol Th 23,181; open int 71,551, +3,802.								
CANADIAN DOLLAR (CME)-100,000 dlrs.; $ per Can $								
June	.7064	.7073	.7051	.7060	− .0003	.7470	.6825	46,257
Sept	.7082	.7090	.7065	.7075	− .0003	.7463	.6845	3,296
Dec	....	....	.7103	....	− .0003	.7400	.6860	1,440
Mr99	....	....	....	.7103	− .0003	.7247	.6875	453
Est vol 4,990; vol Th 7,421; open int 51,476, −1,194.								
BRITISH POUND (CME)-62,500 pds.; $ per pound								
June	1.6592	1.6640	1.6528	1.6620	+ .0030	1.6940	1.5610	35,651
Sept	1.6480	1.6560	1.6480	1.6550	+ .0032	1.6870	1.5690	587
Est vol 6,838; vol Th 5,550; open int 36,251, +112.								
SWISS FRANC (CME)-125,000 francs; $ per franc								
June	.6748	.6764	.6727	.6746	+ .0002	.7304	.6727	57,566
Sept	.6816	.6822	.6798	.6814	....	.7310	.6798	1,233
Est vol 9,184; vol Th 20,501; open int 58,830, +3,157.								
AUSTRALIAN DOLLAR (CME)-100,000 dlrs.; $ per A.S.								
June	.6626	.6673	.6590	.6657	+ .0026	.7050	.6343	12,094
Est vol 564; vol Th 1,907; open int 12,105, −249.								
MEXICAN PESO (CME)-500,000 new Mex. peso, $ per MP								
June	.11240	.11290	.11220	.11270	+ 00032	.11985	.09200	15,633
Sept	.10830	.10875	.10820	.10865	+ 00040	.11680	.80000	4,339
Dec	.10480	.10530	.10470	.10512	+ 00052	.11440	.80000	8,486
Mr99	.10100	.10150	.10100	.10150	+ 00050	.10150	.10050	04
Est vol 2,860; vol Th 4,787; open int 28,562, +351.								

B. Foreign Exchange Futures Contracts

first line of the seven currencies listed). Maturity dates for futures contracts are the third Wednesday of March, June, September, and December. The exchange specifies a standard contract amount; for example, the deutsche mark contract is for 125,000 marks.

SUMMARY

Derivatives allow institutions to take positions in the future that differ from the typical future-oriented decisions banks make every day. The principal difference is that derivatives create monetary obligations in the future without calling for a monetary exchange in the present. Futures and forwards are widely known and used as instruments for trading and for hedging against interest rate risk. Unfortunately, less attention is paid to the easy link they provide between market-derived pricing and the pricing of products banks create through customer relationships. In this chapter we demonstrated the ways futures pricing bridges over into the pricing of bank funding and fixed-rate lending.

END OF CHAPTER PROBLEMS

13.1 The purchasing agent for a large natural gas-powered electrical generating plant expects natural gas prices to fall soon. Unfortunately, she must sign a contract with the gas distributor this week at what she considers a high price for gas. Describe how she might use a forward contract to hedge the plant's cost of fuel.

13.2 In January, Cratchet is advised by his attorney that he will receive payment of $5 million on May 15 from his rich uncle's estate. He plans to invest the funds he receives into long-term bonds, but he is worried that bond interest rates will decline between now (January) and May 15. How can Cratchet hedge this situation using the futures market? Be specific about the position (long or short) and the contract he should use.

13.3 In late March, a corporate treasurer projects the need for a $1 million bank loan starting on June 16. The bank advises that the rate will be 1 percent over the three-month Eurodollar (LIBOR) rate on that date. LIBOR is currently 5.625 percent. He will use the June Eurodollar futures to lock in the forward borrowing rate. The futures are trading at 94.35, implying a forward Eurodollar rate of 5.65 percent (100.00 − 94.35). What transaction should the treasurer make to lock in a borrowing rate for the three-month period beginning on June 16? What borrowing rate will he achieve?

13.4 In this problem, use an appropriate variation of Equation 13.1 provided in the text for pricing Treasury bill futures contracts.
   a. Find the price of $1 million of par value *cash* 91-day Treasury bills trading at an annualized discount from face value of 5.03 percent. (*Hint:* Original three-month Treasury bills have 91-day maturity and, like T-bill futures, are priced on a 360-day year.)
   b. Determine the bond equivalent yield (BEY) for the bill in part (a). (See the conversion from discount to BEY for Eurodollar futures given in Table 13.5.)

13.5 The 90-day Treasury bill futures contract is trading at an index value of 95.40. Assume the discount on this contract declines by one basis point. Calculate the before- and after-contract prices of this contract to show that the value of a .01 "tick" is $25.

13.6 On October 1, Roachamboux National Bank goes short 10 three-month Eurodollar futures contracts at 94.78 and posts initial margin with its broker in the amount of $1,350 per contract; maintenance margin requirements are $1,000 per contract. The Eurodollar futures closes at 94.66 on October 1, at 94.84 on October 2, and at 94.93 on October 3. Determine the amount of margin Roachamboux must have in its account after net settlement each day.

13.7 On June 22, 2000 the September T-bill futures contract is quoted at an index of 95.22. Calculate the futures contract price.

13.8 The futures contract in Problem 13.7 will deliver on September 21, 2000. The six-month Treasury bill with $1 million maturity value sells for $974,700. The borrowing rate for repo and "reverse" repo funds is 5.40 percent. Determine if there is opportunity for arbitrage. If so, how should the arbitrageur proceed in order to clear a profit? How will the market adjust to the actions of arbitrageurs?

13.9 On September 23, 1999, Electro-Mart discount stores asks Enduro Bank for a $5 million nine-month fixed-rate loan to finance new inventories. The loan will mature on June 22, 2000, and interest will be paid quarterly. Enduro Bank raises three-month Eurodollar funds currently paying LIBOR equal to 5.75 percent but will have to roll these funds over in two more successive quarters.

The two quarterly refunding dates coincide with the next two Eurodollar futures contract expirations in December and March, currently priced at 93.90 and 93.50, respectively. Describe how the loan officer at Enduro Bank can hedge the bank's funding rate for the period of the loan. What is the rate she can lock in now for nine months in the futures market?

13.10 In June 2002, Retro National Bank had $500 million in assets. Its assets have a weighted duration of 2.4, and its $460 million liabilities have a weighted duration of 0.8. The current market discount rate is 10 percent. Retro Bank's CFO has heard that bond interest rates will be volatile in the coming six months and wants to protect the bank's balance sheet using the December 20-year Treasury bond futures. He estimates that, owing to basis risk, the correlation of the movement of the bank's equity value will be 70 percent of that of the bond futures contract. At present, the December bond futures contract price is $108^{24}/_{32}$, and the contract's duration is 7.0. Design a proper bond futures hedge for the CFO.

CHAPTER 14

Interest Rate Options: Hedging and Pricing

There is probably no more common banking transaction than selling options. A bank's line of credit sells the customer the option to draw credit when needed. A home mortgage loan sells the customer an option to pay off the loan many years before maturity. A time deposit sells the depositor the option to withdraw the funds, if needed, long before the deposit matures.

These transactions—known as *contingent claims products*—are valuable to customers. As might be expected, banks charge for them in one way or another in the form of commitment fees, higher interest rates, or penalties for early withdrawal. In this chapter, we will portray these charges as the banks' prices for option instruments.

These common transactions have the same elements as formal exchange-traded or over-the-counter options. They convey opportunities without the obligation to exercise them, and they have a price.

Both futures and options normally take explicit positions in the future, but they do not perform their functions in the same way. Futures users take a position in the future without exchanging material value in the present, whereas options users usually pay or receive a present price called the *option premium.*

Futures can *eliminate* risk. Option buyers cannot eliminate risk but only *reduce* it to a known level because a premium must be paid when they establish a position in an option. Option *sellers* take unlimited risk and earn a premium in return. Option buyers should think of options as risk-limiters, and option sellers should view them as risky income generators.[1]

This chapter reviews the basics of options and their pricing. It shows how banks and other institutions use interest rate and commodity options for micro- or macrohedging;

---

[1] Distinctions between options and futures are discussed in Eugene Moriarty, Susan Phillips, and Paula Tosini, "A Comparison of Options and Futures in the Management of Portfolio Risk," *Financial Analysts Journal* (January–February 1981), 61–67.

it describes exchange-traded and over-the-counter interest rate options, including caps, floors, and collars; it demonstrates how to calculate fair prices for products such as real estate mortgages and callable bonds that contain *embedded options*; and finally, it describes the "optionality" of cash market products that are crucial to banking, such as loan commitments and standby letters of credit.

OPTION BASICS

Comparing with Forwards and Futures Contracts

Users of options and of forward and futures contracts take on different obligations. Owners of forward and futures contracts are *required* to buy or sell positions in the underlying assets in the future; they do not have a choice. On the other hand, option users can choose whether or not to buy (*call*) or sell (*put*) an underlying asset in the future at an *exercise price* or *striking price* specified today. The ability to choose produces *asymmetric* payoffs. This means option owners can reject the "opportunity" to buy or sell an asset. That is, they can refuse to *exercise* the option if its price is unfavorable in relation to the option's exercise price, or they can exploit a favorable asset price and exercise the right to buy or sell the asset.

This choice over exercising has "reservation value": Buyers are willing to pay an appropriate price to own this choice (option). Financial experts expend great effort trying to determine the fair price—the option *premium*—to pay for such a choice.

Institutional Background

American options can be exercised at any time up to their maturity dates, whereas *European options* are exercised only on their maturity dates. Options are created in over-the-counter markets as well as in organized exchanges. Financial institutions create customized over-the-counter interest rate and currency options to assist customers hedge particular operations or investment positions.

Options exchanges create standardized option contracts. Each options exchange specializes in certain types of contracts. For example, the Chicago Board Options Exchange (CBOE) began trading options on common stock in 1973. The Chicago Board of Trade (CBOT) introduced interest rate options, including options on Treasury bond futures, in 1981. The Chicago Mercantile Exchange (CME) and the Kansas City Board of Trade began trading stock index options in the 1970s. The Philadelphia Exchange began trading currency options in the same era.

What are the advantages and disadvantages of exchange-traded options versus over-the-counter options? The differences are not unlike those we discussed in Chapter 13 for futures (exchange-traded) versus forward (over-the-counter) contracts. Exchange-traded options are based on underlying assets, contract sizes, and maturity dates that are all standardized. They offer liquidity, low transactions costs, and a continuous market in options contracts. Trading in options on an exchange facilitates closing out a position at any time up to maturity. On the other hand, institutionally created, over-the-counter options normally are not traded. They meet nonstandard needs based on highly specific asset types, contract sizes, and maturities.

There is credit risk in options transactions, but it is one-sided. There is no credit risk on the buying side because option buyers pay an option premium up front and do not take outright losses when the prices of underlying assets move against them. However, option sellers (called option *writers*) may be a source of large credit risk because they may be called upon to make large payouts to option owners. This makes exchange clearinghouses nervous, and it motivates them to closely monitor option writers' positions and require them to post margin.

Option Payoffs

As we have seen, *asymmetric payoffs* result from choices available to option owners. Let's see why these asymmetries occur. A *call option* grants the buyer the choice to *buy* an asset—let's say a common stock—in the future at an exercise price set today. A *put option* grants the future choice to *sell* at a price set today. We can create diagrams of option payoffs called *payoff profiles* such as Figure 14.1. The net payoff at maturity to the owner of a call option is positive if the price of the underlying stock has risen sufficiently above the call's exercise price to offset the cost of the option (shown as *c* in Figure 14.1, panel A, the distance between the horizontal portion of the payoff line and the horizontal axis). If the stock price declines, the option's net value or net payoff remains negative at the level of the price paid for the option.

The payoff profile for the call option seller or writer (who is *short* a call) is shown in Figure 14.1B as the mirror image of the buyer's payoff. When the asset's price rises

FIGURE 14.1   Payoff Profiles for Owning and Shorting Calls and Puts at Maturity

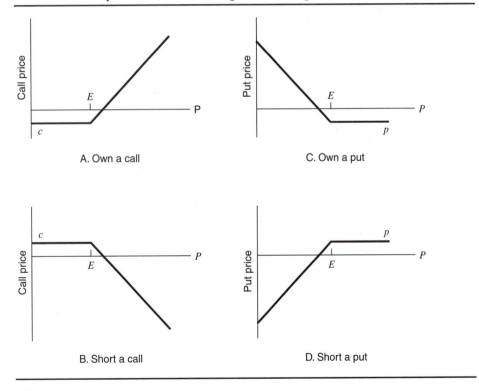

A. Own a call

C. Own a put

B. Short a call

D. Short a put

above the option's exercise price, the seller must deliver the underlying stock at the exercise price.

The payoff profiles to owners and sellers of put options is the mirror image of the call relationships (Figure 14.1, panels C and D). The put option owner profits when the stock price falls below the exercise price by an amount that more than offsets the option price, p. That means the option seller (the short) has to purchase the stock at the exercise price at a time when it is worth less than this price.

Unlike these examples utilizing common stocks, most of the action in financial institutions involves interest rate options. Financial institutions' transactions involve interest-bearing instruments rather than common stocks. Suppose the underlying asset is a fixed-income security such as a U.S. Treasury bond. It now becomes proper to refer to *interest rate* options.

With interest rate options, the relationships in Figure 14.1 appear to be backwards because the price of the underlying asset moves inversely to interest rates. Increases in the interest rate are described as movement from right to left on the horizontal axis, which represents a decrease in the price of the underlying debt.

EXAMPLE   E-Z Bank decides to acquire a Treasury bond option to hedge the value of its Treasury bond portfolio against rising interest rates. Should E-Z acquire a call or a put on Treasury bonds? If interest rates rise as feared, the underlying Treasuries will fall in value, a movement from right to left in Figure 14.1. Thus, an increase in interest rates means negative movement along the horizontal axis. Therefore, in a rising rate environment, E-Z Bank will buy a put option on Treasury bonds, obtaining the right to sell Treasury bonds at an exercise price higher than the market price after interest rates rise. As a practical matter, *a put on bonds is the same as a call on interest rates.*

Pricing: Terminology and Variables

If the exercise price on a call option is equal to or less than the price of the underlying Treasury bond (the bond's price lies to the right of "E" in Figure 14.1A), the option is *in the money.*

EXAMPLE   Santo Securities, Inc. holds a call option on a Treasury bond futures contract with an exercise price of $110. The deliverable underlying bond is priced at $112. Santo's option clearly has value because it is expected that when the option matures, Santo will be able to buy the bond for $110 and immediately sell it for $112, pocketing $2. Contrarily, if the bond is selling for $108, Santo's option to buy at $110 is *out of the money,* and the option could be worth as little as zero.

In the first case of a bond priced at $112, the option is worth a minimum of $2. In either case, if there is still time remaining before expiration, Santo's option will sell for more than its minimum value—that is, either zero or the difference between the bond price and the exercise price. With time remaining, it is always possible that the bond price may increase further.

In general, call option prices are determined by the following variables:

1. t, time to expiration.
2. E, exercise price (lower E produces higher price).
3. P, price of the underlying asset (higher bond price yields higher call price).

FIGURE 14.2 Value of Call Before Expiration

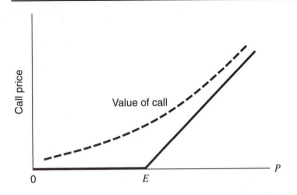

4. σ_P, volatility of the underlying asset's price (greater volatility improves the chances of larger underlying asset values).
5. r_f, risk-free interest rate (higher rates produce a higher price); the owner owns the right to take a position in the underlying asset but does not have to finance the purchase of the asset; avoiding a higher finance charge is more valuable than avoiding a lower one.

The same variables determine the prices of put options except, in the case of puts, a *higher* E as well as a lower P produce higher put prices.

Figure 14.2 depicts the value of a call before its expiration date as a dashed line. The heavy solid lines show the call option's minimum values. A call is in-the-money or *at*-the-money if its exercise price is below or *at* the current price of the underlying asset. A put is in-the-money or *at*-the-money if its exercise price is above or *at* the asset's price.

The slope of the dashed line indicates the amount an option's price will change for a unit change in the underlying asset's price. This rate of change in the option's price for small changes in the underlying asset's price is known as the option's *delta*. For example, a delta factor of 0.5 means that a $1 change in the asset's price produces a $0.50 change in the option premium. This relationship is important for *delta hedging*; a delta factor of 0.5 indicates that the price change in two options will hedge the price change in one unit of the underlying asset. Delta varies from zero to one in the case of calls and from minus one to zero for puts. For calls (puts) delta approaches one (minus one) when it is deep in-the-money and approaches zero as the option goes far *out-of-the-money*.[2]

EXCHANGE-TRADED INTEREST RATE OPTIONS

The most widely traded interest rate options are options on U.S. Treasury bond futures contracts. Options that are directly written on cash bonds also are traded, but the volume

---

[2] Delta hedging requires frequent rebalancing because delta will change constantly as the underlying asset price changes. The delta of an interest rate option is similar analytically to the duration of the price curve for fixed-income securities (see Chapter 4) in the sense that both reveal price sensitivity to small changes in the interest rate. Also, an option's *gamma* factor is a corollary for a bond's convexity. Just as convexity accounted for the curvature of a bond's price curve, gamma shows how the option curve's slope (the hedge ratio) changes with interest rates.

is very small compared to options on bond futures. This may seem strange. One is inclined to assume that a hybrid options-on-futures contract is the far more complicated instrument. The opposite is true: Options on cash bonds are the more complicated of the two types. The complication arises in exercising options on cash bonds. Exercising requires that the actual bonds be delivered, but cash bonds usually are in short supply. To exercise options on them, it is necessary to shop among several dealers in order to find competitive prices on a range of coupons and maturities, when only a small amount of each issue is likely to be available.

In relation to cash bonds, exercising options on U.S. Treasury bond futures contracts is simple. The trading volume of futures contracts is extremely large, which eliminates concern about supply and ensures that they are competitively priced. When the buyer exercises a call option on Treasury bond futures, the exchange clearinghouse simply assigns the buyer a long position in the bond futures contract at the exercise price and creates an offsetting counterposition. The clearinghouse can create an unlimited number of such counterpositions.

In addition to assuming a long position in bond futures upon exercise, the buyer receives a cash settlement equal to the difference in the bond futures price at the time of exercise and the exercise price. When the call option buyer decides to exercise, the call seller or writer is responsible for paying the cash settlement to the buyer via the auspices of the exchange. In addition, the exchange assigns the seller a short position in the futures contract. However, there is no profit in either party's position in the futures contract. At the time of exercise, neither the long nor the short futures position has net value because they are priced at the existing market.

Figure 14.3 gives the quotations for call and put options on futures contracts for

FIGURE 14.3   Quotations on Exchange-Traded Options on Treasury Bond and Note Futures

INTEREST RATE

T-BONDS (CBT)
$100,000; points and 64ths of 100%

Strike	Calls-Settle			Puts-Settle		
Price	Feb	Mar	Jun	Feb	Mar	Jun
109	2-21	....	....	0-03	....	....
110	1-28	2-05	2-56	0-10	0-51	2-07
111	0-46	....	....	0-28	....	....
112	0-17	0-63	1-59	0-63	1-45	3-08
113	0-04	....	....	1-50	....	....
114	0-01	0-23	1-13	2-47	3-02	4-24

Est. vol. 85,000;
Tu vol. 68,847 calls; 88,646 puts
Op. Int. Tues 414,487 calls; 278,357 puts

T-NOTES (CBT)
$100,000; points and 64ths of 100%

Strike	Calls-Settle			Puts-Settle		
Price	Feb	Mar	Jun	Feb	Mar	Jun
107	....	1-55	2-08	0-03	0-21	1-12
108	0-44	1-11	1-36	0-10	0-41	1-40
109	0-11	0-41	1-08	0-41	1-06	2-10
110	0-01	0-19	0-49	1-30	1-50	2-51
111	0-01	0-08	0-32	2-30	2-37	3-33
112	0-01	0-03	0-21	....	3-32	....

Est vol 32,000 Tu 12,067 calls 16,850 puts
Op Int Tues 166,282 calls 132,125 puts

SOURCE: *Wall Street Journal*, January 16, 1997, C19.

U.S. Treasury bonds and notes reported for the market of January 15, 1997 in the *Wall Street Journal.* These option contracts are sold on the Chicago Board of Trade. The report shows strike prices in the left column. The option premiums (prices) for various maturity months are listed for calls and puts. Premiums for options on U.S. Treasury futures are quoted in points and 64ths of a point, even though U.S. Treasury bond futures themselves are quoted in points and 32nds of a point. A 1/64 is the minimum price variation and is equal to $15.63 on a $100,000 contract. For example, an option premium for a June 110 call on "T-bond" futures shown in the report is 2-56 or 2 and 56/64 points, which is $2,875. Each contract is written on $100,000 in bond futures.

EXAMPLE Stock Financial Group (SFG) purchases a June 110 call on Treasury bond futures. Subsequently, the futures price rises to 114-00, and Stock Financial exercises the option. With exercise, Stock Financial is paid $4,000 (based on $114,000 − $110,000) and immediately assumes a long position in the bond futures contract bearing a contract price of 114-00. Gilmer, the option seller, must pay $4,000 and assume a short position in the bond futures at the contract price of 114-00. At this point, neither SFG nor Gilmer has a profit in their respective futures positions, and they can immediately offset their positions with an opposite trade in the futures market.

These relationships are reversed in the case of put options. The buyer of a put option on Treasury bond futures acquires a potential short position in the underlying futures contract. If the put owner decides to exercise, following a decline in the futures price below the exercise price, the owner is paid the difference in the exercise price and the bond futures price at the time of exercise and acquires a short position in the underlying futures contract. The put writer is required to pay the buyer the amount of the settlement and to assume a long position in the futures.

EXAMPLE Stock Financial Group (SFG) buys a June 110 put and exercises when the futures price declines to 109-00. Upon exercise, SFG is paid $1,000 and is assigned a short position in the bond futures contract, again at the exercise price of 110-00. Gilmer, the seller of the put, pays the $1,000 and is assigned a long position on the bond futures contract at 110-00.

HEDGING A BOND PORTFOLIO

Remember the delta factor? We defined it as the change in option premium for a $1 change in the underlying asset value. Hedgers use deltas to determine the number of options—the *hedge ratio*—required to hedge against increasing or decreasing bond prices. The delta for an at-the-money option is usually very close to 0.5. The following example explains simple delta hedging using T-bond futures.

EXAMPLE In January, H. J. Finkelstein Savings Bank (FSB) is preparing to purchase one thousand 8 percent coupon bonds ($10,000 par value each) one week from now. The delta factor for options on Treasury bond futures is 0.5. To create a complete hedge, Finkelstein Savings needs to buy 200 call options. (Recall that options on bond futures are for $100,000 each in bond futures notional value.) Happily, this particular calculation is unusually straightforward because the 8 percent bonds that Finkelstein plans to buy correspond directly to the standardized 8 percent bond underlying the futures contract.

Instead, suppose Finkelstein Savings decides to purchase one thousand 9 percent coupon bonds to mature in 2027. Using the example from Chapter 13 on financial futures, we find that this bond has a conversion factor of 1.063; the number of calls needed now becomes $1.063 \times 200 = 213$ (rounded). Suppose the current Treasury bond yield is 9.0 percent, the futures price is 90-00, and FSB buys 213 March at-the-money calls at a premium cost of $2,000 each.

What happens if one week from now the Treasury bond yield falls to 8.90 percent, raising the futures price to 91-00? Finkelstein now has to pay an additional $100,000 to complete its original goal of buying 1,000 bonds. On the other hand, FSB's call options are increasing. Each call option increases in value by ~$470, producing a total increase in the value of the options of 470×213 calls = $100,110, enough to offset the increased cost of the bond purchase.[3]

OPTION PRICING MODELS

Options have enormous economic and social importance. You don't have to look far into the recent literature of finance to see the significance of research into the economic value of options. The subject ranks among the most compelling for financial economists. The focus of all this activity is, for the most part, theorizing about and modeling option prices.

Option pricing theories and models are constructed from the assumption of no risk-less arbitrage.[4] Researchers initially focused on option pricing models for common stock options. The simplest stock option pricing model is based on the single-period *binomial formula*. In the following, we find a correct option price utilizing a binomial model under the no-arbitrage condition.

EXAMPLE   Reflex Corporation common stock is priced at $100 per share, and it is known that it will be worth either $95 or $110 one period from now.[5] A single-period call option on 100 Reflex Corporation shares with an exercise price of $100 currently trades for a price of $800. There are only two possible payoffs for the call option: (1) $1,000, if Reflex stock rises to $110 (100 shares × (Stock price of $110 − Exercise price of $100)), and (2) $0 if Reflex falls to $95, in which case the call option is worthless because its exercise price is higher than Reflex's stock price.

Figure 14.4A shows the stock price movements emanating from a "*node*" at time 0, and Figure 14.4B shows the corresponding movement in the option price. The market will not sustain an $800 option price because, as detailed below, at this price an arbitrageur

---

[3] Traders apply a more theoretically precise hedge ratio found in the formal Black-Scholes option pricing model discussed in Appendix 14A. We find it hard to give an intuitive interpretation of this formal hedge ratio. While this is not the place to be highly technical, it is roughly a cumulative probability factor that incorporates the price volatility in the underlying bond futures contract as a means of expressing the uncertainty of future price changes. This cumulative probability is the weight assigned to the asset's price in the Black-Scholes formula. It is drawn from the normal distribution function, which is calculated using the standard normal distribution table. In Appendix 14A it is found as the term $N(d_1)$. Most importantly, the expression includes the volatility of the asset price.

[4] See the discussion on arbitrage as the basis for linking forward and futures contracts with spot prices in Chapter 13.

[5] This example is based on Richard M. Bookstaber, *Option Pricing and Strategies in Investing* (Reading, Mass.: Addison-Wesley Publishing Co., 1982).

is guaranteed a profit at either stock price. This is in conflict with the arbitrage-free condition we impose to make sense of option pricing. Consequently, the actions of arbitrageurs force the option's price to its correct level. Let's see how this happens.

Arbitrageurs may write (sell) three Reflex Corporation $100 call options to receive income of $2,400 (3 × $800) and pay out $20,000 to buy 200 shares of Reflex Corporation at $100 per share for a net outlay of $17,600 ($20,000 − $2,400). To avoid investing their personal funds, the arbitrageurs borrow the $17,600 at the going interest rate of 5 percent.

When the three call options expire at the end of the period, the arbitrageurs will receive one of two payoffs. First, as call writers, if Reflex stock goes to $110, they must pay out $3,000 to call owners (3 options × 100 shares per option × ($110 − $100)), receive $22,000 for 200 shares of stock, and repay the borrowings plus interest totaling $18,480 (i.e., $17,600 × 1.05) for a net profit of $520. Second, if Reflex stock drops to $95, they will sell stock worth $19,000 and repay $18,480, again pocketing the difference of $520. (They are not obliged to act on the option which expires worthless.)

This situation cannot continue because, no matter which of the two possible stock prices occurs, an identical profit is guaranteed and arbitrageurs will flood in. Moreover, the profit is riskless, and no net investment is required. It turns out in this case that $635 is the only option price that clears the market of arbitrage opportunities. This is demonstrated in Table 14.1. At an option price of $635, the previous arbitrage strategy is no longer profitable. Profit is eliminated at both the $95 and the $110 stock prices.

Volatility helps to set the option's price. Suppose Reflex Corporation stock is known to be more volatile than the price range of $95 to $110. Larger volatility has the effect of increasing the market-clearing option price. To verify this effect, find the option price if the expected prices for Reflex in Table 14.1 are either $87.50 or $125. You should find that the more volatile future price distribution produces an option price of $1,111.

As you may have guessed by this time, this formulation is rather simple. It suffers from two unrealistic assumptions: First, it assumes only one specific trading period. Second, it assumes only two possible price moves (thus, a *binomial* process), whereas a stock can take on any number of prices. We can improve on the first assumption by expanding to more trading periods—a *multiplicative* binomial process—and allow each trading period to become shorter and shorter as we add more trading periods. With multiplicative models, the simple "fork" diagram of Figure 14.4 quickly becomes a "lattice" or "tree" of price movements emanating from each node as in Figure 14.5.

At the extreme, when we shorten the time intervals enough, the number of trading periods approaches infinity, and we can model trading activity as the near-continuous reality that it is. We can also permit the stock to take on an unlimited number of possible

TABLE 14.1 Arbitrage-Free Price on Reflex Corporation Call Options

	Position at $t = 0$ Stock Price = $100	Position at $t = 1$ Stock Price = $95	Stock Price = $110
Write 3 call options @ $635	+ $1,905	0	−$3,000
Buy 200 shares	−$20,000	+$19,000	+$22,000
Borrow at 5 percent	+$18,095	−$19,000	−$19,000
Net profit	0	0	0

FIGURE 14.4 One-Period Binomial Model, Reflex Corporation Stock

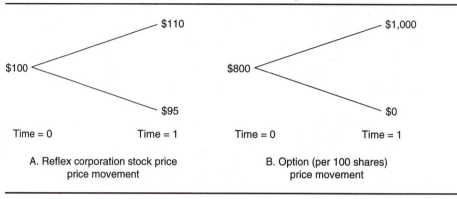

A. Reflex corporation stock price
price movement

B. Option (per 100 shares)
price movement

FIGURE 14.5 Multiplicative Binomial Model of Stock Prices

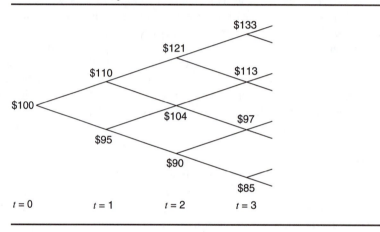

prices. These two changes lead to the renowned Black and Scholes closed-form option pricing formulation. We give a concise explanation of the Black and Scholes formula in Appendix 14A.

INTEREST RATE OPTIONS

Financial institutions transact in interest-bearing assets and liabilities and so focus more on interest rate options than on stock options. Unknown future interest rates are to interest rate options what unknown future stock prices are to stock options. Like stock options, a key factor in pricing interest rate options is the volatility of the debt securities underlying them. It is not feasible, however, to apply a closed-form option pricing model such as Black-Scholes to options that correspond to debt securities.

This is primarily because debt securities have specific maturities, whereas stocks presumably have none. The Black-Scholes model is able to assume—conveniently, as it

FIGURE 14.6 Interest Rate Tree; Subject to Arbitrage (Not Arbitrage-free)

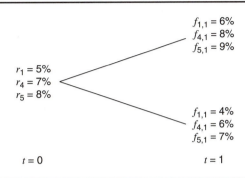

turns out—that the underlying common stock price has constant volatility through time. On the other hand, a bond's price volatility decreases as it ages because its price converges toward its maturity value or par. For example, a 10-year bond's price volatility (or interest sensitivity) is considerably greater earlier in its life than when it is just a few months before maturity. In addition, interest rates, unlike returns on stocks, appear to be *mean reverting*; that is, they tend to revert to a long-term level over time.[6]

Arbitrage-Free Interest Rate Trees

We can represent the evolution of expected future interest rate term structures with an interest rate tree analogous to the stock price tree.[7] We begin the tree by showing the present term structure of interest rates at the $t = 0$ node in Figure 14.6. In the example, zero-coupon bonds with maturities of one, four, and five years produce yields to maturity of 5, 7, and 8 percent, respectively. We will designate this as $(r_1, r_4, r_5) = (5\%, 7\%, 8\%)$.

As zero-coupon bonds, each bond makes a single payment of $1 at maturity. From the $t = 0$ node, we assume only two possible changes in interest rates: in Figure 14.6, the changes are plus or minus 1 percent. Typically, analysts assign equal probabilities to up and down movements, an assumption that turns out to be a reasonable one for short time periods. The model generates a distribution of expected future rates $f_{n,t}s$, where n is maturity and t is the applicable future time, at $t = 1$. We must consider that, because they age by one year, the four- and five-year bonds at $t = 0$ become three- and four-year bonds at $t = 1$. The original one-year bond matures at $t = 1$, and a brand new one is created.

The model in Figure 14.6 presents a naïve and, as it turns out, unacceptable assumption about the future term structure of interest rates. The flaw stems from the generation of expected future rates on a simple constant volatility factor of plus and minus 1 percent up and down movements.

Recall that in our discussion of the term structure of interest rates in Chapter 5 we

---

[6] Furthermore, Black-Scholes assumes that stock price volatility is not related to the level of stock prices, while the mean-reverting property for bonds suggests that bond price volatility is greater the further bond prices diverge from par.

[7] Parts of the discussion in this section are based on Fred Arditti in *Derivatives: A Comprehensive Resource for Options, Futures, Interest Rate Swaps and Mortgage Securities* (Boston: Harvard Business School Press, 1996).

FIGURE 14.7   Arbitrage-free Interest Rate Tree

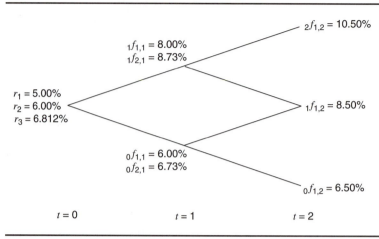

showed that to be free of arbitrage opportunities, alternative maturity strategies must produce the same holding period yields. Unfortunately, the interest change process above cannot be sustained because it does not lead to an arbitrage-free equilibrium.

The one-year yield from purchasing the five-year bond at $t = 0$ and selling it at $t = 1$ always dominates the yield on the one-year bond no matter what happens. Because the original one-year 5 percent bond matures at $t = 1$, it earns 5 percent regardless of the movement of interest rates. In contrast, the original five-year bond, purchased at $t = 0$ for $[1/(1.08)^5] = 0.6806$, gains more than 5 percent in value with either up or down rate movements, and so it is always a superior maturity strategy. If rates rise, it can be sold at $t = 1$ for $[1/(1.08)^4] = 0.7350$ for a rate of return of $[(0.7350 - 0.6806)/0.6806] = 7.993\%$. If interest rates decline, the original five-year bond can be sold at $t = 1$ for $[1/(1.06)^4] = 0.7921$ for a rate of return of $[(0.7921 - 0.6806)/0.6806] = 16.382\%$.

The results indicate that no one would purchase the one-year 5 percent security. This violates the no-arbitrage premise about the equality of different maturity strategies over the same holding period. Under these conditions, arbitrage would force changes in the present ($t = 0$) term structure, and the interest rate tree in Figure 14.6 would not hold up.

The arbitrage-free condition requires that today's bond price equals the present expected (probability-weighted) value of the bond's possible prices one period later. For this to occur requires that a *shift* take place in interest rates in addition to a volatility factor. The interest rate tree shown in Figure 14.7 incorporates a ± 1 percent volatility factor plus a *shift* factor that is properly scaled to ensure that the tree is not subject to arbitrage. The shift factor will be different for different time periods. We assume a 0.5 probability for both up and down movements.[8] The prescript on alternative future rates indicates the number of previous up-moves at future nodes.

---

[8] A rate shift should always occur, unless the term structure is flat (meaning that rates for different maturities are the same), regardless of whether we use a point estimate of future expected rates or a distribution of them. Consider a one-year spot rate of 5 percent and a two-year spot rate of 5.50 percent, which implies an expected future one-year spot rate of 6 percent one year from now. In this case, the *expected* shift in the one-year rate is 1 percent (from 5 percent to 6 percent).

FIGURE 14.8   **Price Tree for Exchange-Traded Call Option**

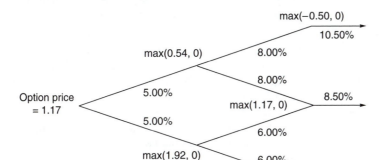

Interest Rate Trees and Interest Rate Options

Traders make wide use of interest rate models to price exchange-traded options as well as to price option features *embedded* in fixed-income securities. We consider both cases using the interest rate expectations described in Figure 14.7. First, we consider a two-period call option written on a three-period bond. To keep it simple, the bond pays no coupons and makes a single payment of 100 at maturity three years from now. The call option has a strike price of 91.00, can be exercised at either $t = 1$ or $t = 2$, and expires at $t = 2$. The bond price is the present value of 100 discounted at the present ($t = 0$) three-year rate and is equal to $[100/(1.06812)^3] = 82.063$.

Figure 14.8 shows the option's price tree, incorporating the values of the call at each node. It shows one-year interest rates on the branches connecting the price nodes. The prices at the end nodes ($t = 2$) are max($P - E$, 0)—that is, the maximum of the bond's price minus the strike price (E), or zero. The option price is solved by "backwardation," that is, the solution starts at the last future node and regresses backward in time to the present. For example, in the highest node at $t = 2$, the price of the underlying bond is $[100/1.1050] = 90.50$ and $(P - E) = (90.50 - 91.00) = -0.50$. The negative value indicates that the option will not be exercised, and so it is valued at max(-0.50, 0) = 0. Similarly, at the middle node for $t = 2$, the underlying bond price is 92.17 (found as $[100/1.0850]$) and $(P - E) = 1.17$.

Working backward, the $t = 1$ node option prices are the probability-weighted prices of the end node prices for $t = 2$, discounted at the one-period interest rates of either 8 percent or 6 percent. For example, the lower $t = 1$ node value is

$$0.5\left(\frac{\max(1.17,\ 0)}{1.06}\right) + 0.5\left(\frac{\max(2.90,\ 0)}{1.06}\right) = \$1.92$$

Working back further to the $t = 0$ node and discounting at 5 percent gives the expected present option value of 1.17.

The case of pricing an embedded option is similar to the case of a call option on a bond. Recall that when we discussed the term structure of interest rates in Appendix 5B we showed how to calculate the option-adjusted spread for a callable bond issued by the Federal Home Loan Bank. It is important not to confuse that exercise from the analysis that follows. The objective of the exercise in Appendix 5B was to determine the market's spread over the risk-free yield curve that is priced into the security. The spread compensated investors for bearing the risk that the security might be called before it matured.[9] A call before maturity exposes investors to surrendering a security on which the yield is above market yields available for reinvestment.

In the present analysis, we determine the *required* spread—that is, what the spread *ought to be,* given the callability of the security. Then we can combine our knowledge of the market's option-adjusted spread with the knowledge of what the spread should be in order to detect whether the security is under- or overpriced.

EXAMPLE A $7\frac{1}{2}$ percent annual coupon, three-year security is issued by the Federal Harley Stabilization Board, a government agency charged with supporting prices for small used vehicles. The note is callable at par after one year. The interest rate outlook is the same as that depicted in Figure 14.7. If it were option-free, the price of the security, discounting its cash flows under the present term structure, would be

$$P_0 = \frac{\$75}{1.050} + \frac{\$75}{(1.060)^2} + \frac{\$1,075}{(1.06812)^3}$$

$$= \$1,020.34$$

As in the earlier example, the value of the embedded option is found by "backwardation." We assume that if the FHSB note's price ever exceeds $1,000 at $t = 1$ or $t = 2$, it will be called. As shown in Figure 14.9, the price at each node is min $(1,000, P_t)$. For example, for the highest node at $t = 2$, the security's price is ($1,000 + $75)/1.105 = $972.85 and min(1,000, 972.85) = $972.85.

Working backward, we see that the $t = 1$ node prices are the probability-weighted prices of the $t = 2$ node prices discounted at the one-period interest rates of either 8 or 6 percent. Working back further to the $t = 0$ node and discounting at 5 percent gives $1,013.58 as the expected value of the agency note based on its exposure to call at $t = 1$ and $t = 2$. In theory, an investor should not pay more than this for the FHSB note. The price of the embedded call option is the difference between the option-free price and this value.

Option-free price = $1,020.34

− Option-embedded value =   1,013.58

Option price = $ 6.76

or the option is valued at ~67 basis points (bps).

Although they are different cases, suppose the market's option-adjusted spread on

---

[9] In Appendix 5B we assumed the spread was unaffected by credit risk because the example security was the obligation of a U.S. government agency. This is not perfectly accurate: agency securities have a modicum of credit risk because, unlike Treasury securities, they do not enjoy the full sovereign power of the government to make good on its debts.

FIGURE 14.9   Price Tree for FHSB Option-Embedded Note

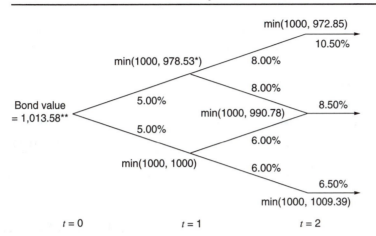

$$* = (0.5)\frac{(972.85 + 75)}{1.08} + (0.5)\frac{(990.78 + 75)}{1.08}$$

$$** = (0.5)\frac{(978.53 + 75)}{1.05} + (0.5)\frac{(1000 + 75)}{1.05}$$

the FHSB note was 90 basis points as we found for a different agency security in Appendix 5B. We conclude that the market compensates investors 90 bps for a call option worth only 67 bps, and the security is, therefore, underpriced. In short, the security would be a bargain purchase.

CAPS, FLOORS, AND COLLARS

Interest Rate Cap Agreements

Borrowers are immensely fond of interest rate caps when interest rates are expected to rise. Caps protect borrowers against rising interest rates by restricting floating-rate loans to a maximum interest rate. Banks sell caps to borrowers either as cap guarantees within loan agreements or as explicit stand-alone cap options.

An interest rate cap is an option on an underlying reference interest rate such as six-month LIBOR. In a capped floating-rate loan agreement, the bank periodically "resets" or "reprices" the loan rate against the loan's reference market rate. When the reference rate rises above the guarantee or striking price, the borrower's rate is capped and the borrower pays no more than the guarantee. If interest rates decline, they still allow borrowers to benefit from the resulting lower costs.

Alternatively, the bank may sell the borrower a stand-alone cap instrument separate from the loan agreement. When the cap's reference rate exceeds its "strike rate" (the cap rate), the buyer is paid the difference between the reference rate and the cap rate multiplied by the "notional amount" of the cap. The notional amount is nominal only and does not refer to an amount of principal changing hands. It is a bookkeeping number used strictly for calculating the payment amount and typically equals the loan principal amount.

TABLE 14.2 Payments, Two-year Cap, Webster Website Wireless, Inc.

	Cap	Reference Market Rate	Difference (Ref. − Cap)	Cap Payment (1-year lag)	Effective Rate
Trade Date					
January 1, 1998	—	5.00%	—	—	5.00%
Reset Dates					
January 1, 1999	7.00%	8.00%	1.00%	$100,000	7.00%
January 1, 2000	7.00%	8.50%	1.50%	$150,000	7.00%
Total		7.17%		$250,000	6.33%

EXAMPLE On January 1, 1998, Webster Website Wireless, Inc. (WWW) obtains a variable-rate $10 million loan for three years. The loan rate "resets" at the beginning of each year at a spread over 12-month LIBOR. At the origination of the loan, the initial rate is set at the market rate and is the basis of interest paid at the end of the first year. The loan rate then resets on the first and second anniversaries of the loan agreement. WWW acquires a rate cap guarantee of 7 percent, establishing the maximum cost of the loan at 7 percent plus the cost of the cap. When the borrowing or actual rate is above the cap on the reset date, a cash payment is made at the end of the year.

Table 14.2 shows the payments made for reference market rates $(r_{1,0}, r_{1,1}, r_{1,2})$ = (5.00%, 8.00%, 8.50%). However, Table 14.2 is not known in advance so we are getting ahead of ourselves.

What is a fair price for Webster Website to pay for this cap? Unfortunately, the charge for the cap is built into the loan up front when future reference rates are unknown. Fortunately, we can account for the uncertainty about future rates using binomial option pricing to value the cap.

The reference for possible interest rates is the arbitrage-free rate structure presented earlier in Figure 14.7. The cap is equivalent to a *strip* of two European call options with maturity dates on $t = 1$ and $t = 2$. If the calls are exercised on these two dates, payments will be made with a one-period lag at $t = 2$ and $t = 3$, respectively. The two-period call is exercised if the rate is either 10.50 percent or 8.50 percent at $t = 2$ and pays either $350,000 or $150,000 with a one-period lag at $t = 3$. It is not exercised if the rate is 6.50 percent. Working backward through the branches of the tree in Figure 14.7, we find that the payments are valued by discounting back to $t = 0$:

$$c_2 = \frac{1}{1.05}\left(0.5\left\{\frac{1}{1.08}\left[0.5\left(\frac{350,000}{1.105}\right) + 0.5\left(\frac{150,000}{1.085}\right)\right]\right\}\right.$$

$$\left. + 0.5\left\{\frac{1}{1.06}\left[0.5\left(\frac{150,000}{1.085}\right) + 0.5\left(\frac{0}{1.065}\right)\right]\right\}\right)$$

$$= \$131,360$$

Similarly, the one-period call will pay $100,000 at $t = 2$ if the rate at $t = 1$ is 8 percent and 0 if the rate is 6 percent:

$$c_1 = \frac{1}{1.05}\left[0.5\left(\frac{100,000}{1.08}\right) + 0.5\left(\frac{0}{1.06}\right)\right] = \$44,092$$

The value of the cap is

$$C = c_1 + c_2 = \$175,452 \approx \$175,000$$

If the cap is part of the Webster loan agreement, the bank builds this price into the loan fee. If the guarantee is sold as a stand-alone, the selling institution simply charges WWW a direct fee of $175,000 (175 basis points on the notional amount). The bank can hedge its cap sale by purchasing put options on Eurodollars, most likely in the form of options on Eurodollar futures.

Prices on caps are sensitive to the length of the agreement and to the level of the cap rate. Longer-term agreements and lower cap strike prices increase the likelihood that the reference rate will exceed the cap rate, leading to higher prices for longer terms and lower cap rates. Banking practice appears to favor a maximum term of about two years, but terms as long as 10 years are not uncommon. Because clients buy stand-alone caps over the counter from their bank, they are not protected by daily settlement procedures used for exchange-traded options. As a result, the integrity of a cap must depend on the bank's credit standing.

Floors and Collars

An interest rate floor guarantee is the opposite of the cap guarantee arrangement. The floor protects the lender against a decrease in loan rate below the floor strike price. The flow of benefits is reversed. When a floor is part of a floating-rate loan agreement, the lender is paid when the market rate falls below the floor rate. The borrower is short a put option and incurs a cost by giving up the benefits of downside interest rate movements below the floor rate. Banks must make other concessions such as reduced loan fees or lower borrowing rates to obtain loan agreements with floors.

Collars simply incorporate both a short or long cap with a long or short floor. Collars confine a borrower's floating rate within a band between the floor and cap rates over the life of the agreement. Borrowers sometimes sell a floor to earn back part of the cost of buying a cap. Floor prices are lower than cap prices because the floor rate is set below the reference rate and is out of the money, whereas the cap rate is normally at the reference rate. Figure 14.10 shows a bank's payoff for a collar in terms of the corresponding cap and floor.

OTHER CONTINGENT CLAIMS PRODUCTS

Options are often called *contingent claims*. This is because owners of options may exercise a claim, *contingent* on the value of an underlying security, service, or product. For example, a borrower whose loan agreement has a cap guarantee may claim a capped loan rate,

FIGURE 14.10 Bank's Payoff Profile for Collar

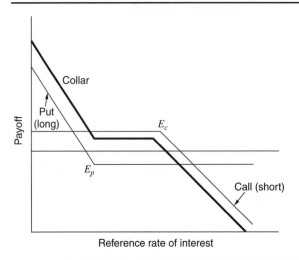

contingent on the reference interest rate rising above the cap. The *contingency* of such a claim has value. In the past, bank managers probably did not recognize that products and services involving contingent claims lend themselves to option pricing concepts and may have priced them in an *ad hoc* way. However, option pricing concepts can be used to sharpen managers' intuition about the value of fee-based products or services and assist in setting fee income in a logical way.

Pricing Loan Commitments

Options are analogous to insurance policies, and option premiums are analogous to insurance premiums. For example, a loan commitment—a valuable product in banking—has an important insurance function. To a bank customer, a loan commitment is credit availability insurance because it insures that the customer will have funds when they are needed. It amounts to selling a put option to the customer because it gives the customer the right to "put" its debt to the bank in the future. The loan commitment fee is analogous to an insurance premium: Functionally, it is the price for the put option. Similar to the insurance one might buy on an automobile, loan commitment "options" transfer the risk of funds availability (damage to the automobile) from the customer (automobile owner) to the bank (insurance company).

Consider the "optionality" of a fixed-rate loan commitment. In a rising rate environment, fixed-rate commitments are more valuable than variable-rate commitments because they lock in the borrowing rate for a period of time in the future. If market borrowing rates decline, the prospective borrower is not obligated to exercise the option to borrow.

As the seller of a fixed-rate loan commitment, the bank's payoff is the same as being short a put option. This payoff is shown in Figure 14.11A. The profit at maturity from selling the loan commitment is plotted on the vertical axis, and the dollar value of the loan commitment is plotted on the horizontal axis. If market interest rates increase (they move from right to left in Figure 14.11) above the guaranteed rate (the exercise price),

FIGURE 14.11   Fixed-rate Loan Commitment

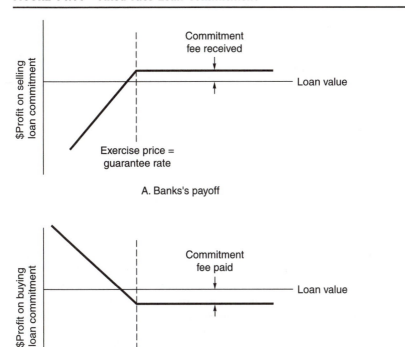

A. Banks's payoff

B. Customer's payoff

the customer may be more eager to borrow because the commitment interest rate is now a bargain compared to the market rate. On the other hand, the loan's prospective value to the bank decreases because the bank is obliged to lend at a below-market fixed rate. The profitability of the commitment, illustrated by the solid line declining to the left in Figure 14.11A, quickly becomes negative.

If market borrowing rates instead fall, the value to the bank of the loan commitment increases (movement to the right in the figure). Now the customer will borrow from cheaper alternative sources and will let the loan commitment expire. This caps the bank's upside profit at the level of the commitment fee (the flat portion of the solid line).

The payoff for the bank's customer is shown in Figure 14.11B and is the mirror image of Figure 14.11A representing the bank's outcome. If interest rates rise, the loan value falls (movement to the left) and the loan option goes in the money because the customer can profit by "putting" underpriced debt to the bank. If market borrowing rates fall below the loan guarantee rate (movement to the right), the customer lets the commitment expire and only loses the commitment fee. As is true for any option, the risk is shifted to the seller (the bank) and the put option buyer (the customer) has no downside risk. However, the customer is guaranteed a modest and known loss if market borrowing rates decline.

FIGURE 14.12   Price and Interest Rate Tree for Loan Commitment

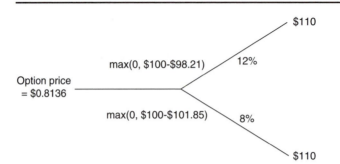

Figure 14.12 shows a simplified single-period binomial model to illustrate the pricing of a fixed-rate loan commitment. Assume the present ($t = 0$) loan rate is 10 percent.[10] Consider a one-year commitment to make a one-year loan of $100 in one year ($t = 1$) at a fixed rate of 10 percent. The loan, if made, would have a repayment obligation of $110 at maturity ($t = 2$). The market borrowing rate initially is 10 percent, and there is a 0.5 probability that the rate will rise or fall by 2 percent of its starting level by the end of the year. If the rate rises to 12 percent, the present value cost of the underlying loan one year from now will fall to $110/1.12 = $98.21. The bank customer exercises the right to borrow because the 10 percent commitment rate is well below the market rate of 12 percent. The commitment value at $t = 1$ is ($100 − $98.21) = $1.79.

If the rate falls to 8 percent, the present value loan cost becomes $110/1.08 = $101.85. Would-be borrowers will not borrow at the commitment rate of 10 percent because it is above the market rate. Instead, borrowers will allow the commitment to expire unexercised. The commitment value at $t = 1$ is zero because the customer can find alternative sources of credit at lower prices and will not exercise the commitment. The minimum price for the commitment at $t = 0$ is

$$\frac{[0.5(\$1.79) + 0.5(\$0)]}{1.10} = \$0.8136$$

or about 81 cents per hundred dollar commitment. For a $1 million commitment at 10 percent, effective at $t = 1$, the bank will charge $8,136 or 81 basis points.

Pricing Standby Letters of Credit

Banks sell standby letters of credit (SLCs) to clients to guarantee clients' payment obligations to third parties. For example, entities that issue debt securities frequently purchase a bank SLC as a *credit enhancement* to improve the rating and reduce the interest cost

---

[10] We simplify the example by assuming the yield curve is flat; that is, loans of all maturities bear 10 percent interest.

FIGURE 14.13 Standby Letter of Credit Relational Triangle

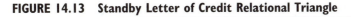
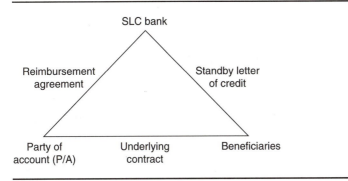

of the securities they issue. If, for any reason, the issuing entity fails to make payment to investors on the securities, the SLC serves as a backup payment source. Figure 14.13 shows the three-way relationships between the participants when an SLC is used. In the terms of our example, we refer to the three participants as the SLC bank, the party of account (the bank's client, or P/A), and the beneficiaries (the investors). We will demonstrate that SLCs are true put options.

As shown in Figure 14.13, the SLC is only one of three contracts that connect the participants. First, there is the original contract between the P/A and the beneficiaries— the debt security instrument in our example. Then, the P/A pays the bank a fee for issuing the SLC, which is a contingent liability to pay beneficiaries in the event the P/A fails to perform: In effect, the bank guarantees the P/A will perform. Simultaneously, the P/A issues a *reimbursement agreement* to the bank promising to compensate the bank if the bank is required to ''make good'' on the P/A's payment obligation to the beneficiaries.

We can apply option pricing concepts to determine how much the bank should charge—the SLC fee—for issuing an SLC. The SLC fee is the option premium earned by the bank for selling a put option to the P/A. It gives the P/A the right to ''put to the bank'' its payment obligation if it cannot perform.

EXAMPLE The City of Altoona (City) decides to issue $10 million one-year notes bearing 6 percent interest to investors. City asks its bank to issue an SLC guaranteeing 100 percent of City's obligation to pay $10 million plus interest to investors at the end of the year.[11] Analysts determine that the probabilities are 0.97 that City will make full repayment of ($10,000,000 $\times$ 1.06) = $10,600,000 one year from now, 0.02 that City will pay 80 percent of its obligation (0.80 $\times$ $10,600,000 = $8,480,000), and 0.01 that it will fail to pay any of its debt. The one-year riskless rate of interest is 5 percent. In each case of payment shortfalls, the bank is responsible for any unpaid balance.

Before solving, let's consider the ''optionality'' of this example. The payment of $10,600,000 is the striking price on a put option, and the different probabilistic estimates of City's ability to pay are the volatility of the underlying asset. The present value of the

---

[11] SLCs usually guarantee somewhat less than 100 percent of the payments due investors. For example, investors may be required to absorb the first 5 percent of losses due to the nonperformance of the ''party of account.'' This results in a 95 percent SLC guarantee.

bank's guarantee is the difference between the exercise price and the underlying ability to pay:

$$P = [0.97 \times (\$10,600,000 - \$10,600,000) + 0.02 \times (\$10,600,000 - \$8,480,000)$$
$$+ 0.01 \times (\$10,600,000 - \$0)]/1.05$$
$$= \underline{\$141,333}$$

The dollar value of $141,333 is 1.413 percent of the amount of the guarantee, indicating that the bank should charge 141 basis points.[12]

Loan Portfolio Insurance

Overall, loan losses tend to increase when the economy is in recession. Losses on loans to firms in particular industries increase when those industries are economically troubled. Losses that are tied to economic distress in the economy as a whole or distress across specific industries are *systemic* losses. Financial institutions can at least partly insure their loan portfolios against such losses by using options.

For example, to insure against losses that correspond to downturns in the economy, lending institutions might purchase stock index put options on the plausible theory that the stock market will do poorly during recessions. As the stock market declines with an economic downturn, index put options go into the money and offset the rise in loan losses. An alternative use of options is for the institution to sell stock index call options and earn enough premiums to cover the increases in loan losses. Here, the lender is counting on the market to decline, causing its sold position in call options to go out of the money and to expire without being called. This strategy takes the risk that the market might rise and force the institution to cover a call.

Lending institutions can use analogous strategies to insure against systematic losses that correspond to poor performance in specific industries. For example, suppose a bank has loans outstanding to several auto industry suppliers. Knowing well the automobile industry's cyclical performance, the bank purchases puts (or writes calls) on the stock of an industry leader such as General Motors or Chrysler on the reasonable presumption that, as the leader goes, so go its suppliers. This insurance strategy should perform similarly to the strategy for general economic recession.

Commodity Options

Loan losses often can be traced to falling prices of real goods such as agricultural commodities and extractive commodities such as petroleum, ores, and minerals. For example, a large number of banks suffered large loan losses in the 1970s and 1980s when crop prices and petroleum prices fell unexpectedly. One conceives of these losses as *systemic regional* losses because the decline in the price of particular commodities impacted not only certain borrowers in a region directly, but also many borrowers indirectly in a broad region dependent on a particular commodity.

Consider how the unexpected sudden decline in oil prices beginning in 1982 affected

---

[12] This fee ignores the additional charge a bank might make for equity capital. As we point out in Chapter 9, banks must have capital on their balance sheets to bear the risk of contingent liabilities such as SLCs.

FIGURE 14.14   Loan Payments Dependent on Oil Prices

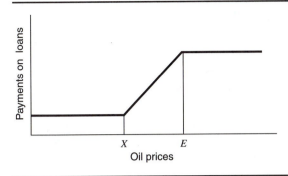

entire communities of western Texas and Oklahoma. The price decline immediately and directly impacted oil-field explorers, producers, and suppliers. In addition, however, the losses suffered by these firms soon damaged local economies. Oil-field jobs disappeared, and spending on new homes, commercial construction, and public infrastructure collapsed along with the collapse in consumption spending. Banks held loans to companies in the oil field and their workers, local builders, merchants, and home buyers and may have thought their loan portfolios were well diversified. Unfortunately, the effects of declining oil prices were systemic and produced catastrophic loan losses for many banks.

Figure 14.14 shows how the loan performance of an oil industry–dependent bank responds to oil prices. Loan payments of principal and interest are plotted on the vertical axis, and petroleum prices are plotted on the horizontal axis. At some critical price E, most borrowers are just able to service their loans. At prices just below E, some borrowers cannot service their debts fully, and loan payments begin to decline. The further prices fall below E, the more borrowers that fail until the bottom is reached at price X, where virtually no borrowers pay their loans and the bank is able to recover only sharply reduced liquidation values. At oil prices above E, nearly all borrowers pay full interest and principal. However, loan payments are constant for all prices above E, and the bank, as a lender, does not benefit from its borrowers' further successes in an environment of increasing oil prices.

Commodities options can protect lenders' loan portfolios against systematic losses that result from such movements in commodity prices. Referring to the example above, we construct a *vertical spread* options strategy to counter decreasing loan payments in an environment of falling oil prices.[13] We buy a crude oil put option with exercise price E and sell a crude oil put with exercise price X. Figure 14.15 shows the payoff profiles of the option positions combined with the loan payoffs of Figure 14.14. The long put goes in the money at E, the oil price that causes the first defaults among bank borrowers. At prices below E, profits on the put option increase as the put goes deeper in the money and offset increasing loan losses. The premium earned on writing the short put is used to offset part of the premium paid for the long put. A second effect is that the short put eliminates excess profits on the long put at prices below X, the point at which loan pay-

---

[13] A *spread trade* is general terminology for any trade consisting of a long position in one instrument offset by a short position in another.

FIGURE 14.15   Loan Portfolio Insurance Using Commodity Options

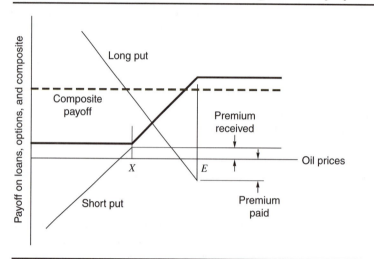

ments bottom out. The combined payoff is the heavy dashed line in Figure 14.15, which indicates that the strategy succeeds in stabilizing cash flows. However, the level of cash flows is somewhat below the unhedged cash flows. The difference in the net cost of the put positions is the cost of the long put minus the income from the short put at a lower exercise price. (Recall that the higher the exercise price, the higher the price of put.) This difference is, in fact, the cost for buying insurance on the portfolio.

SUMMARY

This chapter presented fundamentals of options on stocks, interest rates, and commodities. The intuition behind options is widely applicable to banking situations, both for hedging purposes and for pricing bank products. Buyers of options reserve the choice to either conduct a cash exchange in the future if prices are favorable, or refuse to exchange if prices prove unfavorable. Option holders find that such a choice has reservation value for which they are willing to pay a fair price. We were able to analyze options on the basis of market equilibrium in which the option price should not permit arbitrage opportunities. The pricing procedure applied to both formal (exchange-traded and OTC) options and informal options offered in the course of designing common banking products that include contingent claims. We will further apply this information to the foreign exchange markets in Chapter 16.

END OF CHAPTER PROBLEMS

14.1   Shaunessy acquired a one-year European call option on 100 shares of Intel Corporation common stock with an exercise price of $120. On the expiration date next week, there is a 50 percent chance that Intel will be selling for $145 and a 50 percent chance that it will be selling for $100. What is the expected value (probability-weighted outcomes) of the payoff in dollars to Shaunessy?

14.2 In Problem 14.1, suppose that Shaunessy also held a one-year European put option on 100 shares of Intel with an exercise price of $114. Now what is the expected value of the payoff to Shaunessy?

14.3 In the chart below, enter a $(+)$ or a $(-)$ in each space to indicate the direction of the influence on the price of calls and puts from an increase in each variable's value:

	Call Option	Put Option
t, time to expiration	_____	_____
E, exercise price	_____	_____
P, price of the underlying asset	_____	_____
σ_P, volatility of the underlying asset's price	_____	_____
r_t, risk-free interest rate	_____	_____

14.4 Refer to the example of Reflex Corporation's stock option pricing on pages 566 and 567. Using the arbitrage-free principle, demonstrate that when the stock price will be worth either $87.50 or $125 one period from now, the single-period call option (exercise price = $100) will be worth $1,111.

14.5 (Advanced) Audrey Langtree and Company (ALC), a large Wall Street securities broker, acquired a $100 million inventory in 20-year, 6 percent semiannual coupon Treasury bonds at par. The current bond yield is 6 percent, and the futures price is $120^4/_{32}$. It plans to distribute the bonds during the next two days. ALC's position manager decides to hedge this position using the June put options on $100,000 Treasury bond futures listed below:

Strike Price	Put-Settle Jun
122	2-43

The puts are in-the-money, the delta factor is 0.6, and the conversion factor for the bonds is 0.82.

a. How many put contracts must Audrey Langtree buy to hedge the bonds?

b. Suppose tomorrow the Treasury bond yield rises to 6.10 percent, creating a loss in ALC's inventory. Simultaneously, the futures price falls to $118^{18}/_{32}$. Show how the hedge worked. (*Hint:* The loss on the inventory is the change in value from the rise in yield from 6.00 to 6.10 percent. The put option on bond futures hedge requires you to determine the change in value of the futures. However, you must use the delta factor to relate the change in the option price to the change in the futures).

14.6 At the end of April, Netherwood Insurance realizes it must sell its $100 million position in the $12^1/_2$s of Aug 2014 Treasury bonds. The bonds are priced today at 143:14 asked and the May 110 put option on T-bond futures settled at 0-56. Delta is 0.5. The conversion factor on the deliverable bond is 1.352.

a. How many May 110 put options should NI buy to hedge against expected decline in the bonds' price between now and May 1?

b. Suppose that by May 1 the annualized yield on the bonds rises 0.5 percent, driving the bonds' price to 140.561. Each of the May 110 puts increases in value by $2,045. Show the overall gain or loss of the hedge, utilizing the number of put options you selected in part (a).

14.7 WestFirst Bank is constructing an interest rate tree as follows:

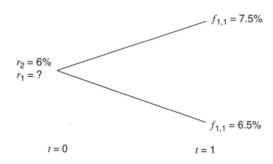

WestFirst assumes a 0.5 probability that the one-year forward rate next year will be 7.5 percent and a 0.5 probability it will be 6.5 percent. What must be the one-year spot rate, r_1, in order for WestFirst to have an *arbitrage-free* model?

14.8 A set of one-period transition interest rates is shown in the following diagram. The transition probabilities for an up and a down movement are equal. Using backward-ation, determine the price of a three-period, 100 par value zero-coupon government agency bond. Invariably, at its maturity $t = 3$ the bond is valued at 100. Enter the price obtained at each node and determine the value at $t = 0$.

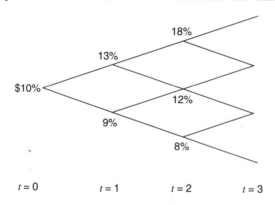

As a check on your results, price the bond looking forward. To do this, calculate the present value of each path (there are eight paths), discounting the $100 value each time by the product of the three relevant one-period rates. (There is a ⅛ probability of each path occurring).

14.9 Determine the price of a two-period American call option with a strike of 88 written on the three-period bond in Problem 14.8. Create a two-period tree, entering the call's alternative values at expiration and working backward to find the price of the call. As in the example in the text, you must compare the computed value with the exercise value of the call; the call's price at a node will be the greater of these two values.

14.10 In January 2000, Penn Circle Bank sold a three-year cap option with an 8.5 percent guarantee (strike price) to Conroy Commercial, Inc., a floating-rate borrower. Conroy was granted a $1 million four-year loan at a loan rate set at 2 percent over one-year LIBOR, to be reset annually on the anniversary of the loan origination date. At origination, one-year LIBOR was 5 percent.

    a. Assume LIBOR is at 7.0, 8.5, and 4.5 percent, respectively, for the first, second, and third loan anniversaries (January of 2001, 2002, and 2003). Recall that the loan rate is 2 percent over LIBOR. Determine the cap payment amounts and timing of the payments during the life of the cap. What is the effective borrowing rate?

    b. In addition, assume Penn Circle purchased a floor with a 7 percent strike price. Determine the payment amounts and timing of the payments on the entire "collar." What is the effective borrowing rate? Create a payoff profile for this collar.

14.11 In Problem 14.10a, assume that the one-year spot and future rates given in the arbitrage-free rate structure of Figure 14.7 represent one-year LIBOR rates. Calculate the option price for the cap. (*Note:* The cap is equivalent to a strip of 2 European call options.)

14.12 Blue Springs National Bank (BSNB) extends a $5 million one-year 8 percent fixed-rate loan commitment to a customer for "take-down" one year from now. The present loan rate is 7.5 percent, and BSNB figures there is a 50–50 probability that the rate will be either 9 percent or 8 percent one year from now. Interest would be paid in arrears, along with principal (two years from now), if the loan is taken down. Using single-period binomial option pricing, determine the fair price Blue Springs should charge for the loan commitment.

14.13 At the end of March, Agro-Bank has a large part of its loan portfolio tied up in loans to cattle feeder lot operators. In the last two years, low cattle prices and slow demand during winter have jeopardized a number of these businesses. The bank believes that, in the coming month or two, for every one-cent decrease below 64 cents per pound in cattle prices it will incur loan losses of 2% of its feeder portfolio. There are no further losses below 60 cents per pound. Agro-Bank decides to hedge its exposure to these customers using CME options on cattle futures. The available options are shown below. Agro-Bank will complete a spread trade in order to cover part of its cost of hedging. Design such a spread trade and diagram it in a payoff profile.

CATTLE LIVE [cme]
40,000 LBS.; CENTS PER LB.

Strike Price	Calls–Settle			Puts–Settle		
	Apr	Jun	Aug	Apr	Jun	Aug
60				0.05	0.17	
62				0.17	0.30	0.40
63	0.72			0.42	0.50	
64	0.30			1.02	0.77	0.77
65	0.10			1.80	1.17	
66	0.05	1.00	2.25	2.75	1.70	1.4

Black-Scholes Model and Put-Call Parity

Black and Scholes produced the path-breaking theory of option pricing in which they determine the price of a call option to be:[14]

$$c = PN(d_1) - Ee^{-rT}N(d_2) \qquad (14.A1)$$

where

$$d_1 = [\ln(P/E) + (r + 1/2\sigma^2)T]/\sigma T^{1/2}$$

and

$$d_2 = d_1 - \sigma T^{1/2}$$

The call price (c) is determined by the five variables described in the early part of Chapter 14. They include the stock price (P), the maturity of the option (T), the exercise price (E), the risk-free interest rate (r), and the variance of the returns on the underlying stock (σ^2). In the formula, ln is the natural logarithm and e is the exponential equal to 2.7183. $N(d_1)$ and $N(d_2)$ refer to the cumulative probabilities for a unit normal variable at the values of d_1 and d_2. The value of $N(\cdot)$ is the cumulative probability from $-\infty$ to $(\cdot)$ standard deviations above the mean in the bell-shaped curve which depicts the normal density function. These values are tabulated in most statistics texts and are easy to use. The most difficult prospective variable to collect is σ^2: the

[14] Fisher Black and Myron Scholes, "The Pricing of Options and Corporate Liabilities," *Journal of Political Economy* (May–June 1973), 637–654.

formula often is solved to obtain volatility information. Using an observed value for c, one can derive the value of σ^2.

The Black-Scholes formula is discomforting in its complex appearance. We can make simplifying assumptions to try to make sense of it. Consider the call's value when σ^2 approaches zero. In this case d_1 and d_2 become very large, $N(d_1)$ and $N(d_2)$ approach one, and the formula breaks down to

$$c = P - Ee^{-rT} \qquad (14.A2)$$

This makes c worth the same as the purchase price of the underlying stock today minus the value of borrowing the exercise price discounted by the risk-free rate over the life of the option. In the absence of volatility, this transaction guarantees that the call will be worth either $P - E$ (when $P - E > 0$ or 0) at maturity where P is also the terminal value of the asset. The decision to exercise is trivial because it is known at the beginning: Exercise if $P > E$.

Now reintroduce volatility and examine the outcome at expiration of the option. The terminal value of the stock will be P^* which is unknown when the call is purchased. If ($P^* > E$), then $c = (P^* - E) > 0$. However, if ($P^* < E$), the equation is no longer valid because ($P^* - E$) < 0 and because the call will not be exercised, $c = 0$. (The equation still works if ($P^* = E$) because both sides of the equation equal zero.) The call option buyer bears the risk that volatility will eliminate any value in the call. This is the risk of *going long on volatility*. In theory, one could *go short on volatility* to eliminate this risk. The logical strategy for doing this is to *sell* a put option with the same exercise price and expiration date. The present value of this position is

$$c - p = P - Ee^{-rT} \qquad (14.A3)$$

Now, at expiration, if $(P^* > E)$, the call is still valued at $(P^* - E)$ because the put expires worthless. If $(P^* < E)$, the new strategy formula is valid because, at expiration, both sides of the equation equal zero.

Value of stock $-$ Repay borrowing $= P^* - E$

Value of call $-$ Value of put

$$= [0 - (E - P^*)] = P^* - E$$

and, therefore, in present value terms

$$c - p = P - Ee^{-rT}$$

Since the terminal values are now the same regardless of the outcome of P^*, the values of each side of Equation 14.A3 must be the same. If not, arbitrage would ensue, driving the values together.

This is the put-call parity relationship derived by Merton[15] and others. The price of any three instruments in the equation determines the price of the fourth.

RELATIONSHIP TO FUTURES

From Equation 13.1 of Chapter 13, we know that futures are related to spot prices according to

$$\mathscr{F}_{n,t} = P_0(1 + r)^t$$

or, solving for P_0 and continuously compounding: $P_0 = \mathscr{F}e^{-rT}$. Substituting in Equation 14.A3,

$$c - p = (\mathscr{F} - E)e^{-rT} \qquad (14.A4)$$

The present value of a futures contract $\mathscr{F}$ can be substituted for a cash asset P to obtain an arbitrage portfolio of puts, calls, and borrowings at the risk-free rate.

---

[15] Robert Merton, "Theory of Rational Option Pricing," *Bell Journal of Economics and Management Science* 4 (Spring year), 183–184.

CHAPTER 15

Interest Rate Swaps: Hedging and Pricing

Interest rate swaps were created in the early 1980s by taking lessons from the currency forward contract. The venerable currency forward (FRA) transactions are merely agreements between banks and their customers to "swap" one currency for another today with the proviso that the transaction will be reversed in, say, 120 days. This transaction, which we review in greater detail in Chapter 16, has been quite common for a very long time. In the early 1980s, banks became aware that the same simple swap mechanism would work in other money markets. A logical extension of swapping currencies was to swap interest payments.

From modest insights like swapping interest streams, mighty markets grow. If ever there was a booming financial market it is the market for interest rate swaps.

Formalized, interest rate swaps are two-party contracts to exchange cash flows on preset dates over an agreed-upon future period. The sizes of the reciprocal cash flows are different and are derived (hence, "derivative") from an interest percentage multiplied by a reference underlying amount known as the *notional principal*.

We can most easily explain the standard fixed-for-floating-rate swap, an instrument that swap market professionals designate "plain vanilla." Two *counterparties* agree that, on scheduled dates, one will pay the other a sum equal to the product of the notional principal—say $1 million—and a *fixed rate* of interest. At the same settlement dates, the other party will pay the first a sum equal to the notional amount multiplied by a *floating rate* of interest such as LIBOR. The notional principal is not exchanged. It is as though the parties had made reciprocal loans to each other of $1 million on which both parties pay, as well as collect, interest. In practice, on the periodic settlement dates the payments due are "netted," meaning that the party owing the largest payment on a given settlement date only pays the difference between the payments due.

The plain vanilla swap is a logical extension of interest rate futures we studied in Chapter 13. There are two sides to both kinds of contracts, and the prices on these two sides are established at different points in time; one is set now and the other is set in the future. In both contracts, the counterparties are exposed to the uncertainty of the price they must pay or receive in the future. For example, a party who buys a futures contract establishes now the price he will pay in the future. However, the party does not know the price on the selling side. The selling price will be unknown until the date in the future on which he offsets his position. Similarly, in a plain vanilla interest rate swap, the fixed-rate payer establishes now the fixed payment it will make on dates in the future, but he or she does not know the future receipts of payments based on future floating rates on the same dates.[1]

In this chapter we describe interest rate swaps and analyze how they are priced in an arbitrage-free market. We examine how financial institutions use swaps to manage risks. For greater insight, we compare swaps with interest rate futures. Based on differences between swaps and futures, we discuss banking applications that are best served by swaps and those that are best served by futures. (We discuss foreign currency swaps and their applications in Chapter 16.)

THE BASICS OF INTEREST RATE SWAPS

Usually, firms enter into interest rate swaps because they need to fix the interest structure of their balance sheets, especially their interest rate-sensitivity gaps. One firm may have fixed-rate assets and floating-rate liabilities, and another firm floating-rate assets and fixed-rate liabilities. These firms can convert the basis of their existing debt service by contracting as counterparties in a plain vanilla fixed-for-floating swap.

EXAMPLE AAA and BBB are two corporations seeking to enter a three-year fixed-for-floating interest rate swap. Table 15.1 shows the borrowing opportunities available to these firms in the cash markets. Of the two firms, counterparty AAA is the more highly rated, and it typically meets its needs for funds in the long-term capital market. At present, AAA can borrow three-year funds at 6.35 percent, which is 25 basis points over the three-year U.S. Treasury note. Were it to borrow in the money market, AAA would have to pay six-month LIBOR. Counterparty BBB, a firm with a lower credit rating, typically borrows at floating rates in the short-term money market for six-month LIBOR plus 50 basis points (bps). If it were to borrow three-year capital market funds, it would have to pay 7.35 percent or 125 bps over the treasury note.

Counterparty AAA wants to convert the fixed basis of $10 million of its debt service to a LIBOR-based floating rate, and counterparty BBB wants to convert $10 million of

---

[1] Swap terminology designates the fixed-rate payer as the swap ''buyer.'' The floating-rate payer is the swap ''seller.''

TABLE 15.1 Borrowing Opportunities, Firms AAA and BBB

Firm	Money Market	Capital Market
AAA	LIBOR	6.35%
BBB	LIBOR + 50 bps	7.35%
AAA advantage over BBB	50 bps	100 bps

FIGURE 15.1   Plain Vanilla Three-Year Interest Rate Swap

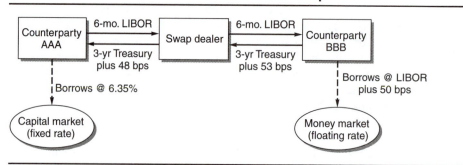

its floating-rate debt to fixed rate. To facilitate a swap for these purposes, on March 15, 2000 they individually contract with a *swap dealer* who completes the two sides of a $10 million three-year swap. Data on the dealer's prices for the swap to each counterparty are presented in Figure 15.1. The terms of the swap require settlement every six months.

At the swap's effective date, the three-year Treasury rate was 6.10 percent. You can easily determine the ''all-in'' costs of borrowing for the counterparties, including the swap, by adding the outbound arrows and subtracting the inbound in Figure 15.1.

$$\textbf{AAA:} \quad 6.35\% - 6.58\% + \text{LIBOR} \qquad\qquad = \text{LIBOR minus 23 bps}$$

$$\textbf{BBB:} \quad (\text{LIBOR} + 50 \text{ bps}) - \text{LIBOR} + 6.63\% = 7.13\%$$

AAA's effective borrowing cost is reset every six months based on the LIBOR rate then existing. Note that its cost is 23 bps cheaper than LIBOR, the rate the firm would have to pay if it borrows directly from the money market. The fixed receipt on the swap more than offsets AAA's fixed obligation to its creditors in the capital market. BBB's cost is fixed at 7.13 percent and is 22 bps below its 7.35 percent cost for borrowing directly in the long-term fixed rate market. By receiving LIBOR, BBB cancels the variability of its LIBOR debt payment to its lenders in the money market.

The swap dealer has contracted to pay AAA Treasury plus 48 bps and receive LIBOR from AAA. This is the *dealer bid* which indicates what the market calls a 48 bps *swap spread* to AAA. In addition, the swap dealer has agreed to pay LIBOR to BBB and to collect Treasury plus 53 bps (the *dealer offer*) from BBB.

$$\textbf{Dealer:} \quad (\text{LIBOR} - (\text{T-note} + 48 \text{ bps})) + (\text{T-note} + 53 \text{ bps}) - \text{LIBOR} = 5 \text{ bps}$$

The dealer clears 5 bps, which is designated the dealer's *bid-offer spread.* This compensates the dealer for its services and for exposure to the risk of nonperformance by one of the counterparties.

Table 15.2 details the series of settlements from the viewpoint of both counterparties AAA and BBB based on the LIBOR rates that apply. The settlement is paid one settlement period in arrears. Thus, the floating-rate fixing of LIBOR is made at the initiation of the swap and is paid at the first settlement date six months later. Settlement payments are based on the notional amount, applicable rates, and number of days in the settlement

TABLE 15.2   Three-Year Fixed-for-Floating Swap Cash Flows

Settlement Date	Day Count	Six-month LIBOR	AAA Pays Dealer	Dealer Pays AAA	AAA Net Payment	BBB Pays Dealer	Dealer Pays BBB	BBB Net Payment
3/15/2000		5.25%						
9/15/2000	184	5.50%	268,333	331,704	(63,371)	334,225	268,333	65,892
3/15/2001	181	6.00%	276,528	326,296	(49,768)	328,775	276,528	52,247
9/15/2001	184	6.25%	306,667	331,704	(25,037)	334,225	306,667	27,558
3/15/2002	181	6.75%	314,236	326,296	(12,060)	328,775	314,236	14,539
9/15/2002	184	6.50%	345,000	331,704	18,704	334,225	345,000	(10,775)
3/15/2003	181		332,222	326,296	5,926	328,775	332,222	(3,447)

period. LIBOR pays on the day count fraction of a 360-day year. Treasury note-based payments pay on a 365-day year basis.

Gains to Swaps

The example swap suggests that all participants win. By structuring a swap instead of restricting financing to conventional borrowing, the participants gained a total of 50 bps: AAA beats its money market borrowing rate by 23 bps, BBB beats its capital market borrowing rate by 22 bps, and the dealer collects a net 5 bps. It appears that the swap exploited market efficiencies that are missing in conventional borrowing. In part, we might explain these gains as a case of comparative advantage.

AAA, with its high credit rating, enjoyed a cost advantage in both long- and short-term financial markets over BBB. However, the significant factor is that BBB's cost in the short-term market is *relatively* favorable (that is, less *un*favorable) to AAA's compared the long-term market. In a sense, BBB shares the benefits of its relative short-term financing advantage, while AAA shares the benefits of its relative advantage in the long-term market. Because of the swap, both firms avoid the market in which they have comparative disadvantages and still manage to transform the interest basis of their debt service.

Several other factors may explain the supposed "gains" to swaps. First, BBB does not acquire a three-year fixed rate loan. Instead, the firm borrows in the short-term market and may not enjoy the liquidity provided by a three-year loan agreement. You would expect the rate on a three-year loan to include an implicit liquidity premium. Unless it can obtain a three-year floating-rate bank loan, probably at a higher spread over LIBOR, BBB still is going to have to reborrow every six months.

Second, interest rates on true bank term loans include a prepayment premium. Borrowers usually can prepay fixed-rate bank loan agreements if interest rates decline sufficiently, whereas swap participants are required to pay a substantial price to terminate an out-of-the-money swap. This prepayment premium further explains cost differences between borrowing long-term capital market funds versus borrowing short-term funds and entering into a pay fixed-receive floating swap. Third, swap dealers charge less because their risk is based only on interest payments, whereas banks' term loan rates are based on the banks' exposure to both interest and principal. Finally, swap participants with lower credit ratings put up collateral or support in the form of standby bank lines of credit; this makes the swap dealer more comfortable and reduces the dealer's swap pricing.

The apparent gains to swaps are not magical. Swaps have less risk than fixed-rate term loans. The participants are protected from liquidity, prepayment, and principal risk and the strongest counterparty often is protected by requiring the weakest to put up collateral. Thus, there are good economic reasons why financing in combination with swaps is cheaper than financing alone.

Swap Credit Risk and Capital Requirements

By matching its positions, a swap dealer offsets its own interest rate or foreign exchange risk. In the example just given, the effects of changes in short-term interest rates are canceled out because the dealer receives as well as pays LIBOR. However, changes in interest or currency rates increase credit risk for one of the counterparties and therefore increase risk to dealers. Movements of interest or exchange rates will be costly for one of the counterparties to a swap and will make the counterparty more prone to default. In option terminology, one of the counterparties is always out-of-the-money in any swap.

In the example, if short-term interest rates fell consistently, BBB would find itself paying an above-market rate on its fixed-rate swap obligation while receiving a decreasing LIBOR-based payment stream. This situation, in addition to BBB's weaker credit standing, raises the prospect of default. If BBB defaults, the dealer fails to collect BBB's 6.63 percent fixed-rate payment. However, the dealer still continues payment of 6.58 percent to AAA and receives LIBOR which, given falling LIBOR rates, produces a net loss. The swap agreement usually requires the weaker party such as BBB to put up collateral, usually in the form of marketable securities or bank lines of credit.

In addition to requiring collateral, the dealer has to set aside capital to support its risk. Commercial banks and investment banks manage swap "books" that often run into the billions of dollars in notional principal, and it is difficult to determine the desired amount of capital required to support the book. Swap intermediaries attempt to run "matched books" in both their interest rate and currency swap books to avoid interest rate or foreign exchange exposure to one side of swaps or the other. However, the increasing credit risk of single swaps from interest or exchange rate movements may be multiplied by a very large number of swaps in these books.

The Federal Reserve and the Bank for International Settlements have attempted to specify how swap risk should be measured and, implicitly, how much capital is required to support the risk. We must understand the valuation of swaps in order to measure their risk, a subject taken up in a later section of the chapter.

BASIS SWAPS

Early swaps were of the fixed-for-floating variety. They appeared attractive because swap parties were said to exploit a form of inefficiency based on "comparative advantage." It appeared that certain parties, for example, large capital-intensive manufacturers, enjoyed an advantage in the capital markets in comparison to money markets and financed themselves at fixed rates. Other parties, for example, U.S. banks, had an advantage in money markets in comparison to capital markets and financed themselves at short-term rates. A fixed-for-floating swap purports to allow parties to share their comparative advantages, resulting in cheaper funds for both parties while improving their match of asset and liability maturities.

It is different for basis swaps. Both parties in a *basis swap* pay floating rates except tied to different indexes. With this structure the parties protect against adverse changes in the difference in the indexes—that is, the basis. For example, a financial institution may fund LIBOR-based assets with deposits (such as money market deposit accounts) tied to T-bill rates. If the institution wishes to hedge against a narrowing of the T-bill/ LIBOR basis and, therefore, protect its natural spread, it may enter into a basis swap to pay three-month LIBOR and receive payments based on three-month T-bill rates.

LIBOR and T-bill rate spreads tend to widen with greater financial market uncertainty because LIBOR includes a default risk premium and T-bills do not. Conversely, this spread narrows when markets enter a period of calm or when bond markets rally. A close proxy for the spread of LIBOR over T-bills is the price spread between Eurodollar futures and T-bill futures called the TED spread. Intermarket spread strategies must pay close attention to the TED spread.

In rising rate environments, banks use basis swaps in conjunction with a cap option to capitalize on the "sticky" nature of banks' deposit pricing. Banks create considerable value by lagging increases in their deposit rates behind increases in market rates. The basis swap-with-cap strategy is designed to capture this value up front. A bank and a swap intermediary might exchange LIBOR-based payments as illustrated in Figure 15.2.

The bank pays three-month LIBOR minus 60 basis points, and the swap intermediary pays either actual LIBOR or a rate capped at the prior payment rate plus 25 basis points. Net settlement is quarterly. The bank may be rewarded a 60 basis point differential. If LIBOR rates are rising rapidly, however, the bank's receipts are capped or temporarily fixed while its payments float upward with LIBOR, thereby reducing the net payoff and eventually generating a loss on the swap.

If the rise in LIBOR is rapid enough, the bank's net settlement on the swap turns negative. In theory, the bank is able to lag increases in its deposit rates to offset any losses that might occur on the swap. The swap intermediary is betting on the rate of increase in LIBOR; the more rapidly LIBOR increases, the more profit it makes. For certain periods of history, short-term interest rates indeed have increased very fast. For the period June 1993 to December 1994, Table 15.3 shows the three-month Eurodollar rate, the minimum receipt of either LIBOR or the previous rate plus 25 basis points, and the net settlement at the end of each quarter based on $100 million notional swap amount. The rates are reset at the beginning of each quarter, and settlement for the quarter is at the end of the quarter. For example, rates are reset with reference to July's LIBOR rate for the third

FIGURE 15.2   Basis Swap with Cap Option

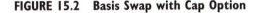

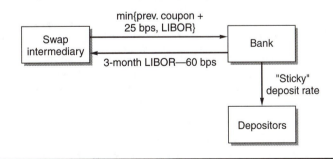

TABLE 15.3 Net Settlement, Basis Swap with Cap

Month and Year	Three-Month Eurodollar	Three-Month LIBOR with 25% Cap	Net Settlement
Jul 1993	3.17%	3.17%	
Aug 1993	3.14%	3.17%	
Sep 1993	3.08%	3.17%	+$150,000
Oct 1993	3.26%	3.26%	
Nov 1993	3.36%	3.26%	
Dec 1993	3.26%	3.26%	+$150,000
Jan 1994	3.15%	3.15%	
Feb 1994	3.43%	3.15%	
Mar 1994	3.75%	3.15%	+$150,000
Apr 1994	4.00%	3.40%	
May 1994	4.51%	3.40%	
Jun 1994	4.51%	3.40%	$0
Jul 1994	4.74%	3.65%	
Aug 1994	4.80%	3.65%	
Sep 1994	5.01%	3.65%	−$127,500
Oct 1994	5.52%	3.90%	
Nov 1994	5.78%	3.90%	
Dec 1994	6.27%	3.90%	−$255,000

quarter of 1993, and third-quarter settlement takes place at the end of September. LIBOR payments are adjusted by subtracting 60 basis points, and receipts are at LIBOR for the first three quarters. Then they are capped for the last three quarters as increases in LIBOR outpace the 25 basis point cap.

SWAPS, FORWARD RATE AGREEMENTS, AND FUTURES

In many respects, interest rate swaps and futures are analogous. (Later in this chapter we show that swaps are no different than a series of futures contracts.) At the same time, swaps—as well as forward rate agreements (FRAs)—overcome certain crucial limitations inherent in futures. Four characteristics of swaps and futures are (1) markets, (2) contracts, (3) credit considerations, and (4) requirements of user organizations.

Markets

We reviewed the futures markets in Chapter 13 and markets for exchange-traded options on futures in Chapter 14. These markets are organized in formal exchanges. Brokers handle all transactions, and, in turn, they must place trades through clearing member firms. Because the exchanges are efficient and process high volumes of standardized products, bid-ask spreads are very small. Both types of contracts are regulated—futures by the Commodity Futures Trading Commission and exchange-traded options by the Securities Exchange Commission.

There is no organized exchange for swaps and FRAs, and they are virtually unregulated by public agencies. Swaps are created and traded over-the-counter through brokers and a network of high-volume dealers, mostly big international banks, who make markets for them. The bid-ask spreads are somewhat larger than they are for futures and might be very large, depending on the uniqueness of the swap or FRA and the credit standing of the counterparties. Most swap volume is conducted through large international bank-dealers. Swaps are less liquid than futures, and counterparties who want to exit an unfavorable swap have to depend on a dealer to set a price the counterparty must pay to reverse (cancel) the swap.

The Contracts

Futures and exchange-traded options on futures are highly standardized contracts. Those that are based on Eurodollars and U.S. Treasury securities trade in large volumes and have large open positions. As a result, they are very liquid and easily traded. For these reasons, position traders prefer to trade in futures and options on futures with Eurodollars and Treasuries because transactions are smooth and instantaneous. Moreover, they can easily reverse their positions to exit the markets.

Hedging with futures contracts instead of swaps and FRAs, however, has three limitations: (1) noncontinuous maturities, (2) lack of underlying security types, and (3) price *nonconvergence*. First, the futures exchanges offer only a limited number of contract maturities and in the process leave "maturity holes"—stretches of time in which there are no futures contract maturities. Traders or hedgers cannot take specific positions in the time gaps represented by maturity holes. Thus, hedgers in particular are forced to mismatch the *tenor* (the length of the positions' lives) of their cash and futures positions. For example, a firm may want to place a hedge during a period spanning next February 15 and August 15. The firm will not find an ideal strip of two three-month futures to match this period. Instead, the firm must contrive a hedge made up of a December futures contract on 90-day Eurodollar deposits commencing on December 15 and maturing on March 15, a March futures contract on Eurodollars starting on March 15 and maturing on June 15, and so forth.

Or suppose a firm expects to issue debt every two years and wants to place a hedge to cover changes in the cost of debt two, four, and six years in the future. The firm might hedge with a strip of 90-day Eurodollar futures, but the "distant" Eurodollar contracts beyond three years or so are illiquid and are not efficiently priced. As another example, suppose a securities dealer wants to hedge an inventory of seven-year government notes. The five-year Treasury note futures is available for five-year positions, but then a "hole" exists between it and the 10-year Treasury note futures. In addition, the denominations of futures contracts are fixed. It would be awkward to hedge a $3.5 million cash position with $1 million par Eurodollar futures contracts that are limited to a size of $1 million per contract. Neither three nor four contracts would create an effective hedge.

In contrast, swaps can be constructed for any denomination. In general, swaps and FRAs offer extreme flexibility to avoid most basis risk. You can create swaps or FRAs across a whole continuum of maturities to exactly match cash exposures, including long-term exposures beyond the most distant futures contracts.

Second, futures contracts are written on only a few securities. Futures hedgers are likely to get burned on basis risk because of the limited number of underlying assets or indexes. The choices of futures hedges are often restricted to Eurodollars and several maturities of Treasury securities because other futures instruments are not sufficiently liquid.[2] For example, a portfolio manager who wants to hedge a position in municipal bonds will not find an acceptable hedge using futures on Treasury securities because changes in Treasury prices correlate poorly with changes in municipal bond prices.[3]

For their part, swaps and FRAs can be written on virtually any index in order to match a cash exposure. For example, indexes might be based on commercial paper, mortgage pools, federal agency securities, Treasury securities of any maturity, and many more. In addition, swaps readily mix indexes. For example, a bank makes a loan earning three-month LIBOR plus 15 basis points and funds the loan with a fixed-rate liability based on a Treasury note rate. The bank hedges this position with a matching "cross-index" swap to receive fixed-rate Treasury and pay floating LIBOR.

Finally, nonconvergence may be the most irreconcilable problem with futures. Nonconvergence of futures and cash prices can present futures hedgers with frightful basis risk. The prices of futures and the cash exposure converge only at maturity. To avoid basis risk, we should match the maturity of a futures hedge with the maturity of our cash exposure. Suppose we hedge a 45-day cash exposure and the closest futures contract maturity is 90 days. When our cash exposure matures, the futures price will still reflect the forward rate in the yield curve for the remaining 45 days beyond the hedge period.[4] This creates what traders call a price *waffle* between the futures and cash positions.

Credit Considerations

The swap market does not have a clearinghouse to guarantee the performance of the counterparties. In contrast, a defining feature of futures markets and the options on futures markets is the absence of credit risk. In these markets, as we described in Chapter 13, the exchange marks-to-market the open positions, and daily gains and losses are immediately settled through clearinghouses. Margin accounts always contain sufficient value to cover daily price movements. If owners or sellers of futures contracts fail to meet their margin calls, the exchange immediately closes out their positions.

Requirements of User Organizations

Swap users must maintain credit lines with their banks to cover counterparty risk. In addition, users are required to hold capital against such risk. Swaps do not require users to handle daily flows of cash into and out of their swap positions. In contrast, futures users are not concerned with collateralizing their positions and do not bear capital charges to support futures risk-taking. However, users of futures have the burden to account for and monitor their futures positions that does not correspond to swaps. A "back office" is needed to monitor margin calls and cash flows into and out of margin accounts. Because futures hedges may be constructed intricately to avoid basis risk or may have nonconvergence risk, they are inherently more difficult to monitor.

---

[2] We are not concerned here with the availability of currency futures, which we discuss in Chapter 16.

[3] The Chicago Board of Trade offers a municipal bond index futures instrument, but its liquidity is inferior to Treasury-based futures.

[4] We demonstrated in Chapter 13 that futures prices are closely related to the implied forward rate found in the yield curve.

SWAP PRICING

Swaps are *zero-sum* instruments. Going forward from the origination (trade date), movements in interest rates generate gains for one swap party at the expense of the other party. However, at the trade date, an interest rate swap has zero expected value to both parties: Neither party would enter into a swap on terms of which initially they bore a loss. As a result, the market sets the terms for the fixed- and floating-rate legs such that the relationship between the two legs produces zero expected value under current financial market conditions. To be sure, the relative credit standings of the counterparties is an additional factor in setting terms.

Swap Valuation—Approximation

Financial market conditions also determine the valuation of swaps beyond the trade date. Changes in interest rates during the life of a swap cause the swap's value to deviate from zero, creating positive value for one party and negative value for the other. Let's reconsider the swap with AAA and BBB detailed earlier in Figure 15.1. Suppose that six months have elapsed since the swap trade date of March 15, 2000 and that interest rates on LIBOR and Treasury securities have risen significantly. The fixed leg of comparable two and a half year swaps for a firm with AAA's standing currently pays 8 percent semiannually compounded. We can approximate (without niceties such as accurate day counts) the amount that AAA's side of the swap has declined in value.

Decreased swap value =

$$\sum_{t=9/15/00}^{3/15/03} \frac{\left(\dfrac{0.0658}{2} \times \$10{,}000{,}000\right)}{\left(1 + \dfrac{0.08}{2}\right)^t} - \sum_{t=9/15/00}^{3/15/03} \frac{\left(\dfrac{0.0658}{2} \times \$10{,}000{,}000\right)}{\left(1 + \dfrac{0.0658}{2}\right)^t} = -\$29{,}678$$

This is the amount that AAA would have to pay a swap dealer to take over its obligation, thereby cancelling AAA's ownership.

Pricing from Eurodollar Futures Strip

In this section we determine the value of a generic fixed-for-floating rate swap from the present value of the payment stream for the fixed-rate leg. We are not concerned about changes in the present value of the floating-rate leg's payments because the floating leg's reference rate is reset to correspond with changing market conditions. Thus, the value of the floating-rate leg's payment stream (including assumed redemption of the notional value at the swap's maturity) should equal the notional value of the swap. As we have noted, swaps behave like a series of futures contracts. Indeed, for the most widely used fixed-for-floating swap, the interest rate on the fixed-rate leg is based on the Eurodollar futures strip.

EXAMPLE On January 15, 1997, a firm arranges a $100 million notional amount swap with a nominal two-year maturity to pay a swap dealer a fixed rate every three months and to receive three-month LIBOR every three months. Think of the value of the firm's

FIGURE 15.3   Swap Payment Timeline

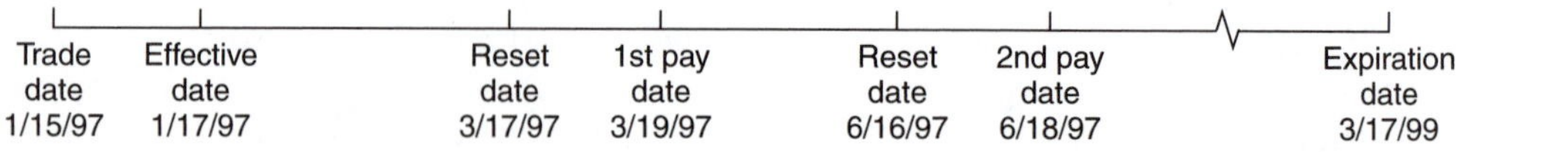

| Trade date 1/15/97 | Effective date 1/17/97 | Reset date 3/17/97 | 1st pay date 3/19/97 | Reset date 6/16/97 | 2nd pay date 6/18/97 | Expiration date 3/17/99 |

long position in the swap as analogous to issuing a fixed-rate bond (to pay fixed) and investing in a floating-rate bond (to receive floating) with the same $100 million notional principal and the same maturity. Our approach is to *determine the semiannual fixed-rate payment that makes the present value of a fixed-rate bond equal to the present value of a (par value) floating-rate bond with the same maturity.* This creates the required zero-value initial condition on the swap's effective date.

To determine the value of a swap requires that we specify the precise timing of payments and reset dates for the floating-rate leg. Figure 15.3 clarifies the timeline and terminology. The initial rate setting is based on spot LIBOR as of the trade date (1/15/97) and applies to the *stub period.* This is the time from the effective date to first payment date following maturity of the Mar 97 Eurodollar futures (the nearest contract). Thus, the stub period spans 1/17/97 to 3/19/97. The floating rate will be *reset* eight times—every three months after the stub period. For purposes of pricing the swap, all of the assumed reset rates beyond the stub period are taken from the implied rates quoted for the series of Eurodollar futures contracts on the trade date, 1/15/97. The implied futures rates correspond to 91 days, or roughly three-month periods.

Interest for the stub period will be paid in arrears on 3/19/97. Then, the floating rate for the first full three-month period is reset at the expiration date of the March 97 Eurodollar contract on 3/17/97 and is effective for a payment period starting two days later on 3/19/97 and ending on 6/18/97. The next reset date is 6/16/97, which coincides with the maturity of the June 97 contract. This sets the rate for the payment period 6/18/97 through 9/17/97 and so forth.

The Eurodollar implied rates are converted to discount factors that are applied to the fixed-rate payments occurring on scheduled payment dates. Table 15.4 lists the applicable Eurodollar contract prices, their implied rates, and the payment periods.

We convert data in Table 15.4 to discount factors. The annual discount factors for the payment period calculated from the implied forward rates that correspond to each payment period in Table 15.4 are shown in column (3) of Table 15.5. For the stub period this is

$$\frac{1}{[1 + 0.0550(0.1964)]} = 0.9893$$

We compound the actual discount rate for the stub period and the implied discount rates for later payment periods to create d_t, the present value discount factor for each payment date. These are shown in column (4) of Table 15.5. For example, the compounded present value discount for 1/17/97–6/18/97 is

$$\frac{1}{[1 + (0.055)(0.1964)]} \times \frac{1}{[1 + (0.0563)(0.2528)]} = 0.9754$$

TABLE 15.4   Implied Futures Rates for Discounting Fixed-Rate Leg of Fixed-for-Floating Swap

Futures Contract	Price on Trade Date 1/15/97	Implied Rate %	Expiration and Reset Date	Payment Period	Number of Days in Pay Period
		5.500[a]	1/15/97	1/17/97–3/19/97[b]	61
Mar 97	94.37	5.630	3/17/97	3/19/97–6/18/97	91
Jun 97	94.19	5.810	6/16/97	6/18/97–9/17/97	91
Sep 97	94.01	5.990	9/15/97	9/17/97–12/17/97	91
Dec 97	93.82	6.180	12/15/97	12/17/97–3/18/98	91
Mar 98	93.74	6.260	3/16/98	3/18/98–6/17/98	91
Jun 98	93.64	6.360	6/15/98	6/17/98–9/16/98	91
Sep 98	93.58	6.420	9/14/98	9/16/98–12/16/98	91
Dec 98	93.48	6.520	12/14/98	12/16/98–3/17/99	91

[a] LIBOR spot rate on 1/15/97 (trade date).

[b] Stub period.

It is convenient to think of these discount factors as the January 15 price of a $1 zero coupon bond that matures at the end of the payment period.

We weight these factors by f_t, the day count fraction of a 360-day year (the Eurodollar convention) to obtain column (5):

$$f_1 d_1 = 0.1964 \times 0.9893$$
$$f_2 d_2 = 0.2528 \times 0.9754$$
$$\bullet$$
$$\bullet$$
$$\bullet$$

TABLE 15.5   Present Value Discount Factors Applicable to Each Payment Date

(1) Payment Period t	(2) Annual Day Count Fraction[b] f_t	(3) Payment Period Discount Factor	(4) Compounded Present Value Discount Factor[c] d_t	(5) d_t Weighted by Day Count Fraction $f_t d_t$
1/17/97–3/19/97[a]	0.1964	0.9893	0.9893	0.1943
3/19/97–6/18/97	0.2528	0.9860	0.9754	0.2466
6/18/97–9/17/97	0.2528	0.9855	0.9613	0.2430
9/17/97–12/17/97	0.2528	0.9851	0.9470	0.2394
12/17/97–3/18/98	0.2528	0.9846	0.9324	0.2357
3/18/98–6/17/98	0.2528	0.9844	0.9178	0.2320
6/17/98–9/16/98	0.2528	0.9842	0.9033	0.2284
9/16/98–12/16/98	0.2528	0.9840	0.8889	0.2247
12/16/98–3/17/99	0.2528	0.9838	0.8745	0.2211

[a] Stub period.

[b] Number of days in payment period divided by 360-day year.

[c] Compounds discount factors in prior column.

The next step is to set the present value of a stream of unknown payments on a nominal fixed-rate bond equal to the swap's par value (say, 100). This is the same as setting the present value of a fixed-rate bond equal to the present value of a floating-rate bond with the same maturity. Payments on the floating-rate leg of the swap are continually adjusted to market, and so this leg remains at par value.

$$100 = 100R \sum_{t=1}^{n} f_t d_t + 100 d_n$$

$$R = \frac{(1 - d_n)}{\sum_{t=1}^{n} d_t f_t} \tag{15.1}$$

$$R = 0.0607748$$

$$R \approx 6.08\%$$

where R is equivalent to the percentage coupon on a fixed-rate bond, $f_t d_t$ is as defined in Table 15.5, and n is the time to expiration of the swap. Note that we assume the exchange of the 100 par values of the nominal fixed- and floating-rate bonds, although these values are not actually exchanged.

The swap dealer considers the creditworthiness of the firm and adds a premium of, perhaps, 10 basis points, bringing the fixed-rate leg to 6.18 percent. On the 1/15/97 trade date of the swap, U.S. Treasury notes trading at near par value and maturing in March 1999 yielded 5.98 percent. Thus, the swap dealer quotes the swap rate as 20 bps over Treasury.

SUMMARY

This chapter briefly reviewed what may be the most successful type of derivative of all—interest rate swaps. The notional value of this instrument held in the largest eight U.S. banks exceeded $17 trillion and represented more than two-thirds of these banks' derivatives portfolios. Interest rate swaps permit users to restructure their debt obligations and to offset interest rate risk. At the same time, swaps do not require the user to alter their balance sheets.

In addition, there appear to be gains to swaps that do not exist in direct borrowing. These gains exist for several reasons, each of which is economic in nature: swaps do not facilitate prepayment, and they do not provide the liquidity protection cash borrowers expect. Moreover, notional principal is not at risk in swap transactions.

Interest rate swaps have advantages relative to financial futures and options, as well as some disadvantages. Most important is the opportunity to create swaps on a wide variety of indexes to match users' cash positions and avoid basis risk. On the contrary, basis swaps are a means of hedging basis risk that might exist in users' cash positions. In addition, swaps are not limited by nonconvergence, noncontinuous maturities, and contract size as are futures.

Swaps are priced in a highly efficient market setting. Their pricing is informed by prices on short-term futures contracts, some of which have exceptionally deep positions and near-continuous trading.

END OF CHAPTER PROBLEMS

15.1 Back Beach Bank uses interest rate swaps to help it penetrate its market for consumer deposits. The bank offers an 18-month certificate of deposit to consumers paying 4.50 percent. Simultaneously, the bank enters into an interest rate swap, receiving 5.40 percent fixed and paying three-month LIBOR.

a. Diagram the swap.
b. Calculate the bank's "all-in cost," considering the CD costs and the swap.

15.2 Alpha Corporation and Gamma Company negotiate a $1 million 10-year interest rate swap in which Alpha will pay 8.5 percent fixed rate to Gamma and Gamma will pay LIBOR to Alpha. (There is no swap dealer involved.) The firms will make net settlement payments semiannually. Ordinarily, Alpha pays LIBOR plus 20 basis points for borrowing, and Gamma borrows at a fixed rate of 8.20 percent.

a. Create a diagram showing the payment responsibilities of each firm.
b. Show the two firms' "all-in" cost of borrowing.
c. Suppose that after two years interest rates have fallen and the market now is offering a swap rate of 6.25 percent against LIBOR. A swap dealer offers to take the swap off of Alpha's hands. How much will Alpha have to pay the dealer?

15.3 On April 20, 2000 (a Thursday), Bank of Baccus arranges a pay fixed-receive LIBOR swap with a nominal maturity of one year. The swap will settle quarterly with LIBOR, being reset according to the implied rate on Eurodollar futures, (cycle months are March, June, September, and December). Reset rates become effective two days after each reset. The swap expires at the expiration date of the last futures contract somewhat more than a year after April 20.

Determine the swap effective date, the dates of the stub period, and all of the reset and settlement dates from year 2000 and 2001 calendars (or by counting forward). Remember that Eurodollar futures deliver on the Thursday after the third Monday of each cycle month (or, if no market on that day, on Friday or the following Monday).

15.4 On April 1, 1994 McGraw Savings entered into a $100 million notional amount, three-year basis swap for quarterly settlement with the investment banker Salmon Brothers. McGraw will pay the weekly prime rate averaged over each quarter minus 225 basis points and will receive capped LIBOR payments according to the formula $\min\{LIBOR_t, LIBOR_{t-1} + 25 \text{ basis points}\}$, payable in arrears, where $LIBOR_t$ is the rate at the date of the swap's origin and settlement dates thereafter and $LIBOR_{t-1}$ is the rate at the previous settlement date. (The LIBOR payments are not averaged.)

Requirement: Determine the net settlement for McGraw for three quarterly settlements from the data below on prime and LIBOR. To simplify matters, assume settlement and reset occur on the same dates (i.e., there is no 2-day lag): these are July 1, 1994, September 30, 1994, and December 30, 1994. The LIBOR rate setting on settlement date is the basis for the next quarter's payment calculation; the prime is averaged weekly over the quarter as the basis for the end of quarter payment.

Date	Weekly Avg Prime Rate	Three-Month LIBOR	Date	Weekly Avg Prime Rate	Three-Month LIBOR
4/1/94	6.25	3.80	8/19/94	7.39	4.85
4/8/94	6.25	3.90	8/26/94	7.75	4.86
4/15/94	6.25	3.89	9/2/94	7.75	4.88
4/22/94	6.39	4.09	9/9/94	7.75	4.88
4/29/94	6.75	4.14	9/16/94	7.75	4.94
5/6/94	6.75	4.33	9/23/94	7.75	5.01
5/13/94	6.75	4.71	9/30/94	7.75	5.26
5/20/94	6.89	4.53	10/7/94	7.75	5.54
5/27/94	7.25	4.49	10/14/94	7.75	5.56
6/3/94	7.25	4.50	10/21/94	7.75	5.45
6/10/94	7.25	4.44	10/28/94	7.75	5.55
6/17/94	7.25	4.45	11/4/94	7.75	5.56
6/24/94	7.25	4.51	11/11/94	7.75	5.74
7/1/94	7.25	4.71	11/18/94	7.96	5.81
7/8/94	7.25	4.76	11/25/94	8.50	5.85
7/15/94	7.25	4.80	12/2/94	8.50	6.06
7/22/94	7.25	4.64	12/9/94	8.50	6.28
7/29/94	7.25	4.73	12/16/94	8.50	6.28
8/5/94	7.25	4.68	12/23/94	8.50	6.24
8/12/94	7.25	4.76	12/30/94	8.50	6.34
			1/6/95	8.50	6.34

15.5 Net interest income, margin, and rate sensitivity for First National Bank of Pittsburgh (FNBP) are as follows.

Interest Revenue

Rate-sensitive assets: $1 billion @ 0.065	=	$ 65,000,000
Nonrate-sensitive assets: $4 billion @ 0.085	=	340,000,000
Total interest revenue		405,000,000

Interest Expense

Rate-sensitive liabilities: $3.5 billion @ 0.045	=	157,500,000
Nonrate-sensitive liabilities: $1.0 billion @ 0.06	=	60,000,000
Total interest expense		217,500,000
Net interest income		187,500,000
Net interest margin		3.75%

FNBP's rate-sensitive assets yield 2 percent over LIBOR, and its rate-sensitive liabilities pay LIBOR. The bank's treasurer projects two rate scenarios for LIBOR in the coming two years. The scenarios are equally probable. Currently, LIBOR is 4.5 percent.

LIBOR Interest Rate Scenarios	Year 1	Year 2
Scenario 1	4.0%	3.0%
Scenario 2	5.5%	8.0%

FNBP negotiates a $3 billion notional pay fixed-receive floating interest rate swap in which it will pay fixed 6.25 percent and receive LIBOR.

a. Determine FNBP's net interest income and margin under the two rate scenarios without the proposed swap. Determine the expected value of net interest income and margin.

b. Determine FNBP's net interest income and margin under the two rate scenarios, including the proposed swap. Determine the expected value of net interest income and margin.

c. Compare and discuss the volatilities of net interest income and margin with and without the swap under the two scenarios.

15.6 (Advanced problem) On December 21, 1999 (the trade date), Bio-Tech, Inc. buys a $50 million two-year pay fixed-receive floating swap (recall that the fixed-rate payer is the swap buyer) to become effective on December 23. The December 23 date coincides with the maturity of the Dec 99 Eurodollar futures contract (so, there is no "stub period"). Bio-Tech will receive LIBOR, and settlement will take place every three months upon expiration of the three-month Eurodollar futures contract that is nearest at settlement time.

Determine the fixed rate to be paid semiannually by Bio-Tech based on the future short-term rates implied in the series of three-month Eurodollar futures shown in the following list. The swap dealer will charge a premium of 12 basis points on the fixed-rate leg.

Contract	IMM Index
Dec 99	94.10
Mar 00	93.85
Jun 00	93.65
Sep 00	93.55
Dec 00	93.45
Mar 01	93.40
Jun 01	93.30
Sep 01	93.20

Adjusting the Swap Rate for Convexity[5]

Pricing the swap off of the Eurodollar futures strip, as described in this chapter, distorts the swap rate. The distortion favors the party with a short position (receives fixed) in a plain vanilla fixed-floating swap. This distortion can be attributed to the difference in timing of swap and futures settlements. On an interest rate swap, in-arrears cash is exchanged only at settlement dates often far in the future; on Eurodollar futures, the futures exchange requires gains or losses to be settled in the present, every day.

This difference in handling payments affects the value of a swap and the value of Eurodollar futures in a different way. In particular, the profit and loss of a fixed receiver of swap payments is a convex function, whereas the function for payments on futures, set at plus or minus $25 per basis point change per contract, is strictly linear (see discussion on convexity in Appendix 5A). To elucidate this point, let us extend the swap pricing example at the end of the chapter, assuming a notional swap amount of $100 million.

To keep it simple, we will consider only the change in the value of the final swap settlement.[6]

For every basis point difference in three-month LIBOR under the fixed rate of 6.18 percent, the party receiving fixed will gain an annualized net $10,000 (equal to $0.0001 \times \$100$ million) on payment date 3/17/99. For every basis point in three-month LIBOR over 6.18 percent, the fixed receiver loses an annualized net $10,000 on 3/17/99. The present value of these per basis point gains or losses on trade date 1/15/97 is found by multiplying this future amount by $f_n d_n$ found in the last column of Table 15.3. This equals $2,211 (equal to $10,000 \times 0.2211$). A futures hedge against present value losses on the swap settlement on 3/17/99 requires $2,211/$25 = 88.44 contracts. (Remember that futures contract prices change $25 per basis point and are settled in the present.)

Let us assume that the spot and all forward rates rise 10 basis points. The December 1998 forward rate that affects the Dec 98 Eurodollar futures settlement increases from 6.52 to 6.62 percent. Working through the effects of a 10 basis point rise in each implied forward rate of Table 15.3 produces a decrease in the compounded discount factor d_1 from 0.8745 to 0.8728. Weighting by the day count fraction produces $f_n d_n = 0.2206$. Table 15A.1 shows the changes in the present values of 88.44 Dec 98 contracts and the receive fixed-pay floating swap.

A 10 bps change in the December 1998 forward rate produces an immediate gain or loss of $22,110 on the 84.44 Dec 98 ED futures contracts. However, the swap loses less than the futures gains or, alterna-

---

[5] Based on the method described in G. Burghardt and B. Hoskins, "The Convexity Bias in Euordollar Futures," *Research Note,* Dean Witter Institutional Futures, September 16, 1994.

[6] The resulting detached swap element is called a *forward swap.*

TABLE 15A.1   Valuation Effects of Interest Rate Shift, Receive Fixed-Pay Floating Forward Swap versus ED Futures

Interest Rate Changes—bps		P/L on Receive Fixed-Pay Floating Swap			Eurodollar	
Forward Rate	Compound Rate $f_n d_n$	on 3/17/99	Compound Discount Factor	Present Value, 1/15/97	Settlement 84.44 Contracts 1/15/97	Net
+10	−5	−$100,000	0.2206	−$22,060	$22,110	$50
0	0	$0	0.2211	$0	$0	$0
−10	+5	+$100,000	0.2216	+$22,160	−$22,110	$50

tively, gains more than the futures loses. The decrease in the swap's price was $22,060 while its price increased $22,160, a clear indication of positive convexity. In either case, the swap performs $50 better than the futures which either gains or loses $22,110. The convexity bias is worth $50. Figure 15A.1 illustrates the pricing relationships.

This favorable aspect of the swap is overlooked when the swap is priced off of the Eurodollar futures strip. Convexity is present in the swap because of the change in the compound discount factor over the whole period from 1/1/5/97 to 3/17/99. We isolated just the final settlement on the swap example described in the last section. Convexity would be present in all of the interim settlements for the example swap, although it becomes progressively less

influential as settlement dates shorten. Convexity introduces progressively larger bias as the maturity of the swap settlement increases.

For the nominally two-year swap described in our earlier example, convexity bias may be worth a couple of basis points or more on the swap yield computed from the Eurodollar futures strip. For term swaps of 10 years, overlooking convexity may add as much as 18 basis points to the swap yield.[7]

---

[7] The analysis for determining the value in basis points on the swap spread is technically beyond our purposes here. See Burghardt and Hoskins, ''The Convexity Bias in Eurodollar Futures.''

FIGURE 15A.1   Gain/Loss Relationships, Forward Swap versus Futures

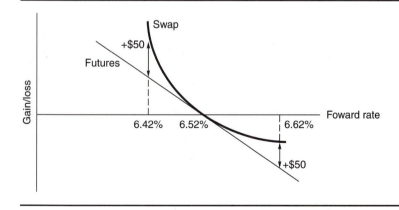

The Swap Curve

The approach behind the *swap curve* is to use swap coupon data from the swap market itself. The objective is to estimate the floating-rate cash flows for future settlement dates of generic interest rate swaps. The swap curve plots the relationship between par coupon swap rates and swap maturities. The curve is based on par coupons observed in the market for swaps. For a given maturity, the present value of fixed payments based on the par coupon swap rate should be equal to the present value of a series of theoretical short-term LIBOR-based payments from the swap's floating-rate leg in effect over the life of the swap. The par coupons therefore embed the market-consensus estimates for future LIBOR rates.

This reverses the approach we took earlier where we used implied floating rates from Eurodollar futures to arrive at the par coupon (equivalently, the value of the fixed-rate leg). We again start from same-maturity fixed-rate bonds and floating-rate bonds whose values are equal to the same notional principal and which have the same maturity. However, instead of determining the par coupon, we wish to *determine the floating-rate payments that make the present value of a hypothetical floating-rate bond equal to the present value of a same-maturity bond bearing the observed par coupon.* Again, the approach is to satisfy the initial condition of a zero value for the swap on the swap's effective date.

The swap curve is used to estimate the spot floating rates for settlement dates beyond the first period. Points on the swap curve are the par coupon swap (fixed) rates of plain vanilla swaps for the maturities on the curve. We cannot directly use these par coupon rates to discount individual cash flows of different maturities; that is, we cannot use them as zero-coupon discount rates. It is necessary to use the bootstrapping procedure (see Appendix 5B) to impute discount rates on hypothetical zero-coupon securities.

EXAMPLE[8] We show the estimated floating payments implied for a $10 million five-year swap with par fixed coupon of 5.85 percent at the swap's effective date, 2/23/96. Table 15B.1 describes the swap and shows the swap curve consisting of market-derived par coupon rates for plain vanilla swaps for maturities from 1 through 30 years. According to the curve, one-year par coupon plain vanilla swaps settled semiannually would have a fixed rate of 5.25 percent; two-year swaps, 5.36 percent; three-year swaps, 5.52 percent; and so on out to 30 years. These values are based on quotes from several active swap intermediaries.

Column 2 of Table 15B.2 displays the spot rates—the theoretical zero-coupon rates—for the settlement dates in column 1. These values are bootstrapped from the swap rates in Table 15B.1. Column 3 of Table 15B.2 lists the swap's floating-rate coupons derived from the spot rates in column 2. Column 4 gives the floating-rate payments on the $10 million notional amount, based on the length of the period in days to the market's convention of a 360-day year for floating rates. Column 5 presents the fixed-rate payments derived from the 5.85 percent par coupon, the length of the period, and a day-

---

[8] This example is adopted from Tom Windas, ''Getting Down to Basics on Swaps,'' *Bloomberg* (April 1996), 57, 59, 61.

TABLE 15B.1   Five-Year Swap Description and Swap Curve as of 2/21/96 (trade date)

Swap Description

Effective date:	2/23/96	
Maturity:	2/23/01	
Notional amount:	$10,000,000	
Market value:	0	

	Fixed	Floating
Coupon:	5.8500%	5.2500%
First payment date:	8/23/96	8/23/96
Day count:	Actual/Actual	Actual/360
Reset:	—	Semiannual
Premium:		0

Swap Curve

Maturity	Swap Rate
1-year	5.250%
2-year	5.360%
3-year	5.520%
4-year	5.700%
5-year	5.850%
7-year	6.090%
10-year	6.360%
15-year	6.600%
20-year	6.720%
30-year	6.750%

TABLE 15B.2   Floating and Fixed Payments for $10 Million Plain Vanilla Swap

1 Date	2 Zero-Coupon (Spot) Rates	3 Floating-Rate Coup.	4 Floating Payments	5 Fixed Payments	6 Net Payments	7 Present Values of Payments
8/23/96	5.337886		265,416.67	290,901.64	25,484.97	24,826.05
2/24/97	5.267745	5.114259	262,816.09	295,937.57	31,121.48	31,438.85
8/25/97	5.313913	5.339874	269,960.29	291,698.63	21,738.34	20,091.60
2/23/98	5.363458	5.429716	274,502.33	291,698.63	17,196.30	15,469.00
8/24/98	5.449182	5.718800	289,117.13	291,698.63	2,581.50	2,256.95
2/23/99	5.531840	5.858097	297,786.59	293,301.37	−4,485.21	−3,807.93
8/23/99	5.630608	6.146958	309,055.37	290,095.89	−18,959.48	−15,613.95
2/23/00	5.725184	6.291769	321,579.29	294,667.64	−26,911.65	−21,472.40
8/23/00	5.811767	6.392626	323,182.77	290,901.64	−32,281.13	−24,950.28
2/23/01	5.8990409	6.497272	332,082.78	294,334.83	−37,747.95	−28,237.88
				Net present value =		0

count convention of actual days in a year (365 or 366) for fixed-rate payments. Column 6 gives the net payments due on each settlement date where positive values indicate positive payoffs to the fixed-rate payer.

Column 7 shows the present values of each net settlement based on discounting by the implied spot rate for the time to the settlement date. As expected, the trade date value of the swap to the counterparties must be zero.

International Banking

Historically, banks that served local and regional U.S. markets had little to do with banking and finance in the international realm. One reason was that the import-export sector represented only a modest share of the U.S. economy compared with the share represented by international trade in most other nations' economies. Among U.S. banks, most international finance was left to a few money center banks that had high volumes of import-export finance, continuous trading in foreign currencies, and the capacity to extend credit to customers or foreigners with business operations abroad.

Today, as business becomes increasingly globalized, regional banks and even community banks no longer are insulated from international financial markets. As these banks' customers find opportunities in international trade, the banks are called upon for international banking services.

The international dollar market—the Eurodollar market—often sets the pricing of credit in U.S. domestic customer relationships. Eurodollar funds have had a large influence on the liquidity of the entire U.S. banking system for many years. Even small banks have investment opportunities in foreign financial instruments, including Eurodollar deposits and loan participations.

International banking, for our purposes, refers to banking transactions that involve one or more parties located outside of the United States. Competition in international banking includes commercial banks that are active international lenders from their headquarters country, or via branches, from foreign locations. Some banks operate investment banking subsidiaries overseas where they underwrite foreign bonds and other foreign securities. International banking has changed from a highly segmented industry in which individual geographic markets were controlled by just a few banks to a highly integrated capital market in which potential competition for major financing includes hundreds of banks.

Banks have several motives to expand internationally. The most straightforward motive is the banks' desire to follow their customers when their customers conduct operations abroad. As American corporations aggressively extended their operations overseas during the 1960s and 1970s, their U.S. banks followed. Similarly, Japanese and European banks followed their domestic corporate customers to foreign markets in the 1970s. This motivation is partly a defensive one, because banks want to maintain and consolidate relationships with domestic corporate customers that develop needs for international banking services. Banks also feel they know more about their customers' particular needs and can serve them more efficiently than local banks, even in a foreign setting.

Another motive for banks expanding internationally is to diversify their business bases. They invest in loan products whose characteristics differ from those of domestic loans. The pattern of demand for foreign loans may offset fluctuations in domestic loan demand and thus help to stabilize overall bank earnings.

In this chapter we (1) present an overview of foreign exchange risk management; (2) describe the foreign exchange market; (3) examine the Eurocurrency markets, especially the Eurodollar market; (4) discuss the financial management of a bank or bank affiliate operating in an international environment; (5) review the international lending activities of U.S. banks; (6) profile the organizational forms used to conduct international banking; and discuss foreign financing by U.S. entities and foreign banks in the United States.

BANK FOREIGN EXCHANGE (FX) RISK MANAGEMENT

Commercial banks may conduct international finance operations in several ways:

- They contract with domestic customers to create assets, liabilities, and off-balance sheet contingency items (e.g., letters of credit) denominated in foreign currencies.
- They contract with foreign customers to create assets, liabilities, and off-balance sheet contingency items in either foreign currency or dollars.
- They purchase and sell foreign currencies for customers and offer hedging services for customers with exposures in foreign currencies.
- They trade foreign currencies on their own account.

EXAMPLE Bountiful Boutique (BB), a specialty artisan-retailer in Scottsdale, wants to import weathered wooden ranch gates from a collector in Torreon, Mexico. BB asks Triad State Bank, its local bank, to assist with financing the purchase. Using the consulting services of a specialist in import-export finance for small businesses, Triad arranges a letter of credit guaranteeing BB's debt to the Torreon exporter, thus allowing BB to complete the transaction.

EXAMPLE Bell Computer Corporation (BCC) decides to extend its computer catalog sales business to Central Europe. Bell will sell its products in local currency, the Polish zloty (PLZ). To supply its new market, Bell applies for inventory financing at the Krakow office of its U.S. bank, and the bank creates a working capital loan to BCC denominated in Polish PLZ.

EXAMPLE Export Corporation sells machinery parts to a German manufacturer for which it will be paid 60 days from now in deutsche marks (DM). Export Corporation is worried that the dollar-to-DM exchange rate may vary unfavorably during the 60 days. Since it will receive DM in 60 days, the firm's regional bank agrees to buy Export Corporation's DMs 60 days forward at today's forward price on a contract that matures in 60 days. Because Export Corporation knows the forward price today, it no longer bears the risk of currency fluctuation.

Each transaction a bank conducts involving a given foreign currency, such as the foregoing examples, affects its overall exposure in that currency. There are two ways to look at foreign exchange (FX) exposure in a given currency: *net exposure* and *total exposure*. Net exposure (NE) is simply the bank's net position in foreign currency-denominated assets and liabilities (including off-balance sheet items), as well as its net bought and sold position in the actual currency itself (including forward contracts). Mathematically, net exposure in currency i is

$$NE_i = (A_i - L_i) + (CL_i - CS_i)$$

where A_i and L_i are assets and liabilities, respectively, denominated in currency i; CL_i and CS_i are purchased and sold positions, respectively, in currency i. When a bank's net exposure in a currency is positive, the bank is said to have a *long book* or is *net long* in the currency; negative net exposure is called a *short book* or *net short*.

The total FX exposure (TE_i) in currency i is found by crossing net exposure with the average durations of assets versus liabilities in the foreign currency-denominated assets and liabilities as well as the durations of the bought versus sold position in the currency itself. Mathematically

$$TE_i = (D_A \times A_i - D_L \times L_i) + (DL \times CL_i - DS \times CS_i)$$

where D_A and D_L are average durations of assets and liabilities, respectively, in currency i, and DL and DS are average durations of purchased and sold positions, respectively, in currency i. For example, a contract to buy DMs 60 days forward has a duration (DL) of 60 days. Because the total exposure measure includes durations, it accounts for differences in exposure to changes in the foreign term structure of interest rates as well as future differences in the timing of exchange rate fluctuations. As we show in the next section, it is not possible to separate foreign interest rates and exchange rate fluctuations.

FOREIGN EXCHANGE RATES

A *foreign exchange rate* is simply the price of one country's currency relative to another country's currency. When there are no restrictions on currency trading, FX rates are set by supply and demand. The price relationship between major currencies changes from minute to minute. In restricted markets, however, governments or central banks attempt to fix the rate and prevent fluctuations for periods of time, although supply and demand seem inevitably to catch up with and upset such attempts. Exchange rates can be stated either in units of foreign currency per unit of the home currency, the *indirect rate,* or in units of the home currency to the foreign currency, the *direct rate.* An indirect rate in U.S. dollars for, say, German deutsche marks is expressed as

DM1.70/$

Because the U.S. dollar occupies a special role as the world's reserve currency, exchange rates are usually expressed with reference to the dollar. By this we mean that exchange rates for most of the currencies of the world express the value of the U.S. dollar in terms of the foreign currency.[1] The direct rate for the above transaction is

$$\$0.558/DM$$

In general, the numerator is known as the *unit of account,* and the denominator is the unit of the currency being priced.

A *cross-rate* transaction involves the purchase and sale of one currency for another without reference to the U.S. dollar. For example, a Dutch subsidiary of a U.S. corporation might buy equipment from a French manufacturer by directly selling Dutch guilders for French francs. Cross rates between two currencies are derived from the exchange rates of each currency in terms of the U.S. dollar. For example, we get the price of Netherlands guilders in terms of French francs as follows:

$$\text{Given:} \quad \frac{NLG2.000}{\$}$$

$$\text{and} \quad \frac{FRF5.920}{\$}$$

We can solve for NLG/FRF:

$$\frac{NLG2.00/\$}{FRF5.92/\$} = \frac{NGL0.3378}{FRF}$$

Banks and nonfinancial firms that have operations involving foreign currencies are exposed to the risk of changing values in the foreign currencies. For example, if a U.S. bank extends a loan denominated in Japanese yen, it cannot be sure that the yen will be worth as much when it is paid back as it was worth when the loan was made. Figure 16.1 shows that the value of the yen fluctuated widely in a recent 39-month period. Between April 1995 and January 1998 the value of the yen fell 61 percent in terms of U.S. dollar value from ¥82.12/\$ to ¥132.49/\$.

Spot Market and Forward Market

There are two types of foreign exchange markets distinguished by the dimension of time. The first type is the *spot market,* which deals in currencies bought and sold for essentially immediate settlement on delivery. Spot market transactions take place at the *spot-exchange rate* and are cleared (payment is made) on the so-called *value date,* normally two days after the buyer and seller agree on the transaction.

---

[1] The main exception is the British pound sterling which is expressed in terms of dollars to the pound. Several currencies of former British Commonwealth nations are also expressed in this way.

FIGURE 16.1   Exchange Rate Fluctuations: Japanese Yen vs. U.S. Dollar

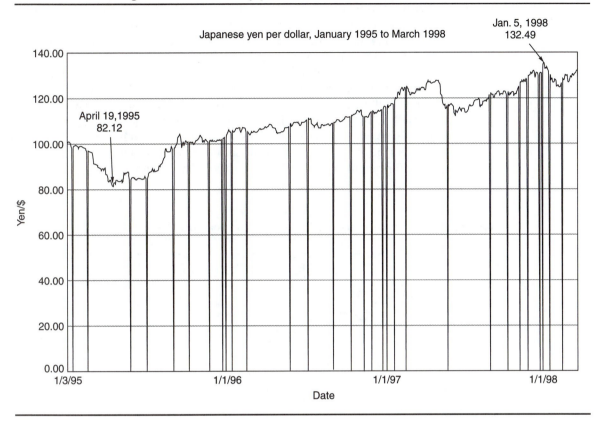

EXAMPLE On June 1, American Bank sells 1 million deutsche marks to Erasmus Corporation at a spot-exchange rate of 1.5200 for value June 3. On June 3, American Bank wires DM1 million from its DM account to Erasmus's DM account. Erasmus Corporation then approves a debit against its dollar account of $657,894.74.

The second type of foreign exchange market is the *forward market*. Participants in the forward market buy and sell currencies for future delivery at the *forward-exchange rate,* that is, for a price at a designated date in the future. The value date is the date of delivery. Contract maturities in the forward market range from several days to months and, in the case of so-called *hard* currencies, even years.

EXAMPLE On September 15, Erasmus Corporation signs a contract with a German manufacturer to purchase machinery to be delivered on June 15 the following year. Erasmus's contract calls for payment of DM1,620,000 upon delivery of the machinery in June. The current spot rate is DM1.6200/$. If Erasmus were to pay today it would cost $1 million. Erasmus believes there is a good chance that the DM/$ exchange rate may fall below 1.6200, meaning the dollar might fall in relation to the DM over the coming nine months. Suppose the exchange rate were to move to 1.5300. In this case, the cost of the machinery would increase from $1,000,000 to $1,058,824 (DM1,620,000 divided by 1.5300). Erasmus decides to protect itself against such a move by locking in the currency rate with a forward contract. American Bank advises the company that it can buy DM forward for delivery on June 15 (270 days) at 1.6690 (a *forward premium* over the spot rate of 490 points). By buying forward DM, Erasmus is fully hedged at 1.6690 and is guaranteed it can buy DM1,620,000 for $970,641 next June.

Table 16.1 is a report that appears daily in the *Wall Street Journal* on foreign exchange selling rates for the spot market in numerous currencies as well as one-, three-, and six-month selling rates for forward transactions in the most active currencies. The pricing of forward contracts can be linked to spot markets by examining opportunities for arbitrage. The spot rate and the interest rates in the currencies involved must be identified.

Another type of foreign exchange transaction is the *swap,* a transaction that bridges the spot and forward markets. One may sell (buy) a foreign currency at the spot rate and

TABLE 16.1   Foreign Currency Trading—Spot and Forward Markets

CURRENCY TRADING

EXCHANGE RATES

Friday, March 20, 1998

The New York foreign exchange selling rates below apply to trading among banks in amounts of $1 million and more, as quoted at 4 p.m. Eastern time by Dow Jones and other sources. Retail transactions provide fewer units of foreign currency per dollar.

Country	U.S. $ equiv. Fri	U.S. $ equiv. Thu	Currency per U.S. $ Fri	Currency per U.S. $ Thu
Argentina (Peso)	1.0001	1.0001	.9999	.9999
Australia (Dollar)	.6650	.6616	1.5038	1.5515
Austria (Schilling)	.07765	.07766	12.878	12.877
Bahrain (Dinar)	2.6518	2.6518	.3771	.3771
Belgium (Franc)	.02648	.02643	37.760	37.830
Brazil (Real)	.8818	.8818	1.1341	1.1341
Britain (Pound)	1.6690	1.6670	.5992	.5999
1-month forward	1.6665	1.6645	.6001	.6008
3-months forward	1.6616	1.6596	.6018	.6026
6-months forward	1.6544	1.6522	.6045	.6053
Canada (Dollar)	.7048	.7051	1.4189	1.4182
1-month forward	.7053	.7057	1.4178	1.4171
3-months forward	.7063	.7067	1.4159	1.4151
6-months forward	.7076	.7079	1.4133	1.4126
Chile (Peso)	.00207	.002211	453.05	452.35
China (Renminbi)	.1208	.1208	8.2792	8.2790
Colombia (Peso)	.0007343	.0007350	1361.87	1360.56
Czech Rep. (Koruna)	....	....	....	....
Commercial rate	.02929	.02940	34.139	34.011
Denmark (Krone)	.1432	.1431	6.9817	6.9875
Ecuador (Sucre)	....	....	....	....
Floating rate	.0002176	.0002176	4595.00	4595.00
Finland (Markka)	.1801	.1800	5.5525	5.5561
France (Franc)	.1630	.1632	6.1360	6.1285
1-month forward	.1627	.1635	6.1474	6.1174
3-months forward	.1638	.1640	6.1041	6.0966
6-months forward	.1646	.1648	6.0749	6.0670
Germany (Mark)	.5459	.5457	1.8320	1.8325
1-month forward	.5468	.5467	1.8287	1.8292
3-months forward	.5487	.5486	1.8224	1.8229
6-months forward	.5514	.5513	1.8135	1.8140
Greece (Drachma)	.003094	.003085	323.20	324.17
Hong Kong (Dollar)	.1292	.1291	7.7420	7.7480
Hungary (Forint)	.004733	.004737	211.30	211.09
India (Rupee)	.02530	.02532	39.525	39.500
Indonesia (Rupiah)	.0001031	.00009756	9700.00	10250.00
Ireland (Punt)	1.3717	1.3704	.7290	.7297
Israel (Shekel)	.2780	.2782	3.5975	3.5940
Italy (Lire)	.0005548	.0005546	1802.50	1803.00
Japan (Yen)	.007666	.007652	130.44	130.69
1-month forward	.007699	.007684	129.88	130.13
3-months forward	.007765	.007750	128.79	129.03
6-months forward	.007866	.007852	127.13	127.35
Jordan (Dinar)	1.4134	1.4134	.7075	.7075
Kuwait (Dinar)	3.2733	3.2723	.3055	.3056
Lebanon (Pound)	.0006570	.0006570	1522.00	1522.00
Malaysia (Ringgit)	.2747	.2692	3.6400	3.7150
Malta (Lira)	2.5221	2.5221	.3965	.3965
Mexico (Peso)	....	....	....	....
Floating rate	.1168	.1167	8.5640	8.5660
Netherland (Guilder)	.4847	.4841	2.0632	2.0656
New Zealand (Dollar)	.5629	.5596	1.7765	1.7870
Norway (Krone)	.1314	.1313	7.6085	7.6143
Pakistan (Rupee)	.02296	.02296	43.560	43.560
Peru (new Sol)	.3600	.3602	2.7775	2.7760
Philippines (Peso)	.02642	.02616	37.845	38.225
Poland (Zloty)	.2912	.2900	3.4340	3.4480
Portugal (Escudo)	.005338	.005332	.18734	187.56
Russia (Ruble)(a)	.1640	.1641	6.0960	6.0940
Saudi Arabia (Riyal)	.2666	.2666	3.7513	3.7511
Singapore (Dollar)	.6217	.6196	1.6085	1.6140
Slovak Rep. (Koruna)	.02847	.02845	35.125	35.150
South Africa (Rand)	.2007	.2010	4.9815	4.9755
South Korea (Won)	.0006904	.0006784	1448.50	1474.00
Spain (Peseta)	.006439	.006439	155.30	155.30
Sweden (Krona)	.1256	.1251	7.9635	7.9960
Switzerland (Franc)	.6671	.6682	1.4990	1.4965
1-month forward	.6696	.6707	1.4935	1.4909
3-months forward	.6744	.6756	1.4828	1.4802
6-months forward	.6814	.6826	1.4675	1.4650
Taiwan (Dollar)	.03051	.03051	32.778	32.772
Thailand (Baht)	.02522	.02497	39.650	40.050
Turkey (Lira)	.00000421	.00000422	237720.00	237150.00
United Arab (Dirham)	.2723	.2723	3.6730	3.6730
Uruguay (New Peso)	....	....	....	....
Financial	.1003	.1003	9.9750	9.9750
Venezuela (Bolivar)	.001913	.001916	522.75	522.00
		———		
SDR	1.3413	1.3432	.7456	.7445
ECU	1.0847	1.0842	....	....

Special Drawing Rights (SDR) are based on exchange rates for the U.S., German, British, French, and Japanese currencies. Source: International Monetary Fund.

European Currency Unit (ECU) is based on a basket of community currencies.

a-fixing, Moscow Interbank Currency Exchange. Ruble newly-denominated Jan. 1998.

The Wall Street Journal daily foreign exchange data for 1996 and 1997 may be purchased through the Reader's Reference Service (413) 592-3600.

SOURCE: *Wall Street Journal*, March 23, 1998, C22.

simultaneously agree to buy (sell) the same currency at a date in the future at the forward rate. The difference between the sell and buy prices is known as the *swap rate.*

EXAMPLE In September, given the previous example, Erasmus Corporation bought the forward contract for the purchase of DM1,620,000 for value nine months from spot (June of next year). On June 13, two days before the DMs are scheduled for delivery, Erasmus learns that the German supplier is running behind on its orders and that it will be three more months before the supplier can deliver the machinery. Erasmus decides to roll its contract forward to the coming September 15 with the use of a swap. At this time (June 13) the spot rate is at DM1.6850/\$. The company takes delivery of DM1,620,000 on its forward contract costing \$970,641 at the contract rate of 1.6690 and sells the DM1,620,000 in the spot market for proceeds of \$961,424 [DM1,620,000/(DM1.6850/\$)] at the June spot rate of 1.6850. Thus, Erasmus takes a loss of (\$970,641 − \$961,424) = \$9,217 on its original forward contract. Erasmus then buys back DM1,620,000 three months forward to avoid exposure to exchange rate movements between June and the next September.

Forward-exchange rates are expressed in terms of *swap rates* or forward *discount* or *premium.* Swap rates are stated in terms of the points of discount or premium from the spot rate. For example, if the three-month forward rate for deutsche marks was DM1.65/\$ and the spot rate was DM1.70/\$, then the discount would be DM0.0500, known in the foreign exchange markets as five hundred points. The forward discount (premium) *rate* is expressed in terms of percent per annum when the forward price is lower (higher) than the spot price. In the foregoing example, we would calculate the forward dollar discount as follows:

$$\text{Forward discount (or premium)} = \frac{\text{Forward} - \text{Spot}}{\text{Spot}} \times \frac{12}{\text{Number of months forward}}$$

$$= \frac{1.65 - 1.70}{1.70} \times \frac{12}{3}$$

$$= -0.1176, \text{ or } 11.76\% \text{ discount per annum}$$

Other Hedging Instruments

Currency Futures Contracts   Currency futures contracts are exactly analogous in foreign currency markets to interest rate futures contracts in domestic money and capital markets (see Chapter 13). They are standardized as to size, quality, and date of delivery. Table 16.2 lists futures contracts trading on the Chicago Mercantile Exchange. Liquidity is ensured for the most active currencies traded by a reasonably deep supply of contracts. As with interest rate futures, currency futures buyers and sellers seldom take or make delivery of the underlying currency but, instead, sell or buy offsetting contracts before the delivery date.

The limitations to hedging with futures contracts are similar to some of those we described in Chapter 15 for interest rate futures. They are not available with continuous maturities, and they are subject to price *nonconvergence.* "Maturity holes" prevent traders or hedgers from taking positions that correspond to the duration of their need for funds and compel them to mismatch the *tenor* of their spot and futures positions. In addition, the longest maturity is just one year and is not suitable for hedging FX exposures of longer periods.

TABLE 16.2 Currency Futures Contracts

						Lifetime		Open
	Open	High	Low	Settle	Change	High	Low	Interest
JAPAN YEN (CME)-12.5 million yen; $ per yen (.00)								
June	.7742	.7830	.7711	.7756	+ .0016	.9090	.7637	79,841
Sept	.7864	.7876	.7856	.7856	+ .0016	.8695	.7735	1,293
Dec	.7950	.7950	.7950	.7957	+ .0016	.8445	.7880	121
Mr99	....	....	....	.8059	+ .0016	.8315	.8065	1,478
Est vol 10,528; vol Th 29,982; open int 82,733, +9568.								
DEUTSCHEMARK (CME)-125,000 marks; $ per mark								
June	.5483	.5498	.5469	.5488	+ .0008	.5995	.5410	69,675
Sept	.5512	.5520	.5497	.5515	+ .0008	.5944	.5490	1,857
Est vol 12,057; vol Th 23,181; open int 71,551, +3,802.								
CANADIAN DOLLAR (CME)-100,000 dlrs.; $ per Can $								
June	.7064	.7073	.7051	.7060	− .0003	.7470	.6825	46,257
Sept	.7082	.7090	.7065	.7075	− .0003	.7463	.6845	3,296
Dec	....	....	....	.7103	− .0003	.7400	.6860	1,440
Mr99	....	....	....	.7103	− .0003	.7247	.6875	453
Est vol 4,990; vol Th 7,421; open int 51,476, −1,194.								
BRITISH POUND (CME)-62,500 pds.; $ per pound								
June	1.6592	1.6640	1.6528	1.6620	+ .0030	1.6940	1.5610	35,651
Sept	1.6480	1.6560	1.6480	1.6550	+ .0032	1.6870	1.5690	587
Est vol 6,838; vol Th 5,550; open int 36,251, +112.								
SWISS FRANC (CME)-125,000 francs; $ per franc								
June	.6748	.6764	.6727	.6746	+ .0002	.7304	.6727	57,566
Sept	.6816	.6822	.6798	.6814	....	.7310	.6798	1,233
Est vol 9,184; vol Th 20,501; open int 58,830, +3,157.								
AUSTRALIAN DOLLAR (CME)-100,000 dlrs.; $ per A.S.								
June	.6626	.6673	.6590	.6657	+ .0026	.7050	.6343	12,094
Est vol 564; vol Th 1,907; open int 12,105, −249.								
MEXICAN PESO (CME)-500,000 new Mex. peso, $ per MP								
June	.11240	.11290	.11220	.11270	+ 00032	.11985	.09200	15,633
Sept	.10830	.10875	.10820	.10865	+ 00040	.11680	.80000	4,339
Dec	.10480	.10530	.10470	.10512	+ 00052	.11440	.80000	8,486
Mr99	.10100	.10150	.10100	.10150	+ 00050	.10150	.10050	104
Est vol 2,860; vol Th 4,787; open int 28,562, +351.								

SOURCE: *Wall Street Journal*, March 23, 1998, C14.

Currency Option Contracts   Not surprisingly, currency option contracts have the same characteristics as the interest rate option products we described in Chapter 14. Participants in this market can purchase contingent claims on foreign currencies that need be exercised only if movements in exchange rates make it profitable to do so. Options on currencies began trading on the Philadelphia Exchange in the early 1980s. Other exchanges, including most prominently the Chicago Monetary Exchange, trade in options on currency futures. Table 16.3 lists the currency futures on which the CME conducts option trading. In addition to the organized exchanges, options on currencies can be purchased over the counter.

A key to the pricing of options on currency futures, as is true for any option, is the expected volatility of the exchange rates. Traders and hedgers can receive guidance on this crucial variable by studying the daily "implied" volatility of options trading at-the-money. Implied volatility is the result of solving a Black-Scholes type option pricing model, given the observations of the option price and the other pricing variables in the model. Table 16.4 gives one day's implied volatilities on currency options of different tenors for the U.S dollar exchange rate for the deutsche mark, Japanese yen, Swiss franc, British pound sterling, Canadian dollar, and Australian dollar. As anticipated in our earlier discussion of the volatility of the dollar/yen exchange rate (see Figure 16.1 above), the

TABLE 16.3   Currency Option Contracts

CURRENCY

JAPANESE YEN (CME)
12,500,000 yen; cents per 100 yen

Strike	Calls-Settle			Puts-Settle		
Price	Apr	May	Jun	Apr	May	Jun
7650	1.46	....	....	0.40	....	1.40
7700	1.12	1.79	2.16	0.56	1.23	1.61
7750	0.84	1.51	....	0.78	1.45	1.85
7800	0.61	1.27	1.67	1.05	1.71	2.10
7850	0.44	....	1.45	1.38	2.00	2.38
7900	0.32	0.88	1.25	1.76	2.31	2.67

Est vol 5,171 Thu 2,074 calls 3,426 puts
Op int Thu 47,155 calls 59,522 puts

DEUTSCHEMARK (CME)
125,000 marks; cents per mark

Strike	Calls-Settle			Puts-Settle		
Price	Apr	May	Jun	Apr	May	Jun
5400	....	....	1.39	0.09	0.35	0.52
5450	0.57	....	....	0.20	0.51	0.71
5500	0.30	0.63	0.83	0.42	0.75	0.95
5550	0.13	0.43	0.63	0.75	1.05	1.24
5600	0.05	0.28	0.48	1.17	....	1.59
5650	0.02	0.19	0.35	1.64	....	1.95

Est vol 2,682 Thu 1,046 calls 9,035 puts
Op int Thu 18,261 calls 32,197 puts

CANADIAN DOLLAR (CME)
100,000 Can.$, cents per Can.$

Strike	Calls-Settle			Puts-Settle		
Price	Apr	May	Jun	Apr	May	Jun
6950	1.12	....	1.31	0.03	....	0.22
7000	0.68	....	0.93	0.08	0.26	0.34
7050	0.33	0.55	0.63	0.23	0.45	0.53
7100	0.13	0.33	0.41	0.53	....	0.81
7150	0.05	0.20	0.27	....	....	1.15
7200	0.02	0.12	0.17	....	....	1.55

Est vol 714 Thu 418 calls 128 puts
Op int Thu 19,806 calls 8,511 puts

BRITISH POUND (CME)
62,500 pounds; cents per pound

Strike	Calls-Settle			Puts-Settle		
Price	Apr	May	Jun	Apr	May	Jun
16400	2.44	....	3.78	0.24	....	1.60
16500	1.66	....	3.18	0.46	....	1.98
16600	1.04	2.10	2.64	0.84	....	2.44
16700	0.62	1.64	2.16	1.42	....	2.96
16800	0.34	1.26	1.76	2.14	....	3.54
16900	0.18	0.96	1.42	....	....	....

Est vol 523 Thu 420 calls 278 puts
Op int Thu 9,820 calls 8,858 puts

SWISS FRANC (CME)
125,000 francs; cents per franc

Strike	Calls-Settle			Puts-Settle		
Price	Apr	May	Jun	Apr	May	Jun
6650	....	....	....	0.12	0.46	0.74
6700	0.69	....	1.38	0.24	0.64	0.93
6750	0.41	....	....	0.45	0.87	1.14
6800	0.22	0.62	0.88	0.75	....	1.41
6850	0.12	....	0.70	1.14	....	1.73
6900	0.06	0.32	0.55	1.60	....	2.06

Est vol 876 Thu 347 calls 486 puts
Op int Thu 9,975 calls 11,176 puts

SOURCE: *Wall Street Journal*, March 23, 1998, C12.

TABLE 16.4   Currency Option Implied Volatilities

Implied Volatility Rates for Foreign Currency Options[a]
February 27, 1998

Currency vs. US$	1 Month Bid/Offer		3 Months Bid/Offer		6 Months Bid/Offer		12 Months Bid/Offer		2 Years Bid/Offer		3 Years Bid/Offer	
DEM	9.1	9.5	9.6	9.9	9.8	10.1	9.9	10.1	9.8	10.2	9.7	10.3
JPY	12.7	13.0	12.7	13.1	12.9	13.2	13.0	13.3	12.9	13.5	12.8	13.4
SWF	9.2	9.8	9.8	10.2	10.2	10.6	10.3	10.8	10.2	11.0	10.2	11.0
STG	8.2	8.6	8.7	9.2	9.0	9.4	9.2	9.5	9.3	9.8	9.3	10.3
CAD	4.3	4.6	4.4	4.6	4.4	4.6	4.4	4.6	4.5	4.9	4.6	5.2
AUD	11.3	11.7	10.2	10.9	9.4	9.9	8.9	9.3	8.5	9.0	8.2	9.1
Cross Rates:												
STG/DEM	7.5	8.0	7.5	8.1	7.5	8.0	7.5	8.0				
DEM/YEN	12.4	12.7	12.3	12.7	12.3	12.7	12.2	12.6				

[a] This release provides survey ranges of implied volatility rates, bid and asked, for at-the-money options as of 3:30 P.M. The quotes are for contracts of at least $10 million with a prime counterparty. This information is based on data collected by the Federal Reserve Bank of New York from a sample of market participants and is intended only for informational purposes. The data were obtained from sources believed to be reliable, but this bank does not guarantee their accuracy, completeness, or correctness.

SOURCE: Federal Reserve Bank of New York.

option market showed that this relationship continued to exhibit the greatest volatility among the six major currencies.

INTEREST RATE PARITY

The relationship between the spot-exchange rate and the forward-exchange rate is based on the relative interest rates in the domestic and foreign currency markets. Suppose the spot DM is DM1.60/$ and the three months forward DM is DM1.65/$. Since the price of a dollar three months forward is higher than at the spot rate, the three-month forward dollar is at a premium. (Alternatively, the three-month forward DM is at a discount.) *The forward dollar premium implies that U.S. interest rates are lower than Germany's.*

It is easy to see why this must be so. Assume the above DM/$ spot and forward rates and suppose three-month interest rates are the same in the United States and Germany, let's say 8 percent per annum. Given these exchange rates, everyone would want dollars. Observe what happens if you buy dollars at spot, invest them for three months at the U.S. interest rate, and sell them for DM three months from now. That is, invest $1 million at spot for three months to obtain $1,000,000[1 + (0.08/4)] = $1,020,000. Now, sell at DM1.6500/$ for DM1,683,000. On the other hand, if you held DM for three months and invested them at the German interest rate, you would obtain (starting with $1 million worth of DM) DM1,600,000[1 + (0.08/4)] = DM1,632,000, an amount that is DM51,000 less than holding dollars for the three months.

Under these circumstances, arbitrage would take place until the relationship between the spot-exchange rate and the forward-exchange rate eventually equalized to accommodate the equality of U.S. and German interest rates. In a perfect world, interest rates would always be the same everywhere. They are not the same, however, and there are several important reasons why. For one, inflationary expectations differ for each nation's currency. Also, there are differences in national economic growth rates, and noneconomic factors, such as government regulations, impede the flow of capital and impact domestic interest rates. The interest rate parity theorem does not suggest that interest rates must be the same everywhere. Rather, it implies that differences between interest rates in one nation versus another should show up in the relationship between spot and forward exchange rates.

The Currency with:	Ought to Have:
Higher interest rate	Discount in forward markets
Lower interest rate	Premium in forward markets

Use of Swaps to Arbitrage Transnational Interest Rates

Speculators, including international banks, may conclude that interest rate differentials between two countries are not justified by economic conditions and that the rates will soon adjust. They will execute swaps through the forward market to attempt to profit from the expected adjustment in the rate differential. Suppose that the spot rate is £0.6700/$ at present and that the one-year forward pound is at £0.6566/$, a difference of 2 percent that reflects the present 2 percent interest rate difference between U.S. and U.K. one-year rates. Suppose, further, that a speculator believes U.S. rates will rise and create a 4 percent differential with the British interest rate.

	12-Month Forward Rate	12-Month Point Premium	Point Premium/Month
2% premium on £	0.6566	0.0134	0.00112
4% premium on £	0.6432	0.0268	0.00223

Spot rate: £0.6700/$

If the forward market has not adjusted to the 4 percent rate differential expected by the speculator, the one-year forward rate will still be £0.6566/$, or a 2 percent premium on the spot rate. If the speculator is correct, the forward market will soon adjust to a 4 percent differential in one-year rates, which infers a one-year forward-exchange rate of £0.6432/$. To collect her profit, the speculator might execute the following swap:

1. Sell forward pounds and deliver in one year.

2. Buy forward pounds to be received in one month.

Assume that the forward markets adjust one month from now to recognize a newly expected 4 percent interest rate differential. Our speculator will have a profit on the original sale of one-year (now 11-month) pounds. The value of this contract will go from £0.6566/$ to £0.6454/$, yielding a profit of £0.6566/$ − £0.6454/$ = £0.0112/$.[2]

---

[2] The new 11-month forward rate is Spot rate − Point premium per month × 11 months × £0.67/$ − £0.00223/$ × 11 = £0.645/$.

Note that, consistent with the definition of a swap, the interest rate speculator held equal positions on the short (sell) and long (buy) sides of the market; only the value dates were different. This protects against the risk of holding a net exchange position in which the spot rate might shift for other reasons. Upon the maturity of the one-month contract, the speculator can close the original 12-month (now 11-month) position and take the profit.

STRUCTURE OF THE FOREIGN EXCHANGE MARKET

Foreign exchange is conducted in a worldwide chain of markets, the largest of which are London, Frankfurt, Zurich, and New York followed by Singapore, Tokyo, Hong Kong, and Paris. The foreign exchange market does not depend on physical marketplaces as stocks do, such as the New York Stock Exchange. As a result, it is difficult to know what volume of foreign exchange occurs in each of the markets. The markets are melded into one global market consisting of telecommunications-linked computers. The major participants' telecommunications and telequote lines access the major trading centers 24 hours each day. Price movements in the major centers are simultaneous with breaking economic and financial news. In short, the markets are highly efficient and immediately absorb and transmit information as it is generated.

The structure of foreign exchange markets is illustrated in Figure 16.2. Most non-bank buyers and sellers of currencies conduct spot and forward transactions through their local bank or primary bank of account. The customer's bank works through upstream correspondent banks or directly through money center banks. These banks, in turn, clear

FIGURE 16.2   Structure of Foreign Exchange Markets

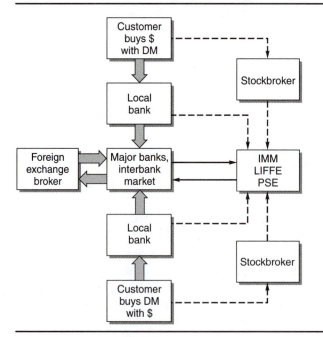

NOTE: The International Money Market (IMM) Chicago trades foreign exchange futures and DM futures options. The London International Financial Futures Exchange (LIFFE) trades foreign exchange futures. The Philadelphia Stock Exchange (PSE) trades foreign currency options.

their foreign transactions through the network of international banks (the interbank market) or through foreign exchange brokers.

Several special exchanges, such as the International Money Market (IMM) in Chicago and the London International Financial Futures Exchange (LIFFE), offer institutionalized access to the forward market (see Figure 16.2). The exchanges deal in *futures contracts,* which are just standardized versions of forward contracts. As noted above, the Philadelphia Stock Exchange (PSE) trades in foreign exchange in the form of *currency options.* Banks are the largest factor in the currency futures and options exchanges. However, individuals can access these markets, mostly for hedging purposes, with or without a bank's assistance.

Contrary to common impressions, outright exchanges make up only a minuscule share of the foreign exchange market. The dominant foreign exchange activity is in interbank spot trading and swaps transactions. Major banks take speculative and hedge positions in various currencies, churning huge volumes of currencies in order to adjust their currency exposures or to profit from short-term movements in exchange rates. Although the largest share of interbank transactions is in the spot market, a substantial volume also occurs as swaps—the forward-to-spot sales (purchases) of a currency coupled with reversing forward purchases (sales) for a different value date as described above. The size of the sale and purchase positions is the same, and both transactions take place between the same two banks; only the value dates differ.

Suppose a bank seeks to increase its short-term exposure to a particular currency, say the British pound. Using the swap mechanism, the bank can short spot dollars for British pounds and go long three-month forward dollars for pounds. The net intended effect would be to increase the bank's exposure to the pound for a three-month period. Financial institutions other than banks, such as investment banks and brokerage houses, are also active in swaps or forward trading.

THE EUROCURRENCY MARKETS

The Eurocurrency markets involve banking units that lend or borrow funds denominated in a currency that is not native to the country in which the banking unit is located. The markets are comparatively unrestricted and unregulated by individual governments; therefore, they freely transcend international boundaries. The volume of Eurocurrencies in the world market is extremely large. In the late 1990s, it consisted of over $5 trillion, measured as the gross foreign currency deposits in banks outside of the United States. The markets have grown dramatically from a base of $100 billion in 1970 to their present size. The Eurodollar accounts for 75 to 80 percent of the market's total size. Belying their name, Euromarket deposits are not restricted to Eurodollars and European-based derivatives, such as Europounds, Eurofrancs, and Euromarks. Also included are non-European currency derivatives such as Singapore dollars and Japanese yen (Euroyen).

The Eurocurrency markets are important to U.S. banking, as evidenced by the fact that over one-half of the transactions of U.S. money center banks are conducted in the Euromarket. Operating through foreign branches and subsidiaries or through international banking facilities (IBFs) (we define these institutions in the next section), U.S. banks accept deposits and make loans in relation to foreign entities and foreign-based U.S. customers. Eurodollar deposits can be taken free of reserve requirements and interest rate limitations. Even though money center banks and many regional banks dominate U.S.

activity in the Eurodollar market, an increasing number of small banks participate in the market by investing in Eurodollar deposits. Finally, the investment banking subsidiaries of the U.S. banks (called merchant banking subsidiaries overseas) participate by underwriting Eurocurrency securities from their foreign locations, principally London.

Eurodollars are defined as dollar liabilities of banks (or U.S. bank foreign affiliates) located outside of the United States or of IBFs. Typically, Eurodollars are created when a customer of a U.S. bank shifts (i.e., wires) dollars from a U.S. bank to a foreign bank or a U.S. bank foreign affiliate. The bank's client, in effect, gives up a dollar deposit and gains a Eurodollar deposit.

The growth of the Eurodollar market can be traced to its universal acceptance in the financing of international trade. In this role, it replaced the British pound, which had been the world trade standard, when it was obvious that the pound had become chronically weak during the 1950s. British banks led the transition to dollars in the 1950s, recognizing that the financing of trade required a plentiful and strong currency. A major stimulus to the Eurodollar's growth and dominance in Eurocurrency markets originated with the rise in oil prices in the 1970s and early 1980s. With this price increase, the Organization of Petroleum Exporting Countries (OPEC) nations earned huge amounts of dollars from their oil exports. The OPEC nations deposited these funds in the Eurodollar market, where the banks of deposit loaned the funds to oil-importing nations to enable these nations to finance massive balance-of-payments deficits. The rate of growth from OPEC nations has slowed as world oil prices have stabilized. The Japanese, with their large current account surpluses, invest part of their earnings through huge trade surpluses from trade in the Eurodollar market since the early 1980s.

BANK FINANCIAL MANAGEMENT IN A FOREIGN ENVIRONMENT

Banks' foreign operations are conducted in two possible currency regimes. One is the Eurocurrency regime, in which the bank takes deposits and makes loans in currencies other than that of the host country. For example, a U.S. bank that manages dollars in its London branch or pounds sterling in its Brussels branch operates in Eurocurrency markets in terms of, respectively, Eurodollars and Europounds. Alternatively, a U.S. bank might manage sterling-denominated assets and liabilities in its London branch. In this case, the bank is competing in a domestic or local-currency market.

In this section we focus mainly on operations in the Eurocurrency sphere, where the vast majority of U.S. bank foreign operations are conducted. Operations in Eurocurrencies are distinct from operations in the local currency. The Euromarket is essentially unregulated and is a true international capital market. Local currency operations, on the other hand, are controlled by the regulatory authorities of the host country.

The position of U.S. bank operations abroad is unique among large international banks because the Euromarket is dominated by the dollar or, more accurately, the Eurodollar. Thus, foreign subsidiaries of U.S. banks conduct much of their operations denominated in their native currency, the dollar, but they do so in foreign lands. In managing their foreign banking operations in Eurodollars, banks must deal with assets and liabilities whose characteristics are different from those on their domestic balance sheet. A bank's portfolio of Eurodollar assets and liabilities is known as its Eurodollar *book*.

Eurodollar Liabilities

Funds in a bank's Eurodollar book are almost all fixed-rate deposits with specific maturities. The deposits usually fall in a maturity range of one week to six months, although some maturities may be as short as one day and others as long as five years. Eurodollar time deposits are mostly interbank liabilities; that is, they are placed on deposit by other banks in a network called the *interbank placement market.* Participating banks usually negotiate directly with one another in arranging for placements, although some interbank placements are arranged by brokers. Eurobankers refer to interbank placements as *redeposits.* The market for redeposits, or interbank placements, permits the participating banks to work out differences in their needs for liquidity and for matching liability maturities with asset maturities.

Eurodollar time deposits can be disadvantageous to depositors because their fixed maturities make them illiquid. As a solution to the problem of illiquidity, large international banks, as well as some midsize banks, offer negotiable Eurodollar CDs. Investors can sell their Eurodollar CDs before maturity in an active secondary market. Because of this liquidity factor, issuing banks can offer Eurodollar CDs at rates below LIBOR.[3] The CD market is thin, however, and Eurobanks cannot issue large volumes of CDs without putting upward pressure on the interest rate. This concern and the easy availability of time deposits from the interbank market make CDs less important than they are in U.S. domestic markets.

In addition to time deposits and CDs, Eurobanks receive funds, known as *call money,* that can be withdrawn on overnight notice. Depositors are willing to take lower rates on call money because they value its high degree of liquidity. Nevertheless, some call money is held on deposit for a while, making some portion of it a long-term and cheap funding source. Foreign banks in local markets, such as U.S. bank branches in London or Paris, do not receive large amounts of call money, for much of it is in local currency deposited in locally headquartered banks.

A final category of deposit is *current accounts,* the foreign equivalent of demand deposits. Current account money is not available to nondomestic banks overseas because this money is in native currency deposited by local firms and individuals in local institutions.

Eurodollar time deposits often carry slightly higher interest rates than comparable U.S. domestic bank deposits, even though the latter are subject to reserve requirements and insurance premiums. One reason is the fear in some cases that authorities in the country where Eurodollars are deposited might block movement of the funds back to a foreign depositor. In addition, some foreign banks that take Eurodollar deposits are less sound than large U.S. banks. In part, this is because the disclosure of financial information on foreign banks is far less complete, and regulatory examinations may be less rigorous.

Eurodollar Assets

Just as Eurodollar deposits differ from U.S. domestic deposits, Eurodollar loans differ from U.S. bank domestic loans. Virtually all Eurodollar loans are priced at some spread over LIBOR, and the spread is typically small. Most of the loans are large wholesale

---

[3] LIBOR is the rate set on term Eurodollar deposits.

credits; essentially none is retail size. Borrowers include U.S. firms that need to finance foreign activities, foreign firms that need to finance activity across their national borders, and foreign governments. Loans may be directly from one foreign banking entity to a borrower, or, as discussed elsewhere, they may be syndicated.

Eurobank loans are almost never made as fixed-rate loans. Occasionally, loans are made for terms as long as 10 years to finance capital projects, but the loan rate is reset at a regular interval, usually every three or six months. Most Eurobank loans are short term, however, and are similarly repriced on so-called rollover dates. The loan agreement is up for renewal on rollover dates, but there is no commitment to a longer term.

Other earning assets that a Eurobank usually holds include interbank placements and foreign currency bonds. The bonds potentially give the bank a longer-maturity asset that might be useful for tailoring a certain interest rate exposure, depending on the bank's outlook for interest rates. In addition, holding a portfolio asset denominated in a foreign currency permits the bank to manage its exposure in that currency, including taking a speculative position on exchange rates if it desires.

Most Eurobank assets and liabilities are renewed and repriced at fixed short-term intervals, unlike U.S. domestic balance sheets, for which many deposit and loan maturities and repricings are uncertain. As a result, Eurobankers have better opportunities than U.S. domestic bankers to control the matching (or mismatching) of asset-liability maturities. Eurobankers can attempt to improve on the narrow spread available on matched funding by carefully managing a mismatch. For example, funding six-month loans with three-month deposits in lieu of six-month deposits (a short book) might prove more profitable, given a positively sloped yield curve where long-term rates are greater than short-term rates. The risk of a short book is that short-term rates might rise by the time the three-month deposit is rolled over. Bankers who mismatch Eurodollar asset and liability maturities or repricing dates clearly must try to "read" the U.S. interest rate outlook with great skill and care, because Eurodollar rates move with U.S. domestic rates. Compared with U.S. domestic banks, Eurobanks have developed a greater propensity for such mismatches, and they seem to have fine-tuned their skills at running a mismatched book.

INTERNATIONAL LOANS

Commercial banks are at the heart of the international financial system. They facilitate world trade and support the international expansion of multinational corporations by financing an array of international transactions. Their major role in short-term finance is to guarantee customers' international trade obligations, discount international paper, and facilitate international payments. Many larger U.S. banks, those with tens of billions of dollars or more in total assets, engage directly in these aspects of international banking. Smaller banks can offer international loan-related services through correspondent relationships with larger banks.

The role of U.S. banks as creditors in international finance consists of direct lending to U.S. customers overseas and to foreign entities, including banks and nonbanks. All U.S. money center banks, as well as many large regional banks, do a significant amount of this type of lending.

Short-Term Finance

International trade credit and the documents associated with it are more complicated than their domestic equivalents. This is because international trade cuts across two bodies of laws and regulations, and because the buyers and sellers (importers and exporters) are less familiar with and less accessible to one another than buyers and sellers in the same country. These complications often require the help of banks to intermediate import-export transactions.

Simple Trade Account   In the simplest form of international trade, the *open-account* basis, banks have only a simple transactions role. In open-account trade, the importer and exporter know each other well and probably have established a successful working relationship. The importer orders goods and promptly pays for them when the goods and title thereto are received.

Almost as simple is the *foreign collection* basis, in which a bank is used to transmit collected funds. Before the goods it has bought can be shipped, the importer must place funds with its bank so that the exporter is assured that payment will be made with collected funds. In this instance, the bank is merely an agent and not a lender.

Bank Drafts   Financial instruments, such as bank drafts and letters of credit, reduce some of the uncertainties of international transactions. A *sight draft* is usually prepared by the exporter and addressed to the importer, ordering the importer to pay on receipt of the goods and the draft. When the draft is signed and "accepted" by the importer and formally acknowledged by the importer's bank, the exporter can use the draft as collateral to borrow funds from his or her own bank, creating, in effect, an international form of accounts receivable financing. A sight draft generally implies only the importer's promise to pay. However, acceptance by the importer's bank makes the draft an irrevocable instrument of payment.

An alternative draft form is the *time draft,* which allows a specified period of time after the goods are delivered and the draft is presented before payment is due. For example, payment terms might be 30, 60, or 90 days' sight. A time draft that has been accepted by the importer's bank is called a *banker's acceptance.* When the bank accepts the draft, the bank guarantees that it will pay the draft on maturity; that is, it effectively replaces the importer's credit with its own credit. As a rule, the exporter, as well as the investment markets, put greater stock in the bank's creditworthiness than in the importer's creditworthiness.

The exporter may attempt to sell the banker's acceptance to an investor at a discount that is consistent with the market rate on banker's acceptances at the time. Alternatively, the bank may effectively extend credit by buying the acceptance from the exporter at the appropriate discount. The bank typically sells it in the banker's acceptance market and later, at maturity, pays off the investor at par as the payment from the importer comes due.

Commercial Letters of Credit   The sight or time draft transactions just described usually involve commercial or documentary letters of credit. The letter of credit (L/C) typically is issued by the importer's bank, that is, the *issuing bank.* The issuing bank's L/C signifies that the bank agrees to pay the importer's obligation to an exporter resulting from a sales agreement, contingent on receiving documentation proving that shipment was made. In return for the L/C, the importer warrants that he or she will pay the bank the sales amount and any fees.

The L/C is crucial to exporters if a foreign customer is not well known or if the customer's credit is suspect for any reason. The L/C substitutes the issuing bank's credit and reputation for those of the importer.

The issuing bank sends the L/C covering the amount of the sale to the exporter's

FIGURE 16.3 **Typical Path of Letter of Credit**

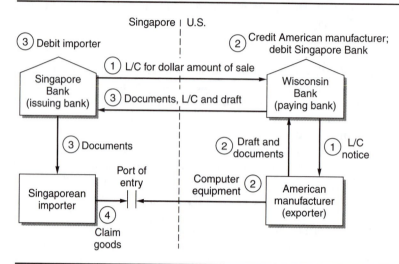

bank (called the *paying bank*) in the exporter's country. The paying bank, in turn, sends the L/C to the exporter. When shipment is made, the exporter presents its sight or time draft along with proof-of-shipment documents to its (paying) bank. The exporter's bank then pays the seller, debits the account of the importer's bank, and sends the shipping documents and draft on to the importer's bank. Upon receipt of the documents and draft, the importer's bank debits the importer's account (in the case of a sight draft; alternatively, with a time draft, the importer's account is debited on maturity) and conveys the documents, representing title to the goods, to the importer.

Figure 16.3, based on an agreement by an American computer manufacturer (exporter) to sell computer equipment to a Singaporean buyer (importer), illustrates the transactions just described. In Step 1, the buyer's bank in Singapore issues its L/C to the computer manufacturer's bank in Wisconsin, which sends it to the manufacturer. In Step 2, the manufacturer in Wisconsin ships the computer equipment to Singapore and presents the sight draft and shipping documents to its bank. The bank in Wisconsin credits the manufacturer's account for the amount of the sale, debits the Singaporean issuing bank's account, and sends the documents to the issuing bank. In Step 3, the Singaporean bank receives the documents, debits the dollar equivalent amount from the buyer's account, and presents the documents to the buyer. Finally, in Step 4, with the shipping documents and effective title in hand, the buyer claims the computer equipment.

L/Cs may be confirmed or unconfirmed and revocable or irrevocable. Confirmed irrevocable L/Cs bear the guarantee of payment by both the issuing and confirming (paying) banks. An unconfirmed irrevocable L/C bears the guarantee of the issuing bank only, and a revocable L/C carries only the importer's promise to pay and does not carry either bank's guarantee.

Direct Loans

Direct international loans take several forms. Private-sector firms in industrial nations borrow long term under guarantees by their respective governments. Governments and private borrowers in less-developed countries (LDCs) borrow large blocks of funds from syndicates of international banks. Many of the latter types of loans are not guaranteed and may represent unusual risks to banks.

Banks with large international credits limit their concentrations of loans in any one country according to the perceived country risk. *Country risk* generally refers to the economic and political conditions of a country. In any case, a loan to the foreign nation's government or its agencies is generally safer than a loan to a private-sector borrower. Even loans to governments may be unsafe, however, because of what is called *sovereign risk.* When foreign governments experience economic or political pressures, there is a risk that they will divert resources to the correction of their domestic problems at the expense of servicing their debts to external lenders. In the 1980s, several LDCs requested the rescheduling of bank loans at considerable sacrifice in interest income to the banks involved. At the extreme, governments may simply repudiate their debts; that is, they may no longer recognize their obligations to external creditors.

The credit analysis process for international lending is a big, sometimes global, task. Banks with major foreign loans must understand the foreign country's history, forecast its future economic performance, and monitor its internal political and structural changes. In addition, because of nations' economic interdependence, banks must recognize how their client nations are affected by changes in the world economy.

Country risk can be evaluated in the same way as domestic credit risk to distinguish between acceptable and unacceptable borrowers. The analysis should break down the country's request for credit into four questions that are analogous to those raised with any borrower: Is the borrower willing to repay? What is the use of funds? What is the primary source of repayment? What is the secondary source of repayment?

A debtor country's willingness to repay has a lot to do with its ability to accept economic discipline in managing its growth. Repayment of external debt may require a nation to slow its growth. If the country uses external debt to fuel its growth at a rate that its citizens demand, it may be unwilling to accept the political risk of an abrupt slowdown. In these circumstances, the debtor nation may prefer to default on its debts. It may find that negotiating to obtain concessions from its creditors to reschedule its debt payments is more palatable than dealing with the political instability that might be associated with retarded growth in the domestic economy.

Banks should analyze a country's use of borrowed funds and the primary repayment source in a straightforward manner. What assets does the country intend to purchase with the funds? Do these assets (such as new industry, education, or public works) promise to produce a rate of return in excess of the interest cost of the subject debt, and will the assets generate increased export earnings? Export earnings, in this sense, are analogous to the net income of a corporation. The debtor nation's ability to earn hard currency, such as the U.S. dollar or the Japanese yen, is crucial in this phase of the analysis. For a U.S. bank lender, the issue is the availability of dollars earned by the country for repayment. Alternatively, other lenders, such as the International Monetary Fund, might be available to take out the bank.

Secondary sources of repayment are significantly different when lending to foreign nations than when lending to domestic corporate borrowers. The secondary source is the nation's ability to reduce its imports in relation to its exports. In a debt crisis, the nation must be able to divert to debt repayment the hard currency used to finance imports. Once again, the key is often the willingness to slow down growth and to let export earnings catch up with or exceed outlays for imports.

TABLE 16.5   U.S. Bank Lending Exposure by Global Region, September, 1997

	(*$Billions*)	
Global Region	**Total Outstanding Cross-Border Exposure**	**Percent of Total**
G-10 nations and Switzerland	262.5	52.6
Non-G-10 developed countries	62.1	12.4
Eastern Europe	13.4	2.7
Latin America and the Caribbean	74.5	14.9
Asia	54.3	10.9
Africa	2.2	—
Banking centers	27.4	5.5
International and regional organizations	2.9	—
Total	499.4	100.0

Source: Federal Financial Institutions Examination Council, Country Exposure Lending Survey of September 30, 1997. E.16 (126), released January 14, 1998.

INTERNATIONAL LENDING BY U.S. BANKS

Total foreign lending by U.S. banks consists of all claims held by U.S. banks in their foreign offices on residents of the country in which the office is located as well as cross-border claims and claims on nonlocal country borrowers. The latter occurs when a U.S. banking office in one country lends to residents of another country; for example, the Singapore branch of Citicorp lends to a firm in Malaysia.

Table 16.5 shows the gross loans outstanding by global region from the foreign offices of U.S. banks. The data include 110 U.S. banking organizations representing 63 percent of U.S. bank assets and 77 percent of capital in U.S. banks.

Table 16.5 reveals that claims on developed nations account for nearly two-thirds of U.S. bank foreign lending. During the 1980s, U.S. bank exposure to developing nations was a much greater concern (see Chapter 1 for a discussion of 1980s banking problems). At its peak in 1982, the ratio of loans to poor developing nations to the banks' capital reached 230 percent. Transforming data in Table 16.5, we see that $144.4 billion in claims on developing countries represented just 45.4 percent of the $317.9 billion in the banks' capital accounts in September 1997. Altogether, foreign loans accounted for 17 percent of loans for all U.S. banks.

LEGAL FORMS OF INTERNATIONAL BANKING ORGANIZATIONS

Banks can adopt several legal forms of organization in entering the international banking arena. The most important of these are listed in the following paragraphs, with comments describing the scope of their activities.

Edge Act and Agreement Corporations

Edge Act and Agreement corporations permit banks to conduct international banking business in the United States from offices in financial centers outside their home states. For example, a Dallas bank might open Edge subsidiaries in cities that are important to international trade, such as New York, Miami, and Los Angeles. Edge corporations are chartered under Section 25(a) of the Federal Reserve Act and are not subject to state banking laws. The state-chartered and supervised counterparts to Edge corporations are called *Agreement corporations* because they must agree to the same restrictions that apply to Edge Act subsidiaries. Edges, but not Agreements, must be capitalized to at least $2 million. Edge corporations conduct international operations abroad through their domestic offices. This permits local corporations to conduct their international financial activities through local banks.

Shell Branches and Representative Offices

Shell branches are overseas offices established to participate in the Eurocurrency markets for booking Eurodollar liabilities for the bank or for issuing foreign loans. They are located in financially obscure places, such as the Bahamas, where they operate virtually free of local taxes; they are not interested in conducting local business. Representative offices are the foreign counterpart to domestic loan production offices. They are minimally staffed, do not take deposits, and essentially do the groundwork on loans made to local borrowers from U.S. headquarters.

Full-Service Foreign Branches

The full-service foreign branch is an extension of the headquarters bank. As such, it can conduct all the same banking activities as the home bank. Some foreign branches, particularly those in London, manage books (balance sheets) that run into many billions of dollars. Branches conduct a wholesale banking business based largely on deposits purchased from the network of international banks known as the *interbank market.* They normally are unable to develop a local base of core deposits. Foreign branches are prohibited in some countries, including Canada and Mexico. In some other countries, branches are not established because they are not safe due to the risk of expropriation.

Merchant Banks

Foreign branches of U.S. banks have a far narrower range of activities than the banks of most other nations, particularly Great Britain, as a result of Glass-Steagall prohibitions on investment banking. Several U.S. money center banks have established investment banking subsidiaries to compete with the merchant banking activities of British banks. British merchant banks are permitted to specialize in investment banking activities such as underwriting stock and bond issues, tailoring mergers and acquisitions, advising customers on portfolio management, and a host of nonlending financial activities. Although they desire this kind of business within the branch proper, U.S. banks are content to segregate it in a separate, nonbanking subsidiary because they feel that merchant banking requires substantially different types of personnel, described as *deal makers,* from commercial banking, where personnel are somewhat more procedure oriented. The investment banking subsidiary may also manage loan syndications, although this activity typically is centered in a department within the branch.

Consortium Banks

Some U.S. banks have joined with banks from other nations to form consortium banks. These banks conduct many of the activities of investment banking subsidiaries. Consortia of large banks can provide a huge capacity for managing and funding syndicated loans. Consortia of smaller banks give the participating banks opportunities to participate in middle-sized Eurofinancings that otherwise would far exceed their individual capacities.

International Banking Facilities

An important organizational form is the international banking facility (IBF). IBFs were authorized in December 1981 by the Federal Reserve to permit banks and other depository institutions to conduct international banking activities from within the United States on a basis similar to that enjoyed by foreign branches and subsidiaries of U.S. banks. In permitting IBFs, the Fed's basic intent was to return such activity to the United States.

IBFs provide banks with a relatively unregulated environment similar to the environment their foreign branches and subsidiaries find overseas. Deposits from foreigners have no reserve requirements and no interest rate limitations. In addition, IBFs are exempt from deposit insurance coverage and the assessments associated with insurance. These exemptions permit IBFs to compete more effectively for foreign deposits and to offer competitive loan rates to foreigners. Deposits must be at least $100,000, and loans can be made only to foreigners.

Most of an IBF's assets consist of loans to foreign-based businesses and foreign governments and central banks for use outside the United States. Their funds come from placements by institutions in the international interbank network and from foreign governments and official institutions.

SUMMARY

The foreign exchange market is central to the operations of the largest banks and is becoming a significant factor in smaller banks as global business reaches into smaller communities. Direct exchange rates are expressed as the price of a foreign currency in domestic currency terms; indirect exchange rates are the domestic currency expressed in terms of the foreign currency.

The foreign exchange market can be divided between spot exchanges and forward exchanges. Domestic persons and firms who must receive or pay a foreign currency at a future date are exposed to movement in the exchange rate. They can protect themselves against such uncertainty by taking forward positions in the foreign currency. Large banks dominate trading in both spot and forward markets. The forward market is an over-the-counter market, typically involving a bank as counterparty.

Other means used by merchants or traders to avoid currency risk include currency forward contracts, futures contracts, currency options (typically on futures), and currency swaps.

The relationship between the spot-exchange rate and the forward-exchange rate is based on the relative interest rates in the domestic and foreign currency markets. In equilibrium, a no-arbitrage condition, interest rate parity ensures that the participant cannot beat the market by transacting in one currency and arbitraging the interest rate differentials between that currency and another. Interest rate parity determines the exchange rate.

Our survey of international banking covered topics and issues that form the background for managing banks with foreign activities. Banks must choose from a variety of organizational forms when they undertake international banking business. International banking can involve a formal organizational presence overseas; on the other hand, it might involve only a special organization within the United States. An overseas organization can be complex, including full wholesale service branches, or simple, such as a shell or representative office, as business activity requires. Alternatively, international banking business can be conducted with only a domestic presence through organizational forms that exempt the bank from certain U.S. domestic banking restraints.

The context of most international banking activity is the Eurocurrency market. International banks conduct most of their foreign operations in nonnative currencies. The market is essentially unregulated and represents a huge, efficient resource in international finance. Eurodollars are the dominant unit of account of most bank assets and liabilities held in nonnative currencies.

The assets and liabilities of a Eurodollar book are different from those of a U.S. domestic banking operation. Most Eurodollar assets and liabilities are repriced at regular and short intervals. The concept of core funds has little meaning to Eurobanks, most of whose funds are comprised of time money of specific duration placed by other banks. An interbank placement market allows banks to resolve their problems of maturity matching of liabilities against assets.

International lending by U.S. banks went through two important phases in the 1970s and up to 1982. In these phases, lending to the developing countries was increasing rapidly. These nations were under pressure to finance large deficits in their balance of payments. These deficits stemmed from the soaring costs of energy and excessive imports used to fuel a high rate of economic growth. Beginning in 1982, a series of defaults by developing nations imperiled the large international loan portfolios of most U.S. money center banks. At the end of the 1990s, U.S. banks' exposure to developing country loans shrank dramatically. Nearly two-thirds of U.S. bank foreign lending was to industrialized nations.

END OF CHAPTER PROBLEMS

16.1 What motives do U.S. banks have for establishing
   a. Edge corporations?
   b. Shell branches?
   c. Full-service foreign branches?
   d. Merchant banking subsidiaries?

What primary types of business do each of these institutions conduct?

16.2 Both Edge corporations and IBFs are formed within the borders of the United States. What are the primary differences between these two entities?

16.3 Foreign exchange can be traded in spot, forward, futures, or option contracts. Define each type of contract and state how it differs from the others.

16.4 From the following, compute the dollar price of deutsche marks:
a. $1.25/£.
b. DM3.00/£.
What is the *direct rate* for dollars in terms of pounds?

16.5 Three-month forward pounds are selling at a 5 percent per annum discount to spot dollars. The spot rate is £0.55/$. Compute the forward rate.

16.6 Critique the following statement: "Traders can use the forward market to guard against deterioration in the spot-exchange rate."

16.7 Define and cite the motivation for interbank currency swaps.

16.8 Suppose that six-month interest rates in Germany and the United States are 6 percent and 7 percent, respectively. The spot-exchange rate is DM1.50/$. If interest rate parity holds, what should be the six-month forward rate?

16.9 Define Eurocurrency markets. Why are Eurocurrency markets dominated by Eurodollars?

16.10 Most U.S. banks operating overseas conduct their activities in Eurocurrencies rather than in the local currency. Discuss some difficulties a foreign branch of a U.S. bank might have operating in a local currency.

EDWARD EDWARDS COMPANY (B)

INTRODUCTION

In March 1998, Edward Edwards, president of the Edward Edwards Company, was both pleased and troubled with the results of his importing business in the past two years. The company had succeeded in doubling its sales between 1995 and 1997; however, the profitability of the additional sales lagged behind the firm's earlier profitability rate (Exhibit 1). Thus, while sales increased 104 percent, net operating income increased only 28 percent.

Edwards had founded the company in 1976 as an adjunct to his career as a manufacturers' representative for domestic producers of kitchenware and other household goods. For many years, Edwards was content to conduct a modest business on the side importing a limited line of low-cost home decorative items. Recently, however, his importing business had grown rapidly, and he was spending an increasing amount of his time and effort in guiding its growth. In the process of expanding the firm's line of household decorative items, Edwards became aware of a group of moderate-sized Japanese exporters whose products were attracting higher volumes of sales. His purchases from these firms were becoming more frequent and were increasing in size.

Recently, Edwards had received the warm interest of two national discount retailers who saw great promise in handling the firm's import line in significantly higher volumes. He concluded that as soon as he could close a few outstanding transactions in his role as a domestic manufacturers' rep, he would shift all of his time into the operations of Edward Edwards Company.

TRANSACTIONS IN YEN

As with many Japanese exporters, Edward Edwards Company suppliers required payment in yen. Trade terms were liberal, and Edwards utilized sight draft letters of credit that were payable 120 days after sight. Invoices from the exporters were fixed at the yen spot rate prevailing on the last day of the month in which Edwards's order was placed. In March 1998, while he wanted to fully utilize the liberal trade terms, Edwards was becoming rather nervous

about his yen exposure during the 120 days allowed by the draft. He knew that if the yen strengthened materially during a period in which he had a large outstanding payable, it would cost him many more dollars when the fixed yen payment became due.

Edwards knew that he had been fortunate that the yen was weakening during 1995 to 1998 when his volume of purchases from Japan was surging. During this period, political leaders in Japan and the United States concurred that a weaker yen would alleviate a financial crisis among Japan's banks and would assist its flagging business climate. In addition, since mid-1997, Japan was believed to have serious exposure to collapsing financial markets in Southeast Asia. Beginning in spring 1995, when it was at its all-time high watermark in relation to the U.S. dollar at ¥81/$, the yen began a steady decline to a low of ¥134/$ at the beginning of 1998. During that period, Edwards often was able to pay for purchase obligations in yen at exchange rates that were more favorable by the time payment was due than the rate in existence when orders were placed. However, Edwards knew that the movement in the yen could become unfavorable and that the firm's exposure with delays in payments of 120 days might involve significant cost. Moreover, the yen appeared to be gaining strength as Japan's problems were placed in a clearer light.

CURRENCY ALTERNATIVES

Edward Edwards called Janos Kraus, the international banker at Third Bank of Dallas, for an appointment to discuss his concern. He advised Kraus that, assuming his firm succeeded in negotiations with the large national retailers, the size of Edwards' import purchases would increase considerably. He noted that these transactions probably would generate the lower margins the firm had experienced lately and that losses on yen exposure could go a long way in wiping out the profits of the business.

Kraus outlined several ways for Edwards to handle the exposure problem. Edwards could continue making payments by buying yen on *the spot market* (currently at an exchange rate of ¥127.43/$) at the payment due date. Suppose, for example, that Edwards completed a ¥12,500,000 purchase today for payment in 120 days and that at the future date the spot-exchange rate was ¥123.00/$. As a result of the yen strengthening during the payment period, Edwards would be hit with a higher cost. Instead of today's dollar price of $98,093 [¥12,500,000/(¥127.43/$)], Edwards would pay $101,626 [¥12,500,000/(¥123.00/$)], an additional cost of $3,533.

Kraus outlined several alternatives. The first was a *money market hedge* which would effectively lock in today's price of yen. Edwards would simply purchase yen at the spot rate from the bank on the order date and put it to work in a Euroyen deposit at about 1.75 percent until payment was due. The bank would lend Edwards the necessary amount to finance the yen purchase and would charge interest at about 8.75 percent, a rate a bit over the prime rate.

Other alternatives involved using currency derivative instruments to hedge this exposure. One alternative was to buy a *forward contract* that would fix today the rate at which the exchange would occur in the future. At today's forward market pricing, the bank would charge a 120-day forward rate based on ¥125.27/$ or, equivalently, $0.00798/¥.

In addition, Edwards could purchase a yen *futures contract*. Futures contracts traded on the International Monetary Market (IMM) in Chicago, and they worked rather like the forward contract hedge offered by the bank. Ideally, Edwards would enter into the appropriate number of futures contracts today to hedge a given transaction. Each contract would deliver ¥12.5 million at today's futures transaction price but at the contract maturity date, say 120 days from now. There was a further complication, however. It was unlikely that the delivery date of the futures contract would coincide exactly with Edwards' payment date to its supplier. As a rule, hedgers acquire a futures contract that matures on a date somewhat beyond the period to be hedged. Futures contracts are highly standardized in contract size and maturity: on the IMM they mature only four times per year in March, June, September, and December, and most probably a maturity is not available to match the end-date of a user's hedge. In that case, to close the hedge, the futures contract would be closed at the end of the hedge period, and the hedger would have exposure to differences in the spot rate on the date of the end of the hedge and the futures contract price at that date. In Edwards' case, if an order was placed on, say March

10, with payment due on July 8, a futures hedge would probably entail a long position in the September yen futures. The futures would be sold on July 8, Edwards would enter the spot market, and the gain (loss) on the futures would offset the stronger (weaker) yen spot price at that date.

Finally, Kraus explained, Edwards could acquire *currency option* contracts either from the bank or from an options exchange. Options convey the right to buy (*call option*) or sell (*put option*) but not the obligation to do so. Option contracts apply to the subject currency at a predetermined price (*exercise price*) and have a specified maturity. A contract acquired through the bank would be a *European-type* option, meaning that it could not be exercised until maturity. Options sold on an exchange such as Chicago's IMM were *American-type* options and could be exercised at any time up to maturity. Most currency options, like those written on the IMM and London LIFFE exchanges, were options on currency futures. For example, in March 1998, a Japanese yen 7900 July call on ¥12.5 million could be acquired for an option price of 2.78. The 7900 exercise (or strike) price was expressed in cents per 100 yen; thus a call on July yen futures at $0.00790/¥ could be acquired for $3,475 ($0.0278 times 12.5 million).

HEDGE EFFICIENCY

Kraus explained that the efficiency of any hedge would be known only after the fact—when the hedge period lapsed and the Japanese billing had been paid. There were pros and cons for each method, and the "best" outcome would be determined by the way exchange rates moved after a hedge position was committed. Certainly, if the yen continued to weaken in the future, a fully exposed unhedged position would be the most profitable. If the yen strengthened over time, an unhedged position would be the costliest. By their nature, each hedge narrowed the range of the potential profit or loss associated with the no-hedge position.

Edwards was a bit dazzled with all of this information. He decided to simulate numeric results for a series of hypothetical transactions. He assumed a sample order to a Japanese exporter for ¥60 million (anticipating larger transactions in the future) on the present date, March 10, 1998, and payable in yen on July 8, 1998. Then he would test and compare the outcomes for various plans by making assumptions about possible movements in the yen–dollar exchange rate. He would ignore all sales commissions on derivative contracts. The plans were:

1. Do not hedge (continue as at present).
2. Conduct a money market hedge with Third Bank.
3. Acquire a 120-day forward contract from Third Bank of Dallas.
4. Acquire September 1998 futures contracts on ¥12.5 million today at a contract price of 0.8055 expressed in cents per yen, that is $0.008055/¥.
5. Buy 7900 call options on July yen futures at ¥12.5 million at an option price of 2.78.

Edwards assumed two scenarios for the yen spot market rate and for the September yen futures price to prevail on July 8. These were:

Scenario A: The July 8 spot is ¥139.00/$ and the September futures is ¥137.00/$.
Scenario B: The July 8 spot is ¥115.00/$ and the September futures is ¥113.00/$.

Edwards felt confident that these results would reveal the volatility of alternative outcomes from the several plans and give him guidance on how he should handle the larger volume transactions he hoped to conduct with Japanese exporters in the future.

EXHIBIT 1   Edward Edwards Company[a]—Statement of Earnings, Years Ended 1996, 1997, and 1998

	1996	1997	1998
Net sales	$501,864	$814,200	$1,025,720
Cost of sales	282,940	478,268	630,713
Gross profit	$218,924	$335,932	$ 395,016
Commission income	193,637	213,763	229,764
Rent subsidy	12,000	12,000	12,000
Miscellaneous income	0	1,142	0
Gross income	$424,561	$562,836	$ 636,780
Expenses	268,295	381,239	436,715
Net operating income	156,266	181,597	200,065
Extraordinary income (expense)	23,058	0	0
Net earnings	$179,324	$181,597	$ 200,065

[a] No provision has been made in this statement for income taxes accruing on the proprietor.

CASE 16

KEYCORP

INTRODUCTION

It was a mid-afternoon in late July 1994, and John Mason felt that he had enough information to review the performance of a special 18-month CD/swap program his employer had been using. He planned to present his analysis of the program's progress to the asset and liability committee (ALCO) at its 8:00 A.M. meeting the next morning. Mason originally had recommended the program to the Community Banking Division and ALCO several months earlier in March, at which time ALCO approved the program.

Mason was senior vice president and funding desk manager for KeyCorp, Incorporated, a $60 billion in assets bank holding company with headquarters in Cleveland, Ohio. The firm concentrated on commercial and retail banking through four primary lines of business: Corporate Banking, National

Consumer Finance, Community Banking, and Key PrivateBank. KeyCorp was proud of operating the second largest banking company in the United States serving small business. In addition, it produced banking services nationwide through over 1,200 full-service banking offices in four regions centered in Albany, Cleveland, Denver, and Seattle and through its "branchless" national telebanking call center. The firm operated nearly 1,500 ATMs in 14 states. KeyCorp provided other specialized services through its bank and nonbank subsidiaries, including personal and corporate trust, cash management, investment banking, and investment management. Exhibit 1 shows year-end 1992 and 1993 financial statements.

When ALCO approved the special CD/swap program in March, several indicators suggested that a stronger economy was emerging in the United States following a period of weak economic performance. Loan demand was becoming robust after a pattern of sluggish growth in 1993 and negative growth in the two prior years. In addition, the Federal Reserve had taken action to head off the inflationary effects of a newly vibrant economy by raising short-term interest rates. At a landmark meeting on February 4, the Federal Open Market Committee (FOMC) raised its interest rate target for fed funds $1/4$ percent to $3 1/4$ percent, reversing a four-year trend of steadily declining and flattening rates. On March 22, the FOMC again raised fed funds another $1/4$ percent.

FUNDS MANAGEMENT AT KEYCORP

KeyCorp participated vigorously in the surge of national loan growth and began to experience pressure on its liquidity. For the month of February 1994, the firm's loans grew at a 12 percent annual rate, and its core deposits decreased by more than a 4 percent annual rate. The outlook was for continued rapid loan growth, which management hoped would continue through 1994 and beyond. With its deposits shrinking in the short run, the firm had no alternative but to fund new loans entirely with wholesale money. Management was concerned that the continuing buildup of loans using wholesale funds while deposits languished was only intensifying liquidity pressures.

Mason's concerns were growing about how KeyCorp would fund its aggressive efforts in lending. He felt it was urgent for the firm to solve its recently lackluster deposit attraction and its ongo-

ing dependence on wholesale funds. Greater competitive pressures made it increasingly difficult to expand the firm's traditional deposit base because other institutions were stepping up efforts to raise such deposits to finance their own expansion in lending. He was particularly concerned about the firm becoming too dependent on purchased funds, and he worried about the premium costs the firm had to pay for wholesale funds in relation to below-market costs for retail deposits.

ORIGINS OF THE CD/SWAP

Mason conceived the use of interest rate swaps to swap wholesale funds for intermediate-term retail funds to attract new deposits. Discussions with managers in the Community Banking Division convinced him of an opportunity to develop the 18-month maturity segment of the market for retail certificates of deposits. Competitors had not shown particular interest in this deposit market segment but, rather, spent most of their effort attracting more conventional money market deposit accounts and short-term time deposits. Given the consensus outlook that interest rates would continue to rise, he believed the firm had an opportunity to "get out ahead of the curve" by lengthening deposit maturities now and locking in deposit costs before market interest rates drove these costs up further. Moreover, he saw an opportunity to "arbitrage" the large difference between expensive 18-month market rates and below-market retail rates on 18-month CDs.

The CD/swap program was implemented in steps. The first step came in March when ALCO approved Mason's proposal for the firm to launch a campaign to market 18-month CDs. ALCO assigned volume targets to the Community Banking Division for raising the 18-month CD money and set a ceiling on rates the Division could pay. The program was limited to the "Great Lakes" group of the Division's banking offices throughout Ohio, Indiana, and Michigan.[1] Community Banking closely tracked the progress of the deposit flows and twice per week reported the volume of new 18-month

---

[1] These states previously comprised the market for Society National Bank (SNB) of Cleveland, Ohio, the primary subsidiary of Society Corporation. The latter changed its name to KeyCorp upon completion of its merger with the "old" KeyCorp on March 1, 1994. Society was the surviving corporation but changed its name to KeyCorp.

CD business written throughout the Division. As these deposits came in, the Division provided estimates of how much of the flows were attributed to internal disintermediation—those funds that were taken from the core deposit accounts of existing KeyCorp customers.

Mason felt that the program had succeeded. Over the period from March to July, the 18-month CD promotion attracted $250 million. In addition, as a result of the promotion, many of the Great Lakes business offices reported significant increases in lobby traffic and cross-selling of other KeyCorp investment and loan products. The Community Banking Division was confident that it would be able to retain and roll over many of the 18-month CDs when they matured in the future.

As the second phase of the program, Mason planned to ask ALCO to enter into interest rate swaps, effectively to swap wholesale funds against the new retail funds. This called for KeyCorp to enter into swaps to receive fixed-rate interest and pay floating-rate interest. The interest rate swaps were booked in a series of steps: When new deposit volumes grew sufficiently and as ALCO became confident that market interest rates were continuing to rise, ALCO would enter an interest rate swap in the notional amount of $50 million. Eventually, ALCO entered five such swaps for a notional total that matched the CD inflows of $250 million.

In July, Mason was conducting his review of the CD/swap program based on the following facts. Working under ALCO's ceiling rate, Community Banking was paying an average of 5 percent for the 18-month CDs. Included in the average cost were rates ranging from 4 to 4.5 percent paid in March to rates of 6 percent or more paid by late July after market rates had increased. KeyCorp was receiving an average fixed rate of 5.84 percent (annualized bond basis) on the swaps and was paying three-month LIBOR (London Interbank Offered Rate) compounded over six-month periods. The average swap spread over like-maturity Treasuries was 22 basis points. As indicated in Figure 1, the all-in cost rate to KeyCorp appeared to be three-month LIBOR minus 84 basis points, a cost well under the firm's costs for wholesale funding.

Mason knew that this cost needed to be modified to take into account a $300,000 expenditure by the Community Banking Division to advertise and promote the intermediate-term CD. In addition, he knew he had to account for internal disintermedia-

FIGURE I   KeyCorp's Receive Fixed-Pay Floating Interest Rate Swap

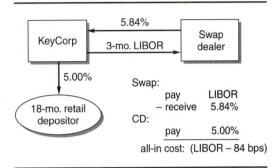

tion, which clearly added to the cost of the new funds. Community Banking estimated that funds that migrated out of lower cost core deposits into the new 18-month CD would have had an average cost of 3.90 percent. In other words, 5 percent money was substituted for 3.90 percent money, albeit while extending the maturity to 18 months. In late July, Community Banking reported that $150 million of the $250 million deposited in the 18-month CD since March had migrated out of the lower cost deposits. This migration was not entirely negative; the rate on lower cost deposits would have continued upward, but now the new CD rate was locked in for 18 months.

LIQUIDITY AND INTEREST SENSITIVITY IN 1994

For the period from November 1993 through July 1994, KeyCorp added the earning assets listed below. These contributed to increasing liquidity pressures, especially because all but $0.3 billion of the funding for these assets came from noncore wholesale funds.

Core Loans	
Commercial	$1.3 billion
Consumer	0.4 billion
	$1.7 billion
Noncore Loans	
Residential mortgages	1.2 billion
Student loans	0.6 billion
Indirect	0.5 billion
	$2.3 billion
Investments	1.4 billion
Total	$5.4 billion

ALCO used the ratio of "adjusted" loans-to-core funding as a key tool to monitor liquidity.[2] As a matter of policy, ALCO sought to adhere to a guideline maximum value of 100 percent. The ratio was stabilized in the low 90 percents during the early 1990s but reached the 100 percent guideline maximum in July and appeared to be headed higher. In addition, the firm's percentage of nondeposit liabilities to deposits, an indicator of its dependence on wholesale funds, had risen from 17 percent in 1991 to a level approaching 30 percent in July 1994.

During the period following approval of the CD/swap program, interest rates continued a strong upward path, supported by the Fed's further increases in the federal funds rate of $1/4$ percent in April and $1/2$ percent in May. The unexpectedly large increases in interest rates added to KeyCorp's problems. Higher interest rates reduced the cash flows from loan payoffs on its large mortgage portfolio as mortgagors with high coupon mortgages found refinancing opportunities less attractive and stopped prepaying their mortgages. Moreover, the rise in interest rates reduced the values of the firm's investment securities, and the firm was not willing to generate liquidity by taking losses through the sale of securities that had gone under water.

In addition, higher interest rates and expensive wholesale funding exposed the firm's liability rate sensitivity, putting pressure on net interest margins. The firm's net interest margin fell from 5.50 percent in January 1993 to 4.40 percent late in the third quarter of 1994. Moreover, ALCO was in danger of violating its primary interest-sensitivity policy guideline. The guideline required that no more than 2 percent of simulated net interest income could be exposed to a gradual year-long rise of 200 basis points in short-term interest rates compared to what net interest income would have been had interest rates not changed.[3]

With the rise in interest rates, KeyCorp's investment security values declined from well above their cost in 1993 to $500 million below cost in July 1994.[4] Finally, KeyCorp held about $10 billion notional amount of *portfolio interest rate swaps*. Of these, over half received a fixed rate and paid a variable rate, thus giving exposure to rising market interest rates.

KeyCorp made a distinction between portfolio swaps and swaps that were entered on customers' accounts. Portfolio swaps were used to modify the repricing or maturity characteristics of specified assets or liabilities. The net interest income or expense associated with portfolio swaps was accrued and recognized as an adjustment to the interest income or interest expense of the asset or liability being managed. Early termination of swaps resulted in gains or losses that were deferred and amortized against the carrying value of the asset or liability to which it is linked.

By late July, ALCO began to discuss steps it would take to reconfigure KeyCorp's balance sheet structure to alleviate the firm's liability sensitivity. Certain investment securities carried at losses were subject to sale. Loans earning low spreads were to be securitized or sold. ALCO would continue to search for means of reducing reliance on wholesale funding. Finally, ALCO would begin to terminate some of the firm's receive fixed-pay floating swaps.

MASON'S RECOMMENDATION

A central issue in the upcoming late July ALCO meeting would be whether or not to continue the CD/swap program. ALCO would want a clear summary of the program's effectiveness and cost. Concerning cost, John Mason suspected that the all-in cost of funds, considering promotion and marketing expense and the disintermediation of low-cost core funds, was not much different from the cost of short-term wholesale funds. He was aware that one or two committee members focused on the fact that the $250 million block of receive fixed-pay

---

[2] Adjusted loans consisted of total loans minus the sum of loans held for sale and loan cash inflows scheduled for the ensuing 90 days. Loans held for sale are shown as noncore loans in the above summary. Core funding consisted of total core deposits plus large certificates of deposit of $100,000 or more over 90 days maturity plus stable wholesale funds over 90 days maturity plus outstanding issues of bank notes.

[3] ALCO relied on a sophisticated computer simulation to measure this exposure. Repricing "betas" were used to differentiate the interest sensitivities of asset and liability accounts. Some betas were "two-directional." For example, a core deposit might have a 0.5 beta with increasing rates and a 0.9 beta with decreasing rates.

[4] On January 1, 1994, KeyCorp adopted new accounting rules established by the recently implemented Financial Accounting Standards Board (FASB) Statement 115. Under the standard, debt securities were classified either as securities held to maturity, trading account assets, or available for sale. Reductions in the value of available-for-sale securities were reflected in a decrease in KeyCorp's equity account, after adjusting for tax effects.

floating swaps added to KeyCorp's liability sensitivity and that KeyCorp's earnings would have been higher in the future without them.

Mason recognized that subjective factors were critical to the analysis of the CD/swap program's performance. For example, while the 18-month CD succeeded in locking in liability rates, the program did not reduce KeyCorp's liability sensitivity because the CDs' maturity effectively was converted to the three-month maturity of the swap's floating rate leg. In other words, in terms of the high interest sensitivity of KeyCorp's liabilities, the program generated CDs that had an effective three-month maturity, not 18 months.

If market interest rates continued to rise, the swaps put on the books under this program threatened to turn "upside down." The pay-floating leg of the swaps would become more expensive, while income on the receive-fixed leg would remain constant. At the time the program was approved, the possibility that the swaps might turn upside down was anticipated because ALCO had been convinced that interest rates would keep rising. ALCO had monitored the performance of these swap positions right along. Admittedly, however, Mason and others on ALCO had been surprised at the magnitude and speed of the interest rate rise.

Finally, continued strong economic growth indicated that recent trends in loan demand and interest rates would continue their upward paths through the rest of 1994 and, most likely, well into 1995.

QUESTIONS

1. Did ALCO make the right decision in March to pursue the CD/swap program? Cite the pros and cons and the strongest arguments for and against. Your answer should be in the context of March's circumstances.

2. Figure 1 shows that the apparent cost for new 18-month CDs was LIBOR minus 84 basis points. Compute the true all-in cost of money generated under the CD/swap program, taking into account the promotional costs and the internal disintermediation of short-term core deposits.

3. The March–July 1994 spread between the average 5.84 percent 18-month receive-fixed rate and the average 4.54 percent pay-floating rate was 1.30 basis points. (The average 18-month CD rate was 5 percent.) As interest rates continue to rise, what will be the effect on future program performance if this spread narrows to, say, 50 basis points? How will such narrowing affect the ability to price the 18-month CD product?

4. Playing the role of John Mason, prepare your recommendations to ALCO on the continuation of the CD/swap program. Should it be continued or closed in late July? Be sure to give your reasoning and be specific about details of your plan.

EXHIBIT I   KeyCorp Consolidated Balance Sheet, as of Dec. 31 ($000)

	1993	1992
Assets		
Cash and due from banks	2,777,438	3,079,700
Short-term investments	107,219	985,500
Mortgage loans held for sale	1,325,338	938,500
Securities available for sale	1,176,828	2,458,700
Investment securities	11,122,093	8,976,300
Total loans	40,071,244	36,021,800
Less: Allow for loan losses	−802,712	−782,600
Net loans	39,268,532	35,239,200
Premises and equipment	912,870	843,300
Other real estate owned	150,362	332,400
All other assets	2,240,471	2,214,800
Total assets	59,631,151	55,068,400
Liabilities		
Total deposits	46,499,148	43,433,100
Fed funds purchased and repurchase agreements	4,120,258	4,207,500
Other short-term borrowing	1,776,192	800
Other liabilities	1,078,116	835,500
Long-term debt	1,763,870	1,790,100
Total liabilities	55,237,584	51,141,100
Total shareholders' equity	4,393,567	3,927,300
Total liabilities and shareholders' equity	59,631,151	55,068,400

Consolidated Income Account, Years Ended Dec. 31 ($000)

	1993	1992
Total interest income	4,213,874	4,198,791
Total interest expense	1,534,897	1,750,118
Net interest income	2,678,977	2,448,673
Provision for loan losses	211,662	338,337
Total noninterest income	1,001,706	925,193
Total noninterest expense	2,385,123	2,170,412
Income before taxes	1,083,898	865,117
Provision for income taxes	373,972	273,019
Net income	709,926	592,098

REGION FINANCIAL CORPORATION

INTRODUCTION

In its meeting of February 7, 1994, Region Financial Corporation Directors' Investment Committee approved the firm's entry into a prime/LIBOR basis swap. The swap was in the notional amount of $500 million with J. P. Morgan Securities, Inc. acting as dealer. Members of Region Financial's finance division had discussed such a swap off and on with the investment committee since the previous summer. The terms of the swap required Region Financial to make payments to Morgan based on the national prime rate. The firm was to receive payments based on LIBOR (London Interbank Offered Rate). The purpose of the swap was to protect the bank's earnings against basis risk.

Region Financial Corporation was a bank holding company headquartered in the western United States, with $7.7 billion in assets in early 1994. The firm's headquarters office was its largest and accounted for 50 percent of corporate assets. Region Financial also operated banking subsidiaries in three other surrounding states. The firm conducted a variety of financial services including domestic commercial banking, investment and funds management, personal banking, trust operations, corporate services, credit life insurance, wholesale real estate lending, and mortgage banking. Operations were conducted through 200 offices and retail branches. Its growth had been assisted by a series of recent acquisitions with still other acquisitions pending in early 1994. Exhibits 1 and 2 present Region Financial's financial statements as of December 31 for the years 1991, 1992, and 1993.

BACKGROUND ON THE BUSINESS PROBLEM

As shown in Exhibit 2, Region Financial's profitability steadily improved from 1991 to 1993, during which time its annual net income doubled. Following problems with bad loans in 1990 and 1991, loan quality improved dramatically and led the way in a robust upward trend in profitability. Nonperforming loans fell from 0.80 percent of assets in 1991 to 0.33 percent of assets by the end of 1993.

The firm's strong profit record in 1993 was boosted by a large "carry" based on a steeply upward-sloping yield curve and a wide "basis" or spread between interest yields on loans and interest costs of deposits. These market factors evolved during a four-year period of steady decline in short-term interest rates in which the three-month Eurodollar rate fell from 8.50 percent in early 1990 to just over 3 percent in August 1993. By early 1994, on the strength of carry and basis, Region Financial's net interest income had improved to an unprecedented rate of 4.4 percent from rates in the low 3 percents in the previous three years. By the summer of 1993, Region Financial's finance division began to explore the feasibility of a prime/LIBOR basis swap to lock in such favorable net interest margins. The division especially wanted to hedge what appeared to be an unusually favorable spread between the firm's prime rate-based assets and its cost of funds. It was this *prime basis hedge* that the division had discussed with Region Financial's board of directors during the months leading up to the February meeting.

Finally, on the approval of the Directors' Investment Committee, Region Financial ("the counterparty") entered into the basis swap transaction with J. P. Morgan ("the dealer") on February 8, 1994. Exhibit 3 presents a diagram of the swap. Terms of the swap are detailed in Exhibit 4.

Basis swaps are floating-for-floating swaps; that is, they are constructed with the two payment legs floating on different short-term interest rates. Basis swaps typically are used to hedge the risk of an unfavorable change in the difference between two money market interest rates. In Region Financial's case, the firm would pay a rate based on daily average prime and receive a "capped" three-month LIBOR rate in return. In presenting the proposal to the Directors' Investment Committee in February 1994, finance division members explained the desirability of locking in the present prime/LIBOR spread which was at "an extremely wide 269 basis points versus the 10-year norm of 158 basis points."

DESCRIPTION OF THE BASIS SWAP

The five-year swap was written on a notional amount of $500 million and had a termination date of February 10, 1999. The $500 million amount would serve to hedge spreads on somewhat less than one-half of the $1.1 billion in prime-based assets finance estimated to be held by Region Financial. The swap provided that Region Financial would pay Morgan the average daily U.S. dollar prime rate minus 253.5 basis points and would receive the minimum of either three-month U.S. dollar LIBOR or the previous quarter's payment rate plus 25 basis points. Net settlements would occur quarterly.

"Sticky" Interest Rate Cap

Region Financial's floating LIBOR receipts potentially were constrained by a schedule of caps. If the LIBOR rate on any reset date exceeded the cap designated for that date, Region Financial would receive only the cap rate and not the actual LIBOR rate for the ensuing quarter. The cap rate on each reset date was equal to the cap rate on the previous reset date plus 25 basis points; in other words, the cap rate increased 25 basis points each quarter.

The cap part of the transaction was a sale by Region Financial of a step-up five-year cap option to Morgan. Finance recognized that, in effect, Region Financial had sold 18 consecutive three-month European call options on LIBOR rates—a sequence known as a "strip" of 18 calls. For each call, the strike price was the cap rate in question, and the maturity of the individual option was the reset date that corresponded to the appropriate cap rate. The swap document in Exhibit 4 lists the cap rates and their matching reset dates. For example, the tenth call had a strike price of 6 percent and a 3-month maturity based on the reset date of August 10, 1996. The call would be in the money if three-month LIBOR was higher than 6 percent on that date because Morgan would have the privilege of paying lower interest costs than it would have paid

if the swap leg had been based on straight LIBOR floating.

For the benefits of owning 18 calls, Morgan expected to "pay" Region Financial an appropriate premium equal to the sum of the values of each of the 18 call options. In actuality, the premiums presumably were reflected in Region Financial's prime-based payments in the form of a larger spread below the prime rate. Without the cap feature, the spread below prime on Region Financial's prime-based floating payment obligations would have been much smaller.

Forward "Mini-Swaps"

In addition to the cap feature, the swap implicitly embedded a strip of three-month floating-for-fixed, forward "mini-swaps." In effect, owing to the method of resetting the prime rate floating leg, a new floating-for-fixed forward swap was created for every LIBOR reset date. The prime rate was reset daily, and the calculation of quarterly settlements made by Region Financial (the prime rate-based payer) was based on the daily average prime rate during the quarter minus 253.5 basis points. In substance, this created the floating-rate leg of a short-term swap with three-month maturity; the exact quarterly payment due was not known until the end of the quarter. On the other hand, LIBOR would be fixed for the ensuing three months on LIBOR reset dates, effectively creating the fixed-rate leg of the embedded short-term swap. This effect was independent of the schedule of cap rates on LIBOR. This "mini-swap" arrangement is shown in Exhibit 5.

To isolate and clarify the influence of the embedded swaps, Region Financial Corporation finance division reconstructed the net settlement at the end of the basic swap's first quarter, May 10, 1994.

	Actual	Hypothetical Fixed Prime[a]	Difference
Daily average prime (2/10/94–5/10/94)	6.268%	6.000%	(0.268%)
Spread under prime	2.535%	2.535%	0
Net	3.733%	3.465%	(0.268%)
LIBOR, 2/10/94	3.563%	3.563%	0
Swap spread	(0.170%)	0.098%	(0.268%)
Swap net settlement, 5/10/94 ($000)	(210.14)	121.14	(331.28)

[a] Actual prime rate on LIBOR reset date, 2/10/94.

This analysis demonstrated that if the prime rate had been fixed along with LIBOR on February 10, 1994 instead of averaged over the ensuing quarter, Region Financial Corporation would have received positive settlement of $121,140. Instead of a fixed prime, however, the payment formula used daily average prime, which required Region Financial Corporation to *pay* net settlement of $210,140. Thus, the embedded mini-swap cost Region Financial Corporation $331,280 in the first quarter alone.

THEORY UNDERLYING THE BASIS SWAP

The finance division's theory in support of the basis swap was straightforward. Many of Region Financial's assets were priced off of prime. Implicitly, the finance division considered three-month LIBOR rates to be highly correlated with, and thus a good proxy for, the firm's cost of funds. In this regard, finance saw the proposed basis swap as a means of protecting the bank against the "inevitable" narrowing of the yield on bank prime-related assets over its cost of funds by hedging against a possible narrowing of prime and three-month LIBOR.

While defending the use of the swap to the Directors' Investment Committee several months after its inception, officers of the finance division cited the analysis and recommendation of a widely known consulting firm:

Banks have about twice as many dollars at risk to changes in interest rate bases as they have to changes in general market rates (levels). The major source of basis risk is the prime/LIBOR spread. Many more assets than liabilities are indexed to prime, while many more liabilities than assets are indexed to LIBOR. The result is that, as the spread between prime and LIBOR widened, bank net interest income greatly increased. In the past two years, for example, the bulge in the prime–LIBOR spread accounted for 10% to 20% of the total after-tax net income of many (banks).

If rates go up, the prime–LIBOR spread is likely to constrict. Now may, therefore, be an appropriate time for banks to reduce some of their outsize basis exposure by doing basis swaps paying prime and receiving LIBOR . . . (although) neutralizing a reasonable portion of a bank's prime–LIBOR basis risk can lower current income. But the reduction in future income volatility may easily warrant this give-up.

The theory underlying the cap on LIBOR rates to be paid to Region Financial by Morgan was based on the "stickiness" of Region Financial's cost of retail deposits. Supposedly, Region Financial's swap receipts would match against the bank's interest expense on retail deposits. The swap receipts were limited to the lesser of either LIBOR or a cap that stepped up 25 basis points per quarter. In general, if LIBOR increased faster than 25 basis points per quarter (100 basis points per year), Region Financial Corporation would receive less than LIBOR. This "sticky" cap was justified by the parallel stickiness of retail deposit rates. Morgan identified the stickiness of deposits, a result of consumer insensitivity to interest rate movements, as a major benefit of retail banking. Morgan offered statistical proof that large urban banks lagged their retail deposit rates behind increases in LIBOR by as much as 78 basis points (see Exhibit 6). Therefore, assuming Region Financial Corporation lagged its retail deposit rates behind LIBOR, it could afford to receive swap payments that similarly lagged increases in LIBOR.

POST-MERGER AUDIT

Early in 1995, Region Financial Corporation was acquired by U.S. Bancorp, a strong regional banking company with headquarters in Portland, Oregon. The acquisition increased U.S. Bancorp's asset base to nearly $30 billion. Soon after the merger of the two companies, the successor company's board of directors was concerned about the large notional amount of the basis swap and ordered its Treasury Division to audit the swap's performance. In early December 1995 the division's asset and liability manager, Tom Rowley, began to gather information to report his assessment. He realized that there were multiple ways to look at it.

First, as a hedge transaction, he felt the primary issue should be how well the swap locked in the bank's spread that existed at the time of the swap's implementation. The base spread at inception on February 10, 1994 was 3.57 percent. Rowley knew that the hedge relationship would not be perfect. The firm's own prime rate differed from national prime, the rate referenced in the swap. Also, at times the bank's CDs did not correlate well with the capped feature of the LIBOR side of the swap. He estimated the bank's balance sheet spread for the quarters the swap had been in existence as follows.

Quarter	Bank Prime Reference Rate Minus Bank Cost of Funds
2/10/94–5/10/94	3.58%
5/10/94–8/10/94	4.36%
8/10/94–11/10/94	4.69%
11/10/94–2/10/95	5.04%
2/10/95–5/10/95	5.32%
5/10/95–8/10/95	5.23%
8/10/95–11/10/95	4.98%

Rowley planned to adjust this spread with the actual swap spread, determined as the difference between the daily average national prime during each quarter minus 253.5 basis points and the LIBOR rate on reset dates. The weekly values of these rates are shown in Exhibit 7.[1] This analysis would show both the rates and dollar flows based on $500 million in prime-based assets as follows:

Net interest income − Swap cash flow

= Hedged net interest income

where net interest income was $500 million times the bank's balance sheet spread.

In addition, Rowley intended to approximate the cost of the embedded mini-swap for each quarter in the manner that Region Financial had done, as described earlier. This entailed finding how the ac-

tual swap spread compared with the hypothetical spread, assuming the swap leg's prime rate were fixed on reset dates and not averaged as in the swap agreement.

Pending the outcome of his analysis, Rowley felt that he was expected to make a recommendation on continuing with the swap for the more than three years to its maturity or if he should recommend exiting the swap. In preparation for this decision, he estimated the swap's value to be a negative $7.9 million to U.S. Bancorp. In other words, to exit the swap, U.S. Bancorp would pay Morgan $7.9 million.

Finally, Rowley could not help but review the original decision of Region Financial Corporation to enter the swap. He appreciated the good intentions of the officers involved in the original transaction and wondered if he would have made the same decision. Hindsight is always 20–20, he thought. Would I do this if similar circumstances arose in the future?

[1] For estimating purposes, absent daily rates, one can average the weekly prime rates within the quarter. The LIBOR rate on reset dates of May 10, August 10, November 10, and February 10 can be interpolated over five business days from the weekly LIBOR on dates around the reset date. For example, the May 10, 1994 reset can be approximated by interpolating between 4.70 percent reported on May 6 and 5.11 percent reported on May 11 in Exhibit 7, or about 5.03 percent.

EXHIBIT 1   Region Financial Corporation Financial Statements —Consolidated Balance Sheet ($000)

	1993	1992	1991
Assets			
Cash and due from banks	450,983	687,662	489,674
Federal funds sold, reverse repurchase agreements	14,055	28,210	30,434
Total securities	1,625,815	1,657,469	1,219,871
Gross loans	5,354,497	4,531,913	3,497,451
Allowance for loan losses	−74,923	−68,243	−53,048
Net loans	5,279,574	4,463,670	3,444,403
Premises and equipment	122,828	120,587	90,491
Other assets	178,098	176,039	142,326
Total assets	7,671,353	7,133,637	5,417,199
Liabilities and Equity			
Noninterest bearing	1,260,869	1,135,967	669,037
Interest-bearing demand	729,247	696,656	438,294
Regular and money market savings	1,971,211	1,717,189	1,129,957

EXHIBIT I   *(Continued)*

	1993	1992	1991
Time certificates < $100,000	1,505,177	1,651,344	1,437,245
Time certificates > $100,000	470,543	435,183	369,875
Total deposits	5,937,047	5,636,339	4,044,408
Federal funds purchased, repurchase agreements	568,295	668,631	618,861
Other short-term borrowing	330,609	141,392	206,284
Long-term debt	116,460	117,649	111,881
Other liabilities	95,376	79,801	68,717
Total liabilities	7,047,787	6,643,812	5,050,151
Shareholders' equity	623,566	489,825	367,048
Total liabilities and equity	7,671,353	7,133,637	5,417,199

EXHIBIT 2   **Region Financial Corporation Financial Statements
—Consolidated Income Statement ($000)**

	1993	1992	1991
Total interest income	497,325	433,788	447,552
Total interest expense	193,435	195,090	249,980
Net interest income	303,890	238,698	197,572
Provision for credit losses	13,383	14,308	29,680
Net interest income after provision	290,507	224,390	167,892
Total noninterest income	102,509	83,461	72,704
Total noninterest expense	272,438	216,524	183,136
Income before taxes	120,578	91,327	57,460
Provision for income taxes	37,391	27,955	16,261
Net income	83,187	63,372	41,199

EXHIBIT 3   **Prime/LIBOR Basis Swap**

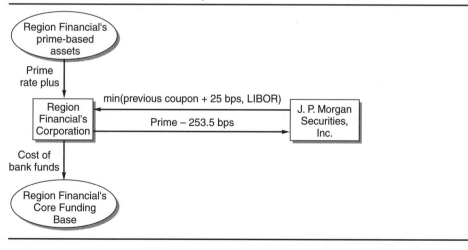

EXHIBIT 4   Swap Transaction, J. P. Morgan Securities, Inc.

Prime/LIBOR Basis Swap

Trade date	February 8, 1994
Effective date	February 10, 1994
Termination date	February 10, 1999
Notional amount	500,000,000 USD
I. Counterparty pays	Floating rate, USD-Prime-H.15
A. Maturity	Daily
B. Spread	− 2.53500 percent
C. Floating-rate day count fraction	Actual/360
D. Reset dates	Daily
E. Method of averaging	Weighted
II. Dealer pays	Floating rate, USD-LIBOR—BBA
A. Maturity	3-month
B. Spread	Inapplicable
C. Floating-rate day count fraction	Actual/360
D. Reset dates	First day, each calculation period
E. Method of averaging	Inapplicable
F. Additional rate formula	The LIBOR rate resetting on the reset dates will be capped at the appropriate levels detailed below:

5/10/94	3.75%	8/10/96	6.00%
8/10/94	4.00%	11/10/96	6.25%
11/10/94	4.25%	2/10/97	6.50%
2/10/95	4.50%	5/10/97	6.75%
5/10/95	4.75%	8/10/97	7.00%
8/10/95	5.00%	11/10/97	7.25%
11/10/95	5.25%	2/10/98	7.50%
2/10/96	5.50%	5/10/98	7.75%
5/10/96	5.75%	8/10/98	8.00%
		11/10/98	8.25%

Business day locations for counterparty	London, New York
Business day locations for dealer	London, New York
Payments will be	Net

EXHIBIT 5   Embedded Three-Month Forward "Mini-Swap"

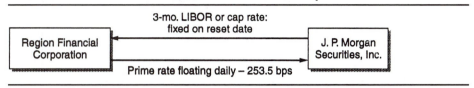

EXHIBIT 6   Retail Deposit Rates at Large Urban Banks Fall Below Alternative Money Market Cost of Funds[a]

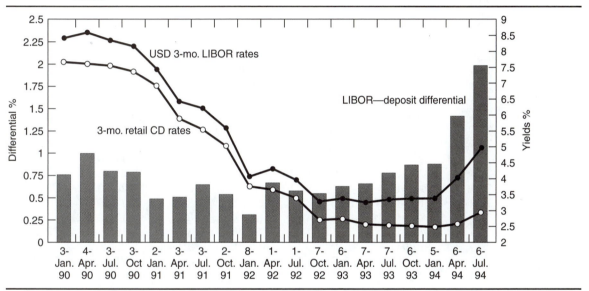

[a] From January 1990 to July 1994, three-month retail CD rates averaged 78.3 basis points less than three-month LIBOR with a standard deviation of 36.3 basis points. Based on this result, Morgan suggested there was a 66 percent chance that this differential would lie between 42 and 114.6 basis points.

SOURCE: *Bank Rate Monitor Index* (TM); Retail CD Rates; APR Averages paid by Commercial Banks that comprise the BRM index.

EXHIBIT 7   Prime Interest and Three-Month Eurodollar Rates

Wednesday Dates	Prime Rate	Friday Dates	Three-Month Euro	Wednesday Dates	Prime Rate	Friday Dates	Three-Month Euro
2/16/94	6.00	2/18/94	3.63	2/1/95	8.57	2/3/95	6.58
2/23/94	6.00	2/25/94	3.76	2/8/95	9.00	2/10/95	6.44
3/2/94	6.00	3/4/94	3/90	2/15/95	9.00	2/17/95	6.45
3/9/94	6.00	3/11/94	4.00	2/22/95	9.00	2/24/95	6.34
3/16/94	6.00	3/18/94	4.00	3/1/95	9.00	3/3/95	6.31
3/23/94	6.00	3/25/94	4.08	3/8/95	9.00	3/10/95	6.43
3/30/94	6.25	4/1/94	4.11	3/15/95	9.00	3/17/95	6.34
4/6/94	6.25	4/8/94	4.28	3/22/95	9.00	3/24/95	6.31
4/13/94	6.25	4/15/94	4.28	3/29/95	9.00	3/31/95	6.35
4/20/94	6.39	4/22/94	4.46	4/5/95	9.00	4/7/95	6.35
4/27/94	6.75	4/29/94	4.51	4/12/95	9.00	4/14/95	6.30
5/4/94	6.75	5/6/94	4.70	4/19/95	9.00	4/21/95	6.24
5/11/94	6.75	5/13/94	5.11	4/26/95	9.00	4/28/95	6.21
5/18/94	6.89	5/20/94	4.90	5/3/95	9.00	5/5/95	6.21
5/25/94	7.25	5/27/94	4.81	5/10/95	9.00	5/12/95	6.06
6/1/94	7.25	6/3/94	4.85	5/17/95	9.00	5/19/95	6.06
6/8/94	7.25	6/10/94	4.75	5/24/95	9.00	5/26/95	6.03
6/15/94	7.25	6/17/94	4.76	5/31/95	9.00	6/2/95	5.91
6/22/94	7.25	6/24/94	4.85	6/7/95	9.00	6/9/95	5.76
6/29/94	7.25	7/1/94	5.08	6/14/95	9.00	6/16/95	5.83
7/6/94	7.25	7/8/94	5.16	6/21/95	9.00	6/23/95	5.76
7/13/94	7.25	7/15/94	5.23	6/28/95	9.00	6/30/95	5.77
7/20/94	7.25	7/22/94	5.08	7/5/95	9.00	7/7/95	5.81
7/27/94	7.25	7/29/94	5.15	7/12/95	8.79	7/14/95	5.65
8/3/94	7.25	8/5/94	5.05	7/19/95	8.75	7/21/95	5.75
8/10/94	7.25	8/12/94	5.19	7/26/95	8.75	7/28/95	5.80
8/17/94	7.39	8/19/94	5.21	8/2/95	8.75	8/4/95	5.81
8/24/94	7.75	8/26/94	5.18	8/9/95	8.75	8/11/95	5.79
8/31/94	7.75	9/2/94	5.19	8/16/95	8.75	8/18/95	5.84
9/7/94	7.75	9/9/94	5.21	8/23/95	8.75	8/25/95	5.86
9/14/94	7.75	9/16/94	5.31	8/30/95	8.75	9/1/95	5.78
9/21/94	7.75	9/23/94	5.49	9/6/95	8.75	9/8/95	5.76
9/28/94	7.75	9/30/94	5.59	9/13/95	8.75	9/15/95	5.73
10/5/94	7.75	10/7/94	5.75	9/20/95	8.75	9/22/95	5.69
10/12/94	7.75	10/14/94	5.76	9/27/95	8.75	9/29/95	5.78
10/19/94	7.75	10/21/94	5.71	10/4/95	8.75	10/6/95	5.81
10/26/94	7.75	10/28/94	5.86	10/11/95	8.75	10/13/95	5.78
11/2/94	7.75	11/4/94	5.88	10/18/95	8.75	10/20/95	5.77
11/9/94	7.75	11/11/94	6.04	10/25/95	8.75	10/27/95	5.79
11/16/94	7.96	11/18/94	6.11	11/1/95	8.75	11/3/95	5.74
11/23/94	8.50	11/25/94	6.19	11/8/95	8.75	11/10/95	5.64
11/30/94	8.50	12/2/94	6.44	11/15/95	8.75	11/17/95	5.63
12/7/94	8.50	12/9/94	6.73	11/22/95	8.75	11/24/95	5.59
12/14/94	8.50	12/16/94	6.80	11/29/95	8.75	12/1/95	5.59
12/21/94	8.50	12/23/94	6.76	12/6/95	8.75	12/8/95	5.52
12/28/94	8.50	12/30/94	6.88	12/13/95	8.75	12/15/95	5.55
1/4/95	8.50	1/6/95	6.88	12/20/95	8.71	12/22/95	5.48
1/11/95	8.50	1/13/95	6.74	12/27/95	8.50	12/29/95	5.42
1/18/95	8.50	1/20/95	6.61				
1/25/95	8.50	1/27/95	6.65				

CASE

18

CITY FEDERAL SAVINGS AND LOAN ASSOCIATION

INTRODUCTION

In January 1984, Reid Nagle was reviewing the hedging program at City Federal Savings and Loan Association. The program involved the use of interest rate futures to hedge the institution's exposure to increases in interest rates. City Federal had been a particularly active user of futures since January 1982. However, up to the present, the firm had experienced losses amounting to $72 million on its futures positions.

Nagle recognized that there are two sides to every futures hedge—the cash side and the futures side. Generally, when one side loses, the other side gains. As a disciplined hedger, the firm must view the $72 million loss only as the inevitable losing side of the hedge. The gain side in this case was the appreciation in value of the cash position under the hedge. Nagle estimated this gain to be $89 million. The difference of $17 million between the cash side gain and the futures side loss resulted from basis risk and had nothing to do with interest rate risk, which was effectively eliminated by the hedge. He considered the fact that the difference was positive and favorable to be simply a matter of luck. He knew that, just as readily, it might have been negative and unfavorable.

BACKGROUND

City Federal, located in Piscataway, New Jersey, was the fourteenth largest savings and loan association in the nation with total assets in excess of $6 billion (see Exhibits 1 and 2 for financial statements). It was the second most profitable publicly owned savings and loan association in the United States during both 1981 and 1982, and its return on assets placed it in the top 25 percent of S&Ls in 1983. The firm had grown rapidly during the past three years as a result of aggressive mortgage lending funded primarily by new retail deposits and, to a lesser extent, by wholesale funds in the form of "jumbo" CDs, wholesale repurchase agreements, and national distribution by brokerage houses of a limited amount of CDs. In addition, City Federal had embarked on an ambitious acquisition program in which it acquired two large savings and loan associations in Florida and two in New Jersey.

The firm also had been moving to diversify its product offerings. Management observed that "the savings and loan business, a two-product industry for so long, today has a wealth of potential product lines." Consumer lending had been recently introduced, and various service corporations within City Federal now offered trust, brokerage, mortgage banking, real estate appraisal, insurance, and other services.

FINANCIAL POLICY

In 1980, Reid Nagle, vice-president of Economics and Planning for City Federal, recognized the threat that rising interest rates posed to the firm's net income. In the savings and loan industry, this threat came from the funding of long-term, fixed-rate mortgages with short-term liabilities. Rising rates forced the cost of funds up, while the yield on mortgages remained constant. By late 1980, the spread on many of City Federal's mortgages in relation to funding costs was negative and was rapidly deteriorating. With this in mind, Nagle successfully urged management to establish an asset and liability management committee (ALCO) to ensure that strict asset and liability management policies would be instituted and observed.

One of the Committee's first policies was to see that new loans were funded at a good spread that was locked in by deposits or borrowings with interest rate sensitivity equivalent to the loans. That is, assets on the margin were to be matched with their funding in rate-sensitivity terms. Thus, the spread on all marginal activity was to be desensitized to interest rate changes. This required lengthening the normal life of liabilities and shortening the life of assets.

The ALCO closely monitored the institution's short-term gap ratio. ALCO defined the gap ratio as rate-sensitive liabilities minus rate-sensitive assets divided by total assets. This measure gave a rough indication of the effect of rate changes on net income. For example, a gap ratio of 40 percent with $2.5 billion in total assets indicates that income before taxes will decrease roughly $10 million for every 1 percent increase in market interest rates (40 percent × $2.5 billion × 1 percent). Because of ALCO's efforts, as shown in Exhibit 3, the gap ratio had been steadily reduced through 1981–1983.

Some of this balance sheet restructuring had come about through the dramatic growth of sensitivity-matched assets and liabilities. The sheer weight of new assets and liabilities restructured the balance sheet by diluting the overall interest sensitivity associated with preexisting assets and liabilities. Thus, City Federal was managing to grow out of its large gap ratio.

In much the same way, City Federal's portfolio of fixed-rate mortgages, which were booked at low interest rates over the years, was being swamped by new loans carrying higher rates or rates that could be adjusted as rates changed in the market. One major source of the growth of new higher rate loans had been the association's acquisitions of other thrift institutions. Exhibit 4 shows a breakdown of the balance sheet in terms of the old, pre-1980 remaining portfolio, the merger portfolio, and the new portfolio remaining since 1980. This breakdown, and the associated yields and rates, demonstrated that City Federal could not rely on its old assets for profitability.

Acquired thrifts were folded into the balance sheet on a purchase accounting basis. Purchase accounting permitted City Federal to mark down or discount the value of loans from an acquired institution to a level that brought their yields up to current mortgage rates. The amount of this discount was then added to income during the roughly 12-year life of the loans.[1]

In general, Nagle believed much of the credit for controlling rate sensitivity was due to the association's system of allocating resources. Nagle's staff prepared a report called the *investment/funding matrix,* which set forth an analysis of all investment and funding opportunities available to the firm. The analysis arrayed and ranked each investment and source of funds by its rate sensitivity and maturity. This innovation pointed out attractive spread relationships along the yield curve. Exhibit 5 presents an example of the matrix and the associated yield/cost spreads on the yield curve.

It also alerted ALCO and management to the feasibility of new products, including consumer lending and the CAMP (City Affordable Mortgage Plan) loan by demonstrating the attractiveness of long-term deposits and borrowing. The CAMP program included many loans that carried attractive below-market interest rates in their early years, resulting in increases in principal or negative amortization.

In addition, City Federal was a major player in secondary mortgage markets, originating and selling nearly $1 billion of loans in both 1982 and 1983.

HEDGING PROGRAM

The asset-liability management program also gave rise to the use of the financial futures markets as a technique for redressing the gap. Beginning in August 1981, the Federal Home Loan Bank Board (FHLBB) permitted FSLIC-insured associations to use financial futures to manage interest rate risk. In general, associations were restricted to short positions, that is, to sell futures contracts; they were prohibited from taking long positions, that is, to buy contracts.[2]

With financial futures, City Federal was able to shorten the rate sensitivity of assets and to lengthen the rate sensitivity of liabilities. The use of futures made it practical to lock in new liability rates for longer periods to better match the rate sensitivity of new assets. Alternatively, futures were used to convert City's deep-discount, fixed-rate mortgages into variable-rate instruments.

Looking back over the nearly two years of using futures, Nagle believed that City Federal had conducted a successful hedging program. Exhibit 6 shows that net interest margin varied less than that of the industry as a whole. It had moved from 35 basis points in 1981 to 58 in 1982 to 136 in 1983. The rise in net interest margin stemmed from City Federal's diversification program and profitable spreads on its huge volume of new assets. But Nagle reasoned that the relative stability of its earnings could be partly attributed to the futures hedging program. This stability could be attributed more generally to the firm's investment/funding analysis that resulted in a huge volume of cash hedges by matching asset and liability maturities in addition to cash/futures hedging.

---

[1] This addition to net income was offset somewhat by a charge against income consisting of amortized goodwill—any excess of the price over market value paid by City Federal. Goodwill was amortized over a period of about 35 years. This increased reported profits artificially, as income was recognized faster than goodwill expense. Subsequent to most of City Federal's acquisitions, this accounting asymmetry was eliminated when regulatory authorities required acquiring firms to amortize goodwill over a time frame that was similar to the life of acquired loans.

[2] However, long positions were permitted in the mortgage banking activities of thrift associations.

TYPES OF HEDGES

City Federal embarked on its hedging program in March 1982 when it was carrying a gap of $1 billion consisting of fixed-rate mortgages funded by six-month money market certificates and other short-term deposits. After watching rates on liabilities surge relentlessly during 1981, ALCO considered three solutions. First, it could absorb the violent swings in profits and do nothing. Second, it could hedge the entire gap against any further rate increases. However, this would ensure that an unacceptably high cost of funds would be locked in at the existing 14.9 percent rate on the firm's six-month money market CDs. Third, it could just hedge part of the gap at different interest rates, locking in positive spreads whenever they could be identified. Then, if interest rates fell, additional hedges would be put on to hedge other portions of the gap. This staggered hedge would not work if interest rates rose further.

After carefully considering these three alternatives, ALCO chose the staggered hedge. ALCO estimated that if rates remained unchanged, the Association would earn $12.7 million in 1982: it ultimately earned $13.2 million. If the entire gap had been hedged, profits would have been much lower at about $8.4 million. In a sense, then, the cost of eliminating the rate sensitivity (except basis risk)[3] with a whole gap hedge instead of a staggered hedge would have been the difference between the actual earnings and estimated earnings under the whole gap hedge—an amount equal to $4.8 million.

Eventually, City Federal's board approved nine types of hedges and set dollar limits on each. The specific hedges and limits in existence in June 1982 are listed in Exhibit 7. In any case, the board limited to $1.1 billion the aggregate cash positions that could be hedged.

EFFECTIVENESS OF FUTURES HEDGING

Although futures were central to the financial policies of the past two years, it was difficult to assess their benefits because they were so intertwined with City Federal's overall risk management program. On the one hand, one could not ignore the fact of a $72 million loss on futures positions since March 1982. The futures position had fluctuated from a high of a positive $20 million to a low of a negative $100 million. Cynics could argue that the firm had bet on increases in interest rates and had lost the bet. Unavoidably, critics pointed out that the losses on futures had been massive and that profits could have been much greater if the Association had simply avoided the futures markets. But Nagle reasoned that without its futures hedging program, the firm would have been a flagrant speculator and would have been exposed to a potential loss with no offsetting gain. His expectation had been that rates would fluctuate; he maintained that there had been no betting on rates moving in a specific direction.

City Federal used *hedge accounting,* in which gains or losses on futures were deferred and recognized over time according to a schedule that was consistent with the hedge purpose. Exhibit 8 shows the adjustment to net interest margin through nine months of 1983 due to hedging activity. At that time (September 1983), a footnote to City Federal's quarterly report read:

As of September 30, 1983, the Association had deferred hedging losses of $71,779,000, which include $64,842,000 of losses on closed contracts and $6,937,000 of unrealized losses on 6,458 open contracts. Through the use of hedging, the Association has converted $456 million of fixed rate assets to variable rate assets and $137 million of short-term liabilities to fixed rate medium-term liabilities. The market appreciation on hedged assets and liabilities totaled approximately $89,438,000 which exceeded the deferred losses by $17,659,000.

As noted previously, futures hedging probably contributed significantly to the stability of City Federal's net interest margin. The Association's board of directors was well versed in the costs and benefits of hedging. In fact, the board had indicated its enthusiastic support of Nagle's initiatives in futures hedging. Nagle was aware, however, that boards of directors of other firms had not understood the nature of hedging with futures and were somewhat intolerant of losses on futures positions.

[3] Basis risk is the potential that movements in futures prices will differ from the movement in prices of the cash position being hedged.

EXHIBIT I City Federal Savings and Loan Association and Subsidiaries—Statements of Consolidated Financial Condition (Unaudited) (dollars in thousands)

	December 31, 1983	December 31, 1982	December 31, 1981
Assets			
Cash	$ 118,537	$ 97,110	$ 49,970
Investment securities	477,816	330,523	247,049
First mortgage loans—net	4,540,426	2,858,981	2,234,263
Consumer loans—net	888,749	748,006	545,073
Accrued interest receivable on loans	63,393	38,264	25,083
Real estate owned or under development—net	57,108	57,939	43,288
Federal Home Loan Bank stock, at cost	38,287	23,287	23,019
Premises and equipment—net	81,354	50,647	38,740
Goodwill	278,773	171,654	79,625
Deferred hedging losses	54,218	88,478	—
Other assets	133,261	89,460	60,914[a]
Total assets	$6,794,586	$4,554,349	$3,347,025
Liabilities and Stockholders' Equity			
Retail funds			
Retail deposits	$4,220,716	$2,630,675	$2,151,590
Retail repurchase agreements	129,118	258,950	42,585
Total retail funds	4,349,834	2,889,625	2,194,175
Wholesale funds			
Wholesale deposits, jumbo and broker CDs	558,118	496,167	251,362
Advances from Federal Home Loan Bank	696,094	427,069	416,697
Securities sold under agreements to repurchase	460,543	283,542	181,716
Other borrowings	99,998	63,747	59,271
Total wholesale funds	1,814,753	1,270,525	909,046
Loans in process	211,915	156,516	105,035
Advance payments by borrowers for taxes and insurance	39,094	20,383	12,064
Accounts payable and other liabilities	122,983	59,595	29,480
Total liabilities	6,538,579	4,396,644	3,249,800
Stockholders' equity			
Preferred stock, $2.20 cumulative conversion, $25 par value	$ 50,000	$ 50,000	—
$2.10 cumulative conversion, Series B, $25 par value	63,500	—	—
Common stock, $0.01 par value; issued and outstanding: 13,014,435 in 1983 and 6,394,164 in 1982	132	64	$ 30
Additional paid-in capital	27,869	28,812	28,759
Retained earnings	114,506	78,829	68,436
Total stockholders' equity	$ 256,007	$ 157,705	$ 97,225
Total liabilities and stockholders' equity	$6,794,586	$4,554,349	$3,347,025

[a] Included deferred hedges losses not separately identified.

EXHIBIT 2 **City Federal Savings and Loan Association and Subsidiaries—Statement of Consolidated Income (dollars in thousands except per share data)**

	Year Ended December 31,			
	1983	**1982**	**1981**	**1980**
Income				
Interest on mortgage loans	$ 417,647	$ 305,545	$ 179,511	$ 149,434
Interest on other loans	116,407	100,340	52,821	20,476
Interest and dividends on investments and deposits	37,052	58,572	57,534	27,105
Loan fees and service charges	81,323	56,093	30,402	15,443
Gain on sale of mortgage loans	36,354	27,209	4,001	4,348
Income (loss) from real estate operations	1,063	2,901	2,330	2,554
Other income	8,470	5,322	2,066	453
Total income	$ 698,316	$ 555,982	$ 328,665	$ 219,813
Expenses				
Interest on retail funds	$ 343,898	$ 292,774	$ 189,372	$ 133,444
Interest on wholesale funds	147,262	150,459	92,001	43,170
Interest adjustment-hedging activity	11,393	1,884	—	—
General and administrative expenses				
Compensation and employee benefits	71,015	43,140	26,500	20,248
Occupancy and office operations	37,172	23,562	12,272	9,052
Advertising	6,070	6,248	5,743	4,568
Other expenses	24,911	16,604	9,498	6,519
Provision for loan losses	1,209	1,255	44	25
Amortization of goodwill	8,364	4,755	—	—
Amortization of other intangible assets	2,499	2,735	—	—
Total expenses	$ 653,793	$ 543,416	$ 335,430	$ 217,026
Income (loss) before income taxes	44,523	12,566	(6,765)	2,787
Income taxes (benefit)	601	(623)	(5,400)	(562)
Net income (loss)	$ 42,554	$ 13,189	$ (1,365)	$ 3,349
Earnings (loss) per share				
Primary	$ 2.50	$ 0.98	$ (0.22)	$ 0.49[a]
Fully diluted	$ 2.11	$ 0.95	$ (0.22)	$ 0.49[a]
Average shares outstanding				
Primary	14,043,585	13,393,574	6,325,154	6,300,000
Fully diluted	20,187,374	13,943,628	6,325,154	6,300,000

[a] This amount represents earnings per share for the six months ended December 31, 1980, which is the period subsequent to conversion to a capital stock association.

EXHIBIT 3   City Federal Savings and Loan Association—Interest Rate Sensitivity

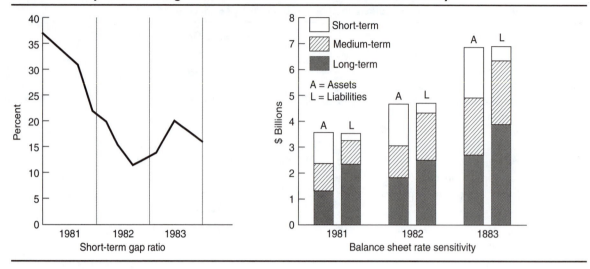

EXHIBIT 4 City Federal Savings and Loan Association—Balance Sheet Composition: Old, New, and Merged Portfolios

	Old Portfolio Remaining (Pre-1980)		Merger Portfolio		New Portfolio		Total 1983	
	Thousands of Dollars	Interest Percentage	Thousands of Dollars	Interest Percentage	Thousands of Dollars	Interest Percentage	Thousands of Dollars	Interest Percentage
Assets								
First mortgage loans	956,000	8.61	569,871	16.93	2,119,834	13.44	3,645,705	12.72
Consumer loans	29,782	14.40	19,951	15.44	859,016	14.74	908,749	14.74
Mortgage-backed securities	98,135	8.33	120,693	13.10	506,642	8.98	725,470	9.58
Investment securities	22,284	6.90	32,121	9.49	516,283	10.30	570,688	10.12
Total earning assets	1,106,201	8.71	742,636	15.95	4,001,775	12.75	5,850,612	12.39
Other assets	56,691	—	304,572	—	370,796	—	732,059	—
Total assets	1,162,892		1,047,208		4,372,571		6,582,671	
Liabilities								
Retail and wholesale funds	1,094,186	10.02	1,047,208	10.02	4,007,671	10.02	6,149,065	10.02
Total interest-bearing liabilities	1,094,186	10.02	1,047,208	10.02	4,007,671	10.02	6,149,065	10.02
Other liabilities	68,706	—	—		364,900	—	433,606	—
Total liabilities and equity	1,162,892		1,047,208		4,372,571		6,582,671	
Ratios								
Adjusted net interest yield spread	(1.21)		0.82		2.56		1.62	
Net interest income	(13,385)		6,090		102,275		94,780	
Percentage of earning asset portfolio	18.91%		12.69%		68.40%		100%	

655

EXHIBIT 5   City Federal Savings and Loan Association—The Investment-Funding Matrix Sample Date: November 18, 1981

Ranking Investments

	Overnight	30-Day	60-Day	90-Day	180-Day	360-Day	Medium-Term	Long-Term
1st choice	13.43 Fed funds	12.86 Fed funds	12.81 Fed funds	12.94 Fed funds	15.80 Alternate mortgage	12.71 GNMA cash and carry	19.77 Equity loan/GPM	18.53 Conventional mortgage
2nd choice	10.42 FHLB-DDA	12.68 Comm. paper	12.67 Comm. paper	12.60 Comm. paper	14.71 Alternate mortgage/GPM	12.24 FHLMC-360	19.08 Equity loan	16.31 FHA/VA
3rd choice		12.38 Bank. accept.	12.35 Bank. accept.	12.13 Bank. accept.	12.63 Fed funds	12.05 FNMA-360	18.99 Interest-only mortgage	15.81 Corporate bond

Ranking Sources of Funds

	Overnight	30-Day	60-Day	90-Day	180-Day	360-Day	Medium-Term	Long-Term
1st choice	12.60 Rev. repo	12.37 Broker reverse	12.37 Broker reverse	11.82 Retail reverse	12.44 Jumbo	10.52 All Savers Cert.	10.08 NOW	15.92 Private sale
2nd choice	13.50 Fed funds	12.69 Jumbo	12.64 Jumbo	12.37 Broker reverse	12.50 Broker reverse	14.38 FHLB advance	12.73 Hedged MMC (6-month)	17.42 FNMA/FHA auction
3rd choice	17.38 FHLB advance	13.07 Comm. paper	13.21 Comm. paper	12.75 Jumbo	12.83 Hedged jumbo (60-Day)		14.89 FHLB advance	17.53 FHLMC auction

Maximum investment yield

Minimum funds cost

X-axis: Overnight, 30 Day, 60 Day, 90 Day, 180 Day, 360 Day, Medium term, Long term

Y-axis: Percent (9–20)

SOURCE: Reprinted from Proceedings of the Seventh Annual Conference, December 10–11, 1981, Federal Home Loan Bank of San Francisco, California.

**EXHIBIT 6   City Federal Savings and Loan versus Industry: Net Interest Income
to Average Assets, 1979–1983**

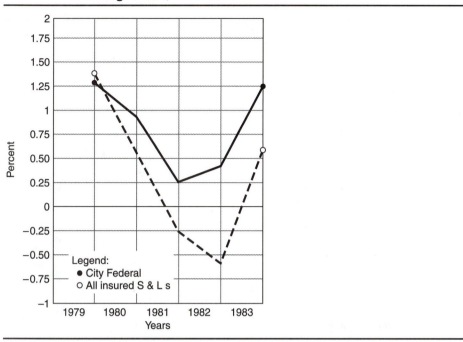

SOURCE: FHLBB Combined Financial Statements.

**EXHIBIT 7   City Federal Savings and Loan Association—Board of Directors
Authorization for Types and Limits of Futures Hedges**

The following types of hedges are specifically authorized:

1. Lock in the rate on six-month money market certificates for beyond the
   original six-months maturity and/or to shorten the effective life of assets.   Limit $200 million
2. Lock in the rate on jumbo CDs for 3 to 60 months.   Limit $150 million
3. Lock in the rate on 30-month money market certificates for beyond
   the original 30 months.   Limit $10 million
4. Lock in the rate on Federal funds for one month or longer.   Limit $5 million
5. Provide fixed-rate construction loans.   Limit $5 million
6. Hedge FHA/VA mortgage production.   Limit $5 million
7. Hedge the market value of fixed-payment mortgages, equity loans,
   and commercial loans.   Limit $650 million
8. Provide fixed-rate or capped-forward commitments for end-loan financing.   Limit $25 million
9. Lock in the rate on FHLB advances during the lag between
   commitment and takedown.   Limit $50 million

Position Limits

Treasury bill futures	$500 million
CD futures (or Treasury bill, if preferable)	$960 million
Treasury bond and note futures and GNMA futures and options	$710 million

EXHIBIT 8   City Federal Savings and Loan Association—Analysis of Net Interest Income, Including Adjustment Due to Hedging Activity (dollars in thousands)

	Nine Months Ended September 30	
	1983	1982
Interest income		
Interest on loans	$374,127	$294,355
Interest on investments	28,817	48,658
Total interest income	402,944	343,013
Interest expense		
Interest on retail funds	240,086	215,241
Interest on wholesale funds	104,697	113,665
Total interest expense	344,783	328,906
Net interest income	58,161	14,107
Interest adjustment hedging activity	(8,765)	(374)
Adjusted net interest income	$ 49,396	$ 13,733
Interest margin	2.51%	1.32%
Interest margin adjusted for the excess of interest-bearing liabilities over interest-earning assets and hedging activity	1.41%	0.49%
Income-earning assets as a percentage of interest-bearing liabilities at September 30	94.98%	92.94%

CASE 19

GRANTLAND NATIONAL BANK

INTRODUCTION

Early in 1991, Mr. Gregory McClure, the recently named president and chief executive officer of Grantland National Bank (GNB), was reviewing his strategic business plan for the years 1991 and 1992 that he had presented to the bank's parent holding company, Grantland Financial Corporation, in the fall of 1990. The plan approved by the holding company's top management projected earnings just over the breakeven level in 1991 and a return on assets (ROA) of 1 percent in the next year that would match the 1990 performance of the average bank in GNB's peer group.

The year just ended, 1990, had been particularly disappointing for GNB because of its sharply deteriorating earnings performance. As shown in the following table, over the last three years, GNB's ROA and return on equity (ROE) measures had declined, while the same profitability measures for the average bank in GNB's peer group had improved.

	1988		1989		1990	
	ROA	ROE	ROA	ROE	ROA	ROE
GNB	1.34%	17.10%	1.09%	14.50%	(0.32%)	(5.00%)
Peer group	0.64%	8.72%	0.81%	10.77%	1.05%	13.96%

CAUSES OF THE EARNINGS DECLINE

The major cause of the earnings plunge was the increase in the loan loss provision, which rose from $2,123,000 in 1989 to $6,647,000 in 1990, as shown in Exhibit 6. After adjustments for loans and leases written off as losses and recoveries, the reserve for loan and lease losses rose from $1,955,000 in 1989 to $3,649,000 in 1990. Despite the increase, the loss reserve fell from about 57 percent of 90-days-and-over past-due and noncurrent loans and leases in 1989 to 26 percent in 1990.

There were several reasons for the substantial increase in the loss provision and loss reserve in 1990. First, the reserve for loan and lease losses had probably been too low in 1989. GNB had believed that its conservative lending policies, high-collateral requirements, and credit review functions would keep the quality of its loans, nearly all of which were made in the local communities within its market area, well above that of most of its peers. Few of the bank's loans were related to agriculture, Third World borrowers, energy, highly leveraged transactions, or commercial real estate, which had led to the severe credit problems of many banks. Many of GNB's loans classified as "other real estate loans" were credits to small business firms based primarily on cash flows or current asset values, with the real estate collateral as a secondary source of repayment. Thus, although many banks in the country were beset with substantial loan delinquencies, renegotiations, and charge-offs, GNB's management was confident that it was correctly reporting only a relatively small volume of credit problems. Mr. McClure, who became GNB's chief executive officer in the summer of 1990, had concluded that GNB's credit underwriting had avoided the adverse effects from the slower economic activity in the bank's market area.

A second reason for the large loss provision in 1990 was the increased scrutiny and critical evaluation of the loan portfolio by the bank's examiners. Because many banks had severe lending problems throughout the country, Mr. McClure believed that the recent examination of the loan portfolio was far harsher than previous examinations. He also thought that GNB would benefit in future years from the examiners' and the bank's own tougher evaluation of loan credit quality with more loss recoveries. But, Mr. McClure wondered, who would provide the financing for the business turnaround needed to get GNB's market area growing again?

The third reason was a decision made by GNB's parent, Grantland Financial Corporation. When the examiners increased the volume of adversely classified loans and leases, which required the bank to raise the loan loss provision and make the loan loss reserve larger, Grantland Financial's senior management decided to "bite as much of the bullet" as it could in 1990 rather than spread the loan problems over several years.

THE BANK

GNB was the smallest of the 11 bank affiliates of Grantland Financial Corporation, a multibank holding company whose banks operated in four midwestern states. At the end of 1990, GNB had total resources of $417 million and served its two-county market area with 17 offices and a staff of 235 full-time equivalent officers and employees (see Exhibit 1).

GNB's business strategy was summarized in its published mission statement: "Grantland National Bank is a community-oriented bank whose skilled and friendly professional people are dedicated to serving the financial needs of its customers today and in the future."

One of GNB's officers observed that the bank's key distinction was how it treated its customers, not how it charged them. By developing a strong interest in community affairs through active participation in many civic organizations and clubs, and by taking a leadership role in programs benefiting youth, GNB paid serious attention to improving its communities.

The attitude of treating customers as friends and of involving the bank deeply in community affairs was embraced by the entire staff. This philosophy was in sharp contrast to the transaction-oriented, highly automated, and more impersonal institutional style of more aggressive banks. The key questions in developing account relationships were: Does the potential customer have a strong reason to want to bank at GNB? Can the bank develop a long-term relationship with the customer? Customer service, not pricing, was viewed as the key to maintaining long-term banking customer relationships. As a consequence, GNB did not usually pursue customers who were overly sensitive to pricing.

The bank's loan committee was convened weekly, and even more frequently if necessary, to accommodate customers and to consider loans in excess of individual officers' loan limits. Lending authorities were based on each officer's experience and seniority, and ranged from $150,000 on a secured basis and $50,000 unsecured for senior loan officers to $25,000 secured and $5,000 unsecured for junior officers. For loans that were presented to the loan committee, a unanimous vote was required to approve the credit.

GNB's commercial business was primarily small, family-owned and -operated firms, a market niche ignored by many competitors. The bank's officer calling program was directed at small industrial companies operating within its market area with annual sales between $5 million and $15 million. Selected businesses with sales below $5 million were also targeted. The bank provided financing primarily for working capital purposes. Potential losses seemed reasonably anticipated, but new loans of acceptable quality were proving increasingly hard to find.

Although GNB showed a concentration of real estate loans, problems had been avoided until 1990 by the absence of larger development and commercial real estate loans. As already noted, most of the bank's "other real estate loans" were related to credits to small operating companies, with the real estate collateral serving as a secondary source of repayment.

MANAGEMENT ISSUES

Mr. McClure realized that one of the issues central to GNB's successful turnaround in 1991 would be the attitude of the bank's officers and employees in dealing with an operating loss for the first time in the bank's recent history. Facing a difficult economic situation both locally and nationally presented an additional challenge. The bank's low staff turnover rate and the continuity of senior management were essential ingredients for achieving forecasted goals. To replace and retrain personnel was a time-consuming but relatively easy task. However, to find employees with the abilities and personalities to embrace GNB's philosophy of dedication to customers and communities served was much more difficult.

As he looked at 1991 and beyond, Mr. McClure hoped for improvements in the bank's net interest margin, which, as a percentage of average total assets, had declined from 4.57 percent in 1989 to 3.84 percent in 1990. He pondered how to achieve this improvement. He knew that loan quality must

be kept high so that the provision for loan losses would not require an increase. He was also concerned that the bank not take excessive interest rate or liquidity risks. Mr. McClure also wondered how GNB could increase noninterest or fee-based income while controlling noninterest expense.

Many courses of action were limited by existing requirements. For example, Mr. McClure estimated that the provision for loan and lease losses would probably have to be close to $4 million in 1991 to keep the examiners happy. Growth was also constrained by a relatively low-capital position at the beginning of 1991. Furthermore, GNB would have to pay its holding company $900,000 in cash dividends so that Grantland Financial Corporation could meet its debt repayments. Mr. McClure had studied the risk-based capital rules coming in 1992 so that GNB would also meet these guidelines.

As he looked out of his third-floor window on a gray winter's day early in 1991, Mr. McClure wondered if GNB could achieve its performance targets of a slight profit in 1991 and an ROA of about 1 percent in 1992 within these constraints without taking excessive risks.

To assist Mr. McClure in his evaluation of GNB's recent performance and profit goals for the next two years, Ms. Helen Rajak, senior vice-president and chief financial officer, prepared Exhibits 1 through 7. These statements contain balance sheet and income statement data for the bank and its peer group of banks, with total assets of $300 to $500 million and three or more banking offices.

QUESTIONS

1. Ignore the year 1990 just ended. Consider the two-year period 1988–1989, when the earnings performance of GNB was significantly better than that of the average peer group bank, as shown by the ROA and ROE measures.
   a. Explain how GNB achieved its superior earnings performance.
   b. Compare GNB's risk exposure with that of the average peer group bank. Evaluate the bank's relative credit risk, interest rate risk, liquidity risk, and capital-risk exposures.
   c. Summarize GNB's relative strengths and weaknesses as of the end of 1989.

2. Consider the year 1990.
   a. How do you explain the loss suffered by GNB?

b. Evaluate the risk exposure of GNB at the end of the year compared with the risk position of the average peer group bank.

c. What were the strengths and weaknesses of GNB at the end of 1990?

3. Under the risk-based capital guidelines, as of the end of 1990, GNB's risk-adjusted assets (in millions of dollars) were as follows:

Risk Category	Risk Weight	Total Assets	Risk-Adjusted Assets
Category 1	0%	$102.9	$ 0.0
Category 2	20%	78.4	15.7
Category 3	50%	38.2	19.1
Category 4	100%	200.9	200.9
Off-balance sheet	Varies	0.0	6.1
Totals		$420.4	$241.8

Under the risk-based capital rules, half of total required capital (known as *Tier I capital*) must be composed of common stockholders' equity and noncumulative perpetual preferred stock less goodwill. The other half (known as *Tier II capital*) may include subordinated debt, limited-life preferred stock, and loan loss reserves (up to 1.50 percent of risk-adjusted assets at the end of 1990 and 1.25 percent at the end of 1992). Total Tier II capital cannot exceed total Tier I capital.

As of year-end 1990, banks were required to comply with a minimum ratio of capital to risk-adjusted assets of 7.25 percent (3.625 percent of which had to be Tier I). When the capital rules became fully effective at the end of 1992, the minimum required capital ratio would be 8 percent (4 percent for Tier I capital).

Evaluate GNB's position against the risk-based capital guidelines.

4. GNB's profit targets are to operate just over the breakeven level in 1991 and to earn an ROA of about 1 percent in 1992. Are these goals attainable? Recommend steps that the bank should take to restore its profitability.

EXHIBIT I   Grantland National Bank—Balance Sheet as of December 31 (dollars in thousands)

	1990	1989	1988
Noninterest cash and due from banks	$ 22,022	$ 14,282	$ 14,796
Money market investments			
Interest-bearing bank balances	31,400	32,800	40,600
Federal funds sold	16,800	14,820	11,000
Total money market investments	48,200	47,620	51,600
Investment securities			
U.S. Treasury and agency securities	86,912	54,482	44,516
State and local government securities	33,496	34,498	33,026
All other securities	1,228	1,600	1,472
Total investment securities	121,636	90,580	79,014
Loans and leases			
Commercial and industrial	78,848	99,638	58,390
Real estate loans	96,958	91,864	94,432
Consumer loans	28,042	20,220	20,456
All other loans and leases	3,479	3,084	2,741
Total loans and leases	207,327	214,806	176,019
Less reserve for loan and lease losses	3,649	1,955	1,514
Net loans and leases	203,678	212,851	174,505
Bank premises and equipment, net	13,370	12,610	11,228
Other assets	7,904	6,836	6,122
Total assets	416,810	384,779	337,265
Total earning assets	$377,163	$353,006	$306,633
Noninterest-bearing demand deposits	$ 65,536	$ 53,604	$ 51,498
Interest bearing deposits			
Transactions accounts	36,544	33,352	29,748
Money market deposit accounts	31,950	38,100	32,588
Regular savings	34,344	32,548	30,232
Time deposits under $100,000	144,856	122,976	105,106
Time deposits $100,000 and over	70,740	70,038	53,336
Total interest-bearing deposits	318,434	297,014	251,010
Total deposit liabilities	383,970	350,618	302,508
Short-term borrowings	3,118	3,345	5,200
Other liabilities	4,228	3,112	3,104
Total liabilities	391,376	357,075	310,812
Shareholders' equity	25,434	27,704	26,453
Total liabilities and shareholders' equity	$416,810	$384,779	$337,265

EXHIBIT 2   Grantland National Bank—Year-End Loan and Investment Portfolios

	1990		1989		1988	
	GNB	**Peers**	**GNB**	**Peers**	**GNB**	**Peers**
Loan Mix as a Percent of Total Loans						
Commercial and industrial	39.05	27.28	34.36	29.39	28.34	30.41
Real estate						
Construction and development	5.44	4.84	6.52	4.15	7.32	5.65
1–4-family residential	13.35	25.45	17.40	24.04	19.98	22.03
Home equity	4.14	5.03	3.10	3.49	1.26	2.21
Other real estate	22.93	15.84	24.36	17.66	27.88	17.61
Total real estate	45.86	51.16	51.38	49.34	56.44	47.56
Loans to individuals	13.24	19.25	12.63	18.61	13.46	19.51
All other loans and leases	1.85	2.31	1.63	2.66	1.76	2.52
Total loans and leases	100.00	100.00	100.00	100.00	100.00	100.00
Investment as a Percent of Total Investments						
U.S. Treasuries and federal agencies	70.34	69.38	59.73	68.88	56.54	63.09
State and local government securities	27.55	21.68	38.11	22.58	41.07	29.46
Other securities	2.11	8.94	2.16	8.54	2.39	7.45
Total investment securities	100.00	100.00	100.00	100.00	100.00	100.00
Investment Maturities as a Percent of Total Investments						
Under one year	31.27	34.87	33.75	33.78	37.49	28.42
One to five years	41.47	39.42	28.93	43.51	31.93	42.25
Over five years	27.26	25.71	37.32	22.71	30.58	29.33
Total investment securities	100.00	100.00	100.00	100.00	100.00	100.00

EXHIBIT 3   Grantland National Bank—Average Balance Sheet (dollars in thousands)

	1990	1989	1988
Noninterest cash and due from banks	$ 18,188	$ 12,879	$ 12,508
Money market investments			
Interest-bearing bank balances	29,239	34,531	51,289
Federal funds sold	14,354	14,010	11,766
Total money market investments	43,593	48,541	63,055
Investment securities			
U.S. Treasury and agency securities	78,827	49,744	36,653
State and local government securities	30,870	31,736	26,627
All other securities	2,365	1,804	1,547
Total investment securities	112,062	83,284	64,827
Loans and leases			
Commercial and industrial	84,292	66,229	47,322
Real estate loans	99,012	99,035	94,228
Consumer loans	28,586	24,344	22,469
All other loans and leases	3,996	3,142	2,934
Total loans and leases	215,886	192,750	166,953
Less reserve for loan and lease losses	2,977	1,804	1,547
Net loans and leases	212,909	190,946	165,406
Bank premises and equipment, net	13,457	11,817	10,864
Other assets	7,585	6,333	5,706
Total assets	$407,794	$353,800	$322,366
Total earning assets	$371,541	$324,575	$294,835
Noninterest-bearing demand deposits	$ 60,598	$ 49,885	$ 46,808
Interest-bearing deposits			
Transactions accounts	34,581	30,356	28,658
Money market deposit accounts	33,521	34,496	37,298
Regular savings	34,459	32,019	29,077
Time deposits under $100,000	138,691	113,994	98,677
Time deposits $100,000 and over	72,260	60,394	50,450
Interest-bearing deposits	313,512	271,259	244,160
Total deposit liabilities	374,110	321,144	290,968
Short-term borrowings	3,181	2,830	2,934
Other liabilities	4,119	3,397	3,191
Total liabilities	381,410	327,371	297,093
Shareholders' equity	26,384	26,429	25,273
Total liabilities and shareholders' equity	$407,794	$353,800	$322,366

EXHIBIT 4 Grantland National Bank—Asset and Liability Distribution as a Percentage of Average Total Assets

	1990		1989		1988	
	Grantland	Peers	Grantland	Peers	Grantland	Peers
Noninterest cash and due from banks	4.46	5.47	3.64	5.37	3.88	5.65
Money market investments						
Interest bearing bank balances	7.17	3.01	9.76	2.76	15.91	3.87
Federal funds sold	3.52	4.49	3.96	6.29	3.65	8.16
Total money market investments	10.69	7.50	13.72	9.05	19.56	12.03
Investment securities						
U.S. Treasury and agency securities	19.33	16.45	14.06	17.11	11.37	14.22
State and local government securities	7.57	5.14	8.97	5.61	8.26	6.64
All other securities	0.58	2.12	0.51	2.12	0.48	1.68
Total investment securities	27.48	23.71	23.54	24.84	20.11	22.54
Loans and leases						
Commercial and industrial	20.67	16.39	18.72	16.91	14.68	17.16
Real estate loans						
Construction and development	2.88	2.91	3.55	2.39	3.79	3.19
One- to four-family residential	7.07	15.29	9.48	13.83	10.35	12.43
Home equity	2.19	3.02	1.69	2.01	0.65	1.24
Other real estate	12.14	9.52	13.27	10.16	14.44	9.97
Total real estate	24.28	30.74	27.99	28.39	29.23	26.83
Consumer loans	7.01	11.57	6.88	10.71	6.97	11.01
Other loans and leases	0.98	1.39	0.89	1.53	0.91	1.42

EXHIBIT 4 *(Continued)*

	1990		1989		1988	
	Grantland	Peers	Grantland	Peers	Grantland	Peers
Total loans and leases	52.94	60.09	54.48	57.54	51.79	56.42
Less loan and lease loss reserves	0.73	0.81	0.51	0.82	0.48	0.76
Net loans and leases	52.21	59.28	53.97	56.72	51.31	55.66
Bank premises and equipment, net	3.29	2.01	3.34	1.88	3.37	1.87
Other assets	1.86	2.03	1.79	2.14	1.77	2.25
Total assets	100.00	100.00	100.00	100.00	100.00	100.00
Total earning assets	91.11	91.30	91.74	91.43	91.46	90.99
Noninterest-bearing demand deposits	14.86	15.27	14.10	15.47	14.52	15.70
Interest-bearing deposits						
Transactions accounts	8.48	9.62	8.58	8.96	8.89	8.38
Money market deposit accounts	8.22	13.38	9.75	14.99	11.57	15.84
Regular savings	8.45	9.46	9.05	8.79	9.02	8.10
Time deposits under $100,000	34.01	29.41	32.22	24.74	30.61	24.68
Time deposits $100,000 and over	17.72	12.48	17.07	16.94	15.65	17.96
Total interest-bearing deposits	76.88	74.35	76.67	74.42	75.74	74.96
Total deposit liabilities	91.74	89.62	90.77	89.89	90.26	90.66
Short-term borrowings	0.78	1.76	0.80	1.57	0.91	1.55
Other liabilities	1.01	1.10	0.96	1.02	0.99	1.05
Total liabilities	93.53	92.48	92.53	92.48	92.16	92.66
Shareholders' equity	6.47	7.52	7.47	7.52	7.84	7.34
Total liabilities and equity capital	100.00	100.00	100.00	100.00	100.00	100.00
Average total assets ($ in thousands)	407,794		353,800		322,366	

EXHIBIT 5 Grantland National Bank—Income Statement, Taxable-Equivalent Basis, Percentage of Average Total Assets (dollars in thousands)

	1990			1989			1988		
	Grantland		Peers	Grantland		Peers	Grantland		Peers
	$	%	%	$	%	%	$	%	%
Interest income									
Loans and leases	24,913	6.11	7.12	22,956	6.49	6.10	19,330	6.00	5.81
Investment securities	10,736	2.64	2.34	7,936	2.24	2.28	6,793	2.11	2.20
Interest-bearing bank balances	2,254	0.55	0.25	2,569	0.73	0.21	3,606	1.12	0.28
Federal funds sold	1,062	0.26	0.35	1,020	0.29	0.47	824	0.25	0.58
Total interest income	38,965	9.56	10.06	34,481	9.75	9.06	30,553	9.48	8.87
Interest expense									
Interest on deposits	23,043	5.65	5.25	18,091	5.12	4.77	15,591	4.84	4.70
Interest on short-term borrowings	264	0.07	0.14	211	0.06	0.11	192	0.06	0.10
Total interest expense	23,307	5.72	5.39	18,302	5.18	4.88	15,783	4.90	4.80
Net interest margin	15,658	3.84	4.67	16,179	4.57	4.18	14,770	4.58	4.07
Provision for loan and lease losses	6,647	1.63	0.37	2,123	0.60	0.53	967	0.30	0.70
Adjusted net interest margin	9,011	2.21	4.30	14,056	3.97	3.65	13,803	4.28	3.37
Noninterest income	3,874	0.95	0.87	3,290	0.93	0.85	2,901	0.90	0.82
Noninterest expense									
Personnel	6,729	1.65	1.69	5,661	1.60	1.51	4,997	1.55	1.47
Occupancy and equipment	1,427	0.35	0.57	920	0.26	0.46	774	0.24	0.45
Other noninterest expense	6,729	1.65	1.32	4,918	1.39	1.30	4,384	1.36	1.30
Total noninterest expense	14,885	3.65	3.58	11,499	3.25	3.27	10,155	3.15	3.22
Net overhead burden	11,011	2.70	2.71	8,209	2.32	2.42	7,254	2.25	2.40
Income before income taxes	(2,000)	(0.49)	1.59	5,847	1.65	1.23	6,549	2.03	0.97
Applicable income taxes	(680)	(0.17)	0.54	1,988	0.56	0.42	2,227	0.69	0.33
Net income	(1,320)	(0.32)	1.05	3,859	1.09	0.81	4,322	1.34	0.64
Cash dividends	950			2,608			3,240		

EXHIBIT 6   **Grantland National Bank—Analysis of Loan and Lease Loss Reserve and Problem Loans (dollars in thousands)**

	1990	1989	1988	1987	1986
Balance, beginning of the year	1,955	1,514	1,617	1,385	1,716
Gross loan and lease losses	5,409	2,013	1,224	974	1,741
Recoveries	456	331	154	347	453
Net loan and lease losses	4,953	1,682	1,070	627	1,288
Provision for loan and lease losses	6,647	2,123	967	859	957
Balance, end of the year	3,649	1,955	1,514	1,617	1,385
Problem loans					
Past due loans 30–89 days	7,548	11,665	4,127	4,050	3,196
Past due loans 90 days and over	439	690	1,005	708	710
Nonaccrual loans and leases	13,493	2,758	289	168	1,224
Renegotiated	1,431	1,230	0	0	0

EXHIBIT 7 Grantland National Bank—Interest Rate Sensitivity Report
Maturity and Repricing Distribution of Earning Assets and Interest-Paying Liabilities
Cumulative Amount and as a Percent of Assets, December 31, 1990 (dollars in thousands)

	Repriced Within 3 Months			Repriced Within 12 Months		
	Grantland National		Peers	Grantland National		Peers
	$	%	%	$	%	%
Earning assets						
Money market investments	26,220	6.29	6.16	48,200	11.56	8.18
Investment securities	11,264	2.70	2.48	38,036	9.13	8.27
Loans and leases	78,841	18.92	27.61	101,730	24.41	36.04
Total earning assets	116,325	27.91	36.25	187,966	45.10	52.49
Interest-paying liabilities						
Transactions accounts	36,544	8.77	9.62	36,544	8.77	9.62
Money market deposit accounts	31,950	7.67	13.38	31,950	7.67	13.38
Regular savings			0.15	3,435	0.82	0.95
Time deposits under $100,000	50,700	12.16	10.29	108,642	26.07	22.06
Time depsits $100,000 and over	45,981	11.03	7.49	63,666	15.27	10.61
Short-term borrowings	3,118	0.75	1.80	3,118	0.75	1.80
Total interest-paying liabilities	168,293	40.38	42.73	247,355	59.35	58.42
Gap (Earning assets − Interest-paying liabilities)	(51,968)	(12.47)	(6.48)	(59,389)	(14.25)	(5.93)

INDEX

A

Ability risk, 91
Acceptable collateral, and lending policies, 400
Acceptance participations, as off-balance sheet information, 49
Accounting classification, and security portfolio management, 296–298
Accounts receivable, as collateral, 435–436
Accounts receivable financing, 437, 438
Accrual accounting, converting to cash basis, 467–471
Acquisitions, *see* Mergers and acquisitions
Activity ratios, 455
   defined, 456–457
Actuarial method, for computing prepayment charges, 482
Add-on rates, 480
Adjustable-rate mortgage backed securities, 312
Adjustable-rate mortgages, 497–499
Adjustable-rate preferred stocks, 285, 345
Affirmative covenants, 423
Africa, lending to, 628
After tax income, as income statement line item, 43
Age, and credit scoring systems, 488
Agency obligations, 282
Agreement corporations, 629. *See also* Edge Act Corporations
Agricultural loans, 443–446
   farm credit evaluation, 443–445
   farm loan competition, 445–446
Almanac of Business and Industrial Financial Ratios, 458
Alternative investments, *see* Nontraditional investments
American Banker, 52, 53
American Bankers Association, 52, 53
American Express, 19
American options, 560
Annual fees, credit cards, 492, 493
Annual SEC filing Form 10-K, 53
Annual percentage rate, and Truth in Lending Act, 504–505
Anticipatory hedging, 544–545
Applicable income taxes, as income statement line item, 43
Appraisals, and lending policies, 400

Arbitrage, 134, 148, 543–544
   of international interest rates, 619–620
   pure, 542
   riskless, 542
Arbitrage-free interest rate trees, 569–570
Arbitrage-free markets, 542
Arbitrageurs, 134
ARMs (adjustable rate mortgages), 497–499
ARM securities, 312
Asia, lending to, 628
Aspict Bankshares Corporation: case study, 379–386
Asset-based lending, 434–435
Asset composition, 36, 77, 84
Asset growth, capital adequacy for, 339–343
Asset hedges, 544
Asset-liability management, *see also* Interest rate risk
   duration concept for, 111–115
   convexity and higher order duration, 118–119, 126–128
   multipayment assets, 112–113
   single-payment assets, 111–112
   duration gap model, 115–118
   earnings simulation, 138–141
   gap management for, 134–144
   mismatch risk, 108
Asset priority model, 274–275
Asset quality risk, *see* Credit risk
Assets
   as balance sheet line items, 37
   of commercial banks, 9
   mark to market value, 111
   rate sensitivity of, 228–230
   return required, 228
   utilization ratio, 60, 61, 62, 63, 75, 78
Asset/Liability committees, 395–396
Asymmetric payoffs, 561
Attracting deposit funding, 235–240
Attracting nondeposit funding, 240
Automated teller machines (ATMs), 28, 478
   for attracting deposits, 237, 241
Automobile loans, 477–478. *See also* Consumer lending
Available-for-sale securities, 37, 281, 297–298
Average collection period ratio, 457

B

Balance sheet control covenants, 424
Balance sheets, 35–41
   assets line items, 37–39
   for credit investigations, 459–464
   liabilities line items, 39–41
   market value, 110–111
   maturity mismatching, 107–111
Bank Administration Institute, 52, 53
Bank discount rate, 480
Bank drafts, in international lending, 625
Banker's acceptances, 215, 280, 625
Banker's banks, 33
Bankers Trust, 451
Bank examination, 25–26
   for loan quality, 412–414
Bank failures, 10–12, 15–19, 27
   credit risk and, 389, 390, 391. *See also* loan quality
Bank holding companies, 29–31
   permissible/nonpermissible activities, 30
Bank Holding Company Act of 1956, 21, 22
Banking, *see also* Banks
   changing environment of, 21–22
   combinations, 27
   competition with brokerage firms, 14, 416–417
   computer's role in, 13–14
   emphasis on safety, 10–12
   financial management in a foreign environment, 622–624
   legislation, 22–23. *See also* Regulatory structure: specific acts affecting banking
   new charters, 27
   new powers and technologies, 21–22
   number of, 9
   problems, 16–19
   regulations, *see* Regulatory structure
   resulting regulations, 23–25
   role in U.S. economy, 3–6
   structure, 26–33
   trends in, 28–29
   unit *vs.* branch, 27–29
Banking centers, lending to, 628
Bank Insurance Fund (BIF), 19

Bankruptcy code
abuses of, 502–503
Chapter 8, 501
Chapter 12, 502
Chapter 13, 501–502
reform, 501–502
''substantial abuse'' test, 502
Bankruptcy Reform Act of 1978, 501, 502
Banks, *see* Banking
Barbell maturity portfolio distribution, 291–293
Basic loan agreement, 402
Basis risk, 137
of ARM securities, 312
and hedging, 546, 555
Basis swaps, 592–594
Benchmark interest rates, 142–144
Bergner Construction Company: case study, 517–522
Binomial model, of interest rate changes, 566–568
Black-Scholes option pricing model, 586–587
Bonds, *see also* specific types of Bonds
interest rate sensitivity, 105–107
value of, 104–105
vs. term loans, 436
Bond swapping, 294–296
Bootstrapping, 153
Borrowed funds, types of, 214–215
Borrowing base formulas, 435
Borrowing from Federal Reserve, 215
Branch banks, *vs.* unit banks, 27–29
Bridge loans, 434
Brokerage firms, competition with commercial banks, 14, 416–417
Broker call loans, 280–281
Brokered deposits, 16, 213–214
Bullet loans, 409
Burden risk, 92
Business finance, applying to banking, 58–63
Business Information Report, 422
Business Periodical Index, 422

C

Calbank Leasing Corporation: case study, 522–529
Call loans, 280–281
Call money, 623
Call option, 561. *see also* Options
Capital acquisition, 343–354. *see also*
Capital management; Funding
common stock, 352–354
convertible debt, 345, 350–352
external equity/senior capital choice, 343–347

senior capital, 347–352
financial effects of, 347–350
newer forms of, 350–352
Capital adequacy, 322–331
functions of capital, 323–324
leverage and returns, 324–327
ratios, 83
regulatory criteria, 327–331
risk-based capital ratios, 328–331
for sustainable internal growth, 339–343
calculating, 341–342
Capital allocation, 332–334
Capital debentures, 345
Capitalization value, 110
Capital management, 331–339
capital allocation, 332–334
capital required, 334–335
by dividend policy, 336–337
risk based capital ratios for, 328–331
Capital notes, 345
Capital planning, role in financial planning, 356–359
analyzing a bank's performance, 356
determining capital needs, 359
predicting selected variables, 356–358
sensitivity analysis, 358–359
Capital ratios, 83
Capital risk, *see* Leverage risk
Cap options, 474
for ARMs, 499
Capital to risk assets ratio, 83
CARDs (certificates for amortizing revolving debt), 447–449
CARs (certificates of automobile receivables), 447–449
Case studies:
Aspict Bankshares Corporation, 379–386
Bergner Construction Company, 517–522
Calbank Leasing Corporation, 522–529
City Federal Savings and Loan Association, 649–658
Edward Edwards Company (A), 529–532
Edward Edwards Company (B), 633–635
First National Bank of Park Cities, 157–173
Global Machinery and Metals Company, Inc., 513–517
Grantland National Bank, 658–669
Hillside Bancorp (A), 368–375
Hillside Bancorp (B), 376–378
Keycorp, 635–640
Lincoln National Bank, 173–183
Lobo Mill Products Company, 507–509
Norwest Corporation, 200–205

Peralta National Bank, 191–199
Quaker National Bank, 183–191
Questor, Inc., 509–513
Region Financial Corporation, 641–648
Shawnee National Bank, 360–367
Cash and due from institutions, as balance sheet line item, 37
Cash basis accounting, 467–471
Cash flow analysis, for credit analysis, 485–486
Cash flow control covenants, 424
Cash flow from operations, 467–471
Cash items in process of collection, 37
managing, 248
Cash Management Account (CMA), 14
Cash position, 360
Cash-to-cash cycle, 457–458
Certificates for amortizing revolving debt (CARDs), 447–449
Certificates of automobile receivables (CARs), 447–449
Certificates of deposit (CDs),
as balance sheet line item, 40
large CDs, 213, 214, 238–239
security interests in, 404
variable-rate, 232
Chapter 8 (bankruptcy code), 501
Chapter 12 (bankruptcy code), 502
Chapter 13 (bankruptcy code), 501–502
Checking overdraft lines, 483
Chicago Mercantile Exchange (CME), 556
Citi Credit Card Trust (Citibank), 448
City Federal Savings and Loan Association: case study, 649–658
Clean-up rules, 453
Co-agents, 439
Code of Ethics for the Exchange of Credit Information (Robert Morris Associates), 409
Collars, 575
Collateral, 421. *see also* Security interests
commercial loans:
bridge loans, 434
revolving credit loans, 435–436
short-term loans, 433–434
term loans, 437
market value decrease of, 408
Collateral and note department, 395
Collateralized mortgage obligations (CMOs), 285, 313
IO/PO, 285, 316
PACs, 285, 316
REMICs, 313
SMBSs, 313, 316
STRIPS, 285
TACs, 316
Tranches, 313

Co-makers, 421, 437

Commercial banks, *see* Banking

Commercial lending, *see also* Financial analysis; Working capital analysis
commitment fees, 428
compensating balances, 427–428
competition for business loans, 416–417
credit analysis, 418–421
credit investigation, 421–423, 455–472
loan covenants, 423–424
affirmative vs. negative, 423
loan types:
bridge loans, 434
revolving credit loans, 434–436
short-term loans, 432–434
term loans, 436–437
nonresidential mortgages, 499
pricing:
basic concepts, 424–429
commitment fees, 428
compensating balances, 427–428
cost accounting systems, 426
noninterest aspects of, 427, 428–429
spread pricing model, 425–426
security interests, *see* Security interests

Commercial loan sales, 449–450
stripping, 449–450

Commercial paper, 280
competition with commercial banks, 416–417

Commitment fees, in commercial lending, 428

Commitments, as off-balance sheet information, 48–49

Commodity Credit Corporation (CCC), 446

Commodity options, 580–582

Common equity capital, 343–347

Common shares, number of, as supplementary information, 45

Common size ratios, 455

Common stock, 40, 345
for capital acquisition, 352–354
market price: strategies for increasing, 352–353
vs. senior capital, 347–350

Community Reinvestment Act, 18

Compensating balances, in commercial lending, 427–428

Compensation risk, 91

Competitive Equality Banking Act, 19

Competitiveness, of banks in commercial lending, 416–417

Competitive risk, 91

Compliance officers, 503

Composition of assets, 36, 77, 84

Composition of liabilities, 36, 77, 84, 85

Comptroller of the Currency, 23
capital notes and long-term debentures, 343
and capital requirements, 328
and loan policies, 397–398
proposed risk-based capital ratios, 328–331

Computers, role in banking trends, 13–14

Concentration risk, 393, 432

Conflict of interest, and lending, 409

Consortium banks, 630

Constant payment rate (CPR), 307, 308, 311–312

Construction loans, 499–500
risks, 500

Consumer lending, *see also* specific types of Consumer credit
and bankruptcy code, 500–501
automobile lending, 477–478
bank credit cards, 491–493
growth of, 491–492
issues in pricing, 492–493
basic types, 483
typical interest rates, 480
cash flow and statement analysis, 485–486
commercial bank consumer credit, 476–477
credit analysis, 482–490
empirical credit analysis, 487–490
equal credit opportunity, 484–485
information gathering, 483–484
judgmental credit analysis, 486–487, 489–490
credit scoring systems, 487–489
debit cards, 493–494
depository *vs.* nondepository institutions, 477
growth relative to personal income, 475
history of, 475–476
home equity credit, 478–479
interest charge considerations,
add-on rates, 480
bank discount rate, 480
prepayment penalties, 481–482
state usury ceilings, 481
variable-rate loans, 481
mobile home financing, 479
real estate loans, 494–500
regulations, 503–505
reporting credit decisions, 490–491
revolving credit, 478
securitization, 479–480. *See also* Securitization

Consumer loan sales, 447–449

Continental Illinois National Bank, 17–18

Contingent claims,
defined, 575
as off-balance sheet information, 48–49
option pricing, *see* Option pricing

Contingent claims products, 559

Contingent liquidity needs, 261

Continuing guarantees, 403

Convertible debentures, 346

Convertible debt, 345
advantages/disadvantages, 350–352
calling, 351

Convertible preferred stock, 345

Convertible securities, 351–352

Convexity, 118–119, 126–128
and the swap rate, 604–605

Cook, Scott, 29

Core deposits to assets ratio, 80

Corporate bonds, 284
with put options, 286
zero coupon, 285–286

Corporate borrowing resolution, 402

Corporate demand deposits, attracting, 236–237

Correlated interest rate risk, 140

Correlation coefficient, 138

Correspondent banking, 32–33

Correspondent debt, 346

Correspondent deposits, 214
attracting, 240

Cost accounting, for bank services, 426

Cost of funds, *see* Funding, cost measures

Cost rate on interest bearing deposits, 79

Cost rate on total funds, 79

Country risk, 627

Coupon effect, 114–115

Credit analysis, agricultural loans, 443–445

Credit analysis, commercial loans,
bridge loans, 434
character/soundness of borrower, 419–420
migration analysis, 431
use of loan funds, 420
primary repayment source, 420
revolving credit loans, 435
risk rating and monitoring, 429–431
risk rating systems, 429
secondary repayment sources, 421
short-term loans, 433
term loans, 436
watch list, 429–430

Credit analysis, consumer loans,
  cash flow analysis, 485–486
  equal credit opportunity, 484–485
  evaluation errors, 486
  evaluation systems,
    empirical credit analysis, 487–490
    judgmental credit analysis, 486–487,
      489–490
  information gathering, 483–484
  investigation and verification, 484–485
  loan types and, 483
  steps in, 482
Credit bureaus, 422
Credit card banks, 492
Credit cards, 478, 491–493
  pricing, 492–493
  shifting operations to states without
    rate ceilings, 492
  usury laws and, 478
Credit crunch, 13
Credit culture, 392
Credit department, 395
Credit files, and lending policy, 402–403
Credit Interchange Service, 422
Credit investigation, 418–423
  consumer loans, 484
  customer interview, 421
  financial analysis for, 455–458
  information sources:
    external, 422–423
    internal, 421–422
Credit lines, 433
  checking overdraft, 478
  home equity, 478–479
  as off-balance sheet information, 49
  seasonal, 433
Credit philosophy, 391–392
Credit quality ratios, 81
Credit risk, 67, 68, 75, 91, 92. See also
    Lending
  assessment of, see Credit analysis
  and bank failures, 390–391
  of debt securities, 277
  elements of, 393–394
  of fund sources, 232
  lead indicators for, 93
  management techniques, 93
  managing strategy, 393–394
  and swaps, 592
  traditional measures of, 93
Credit scoring systems, 486–490
Credit spread, 88, 89, 90
Credit standards, and lending policy,
    399–400
Crocker National Corporation, 354
Cross rate, 612
Currency, Comptroller of the, see Comp-
    troller of the Currency

Currency and coin, 37, 246
Currency futures contracts, 615
Currency option contracts, 616–618
Currency swaps, as off-balance sheet
    information, 49
Current accounts, 623
Current ratio, 456
Cyclical liquidity needs, 257–258
Cyclical maturity portfolio distribution,
    291

D
Dealer bid, 590
Deal makers, 629
Debentures, 343–346. See also specific
    instruments
Debit cards, 493–494
Debt-assets ratio, 444
Debtor nations, 627–628
Debt ratio, 456
Debt securities, 277–278
  long-term, 281–284
  mortgage- and other asset-backed,
    284–286
  risks, 277–278
  short-term, 278–281
Debt securities mutual funds, 320–321
Debt-to-income ratio, 485
Defalcation risk, 91
Default risk, see Credit risk
Deficit units, 4
Delivery risks, 91
Delivery systems, as funding strategy,
    233
Delta hedging, 563
Demand deposits, 210–211
  attracting, 236–237
  as balance sheet line item, 39
Deposit insurance, see Federal Deposit
    Insurance Corporation (FDIC)
Depository Institutions Act of 1982, see
    Garn-St. Germain Depository Insti-
    tutions Act of 1982
Depository Institutions Deregulation and
    Monetary Control Act of 1980,
    15, 22
  and reserve requirements, 242–244,
    246
Depository Institutions Deregulation Com-
    mittee, 22
Deposits, see also specific types of depos-
    its, i.e., Demand deposits and
    NOW accounts
  attracting, 235–240
  future product possibilities, 240–241
  risks associated with, 230–233
  types of, 209–214
Deposits with the Federal Reserve Bank, 37

Deposits with correspondent banks, 37
Deposit service charges, as income state-
    ment line item, 43
Derivative instruments, 136, 535–537
  reasons for use, 537
Derivative securities, 285
Developing countries, lending to,
    627–628
Director's loan committee, 395–396
Direct rate, 611
Discrimination, and ECOA, 484–485
Disintermediation, 13
Distant contracts, 540
Diversification, 398–399
  of security portfolios, 288
Dividend policy, and capital manage-
    ment, 336–337
Divorced persons, discrimination against,
    484–485
Documentation, for loans, 402–403
Dollar gap, 82
Doubtful loans, 413
Dual banking system, 10
Due from Federal Reserve, 246–248
Due from other commercial banks, 248
DuPont system, for ratio analysis,
    458–459
Duration, 111–115, 126–128
  arithmetic calculation of, 113
  and gap, 115–118, 551–552
  and interest rate sensitivity, 111–113
  and MBS, 308–311
  multipayment assets, 112–113
  single-payment assets, 111–112
Duration based hedging, 554
Duration gap, 115–118, 551–552. See also
    Gap management defined, 115
Duration structure of interest rates, 130
Dynamic interest sensitivity gaps, 141

E
Earning assets,
  as supplementary information, 44
  yield on, 77, 84
Earnings power, 78
Earnings risk, 135
Earnings simulations, 138–141
Eastern Europe, lending to, 628
Economic risk, 91
Economy,
  banking's role in, 3–8
  financial flows in, 4
Edge Act and Agreement Corporations,
    22, 629
Edward Edwards Company (A): case
    study, 529–532
Edward Edwards Company (B): case
    study, 633–635

Efficiency ratio, 79
Electronic banking, 27–29
Embedded option risk, 551
Embedded options, 560
Emergency Agricultural Credit Act of
    1979, 446
Emergency Banking Act, 11
Empirical credit analysis, 487–490
Employees, number of, as supplementary
    information, 45
Employee stock option plans (ESOPs),
    345
Employee stock option trusts (ESOTs),
    345
Environmental risks, 91
Equal Credit Opportunity Act (ECOA),
    484–485
Equity capital, 343–347
    as balance sheet line item, 40
Equity-capital ratio, 83
Equity-capital ratio for sustainable
    growth, 342
Eurocurrency markets, 621–622
Eurodollars, 215
    attracting, 240
    defined, 13, 622
Eurodollar assets, 623–624
Eurodollar liabilities, 623
    for hedging cap agreements, 575
    as liquidity source, 263
    market in, 621–622
Euronotes, as off-balance sheet informa-
    tion, 41
European options, 560
Evergreen credit, 437
Examination, *see* Bank examination
Exercise price, 560
External equity, 343
Extraordinary gains (losses), as income
    statement line item, 43

F

Facility, *see* Loan facilities
Factoring, 437–438
Failures, *see* Bank failures
Fair Credit Reporting Act, 504
    denial of credit reporting, 490–491
Fair Housing Act, 504
Fannie Mae, *see* Federal National Mort-
    gage Association
Farm Credit Administration, 445
Farm Credit System, 445
Farmers Home Administration (FmHA),
    446
Farm loans, *see* Agricultural loans
FDIC, *see* Federal Deposit Insurance Cor-
    poration
FDIC Information Service, 52, 53

Federal agency notes, 279
Federal Deposit Insurance Acts of 1933
    and 1934, 11, 22
    statutory requirements for bank char-
        ters, 170–172
Federal Deposit Insurance Corporation
    (FDIC), 11, 22, 24–26, 27
    and capital requirements, 327–331
    competitiveness of banks in commer-
        cial lending, 416–417
    premiums, 26
    proposed risk-based capital ratios,
        328–331
Federal Deposit Insurance Corporation
    Improvement Act (FDICIA),
    19–20, 22, 26
    insider abuse clause, 411
    risk-based capital requirements,
        329–331
Federal Financial Institutions Examina-
    tion Council (FFIEC), 26, 52
    securities policy statement, 304
Federal Financial Institutions Examining
    Committee Schedule RC-L, 50
Federal funds purchased, 214, 215
Federal funds sold, 279
Federal Home Loan Bank Board
    (FHLBB), 15
Federal Home Loan Mortgage Corpora-
    tion (FHLMC or Freddie Mac),
    284, 307–312
    mortgage participation certificates, 284
Federal Housing Administration (FHA),
    284–285, 496
Federal National Mortgage Association
    (FNMA or Fannie Mae), 307–312
    pass-throughs, 447
Federal Reserve Act of 1913, 10, 22
Federal Reserve Act of 1935, 11–12
Federal Reserve System, 10. *See also* en-
    tries under "Regulation", i.e.,
    Regulation Q
    Board of Governors, 22, 24, 25, 29
    borrowing from, 215
    capital notes and long-term debentures,
        343
    capital requirements, 327–331
    creation, 10
    funds mobilization, 236
    loan limits, 411
    proposed risk-based capital ratios,
        328–331
    reserve requirements, 242–246
    day-to-day balances, 360–367
Federal safety net, 11–12
Federal Savings and Loan Insurance Cor-
    poration (FSLIC), 16
Field warehouse, 438–439

Finance charges, and Truth in Lending
    Act, 504–505
Finance companies, competition with
    commercial banks, 416–417
Financial Accounting Standards Board
    115 (FASB 115), 296–298
Financial analysis,
    for credit investigations, 459–464
    financial statements, 35–43
    information sources and quality,
        51–54, 458
    nonfinancial information, 51
    off-balance sheet information, 48–51
Financial flows in the U.S. economy, 4
Financial futures, 537–540.
    as off-balance sheet information, 49
    and pricing of commercial lending,
        546–550
Financial guarantees, as off-balance sheet
    information, 49
Financial Information, Annual Financial
    Report, 53
Financial Institutions Reform of 1989, Re-
    covery, and Enforcement Act of
    1989 (FIRREA), 19, 22
    appraisal regulations, 400
Financial Institutions Regulatory Act of
    1978, 411
Financial intermediaries, 4–5
Financial intermediation, 6–8
Financial leases, 442
Financial leverage ratios, *see* Leverage
    ratios
Financial planning, 356–359
    analyzing a bank's performance, 356
    determining capital needs, 359
    predicting selected variables, 356–358
    sensitivity analysis, 358–359
Financial ratios, *see also* numerous spe-
    cific financial ratios
    for credit selection, 455–458
    DuPont system, 458–459
    ratios defined, 455–458
    sources of comparative data, 458
Financial risk, 91, 93
    lead indicators for, 91–94
    ratios, 80
Financial statements
    balance sheets, 35–41, 46
    of borrowers, and lending losses, 408
    income statements, 41–43, 46
    supplementary information, 44–45, 46
    as tool for return analysis, 64–66
First Bank of the United States, 8
First National Bank of Park Cities: case
    study, 157–173
*First of Omaha Service Corporation vs.
    Marquette National Bank,* 492

Fisher, Irving, 148
Fixed assets, as collateral, 437
Fixed-asset turnover ratio, 61, 457
Fixed-charge coverage ratio, 456
Floating liens, 438
Floating-rate notes, 285
Floating rates, 474
Floor limit, 492
Floor-plan financing, 438
   auto loans, 478
Floors, 575
Foreign branches of U.S. banks, 629
Foreign collection basis, for international
   trade, 625
Foreign exchange markets, 620–621
   interest arbitrage, 619–620
   spot and forward markets, 612–615
Foreign exchange rates, 611–612
Foreign exchange risk, 555
   management of, 610–611
Foreign fund sources, 474. *See also* Euro-
   currency markets: Eurodollars
Form 2900, 243, 245
Forward commitments, as off-balance
   sheet information, 49
Forward contracts, 537–540
   vs. cash transactions, 537
   characteristics of, 537–538
   pricing, 541–543
Forward data, 138
Forward exchange rate, 613
Forward gap, 141
Forward interest rates, 132–134,
   148–150
Forward market, in foreign exchange,
   613
Fractional reserve banking, 11
Fraud,
   and lending, 408, 419
   and warehouse financing, 439
Freddie Mac, *see* Federal Home Loan
   Mortgage Corporation
Full-service banking, 238
Full-service foreign branches, 629
Funding,
   composition of, 217–219
   cost measures, 219–228
     historical average cost, 222–225
     marginal cost, single source,
     225–226
     pooled marginal cost, 226–227
     utilizing, 228–230
     weighted average projected cost,
     227–228
   cost of, 77, 84
   deposits, 209–214. *See also* specific
     types of deposits, i.e., Demand
     deposits and NOW accounts

   attracting, 235–241
   double-counting value of, 236
   future product possibilities, 240–241
   nondeposit sources of, 214–215
     attracting, 240
   principal sources of, 209–214
   rate sensitivity of assets, 228–230
   required return on assets, 228
   risks associated with, 230–233
   strategies, 233–241
     delivery systems, 233, 234
     image, 235
     market segmentation, 234–235
     product attraction, 235–236
     product development, 233–234
     product differentiation, 235
Funding risk, *see* Liquidity risk
Funding spread, 88, 89, 90
   as source of profitability, 216–217
Funds management committee, 191
Funds mobilization, 236
Funds transfer pricing, 88, 335
Futures, *see* Financial futures
Futures contracts, 537–540, 595–596
   vs. cash transactions, 537
   characteristics of, 537–538
Futures settlement procedures, 540–541

G

G-10 nations and Switzerland, lending to,
   628
Gap management, 134–144
   and basis risk, 138
   concerns about traditional gap models,
     136–138
   dynamic gap, 141
   simulation systems, 138–141
   strategies and interest rate benchmark-
     ing, 141–144
Gap report, 135
Gap risk, 137
Gap-to-assets ratio, 82
Gap-to-equity ratio, 82
Garn-St. Germain Depository Institutions
   Act of 1982, 15, 22
   and competitive environment, 159
   exemption for reservable deposits, 312
   loan limits and, 411
   and reserve requirements, 244
Gates, Bill, 29
General obligations, 283
General security agreements, 404–405
Gilbert, R. Alton, 216–217
Ginnie Mae, *see* Government National
   Mortgage Association
Glass-Steagall Act, 11, 21, 22
Global Machinery and Metals Company,
   Inc.; case study, 513–517

Goodwill and other intangibles, as bal-
   ance sheet item, 39
Government-backed mortgages, 307–312
Government-guaranteed SBA loans,
   439–441
Government National Mortgage Associa-
   tion (GNMA or Ginnie Mae),
   279, 284, 307–312
   mortgage-backed pass-through securi-
     ties, 284
Grace period, credit cards, 491
Grantland National Bank: case study,
   658–669
Green Line program, 440
Gross margin ratio, 60, 61
Growth, sustainable, 339–343
Growth rates, annual, 84, 85–86
Guarantees as security interest, 437
Guarantors, 421, 437

H

Hard currency and ability of debtor
   nations to pay, 627
Hedge ratio, 546, 565
Hedging, 544–546
   anticipatory hedge, 544–545
   bond portfolios, 565–566
   cash, 544–545
   delta hedging, 563
   IOs for, 319–320
   and pricing of commercial lending,
     546–550
Hillside Bancorp (A): case study,
   368–375
Hillside Bancorp (B): case study,
   376–378
Historical average cost of funds,
   222–225, 228
Holding companies, *see* Bank holding
   companies
Hold to maturity securities, 37, 281, 297
Home equity credit, 478–479
Home Mortgage Disclosure Act, 18,
   504
Housing authority bonds, 283
HR 4986, *see* Depository Institutions De-
   regulation and Monetary Control
   Act of 1980
HR 6267, *see* Garn-St. Germain Deposi-
   tory Institutions Act of 1982

I

Image, as funding strategy, 235
Income statements, 41–43
   for credit investigation, 459–464
Indirect rate, 611
Individual retirement accounts (IRAs),
   213, 239

Information,
    off-balance sheet, 48–51
    sources and quality, 51–54
    sources for credit investigations,
        421–423, 458
    supplementary, 44–45, 46
INNERLINE, 52, 53
Innovative investments, *see* Non-
        traditional investments
Insider abuse clause (FDICIA), 411
Insider loans, as supplementary informa-
        tion, 45
Insurance,
    and lending policy information,
        401–402
    loan portfolios, 580
    as secured collateral, 404
Interbank deposits, 33
Interbank markets, 629
Interbank placement market, 633
Interest coverage ratio, 456
Interest expense on NOW and other trans-
        action accounts, as income state-
        ment line item, 41
Interest income, as income statement line
        item, 41
Interest margin ratio, 62, 75, 79
Interest only-principal only (IO-PO), 316,
        318–320
Interest rate arbitrage, 619–620
Interest rate cap agreements, 573–575
Interest Rate Expectations Theory, 148
Interest rate forecast, and liquidity needs,
        267–268
Interest rate options, 562, 563–565,
        568–569
Interest rate parity, 618–619
Interest rate risk, 67–68, 75, 91, 92, 111, 134
    accounting perspective, 201
    of debt securities, 277
    economic perspective, 201
    of fund sources, 232
    lead indicators for, 93
    management, *see* Asset-liability man-
        agement
    management techniques, 93
    spread, 88, 89, 90
    traditional measures of, 93
Interest rates, option pricing, 571–573
Interest Rate Sensitivity Report, 135
Interest rate swaps, 589–591
    basics of, 589–591
    in foreign exchange market, 614–615
    gains to swaps, 591–592
    as off-balance sheet information, 49
Interest sensitivity,
    and maturity, 106
    asymmetry of, 106

    demonstrated, 105–107
    as supplementary information, 45
Interest-sensitivity ratios, 82
Intermediation process, 5
International banking, *see also* Interna-
        tional lending
    arbitrage of transnational interest rates,
        619–620
    currency futures contracts, 615
    currency options contracts, 616–618
    eurocurrency markets, 621–622
    foreign exchange markets, 620–621
    foreign exchange rates, 611–612
    foreign exchange risk management,
        610–611
    forward market, 612–615
    interest rate parity, 618–619
    management in foreign environment,
        622
International banking facilities (IBFs),
        630
International lending, 624–628. *see also*
        International banking
    bank drafts, 625
    commercial letters of credit, 625–626
    developing countries, 626–628
    direct loans, 626–627
    hard currency and repayment ability,
        627
    repayment sources, 627
    risks of, 627
    short-term finance, 624–625
    simple trade account, 625
International Monetary Fund (IMF), 627
International Monetary Market (IMM),
        556
International and regional organizations,
        lending to, 628
International risk, 91, 92
Interstate Banking and Branching Effi-
        ciency Act of 1994, 20, 22
Intrinsic risk, 393, 431–432
Intuit, 21, 29
Inventory, 465
    as collateral, 435
Inventory financing, 438
Inventory turnover ratio, 61, 457
Investment account, 303
Investment activities, as off-balance sheet
        information, 49
Investment bankers, competition with
        commercial banks, 416–417
Investment/funding matrix, 650
Investment portfolios, *see* Security portfo-
        lios
Investments, nontraditional, *see* Nontradi-
        tional investments
Issuing bank, 625

J
Judgmental credit analysis, 486–487,
        489–490
Junk bonds, 15

K
Keogh accounts, 213, 239
*Key Business Ratios in 125 Lines of Busi-
        ness* (Dun and Bradstreet), 458
Keycorp: case study, 635–640
Key-man life insurance, 401
Knapp, Michael, 51

L
Latin America and the Caribbean, lend-
        ing to, 628
Lease financing, 441–443
    financial *vs.* operating leases, 442
    leveraged leasing, 443
    straight leasing, 442–443
Leases, as balance sheet item, 38
Leasing arrangements, 345
Legislation, 9–25. *See also* regulatory
        structure; specific laws
Legislative risk, 91
Lending, 387. *See also* Credit risk; Loans
    agricultural, 443–446
    and bank failure, 391
    to businesses, *see* Commercial lending
    to consumers, *see* Consumer lending
    government-guaranteed (SBA pro-
        gram), 439–441
    international, *see* International lending
    lease financing, 441–443
    loan examination, 412–414
    loss control, 403–409
        borrower financial statements, 408
        common reasons for losses, 409–410
        loan review function/procedures,
            405–407
        problem loans: identifying and cor-
            recting, 407–408
        securing collateral, 403–405
        unethical conduct/conflict of inter-
            est, 409
    organizational structure of credit func-
        tion, 394–395
    policy and procedures formulation,
        397–403
        changes over time, 397
        credit standards, 399–400
            acceptable collateral, 400
            appraisals, 400
            short-term credit, 399
            speculative loans, 399–400
            trade area, 400
            undesirable loans, 399–400

Lending (*cont'd*)
  documentation standards, 402–403
  insurance protection, 401–402
  loan authority/approvals, 399
  objectives, 398
  outline, 398–400
  risks and losses, 390–391
  strategies, 398–399
  pricing policy, 409
  real estate, *see* Real estate loans
  regulatory controls on, 410–414
Less-developed-countries,
  lending to, 14, 16, 397
  loan failures, 17, 397
Letters of credit, 625–626
  as off-balance sheet information, 49
  standby, option pricing of, 578–580
Leverage and capital requirements,
    324–327
Leveraged leasing, 443
Leverage multiplier, 60, 61, 62, 75, 78
Leverage ratios, 455
  Defined, 456
Leverage risk, 67, 68, 75, 91, 92
  of fund sources, 232–233
  lead indicators for, 93
  management techniques, 93
  traditional measures of, 93
Liabilities
  balance sheet line items, 39–41
  mark to market values, 111
Liability composition, 36, 77, 84, 85
Liability hedges, 544
Liability sensitive, 109
Life insurance,
  on key personnel, 401
  as secured collateral, 404
Lifo basis, for participation agreements, 439
Lincoln National Bank: case study,
    173–183
Lines of credit, *see* Credit lines
Liquid assets to earning assets ratio, 80
Liquidity, net working capital as indica-
    tor of, 464–465
Liquidity needs, 253–255
  characteristics of sources, 266–267
  charting, 260
  coordinating with security portfolio,
    287
  cost of sources, 266–267
  crisis management, 268–269
  deposit classification conflicts, 262
  interest rate forecast, 267–268
  money market access, 265–266
  managerial philosophy, 266
  measuring, 253–261
    contingent liquidity needs, 261
    cyclical liquidity needs, 257–258

seasonal liquidity needs, 255–257
short-term liquidity needs, 255–257
trend liquidity needs, 258–261
meeting, 262–270
  asset sources, 263
  contingency needs, 268–269
  emerging sources, 262–264
  future needs, 269–270
  matching sources to needs, 264–268
  purchased sources, 263
  source diversification, 266
  traditional sources, 262
purpose of, 264–265
Liquidity premium, 150–151
Liquidity ratios, 455
  defined, 456
  supplemental, 85
Liquidity risk, 66–67, 75, 91, 92
  of fund sources, 230–232
  lead indicators for, 93
  management techniques, 93
  traditional measures of, 93
Liquid Premium Theory, 150–151
Loan approval process, 396–397
  delegation of authority, 396
  loan decision, 397
  uniform presentation format and stan-
    dards, 396–397
Loan commitments, 433
  option pricing, 576–578
Loan committees, 395–396
Loan covenants, 423–424
  affirmative *vs.* negative, 423
  objectives of, 423–424
Loan divisions, 394–395
Loan examination, 412–414
Loan facilities
  bridge commercial loans, 434
  defined, 432
  revolving credit commercial loans,
    434–436
  short-term commercial loans, 432–434
  term commercial loans, 436–437
Loan loss accounting, 47–48
Loan losses, common reasons for, 410
Loan losses less recoveries, as supplemen-
    tary information, 45
Loan memorandum, 510
Loan portfolio insurance, 580
Loan pricing, 424–429
  commitment fees, 428
  compensating balances, 427–428
  cost accounting systems, 426
  floating rates, 473
  noninterest aspects of, 427, 428–429
  prime rate, 473
  spread pricing model, 425–426
Loan reviews, 405–407

Loans, *see also* Lending
  as balance sheet line item, 38
  and bank failure, 389
  floors and collars, 575
  interest rate cap agreements, 573–575
Loan sales and securitization, 446–452
  benefits, 450–451
  commercial loans, 449–450
  consumer loans, 447–449
  mortgage-backed securities, 447
  regulatory considerations, 452
Lobo Mill Products Company: case
    study, 507–509
London Interbank Offering Rate
    (LIBOR), 474
Long position, 544. See also Financial
    futures
Long-term debentures, 343–346
Long-term debt securities, 281–284
Long-term financial requirements, de-
    termining in credit investigation,
    471–472
Loss control, *see* Lending, loss control
Loss loans, 413
Loss reserves to gross loans and leases
    ratio, 81
Loss reserves to noncurrent loans ratio, 81

M

Macrohedging, 550–554
Maintenance margin, 541
Maintenance period, 243
Managed liabilities, 13
Management, philosophy and liquidity
    needs, 266
Management risks, 91, 92
Managing agents, 439
Margin, 541
  maintenance, 541
  requirements, 540–541
  variation, 541
Marginal cost of funds, 225–226, 228
Margin call, 538
Marketability risk, debt securities, 277
Market price per share, as supplementary
    information, 45
Market risk, 104
Market segmentation, as funding strategy,
    234–235
Market Segmentation Theory, 151
Market value accounting, 110
*Marquette National Bank v. First of
    Omaha Service Corporation*, 492
MasterCard, 491, 492, 494
Maturity,
  strategies for, 107–111, 290–293
  of securities, as supplementary informa-
    tion, 45

Maximization of value to owners, 95
McFadden Act, 22
Merchant banks, 629–630
Merrill Lynch, 14
Microhedging, 544–546
    anticipatory hedge, 544–545
    asset hedges, 544
    liability hedges, 544
Microsoft, 21, 29
Migration analysis, 431
Mismatch risk, 108
Mobile home financing, 479. *See also*
    Consumer lending
Modified duration, 114
Monetary policy, banks as instrument of,
    410–411
Money market access, and liquidity
    needs, 265–266
Money market accounts, attracting, 238
Money market funds, competition with
    commercial banks, 14
Money market monitor, 52, 53
Money market mutual fund (MMMF), 14
Money position, managing, 246–253
Moody's Industrial Manuals, 422
Moral hazard, 16
Morris Associates Code of Ethics for the
    Exchange of Credit Information,
    see Robert Morris Associates
    Code of Ethics for the Exchange
    of Credit Information
Morris Associates *Statement Studies, see*
    Robert Morris Associates *State-
    ment Studies*
Mortgage-backed pass-through securities,
    284
Mortgage-backed securities (MBS),
    307–320
    adjustable-rate, 312
    analysis, 312
    as callable investments, 307
    investment analysis, 308–312
    market, 447
    mortgage guaranteed or insured by the
        federal government, 285
    multi-class securities, 312
    and prepayment effects on yields,
        308–312
    stripped, 313, 316–320
Mortgage participation certificates, 284
Mortgages,
    government-backed, 307–312
    nonresidential, 499
    residential, *see* Residential mortgages
Multiclass securities, 312–320
Multilender loan agreements, 439
Multiple discriminant analysis (MDA),
    488

Mutual funds, 320–321
Mutual fund sales, as supplementary
    information, 45

N

NASDAQ, 353
National bank charters *vs.* state charters,
    170–173
National Banking Act, 10, 22
Nearby contracts, 540
Negative covenants, 423
Negotiable Certificates of Deposit
    (NCD), 12, 280
Negotiable Order of Withdrawal (NOW)
    accounts, 39
Net burden, 63
Net charge-offs to gross loans and leases
    ratio, 81
Net income, as income statement line
    item, 43
Net interest income after provision, as in-
    come statement line item, 43
Net interest income, as income statement
    line item, 41
Net interest margin, 87–91, 216
Net operating income before taxes, as in-
    come statement line item, 43
Net liquid assets, 465
Net loan losses, 390–391
Net loans to assets ratio, 80
Net loans to core deposits ratio, 80
Net loans to deposits ratio, 80
Net loans and leases, as balance sheet
    line item, 38
Net margin, 60, 61, 62, 63, 75, 78
Net non-core funding dependence ratio, 80
Net noninterest expenses to total assets
    ratio, 79
Net working capital, 464–465
New Deal banking, 11–12
    erosion of, 12–15
New-product risk, 91, 92
Nominal contracts, 104
Noncore funding dependence ratio, 253
Noncore funding, as supplementary infor-
    mation, 45
Noncurrent loans + OREO to gross loans
    and leases + OREO ratio, 80
Noncurrent loans, as supplementary infor-
    mation, 45
Nondeposit fund sources, 214–215
    attracting, 240
Nonfinancial information, 51
Non G-10 developed countries, lending
    to, 628
Noninterest aspects of loan pricing,
    direct factors, 427
    indirect factors, 428–429

Noninterest expenses to total assets ratio,
    78
Noninterest income, 77, 84
Nonreserve correspondent balances, 248
Nontraditional investments,
    mortgage derivatives, *see* Collateral-
        ized mortgage obligations: mort-
        gage-backed securities
    need for, 307
Norwest Corporation: case study,
    200–205
Note-issuance facilities, as off-balance
    sheet information, 49
Notional amount, 535
Notional principal, 588
NOW and other transaction accounts, 211
    Attracting, 237–238
    as balance sheet line item, 39
    interest expense on, as income state-
        ment line item, 41
    NOW–Super NOW distinction, 211

O

Off-balance sheet derivatives, as supple-
    mentary information, 45
Off-balance sheet information, 48–51
Office of the Comptroller of the Cur-
    rency, *see* Comptroller of the Cur-
    rency
Officer's loan committee, 395–396
Offices, number of, as supplementary in-
    formation, 45
One-stop banking, 238
OPEC (Organization of Petroleum Ex-
    porting Countries), 622
Open account basis, for international
    trade, 625
Open financial markets, 4–5
Open interest, 538–540
Open-market commercial borrowing *vs.*
    commercial banks, 416–417
Open Market Committee, 22
Operating leases, 442
Operational risk, 91, 92, 393
Optimization, of risk-return trade-offs,
    94–96
Option-adjusted spread, 156
Option premium, 559
Option pricing, 566–582
    arbitrage free interest rate trees,
        569–570
    commodity options, 580–582
    floors and collars, 575
    interest rate cap agreements, 573–575
    interest rate trees, 571–573
    loan commitments, 576–578
    and loan portfolio insurance, 580
    for standby letters of credit, 578–580

Option-rate debt, 345
Option risk, 137, 152
Options, 136
  call *vs.* put, 561
  as contingent claims, 575–576
  and credit risk, 560–561
  defined, 559
  exchange traded, 560
  vs. forwards and futures contracts, 560
  institutional background, 560–561
  interest rate options, 562, 563–565, 568–569
  in the money *vs.* out of the money, 562–563
  as off-balance sheet information, 49
  over-the-counter, 560
  payoff profiles, 561–562
Organizational risk, 91
Organization of Petroleum Exporting Countries (OPEC), 622
Other assets, as balance sheet line item, 39
Other assets especially mentioned (OAEM), 413
Other interest bearing deposits, as balance sheet line item, 40
Other liabilities, as balance sheet line item, 40
Other noninterest expense, as income statement line item, 43
Other noninterest income, as income statement line item, 43
Other real estate owned, as balance sheet line item, 38–39
Other short-term borrowing, as balance sheet line item, 40

P
PAC band, 316
PACs (planned amortization classes), 285, 316
Participation agreements, 439
Participation certificates, 284, 447
Partnership agreements, 402
Passbook savings deposits, attracting, 238
Pass-through securities, 284
Paying bank, 626
Payoff profiles, 561–562
Penney, J.C., 19
Penn Square Bank failure, 213
Peralta National Bank: case study, 191–199
Perfection of security interests, 395, 402
Performance evaluation, 63–87. *See also* Financial statements: Information; Returns; Risks
  supplemental measures, 77, 85

Personal property, as security interest, 404–405
  in bank's possession, 404
  in borrower's possession, 404–405
Planned amortization classes (PACs), 285, 316
Pledge agreements, 404
Point-of-sale terminals, 28, 241, 478
Polk's city Directories, 422
Pooled marginal cost of funds, 226–227, 228
Portfolio risk, 393
  managing, 431–432
  profile, 432
Preferred Habitat Theory, 151
Preferred stock, 40, 285, 345
  and taxes, 350
Premises and equipment expense, as income statement line item, 43
Premises and fixed assets, as balance sheet line item, 38
Prepayment of mortgages, 308–312
  CMOs, 312–313
Prepayment penalties, consumer loans, 481–482
Prepayment risk, 313
Price curve, 106, 107
  convexity of, 106, 107
Pricing, of commercial loans, 424–429
Prime rate, 473
  legal challenges to, 409
  moves away from use of, 409
Private mortgage conduit, 447
Problems, in the banking system, 10–12, 14–19
Product attraction, as funding strategy, 234–241
Product development, as funding strategy, 233–234
Product differentiation, as funding strategy, 235
Production credit associations (PCAs), 445
Profitability analysis,
  banking-business parallels, 58–63
  business example, 58–61
Profitability ratios, 78–79, 455–456
Profit margin, 456
Prompt intervention, 20
Pro rata basis, for participation agreements, 439
Provision for loan losses, as income statement line item, 41
Provision for loan losses to gross loans and leases ratio, 81
PSA speed, 316
Public deposits, 214
  attracting, 240

Public warehouse financing, 438
Purchased mortgage service rights, as supplementary information, 45
Purchasing power risk, of debt securities, 277–278
Pure discount securities, 130
Put option, 561. *See also* Options

Q
Quaker National Bank: case study, 183–191
Quarterly call report, 53
Questor, Inc: case study, 509–513
Quick ratio, 456

R
Racial discrimination, and ECOA, 485
Rate ceilings, 270
Rates, *see* Interest rate risk; Interest rates
Rate sensitivity of assets, 228–230
Ratios, *see* Financial ratios
Real estate, as security interest, 403–404
Real estate loans, 494–500. *See also* Residential mortgages
  adjustable rate mortgages, 497–499
  construction loans, 499–500
  credit standards, 497
  government backed mortgages, 495–496
  legal restrictions, 495
  nonresidential mortgages, 499
  residential mortgages, *see* Residential mortgages
  secondary markets, 496–497. *See also* Collateralized mortgage obligations; Mortgage backed securities
Real Estate Settlement Procedures Act, 504
Receivables, *see* Accounts receivable
Receivables turnover, 61
Reciprocal coverage ratio, 444
Redeposits, in Eurodollar market, 623
Refunding risk, 137–138
Region Financial Corporation; case study, 641–648
Regulation AA, 504
Regulation B,
  age and scoring systems, 488
  discrimination, 484–485
  statement of, 504
Regulation BB, 504
Regulation C, 504
Regulation DD, 235
Regulation E, 504
Regulation Q, 12, 14, 15
  and compensating balances, 427–428
  lifting of, 15, 213, 231

Regulation U, 404, 411
Regulation Y, 441
Regulation Z, 504
Regulatory Accounting Principles (RAP), 15
Regulatory forbearance, 18
Regulatory risk, 91–92
Regulatory structure, 8–26
    See also Deregulation; specific regulatory agencies, such as Federal Reserve System
    consumer lending, 503–505
    functions of, 23–25
    and lending, 410–414
    loan sales and, 452
    responsibility overlap, 23, 25
    and security portfolio management, 304
    uncovered banks, 24
Reinsurance, 401–402
Reinvestment risk, 137–138
REMICs, 313
Repayment sources
    bridge loans, 434
    international lending, 627
    primary, 420
    revolving credit loans, 435
    secondary, 421
    short-term loans, 432–433
    term loans, 436
Repos, 214–215
    attracting, 240
Representative offices, 629
Repriceable assets to total assets ratio, 82
Repriceable liabilities to total assets ratio, 82
Repricing risk, 137
Repurchase agreements, 40, 279
Required expense coverage, 61
Requirements, reserve, *see* Reserve requirements
Reserve for loan losses, 413
    as balance sheet line item, 38
Reserve requirements, 242–246
    as ''dues'' required to be in business, 248
    holidays, 251
    managing, 248–249
    money position management, 246–253
    worksheet for computing, 250
Residential mortgages, 494–495
    adjustable-rate, 497–499
    government-backed, 495–496
    prepayment rate, 308, 309
    secondary markets, 307, 496–497
    See also Collateralized mortgage obligations; Mortgage-backed securities

Resolution Trust Corporation, 19
Rest period, 433
Return on assets, 60, 61, 62, 75, 78, 455, 458
    defined, 455
    required, 228
    for sustainable growth, 342
Return on equity, 59, 60, 61, 62, 75, 78, 455, 458
    defined, 455
    model for, 61
Returns, 59–64. *See also* Risks
    accounting perspective, 111
    business as parallel with banking, 59–61
    economic perspective, 111
    evaluating: First National Bank example, 74–86
    financial statements as analysis tool, 64–66
    measuring, 66
    performance objectives for, 68–69
    supplemental measures, 77, 85
    trade-offs with risks, 69–70, 94–96
        effect of improving return, 71
        effect of lower risk, 70
        liquid low-capital situation, 72–73
        optimizing, 94–96
        profitable high-capital situation, 73
        rapid purchased-growth situation, 74
        shifting fund sources situation, 73
Revenue bonds, 283
Revolving consumer loans, 478. *See also* Consumer lending
Revolving credit commercial loans, 434–436
Revolving loan commitments, as off-balance sheet information, 49
Revolving underwriting facilities (RUFs), as off-balance sheet information, 49
Risk assets, as supplementary information, 44
Risk-based capital ratios,
    and capital adequacy, 327–331
    and capital management, 335–339
Risk premiums, and the term structure of interest rates, 152–156
Risks, 91–94. *See also* Returns
    classification: classes and categories, 91–94
    of debt securities, 277–278
    delivery, 91
    environmental, 91
    evaluating: First National Bank example, 74–86
    financial, 91
    of funding sources, 230–233
    management, 91

    measuring, 66–68
    performance objectives for, 68–69
    security portfolios, 287–288. *See also* specific instruments for discussion of risks
    supplemental measures, 77, 85
    trade-offs with returns, 69–70, 94–96
        effect of improving return, 70
        effect of lower risk, 70
        liquid low-capital situation, 72–73
        optimizing, 94–96
        profitable high-capital situation, 73
        rapid purchased-growth situation, 74
        shifting fund sources situation, 73
    types of, 66–68. *See also* specific types of risk
Robert Morris Associates Code of Ethics for the Exchange of Credit Information, 409, 422
Robert Morris Associates *Statement Studies*, 458, 462, 472
Roosevelt, Franklin D., President, 11
Rule of 78s, 481

S

Safety net, 12
Salad oil scandal, 439
Salaries and benefits, as income statement line item, 43
Savings accounts,
    as balance sheet line item, 39
    security interests in, 404
Savings and loan associations. *See also* Resolution Trust Corporation; Thrift supervision, Office of,
    failures of, 15–16
    FIRREA and, 19, 22
    problems with, 15–16
Savings Association Insurance Fund (SAIF), 19
SBA loan guarantee program, 440–441
SBA loan pools, 320
Sears, 19
Seasonal liquidity needs, 255–257
Secondary markets, 5
    in mortgages, 307
        See also Collateralized mortgage obligations; Mortgage-backed securities
    SBA loans, 440–441
Securities. *See also* Security portfolios; specific types of securities, i.e., mortgage-backed securities
    accounting classification of, 296–298
    as balance sheet line item, 37
    available-for-sale (AFS), 37, 297
    defined, 130
    held-to-maturity (HTM), 37, 297

Securities (*cont'd*)
  maturities of, 45
  trading, 37, 298
Securities and Exchange Commission
  10-K forms, as information
  source, 54
Securities Exchange Acts of 1933 and
  1934, 11
Securities gains and losses, as income
  statement line item, 43
Securities maturing < 1 year, 80
Securities sold under agreement to repurchase (repos), 214, 215
Securitization, 446–449
  See also Mortgage-backed securities
  benefits of, 450–451
  consumer loans, 479–480
  credit cards, 447–449
  as liquidity source, 262, 264
Securitization with recourse, as off-
  balance sheet information, 49
Security agreements, 404–405
Security interests. *See also* Collateral
  accounts receiving financing, 437
  factoring, 437–438
  guarantees, 437
  inventory financing, 438
  participation agreements, 439
  perfection of, 402
  personal property in bank's possession,
  404
  personal property in borrower's possession, 404–405
  real property, 403–404
  trust receipt financing, 438
  warehouse finance, 438–439
Security portfolios, 274–276
  asset priority model, 274–275
  contribution to earnings, 275–276
  coordinating with external environment, 287
  coordinating with liquidity needs, 287
  core portfolio, 289
  debt securities, *see* Debt securities
  diversification, 288
  forecasts and, 287
  managing, 286–293
  managing for total return, 293–296
  objectives, 275–276, 286
  pledging requirements, 287
  policy/strategy formulation, 289–293
    implementation, 303–304
    maturities, 290–293
    trading and swapping, 293–296
  risk assessment, 287–288
  tax assessment, 288
  uncertain cash flows, 303
Selection risk, 393

Senior capital, 343–347
  financial effects of, 347–350
  new forms of, 350–352
Sensitivity analysis,
  and gap management, 138, 139
  in capital planning, 358–359
Sensitivity ratio, 82
Separate Trading of Registered Interest
  and Principal Securities (STRIPS),
  285
Settlement Wednesday, 360
Settlement risk, 538
Sexual discrimination and ECOA, 485
Shawnee National Bank: case study,
  360–367
Shell branches, 629
Short book, in Eurodollar market, 624
Short position, 544. *See also* Financial fu-
  tures
Short-term borrowing, as balance sheet
  line item, 40
Short-term commercial loans, 432–434
Short-term debt securities, 278–281
Short-term instruments, as balance sheet
  line item, 37
Short-term international loans, 624–626
Short-term liquidity needs, 255–257
Sight drafts, 625
Simple trade accounts, 625
Single-payment loans, 483
Size of banks and leverage, 326–327
Small Business Administration (SBA)
  loan guarantee program, 440–441
  secondary market in, 440–441
Small Business Administration (SBA)
  loan pools, 320
Smithville Bank, 63–74
Solicitation lines of credit, 237
Sources and uses of funds analysis, 465
Sources of repayment, *see* Repayment
  sources
Sovereign risk, 627
Special assets committees, 395–396
Speculative loans, and lending policy, 400
Splitting deposits, 214
Spot exchange rate, 612
Spot market, in foreign exchange, 612
Spot interest rates, 133–134, 148–150
Spread, 6, 79
Spread pricing model, 425–426
Spreadsheets, for credit investigations,
  459–464
Staggered maturity portfolio distribution,
  291–293
*Standard and Poor's Corporation Rec-
  ords,* 422
Standby letters of credit, 578–580
  as off-balance sheet information, 49

Standby note issuance facilities (SNIFs),
  49
State and local government bonds,
  282
  legislative changes, 283
  zero coupon, 285–286
State and local notes, 279–280
State bank charters *vs.* national charters,
  170–173
State banks, reserve requirements,
  242–243
Statement Studies (Robert Morris Associ-
  ates), 458, 462, 472
State usury laws, *see* Usury laws
Statistical credit scoring, 482
Stock power assignments, 404
Straight leasing, 442–443
Strategic risk, 91, 92
Striking price, 560
Strip hedge, 546–550
Stripped mortgage-backed securities
  (SMBSs), 313, 316–320
Stripping, 449–450
STRIPS (Separate Trading of Registered
  Interest and Principal Securities),
  285
Subordinated debt, as balance sheet line
  item, 40
Subordination agreements, 402–403
Substandard loans, 413
Supplemental performance measures, 77,
  85
Supplementary information, financial
  statements, 44
Suretyship, 403
Surplus, as balance sheet line item, 40
Surplus units, 4
Sustainable growth, and capital, 339–343
Swap curve, 606–608
Swap rate, 614
Swaps, 136
  arbitrage of transnational interest rates,
  619–620
  basis swaps, 592–594
  contracts, 595–596
  credit considerations, 596
  credit risk and capital requirements,
  592
  dealers, 590
  from Eurodollar futures strip, 597–600
  in foreign exchange, 614
  markets, 594–595
  pricing, 597–600
  requirements of user organizations,
  596
  spread, 590
  valuation, 597
Swapping, of bonds, 294–296

T

TACs (targeted amortization classes), 316
Takeout funds, 420
Targeted amortization classes (TACs), 316
Tax assessment, security portfolios, 288
Taxes, and debt securities, 277
Tax rates, and choice of capital sources, 350
Tax Reform Act of 1986
　as boost to home equity credit, 478
　and REMICs, 313
Tax returns, in credit investigations, 422
Teasers, 498–499
Technological risk, 91, 92
Telephone banking, 237
Term commercial loans, 436–437
　vs. bonds, 436
Term structure of interest rates, 119, 130
　and risk premiums, 152–156
　theories of, 148–151
　　Interest Rate Expectations Theory, 148–150
　　Liquidity Premium Theory, 150–151
　　Market Segmentation Theory, 151
　　Preferred Habitat Theory, 151
Third party credits, 437–439
　accounts receivable financing, 437, 438
　factoring, 437–438
　guarantees, 437
　inventory financing, 438
　participation agreements, 439
　trust receipt financing, 438
　warehouse finance, 438–439
Thomas Registers, 422
Tier I capital, 330–331, 343, 379–380
　ratio, 83
Tier II capital, 330–331, 343, 379–380
　ratio, 83
Time certificates, 239
　as balance sheet line item, 39
Time deposits, 213
　attracting, 238–240
Time drafts, 625
Title insurance, 403
Too-big-to-fail, 17
Total assets turnover, 458
Trade accounts, 625

Trade area, and lending policy, 400
Trade finance, as off-balance sheet information, 49
Trading, of security portfolio, 294–296
Trading account assets, as balance sheet line item, 38
Trading securities, 37, 281, 298
Tranches, 313
Transaction deposits, attracting, 237
Transaction risk, 393
　See also Credit risk: Lending
Treadwater Bank, 108–111
Treasury bills, 130, 279
Treasury notes and bonds, 130, 282
　interest rate futures in, 540–541
Treasury securities,
　compared to mortgage-backed securities, 312
　as liquidity source, 263
Treasury strips, 130, 131
Treasury tax and loan accounts, 240
Trend liquidity needs, 258–261
Trigger covenants, 424
Trust receipt financing, 438
Truth in Lending Act, 503–505
Truth in Lending Simplification and Reform Act, 505
Turnover ratios, 455
　defined, 456–457

U

UBPR, *see* Uniform bank performance reports
UBPR *User's Guide,* 97
Udell, Gregory F., 405
Underwriting risk, 393
Undesirable loans, and lending policy, 399–400
Undivided profits, as balance sheet line item, 41
Unethical conduct, and lending, 409
Uniform bank performance reports (UBPR), 52, 53, 96–97
　for Lincoln National Bank, 176–181
　typical contents, 97
　User's Guide, 97
Uniform commercial Code,
　Article 1, 402

Uninsured depositors, 324
Unit banks *vs.* branch banks, 27–29
Unit of account, 612
Unused commitments, as supplementary information, 45
User's Guide, to UBPR, 97
Usury laws, 409
　consumer credit, 481
　credit cards, 478, 492–493

V

Value date, 612
Variable-rate CDs, 232
Variable-rate consumer loans, 481
Variable-rate debt, 345
Variation margin, 541
Veteran's Administration (VA), 284–285, 496
VISA, 491, 492, 494

W

Wage earner plan, 501
Warehousing finance, 438–439
Wealth position, of shareholders, 94–96
Weighted average projected cost of funds, 227–228
Working capital, as primary reason for business borrowing, 420
Working capital analysis, 464–472
　cash flow from operations, 467–471
　long-term financial requirements, 471–472
　net working capital, 464–465
　sources and uses of funds analysis, 465
　　financial projections using, 465–467
Working capital cycle, 433
Workout specialists, 415

Y

Yield curve, 88–89, 130–132, 133, 134
Yield curve interpolation, 153–156
Yield curve risk, 137
Yield on earning assets, 79
Yield to maturity, 119–121

Z

Zero coupon bonds, 106, 285–286